AND TYLER TOO

and Tyler too
A BIOGRAPHY OF JOHN &
JULIA GARDINER
TYLER

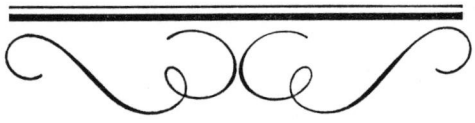

BY ROBERT SEAGER II

12373

McGraw-Hill Book Company, Inc.
New York   Toronto   London

AND TYLER TOO

Copyright © 1963 by Robert Seager II. All Rights Reserved. Printed in the United States of America. This book, or parts thereof, may not be reproduced in any form without permission of the publishers.

Library of Congress Catalog Card Number: 63-14259

First Edition

55890

M02 40001 02715

E
397　　　　　　　　　　　　　　　12373
S 4　　　　　　Seager, Robert

and Tyler too

DATE DUE			
JUL 2 8 1982			
NOV 2, '84			

Waubonsee Community College

To the memory of my father

Warren Armstrong Seager

1898–1952

ACKNOWLEDGMENTS

Mr. Howard Gotlieb, Curator of Historical Manuscripts in the Sterling Memorial Library and Archivist of Yale University, is chiefly responsible for this volume. He first brought to my attention the extensive Gardiner Family Papers in the Yale Library on which the book is largely based and suggested a joint biography of John and Julia Gardiner Tyler. Throughout the entire period of research and writing he has been a constant source of information, encouragement and assistance. Without his kind help and continuing interest there would have been no book.

Mrs. Gail Grimes Mirabile, formerly of Yale University Library, taught me to read Gardiner handwriting and introduced me to the peculiarities of Julia Gardiner's punctuation system. Mrs. Carolyn Strauss of New Haven, Connecticut, discovered valuable Tyler materials reposing in the Pequot Collection in the Yale Library. Mrs. Amy Osborn Bassford, Curator of the Long Island Collection in the East Hampton Free Library, brought important Gardiner data to my attention and assisted me in other ways. To no less degree am I grateful to the following librarians and curators of manuscripts for putting Gardiner and Tyler and related manuscript materials in their charge at my disposal: Mr. Peter Draz of the Manuscript Division of the Library of Congress; Miss Mattie Russell, Curator of Manuscripts, Duke University Library; Mr. Robert E. Stocking of the Manuscripts Division, Alderman Library, University of Virginia; Mr. James A. Servies, Librarian of William and Mary College, Williamsburg, Virginia; and Mr. Randolph W. Church, Librarian of the Virginia State Library, Richmond.

I am indebted in other important ways to Miss Lois Engleman, Librarian of Denison University, Granville, Ohio; Mrs. Jane Secor, Reference Librarian, Denison University Library; Mr. Vernon Tate, Librarian of the United States Naval Academy; Mr. Francis Allen,

Librarian of the University of Rhode Island; the Reference Staff of the New York City Public Library; Mr. Marcus C. Elcan, editor of *The Iron Worker*, Lynchburg Foundry Company, Lynchburg, Virginia; and to my brother-in-law, Mr. Deane M. Parrish, Jr., formerly of the Richmond, Virginia, *Times-Dispatch*.

The book would have been far less accurate and factually complete had it not been for the Tyler and Gardiner descendants who gave me their time and patiently answered my many questions. They were: Mrs. Alexandra Gardiner Creel of Oyster Bay, New York, grandniece of David Lyon Gardiner and donor of the Gardiner Papers to Yale Library; Judge J. Randall Creel; Mrs. Julia Tyler Wilson and Mrs. Elizabeth Tyler Miles of Charlottesville, Virginia, granddaughters of John Tyler; Miss Pearl Tyler Ellis of Salem, Virginia, and Mrs. Cornelia Ellis Booker of Washington, D.C., also granddaughters of John Tyler; Mr. J. Alfred Tyler of Sherwood Forest, Charles City, Virginia, grandson of John Tyler, and Katherine Thomason Tyler, his gracious wife; Mrs. Arthur Costello of Sahuarita, Arizona, granddaughter of J. Alexander Tyler; and Mrs. Priscilla G. Griffin of Wawa, Pennsylvania, granddaughter of Robert and Priscilla Cooper Tyler. Elizabeth Tyler Coleman and her publishers, the University of Alabama Press, have permitted me to quote extensively from Miss Coleman's excellent *Priscilla Cooper Tyler and the American Scene, 1816–1889*, published in 1955. Miss Coleman is the great-granddaughter of Priscilla Cooper Tyler. These people were all unfailingly kind and helpful, providing me with recollections, anecdotes, letters and pictures of the various Tylers and Gardiners who figure in these pages. This is not, however, an "official" family biography in any sense.

Professor Henry H. Simms of the Ohio State University and Professors Lionel U. Ridout and James C. Hinkle of San Diego State College provided me with information and insights that enabled me to avoid many factual and interpretive pitfalls. So too did Professors Frederick W. Turner III of Haverford College; Tristram P. Coffin of the University of Pennsylvania; Robert Sorlein of the University of Rhode Island; and my former colleagues at Denison University, G. Wallace Chessman, William P. T. Preston, Jr., and John K. Huckaby. Needless to say, the author is alone responsible for all errors in fact and interpretation that may remain in the work.

I am indebted to Denison University, particularly to Dean Parker E. Lichtenstein, for the leave of absence from my teaching duties there that allowed me to commence research on the book. And I am grateful to my colleagues in the Department of History of the United States Naval Academy, mainly Professors William W. Jeffries, E. B. Potter and Neville T. Kirk, for creating the scholarly atmosphere in the Department that enabled me to complete the manuscript and see it through press.

I am especially in the debt of Mrs. Ruth-Ellen K. Darnell of Baltimore, Maryland, formerly of Yale University Library, who read the manuscript in its various stages and suggested numerous stylistic and organizational improvements. Her assistance throughout has been invaluable.

I am also grateful to my sister-in-law, Mrs. Ann Brock Parrish of Richmond, Virginia, for her many benevolences to me during my several extended visits to the Richmond-Williamsburg area for research. Her culinary kindnesses enabled me to subsist for long periods of time on an academic leave of absence without salary. My aunt, Mrs. Lillian Hales Didenhover of Raleigh, North Carolina, similarly rescued me from malnutrition when research carried me to Durham.

But most of all I am indebted to my wife, Caroline Parrish Seager. It was she who did all the backbreaking clerical work on this book over a period of three years. She transcribed fifteen hundred single-spaced typed pages of recorded notes; typed the entire manuscript four times; labored over my grammar, style and punctuation; checked all the footnotes; and read and corrected the galley and page proofs. How she managed to do all this and maintain an efficient household, I will never know.

Annapolis, Maryland

Robert Seager II

CONTENTS

Acknowledgments vii
Foreword xiii
1 True Love in a Cottage 1
2 The Gardiners of East Hampton 17
3 John Tyler: His Father's Son, 1790–1820 48
4 The Dilemmas of a States' Rights Politician, 1822–1834 73
5 John Tyler: The Middle Years 102
6 And Tyler Too 127
7 His Accidency: The Disadvantages of Conscience 147
8 Courtship and Catastrophe 172
9 Tyler and Texas—And Tammany 209
10 Julia Regina: Court Life in Washington 243
11 Alexander Gardiner: Sag Harbor to the Rio Grande 266
12 Retirement to Sherwood Forest 289
13 Tyler and Polk: A Question of Reputation 312
14 Sherwood Forest: The Good Years 334
15 And the Pursuit of Property 361

16	Black Men and Black Republicans	387
17	Rumors of War: An End to Normalcy, 1855–1860	417
18	From Peace to Paradise, 1861–1862	447
19	Mrs. Ex-President Tyler and the War, 1862–1865	473
20	Reconstruction and Epilogue, 1865–1890	511
	Notes	557
	Bibliography	647
	Index	655

FOREWORD

This book does not pretend to be a definitive study of President John Tyler and his times (1790-1862). Nor, obviously, is it the last word on his wife, the vivacious Julia Gardiner Tyler (1820-1889). It is, instead, an attempt to humanize John Tyler and bring him out of the shadow into which history has cast him; to see him as his wife, his family and his intimate friends saw him, and as he saw himself. The book is therefore an informal social history of the Tylers and the Gardiners, two proud families who numbered in their midst many able and ambitious people. Not the least of these were the tenth President of the United States and his second wife. The backdrop against which the Tyler-Gardiner family alliance is viewed is the political and sectional history of the United States from 1810 to 1890.

Few Americans today know much about Tyler save that he was the "Tyler too" who ran for the Vice-Presidency on the ticket that elevated someone nicknamed "Tippecanoe" to the White House back in the distant reaches of the 1800s. That Tyler became the first Vice-President to succeed to power when an elected President died in office is also not as well known as it might be among contemporary Americans. Ironically, few American Presidents have so wanted to be remembered to posterity for their deeds. Yet John Tyler has become one of America's most obscure Chief Executives. His countrymen generally remember him, if they have heard of him at all, as the rhyming end of a catchy campaign slogan. Only one solid biography of him has appeared in the century since his death—Professor Oliver P. Chitwood's fine study which was published twenty-five years ago. Unfortunately, it has long been out of print and is virtually unobtainable today.

When I began the research for this volume there seemed to be a place for a new evaluation of Tyler that, insofar as possible and practicable, would emphasize the human side of the man—his fears, frustrations, ambitions, joys, sorrows and loves. The recent appearance of some ten thousand new Gardiner and Tyler family letters, many of which include revealing insights into the private lives of Tyler and his intimates, fixed my decision in the matter of emphasis. These valuable letters have never before been employed by an historian. They are the foundation upon which this book has been based. They help fill the vacuum of primary source material created when the bulk of Tyler's private papers were burned in the fires set by the retreating Confederate Army during Lee's evacuation of Richmond in April 1865. In addition I have employed several thousand Tyler and Gardiner letters reposing in known manuscript collections and in the three volumes of Tyler papers and letters published by the late Dr. Lyon Gardiner Tyler in the mid-1880s. The intense personal quality of much of the available material has encouraged an effort to convert the bronze statue of the forgotten President into a flesh and blood creature. The reader will discover that I am as interested in Tyler the husband, the father and the planter as I am in Tyler the President, the states' righter and the secessionist.

This is as much the story of the New York Gardiners as it is of the Virginia Tylers. It details the love of a widowed President for a woman thirty years his junior, their courtship, their marriage, and their life together in the White House and afterwards at Sherwood Forest plantation. It is largely through Gardiner eyes, especially those of the incomparable Julia and her delightful sister Margaret, that we see John Tyler the family man and the statesman. Surely the nineteenth century produced few American women as fascinating, attractive and forceful as Julia Gardiner Tyler. Whether she was flirting with politicians, "reigning" as First Lady over her White House "Court," lobbying for Texas annexation, advising the President on patronage, raising her seven children, presiding over a James River plantation house, demanding secession, or running the Union blockade, her every action and activity revealed her boundless energy. Like her domineering mother Juliana and her ambitious brother Alexander Gardiner, Julia Tyler was a positive and dynamic personality who usually got what she wanted. Fortunately for the historian, the members of the loquacious Gardiner clan liked nothing better than to write each other long, candid, and gossipy letters. Because of this, nearly half of the book turns on the intimate history of the Gardiner family before, during and after its connection with the ill-starred tenth President.

As for Tyler the politician, it seemed presumptuous for me to attempt to rewrite Professor Chitwood's excellent *John Tyler: Champion of the Old South* (1939), which deals primarily with Tyler's public life until 1845, or to rework the materials in two first-rate scholarly monographs on the subject—Robert J. Morgan's *A Whig Embattled: The Presidency under John Tyler* (1954), and Oscar D.

Lambert's *Presidential Politics in the United States, 1841–1844* (1936). For this reason, I have treated cursorily those sectors of Tyler's political career about which Chitwood, Morgan and Lambert have already written in great detail. Only when the new documentary evidence has warranted a closer look at Tyler's motives and attitudes on crucial public issues have I discussed that side of his life with any completeness at all. For example, I have gone rather extensively into his third party movement in 1843–1844 and the patronage questions involved, and into his motives in Texas annexation. The Gardiners were quite close to these developments and their private correspondence throws much new light on the problems encountered. Otherwise, many of the activities of Tyler's long and controversial public career have been drastically compressed, mentioned only in passing, or slighted altogether.

Similarly, it proved impossible to provide as historical background more than a cursory account of the many issues and personalities in American history from Tyler's birth in 1790 to Julia's death in 1889. Consequently, I have sketched in only enough of this material to make Tyler's actions and reactions, and those of the members of his family, intelligible to the reader whose college course in American history may have become hazy over the years. In doing so, I have made no particular effort to resolve the great national controversies with which Tyler concerned himself—the Bank of the United States, the tariff, internal improvements, slavery, secession and the Civil War. I unlimber little of the available scholarly artillery—the hundreds of biographies, monographs, Ph.D. theses, memoirs, and articles—that might be brought to bear on every nuance of each of these complex and controversial issues. It was clear to me at the outset that I would have the space in a single volume to do little more than state the basic nature of these problems, provide a few passing references to each in the backnotes and bibliography, and move on to emphasize the Tyler-Gardiner view of the matter as it personally affected them and as it was revealed in their private correspondence. This decision may have made for some imbalance in my interpretation.

Nor have my personal biases always been well camouflaged in these pages. Tyler owned Negroes and he accepted the institution of human slavery. He believed in rigid states' rights, strict construction of the Constitution, the territorial dismemberment of the Mexican Empire, and secession. I have little confidence that any of these ideas and policies were in the best interests of the United States at the time, although I try to treat Tyler's view of them in a manner which is neither hostile nor patronizing. He opposed the Bank of the United States, the protective tariff and popular democracy. My twenty-twenty hindsight tells me that the nation needed a national bank, a moderate tariff, and an expansion of the democratic process in the ante-bellum period. I can not accept human slavery in any form although I think I can appreciate and sympathize with Tyler's moral dilemma on the agonizing questions of abolition and secession. To the Gardiners money and social position were the root of all good and the measure of all worth; I think not. Both families were Anglophobes; I am not. While I have tried to suspend my biases the better to appreciate and understand theirs, I am certain that mine remain and push through to the surface. The reader should therefore be aware of these fundamental conflicts between the biographer and his subjects and make allowances accordingly.

Nevertheless, the reader will learn very quickly that I like John and Julia Tyler and most of the members of their immediate families. By and large they were engaging people. Tyler made many mistakes, and his intellectual window on the world of his day appears a clouded one to me a hundred years removed from the period in which he lived and worked. He was somewhat too thin-skinned about personal criticism; he could be maddeningly self-righteous; he managed money casually. Yet I find him to be a courageous, principled man, a fair and honest fighter for his beliefs. He was a President without a party. Considering this overriding political fact, his achievement of Texas annexation by manipulating Polk and the Democracy was the intrepid and successful playing of a weak hand. He was a skillful politician in the best sense of that often misused word. The inherent rebel in Tyler's stubborn nature also impresses me as a laudable characteristic. It seems a refreshing quality in this era of social and political togetherness. When the majority said, "Yes... how true... you're so right," John Tyler could generally be counted upon to say, "No, gentlemen, it won't do." He seldom compromised his principles. If anything, he was too rigid in them. He lived in great psychological fear of historical obscurity and economic insolvency. Yet on more than one occasion he accepted economic hardship and the prospect of certain obscurity rather than take what he considered the hypocritical road to political popularity. He died insolvent and unsung.

True, he was neither a great President nor a great intellectual. He lived in a time in which many brilliant and forceful men strode the American stage—Clay, Calhoun, Benton, Webster, Jackson, Douglas and Lincoln—and he was overshadowed by all of them, as was the office of the Presidency itself. The leading issues with which he grappled, relatively few in number by today's standards, ultimately required a bloody civil war to resolve. Save for the success of his Texas policy and his Maine Boundary treaty with Great Britain, his administration has been and must be counted an unsuccessful one by any modern measure of accomplishment. Had he surrendered his states' rights and anti-Bank principles he might have salvaged it. He chose not to surrender and the powerful Henry Clay crushed him. From then on he administered a caretaker government amid mounting threats of impeachment and assassination.

He was, however, a good lawyer, a fine farmer, an excellent husband to two wives, and an understanding father to fourteen children. In Julia Gardiner he had one of the great belles of the nineteenth century for a wife. She cured him of an inherent prudery and brought his best personal qualities to the fore. In a word, she made him happy. She was an able, bright, determined, and socially ambitious woman, and the reader will soon discover that I am both impressed and amused by her sheer drive and her immense extrovertism. Her will power was exceeded only by her personal charm and her often cynical sense of humor. As a hostess she was without peer. She remains, with few real challengers, one of the most interesting First Ladies in White House history. I like her and her numerous children and the essentially tragic figure who was her husband. I hope the reader does too. It is a bias for which I make no apology.

1

TRUE LOVE IN A COTTAGE

You must not believe all the President says about the honeymoon lasting always—he has found out that you in common with the rest of Eve's daughters are fond of flattery.
—JULIANA MC LACHLAN GARDINER, 1844

The Right Reverend Benjamin Treadwell Onderdonk, fourth Bishop of the Episcopal Diocese of New York, was a busy man. But not too busy to see Alexander Gardiner, the twenty-six-year-old lawyer and Tammany politician who had requested an appointment at noon on that hot Saturday of June 22, 1844. No time was wasted after young Gardiner strode into the Bishop's chambers. Characteristically, he came right to the point. His mission, he explained, was as simple as it was confidential. Would the Bishop officiate at the marriage of his younger sister, Miss Julia Gardiner, to John Tyler, President of the United States? Taken aback, Onderdonk pressed Gardiner for the details, and Alexander briefly explained that the proposed ceremony was being planned for the Church of the Ascension on Fifth Avenue at Tenth Street at 2 P.M. on Wednesday, June 26. The Reverend Dr. Gregory Thurston Bedell, rector of the church and clergyman to the family when the Gardiners were resident at their Lafayette Place town house, would assist the Bishop at the ceremony. Gardiner impressed on Onderdonk the importance of absolute secrecy in the matter, pointing out that the wedding date had been hastily arranged and that President Tyler would arrive incognito in the city late on Tuesday evening, June 25. Only four months had elapsed since the tragic death of David Gardiner, the bride's father. He had been among those struck down when the great experimental gun aboard the steam frigate *Princeton* exploded the preceding

February. The family was still in deep mourning. For this reason, explained Alexander, the Gardiners were planning a very small ceremony. There was to be no publicity of any kind. With that admonition, Alexander Gardiner departed.[1]

Aside from the Bishop's ready assent to perform the nuptials, no record of his reaction to this brief interview has survived. But Benjamin Onderdonk was a worldly man. He lived in no stained-glass tower and several practical thoughts undoubtedly crossed his mind after Alexander had left. He knew that the Gardiners were a long-established, wealthy, and prominent family, residents at various times of Gardiners Island, East Hampton, and New York City. They were the direct descendants of Lion Gardiner, the professional soldier who had first come to America in 1635 under contract to the Connecticut Company as a fortifications engineer. He was aware that Julia Gardiner was an attractive and accomplished woman, for several seasons one of the reigning belles at Washington and Saratoga Springs. Surely he wondered at the propriety of so conspicuous a wedding following hard on the heels of so publicized a family funeral. He could imagine what the gossips would do with that (as they did). And he may have ruminated on the plain fact that John Tyler was fifty-four and his bride-to-be fully thirty years his junior. If such were his thoughts, however, he kept them to himself.

The courtship of John Tyler and Julia Gardiner had begun in Washington in January 1843, four months after the death of the tenth President's first wife, the beautiful Letitia Christian Tyler of Virginia. It matured quickly during the early spring of 1843 amid a storm of rumor, speculation, and gossip, much of the latter salacious and vicious. In March 1843 a "definite understanding" had been reached, although no formal engagement was then announced. Julia's mother had blocked that. The sudden death of David Gardiner on the *Princeton* necessitated a further delay in plans. Thus it was not until April 20, 1844, seven weeks after the tragedy aboard the *Princeton,* that the President of the United States, using a second-hand envelope (John Tyler was a frugal man), wrote to Juliana McLachlan Gardiner, mother of the intended bride, asking formally for Julia's hand in marriage:

I have the permission of your dear daughter, Miss Julia Gardiner, to ask your approbation of my address to her, dear Madam, and to obtain your consent to our marriage, which in all dutiful obedience she refers to your decision. May I indulge the hope that you will see in this nothing to object, and that you will confer upon me the high privilege of substituting yourself in all that care and attention which you have so affectionately bestowed upon her. My position in Society will I trust serve as a guarantee for the appearance which I give, that it will be the study of my life to advance her happiness by all and every means in my power.[2]

Juliana Gardiner knew perfectly well what Tyler's "position in Society" was. In answering the President's letter on April 22 she implied that this fact was not sufficient to dull her sense of judgment on so important a matter. She must insist that her daughter receive from Tyler's hands "all the necessary comforts and elegancies of life" to which the Gardiners had been long accustomed. It would have been impolite to look the Presidential gift horse straight in the mouth, but Juliana did want to make certain that the Tylers had a horse of some value:

> In reply to your letter received day before yesterday I confess I am at a loss what answer to return. The subject is to my mind so momentous and serious, rendered doubly so by my own recent terrible bereavement, that I know of no considerations which this world could offer that would make me consent without hesitation and anxiety, to a union so sacred but which death can dissolve. The deep and solemn emotions of my mind are not to be regarded as a criterion of the mind of others neither do I desire by any reference to my own feelings to cast a shade over the future hopes of those whose anticipations of life are comparatively unclouded. Your high political position, eminent public service, and above all unsullied private character command the highest respect of myself and family and lead me to acquiesce in what appear to be the impulse of my daughter's heart and the dictates of her judgment. In cases of this kind I think the utmost candor should prevail and I hope you will not deem the suggestions I consider my duty as a mother to urge otherwise than proper. Her comfortable settlement in life, a subject often disregarded in youth but thought of and felt in maturity, claims our mutual consideration. Julia in her tastes and inclination is neither extravagant nor unreasonable tho' she has been accustomed to all the necessary comforts and elegancies of life. While she remains in the bosom of my family they can be continued to her. I have no reason to suppose but you will have it in your power to extend to her the enjoyments by which she has been surrounded and my reference to the subject arises from a desire to obviate all misunderstanding and future trial.[3]

For a woman torn emotionally by the sorrows and psychological readjustments of early widowhood, Juliana Gardiner had a canny ability to penetrate to the core of the practical economic realities of life, particularly those relating to its "enjoyments" and "elegancies." Her concern was a natural one, conditioned by the fact that for two centuries the Gardiners had held high status in fashionable New York society. Thus when Juliana Gardiner questioned the President of the United States on his ability to provide adequately for young Julia it was an ingrained family reflex action. Unfortunately, Tyler's reply to her interrogatory (if indeed he did reply) is not extant. The important point was that his future mother-in-law—nine years younger than himself— had consented to the union.

Tyler's party arrived in New York by rail from the capital at 10:30 P.M. on Tuesday, June 25, and slipped unobserved into Howard's Hotel. His traveling companions from Washington included John Lorimer Graham, Postmaster of the City of New York and patronage dispenser for the Tylerite political forces in the area; John Tyler, Jr., his second son and private secretary; and Robert Rantoul, prominent Boston politician, sometime Collector of Customs there, twice unsuccessfully nominated to high public office by the President. So insistent was Tyler on secrecy that he persuaded D. D. Howard, the proprietor of the establishment, to lock up his servants for the night lest they leak the news of his arrival in the city. In the best tradition of a Renaissance poisoning, the secret was kept.

At two o'clock on the sultry Wednesday afternoon of June 26 the ceremony was held, Bishop Onderdonk and Dr. Bedell presiding. Present in the small wedding party at the Church of the Ascension were the immediate family: Juliana, the bride's mother; Margaret Gardiner, Julia's twenty-two-year-old sister; Alexander and David Lyon Gardiner, her older brothers. Of the numerous Tylers, only John, Jr., accompanied his distinguished father. Nonfamily guests included United States Postmaster General and Mrs. Charles A. Wickliffe, their daughters Mary and Nannie, Miss Caroline Legaré, daughter of Hugh S. Legaré of South Carolina, the late Attorney General and Secretary of State in the Tyler administration, and Colonel and Mrs. John Lorimer Graham. Margaret served her sister as bridesmaid and Alexander was her groomsman. The bride wore a simple white dress of lisse "with a gauze veil descending from a circlet of white flowers, wreathed in her hair." Since she was in mourning for her father she wore no jewelry. As the New York *Herald* remarked, "In her form and personal appearance, she is beautiful; and we should be proud to have her appear at the Court of Queen Victoria." This gratuitous remark was an oblique reference to the groundless rumor that Tyler was about to withdraw from the 1844 Presidential canvass, throw his strength to Democrat James K. Polk, and receive in return the ambassadorship to the Court of St. James's.[4]

Julia *was* pretty. By the standards of her day she was considered beautiful. Her raven-black hair was parted in the middle and pulled back into neat, tight buns covering her ears. Her dark oval eyes were large and expressive, the flashing beacons of an animated and extroverted personality. Firm chin, full lips, and a straight nose perhaps a trifle too large for her small round face completed a picture of charm and attractiveness. She was five feet three inches in height with a tiny hourglass waist and a full bust. Tending to plumpness, Julia (like all women) would always complain of her tendency to gain weight. But on her wedding day in June 1844 her light complexion, white dress, and gauze veil contrasted effectively and strikingly with her dark hair and eyes to produce a trim appearance of radiance and loveliness. Indeed, her bright face, shapely figure, and pleasing manner were enough to excite the envy of any man for John Tyler's good fortune. In the homage of one newspaperman the President was "Lucky honest John."[5]

Following the brief Episcopal ceremony five carriages transported the wedding party from the church to the Gardiner residence on Lafayette Place. After a light wedding breakfast the guests repaired to the foot of Courtland Street, where they boarded the ferryboat *Essex* for a cooling turn around the harbor. Julia meanwhile had changed into a plain black baize traveling gown. Waiting aboard the ferryboat to greet and congratulate the radiant couple was a noisy group of local politicians and Tyler supporters. Chief among them were William Paxton Hallett, Silas M. Stilwell, George D. Strong, and Louis F. Tasistro. A band entertained the happy cargo as the *Essex* moved among the ships anchored in the harbor. Thundering salutes were received from the warships *North Carolina* and—ironically—*Princeton,* and from the guns of the fort on Governors Island. Within an hour the President and Julia were debarked at Jersey City. There they entrained for Philadelphia and a honeymoon trip that would lead them to Washington, Old Point Comfort, and to the President's recently acquired estate, Sherwood Forest, in Charles City County, Virginia. Margaret accompanied the newlyweds as far as the capital, an arrangement not considered unusual in Victorian days. A maidservant completed the wedding party. The plan was to stop a few days at the White House to permit Tyler to attend to official business that had piled up during his absence, and then to proceed to Old Point Comfort and Sherwood Forest for the remainder of the honeymoon.

When news of the wedding was published the next day in the New York papers, the effect was electric. Alexander, who thoroughly enjoyed intrigue, was particularly pleased with the *coup* he had so skillfully arranged:

The city continues full of the surprise [he wrote Julia], and the ladies will not recover in some weeks. At the corners of the streets, in the public places and in every drawing room it is the engrossing theme. The whole affair is considered one of the most brilliant *coup de main* ever acted; and I can not but wonder myself, that we succeeded so well, in preserving at once the President's dignity, and our own feelings, from all avoidable sacrifice.[6]

For a day or two even the sensational murder trial of the notorious Polly Bodine was pushed to the inside pages of the papers. The *Herald,* among other newspapers, enjoyed the heaven-sent opportunity to juxtapose the wedding story with Tyler's vigorous fight for the annexation of Texas and his campaign for re-election on that issue. The puns were bad but the spirit was good:

Miss Julia Gardiner [wrote a *Herald* reporter] is known as one of the most accomplished daughters of the State of New York. It is said that the ladies of this Country are all in favor of annexation, *to a man*. Miss Gardiner is an honor to her sex, and goes decidedly for Tyler and annexation... the President has concluded a treaty of immediate annexation, which will be ratified without the aid of the Senate of the United States... if we have lost

Texas by the recent vote of the Senate, the gallantry of the President has annexed Gardiners Island to the "Old Dominion."... Now, then, is the time to make a grand movement for Tyler's re-election. Neither Polk nor Clay can bring to the White House such beauty, elegance, grace, and high accomplishments as does John Tyler, and meetings should be at once convened—committees appointed—and all proper measures taken to ensure the reign of so much loveliness for four years longer in the White House.[7]

The secrecy with which the Chief Executive's wedding had been arranged and executed produced some understandable embarrassment. John Jones, editor of *The Madisonian*, the Tyler newspaper in Washington, was only one of many administration insiders caught by surprise. On the day before the ceremony Jones had run a routine announcement of the President's temporary departure from the capital to rest from his "arduous duties" and seek a few days' "repose." At this unintended *faux pas* the *Herald* chortled with good-natured glee: "John don't know what's going on. We rather think that the President's 'arduous duties' are only beginning. 'Repose,' indeed!"[8]

Most distressed by the suddenness of the wedding were the numerous intimate friends and relatives of the Gardiners in New York City who had received neither intimations of nor invitations to the important social event. They were particularly critical of the fact that the President had seen fit to surround the wedding party with such socially unacceptable political hacks as John Lorimer Graham, William Paxton Hallett, and Louis Tasistro and that the Gardiners had acquiesced in this disgraceful arrangement. Following the departure of the President and Julia for the South it fell to Alexander Gardiner to pacify the injured sensibilities of this group. In this delicate task he claimed complete success. He reported to Julia on June 28 that the "presence of so many persons at the solemnization, and the announcement that they constituted the bridal party, and were our guests after the ceremony, awakened some unpleasant feelings among our relations and friends, but these have been entirely quieted... there were some names introduced to the public as part of your party, in which you would have taken no great pride in such a connection." Nevertheless, as late as mid-July family friends in the city were still bitterly complaining about the way the whole thing had been handled.[9]

At East Hampton, Long Island, the news was received with surprise and delight but with little of the causticity displayed by the bride's friends in the city. Julia had grown up in the hamlet and her friends, neighbors, and kinsmen there absorbed the fact of her marriage in the unsophisticated manner of all villagers. They were too proud of East Hampton's sudden prominence in the world to worry about the social structure of the wedding party.[10]

Relatives on the Tyler side were also stunned by the suddenness of the event, particularly the President's four daughters by his first wife.

These ladies were well aware of their father's desire to marry Julia Gardiner. While they felt some concern about the sharp age difference involved in the match, they all had accepted the inevitability of the union. Throughout the difficult readjustment period that followed the ceremony, their attitude toward their new young stepmother was influenced by the fact that they had all been extremely close to Letitia Tyler, their own mother. Her death in September 1842 was still very much on their minds and in their hearts. Hence it was the timing of the wedding and its near-elopement character that produced their initial pique. They were certainly not made privy to their father's specific plans. Three weeks before the wedding the President had told his eldest daughter, Mary Tyler Jones, who was five years Julia's senior, that he had "nothing to write about which would be of any interest to you." He merely mentioned in passing that "whatever I may do *on any subject* be assured my dear daughter that your happiness will ever be near to the heart of your Father." This was the only hint of the approaching nuptials any of his daughters received. Thus when the President announced the actual occurrence of the event to Mary on June 28 it was really a plea for her approbation:

Well, what has been talked of for so long a time is consummated and Julia Gardiner, the most lovely of her race, is my own wedded wife. If I can lay my hand on a paper containing a proper account of the ceremonial I will send it. Will not my dear child rejoice in my happiness! She is all that I could wish her to be, the most beautiful woman of the age and at the same time the most accomplished. This occurrence will make no change in aught that relates to you. Nor will new associations produce the slightest abatement from my affection for you.... Will you not also write a suitable letter to Julia... expressive of your pleasure to see her? [11]

Mary was a mature and sensible woman and she soon adjusted to the idea of a young stepmother. Her sister, twenty-one-year-old Elizabeth Tyler Waller, required more time. So hurt and upset was she by the news that it was nearly three months before she could bring herself to write Julia and acknowledge the event. Addressing her letter to "My dear Mrs. Tyler," Elizabeth begged for time to absorb the implications of the new situation:

My reasons for not having written you before will I hope be appreciated, and I shall endeavor in giving them to you to be as candid as I would wish you to be to me. For weeks after your marriage I could not realize the fact, and even now it is with difficulty that I can convince myself that another fills the place which was once occupied by my beloved Mother. I had ever been taught to love that Mother above all else on Earth and surely you must feel that the short space of two years could not have obliterated her memory sufficiently for me to have been enabled to greet *any* one whom my father might have married with a great deal of affection. We are strangers to each other now which renders it impossible for either of us to entertain that affection which

I hope in after years we may feel. It would be impossible for me to regard any one in this world in the lights of a Mother were they many years your senior —but I shall endeavor to love you with the affection of a sister and trust it may be reciprocated on your part.[12]

Mary and Elizabeth did finally come to love and admire Julia. Tyler's second daughter, Letitia Tyler Semple, did not. Hers was a quiet vendetta with Julia that lasted through the years. She disliked her new stepmother instantly. After a while her unreasonable hostility was reciprocated by Julia—whose several attempts at peacemaking were all rudely rebuffed. Alice Tyler, the youngest of the President's daughters, seventeen at the time of the wedding, also proved difficult about the new order of things. Although she thawed considerably while serving as a member of the First Lady's "Court" during the brilliant 1844–1845 social season in Washington, she and Julia would have some tense moments in the years ahead. But by the time of her own marriage in 1850 she had come to respect, if not love, her beautiful stepmother.

With Tyler's three sons there was never a problem. Fourteen-year-old Tazewell was too young to grasp fully the implications of what had happened. His memory of Letitia was fairly dim and he was pleased to have a new mother. Both of Tyler's grown sons, Robert and John, Jr., were extremely fond of Julia. And while she in turn was often privately critical of their political behavior and personal habits (particularly those of the erratic John, Jr.), their relations over the years were generally warm and cordial. Save for the continuing hostility of Letitia Semple, Julia fitted easily and quickly into the Tyler family complex.

Julia's honeymoon trip to the South was a bit like Caesar's triumphal return from Gaul. The wedding night was spent in Philadelphia. Following a brief stopover in Baltimore, the honeymoon party reached Washington on the evening of June 27. "Wherever we stopped, wherever we went, crowds of people outstripping one another, came to gaze at the President's bride," Julia exclaimed ecstatically; *"the secrecy of the affair* is on the tongue and admiration of everyone. *Everyone* says it was the best managed thing they ever heard of. The President says I am the best of diplomatists."[13]

On Friday afternoon, June 28, there was a wedding reception in the flower-laden Blue Room of the White House attended by "a throng of distinguished people." Julia, Margaret, and the President received the guests. In the center of the oval room stood a tastefully decorated table on which was placed the wedding cake "surrounded by wine and bouquets." John C. Calhoun, Tyler's energetic and controversial Secretary of State, escorted Julia to the bride's table and, in the approved South Carolina feudal manner, gallantly helped her cut the great cake. The reception lasted two hours. To the young bride it was all "very brilliant—brilliant to my heart's content." Julia was truly in her element. "I have commenced my auspicious reign," she confided to her mother, "and am in quiet possession of the Presidential Mansion." [14]

In spite of this triumphant declaration it took the pragmatic Juliana another week to comprehend fully the fact that her new son-in-law was in truth the President of the United States, and that Julia had begun her "reign" at his side:

> My mind has been so absorbed with you [she wrote to Julia on July 4] that the idea never occurred to me until this morning at the breakfast table it seemed suddenly to break upon me that I had a son President of the United States—as I was alone and no person to communicate this sudden conviction to I enjoyed it by myself. To my mind however it is more like poetry than reality. I used to indulge a fancy when David and Alex. were little children perhaps one of these may be President—yet the idea in truth appeared so improbable to my mind as to render it absurd.[15]

One disquieting bit of news about Julia's married life soon drifted north to Juliana Gardiner. Within a few days of their arrival at the White House, Margaret reported Tyler's good-natured complaint that Julia's demand for his constant attention prevented him from working. He had great difficulty getting his sleepy wife out of bed in the morning, and he observed that in other ways she was "a spoilt child." Margaret agreed with the President, conveying to Lafayette Place her own opinion that if the honeymoon lasted much longer Julia would be spoiled beyond redemption. After all, she confided to her mother, the President's job required a great deal of difficult and complex work, a burden made no lighter for him by his strong political "hope of returning to the White House in '48." [16]

Juliana reacted quickly and positively to this adverse report from the capital. She told Julia bluntly that her reign in Washington would likely be short enough, and that she had better not "interrupt the President in his business." Instead, she should "urge him on" in order to help effect his re-election in November. Her advice on the more personal question involved was equally straightforward: "Let your husband work during all business hours," she ordered. "Business should take the precedence of caressing—reserve your caressing for private leisure and be *sure* you let no one see it unless you wish to be laughed at." Specifically, she suggested that Julia busy herself with putting the White House in order. She had heard from Julia's maidservant Elizabeth, and she knew from personal observation, that it was a dirty and run-down establishment. She pointed out that "the President should make the government clean it forthwith.... You know how I detest a dirty house. Commence at once to look around and see that all things are orderly and tidy. This will amuse and occupy you...." [17]

To this recommendation of occupational therapy Margaret, after she had returned to New York, added the practical suggestion that Julia might well start doing something constructive and useful for the Gardiner family in her new position as First Lady. "You spend *so much* time in kissing, things of more importance are left undone," she complained. There was, for example, their brother Alexander, whose recently launched political career in New York City needed a sharp Presidential nudge. "Recollect that A— too would like to have you make *hay* for him while the Sun shines," she reminded her sister. "In truth you must be a politician." Julia's reaction to the family advice which descended from New York was one of contrition. "I very well know every eye is upon me, my dear mother, and *I will behave accordingly*." [18]

As it turned out, Julia would have more effect on her brother's political fortunes than on the White House dirt. The President's House was in appalling condition in 1844, a slumlike casualty of the running three-year battle between Tyler and the Congress. The hostile House of Representatives had stubbornly refused to appropriate the funds necessary to keep the mansion in even a minimum state of cleanliness. Its white pillars were stained with tobacco juice, its draperies and rugs were threadbare and worn, its walls and ceilings cried for paint, and in its windows and remote corners one might observe "spiders amusingly playing at beau-peek for a naughty fly." Juliana McLachlan Gardiner was a forceful and persuasive woman, as was her young daughter, the new First Lady; but the two of them together, supported by all the power and prestige of the Executive branch, were unable to move the Congress of the United States to redecorate the White House during the remaining seven months of the Tyler administration. Nothing was done by Congress toward basic redecoration until the Polks took possession in March 1845. Before she left Washington for Old Point Comfort, however, Julia satisfied herself that the President at least appreciated the sad condition of the domicile, and she exacted from him a promise that when they returned in August she would find the premises "in prime order." [19]

Margaret returned to New York on July 1, although Tyler strongly urged her to accompany them on to Old Point Comfort. He feared his bride would "grow gloomy through the separation" from her beloved sister, as for a brief time she did. But Margaret demurred, and the honeymooners left Washington alone by boat on July 3, arriving at Old Point at one o'clock the next morning. They were met at the landing by Colonel Gustavus A. De Russy of New York, commanding officer of Fortress Monroe, who conducted them to their cottage. Julia was delighted with the comfort and beauty of the honeymoon retreat, and the separation from Margaret was soon forgotten. As Tyler's confidential agent in the matter, De Russy had done well in tastefully selecting and purchasing the furniture in Norfolk, and Julia described the arrangements he had made with genuine enthusiasm:

Col. De Russy is one of the first officers of the country and a perfect gentleman. His taste, and I believe, his own hand, arranged our sleeping apartment. ... A richly covered high post bedstead hung with white lace curtains looped up with blue ribbon, and the cover at the top of the bedstead lined also with blue—new matting which emitted its sweet fragrance, two handsome mahogany dressing tables, writing table, and sofa, the room was papered to match, and the whole establishment *brand new*—True love in a cottage—and quite a contrast to my dirty establishment in Washington. It seemed quite as if I had stepped into paradise.[20]

The next two days were filled with a ceaseless round of social activities. All the officers of the garrison were marched in a body to the honeymoon cottage to pay their respects to the Commander-in-Chief and his bride, "a really imposing scene," wrote Julia. The troops were solemnly reviewed, a duty which Julia thought "all very fine and imposing but I was so annoyed by the *mosquitos* [*sic*] which positively *devoured* me." In addition, there was a dinner aboard a Revenue cutter, endless toasts to the happiness of the President and his lady, and a flying visit from the swashbuckling John Tyler, Jr. An inspection tour of the USS *Pennsylvania* (the largest sailing warship ever built in America), lying in Hampton Roads, was marred somewhat when the flustered and confused Commodore William C. Bolton lost count of the formal salute and fired only nineteen guns instead of the customary twenty-one for a President of the United States. Flowers and wine, marching men and gallant officers, booming salutes, compliments and flattery made these days memorable for the young lady of East Hampton, thrust suddenly into the national spotlight.[21]

Never had Julia been so completely happy. "The P. bids me tell you the honeymoon is likely to last *forever*," she breathlessly told her mother, "for he finds himself *falling in love* with me every day." This was a bit too lyrical for the practical Juliana. "You must not believe all the President says about the honeymoon lasting always," she wrote her starry-eyed daughter, "for he has found out that you in common with the rest of Eve's daughters are fond of flattery." It was a charge Julia could not easily deny. She was a woman, and she was a Gardiner. Flattery, when it flowed freely and abundantly, was the very fountain of her emotional strength and happiness. At Old Point Comfort in July 1844 it flowed in torrents.[22]

While Julia thoroughly enjoyed the deference and attention that came with being the First Lady of the land, she was not insensitive to the fact that her husband was under great political strain during the entire honeymoon. For him it was a time of decision. As Julia explained it from Sherwood Forest in early July, "In this region of the country the President's friends are *strong and true,* but whether he shall continue as a candidate is a question upon which he is now deliberating. As to his views the President will soon write to Alexander." This was the first indication anyone in the Gardiner family had that the President was contemplating withdrawing himself and his Democratic-Republican third party from the 1844 campaign. The Gardiners had simply assumed, as had most of the President's close friends, that Tyler would continue in the race, win or lose. There is considerable evidence that they were confident of his success in the tricornered contest with Polk and Henry Clay. Nonetheless, it was reassuring to know that the Gardiners would instantly be privy to the President's innermost political thoughts, whatever his decision in this instance would be. The Tyler–Gardiner marriage alliance was destined to be one that was political as well as social and economic. Because of this, the redoubtable Juliana could insist with good reason that her daughter learn to "be a *politician* and look deep into the affairs of State." Julia learned to be a politician—rapidly—and her later contribution to the social and political success of the Tyler administration was no small thing.[23]

On the sixth of July the President and his bride went up the James River for a five-day inspection visit to Sherwood Forest, located on the north bank twenty-seven miles southeast of Richmond. It was a magnificent sixteen-hundred-acre plantation which Tyler had purchased in 1842 as his place of retirement. When Julia first saw it, the ninety-by-forty-two-foot house, located in a large grove of oaks, was undergoing the extensive remodeling and enlargement that would bring it to its present length of three hundred feet. The President's son-in-law, Henry Lightfoot Jones, and his daughter, Mary Tyler Jones, were temporarily managing the estate and supervising the construction work of the slave gangs. The basic work was not scheduled for completion until December 1844 and it would be a full year after that before all the detail work was finished. When at last it was finished in 1845 it was one of the most beautiful and impressive homes in Tidewater Virginia.

The morning after their arrival at the plantation, Tyler called the sixty-odd slaves to the house to greet their new "missus." It was a solemn moment. The Negroes shuffled their feet and tugged self-consciously at their caps. For a few embarrassed minutes no one spoke.

"Well, how do you like her looks?" the President finally called to one of his oldest Negroes.

"Oh, she is *mighty handsome*—just like one *doll-baby*, by Gov.," said the old-timer. The slaves laughed uproariously, the remark being what Julia correctly recognized as "the quintessence of a negro compliment." [24]

While Tyler talked politics with his friends and constituents in the area, still contemplating his course of action in the Presidential canvass, Julia wandered over the house and grounds, trying to decide what furniture and shrubs would be needed,

> ... directing the Carpenters and mechanics where to make this change and where this addition. The head carpenter was amazed at my science and the President acknowledged I understood more about carpentry and architecture than he did, and he would leave all the arrangements that were to be made

entirely to my taste. I intend to make it as pleasant as I can *under the circumstances*. A new house I would have arranged and built differently of course. It will be the handsomest place in the County and I assure you there are some very fine ones in it. The grove will be made into a park (twenty-five acres) and stocked with deer.... The President says when we walk about the house "This is for your mother to occupy, this for Margaret, and that for David and Alexander."... How I wish I had you here to talk over my *arrangements* for I am sure I don't know what to propose, and in everything the President appeals to me. In the world, as here, wherever he goes and whatever is done it is *me* in all situations he seems only to consider.[25]

That Tyler was supremely happy with his new bride there is no doubt. Her beauty, vivacity, good humor, and poise delighted him; her stamina amazed him. Julia correctly represented his feelings when she said that "Nothing appears to delight the President more than to notice the admiration, and to hear people sing my praises." He was completely captivated by Julia. When John Tyler was happy poetry invariably flowed from his lips and from his pen. Thus from his honeymoon with Julia came a final version of the verse "Sweet Lady, Awake!" which he had originally written during their courtship. Subtitled "A Serenade Dedicated to Miss Julia Gardiner," the President revised, polished, and reworked it at the honeymoon cottage at Old Point Comfort. Julia, her considerable musical talents unimpaired by her new title and responsibilities, set it to music:

> Sweet lady awake, from your slumbers awake,
> Weird beings we come o'er hill and through brake
> To sing you a song in the stillness of night,
> Oh, read you our riddle fair lady aright?
> We are sent by the one whose fond heart is your own,
> Who mourns in thy absence and sighs all alone.
> Alas, he is distant—but tho' far, far away,
> He thinks of you, lady, by night and by day.
>   Sweet lady awake, sweet lady awake!
>
> His hearth, altho' lonely, is bright with your fame,
> And therefore we breathe not the breath of his name.
> For oh! if your dreams have response in your tone,
> Long since have you known it as well as your own.
> We are things of the sea, of the earth, and the air,
> But ere you again to your pillow repair,
> Entrust us to say you gave ear to our strain,
> And were *he* the minstrel you would listen again.
>   Sweet lady awake, sweet lady awake!

While it is hardly Gilbert and Sullivan in quality, the ballad remains the only known musical collaboration of a President and his First Lady. Although the team of Tyler and Tyler was destined to pose no serious threat to that of Rodgers and Hart, the sentiment of the President's love for his young wife was sincere.[26]

Before the return of the honeymooners to Old Point Comfort from Sherwood Forest on July 10, and well before the honeymoon trip finally ended at Washington in early August, the gossips were hard at work discussing the suitability of a marriage between a fifty-four-year-old man and a twenty-four-year-old woman. Julia's mother reported a typical exchange among several ladies at a resort hotel in Rockaway, Long Island, which seemed to sum up all the vicious possibilities. As one of the gossips put it, "Well I never would *like* to interfere much with inclinations of my daughter in such cases, but I can't help thinking it was a great sacrifice for such a young and beautiful belle to make in marrying a man so much older than herself." Others chimed in with the observations that the President was "not rich either" and that he had "a large family besides."

It was not enough to label this, as Juliana promptly did, the "ignorant gossip... of our enlightened fashionable society such as congregate at the watering places in this region." Privately and subconsciously the age question also disturbed the Gardiners, the Tylers, and many of their intimate friends. Elizabeth Tyler Waller had this in her mind when she wrote to Julia in September of her difficulty adjusting to any stepmother, even one "many years your senior." J. J. Bailey, a Gardiner family friend, had teased Julia in 1843 about her developing romance with the President, repeating a widely held conviction in Washington society that such a match "would appear like green tendrils round a gnarled oak or like a wreath of roses on the brow of Saturn— Julia Gardiner and John Tyler indeed!"—a remark the socially sensitive Juliana had relayed to her son Alexander in New York with great concern. Indeed, when Margaret Gardiner first met the President at a Washington reception in December 1842, she described him to her brother David as a "most agreeable old gentleman." Subconsciously, Margaret never overcame this initial impression of Tyler. In a "funny dream" she reported to Julia in November 1845, she

... thought we were all at Newport together with you—awaiting his arrival. In the midst of the crowd he presented himself just emerged from a regular spree, so bloated as to be quite unrecognizable. You were so ashamed and provoked as to take no notice of him. But David went to shake hands and told him he always thought he was a young looking man but he was anything but that now. "Yes," replied the P— in melancholy tones, "I have grown old in a few days...." Was there ever anything so ridiculous? [27]

At one point Tyler himself wondered whether the age gap might not be too broad. Riding in his carriage one day in March 1844 with his good friend Henry A. Wise, he decided to confide to the Virginia politician his intention to marry a much younger woman. He named Julia Gardiner and watched closely for Wise's reaction.

"Have you really won her?" asked his friend in amazement.

"Yes," replied the President; "and why should I not?"

"You are too far advanced in life to be imprudent in a love-scrape," countered the cautious Wise.

"How imprudent?" Tyler pressed him.

"Easily," said Wise. "You are not only past middle age, but you are President of the United States, and that is a dazzling dignity which may charm a damsel more than the man she marries."

"Pooh!" laughed the President. "Why, my dear sir, I am just full in my prime!"

Wise was not convinced. To make his point stronger, he told Tyler the story of a James River planter who had also decided to marry a much younger woman. The planter finally asked his house slave, Toney, what he thought of the match.

"Massa, you think you can stand dat?" asked the servant in awe.

"Yes, Toney, why not? I am yet strong, and I can now, as well as ever I could, make her happy."

"Yes; but Massa," replied Toney, "*you* is now in *your* prime, dat's true; but when she is in *her* prime, where den, Massa, will *your* prime be?" Tyler burst into laughter.[28]

If Julia or the President ever worried about the thirty-year difference in their ages, none of their surviving personal letters give any indication of it. Nor is there any evidence to suggest that Julia tortured herself psychologically with fears of a lengthy widowhood. On the contrary, she passed off the age question with good humor. There is no better illustration of this than the lines of a poem she wrote for her husband in March 1852, on the occasion of his sixty-second birthday:

> There may be those with courtier tongue
>   Who homage pay to me—
> But deep the tribute love compels,
>   With which I bend to thee!
> Let ruthless age then, mark thy brow—
>   It need not touch thy heart—
> And what e'er changes time may bring,
>   I'll love thee as thou art! . . .
>
> Then listen, dearest, to my strain—
>   And never doubt its truth—
> Thy ripen'd charms are all to me,
>   *Wit* I prefer to *youth!* [29]

The fears of Henry A. Wise were never realized. Returning from his ambassadorship to Brazil in the fall of 1847, he saw Tyler again for the first time since their carriage ride and conversation in Washington in March 1844. Wise immediately noticed that included in the former President's baggage on the river boat that day was a double-seated wicker baby carriage.

"Aha! it has come to that, has it?" laughed Wise, lifting his eyebrows.

"Yes," said Tyler; "you see now how right I was; it was no vain boast when I told you I was in my prime. I have a houseful of goodly babies budding around me...." At the time he had but two, but more would come along—five more, to be exact.[30]

In early August the all-too-brief honeymoon ended, and Julia and the President returned reluctantly to Washington. Tyler had important political business to attend to, the day-to-day work of the Presidential office having accumulated during his trip. There was the November election to think about, an Annual Message to Congress to write, and the Texas annexation question to reconsider. He had finally decided to withdraw from the campaign in favor of Young Hickory, and confidential negotiations with the Polk forces to effect this with maximum advantage to the Tylerites were already under way and would require his personal attention.

More and more of his time was taken up with his official duties, and Julia saw little of him for the next few weeks. Since her own social duties as First Lady would not commence until the Congress reconvened in early December, the President suggested she visit New York in September for a short rest. The coming social season would demand all her energies. Julia agreed and alerted her mother to her projected homecoming with the plea, "Can't it get into the New York papers that Mrs. President Tyler is coming to town accompanied by Mrs. Ex-President Madison, the Secretary of War and lady?"[31]

Julia, it was clear, was beginning to live her exciting new role. The honeymoon with John Tyler was over. The honeymoon with the idea of being "Mrs. President Tyler" was just beginning. It would last for forty-five years.

2

THE GARDINERS OF EAST HAMPTON

You must be more cautious in expressing your opinions so freely as it will certainly give you trouble.
—JULIANA MC LACHLAN GARDINER, 1835

The marriage of the aristocratic John Tyler of Virginia to the vivacious Julia Gardiner of New York brought together two proud and prominent families, each with roots deep in the history and tradition of America. Whether a Gardiner had married into the Tyler family or a Tyler into the Gardiner family was a status question each gossiper decided for himself. To George Templeton Strong, prince of New York snobs, the point was irrelevant. "I've just heard a rumor," he confided to his diary, "that infatuated old John Tyler was married today to one of these large, fleshy Miss Gardiners of Gardiners Island. Poor unfortunate, deluded old jackass." To others in New York, especially to those family-conscious souls at or near the Gardiners' social level, the social and financial "suitability" of the alliance remained a subject of parlor conversation for months.[1]

Certainly Julia had no cause to feel social or economic inferiority in the presence of the Tylers. Nor did she. The Gardiners had far more material wealth than the Tylers. And while they had produced no Presidents or even governors, they were secure in the knowledge of having arrived in America in 1635, a good fifteen years before the first Tyler reached Virginia. As early as May 3, 1639, they had acquired Manchonake Island (later called Gardiners Island), the thirty-three-hundred-acre property in Block Island Sound lying off the eastern tip of Long Island. Not until January 7, 1653, fourteen years later, had Henry Tyler, the first of his clan in the New World, received his relatively modest two-hundred-fifty-four-acre grant at Middle Plantation, Virginia. From the Gardiner standpoint the Tylers were recently arrived immigrants—and poor ones at that. As a close student of genealogy, Julia was confident that none of the Tylers, save Governor John Tyler of Virginia and his son, the President, had matched the timely and impressive contributions to the nation's history of Lion Gardiner (1599-1663), founder of the Gardiner line in America.

The European background of Lion Gardiner is blurred. Aside from his birth in 1599 no detail of his childhood has survived. The names of his parents are unknown. His social status can only be guessed at. One English genealogist, Sir Thomas Banks, linked the Gardiners with a descendant of Robert Fitzwalter, baronial leader in the great struggle against King John. This generous act had the advantage of identifying the otherwise obscure Gardiners with the English nobility, the Battle of Runnymede, and the Magna Charta. Julia naturally favored this version of her ancestry, and she sought to perpetuate it by naming her sixth child Robert Fitzwalter. Nonetheless the Banks theory remains a doubtful hypothesis, no better or worse than the less-impressive tradition that Lion was descended from a family of bellmakers named Gardiner who lived near Heddingham Castle in Kent in the early sixteenth century. It was from Kent that many of the English soldiers who fought in the Netherlands during the Thirty Years' War were recruited. In 1635 one of these soldiers was certainly Sergeant Lion Gardiner, who, in his own words, was "an engineer and master of works of fortification in the legers of the Prince of Orange in the Low Countries." Still, the evidence of his humble Kentish origin is scarcely more than suggestive. Not until 1635, when Lion Gardiner was thirty-six and on military duty in Holland, does his career take on the solidity of historical fact.[2]

In that year he was employed by the Connecticut Company on a four-year contract at £100 per annum to migrate to Connecticut, there to build forts and fortifications to protect the threatened colonists from the Pequot Indians and stem the expansion of the Dutch eastward from New Amsterdam. Before departing for the distant wilderness he took as his wife Mary Wilemson of Woerdon, Holland. So impressed was he with her solid bourgeois background (she was, he later boasted to posterity, a kinsman of prominent Dutch "burger meesters"), one might hazard the guess that the general social direction of the adventuresome sergeant's marriage was rather more up than down.

In any event, Lion Gardiner arrived in Boston from Rotterdam aboard the 25-ton bark *Batcheler* on November 28, 1635, having passed through "many great tempests." He was at once assigned to building a fort at what is now Saybrook, Connecticut. For the next few years, principally during the great Pequot War of 1636-1637, he slaughtered the Indians scientifically. In these engagements he sustained painful arrow wounds and experienced many other hardships. He was also forced to endure the multiple stupidities of his God-fearing Massachusetts superiors who fell on their knees and on the aborigines with equal frequency and élan. Always an outspoken individualist (a trait Julia would inherit from him honestly), he came to reject the official Boston line that the only good Indian was a dead Indian. Instead, he made a genuine and successful effort to learn the Indian tongue and understand their culture and their point of view. It was during this somewhat subversive program of self-education that Lion established a close personal friendship with Waiandance, a Montauk chief from eastern Long Island. Indeed, when Gardiner published his critical *Relation of the Pequot War* in East Hampton in 1660, he reserved the main bolt of his wrath not for the ignorant, diseased, half-starving Indians but for the arrogance of the Massachusetts Bay officials who provoked the confused savages to war and then made no military preparations to protect the white settlers. "The Lord be merciful to us for our extreme pride and base security, which cannot but stink before the Lord," said Lion in disgust.[3]

When his contract with the Connecticut Company expired in July 1639, Lion settled down on Manchonake Island. He had purchased the island from the Montauks through the good offices of his friend Waiandance in May of that year "ffor ten coates of trading cloth." The beautiful property contained large fertile fields, a pond, harbor, inlets, beaches, woods, and breathtaking scenery. It was alive with ducks and deer. For ten pieces of cloth it was one of the great real estate bargains of colonial times. In March 1640 the Montauk contract was supplemented by a deed from the Earl of Stirling, grantee of Charles I, transferring the island to Lion Gardiner for an annual consideration of £5. This action marked the formal planting of the Gardiner tree in America. For more than three hundred twenty years, thirteen generations of Lion's descendants have, with uncommon tenacity—through wars, depressions, and taxations—preserved and maintained Gardiners Island. It remains today the only seventeenth-century royal land grant in America to come down intact in the hands of the same family.

When Lion moved Mary and his two children from Saybrook to the island in 1639 it marked the first English settlement in what is now New York state. There in 1641 was born the first English baby in New York, his third child and second daughter, Elizabeth. She was a strange girl who died in childbirth in 1658 muttering semicoherent witchcraft charges against one Goodie Garlick of East Hampton, Long Island.[4]

By 1663, the year he died, Lion Gardiner was full of honor, dignity, and real estate. Throughout the 1650s he had acquired by gift and purchase from the friendly Montauks extensive lands around East Hampton and in eastern Long Island. In 1653 he moved his family to East Hampton to escape the isolation of the offshore island, leaving his farm there to be run by tenants. On the day of his death he was a man of substance. Builder of forts, conqueror of Indians, historian of the Pequot War, soldier, engineer, linguist, individualist, Lion Gardiner was no ancestor to scorn.

Julia Gardiner Tyler had no need to apologize for her family origins. Although a full century and a half separated his death and her birth, she was a worthy child of old Lion. The Gardiner individuality, outspokenness, and love of life and adventure ran strong in her. So too did the material acquisitiveness of the Gardiners and the inordinate concern of all the family for proper marriage alliances. Her physical stamina and will to prevail over all adversity had a firm genealogical basis. Indeed, when Lion was disinterred for reburial in 1886, two and a quarter centuries after his death, his massive six-foot skeleton was still intact, bones white and hard, teeth still firmly set in powerful jaws. Like the great family he had launched, he too had prevailed.[5]

Gardiners Island remained the emotional home of all the Gardiners in America as they married, multiplied, and moved away from the island and from East Hampton to various parts of Connecticut, Massachusetts, and New York. Most of the island's numerous proprietors tended its rich fields and large flocks with care and concern. Some of the descendants of Lion were wastrels and spendthrifts who exploited, scarred, or neglected the property. Some were psychological incompetents and alcoholics. But the majority were respected farmers, businessmen, and lawyers. And all regarded the island as the symbol which gave the family its unity and identity.

With careful planning and genealogical exactitude the island was passed from eldest son to eldest son down through the centuries. When a transfer could not be accomplished legally, or if the logical recipient of the proprietorship refused the bequest or was too young to exercise it responsibly, family conferences determined in what manner the next eligible son should become proprietor, or "Lord of the Isle" as the owners began styling themselves grandly in the mid-eighteenth century. There were, to be sure, some frictions in this, but the complex process of title transference was accomplished over the years with an amazing smoothness and lack of rancor. Happily, each generation produced sons.[6]

Other problems arose. Not the least of these was the supply of labor to work the island. Lion had tended his fields with white farm hands hired in Saybrook. When the Indians were expelled from Long Island, New England, and eastern New York state and the march of the frontier westward opened up cheap and ample lands to white farm laborers, a grave shortage of help developed on Gardiners Island. Some time during the seventeenth century (no firm date is possible) Negro and Indian slaves were imported to work the land and tend the large herds of sheep and cattle. Thus David Gardiner (1691–1751), the fourth proprietor, could and did stipulate in his will that his wife,

Mehetable, receive from his estate "one negro wench as she shall make choice out of all my negro slaves." At least sixteen Negro and Indian slaves were on the island at the time of the American Revolution, and as late as 1816 the will of John Lyon Gardiner (1770–1816), seventh proprietor, showed fourteen slaves on the property. All evidence points to the Gardiners as conscientious and paternalistic slavemasters; but they were slavemasters nevertheless. Only when slavery was outlawed in New York state in 1817 were the slaves on the island gradually manumitted. Exactly when the last slave there received his freedom is not known, certainly by 1827, at the end of the grace period allowed for emancipation. During the 1820s, therefore, the work of the estate came to be performed by resident white tenants and by farm hands hired seasonally from the Long Island mainland. This arrangement survived well into the twentieth century.[7]

Given this background, there was understandably little hostility toward slavery in the Gardiner family at the time of Julia's birth in 1820. The New York *Herald* correspondent who described the President's new wife in 1844 as a "Northern bride with Southern principles," called attention not to a conversion in Julia's thinking occasioned by her marriage to John Tyler but to a fixed attitude toward slavery that was part of her family heritage. On the great slavery question that tore the nation asunder in 1861 the Rebel Julia was never a "traitor" to her background or upbringing. Ten years before her birth on Gardiners Island the property was operated in much the same manner as any large and prosperous Virginia plantation. A thirty-three-hundred-acre farm that boasted thirty-five hundred sheep and a hundred head of cattle, stabled sixty horses, produced annually one hundred hogs, two thousand loads of hay, and thousands of pounds of wool and required a labor force of eighty to a hundred men during the harvest and shearing season was, indeed, a plantation comparable to the great establishments in the South.[8]

By 1820 the island had developed a history and a folklore peopled with pirates and naval captains. In 1699, during the proprietorship of the jovial and much-married third "Lord of the Isle," John Gardiner (1661–1738), the famous Captain William Kidd dropped anchor in Gardiners Bay, and was entertained by the proprietor while his men were secreting a treasure valued at £4500. Although the booty was recovered after Kidd's arrest, the island long remained a mecca for gullible treasure-seekers who regularly hacked away at the earth in pursuit of Kidd's gold. In 1728 the celebrated Block Island pirate, Captain Paul Williams, visited the island, sacked the main house, wounded the proprietor, and made off with the family silver. No less costly was the visit in 1774 of Captain Abijah Willard's squadron en route to Boston to supply General Thomas Gage. The British commander sent ashore a provisioning party which seized $4000 worth of livestock and food. Similarly, British Admiral Marriot Arbuthnot requisitioned provisions on the island with such vigor in 1780 that by war's end the seventh proprietor, John Lyon Gardiner, reported that there was "scarcely personal property left sufficient to pay back taxes." Nor did the island fare much better during the War of 1812. At the outset of that contest Lord Nelson's great Captain, Sir Thomas Hardy, hove to in Gardiners Bay and again plundered the island's livestock. "It is not my wish," he politely wrote John Lyon Gardiner in July 1813, "to distress the Individuals on the Coasts of the United States who may be in the power of the British Squadron." But the sheep and cattle were seized nonetheless. Stories of pirates, treasure, and British depredations fascinated Julia Gardiner as she grew to young womanhood in East Hampton.[9]

Julia's father, David Gardiner, was the great-grandson of David Gardiner (1691–1751), fourth proprietor of the island. Little is known of his early life save that he was born in East Hampton in 1784. He was the second of the five children of Captain Abraham Gardiner and his wife, Phoebe Dayton, both of East Hampton. Throughout his childhood the reigning "Lord of the Isle" was his cousin, John Lyon Gardiner, the seventh proprietor. As a young boy and student at the local Clinton Academy David often sailed out to the island to hunt ducks and search for Captain Kidd's nonexistent treasure. In 1800 he went to Yale and was graduated in the famous class of 1804 which numbered among its members the brilliant young John C. Calhoun of South Carolina. Later that year he was in New York City reading law in the office of Sylvanus Miller. From 1807 until his marriage in 1815 David Gardiner practiced law in New York.[10]

Practically nothing is known of these early New York years in the life of Julia's father except that he maintained a profound interest in Gardiners Island, escaped the yellow fever epidemic which struck the city in 1809, and opposed the embargo and non-importation economic foreign policies of Presidents Jefferson and Madison as disastrous to business. In 1814 he marched out with the local lawyers when they contributed, as a professional group, two days' voluntary labor on the Brooklyn Heights fortifications. This duty was demanded when it appeared that a British fleet might descend on the city. David thoroughly enjoyed the excitement and the patriotic fervor the enemy threat stimulated. But he was not skilled with spade, shovel, and pickaxe, and his two twelve-hour manual-labor stints on Harlem Heights and Brooklyn Heights left him blistered and exhausted.[11]

It is known that David Gardiner worried a great deal about his financial future during his days as a young lawyer. In 1809 he wrote that his prospects are more promising than they have appeared at any other time—and should they be realized I hope to escape the trammels of dependence—for I believe that as long as a person is in such a situation it is impossible to be happy, and for the last two years my feelings have been more tortured with the idea of dependence than all the pain I have ever before experienced.... My thoughts have been so continually and imperceptibly drawn to the subject that it has fixed a gloom upon my mind which every exertion has been frequently unable to move.... I have never possessed that nerve or that indifference to look with contempt upon the superciliousness of a creditor whom *the emptiness of my pocket placed above me*.... Indeed the day which finds me able to satisfy my pecuniary demands, or as the phrase is, *places me above the world,* shall be kept by me as a day of Jubilee.[12]

This deep-rooted fear of economic insolvency was one David Gardiner passed, only slightly diluted, to his four children. They too were often inclined to regard human worth and social acceptability in terms of money. And like their father, their own fear of material insecurity was a strong, constant, and dominant force in their lives—so strong that David Lyon and Julia were willing in 1865–1868 to tear the Gardiner–Tyler family alliance apart in a jackal-like struggle over their mother's will.

David Gardiner's patiently awaited "day of Jubilee" finally arrived in 1815 when he married the wealthy young Juliana McLachlan, the sixteen-year-old daughter of Michael McLachlan, a Scots émigré to Jamaica in the West Indies following the Battle of Culloden in 1746. The clan McLachlan had chosen the wrong side in that civil struggle, and young Michael's change of hemisphere was not entirely voluntary. How long he remained in Jamaica, what business he undertook there, and what year he arrived in New York City is not known. It is established only that his wife gave birth to two children, Alexander, birthdate unknown, and Juliana. Juliana was born in New York on February 8, 1799.

It is also recorded that Michael McLachlan prospered as the owner of a brewery in Chatham Street and that he wisely invested his profits in real estate in lower Manhattan. Thus, when Alexander McLachlan died in 1819, Juliana came into possession of thirteen valuable pieces of commercial and residential property located on Chatham, Oliver, Greenwich, and Harrison streets. These produced at the time an annual rental income of $6000 to $7000, and during Juliana's long tenure of ownership they steadily increased in market value from $130,000 to $182,000. Used to material comfort as she was, Juliana would spend her lifetime advising young ladies of her acquaintance, especially her own daughters, not "to marry *any* man without *means*. It would answer very well for a young lady who had a fortune in her own right but not otherwise." [13]

Juliana McLachlan Gardiner was a forceful, opinionated young lady who completely dominated her husband. An excellent mother to the four children who made their appearances, and much loved by them, she nevertheless ran her home and her offspring with an iron hand. Possessed of a sharp sense of social propriety and an ear keenly tuned to imagined snubs, she regarded as perpetual occupations the maintenance of social exclusiveness and the consolidation of social gains. Her interest in cleanliness, precision, and order amounted to a passion. Spring cleaning in her home was a ritual conducted with religious overtones. She hired and fired her terrified Irish servants with monotonous regularity. She was sharp and short-tempered with those she considered inferior, firm and fair with those she regarded her equals. She considered no one her superior. Her morality was of the strict Calvinist variety, intolerant and absolute. She had a quick temper and a testiness that stemmed from a lifelong struggle with migraine headaches which could prostrate her for days at a time. Still, she was something of a hypochondriac. She constantly experimented with unnecessary medications, often with painful results. She was also the family's amateur physician, consulted on every illness. Difficult and cantankerous as could be, she would do anything to advance the interests and comforts of her children. She loved them, worried about them, and toward them she was utterly selfless. They were permitted, however, to make no decision, however minor, without her advice and counsel. A peculiar mixture of tyrant and chaperone, autocrat and nursemaid, Juliana McLachlan Gardiner was the dominant force in the lives of her children and in the life of her placid husband.

Following her marriage to David Gardiner, Juliana turned over to him the management of her Manhattan properties. He in turn employed various agents, notably Jacob G. Dychman, to collect the rents and look after the necessary maintenance. Within a few months after his wedding he abandoned the practice of law and moved his bride to East Hampton, preparatory to taking up residence on Gardiners Island. Except for managing his wife's business affairs in the city and occasionally providing legal advice for other members of the Gardiner family, David Gardiner retired at the age of thirty-two. Julia accurately described him after 1822 as a man "possessing means and leisure." The only known gainful activity he subsequently undertook was the management of Gardiners Island. This was a temporary occupation which began in 1816. It terminated in 1822 when he purchased a house in East Hampton and settled his family there.[14]

The Gardiners Island opportunity was presented when the seventh proprietor, John Lyon Gardiner, died in 1816. His widow, Sarah Griswold Gardiner, offered to lease the island to her cousin David. The heir apparent, David Johnson Gardiner, was a boy of twelve at the time, still a student at Clinton Academy in East Hampton. The lease price ranged from $2500 to $2900 per annum, a nominal figure considering the agricultural potential of the island. David Gardiner thus became the regent of the island until the eighth proprietor reached maturity. As his farm manager and overseer he hired Burnet Mulford of East Hampton. Mulford did the work.

Just how David fared financially in his agrarian undertaking cannot accurately be determined, although it is doubtful that he profited from his stewardship. These were difficult years for the island. Livestock appropriated by British naval commanders during the War of 1812 had not been fully replaced, and after 1817 the island labor-supply system experienced the shock of manumission. That Gardiner poured more capital into the project than he took out is suggested by his mortgage and account records. As late as 1828 he was still involved in a nagging correspondence over the unpaid debts and confused inventory balances of his period of tenure. It seems probable, then, that David Gardiner's brief career as a gentleman farmer cost him more than he earned. Certainly he was not a very efficient agriculturist. His most significant crop during his six years' residence on the island was three of his four children: David Lyon was born there on May 23, 1816; Alexander on November 3, 1818; and Julia on either May 4 or July 23, 1820. Margaret, the youngest, was born in East Hampton on May 21, 1822.[15]

Turning from gentleman farming to gentleman politics after his removal from Gardiners Island to East Hampton in 1822, David was elected to the New York state senate in 1824 to represent the First District of New York (Suffolk County). At Albany he identified himself with the John Quincy Adams political faction, and he was re-elected to the senate in 1825, 1826, and 1827 on his record of conservative opposition to the emerging Martin Van Buren brand of popular democracy based on machine politics, patronage manipulation, social reform, and state-financed public works. His four-term career as a state senator was, on balance, undistinguished. In general, he upheld the rights of the individual and his property against all encroachments, real or imagined, by the state. Thus he supported the exemption of conscientious objectors from militia duty, and he opposed legislation reducing the legal interest rate in New York state from 7 to 6 per cent. As a junior member of the state senate his committee assignments were not important, nor did they afford him an opportunity to influence legislation at the committee level. On one occasion, however, he was instrumental in killing in committee a bill that sought to control wolves and panthers through a bounty incentive system. He voted for the panthers, presumably on the ground that bounty payments were crude subsidies which interfered with the inalienable rights of citizens to be eaten by wild animals. Not surprisingly, the popular Jacksonian upheaval of 1828 swept him from office. Nevertheless, for the rest of his life he called himself Senator Gardiner and he always listed his occupation as "Senator."[16]

Following his involuntary retirement from the New York senate in 1828, little is known of David Gardiner until his re-emergence in Washington in 1842 as the father of the celebrated Julia. Occasional glimpses during these fourteen years reveal a country squire expensively dressed in moleskin shooting coat and black velvet vest, an anti-Jacksonian complaining to Washington officials of poor postal service in East Hampton, and a devoted trustee of Clinton Academy, the school at which his sons David Lyon and Alexander received their preparation for Princeton. During this period he also began his research into Gardiner family genealogy and into the history of East Hampton. From this contemplation of the family navel he derived great satisfaction, Margaret once reporting him in his study on a rainy Monday afternoon happily "buried in old writings, records, deeds, wills, etc."[17]

David Gardiner's active interest in politics never waned. In 1832 he ran again for the state senate, entering vigorously into the Whig campaign against Jacksonianism on Long Island. During the canvass he was called upon to distribute $200 in party slush funds among the Whig faithful in Suffolk County in an attempt to get the entire anti-Jackson vote to the polls. He was therefore dismayed to learn in November that in spite of his handouts the Whigs had "lost the county stock and fluke," the popularity of Jackson having "carried all before it." His own candidacy for the senate was unsuccessful by some two hundred votes. "I extremely regret," said his cousin Sarah Dering, whose father was Jackson's Collector of Customs in Sag Harbor, "that some of my best young friends here and elsewhere, such as the Gardiners... are so far led astray by their aristocratic newspapers."[18]

Gardiner's distrust of Andrew Jackson and the new popular democracy of the 1830s deepened with the President's removal of the federal Treasury deposits from the Bank of the United States in October 1833. The act severely shook the credit structure of the Manhattan Bank in New York where David Gardiner normally borrowed money which was secured on expected rents from Juliana's properties. Jackson's move inconvenienced and angered him. In the off-year elections of 1834 he again worked vigorously for the Whigs on Long Island. In 1838, however, he turned down a projected Whig nomination for a Suffolk County judgeship with the plea "It is now nearly or quite twenty years since I left the bar and I have grown rusty in all its proceedings... new principles of law have been adopted and old principles set afloat." His rejection of office in no way compromised the continuing political education of his sons. By 1840 he had succeeded in conveying intact his conservative political principles to both David Lyon and Alexander.[19]

Two years apart in age, the sons of David Gardiner were quite different in temperament and character. Alexander was quick, bright, extroverted, and outspoken. Attractive to women, he thoroughly enjoyed mingling in the social world. He had a sharp sense of humor and a first-rate mind, and he became an excellent lawyer. In addition, he had a natural talent for business and for financial speculation. He enjoyed the excitement and the pressures of politics, and when given the opportunity by John Tyler in 1844 he entered into the New York political arena with skill and enthusiasm. He was an energetic, ambitious, effervescent, dynamic, and sometimes impetuous human being. Intellectually he was the most capable member of the family. He and his sister Julia had much in common. They had the same interests, laughed at the same things, shared the same sense of the ridiculous, and reacted in much the same manner to the foibles and pretensions of people around them.

David Lyon was quite the opposite. He was quiet and introverted. In the presence of women he was shy and backward. He preferred shooting ducks on Montauk Point to practicing law in New York or to flirting with the Gotham ladies. He had little skill and no interest in the law. And while he did have some feeling for business, he thoroughly disliked managing the family real estate in New York. As a part-time gentleman farmer he was unsuccessful. Stolid and stable, sometimes pompous and stuffy, he lacked imagination and incisiveness of mind. He also permitted his strong-willed mother to dominate his private life rather than create family tensions by opposing her desires. Like all the members of the Gardiner family, economic security was vitally important to him. But he insisted on life's material comforts without displaying any militant acquisitiveness. On only one occasion in his life did he truly bestir himself, traveling to California in 1849 to mine gold, and that failing (as it did), to mine the miners. As a shopkeeper and real estate speculator in San Francisco and San Diego he had modest success. This was the only real work he ever tried. Most of his seventy-six years on earth were years of semi-retirement. When he finally married in 1860, at forty-three, it was to a lady of great wealth and property. At that point he ceased doing anything at all. With all his impassiveness, however, David Lyon Gardiner was no dolt. Julia discovered this to her sorrow in 1865 when, much to her surprise, he energetically contested his mother's deathbed will which, under suspicious circumstances, had named Julia the principal beneficiary.

David Lyon was more like his sister Margaret than his brother Alexander. While he had none of Margaret's sense of humor or devilishness and little of her independence and charm, he was closer to her in temperament than either of them was to the personality whirlwind that was Julia or the Roman candle that was Alexander. David followed in his father's footsteps in his lack of any urgency or sense of direction, his uncritical acceptance of the alleged privileges of wealth and family background, and in his willingness to play the role of the English country squire. Within the immediate family circle, then, Alexander was the brilliant and extroverted, Julia the unpredictable stormy petrel, Margaret the quiet freethinker, gracious and dependable, and David Lyon the phlegmatic and retiring.

David Lyon and Alexander both attended Princeton. David entered the college in 1833; Alexander followed him to Nassau Hall a year later. David Lyon's career at the school was neither eventful nor memorable. He liked the place well enough, but he missed his duck hunting, stood apart from his classmates, and—like all college students in all eras of history—he constantly pleaded for and spent more money than his father thought necessary. When the more imaginative Alexander reached Princeton in 1834 the two collegians planned and executed joint raids on the parental money bag with the precision of general staff officers. Scarcely a letter moved from East Hampton to New Jersey without containing extra spending money for some allegedly vital project dreamed up by the brothers. Naturally, each ten-dollar check from home was accompanied by the fatherly lecture, likewise as old as formal education itself, on the values of thrift and frugality and the need for greater academic effort. "Bend down to your studies with a resolution to accomplish whatever industry well directed can effect in scholarship," their father demanded. "Do not be content with a medium standing— if you cannot reach the top at least strive to approach it." [20]

The Princeton of the mid-1830s offered no academic frills and few material comforts. The physical task of reaching the college from New York was itself difficult and harrowing. Juliana angrily reported herself "be-splattered with mud by the time we reached here" on one of her infrequent visits to Princeton while her sons were in residence. The rooms in the dormitory and in boardinghouses in town were scarcely luxurious and the Gardiner boys complained continually of cold quarters, plugged fireplaces, and Spartan surroundings. The academic regimen was as rigorous as the weather, the curriculum as bare and classical as the room furnishings. Alexander found his studies "difficult and tedious" and wished that instead of theoretical mathematics, which "agrees badly with me," he could study navigation and surveying, "something that would be far more useful to us hereafter." Happily, the social life of Princeton agreed with him better. He took part in various student pranks and capers, and he flirted outrageously with the young ladies imported to the campus for the dances. From these undergraduate releases the dour David Lyon remained aloof.[21]

Politically, the college community, town and gown, was conservative, Whig, and anti-Jackson. In March 1834, for example, students joined townspeople to protest Old Hickory's removal of the Treasury deposits and to urge their immediate restoration. This political-economic orientation was quite in keeping with what the young Gardiners had learned in their own parlor at home, and they were exposed to nothing in the Princeton curriculum that caused them to doubt the tenets of their Whig catechism. "Old Jackson is playing the mischief with the banks in this State," complained an exercised David Lyon to his equally exercised father.[22]

The intellectual safety of the curriculum was guaranteed the patrons of the college. Save for Alexander's quaintly dissonant opinion that modern American women could "learn many useful, becoming and profitable lessons from the females of the barbarian nations" (a view he derived from a reading of Tacitus and Caesar), there is little evidence that either of the undergraduate Gardiners experienced any significant challenge to the ideas and attitudes they brought to Princeton with them. Thus Alexander in his Fourth of July oration at the college in 1838 could point boastfully to the decisive impact of the American Revolution on struggles for human freedom in Ireland, Poland, France, Greece, Canada, Texas, and Belgium and predict that in the future these same principles "must, and will extend over the whole surface of the globe." In the same breath, however, he chastised Americans who demanded the abolition of Negro slavery as dupes of "cunning and disorganizing demagogues from other lands," and charged that their agitations "violated the rights of property and person, and trampled upon the laws of this country." To Alexander Gardiner, at the age of twenty, the educational process had no relevance or application to such highly controversial subjects as the slavery question. Formal education was the key that unlocked the golden door to status, power, and wealth—no more. "Be not deceived as to the importance of knowledge," he stoutly maintained. "Who are they that govern the land? Who are they that direct enterprise? Who are they that accumulate wealth? Behold the triumphs of the educated!" Nothing at Princeton in 1834–1838 disabused him of this notion, and the viewpoint is not unknown among Nassau undergraduates even today.[23]

While her brothers endured the rigors of Princeton, Julia made her own way in the educational and social world at Madame N. D. Chagaray's Institute for young ladies on Houston Street in New York City. It was a fashionable finishing school for the daughters of wealthy and socially prominent New York families. If Princeton shielded the young men of these proud clans from the raw realities of contemporary American social, political, and economic life, Madame Chagaray shielded their sisters from life itself. At 412 Houston Street the world of sex, poverty, sin, and exploitation was officially nonexistent. Instead, the curriculum turned delicately on music, French, literature, ancient history, arithmetic, and composition—nothing controversial, nothing transcending the superficially literate polish the young ladies were specifically sent there to acquire.

Julia was entered at Madame Chagaray's in April 1835. There she remained as one of the forty boarding students through the 1836–1837 school year. She very likely attended the 1837–1838 session as well, although there is no certain evidence that she did. Throughout this period, Eliza Gardiner Brumley, a "naturally refined" family cousin, formerly of East Hampton, looked after young Julia's progress and helped her with her problems. When the rules permitted absence from the school premises, Julia regularly visited the Reuben Brumley home on Bleecker Street. And when her brothers came through town from Princeton en route home for visits or vacations they would stop to see their sister and take her on shopping expeditions. In spite of these family contacts Julia was desperately homesick at first, and she pleaded to be allowed to return to East Hampton. This feeling soon passed, and within a few months she found herself more bored and lonesome at home than in the bustle and activity of the school.[24]

From East Hampton to the Chagaray Institute came a steady stream of detailed maternal advice. Juliana was not one to leave much to young Julia's imagination. A fifteen-year-old girl needed constant counsel from home, even down to advice on ten-cent purchases:

You must be more cautious in expressing your opinions so freely as it will certainly give you trouble. Do not say anyone is not good looking. Nothing is more offensive or unlady-like.... You must engage yourself about your studies and make all the progress you possibly can. You must also aim at being correct and take an independent stand as it will never answer for you to lean too much upon your companions—be polite and pleasant to them all. ... When you walk out take no money except what you will want to use as you may lose it.... I place great confidence in your propriety but you cannot be too cautious. If you accept the invitations of your friends and they inquire with interest how you like your school if you cannot approve of everything do not condemn anything. Open your heart to your parents only.... The account you gave of your expenses I must say was not altogether satisfactory.... I think [the hair net] was a foolish purchase although I excuse it as everybody has something to learn by experience.[25]

With all her nagging, Juliana was as excited as her daughter by the approach of young Julia's first formal dance. She entered into the preparation of the necessary clothing with zest. Since she and Julia were about the same size she decided to contribute one of her best white formal dresses to the cause. And after the obliging Eliza Brumley had taken it in a bit at the waist, Julia was ready for her social debut. Her breathless description of the event of Friday evening, May 21, 1835, revealed it as the high point of her teens. At the age of fifteen Julia was already beginning to evidence something of the poise and sophistication John Tyler later found so attractive:

The 21st was a memorable evening. Our Soirée has taken place and is finished to my great comfort for I was tired of *thinking about it*. You would have been surprised to have seen how very much the young ladies [day scholars] were dressed. The boarders were not decked off in *quite such style* but *sufficiently* so I assure you. I presume you would like to know how *I* was dressed. I will begin. Pearl earrings, your buckle, and a beautiful *bouquet of flowers* in my bosom. It was composed of *minunet* [sic], lily of the valley, lover's wreath, a geranium flower and leaf. Mrs. Cowdrey (Mrs. B[rumley]'s next door neighbor) and herself made it. There was also a rosebud—it was beautiful! None in the room could compare with mine. I was the only one in the room that had the lily of the valley and minunet [sic]. My dress looked very well indeed among white satins, silks and lace dresses. Five hundred were invited but between three and four hundred *only* made their appearance as the night was stormy. The company did not break up til *half past three* at night and we were none of us in bed before *five*. There was an entire band of music consisting of Harp, piano, viola, cello, etc., etc., etc. I was perfectly delighted, dancing every cotillion but *one*. It is a long time since I have enjoyed myself so much....[26]

It was during these years at Madame Chagaray's that Julia came gradually to understand the complicated mores of intricate maneuver, ambiguous pursuit, and feigned artlessness that comprised the flirtation-courtship-marriage strategy of mid-nineteenth-century American women. There was nothing in the Chagaray curriculum that dealt with this. It just came naturally to Julia, who discovered at the age of fifteen that it was important to a woman of her social class that her prospective husband be "a very fine young man and have considerable property"; but she also insisted that he be "good looking" and possess great "conversational powers." She was still very young. By the time she was seventeen she had become far more sophisticated about the economic realities of the tribal mating dance. When she was twenty she was so adept at attracting hot-blooded suitors that her family whisked her off to Europe for a cooling-off period. Nothing like a damp cathedral to cool reciprocated ardor.

Margaret did not experience the social advantages of Madame Chagaray's Institute. She was, as a result, less cynical about men and marriage, and she naïvely insisted that love should play a major role in the process. She would always feel this way. At her own boarding school she made few friends and she attracted no beaux of suitable demeanor. Juliana was wholly dissatisfied with the institution. "I believe the company [there] is only a middling one," she told Julia in 1837. "I shall not desire her return after this term." [27]

By 1839 Julia and Margaret had completed what formal education they were to receive and were at home again in East Hampton. Alexander and David Lyon were in New York City reading law. David Lyon had drifted into law rather casually after leaving Princeton in 1837. As an undergraduate he had shown no interest in the subject and his decision to pursue it professionally was an arbitrary one. Alexander, on the other hand, took it seriously, worked hard at his books, and prepared with diligence for the difficult bar examinations. When he passed these with distinction in May 1842 and modestly conveyed the news of his success to East Hampton, Julia reported the entire family "very agreeably relieved." She could not, however, resist the temptation to chide her brother: "How over-modest were you in your account of the examination.... I think when one produces a sensation there is no harm in blowing the trumpet to one's family ... this is the principle upon which I always act." [28]

The financial burden of his sons' legal educations was undertaken by David Gardiner. He sent them money for their room, board, and clothing; and when their perpetual pleas of dire poverty became too heartrending, he provided spending money as well. When the two brothers finally opened their own law office in Wall Street in June 1842 they attracted so little business they were forced to rely further on their father's bounty. Not until May 1843 did the young lawyers begin to command even a minimum living wage, and this modest success so impressed Alexander that Margaret warned him he "must not get too much excited but be as composed as possible." [29]

During these three years of legal study and enforced financial prudence, David Lyon and Alexander moved from boardinghouse to boardinghouse searching for inexpensive accommodations consistent with their mother's insistence on the cultural advantages of a socially agreeable company. Variously they lived on Dye, Houston, and Chambers streets, and at one point in 1842 they contemplated a move to Madame Garcia's boarding establishment on Leonard Street because French was spoken at table. Juliana had very positive opinions about New York City boardinghouses. She urged the proposed move to Leonard Street because she had heard that Commodore Charles Stewart's son and other acceptable people boarded there and that skill in conversational French could be rapidly acquired. "Don't be too sharp about your bargaining" with Madame Garcia, she warned, "as it may give an unfavorable impression and nothing is gained by it." She felt that her young sons, now in their early and middle twenties, required her constant advice on the wicked ways of the world, and nowhere more needfully than in the area of boardinghouse morality. "Those houses are not always entirely select," she cautioned Alexander. "There is a great mixture and a great many husbands seeking young ladies.... A very general and rather distant politeness is all that is necessary until you find them out and then very likely you will wish to be still more distant." [30]

Alexander was not interested in ladies of the sort pursued and caught by boardinghouse Lotharios—or if he was he wisely kept the information from his hidebound mother. But he was interested in girls and he pursued them relentlessly. One of these was Mary Livingston.

Encouraged in his efforts by Juliana, he called at the Livingston house time after time only to be told that Mary was busy or "out." When he did manage to see her she would tell him she had "been out of town engaged in a little business," an explanation Alexander rightly regarded as "very mysterious." So persistent was the young swain and so attentive and polite was he to her mother (always sound strategy) that Mrs. Livingston finally told him confidentially, "Yes, Mary is out sometimes, Mr. Gardiner, but then you know the ladies often say they are out when they are not—you've lived in the City long enough to find this out." She conveyed this hint to Alexander "as full as ever of smiles, winks, nods, craft and mystery." A passing interest in Miss Ann Ware was quickly dashed when Julia observed that she had "a fine head of hair and a quite symmetrical petite figure," but "as for her wealth Pa does not believe a word of it." Next in an unending line came Miss Julia Lane, who elicited from Alexander love letters strewn with such deathless phrases as "To share with thee prosperity and adversity ... to have thee to cheer, to inspire ... oh! priceless treasure!"[31]

Alexander's social life in the city was a strenuous round of formal calls, cotillions, and suppers, most of which the bashful David Lyon avoided. "I have not yet joined the dance," David Lyon confessed, "my time having generally been otherwise occupied." To Julia and Margaret, marooned in distant East Hampton, Alexander boastingly recounted his social and romantic conquests and sent to his sisters a steady stream of local gossip—what beaux were pursuing what belles; who was engaged, married, or divorced; friends seen and greeted in lower Broadway; and the financial status of various eligible maidens and bachelors. Most of this was trivia. Some of it was caustic and snobbish. But all of it was extremely important to the isolated sisters.[32]

To be sure, some of the gossip Alexander overheard in the city was extremely vicious. As he came to learn "the social secrets of the fashionable cliques," he was distressed at how malevolent the in-fighting could be, how like a barracuda tank was the social maneuvering of the New York elite. Gradually he came to hate the "ill-feeling in which they habitually indulge," and the "under-hand whispering by which they endeavor to put down those whom envy and fear prompt them to hate." His mother's opinion on the ceaseless backbiting was less troubled and more philosophical. It was, she told him, "exactly in character with that set of New Yorkers and always has been." Alexander must learn to live with it.[33]

The detailed reports of the goings and comings of the fashionable set in town caused Julia and Margaret to feel even more removed from the mainstream of passing events. They begged their brothers to send them the New York newspapers and magazines and every fragment of gossip they could collect. Every social scandal and every character

33

assassination they instantly devoured and commented upon by return mail, demanding more. "Tell us all the news," Julia implored, "even the tidbits." In 1839–1840 theirs was a vicarious social life.[34]

In return for the edifying services of their brothers the girls could offer little. There was simply no news available of comparable titillation in East Hampton. Margaret lamented on one occasion that she could not fill a single page since absolutely nothing had happened in the sleepy village. Julia, on another occasion, confessed that she had "drained the weekly stock of news most completely. It is indeed flat and stale and unprofitable. You must read it with good grace and upon the principle of 'take what you can get,' for I certainly *get what I can.*" The Sunday sermons at the local Presbyterian church provided the girls no conversational ammunition beyond the laconic report that the Reverend Mr. Samuel R. Ely's homiletics ranged from "so-so" to "perfectly intolerable." Thus when a group of white toughs beat an East Hampton Negro half to death in the street in front of the Gardiner home for an alleged impertinence, Julia was grateful for the opportunity to write a detailed account of the rare excitement, concluding with the observation that the Negro had received a good thrashing "for his impudence which taught him to his sorrow that he must mind his Ps and Qs here." [35]

Time dragged slowly for Julia and Margaret. A semiannual trip to the city for necessary shopping, an occasional visit to the Samuel Gardiner home on Shelter Island, Julia's August 1839 invitation to a ball at West Point as the guest of Cadet Daniel G. Roberts, and a few poetic letters from casual beaux in New York scarcely sufficed to break the monotony.[36]

Keeping abreast of clothing styles in the city was a difficult enough task, and few letters reached David Lyon or Alexander that did not contain urgent "emergency" pleas for thread, lace, ribbon, hats, gloves, silks, and fashion magazines. Swatches were sent to be matched, detailed and technical tailoring instructions were given. When the hard-pressed brothers botched one of their numerous purchasing commissions (which was not infrequently) a sharp reprimand would arrive from Julia in East Hampton: "I intend returning you those *exquisite pink* gloves for you to change.... I think Taste hid herself in your pocket when they were selected." Speed was always essential in these matters. "My dear child," she scolded Alexander on another occasion, "you must learn to execute commissions in the twinkling of an eye." Nor was any detail left to the imagination. "If you find you can not get silk in any store then please go back and purchase the Tarlatan muslin—*Have I made you understand?*" [37]

To while away the tedious hours and to give vent to a naturally romantic nature, Julia learned to play the guitar. On warm moonlit evenings in East Hampton "as the dew falls with perfume from the honeysuckles," she would sit for hours on the piazza and strum her guitar, singing of home and heaven, love and chivalry, and romantic lands far away. She had a sweet, clear voice and her impromptu concerts were much admired by her family and friends. For her brothers it simply meant more tiresome shopping commissions. Julia sent them scurrying around to the music stores of the city to fill her needs for sheet music. Her repertoire grew rapidly and she soon mastered such ballads as "Oh, Why Hast Thou Brought Me No Love," "There's Nothing Nice But Heaven," "Moonlight! Moonlight! or, What An Hour Is This!," "The Home of My Childhood," *"Chi Bene Ama Non Obblia"* ("It is an Italian song," said Julia helpfully), and "Thou Art Gone." This was all very sweet, but the twenty-year-old Julia wanted more from life. As she explained her plight to Alexander, "I generally hail the approach of [night], as in the Land of Dreams I can at least experience variety." There was very little variety in East Hampton, Long Island.[38]

It was Julia's boredom, her restlessness, her strong desire to escape East Hampton, and her hunger for excitement that explains her involvement in the embarrassing "Rose of Long Island" incident of 1839–1840. It would almost seem she provoked it. If indeed she did, her strategy was successful. At least it got her out of East Hampton. And had she not been taken first to Europe and then to Washington she would never have met John Tyler.

Late in 1839 a cheap throwaway advertising lithograph was distributed throughout New York City by Bogert and Mecamly, a semi-fashionable dry goods and clothing establishment on lower Ninth Avenue. The advertisement pictured Julia Gardiner strolling in front of the store carrying on her arm a small sign, shaped like a lady's handbag, which boldly proclaimed: "I'll purchase at Bogert and Mecamly's, No. 86 Ninth Avenue. Their Goods are Beautiful and Astonishingly Cheap." In the manner of a professional model Julia was magnificently overdressed in a sunbonnet which trailed large ostrich feathers. She wore a heavy fur-hemmed winter coat. Depicted at her side was an unidentified older man, clad like a dandy in top hat and light topcoat and carrying an expensively wrought cane. The advertisement was captioned with the abstruse identification, "Rose of Long Island." It was one of the first, if not the first, endorsed advertisements to appear in New York City. Certainly it was the first personal endorsement of a mercantile house by a New York lady of quality. That Julia posed for the lithograph, or approved the use of her likeness in connection with it, cannot be doubted.[39]

The Gardiners were embarrassed and humiliated that a proper daughter of theirs could have become involved in such a crass, commerical display. Not only did the family shop at the more fashionable Stewart's, but their own daughter had now been pictured to the general public in the company of an older man who was dressed like a swell.

Something had to be done. Convinced that idleness was Satan's ally, David Gardiner began thinking of a European tour for his restless daughters. No surviving family letter ever mentioned the mortifying incident. The memory of it and all reference to it were buried with the speed of an unembalmed corpse.

Were this not awkward enough, the Gardiners were further embarrassed a few months later with the publication of "Julia—The Rose of Long Island," an eight-verse, sixty-eight line effort by one "Romeo Ringdove," which appeared on the front page of the Brooklyn *Daily News* for May 11, 1840. A copy of the paper was sent anonymously to Julia. It was definitely not great poetic literature, as an excerpt will indicate. It was, however, in the nature of distinctly unwanted publicity. As "Romeo Ringdove" phrased his love for "The Rose of Long Island":

> In short, I was bedeviled quite,
>   Bewitched's a prettier word!
> She stole my heart that luckless night,
>   This gentle singing bird.
> She sang about "The Rustling Trees,"
>   "The Rush of Mountain Streams,"
> About "The Balmy Southern Breeze,"
>   The "Sunlight's Radiant Beams." ...
>
> I grieve my love a belle should be,
>   The idol of each beau;
> It makes it idle quite, for me
>   To idolize her so.
> When gallants buzz like bees around
>   Who sweets from flowers suck,
> Where shall the man so vain be found
>   As hopes this rose to pluck?
> And since, to end my cruel woes
>   No other mode I see;
> I'll be a hornet to her beaux,
>   To her a bumble-bee.

To a less Victorian generation all this would seem quite innocent. But 1840 was not a good year for buzzing around on the front page of a metropolitan newspaper. Julia's renewed notoriety as the "Rose of Long Island" was more than her parents could tolerate. "Pa still talks of taking me to Europe in October—I think seriously," wrote Julia. Some basic decisions were indeed being made in the Gardiner home.[40]

David Gardiner had discussed the European trip before the poetic phase of the double-barreled "Rose of Long Island" incident. He now began planning it as an imminent event. His brother, Nathaniel Gardiner, was engaged to manage Juliana's properties during the absence of the family. David Lyon and Alexander, it was decided, would remain at their law studies in New York. Letters of introduction were secured. Benjmin F. Butler, Attorney General of the United States, supplied one to Lewis Cass, American ambassador to the Court of Louis Philippe; and Charles King of New York wrote to Georges W. Lafayette introducing David Gardiner as a former member of the New York senate and "a man of education and fortune." The departure date was set for September 1840.[41]

In the meantime the girls were taken on a short trip to Washington and to White Sulphur Springs in Virginia—a practice run of sorts for the social trials of the coming jaunt to Europe. On August 3, 1840, the family left East Hampton for the capital. It was a rigorous trip by steamboat from Sag Harbor to New Haven (Juliana feared the noisy boilers would explode at any minute), and thence by rail to New York and Washington. By the time they reached Washington on August 9 Juliana was exhausted and quite ready to return to East Hampton. "I think I shall keep on as it is for Julia's advantage, but for myself it is a great effort even to think of it," she complained. As usual, Juliana found the strength to go on. She always did. The single day in Washington was profitably spent. The senator had an interview with President Martin Van Buren and Juliana took her daughters to view the White House. She found the furniture in the East Room "rich and elegant." The family left the capital on August 10 for a short stay at White Sulphur. Just what "advantage," social or physical, Julia derived there is not known, although the Gardiners were "very much pleased" by the trip to the spa. As Juliana summed it up, "We have traveled a long distance and seen a great variety of people. All seem to think we have a feast before us in going to Europe."[42]

David Gardiner, his wife and daughters sailed from New York aboard the packet ship *Sheridan,* Captain de Peyster, on September 27, 1840. Margaret's diary entry for the day of departure conveyed the intense excitement the sisters felt. "A new world is opening before us!" she wrote. "Bright are our anticipations! I was awakened by the songs of the sailors whilst hoisting sails and preparing for sea." The voyage across was an interesting one for the girls, particularly for Margaret, who flirted rather openly with Captain de Peyster.[43]

Arriving in London on October 29, the Gardiners found that they could "perceive no difference in the appearance of the people from those of New York." They toured the churches, found the country "cold and dreary," ogled the public buildings, and predicted that New York would soon outstrip London. It was par for the course.[44]

The Channel crossing to France on the steamer *Waterwitch* was "exceedingly turbulent." Nonetheless, Julia was in fine form and she soon managed to beguile and captivate one of the passengers, Sir John

Buchan, who was "extremely gallant, and quite enveloped J. in his macintosh to keep off the spray." This little fling under the macintosh was quickly terminated by violent seasickness which sent Julia scurrying to her cabin, a clear victory for Poseidon over Aphrodite. Unfortunately, Sir John's attempts to see Julia again were smashed on the rocks of divergent itineraries.[45]

In Paris it was a strenuous round of cathedrals, galleries, museums, and receptions, French lessons for Margaret, a new guitar for Julia, a visit to the Chamber of Deputies for Senator David, and a sick headache for Juliana. The pace was killing. The Parisian high point, and for the Gardiner sisters the outstanding event of the entire grand tour, was their presentation at the French court of Louis Philippe on January 7, 1841. This treat was arranged by Ambassador Lewis Cass. As Margaret described it:

Twenty-eight American ladies were presented, besides a large number of English and French.... The dresses of the ladies were rich and splendid, while many of the English were emblazoned with diamonds, and with the gay and elegant uniforms of the gentlemen presented a *tout ensemble* which far surpassed my most brilliant imaginings.... The King looks old, is very affable in manners, and resembles his paintings, except in stature. In this he is given too much height. He was dressed in the uniform of an officer of the army, and wore an auburn wig, which but half concealed his snow-white hair. He principally addressed the married ladies—asked J. and myself if we were sisters, and passed on.... In a short time followed the Queen, attired in scarlet velvet robe and cloak, confined at the waist with a band, and diamond clasp. Her head-dress was fancifully arranged with diamonds of great brilliancy, and a bird of paradise. She is tall and thin. In short, a perfect anatomy, and there's a striking contrast, in this respect, to the King. Her conversation was a mixture of French and English, which I could not comprehend, and only bowed in reply.... The salons were insufferably warm, and I was obliged to retire twice, in consequence of faintness. I was attended by the King's physician and two or three maids in waiting, and furnished with cologne, salts, orange flower water, etc.[46]

When Julia later spoke of her "reign" as First Lady she had this recollection of royal splendor as a guide and a goal. Having observed the etiquette, posturing, and regal brilliance of the Tuileries, Julia undertook to transplant to the White House something of its opulence and its studied deference to reigning monarchy. She would even surround herself with "ladies in waiting" and insist on many court procedures. David Gardiner was equally impressed with the magnificence of the French court. His detailed analysis of its brilliance and the social advantages of Americans' being presented there was dispatched to the editor of the New York *American* and printed in the edition of May 25, 1841.[47]

In Rome the family was disappointed to find "very few Americans," but there was some compensation in obtaining rooms in the Hotel de Londres just below those of Christina, the former Queen of Spain. And an audience with Pope Gregory XVI impressed them. They found the reactionary old Pontiff's "affability of manner and pleasant conversation very gratifying." Margaret was thoroughly repelled, however, by some Roman Catholic practices:

We all witnessed the washing of feet, and serving at table, of thirteen poor priests, of different nations, by the Pope in imitation of the washing of the apostles' feet by our Saviour... we went to the Hospital Pellegrini, and saw the washing, and serving at table, of a host of poor pilgrims, by the noble ladies of Rome. It is a disgusting act of humility! These ladies actually washed and kissed the feet of the filthy miserable people.

She was relieved, on her arrival back in England three months later, to find herself "in a Christian land once more." Julia was less concerned with the ecclesiastical side of Rome. Instead, she engaged in a fleeting romance with Baron von Krudener, a young German nobleman then visiting in the city. How involved each became with the other can only be surmised by Julia's recollection that he had worshiped her "in secret, in silence, in tears." Twenty-five years later she still remembered him fondly, and when her sons went to Germany to college after the Civil War she urged them to discover what had become of him.[48]

The Roman holiday was followed by an exploration into the smoking crater of Vesuvius. During her descent into the volcano Julia became extremely frightened and nearly fainted. It was one of the very few times in her life her poise and self-assurance deserted her. It took a volcano to do it. She rallied quickly, however, and enjoyed the next stages of the trip as the family moved leisurely northward from Pompeii to Florence, Venice, Leghorn, and Genoa. Then traveling through Switzerland, into Germany, down the Rhine, and on to The Hague, Amsterdam, and Brussels (where Julia treated herself to a brief romantic fling with a Belgian count), they finally reached London again on July 3, 1841.[49]

Sightseeing trips to Scotland and Ireland occupied the family in July and August. Julia was occupied too. This time it was with a Mr. Delebarger of London, an employee of the War Ministry who, according to Juliana, "foolishly became very much *taken* with Miss Julia without any encouragement from any quarter." Julia did not have to provide much overt encouragement. A glance over her fan generally served to start the chemical reaction. The Delebarger involvement was quickly terminated by Juliana. The Gardiners left England in early September in the *Acadia,* and after an extremely rough crossing they reached Boston at the end of the month. They had been gone a full year.[50]

It had been an exciting and educational experience for Julia and

Margaret. If Julia had attracted ardent young men to her side in London, Rome, and Brussels, the incidents were less disastrous from the Gardiner standpoint than having her paraded in lithograph and verse through the public prints of New York. At the same time, however, it was certain that after having seen the wonders of the Tuileries, the Vatican, and Westminster Abbey, East Hampton would seem tame indeed to the Gardiner girls.

Throughout the European tour the letters of David Lyon and Alexander to the family had described in detail the swiftly changing political scene at home. Their sympathies, of course, were Whig. In November 1840 both of them voted for "Tippecanoe and Tyler Too" in preference to President Martin Van Buren and the egalitarian policies he favored and the Gardiners so detested. When news of the sudden death of President William Henry Harrison on April 4, 1841, reached the Continent, the Gardiner girls, in common with other American ladies then touring in Europe, carefully wrapped their left wrists in black crêpe as a testament "to the sense of grief universally felt by Americans... for the death of the good man and soldier, the Hero of Tippecanoe." [51]

Alexander's April 9, 1841, letter to his father provided the absent family a full account of the shocking news of General Harrison's death after one month in the White House:

This melancholy event, which has really cast a gloom over the country, was the result of an illness of only a week. His disease was the *bilious pleurisy*. ... His enemies have asserted that he was infirm from age, and this doubtless led him to exert himself more than he would otherwise have done. He was accustomed to walk before breakfast in the morning, and it was on one of these occasions that he caught his death. The labours he was obliged to undergo about the time of his inauguration were prodigious; and since, his house has been beset from morning til night by office beggars and others....

Alexander described the suddenness with which Vice-President Tyler had been "drawn from the bosom of his family" in Williamsburg "to assume the direction of affairs" in Washington, the funeral arrangements for the dead President, and the deep mourning into which the nation was plunged. Like thousands of other Americans, Alexander Gardiner also posed the crucial question of the hour. Who *was* the enigmatic John Tyler, and for what did he stand?

In the midst of these scenes Mr. Tyler has assumed the government, and retained the Cabinet selected by Gen. Harrison. Yet some doubts are entertained whether he may not strike out a new course of political policy. He is of the Virginia school, and has been very decidedly anti-bank, anti-tariff, and anti-distribution of the public lands. The party insists that his opinions are now altogether Whig, and that he will carry out the measures proposed by the Harrison administration. Time will decide, but it would be stranger indeed if he were not orthodox.[52]

As the nation and the Gardiners soon discovered, John Tyler was very definitely of the "Virginia school" and, from the Whig standpoint, he was certainly not "orthodox." Indeed, by the time the Gardiners had landed safely again in Boston in September 1841 these facts had become clear. John Tyler's voyage through the turbulent seas of the bank crisis had just ended in disaster, and waves of Whig criticism crashed heavily onto the decks of his sinking Ship of State. In this assault few critics pounded the renegade Tyler administration with less mercy than the brash young Alexander Gardiner.[53]

The political explosion in Washington in 1841 was a dramatic spectacle, educational enough to warrant closer study. Julia and Margaret had already seen the capitals of Europe, visited the public buildings of London, Paris, Rome, and Brussels, consorted and flirted with the statesmen and nobility of half a dozen nations. It was past time, David Gardiner reasoned, for his sprightly daughters to glimpse the wonders of American democracy in action, however chaotic that action might be. It was decided, therefore, that the family should proceed to Washington for a short visit. In this way the sadly neglected political education of Julia and Margaret could be advanced. The European trip had polished and readied them for an introduction to Washington society. Now they needed an introduction to politics. So it was that the young ladies and their parents departed by train from New York in mid-January 1842 bound for the sprawling, mud-caked capital on the Potomac.

The girls began to attract admiring male glances immediately. As the train rolled south toward Washington, a "handsome, portly gentleman" came several times into the car where Julia and Margaret were seated and self-consciously adjusted his cravat at the ornate mirror, casting, as he did so, "several furtive glances" at the attractive Gardiner sisters. Only after she reached Washington did Julia discover that the handsome, forty-two-year-old stranger with the large cravat and the roving eyes was Congressman Millard Fillmore of Buffalo, New York, political protégé of Thurlow Weed and later President of the United States. He was, Julia learned to her dismay, quite married.[54]

The family took up residence at Mrs. Peyton's well-known boardinghouse on the corner of Pennsylvania Avenue and Four-and-a-Half Street. It was as comfortable and fashionable a place of its sort as the backward capital afforded, and it served as a residence and eating club for a bevy of congressmen and government officials. Among those present at Mrs. Peyton's place in January 1842 were Congressmen Edmund Hubard and Francis Mallory of Virginia, John McKeon and Richard Davis of New York, Caleb Cushing of Massachusetts, Thomas D. Sumter of South Carolina, and Thomas Butler King of Georgia.

Within a few days of their arrival the Gardiners were caught up in the social swirl of the town. Congressman Sumter, who was a retired United States Army colonel, was particularly attentive to Julia and Margaret. He squired the young East Hampton ladies from reception to reception with a gracious chivalry that matched anything the girls had experienced in Europe. Millard Fillmore and Senator Silas Wright of New York soon called on the Gardiners, as did Congressman Fernando Wood, later mayor of New York City. Senator David Gardiner was no ordinary tourist. Formerly a leading Whig politician in Suffolk County, he was worth cultivating politically and socially. Luckily for his daughters, his position and wealth assured the family immediate absorption into the top circles of Washington society.[55]

Julia and Margaret reveled in the excitement of the Washington social scene and in the opportunity to meet the great and the near-great of the American Republic. Julia was quickly singled out by young Richard R. Waldron of New Hampshire, a purser in the United States Navy. He became her constant escort and guide. Through Waldron and Colonel Sumter the girls met Postmaster General Charles A. Wickliffe and his attractive daughters. The Wickliffes, reported Margaret, were a lovely family who had "remained long enough at their home in Kentucky not to be easily contaminated by mingling with the worldly." It was the beginning of a friendship that would last for many years.

Waldron obligingly escorted the Gardiners to the House and Senate to hear the debates, and to the weekly Assemblies or balls patronized by the rich, the well-born, and the politically important people of the capital. At a reception on January 18, 1842, Julia first met Robert Tyler and enjoyed "quite a critical discussion ... of the poets" with him. The thrill of meeting the President's eldest son was almost overwhelming, and when the girls reached Peyton's later that evening they eagerly "talked over the proceedings until after one."

At a private dance in the home of General John P. Van Ness a few nights later, where "the wine flowed like water," they saw a less attractive side of Washington society. They were shocked at the behavior of General Aaron Ward, a New York congressman. Ward got quite drunk and insulted Madame Bodisco, the beautiful and shapely wife of the Russian ambassador. According to Margaret's pristine description of the incident, the tipsy congressman introduced Madame Bodisco to David Gardiner and then "told her to show the gentleman her eyes. Asked Pa if he did not think she had a nice figure, etc." That the popular Madame Bodisco had clearly visible charms could not be denied. The low-cut bodice of her dress left little to the imagination. But the ground rules of polite society in 1842 did not include drunken references to a lady's endowment. This was the stuff of duels.[56]

These social activities were of little importance when compared with the much anticipated moment on the evening of January 20, 1842, when Julia and her parents were first invited to the White House to meet President John Tyler. Margaret, unhappily, had a severe cold that night and was forced to remain in her chambers. "The President's break with the Whigs," Julia recalled, "had been the occasion of unprecedented political excitement, and his name was on all lips." She was curious to meet the controversial Chief Executive. Young Waldron obligingly escorted the family to the President's reception.

As usual, the First Lady, Letitia Christian Tyler, made no appearance downstairs that Thursday evening. Half-paralyzed by a stroke three years earlier, she took no part in the social life of her husband's administration. Instead, the guests crowding into the White House were greeted by the President and his daughter-in-law, Priscilla Cooper Tyler, who acted as the Chief Executive's official hostess. Julia's formal introduction to the politically harassed tenth President of the United States was performed by Congressman Fernando Wood. For the young lady of East Hampton it was a personal triumph. So cordially was she greeted by John Tyler, so gracious and effusive were his "thousand compliments," that those standing nearby "looked and listened in perfect amazement." Years later when she recalled that most important moment in her life Julia still remembered in Tyler's deportment an "urbanity" so pronounced "we could not help commenting, after we left the room, upon the silvery sweetness of his voice... the incomparable grace of his bearing, and the elegant ease of his conversation." [57]

John Tyler may not have been America's most successful President, but the courtly Virginian was certainly one of America's most gracious and socially engaging Chief Executives. So polite and courteous was he with strangers, so warm and genuine was he in his greeting and in his concern for the comfort and well-being of his guests, that few who met him escaped his personal magnetism. No suggestion of his many personal trials, political disappointments, and private worries, family or financial, ever publicly escaped his lips. Surrounded by the inadequate lights, shabby furniture, unpainted walls, and grimy appointments of the President's Mansion, Tyler gave off a personal charm, dignity and regality that transformed his surroundings.

Julia's brief visit to Washington in January–February 1842 ended much too quickly to suit her. When, in early March, the Gardiners were again at their East Hampton home the boredom of that pleasant hamlet seemed all the more oppressive after the wonders of Europe and the delights of the capital. Julia was soon plunged once more into the depression of isolation. Gathering the local gossip for David Lyon and Alexander scarcely compared with the excitement of the previous eighteen months—even when the gossip concerned the erratic behavior of her colorful cousin, John Griswold Gardiner, ninth proprietor of Gardiners Island.

John was the black sheep of the family. In March 1842 he went berserk while engaged in what Julia termed a "regular frolic" and before he was finally locked up in the East Hampton jail he had wrecked a farmer's kitchen in Sag Harbor, disturbed the peace in Montauk, created a drunken scene in Acabonack, and fired his shotgun at a cornhusker named Bennet in the grain barn on Gardiners Island. Bennet escaped death only by lunging at the proprietor and spoiling his aim. Whereupon crazy John calmly reloaded and was again taking aim at his antagonist when Henry Davis, a Negro agricultural laborer on the Island, seized the gun. "Amid such a number of white companions," remarked Julia, "the intended victim owed his life at last to a negro—I think abolition a good cause." Whether the "Lord of the Isle" was under the influence of whiskey or opium or both during his two-day spree, the sisters could not ascertain. They were fairly certain he was under the influence of something. The subsequent trial of John for assault with intent to kill occupied the summer months and stimulated conversation for a time in the otherwise torpid town. Gardiner was eventually fined $33 for disturbing the peace, a judgment the proprietor himself considered pretty lenient for "a man who has been a drunkard all his life." [58]

Even with John Griswold Gardiner to liven things up occasionally, life in East Hampton was incredibly dull. The usual Fourth of July celebration was called off in 1842 when the eligible toastmasters quarreled over whether wine should be used to drink the toasts at the dinner. The drys won the argument and local patriotism received a body blow. When a gang of boys broke into the general store, smashed the windows, and hurled rotten eggs at the merchandise, the incident, big news in East Hampton, interested the twenty-two-year-old Julia not at all. It was a far cut below her presentation at the court of Louis Philippe and her discussion of the poets with Robert Tyler in Washington. "We have been stationary nearly five months," she complained to Alexander in July. "Dear me! Sometimes I feel dolefully *ennuyée.*" Few days passed that the sisters did not frantically write their brothers in New York to send them the news of the fashionable set in the city or demand of them that they execute some trifling purchasing commission. While Julia was certain that the "innocent pleasures of a country life" were adequate for "the *evening* of life," the point was that she was still young. "We *can* make our lives sublime," she insisted to Alexander, with more hope than conviction. There was not much sublimity in East Hampton.[59]

During the early summer months of 1842 Julia began agitating for a trip to Saratoga Springs or Newport. She had heard there was a "considerable company" at both spas. When this effort to escape East Hampton failed, she then urged her father to lease or purchase a town house in New York City. The sharp sag in the real estate market in New York not only made this suggestion an economical one, but it had the further advantage of putting David Gardiner's increasingly eligible daughters where the boys were. For these reasons he began to consider the idea seriously. Meanwhile Julia pleaded for a return to Washington when Congress convened again in December 1842. So piteous were her entreaties with her father that he could scarcely resist them. By November the parental promise of another trip to the capital had been reluctantly given, although the harassed senator confessed to Alexander that "were it not to gratify your sisters I must confess I should prefer a more quiet winter." Alexander sided with Julia in the matter, assuring his father that he would "derive more pleasure from a winter in Washington than you seem to anticipate." [60]

Her spirits raised considerably by the combined prospects of moving into town and returning to Washington in the winter, Julia's cup of joy very nearly overflowed when she learned that the Gardiners had been conspicuously included in Moses Y. Beach's little volume, *Wealth and Pedigree of the Wealthy Citizens of New York City*. First published in the summer of 1842, the book set out "to define the true position of sundry individuals who are flourishing under false colors. . . . In a country where *money*, and not *title*, is the standard by which merit is appreciated, it is desirable to adjust the standard with as much exactitude as possible. . . ." Beach included only the names of families with resources in excess of $100,000. The accuracy of some of his figures was questionable, but at least he provided a rough guide to the tricky New York marriage market. For this invaluable service the Gardiners were grateful.[61]

The entry under the name of David Gardiner was brief and to the point: "$150,000. To the ancestors of this distinguished family belonged Gardiners Island, Suffolk Co., L.I. One was called 'Lord Gardiner,' by some of his poor tenantry." Julia's erratic cousin, John Griswold Gardiner, the ninth proprietor of Gardiners Island, was rated at $100,000, although at the very moment of his triumph, if triumph it was, he was drunkenly celebrating the birthday of his horse by riding the animal into his mother's parlor where the astonished lady sat sewing. It was just another "high frolic," said Julia, similar to the spree that had put the latter-day Caligula in the East Hampton jail two months earlier.[62]

Julia could hardly wait to get her hands on Beach's volume. She learned of its existence from her Uncle Samuel while attending the funeral of her Uncle Nathaniel's wife, Elizabeth, at East Hampton in June 1842. The news livened up an otherwise dreary afternoon. She was elated to hear that editor Beach considered the Gardiners to be "a very respectable family who used to be styled Lords by their poor tenants." Her father, no less eager to see the book, ordered son David Lyon in New York to procure and send a copy "by the first opportunity by water." The little volume was a gold mine of information and Julia spent many pleasant hours researching the financial situations of her New York friends and acquaintances. She learned, for example, that the families of her friends Mary Conger and Mary Corse weighed in at $200,000 and $250,000, respectively; and that the family of Catherine Hedges was rated at $200,000. Even the unattractive and obnoxious young Jacob LeRoy who would chase after Margaret in Washington in 1843 could look forward to a $300,000 inheritance. None of this information proved very valuable to the Gardiner sisters in the long run. Julia married a man who could never have aspired to the Beach register, and Margaret married one who had not two dimes to rub together.[63]

The only damper on Julia's spirits as she anticipated a brighter social future came in the knowledge that her brother Alexander had renounced the Whig Party and voted for the Democrats in the November 1842 elections in New York City. A trip to depression-ridden Norwich, Connecticut, in June 1842 had shown him that a stone's throw from closed mills and breadlines were all the evidences of the conspicuous consumption in which the wealthy indulged. Perhaps this sight influenced his sudden conversion. It would be encouraging to think so. More likely, Alexander Gardiner became a Democrat in 1842 for pragmatic reasons. As a struggling young lawyer in New York City he sorely needed clients and contacts. To further his career in the law he had decided to dabble in local politics at the ward level and the best way to do this was through Tammany Hall. Tammany was basically anti-Van Buren in 1842, locked as it was in bitter patronage struggles with the Little Magician's Albany Regency. Within its tattered folds were also members of the old Workingmen's Party of the middle 1830s. These white proletarians, native-born and immigrant, feared the abolition of slavery. They viewed the economic implications of abolition on the white labor market of New York City with undisguised horror. Alexander had no difficulty adjusting to the ideological orientation of Tammany Hall on the Negro question. The Hall was also controlled by pragmatists who had small respect for either Martin Van Buren or liberal Jacksonian democracy. These men were Conservative Democrats. They were corrupt, but they could deliver the street vote and win local elections. The town's self-satisfied Whigs generally could not. From Alexander's standpoint it was as simple as that.

Still, Margaret voiced the collective Gardiner opinion of Alexander's heresy when she told her brother that she "could scarce reconcile myself to the idea of your voting the Democratic ticket. At any earlier period it would certainly have overthrown any resolutions I *might* have formed of conferring a Dukedom upon you. You might better not have voted at all, I think; and so does Pa, but for another reason— you would then escape your indefatigable *military* friend, Mr. Jackson." Margaret had missed the point. Her brother had not become a Jackson Democrat. And to her irrelevant criticism Alexander replied wearily that Tammany's "triumphant success" in the election had reinforced him in the rightness of his decision. There was no point in going into it further.[64]

In choosing the Democratic Party in 1842 Alexander Gardiner gained one distinction to which no one else in the immediate family could aspire. He was a Democrat *before* his sister's courtship by John Tyler began. He was in Tyler's party before Julia was in Tyler's family. And John Tyler in 1842 needed all the help he could command.

3

JOHN TYLER:
HIS FATHER'S SON, 1790–1820

For myself, I cannot and will not yield one inch of the ground.
—JOHN TYLER, 1820

Few American Presidents have left a record of their childhood so scanty as that of John Tyler. Much of what has survived—the anecdotes and the distant recollections—is tinged with myth and fantasy. It is known that the tenth President was born the second of three sons (there were five daughters) to John and Mary Armistead Tyler on March 29, 1790, at Greenway, a twelve-hundred-acre family estate on the James River in Charles City County, Virginia. Beyond that, little can be said about John Tyler until he entered the preparatory division of William and Mary College in 1802. As a youth he was very slight in build; his long, thin patrician face was dominated by the high cheekbones and the prominent Roman nose he would later joke about —the "Tyler nose," Julia called it. His lips were thin and tight, his dark brown hair was silken. Physically, he was never robust. He was always much too thin and throughout his life he was highly susceptible to colds, to severe gastric upsets, and to frequent attacks of diarrhea. As a child and young man he was serious-looking, inclined to moodiness. When he was seven, in April 1797, his mother died of a paralytic stroke. He thus grew to adulthood without the comforting guidance of a woman.

Judge John Tyler raised young John to manhood and by all surviving accounts he did an excellent job of it. The future President would always recall with tenderness a picture of the old Judge as he sat on the front lawn of Greenway playing his violin for the plantation youngsters or telling them tall stories of the great revolution against

Britain. He was a great favorite of the local small fry, white and Negro. Young John inherited his father's love of music and he learned to "fiddle," as he called it, at an early age. It was a relaxing hobby to which he returned after the frustrating White House years. It is doubtful, however, as one story has it, that he played the instrument so movingly at the age of ten that mice emerged from the baseboard to dance to his tunes.

Given the paucity of details of Tyler's childhood it is not surprising that the biographical gap has been filled with the standard motifs of a precocious and foreordained youth which Americans demand of their Presidents—myths assiduously propagated by eager campaign biographers at election time. Hence if John Tyler cannot in all honesty be placed in a log cabin at birth (there were rude log cabins at Greenway plantation but they were inhabited by Judge Tyler's forty slaves), his biographers have linked him with the Child-of-Destiny motif and with the David-and-Goliath theme.

The first of these harmless little stories has his mother holding him in her arms on a bright moonlit night at Greenway in 1791. The baby caught sight of the shining orb through the branches of an old willow tree, eagerly stretched his chubby arms heavenward, and cried bitterly for the moon. At this point, according to the legend, the mother quietly whispered, "This child is destined to be a President of the United States, his wishes fly so high."

The second tale pits young John Tyler against the local Goliath symbol, Mr. McMurdo, a cruel Scottish schoolmaster who held forth, birch in hand, at the little school on the River Road near Greenway. According to this legend, the tyranny of the rod finally became so oppressive and unjust that John led a schoolboy revolt which resulted in the physical overpowering and manacling of the giant, much to the satisfaction of his father, who shouted *"Sic semper tyrannis!"* on learning of the classroom revolution. Tyler did later recall that it was a wonder McMurdo "did not whip all the sense out of his scholars," but he never verified the specific fact of the revolt or mentioned his alleged role in it.

Nevertheless, the McMurdo yarn probably has a larger grain of truth in it than one which pictures Vice-President Tyler down on his hands and knees at sunrise one morning in April 1841 playing marbles with his sons when sweaty couriers from Washington ride up to inform him that General Harrison has died and that he has become the President of the United States. This, of course, is the homey-touch theme which is also required of American Presidents by their constituents, and it would be somewhat more believable in this instance were it not known that in 1841 two of Tyler's sons were married men in their twenties and only the third, Tazewell, was at the marble-playing age.[1]

Only in 1802 does John Tyler emerge from the shadows of mythology. In that year he traveled from Greenway to Williamsburg to enter the secondary division of the College of William and Mary. The twelve-year-old boy boarded in town with his brother-in-law, Judge James Semple. In 1806 his name first appeared on the roll of the collegiate students, although it is probable he began college-level studies a year earlier. The college curriculum at the time was a narrow one—classical languages and English literature predominating—but in his undergraduate years Tyler was also introduced to history and political economy. The text used in the economics course was Adam Smith's recently published *Wealth of Nations,* and Tyler seems to have committed its concepts and leading arguments to memory. His subsequent speeches on the tariff and free trade were drawn almost verbatim from this influential work. Indeed, Smith's persuasive arguments for government noninterference in the sphere of individual enterprise neatly complemented emerging states' rights arguments in the field of economic policy, and Tyler was quick to enlist them in the South's struggle against any and all latitudinal constructions of the Constitution on tariff and trade questions.[2]

By all reports Tyler's academic career at William and Mary was a brilliant one, and his subsequent devotion to his alma mater would gladden the heart of any present-day alumni secretary. In 1807, at the age of seventeen, he was graduated from the little college he loved so much. He returned to Charles City and began the study of law, first under his father's direction, then under that of his cousin, Chancellor Samuel Tyler. Finally, when his father became governor in 1809, he studied in the Richmond office of the brilliant Edmund Randolph, former United States Attorney General in the Washington administration. His work with Randolph he remembered as the least satisfactory. He recoiled with distaste from the Federalist principles to which Randolph exposed him, principles which undercut the states' rights teachings of his father and his William and Mary professors. Randolph's loose construction of the Constitution and his advocacy of a strong central government pained Tyler greatly. "He proposed a supreme national government," Tyler recalled in horror, "with a supreme executive, a supreme legislature, and a supreme judiciary, and a power in Congress to veto state laws." It was shocking.[3]

The most important single fact that can be derived from John Tyler's formative years is that he absorbed *in toto* the political, social, and economic views of his distinguished father, John Tyler, Sr., Revolutionary War patriot, governor of Virginia (1809–1811), and judge of the United States Circuit Court. Judge Tyler was a congenital rebel and individualist, an intellectual child of the French Enlightenment, devoted in person, idea, and political loyalty to his friend and contemporary, Thomas Jefferson. These qualities and attitudes he passed undiluted to his son, and the William and Mary faculty saw that they stuck.

Born in 1746, Judge Tyler was a direct descendant of Henry Tyler, first of the family in America, who had arrived in Williamsburg from England in 1653. The English background of Henry Tyler is as obscure as the origin of Lion Gardiner. Lyon G. Tyler, the family biographer, once argued that Henry Tyler was an aristocratic Cavalier in flight from Puritan despotism, and that the whole Tyler clan was directly descended from the famous Wat Tyler, the fourteenth-century revolutionist against the tyranny of Richard II. To further this dubious connection Judge Tyler named one of his sons Wat. But like the wished-for Gardiner alliance with Robert Fitzwalter and the Barons of Runnymede, the claim can be established neither historically nor genealogically. It is probably just as well. Wat Tyler had a conception of private property and social equality scarcely acceptable to his slaveowning descendants on the Tidewater Virginia plantations. He was, in truth, an egalitarian socialist. Nevertheless, John Tyler himself accepted the alleged family connection with Wat the Red and gloried in it, defending its legitimacy against all doubters. "I am proud of Wat Tyler and cannot let him go," he once confessed. So it passed into the family tradition.[4]

More solidly based in historical certainty than the Wat Tyler connection is the Revolutionary career of Judge John Tyler. Not only did he serve with distinction in the Virginia legislature during the unpleasantness with the Redcoats, risking his life and his property in the great cause throughout its darkest and most discouraging days, he also emerged from the contest as one of the Old Dominion's leading voices for a strengthening of the wartime Articles of Confederation. As a member of the Virginia House of Delegates in 1785–1786, the Judge helped draft the resolutions appointing Virginia's delegates to the famous Annapolis Convention. This meeting, a preliminary to the Constitutional Convention in Philadelphia in 1787, was called to consider the propriety of investing the Confederation Congress with enough additional power to regulate and promote interstate commerce. This limited function by a weak central authority Judge Tyler favored. He did not support the corollary idea that commerce regulation should expand into or take on the form of a whole new constitutional and federative political system. "I wished Congress to have the regulation of trade," he recalled in stunned disbelief at what eventually happened in Philadelphia in 1787–1788, "but it never entered my head that we should quit liberty and throw ourselves into the hands of an energetic government. When I consider the Constitution in all its parts, I cannot but dread its operation. It contains a variety of powers too dangerous to be vested in any set of men whatsoever." [5]

To Judge Tyler, the Constitution of the United States was little less than the beginning of tyranny in America, and as a member of Virginia's 1788 convention to consider the new document he worked vigorously, albeit unsuccessfully, to block its ratification. "Little did I think that matters would come to this when we separated from the mother country," he told the convention sadly. Clearly, he missed the point that the Constitution was actually a very conservative document. While under its subsequently adopted Bill of Rights (which Judge Tyler strongly favored) it guaranteed certain individual liberties to all white male adults, it then effectively removed real power from the hands of these same people with a system of political filters and a provision permitting the states themselves to determine the conditions of suffrage. A complicated arrangement of checks and balances within the federal authority was skillfully designed to render the government virtually impervious to pressures and manipulations by any man, special-interest group, state, or section. Its theory of residual state power and its complex amending clause also contributed to its conservative stability. In its final form it was a brilliantly contrived monument to the *status quo* that over the years would demand the most elastic judicial interpretation to make it function at all. Indeed, it would ultimately require the bold decisions of Chief Justice John Marshall and the near-revolutionary agitations of Andrew Jackson's unwashed multitudes to blast it into the evolution that gave it life and preserved it. At the moment of its birth, however, the Constitution of the United States was hardly a radical, a dangerous, or even a democratic document.

The Tylers, father and son, were determined to keep it that way. Initially they were not fearful of the rise of the masses; they feared the use of the federal machinery by one sector of the propertied class to exercise a tyranny over the other—the Northern merchants over the Southern planters. Only by maintaining the power of the individual states over their own internal affairs could the nationalistic implications of the document, weak as these were, be cribbed and the prerogatives of the Virginia planter and his feudal way of life be preserved. This in essence was what Judge Tyler and John Tyler meant when they invoked "states' rights" as the key to "individual liberty." It was not a theoretical abstraction. Instead, the states' rights idea in the South was the main foundation of a society dominated by slaveowning white men of property. The alternative was a powerful central government run by and for the merchant classes—or those with no property at all. To prevent the capture, consolidation, and manipulation of the machinery of the federal government by such untrustworthy people, the Constitution had to remain the static document it was. Any interpretation that rendered it more democratic, more responsive to the popular will, more relevant to the revolutionary theory of the equality of men, or more powerful and efficient in its practical operation in relation to the states had to be opposed with all the vigor of Horatio at the bridge. For this reason John Tyler, like his father before him, would spend the greater part of a political lifetime demanding a starkly literal interpretation of the written words of the conservative document, voicing these demands with all the fervor of a Bible Belt Fundamentalist elucidating the Book of Exodus to a backwoods congregation. In sum, he insisted that the rules of the game not be changed while the game was in progress. The original rules would do nicely.

Given the gradual broadening of white male suffrage in the 1820s–1830s under the impact of Jacksonian democracy, strict construction also seemed the only alternative to the potential political tyranny of a Northern and Western majority over the "peculiar institution" of human slavery. Thus John Tyler, tutored at his father's knee, would view nationalistic phrases in the Constitution like "We the people of the United States" and "the *general* welfare" as semantic booby traps requiring constant defusing and disarming in the interest of states' rights and the maintenance of slavery as a legal form of private property. He consistently eulogized the "primitive simplicity" of the document, noting frequently that he was "a republican after the strictest sect," a true keeper of the original flame.[6]

As a young man John Tyler was less certain of his relationship to the slave institution. In general, he followed his father in accepting the fact of slavery. And, like his father, he was a slaveowner all his life. Nevertheless, he opposed a continuation of the African slave trade. As a United States senator in 1832 he fought for legislation to end the actual buying and selling of human beings within the shadow of the Capitol. The sight of this made him physically ill. He never attended a slave auction. As President he signed in 1842 the treaty with Britain which obligated the United States to maintain naval units on the African coast to enforce the nation's anti-slave-trade laws.

At the same time he never advocated or supported an effective program of slavery abolition; nor would he ever acknowledge the right or duty of the federal government to interfere in the brutalizing institution at the state, local, or personal level. He never manumitted any of his own slaves. Instead, he found comfort of sorts supporting the notion of "gradual abolition" in Virginia though the impractical African Colonization scheme. He also advocated a diffusion or "bleeding" of the Old Dominion slave population into and throughout the territories—a form of abolition by anemia. In moments of candor he admitted that the removal of Negroes to Liberia was little more than a utopian solution to slavery, "a dream of philanthropy, visiting men's pillows in their sleep, to cheat them on their waking." Since both "solutions" to the problem were impractical, and gradual to the point of being glacial, Tyler in effect upheld the slavery institution throughout his life. Still, he wished sincerely that slavery would just go away somehow, quietly and without fuss. He hoped for this in spite of the fact that his own economic welfare and that of his large family became inexorably linked with the slave-labor system after his retirement from the White House to Sherwood Forest in 1845.

At Sherwood Forest he conducted a slavery operation that was humanitarian, gentle, and paternalistic. There were no whips, lashes, split families, or runaways. On Sherwood Forest plantation the Negroes *did* sing and dance and play their banjos and clack their bones. But the realization that he was a kind master brought John Tyler no closer to a moral evaluation of the system. He simply borrowed Judge Tyler's view that slavery had been fastened on the United States by the colonial policy of Great Britain. This conveniently identified the embarrassing institution with a hated foreign symbol and glossed over his moral confusion on the issue. It was a weak rationalization, but it was an important contributing factor to the intense Anglophobia he carried with him through life. As late as 1851, on a visit to Niagara Falls, John Tyler would refuse so much as to set foot on British soil.[7]

The slavery problem was still a small black cloud on a distant horizon in 1811 when Tyler attained his majority and began the practice of law in Charles City County. That year he was also elected to the Charles City seat in the Virginia House of Delegates. As a lawyer and a state legislator he exhibited all the characteristics of a young man in a hurry. He loved the law, which he regarded as the "high road to fame," and he quickly became a brilliant courtroom performer. At the outset of his legal career he took many near-hopeless criminal cases because they gave him an opportunity to develop and polish that feeling for the grandiloquent which ultimately placed him in the very first rank of American orators. At his best, Tyler was the rhetorical equal of Webster, Clay, Benton, and Calhoun in his ability to move and manipulate an audience. This mastery of the spoken word he first learned in the Charles City courthouse. As a young lawyer he discovered that the way to a juror's heart was often not through the law but through the emotions. Like the clergyman who pounds the pulpit harder as his theology becomes weaker, Tyler developed a forensic style that permitted him to play on the emotions of jurors as though they were strings of his violin. Jefferson Davis once said that "as an extemporaneous speaker, I regard [Tyler] as the most felicitous among the orators I have known."[8]

As a tyro legislator young Tyler made an instant impact in the House of Delegates in 1811. The point at stake was the national-bank question, the issue on which John Tyler rode into national prominence in the 1830s and the one that would ultimately break the back of his Presidency in 1841. In 1791 the first Bank of the United States had been chartered by Congress for a twenty-year period. The Bank was a privately owned and operated institution (in which the federal government held only 20 per cent of the stock) designed to act as a fiscal agent for the government. It was also a depository for government funds, and it was further empowered to issue currency secured by government deposits and by its own capital resources. Alexander Hamilton and other Federalist economists of the period hoped that this currency would provide the new nation a much-needed, stable, and standardized medium of exchange. The charter also permitted the establishment of branch banks in the principal commercial cities of the several states. It was, then, essentially a private corporation with monopolistic power to do the banking business of the federal government throughout the states. As such it had no specific constitutionality, and the incorporation bill passed the Congress in a welter of sectional controversy, the South vigorously in opposition. For this reason President Washington hesitated signing the measure.

Soliciting the written opinions of his Cabinet members on the constitutionality of the Bank, the President received from Jefferson the positive view that the Constitution nowhere empowered the Congress to incorporate a bank. Alexander Hamilton, on the other hand, in a brilliant and seminal state paper, set forth the doctrine of "implied powers," arguing that the constitutional power of Congress to collect taxes and regulate trade also *implied* the constitutionality of a bank in which to deposit the tax and tariff receipts. As he put it (firing the shot which thenceforth in American history separated the Hamiltonian "loose constructionists" from the Jeffersonian "strict constructionists"), "If the *end* be clearly comprehended within any of the specified powers, and if the measure have an obvious relation to that *end,* and is not forbidden by any particular provision of the Constitution, it may safely be deemed to come within the compass of the national authority." Washington accepted this interpretation, rejected Jefferson's protests, and signed the controversial bill into law.[9]

It was the possibility of just such semantic taffy-pulling within the framework of the Constitution that Judge Tyler had protested in 1788. When the Bank charter came up in Congress for renewal in 1811, both the Judge and his son carefully watched Virginia's reaction to the menace from Washington. The issue was thoroughly debated in the Virginia legislature during the 1810–1811 session, the year before young Tyler arrived on the scene. At that time the legislature had overwhelmingly voted to "instruct" Virginia's United States senators, William B. Giles and Richard Brent, to work against and vote against the renewal of the Bank charter when it came before the Senate. Both senators had, however, disobeyed these instructions from Richmond, Brent outright and Giles partially.

Although the Bank renewal bill was killed in the Senate in February 1811, forcing the institution temporarily out of existence, young Tyler decided that Virginia's erring senators should be signally punished. Not only was he convinced of the absolute unconstitutionality of a national bank, but he was also angry that the senators the legislature had elected and sent to Washington had defied the authority of that legislature and hence the authority of the "sovereign" state of Virginia. Thus when he reached the House of Delegates late in 1811 Tyler introduced three spot resolutions, "without conference or consultation with any human being," censuring Giles and Brent for their failure to obey the specific instructions of the legislature on the Bank question. This action, as precocious as it was brash, drew immediate attention to the ambitious young man from Charles City. The Tyler motions were referred to a select committee. From this ordeal they emerged in watered-down form, but the basic idea asserting the right of the legislature to instruct its United States senators survived intact, and the Tyler resolutions were passed by the House of Delegates 97 to 20. For the new member from Charles City it was a heady victory.[10]

His legal and political careers signally commenced, John Tyler felt prepared to take a wife. He had thought the matter through carefully. "The very moment a man can say to himself, 'if I die tomorrow, my wife will be independent,' he is fully authorized to obey the impulse of affection," he maintained. Convinced that he was ready for the step, he obeyed his own impulse, and on March 29, 1813, his twenty-third birthday, he married Letitia Christian of Cedar Grove plantation in New Kent County. She was the daughter of Robert Christian, and from a material standpoint the match was an advantageous one for the groom, even though he had inherited part of the Greenway estate from his recently deceased father and now had property and slaves of his own. The Christians were a numerous, politically prominent, and wealthy tribe, and when the bride's parents died soon after the wedding, Letitia came into a sizable competence. In the single surviving love letter Tyler wrote her before their marriage, dated December 1812, he made the point that while his own financial situation was clearly not equal to hers, that fact alone made him realize that she truly loved him:

You express some degree of astonishment, my L., at an observation I once made to you, "that I would not have been willingly wealthy at the time I addressed you." Suffer me to repeat it. If I had been wealthy, the idea of your being actuated by prudential considerations in accepting my suit, would have eternally tortured me. But I exposed to you frankly and unblushingly my situation in life—my hopes and my fears, my prospects and my dependencies—and you nobly responded. To ensure to you happiness is now my only object, and whether I float or sink in the stream of fortune, you may be assured of this, that I shall never cease to love you.[11]

There is no evidence that the gentle Letitia thought Tyler himself might have been "actuated by prudential considerations." She was a quiet and introverted girl, more beautiful in facial features than Julia Gardiner. Socially reserved in manner, domestic in her interests, she was unconcerned with the subtle economics of marriage alliances within the planter aristocracy. She was in love with the young lawyer and legislator from Greenway, and she wanted him as he was. Their courtship was a calm, undemonstrative affair. Tyler confessed that until three weeks before the wedding he had not even dared kiss Letitia's hand, "so perfectly reserved and modest" was she. A few sonnets addressed to her, a few books lent and discussed, and they were married. Not surprisingly, Tyler regarded the approaching ceremony with a certain impassivity. Six days before the wedding he wrote his friend Henry Curtis, "I had really calculated on experiencing a tremor on the near approach of the day; but I believe that I am so much of the *old man* already as to feel less dismay at a change of situation than the greater part of those of my age." [12]

The Tyler–Christian marriage was a tranquil relationship throughout. It gave off none of the sparks of Tyler's later marriage to Julia Gardiner. It was, however, a happy marriage, and it remained so for twenty-nine years. Letitia Christian Tyler was a lovely woman. Every surviving account of her, every recollection, emphasizes her domestic virtues, her sweetness of manner, her devout religious life, and her selflessness. Her seven children were devoted to her. Still, Letitia Tyler never really emerges from the mists of history, perhaps because none of her own letters survived. She preferred to remain wholly in the background of Tyler's public career as he moved steadily from the House of Delegates upward through the House of Representatives, the governorship of Virginia, the United States Senate, and into the White House. She had no known political interests and no desire to live in Washington. So wretched were living accommodations in the mudhole that was the capital, and so comfortable did she make her successive homes at Woodburn, Greenway, Gloucester, and Williamsburg that she accompanied her husband to Washington only once before his elevation to the Presidency. This was in the winter of 1828–1829. During this brief exposure in the capital she was remarked upon for her "beauty of person and eloquence of manner." On only one occasion did she visit the fashionable watering places of the North, preferring instead, when she left home at all, the various Virginia springs. She knitted and stitched and gardened (she loved flowers), supervised her household slaves with humanity and kindness, raised her seven children, and minded her own business. Hers was a quiet and useful life, filled with domestic interests. She remained, by choice, well removed from the limelight of her husband's political career.[13]

After Letitia was semi-invalided by a paralytic stroke in 1839 she lived out her few remaining years in the seclusion of her bedchamber, demanding no special attention, creating no special problem. When Priscilla Cooper Tyler, wife of Letitia's oldest son Robert, first met her new mother-in-law in 1839 she noted that Letitia, then forty-seven,

...must have been very beautiful in her youth, for she is still beautiful now in her declining years and wretched health. Her skin is as smooth and soft as a baby's; she has sweet, loving black eyes, and her features are delicately moulded; besides this, her feet and hands are perfect; and she is gentle and graceful in her movements, with a most peculiar air of native refinement about everything she says and does. She is the most entirely unselfish person you can imagine. I do not believe she ever thinks of herself. Her whole thought and affections are wrapped up in her husband and children.... The room in the main dwelling furtherest removed and most retired is "the chamber," as the bedroom of the mistress of the house is always called in Virginia ...here Mother with a smile of welcome on her sweet, calm face, is always found seated on her large arm-chair with a small stand by her side, which holds her Bible and her prayer-book—the only books she ever reads now— with her knitting usually in her hands, always ready to sympathize with me in any little homesickness which may disturb me.... Notwithstanding her very delicate health, Mother attends to and regulates all the household affairs, and all so quietly that you can't tell when she does it. All the clothes for the children, and for the servants, are cut out under her immediate eye, and all the sewing is personally superintended by her. All the cake, jellies, custards, and we indulge largely in them, emanate from her, yet you see no confusion, hear no bustle, but only meet the agreeable result.

When she was dying in the White House in September 1842, her last act was to take from a bedside vase a damask rose. She was still holding it in her hand when she was found dead. She died as she had lived, without fuss or ostentation, always in the shadow of John Tyler's ambition.[14]

No sooner had Tyler settled with his bride at Mons-Sacer, a beautiful five-hundred-acre section of the Greenway estate he had inherited from his father, than he was called to arms against the British. Once again the Redcoats were marching, and during the 1812 session of the House of Delegates the young legislator vigorously upheld the war measures of the federal and state governments against the English. Every resolution designed to throw Virginia's military and economic weight effectively onto the balance received Tyler's enthusiastic support. He was convinced that Britain's policy of impressment and search on the high seas, and her interference with American shipping, were the real causes of the War of 1812. That the United States had intervened in the larger European war on the side of the Napoleonic military dictatorship; that the desire of the "War Hawks" for territorial expansion at the expense of British Canada and Spanish

Florida might have been a fundamental reason for the conflict; or that British impressment of American seamen had been surrendered in practice if not in principle well before 1812 were thoughts that concerned Tyler not at all. He wanted war. Judge Tyler wanted war. Indeed, the infirm Judge, lying on his deathbed at Greenway in January 1813, cursed the fates that would not permit him to "live long enough to see that proud English nation once more humbled by American arms." The father's hatred of the ubiquitous Redcoats was the son's hatred, and young Tyler undertook to discomfit the traditional enemy in every conceivable manner, legislatively and militarily.[15]

The War of 1812 was not a glorious passage in American arms. Tyler's own military experience was rather typical of the amateurish performance of American militia which led directly to the greatest military disaster ever sustained by the United States. In the summer of 1813, a British raiding party landed at Hampton, plundered the town, and for a time appeared poised and ready to march up the James River to Richmond. The Virginia legislature had adjourned for the summer and Tyler was home in Charles City with his bride of four months. The British threat at Hampton fired his patriotism. He immediately joined a local militia company, the Charles City Rifles, raised for the defense of the state capital and its river approaches. In this raw and disorganized little unit Tyler was commissioned Captain, and he set to work to produce something in the ranks resembling military discipline. Although wholly ignorant of the military arts, he improvised a simple system of drill which the unskilled farmers were able to master. Thus when the Charles City Rifles were attached to the Fifty-Second Regiment of the Virginia Militia and ordered to Williamsburg they managed, thanks to Captain Tyler, to get there in some sort of order. They were quartered upstairs in the William and Mary College building, there to await the approach of the enemy. One night when all were asleep a rumor was broadcast that British forces had suddenly entered the town. Panic struck Captain Tyler's men. In their eagerness to quit the dark building the entire group, officers and men, tumbled head over heels down a long flight of stairs and landed in a struggling heap at the bottom. Following this self-inflicted rout, Tyler's intrepid band was attached to a new unit, hopefully titled the Second Elite Corps of Virginia, General Moses Greene commanding. This assignment lasted one month and was fortunately uneventful. The British raiding force soon withdrew from the Hampton area, and the Charles City patriots returned triumphantly to their farms. Their little war was over.[16]

Tyler had a good sense of humor and he often laughed over the ludicrousness of his brief military career. When his political enemies later referred to him derisively as "Captain Tyler" or "The Captain," he took no offense. He frequently joked about his "distinguished military services during the War of 1812," and he thought the whole experience made a delightful parlor story. Nevertheless, for his heroic contribution to the defense of Williamsburg he later qualified for a war bonus of one-hundred-sixty acres of land. He first considered a plot in St. John's County, Florida, but finally elected to take a quarter-section in what is now Sioux City, Iowa. In the difficult days of Reconstruction Julia was happy to have the monthly bonus of eight dollars later allotted by Congress to the widows of War of 1812 veterans. So Tyler's military service was not a waste of time and effort after all.[17]

The fact remained, however, that John Tyler had little feeling for the martial life. He distrusted the military mentality and he feared the appearance in American politics of an American Napoleon, a Man on Horseback. Men of destiny like General Andrew Jackson frightened him. He consistently opposed the creation of a standing army. Instead, he became a partisan of the infant United States Navy. This toothless force, mainly stationed abroad, was unlikely to overthrow the government and Constitution by force and violence. When it appeared in 1832 that two erstwhile military heroes, Andrew Jackson and Richard M. Johnson (the alleged slayer of Tecumseh), might run together on the Democratic ticket, Tyler remarked with discouragement that "the day is rapidly approaching when an *ounce of lead* will, in truth, be worth more than a pound of sense." [18]

In 1816, following the close of the unfortunate War of 1812, John Tyler was elected to the United States House of Representatives from the Richmond district, defeating his good friend Andrew Stevenson in a special election for the vacant seat. Since he and his opponent both ran on states' rights platforms, the campaign was little more than a popularity contest. Tyler's arrival in Washington in 1817 was not, of course, that of a raw freshman congressman from a frontier district. Member of a prominent Virginia family, son of a former governor, master of Woodburn, and husband to a daughter of the powerful Christian clan, Tyler moved swiftly and surely into the most exclusive social life of the capital. Within a few weeks he was dining at the "Seven Buildings," the makeshift home of James and Dolley Madison during the period of the rebuilding of the White House. Dinner at the Madisons' was a gastronomical experience that produced a grave shock to his system. The gracious Dolley took great pride in the table she set. Foods were sharply spiced in the French manner and the champagne always flowed. "They have good drink," he wrote Letitia, "champagne, etc., of which you know I am very fond, but I had much rather dine at home in our plain way ... what with their sauces and flum-flummeries, the victuals are intolerable." [19]

Equally intolerable were living conditions in the capital in those years. Cows and hogs wandered about the muddy lanes that passed for streets. Malaria-infested swamps were cheek by jowl with the few scattered private residences. Sidewalks were virtually nonexistent. The town was dirty, sprawling, and fever-ridden. In the summer it was a stinking oven. Even on the main thoroughfare, Pennsylvania Avenue, the street lamps were extinguished in 1818 because the District treasury had no funds for fuel. It was a city of mediocre boardinghouses and crowded hotels. Like most of the members of Congress, Tyler lived in a boardinghouse. At these places the food was dreadful. On one occasion he was served bad fish and was seriously ill for several days. Dolley Madison's fare may have been too "flum-flummery" for Tyler's taste but he did not get ptomaine poisoning at her table. At the local boardinghouses any meal could be a wild gamble with destiny. Washington was obviously no place for Letitia.[20]

Tyler's career in the House of Representatives during the years 1817 to 1820 was not distinguished. It remains of interest only because the freshman congressman from Charles City made clear the ideas he would support for most of the remainder of his life. In his maiden speech in the House he laid down the political principle which would govern his voting on important issues. He would never, he said, attempt to court popular favor. "Popularity, I have always thought, may aptly be compared to a coquette—the more you woo her, the more apt is she to elude your embrace." On the contrary, he would listen to no "mere buzz or popular clamour" from the voters of his district, only the "voice of a majority of the people, distinctly ascertained and plainly expressed." And he would close his ears to the majority voice if his constituents ever demanded that he violate the Constitution. "If instructions go to violate the Constitution,—they are not binding—and why? My constituents have no right to violate the Constitution themselves," he said, "and they have, consequently, no right to require me to do that which they themselves of right cannot." [21]

Like many of his planter-politician contemporaries in the South, especially those from "safe" districts like Charles City, Tyler developed no rapport with the masses of people. Nor did he attempt to develop a common touch. He shunned the people, avoided their importunities, and defied their proclaimed champions. "The barking of newspapers and the brawling of demagogues," he once said, "can never drive me from my course. If I am to go into [political] retirement, I will at least take care to do so with a pure and unsullied conscience." The warmest of men in his private life, he was incapable of projecting his warmth, good humor, and camaraderie to people of humble station; in this regard he was a great deal like Woodrow Wilson. A brilliant speaker in the presence of other statesmen or to groups of his social and intellectual peers, he quailed before the indiscriminate mass of men. He invariably preferred to address them in pamphlets or through the columns of newspapers rather than from the stump. During the campaign of 1840, forced to tour the West to carry the Whig message to the decisive coonskin-cap element, his speeches took on a nervous, unconvincing ring as though he were half-afraid some rough and hearty citizen would interrupt him, hand him a cup of hard cider, slap him on the back, and call him "good old Jack Tyler."[22]

After the emergence of Andrew Jackson onto the American political stage, Tyler came to fear the potential power of the people. Throughout the remainder of his long political life he worried lest the establishment of a "mere majority principle" in government wreck the country, subvert the Constitution, and reduce the social order to mobocracy. As he summed it up in 1851, in opposing a further broadening of the suffrage in the Old Dominion:

> One word more. The opinion is deeply seated with me that no government can last for any length of time, in consonance with public liberty, without checks and balances. Without them we rush into anarchy, or seek repose in the arms of monarchy. We can neither trust King *Numbers* or King *One* with unlimited power. Both play the despot. By the first, the minority is made the victim; by the last, the whole people.... The majority principle may lead to the establishment of a branch of the Legislature in which the full voice of the "political people" may be heard, while at the same time those having the deepest stake in the community [the property holders] ... may very well insist upon being protected by some wholesome check over the action of the mere numerical majority.

Resisting "King Numbers" and "King One," Tyler advocated instead the reign of King Few, a paternalistic oligarchy of influential property-owners. In his view, this was the only answer to the dictatorship of the One or the tyranny of the Many. Understanding the aspirations of the people was not John Tyler's strong suit. And his inability to do this caused contemporaries like Edmund Ruffin to conclude that "Mr. Tyler has always been a vain man." This charge misses the point. Vanity was not Tyler's problem. He was no more or less vain than any other of the ambitious men of his time. What appeared to be vanity was an ingrained shyness and discomfort in the presence of people with dirty fingernails. He had difficulty communicating with citizens who moved their lips when they read, if indeed they could read at all. He had never had any experience with these people, and he was too diffident to gain any. It is extremely doubtful that John Tyler could ever have won the White House in his own right after Andrew Jackson revolutionized and democratized the American image of the Chief Executive in 1828–1836. Tyler simply did not have the common touch, and no campaign biographer could create what was not there.[23]

What Tyler could do best, and what he did do with great energy during his first years in Washington, was to protect his stark version of the Constitution from the onslaught of the proponents of the so-called American System. This program, most prominently and consistently sponsored by Henry Clay during the decades after the War of 1812, linked a protective tariff with a national system of government-financed internal improvements and a national bank. Designed to bind the sprawling and expanding country together, to increase the domestic consumer market, subsidize infant home industries, stabilize the currency, and render the United States less dependent commercially and economically on a war-prone Europe, the American System sought to bring the Northern manufacturing interests into a political and economic alliance with the turnpike- and canal-conscious frontier West. From this arrangement the interests of the Tidewater and coastal South seemed virtually excluded.

It was a program which stemmed naturally and reactively from the humiliation of the War of 1812. Its proponents hoped that by bringing together the political and economic interests of two of the three great sections, the North and the West, something resembling a nation might be created out of a loose confederation of individual states. The lesson of American involvement in the Napoleonic Wars was plain enough. The United States could not exist in a world of competitive nation-states as a vague and contentious confederacy. Nothing discredited the original constitutional conception of a United States more swiftly and positively than the state jealousies, sectional squabbling, and lack of central economic and military direction that had characterized the prosecution of the war. A seagoing and agrarian people whose economic health turned on foreign trade either had to make themselves self-sufficient economically, and less dependent on foreign manufactures, or maintain larger standing armed forces and accept the necessity and inevitability of fighting for their trade on the high seas in each future European war. In this sense, the American System was a decision for and a step toward a national economic self-sufficiency bordering on economic and commercial isolation from Europe. It was a sensible concept at the time. In 1816–1836 the country needed a national bank, a moderate protective tariff, and a system of government-sponsored internal improvements. John Tyler and most Southern states' righters strenuously disagreed. To them, the constitutional price was too high to pay. The United States was a confederacy of states, not a nation, and it should stay that way. The alternative was tyranny.

At no project did young Congressman Tyler work harder than in his effort to bring the second Bank of the United States to defeat and ruin. Chartered by Congress in 1816 for a twenty-year period, the new national bank, like the old, was essentially a private corporation monopolistically empowered to do the government's banking business and provide a depository for its revenues. The need for it, or something like it, seemed obvious in 1816 when postwar inflation, currency dislocations, and the proliferation of unsound private banks (many of them little more than wildcat operations) threatened to bring the fiscal integrity of the nation to grief. By 1819, however, the new Bank was in deep trouble.

Mismanagement, corruption, and favoritism had stained its three years of operation and the resulting congressional investigation was perhaps inevitable. Demands in the South to repeal the Bank's charter altogether were voiced more loudly as a sharp break in grain prices in the European market in 1819 produced widespread depression and economic discontent in the United States. The search for a scapegoat began almost at once. The Bank was it.

Against the background of the depression an investigation of the Bank was ordered and launched, and John Tyler was appointed to the five-man congressional committee to carry it out. His specific task was to evaluate the operations of the Bank's branches in Washington and Richmond. This he did over the Christmas recess of 1818. The job was difficult and highly technical. "To have to wade through innumerable and huge folios in order to attain the objects of our enquiry; to have *money* calculations to make; and perplex one's self with all the seeming mysteries of bank terms, operations and exchanges," was a task so complex, he confessed, that "the strongest mind becomes relaxed and the imagination sickens and almost expires." Yet he stuck doggedly at it, and the experience made him an expert on banking matters in short order. He did not commence his investigatory labors entirely free of bias. To his brother-in-law Henry Curtis, who had married Tyler's sister Christiana in 1813, he wrote:

Our wise men flattered us into the adoption of the banking system under the idea that boundless wealth would result from the adoption.... Mountains were to sink beneath the charm, and distant climates, by means of canals, were to be locked in sweet embraces. Industry and enterprise were to be afforded new theaters of action, and the banks, like Midas, were to turn everything into gold. The dream, however, is over—instead of riches, penury walks the streets of our towns, and bankruptcy knocks at every man's door. They promised us blessings and have given us sorrows; for the substance they have given the shadow; for gold and silver, rags and paper. The delusion is over....[24]

The report the committee submitted to Congress in January 1819 was a model one. Well researched, well organized, and fair, it made several specific criticisms of the loose management of the Bank and pointed out several violations of the institution's charter. The most damaging of these was the accurate charge that the directors of the Bank had encouraged outright stock-jobbery.

In the subsequent debate on the floor of the House Tyler pressed home a slashing, wide-ranging attack on the institution. He argued that the chartering of a national bank was unconstitutional to begin with, that the institution was shot through with corruption and speculation (which was true), and that the violation of a single article of its charter should invalidate the whole charter. "If any one member of the human body offends," he said, "the whole body bears the punishment. If my finger violates the law, my body pays the penalty. If my hand commits murder, the hand is not lopped off, but the ligaments and arteries of the whole system are cut asunder." He blamed the deepening national depression on speculative stock-jobbing (this was an oversimplification of an extremely complex set of economic factors), and he called attention to the fact that "Gloom and despondence are in our cities. Usury stalks abroad and boasts of its illicit gains, while honesty and industry are covered with rags." All this he blamed on the second Bank of the United States. Specifically, he recommended abandoning the national-bank concept entirely. He suggested that government revenues be deposited instead in several "notoriously solvent" state banks. As to the possible political repercussions of his vigorous opposition to the Bank, his attitude was characteristic: "Whether I sink or swim on the tide of popular favor, is a matter to me of inferior consideration." [25]

It was an able speech which summed up states' rights objections to the national bank and offered a solution which was worth a try. Its weakness lay in its naïve analysis of the causes of the existing national depression and in Tyler's willingness, given proven violations of the Bank charter, to throw the baby out with the bath water. His was a narrow view, one rejected by the majority of the Congress.

The states' rights position on the Bank was legally undercut two months later when Chief Justice John Marshall, speaking for an unanimous Supreme Court, announced his opinion in *M'Culloch* v. *Maryland*. In this famous decision Marshall denied the right of Maryland to tax a branch of the second Bank of the United States—"the power to tax involves the power to destroy," he argued in one of the best-remembered sentences in American history. Specifically, he upheld the constitutionality of the Bank's 1816 charter. Drawing heavily on Hamilton's 1791 doctrine of implied powers, Marshall further stated: "Let the end be legitimate, let it be within the scope of the constitution, and all means which are appropriate, which are plainly adapted to that end, which are not prohibited, but consistent with the letter and spirit of the constitution, are constitutional." This view was supplemented by Marshall's broader contention that the powers of the government stemmed from the people themselves, not from the voluntary act of confederation of the several states. "The government of the Union," he maintained, "is emphatically, and truly, a government of the people. In form and in substance it emanates from them. Its powers are granted by them, and are to be exercised directly on them, and for their benefit." Needless to say, this was not what many of the Founding Fathers had had in mind three decades earlier.[26]

Re-elected to the House in 1819, Tyler returned to Washington to enlist for the duration in the South's cold war against the American System nationalists. First he lashed out at the tariff of 1820, which sought to raise existing import duties on textiles and metals by some

40 per cent, ostensibly to protect domestic manufacturers from ever-increasing European competition. This protection, argued Clay and others, would help struggling American manufacturers through the period of national depression. Tyler did not challenge the constitutionality of the tariff; that was beyond question. He did, however, challenge its wisdom, pointing out that the deepening depression was related to the outbreak of peace in Europe which had temporarily dried up markets supplied by the neutral Americans during the Napoleonic Wars. Tyler was sure that the European powers would soon be at each others' throats again and that to continue a policy of tariff protection would only result in sealing America off from what would soon be a thriving market once more:

> Who can tell how long the causes which now operate to our injury may continue to exist? All human affairs are constantly undergoing a change; and even while I am addressing you, new causes of dispute among the powers of Europe may be unfolding themselves. The speck which is now scarcely discernable on the horizon, the next moment may swell into a cloud, dark and portentous. Will you not, by this system, deny to us all benefits from any change which may occur? Yes, sir, you will have done so. Society lives on exchanges; exchange constitutes the very soul of commerce.... Can you expect that foreign nations will buy of you for any length of time, unless you buy of them? [27]

If this idea had a certain ghoulish quality, if frequent European war was indeed the key to the economic health of the American state, the morality of the notion did not disturb Tyler. In common with the free-trade viewpoint of most Southern agriculturalists, he argued that cotton and tobacco needed no tariff subsidy, that these commodities could find their way easily and profitably into the markets of the world without government protection or stimulation of any sort. Projected tariffs on sugar, coffee, molasses, and salt, on the other hand, represented a direct tax on those who must use these staples. "Who will have to pay it?" Tyler asked. "Inasmuch as the agricultural class is the most numerous, they will have to pay the greater portion of it. It operates as a direct tax on them." Southerners asked no tariff protection for their own commodities. Yet they were expected to shoulder the higher prices tariffs caused in order to stimulate the growth of Northern manufactures. The protective tariff in this sense was little more than a form of sectional economic exploitation.

Congressman Tyler felt that the whole American System concept of making the agrarian United States over into an image of industrial Britain was dangerous and wrongheaded. He preferred to see his country remain agricultural, the supplier of the warring world's foodstuffs. A profitable neutrality in European power politics could best be preserved in the future, he was convinced, through a condition of agrarianism:

A manufacturing nation is, in every sense of the word, dependent on others. Look to England! Cut off from the markets of the world, misery and ruin await her. Threaten to close your ports against her, and she becomes forthwith alarmed. Close them and a great portion of her population are thrown out of employment, and reduced to beggary. How is it with an agricultural nation? Other nations are, in great measure, dependent on it for food. They may dispense with your silks and gee-gaws, but bread they must have. And when its foreign trade is destroyed, that very circumstance operates beneficially to the poorer classes, for they are then enabled to obtain the necessaries of life in greater abundance, and on much cheaper and much better terms.... Let other nations press on, if they please, to that point where they will lose their agricultural, and assume a manufacturing character; so much the better for us; our markets will thus be increased for the products of our soil, and wealth and happiness will await us....[28]

In proposing a free-trade alternative to protectionism, Tyler accepted Adam Smith's idealistic notion of a great world market controlled and ordered by a mystical law of supply and demand. He followed Smith's suggestion that each nation should sell in that market those commodities it was most cheaply and efficiently capable of producing while buying from that market those commodities most cheaply and efficiently produced elsewhere. American commodities in this first category were obviously cotton, tobacco, and grains. To attempt to produce in America those goods more cheaply manufactured abroad was sheer madness. And to stimulate such production at home artificially through tariff protection was at best a form of robbery practiced by Northern manufacturing interests on the vast mass of American consumers. He was jubilant, therefore, when the 1820 tariff bill was defeated by a narrow margin, although he could see that the sectional conflict on the tariff issue, like the Andrew Jackson problem, was just beginning.

John Tyler's fear of the colorful Jackson began in 1818 in profound shock over the General's military irresponsibility in a command situation. It lasted until a few months before Old Hickory's death in June 1845. Throughout this period the two strong-willed men disliked each other with a passion bordering on the unreasonable. In fairness to Tyler, however, it must be pointed out that Jackson gave some cause for alarm in 1817 when he undertook his celebrated invasion of Spanish Florida to chastise the Seminoles. In this self-generated punitive expedition he assumed for himself a power to make and levy war clearly delegated to Congress by the Constitution. When he captured, court-martialed, and executed two pro-Seminole British citizens, Alexander Arbuthnot and Robert C. Ambrister, during the course of his foray, he arrogated a judicial power without precedent or antecedent in American history. From a purely legal standpoint, his was the unique case of an American military commander on an unauthorized foreign invasion, arresting two British subjects on Spanish soil and bringing them to trial there under American military law. He then executed both of them, even though the officers of his own hand-picked military court had only sentenced Ambrister to six months at hard labor. Finally, when the rampaging General seized and deported Spanish colonial officials in Florida and proclaimed in force there the revenue laws of the United States, he usurped a quasi-diplomatic function clearly not his under the Constitution. It was an amazing performance. That both Britain and Spain were nations with which the United States was at peace in 1817 created severe embarrassment and a threat of war.

It was too much for Congressman Tyler. When a motion to censure Jackson was brought to the floor of the House of Representatives in January 1819, Tyler was angrily on his feet. He reviewed the facts in the case, observing pointedly that

> ...however great may have been the services of General Jackson [in the past], I cannot consent to weigh those services against the Constitution of the land.... Your liberties cannot be preserved by the fame of any man. The triumph of the hero may swell the pride of your country—elevate you in the estimation of foreign nations—give you a character for chivalry and valour; but...the sheet anchor of our safety is to be found in the Constitution of our country.... It is the *precedent* growing out of the proceedings in this case that I wish to guard against.... I demand to know who was authorized, under the Constitution, to have declared the war—Congress or the general?... I cannot imagine a more formidable inroad on the powers of this House.... Under what laws have these [British] prisoners been deprived of their existence? We live in a land where the only rule of our conduct is the law. The power of promulgating those laws is vested in Congress. They are not the arbitrary edicts of any one man, nor is any so high as to be above their influence.[29]

Tyler's was a vigorous and, in the circumstances, legitimate indictment of the rampaging general, but it was to no avail. The dashing Jackson, hero of New Orleans, was too popular on the Western frontier. The fact that he had killed a few hundred Indians, executed two subjects of insane old George III, and inconvenienced the colonial administration of the hated Spanish Don merely increased his stature in the boondocks as American Hero, First Class. "Among the people of the West," one journal observed, "his popularity is unbounded—old and young speak of him with rapture, and at his call, 50,000 of the most efficient warriors of this continent would rise, armed, and ready for any enemy." Given these circumstances, no resolution of censure could be passed through Congress, and Tyler was left to worry over the prospect of a Man on Horseback riding roughshod over the Constitution while the ignorant frontier element went wild with joy. He never trusted Jackson thereafter.[30]

An even greater threat to domestic tranquility in America soon pushed Jackson's dangerous heroics into the back of Tyler's mind. This was the 1819–1820 Missouri Compromise debate, a political watershed in American history and in the personal life of John Tyler. In its larger meaning it marked the first concerted attack from the North on the South's "peculiar institution." It produced in the South a comprehensive defense of human slavery as a positive moral good. In the life of Tyler it added to a growing feeling of frustration and inadequacy that led him to resign his congressional seat and retire to private life. His was a leading voice in opposition to the Compromise on the floor of the House. In great alarm he pointed out the long-range danger to the South of granting to Congress the power to prohibit or regulate slavery in the territories. The Missouri Compromise was the camel's nose under the tent flap so far as the ultimate end of slavery was concerned. Or so Tyler argued.[31]

The question at issue was whether Congress under the Constitution had the right to determine where and whether slavery should be legal in territories not yet ready for statehood. The debate took an ugly turn in 1819 when the Congress attempted to admit Maine and Missouri into the Union simultaneously with a view toward maintaining the exact balance existing in the Union between free states and slave states. The intent, laudable in itself, demanded nevertheless an acceptance of the idea that Congress had the right to set territorial limits on the location and expansion of slavery, a right nowhere made specific in the Constitution. To be sure, a precedent for this right did exist. In 1787 the Confederation Congress had passed the Northwest Ordinance, setting forth the conditions for territorial organization in the lands north of the Ohio River. The first Congress under the Constitution had re-enacted this legislation. Under its provisions slavery was specifically prohibited in these territories. But whether this had any applicability to the Maine-Missouri problem was another question. As the debate progressed, tempers flared, insults were flung, and pistols were packed on the floor. "Missouri is the only word ever repeated here by the politicians," Tyler wrote Henry Curtis in alarm. "You have no possible idea of the excitement that prevails here. Men talk of a dissolution of the Union with perfect nonchalance and indifference." He was not much less agitated himself, however. "For myself," he said, "I cannot and will not yield one inch of the ground." [32]

The main Southern argument that Missouri should be admitted slave and Maine free to preserve the political balance of power in the Union struck Tyler as an extremely dangerous one in that it threatened eventual sectional strife and definitely beclouded the essential point that Congress had no specific power to prohibit slavery in the territories, either under the Constitution or under the 1803 Louisiana Purchase treaty. The treaty by which the vast Louisiana Territory had been acquired from France had specifically upheld slavery in the area, and, presumably, in any state or territory subsequently carved from the extensive domain. But it was the sectional-balance-of-power concept that most distressed Tyler:

> Look at the page of history and tell me what has been the most fruitful cause of war, of rapine, and of death? Has it been any other than this struggle for the balance of power? ... Sir, it is the monster that feeds on the bodies of mangled carcasses, and swills on human blood. And has it come to this, that we are now to enter into this struggle for power? ... Equality is all that could be asked for, and that equality is secured to each state of this Union by the Constitution of the land.[33]

Tyler's counterargument was that slavery should be permitted to spread into any territory where it could competitively maintain itself as an economically viable institution. It would therefore limit its own expansion if Congress would obey the Constitution and maintain a hands-off policy toward it. This occurring, he felt that the problem of the South's political power within the Union would solve itself. In his speech attacking New York Representative James Tallmadge's amendment prohibiting the further introduction of slavery into the Missouri Territory, Tyler maintained that a diffusion of the slave population into frontier territories would be beneficial to master and slave alike and would mark a step toward gradual abolition.

Admittedly, his reasoning on this point had a certain unreal quality about it. He held that the opening of Missouri and other territories to slavery would benefit slaves in the slave states by reducing Negro overcrowding there and by expanding the market for slaves west of the Mississippi. This would drive the price of slaves upward (benefiting the slaveowners and dealers) and cause masters to treat their now more valuable slaves with greater kindness and humanity (benefiting the slaves). As the number of slaves in the slave states was thus proportionately reduced, opposition in the South to the idea of compensated emancipation would wither, the ultimate financial cost of such emancipation to the federal or state government would be lessened, and the importance of slavery in the total economy would decline. Thus a gradual and orderly abolition would be brought within the range of possibility. "You subserve, then, the purposes of humanity by voting down this amendment," Tyler informed his colleagues. "You advance the interest and secure the safety of one half of this extended Republic: you ameliorate the condition of the slave, and you add much to the prospects of emancipation and the total extinction of slavery." [34]

The final compromise on the heated Missouri question was really no compromise at all, from Tyler's standpoint. The so-called Thomas Amendment, sponsored by Illinois Representative Jesse B. Thomas in February 1820, admitted Missouri as a slave state. This satisfied the South that the Tallmadge Amendment had been defeated and that slavery had at least hurdled the Mississippi. But this gain came at the expense of prohibiting slavery forever in the Louisiana Territory north of 36°30′. In accepting this less-than-half-a-loaf the South won a battle and lost a war. The precedent for congressional regulation of slavery in the territories was established, the geographic extent of slave territory was limited to a much smaller area than that which lay north of 36°30′, and the political balance of power between slave and free states in Congress was potentially, if not actually and immediately, upset. The Compromise had, however, prevented possible dissolution of the Union.

Tyler was heartsick at the outcome. He wanted neither the breakup of the Union nor the Compromise. Just what he did want is not entirely clear. In the final vote in the House, the Missouri Compromise was adopted 134 to 42. Of the 42 nays, 37 were from the South and 17 of these were from Virginia. Tyler, of course, was one of the 17. On the eve of the Civil War, forty-one years later, Tyler could still say of the Missouri Compromise:

I believed it to be unconstitutional. I believed it to be ... the opening of the Pandora's box, which would let out upon us all the present evils which have gathered over the land.... I want, above all things, to preserve the little space I may occupy upon the page of history legibly and correctly written. I never would have yielded to that Missouri Compromise. I would have died in my shoes, suffered any sort of punishment you could have inflicted upon me, before I would have done it.[35]

Everything seemed to be going badly for John Tyler in 1820. Four years of hard labor in Congress had taken its toll, emotionally, physically, and economically. He was sick, tired, overworked, and discouraged. The income from his neglected law practice had dropped to half what it had been in 1816. Children were coming along now with distressing regularity (Mary in 1815; Robert in 1816; John, Jr., in 1819; and Letitia in 1821) and Tyler was worried about his ability to provide them with proper educations and the material comforts of life. Most importantly, his vigorous efforts to preserve the Constitution had apparently failed. The corrupt and hated Bank had not lost its charter, the Man on Horseback had not been censured, the disastrous Missouri Compromise had been adopted. The victory on the tariff proposal of 1820 was at best a temporary one. The great test on that issue was still to come.

In December 1820 Tyler decided to resign from Congress. He saw no reason to continue the unequal struggle against the American System nationalists, Federalists, and loose constructionists. A letter to Dr. Henry Curtis indicates that 1820 was one of the psychological low points of his life:

I have become in a great measure tired of my present station, and have brought my mind nearly to the conclusion of retiring to private life, and seeking those enjoyments in the bosom of my family and in the circle of my friends, which cannot be found in any other condition of existence ... the truth is, that I can no longer do good here. I stand in a decided minority, and to waste words on an obstinate majority is utterly useless and vain. ... To my last breath I will, whether I am in public or private life, oppose the daring usurpations of this government—usurpations of a more alarming character than have ever before taken place. ... How few are there who ever pass beyond my present condition? Not more than one in a thousand. By remaining here, then, I obtain for myself no other promotion; for were I to remain all my life, I should still die only a member of Congress ... the honor of the station is already possessed. ... [By resigning] I should promote my peace of mind, and with it my health ... which is now very precarious.

On January 15, 1821, Tyler drafted an open letter to his constituents resigning his seat for reasons of health. In February of the previous year he had experienced a serious gastric upset—probably food poisoning—which, he informed Curtis, "was so severe as to render my limbs, tongue, etc. almost useless to me. I was bled and took purgative medicine. ... The doctor here ascribed it to a diseased stomach." He was still feeling the after-effects of this upheaval a year later. Indeed, one medical historian has suggested that Tyler may have had a cerebral vascular accident from a thrombosis, so slow was he in recuperating from this illness. Whatever his malady, his plea of poor health was sincere. He was a sick man. Returning to Charles City, he again took up the practice of law. His old friend Andrew Stevenson was nominated for and elected to Congress in his place with Tyler's support and endorsement.[36]

Tyler's health slowly improved, although in mid-1821 he could still complain of a severe "dyspepsia" which "not only affects my body, but often my mind. My ideas become confused, and my memory bad while laboring under it." What the despondent thirty-one-year-old Virginian could not know was that his life was about to enter a new and useful cycle; nor, of course, could he know that the year 1820 had provided him a future wife. In that year Julia Gardiner was born on Gardiners Island.[37]

4

THE DILEMMAS OF A
STATES' RIGHTS POLITICIAN, 1822–1834

> *Speak of me always as a Jackson man whenever you are questioned.... In this way those who make enquiries will be readily satisfied and be no wiser than they were.*
>
> —JOHN TYLER, 1832

John Tyler at last recovered his health and self-assurance, a fact Colonel John Macon ruefully discovered for himself one afternoon in June 1822 outside the New Kent County courthouse. Macon was a hotheaded Tidewater cavalier quick to take affront when any insult, real or imagined, came his way. In this instance it was imagined. Tyler had given him no cause to be offended. But Macon, a witness in a suit Tyler was contesting, considered his delicate sense of honor somehow injured by the lawyer in the course of a routine cross-examination. When Tyler emerged from the building at sunset Macon strode rapidly up to him.

"Mr. Tyler," he said belligerently, "you have taken with me a very unjustifiable liberty."

Tyler eyed his antagonist narrowly, replying only that he was not aware he had offended the Colonel.

"You have not acted the part of a gentleman, Sir," Macon continued.

Tyler's own boiling point was not high when it came to personal imputation and he promptly struck Macon in the face with his fist. A wild brawl ensued, the Colonel laying on hard with a riding whip. Tyler finally wrested the whip away and slashed Macon several times. That ended the fight. Tyler happily reported that he had received no injury and that he had marked the Colonel's face severely.[1]

If Tyler's fighting spirit had revived by 1822, so too had the compelling lure of public life. In 1823 he was elected again to the Charles City seat in the Virginia House of Delegates. Immediately he threw himself into the fight to block Old Dominion endorsement of the so-called Tennessee Resolution which was designed to democratize the party caucus system of nominating Presidential candidates. The Tennessee Resolution asked that the people be given a voice in the nominating process, a reform Tyler considered dangerous since the candidate for the White House it would benefit most in 1824 was the popular hero, Andrew Jackson. Tyler favored the candidacy of the Virginia-born Georgian, William H. Crawford. For this reason he unwisely linked his support of Crawford with his opposition to the Tennessee Resolution. So diligently and openly did he labor for Crawford that the legislature reluctantly abandoned its support of the caucus system rather than see Virginia's congressional delegation instructed to support any one of the five contenders for the prize. Crawford, Clay, Jackson, Calhoun, and John Quincy Adams all had vigorous partisans in the House of Delegates. Tyler thus sustained a stinging defeat on the Tennessee Resolution; he emerged from the fight "covered in sackcloth and ashes." With the undemocratic caucus system in its death throes, Presidential nominations for a time were made by various state legislatures.[2]

As the 1824 Presidential campaign unfolded, Tyler found himself supporting the candidacy of John Quincy Adams after a paralytic stroke virtually removed states' rights hopeful William Crawford from the canvass. Clay and Calhoun were too closely identified with the American System heresy to suit Tyler, and Calhoun had made the additional mistake of supporting the Missouri Compromise. Senator Jackson, on the other hand, was erratic and unpredictable, the mystery candidate of the 1820s. Just what he stood for in 1824 was difficult to ascertain. About the most that could be said for him was that he wanted very much to be President. To achieve this laudable ambition he charged boldly down from the hills of Tennessee damning "King Caucus" and extolling the democratic virtues. His appeal, much to Tyler's disgust, was to the illiterate frontier element, to the newly enfranchised, and to those patriots dazzled by his military reputation as scourge of Redcoat and Redskin. To sharpen this vote-catching image his managers shrewdly converted the Andrew Jackson who was planter, land speculator, and aristocrat by taste into "Old Hickory," backwoods democrat and champion of the Common Man. Since at various times in his career Jackson had both supported and opposed national banks, protective tariffs, and internal improvements, he could be—and was—all things to many men. Tyler considered him an unstable opportunist, a greater danger by far to American institutions than Adams. True, Adams was noted as a loose constructionist, a friend of the American System, and no lover of human slavery. But Tyler rationalized his vote for the former Federalist on the grounds that Adams actually in office would be more moderate, responsible, malleable, and predictable than any of the other heretical candidates. It was Tyler's first major exercise in political clairvoyance and the result was a disaster. He should have supported the infirm Crawford, paralysis or no paralysis.[3]

The result of the election of 1824 pointed up the poverty of a political system based on warring factions led by strong men nominated by various state legislatures. Of the four major candidates Jackson received a plurality of the popular and electoral votes, running well ahead of Adams, Crawford, and Clay. He did not, however, command a majority in the Electoral College and the decision was thrown into the House of Representatives, where each of the twenty-four states had one vote. Under the constitutional provision relevant to this confused situation only the three leaders in the electoral vote could be considered further. Clay's name was thus dropped from consideration at the outset even though he had outpolled Crawford in the popular vote. Eliminated from contention as he was, Clay nevertheless held the balance of power in his hands and with it the real key to the White House door. Following a confidential talk with Adams, the details of which have never come to light, the ambitious Kentuckian advised his supporters in the House to vote for Adams. That endorsement did it. The final outcome was thirteen votes for Adams, seven for Jackson, and four for Crawford. By polling 30 per cent of the electoral and popular vote John Quincy Adams of Massachusetts had become the sixth President of the United States. John C. Calhoun of South Carolina, Vice-Presidential candidate on both the Adams and Jackson tickets, became Vice-President. The whole thing was a mockery of the American electoral process and a fraud against democracy. This aspect of it did not disturb Tyler. On the contrary, throughout the remainder of his political life he never lost sight of the fact that one way to deal with the menace of King Numbers in a Presidential canvass was to force the decision into the House of Representatives.

The pyrotechnics of the 1824 election came a few days later, when Adams suddenly announced Clay's appointment as Secretary of State—traditionally the post of succession to the Presidency itself. With the release of this stunning news, a plump little Pennsylvania congressman named George Kremer waddled briefly into the pages of history. In an anonymous letter to a Philadelphia newspaper Kremer charged that Clay's support of Adams in the House election and his subsequent appointment to the Adams Cabinet were part of a "corrupt bargain." Clay was furious at the imputation. Oiling his dueling pistols, he demanded satisfaction for the "base and infamous calumniator, a dastard and a liar" who had sullied his honor. When the guileless Kremer identified himself as the author of the "corrupt bargain" charge, the idea of a duel became ridiculous. Kremer was not worth shooting, and Clay put away his weapons, convinced that powerful Jackson forces had secretly employed Kremer as their mouthpiece. If Kremer was not worth the lead it would take to kill him, the erratic and imperious Senator John Randolph of Virginia was. When the lanky Virginian repeated the "corrupt bargain" indictment on the floor of the Senate in 1826 in a wild tirade against the President, suggesting that the Adams-Clay administration was at best a "coalition of Blifil and Black George," a cynical alliance of "the Puritan with the blackleg," Clay promptly challenged him. Fortunately, both men were mediocre marksmen and honor was satisfied bloodlessly after each had fired a shot.[4]

Tyler never believed that the Adams-Clay relationship involved a "bargain" of any kind. Although Clay carried the charge with him to his grave, no historical evidence has ever been adduced to support the accusation. Tyler had quietly supported Adams in the campaign and he realistically accepted Adams' appointment of Clay to the Cabinet as part of the normal political process. The thought of General Jackson still hovering in the political wings frightened him. He also entertained the hope, one soon to be blasted, that the Adams administration would prove less nationalistic in its policies than some states' righters feared. It was in this spirit of wishful thinking that he wrote the Virginia-born Clay in March 1825 saying that he personally considered the bargain and corruption charges groundless. Only Clay's ready and patriotic support of Adams' candidacy in the House had brought about the "speedy settlement" of the "distracting subject":

Believing Mr. Crawford's chance of success to have been utterly desperate, you have not only met my wishes... but I do believe the wishes and feelings of a large majority of the people of this your native State. I do not believe that the sober and reflecting people of Virginia would have been so far dazzled by military renown as to have conferred their suffrages upon a mere soldier—one acknowledged on all hands to be of little value as a civilian. I will not withhold from you also the expression of my approval of your acceptance of your present honorable and exalted station.

This friendly, unsolicited letter arrived in Washington in the midst of one of the great crises of Clay's political life. He was grateful for Tyler's moral support, and his subsequent friendly relations with the Virginian, until their dramatic break in 1841, reflected something of his continuing gratitude. If they had little else in common, both men feared and hated Andrew Jackson.[5]

In 1825 John Tyler was elected governor of Virginia by the state legislature. The office was ceremonial in character and little political significance attaches to Tyler's elevation to it. Virginia in 1825 was still operating under a 1776 state constitution which reflected the bias of the state's Revolutionary leaders against any centralization of administrative authority. In addition, the party situation within the Virginia legislature in 1825 was in flux, just as it was at the national level. Each of the great sectional leaders—Clay, Adams, Jackson, and Calhoun—commanded strong personal support in Richmond. At no time, therefore, did Tyler have a disciplined political organization with which to work. Nor during his thirteen-month tenure of office did he work to build one. He sought no changes in the constitutional structure that reduced the governorship to little more than the exercise of verbal masonry at cornerstone dedications. Governor Tyler proposed legislation and the legislature disposed of it. As a training ground for executive leadership the governorship of Virginia was deficient in every respect.

Tyler urged, for example, that the legislature create a system of public schools for all classes of people. But he submitted no plan for financing the scheme and left the question of implementation to the General Assembly. While the idea was sound and farsighted, there was no executive follow-through and no willingness to ask for or fight for the higher taxes the school plan would require. Similarly, Tyler was convinced that something should be done to bring the transmontane counties into a closer political and commercial relationship with the Piedmont and Tidewater. A canal- and road-building program to bind the state together was recommended. But he preferred to leave the details of this to "the wisdom of the General Assembly," noting only that unless Virginia got into the internal-improvements business soon, pressure in the western counties to invite the federal government to do the job would become irresistible.[6]

Also less than energetic was Tyler's circuitous effort to convince the General Assembly that the governor's salary was inadequate to sustain the social demands of the office. During his term as governor the expenses incurred in entertaining the exclusive society of Richmond and the state legislators and their ladies mounted steadily. In spite of Letitia's heroic efforts to maintain simplicity at official social functions the costs invariably exceeded the cash income of the governor. To suggest this point as delicately as possible to the members of the legislature, Tyler wryly invited them all to a banquet at the Mansion at which he served only Virginia ham and huge quantities of cooked corn bread; cheap Monongahela whiskey was ladled out in copious amounts to wash down the glutinous fare. Whether the lawmakers became sick or drunk or both is not recorded. Nonetheless, the tactic failed. Tyler's salary was not raised, and by the time he resigned the office in January 1827 to accept election to the United States Senate he was in serious financial difficulty.[7]

Still, Tyler enjoyed his gubernatorial career—at least he said he did. Sterile as it was from the standpoint of his political education or the possibility of truly constructive accomplishment, it did give him the psychological satisfaction of following in the footsteps of his revered father. He once remarked that the honor of being a member of the United States Senate could scarcely compare to that afforded by the governorship of Virginia. Nevertheless, when an opportunity to leave the Governor's Mansion in Richmond was presented to him early in 1827, Tyler jumped at the opportunity to return to Washington.[8]

Tyler's promotion to the Senate in 1827 was accomplished only after a bitter and controversial fight with incumbent Senator John Randolph in the General Assembly. The issue between them was not political; it was entirely personal. Randolph was a brilliant and caustic advocate of states' rights. He had loyally supported William H. Crawford in 1824—long after John Tyler had abandoned the stricken Georgian for John Quincy Adams. So orthodox was he on states' rights that Governor Tyler himself publicly urged his speedy re-election to the Senate and stated his hope that there would be no opposition to the Randolph candidacy in the General Assembly. Privately, however, Tyler had serious objections to Randolph's erratic personal behavior and to the Senator's tendency to indulge in public proclamations unbecoming a Virginia gentleman. Many Virginians shared the governor's concern. It was true that Randolph had an unhappy facility for verbal provocation. Henry Clay once reminded him of a rotten mackerel lying in the sun shining and stinking and the charge of Clay's "corrupt bargain" with Adams had produced the celebrated duel with Harry of the West. On another occasion the colorful senator was reported to have undressed and dressed in the Senate chamber. When angry he indulged in character assassination; when depressed he sought solace in liquor. His hatred of the Adams-Clay administration was so passionate that he was willing to make common legislative cause with the Jacksonians against it. This alliance proved quite disturbing to conservative states' righters in Richmond, Tyler among them.

On January 12, 1827, the day before the balloting was to take place in the General Assembly, Governor Tyler suddenly became a candidate for the Randolph seat. Offered a last-minute nomination to the post by a group of anti-Randolph legislators, Tyler replied to their importunity with a skillfully worded statement that denied any interest in the position while strongly implying that he might indeed respond to a draft. Not surprisingly, he was promptly placed in nomination for the Senate the next day. Publicly he maintained that he had absolutely no interest in the nomination. But he would not withdraw his name from consideration. Randolph's partisans were outraged. Richard Morris of Hanover County construed the unexpected Tyler candidacy as a clever plot in which the wily governor had lulled Randolph's supporters into a sense of false security while secretly conniving to have his own name placed in contention. Tyler of course denied this. He called the Morris charge "slanderous and false" and bluntly stated that he was fully prepared to meet "all the consequences which may result from such declaration." Neither Morris nor Tyler was a duelist at heart and it was well that the matter ended there. The fact remains, however, that in the sandbagging of Randolph, Tyler was forced to accept the votes of some thirty Virginia legislators who actively supported the Adams-Clay party and who were openly hostile to states' rights. Joining with those members who thought Randolph lacked the decorum befitting a Virginia senator, this ideologically suspect group gave Tyler the necessary margin of victory. By the slim count of 115 to 110 Randolph was retired and Governor John Tyler became a United States senator.[9]

When Tyler reached Washington in December 1827 to take his seat in the United States Senate he returned to the arena of familiar battles still raging. He had already informed Virginians of his attitude toward the Adams administration. Shortly after his election he told a group of his political friends at a Richmond dinner in his honor that his complete disillusionment with Adams began as early as December 6, 1825, when the new President had delivered his first Annual Message to Congress. The Message was a paean to nationalism. Adams recommended a vast federal internal-improvements program, called for a uniform national militia law, a national university, a national astronomical observatory, and the national standardization of weights and measures. He also urged national laws to promote manufacturing, commerce and agriculture, the arts, sciences and literature. The implications of the speech took Tyler's breath away:

I saw in it an almost total disregard for the federative principle—a more latitudinous construction of the Constitution than has ever before been insisted on.... From the moment of seeing that message...I stood distinctly opposed to this administration.... I honestly believe the preservation of the federative principles of our government to be inseparably connected with the perpetuation of liberty.... A war for [our principles] I shall be ready to prosecute under any banner, and almost under any leader. It is a cause calculated to awaken zeal, for it is that of liberty and the Constitution; and in such a cause I will consent to become a zealot.[10]

The Tariff Bill of March 1828 gave Senator Tyler his first opportunity for zealotry. It was a grotesque, cynical bill. As Calhoun admitted a decade later, it was little more than a complicated Jacksonian plot designed to wreck the Adams administration on the eve of the 1828 election and advance the political prospects of Old Hickory. Its essential feature was a proposed tariff schedule which at one stroke would discriminate against New England wool manufacturers, subsidize the iron-manufacturing interests of the politically vital Middle Atlantic states, make the South's free traders happy, and provide the frontier states with higher protection on those articles in which they were most interested. The political strategy behind the new tariff was crude. Given the proposed lower wool schedules, its sponsors were certain that New England would oppose the legislation and that Adams would surely veto it if it passed. Actually, the floor managers of the legislation did not want it to pass. What they wanted was a campaign issue with which to flay Adams.

Thus they designed the protective clauses in such a way that if the bill happened to pass and the President signed it, he was politically ruined in the South and in New England. If it passed and he vetoed it, he was damaged in the Middle Atlantic states and in the West. In either event the Jacksonians would gain politically at his expense. As John Randolph correctly sized it up, "The bill referred to manufactures of no sort or kind, except the manufacture of a President of the United States." [11]

Something in the Jacksonian strategy went wrong. Many New Englanders, Webster among them, voted for the bill on the grounds that it maintained the broad concept of protection even if it lowered temporarily the protective tariff shield on woolens. In its final form the bill was a high-tariff monstrosity spiced with sectional sweeteners. Few legislators really wanted it. Nevertheless, it slipped through the House 105 to 94 and through the Senate 26 to 21. Adams promptly signed it, and wails of anguish swept the nation, particularly in the South. It was immediately and accurately dubbed the "Tariff of Abominations" in the South and it was destined to trigger a series of events which nearly disrupted the Union in 1833.

Tyler participated only peripherally in the 1828 tariff debate. He wanted to see Adams destroyed and he did not inquire into the ethics or tactics of those of his colleagues who worked toward the same end. He had come to Washington a few months earlier prepared to enlist "under any banner, and almost under any leader" to break the President. Within a few days of his arrival in the capital, after great soul-searching, he cast his political lot with General Jackson and his devious lieutenants. He was thoroughly convinced that the American System nationalism of the Adams administration, supported as it was by Henry Clay, was aimed at the political and economic consolidation of the Northeast and West at the expense of the South. Adams, he bluntly charged, "seeks to win us by roads and canals." The immediate future, filled as it was with internal improvements and higher protective tariffs, looked black indeed. Moreover, he feared that the re-election of Adams in 1828 would surely result in Secretary of State Clay's succession to the Presidency in 1832 and 1836. "And what possible chance have we of making a stand for the Constitution during that period?" he asked Curtis. "Rely upon it, none." In the long run he felt that "the Jackson men will alone arrest" the march to higher tariffs and other American System schemes favored by Adams and Clay. Thus when the 1828 bill emerged from committee Tyler supported the measure. He too hoped that by cramming it with features unacceptable to New England manufacturing interests the whole thing would go down in massive defeat. He therefore opposed all "sundry villainous amendments"; and, he pointed out, "Its fate rests on our ability to preserve the bill in its present shape. If we can do so it will be rejected." When it was passed and then signed by Adams, Tyler was stunned. Again he had outwitted himself.[12]

Tyler's decision to support Andrew Jackson for the Presidency in 1828 was not a reckless plunge. It was forced by the fact that Jackson now seemed to be the only alternative to the hated Adams just as Adams had been in 1824 the best alternative to the then-hated Jackson. Tyler personally preferred the nomination of Governor DeWitt Clinton of New York, who, he felt, was the kind of Northern leader Virginia could trust and support. He had built the great Erie Canal with state funds, proving to Tyler's satisfaction that large-scale internal improvements could be constructed without federal money and interference. But Clinton proved uncooperative. In 1827 he announced for Jackson and Tyler was left without a candidate. Again Tyler was faced with a dilemma. It was Adams or Jackson, "and we must make the best of our situation. The people will choose between two latitudinarians...." Nor did the senator make his reluctant choice of Jackson without embarrassment. News of his congratulatory March 1825 letter to Clay leaked into the Virginia press. "John Tyler identified with Henry Clay," screamed the *Virginia Jackson Republican*. "We are all amazement!! heart sick!! chop fallen!! dumb!! Mourn, Virginia, mourn!!" Tyler was furious at the revelation of his indiscretion. "Mr. Clay has betrayed me!" he shouted.[13]

The Virginia Jacksonians need not have pounded their breasts in such anguish. Tyler had already rationalized his support of Old Hickory though he was obliged to cling to some very soggy straws in doing so. As early as December 1827 he had reported as fact a confused mixture of hearsay, rumor, and supposition to the effect that Jackson was, deep down inside, a strict constructionist and a states' rights man. The General's "ardent advocates from Tennessee are decidedly, as far as I can gather, in favor of a limited construction of the Constitution," said Tyler. He was also convinced, although he had little evidence to support the notion, that Jackson would "surround himself by a cabinet composed of men advocating, to a great extent, the doctrines so dear to me." He therefore decided that the prospects of a Jackson administration were "bright and cheering" and he urged Virginia's states' rights men into an "active support" of Jackson's candidacy. While there were "many, many others whom I would prefer," he confided to Curtis, "every day that passes inspires me with the strong hope that his administration will be characterized by simplicity—I mean Republican simplicity." Basically though, it was still a choice of evils. "Turning to [Jackson] I may at least indulge in hope," Tyler confessed; "looking on Adams I must despair." He decided to vote for Old Hickory in 1828 on the basis of the same rationalization he had employed in 1824 when he opted for Adams. In neither instance was he deceived by others. He deceived himself.[14]

The Jackson cause in the South in 1828 was strengthened by the appearance on the Democratic ticket of John C. Calhoun as Vice-Presidential nominee. Calhoun, his long honeymoon with Clay and the American System ended on the rocks of the Tariff of Abominations, was now a staunch states' rights advocate. He shifted from Adams' faction to that of Jackson with all the skill and finesse of a Talleyrand. Vice-President under Adams, he would soon become Vice-President under Jackson. The so-called National Republicans, an amalgamation of the followers of Adams and Clay and the remnants of the old Hamiltonian Federalists, met in convention at Harrisburg and predictably renominated Adams. His Secretary of the Treasury, Richard Rush of Pennsylvania, was given the second place on the ticket.

The campaign began in the gutter and remained there. The issues of the day received scant attention. The National Republicans portrayed Jackson as an ignorant, drunken, quarrelsome, trigger-happy duelist, murderer, and militarist who had committed bigamy with his wife Rachel. The Democracy shrilly countered with the old charge of the "corrupt bargain" and added the accusation that Adams had misappropriated public funds for his personal use and had kept a "gaming table" in the White House. To counteract the bigamy charge, one of Jackson's more creative campaign managers, Duff Green, concocted the story that Adams, while Minister to Russia, had encouraged the Czar to seduce a friendless American girl there.

All this was hokum. It stirred up the voters, however, tens of thousands of them recently enfranchised, and some 1,155,000 Americans turned out to give the alleged bigamist a 647,000-to-508,000 margin over the alleged procurer. Compared with the 361,000 Americans who had cast ballots in 1824, the election of Jackson represented a major democratic upheaval. His personality excited both love and hate, but it did excite. And with suffrage coming to most white American males who wished to exercise it, a revolution toward what Tyler later called "King Numbers" was well under way. The masses swept Old Hickory into office.[15]

Tyler took no active part in the campaign. He paid no attention to the scurrility employed by both sides. He voted for the Jackson-Calhoun ticket and sat back to await developments. "We are here in a dead calm," he wrote a Charles City neighbor from Washington in December 1828. "When the General comes we may expect more bustle and stir." It was one of John Tyler's greatest understatements.[16]

Tyler had hoped that Jackson's administration would be characterized by "Republican simplicity," but he was scarcely prepared for the arrival of the drunken, fighting, unwashed hordes that descended on the capital when Old Hickory rode into Washington. The streets, the boardinghouses, the hotels—every available space—was filled with rough, plain people come to see their champion safely installed in the White House. "I have never seen such a crowd before," wrote Daniel Webster. "Persons have come five hundred miles to see General Jackson, and they really seem to think that the country has been rescued from some dreadful danger." [17]

The details of the reception at the White House following Jackson's Inaugural Address have long been part of America's democratic folklore. Scrambling, surging, and elbowing, the crowd flooded into the Executive Mansion to glimpse, to touch, to admire the Hero. Muddy boots, crashing glass, fainting women, bloody noses, and ruined furniture contributed to the pandemonium. Until the punch bowl was moved out onto the lawn, followed closely by the thirsty frontier citizenry, it seemed that Jackson would be crushed to death and the White House laid waste. On March 4, 1829, the Voice of the People breathed the strong odor of raw whiskey. To one dignified aristocrat the reception seemed to herald the "reign of King Mob"; to another the General's cheering section was a "noisy and disorderly rabble" reminiscent of the French Revolution.[18]

There was nothing in Jackson's inaugural speech to stir men's souls to this boisterous extent. It was a pedestrian address promising economy in government, a proper regard for states' rights, and an overhauling of the federal civil service. The main issues of the day—tariffs, internal improvements, the Bank of the United States—were buried in verbal fog. The General was not yet ready to tip his political hand. Behind the scenes he was busily engaged in forging his "Kitchen Cabinet," those practical politicians, publicists, and advisers who would build the Jackson party, organize the rural and urban masses behind it, and revolutionize the whole conception of the role of the Executive in American government. These insiders—Francis P. Blair, Duff Green, Isaac Hill, Amos Kendall, Andrew J. Donelson, and William B. Lewis—were all ambitious Democrats, men willing to employ intrigue and ruthlessness in their desire to crush the political power of the moneyed and landed aristocracy in America. In their prejudices, ideas, and actions they nurtured the first seeds of a concentrated attack on entrenched class privilege in the United States. It is little wonder that the aristocratic John Tyler would soon find himself, like Ali Baba, fallen among political thieves.[19]

The first sure indication Tyler had that Jackson planned a major assault upon the old order of things came in 1830 with the so-called Spoils System, Old Hickory's policy of frankly bending the power of patronage to party purposes. It was not a new idea. Thomas Jefferson had employed patronage in this manner, with considerable restraint to be sure, during his White House years. By 1830 it had become standard operating procedure in the governments of several states, notably New York and Pennsylvania. What Jackson did was to introduce the system openly and boldly into federal administration. He fired civil servants friendly to the old Adams administration and he removed others who were engaged in sabotaging the policies of his own. During his first year in the White House he removed from office, for political reasons alone, 9 per cent of all federal officeholders, replacing them with men personally loyal to himself. Proportionately, this was no greater number than Jefferson had removed, but it looked like a vast purge. Jackson's intention in all this was to narrow the gap between the government and the people. Official duties, said the President, should be made "so plain and simple that men of intelligence may readily qualify themselves for their performance." Only in this way could the educated leisure class be shaken from its firm grip on the engines of government.[20]

Tyler's principal objection to Jackson's appointment policy hinged on the professional background of some of the appointees. He did not oppose the use of patronage for party purposes as such; indeed, he embraced the idea affectionately when he himself was in the White House. His primary criticism of administration patronage policy centered upon Jackson's appointment of a group of pro-administration newspaper editors and journalists to public office. Tyler's feeling was that "the press, the great instrument of enlightenment of the people, should not be subjected, through its conductors, to rewards and punishments." He did not consider the fact that many of the great newspapers in the nation were already at the service of aristocratic elements hostile to Jackson. Nevertheless, he feared that the free press would swiftly be reduced to a mere trumpet of party by Jackson's policy. For this reason Tyler voted in the Senate against the confirmation of pro-Jackson journalists Amos Kendall, Henry Lee, James B. Gardner, Mordecai M. Noah, and Isaac Hill.[21]

He similarly opposed Jackson's right to utilize recess appointments of American diplomats as a device to avoid the problem of Senate confirmation. The appointment power was clearly the President's under the Constitution, but Jackson had not subsequently submitted the names of his recess appointees to the Senate for its "advice and consent." The President's position was that the work of the nation had to go forward whether the Senate was in session or not and that the submission of the names of diplomats to the Senate after the completion of the work they were appointed to do was an irrelevancy and a waste of time. In this attitude Jackson was in violation of both the spirit and letter of the Constitution, and Senator Tyler was quick to pounce on him. In an able speech on the floor of the Senate in February 1831, Tyler carefully read the wording of Article II, Section 2, Paragraph 2, dealing with "advice and consent." Semantics were with him on this issue and he knew it:

Sir, I take the simple, unambiguous language of the Constitution as I find it. I will not inquire what *it should be,* but *what it is,* when I come to decide upon it.... For myself the path of duty is straight, and I shall walk in it. Shall I displease the President by doing so? If I do, I cannot help it.... I have seen much in his career to applaud.... But if we were now forming the government, I would add to the power of the President not even so much as would turn the scales by the hundredth part of a hair. There is already enough of the spice of monarchy in the presidential office. There lies the true danger to our institutions. It has already become the great magnet of attraction. The struggles to attain it are designed to enlist all the worst passions of our nature. It is the true Pandora's box. Place in the President's hands the key to the door of the treasury, by conferring on him the uncontrolled power of appointing to office and liberty cannot abide among us.

A majority of the Senate agreed with Tyler, and Jackson's knuckles were sharply rapped.[22]

Senator Tyler was not yet in opposition to Jackson. On the contrary, he found much in the Jackson administration in 1829–1831 to command his support, and he was sincere when he said in February 1831 that he had seen much in Jackson's career to applaud. He feared Clay and his American System more than he distrusted Jackson. In March 1830 he had written his friend John Rutherfoord that while a polyglot opposition to Jackson was beginning to form in Congress behind the leadership of Henry Clay it was to the advantage of the South to continue supporting the President:

... the South sustains him from the fear of greater ill under the auspices of another. The opposition is united to a man and will carry on the most unsparing warfare. They produce the effect, which may be salutary, of holding our heterogeneous materials together.... At this time too the country is peculiarly excited by the alarmists and fanatics, anti-Sunday mail, anti-masonic, abolition societies, and last, tho' not least, the sympathy and mock sensibility attempted to be created in behalf of the Southern Indians, all conspiring to one end, viz: the overthrow of Jackson and the elevation of Clay.

Nor in their personal relations was Tyler yet ready to fault Old Hickory. A dinner at the White House in 1830 frankly impressed him. "Would you old-fashioned Virginian believe it," he remarked in good humor to Rutherfoord, "he even went so far as to introduce his guests to each other—a thing without precedent here and most abominably unfashionable. At dinner he seemed to me to have laid aside the royal diadem, and to have fancied himself at the Hermitage.... All satisfied me that I stood in the presence of an old-fashioned republican." [23]

More important than social graces, Jackson's veto of the Maysville Road Bill on May 27, 1830, drew Tyler and other states' rights politicians to his banner with positive enthusiasm. The veto was a sharp blow at the National Republicans and at Henry Clay, whose supporters in the West and Northeast had rammed the proposal through Congress. It was also an attempt by Jackson to bring the South more closely to his support and head off defections in that section threatened in the growing personal tension between himself and Vice-President Calhoun. It represented, finally, the beginning of Jackson's shift, under the urging of Martin Van Buren and others, to a more radical position of attacking privilege by denying federal subsidies to private corporations.

The bill authorized the government to buy $150,000 worth of stock in the Maysville Turnpike Road Company to permit the company to construct a sixty-mile stretch of highway located entirely within the state of Kentucky. The President argued in his veto message that since the proposed road lay entirely within the limits of Kentucky and was not connected with any existing transportation system of an interstate character, it was not properly a matter for federal concern. He also suggested that the question of the constitutionality of future internal-improvement proposals might well be solved by a constitutional amendment specifically permitting federal expenditures for such purposes.

Tyler was extremely encouraged by the veto message. "This action of the President," he exulted, "is hailed with unbounded delight by the strict constructionists, and the two Houses of Congress resound with his praise." Well might Tyler have been pleased with the veto. His own speech in the Senate in April 1830 in opposition to the Maysville Bill was a slashing attack on the whole concept of government-financed internal improvements. The twisting of the Constitution had reached the point in the Maysville proposal, he argued sarcastically, whereby the dirt lane running past his Gloucester farm could be designated a "national" road because it ultimately intersected a road that later joined another road that ran from Virginia to Alabama.[24]

If Tyler remained reconciled to the Jackson administration, the spring of 1831 found many states' rights politicians in the South searching for greener pastures. Chief among these was John C. Calhoun. Following the passage of the hated Tariff of Abominations in 1828, a troubled Calhoun returned to his Fort Hill plantation at Pendleton, South Carolina, to ruminate on the sad state of the nation and his future role in it. While the citizenry was electing him once again to the Vice-Presidency, Calhoun was calmly producing the explosive pamphlet "South Carolina Exposition and Protest." In this revolutionary work the Vice-President coldly and brilliantly argued the thesis that South Carolina, as a voluntary member of the original compact of states, retained the right under the Constitution of that compact to nullify and declare void within her borders the operation of any federal law that was unconstitutional—in this instance the Tariff of 1828.

Armed with this sputtering ideological bomb, Calhoun returned to Washington to fight the states' rights cause. During the next two years he permitted his personal and political relations with Jackson to deteriorate to such a point that by 1831 the two men were scarcely speaking. In the first place, Jackson was distressed to learn that Calhoun had covertly criticized his conduct in Florida in 1818. The split was widened when Calhoun and his haughty wife, Floride, refused to mingle socially with Peggy O'Neale Eaton, the former Washington barmaid who had married Jackson's Secretary of War, John H. Eaton, in 1829. Jackson's decision to champion the controversial Peggy disrupted the Cabinet and all Washington society. Only the urbane widower, Martin Van Buren, Secretary of State, sided with his chivalrous chief and maintained social intercourse with the outcaste Eatons.[25]

The political vacuum in the Jackson administration created by Calhoun's break with the President was filled by Van Buren. Indeed, Tyler watched with fascination as the leader of the New York Democracy and champion of the common man in the Empire State ingratiated himself with Old Hickory and overnight maneuvered himself into the position of chief heir to the Presidential succession. Tyler was no admirer of the Little Magician. He considered Van Buren little more than a slick opportunist. "I like not the man overmuch," he confessed to his brother-in-law, John B. Seawell, in January 1832. He could see, however, that as Calhoun and his friends marched out of the Jackson administration the New York liberals under Van Buren were marching in. The political alliance of frontier agrarians and urban artisans which would sweep all before it in 1832, and again in 1836, was beginning to take form in the Jackson-Van Buren amalgam. "What deeper game could any man have played?" Tyler asked. Nevertheless, he was impressed with the New York politician's skill in moving his cohorts into Jackson's inner circle.[26]

Tyler was unwilling in 1831-1832 to carry his states' rights orientation to the extreme of Calhoun's radical nullification doctrine. Nor was he prepared to flail the Jackson administration without good cause. For him, the glow of the Maysville veto lingered on. When Jackson also vetoed the Bank Bill in July 1832, Tyler had no choice but to come again to Old Hickory's support in the November canvass. As he explained his decision to his daughter Mary in April 1832:

You say that enquiries are often made of you as to my opinions on various political subjects. If you knew them, upon many it might be improper to divulge them. There are enough persons who would be inclined to turn your declarations to bad account in reference to myself. Speak of me always as a Jackson man whenever you are questioned, and say that in regard to Van Buren, Calhoun, etc., etc., they are matters with which I do not deal; that you have reason to believe that I am directed exclusively by reference to the public interests, and not by men. In this way those who make enquiries will be readily satisfied, and be no wiser than they were before questioning you.[27]

Following the investigation of the second Bank of the United States, in which Tyler had participated in 1819, the controversial institution had grown and flourished under the able leadership of Langdon Cheves of South Carolina. Honesty and conservatism had characterized its operations for a decade. It had provided a stable currency and had served as a safe repository of Treasury receipts. Nevertheless, considerable ideological and political hostility to the Bank remained. States' rights theorists still considered the institution unconstitutional. Western debtors and land speculators favoring inflation and cheap money objected to the Bank's conservatism and its deflationary policies. Private banking interests throughout the nation resented the Bank's monopolistic features. Jackson himself harbored the unsophisticated frontier notion that paper money was a dangerous thing to have floating around. Less naïve was his view that the Bank was a monopolistic private corporation of great power, wealth, and influence. Operating partially in the public interest without public controls upon it, it was an octopus among financial porpoises. Its leader after 1822 was the haughty Nicholas Biddle, a snobbish patrician from a social background the Old Hero felt he could not trust. The more Jackson thought about the potential threat of the rising moneyed aristocracy in America, symbolized by Biddle, his rich friends, and the stockholders of the Bank, the more convinced he became that a cancer of privilege was spreading among the healthy tissues of the republican body social.

Nicholas Biddle wanted desperately to keep the Bank out of partisan politics. Yet its charter would expire again in 1836 and he felt it imperative to the economic well-being of the nation that it be renewed. Conversations with Henry Clay convinced him that he should push for charter renewal in 1832, four years in advance of the expiration date—before Jackson could effectively organize anti-Bank forces behind his own party. A lightning campaign for the Bank might prove successful in Congress. But what if the unpredictable Jackson vetoed a new Bank bill, Biddle wondered. "Should Jackson veto it," exclaimed Clay, "I shall veto him!" [28]

Clay's motives in urging a premature renewal of the Bank charter were political. As a longstanding champion of the institution in the political arena, he felt that a revival of the Bank issue in 1832 might be used to defeat Jackson in the November campaign. This, as it turned out, was a serious miscalculation. Nevertheless, beginning in May 1832, Biddle and Clay launched a massive propaganda campaign for immediate charter renewal. All that money, pamphlets, newspaper editorials, and crack lobbyists could accomplish was done. On June 11 the Bank Bill passed the Senate 28 to 20, and on July 3 it cleared the House 107 to 85. The General was outraged at the crude machinations of the Clay-Biddle campaign. "The bank is trying to kill me," he told Van Buren grimly, *"but I will kill it!"* [29]

With his usual vigor Senator Tyler joined the new fight over the Bank. He had fought the institution and its predecessor steadily since 1811. Twenty years' service in the anti-Bank ranks had made him an expert on the question. His Senate speech of May 1832 revealed a firm grasp of banking economics. He voted for every amendment brought to the Senate floor designed to weaken the Bank and he opposed every proposal aimed at strengthening the institution. Specifically, Tyler spoke for a crippling amendment that would limit to 5 per cent the legal interest rate the Bank might charge on loans. On the moral side of the question he argued that any allowable interest rate above 5 per cent was a federal endorsement of usury. He spoke feelingly of the

> vital importance of laws regulating the rate of interest; without them a nation becomes a nation of money-lenders.... The Mosaic regulation which permitted usance to be taken of strangers, aided by the oppressions under which they laboured, converted the Jews into a nation of money-lenders. I mention this not to their discredit. They are like all the rest of the human family—no better and no worse—devoting themselves to the acquisition of money, and seeking for their money such investment as yields the greatest return. Into the same condition may the people of any country be changed. Only make the profits on loans high enough: if six per cent will not do, take ten; if ten does not, take twenty; in other words, make it more profitable for the capitalists to loan out their money than to invest it in lands, ships, or machinery, and the work is accomplished. Government will have converted the community into a nation of usurers.[30]

So eager was Tyler to expel the Northern moneychangers from the cool temples of Jeffersonian agrarianism he could only cheer Jackson's veto message. Written by the President with the assistance and advice of Martin Van Buren, Amos Kendall, Andrew J. Donelson, and Roger B. Taney, the veto had, a stunned Biddle explained to Clay, "all the fury of a chained panther biting the bars of his cage. It is really a manifesto of anarchy ... and my hope is, that it will contribute to relieve the country of these miserable people. You are destined to be the instrument of that deliverance." Jackson's message indeed rang with defiance and challenge, appealing to the economic and class interests of the farmers and workers. If it was short on fiscal analysis it was full in its condemnation of the moneychangers so hated by Tyler. "It is to be regretted," said the President, "that the rich and powerful too often bend the acts of government to their selfish purposes ... but when the laws ... make the rich richer and the potent more powerful, the humble members of society—the farmers, mechanics, and laborers—who have neither the time nor the means of securing like favors to themselves, have a right to complain of the injustice of their Government." Jackson was well on his way toward a more radical democracy. Thanks to the vigor of the veto and the skill of Jackson's campaign managers the Bank question became the central one in the Presidential canvass. The

President rode it hard. "The veto works well everywhere," he announced in August; "it has put down the Bank instead of prostrating me."[31]

Tyler supported Jackson in the November election even though the President's effort to ingratiate himself with the nation's small farmers and mechanics was an appeal to American social classes with which the planter aristocracy had little in common. Nonetheless, the record of Old Hickory's first administration on internal improvements and the Bank made the President eminently preferable to National Republican Henry Clay. And while the slippery Van Buren was Jackson's running mate on the Democratic ticket, Tyler felt that the Maysville and Bank vetoes left him not much choice in the matter. There was also the practical consideration that Clay had small prospect of victory. "Clay stands no chance," said Tyler in April 1832. "Jackson is invincible." For Tyler it was again largely a choice of the lesser of evils and once more he held his considerable nose, voted, and went home to disinfect himself.[32]

Jackson ran hard against the "Money Monster" while Biddle and his wealthy friends poured their money and time into the Clay cause. The result was a Jackson landslide. The President received 687,502 popular votes and 219 electoral votes to Clay's 530,189 popular and 49 electoral votes. Clay carried only his own Kentucky and the high-tariff states of Massachusetts, Rhode Island, Connnecticut, and Delaware. Jackson swept the rest. If an American election was ever a popular mandate for anything (the point is debatable), the election of 1832 was a mandate against the second Bank of the United States.[33]

Soon after the election of 1832 states' rights radicals in South Carolina brought the nation to the brink of a civil war. On November 24, 1832, a state convention (elected in October) officially nullified the Tariff Act of 1828 and its milder brother, the Tariff Act of 1832, and threatened secession if the federal government attempted to use force to collect tariff revenues within the state. On November 27 the legislature authorized the raising and arming of a military force to resist any federal encroachments. To punctuate these provocative moves, John C. Calhoun resigned the Vice-Presidency on December 28 and left for Washington to assume the Senate seat he had won two weeks earlier in the juggling of offices which sent Robert Y. Hayne from the Senate to the Governor's Mansion. From his Senate vantage point Calhoun immediately launched South Carolina's defense of nullification.

Jackson's reaction to the threat from Charleston was that of the carrot and the stick. The carrot was the recommendation in his Annual Message of December 4 to lower tariffs below the 1832 level. This would put tariff schedules far below the 1828 levels that had outraged the South four years earlier. The stick was brandished in his Proclamation to the People of South Carolina, issued on December 10. The Proclamation minced no words. The whole doctrine of nullification, said the President, was an "impractical absurdity." Drawing on the views of John Marshall, Alexander Hamilton, and Daniel Webster, he maintained that the federal government was sovereign and indivisible. No state could refuse to obey the laws of the land; nor could a state withdraw from the Union. "Disunion by armed force is treason," the President stated bluntly. He thus made it perfectly clear that South Carolina would be crushed by federal arms if necessary. On January 16, 1833, he asked Congress for the authority to use military force if necessary to uphold the federal revenue laws in South Carolina. Angry and frustrated, he confided to his closest aides that he would see that the leading nullifiers were "arrested and arraigned for treason." Jackson was no man to trifle with when he was annoyed.[34]

The major political effect of the President's Proclamation and his Force Bill was to split the dominant Jackson party, so recently triumphant at the polls, down the middle. States' rights advocates in Virginia were shocked to see their hero of the Maysville and Bank vetoes now embrace extreme nationalist doctrine. Jackson's threat to use armed force went far beyond anything the Founding Fathers had visualized in the legitimate relationships between the states and the federal government. The Virginians were not agreed, however, on the constitutionality of nullification or secession. Theoretical confusion stalked their ranks. Some, like Tyler's friend Henry A. Wise, argued that the nullification of a tariff was illegal since the levying of a tariff was obviously constitutional. Others accepted the nullification as a legitimate form of remonstrance but denied the related right of secession. Some upheld both; some denied both. Still others denied nullification and maintained the right to secede. Thomas Ritchie, editor of the Richmond *Enquirer* and a strong Jackson man, thought secession legal but called nullification a "mischievous and absurd heresy ... seeking to place a State *in* the Union and *out* of it at the same time." [35]

Tyler was placed in an intellectual quandary by South Carolina's revolutionary action and Jackson's militaristic reaction. He agreed that the Tariff of 1832 was a bad business. Even though duties had been scaled back to the 1824 levels, Tyler had opposed the legislation in the Senate because there was in it no retreat from the basic principle of tariff protection. And while he saw it as an improvement over the 1828 Tariff of Abominations, he had delivered an impassioned three-day speech in February 1832 attacking it. The protective tariff, he again argued, was a form of robbery in which the mercantile class of the North picked the pockets of agrarian consumers in the South. Indeed, the whole conception of protectionism was evidence of the new materialism that was overtaking the nation, threatening to reduce Americans to mere moneychangers. "Man cannot worship God and Mammon," Tyler cried. "If you would preserve the political temple pure and undefiled it can only be done by expelling the money-changers and getting back to the worship of our fathers." [36]

But when it came right down to the legality of nullifying the Tariff Acts of 1828 and 1832 Tyler was far less sure of himself. What he attempted to do was discover and occupy a middle ground on an issue which had no detectable middle. On one extreme of the question Calhoun maintained the legality of both nullification and secession and the unconstitutionality of Jackson's Force Bill. Webster, on the other extreme, consistently upheld the illegality of secession and nullification and argued the propriety of using force in the circumstance. Tyler upheld the right of secession while denying the right of nullification. But he also denied the right of the federal government to employ force against nullification when it occurred. Even firm states' rights Virginians like Henry St. George Tucker could not accept this peculiar dichotomy in Tyler's thinking. As long as South Carolina was actually in the Union, argued Tucker, there was no such thing as nullification. It was a question of either submitting or seceding, and since South Carolina had not seceded, the federal government had no alternative but to compel the state to comply with federal legislation. Anything less than this made the whole idea of federal government a "farce." But Tyler's middle way, however logically inconsistent it was, was supported in part by a resolution of the Virginia legislature on January 26, 1833. The resolution strongly urged compromise, pledged Virginia to a continuing support of state sovereignty, and denied Jackson's right under the Constitution to use armed force against South Carolina. When news of this action reached Tyler in Washington he and his friend William F. Gordon "both sprang up, caught each other in their arms and danced around the room like children in a delirium of joy." [37]

If the theoretical considerations remained complex for the terpsichorean Tyler, the personality factor became clear to him. Even though the Virginia senator was willing to admit that South Carolina's nullification decree had been a terrible tactical blunder, he finally decided that Andrew Jackson was the real villain of the piece. Thus Tyler informed Virginia's Governor John Floyd on January 16, the day Jackson asked for a congressional authorization of force, that

> If S. Carolina be put down, then may each of the States yield all pretensions to sovereignty. We have a consolidated govt. and a master will soon arise. This is inevitable. How idle to talk of me serving a republic for any length of time, with an uncontrolled power over the military, exercised at pleasure by the President.... What interest is safe if the unbridled will of the majority is to have sway?

By February 2 Tyler had warmed further to the theme that General Jackson was seeking to establish a military dictatorship in America. The old 1819 vision of the Man on Horseback returned. "Were ever men so deceived as we have been...in Jackson?" he asked Littleton Tazewell. "His proclamation has swept away all the barriers of the Constitution, and given us, in place of the Federal government, under which we fondly believed we were living, a consolidated military despotism.... I tremble for South Carolina. The war-cry is up, rely upon it.... The boast is that the President, by stamping like another Pompey on the earth, can raise a hundred thousand men." [38]

A few days later, on February 6, 1833, Tyler delivered his Senate speech against the Force Bill. The visitors' galleries were packed. From beginning to end the speech was an appeal to emotion. The oratory was brilliant, but at no point in his address did he suggest to Jackson how the Union might be preserved without the use of force. Faced with the nullification of constitutional federal legislation, how else could Jackson approach South Carolina save by force? That was the question. Either the Union was or it was not. There could be no partial Union some of the time when it suited the convenience of some of the parties to it. Jackson, of course, wanted no civil war. But he could not permit the Union to degenerate into a part-time half-Union. He had taken an oath to "preserve, protect and defend the Constitution of the United States." Whatever that Constitution was, whether it had created a nation or a confederation, there was nothing in it specifically permitting nullification. His was much the same problem Lincoln would face on secession in 1861.

Tyler wanted no dissolution of the Union either. Unlike Jackson, though, he had no plan to prevent dissolution. Instead, he spoke to the Senate of preserving the Union by restoring mutual confidence and affection among the states. He suggested the passage of a compromise tariff act that would allow both sides to save face. He shied away from the theoretical implications of nullification. At the same time he ripped into the Force Bill with a ferocity unequaled in any other public speech in his career. It was a speech aimed as much at the political factions in Virginia as at those within reach of his voice. A few days later he would stand for re-election to the Senate before the General Assembly in Richmond. This test he won handily, defeating James McDowell, candidate of the Virginia Jacksonians, 81 to 62 on the first ballot. Nevertheless, he wanted to make his position on the Force Bill absolutely clear to Virginians as well as to the senators who sat before him:

Everything, Mr. President, is running into nationality. You cannot walk along the streets without seeing the word on almost every sign—National Hotel, National boot-black, National black-smith, National oyster-house. The government was created by the states, it is amendable by the states, it is preserved by the states, and may be destroyed by the states; and yet we are told that it is not a government of the states.... The very terms employed in the Constitution indicate the true character of the government. The terms "We, the people of the United States," mean nothing more or less than "We the people of the states united." The pernicious doctrine that this is a national and not a Federal Government, has received countenance from the late proclamation and message of the President. The people are regarded as one mass, and the states as constituting one nation. I desire to know when this chemical process occurred... such doctrines would convert the states into mere petty corporations, provinces of one consolidated government. These principles give to this government authority to veto all state laws, not merely by Act of Congress, but by the sword and bayonet. They would place the President at the head of the regular army in array against the States, and the sword and cannon would come to be the common arbiter.... To arm him with military power is to give him the authority to crush South Carolina, should she adopt secession.

He was convinced that if the crisis came to outright secession, economic pressures alone would bring South Carolina back into the Union more swiftly than the "employment of a hundred thousand men." As he would do again in 1861, Tyler painted a grim picture of the bloodshed and property destruction of civil war. He pleaded that Jackson not be given the power to coerce South Carolina and thereby precipitate a civil war. It was Jackson's decision, said Tyler, not South Carolina's:

If the majority shall pass this bill, they must do it on their own responsibility; I will have no part in it.... Yes, sir, "the Federal Union must be preserved." But how? Will you seek to preserve it by force? Will you appease the angry spirit of discord by an oblation of blood?... Glory comes not from the blood of slaughtered brethren. Gracious God! Is it necessary to urge such considerations on an American Senate? Whither has the genius of America fled? We have had darker days than the present, and that genius has saved us. Are we to satisfy the discontents of the people by force—by shooting some, and bayoneting others?... I would that I had but mild influence enough to save my country in this hour of peril.... I have no such power; I stand here manacled in a minority, whose efforts can avail but little. You, who are the majority, have the destinies of the country in your hands. If war shall grow out of this measure, you are alone responsible. I will wash my hands of the business; rather than give my aid, I would surrender my station here....[39]

On February 20 the Force Bill came to a Senate vote. Several Southern senators left the floor rather than be recorded in favor of a measure they could not stomach. It was clear by this time, however, that a compromise tariff might be worked out that would stay the hands of both South Carolina and General Jackson. Neither side wanted bloodshed. No one wanted to die for an *ad valorem* tariff. Better then, reasoned the practical politicians of the South, not to be counted on either side of the Force Bill. Only John Tyler among them retained his seat, and only Tyler had the courage to vote his convictions. Even Calhoun was conveniently absent, as was Clay, who was leading the compromise tariff movement behind the scenes. Senator William C. Rives of Virginia, Tyler's colleague, abstained from voting although he had reluctantly supported Jackson's course throughout the crisis, being, in his own words, "anti-bank, anti-tariff and anti-nullification." The final vote for the Force Bill was thirty-two; the vote against it was one. John Tyler cast the only recorded dissenting vote—the vote he was proudest of for the rest of his life. In 1839 he boasted in the Virginia House of Delegates that "Against that odious measure my name stands conspicuously recorded. I say conspicuously, since it is the only vote recorded in the negative on . . . that bloody bill." [40]

It was a courageous vote, but it was not quite so conspicuous as Tyler later remembered it. The chronology of events indicates that the prospect of a bloodless compromise was well advanced by February 6 when Tyler made his ringing speech against the measure. Although the Virginian did not know the extent to which compromise negotiations had proceeded in the cloakrooms and boardinghouse parlors, he did know that South Carolina, in a gesture of conciliation, had temporarily suspended the Ordinance of Nullification on January 21. By February 20, when Tyler cast the lone vote against the Force Bill, the crisis had largely passed. His concern for citizens being shot and bayoneted while blood flowed in the gutters of Charleston was therefore a bit theatrical. His role in the compromise tariff that averted bloodshed was far more constructive than either his ringing speech or his stubborn vote. It was actually one of his greatest services to his distracted country.

Throughout the entire agitation and debate on the Force Bill there existed the underlying assumption, made clear at the outset by Calhoun and other nullifiers, that a sharp reduction of the tariff duties of 1832 would provide the path of compromise through which all parties to the dispute might exit gracefully and bloodlessly. Tyler was aware of this, and he was a prime mover in the search for a compromise plan. As early as January 10 he wrote John Floyd that the battle for tariff compromise "is fought and won. My fears for the Union are speedily disappearing." Some time earlier Tyler had seen Henry Clay privately. He "appealed to his patriotism" and asked him to sponsor a tariff bill that would save the Union. He urged Clay, who was openly supporting the Force Bill, to consult with Calhoun, "the only person necessary to consult," and work out something agreeable both to Northern protectionists and states' rights free traders. Tyler's patient efforts were successful. The two statesmen were brought together for negotiations. The details of a compromise tariff settlement could not quickly be ironed out, and by January 16 Tyler was again beginning to despair. Jackson called for his Force Bill that day, and Tyler told Floyd that "all prospect of settling the tariff except through Clay is gone. From him I still have hope. If he strikes at all, it will be at a critical moment." [41]

Tyler was not disappointed. On January 21 rumors flooded Washington and reached South Carolina that a compromise tariff was in the making. To facilitate this hopeful development the Charleston radicals uncocked the pistol it held to the head of the nation by suspending the

Ordinance of Nullification. It was probably on this day, or the day before, that Clay and Calhoun reached a final understanding. Clay agreed to a gradual reduction of all tariff duties over a ten-year period, and a relinquishment of the entire principle of protection by 1842. Calhoun in turn pledged South Carolina's acceptance of this arrangement and a repeal of the Ordinance of Nullification. Tyler was not privy to this agreement nor was he told about it. But he had done much to bring the negotiators together. And he breathed a sigh of relief when, on February 11, the theatrical Clay, his eyes still riveted on the White House, rose in the Senate and announced to a breathless chamber that he would, the following day, introduce a compromise tariff bill. As Tyler recalled that dramatic moment in the Senate from the vantage point of 1860: "Now that years have gone by—now that my head is covered with gray hairs, and old age is upon me, I recall the enthusiasm I felt that day when Mr. Clay rose in the Senate to announce the great measure of peace and reconciliation. I occupied the extreme seat on the left; he a similar one on the right of the Senate Chamber. We advanced to meet each other, and grasped each other's hands midway the chamber." [42]

On the next day, to a cheering audience, Clay introduced a bill that would progressively reduce tariff duties year by year until a level of 20 per cent *ad valorem* was reached in 1842. At that point all further duties would be imposed only "for the purpose of raising such revenue as may be necessary to an economical administration of the Government." Calhoun followed Clay's proposal with a speech extolling the beauties of the Union. With this, the Compromise Tariff Bill of 1833 passed the House 119 to 85 on February 26 and the Senate 29 to 16 on March 1. Tyler voted for it with enthusiasm. So the crisis passed.

Just who won the contest cannot be stated with certainty. By nullification and threatened secession South Carolina had blackjacked the federal government into an immediate reduction of the tariff and a promise to repeal the entire protective system a decade hence. On the other hand, Jackson was satisfied that he had made his no-nullification, no-secession point crystal clear by approaching the brink of military coercion. What it seemed to prove to Calhoun and the Charleston hotheads was that a little bit of blackmail, judiciously exercised, could accomplish for the South in Washington what an orderly legislative approach there could not. This dangerous notion was still tragically alive in 1860–1861.

The Senate adjourned on March 2 and Tyler returned to the Tidewater in triumph. His constituents gave him a boisterous dinner at the Gloucester County courthouse. Toasts were quaffed in happy celebration of the great victories of states' rights on the Bank and tariff questions. A toast to Tyler's lone vote against the Force Bill was eagerly proposed and drunk. Tyler rose to his feet and gave a short and gracious speech in reply. He reviewed his course of action on the nullification question in Congress and reminded the celebrators again that he was "not the apologist of South Carolina." He simply objected, he said, to Jackson's policy of armed coercion. The issue was not South Carolina's nullification. It was Jackson's threatened military dictatorship.

The charge was overdrawn and alarmist, even wrongheaded, but it was slowly and surely carrying Tyler into the anti-Jackson opposition forming under the banner of the opportunistic Henry Clay. Tyler did not know in March 1833 that he was becoming a Whig. He knew only that he could no longer stomach Andrew Jackson. By November 1833 he could eulogize the once-feared Clay as the statesman and patriot who had "rescued us from civil war, when those who held or ought to have held our destinies in their hands talked only of swords and halters. Such is my deliberate opinion." His gradual rapprochement with Harry of the West was to make John Tyler Vice-President of the United States.[43]

It was only a question of time until Tyler faced an issue which would make his break with the Jacksonian Democracy clear and final. That issue was Jackson's removal of government deposits from the Bank of the United States in an effort to undermine and crush the institution even before its charter expired in 1836. He announced his decision on the matter in September 1833 while Congress was in recess. Angered at the Bank's intervention against him in the 1832 campaign, and convinced that his landslide victory in 1832 was an anti-Bank mandate from the people, Old Hickory began juggling Secretaries of the Treasury into and out of his Cabinet like so many sacks of wheat until he found in Roger B. Taney one who would sign the removal order and defend its legality. By the end of 1833 the withdrawn federal funds had been distributed in twenty-three state banks which were promptly dubbed "pet banks" by the anti-Jacksonians. Whatever the economic wisdom of this move, it was not unconstitutional and it was very close to what Tyler had urged in 1819 when he characterized withdrawal and distribution as a sound states' rights solution to the banking question. But this was not 1819.[44]

When the Senate convened early in December 1833, Tyler returned to Washington in an ugly mood. The idea that Andrew Jackson was a dangerous dictator now possessed him above all others. He was convinced that if Taney could "locate [the] Treasury where he pleases there can exist no security or safety for the public monies." Indeed, Taney might even decide to locate public funds in "either his own or the President's pocket." This unworthy suggestion pointed up the fact that John Tyler once again found himself in a cruel dilemma. He hated and feared what he felt were the dictatorial pretensions of Andrew Jackson. He also feared and hated the Bank of the United States and the moneyed aristocracy that was rapidly reducing America to a counting house. To his way of thinking, the victory of either Biddle or the President in the Bank struggle would mark a defeat for the national interest. An opportunity to ponder this dilemma and think matters through calmly was presented Tyler by an illness which kept him in his quarters for ten days in late December and early January. During this confinement Henry Clay delivered a slashing speech in the Senate which established the political line the anti-Jacksonians, Tyler among them, would follow for the next few months. To a hushed chamber and packed galleries Clay threw down the gauntlet to Jackson in terms the states' rights men could understand and applaud:

We are in the midst of a revolution hitherto bloodless, but rapidly tending towards a total change of the pure republican character of the Government, and to the concentration of all power in the hands of one man.... If Congress do not apply an instantaneous remedy, the fatal collapse will soon come on, and we shall die—ignobly die—base, mean and abject slaves; the scorn and contempt of mankind; unpitied, unwept, unmourned.

Clay concluded by introducing two resolutions of formal censure. The first condemned Taney's role in the removal of the deposits; the second and most important charged that "the President, in the late Executive proceedings in relation to the public revenue, has assumed upon himself authority and power not conferred by the Constitution and laws, but in derogation of both." It was a damning indictment but one supported by such diverse political personalities as Webster and Calhoun.[45]

When Tyler returned to the political wars on January 9, 1834, he informed Littleton W. Tazewell that his opinion was "... decisively made up on the subject of the deposits." He would support censure of Jackson and the restoration of the deposits even though this would strengthen the Bank and "render its spasms more disturbing and hurtful to the country." This decision was strongly urged upon him by a flood of petitions and memorials from Tidewater merchants and by specific instruction from the Virginia General Assembly. He was encouraged by the intense hue and cry raised by Biddle and mercantile newspapers throughout the country against Jackson. On February 17 he wrote Letitia his opinion that "the Administration is evidently sinking, and I do not doubt that in six months it will be almost flat.... I have not yet spoken, but everybody seems anxious to hear me...."

If he was somewhat premature in reading final services over the grave of Jacksonian Democracy, he was not wrong in his estimate of Senate anticipation. The Senate was indeed anxious to hear Tyler's indictment of Jackson. He was recognized as one of the most articulate of the states' rights spokesmen. When he rose to speak on February 24 the chamber was filled. He made it clear at the outset that he was no friend of the Bank and had never been; he had always regarded its establishment an unconstitutional act, and he was certain the nation would survive its demise. The only question was *how* the Bank should die:

For one, I say, if it is to die let it die by law. It is a corporate existence created by law, and while it exists, entitled to the protection which the law throws around private rights. If its privileges can be lawlessly seized upon, what security exists for individual rights? The rights of the bank are the rights of individuals.... If the President had rested on his veto, the Bank was dead, dead beyond the reach of surgery ... was it necessary after the Pursey [sic] was dead for the President to imitate the conduct of Falstaff, and inflict a new wound upon its lifeless body, lest it should rise again? Yes, sir, this was esteemed necessary; more justly speaking, he saw it in its agonies, produced by the exertion of his constitutional authority, and yet he was not content. He rushes upon it—seizes upon one of its privileges, one of the limbs of this corporate existence, and throws it into convulsions.... My answer is that of Virginia, spoken through her Legislature: if the Bank must die, let it die by law then, sir.... By that I will stand.[46]

The opportunity to link the deposits question with a condemnation of Jackson's use of patronage was too good to pass up and Tyler could not let it slide by:

I ask if it be true that [Jackson] has used none of the public money for the advancement of presidential power. Sir, all the revenues of the country are devoted to this object by these proceedings; an army of retainers is created in the officers and stockholders of the state banks.... Is the presidential power only to be considered dangerous when he is at the head of an army? Patronage is the sword and cannon by which war may be made on the liberty of the human race.... They work silently, and almost unseen. They make sure their advances by corruption.... Sir, give the President control over the purse—the power to place the immense revenues of the country into any hands he may please, and I care not what you call him, he is "every inch a king."

Mercifully, it would seem, no one flung these words back in Tyler's face in 1843 when he too, as President, attempted to build a personal party with patronage and, like Jackson, insisted on an absolute conformity of opinion between himself and his Cabinet officers. If patronage was indeed "the sword and cannon by which war may be made on the liberty of the human race," Tyler would soon fondle the hilt of that sword himself.[47]

Tyler suggested that the only way to remove the vexing Bank question from partisan politics once and for all was by a constitutional amendment specifically legalizing or proscribing the institution. "The question of bank or no bank has been always made a political stepping-stone ... it is the last subject which ought to be handed over to politicians." In the meantime, he thought the deposits should be restored. Because there was no likelihood that a constitutional amendment on the subject could be passed through the Congress by a two-thirds majority or through three-fourths of the state legislatures, Tyler's somewhat impractical solution to the problem was less significant than the political implications of his speech. Throughout his long address there were clear suggestions that Henry Clay was really a great patriot after all and that the Democratic Party, dominated by the "despotism" of King Andrew I, could no longer serve as the Tyler political home. Without hesitation, Tyler at last walked boldly into the Whig opposition forming under the leadership of Clay, Calhoun, and Webster. He spoke openly now of his "Whig principles," a phrase beginning to circulate in Washington to designate the views of the anti-Jackson bloc. As for the Democratic Party dominated by Jackson and the spoilsmen, Tyler renounced it:

> To this party do I belong, not to that nondescript, patch-work, mosaic party which meets in conventions, and calls itself *the Republican party;* not to that party which changes its principles, as the chameleon its color, with every cloud or ray which proceeds from the presidential orb—which is one thing today, another tomorrow, and the third day whatever chance may make it; nor, to the Republican party which ... denounces the tariff, and yet votes for and sustains the tariff of 1828—that Bill of Abominations; not that Republican party which denounces the Bank and upholds the proclamation [to South Carolina]; which denounces the Bank and sustains the Force Bill; which denounces the Bank, and even now sustains the President in his assumption of power conferred neither by the laws nor Constitution. No, sir, I belong not to that "Republican party"; its work is that of president-making. Even now it is in motion. Before the President is scarcely warm in his seat, not yielding to what decency would seem to require, not even permitting one short year to elapse, that party is in full march, calling conventions, organizing committees, and seeking by all manner of means, at this early day, to commit the people.[48]

Tyler could not have made his secession from the Democracy more plain. The Democratic-Republican Party of Jefferson had been subverted by Andrew Jackson. The new democratic political techniques introduced by Jackson—national nominating conventions, political organization and agitation at all levels, pragmatic accommodations to appeal to the greatest number of voters, and the sagacious use of patronage—were not to the aristocratic tastes of John Tyler. The dawn of the new democracy, the advent of King Numbers, was not for him. It was not the way of gentlemen.

Nor was it a way for the Commonwealth of Virginia in 1834. Statewide elections in the Old Dominion in March produced the elevation of Littleton W. Tazewell to the Governor's Mansion and the routing of the Jackson faction in the new General Assembly. Tyler was pleased and encouraged by this result. He was close personally to Tazewell and had done much to engineer his nomination and election. The defeat of the Jacksonians in Virginia also buoyed the hopes of the informal Whig grouping in Washington. Clayites, Calhounites, and Websterites alike sounded "notes of triumph" in the capital. But Jacksonianism in Virginia was not yet dead and Tyler cautioned Tazewell, lest the new governor grow overconfident, that "it requires numerous strokes of the axe to bring down the oak, and the exposure of every encroachment committed by a popular administration on constitutional rights is absolutely necessary for preserving free government." [49]

When the new General Assembly in Richmond instructed Tyler and his colleague, Senator William C. Rives, to vote for Clay's resolutions censuring Taney and Jackson, an order which caused Rives to resign his seat rather than comply and Benjamin W. Leigh to be appointed in his stead, Tyler was sure that sanity was returning to America. He voted for the censure of Jackson with enthusiasm and he has was cheered when the Senate condemnation of King Andrew I passed on March 28 and was formally entered in the Senate *Journal*. He paid no heed to the solemn oath taken at that portentous moment by Senator Thomas Hart Benton of Missouri. "Old Bullion" Benton, leading Jacksonian in the upper chamber, swore he would never rest until the censure of the President of the United States had been expunged from the *Journal*.

Benton's wordy gesture impressed Tyler not at all. Senate censure was the least punishment he had a right to expect. Jackson, after all, had converted the federal government into a "mere majority machine," and Tyler was certain that the continued growth of the "mere majority principle" could lead only to many political embarrassments and defeats for the South in the years ahead. Nevertheless, by June of 1834 Tyler began dimly to realize that politics in America would never be quite the same after Andrew Jackson. He began to see that the real and lasting source of Jackson's strength lay with the power of the unwashed as expressed in the ballot box. "We have a great work before us," he told Tazewell, "a work of real reform. Without the *people* we can do nothing. . . ." Just how a majority of the people were to be alerted to the dangers of the "mere majority principle" Tyler did not say. It was another dilemma.[50]

5

JOHN TYLER: THE MIDDLE YEARS

> *In the consciousness of my own honesty, I stand firm and erect. I worship alone at the shrine of truth and honor.*
>
> —JOHN TYLER, 1834

Throughout these years of political advancement from the House of Delegates to the Governor's Mansion and on to the United States Senate, John Tyler's private life was complicated by too many children and too little money. Between 1820 and 1830 Letitia bore him five more children, bringing to eight the mouths to be fed, bodies to be clothed, and minds to be educated in the burgeoning Tyler household. Letitia came along in 1821, followed by Elizabeth ("Lizzie") in 1823, Anne Contesse in 1825, Alice in 1827, and, finally, Tazewell ("Taz") in 1830. In spite of the added burden each new arrival brought Tyler great joy. When the sickly Anne Contesse died in July 1825 after a bare three-month hold on life, Tyler was crushed. Retiring to the quiet of his study he wrote a lament for the dead child which began:

> Oh child of my love, thou wert born for a day;
> And like morning's vision have vanished away
> Thine eye scarce had ope'd on the world's beaming light
> Ere 'twas sealed up in death and enveloped in night.
>
> Oh child of my love as a beautiful flower;
> Thy blossom expanded a short fleeting hour.
> The winter of death hath blighted thy bloom
> And thou lyest alone in the cold dreary tomb....[1]

As the decade of the Tyler population explosion opened, the young lawyer and politician was "so cashless and really straitened for resources" that he was reduced to dunning his friends and relatives for payment of debts as trifling as thirty dollars. Much of his financial problem was of his own manufacture: Tyler was not a brilliant steward of money. In 1820, for example, he lent his brother-in-law Henry Waggaman almost all his available cash reserve. In the same year he advanced other relatives upward of six thousand dollars borrowed from the various estates he managed as legal trustee. This was a dangerous practice since Tyler was invariably forced to stand personal surety for these loans. Like so many other Tidewater planters, Tyler was land-rich and cash-poor. Most of the cash income from his law practice and from the salaries of his public offices was poured back into the Greenway plantation and —after 1829—into his 630-acre farm on the York River in Gloucester County. His need for additional livestock and for slaves was constant. Even under the best conditions, most of the James and York River planters experienced seasonal shortages of cash; John Tyler was certainly no exception.[2]

But unlike many of his more prudent neighbors, Tyler managed money loosely and he often lent his cash to friends and relatives at the drop of a tear. In May 1828 he experienced "unfortunate bank transactions" which prompted an appeal to Henry Curtis for a loan to tide him over. He told Curtis at that time that he was "fixed immutably in my determination to get clear of the world . . . in other words to be my own Executor. I do not feel as a free man should, with these encumbrances hanging over me. Nay, I am ready and willing to sell slaves . . . if I could find a purchaser." [3]

Unhappily for John Tyler, his entire life was spent under the shadow of various "encumbrances." Until Julia brought her own financial reserves into his life in 1844, Tyler's personal economic existence was a marginal proposition. And save for the brief 1845–1851 period, when the businesslike Alexander Gardiner took over the supervision of his financial affairs, it remained marginal until his death, in debt, in 1862.

The necessity of having to sell a favorite house slave, Ann Eliza, to raise cash to move to Washington in 1827 was a sad experience for Tyler. He had a genuine fondness for the Negro woman, and he sincerely regretted having to part with her. But he had no choice. "My monied affairs are all out of sorts," he confessed to Curtis; "my necessities are very pressing, more so than at any previous period, and the time has arrived when I must act definitely." First he tried to sell Ann Eliza to Curtis, knowing that with him she would have a good home. When Curtis declined the purchase, Tyler tried without success to sell her in the immediate neighborhood. Under this arrangement either he or Curtis would be certain to learn of any ill-treatment at the hands of her new owner. Only as a last resort did Tyler finally instruct Curtis "to put her in the wagon and send her directly to the Hubbards" auction block in Richmond.[4]

While the ultimate fate of Ann Eliza is not known, it is certain that Tyler did not have the heart to accompany the poor woman to Hubbard's pens. When he felt he had to deal in human flesh he usually bought slaves from his friends, relatives, or neighbors. When necessary, he quietly disposed of them among the same intimate group. He often preferred to hire seasonal labor from his friends rather than buy new slaves on the market. Another Tyler practice was to lend and lease slaves within the family. As noted, his treatment of his Negroes was uniformly kind and considerate. His philosophy of slave management was best summed up in 1832, a year after the bloody Nat Turner slave revolt in Southampton County resulted in the wanton butchering of fifty-seven whites and the retaliatory slaughter of nearly a hundred Negroes. "I trust that all will go on smoothly in harvest," he wrote. "My plan is to *encourage* my hands, and they work better under it than from *fear*. The harvest is the black man's jubilee." [5]

No statement from Tyler on the tragic Nat Turner affair has survived. Nor did Tyler participate in the Virginia Convention of 1831–1832 which debated the slavery question and narrowly voted down several emancipation schemes. It is clear, however, that Tyler identified himself with those Virginians who interpreted slave unrest within the Commonwealth in terms of abolitionist propaganda filtering into the state through the United States mails. Speaking in Gloucester in 1835, Tyler lashed out at this menace by mail. In his most intemperate speech on the slavery question he pointed out that

The unexpected evil is now upon us; it has invaded our firesides, and under our own roofs is sharpening the dagger for midnight assassination, and exciting cruelty and bloodshed. The post-office department ... has been converted into a vehicle for distributing incendiary pamphlets, with which our land is at this moment deluged. A society has sprung up whose avowed object is to despoil us of our property at the hazard of all and every consequence.... It has established numerous presses.... [In these publications slaveowners] are represented as demons in the shape of men; and by way of contrast, here stands Arthur Tappan, Mr. Somebody Garrison, or Mr. Foreigner Thompson, patting the greasy little fellows on their cheeks and giving them most lovely kisses. *They* are the exclusive philanthropists—the only lovers of the human race—the only legitimate defenders of the religion of Christ....

As a Christian Tyler was particularly disturbed, he said, to learn that some Northern clergymen had taken up the cry for slavery abolition:

Standing as pastors at the head of their flocks, teaching the divine truths of religion, they are entitled to all respect and reverence; but when abandoning their proper sphere, they rush into the troubled waters of politics—when, instead of a mild and meek observance of their religious rites and ceremonies, they seek to overturn systems—when, instead of being the ministers of peace and good will, they officiate at the altar of discord, and contribute their influence to excite general disturbance and discontent, they deserve the scorn and contempt of mankind. Did their and our Divine Master commission them upon such an errand? When He bade His followers to "render unto Caesar the things that were Caesar's," He taught a lesson to rebuke the present agitators.

But when all was said and done the fate and welfare of Virginia's Ann Elizas troubled Tyler deeply.[6]

He was also troubled, in quite a different way, by the cheerless existence afforded him by Mrs. McDaniel's boardinghouse in Washington. After his return to Washington in 1827, Senator John Tyler of Virginia was often a homesick man. Letters from his beloved Letitia and his growing children were eagerly awaited, gratefully received, and speedily answered. Enforced separation for long months on end brought Tyler closer to his children. He did not take them for granted, and in his letters to them he entered into their many adolescent problems with patience and understanding. "My children are my principal treasures," he confessed to his daughter Mary, "and my unceasing prayer is that you may all so conduct yourselves as to merit the esteem of the good. In that way you will crown my declining years with blessings, and multiply my joys upon earth." The family was always a close-knit one. When the youngest of his children, Tazewell (named for his friend Littleton W. Tazewell), was born in 1830, he solicited suggestions for a name from the older children. He watched sympathetically as his two older sons, Robert and John, Jr., navigated the stormy waters of their first loves. He encouraged them to participate fully in the social life of Williamsburg and Richmond and he sent them extra money to pay for subscriptions to parties and balls. He was certain that such social experience would give them that "polish and shape to manners which constitute one-half the concern in our journey through life. I have known persons possessing only ordinary capacities getting on better than others who were in intellect greatly superior, simply for force of manners."[7]

The proper education of his children concerned Tyler above all other family considerations. Private tutors were engaged to instruct them at early ages; evidence of sloppy penmanship, academic malingering, and superficial thought brought instant paternal condemnation. The education of his daughters was no less important to him than the education of his sons. In 1830 he told Mary, then fifteen, that

Your resolution to attend to your studies and not to be led away by the vanities of the world affords me sincere pleasure. Without intellectual improvement, the most beautiful of the sex is but a figure of wax work. The world is but a sealed book to such an one; and to eat, to drink, to dance, to sleep, to gaze upon objects without seeing them, and to move in creation with scarcely a sense of anything, is the poor existence which they pass. The mind has been compared to the marble in the quarry, ere the light of science has shed its rays upon it; but when instructed and informed, like that same marble formed into a beautiful statue and polished by the hand of the artist.

So insistent was he with his children on the importance of education that his second daughter, Letitia, felt it politic to link an urgent request that she be permitted to attend a ball in Williamsburg (she desperately wanted to wear her "new silk") with assurances that her studies in philosophy and chemistry were progressing well.[8]

Both Robert and John, Jr., were urged by their father to attend William and Mary, and, following that, to read law. It was Tyler's subconscious desire to recreate his older sons in his own intellectual and professional image. With Robert he was more successful than he was with John, Jr. Indeed, his namesake eventually rebelled against the parental regime imposed on him and for a number of years in the 1840s and 1850s he led a checkered existence that brought no credit to the family.

Robert was his father's favorite. This bias, however innocent its origin, was sensed by John, Jr. Certainly Robert received more attention from Tyler than did his younger brother. While he was at William and Mary he was the recipient of many special favors. He asked for and received extra spending money from his father even when Tyler was under extreme financial pressure and unable to meet bills he owed the college. In 1836, when Robert precociously decided he would write a history of the American Revolution, Tyler encouraged him with a promise to pay the cost of publication. Yet he instructed his historiographically inclined son that he "should by no means suffer it to interfere with your college studies, nor should any more time be devoted to it than cannot be otherwise more usefully employed." Under such strictures, it is not surprising that he never wrote the book, though he later wrote some competent poetry. He was a good student and Tyler followed his progress in philosophy, metaphysics, chemistry, and mathematics with interest and pride. "I would have you go into genteel company," he advised his son, "when you can do so without neglecting your studies. They must go on at all events." In spite of Robert's close attention to his studies he did somehow find time enough to involve himself in a quarrel with a classmate, one in which the words *duel, honor,* and *challenge* were loosely bandied about. When Tyler heard of it, he instantly quashed any bellicose plans his son entertained. "In advanced life," he told Robert, "very few occurrences can justify a resort to pistols or duels; but at college nothing short of absolute disgrace can do so ... if you should unfortunately be involved in a serious quarrel, let me know the circumstances connected with it before things are pushed to any extremity. Your honor will always be safe in my hands."[9]

Tyler insisted that his sons abide by all the disciplinary rules in force at Willam and Mary. As a member of the Board of Visitors he could scarcely expect them to do less. He was also a personal friend of Thomas R. Dew, William and Mary's prominent president and the South's leading apologist for the idea that human slavery was a positive good. Thus Tyler was thoroughly embarrassed in November 1836 to learn that his own sons had joined their names in a student memorial to the president and the Board of Visitors protesting a new series of disciplinary regulations. Tyler's reaction to this distressing news suffered nothing in translation:

> I regard you as lying under the strongest obligations of honor to abide rigidly by the college laws. Surely it is no great matter to acknowledge their restraint for the few months you have to remain at college. Remember always that I am a visitor, and that the late enactments have emanated chiefly from me. Surely, if my own sons cannot conform, obedience should not be expected from others.... Be affable and polite to all the students, without cultivating extreme intimacy with any. Do not be too captious or prone to take offense ...a suavity of manners—a constant respect for the feelings of others, is indispensably necessary for success in life. These remarks are designed for you both, and I trust you will give them full weight.[10]

During the years he sat in the Senate, Tyler regularly described the social and political life of Washington to Letitia and the children. The dull social seasons were compared with the lively ones, and the weddings, dinners, and parties he attended were commented upon with good humor and a flair for the descriptive detail he knew the family would enjoy. He described the beautiful and diminutive Emily Donelson, Jackson's official White House hostess, who attempted to add to her height by wearing "three waving ostrich feathers" in her bonnet. Henry Clay carried his head "very loftily" although "age has bleached it very much." When Washington Irving visited the capital in June 1832 Tyler sketched him for Mary's benefit: "His face is a pretty good one, although it does not blaze with the fire of genius. It is deeply marked with the traces of hard study, and although sometimes lighted up with a smile, is for the most part serious and contemplative." The senator moved through the relentless cycle of Washington society, from party to party, reception to reception, dinner to dinner. Much of the social life of the capital bored him. Yet he made the expected rounds. "I must see the folks, you know, and make myself agreeable." [11]

There were times Tyler was shocked at what he considered the loose morality of Washington society. During the 1827 Christmas season he attended a dinner dance at the home of Cary Selden, brother of a James River friend and neighbor, residing in Washington. There he saw the waltz danced for the first time and the sight disgusted him. He told Mary that it was "a dance which you have seen, and which I do not desire to see you dance. It is rather vulgar, I think." He constantly worried lest some breath of scandal besmirch the reputations of his young daughters. "The world is so censorious," he reminded Mary, then sixteen, "that a young lady cannot be too particular in her course of conduct." He missed few opportunities to alert his girls to the existence of that "swarm of busybodies, who are found everywhere, and whose whole concern and chief delight consist in talking slander and indulging in injurious whispers." He constantly advised them to emulate their mother ("You never see her course marked with precipitation ... her actions are all founded in prudence"), avoid vanity, and watch their tempers. Thus when Anne Royall, in her book *Letters From Alabama,* described Mary in 1830 as a "little sylph" with a "smooth fascinating way" who "fairly beguiled me of my senses," Tyler told her bluntly that "Mrs. Royall's praise is of very little value; and, therefore, you are not to be rendered vain by it." Young ladies of good breeding, he instructed Mary, should also exhibit no temper. "Remember the maxim of Mr. Jefferson, in which he bids you, 'if you are angry count ten, if very angry count an hundred,' before you speak." Mary Tyler absorbed all this advice; she was delivered to her bridegroom unencumbered by scandal. When she married Henry Lightfoot Jones in December 1835, in an elaborate wedding that rocked Tyler financially, the senator warmly approved her choice. Jones was a young Tidewater planter of comfortable means who possessed inherited lands in North Carolina.[12]

At no time during his career in the Senate did Tyler permit his children to be uninformed about the great political issues of the day. He patiently explained to them his thinking on all questions. His growing distrust of Andrew Jackson was constantly made explicit to them. He did not, however, solicit family advice or opinion on political matters. His letters home were mainly an opportunity for him to think aloud before a friendly audience. When he felt that the Virginia press had done him an injustice on some issue or underestimated the importance of his personal role in some Senate decision, he would hastily correct the impression in a letter to the family. It is not surprising, then, that the Tyler children grew up firm in their father's states' rights political faith. He took them into his confidence at an early age, and he patiently explained his political decisions and actions, even the sacrifice of his Senate seat, to their satisfaction. "Retirement has no horror for me," he wrote Robert of his struggle with Jackson and Benton in December 1834; "for, come when it may, I have the satisfaction to know that I have been honest in the worst of times."

Indeed, his personal sense of political honesty was so stringent that he would not allow his franking privilege to be used for private mail within the family. Yet he was perfectly willing to use his influence to secure patronage jobs for members of his clan. He pushed his brother-in-law, John B. Seawell, for a clerkship in the Land Office, and he was instrumental in getting his nephew, John H. Waggaman, clerkships in the Postmaster General's Office and in the Land Office. Still, he prized the nickname "Honest John" throughout his political career, and it seemed no contradiction to him that he spent much of his public life herding a small army of his relatives, in-laws, and personal friends into public office.[13]

Like his political views, Tyler's religious views were also transmitted to his children. That he was a firm and lifelong believer in Jefferson's doctrines of religious toleration and the separation of church and state there is no doubt. Any connection between church and state he felt was "an unholy alliance, and the fruitful source of slavery and oppression." While he was nominally an Episcopalian, there is no evidence that his was ever a denominational approach to God. Nor did his Protestantism choke off a tolerant curiosity about the Roman Catholic Church and its doctrines; he was, if anything, somewhat pro-Catholic. Certainly John Tyler joined no holy crusade of one Christian group against another. He had nothing but contempt for hate-filled movements like the Anti-Masons of the 1830s, the Native Americans of the 1840s, and the Know Nothings of the 1850s. He preached religious toleration—and he practiced it. He believed the church and the clergy should stay strictly out of politics, particularly the politics of the slavery question. He saw nothing in Christian theology that justified making the slavery controversy the business of institutional religion, and he rather thought that the African Colonization Society, by restoring Christianized American Negro slaves to Africa, could provide more spiritual and moral uplift for all African Negroes than "all the foreign missionary societies combined." [14]

Like Jefferson before him, John Tyler was essentially a deist. He accepted the Newtonian concept of a mechanistic universe in motion, bound together by immutable natural laws. His interest in the new physical sciences was profound, and he believed firmly in the existence of "that invisible power which puts all things in motion, and sustains them in their respective orbits." As he once told Mary, "the person who justly contemplates the wise order of Providence [in the universe] can alone possess a just idea of the Deity." This view of the cosmos led Tyler to the corollary notion, almost fatalistic in its implications, that while man was an integral part of the Creation, he had little or no control over his own destiny. The truly good man, thought Tyler, could only strive to attain pure morality, and in so doing he could expect to be reviled and abused by men who sought not. As he explained this attitude in 1832:

The person who is a stranger to sickness is equally a stranger to the highest enjoyments of health. So that I have brought myself to believe that the variableness in the things of the world are designed by the Creator for the happiness of His creatures. In truth, what exists but for some wise purpose? All our crosses and the numerous vexations which assail us are designed to improve our moral condition.... The purest and best of men have been neglected and abused. Aristides was banished and Socrates was poisoned. We should rather rely upon ourselves, and howsoever the world may deal with us, we shall, by having secured our own innocence and virtue, learn to be happy and contented even in poverty and obscurity....[15]

These theological views permitted Tyler to accept the order of things as he found them in the world in which he lived—human slavery, sharp class differentiations, prosperity and depression. His was not a theology of revolutionary change. Instead, his philosophical attitudes undergirded his acceptance of the *status quo* in America and justified his own political efforts to maintain it. At the same time, it permitted a battered psyche to withdraw occasionally from the arena of political and sectional controversy with flags flying, secure emotionally and psychologically in the belief that men as virtuous as Aristides had also been forced from politics, and that even the immortal Socrates had been compelled to drink the hemlock. It was not accidental that he used the image of Socrates and the chalice of poison when he told Clay and Calhoun in February 1836 that he must resign his Senate seat on the instructions question.[16]

Tyler knew he was in for political trouble as early as the spring of 1835, when Virginia's Jackson Democrats scored important gains in the statewide elections. Thanks to an impressive demonstration of how to organize and deliver votes at the grass-roots level, the Jacksonians and their allies in the Old Dominion forged a working coalition of agrarian and artisan voters and used it successfuly to seize control of the House of Delegates and the state senate. With the radicals firmly in the saddle in the General Assembly, they determined to "instruct" the aristocratic John Tyler and his junior colleague, Benjamin W. Leigh, right out of their Senate seats on the expunction question and replace them with two senators more friendly to the Jackson administration—a power play pure and simple.

On March 28, 1834, Senator Thomas Hart Benton first sought to make good his pledge that he would not rest until Clay's resolution of December 26, 1833, censuring Andrew Jackson for removing the Bank deposits, was stricken from the written record of the Senate. On that day he introduced a motion to "expunge" the censure resolution from the Senate *Journal.* Defeated on the resolution in 1834 and again early in 1835, Benton tenaciously reintroduced his motion in December 1835. To the senator from Missouri, "expunge" meant the physical mutilation of that page of the *Journal* on which the censure appeared. The Constitution explicitly stated, however, that "Each House shall keep a journal of its proceedings, and from time to time publish the same...." Thus to emasculate that *Journal,* or to establish a precedent for emasculation, states' rights senators argued, was unconstitutional. Technically it represented a denial of the absolute constitutional command to "keep a journal." Rescind or repeal a resolution, yes; physically expurgate an entry, no. This argument may have added up to so much semantic nonsense, but throughout human history semantic nonsense has split churches, launched crusades, and triggered great wars.

Since his enthusiastic vote to censure Jackson in the first place, Tyler had done nothing to ingratiate himself with the Jacksonians or with "Old Bullion" Benton, the President's strong-willed hatchet man on Capitol Hill. On the contrary, he had antagonized Benton and his friends further in 1834 by participating in another of the interminable congressional investigations of the Bank. This particular investigation was politically motivated from start to finish. The five-man committee, which Senator Tyler headed, was stacked four to one against the administration. There was much truth, therefore, in Benton's angry charge that it was a "whitewashing committee," little more than "a contrivance to varnish the bank" and blacken the Jackson administration. Not unexpectedly, the Tyler committee brought in a report mildly favorable to the second Bank of the United States. This lengthy document admitted that there was evidence to substantiate the meddling-in-politics charge (the point on which Jackson had built the essence of his anti-Bank case in 1833); but it denied that the Bank had attempted to bribe and corrupt newspaper editors. This charge Tyler had earlier voiced himself. The report argued too that the Bank was financially stable and safe, that there had existed no cause for withdrawing government deposits on the grounds that it was weak and mismanaged. It also accepted at face value Biddle's contention at the time that Bank credit had been tightened in 1833 solely to prepare the institution for winding up its affairs and going out of business in 1836, not as a device to produce a recession politically embarrassing to Old Hickory.[17]

Benton's reaction to the Tyler report was to denounce the members of the committee as pliant tools of Nicholas Biddle and to charge that the criticisms of Jackson in the document were "False! False as hell!" Tyler was quick to deny the imputation. Reminding the Senate of his long hostility to the Bank, he declared that "I can not be made an instrument of the bank, or by a still greater and more formidable power, the administration.... In the consciousness of my own honesty, I stand firm and erect. I worship alone at the shrine of truth and honor." Profane allegations and pompous denials aside, it is clear that John Tyler had become no tool of Biddle and the Bank. He had, however, become so antipathetic toward Andrew Jackson that what the President opposed Tyler could almost support. For this reason he appended his name to what was indeed a whitewash of Biddle and the Bank. In so doing he clouded his long-standing attitude toward the Bank question.

Nevertheless, his apparent pro-Biddle stance on the Bank investigation in 1834 gave rise to suggestions that Tyler might make an acceptable Vice-Presidential nominee on the Whig ticket in 1836. In fact, the Whig-dominated Maryland legislature formally made such a nomination in 1835. But whatever his motives in the Biddle whitewash and the relation of these motives to his personal future political ambitions, his role in the original censuring of the President was enough by itself to make the Virginia senator fair game for the Jacksonian counterattack that came from Richmond in December of that year, when the Benton expunging resolution came up again.[18]

On December 14, 1835, Colonel Joseph S. Watkins, a leading Goochland County Democrat, introduced a resolution in the House of Delegates instructing Senators Tyler and Leigh to vote for Benton's expunging resolution. It was a neolithic political move, so transparent in intent that some Virginia Democrats saw it could make a political martyr of Tyler and force him irrevocably into the outstretched arms of the growing states' rights Whig faction in Virginia. With the Watkins resolution, therefore, came covert feelers from Richmond suggesting to Tyler that if he resigned his Senate seat without a fuss he might have permanent assignment to the circuit court judgeship temporarily being occupied by Letitia's brother John B. Christian. This attempted bribe, aside from the family considerations involved, outraged Tyler. "To accept any retreat from my station would be dishonorable," he thundered. "I throw the offer from me, and am ready to abide any storm which may come." [19]

The storm was coming, and Senator Benjamin W. Leigh had already decided how to weather it. As early as July 1835, when it was apparent that the Jacksonians would control the next House of Delegates, Leigh had written Tyler that he would not resign if instructed to vote for expunction. Like Tyler, he had long supported the concept of instruction, but he was determined he would not supinely hand his seat over to the Jacksonians. "I will not obey instructions which shall require me to vote for a gross violation of the Constitution," he said bluntly. He would vote for the Benton resolution only "when I shall be prepared to write myself fool, knave and slave, and not before." Leigh stood firmly by his guns. He refused to be instructed to support a measure that in his view was unconstitutional; he also refused to resign.[20]

Tyler might very easily have taken the same position. He had little to gain and much to lose by resigning his seat. Psychologically, he enjoyed being a United States Senator. He also needed the salary the position paid. He could certainly have rationalized a decision to follow Leigh's course. He had long held that his constituents had no right to require him to violate the Constitution, and he had often argued that he alone reserved the right to decide when a violation was being demanded. In this instance he fully agreed with Leigh that Benton's resolution was unconstitutional.

There were several considerations that caused Tyler to postpone a decision on what he would do in the matter until January 20, 1836, and then to withhold announcing that decision publicly until mid-February. Pleas from friends in Virginia to follow Leigh's course, to consider the larger political interests of the state's anti-Jacksonians in the November 1836 elections, gave him pause. So too did his personal financial worries. His eldest daughter Mary had just married Henry L. Jones during the Christmas holidays of 1835. "I have large debts to pay," he told his son Robert, "and your sister's marriage has drained me pretty well of money." Therefore during early January he remained silent about his intentions. When asked by his friends whether he planned to "abandon the Constitution" by resigning, he kept his answers "enigmatical." He toyed with a suggestion that he and Leigh retain their seats and appeal their decision directly to the people of Virginia in the April 1836 state elections. But he abandoned this idea as "extremely hazardous" for two reasons: He feared the effect an April defeat on the issue might have on the anti-Jackson cause in Virginia in November; and he did not like the precedent that would be set, too democratic to suit Tyler, of by-passing the legislature that had elected him by going directly to the people. So he hesitated and he pondered. While he leaned strongly toward resignation by mid-January, he would tell Robert little more than not to repeat his thinking on the question "out of the family" and to "rely upon my firmness, unmixed with obstinacy." [21]

The advice that poured it upon him emphasized the point that Tyler and Leigh should act in concert whatever their decision might be. If the two men divided on the issue, the whole doctrine of instructions, a popular one among states' rights politicians in Virginia, would be brought into disrepute. Nor would the Virginia Whigs (as the anti-Jackson Democrats in the Old Dominion were now being called) be able to present a united front on the expunging-bill question against the Jackson party in November. Maryland Whigs even threatened to rescind their Vice-Presidential nomination unless Tyler followed the position chosen by Leigh. Typically, Tyler absorbed all this advice, weighed it, and remained the individualist. As will become apparent, he did not act in concert with Leigh, he did resign, and his decision to surrender his seat seriously embarrassed the Virginia Whigs in the November 1836 elections. Van Buren carried the state.[22]

By January 20, 1836, he had made up his mind to stand with his principles regardless of cost. He had favored the doctrine of instructions since 1811 and he could not now easily or with consistency shift his position. He wrote Mary Tyler Jones on January 20 that his inclination was "to quit promptly and at once." He doubted that anything would "turn up to vary my present resolves." As for pending legislation in the Senate in which he was interested, he would simply have to "make hay while the sun shines" and let it go at that. Flattering talk of a possible nomination for Vice-President by Virginia Whigs, on a ticket with Senator Hugh L. White of Tennessee, failed to stay his decision to resign. While he thought such a nomination might garner him a "good vote," he knew that he could not carry Pennsylvania. And he would need that state to make any respectable showing. With a characteristic shrug, he decided to "make no calculations, but leave things to take care of themselves." [23]

On February 10 the punitive Watkins motions cleared the Virginia House of Delegates and senate and Tyler was formally instructed by the General Assembly to vote for the Benton resolution. To discourage his resignation and to persuade him to stay on in Washington, the Virginia Whigs that same day nominated Tyler for the Vice-Presidency. Again advice descended upon him. Most of it pointed out that the prospects of his election to the Vice-Presidency in 1836 were "very flattering" and that his friends were "quite sanguine" of his success. Since Vice-Presidential nominations for Tyler on Harrison and White tickets were expected in several states, he was urged to delay his resignation until some face-saving unanimity with Leigh could be arranged.[24]

These importunities failed to move Tyler. His decision to resign was firm and absolute. On February 10 he informed Robert Tyler that "My resolution is fixed, and I shall resign.... I cannot look to consequences, but perhaps I am doomed to perpetual exile from the public councils." Three days later he was looking beyond politics, praying that his health would permit him ten years of activity "which can be devoted to making worldly acquisitions." His immediate hope was that his sons Robert and John would join him in a family law practice from which all three might prosper. As for the Vice-Presidency, he professed little interest in it and no "hope of success," were he to become a serious candidate for the post. He would therefore observe the coming national campaign with "as much nonchalance as I can assume," and he urged Robert to adopt a similar course of silent reserve with regard to it. "Say as little about it as needs be," he counseled. Nevertheless, he suggested that Virginia Whigs and anti-Jackson Democrats should arrange a mass rally to condemn the instructional act of the General Assembly, one that would trigger a "general burst of indignation from the Ohio to the Atlantic." Such mass activity, he felt, would ensure Whig success throughout the state in November.[25]

When it became generally known in Washington that Tyler would resign and that Leigh would pay no attention to the General Assembly's instruction, Whig senators in the capital expressed their "decided opposition" to a decision they believed unnecessarily sacrificial. Clay and Calhoun were quickly deputized to see the stubborn Virginian and persuade him to change his mind. The two statesmen called upon Tyler, carefully marshalled the case for nonresignation and waited hopefully for his response. "Gentlemen," Tyler said firmly, "the first act of my political life was a censure of Messrs. Giles and Brent for opposition to instructions. The chalice presented to their lips is now presented to mine, and I will drain it even to the dregs." Calhoun stared incredulously at the Charles City Socrates. "If you make it a point of personal honor," he said finally, "we have nothing more to say." [26]

On February 29, 1836, Tyler wrote his formal letter of resignation to the General Assembly of Virginia. In this lengthy epistle he argued that the expunging resolution was entirely unconstitutional and that he could not lift his hand against the Constitution by supporting it. To do so would require sheer hypocrisy. Rather than do this, he would resign, whatever the personal and professional costs. He was certain that the precedent of expunging the Senate *Journal* was the first step toward converting the Senate into a "secret conclave, where deeds the most revolting might be performed in secrecy and darkness." The doctrine of instructions, he predicted, would soon "degenerate into an engine of faction—an instrument to be employed by the outs to get in." With this "salvo," as he liked to called it, Tyler returned to Virginia.[27]

In many ways he was happy to retire again to the quiet of his Gloucester farm and to his long-neglected law practice. Eight years in Washington was too long. He felt he hardly knew his children or his wife. It was nice to be home again for good. A few months after his return to Gloucester he sold his farm, moved his family to Williamsburg, and began practicing law in town again. His attention to the public business since 1828 had produced such "utter disorder" in his private affairs that for six months they required his "unremitting and undivided attention." His personal financial situation in 1836 was desperate, a fate, he complained, shared by all "who like myself have made themselves a voluntary sacrifice to public service, for the entire period of their manhood." He was almost grateful that his political enemies had forced his resignation from the Senate, thus allowing him a "fit season to put my house in order." [28]

In Richmond meanwhile, the confused Whigs and anti-Jacksonians tried to devise a means of honoring both Leigh and Tyler for their contradictory stands. The General Assembly had appointed William C. Rives to replace Tyler in the Senate. That the anti-Jackson cause in Washington was one vote weaker was a fact all Virginia Whigs could understand. Thus the hilarity was forced and the embarrassment profound when the Whigs collected at a dinner in Richmond in March to cheer Tyler's great courage in resigning and praise Leigh's courage in not resigning. This obvious contradiction was not allowed to pass unnoticed by Thomas Ritchie, editor of the Richmond *Enquirer*. Ritchie sarcastically skewered the hydra-headed Whig leadership in the Commonwealth, pointing out that it was a peculiar and opportunistic grouping of hostile personalities and contradictory principles. Indeed it was. But if the dilemma of the Virginia Whigs at the Tyler-Leigh banquet was great, it was no greater than that faced by the emerging Whig Party at the national level.[29]

To call the Whig coalition a political party is to do it a service above and beyond the call of historical accuracy. It was not a party—not in the European sense, certainly, and probably not in the modern American sense. It was, instead, a loose confederacy of warring factions bound vaguely together by a common hatred of the new popular democracy in general and of General Andrew Jackson and Martin Van Buren in particular. The party grew out of that hatred in 1833–1835 and it collapsed in the confusion of its own internal intellectual and factional contradictions in 1853–1854. During its twenty-year history it elevated two bewildered generals to the White House, William Henry Harrison in 1840 and Zachary Taylor in 1848, and it nominated another—General Winfield Scott—in 1852. These leaders were chosen to head the Whig coalition primarily because they stood for nothing controversial, antagonized no one, and because they could be sold to the voters, as Andrew Jackson had been marketed in 1828, wrapped in an aura of military glory. Both of the aging Whig generals died in office, bringing into power their Vice-Presidents, Tyler and Millard Fillmore. These men had little in common politically with their chiefs, and they were in both instances considerably more able than their predecessors. When in 1844 the Whigs did nominate a man who stood for something, Henry Clay, the Democrats beat him with James K. Polk, a political unknown. Party platforms and statements of political principles were scrupulously avoided by the Whigs for fear the brawling factions would disintegrate the party in a gigantic internal explosion. It was on this unstable vehicle that John Tyler of Virginia, no Whig himself really, backed into national politics and into the White House.

The Whig Party was an opportunistic amalgamation of two major factions. Foremost in its councils were the National Republicans, descendants of Hamiltonian Federalism. Led by Henry Clay, Daniel Webster, and John Quincy Adams, they supported the nationalistic American System—tariff protection, internal improvements, national bank—and they were generally loose constructionists of the Constitution. They had no use for slavery. Within the Whig Party the National Republicans were the best-organized, best-led, and most influential faction. The humiliation of their overwhelming defeat under Clay in 1832 ripened them for alliances and arrangements that would give them a broader political base. They most consistently represented the interests of the merchants, shippers, and the new industrialists of the North and Northeast.

Second in power and prestige within the Whig coalition were the states' rights Whigs of the South. Former Jeffersonian Democrats, they were variously disenchanted with Andrew Jackson for his spoils system, his Force Bill, and his removal of the Bank deposits, and they streamed into the Whig coalition in 1833–1835 in search of a new political home. They were much mollified by Clay's unexpected moderation during the nullification crisis, by his work on the Compromise Tariff of 1833, and by his statement that much of Jackson's proclamation against South Carolina was "too ultra." They remained, however, strict constructionists, free-traders, and antinationalists, and they looked to the continued domination of the national political process by gentlemen. Led by John Tyler, Willie P. Mangum of North Carolina, and Hugh L. White of Tennessee, the Southern Whigs chiefly represented the interests of the slaveowning plantation aristocracy. They feared the growing political power of the newly enfranchised white hill farmers, the upcountry agrarians and "poor whites" in the South who rallied around Jackson. Like Jefferson, most of them feared the propertyless urban artisans to whom both Jackson and Van Buren appealed. Indeed, in Virginia it was said that the "Whigs know each other by the instinct of gentlemen." Their hatred of the egalitarian Jackson and all his works was summed up in Mrs. John Floyd's heated characterization of the General as a "bloody, bawdy, treacherous, lecherous villain." [30]

Lesser adherents to the Whig coalition in 1834 were the out-and-out slavers and nullifiers led by John C. Calhoun and a small coterie of extremist South Carolina statesmen including Robert Y. Hayne, Francis W. Pickens, and William C. Preston. There was also an anti-Jackson contingent of Conservative Democrats, centered primarily in New York, Pennsylvania, and Ohio, who had broken sharply with the General on the threat of dictatorship they thought they detected in his Bank policy. While most of the leadership element in this faction opposed slavery, free trade, and strict states' rights, they were opposed even more strenuously to Van Buren and to the machine politics of the urban workingmen's democracy known in New York as Locofocoism. Led by such politically diverse and ambitious champions as John McLean of Ohio, Lewis Cass of Michigan, and Nathaniel P. Tallmadge of New York, theirs was an opportunistic movement of Democratic outs seeking to make themselves Whig ins.

Finally, there were the Anti-Masons, that strange and emotional sect that came bursting out of western New York and onto the American political scene in 1831 with little more for a program than the naïve and half-crazy belief that Freemasonry and Americanism were somehow incompatible. Skilled and practical politicians like Thurlow Weed, William H. Seward, and Francis P. Granger quickly moved in on this lunatic fringe and made of it an anti-Jackson, anti-Van Buren faction in the Empire State, dedicated in its principles to the protective tariff and to internal improvements.[31]

The practical problem in 1836 was how to bring the diverse Whig elements together against Martin Van Buren, hand-picked by the General to carry on the Jackson revolution. Crowding protectionists and free traders, Bank men and anti-Bank men, moderate and extreme states' righters, nullifiers, American System nationalists, Anti-Masons, planters and manufacturers, businessmen and farmers into one political tent was a trick John Tyler and the other Whig leaders pondered. Tyler's idea was to nominate a man who could at least unite the entire South and who would not be too offensive to anti-Van Buren Democrats and National Republican Whigs in the North. His personal candidate was his good friend Littleton W. Tazewell, a "Virginia Gentleman" who could, he was sure, unite and carry the South. Tyler thus undertook in November 1834 to launch a Presidential boom in Tazewell's behalf, certain that "no matter where his name may be first brought out, it will spread like lightning." When the Tazewell boom failed to spread at all, in Virginia or elsewhere, Tyler began reluctantly to consider the possibility of nominating Judge Hugh L. White of Tennessee. To be sure, White's estrangement from the Jackson administration was of recent date. But, as Tyler pointed out to James Iredell, Jr., in January 1835, White was certainly more desirable than Van Buren, and through White a united South might hope to control the situation. "We could only take him as a choice of evils," Tyler explained, "[but] I desire to see the South united, and to accomplish this I would yield much." [32]

Events were moving swiftly. In May 1835, at a Baltimore convention packed with federal officeholders, the Jackson Democrats nominated Van Buren for the Presidency and Colonel Richard M. Johnson of Kentucky for the Vice-Presidency. The nominations triggered a rush of states' rights Whigs in the South to the candidacy of Judge White. White had supported much of the Jackson program including the Force Bill ("He has voted to support the admin. in all its measures," admitted Tyler) while insisting that his states' rights remained orthodox. It was hoped that the very fogginess of this record might cut into Van Buren's strength in the North. The fact that the controversial Richard M. Johnson appeared with Van Buren on the regular Democratic ticket also gave the Southern partisans of Hugh White considerable hope.

Johnson's nomination was designed to give the Jacksonless ticket a genuine frontier flavor. Veteran of the War of 1812, comrade in arms of General William Henry Harrison in the Indian campaigns in Ohio, Michigan, and Ontario, Johnson's main claim to fame rested on his dubious assertion that he had personally and heroically delivered the death blow to the Indian chief Tecumseh at the Battle of the Thames in October 1813. Whether the reputed "Slayer of Tecumseh" was a simulated hero or not, it was a fact that he had long lived with a mulatto woman, fathered two quadroon daughters by her, and had boldly sponsored the girls in polite society. Miscegenation was scarcely a popular concept in the South in 1835, and when Johnson's nomination to the Vice-Presidency was confirmed at Baltimore, the Virginia Jackson Democrats at the convention broke into catcalls and hisses. The United States *Telegraph* sounded the alarm, calling attention to Johnson's "connection with a jet-black, thick-lipped, odoriferous negro wench, by whom he has reared a family of children whom he had endeavoured to force upon society as equals." [33]

The anti-Jackson Virginians struck back at the Baltimore nominees with speed. A meeting of Old Dominion Whigs was promptly held at Charlottesville; it denounced the United States Bank, internal improvements and the protective tariff, called Van Buren a "Federalist" (still a dirty word in Jefferson's Virginia), drew up a states' rights platform, and nominated Hugh L. White for the Presidency. Within a few days, in a letter to Colonel Thomas Smith dated May 8, 1835, Tyler endorsed White. The Tennessee senator, whom Tyler had accused four months earlier of having "voted to support the admin. in all its measures," was transformed in Tyler's mind into a magnolia patriot who had "been against the Old Democracy for two years only, and [only] on two or three important subjects." Tyler's conversion to White was speedy, but it was not related to rumors circulating in Virginia in May 1835 that linked his own name with White's as Vice-Presidential nominee on a states' rights Whig ticket. "I learn that there is an idle rumor afloat relative to myself," he told Colonel Smith. "I need scarcely say to you, believe it not." [34]

Meanwhile, the Whig campaign strategy, if strategy it can be called, was beginning to emerge. It eschewed both a national nominating convention and a platform statement of principles for fear the anti-Jackson bloc would disintegrate. Thus the Whig leadership fell back on the device of having various state legislatures and state nominating conventions put forward sectional candidates. The idea was to repeat the history of 1824. By preventing any candidate from receiving an electoral majority, the decision would be plunged into the House of Representatives—where bargaining by professional politicians might produce a Whig choice without further reference to the people. Three Presidential candidates were nominated with this plan in mind: Daniel Webster to appeal to the Northeast and the old National Republicans in that section; Hugh L. White to draw the South's anti-Jackson and states' rights groups together; and General William Henry Harrison, "Old Tippecanoe," a Virginia-born Ohioan to appeal to the West.

Of the three major Whig candidates Harrison was by far the least able and the most manipulatable. He was also perhaps the least controversial. A soldier of mediocre talents, a failure in business, and a regular suppliant at the fountain of public office, elective and appointive, Harrison had made obscure public speeches and statements over the years that had had that valuable political quality of saying nothing at great length on all sides of many issues. It is doubtful that he knew himself where he really stood on anything. One of his most perceptive insights came in January 1835 when he informed a friend "I have news more strange to tell you. Some folks are silly enough to have formed a plan to make a President of the United States out of this *Clerk* and *Clodhopper!*" It *was* silly but it was good politics. A myth was being built around the Clodhopper by his Ohio managers. Just as Jackson's propagandists had created the image of Old Hickory a decade earlier, so now did Harrison's associates create the legend of Old Tippecanoe, slayer of Redcoats and exterminator of red Indians. A mantle of rugged frontier simplicity and military glory was skillfully woven by Western Whigs and Anti-Masons and draped on his threadbare shoulders. All this on the theory, so often proved sound in American Presidential politics, that the packaging tends to be more important than the product. In William Henry Harrison the Western Whigs had an inferior product. But they presented him in a bright and sparkling package borrowed from the shelf of Andrew Jackson. Harrison was all things to all men, the all-American candidate.[35]

Tyler was not overwhelmed with enthusiasm for Harrison. Nor was he at all convinced that the multiple-candidate approach was the wisest one. But, given the nature of the Whig Party in 1835-1836, there seemed no alternative. At the same time, however, he did nothing in 1836 to advance his own political fortunes within the Whig alliance. He watched the movement for his nomination to the Vice-Presidency with detachment, neither encouraging nor discouraging the efforts of those who were working to get his name on the ballot in various states. He had no hope of his own election and little confidence in the chances of any of the various Whig Presidential candidates. He evidenced no elation when he was nominated on a Harrison-Tyler ticket in Maryland and on White-Tyler tickets in Virginia, Tennessee, North Carolina, and Georgia. He apparently felt no particular depression when he lost a possible spot on a Harrison ticket in Pennsylvania to Anti-Masonite Francis P. Granger. Nor was he angered when he learned that Henry Clay, in a characteristic backstage maneuver, had quietly severed the Tyler jugular at the Whig state convention in Ohio, slipping Granger's name onto the Buckeye ticket with Harrison instead of Tyler's. The Clay operation in Ohio was pure "humbug and trickery," snorted John G. Miller from Columbus. Miller was more outraged by Clay's double-dealing than was Tyler. Urged by his friends to campaign in "every man's house, talk to him as tho' everything was in his power—flatter the wife and daughters and praise the hogs," the Virginian was unresponsive. He was simply not a wife-flatterer, baby-kisser, or hog-praiser.[36]

The Whig chaos of multiple Harrison-Tyler, White-Tyler, Harrison-Granger, and Webster-Granger tickets in various sections produced confusion throughout the entire nation—nowhere better revealed than in Virginia. Having endorsed a White-Tyler nomination in February 1836, the Virginia Whigs were soon deluged with demands from the western counties for a Harrison nomination as well. This sentiment they happily accommodated. A second Whig convention was called in July 1836 which nominated Harrison and Tyler. In Virginia, therefore, there were two Whig tickets, White and Tyler and Harrison and Tyler, the arrangement being that in the event the Whigs carried the state, Virginia's electoral votes would go to the Presidential candidate, Harrison or White, who polled the highest popular vote. The combined ticket in Virginia was called the "Union Anti-Van Buren Harrison ticket," and the party there labeled itself "Republican Whig."[37]

The surprising thing about the election of 1836 was that the multiple-candidate approach very nearly succeeded. Voters in Ohio and

Pennsylvania went to the polls earlier than in some of the other states and by October 27 it was certain that the Whigs had carried Ohio and were running strong in Pennsylvania. Tyler was greatly encouraged. For a brief moment he felt that Johnson's Vice-Presidential candidacy was doomed and that his and Francis Granger's names would be the two submitted to the Senate for a final decision. "If the Virginia vote be sustained by the South, then my individual cause is neither desperate or hopeless." It was the only time during the campaign Tyler believed that a combination of fortuitous circumstances might conceivably bring about his election. Two weeks later he confided to James Iredell, Jr., that while the vote in Virginia would be close, "I fear we shall be beaten by a small majority." [38]

Tyler did nothing to aid his own cause. He did not campaign personally; he made no statements of a political nature; he praised no hogs. He simply sat on his front porch in Williamsburg and waited to see if the Vice-Presidential lightning would strike. It did not. Virginia rejected the Whig coalition and went for Martin Van Buren, whose appeal in the western mountain counties was powerful enough to offset divided White and Harrison sentiment in the Tidewater and Piedmont. In the final national count Van Buren received 170 electoral votes to Harrison's 73, White's 26, and Webster's 14. Among the Vice-Presidential candidates Richard M. Johnson received 147 electoral votes, just one less than a majority; Anti-Mason-Whig-Democrat Granger collected 77, and states' rights Whig John Tyler picked up the 47 electoral votes of South Carolina, Maryland, Tennessee, and Georgia. Rather than cast Virginia's 23 electoral votes for the miscegenist Johnson, Virginia's Democratic electors cast their vote for William Smith of Alabama. For the first and only time in American history, the Vice-Presidential decision was thrown into the Senate. There, on February 8, 1837, to the surprise of no one, the Democratic upper chamber chose Johnson over Granger by a margin of 33 to 16. "The double-shotted ticket killed us," said Tyler sadly.

Still, he was not long disappointed in the outcome. The total Whig popular vote was 736,000, only 27,000 shy of Van Buren's total and 206,000 better than Clay had done in 1832. A shift of 1200 votes in Pennsylvania would have thrown the election into the House as Whig leaders had planned. In addition, Tyler derived much from his losing effort. Not only did he gain national exposure, but he ran well ahead of White throughout the South. All in all, his performance and that of the new Whig grouping was impressive. True, Tyler's decision to resign his Senate seat on the expunging resolution had hurt the Whig cause in Virginia—as Whig leaders there had predicted. So too had the peculiar "double-shotted ticket." Yet in Maryland, the only other state in which he ran on a Whig ticket with Harrison, Tyler won. Indeed, Harrison and Tyler carried the Free State by a better margin than Clay had in 1832. Nor had Tyler compromised his states' rights ideals during the canvass. He simply kept quiet about them.

Tyler chose to remain with the Whigs after the election although he knew that the new party was dominated by its Northern nationalist faction. No surviving word from his pen explains his decision. It can only be surmised that he saw the Whig party in Virginia as the safest political redoubt for propertied gentlemen, a bulwark against egalitarian Jacksonianism and King Numbers in the Old Dominion. Certainly he had little confidence in the political sagacity of Virginia's "mountaineers," those hill farmers west of Lexington who had rallied first to the popular democracy of Jackson. It was his dedication to the political and economic interests of the Tidewater aristocracy that very likely caused him to remain a Whig when solid anti-Jacksonians like his friends Tazewell and Gordon were returning to the Democracy. Ironically, Tyler's class bias would make him President of the United States. He would owe the office to hundreds of thousands of these same unwashed "mountaineers" who swept "Tippecanoe and Tyler too" into the White House in 1840.[39]

Whether Tyler personally voted for White or for Harrison in 1836 is not entirely clear. In 1840, when he and Harrison were running together on a unified Whig ticket, Tyler vaguely demurred when it was charged that he had voted for Hugh White in 1836. But he never claimed that he had voted *for* Harrison. It was an embarrassing question in 1840 and Tyler, for good reason, preferred to remain as foggy as possible on the subject. In all likelihood, however, he did vote for White, although the evidence on the point is more suggestive than conclusive. His correspondence in 1835–1836 shows a willingness to support White. None of his surviving letters indicate any interest whatever in Harrison. His May 8, 1835, letter to Colonel Smith specifically endorsed White, it will be recalled. His statement in January 1835 that he would "yield much" to see the South united in the campaign would also seem to preclude his later support of Tippecanoe. Harrison's candidacy not only split the anti-Jackson vote in Virginia in 1836, it hurt the entire Whig cause in the South. Shortly after the election Tyler complained to Henry A. Wise that several leading Whig newspapers in the South had "dropped" White and taken up Harrison, and he blamed the loss of Virginia and North Carolina to Van Buren on this development. This is not the protest of a man who had voted for Harrison.[40]

The loss of the Vice-Presidency in 1836 at least enabled Tyler to remain at home with his family and rebuild his law practice. The next few years were happy ones in Williamsburg, and Tyler's practice grew steadily. His older children began to marry and produce Tyler grandchildren. Unfortunately several of these unions were unhappy ones, and it took all the power of Tyler's near-fatalistic deism to reconcile him to the ensuing disasters. What would be would be, his theology told him.

A case in point was the wedding of Letitia Tyler to James A. Semple in February 1839, a joyous occasion at the time in the Williamsburg household. Semple was a James River neighbor well known to Tyler. When he and his bride, a girl who was thought "very handsome, full of life and spirits," settled down at Cedar Hill plantation in New Kent County it seemed scarcely possible that within a few years the marriage would amount to little more than an armed truce. In May 1844 Semple went into the Navy as a purser (Tyler appointed him to the commission) and remained at sea much of the time thereafter. Shortly after the Civil War a separation was effected.

Similarly, the October 25, 1838, marriage of John, Jr., to Mattie Rochelle of Jerusalem (now Courtland), near Franklin, Virginia, began well and ended in failure. John Tyler encouraged the union, and he did everything in his power to salvage it once the fact became apparent in 1842 that it had moved onto shaky ground. Where the fault lay is difficult to ascertain. It seems clear that young Tyler drank too much and was unable to complete his law studies or much else that he set out to do. In any event, Mattie refused to live in Washington with him while he served Tyler as White House private secretary. Tyler in turn objected to having John, Jr., "live in a state of daily dependence" upon the Rochelle family. "I desire therefore to see them placed in a different situation," he informed the Rochelles in October 1843. He proposed specifically that the two families share the expense of purchasing a small estate for John and Mattie near Washington, even stocking it for them with a few slaves. He pointed out to Martha Rochelle, Mattie's mother, that while his own large family made it impossible for him to make a "heavy advance," he was willing to bear a fair share of the burden. Meanwhile, he was paying his son a salary as Presidential secretary. Tyler had already accommodated the Rochelles by appointing Martha's son James a midshipman in the Navy in September 1841. Neither this gesture nor Tyler's recommendations to Martha bore fruit. The Rochelles proved uncooperative, and by 1844 the couple were spending more time separated than together. In September of the same year the President fired John, Jr., from his secretarial post for his general inefficiency.[41]

Much more happily founded was the marriage of Robert Tyler to the lovely Priscilla Cooper of Bristol, Pennsylvania. The ceremony took place in Bristol on September 12, 1839. Priscilla was a magnificent woman with fine features, beautiful skin, and dark brown hair. She had a wonderful sense of humor and a flirtatious devilment about her which fascinated men. From 1841 to 1844 she graced the White House as her father-in-law's official hostess, the only professional actress ever to serve in such a capacity in the President's Mansion. Always a tower of strength in the Tyler family, she had seen much hardship when she first met Robert Tyler in March 1837.

Priscilla's background was anything but normal, although on her mother's side she was directly descended from the prominent Major James Fairlee of New York, staff officer with Baron von Steuben during the Revolution, and from Chief Justice Robert Yates of the New York Supreme Court. Her father, however, was Thomas A. Cooper, adopted son of the English freethinker and social reformer William Godwin. Actor, gambler, drinker, Cooper was one of America's leading tragedians when he married the respectable Mary Fairlee in 1812. The marriage virtually severed her connection with her outraged family.

 To this strange union Priscilla was born on June 14, 1816, the third of nine children who arrived with annual regularity. She grew up in Bristol in a house her father had won in a card game. There she lived until her mother died in 1833. By this time a whole new generation of actors—Edmund Forrest, Tyrone Power, and Edmund Kean among them—trod the boards, cutting into Cooper's fame and earning power with such severity that the large brood of motherless Cooper children faced privation. Tom Cooper had no savings, of course, only sour memories of bad cards. Faced with this situation, Priscilla decided that she too must go on the stage. Coached and trained by her father who reasoned that a father-daughter team might revive public interest in the Cooper name, Priscilla opened to mixed reviews at the Bowery Theater on February 17, 1834, in *Virginius*, a tragedy by Sheridan Knowles. The next three years of her life added up to a dreary succession of grimy boardinghouses, dirty theaters, and dwindling audiences. She was not a great actress. She was pretty and competent and tireless, but she was no Charlotte Cushman. Constantly on tour, she played the coastal cities from Boston to Charleston—as Juliet in *Romeo and Juliet,* Beatrice in *Much Ado About Nothing,* Juliana in *The Honeymoon,* Mrs. Beverly in *The Gamester,* Virginia in *Virginius,* and Desdemona in *Othello.* When the panic and depression of 1837 virtually wrecked the American theater, the Coopers experienced real hardship. On May 17 of that black year Priscilla wrote her sister Mary Grace that

We had radishes and salad—not roses and strawberries. The latter I shall not hope to taste this year, for economy is the order of the day. One pound of butter lasts us two days. We eat rye bread, burn one candle. Pa gets shaved once in two days and by the month. We wash ourselves only once a week as the Delaware is red [muddy], eat nothing but bacon and potatoes for dinner, with an occasional lone dumpling to give weight to the repast. Our business in Baltimore was so utterly wretched that Papa could not afford to go for you ... our houses were most miserable.... Hard times, banks breaking, merchants failing and strong fear of negro and Irish mobs. This latter keeping all the fathers of families in their houses after nightfall....[42]

 By the time Priscilla and her father reached Richmond on March 18, 1837, to play *Othello,* the young actress was tired and discouraged. She confided to Mary Grace, half hopefully, half wistfully, that if someone "with a large country establishment in Virginia, a good family name, and a handsome and good natured person," were to fall in love with her and ask her to marry him, she would not think his proposal "to be sneezed at"—a remark that was almost clairvoyant. The same evening she met Robert Tyler. Robert had finished at William and Mary in 1835 and was engaged in the reading of law in the Williamsburg office of Professor Nathaniel Beverley Tucker. The prospect of seeing the great Thomas A. Cooper play *Othello* had lured him up to Richmond for the evening. When Priscilla came on the stage as Desdemona, the patrons rose to applaud. This was a mark of respect frequently paid young actresses by courtly Southern audiences. Robert was transfixed at the sight of the beautiful Desdemona and remained standing and staring at Priscilla after everyone else sat down. After the play he went immediately backstage, introduced himself to Tom Cooper, and asked permission "to pay his addresses" to his lovely daughter.[43]

So began the romance which, after six proposals and a bundle of poetic love letters, culminated in marriage at St. James' Episcopal Church in Bristol in September 1839. All the Tylers encouraged Robert in his anxious quest. There was no foolishness about taking an impoverished actress into the family. As Robert told Priscilla, his mother was "more glad that I shall marry you than anyone else in the world." John Tyler was his son's best man at the ceremony and John Tyler, Jr., served as a groomsman. Because of her recent stroke, Letitia Christian Tyler could not attend her son's wedding. After a honeymoon at Woodlawn plantation, home of Henry and Mary Tyler Jones, the couple returned to Williamsburg.[44]

Priscilla fitted easily and happily into the bosom of the Tyler family. She truly loved Letitia, got on very well with John Tyler, and enjoyed the Tyler children. She was a happy bride. She never looked back to her grim days in the theater. It worried her sometimes that her father, working alone again, was reduced in 1839 to playing such backwoods tank towns as Montgomery, Alabama. But she had her own life to lead now, and she threw her energies into her husband's career. She helped him prepare his law cases and write his speeches to the juries. "I write all the pathetic and romantic parts, and Mr. Tyler, the law and reason," she informed her sister. She also transcribed his somber poetry, mended his shirts, and tried to save money by making some of her own dresses. Her clumsy efforts as a seamstress reminded her of the two French towns, "Too Long" and "Too Loose." Nor did it take her long to discover that the management of money in the Tyler household was a casual affair. In August 1840 she wrote Mary Grace that

At present the situation is anything but comfortable. Mr. [Robert] Tyler has nothing to do scarcely in Williamsburg, and his father won't send him away. The family are *very* extravagant. The governor [Tyler] pressed for money; consequently I never think of indulging in any little elegant superfluities, even to a yard of blue ribbon; in fact, never get a paper of pins without waiting a week or two to see if I *can* do without them. The governor is very generous though and has given me permission to have an account in every store in Williamsburg, which of course I do not avail myself of.[45]

Priscilla was understandably worried. When she wrote this letter she was five months pregnant, and she was beginning to wonder when her husband was ever going to commence his law career seriously. For all practical purposes he had given up the law early in 1840 to assist in his father's campaign for the Vice-Presidency. Thus, when she and Robert visited Tom Cooper in Bristol in August 1840, two months before the election, she saw the two men she loved most in the world staring poverty in the face.

It was not a successful homecoming. Robert did not get along well with his crusty father-in-law, who was a staunch Van Buren Democrat. "The Whigs stand no more chance than a cat in hell without claws," he told Robert. "Damn their bloods. They will cut their own damn throats." While Robert laughed politely at these profane little sallies, the fact remained that the men mixed, as Priscilla put it, "about as much as oil and water." Fortunately for the economic well-being of both of them, the Whigs did win the election. Thus when Tyler became President in 1841 Robert promptly received a fifteen-hundred-dollar-a-year sinecure in the Land Office and Tom Cooper was appointed storekeeper at the Frankford Arsenal in Pennsylvania with the pay of an Army captain. Priscilla finally caught the spirit of the Presidential campaign to which her husband had sacrificed his budding law career. She wrote to everyone she knew urging them to support the Whig ticket. And when Harrison and Tyler were swept into office she literally danced for joy.[46]

6

AND TYLER TOO

*And we'll vote for Tyler, therefore,
Without a why or wherefore.*
—WHIG CAMPAIGN SONG, 1840

Tyler's return to active politics in April 1838, after an absence of two years, was as predictable as it was inevitable. He could not long bear being out of the political stream. He had a real addiction to politics. On April 26, 1838, he stood as a Whig for the Virginia House of Delegates from the Williamsburg district and was swept into office. Already talk and speculation had revived throughout the South that linked Tyler's name once more to the Vice-Presidential nomination for 1840 on the Whig ticket. The Virginian's election to the speakership of the House of Delegates in January 1839 only increased this speculation. But Tyler did not return to the political arena in 1838 to run for the Vice-Presidency in 1840; he felt he had no chance in that direction. As he confided to Henry A. Wise in December 1838, "I dream not that any Southern man with *Southern* principles is to be selected. This has already been tested in my case. My election was certain [in 1836] if Northern and Western men had come to my aid." [1]

Nevertheless, 1840 had all the earmarks of a Whig year. The depression which stalked the nation had, by 1839, stimulated widespread popular demands to throw the ins bodily out. Most Americans did not understand just how Andrew Jackson's fiscal policies had triggered the economic crisis, but they did understand seven-cent cotton, five-cent sugar, and sixty-eight cents' wages for a fourteen-hour day at common labor. They could not appreciate the fact that Jackson's destruction of the Bank of the United States and the subsequent deposit of Treasury funds in "pet" state banks had introduced a wild period of credit expansion, paper-money inflation, and speculation in 1835–1837. Centering in the speculative buying and selling of public lands, the inflationary boom sent food prices spiraling upward and soon caused great hardship among urban workingmen in the North. This politically undesirable development eventually encouraged Jackson to issue the ill-timed if not ill-advised deflationary Specie Circular of July 1836 which demanded that all public lands forthwith be paid for in silver and gold. The resulting dislocation in banking and currency circles quickly set off the dreary cycle of depression—banks collapsed, credit dried up, commodity prices dropped, wages declined, businesses folded, factories shut down, and more banks collapsed. By 1838 some fifty thousand unemployed men walked the streets of New York City alone.

The Van Buren administration inherited the deepening economic crisis and could come up with nothing more inspiring to counter it than the Independent Treasury plan, which, after two years of bitter political wrangling and maneuvering, the distracted Democracy managed finally to push into law in June 1840. The Independent Treasury had no appreciable effect on the depression. It was a Democratic hard-money scheme which sought to divorce the Treasury from the state banking system once and for all by placing all government revenues in special federal depositories. While this plan had the advantage of removing government deposit funds from the speculation-crazed hands of irresponsible state-bank officials, its corollary stricture that obligations due the government be paid only in specie threatened further to reduce the supply of currency (and credit) at a time when the depressed state of the economy called for a policy of controlled inflation.

Meanwhile, conservatives like Tyler were shaken by the rise of Locofocoism within the Northern Democracy. Centering in the urban areas, particularly New York City and Philadelphia, the movement began as the Workingmen's Party in the late 1820s. At that time it advocated nothing more radical than free public education, protection of workers from the competition of prison contract labor, and the abolition of imprisonment for debt. But when it emerged again in New York in 1834 as the Equal Rights party, its leadership was demanding in addition abolition of business monopolies, legalization of trade unions, the right to strike, hard money, stable prices, free trade, and a strict construction of the Constitution. Enamored neither of inflation nor deflation, the workingmen of the North who complained bitterly about the rising cost of bread during the inflation of 1835–1837 were, by 1839, an angry mob of unemployed ready to heed the Whig campaign slogan: "Matty's policy: Fifty cents a day and French soup—Our policy: Two dollars a day and roast beef."

The rise of these radicals and levelers (or so they seemed at the time to the comfortable classes) in the mid-1830s split the Democratic Party in New York into two factions. The Locofoco wing, led by Martin

Van Buren and Senator Silas Wright, mainly supported the aims of the urban Equal Rights movement; the Conservative wing, led by Senator Nathaniel P. Tallmadge, largely represented the Empire State agrarian community. The Conservatives were willing to cooperate with the Whigs on most matters of fiscal and economic policy. Both factions vied for control of patronage-rich Tammany Hall, key to the New York City political situation.

With the onset of the depression years in 1837, the miserable, the hungry, and the jobless flocked to the Locofoco banner and marched through the streets of New York, Philadelphia, Boston, and Baltimore chanting angry demands for bread and work. The picture they presented was indeed a frightening one to conservative Democrats. That these same workingmen also supported the deflationary policies of the Jackson and Van Buren administrations (foolishly, it would seem) was proof enough to the conservatives that the entire Democracy had been captured by its radical element. Actually, the Van Buren administration did little to earn the allegiance of the unemployed workingman, and it certainly had no solution to his problem. Suggestions that the federal government intervene to combat the depression and alleviate human suffering fell on deaf ears in the capital. Indeed, Martin Van Buren in his Annual Message of December 1837 criticized those who were "prone to expect too much from the Government." Nor did the Whigs of 1840 have any idea how to produce "two dollars a day and roast beef" either. But they were out and Van Buren was in and it was in a fine slogan.[2]

As it became apparent that the Van Buren administration was destined to wrestle unequally and unsuccessfully with the disaster, and that the Northern Democracy was fracturing into two hostile wings, the Whig nomination for the Presidency became a prize eagerly sought. Congressional elections in 1838 produced sharp Whig gains in the South, particularly in Virginia, North Carolina, Georgia, and Louisiana. No one appreciated the rosy future of the shaky Whig coalition more than Henry Clay. Denied in 1824, passed over in 1828, beaten in 1832, neglected in 1836, the Sage of Ashland confidently looked to 1840 as the year he would at last walk triumphantly into the White House. As a charter member of the anti-Jackson crusade since 1828, no Whig deserved the honor more than he. Yet the key to the nomination was held by the states' rights Whigs of the South. Without the support and good will of men like Tyler, William C. Preston, and Hugh L. White he could not hope to capture either the Whig nomination or the election. So it was that Clay's slow canter toward an accommodation with the states' rights Whigs, which began with the Compromise Tariff of 1833, became a fast gallop after the elections of 1836 and 1838 demonstrated that the strength of Jackson and Van Buren in the South was not that of Hercules.

As early as September 1837 Clay commenced unloading much of

the American System ideological baggage that prevented the full consummation of a political love feast with the Southern Whigs. Speaking on the expediency of re-establishing a Bank of the United States, he retreated to the view that the Bank question was a closed issue until it became demonstrably certain that a clear majority of the American people desired the revival of such an institution. In February 1838 he attacked the Independent Treasury from a states' rights standpoint. In January 1839 he finally secured Judge Hugh White's support for his candidacy in a secret alliance negotiated through Henry A. Wise. By the terms of this treaty Clay abandoned his entire American System—Bank, tariff, and turnpike. As the Great Compromiser began to compromise his principles, Tyler could confide to Wise that in comparing the abilities of Clay and Harrison, he felt the Kentuckian was by far the more distinguished of the two leading Whig candidates for the nomination. "Amid numerous errors," said Tyler in December 1838, Clay had "yet contrived to build for himself a fame which will greatly outlast the times in which we live. I have admired him always, and he knows it." [3]

In sum, John Tyler returned to active politics in 1838 as a supporter of Henry Clay. Given the necessity of a sectionally balanced ticket, Tyler knew that the Kentuckian's nomination for the Presidency would preclude any possibility of his own nomination for the Vice-Presidency. The selflessness of his stand for Clay (indeed the irony of it) was shown by the fact that Tyler remained a Clay supporter even *after* Harry of the West had firmly planted a knife in his back during the Tyler-Rives struggle of January 1839 in the Virginia General Assembly.

The issue at stake was the United States Senate seat Tyler had resigned in February 1836 and to which William C. Rives had been promptly elected as a Jackson Democrat. With no prospect of a Vice-Presidential nomination in the offing, Tyler announced his candidacy for his old seat, partly as a vindication of his earlier stand on the expunging resolution, partly because he wanted the position and needed the salary. Meanwhile, in 1838, Rives had abandoned the Jackson-Van Buren Democracy on the Independent Treasury question and was now calling himself a Conservative Democrat. The state elections that year produced in the Virginia General Assembly a count of eighty-one Whigs, sixty-nine Van Buren Democrats, and sixteen Rives Conservative Democrats. The latter group comprised men, like Rives, who had split with Van Buren in 1838, but who had not yet become politically integrated into the Virginia Whiggery. To Henry Clay and to other Whig leaders, it was vital that the Rives Democrats be speedily incorporated into the Whig coalition. In a crucial swing state like Virginia, their support of a Clay ticket in 1840 would be the key to success there. For this reason Clay quietly passed the word to his Virginia friends in

December 1838 that he was for Rives in the coming contest with John Tyler. From Tyler's standpoint, Rives was a Johnny-come-lately to the Whig persuasion, a man who had "sustained Gen'l Jackson in all his high handed usurpations and openly proclaimed that the executive power was a unit, and who sustained that unit even unto the point of blotting out the just censure of the Senate." Tyler could not bring himself to believe that Virginia Whigs could support a man whose political conduct had been so "obnoxious." [4]

But support him they did, a fact which became quickly apparent to Tyler when on the first ballot Rives polled 29 votes, twelve more than his known strength. When Rives' vote increased to 43 on the fourth ballot while Tyler's dropped steadily from 62 to 47 (Democrat John Y. Mason holding at 68), it was clear that treachery of some sort was afoot within the Whig fraternity. At this point Tyler's brother-in-law, Judge John B. Christian, got in touch with Henry A. Wise in Washington and instructed Wise to put the matter bluntly before Clay. In a stormy interview with Harry of the West, Wise learned that Clay was indeed secretly supporting Rives in the hope of carrying Virginia in 1840. Then came Clay's *quid pro quo*. In Wise's words, Clay "agreed that if Mr. Tyler's friends, who withheld Mr. Rives' election by the legislature, would yield his reelection, Mr. Tyler should be nominated on the Whig ticket for the Vice Presidency." [5]

Tyler rejected the proffered bribe out of hand. He did not seek and was not seeking the Vice-Presidency, and for personal reasons he would not permit Rives' re-election. Rather than release his friends to the Rives candidacy, Tyler decided to hold fast and thus deadlock the contest. Under the circumstances, Rives could not command a majority and the stalemate continued until February 23 when the General Assembly, after twenty-eight indecisive ballots, at last voted the indefinite postponement of the election. So angry were Virginia Whigs with Tyler over the Rives matter that they withheld from him their favorite-son Vice-Presidential nomination. At their Staunton state convention in September they endorsed instead New York Senator Nathaniel P. Tallmadge for the second spot on a ticket with Clay.[6]

There is no evidence that Clay's patent double-dealing on the Rives question angered John Tyler. On the contrary, Tyler apparently accepted the situation as all in a good day's work, part of the political game. Indeed, in mid-September, at the moment Virginia Whigs at Staunton were pointedly passing him over for a Vice-Presidential nomination, he wrote Clay a friendly letter reiterating his support. He told the Kentuckian "I always regarded you as a republican of the old school on principle—who had indulged, when the public good seemed to require it, somewhat too much in a broad interpretation to suit our Southern notions." Such venom as Tyler had stored in him in the summer of 1839 (and with family wedding-bells ringing all around he was in a cheerful frame of mind) was reserved for Martin Van Buren for not having countermanded the removal of Tyler's nephew, John H. Waggaman, from the position in the Land Office Tyler had earlier obtained for him.[7]

Nor did Tyler give any indication that his disappointment in the contest with Rives, if indeed there was any, would take the form of a long sulk in Virginia's political tent. In the months preceding the national Whig convention at Harrisburg in December 1839, Tyler was extremely active in the Whig cause in spite of the fact that only one state (Mississippi) had seen fit to tender him a Vice-Presidential nomination. The Southern Whig tide was running strong for Henry Clay—Virginia, Louisiana, Mississippi, Alabama, and North Carolina all announced for him—and Tyler gave his time and energy unstintingly to the Clay cause. In various precampaign speeches he ridiculed the excesses to which internal improvements had been carried, rang the tocsin for states' rights, belabored the Force Bill, and eulogized the Compromise Tariff of 1833. In April 1839 he joined in a statement issued by Whig members of the Virginia Assembly to the effect that internal improvements, protective tariffs, and the Bank had all "ceased to be practical questions." In July he addressed an open letter to the Whigs of Louisville in which he variously criticized the Independent Treasury, Van Buren's use of patronage, the lack of and need for economy in the government, and the Expunging Act.[8]

Thus when what was called the "Democratic Whig National Convention" convened in Harrisburg on December 4, 1839, Tyler was little more than an interested spectator and Clay supporter attached to the Virginia delegation. Early in the proceedings Benjamin W. Leigh informed the Virginia delegates that if Clay was passed over and either Harrison or Winfield Scott nominated in his stead, Tyler would be acceptable to the convention for the Vice-Presidency. This prospect did not excite Tyler. He publicly "disclaimed *all* wish upon the subject." He was present, he said, only to see that Clay got the nomination; he was not himself a candidate for anything.[9]

That Clay was not going to get the nomination for which he had labored so hard and compromised so much soon became apparent. He had a strong plurality of the votes in the convention but not the necessary majority. So identified had he become with the Southern Whigs since 1837 that he had alarmed and antagonized the Northern wing of the party. Indeed, by December 1839 the Northern and Western Whigs were ready to nominate almost anyone *but* Henry Clay. Led by Thurlow Weed, William H. Seward, Thaddeus Stevens, and Daniel Webster, they proceeded to do just that. No slaveowning states' rights-oriented Whig nominee like Henry Clay could possibly hope to carry New York or Pennsylvania, they argued. Their alternatives to Clay were two amiable hopefuls: the ever-available Whig generals, William Henry Harrison of

Ohio and Winfield Scott of Virginia. Old Tippecanoe was still popular in the West and he had done nothing since 1836 to jeopardize his continued availability. General Scott, a mediocrity on the order of Harrison, although more of a pompous windbag, also had the advantage of having said little in public that was controversial about anything. He had a personal following in western New York state and a scattering of supporters in New Jersey and Vermont. "The General's lips must be hermetically sealed, and our shouts and hurras must be long and loud," said Millard Fillmore to Weed. Sealed or gushing, Scott was not really a major candidate. He had been temporarily embraced and used by Thurlow Weed only as a stalking horse to hold the New York Whig delegation together until such time as some reasonable anti-Clay coalition could be forged at the convention.[10]

A coalition was quickly cemented by the supporters of Scott and Harrison on the opening day of the convention. Their first victory—a decisive one—was to secure adoption of a unit rule. Under this arrangement all the balloting would be done secretly in a central committee composed of three delegates from each state. The total vote of each state delegation would be cast for the candidate favored by the majority of the delegates of each state sitting in the central committee. In this manner, Clay's considerable minority vote within the Ohio, Pennsylvania, and New York delegations was completely nullified. Still, on the first ballot the voting showed Clay with 103, Harrison with 91, and Scott with 57. Several subsequent ballots failed to produce any substantial change except that Clay dropped to 95 while Scott climbed slowly to 68. The vainglorious Scott began to look more and more like a compromise candidate in the likely event of a Clay-Harrison deadlock.

It was fear of Scott as a compromise choice that caused Thad Stevens of Pennsylvania, Harrison's floor manager, to deliver the great *coup* of the convention. Harrison's strength was derived principally from the 30 votes of Pennsylvania and the 21 of Ohio. Clay's strength lay largely in the South, where it was solidly underpinned by Virginia's 23 votes. Early in the proceedings the Virginia delegation had reluctantly decided that their second choice, if Clay could not be nominated, would be Scott. At least he was a graduate of William and Mary and had been born near Petersburg. Of course, Clay and Harrison had also been born in Virginia. To prevent any break by Virginia from Clay to Scott, an act that would surely have stampeded the convention to the General, Stevens casually showed the Virginia delegates a letter the foolish Scott had written to Francis Granger earlier in the year. When or how Thad Stevens came into possession of this blockbuster is not known. It is known, however, that the letter had enough antislavery sentiment in it to cause the influential Virginia delegation to announce that their second choice for the nomination was now Harrison. This announcement triggered a stampede to Tippecanoe as the Scott candidacy swiftly collapsed. Weed worked quickly to shift the New York delegation from his stalking horse to Harrison, and on the next ballot the old Indian fighter received a majority of 148; Clay had 90 and Scott garnered 16.[11]

Virginia and Tyler stuck with Clay to the bitter end. They shifted to no one. The report soon went around the convention that when Tyler heard the outcome of the final ballot he broke down and wept. Tyler did no such thing, but the story became part of the Tyler myth. It may even have aided his Vice-Presidential candidacy among disgruntled supporters of Clay. In any event, it is clear that John Tyler worked for and voted for Henry Clay on every ballot. It was this practical evidence of loyalty to Clay (greater loyalty than Clay had ever shown him), not alleged tears, that brought Tyler the support of grateful Clay forces at Harrisburg for second place on the ticket.[12]

Less legendary were Clay's tears of anger and frustration when he learned that the convention had nominated Harrison, that the grand prize had eluded him once again. Henry Wise was with him in his room at Brown's Hotel in Washington when the unexpected news arrived from Harrisburg. Clay had been drinking heavily in a somewhat premature celebration of his certain nomination, and the shocking intelligence of Harrison's success sent him into a half-drunken rage. Stamping, cursing, and gesticulating, Clay paced the room hurling obscenities at his enemies. "My friends are not worth the powder and shot it would take to kill them!" he screamed. "It is a diabolical intrigue... which has betrayed me. I am the most unfortunate man in the history of parties: always run by my friends when sure to be defeated, and now betrayed for the nomination when I, or anyone, would be sure of an election." [13]

With Harrison as the Whig nominee, Tyler's selection as his running mate became a distinct possibility. He had run with the General on Whig tickets in Maryland and Virginia in 1836, he had a national political reputation, and his states' rights ideology and Southern background gave the ticket of the Whig coalition a sectional balance it sorely needed. Of equal importance was the fact that there was a serious shortage of available Vice-Presidential candidates other than Tyler. John Tyler was also a powerful force in Virginia politics. He still held the key to Rives' re-election to the Senate, that same key Clay and other Whigs thought must be turned if the party expected to carry the Old Dominion in 1840. But mainly it was a lack of other Vice-Presidential hopefuls that attracted the lightning to Tyler's graying head.

The name of John M. Clayton of Delaware, a Clay stalwart, was briefly considered by the convention managers, Stevens and Weed, in their desire to pacify the Clay forces with the Vice-Presidency. Clayton made it clear that he was not interested. Nathaniel P. Tallmadge of New York was from the wrong state. So too was Daniel Webster, who had no interest in the dead-end job anyway. Benjamin W. Leigh of

Virginia was apparently approached (how forcefully is not clear), but he too declined the dubious honor. The name of Senator William C. Preston of South Carolina was suggested but caused no ripple. And so it finally worked down to Tyler, for whom there was little enthusiasm even within the Virginia delegation. Certainly there was no effort on the part of Virginia to obtain the nomination for him. Most of the members of the delegation preferred Tallmadge; they had no second choice. Leigh, the nominal leader of the Virginia delegation, favored Willie P. Mangum of North Carolina. As Thurlow Weed later confessed, the nomination went to Tyler by default. When his name was brought before the apathetic convention, the Virginia delegation pointedly abstained from voting for him; it "looked" better that way, several of them later explained in obvious embarrassment. The Rives matter still rankled them.[14]

In accepting Tyler, the Whigs at Harrisburg asked him no questions about his views and required him to make no pledges. There was no deal in any smoke-filled room. Tyler did, however, obligingly withdraw from the deadlocked Senate race in the Virginia General Assembly and permit the re-election of Rives. This act mollified Clay and eventually brought him into Virginia to stump for the Whig ticket. But at no time was Tyler asked to define or change his opinions. On this point he recalled later that he was "perfectly and entirely silent in that convention. I was ... wholly unquestioned about my opinions. ... In the presence of my Heavenly Judge ... the nomination given to me was neither solicited nor expected." The Whig charge leveled against him in 1842 that he had surreptitiously sought the Harrisburg nomination by whispering to some of the delegates of his conversion to the expediency and constitutionality of a national bank was false. Tyler said nothing at the convention and he did nothing there to advance his candidacy. He was put on the ticket to draw the South to Harrison. No more, no less. In asking him nothing of his views on the political questions of the day the convention managers carried to a logical conclusion their decision to avoid any formal statement of Whig principles for fear the party would explode like a chameleon on Scotch plaid. Both Clay and Tyler agreed with this tactic. "It is a safe general rule," Clay said, "that it is best to remain silent." So it was that the Whigs, their lips "hermetically sealed," left Harrisburg to do battle for "Tippecanoe and Tyler too." It was a great slogan. "There was rhyme but no reason in it," said Philip Hone. Young Abraham Lincoln was less critical. He thought the Whig slate "first rate." [15]

Hone's "rhyme but no reason" remark sums up the history of the Whig "Log Cabin and Hard Cider" campaign of 1840. Never before in the United States, and seldom since, has a major political party taken such cynical advantage of the political naïveté of the population. If it proved anything at all, it demonstrated to generations of politicians who would follow the Whigs of 1840 that most of the people can be fooled some of the time. They were fooled in 1840 by one of the greatest political shell games in American history. It was a sleight-of-hand approach which so embarrassed John Tyler that he made an honorable effort to detach himself from it. Failing, he retreated to saying nothing specific enough to damage the Whig cause and nothing at basic variance with the states' rights principles for which he stood. In fine, John Tyler walked a semantic tightrope during the great circus of 1840, but in so doing he too contributed something to the intellectual fog that enveloped and sustained the Whig effort.

At the outset of the campaign Whig strategy was to keep Harrison vague and Tyler quiet while the party managers whipped up enthusiasm for their Janus in a carnival atmosphere of torchlight parades, slogans, catchy campaign songs, and semi-drunken political rallies. That Harrison and Tyler were not of the same mind on most of the basic issues of the day was simply glossed over with

> And we'll vote for Tyler, therefore,
> Without a why or wherefore.

In the South the Whigs were for states' rights; in the North they were for American System nationalism; in the West they stressed Harrison's military record and fleshed out the 1836 image of the log-cabin-born man of the people, Cincinnatus of the West, wearer of coonskin and drinker of hard cider. They contrasted this portrait of their hero with a picture of Van Buren as an effete, cowardly, champagne-drinking fop living in the regal splendor of the White House. For the poor there were promises of "two dollars a day and roast beef" and stirring damnation of "Martin Van Ruin." For the rich there was the charge that Van Buren was a Locofoco leveler. Whig businessmen warned their hard-pressed workers that there would be fewer jobs if Van Buren were elected. In Protestant areas the rumor was circulated that Van Buren was secretly a Catholic; in Roman Catholic areas it was hinted that there would be state funds for parochial schools if the Whigs won. And in the West it was even reported that as the hens laid their eggs they cackled *"Tip-tip! Tip-tip! Tyler!"* [16]

Keeping Harrison vague was no problem at all. The man was born vague. His campaign up and down the country was a schizoid performance, a tiresome repetition of hazy clichés which looked North, South, and West in bewildering succession. Vague on the Bank, fuzzy on slavery, contradictory on the tariff and on internal improvements, Tippecanoe said he favored "sound Democratic Republican Doctrines, upon which the Administration of Jefferson and Madison were conducted"—whatever that meant. He condemned Executive use of the veto power, declared that he would serve one term only, promised that as

President he would initiate no legislation, and maintained that corruption in government was really a very bad thing. Motherhood, morality, God, and the flag he vigorously endorsed. All in all, his performance was that of an acrobatic octopus doing eight simultaneous splits.[17]

Keeping Tyler silent was not much more difficult than keeping Harrison vague. The Virginian preferred not to campaign at all. Better to sit quietly on his porch in Williamsburg and wait for the Vice-Presidency to come to him than to mix with the unwashed multitudes in the wild carnival atmosphere that was the Whig canvass of 1840. It was not the kind of campaign a gentleman could get very enthusiastic about. Thus as late as June 1840 Tyler turned down an invitation from his friend, former Governor James Iredell, Jr., of North Carolina, to aid the Whig cause in North Carolina with a speech at Raleigh. He could not come to Raleigh, he said

without being subjected to assaults from the newspaper press which at this time I feel desirous of avoiding. You have a warm political canvass going on in your State for public offices which to a great degree is associated with the presidential election. The desperation of party would cause ascriptions to be made to me of objects and purposes in connexion with my visit, which however unjustly, would be made to bear on the politics of the country.[18]

In this decision Tyler had the full support of Whig campaign managers. Early in the canvass, during the spring of 1840, they made it quite clear to him that he was to say nothing on any controversial issue. This decision was prompted when a group of Pittsburgh Democrats wrote Tyler and asked him point-blank whether he could, under any conditions, sanction the incorporation of a third United States Bank. Tyler honestly answered that he had always thought the Bank unconstitutional and that he would not and could not sanction one without a specific amendment to the Constitution permitting it. This reply he sent to Wise in Washington for clearance. Wise showed it to horrified Whig members of Congress, who quickly decided it would be "impolitic to publish it." Their argument was, as Wise later explained it, "that Mr. Tyler's opinions were already too well known, through his speeches and votes, to need a response, and that it would be unwise to array them directly against the opinions of many Whigs, perhaps a majority of the party, who were in favor of a bank." By suppressing his views during the campaign, the Whig managers were quite willing to risk the later charge that Tyler "had practiced concealment and deception." Unhappily, Tyler went along with this fraud, and from this point forward in the campaign he adjusted himself to the Whig strategy of remaining as silent and noncontroversial as possible.[19]

Had it not been for an exceptionally successful speaking tour through the West by Democratic Vice-Presidential candidate Richard

M. Johnson, Tyler might have remained quietly and comfortably in Williamsburg until the end of the campaign. As it was, Johnson's impact in the West momentarily frightened the Whigs and caused them to dispatch Tyler to Columbus to address a rally of Ohio Democrats For Harrison. The main purpose of the trip, as the Whig top command visualized it, was to demonstrate in the West that Harrison and Tyler were really one and united in their political viewpoints.

From Tyler's standpoint it was a harrowing and distasteful experience. Moving slowly through western Virginia in late August and September, he entered Pennsylvania and Ohio in early October. Politically, the tour went well on the Virginia side of the Ohio River. He remained carefully noncontroversial.

But after leaving the state he was increasingly harangued and heckled by Democrats in his audiences. Finally he was badgered into firm statements, in Pittsburgh and in Steubenville, that he favored the nonprotectionist Compromise Tariff of 1833. At St. Clairsville, Ohio, he was forced to grapple publicly with the inescapable bank question. Rather than be sandbagged as he had been at Pittsburgh and Steubenville on the tariff, he retreated to quoting the vapid language employed by Harrison in an earlier speech at Dayton in which Tippecanoe had declared ambiguously, like a squid squirting ink, that "There is not in the Constitution any express grant of power for such a purpose, and it never could be constitutional to exercise that power save in the event the powers granted to Congress could not be carried out without resorting to such an institution." In a two-hour speech at Columbus Tyler managed to avoid the bank issue altogether.[20]

In a final, almost humorous, effort to force Tyler to commit himself on the issues of the campaign and to demonstrate the broad ideological gap between the Southern Whigs and the Northern Whigs, a group of Virginia Democrats publicly directed ten skillfully loaded questions to Tyler and demanded answers to them. Tyler was never more cautious. He either pronounced the queries irrelevant to the canvass or noted his general agreement with foggy Harrison statements covering the same points. His response to the inevitable bank question was typical. Asked whether, as President, he would veto a bank bill, Tyler referred the questioning Democrats to his congressional speeches and votes on the Bank in 1819, 1832, and 1834. He then quoted Harrison's elusive Dayton statement on the bank, said it was his own view, and went on to explain the meaning of Harrison's language:

The Constitution confers on Congress, in express terms, "all powers which are necessary and proper" to carry into effect the granted powers. Now, if "the powers granted" could not be carried into effect without incorporating a bank, then it becomes "necessary and proper," and, of course, expedient: a conclusion which I presume no one would deny who desired to see the existence of the government preserved, and kept beneficially in operation. Whether

I would or would not exert the veto, it will be time enough for me to say when I am either a candidate for, or an expectant of, the presidential office—neither of which I expect ever to be.²¹

So confusing were the Whigs on the bank issue in the campaign of 1840 that when the question came up again in early 1841 they could not decide whether it had been an election issue or, if it had been, just where the Whig Party had taken its stand. In the North, Webster had campaigned for a United States Bank. In the South, Henry A. Wise had campaigned against it. Harrison and Tyler had tiptoed around it, and Clay had tried to bury it with the observation that "I have no thought of proposing a national bank, and no wish of seeing it proposed by another, until it is demanded by a majority of the people of the United States." ²²

If the Whigs were successful in confounding the issues, the Democrats were utterly frustrated in their efforts to point up the fact that Whiggery was more a confused state of mind than a political party. The Democracy was constantly on the defensive throughout the 1840 campaign. Their renomination of Van Buren had been a foregone conclusion. The presence of Richard M. Johnson on the ticket helped very little. Still consorting openly with his mulatto paramour, Johnson did not stir many souls in the Southern Democracy. Unable to keep him off the ticket, Southern Democrats did have the satisfaction of seeing their Baltimore convention produce a pro-South platform which forthrightly opposed internal improvements, the protective tariff, and the Bank of the United States. It also endorsed states' rights and denied the right of the federal government to interfere in any way with slavery in the states. The appeal of this platform in the South was badly diluted by Johnson's candidacy, whereas in the North Van Buren's proclaimed anti-abolitionism condemned him as a "Northern man with Southern principles." Throughout it all the depression and widespread unemployment continued.²³

The Democratic campaign never got off the ground. They laughed at "General Mum," quoted General Harrison to Candidate Harrison, and complained that the whole Whig Party was a fraud. It was, said Thomas Ritchie in the Richmond *Enquirer,* a "motley multitude, like the monstrous image of Nebuchadnezzar...made up of such heterogeneous and ill-sorted materials, that they have no great principles on which they can agree." Attempts to transfer the mantle of Andrew Jackson to the shoulders of Van Buren and Johnson were not successful. The charge that Harrison was a tired old man, physically and mentally unsuited for the Presidency, struck no fire. When it became apparent that Harrison would commit himself on absolutely nothing, the Democrats frantically stepped into the gutter, producing an Indian squaw who claimed that Harrison had fathered her children. It was difficult to set slime to music, and the Democrats at no time matched the catchy Whig fight song which asked:

> What has caused this great commotion, motion,
>   Our country through?
>   It is the ball a-rolling on,
> For Tippecanoe and Tyler too, Tippecanoe and Tyler too
> And with them we'll beat the little Van, Van, Van
>   Van is a used up man.[24]

When the ballots were counted, Van was a very used-up man. He carried a mere seven of the twenty-six states—Virginia, South Carolina, Arkansas, and Alabama in the South; Missouri and Illinois in the West; and New Hampshire in the North. In popular votes, however, he trailed Harrison by only 150,000 of the 2,400,000 votes cast. He polled 400,000 more votes in defeat than he had polled in victory in 1836. Thanks in part to a campaign in which both sides appealed to the lowest common denominator, one which was carried out with all the color and buffoonery of Mardi Gras, the popular vote was 54 per cent higher than it had been in 1836. The key to Whig victory lay in entertaining and bringing out to the polls hundreds of thousands of new voters; Whig tacticians called them the "hurrah boys." In sum, they expropriated the electoral techniques developed by the Jacksonian Democracy, embellished and polished them, and hurled them back at Van Buren with all the speed and deception of a fast-breaking curve ball. The effectiveness of this strategy was demonstrated with particular clarity in the South, where the Whigs cut deeply into the rural white-farmer vote which had been largely Jacksonian since 1828. In the West the Whigs were able to replace the frontier image of Old Hickory with that of Old Tippecanoe. In fact, Old Tippecanoe outhickoried Old Hickory. The Whig victory was therefore produced by holding the North while making deep inroads into the Jacksonian West and South. Ironically, Harrison and Tyler, both born in Charles City County, Virginia, failed to carry their native state. Van Buren also lost his native New York.[25]

Alexander Gardiner, who labored for the Whig cause in Suffolk County during the campaign, was disturbed that the Whig margin of 11,000 was not larger in New York. He ascribed this to the fact that Governor William H. Seward had meddled and muddled in the religious issue, recommending "that the Catholics be allowed a portion of the School fund," and by "hiring a pew in a Catholic church." Happy though he was with the Whig victory, Alexander, like most politically literate Whigs, saw serious storms ahead for the party—specifically, a struggle between Clay and Webster for the succession and a new fight over the Bank. "General H. has declared that he considers the old U.S. bank in some of its features repugnant to the Constitution," he wrote his father in Europe, "and that he will not favor another national bank institution unless it is very plainly demanded by the will of the people. How far he will consider his new election a demand of that nature is of course problematical. It seems as though some new scheme must be brought forward...."[26]

John Tyler also worried about the Whig future. He had predicted a Whig victory of 10,000 in Virginia and was much embarrassed when the state fell to the Democracy. He correctly blamed the defeat of the party in the Old Dominion on inadequate support from Rives' Conservative Democrats and on the inability of the Tidewater to balance Van Buren's popularity in the western counties. It particularly chagrined him that Virginia had "wheeled out of line" and joined New Hampshire in sustaining Van Buren rather than following Southern brethren like Maryland, North Carolina, Georgia, Mississippi, Tennessee, and Louisiana into the Harrison-Tyler fold. Disturbing also to Virginia Whigs was Clay's postelection remark in December that "it is not to be lamented that old Virginia has gone for Mr. Van Buren, for we will not now be embarrassed by her peculiar opinions!" But most worrisome to Tyler was the unstable and eclectic nature of the Whig party on the eve of its taking power. Which of its several factions would dominate the new administration? He explained his fears to Henry A. Wise:

There are so many jarring views to reconcile and harmonize, that the work is one of immense difficulty, and in your ear let me whisper what you already know, that the branch of the Whig party called the Nationals is composed of difficult materials to manage—they are too *excessive* in their notions, I mean many of them, and are accustomed to look upon a course of honest compromise as a concession of something which they call principle, but which dissected is nothing more than mistaken conviction.... I agree with you fully in the importance you attach to General Harrison's first step. It is one, however, of great difficulty. I hope he may meet and overcome it. His language should be firm and decisive to one and all. There should be no caballing, no intriguing in his Cabinet. Every eye should be kept fixed upon the official duty assigned, and never once lifted up to gaze at the succession.[27]

Tyler realized at the outset that the Whig Party might well be dominated by its Northern wing. He was correct in seeing the difficulty the states' rights faction would have preventing excesses on the part of the "Nationals." But he was wholly unrealistic in his hope that Harrison would prove strong enough to hold the factional alliance together and prevent the explosion that was implicit in the Whig mixture. Harrison had made it quite clear in 1836, and again in 1840, that he did not intend to be a strong Executive—that so far as he was concerned the Congress should and could run the country. The question, then, was how long could the lingering hatred of Andrew Jackson and the democratic principles he represented, principles actually congenial to a majority of the voters, serve as a cement for a coalition of ambitious leaders, competitive factions, and contradictory ideas? And how would this coalition, now that it had power, exercise that power evenly and responsibly without the benefit of competent or powerful leadership? The sudden death of Old Tip in April 1841 answered these questions by bringing swiftly to the surface the political, personal, and sectional chaos that was Whiggery. Nor when the explosion came could it be denied that John Tyler had helped fashion the unstable anti-Jackson compound and fasten it on the country. It was Tyler, not Harrison, who would be blown up in the detonation.

These considerations seemed remote as Harrison prepared to take office. That he was popular with the common people, if not with Whig politicians who covetously eyed the succession, cannot be denied. When he arrived in the capital on February 9, 1841 (his sixty-eighth birthday), to commence the ticklish task of selecting a Cabinet, so large a throng turned out to greet him that the pickpockets on Pennsylvania Avenue had a field day. They, perhaps, were the only group to benefit economically from the short-lived Harrison administration.[28]

The state of Harrison's health had been much commented upon during the campaign by friend and foe alike. Clay saw the President-elect in Kentucky shortly after the election and remarked that the aging Indian fighter looked "somewhat shattered." Littleton W. Tazewell had predicted to Tyler before the canvass that were Harrison elected he would not have the stamina to live out his term of office. And Alexander Gardiner agreed with John Quincy Adams' view that "no man of the General's age, without a constitution of most extraordinary vigor, could survive so great a change of habits, and the cares, burdens and anxiety of the office." The consensus within the Tyler circle seemed to be that William Henry Harrison could not survive the Battle of Washington. Indeed, when the General took leave of his neighbors in Cincinnati to go to the capital he had some of the same forebodings.[29]

Whatever stamina the old man had in reserve was quickly used up in the raging menagerie that then characterized the process of appointment to federal office. Whig office-seekers, sniffing the fragrant patronage trough for the first time, pressed in upon the General like a wave of screeching Shawnees. Meanwhile, Henry Clay arrived from Kentucky, confident that he would be the real power behind a fumbling throne. So arrogantly did he urge the appointment of John M. Clayton for the Treasury post that an exasperated Harrison finally exploded, "Mr. Clay, you forget that I am President!" Clay *had* forgotten, and so had most of the imperious Whig office-seekers. They surrounded Harrison in such numbers and pressed their demands that holdover Democrats be purged instantly from office with such shrill insistence that the placid General was stunned. "So help me God," he finally shouted to a group of them, "I will resign my office before I can be guilty of such iniquity." On two occasions he consulted Tyler about removal of incumbent Democrats from minor posts. Tyler rendered judgments from Williamsburg that enabled the harassed Harrison to outflank a few of his Whig tormentors with the remark: "Mr. Tyler says they ought not to be removed, and I will not remove them." Harrison wished the office-seekers would go away and leave him alone. He wanted to stir up no trouble with purge and patronage controversies. He hoped to be the respected head of a quiet, peaceful, orderly administration. Nothing more. As he expressed his political pacifism to Senator Benton, "I beg you not to be harpooning me in the Senate; if you dislike anything in my Administration, put it into Clay or Webster, but don't harpoon me." [30]

Out of all the confusion in the White House a Cabinet finally emerged. As a series of compromises looking toward all factions in the Whig constellation, it fully satisfied no one. Offered the State Department, Clay turned it down to remain in and control the Senate. Webster, who received State, was anathema to Southern Whigs. "He is a Federalist of the worst die, a blackguard and vulgar debauchee," cried Governor Thomas W. Gilmer of Virginia. The appointment of North Carolina Whig George E. Badger to the Navy Department quieted some of the Whig grumbling in the South. Whig abolitionists in the North were thrown a bone in the appointment of Francis Granger of New York to the office of Postmaster General. Former Jacksonians who had defected to the Whigs in 1840 were rewarded with the appointment to War of John Bell of Tennessee. Thomas Ewing of Ohio was given Treasury, partly to head off the capture of that post by Clay's candidate, John M. Clayton of Delaware, who was known to be a more belligerent Bank man than Ewing. To pacify the Clay contingent, John J. Crittenden of Kentucky was made Attorney-General. This blocked the aspirations of former Kentucky governor Charles A. Wickliffe, whose appointment to the Justice Department would have been a direct slap at Clay. And so it went. The Harrison Cabinet was a political polyglot.[31]

In all this patronage manipulation Tyler played no role. Harrison neither consulted the Vice-President-elect on Cabinet appointments nor was he offered any suggestions on the subject by Tyler. So far as appointments to key federal offices were concerned, it was Tippecanoe, not Tyler too. Tyler hoped only that the Harrison Cabinet "be cast of the proper material," and that within it "the voice of faction will be entirely silenced, [and] ... the question of the succession ... be shunned." Contrary to Tyler's hope, faction had been rewarded, not silenced; and with the aging Harrison in the White House the vital question of the succession loomed large indeed. Nevertheless, Tyler offered no criticism of the General's patchwork Cabinet. He had had no direct contact with the President-elect during the campaign, and when Harrison visited Richmond briefly in late February 1841 the two men had spoken nothing of politics. So far as minor patronage posts were concerned, the Vice-President-elect spoke only when spoken to. He pushed no one upon Harrison. Thus Tyler lingered in Virginia after the election, casually making his arrangements to move to a Washington hotel in time for the inauguration. Had William Henry Harrison lived, John Tyler would undoubtedly have been as obscure as any Vice-President in American history. As it was, he became the first American elected to that lightly regarded post who succeeded to the President's Mansion.[32]

On a cold, brisk Inauguration Day some fifty thousand excited, cheering citizens jammed the frozen streets as the venerable General rode "Old Whitey" up Pennsylvania Avenue to the Capitol. Hat in hand, without overcoat or gloves, the Old Hero waved and bowed to the crowd. He was in fine spirits, "as tickled with the Presidency as a young woman with a new bonnet." As the attention of the throng focused on the General's triumphal progress to Capitol Hill, John Tyler made his unnoticed way quietly from Brown's Hotel to the Senate chamber. There, shortly after the noon hour on March 4, 1841, he was sworn in as Vice-President of the United States. His speech lasted barely five minutes. It was a standard Tyler appeal for states' rights. Uninspired and largely unheard, it was not one of the articulate Virginian's better performances. It is just as well he put no more effort into it than he did, for while he spoke Harrison circulated noisily through the chamber exchanging greetings with well-wishers. No one was paying any attention to John Tyler. He was like the clergyman at a fashionable wedding. When he finished his brief remarks the assemblage moved outdoors into the chilled air. There, on a hastily constructed frame platform, William Henry Harrison, ninth President of the United States, delivered the worst inaugural address in American history to the assembled throng.[33]

Reduced to its thin essentials, Harrison's rambling, two-hour speech promised the nation four years of government by Congress. Not only did the President renounce a second term as a step toward checking the growth and abuse of Executive power, but he also specifically promised no Executive interference in the business of Congress during his term of office. The currency question, he felt, was strictly the business of Congress. Nor would the Chief Executive interfere in any way in the electoral process. On and on he maundered, abdicating the power of his throne at the moment of his coronation. Nowhere did he suggest what might be done about the depressed state of the economy. This too was up to Congress. Bored politicians left their seats and roamed around the platform, stamping their feet to restore circulation. When the Old Warrior finally finished, when the last windblown cliché was wafted mercifully heavenward, he returned to the White House, took to his bed for half an hour, and had his forehead and temples rubbed with alcohol. He was very tired. Meanwhile, John Tyler returned to Brown's Hotel, gathered together his belongings, and slipped unobtrusively out of Washington and back to Williamsburg.[34]

At the instant he took power Harrison was already in trouble, a trouble centering on Henry Clay's vaunted ambition to run the administration from behind the scenes. Specifically, Clay had decided that it would be he who would appoint the Collector of the Port of New York, not Harrison or anyone else. Clay's candidate for the lush patronage post was Robert C. Wetmore of New York. Webster had a candidate in mind for the spot too, Edward Curtis. Curtis, however, had worked for Winfield Scott at the Harrisburg convention and he was distinctly *persona non grata* in the Clay camp. Unfortunately for Clay and Wetmore, Abbott Lawrence of Massachusetts also supported Curtis. The fact that the powerful cotton-mill capitalist had personally lent the impoverished Harrison $5000 shortly after the inauguration somewhat strengthened his influence at the White House. Not surprisingly, therefore, Edward Curtis got the lucrative post. But not before Clay's continued insistence on Wetmore produced a Harrison explosion: "The federal portion of the Whig party are making desperate efforts to seize the reins of government," he charged. "They are urging the most unmerciful proscription, and if they continue to do so much longer, they will drive me mad!"[35]

Clay struck back at the President with a patronizing note to the White House, dated March 13, 1841, in which he insisted that Harrison call a special session of Congress to deal with the nation's problems. Without such a session there was no good reason for kingmaker Clay to remain longer in the capital. Again Harrison erupted: "You use the privilege of a friend to lecture me and I take the same liberty with you," he wrote the Kentuckian. "You are too impetuous... there are others whom I must consult and in many cases to determine adversely to your decision."[36]

Now it was Clay's turn to be outraged. A friend found him pacing the floor of his rooms. Harrison's note was crumpled in his hands. "And it has come to this!" he shouted. "I have not one [office] to give, nor influence enough to procure the appointment of a friend to the most humble position!" Taking pen in hand he composed another unfortunate letter to Harrison denying that he was attempting to dictate to the administration. "I do not wish to trouble you with answering this note," he snarled in conclusion. With that parting shot Clay left town for Kentucky. Only when he was safely en route home did Harrison finally decide to call a special session of Congress to meet May 31. Fortunately for the President he was seven weeks in his grave when Congress convened. It was one of the stormiest and most disorderly in the legislative annals of the nation.[37]

Overwhelmed by office-seekers, fatigued by social activities, discouraged by his break with Clay, the Old Hero steadily lost strength during his first weeks in office. On March 27 during his usual early morning stroll he was caught in a rain shower. By evening he was sick and a physician was called in. Within a day the malady was diagnosed as pneumonia. More doctors were called in. The diagnosis was cautiously changed to "bilious pleurisy," a catch-all designation covering every respiratory ailment from lung cancer to bronchitis. Various remedies were tried. The President was bled, blistered, cupped, leeched, massaged, poked, and otherwise battered. At 12:30 A.M. on April 4, precisely one month after taking office, William Henry Harrison died. What the armies of Tecumseh and the Prophet had failed to accomplish in a dozen campaigns the medical profession had managed in one short week. No more accurate a parting judgment was rendered on Old Tippecanoe than Henry A. Wise's prescient remark that had poor Harrison lived until the Congress met he would have been "devoured by the divided pack of his own dogs." [38]

7

HIS ACCIDENCY:
THE DISADVANTAGES OF CONSCIENCE

Go you now then, Mr. Clay, to your end of the avenue where stands the Capitol, and there perform your duty to the country as you shall think proper. So help me God I shall do mine at this end of it as I shall think proper.
       —JOHN TYLER, 1841

As Henry Wise had correctly predicted, the cannibalistic Whig feast was soon to come, but fate willed that the victim be John Tyler, at fifty-one the youngest man to reach the White House in the brief history of the Republic. Service in the Virginia House and Senate, in the House and Senate of the United States, and in the Governor's Mansion in Richmond had given him training in the art and science of government unmatched by any other American President before or since. That he became the missionary in Henry Clay's kettle can be traced almost exclusively to an odd quirk in his character: Faced with a choice between political popularity and the principles in which he sincerely believed, he chose the principles. It matters little that those principles would become quaint anachronisms in American history; it matters a great deal that he elected to stand firmly for his beliefs when it was clear to him that his posture would likely lead him down the road to political suicide and historical obscurity. With John Tyler it was a question of conscience—and a touch of stubbornness.

During the week of Harrison's illness no word was sent Tyler appraising him of the gravity of the situation in the capital. Not until Harrison had actually expired was Fletcher Webster, Chief Clerk of the State Department and son of the Secretary of State, dispatched hastily to Williamsburg to inform Tyler that by act of God he had become

President of the United States. At sunrise on the morning of April 5, 1841, young Webster reached Williamsburg after an all-night journey, and banged impatiently on the door of the Tyler home. A sleepy Vice-President descended the stairs to find out what the commotion was about. So it was that John Tyler, clad in nightshirt and cap (*not* playing marbles), learned that he had become the tenth President of the United States and the first Vice-President to reach the White House.

Out of such tense situations mighty myths grow. One has pictured Tyler bursting into tears on hearing the news, so great was his affection for the fallen President. Actually, Tyler scarcely knew Old Tippecanoe; what little he did know he did not much like. Another story has Tyler tarrying a full day in Williamsburg attempting to borrow several hundred dollars from a friend to finance his journey to Washington. He was always short of cash, but did not worry about it on this occasion; Tyler did what any sensible man would have done in the circumstances. He awoke the household, conveyed the news to one and all, ate his breakfast, and then convened a family conference. At this conference it was determined that Tyler should proceed immediately to Washington and that Robert and Priscilla should follow northward within the week. Time permitted no immediate decision on whether the partially paralyzed Letitia should go to Washington or not. At 7 A.M., barely two hours after receiving notification of General Harrison's death, Tyler left Williamsburg for the capital. Twenty-one hours later, at 4 o'clock on the morning of April 6, he reached Washington, having covered the two hundred thirty miles by boat and horseback in near record time.[1]

The new President found the capital swirling in confusion and turmoil. Since no Chief Executive had ever died in office before, the constitutional situation was extremely fluid. Whatever Tyler elected to do in the crisis would establish many important historical precedents. Later Vice-Presidents who found themselves in the same unstrung situation—Fillmore, Johnson, Arthur, Theodore Roosevelt, Coolidge, and Truman—would be indebted to John Tyler for his swift and sure handling of the basic constitutional question involved.

The Constitution provides that "in case of the removal of the President from office, or of his death, resignation, or inability to discharge the powers and duties of the said office, the same shall devolve on the Vice President...." Like so many other phrases in that wondrously exact and inexact document, the words *the same* could be interpreted to refer to the office itself or, more narrowly, solely to the duties of the office. John Tyler, one of the nation's most prominent strict constructionists, chose the broader of the two possible interpretations. He assumed that the office itself had devolved upon him from the moment he arrived in Washington, and from the beginning he claimed all the rights and privileges of the Presidency.

This was more than the resolution of a nagging semantic problem.

It defined for Tyler (and for all future Vice-Presidents) the exact status of a Vice-President in the event of an elected President's death. Tyler even insisted that there was no need for him to take a new oath of office, arguing that his oath as Vice-President covered the new situation legally and constitutionally. Nevertheless, he was persuaded to take another oath to forestall any public doubts on the question. At noon on April 6, in Brown's Hotel, Chief Justice William Cranch of the United States Circuit Court of the District of Columbia, swore Tyler in. Nonetheless, there were still those who argued that John Tyler was only the "Acting President," or the "Vice-President-Acting President," or, after he left the office in 1845, the "Ex-Vice-President." Tyler paid no attention to these degrading designations (he returned mail so addressed unopened) and they all quickly dropped from usage.[2]

The political situation in Washington on April 6 was equally fluid. At a lengthy Cabinet meeting that morning and afternoon, devoted chiefly to the multitudinous details of Harrison's funeral (scheduled for the following day), Tyler made a decision he lived to regret. He decided to retain Harrison's Cabinet intact. His motive was to avoid adding further to the confusion that already prevailed in the novel transition of power from one administration to another. His decision also had the immediate advantage of holding together the various factions of the Whig party until the chaos engendered by Harrison's death could be resolved. Yet when Webster informed the President that Harrison's practice was to have all policy decisions determined by a majority vote in the Cabinet, Tyler quickly rejected continuance of the procedure. "I am the President, and I shall be held responsible for my administration," he told the Cabinet bluntly. "I shall be pleased to avail myself of your counsel and advice. But I can never consent to being dictated to as to what I shall or shall not do.... When you think otherwise, your resignations will be accepted." In spite of his declaration of independence to them, Tyler's retention of the Harrison group was an error in that he retained in his official family a political cancer that had already commenced gnawing on the vitals of the Old Hero and would soon turn on the new President. "He has not a sincere friend in [the Cabinet]," Abel P. Upshur worried.[3]

Tyler knew perfectly well that he had reaped the Whig whirlwind. He was, in his own words, "surrounded by Clay-men, Webster-men, anti-Masons, original Harrisonians, Old Whigs and new Whigs—each jealous of the others, and all struggling for the offices." Under the circumstances he felt he had no choice but to proceed cautiously in an attempt to "work in good earnest to reconcile ... the angry state of the factions towards each other." As he expressed his problem to Senator William C. Rives on April 9:

I am under Providence made the instrument of a new test which is for the first time to be applied to our institutions. The experiment is to be made at the moment when the country is agitated by conflicting views of public policy, and when the spirit of faction is most likely to exist. Under these circumstances, the devolvement upon me of this high office is peculiarly embarrassing. In the administration of the government, I shall act upon the principles which I have all along espoused... derived from the teachings of Jefferson and Madison... my reliance will be placed on the virtue and intelligence of the people.

Considering the political climate of 1841, the "virtue and intelligence of the people" was a weak reed, as Tyler would discover to his sorrow.[4]

At Harrison's funeral in the East Room of the White House on April 7 Tyler was observed to be "visibly affected." He was also confused as to how he might best proceed with his new duties. Indeed, he was so upset by the stark suddenness of his new situation that he toyed briefly with the idea that national political harmony might best be assured if he, like Harrison, utilized his inaugural address to announce that he would not be a candidate for re-election in 1844. But as his friend and confidant, Duff Green, correctly pointed out, such a statement "would be taken as a plea of weakness" and would only be the "signal for the organization of parties in reference to the next election." Thanks to Green's intervention, no such self-denying remark appeared in the final draft of the speech.[5]

Tyler's hastily written inaugural address of April 9 was both an olive branch to the various Whig factions and a cautious trial balloon to test the general political atmosphere. Couched in guarded language, Tyler agreed that the depressed state of the economy demanded some change in the fiscal policies of the government. He suggested no specific changes, only that any approach to the problem be entirely "constitutional."

As his thoughts on the matter took substance and form he decided to adopt a defensive posture with reference to any fiscal changes. "Coming so recently into power," he wrote Judge Nathaniel B. Tucker on April 25, "and having no benefit of previous consultation with Gen. Harrison as to the extra-session, the country will not expect at my hands any matured measure, and my present intention is to devolve the whole subject on Congress, with a reservation of my constitutional powers to *veto* should the same be necessary in my view of the subject." In a candid though friendly letter to Clay a few days later, he agreed that Van Buren's Independent Treasury should be repealed. This did not suggest to him, however, that the old Bank of the United States should necessarily be re-established in its stead. "As to the Bank, I design to be perfectly frank with you," he told the Whig leader; "I would not have it urged prematurely." If Clay insisted on pushing ahead with a new Bank project, Tyler hoped that he would

consider whether you cannot so frame a Bank as to avoid all constitutional objections—which of itself would attach to it a vast host of our own party to be found all over the Union.... I have no intention to submit anything to Congress on this subject to be acted on, but shall leave it to its own action, and in the end shall resolve my doubt by the character of the measure proposed, should any be entertained by me.

That Henry Clay could be trusted to devise a Bank plan which avoided "all constitutional objections" was more than Tyler had a right to expect. The Great Compromiser was not that great and he was in no mood for compromise. Nor was he blind. He saw at once that Tyler was willing to surrender much of his Executive power to Congress on the crucial financial question, retaining only the negative power of a veto.[6]

In sum, Tyler's excessive caution in the opening weeks of his administration, his unwillingness to agitate the factional situation in an unprecedented transition of power added up to the creation of a political vacuum into which the ambitious Clay walked boldly. The Kentuckian was already convinced that "Vice-President" Tyler's administration would be little more than a "regency," and that serious objection to the constitutionality of a national bank was "confined to Virginia." To him the accidental President was but a "flash in the pan," to be neither feared nor followed.

Nor was Clay disabused of this denigrating opinion when Tyler sent a set of vaguely worded fiscal recommendations to the special session at the end of May urging the Congress to repeal the Independent Treasury and "devise a plan" for a new financial system themselves. Having no clear program of his own to suggest, his function in the matter would be limited, he said, to "rejecting any measure which may in my view of it conflict with the Constitution or otherwise jeopardize the prosperity of the country—a power which I could not part with even if I would...." While he did favor what he termed a "suitable fiscal agent capable of adding increased facilities in the collection and disbursement of the public revenues," he hoped that "the Southern members" of Congress would be able to "mature a system void of offense to the Constitution." Having thus opened Pandora's box, Tyler settled back to see what Clay and Congress might devise. Within a few weeks he knew. Thanks to the parliamentary skill of Clay, the specter of the old Bank of the United States rose from its grave, took on flesh, and ascended to the Presidential desk.[7]

In considering the Bank crisis of 1841 which led to Tyler's expulsion from the Whig Party, the resignation of his Cabinet, and the virtual collapse of his administration, it is well to remember that the economics of the Bank issue was always a secondary consideration. The issue was essentially political, and it turned fundamentally on Clay's attempt to seize control of the Whig leadership and drive Tyler back into the political exile from which he had unexpectedly re-emerged in 1839. In this sense, the Bank crisis was a test of strength, prestige, and personality between two strong and willful men, each loath to lose "face" in the struggle as it developed and waxed hotter. No convincing evidence has ever been offered to show that the depressed state of the national economy in 1841 demanded a national bank or any variation of one. Nor can it be demonstrated that the general economic recovery of 1844 was related to the fact that there was no Bank. Certainly there was no grass-roots expression either for or against the institution. It had not been a clear-cut issue in the campaign of 1840. The people seemed to understand neither the technical questions involved nor the complex mechanics of the various Bank proposals that were brought forward. The Bank crisis was manufactured solely for political purposes by Henry Clay. And, although his audacity might be traced to the loose grip with which Tyler picked up the Presidential reins, the fact remains that the crisis of 1841 was at bottom a personal and factional political battle in which Clay had the votes and Tyler the vetoes. Tyler's moral position would have been stronger, and more sympathy might have been his to command, had he seen fit to reaffirm his ancient hostility to the Bank in clear and definite terms during the 1840 campaign. Instead, he permitted the Whig managers to gag him on the question, and in so succumbing to their vote-greedy importunities he compromised himself on the whole issue. When the bitter game with Clay was over, the end result was a scoreless tie from which the nation had gained little but new sectional animosities. Less than two years after the celebrated Bank upheaval of 1841 Daniel Webster could ask of it: "Who cares anything now about the bank bills which were vetoed in 1841?" Nobody cared.[8]

Tyler's personal feelings for Clay in May 1841 were not hostile. As Secretary Ewing reported to the Sage of Ashland at the outset of the crisis, "No man can be better disposed [toward you] than the President. ... He speaks of you with the utmost kindness and you may rely upon it his friendship is strong and unabated." This was not the viewpoint of the "Virginia Clique," a small coterie of extreme states' rights men from the Old Dominion who were soon to dominate the inner councils of the administration. They would also become key figures in what would become the President's "Corporal's Guard" in the Congress. Such Virginians as Thomas W. Gilmer, Abel P. Upshur, and Henry A. Wise had little but contempt and hatred for Clay, and they were willing to force the impending Clay-Tyler struggle to a bitter showdown in order to destroy the Whig sectional coalition within which they felt Southern constitutional principles were being steadily eroded. "I shall see Tyler and urge him to tread the deck like a man," promised Gilmer. "Let the factions devour each other," added Wise, "and let the Republicanism left among us thrive by the contest!"[9]

Clay's power position was the superior one as he girded for contest with Tyler. The Whig majority in the Senate was 29 to 22; in the House it was a comfortable 122 to 103. While Clay controlled the bulk of the Whig vote in the lower chamber, there were in the Senate four or five states' rights Whigs to whom he could not dictate. He was confident, however, that he could balance the defections of this group by garnering a few Democratic votes from the North and the West. As the special session opened, the Kentuckian was confident and cocky. One observer reported that he was "much more imperious and arrogant with his friends than I have ever known him and that you know is saying a great deal." So overbearing did the free-wheeling Clay become during his conflict with Tyler that his friends became alarmed. "He must hereafter remain a little quiet and *hold his jaw*," said R. P. Letcher. "In fact, he must be *caged*—that's the point, *cage* him!" Unfortunately, Clay's arrogant manner was not containable. On the contrary, he was convinced that he had the power and skill to unify the great bulk of the Whig Party on a platform of national bank and protective tariff. With this organic and ideological unification the creaky Whig vehicle would become stable enough, he felt, to carry him into the White House in 1844.[10]

The Bank feature of Clay's program was unacceptable to the President. In March 1841 Tyler had emerged from the fog of the 1840 campaign to reiterate his Bank views to prominent Whigs. Conversations with them took place in his room in Brown's Hotel when he was briefly in the capital for the Harrison inauguration. During the course of these informal exchanges he indicated a willingness as Vice-President to support the White plan for a District Bank. First suggested by Hugh L. White in 1836, this plan was unquestionably constitutional in that it proposed a bank incorporated by Congress in the District of Columbia under that provision of the Constitution empowering Congress to legislate for the District. Such a bank, thought Tyler, might even take on a pseudo-national character by establishing branches in the several states, but only within those states whose legislatures specifically assented to the presence of the branches. The irreducible-minimum criterion, then, was the *voluntary* nature of the branching process. Beyond this compromise, Tyler could not and would not go. As he told Wise a few days after Harrison's death, he was just "too old in his opinions to change them" more radically than this.[11]

Not until Senator Clay intimated an interest in reviving the old Bank of the United States did Tyler in mid-June finally set himself to the "task of devising some plan which would lead to conciliation and harmony." What he devised to fill the vacuum in the administration into which Clay was moving was the White plan for a District Bank with power to branch in states requesting branches. Tactically speaking, Tyler might well have blanketed Clay's fire with such a scheme two months earlier instead of waiting for the Kentuckian to seize the initiative in the matter. Had the District Bank plan been vigorously sponsored by the Chief Executive in the first weeks of his administration its probable adoption would have calmed things considerably in the capital. Its existence would have had no more deleterious effect on the national economy than a new Bank of the United States or no Bank at all. And in addition to its essential harmlessness it had the advantage of being politically and constitutionally acceptable to Southern Whigs. But to Henry Clay, the Great Compromiser now threatened with compromise, Tyler's District Bank proposal was a red flag. In a stormy interview in the President's office, Clay made it brutally clear to the Chief Executive that the Whigs could not accept a Bank plan so hedged with states' rights qualifications. Tyler's patience snapped: "Go you now, then, Mr. Clay, to your end of the avenue, where stands the Capitol, and there perform your duty to the country as you shall think proper. So help me God, I shall do mine at this end of it as I shall think proper." [12]

With the support and encouragement of his entire Cabinet, Tyler submitted his Bank plan to the Congress. Promptly taken up in the Senate by a select committee, chaired by Clay, the administration's District Bank bill was quickly mangled beyond recognition. The chief feature of the Clay committee's counterproposal, dated June 21, was that the assent of individual states *not* be required preceding the branching process. The District Bank could establish its branches where and when it wished. As Alexander Gardiner accurately evaluated Clay's handiwork, it was "synonymous with National Bank." [13]

Tyler could not accept the involuntary branching feature of Clay's revised District Bank concept. He knew too that banking legislation as such was no longer the real issue anyway. "I am placed upon trial," he wrote John Rutherfoord in Richmond on June 23. "Those who have all along opposed me will still call out for further trials, and thus leave me impotent and powerless.... Remember always that the power claimed by Mr. Clay and others is a power to create a corporation to operate *per se* over the Union. This from the first has been the contest." Tyler remained convinced that to depart from the White plan or "to propose a scheme on my own would be the height of folly since I have no party to sustain it on independent principles." He therefore looked to his Cabinet to produce a new plan that would be constitutional.[14]

As Tyler began to search for an entirely different solution to the Bank problem, Clay discovered that he lacked two votes in the Senate to enact the legislation incorporating his involuntary branching concept. To secure these votes he offered on July 27 a somewhat softer version of the District scheme based on a compromise suggested by Whig Representative John M. Botts of Richmond. Endorsed by a Whig congressional caucus, the Botts compromise called for a District Bank which could establish its branches only with the assent of the individual states. But such assent would be presumed automatically given unless the legislature of each state, during its first session following the passage of the bill, specifically expressed opposition to having a District Bank branch within its borders. Once they were established, however, the branches could be expelled by the states only with the consent of Congress. On July 28 the Senate passed the bill 26 to 23 and sent it to the House. The lower chamber approved the measure on August 6 by 131 to 100.

The Botts compromise went far toward meeting Tyler's states' rights objections; hindsight suggests that he should have accepted and signed the measure then and there and been rid of the problem. The Cabinet unanimously urged this course upon him. But in a private conversation with Botts before final Senate action on the bill, Tyler characterized the compromise feature of the legislation as "a contemptible subterfuge behind which he would not skulk." This, it now seems clear, was a hasty and not carefully considered evaluation of the Botts proposal. As it stood the measure was certainly no great threat to states' rights. States objecting to the establishment of District Bank branches could prevent such establishment without undue difficulty or inconvenience.[15]

Tyler felt the issue had now become solely a political reconnaissance by the Whigs and he was adamant. No longer was it a question of acceptable fiscal legislation; it was now a personal power struggle with Henry Clay. "My back is to the wall," he wrote Judge Tucker on July 28; "and ... while I shall deplore the assaults, I shall, if practicable, beat back the assailants." Nor would the President entertain pleas from his friends to compromise on the Bank question so that there would not remain "a ripple to disturb its smooth current during your term of service." [16]

The capital was rife with speculation as to whether or not Tyler would veto the Botts-Clay version of the District Bank bill. The New York *Herald* reported: "Politicians discuss it morning, noon and night—in the Avenue, in the House, over their lunch ... their coffee, their wine. ... It is a favorite topic with the hackney coachmen." Representative Thomas W. Gilmer, charter member of the Virginia Clique, was convinced that "The President will veto the Bank bill" and that "a dreadful tornado will blow for a time." He was eager to see the Whig Party disintegrate on the issue. Then there could be a general reorganization of its disparate factions along states' rights lines. On August 12 Robert Tyler told a New York congressman in the lobby of the House that "to suppose that my father can be gulled by such a humbug compromise as the bill contains is to suppose that he is an ass." The President's brother-in-law, Judge John B. Christian, had "no doubt he will veto it." On the other hand, Whig Representative A. H. H. Stuart of Virginia saw the President the evening before the veto message was submitted and received from Tyler the impression that a "fair ground of compromise might yet be agreed upon." He thought it a "rather bad omen," however, to discover the President then in conference with a "distinguished *Democratic* senator." Tyler himself said only that he would go to church on Sunday, August 15, and "pray earnestly and devoutly to be enlightened as to his duty." (On that same day he did sign the bill repealing Van Buren's Independent Treasury, a repeal dear to Whig hearts). He knew the consequences of a veto. As John M. Botts wrote him on August 10, "if you can reconcile this bill to yourself, all is sunshine and calm: your administration will be met with the warm, hearty, zealous support of the whole Whig party, and when you retire from the great theater of National politics, it will be with the thanks, and plaudits, and approbation of your countrymen." [17]

The announcement of the veto on August 16 triggered a political explosion of massive proportions. While the message was being read in the Senate, disorder broke out in the gallery. Democratic Senator Benton of Missouri, seldom a Tyler ally, leaped to his feet demanding that the Sergeant-at-Arms "arrest the Bank ruffians for insulting the President of the United States." In Democratic circles there was jubilation. A group of Democratic senators, among them Benton, Buchanan, and Calhoun, called at the White House on the evening of the sixteenth to congratulate Tyler on his "patriotic and courageous" action. A brandy bottle appeared and the congratulations "gradually degenerated into convivial hilarity." Less hilarious was the appearance later that evening of a drunken mob of Whig demonstrators who arrived at the White House armed with guns, drums, and bugles. The clamor they raised in their denunciations of Tyler and the veto awakened the household, frightened the ladies within, and contributed little to the health and welfare of the stricken First Lady. After rousing the family they paid Tyler the supreme political compliment. They burned him in effigy, an incident which led directly to the passage of legislation establishing a night police force in Washington.[18]

Against a background of these and other disorders Henry Clay arose in the Senate on August 18 to castigate John Tyler. He demanded that Tyler accede to the will of the nation as expressed in the congressional vote on the Bank measure or do again as he had done in 1836 and resign his post. He then introduced a motion to override the veto. Sustained 25 to 24, it was well below the necessary two-thirds margin required to set aside a veto. The following day, August 19, Clay demanded an amendment to the Constitution to permit the overriding of Presidential vetoes by simple majority vote. This too came to nought. While these heavy-handed blows were being delivered on the Senate floor, Clay blandly maintained that there was no bad blood between the President and himself. Any rift that might seem to be developing among the Whig leadership he blamed on unnamed conspirators who were "beating up for recruits, and endeavoring to form a third party, with materials so scanty as to be wholly insufficient to compose a decent corporal's guard." [19]

Tyler expected the venom of Clay. He was more disturbed personally by the August 21 publication of the "Coffee House Letter" written by his old political ally, John M. Botts. It came at the very moment a second Bank bill—the Fiscal Corporation bill—was being introduced in the House. Indeed, the temper and the timing of the Botts letter convinced Tyler once and for all that all Whig fiscal proposals were designed to accomplish no more than his political destruction. Addressed to the patrons of a Richmond coffee house and dated August 16, the Botts communication was a savage attack on the President. It predicted that "Captain Tyler" would veto the District Bank bill in an effort to curry favor with the Democrats. Insulting in both tone and content, it suggested that the President would be "headed" and would soon become "an object of execration with both parties." Botts charged further that Tyler had "refused to listen to the admonition and entreaties of his best friends, and looked only to the whisperings of the ambitious and designing mischief makers who have collected around him." This was a reference to the same shadowy group Clay would sarcastically designate a Corporal's Guard in his anti-Tyler tirade a few days later.[20]

The letter stunned the President. Botts had been a trusted lieutenant in the Virginia legislature in 1839 during the fight against the election of Rives to the Senate. While Tyler was trying to understand the reason and motive behind the unexpected outburst, Botts went a step further. On September 10 he delivered a wild speech in the House charging Tyler with having supported the principle of a national bank during the Harrisburg convention and in various speeches in western Virginia and western Pennsylvania during the 1840 campaign. He claimed he had had a personal interview with Tyler in June 1841 during which the President had assured him that he favored a national bank. An allegation that Tyler had attempted to bribe him to join in an effort to stretch his Presidential span to twelve years completed the list of patent falsehoods to which the irresponsible Botts treated a credulous House of Representatives.[21]

Given the political and emotional context of the situation, Tyler's veto of the Fiscal Corporation bill on September 9 was not wholly unexpected. The new bank measure had appeared a few days after Tyler's August 16 veto of the District Bank bill as amended by Clay and Botts. In his first veto statement he had suggested that certain changes in the District Bank concept might make similar legislation acceptable to him. Hasty consultations between Whig emissaries and the President brought forth legislation complexly titled "A bill to incorporate the subscribers to a fiscal corporation of the United States." The actual framing of the bill and the details of its submission and passage Tyler unwisely left to his Cabinet. He made it clear to them, however, that he would approve no banking legislation that did not clearly require state assent for the establishment of branches (called "agencies" in the new legislation). He specifically instructed Ewing and Webster to see to it that the Fiscal

Corporation bill incorporated this provision and retained it in its journey through Congress. He even took the precaution of jotting down this crucial reservation on the margin of the working paper that became the basis for the Cabinet draft. He insisted also that he be shown the final wording of the bill before it was sent up to the House.

By a failure in communication within the top echelons of the administration (whether accidental or intentional remains a mystery), the finished bill reached the House before Tyler saw it. This slight infuriated him and contributed to his developing thesis that a full-blown Whig conspiracy was in operation against him. He was especially upset when members of his Cabinet, notably Webster and Ewing, stated publicly that the new bill conformed to the President's opinions and bore his imprimatur, although it was obvious that his marginal notations had received no serious consideration within the Cabinet or in the Whig caucus that endorsed it. Nor did the final form suit Tyler. In his opinion, the right of the states to interdict the branches was not adequately protected, and the powers given the Fiscal Corporation in the area of discounting and renewing notes were excessive in scope and inflationary in intent. More important, the Fiscal Corporation would be chartered by Congress acting as the national legislature and not as the legislature of the District of Columbia. From Tyler's standpoint the new legislation, ostensibly the brainchild of his own Cabinet, was as unsatisfactory as the vetoed District Bank bill had been.[22]

Nevertheless, the Fiscal Corporation bill sailed through the House in late August by a 125-to-94 vote in spite of attempts by Henry A. Wise and George H. Proffit of Indiana to amend it to reflect Tyler's objections. "It will be vetoed," Wise predicted. "Tyler is more firm than ever.... A second veto will strengthen him. Ten days will bring about the denouement." Similarly, the measure passed the Senate on September 2 by a margin of 27 to 22. Although the Fiscal Corporation was not national enough to suit Clay, the Kentuckian supported the measure, eager to see if Tyler had the courage to veto it. "Tyler dares not resist," Clay exulted to James Lyons of Richmond; "I will drive him before me!" Lyons could see that Clay was "very violent" on the subject. "You are mistaken, Mr. Clay," the Virginian replied. "Mr. Tyler wants to approve the bill, but he thinks his oath [to support the Constitution] is in the way, and I, who know him very well, will tell you that when he thinks he is right he is as obstinate as a bull, and no power on earth can move him." Lyons understood Tyler better than Clay did.[23]

To head off the expected veto Clay combined liquor, persuasion, and subtle threat in the hope of bringing Tyler around. On the evening of August 28, as the legislation was making its way through the House, a supper party was given at the home of Attorney-General John Crittenden. Tyler had been invited but had politely declined. Late in the evening, as libations melted inhibitions and as the party became gay, a tipsy delegation was dispatched to the White House to persuade Tyler to join the mellowing group. Although the hour was late, Tyler consented. Arriving at Crittenden's, he was met at the door by Henry Clay. "Well, Mr. President," Clay shouted, with obvious political implication, "what are you for, Kentucky whiskey or champagne?" Tyler chose aristocratic champagne. Slowly sipping it, he found himself regaled by Clay with the lines from Shakespeare's *Richard III* on the dangers of conscience:

> Let not our babbling dreams affright our souls;
> Conscience is but a word that cowards use,
> Devis'd at first, to keep the strong in awe.

The political meaning of the gathering and the poetry was clear. In a pleasant, half-drunken way Clay warned Tyler to abandon his friends in the Virginia Clique and in his Corporal's Guard on Capitol Hill and sign the Fiscal Corporation bill.[24]

As he considered the pending legislation in all its ideological and political ramifications, Tyler decided to lift the whole issue above partisan politics by including in his veto message a statement that he would not be a candidate for re-election in 1844. However laudatory this thought of flying up and out of the political jungle, Webster and Duff Green dissuaded Tyler from making a statement that could only weaken him further with the Whig leadership. Angered by the Coffee House Letter, hurt by what appeared to be sabotage within his own Cabinet, stung by Whig vilification of his first veto, importuned by his supporters in the Virginia Clique and Corporal's Guard to hold firm, and convinced that the Fiscal Corporation bill was at bottom unconstitutional, Tyler vetoed the measure. He did this with full appreciation of the political implications of his decision. "Give your approval to the Bill," John J. Crittenden had written him, "and the success of your Administration is sealed ... all before you will be a scene of success and triumph." Veto the bill, continued the Attorney-General, and "read the doom of the Whig party, and behold it and the President it elected, sunk together, the victims of each other, in unnatural strife." [25]

In his second veto message of September 9, the President pointed out that he was pained to be "compelled to differ from Congress a second time in the same session." He noted that he had not had time enough in office to fashion a financial plan of his own, and he hinted that he would offer such a plan at the opening of the regular session in December. He deplored the speed with which the special session had brought the bank question to the fore. The veto message was a polite, almost apologetic document which emphasized Tyler's objection that the Fiscal Corporation was designed to operate *"per se* over the Union by virtue of the unaided and assumed authority of Congress as a national legislature, as distinguishable from a bank created by Congress for the District of

Columbia as the local legislature of the District." As such it was clearly unconstitutional. He would rather uphold the Constitution, Tyler concluded, "even though I perish ... than to win the applause of men by a sacrifice of my duty and my conscience." Where government moneys might legally be deposited, given the repeal of the Independent Treasury and the vetoes of the District Bank and the Fiscal Corporation, was an academic question to Tyler. "We have no surplus, nor are we likely to have for some years, and may be regarded as living from hand to mouth," he told Webster.[26]

The response to the second veto was even more violent, more politically inspired, than the reaction to the first. Demonstrations and protest meetings were whipped up by Whig leaders all over the country. The President was burned in effigy a hundred times; scores of letters poured in threatening him with assassination. Whig editors outdid one another in contests of personal vilification. Editor John H. Pleasants of the Richmond *Whig*, for example, told his readers that he "knew Mr. Tyler well, personally, and had known him long, and I could not believe that a man so commonplace, so absolutely inferior to many fifteen shilling lawyers with whom you may meet at every county court in Virginia, would seriously aspire to the first station among mankind." [27]

On September 11, two days before the special session was to adjourn, the entire Cabinet, excepting Daniel Webster, resigned in a body. Between 12:30 and 5:30 P.M. on that fateful day, five Cabinet officers marched into Tyler's office and laid their resignations on his desk while John Tyler, Jr., the President's secretary, stood by, watch in hand, recording for posterity the exact moment of each resignation. The reasons given by each departing Secretary varied in tone, clarity, and conviction, but taken together they added up to a vote of no confidence.

This massive walkout was planned, calculated, and coordinated by Henry Clay to wreck the Executive branch, punish John Tyler for his Bank vetoes, and force his resignation. The latter result, if accomplished, would bring Clay-adherent Samuel L. Southard, president of the Senate, to the White House under the succession pattern then operating. The resignations did not take Tyler entirely by surprise. As early as August 16 he had received intimations from Whig Representatives James M. Russell of Pennsylvania and John Taliaferro of Virginia that the underlying purpose of the first Bank bill was to trigger the expected veto that would isolate him from the Whigs, force a dissolution of his Cabinet, and bring the Executive department to ruin. By the time the second Bank bill was being forced upon Tyler, newspapers like the New York *Herald* were saying of his Cabinet: "What treachery! What ingratitude! Why do they not act like men, and at once give their resignations, and suffer the President to bring to his aid such men as he has confidence in?" Whatever Clay's object in producing the great Cabinet stroll, the resignations did not paralyze Tyler's will to continue as President. "My resignation," he wrote in 1844, "would amount to a declaration to the world that our system of government had failed ... that the provision made for the death of the President was ... so defective as to merge all executive powers in the legislative branch of the government...." [28]

Webster had not joined the conspiracy or the resulting exodus. He had no hand in the Cabinet disruption. He admired Tyler's integrity and distrusted Henry Clay, whose fine Italian hand he saw behind the Cabinet crisis. More significantly, he and Tyler were at that moment deeply involved in the complex diplomatic negotiations with Britain that would lead to the 1842 Webster-Ashburton Treaty, settling the Maine boundary and other questions. Studies looking toward the dismemberment of the Mexican Empire in California as part of an Anglo-American settlement of the Oregon boundary problem were also under review. It was no time for upheaval in the State Department.

"Where am I to go, Mr. President?" Webster asked his chief during the course of that hectic afternoon of September 11.

"You must decide that for yourself, Mr. Webster," Tyler replied.

Webster considered the choice for a brief moment and made his decision. "If you leave it to me, Mr. President, I will stay where I am."

Tyler rose from his chair and leaned forward, eyes flashing. "Give me your hand on that, and now I will say to you that Henry Clay is a doomed man." [29]

Webster's patriotic decision to remain on in the Cabinet distressed New England Whigs and the Virginia Clique alike. Not only did his continued association with the administration give it a political anchor northward, it placed near Tyler a statesman of great national prestige at a time when the renegade President desperately needed friends. The embarrassment of the Massachusetts Whigs was therefore understandable. To Virginians like Wise, Tucker, Upshur, and Gilmer the retention of Webster was a political blunder. "We are on the eve of a cabinet rupture," Wise informed Tucker on August 29. "With some of them we want to part friendly. We can part friendly with Webster by sending him [as Minister] to England. Let us, for God's sake, get rid of him on the best terms we can." In spite of this sentiment within the Clique, Webster stayed on. He was a bulwark in an unpopular administration until his resignation in May 1843. By that time he and Tyler were in sharp disagreement on the Texas annexation issue and on the President's use of patronage to build a third party to be employed as a foreign-policy lever in the 1844 campaign. Nevertheless, they parted in 1843 on the friendliest personal terms.[30]

The speed with which Tyler assembled a new Cabinet indicated that he had given considerable thought to the matter before the crisis matured. From a political standpoint, his appointments marked the beginning of the President's effort to link the Conservative Democracy of New York and Pennsylvania with states' rights Whigs who, like Tyler himself, were inexorably moving back toward the Southern Democracy from which they had parted in 1833–1836. The next three years would see fourteen different men involved in the game of musical chairs which characterized the unstable history of the Cabinet under John Tyler. But in all these changes, shiftings, comings, and goings, the Tyler Cabinets increasingly reflected a states' rights-Democratic orientation.

Dominating these alterations and mutations was Tyler's philosophy that a Cabinet should be totally subordinate to the President and in absolute intellectual harmony with him. There was to be no maneuvering for the succession. Differences of opinion were neither encouraged nor tolerated. Cabinet meetings would involve no more than friendly discussions on how best to implement commonly agreed-upon principles. "The new cabinet is made up of the best materials," Tyler happily wrote Thomas A. Cooper in October 1841. "Like myself, they are all original Jackson men, and mean to act upon Republican principles." There would be "no more jarring" within the official family; Tyler made this clear to prospective appointees. He insisted that they "conform to my opinions" on all subjects. As he explained his wishes to Webster, "I would have every [Cabinet] member to look upon every other, in the light of a friend and a brother." That this ideological togetherness would have its limitations the President was soon to discover. By August 1842 he was complaining to his friend Tazewell that "I have been so long surrounded by men who have now smiles in their eyes and honey on their tongues, the better to cajole and deceive, that to be shown the error of my ways, whensoever I do err, after a plain and downright fashion, is a positive relief." [31]

One final and curious indignity awaited the truculent President. On September 13, 1841, two days after the Cabinet resignations, he was formally and officially expelled from the Whig Party. To effect this comic-opera touch some seventy Whig congressmen caucused in Capitol Square and in all solemnity repudiated Tyler. In many ways it was like firing a worker who had already walked off the job, since Tyler's transient Whiggery had been born and reared in anti-Jacksonianism and little else. Nevertheless, his expulsion from the party marked the first and only time in American history a President was thrown bodily out of the political organization which had nominated and elected him. In Clay's triumphant words, Tyler was now "a president without a party," an observation which impelled young Julia Gardiner Tyler to remark two years later that "If it is a party he wants, I will give him a party." She did.[32]

The expulsion did, however, encourage Whig pamphleteers to launch a war of words on Tyler which lasted until his departure from the White House in March 1845. While the pamphlets contributed little that was constructive to the political crisis, they provided a therapeutic outlet for splenic Whigs who saw Tyler as a "reptile-like" man who had "crawled up" into the Presidency, there to betray the party that had given him power. On the other side of the battle line, pamphleteers of the states' rights persuasion saw in Henry Clay the snake-in-the-grass and maintained that John Tyler was leading America's fight for true democracy against the corroding influences of nationalism, Federalism, and centralism. Called by his enemies an "Executive Ass," the "Accident of an Accident," "a famished Charles City pettifogger," the "synonym of nihil," or simply a man who should be lashed "naked through the world," Tyler at least had the distinction of exciting a strong point of view.[33]

Actually, the vituperation angered and disturbed him. Tyler did not have the political hide of an elephant. The Whig darts stung him severely and had the predictable effect of driving him more rapidly back to the not eagerly outstretched arms of the Southern Democracy. At a different level, the anti-Tyler campaign had the consequence of welding the Tyler family into a solid phalanx. Throughout his trials and political tribulations his kin stood solidly and protectively with him, strengthening his sword arm against the Whig assaults. Some of this was automatic clan defensiveness; some of it was related to an attempt by the entire family to shield the sensibilities of the failing First Lady. Priscilla Cooper Tyler was particularly helpful to the President during these trying months. Tyler's brother-in-law Judge John B. Christian and his distant kinsman Major Washington Seawell, then serving against the Seminoles in Florida, wrote encouraging letters which buoyed Tyler considerably. John Tyler, Jr., became an active pamphleteer and publicist for the President's views and on one occasion walked to the field of honor to defend his own and his father's reputation. Robert Tyler also aided his father in many ways, most significantly as the Chief Executive's principal political liaison man with the Conservative Democracy in Philadelphia and New York City. In this task Alexander Gardiner enthusiastically joined after his sister's marriage to the President in June 1844. Like the new Cabinet, the family functioned as a close-knit political unit as Tyler's struggle with the Whigs broadened and deepened.[34]

Having vetoed two Whig Bank bills, Tyler felt a strong personal obligation to devise a fiscal scheme of his own which would facilitate interstate banking operations while remaining entirely constitutional in structure and function. He was also under pressure from his friends to produce a "substantive plan which [would] provide for the permanent settlement of this question," a solution they hoped would make the Tyler administration politically "impregnable." Thus the President left the capital in mid-October for a much-needed rest in Williamsburg, where he planned "to meditate in peace over a scheme of finance." By December 1841, after considerable correspondence with Littleton W. Tazewell on the subject, Tyler had worked out a plan which was basically a version of one Andrew Jackson had proposed in 1830. It was a system in which state banks would play an important role, and Tyler confessed to Tazewell that from a purely political standpoint he was "greatly influenced by a desire to bring to my support that great interest." [35]

Tyler's idea envisioned a public banking institution directed by a nonpartisan Board of Control in Washington, with agencies (some of them state banks) located in principal financial centers throughout the country. No capital was to be raised by private subscription, so there would be no private stockholders. The agencies (branches) would facilitate interstate commerce in being authorized to buy and sell domestic bills and drafts. The branches could also receive deposits of silver and gold from individuals and issue negotiable certificates for these metals that would circulate as currency. Government moneys would be deposited in the agencies and these deposits would permit the government, through the issuance or recall of Treasury notes, to increase or decrease the amount of sound paper currency in circulation at any given time. It was a well-conceived system. It did not confine the currency exclusively to specie as Van Buren's Independent Treasury system had, and the sovereignty of the states was protected in the provision that forbade the branches to transact any business of a private character in conflict with the laws of the states in which they functioned. In sum, the Tyler proposal combined a states' rights approach with a national approach that would "relieve the Chief Executive ... from a controlling power over the public Treasury."

Tyler called it the Exchequer Plan and presented it to the Congress in his Annual Message on December 7, 1841. The new Cabinet (particularly Webster and Secretary of War John C. Spencer of New York) was enthusiastic about it. But by falling somewhere between the Democrats' Independent Treasury and Clay's Bank of the United States it satisfied the partisans of neither approach. Both attacked it, as did the Wall Street lobby. "This city is filled with agents from Wall Street," reported Secretary of the Navy Abel P. Upshur, "who are endeavoring to defeat every arrangement of the currency question. So long as they can keep things in their present state, money will be valuable, and they have money. This is another sore evil against which the administration has to contend." The Exchequer Plan had no chance politically, although it represented that vain search for a middle course that would characterize the remainder of the Tyler administration. In spite of a vigorous fight for the Exchequer by congressmen Caleb Cushing, Henry Wise, George H. Proffit, and others of Tyler's minuscule Corporal's Guard in Congress, the project was tabled without adequate discussion in the 1841–1842 session. It was soundly defeated the following year. Tyler thus dropped the plan entirely in 1843, and that was the end of it. Public moneys, such as existed, continued to repose in selected state banks, much to the delight of old Jacksonians.[36]

By July 1842 the relationship between the Executive and legislative branches had reached a stalemate. Whig strategy was to produce legislation the President could not approve and then charge perfidy and treason and Executive dictatorship when the expected veto was delivered. Tyler, in turn, continued to veto legislation he could not stomach while vigorously defending his right to do so. "Executive dictation!" he excitedly wrote a group in Philadelphia:

I repel the imputation. I would gladly harmonize with Congress in the enactment of all necessary measures if the majority would permit me.... Each branch of the government is independent of every other, and Heaven forbid that the day should ever come when either can dictate to the other. The Constitution never designed that the executive should be a mere cipher. On the contrary, it denies to Congress the right to pass any law without his approval, thereby imparting to it, for wise purposes, an active agency in all legislation.

In his relations with the Congress in 1842 Tyler constantly searched for that "moderation, which is the mother of true wisdom," and found little. "We have reached the turning point in our institutions," he remarked to Nathaniel B. Tucker in June 1842 with sadness tinged by frustration. "I fear that more firmness and wisdom are necessary to carry us safely through the trial than I can in any way lay claim to." [37]

The Clay-dominated Congress was, Tyler fumed, a "do-nothing" body whose sole function and aim was the destruction of the administration in preparation for the coming midterm elections. In his Annual Message of December 7, 1841, Tyler had called for his Exchequer Plan, a new tariff for revenue bill which would "afford the manufacturing interests ample aid," and an expansion of the Army and the Navy. By July 1842 none of these vital projects had been acted upon. "If nothing has been done to accomplish any of these objects," Tyler said, "the fault is not with the Executive." He thought it "particularly abominable that this miserable Congress should not even yet [July] have passed the Army or Navy appropriation bill," thus "subjecting the country to be browbeat" by the Mexican dictator, Santa Anna. The Congress had not "matured a single important measure," agreed Upshur in disgust. On the contrary, theirs was the "deliberate purpose to make Henry Clay President of the United States, even at the hazard of revolution." The time had finally come, thought Upshur, for patriots in both parties to "shake off their leaders, and come at once to the rescue of the country."

Intelligence reaches us from all parts of the country proving that our do-nothing Congress is fast falling into contempt with the people. It is the most worthless body of public men that I have ever known or heard of. Clay is the great obstacle to wholesome legislation. When he retires something may be done, and not before.[38]

By the time David Gardiner brought Julia and Margaret to the capital again in December 1842, the degree to which legislative decay and partisan chaos had proceeded was a public scandal. Congressional activity, such as it was, seemed to the East Hampton visitor designed only to advance "some man in respect to a presidential candidate." Both parties were "greatly divided." The Congress had become impotent. As David Gardiner expressed it to his sons:

Of the different [banking] plans none will probably be adopted and Congress after having undone all they have done during the last session will be ready to adjourn without much hurry.... Most of the speakers are blessed merely with a capacity of uttering sound and connecting most disconnected sentences. Mr. Adams stands alone among them for ... great powers of mind. ... It seems to be the fashion even on the most trifling subjects, to rage with violence.... A speech of Cushing has called forth much political debate, but I do not think has been fairly met, although most severely denounced by both of the great political parties. The President was abandoned by the Whigs for vetoing the Bank bill while they without reason ... have protested with greater inconsistency the bankrupt bill.... I am heartily tired of listening to the debates.... I think the Senate of New York when I was acquainted with it, possessed in proportion to its numbers a far greater amount of talent.... Those who loom the largest here from the distance diminish wonderfully on contact.... I see here all the old corrupt political lobby which in former years infested Albany.[39]

As the government of the United States virtually ceased to function, Tyler became increasingly aware of the painful fact that the Treasury was bare. A national debt of $5,650,000 had been left by the Van Buren administration, along with an unbalanced budget for 1840–1841 which ultimately raised the debt to $17,736,000 by January 1, 1842. Indeed, the pay of the military and the civil service had on occasion in 1841 been suspended by Tyler because the public coffers were empty. Treasury notes declined steadily in value throughout 1842, and the Home Squadron of the Navy was tied up as an economy measure.

Faced with this critical financial situation, the President was not averse to raising the tariff for the purpose of providing badly needed revenue. He was loath, however, to tamper with the delicate economic and political arrangements hammered out in the Compromise Tariff Act of 1833 and he was vehemently opposed to the Whig plan to link distribution to a higher tariff. Under the distribution scheme income realized by the Treasury from the sale of public lands would be "distributed" to the several states. This, of course, would aid the financially hard-pressed states survive the impact of the depression. The giveaway would also reap obvious political benefits for the munificent Whig distributors. But by dissipating sizable portions of the federal revenue, distribution would inevitably force hikes in the tariff schedule to raise revenues for the near-bankrupt government. The Whigs thus hoped that by depleting the shaky Treasury with their politically negotiable distribution plan they could then logically call for higher tariffs. In this manner they could gradually force the tariff schedule upward to the point of outright protectionism—in the holy name of tariff for revenue only. Tyler was not opposed to significantly higher tariffs in 1842 so long as they were strictly revenue-raising in intent. The Compromise Tariff of 1833 had made it plain that after 1842 any duties above 20 per cent *ad valorem* would be levied only "for the purpose of raising such revenue as may be necessary to an economical administration of the Government." Nor was he opposed to the distribution of public-land revenues so long as this did not force tariffs clearly into the protectionist range. Indeed, he had willingly signed Clay's Distribution Act of 1841 when the legislation included a cut-off proviso that distribution would cease if and when the tariff schedule went above 20 per cent *ad valorem*. His attitude toward a tariff for protection as such had not changed since 1832. He had always been a free-trade, tariff-for-revenue man and would remain one until he died.[40]

For the purpose of embarrassing Tyler politically at a time when the Treasury was bare, the Whigs on two occasions during the summer of 1842 brought forth tariff bills which raised rates above 20 per cent while providing for the continued distribution of government revenue from public-land sales. Tyler promptly vetoed both measures, much to the jubilation of Clay partisans. "If we can only keep up the feeling that now exists," Crittenden wrote Harry of the West, "your election is certain. Tyler is one of your *best friends;* his last veto has scored us all well; it has just reached the convention in Maine, which nominated you and denounced him."

The Whig policy, designed to raise more Clay than revenue, quickly shifted to the appointment of a House select committee to investigate the reasons given by Tyler for his latest veto of the tariff-distribution bill. Needless to say, the committee was carefully packed to produce a predetermined result. Chaired by John Quincy Adams and numbering in its heavy Whig majority such proven anti-Tylerites as John M. Botts, the committee reported its findings on August 16, 1842. The document went far beyond a *pro forma* criticism of the President's veto of the tariff-distribution bill. It was a wide-ranging, free-swinging attack on the Tyler administration and all its negative works from the moment it came to power. It recommended an amendment to the Constitution that would permit the overriding of a White House veto by a bare majority vote, and it concluded with the observation that John Tyler was a fit subject for impeachment proceedings. A dissenting minority report, signed only by Democratic congressmen Charles J.

Ingersoll of Pennsylvania and James I. Roosevelt of New York, defended the President's stewardship of the nation for the preceding seventeen months.[41]

Against a background of violent Whig editorial attacks—"Again has the imbecile, into whose hands accident has placed the power, vetoed a bill passed by a majority of those legally authorized to pass it," shouted the *Daily Richmond Whig*—Tyler dispatched a defense of his behavior to the House on August 30 with a request that it be printed in the House *Journal*. The entreaty was refused, gleeful Whigs pointing out that Tyler himself had voted to deny Jackson the same privilege in 1834.[42]

In the midst of this renewed assault, Tyler signed into law on August 30 the controversial Tariff Act of 1842, a bill pushed through by an alliance of protectionist Whigs and Democrats who pointed with real alarm to the stark emptiness of the Treasury. In this sense it was regarded by its proponents as a tariff for much-needed revenue although it did in fact return the tariff schedule to the high protectionist rates of 1832. And while no distribution rider was attached to it (Clay's friends fought it for this very reason), Tyler's approval of the measure was at variance with his longstanding hostility toward high tariffs. To be sure, the Treasury was desperate for a new infusion of funds and this consideration alone probably swung Tyler over. He undoubtedly regarded it at the time as a tariff for revenue, even though the rates *were* protectionist in 1832 terms. Unfortunately, he never explained his reasons for approving the "Black Tariff," as noxious to Southern antiprotectionists as it was gratifying to American System Whigs. Or if he did explain his thinking on the matter, the knowledge was lost to history when most of his private papers were burned in Richmond in 1865. Lyon G. Tyler accounted for his father's apparent surrender on the tariff question of 1842 as part of the President's desire to build a coalition of moderates to carry him politically and placidly between the Scylla of Clay and the Charybdis of Benton. It was, he wrote in 1885, "the first legislative fruits of the policy of the President to depend upon the moderates of both parties." This neat explanation has some obvious defects. A broader basis of interpretation would include Tyler's fear of the approaching bankruptcy of the federal government, his psychological reaction to continued Whig poundings, his distress at talk of his impeachment, concern for Letitia's peace of mind in her last days (she died September 10, 1842), and a willingness—after eighteen months of continual wrangling over banking and tariff matters—to move on to other and more fruitful subjects. By August 1842 he had matured the great Texas annexation plan by which he hoped to put an end to faction, unify the nation, and rescue his historical reputation. This object came to dominate his hopes and ambitions almost exclusively after January 1843.[43]

Whatever his motives in signing the 1842 Tariff Act, Tyler was clearly unsettled and hurt by concurrent Whig talk of impeachment. He knew that the Whigs did not have the votes to accomplish such a radical solution to their frustrations, but the chattering itself angered him, frightened him a bit, and drove him ever closer to the Southern Democracy for aid and comfort. The impeachment movement began on July 10, 1842. On that date a resolution was introduced in the House by John M. Botts, calling for the appointment of a special committee to investigate the President's conduct in office with a view toward recommending impeachment. Henry Clay agreed that "the inevitable tendency of events is to impeachment," but he felt that the timing and introduction of the Botts motion was unfortunate. He held that the politics of the situation called for a lesser punishment—a House vote of "want of confidence" in Tyler rather than the institution of formal impeachment proceedings. While he certainly encouraged the impeachment movement from behind the scenes, Clay urged that it proceed with great care. It had proceeded practically nowhere at all when Tyler learned of it and fairly exploded. "I am told that one of the madcaps talks of impeachment," he wrote a friend:

> Did you ever expect to see your old friend under trial for "high crimes and misdemeanors"? The high crime of sustaining the Constitution of the country I have committed, and to this I plead guilty. The high crime of arresting the lavish donation of a source of revenue [distribution], at the moment that the Treasury is bankrupt, of that also I am guilty; and the high crime of daring to have an opinion of my own, Congress to the contrary notwithstanding, I plead guilty also to that; and if these be impeachable matters, why then I ought to be impeached.... I am abused, in Congress and out, as man never was before—assailed as a traitor, and threatened with impeachment. But let it pass. Other attempts are to be made to head me, and we shall see how they will succeed.[44]

The ill-contrived impeachment attempt did not, of course, succeed. On January 10, 1843, Botts' resolution of the previous July was finally brought to a vote in the House. It was soundly defeated—127 to 83, only the most extreme Clay and Van Buren men supporting it. "There was," reported Senator David Gardiner, who witnessed the vote, "no excitement and little debate, and this ... foolish attempt will only result in increasing the number of the President's friends." [45]

If the Botts assault did not actually increase Tyler's friends, it did obscure the fact that the President was not unwilling to accommodate the Whigs on several important legislative matters. John Tyler, in truth, made a genuine attempt in 1841–1842 to reach some accommodation with the Whigs, consistent with his constitutional principles. On most issues he was willing to meet them halfway or better. His signings of the 1842 Tariff Act and the Bankruptcy Act of 1842 were clearly pro-

Whig. His acceptance of Clay's 1841 Distribution Act and his willingness to see the Independent Treasury Act repealed in 1841 were also pro-Whig gestures. On the controversial tariff question he agreed with Upshur that "the free trade men of the South must relax their principles a little." Indeed, Tyler's approval of the Bankruptcy Act, liberalizing the laws governing that unhappy condition, benefited the depressed Whig business community to the extent that in November 1842 Alexander Gardiner, a recently converted Tammany Democrat, could cry out that the legislation should be repealed immediately. It was, said the President's future brother-in-law, a mockery of "the great Democratic doctrines of individual enterprise and freedom," destined only to subsidize the improvident and speculative classes.[46]

The results of the midterm elections of 1842 seemed to Tyler to support his side of his struggle with Clay and the Whigs. He interpreted the Democratic sweep as the "greatest political victory ever won within my recollection ... achieved entirely upon the vetoes of the Bank bills presented to me at the extra session." The Whig majority of sixty in the House of Representatives gave way to a Democratic majority of eighty. Whig reverses in New York, Pennsylvania, Georgia, Mississippi, Michigan, Virginia, and Louisiana caused John Quincy Adams to moan that the Whigs were "overwhelmed and the Democracy altogether in the ascendant ... the Tyler party are much stronger than I could have imagined." Still, Tyler's loyal little Corporal's Guard was all but wiped out in the election. Their support of the unpopular President had endeared them to the leadership of no faction or party. Thus Representatives James I. Roosevelt, Henry A. Wise, George H. Proffit, Francis Mallory of Virginia, and Caleb Cushing of Massachusetts all decided that retreat was the better part of valor and declined to stand for renomination or re-election. Tyler appreciated immensely their great sacrifices for him and made every effort to place them all in appointive offices. Years later he still referred to them warmly as the "half dozen gentlemen" who had stuck with him "when I had to sustain the combined assaults of the ultras of both parties." In his memory they remained the "six [who] stood by and beat back all assailants. Yes, beat them back and foiled all their efforts." John Quincy Adams notwithstanding, these doughty White Knights did not constitute a "Tyler party" or any segment of one.[47]

There was as yet no Tyler party. Nor had the President's attempt to unify moderates in both major parties on a domestic program that sought a middle road between states' rights and nationalism met with conspicuous success. Pro-Whig gestures had distressed the states' rights group and pro-states' rights vetoes had triggered a Whig impeachment movement. Thus the popular swing away from the obstructionist Clay Whigs and their "do-nothing Congress" in November 1842 convinced Tyler that the time was at hand for launching a third party "for the sole purpose of controlling events by throwing in the weight of that organization for the public good" during the 1844 campaign.

He had considered the possibility of a third-party movement as early as October 1841. At that time he had discovered an issue on which he hoped he might unite all moderate factions under his leadership and, in so doing, salvage the prestige of his faltering administration. The Tyler party, as he conceived it, would undertake nothing less ambitious than the annexation of Texas and the filling out of America's continental boundaries to the Pacific. So it was that on October 11, 1841, while vacationing at his home in Williamsburg, where he had retired to "meditate in peace" over what became his Exchequer Plan, the Texas thought struck him. "Could anything," he inquired of Webster,

...throw so bright a lustre around us? It seems to me the great interests of the North would be incalculably advanced by such an acquisition. How deeply interested is the shipping interest. *Slavery*, I know that is the objection, and it would be well founded, if it did not already exist among us; but my belief is that a rigid enforcement of the laws against the slave-trade would in time make as many free States South as the acquisition of Texas would add of slave States, and then the future (distant as it might be) would present wonderful results.[48]

The happy results of the 1842 elections coupled with a growing confidence in the patriotic rightness and political possibilities of his Texas policy helped Tyler sublimate the great sorrow he experienced when Letitia finally passed away in September 1842. The excitement and activity involved in organizing his third party also proved therapeutic in this regard. Thus when Julia Gardiner walked into his life in December of that year he was politically more confident and self-assured than he had been since the beginning of his ill-starred administration.

Nevertheless, with the exception of Texas annexation (a large exception, to be sure), the Tyler administration in 1843–1845 was a caretaker government. Thanks in part to the increased revenue under the Tariff Act of 1842, the budget was balanced and the public debt significantly reduced. Efficient fiscal administration also permitted a reduction in the size of the annual budget. In truth, "Mr. Tyler found the currency 'shin-plasters'; he left it gold and silver and Treasury notes at par." Well-managed as it was, his administration still remained a caretaker operation. No significant domestic legislation was passed. Nothing more important emerged from Congress than the $30,000 appropriated in March 1843 to assist Samuel F. B. Morse test his telegraph. And from the White House came no act more stirring than the appointment of writers Washington Irving and John Howard Payne to diplomatic posts abroad. In foreign affairs, however, it was a much more successful story. So too was it in the social life of the White House.[49]

8

COURTSHIP AND CATASTROPHE

> *Shall I again that Harp unstring*
> *Which long has been a useless thing,*
> *Unheard in Lady's bower?*
> —JOHN TYLER, MARCH 1843

While John Tyler's administration collapsed noisily about his ears, the social life of the White House went forward from triumph to triumph under the able direction of Priscilla Cooper Tyler. Priscilla had not sought the post. Indeed, Tyler's elevation to the Presidency had come so suddenly and unexpectedly that no provision had been made, or even contemplated, for the purely festive and ceremonial side of White House living. But within a week after Tyler's hasty departure from Williamsburg in April 1841 to take up his new duties in the capital, it was decided that Letitia should join her husband in Washington even though she could do little to help his administration in a social sense. Priscilla, Tyler determined, would perform the First Lady's duties as White House hostess. Letitia was far too weak to take on this burden. On only one occasion did she feel strong enough to be helped from the privacy of her bedchamber and downstairs to the White House reception rooms.

Actually, the beautiful Priscilla inherited her responsible station by default. Letitia's older daughters, Mary Tyler Jones and Letitia Tyler Semple, had husbands and homes of their own to maintain in Virginia. Thirteen-year-old Alice Tyler was too young to assume the duties of hostess, and eighteen-year-old Elizabeth was too inexperienced socially to do much more than assist Priscilla.

Happily, Priscilla was ideal for the demanding task. As an experienced actress she knew how to play a role with dignity, restraint, and good humor. For her the White House became a great stage. She set the scenery, chose the cast, and read her lines with consummate skill. In all this she sought the advice of the elderly Dolley Madison. Throughout the sixteen years of the Jefferson and Madison administrations Dolley had served as White House hostess. She knew everything worth knowing about social Washington. She was a jolly, buxom woman who dipped snuff and rouged her face like a Paris streetwalker. But she was much loved by the Tylers and was quickly taken into their confidence. Her assistance to Priscilla as producer-director of the White House theater was invaluable. Elizabeth Tyler also helped her sister-in-law until her marriage to William N. Waller in January 1842, when her departure left Priscilla with the sole responsibility of the post until March 1844. At that time Robert Tyler gave up his patronage slot in the Land Office and moved his wife and their two daughters to Philadelphia to begin a belated practice of law. With Priscilla's departure in March 1844 the vacancy as acting First Lady was temporarily filled by Letitia Tyler Semple, whose semi-estranged husband James had been helped off to sea as a purser in the Navy by Tyler. Julia, of course, inherited the position in the summer of 1844 and filled it until the Tyler administration ended in March 1845. Like her immediate predecessors in the post, she depended much on the experienced Dolley Madison for advice and counsel.[1]

Priscilla enjoyed every minute of her novel role in spite of the fact that the First Family was always surrounded by a genteel poverty and the grim realization that Letitia was slipping toward her grave. This was an intimate, depressing side of the Tylers' life in the White House that was kept strictly private. Julia, for instance, neither saw nor suspected it during her first extended visit in the capital in January and February 1842. But it was there nonetheless, and Priscilla learned to live with it. Her general attitude was not unlike that of Pope Alexander VI: Now that we have the Presidency, let us enjoy it—as best we can. Shortly after her arrival at the White House from Williamsburg she marveled at what fate had cast before her:

Here am I [she told her sister], *nee* Priscilla Cooper... actually living, and —what is more—presiding at the White House! I look at myself like a little old woman, and exclaim: Can this be I? I have not had one moment to myself since my arrival, and the most extraordinary thing is that I feel as if I had been used to living here always; and receive the Cabinet, ministers, the diplomatic corps, the heads of the army and navy, etc. etc., with a facility which astonishes me. "Some achieve greatness—some are born to it." I am plainly born to it. I really do possess a degree of modest assurance that surprises me more than it does anyone else. I am complimented on every side; my hidden virtues are coming out. I am considered "charmante" by the Frenchmen, "lovely" by the Americans, and "really quite nice, you know," by the English.

It was quite a new world for a struggling young actress who a scant four years earlier had bathed in the muddy Delaware and had eaten "nothing but bacon and potatoes for dinner, with an occasional lone dumpling to give weight to the repast." [2]

Priscilla's new position as White House hostess entailed coping with incredible pressures. While Congress was in session she was expected to supervise and preside over two formal dinner parties each week. At the first of these twenty guests were regularly invited, men who were visiting Washington and who had shown "respectful attention to the President and his family." At the second there were usually forty at dinner, drawn from the upper echelons of the government, the military, and the diplomatic corps. Each evening until ten o'clock the White House reception rooms were opened to informal visitors. These too required Priscilla's presence although Tyler frequently escaped by pleading the demands of his office. In addition, the Tylers occasionally sponsored small private balls. And once a month during the congressional session the White House was the scene of a grand public levee. Well over a thousand people generally attended these affairs; the crush of bodies made dancing almost impossible. The company at the levees was, recalled John Tyler, Jr., "less select as to true worth than was altogether agreeable." Select or not, Priscilla enjoyed them. Special receptions on New Year's Day and on the Fourth of July and weekly Marine Band concerts for the public on the south lawn of the White House on mild evenings rounded out the formal events over which the official hostess was expected to preside. For Priscilla it was a grueling schedule. With one exception, the young lady whom Tyler lauded as the "presiding genius of the White House for more than two years" rose to every occasion.[3]

Her lone failure occurred one evening in May 1841, early in her White House tenure. It was the night of her first formal dinner for the officers of the Cabinet. Priscilla was fatigued with the strain of managing her four-month-old daughter, Mary Fairlie, and she was already pregnant with her second child. The baby was sick and had been squalling and fretting all day, as Priscilla rushed about the Mansion trying to supervise the extensive dinner preparations and comfort her unhappy offspring at the same time. By evening she was exhausted. When the guests finally arrived, Secretary of State Webster escorted her in to dinner. Priscilla was the only woman present. For a time she chatted easily and amiably with the great Webster, whose imposing countenance and booming voice often reduced less poised acquaintances to awed silence. Priscilla was nervous and she was bone-tired, but she was not overwhelmed by the commanding presence of the "godlike Daniel." She was, after all, a woman who had often been strangled in her bed by Othello. It took more than a mere Secretary of State to faze the onetime Desdemona.

Yet on this particular evening, as the dessert was being served, Priscilla grew deathly pale. Suddenly she fell back from the table in a faint. Webster moved quickly from his seat, gathered her in his arms, and gallantly carried her away from the table. At this point Robert Tyler converted mere confusion into absolute chaos by impetuously dumping a pitcher of ice water on both the hero and the swooning heroine. As Priscilla recounted her embarrassment a few days later, the ice water ruined her "lovely new dress, and, I am afraid, produced a decided *coolness* between myself and the Secretary of State. I had to be taken to my room, and poor Mr. Webster had to be shaken off, dried and brushed, before he could resume dinner." The generous Webster quickly forgot the incident and soon became Priscilla's favorite person in the Cabinet. They chatted and gossiped every time they met and he undertook the education of her palate, advising her on foods and wines he thought she might enjoy.[4]

Following the opening-night disaster, Priscilla's social productions as White House hostess were an unbroken series of successes. She managed to tame—indeed charm—the haughty Chevalier de Bacourt, France's ambassador to the United States and one of his nation's most distinguished and accomplished snobs. The fine party she arranged in June 1842 for the British plenipotentiary, Lord Ashburton, may not have advanced the tedious Webster-Ashburton conversations on the Maine boundary dispute one whit, but it was proclaimed—even by the crusty John Quincy Adams—a great and glittering affair, "all that the most accomplished European courts could have displayed." So too was the White House reception in October 1841 for the Prince de Joinville, son of King Louis Philippe. At this time Priscilla was six months pregnant with her second daughter. So uncomfortable was she that Letitia Tyler Semple came up from Virginia to help out. The whole thing finally went off with great éclat.[5]

Priscilla's greatest triumph came early in 1843. On the shortest possible notice she hastily organized a White House reception for Count Henri Bertrand, former aide to Napoleon Bonaparte and onetime Grand Marshal of the Emperor's court. It was a solo performance. The President was visiting in Virginia. Robert Tyler was on hand to assist in the preparations, but he was, said Priscilla, "only Prince Consort." The Cabinet was hurriedly summoned to the White House at eight o'clock to greet the distinguished Count, who was a hand-kisser of the most impulsive continental sort. Priscilla was so amused by his exaggerated caricature of feudal chivalry that upon his departure, "as the last mustachioed Frenchman left the room, I turned a pirouette on one foot, and then dropping a low curtsey, said I begged the cabinet's pardon; whereat Mr. [Robert] Tyler was exceedingly wrathy, though everyone else said it was the sweetest thing I had done all evening." [6]

A few days later a more formal social gesture was extended Count Bertrand and his mustachioed entourage. Again Priscilla was equal to the occasion. She prepared a glittering state ball for two hundred carefully selected guests. Clad in a "rose-colored satin trimmed in blond lace flowers and a charming headdress of white bugles," she stationed herself

...at the head of the blue centre room near the window. As the Marshal arrived and walked through the hall, the band struck up the Marseillaise. The guests fell back on either side of the end of the room, leaving a wide path for Bertrand to advance to where Josephine—I mean, I—stood surrounded by the Cabinet. To describe the references he made, followed by his son and each of his suite in turn would be vain. I returned them with grandmama's old-fashioned curtseys, such as must have existed in the days of the Empire. ... No party ever went off better. Father with his usual kindness had given me carte blanche before he left. My supper was splendid. (It is so easy to entertain at other people's expense.) ... When the Marshal led me into supper, he seemed completely overcome, and putting his hand over his heart, said, "Ah, madame...all zis for me?" The only contretemps that occurred was that I gave him with a sweet smile a most splendid looking sugarplum without looking at the picture on it, which I afterwards discovered to my horror to be that of an ape.[7]

The official social events at which Priscilla performed so graciously and efficiently set a high standard for Julia and First Ladies after her to follow. Some of these functions were not always as pleasant as the Bertrand reception and ball. At the White House reception on New Year's Day, 1842, for instance, Priscilla stood for three wearying hours in the Blue Room shaking hands with the thousands of citizens who trooped in to catch a glimpse of their controversial President. "Such big fists as some of the people have," she remarked, "and such hearty shakes as they gave my poor little hand. ... One great hearty countryman gave me a clutch and a shake I almost expired under." [8]

Tyler also ran the risk of being crushed at these public affairs. He generally stationed himself in the center of the oval Blue Room to receive his guests, the ladies of the White House retiring to the comparative safety of the side walls. Centrally located as he was, he became the focal point of a milling throng which seethed and writhed like a gigantic octopus. It was what Priscilla termed the "rush of the sovereign people," and the President was thoroughly jostled and pushed about as the citizenry sought to shake his hand or even touch his coat. In all this physical contact Tyler maintained his equanimity and good nature, much as a victorious prizefighter surrounded by his fans must do at the end of an important bout. Still, it was a trying experience. When Julia became First Lady in 1844 one of her first reforms was to move her husband from the direct line of fire to the protective custody of a side wall. There he received and shook hands with his guests as they filed by in an orderly line. During Priscilla's tenure, however, Tyler took his chances. With all the Whig talk of assassination going around, the wonder is he was not shot down by his enemies or mashed to death by his friends.⁹

Behind the surface glitter of these formal receptions for important diplomats, dashing noblemen, bejeweled ladies, and brocaded officers stood the harsh fact that the Tyler family was, as usual, in serious financial difficulty during the White House years. Tyler was not a poor man, but the social obligations of his office created financial demands well above the capacities of a Virginia lawyer and planter. Money, or the lack of it, was a constant concern. When Priscilla on one occasion saw Madame Bodisco magnificently attired in a pink satin and lace dress, her throat all but hidden by "splendid diamonds," she could say of the magnificent stones that she "really envied them, not for their luster but for their value. Mary Fairlie's education might be purchased by them." [10]

Thanks to a politically vindictive Congress, the sums normally appropriated for the upkeep of the President's Mansion were not forthcoming. As a result, the President himself bore much of the cost of the lighting, heating, and essential maintenance of the establishment out of his own pocket. And since his pockets were scarcely overflowing, the New York *Herald* in November 1844 could correctly say of the White House that

This building bears the name of the "White House"; but, alas! how changed since the days of yore: its virgin white sadly sullied—its beautiful pillars disgustingly besplattered with saliva of tobacco—its halls deserted by day—and gloomily illuminated triweekly by night—the gorgeous East Room reflecting, from its monstrous mirrors, patched carpets, the penury of "Uncle Samuel"—and the three inch stumps of wax lights in the sockets of magnificent chandeliers, attesting to the rigid economy observed by its present possessors—the splendid drapery falling in tatters all around time's rude hand, the fingers of visitors having made sad havoc with their silken folds.[11]

The furniture also deteriorated during Tyler's tenure of office. It was, said F. W. Thomas, the New York *Herald*'s irate Washington correspondent, "a disgrace—a contemptible disgrace to the nation. Many of the chairs in the East Room would be kicked out of a brothel." Even when Gardiner money was added to the President's modest resources in 1844 it was spent on more opulent entertaining rather than on needed refurbishing. Tyler, of course, had no private funds for renovating or reupholstering the mangy furniture. The cost of food alone was a burden to him. "I am heartily tired of the grocers here who exact extravagant prices for everything," he complained. So high was the relative cost of living in Washington that he was ultimately reduced to ordering groceries in wholesale lots and at wholesale prices from New York and from his relatives in Charles City.[12]

Additional demands within the family circle increased the President's numerous financial burdens. Thomas A. Cooper, Priscilla's father, was given a patronage position, that of military storekeeper at the Frankford, Pennsylvania, Arsenal. This prevented him from becoming entirely dependent upon the Tylers, but the prodigal old actor would not or could not make ends meet on the pay of an Army captain. The standard of living he furnished those of Priscilla's younger sisters still at home was so marginal that she was forced to invite them to the White House for frequent and extended visits to keep them from going hungry. Tyler accepted this added cost of running the Mansion without complaint. Nonetheless, he attempted to ease his financial situation by appointing his son Robert to a fifteen-hundred-dollar-a-year position in the United States Land Office. At no time did the financially harassed President consider the appointment of Tom Cooper or Robert Tyler as nepotistic raids on the public treasury. Their patronage positions were absolute economic necessities to the family.[13]

To the Gardiners and to the American public in general nothing of this constant financial concern ever appeared on the surface. The Tylers graciously played their expected social roles in the White House without giving outward signs of the scrimping that was always going on within the bosom of the family. Nor did Tyler give any indication of his despair as he watched Letitia die. Instead, he buried himself in his work, arising at sunrise and remaining at his desk without break until 3:30 P.M. After a midafternoon family dinner he returned to his desk until dusk. Interviews, social functions, and more desk work occupied the evening hours until he retired at ten o'clock. It was a punishing schedule. Abandoned by many of his old friends, castigated by his political enemies, pilloried in the press, threatened with assassination, John Tyler was faced with the varied emotional and physical pressures of an administration in crisis, a wife who was dying, and a personal life of financial discomfort. It is not surprising that he often searched for solace in frantic attention to his official duties.

When there were few duties to perform, or when his desk was momentarily clear, he turned to correspondence with his children. This was something in the nature of therapy, and it served to bring father and daughters closer together during the months preceding and following Letitia's death. Thus on one occasion he urged daughter Mary not to concern herself with the vicious anti-Tylerism that spilled over and threatened to engulf all the members of the family. "Never give a thought to them," he advised her of his political critics. "They are entirely unworthy of giving you the slightest concern... go along as if they did not exist. In that way you obtain mastery over them."[14]

There were, of course, light and happy moments within the family circle during 1841–1843, although they were relatively few. One of these was the White House wedding of Elizabeth Tyler to William Nevison Waller of Williamsburg on January 31, 1842. Save for the presence of

Dolley Madison, members of the Cabinet, and a few intimate friends, it was a family affair. It marked the only occasion Letitia emerged from her sickroom to make an appearance downstairs in the President's Mansion. Tyler knew little about young Waller. But he approved the match on learning that the prospective bridegroom was an "artless, unsophisticated, generous, honorable man of pure and sound principles—ardent and affectionate in his attachment to all his Relatives." He would, in sum, make a good husband. Lizzie looked "surpassingly beautiful" on her wedding day, "lovely in her wedding dress and long blond-lace veil; her face literally covered with blushes and dimples." The affair pleased everyone.[15]

When Letitia finally died on September 10, 1842, the White House was plunged into the deepest gloom. Priscilla had gone to New York for a brief visit with her sister and Letitia, sensing that she was dying, hurriedly sent Robert north to bring her home. They both arrived back in Washington too late. "My poor husband suffered dreadfully when he was told that Mother's eyes were constantly turned to the door watching for him," Priscilla agonized. "Nothing can exceed the loneliness of this large and gloomy mansion, hung with black, its walls echoing with sighs." In the words of the Washington *Intelligencer,* Letitia Christian Tyler was "loving and confiding to her husband, gentle and affectionate to her children, kind and charitable to the needy and afflicted." Few obituaries have been so accurate. She was sorely missed.[16]

Crushed by grief, the President plunged himself even more vigorously into the everyday duties of his exacting office, into his Texas idea, and into his third-party plan. When the Gardiners returned to Washington in December 1842 for their second season in the capital they found the somber household in deep mourning. Priscilla gave no parties. Instead, she invited Julia and Margaret to the White House for a "quiet whist game," and to help roll back the surrounding gloom she implored Julia on one occasion to "bring her guitar with her." [17]

Following the death of his wife Tyler increasingly concerned himself with the life he would lead after his departure from the White House. Letitia's terminal illness turned his thoughts more positively to his eventual retirement and in the fall of 1842, after she was buried, he purchased from his neighbor, Collier Minge, for $10,000, the property in Charles City County known as Walnut Grove. It was located within two miles of Greenway, the old Tyler estate where the President had lived as a boy. No sooner had the purchase been effected than Tyler began extensive remodeling and expansion. No detail of this architectural transformation escaped his interest. It was a good diversion for him from his grief, although the added financial burden was a great one. The location of rooms, the construction of chimneys, the pitch of stairways all captured his attention. Plans, sketches, drawings, and suggestions were sent regularly to the site. By early 1843 Tyler had renamed the property Sherwood Forest in whimsical reference to his outlaw status in the Whig Party. He loved the place from the beginning, and during his courtship of Julia in 1843 his letters to her were filled with word-pictures of the emerging beauty of the estate, the magnificent view of the James River from his lawn, and his plans for the continued expansion and improvement of the plantation.[18]

Such was the situation at the White House and in the personal life of John Tyler when the Gardiner family arrived in Washington again on Sunday, December 4, 1842, occupied their chambers at Mrs. Peyton's boardinghouse, and began preparations for the coming season. The following Wednesday, James Keating, a servant brought along from East Hampton for the campaign, carried the Gardiners' cards to the White House, to the homes of all the Cabinet members, and to the residences of New York friends and acquaintances known to be in town. This was accepted etiquette and little could be expected to happen until these small billboards had been posted around the city.[19]

Within a week Mrs. Peyton's parlor was filled with callers who came to welcome the Gardiners. Among the first to pay their respects were General and Mrs. John P. Van Ness, Secretary of State and Mrs. Daniel Webster, Jessica Benton, congressmen James I. Roosevelt and John McKeon of New York, Senator James Buchanan of Pennsylvania, and Richard R. Waldron, the young naval officer from New Hampshire. Julia thought James Buchanan particularly engaging. Not only was he "a candidate for the presidency," he was also "a young bachelor of 50 ... a great beau among the young ladies; one of the first families and very wealthy." At the ripe old age of fifty James Buchanan was obviously too ancient for Julia, who was much more titillated by the attentions again paid her by young Waldron. A protégé of New Hampshire Senator Levi P. Woodbury, he had sailed with the famous Wilkes Expedition. He was a man of charm and intelligence, widely traveled and well read. Without too much encouragement from Julia's ever-flirtatious eyes, Richard Waldron again volunteered for the happy shore duty of escorting the Gardiners about town.[20]

In some respects life at Mrs. Peyton's house was not satisfactory. While the family could take their meals in their own rooms (the obliging James Keating carrying the steaming dishes up from the kitchen), they were forced to use the downstairs public parlor to entertain their neighbors and callers. Julia and Margaret considered this a wonderful arrangement. "There are quite a large number of gentlemen boarders," Julia explained. But Juliana was not so sure. "Society here is a strange medley when you come to analyze it," she informed her sons in New York. "Many are introduced and called that we know nothing about except the names and dare not ask lest exceptions should be taken to the question.

In company you must be as civil to one as another and dance with those who ask first without respect to persons otherwise you will make enemies enough. Pride must be laid aside as liberty and equality and true democracy prevail and make no mistake." [21]

Julia and Margaret were quite willing to lay aside as much pride as the situation demanded. They enjoyed nightly whist games in the parlor with their visitors and fellow boarders, and they enthusiastically joined in the spontaneous informal dances which developed when Mrs. Peyton engaged a violinist for an evening's entertainment. "These little dances are kept a profound secret so that none may go in but the boarders and their friends," Julia reported. She found them "perfectly delightful" if for no other reason than that "I had more than half the beaux in the room surrounding me all the while." Occasionally Julia would produce her guitar and sing. The common parlor thus provided excellent opportunities to see and be seen. Clear weather permitted casual promenades on Pennsylvania Avenue and afforded still another means of social exposure, as did regular appearances in the galleries of the House or Senate. Senator Gardiner enjoyed the high-level political conversation in the parlor with the "influential politicians" who resided at Peyton's, particularly with Duff Green of South Carolina, formerly a prominent Jacksonian, now a Tyler partisan.[22]

Nevertheless, from a purely social standpoint Mrs. Peyton's establishment was not adequate, especially after Julia's name was romantically linked with John Tyler's. The crush of callers became so great by late January 1843 that the Gardiners were obliged to engage an additional room which they used as a private parlor. This enabled the family to return their social obligations with a bit more style. "We did not find the public parlor as pleasant as we anticipated," Margaret finally explained to her brothers. "The ladies not as agreeable, the company not as *select*." The change also afforded the Senator some privacy. The additional room did not, however, solve the noise problem. The walls were so thin at the boardinghouse that Julia and Margaret were "sometimes regaled" with the activities and conversations of the gentlemen in the adjoining rooms. While this unintentional eavesdropping undoubtedly provided certain educational advantages for the girls, it was distracting.[23]

Nor, after some contact, did the family find all the male boarders at Peyton's socially eligible—or available. Maxwell Woodhill, a young naval officer from New Jersey, owned property enough, but he was frightfully ugly and, more relevant, he was about to be married. "You cannot conceive the horrors of his visage!" exclaimed Julia, writing him off as a hopeless case. John Haines of South Carolina was a well-traveled young man who played a good hand of whist, but Margaret's determination to charm him by being "very insinuating" came to nought. He soon left town, anyway. Too bad. He had been entertained in some of the best castles in France and England and was, thought Juliana, "a perfect little gentleman," although he was small, asthmatic, and he sniffled. Colonel Thomas Delage Sumter, on the other hand, was a Peyton resident all the Gardiners liked instantly. His many services to them the season before were gratefully remembered. The thirty-three-year-old West Point graduate and South Carolina congressman was an obliging escort on many occasions.[24]

Some of the young lady boarders at Peyton's were predatory and otherwise ill-behaved by Juliana's puritanical lights. Ruth Woodbury, daughter of Senator Levi Woodbury of New Hampshire, for example, was jealous of the attention paid Julia and Margaret, and they in turn thought her "not very refined." She attended rowdy parties at the homes of various Locofoco Democrats, a political species well beneath the contempt of the Gardiners, and she tried to "monopolize the beau[x]" in the Peyton parlor. In addition, she had numerous gentleman callers, so many that Julia and her sister "never knew who called to see us and who the W[oodbury]s." The private-parlor arrangement finally solved this dilemma.[25]

Refined or not, Miss Woodbury was not considered wanton by the Gardiners. That dubious honor was accorded solely to Miss Sarah Low of New York. She and her merchant father had rooms at Mrs. Peyton's and when Low was called back to New York on business, often for several weeks at a time, it was his practice to leave his daughter in the charge and care of his friend, Representative Thomas Butler King of Georgia. King, however, was soon observed to be "carrying on such a desperate flirtation" with the lady that "very few gentlemen pay her much attention." Since King had a wife and seven children at home, and because Miss Low was of "low origin" (her father had once kept a needle-and-thread shop in New York City), Juliana naturally assumed the worst. The King-Low relationship raised a "great talk" in Washington, so great in fact that the Gardiners were determined to have "nothing to do with her." More than that, they shunned anyone who maintained social contact with the lowbrow Lows. Those who conformed to the Gardiner boycott of the much-gossiped-about New Yorkers, like Colonel Sumter, were thought to possess great "penetration in having a respect and admiration for us and hatred of Miss Low." Even Mrs. Peyton ultimately got revenge for the odium brought upon her establishment by the Lows. She sharply overcharged them for their stay.[26]

The alleged indiscretions of Congressman King and the New York belle were among the subjects discussed excitedly behind fans in the galleries of the House and Senate. The Gardiner girls frequently attended the congressional debates, not so much to listen to the death rattles of the Tyler administration as to be seen and to exchange the social patter of the day. Actually, there was not much worth hearing on Capitol Hill. The lame-duck session of the Twenty-seventh Congress was a dreary affair, devoid of political significance and interest. Nevertheless, Julia's visits to the Senate and House of Representatives were mystifying experiences. "I was about as wise when the speaker finished as to who voted upon either side as when he commenced," she commented on one occasion. She was intrigued, however, by the appearance and the forensic energy of John Quincy Adams and Henry A. Wise. "They are unsparing in tender epithets," she remarked, "and I understand nothing but the age of Mr. Adams prevents them at times coming to blows on the floor. Mr. A[dams] has the reputation of professing every sense but Common Sense and the personal appearance of Mr. Wise I think vastly unprepossessing." [27]

Margaret agreed that the debates were dull and the excited exchanges on the floor transparently contrived. She found only Caleb Cushing to her liking. At forty-two, the tall, handsome congressman from Massachusetts was "mild and agreeable," with a voice "manly and distinct." She was impressed that Cushing "does not allow himself to become excited like Wise who looks as if he had one foot in the grave." After she met Cushing socially, however, she decided he had a "handsome face but bad figure, and is very awkward in company." It surprised her, therefore, to hear the rumor that the maladroit Mr. Cushing was engaged to a Baltimore belle, "rich and thirty." When the rumor proved false, Julia moved in herself for a casual flirtation with Cushing. In return for singing him a song, she received a sonnet from him—"a fair exchange," she termed it. She found him very personable and quite brilliant, "the most studious member in the House . . . high on the road to fame—a widower with no children." He would do. Not so Henry A. Wise, the homely Virginian. While Margaret discovered that Wise was "quite disposed to have a *flirtation*," his face was "as wrinkled as an old man's of seventy and he looks as if he had actually worn himself out." The thirty-six-year-old Wise was scarcely worn out. Twenty-two years later he was energetically commanding the Confederate defenses at Petersburg. He lived until 1876. Appearances could be deceiving.[28]

When the debates were not actually boring to the sisters, they were incomprehensible. Julia had no luck whatever following the exchanges on the resolution to repeal the Bankruptcy Act of 1842; and Margaret had too little background in American history to make much sense of the Senate debate on a motion to end the joint Anglo-American occupation of Oregon. She was impressed only with the fact that Senator George McDuffie of South Carolina spoke humorously and eloquently on the Oregon question while holding himself painfully upright at the side of his chair "owing to his having received a ball in a duel which has never been extracted." [29]

To counteract their boredom and their ignorance of the political issues of the day, Julia and Margaret chatted with congressmen who circulated in the galleries while the debates dragged on below. Representatives Cushing, Edmund W. Hubard of Virginia, Ira A. Eastman of New Hampshire, Richard D. Davis of New York, and Francis Marion Ward of New York frequently made their way to the side of the Gardiner sisters to exchange pleasantries while "the orators of the day ... jumped and screamed and perspired and foamed and as usual made much ado about nothing." If the lawmakers were too busy to pass the time of day in gallery gossip, Purser Waldron could always be counted upon to produce an admiring coterie of young naval officers to surround and amuse the ladies. For Julia and Margaret the House gallery became a virtual reception parlor for their friends and acquaintances. It was a pleasant place to pass a "delightful morning." The social advantages were obvious even if they learned little about the American political process. When Congress adjourned on the evening of March 3, 1843, and ladies were admitted directly to the floor of the House for the first time in many years, Julia and Margaret were conspicuously present. Taking seats near that of their friend Representative Thomas F. Marshall of Kentucky, the girls soon "had no less than twenty-one gentlemen" clustered around them. These included Representative Francis W. Pickens of South Carolina and Supreme Court Justice John McLean of Ohio, both of whom were desperately in love with Julia at this time. In spite of the romantic distractions Margaret reported that the "admittance of the Ladies to the floor ... kept the house in excellent order." [30]

These occasional visits to the House and Senate gallery produced great social dividends. Within a month of the Gardiners' arrival in the capital the Peyton parlor was filled with congressmen and senators who came to flirt, dance, and play whist with the young ladies from East Hampton. By December 16 the Washington correspondent of the New York *Herald* could write of Julia, much to her delight, that

> ... the beautiful and accomplished Miss Gardner [*sic*] of Long Island, one of the loveliest women in the United States, is in the city, and was the "observed of all observers" during her promenade on the avenue today. She had a very distinguished escort from the Capitol to her residence after the adjournment, of members of the House, grave Senators not too old to feel the power of youth and beauty, Judges, officers of the Army and Navy, all vieing [*sic*] with each other to do homage to the influence of her charms.

This flattering notice produced a decided "sensation" among the fashionables in New York City—or so brother David Lyon reported.[31]

In spite of her exposure to Washington's sophisticated political set, Julia's political views remained naïve and superficial. To be sure, Madame Chagaray's quaint curriculum had ill prepared her to wrestle with the subtle intricacies of fiscal and foreign-policy legislation; but maneuverings of various hopefuls for the Presidential succession were not subtle. Julia nonetheless exhibited nearly total ignorance of this phase of the political life of the capital. Her candidate for the White House in 1844 was invariably the last aspirant she had spoken or danced with. First it was Buchanan. After meeting Senator Benton at a Christmas Eve party she came out enthusiastically for "Old Bullion." For a brief week in mid-December she was for "Capt. Tyler." This endorsement she soon shifted to the urbane John C. Calhoun. When Calhoun heard Julia had "nominated" him he was amused and flattered to the extent of hurrying around to Peyton's to pay his respects to such a lovely and politically perceptive lady.[32]

Richard Waldron agreed with Calhoun's analysis of Julia's charming qualities, but from motives indicating that he was in love with the young woman from Long Island. He had squired her about town the previous season, it will be recalled. She had enjoyed his company and had appreciated his social usefulness. But that was as far as their relationship had gone. Waldron was a youth of twenty-three who had followed the sea since the age of fourteen. In June 1837 he had been appointed midshipman in the United States Navy, and in January 1840 he had been aboard the frigate *Vincennes* when she attempted to put an exploring party ashore in Antarctica. He was a fine seaman and an interesting person and he had a wealth of stories to tell. By December 1842 he had decided he would like to marry Julia and he launched a serious romantic campaign to that end.

Waldron's whole approach, however, was boyish and unsophisticated. Perhaps he had been too long at sea. In any event, his endeavor of the heart turned on introducing Julia to important and interesting people in Washington. It was an attempt to overwhelm a small-town girl. Among these notables was Prince Timoleo Haolilio of Hawaii—"Timothy Hallelujah," Julia called him—who was briefly in the capital in December 1842 for the purpose of alerting the Tyler administration to the Machiavellian designs of the French on the Sandwich Islands. He also discussed with Tyler the possibilities of Hawaiian annexation to the United States. Accompanied by a dour American missionary who served as his interpreter, Prince Haolilio was a unique visitor to the city and he was much sought after socially. Waldron had met the Prince in the islands while attached to the Wilkes Expedition, and it was quite a *coup* for him to be able to bring "Hallelujah" to Peyton's parlor to meet young Julia. She was impressed. "His complexion is about as dark as a negro," she reported, "but with Indian hair though at a distance being short and thick it seems the *true wool*. He was in an undress military uniform and his manners were modest and graceful—quite the man of the world in comparison with his Interpreter." [33]

Continuing to employ the travelogue route to Julia's heart, Waldron escorted her to the Patent Office to see the collection of curiosities brought home by Captain Charles Wilkes. Again Julia was impressed, but Waldron's gesture was like that of a small boy showing a little girl his pet caterpillar. "The scalp of the Fijee [sic] cannibal who was brought to this country is there exhibited—his head must have been three times the size of an ordinary man. A perfect Cyclops!" she exclaimed. Since Waldron had had an island in the Fiji group named for him, he was understandably partial to this particular exhibit.

Somewhat more conventionally, Waldron danced with Julia at the Peyton parlor informals, sent her flowers, dropped in for evening whist games, escorted her to the Assembly balls, and made himself generally useful to Julia's father in arranging his invitations to the White House. "I 'opened the ball' with Mr. Waldron," Julia wrote of one of the small dances at Peyton's. "Mr. W. has it in his power to be very useful. He is intimately acquainted with all the people of influence here, particularly with the President's family and the Websters."

Waldron was useful—and he was used. He was genuinely in love with Julia, and it was unkind of her to say of him after her return to East Hampton in March 1843 that he had been "very presuming"; that his continued pursuit of her after her connection with Tyler had become general knowledge was designed merely "to make himself of some importance—nothing like the cunning of a New Hampshire Yankee!" Waldron, it would seem, was never in serious contention, a fact it took him some time to discover. Nevertheless, Juliana liked him and she encouraged his attentions to Julia. At one point, in December 1842, she was fairly certain that "an engagement" to Julia was in the offing.[34]

Less seriously in contention than Waldron was Representative Richard D. Davis of Saratoga County, New York. "Old Davis," as Julia dubbed him, was a creaky forty-three (Julia spoke of him as an "invincible old bachelor of 50!") but still spry enough to follow her around like a frisky bird dog. He pursued her relentlessly at the informal little dances in Peyton's parlor. His attentions embarrassed Julia greatly, although the other congressmen who attended the affairs laughingly encouraged Davis in his eager quest. "His deferential manner of approaching me is the greatest source of amusement," Julia complained. "One would think he was addressing a Goddess." Still, the practical Juliana thought it would be a good idea to "make particular inquiries concerning him as he has the reputation here of being very wealthy." One had to be sure of such things. Alexander was thus commissioned to run a confidential Dun & Bradstreet on Richard D. Davis. While this was in progress Representative Davis became the bane of Julia's existence. No sooner would she take her seat in the House gallery than the homely New Yorker would leave the floor and appear at her side. "I was *bored to death* ... by old Davis," she protested on one occasion. "I wish him in Africa a hundred times." It became a joke among other congressmen on the floor to see Davis scurry up to the gallery to talk to Julia whenever she attended the debates. One day when she appeared in the House wearing a lavishly plumed hat, designed something on the order of a frightened flamingo, Davis, as usual, departed his legislative station and headed for the gallery. A few minutes later the ayes and nays were taken on a minor bill. "Mr. Davis?" intoned the teller. No answer. "Mr. Davis?" he repeated. At this point all eyes turned to the gallery. There was Davis chatting with Julia, her untamed hat nearly covering both of them. "Mr. Speaker," said Representative Roosevelt, "Mr. Davis has gone to the gallery to study horticulture." This produced much merriment in the chamber, and for Julia much embarrassment. Snubbing the gentleman produced no relief from his unwanted attentions. As Margaret explained the problem to her brothers:

On Wednesday evening we had a little dance in the Parlour, in which as luck would have it (Davis said) he was a participator, and danced with *Julia* and I [*sic*]. She put him off three cotillions, but he very quietly waited. We understand he says he cannot sleep at night from *excess* of *love* and having inquired about our family, with a satisfactory result, intends popping the question. The requisites are beauty, riches, youth, and family, in return for which he offers a rabbit face, with one foot of shirt-collar, comical figure, *two* front teeth, and *two* hundred thousand dollars. I am sure it will kill you, to witness his movements in the dance. He created a fund of merriment among the gentlemen.

If Davis ever did "pop the question" the fact is not a matter of record. It can be safely asserted, however, that Julia demanded more in a husband than a rabbit face and two front teeth, even when the deal included "two hundred thousand dollars." [35]

Representative Francis W. Pickens did ask for Julia's hand. He was a handsome, cultured, wealthy plantation owner from Edgefield, South Carolina. At thirty-seven he was already a nationally prominent states' rights legislator and a leader of the Calhoun faction in the House. His principal drawback, as the Gardiners collectively assessed him, was that he was a widower with four children. That Tyler was a widower with seven children would later seem not quite so important. Whether Julia seriously considered Pickens as a prospective husband cannot be determined with certainty. She did, however, skillfully use his love for her as a lever in her courtship with John Tyler. She used Justice John McLean in much the same manner. And she constantly pitted Pickens against McLean and both of them against the President. It was the way these things were (and still are) done.

Julia met the courtly South Carolinian at a reception at the Daniel Websters' on January 2, 1843. Introductions were performed by her escort, Colonel Thomas Sumter, a friend and colleague of Pickens. On the way back to Peyton's in Sumter's carriage they passed Pickens on Pennsylvania Avenue.

"There goes Mr. Pickens," said Sumter, pointing him out.

"I see," Julia replied, "but I should not know him again. I am such a miserable hand to recollect faces."

"Oh, but I just introduced him to you at Mrs. Webster's," protested the Colonel. "You must remember him, for he said one of the prettiest things of you today I ever heard." [36]

From then on, Julia remembered. Within a few days Pickens had become one of the regular visitors at Mrs. Peyton's. By mid-February the South Carolinian was reputed "dead in love with Julia." He certainly missed none of the "whisto-musicales" sponsored by the Gardiners in their chambers. These were informal evenings at cards which ended with Julia playing her guitar and singing such ballads as "A Soldier's Tear" while the guests consumed great quantities of champagne, hot whiskey punch, and raw oysters. By early March the perceptive Pickens realized that he had a great deal of competition for Julia's hand and he pressed his attentions on her more vigorously. Not only was there the formidable challenge of the President of the United States, but there was also that of Supreme Court Justice McLean. Pickens was "exceptionally jealous" of McLean, Margaret reported; and on one occasion when the two men were monopolizing Julia, he "interrupted the conversation continually for fear [McLean] might prove too entertaining." [37]

In spite of the competition, or because of it, Pickens pushed his suit with great energy and determination. On March 4, the day after Congress adjourned and just before his scheduled departure for South Carolina, he proposed marriage to Julia. He had waited too long. By that time Julia was involved with John Tyler, and she was still flirting conspicuously with Justice McLean. She politely but firmly declined the offer. Margaret relayed the news of the Pickens proposal to her brother Alexander with a rare economy of words: "Mr. P. has offered and been rejected—*of course*. The particulars when we meet. Today we are going to the Supreme Court, Julia to *court* in earnest. She is resolved to lay siege to Judge MacClean [sic]." [38]

Pickens did not give up so easily. After Julia had returned to East Hampton in March, Pickens repeated his proposal, suggesting in a lengthy and tender letter on May 8 that Julia come share his "southern home where flourishes the pomegranate and orange, where luxury surrounds, and reign Queen." He assured her that as mistress of Edgewood plantation she would be waited upon and made happy by *"ever so many niggers and step-children."* From the perspective of East Hampton it was indeed an attractive offer, and everyone in the family gratuitously voiced an opinion on it. "It's one of the best," said Senator Gardiner flatly. "Such an offer is not presented every day." Juliana was less enthusiastic: "I don't like his principles altogether or his three or four children," she snorted. Brother David Lyon decided that "Distinguished Southerners are more than common, and if it was not for his principles and his children I should advise [acceptance], but as the case stands it's another affair." Margaret simply told Julia to "do just as you please." And Julia did precisely what she pleased; she always did. She was still not interested in Pickens' offer. She had a better one from John Tyler.

"What think I?" she asked her brothers. "Just nothing at all and think about [it] as much." She finally wrote Pickens that while she would "fain preserve" his valuable friendship, her own "friendly esteem" for him would be considerably strengthened were he to "change the tone of his consideration." She hoped this would prove "no difficult task" for him, and that he would not "eradicate my image entirely from [your] mind." A later generation would call it a "Dear John" letter. In this polite brush-off of Pickens she had Margaret's full approbation. Her sister, it seemed, did "not exactly consider him a man of the world." [39]

A fresh barrage of poetry-filled letters from Edgewood plantation failed to change Julia's mind in the matter. Not that Pickens was much of a poet:

> Oh! come to the South,
> The land of the sun;
> And dwell in its bower,
> Sweet, beautiful one.

"He at least deserves the credit of being persevering," Margaret granted. At length the poetic Pickens tired of his hopeless quest. By August 1843 Alexander was curious to learn if he "gives up the ghost, or only the pursuit—whether he makes further overtures or asks a return of missives—whether he is offended, determined or resigned." Three months later it was clear that Pickens had graciously given up the ghost. He was neither offended nor embittered. He was a South Carolina gentleman; as a gentleman he was an affable loser in an affair of the heart. His relations with the Gardiners remained cordial and friendly.[40]

Judge John McLean was also a good loser, although he had the advantage of his age (fifty-seven) as a rationalization when he too stepped out of Julia's life. She in turn had never had more than a passing interest in the distinguished Ohio Democrat who had served as Secretary of War in Jackson's Cabinet. He was a charming and sophisticated man, a perennial candidate for the Presidency, and he was naturally flattered by the attentions of an attractive and sought-after woman of twenty-two. She flirted with him outrageously during the 1842–1843 season and he returned the courtesy. Actually, Julia was using McLean only to pique and sustain the interest of Tyler and Pickens. She also flirted with Supreme Court Justices Smith Thompson and Henry Baldwin, but of the three jurists who were treated to her wiles only McLean "laughed bewitchingly" back at her. Indeed, McLean was soon telling Baldwin that were he "twenty-five years younger he'd cut the P[resident] out if he could." [41]

After Julia's return to East Hampton McLean tried to put into writing what he had apparently had difficulty putting into words in Washington. His first letter to Julia, containing "some tender traits if no open avowal," was read aloud around the family tea table and "made the house resound with laughter." It titillated them all to learn that McLean was "quite jealous of his rival the President." Julia's carefully phrased response to him was less cruel than the tea-table hilarity. In his reply to her, dated April 19, McLean sadly noted

If it were not sinful, I should rebel against the law of my species and ask, why is it that a disparity of years makes so little change in the susceptibilities of our nature.... To overcome this powerful tendency and follow the dictates of a sober judgment all the firmness of the highest mental attitudes are required. Miss Julia saw something of this struggle at our last interview when I signified to her the concern I felt at my being more than twenty five or thirty years of age. For the first time in my life I desired to be young. This I know was a selfish and a vain feeling, that I should not have indulged. The temptation to the wrong, if it was a wrong, was so strong, indeed, so overwhelming, that I could not resist it. Ah! Julia suffer me to say to you that in my eyes you are the most fascinating and lovely creature that exists on earth ... if I had it in my power to gain more than your friendship, which I have never imagined, it would be improper in me to do so. I did not bring myself to this conclusion without many wakeful and anxious hours of the deepest feeling; and at last I yielded to the imperious conviction of propriety which should never be disregarded. Were I only thirty years of age, there is no being this side of heaven that could be so important to my happiness. In ten years I shall be quite an old gentleman while Miss Julia will be still rising in the beauty and bloom of her nature. I have therefore on the fullest consideration made it the greatest sacrifice of feeling to principle in coming to the above conclusion that I have ever done. Miss Julia will not suppose that I have for a moment been vain enough to believe that however recent my aspiration for her affections might have been, I could have succeeded. Such a calculation did not enter into my mind or influence my decision. I could not under the circumstances have been so presumptuous. After saying this much in the utmost frankness, Miss Julia will suffer me to say that I am solicitous to be numbered among her best friends—nay will she not give me in this pre-eminence.... To be remembered kindly by one who stands pre-eminent among the most intelligent, elegant and beautiful young ladies of the age cannot but be highly appreciated....

Julia was deeply touched by McLean's kind and pensive remarks: "A more beautiful letter, more honorable for himself or more flattering to me could not have been written, as all acknowledge—it was great throughout." A century and a quarter later it was still among her papers, carefully preserved.[42]

A month later news reached East Hampton via the New York *Express* that McLean had suddenly married. Julia thought the idea terribly amusing, especially since her consolatory answer to McLean's tender missive of withdrawal must have reached the Justice within a few days after his wedding to the widow Sarah Bella Garrard. "Ah! Alexander, and now who do you think is married—yes, *married*.... Hymen's torch is consumed and I have dropt an hysterical tear on its ashes... it is *Judge McLean!!!* He has married a widow and I conclude a rich one.... Three days a bridegroom and he must have received my reply. ... What was his expression when he recognized the handwriting! Oh, what wouldn't I have given to have witnessed it at such a time—do you think he let his wife read it?" [43]

To Julia it was very humorous. Indeed, her rather callous flirtation with the aging McLean revealed her one of Eve's truly extroverted daughters. She tripped lightly through her young life leaving behind a trail of broken hearts—aged twenty-three to fifty-seven. She was a great belle in an era of great American belles. Her conquests were legion. The fields of romantic combat on which she jousted were strewn with the bodies of old men and boys. McLean was merely another notch on her parasol handle. At every ball she attended in Washington she was a sensation, her presence immediately felt. Her appearance, dress, and popularity, combined with her wealth and social background, made her the marriage catch of the season. She represented a challenge John Tyler could scarcely resist.

Paced by their home-grown Aphrodite, the entire Gardiner family made a decided impression on the capital. Dress was vitally important in this effort and no economy was practiced by the Senator when it came to clothing the Gardiner women for their ostentatious sallies into society. "J[ulia] and I with Ma and Pa went to the Assembly," Margaret wrote of the ball of January 12. "J. was dressed in white with her Greek [headdress]. Ma in velvet with white toke and I in white with silver ornaments. I never saw a more perfect display of taste, rich dresses and beauty... the company was unusually select." When Alexander came down from New York for the fourth and final Assembly ball of the season on February 27, he was first given detailed instructions on how he should clothe himself. It was important also that reigning belles not be seen at social functions sponsored by those of dubious social or political background. For this reason the Gardiners would attend no parties given by such Locofoco Democrats as editor F. P. Blair; nor would they risk being linked with the likes of the controversial and celebrated Peggy Eaton. "We shall not attend Mrs. Eaton's ball until we hear a favorable account of her standing here. Previously to her residence... it was not very fair." [44]

Instead, they limited themselves to the subscription Assembly balls —Julia and Margaret were escorted to these sparkling affairs by acceptable Army and Navy officers, congressmen, and diplomats—and to private dances and receptions at the homes of the Websters, Upshurs, and Wickliffes. At the more exclusive private functions the young Gardiner ladies were accompanied by or received the flattering attentions of Robert Tyler and John Tyler, Jr. Frequent invitations to the White House rounded out the pattern of their social life in the capital during the early months of 1843.[45]

This rarefied social atmosphere produced in Juliana no feeling that

Washington society was in any way superior to New York society. "The society here is quite provincial," she confided to Alexander, "tho'... I think it is perhaps the best place for young ladies who wish to mingle in the gaieties of the new coast." Matchmaking aside, she was amazed that people with no social background in New York could make such a splash in Washington because of their political importance back home. There was, for example, Silas M. Stilwell, the United States Marshal in New York City, much sought after when he visited the capital, who "kept but a few years since a *shoe store* in the Bowery." It distressed her to pass New York acquaintances on Pennsylvania Avenue and discover that the women they were with were not their wives. And it angered her that a lady of the quality of Mrs. Charles Stewart, wife of the famous Commodore, would attempt in Washington what would never have been undertaken by any fashionable person in New York—the use of teatime in her parlor to negotiate a loan for five hundred dollars from David Gardiner. There was a provincial streak in Washington to which Juliana never really adjusted. "I don't think I should like Washington as a residence," Margaret agreed. "It's very well for a winter or so but wonderfully provincial." [46]

The least provincial features of the capital were the White House and the Tylers. Within a week of the Gardiners' arrival in Washington John Tyler, Jr., had called at Peyton's to pay his respects to the much-talked-about Gardiner ladies. Two days later, December 15, Waldron escorted the Senator to the President's Mansion for an interview. The President was busy that day, but Gardiner spoke with John, Jr., who urged him to return the following afternoon and greet the President. When he returned he found the President looking "very unwell." But their chat was a pleasant one, and Tyler invited the Gardiner family to take dinner at the White House on Christmas Eve. Accompanied by Representative and Mrs. Robert McClellan of New York, Purser Richard Waldron, and Colonel Thomas Sumter, the family was received in the "most modest, affable, unassuming manner." Julia found John, Jr., to be "quite handsome and distingué in his person—and ah! how interestingly sentimental was his conversation. He laid quite a siege to my heart." So intensely did young John flirt with Julia that he quite forgot to mention to her that he was married. The fact that he had lived with Mattie Rochelle only a few months after their marriage in 1839, and had since tried to arrange a divorce was, however, common gossip in Washington which Julia had already heard. She was not swept away by his performance. He was soon bombarding her with bad poetry ("I excuse all bad poetry where I am the subject," Julia allowed) and sending the Gardiners "very handsome French confectionaries" from the White House kitchen. Julia was still cautious. On the other hand, she found Priscilla Cooper Tyler "pretty and interesting" and Mrs. William Tyler, the President's sister-in-law, "a little country looking." So many various Tylers seemed to be present that Christmas Eve that Waldron guessed "there [are] some fifty country cousins 'come to town' to spend holidays with their great relations and [are] . . . stowed away in some of the closets to await New Year's." Entertaining his numerous "country cousins" at the White House was another expense John Tyler bore uncomplainingly.[47]

The Christmas Eve dinner went very well. Three days later Robert and Priscilla Tyler called on the Gardiners at Peyton's, and the Senator, thanks to the manipulation of John, Jr., was signally honored by an invitation to another White House dinner. At this affair the President made a special effort to flatter him. On New Year's Day the family "attracted universal attention" at St. John's Episcopal Church. Like most good and fashionable Episcopalians, they arrived at the church after the services had begun. Looking for an unoccupied pew, they were "perfectly astonished" to see the President rise from his seat, bow several times, move into the aisle, and graciously usher them into his own pew. "Even the minister stopped his proceedings and lost his place," so great was the general astonishment. Unfortunately, Julia was not present for this *coup,* being confined to her room with a bad cold. Margaret was certain that the affair had created "bitter envy among our young lady boarders," and for this she was extremely grateful.[48]

Julia recovered her health quickly. On January 2, 1843, she was well enough to attend the public levee at the White House. After a great effort to get herself "sufficiently festooned" for the occasion, she sallied forth on the arm of Colonel Sumter, he "sumptuously equipped—whiskers brushed to a turn—[in] a dashing vest of black velvet." The rooms were jammed. It required a full hour before she and the Colonel could make their way into "the presence of his majesty." As the moment of truth approached, Julia worried to Sumter that "He surely will not recognize me, you know I have seen him but once in the evening and then with a different hat." But Tyler did remember her, and he reached over several shoulders to grasp her hand. "I hope you are very well," he said warmly. Julia was highly flattered, and as she moved on to chat with Calhoun and Lewis Cass the climax of the evening had already passed for her. She took no offense when Ambassador Bodisco, "the old representative of all the Russias, scanned me from head to foot with the eye of a conneissuer [*sic*]." The ambassador's reaction to her appearance she never learned. Margaret could only hear Bodisco say, as Julia passed him, "She has nice teeth, *but.* . . ." Remarks like this apparently worry women, and Julia worried.[49]

She need not have. The Gardiners had arrived, been seen, and had conquered. Family calls at the White House and return calls at Peyton's by Robert and John, Jr., became regular events. By late January the two families had become so intimate that Juliana had to warn Alexander that his appearance in town at that moment would only be construed as a crude "pursuit of office." And Robert paid so much attention to Margaret at the Wickliffe ball on January 31 that a dozen young men crowded forward seeking introductions to the popular sisters, apologizing profusely for not having called upon them earlier. "The *influence* of power was very apparent," remarked Juliana, who was at last convinced that the Tylers measured up socially. "We all like the Tylers," she confessed to her son David. "They are noble in their mien and possess much genius and gallantry. They are superior to political trickery, and I sincerely hope John Tyler will be re-elected President."[50]

Robert Tyler was a particular favorite of Julia and Margaret. During February he became a fixture at the Gardiner whisto-musicales. He played whist indifferently enough to permit the sisters to win numerous pairs of gloves from him, and he invariably brought along his latest poem to read to Margaret. She in turn listened and frankly gave her opinion of his efforts. He was a competent poet in the incompetent Victorian manner. Much of his work turned on somber death themes. As he read to Margaret and Julia from his *Death; Or, Medorus' Dream*, which *Harper's* published the following month, he consumed whiskey punch and oysters in great quantity. The next morning he complained of what he delicately described as a "nervous headache." Margaret found Robert "not handsome." He possessed, however, a "pleasant countenance" and his manner was "subtly amiable and agreeable." When Robert appeared in the Gardiner parlors on February 6 to read from his recently published *Ahasuerus. A Poem,* Margaret made the same political decision her mother had made a week earlier. She too "adopted the Tyler banners" for 1844.[51]

So it was that when the Gardiners went to the White House on the all-important evening of February 7, 1843, the political tide in the family was running strong for the President. It was a small gathering of thirteen. Quite mixed socially, the group was dominated by New York politicians chosen, thought Margaret, "from the *unavoidables,* from *politicals*." Only the James I. Roosevelts and the Gardiners were invited, she felt, from "congenial motives." Also present that evening were Robert and Priscilla and Priscilla's father, Tom Cooper. The Red Room of the White House was ice-cold and the sisters had all they could do to maintain circulation in their fingers. Two tables of whist were organized, but the frigid air made it difficult to hold the cards. Tyler finally came in at nine-thirty to chat with his guests. He was in an exceedingly good mood. First he teased Margaret to tell him how many beaux she had. When she coyly demurred, he jestingly demanded an official answer in the name of "the President of the United States." Margaret replied that she had "a dozen or more," but that Julia had even more than that. Turning to Julia, the President began teasing her about her numerous beaux. Then he asked her to play cards with him. Just the two of them. "He had quite a flirtation with J[ulia]," Margaret reported, "and played several games of *All fours* with her." The sight of this easy familiarity on the part of the graying President toward the twenty-two-year-old Julia was too much for the worldly Thomas Cooper. "Do see the President playing *old sledge* with Miss Gardiner," he exclaimed. "It will be in the *Globe* tomorrow." It did not appear in the Washington *Globe* or any other newspaper. Perhaps it should have. The resulting humanization of John Tyler might well have commanded the votes of all those humble citizens who enjoyed a good fast game of old sledge.[52]

After the other guests had departed the Gardiners were invited into the warmth of the President's chambers upstairs. For several hours they sat and chatted in front of the fire. It was at this moment that John Tyler decided he wanted to know Julia Gardiner much better. Late that night, as the family was taking leave of the courtly President, "What does he do but give me a *kiss*," Margaret wrote excitedly.

He was proceeding to treat Julia in the same manner when she snatched away her hand and flew down the stairs with the President after her around chairs and tables until at last he caught her. It was truly amusing. Putting the cold out of the question we had a delightful evening...the President escorting us quite to the carriage, and Mr. [Robert] Tyler promising to call today and read to us his new poem....[53]

It had been very amusing. More importantly, it marked the beginning of still another serious courtship for Julia. Waldron, Pickens, McLean—now Tyler. The social life of the Gardiner sisters was moving into high gear. In fact, the young ladies began to experience real fatigue. By mid-February their father worried about their ability to maintain the killing pace. "We were out four evenings last week and up until after one o'clock every night this," Margaret reported. "Every day and every evening is occupied in these gay scenes," the Senator wrote Alexander. "I think your sisters when the spring passes will not object to the quietness of our summer residence." The girls were of different mind. They had no doubt of their ability to cope with their demanding social calendar and the thought of returning to sleepy little East Hampton was not a congenial one. The morning after the "All fours" party at the White House they began imploring their father to let them remain on for a while in Washington after Congress adjourned on March 3 and the social season more or less ended. Meanwhile, to prepare themselves for each evening's new tax on their energy they adopted the simple device of staying longer and longer abed in the morning.[54]

Tyler was fascinated by Julia and he pushed his suit as relentlessly as was proper for a widower of five months. He was a lonely man after Letitia's death, and he responded eagerly to the sparkle and excitement of the winsome Julia. On Sunday, February 12, he walked the Gardiners home from church, the first time he had appeared publicly on the Avenue with them. This courtesy naturally caused a great deal of speculation and gossip. "Many jokes are already being passed around about our being in such favor at the White House," Juliana informed Alexander. "The President is a fine man," she continued, "amiable and agreeable and independent. He has been shamefully abused by those not to be compared with himself in any respect. You must be a Tyler man as I believe his measures are wise." [55]

Whether his measures were wise or not, the President had come to the conclusion in mid-February that he wanted to marry Julia Gardiner. To court her properly he was forced to contrive various stratagems to be with her—meetings that would occasion a minimum amount of gossip. Thus he insisted that the sisters stop at the White House en route to the Webster ball on February 13 that he might see their new dresses. He was still in mourning for Letitia and thus was not yet going out socially himself. When they arrived that evening for inspection the President, in Margaret's words, "admired our dresses and passed innumerable compliments. He was extremely affectionately inclined—Julia declared he was rather too *tender* for he gave her *three* kisses while I received only *two*. In truth we did look very well for our dresses were entirely new for the occasion." [56]

On the evening of the Washington's Birthday ball at the White House, February 22, 1843, Tyler could contain himself no longer. Julia was dressed in a white tarlatan and on her head she wore a crimson Greek cap with a dangling tassel. She was radiant. The President spied her dancing with Waldron. When the music stopped the young naval officer was on the verge of leaving the floor with his partner when the President suddenly appeared at his side. "I must claim Miss Gardiner's company for a while," he said, drawing Julia's arm through his own. Waldron gave his Commander-in-Chief a black look, but wisely gave no voice to his injured feelings. For a few minutes the President and Julia promenaded the rooms. Then John Tyler asked her straight out to marry him. "I had never thought of love," Julia recalled years later, "so I said, 'No, no, no,' and shook my head with each word, which flung the tassel of my Greek cap into his face with every move. It was undignified, but it amused me very much to see his expression as he tried to make love to me and the tassel brushed his face." Julia was probably not as surprised by the President's declaration as she later remembered. In any event, she decided not to tell her father about Tyler's proposal. "I was his pet," she explained, "yet I feared that he would blame me for allowing the President to have reached the proposing point, so I did not speak of it to anyone." [57]

It was impossible, of course, to halt the rapidly mounting gossip however close-mouthed Julia chose to be about Tyler's address. Robert Tyler called so frequently at Peyton's, relaying messages and invitations from his father, that the boarders there began buzzing that the President was "doing business by *proxy*." Representative Hubard had informed the family on February 15 that the House was "in an uproar all day in consequence of news having reached there of the President's having fallen in love with Julia." And as the rumors spread, old New York friends eased forward in hope of using the growing Gardiner influence at the White House for political purposes. Ogden Edwards of New York, for example, insisted that the Gardiners help him gain appointment as a bearer of diplomatic dispatches to Mexico, a thought the family found "provoking." J. J. Bailey was ready "to fill any office, where I may enjoy a great deal of dignity and honor, with plenty of money and nothing on Earth to do." To the wry amusement of East Hamptonians and the mild embarrassment of the family, distant Gardiner cousins from Long Island suddenly appeared in Washington to share the limelight.[58]

From the family's standpoint, if anyone was to benefit politically from the Tyler connection it was to be young Alexander. There was no substance to rumors in Washington that David Gardiner was interested in the Collectorship of the Port of New York for himself. He did, however, push Alexander forward and his son was not reluctant. Urged also by his mother to be "a Tyler man," Alexander wasted no time. On February 15 the New York *Post* carried his anonymous letter to the editor praising the Tyler administration. Two copies were clipped and sent to Senator Gardiner in Washington, who in turn gave one to Robert Tyler. Robert had already received a copy of the article from John Lorimer Graham, Postmaster of the City of New York. He had shown it to Tyler and the President had ordered it reprinted in the Washington *Madisonian* of February 17. When he discovered that Alexander Gardiner was the author of the piece he was "surprised and gratified" and remarked that it was written by one "who understands the course of politics well." The time had finally come, thought David Gardiner, for his son to come to Washington. Alexander arrived on February 24, in time for the last Assembly ball three days later. He immediately began making himself known to the key figures in the Tyler administration.[59]

He accompanied his parents and sisters to the White House for tea *en famille* on the twenty-fifth and witnessed in amusement what Margaret called "a real frolic with the P[resident]":

Julia and I raced from one end of the house to the other, upstairs and down, and he after us. Waltzed and danced in the famous East Room, played the piano, ransacked every room and in fact made ourselves as much at home as the occupants. At half past seven we went to the concert and prevailed upon the P[resident] to accompany us.... It was the first time he had been out this winter, and to be seen gallanting Julia was a matter of great speculation... we were seated in the most conspicuous part of the room with the eyes of all directed to us.[60]

Tyler had wisely decided to drop all pretense and subterfuge. He would be seen publicly with Julia regardless of the gossipmongers. By

March 8 rumors that he and Julia were engaged swept Washington, and the subject was being openly discussed, even in Tyler's presence. Both Pickens and McLean were frantic to learn the truth of the matter. Actually, the reports were premature. While his ultimate intentions were known to Julia, they were not yet public property. They soon entered that realm, however, or very near it. On March 8 Tyler penned a verse in Julia's autograph album which rhetorically asked:

> Shall I again that Harp unstring,
> Which long hath been a useless thing,
> Unheard in Lady's bower?
> Its notes were once full wild and free,
> When I, to one as fair as thee,
> Did sing in youth's bright hours.
> Like to those raven tresses, gay,
> Which o'er thy ivory shoulders play,
> Were those which waked my lyre.
> Eyes like to thine, which beamed as bright
> As stars, that through the veil of night,
> Sent forth a brimy fire.
> I seize the Harp; alas! in vain,
> I try to wake those notes again,
> Which it breathed forth of yore.
> With youth its sound has died away:
> Old age hath touch'd it with decay;
> It will be *heard* no more!
> Yet, at my touch, that ancient lyre
> Deigns one parting note respire.
> Lady, it breathes of heaven....

The secret might still have been kept had not Julia foolishly (or purposely) permitted Supreme Court Justice Baldwin to carry her autograph album (and the President's poem) to Capitol Hill. She wanted to add a few more important autographs before the Justices and legislators left town for the summer recess. Knowledge of the President's romantic exercise in iambic tetrameter thus spread quickly around Washington. McLean read it, wrote in the album a "few *prozy* lines" of his own, and fervently wished he were thirty again. "The Judges have resolved to put their heads together next winter and try to outdo the P[resident] in writing poetry. It is not amusing," snapped Margaret.[61]

During the first two weeks of March Congress adjourned, the social season ended, and the capital took on a "deserted air, quite melancholy." Robert Tyler departed to the South with Priscilla, and a thoroughly fatigued David Gardiner, longing for the peace and quiet of East Hampton, said he felt like the "last man." Even Margaret began to "think of the north." But on March 15 Tyler again spoke of marriage to Julia, this time in Margaret's presence. Julia's proposal from the President could no longer be kept secret from her parents. At last they were told. They were extremely pleased with the news and they determined to linger on in the deserted capital until some definite understanding had been reached between Julia and the President. Plans to leave Washington on March 17 were set aside, and the family did not actually depart for East Hampton until March 27.[62]

On the afternoon of March 15 the President conducted Julia and Margaret to King's Gallery to view the paintings and other *objets d'art*. Driving back to Peyton's in the Presidential carriage an enboldened Tyler

> ... began to talk of resigning the Presidential chair *or at least sharing it with J[ulia]*. J[ulia], to excite his jealousy, whispered that he must drink to the health of Judge McLean. It had the desired effect, and made him as uneasy as you please—but the drollest part is to come. On reaching Mrs. Peytons the P[resident] alighted to help us out and just at that moment the door opened and out came Col. S[umter], Mr. Stevens and another gentleman. The P[resident] colored up to his eyes. They looked astonished and bemused. Scarcely waiting to say good bye in he jumped and hid himself behind the curtain, and when we turned to give a parting nod not even his shadow was to be seen. To cap it all, who should call this afternoon but Judge McL[ean]! to invite us to accompany him to the self same picture gallery! We told him the P[resident] had anticipated him; nevertheless we said we would go and now what do you think the P[resident] will say when he hears of it? [63]

Just what the jealous President did say of McLean's continuing pursuit of Julia is not known. There is, however, evidence that before the family's departure for Long Island on March 27, Tyler again proposed marriage to Julia and suggested to her that the wedding take place before the beginning of the next social season in Washington—probably in November 1843. It is definitely known that Juliana blocked this proposed schedule of events. She insisted that her daughter wait a few more months to make sure of her feeling for the President, and in this advice Julia reluctantly concurred. In any event, the family returned to East Hampton secure in the knowledge that an informal "understanding" had been reached between Julia and the President of the United States. The only remaining question was the exact date of the wedding. The season had obviously been a great success. "When I think of all that has occurred," wrote Margaret, "... I feel highly gratified with the attention we have received. We have certainly great inducement to return." [64]

Margaret had had nowhere near the good romantic fortune of the more extroverted Julia. Her most constant companion in Washington was Robert Tyler. He was happily married, although he did from time to time during the summer of 1843 write her mildly flirtatious letters to buoy her spirits. While she was definitely on the prowl for a husband, none of Margaret's "insinuations" in Washington bore fruit. It was her bad luck to get stuck at dances with highly ineligible men like Senator

Ambrose H. Sevier of Arkansas, or be pursued by the likes of a Mr. Marsh of New York who had "light hair and lisps," or a Mr. Fry of New York who was a "decided bore." Her flirtations with eligible widowers and bachelors like Henry A. Wise, Caleb Cushing, and Colonel Thomas Sumter led nowhere. There was, briefly, a Mr. May of Boston, "tall, with a splendid figure and handsome face," but after one or two calls at Peyton's he stopped coming. It was Margaret Gardiner's great misfortune in life to be hidden in the shadow of the effulgent Julia.[65]

The Gardiners arrived back in East Hampton on March 30 to find the little village agog with speculation about Julia's romantic triumph in Washington. Rumors linking the local beauty with the President of the United States circulated everywhere. Parson S. R. Ely's wife was so impressed with Julia's new status she was literally rendered speechless; and Mrs. Dayton told Margaret "it was generally believed around town that Julia was to be mistress of the *White House* next winter and that she had heard of it a half a dozen times during the last fortnight." To Julia's delight the same speculations also made the rounds of the fashionable set in New York City.[66]

It was rumored too that the President and his family would visit East Hampton during the summer of 1843. In these reports there was some truth. The Gardiners had invited Priscilla and Robert to visit them after Priscilla's return from Alabama in June. Priscilla accepted the invitation, but the Gardiners rather hoped the proposed visit would not occur. Julia had also invited the President and his daughter, Mary Tyler Jones, to stop in East Hampton when the Chief Executive came north in June en route to the dedication of the Bunker Hill monument in Boston. She promised him "pure air with sea bathing that can not fail to invigorate." In extending the invitation she was fairly certain that the ailing Mary would feel too weak to make the trip, and that once in New York City Tyler would not be able "to break from his friends." As it turned out, none of the Tylers made an appearance in the hamlet that summer, much to the disappointment of the townspeople. Of the Gardiners, only Alexander saw the President when he passed through New York on his way to Boston.[67]

Tyler's love letters to Julia that summer were read aloud to the whole family and then sent "for perusal" to David Lyon and Alexander in the city. In these, the President spoke of Julia as his "fairy girl." All of his communications were filled with romantic sentiments, said Julia, about "setting suns, stars peeping from behind their veils, the soul, music and memories, my raven tresses, brightest roses, gay morning of life, summit of the hill of life, his feet directed to its base, view of the setting sun, and James River from his house ... etc." He spoke too of the "faery spell" Julia had left behind her in Washington and of his "dreamy anticipation" of her letters to him. He still worried about Pickens and the dogged efforts of the South Carolinian to "transplant the fair rose of East Hampton to that sunny clime." As for himself, the President felt that a summer of quiet repose at Sherwood Forest would "compensate in some degree for the abuse I have met with at the hands of vile politicians." These declarations of his love raised Julia's spirits considerably. "We drank his health in a glass of champagne today at dinner," Margaret reported. "We don't *often* indulge in such luxuries but were testing it." [68]

Knowledge of Julia's correspondence with Tyler soon spread through East Hampton, the hangers-on at the post office keeping a careful check on the number of letters flowing between East Hampton and Sherwood Forest. "Yesterday evening I sent off a letter of 5 pages to the President," Julia informed Alexander in early April. "They have had all today at the taverns to talk about it. I am curious to know the surmises." There was naturally much local speculation about her plans. She was amused to learn, for instance, that rumor in New York City and Washington had it that she had accepted an offer of marriage from Tyler but only on the condition that he be re-elected in 1844. Her part of the bargain, so the story went, would be to campaign for Tyler at Saratoga and in other of the fashionable watering places in the North where her specific job would be to "win hearts" and "gain popularity" for the President. At the same time, two Tylerite politicians in New York, Mordecai M. Noah and Collector of the Port Edward Curtis, together with all the New York Customs House officials, would invade the South to "drum up recruits there." [69]

As Julia moved closer to the bosom of the Tyler family she began to take an increasing interest in the administration's political problems and activities. She was stunned, for example, to learn that Robert Tyler was instrumental in the appointment of one Jeremiah Miller to a clerkship in the New York City Post Office. She knew the gentleman as "that dissipated Jerry Miller," and she was certain he was dishonest. "What a nice opportunity he will have to pocket a *few* thousands if any of the letters feel particularly heavy," she protested to Alexander. Juliana was more tolerant of such appointments than her daughter, understanding somewhat better the difficulties Tyler was experiencing in launching his third party. By her pragmatic standards all the President's appointments were "*great appointments.*" Julia finally saw the logic in patronage. And, since ripe political plums were being handed out by John Tyler, it was her speedy reasoning that Alexander might as well have one of them. "Why won't you write another piece for Capt. Ty.?" she suggested to her ambitious brother. "It would not be trying *very hard* for a Secretaryship." Alexander accepted her sensible suggestion and within a few days was hard at work on another pro-Tyler piece which predictably began: "The Administration of John Tyler is destined to be one of the most remarkable in the civil history of this government...." Etc.[70]

The summer of 1843 sped swiftly by. The law business engaged in by Alexander and (occasionally) David Lyon picked up enough to give promise of becoming self-sustaining. This relieved their father of the necessity of paying the office rent. For a moment it even appeared that Cousin John Gardiner, the wild man of the clan, was going to mend his ways. A touring temperance lecturer sailed out to Gardiners Island and persuaded him to sign *"The Pledge,"* but John's reform lasted only a few sober days. "He is a hopeless case," sighed Margaret. James Keating, the family servant in Washington, had to be discharged for forgetting his proper station in life once the Gardiners had returned home. A new Irish maid was engaged in New York and brought out to East Hampton after being assured there were "no wild beasts about." [71]

The sisters spent the summer preparing their already extensive wardrobes for an August trip to Saratoga and for their return to Washington in the winter. A torrent of letters were poured forth to Alexander in the city instructing him to buy this, buy that, and return the other. So many purchasing commissions were piled upon him that his mother began fearing for his physical ability to execute them all. "Do not run about the city in the heat," she advised him. "Hire a cab to do your business." When not bothering Alexander with cloth, lace, dress, and shoe commissions, the sisters bothered their father about moving into New York. They insisted that he follow through on his earlier intention to buy or lease a house in town. As Gardiner carefully negotiated for a property on Lafayette Place, the girls urged more speed in the matter and complained that the Senator would not let them exercise a vote on the question. Not until November 1843 was it finally settled—a lease for $1000 per year. Late that month the peripatetic family moved into the house at 43 Lafayette Place.[72]

Julia was not nearly so interested now in the attractions of a town house in New York as she had been before her conquest of Washington and the White House:

I can now only judge from past experience [she wrote]. Place three winters in New York and one at Washington in the balance and which will weigh heaviest with agreeability? Whoever spent a more brilliant winter in W.— brilliant in the first degree—than we? And next winter promises to be even more so. The White House will be constantly thrown open—a new set of members—and a long session.... New York contains the most abominable set of people of any city in the world! Though I would not tell them so, there are several exceptions. We'll see what Saratoga will bring forth.[73]

Saratoga brought forth very little. The family stayed at the Tremont. There were the usual fancy-dress balls, the games of tenpins on the lawns, and the interminable gossip on the verandas. Julia made her usual stunning impression, and Tyler wrote to say he had heard in faraway Virginia that she was the "observed of all observers" there. There was, of course, some pleasure in discovering at Saratoga that the

Gardiner connection with the Tylers was beginning to excite increasing envy among the elite families of New York. But the vacation was clouded when the Gardiner family learned of the attempt on the life of their good friend, Postmaster General Charles A. Wickliffe. The would-be assassin was J. McLean Gardner, an unstable young man who had read law in the same office with Alexander in New York in 1841–1842 and whom the Gardiners again had seen briefly in Washington the preceding winter. Wickliffe sustained a minor knife wound in an attempt to protect the person of his daughter Mary, who was with him at the time. While both Alexander and David Lyon were certain that the thwarted assassin was an attention-seeking mental case, the episode was no less distressing. Equally upsetting was the fact that the Saratoga jaunt produced no husband for Margaret. "The harvest is finished, the summer ended, and we not married!" she complained.[74]

———◆———

No sooner was the summer over than the President began urging the Gardiner sisters to return again to Washington. "Are you coming to Washington this winter?" he implored Julia. "I am selfish in desiring that you should, as I wish my levees attended by the fairest forms from all parts of the country and who [are] brighter and fairer than you and Margaret? Do you not make a *curtsy* for that?" Julia replied that there would be a considerable delay in their leaving for Washington occasioned by the projected move of the family from East Hampton to Lafayette Place, but that they did hope to reach the capital by mid-February at the latest. The Washington visit would be followed by another Grand Tour of the Continent, preliminary plans for which the Senator had already made. To raise the necessary cash for these ventures and other expenses he negotiated mortgage loans on several of his wife's New York properties for $6800.[75]

The Senator and his excited daughters reached Washington once again on February 24, 1844. As usual, Alexander and David Lyon remained in New York to attend to their law business. Juliana also remained behind. A series of painful migraine headaches had plagued her throughout the winter. She was not feeling at all well. For Julia and Margaret a vigorous social schedule began immediately. On the twenty-seventh they attended a public levee in the East Room of the White House at which they danced and flirted with their acquaintances of the previous seasons.

The President was in a particularly fine mood that evening, "his thin long figure and prominent proboscis were everywhere amid the throng wheeling in ready obedience to the slightest pull of his coat-tail." As he watched his beloved Julia swirl across the floor with her many attentive partners he felt mellow and satisfied, for a moment almost democratic. His political future looked brighter than it had for months. Thus when the Washington correspondent of the New York *Herald* congratulated him on the truly public nature of the company present, Tyler said:

> Yes, sir, I am somewhat proud of the innovation. I believe it has had an ameliorative influence upon society here.... It is a Virginia notion, sir, a Virginia abstraction, if you please, but not a bad one, I think. It brings all classes of people together—and at least for the time, it Americanizes them. We must Americanize the people socially, as well as politically, if we would escape the evil distinctions and false notions of the European monarchies. We must subject their notions of superiority to our ideas of equality, to give them the proper illustration of our free institutions.[76]

Amid all the gaiety and laughter of the levee no one could suspect that the bloodiest tragedy of the Tyler administration was less than twenty-four hours away. Julia and Margaret, in company with a great number of those present at the ball that evening, were looking forward to a gay excursion next day down the Potomac aboard the new steam frigate *Princeton,* pride of the United States Navy. Robert F. Stockton, captain of the *Princeton,* was present at the White House levee on February 27, as were many of the 150 ladies and 200 gentlemen he had invited to make the gala voyage. There was much talk and anticipation of the morrow's treat. A high point of the outing would be the firing of the great "Peacemaker," the world's largest naval gun.

A large and expectant throng boarded the *Princeton* late the following morning. The President, his son-in-law William Waller, Senator David Gardiner and his daughters, Cabinet members, senators and representatives, Army and Navy officers, foreign diplomats, and the elite of Washington society (among them Dolley Madison) all packed themselves into the below-deck area which had hastily been converted into a salon for the occasion. There they found food and drink in great quantities. At 1 P.M. the vessel weighed anchor and proceeded slowly down river toward Mount Vernon. Twice the huge "Peacemaker" was fired, to the accompanying cheers of the guests who crowded tightly around the great gun. It was quite safe. The weapon had been fired several times before on the *Princeton*'s test runs down the Potomac, the President himself having been aboard to witness one of the experiments.

Shortly after 3 P.M. the guests were gathered again in the salon for a "sumptuous collation." Julia tarried on deck until a gentleman approached her and said: "The President wishes to take you into the collation which is just served. I suppose you will have to obey orders." Julia laughed, bidding her father to follow her below. Reaching the salon, she was met by Tyler, seated, and given a glass of champagne. The toasts began. Champagne flowed as the President toasted the Navy, the "Peacemaker," and Captain Stockton. Other toasts followed in rapid order. There was much hilarity. Some of the guests began to sing. When "wit and mirth, and every circumstance of gratification pervaded," someone suggested to Captain Stockton that the mammoth gun be fired just once more—in honor of George Washington, whose estate the vessel had just passed. Stockton agreed and went up on deck, followed by a group of gentlemen. The President rose from his chair to follow. Senator Gardiner paused for a moment to chat with Mrs. Madison, with whom Margaret was sitting. Then he went up on deck with the others. Tyler reached the foot of the ladder and stopped. Waller had broken into song and the President tarried briefly to hear him out—a momentary hesitation that may well have saved his life. Julia meanwhile was flirtatiously engaging the rapt attention of John Potter Stockton, the captain's young son. As Waller reached a line in his ditty which ran "Eight hundred men lay slain," the "Peacemaker" was again fired on the deck above. The coordination of the blast with the words of Waller's song seemed "so appropriate that the company joined in cheers." But within a few seconds a distraught officer, "blackened with powder, rushed through the gangway and called loudly for a surgeon." Great billows of black smoke began drifting into the suddenly sobered salon.

The breech of the great "Peacemaker" had exploded, spraying jagged chunks of red-hot iron around the deck like buckshot. Then came the shout, "The Secretary of State is dead!" During the confused moments of "woe, agony and despair" which followed, Julia tried without success to make her way through the surging throng to the deck.

"Let me go to my father!" she shouted in panic.

"My dear child, you can do no good. Your father is in heaven," a comforting voice said. Julia fainted.[77]

David Gardiner of East Hampton was indeed dead. So too were Virginians Abel P. Upshur, the Secretary of State, and Thomas W. Gilmer, Secretary of the Navy. Also lying dead near the twisted gun were Virgil Maxcy of Maryland, former American *chargé d'affaires* at The Hague; Commodore Beverly Kennon, Chief of Construction, United States Navy; Tyler's Negro body servant; and two seamen. Wounded were Captain Stockton, who suffered powder burns, Senator Thomas Hart Benton, whose right eardrum was punctured, and nine seamen. The bodies of Upshur, Kennon, and Maxcy were badly mutilated. Gilmer, however, retained a "natural countenance" in death. So did David Gardiner, who was "comparatively little injured in his person or altered in any respect." His glasses were unbroken. His watch had stopped at the moment of the explosion. It read 4:06; Upshur's read 4:15.

As Tyler reached the scene of the tragedy above, the dead were already being covered with flags and blankets. The wounded were taken below, where physicians attended them. At 4:20 the *Princeton* was standing off Alexandria. Additional medical aid was summoned, and the small steam vessel *I. Johnson* came alongside to take the shaken and panicky survivors ashore. Tyler himself carried Julia across the gangway to the rescue boat. At this point she regained consciousness and, dazed, began to struggle so violently in Tyler's arms that "I almost knocked us both off the gang-plank. I did not know at the time... that it was the President whose life I almost consigned to the water." Tyler and Secretary of War William Wilkins and other friends of the victims remained aboard the *Princeton* until eight-ten that evening, keeping vigil over the bodies of the dead. Julia and Margaret were taken to the White House where they spent the night.

News of the disaster was dispatched quickly by courier to New York and to other sections of the nation. Juliana learned of her husband's death the following evening. The initial reports reaching New York included no mention of the fate of Julia and Margaret, only that David Gardiner was among the dead. With characteristic fortitude Juliana drove in her carriage to the home where her sons were dining that evening and personally conveyed to them the sad news of their father's sudden passing. Alexander and David Lyon immediately excused themselves and prepared to depart for Washington. They arrived in the capital on Friday afternoon, March 1. There they found their sisters "though greatly afflicted and enervated, bearing our deep misfortune much better than could have been anticipated." Alexander himself had not eaten or slept for twenty-four hours.[78]

The bodies of David Gardiner and the other victims of the *Princeton* disaster lay in state in the East Room of the White House. It seemed scarcely possible that a few days earlier this same black-hung room had been the scene of such gay festivities. Throughout Friday some 20,000 people filed by the caskets. The following morning a great funeral procession two miles in length was formed. Stores closed, bells tolled, black cloth was everywhere evident. The President, joined by all the civilian officials of the government, military officers, the diplomatic corps, and thousands of private citizens, conveyed the remains of the fallen to Capitol Hill where impressive funeral services were held. David Gardiner, his son reported, "was indeed buried with such honors as perhaps never before fell to the lot of a private citizen." His body was placed in the vault of Congress until arrangements for final burial in East Hampton could be made. Returning to the White House from the funeral, the President's horses ran away at full speed and the nation was "again well nigh deprived of its noble-hearted Chief Magistrate." Everything seemed out of joint. March 2, 1844, the day of the funerals, was a dark day in the history of the Gardiner family. "Oh!... what were all the pomp and circumstance of even such funeral rites to us...?" lamented the broken-hearted Alexander. The sudden, tragic affair had badly shaken everyone in the tightly knit family. Twelve years later John Tyler could still not "revert to that awful incident without pain amounting almost to agony." [79]

David Lyon and Alexander solemnly escorted their grief-stricken sisters back to New York. It had been a short season in Washington for them—less than two weeks. Letters of condolence flooded in. "Would that I could come to you and mingle my tears with yours," wrote Pastor Ely from East Hampton, "but that cannot be. I can only say to you as one who knows how rich the consolation, go and tell *Jesus*." In Washington, Tyler was faced with the always awkward task of comforting the widows of the deceased. This he accomplished with skill and in good taste. He arranged with Washington morticians the grim details of preparing David Gardiner's body for removal to East Hampton. He urged Alexander to "perform this last pious duty at as early an hour as possible," and offered him the hospitality of the President's Mansion when he returned to Washington to escort the Senator's remains to Long Island for interment. To Juliana he sent a small volume of poems, a gift of condolence, together with a resolution of grief and regret passed by the Michigan legislature. In every way he was tender and helpful.[80]

The fact that David Gardiner died far from poor, that his family was left in comfortable circumstances, in no way lessened the shock of his passing or shortened the period of grief felt by his wife and children. Juliana went into deep mourning.[81]

Julia dreamed frequently of her father in the fortnight that followed. She imagined him at her bedside so often and "saw" him so clearly that she would "sigh away the night in watching" for him. Within a few weeks she decided that an early marriage to John Tyler might help blot out the recurring image of her dead parent and transport her mind to happier thoughts. Within seven weeks of the *Princeton* disaster, a month after David Gardiner's burial in East Hampton, Julia let John Tyler know that she was ready to marry him. Perhaps she needed a new father image to sustain her. "After I lost my father I felt differently toward the President," she remarked many years later. "He seemed to fill the place and to be more agreeable in every way than any younger man ever was or could be." Whatever the Freudian implications of Julia's decision, Tyler needed no urging. He talked the matter over with Priscilla, John, Jr., and Henry A. Wise, received their approbation, and after careful consideration decided to write Juliana the formal letter of April 20 asking for Julia's hand.[82]

Saddened as he was by David Gardiner's death, vexed by gossip about the state of his private relations with Julia, Tyler made haste to the altar. His decision was conditioned by his own loneliness. Julia's sudden departure from Washington on March 5 left him emotionally depressed. His financial affairs were in disarray. His spirits had seldom been lower. On March 24, two days before David Gardiner was buried at East Hampton, he wrote his daughter Mary from the White House that he had decided

to keep a bachelor's establishment for this year dismissing the Steward and House Keeper on the 4 April—so that I might save as much money as possible. In that way I could live for $5000 whereas the moment a Lady is here the House becomes full and the expenses heavy. Our family connexion is so extensive that they flock to us always in numbers.... I shall have a lonesome time unless *someone is with me*. This gossiping people have filled the whole country with rumors as to myself and Miss G———. They have had me at one time in New York. Then I was to meet her in Philadelphia and on two occasions they have had me married—and all this too before the remains of her father had been buried and while she was laboring under an agony of grief. How excessively cruel and stupid. I will not deny to you my great admiration of her, but to this moment there exists no sufficient foundation for all this, and I wish you and Letty to be assured that whatever might come of it I should never forget my love for either of you, or fail to make some suitable provision for you both. I say these things to put you entirely at ease.... We are all recovering from the shock of the *Princeton*—and the City becoming less gloomy.

When Julia suggested an early wedding date, June 26, Tyler agreed. He had no desire to live in a "bachelor's establishment." [83]

Julia's depression passed quickly after her wedding. Visions of her father stopped haunting her. In November 1844 she alarmed her mother with the suggestion that she be allowed to trim her black velvet mourning coat in fur. During her "reign" in the White House she usually wore black during the day and white or black lace over white for evening wear. The diamond star she normally wore on her forehead on formal occasions was replaced with a black onyx. By March 1845 she was shopping for "something pretty in the way of mourning silks." Three months later she was complaining that the hot weather in Virginia was causing the black dye of her clothes to stain her neck and arms. Protracted mourning could be very inconvenient.[84]

Alexander overcame his gloom by throwing himself wholeheartedly into the politics of the struggling Tyler party. Beginning in April 1844 he became a leading, though often anonymous, publicist for the President and for those "independent Democrats" in New York state who "in the midst of the contentions of parties yet retain minds free and unshackled, patriotic and self-sacrificing, holding the public good superior to pre-conceived opinions and personal associations." This particular effort for his future brother-in-law was penned on April 27, 1844, the day the President was nominated by a convention of his friends in Baltimore on a ringing platform of "Tyler and Texas!" Only a week had passed since he had asked Juliana for Julia's hand in marriage. With a young new wife in prospect and a nomination for the Presidency in hand, John Tyler looked to the future with confidence. Shortly after the explosion aboard the *Princeton*, Tyler had lamented the "loss I have sustained in Upshur and Gilmer. They were truly my friends, and would have aided me for the next twelve months with great effect." Alexander Gardiner was determined to provide Tyler something of that lost aid.[85]

9

TYLER AND TEXAS—AND TAMMANY

> *If the annexation of Texas shall crown off my public life, I shall neither retire ignominiously nor be soon forgotten.*
> —JOHN TYLER, 1844

John Tyler first broached the Texas question in October 1841 in terms of the "lustre" it might throw around an administration in serious political difficulties. He did not, of course, originate the Texas problem, nor did he write *finis* to it. It began in 1836 when Texas threw off the Mexican yoke in a revolutionary war; it ended only when General Winfield Scott's army finally stormed into Mexico City in 1847. What Tyler did do was move the annexation issue off the dead center it occupied in 1843–1844. Since 1837 a Texan request for annexation had languished in Washington, unattended for fear the whole subject would further agitate the slavery issue. For reasons other than any personal interest in slavery expansion—reasons that were essentially psychological—Tyler was determined to bring the annexation proposition to a head. The Texans wanted annexation, and it was clearly in the national interest that annexation be effected. To accomplish this desirable goal Tyler was convinced he must first have a sound political foundation from which to proceed. It was therefore no accident of chronology that Tyler founded his third-party movement in January 1843, in February was nominated for the Presidency by a small group of his friends in Trenton, and then in March informed Isaac Van Zandt, Texan *chargé* in Washington, to "encourage your people to be quiet and to not grow impatient; we are doing all we can to annex you, but we must have time."[1]

Unfortunately, the Texans grew quite impatient. In July 1843 they abruptly withdrew their offer of annexation and began ostentatious negotiations with both the Mexicans and the British. Those with Mexico turned on the possibilities of an armistice, a Mexican recognition of Texan independence, and an end to the sporadic hit-and-run border warfare that had dragged along since 1837. Those with London represented a snuggling up to Britain for the purpose of alarming Tyler and forcing him into more positive and speedy action on the annexation question. The strategy was successful. Tyler later remarked that President Sam Houston's "billing and cooing" with England was much more than the "coquetry" the Texan called it; it was, he said, "a serious love affair." Fearful that real peace might break out along the Rio Grande with Mexican recognition of Texan independence and concerned that British machinations in Texas might lead, as part of a rumored Anglo-Texan alliance, to British commercial hegemony and the abolition of slavery in the Lone Star Republic (although the White House knew there was scant danger of abolition), Tyler and Secretary of State Abel P. Upshur moved swiftly. In September 1843 they decided to open secret negotiations with Texas looking toward an annexation treaty. The following month Tyler secretly made a firm annexation offer in spite of a strong Mexican note in August identifying annexation consummated as *ipso facto* an act of war. By early fall, however, Tyler was sure his third-party movement was well launched. He was ready for any eventuality, war included.[2]

The Texas annexation issue was not drummed up to serve selfish political ambitions. Tyler's hand-fashioned Democratic Republican Party with its famous "Tyler and Texas!" slogan was not designed by the President to secure his re-election on the Texas question. He never had any hope of re-election. Instead, the party was created only to force the Democrats to adopt a pro-annexation stance in the 1844 canvass. That accomplished, it was designed that the new party would go swiftly and willingly out of business, pausing only to secure from the Democratic nominee, whoever he might be, a guarantee that Tyler's friends, particularly those who had fought most vigorously for annexation, would not be proscribed by the new administration. Nor did Tyler rip the controversial Texas issue from an ideological context foreign to his longstanding personal views on American diplomacy. If he wanted annexation for the "lustre" it might throw upon an otherwise unimpressive administration, his personal psychological motive was not in conflict with the fact that he had long supported Manifest Destiny.

As early as 1832 he had maintained that the destiny of America was to expand westward to the coast and into the Pacific, "walking on the waves of the mighty deep...overturning the strong places of despotism, and restoring to man his long-lost rights." He was convinced that the future greatness of the United States lay in its ability to penetrate the markets of the world, to compete successfully with Great Britain for commercial empire. His free-trade views turned largely on this consideration, and few projects occupied his attention as President to a greater extent than the negotiation of commercial agreements abroad. When, for example, the Senate turned down such a treaty with the German *Zollverein* in 1844, he boldly took it up again as a campaign issue. He was particularly pleased when Caleb Cushing negotiated the Treaty of Wanghia with China, opening the commercial doors of the Middle Kingdom to American enterprise. Indeed, when news of the Cushing Treaty reached the White House in December 1844, Julia shouted, "Hurrah! The Chinese treaty is accomplished.... I thought the President would go off in an ecstasy a minute ago with the pleasant news." Similarly, he looked forward to the possibility of opening trade with Japan as early as 1843. And when Commodore Matthew C. Perry finally pried Japan open in 1854 Tyler accurately regarded his earlier success with China as "the *nest* egg of the Japan movement." His attentions to Prince Timoleo Haolilio in Washington in 1842, and his bold extension of the Monroe Doctrine to the Sandwich Islands at that time, indicated a ready appreciation of Hawaii as a steppingstone to the markets of East Asia. If any nation sought "to take possession of the islands, colonize them, and subvert the native Government," he warned the powers on December 20, 1842, such a policy would "create dissatisfaction on the part of the United States." So was born the Tyler Doctrine which found its way into the ideological arsenal of American diplomacy where it was stored for future use by the United States in the Pacific.[3]

It is not surprising, then, that he viewed the annexation of Texas in commercial terms that would benefit the whole nation. Indeed, the dismemberment of the rich Mexican Empire came to occupy his hopes and his dreams almost exclusively in 1842. Stretching from the jungles of Central America northward to the forty-second parallel, it was a corrupt, weak, misgoverned nation, exploited by venal dictators and milked by a decadent aristocracy. Like most Americans of the period, Tyler had little but contempt for the backward Mexicans. In his view, Dictator-President Santa Anna was never more than "the captive of San Jacinto." Tyler also knew that Mexico was in no position to defend its vast territories which hung waiting to be plucked. The only question was when and how the harvest would be gathered. In May 1842 Tyler attempted to gather in the Mexican province of California. This would bring him just as much "lustre" as Texas annexation. As a "window" on the Pacific, and from the standpoint of American commercial expansion, it had much to recommend it.

With Webster's assistance he matured a scheme to partition Mexico. Based upon an expectation of British good offices in the matter, Tyler's plan visualized an exchange of two million dollars in American claims against Mexico for all of California north of the thirty-second parallel. This would give the United States the harbors of Monterey and San Francisco, the "windows on the Pacific" so important to American commercial penetration of the Pacific. In addition, the United States and Mexico would agree jointly to recognize the independence of Texas. This trade consummated, Tyler demonstrated his willingness to abandon the prospect of future Texas annexation. In payment for British pressure on Mexico City to accept this uneven exchange, Tyler was prepared to settle the Anglo-American Oregon partition question at the Columbia River line, although this would give Britain a chunk of Oregon between the waterway and the forty-ninth parallel to which she had no firm claim. "I never dreamed of ceding this country [Oregon] unless for the greater equivalent of California which I fancied Great Britain might be able to obtain for us through her influence in Mexico," Tyler later explained. He proposed that the whole California-Texas-Oregon deal be wrapped up neatly in an Anglo-American-Mexican tripartite treaty. "The assent of Mexico to such a treaty is all that is necessary," the President maintained blandly; "a surrender of her title [to California] is all that will be wanting. The rest will follow without an effort." [4]

There was not much likelihood that Mexico would agree to such a lopsided deal, but as long as the project was under discussion it was imperative that outstanding differences between the United States and Great Britain be resolved while London was being encouraged to play the role of dishonest broker in Mexico City. For this reason Tyler and Webster handled the complex negotiations on the potentially explosive Maine boundary dispute with great delicacy. While they undoubtedly gave to Britain somewhat more territory in the Northeast than London was entitled to receive, the Webster-Ashburton Treaty of October 1842, approved overwhelmingly by the Senate, at least put an end to talk of war on the American-Canadian frontier. By smoothing Anglo-American relations it served to isolate Mexico diplomatically. Only when his tripartite-treaty plan disintegrated on the rocks of Mexican opposition did Tyler abandon his California dream and return to the annexation of Texas, secure now in the knowledge that Texas might be incorporated into the Union without serious British interference. The Webster-Ashburton *coup*, thought Tyler, was the high point of his administration to date, and for it he felt himself entitled to "some small share of praise as a set-off to the torrents of abuse so unceasingly and copiously lavished upon me." [5]

With the tripartite partition scheme in ruins, Anglo-American relations pacified, Mexico isolated, and his third-party movement gaining sufficient headway to cause alarm among Democratic leaders, Tyler boldly took up the Texas annexation question again in September 1843. His renewed effort was facilitated by the departure of Webster from the State Department in May 1843 and the arrival there of Abel P. Upshur in July. Webster had no heart for Texas annexation and the slavery-extension implications his New England constituency would certainly see in it. Upshur was all heart on the matter. As the Texan *chargé* in Washington explained this crucial shift in Department personnel, "Though friendly to us [Webster], is very much in our way at present. He is timid and wants nerve, and is fearful of his abolition constituents in Massachusetts. I think it likely Upshur will succeed him... it will be one of the best appointments for us. His whole soul is with us. He is an able man and has nerve to act." It was an accurate analysis.[6]

To advance the Texas project more safely *vis-à-vis* Great Britain, Tyler accepted the forty-ninth parallel as the boundary for an Oregon settlement since a territorial equivalent in California for the Columbia River line now seemed out of the question. At no time did he seriously embrace the irresponsible "Fifty-four forty or fight!" nonsense that swept the nation after the campaign of 1844. He knew perfectly well that American title to any part of Oregon north of the forty-ninth parallel was nonexistent, and he wanted no unnecessary embroilment with Britain in that quarter while gathering the Texas fruit on the Rio Grande. Thus his carefully worded statement to Congress in December 1843 that "after the most rigid and... unbiased examination of the subject, the United States have always contended that their rights" extended north to 54°40′ was purely a political gesture designed to allay abolitionist opposition to Texas annexation by presenting to Northern and Western expansionists the prospect of additional free territory in the Northwest. Tyler did not say that he believed in 54°40′ personally, because he did not. Nor did he say that past contentions on the subject were necessarily those of the present or future. On the contrary, he suggested no particular action on Oregon at the time save the continuing need for peace in the Northwest. In the same speech he did maintain that in the interests of "humanity" the United States had the right and the duty to intervene in the sputtering Mexican-Texan war in order to bring it mercifully to a close.[7]

Breathing fire on the Rio Grande and peace on the Columbia, Tyler pushed forward with the secret negotiations for a Texas annexation treaty. In December 1843 Upshur took a quiet poll among the senators and reported to the President that two-thirds of them favored annexation and would vote for it. All that remained to complete the final draft of the treaty agreement were assurances to the Texas government that the land and sea forces of the United States would be deployed near the borders and coasts of the Republic to offer aid and protection should the Mexicans undertake to invade Texas during the brief period between the signing of the treaty and the exchange of formal ratifications. President Sam Houston was understandably tender on this point, and two crucial months passed before Tyler and Upshur could convince him that his demand to have these American forces placed under the tactical command of Texas officials was an impossible one from a constitutional standpoint. The Constitution nowhere permitted the Commander-in-Chief to "lend" the military forces of the United States to another nation, and no amount of loose construction could deny that obvious fact. It was not until February 17, 1844, that Upshur finally agreed to military dispositions that the security-conscious Houston deemed adequate. With this, the last hurdle toward the treaty was cleared. In none of these confidential arrangements was there any concern in the White House for the morality of annexation. It was simply a question of coordination, logistics, and timing.[8]

Tyler deemed the Mexican position on Texas annexation specious and legalistic. From the point of view of Mexico City, the battlefield Treaty of Velasco ending the Texas Revolution and recognizing the independence of Texas in 1836 had been extorted from the captured Santa Anna under duress. For this reason it had been promptly renounced by the Mexican legislature. After 1836, therefore, Texas was still technically a Mexican province in a continuing state of rebellion. While the Texas Republic had received *de facto* recognition from Britain, France, and the United States, that did not alter the fact—said the Mexicans—that American annexation would constitute from a strictly legal standpoint a hostile and unwarranted intervention in Mexican internal affairs. Indeed, the Mexicans argued that annexation would be little less than an act of aggression against their nation and under international law a positive act of war.

To counter these arguments, and to put a somewhat better moral face on what was essentially a territory grab, Tyler and other spokesmen of the Manifest Destiny fraternity came up with the strained idea that the annexation of Texas was really the "reannexation" of the territory, since Texas had originally been included in the Louisiana Purchase. This was of course patent nonsense. Texas was no more part of the Louisiana Territory than was Manchuria; even if it had been, the claim had long since been specifically surrendered in the 1819 Adams-Onís Treaty with Spain. With more cogency Tyler and Upshur also argued that since Mexico had been unable to subdue her rebellious province militarily, Texas was by definition a free agent to contract such international obligations as she pleased. Continuing bloodshed along the frontier, Tyler maintained, was little more than an affront to all humanity.

In sum, the Mexicans had numerous legal arguments and few guns, while the Americans had dubious historical arguments and the potential of many guns. This, then, was the unsettled situation as Tyler's secret treaty negotiations with the Texas government came to a head early in 1844. At this moment the explosion aboard the frigate *Princeton* removed the brilliant Upshur from the scene. Upshur's death brought John C. Calhoun into the State Department. This disastrous change, cunningly foisted on Tyler by Henry A. Wise, introduced the extraneous slavery issue more forcefully into the Texas debate and ultimately destroyed any hope Tyler had of obtaining a two-thirds majority for this Texas treaty in the Senate in 1844.

Admittedly, Tyler was surrounded by men who viewed Texas annexation as an opportunity to expand the "peculiar institution" of slavery into new territories. Ritchie, Wise, Gilmer, Upshur, Calhoun, and (in Upshur's view) the "entire South" viewed annexation from a sectional standpoint. Tyler later complained that the slavery feature of annexation possessed Calhoun and Upshur *"as a single idea,"* and it is true that Calhoun foolishly put the issue before the nation on this narrow basis. This was not Tyler's view, however. If there was what the Northern abolitionists liked to call an "aggressive slavocracy" operating in Washington in 1844, John Tyler was not part of it. He had no confidence in Calhoun's view that slavery was a positive moral good. He did not believe that the slave institution must expand or die. He did not share the South Carolinian's fear that unless Texas was speedily annexed growing British influence in Washington-on-the-Brazos would lead to the abolition of slavery there, although he did admit that were abolition accomplished in Texas that fact would further agitate the slavery question in the United States. It would also provide a convenient new haven for runaway Negroes. So far as it can be determined, Tyler never endorsed Mississippi Senator Robert J. Walker's comforting "safety valve" theory that a Texas annexed would, like some giant magnet, actually solve the slavery question by draining the Negroes out of the Old South and onto the virgin cotton lands of Texas. As soon as the Texas cotton lands also began to wear out, Walker argued, the simple economics of the situation would dictate the gradual manumission of the slaves. Liberated, they would cross the border into the torrid zones of Mexico and Central America where they would disappear into the predominantly colored populations there. Thus in seventy-five to a hundred years the problem would solve itself.

While Walker's far-fetched hypothesis had elements of the abolition-by-anemia argument Tyler himself had advanced in 1820 during the Missouri Compromise debates, the President nonetheless deplored the employment of any slavery-oriented argument, pro or con, in relation to the Texas issue. He did everything in his power to keep such considerations out of the debate. He took instead a broad national view of the matter. Again and again he emphasized the commercial and economic advantages that would accrue to the entire United States with the annexation. He stressed specifically in this regard the inevitable expansion of America's foreign and domestic commerce and the increase of her coastwise carrying trade. American monopoly of world cotton production was also a fundamental consideration in the President's thinking. In 1847 he said flatly that "so far as my agency in the matter extended, I looked to the interests of the whole Union. The acquisition of Texas gave to the U. States almost a monopoly of the Cotton plant, and thus secured to us a power of boundless extent in the affairs of the world." This monopoly would permit Americans, said Tyler, "to hold control over the issues of peace and war" throughout the world. In more extreme versions of the cotton-monopoly theme, which he repeated in 1850 and again in 1861, Tyler contributed to the evolution of the "King Cotton" myth later so disastrous to Confederate States diplomacy: that the cotton monopoly achieved by Texas annexation would permit the South, merely by withholding or shipping the precious commodity, to control European diplomatic behavior in the event of a civil war. But the speciousness of this subsequent argument does not detract from the point that in 1844 Tyler viewed Texas annexation in national-commercial rather than in sectional-slavery terms.[9]

To a lesser extent Tyler also concerned himself with what would later be termed the geopolitical implications of British machinations in Texas. While he was not interested in slavery expansion into Texas *per se,* he did fear an Anglo-Texan treaty of alliance which would bring Texas into Britain's diplomatic and economic orbit. This, he felt, might effectively prevent all future American territorial expansion into the West and Southwest. He worried that with Texas in British leadstrings the economic encirclement of the United States would be effected. "The Canadas, New Brunswick, and Nova Scotia, the [British] islands in the American seas with Texas ... would complete the circle," he warned. To prevent this there was no alternative save American annexation. Anything less would only force a war-weary Texas, perpetually threatened by Mexico, to "seek refuge in the arms of some other power." Frequently, therefore, the ever-Anglophobic Tyler pointed with alarm to the British "menace" in the Southwest. Actually, there was not much of a menace there, but Americans could always be roused to furious action by the suggestion that the Redcoats were coming.[10]

Unhappily for Tyler, the arrival of Calhoun in the Cabinet stamped the word *slavery* all over the controversial annexation issue. On February 29, 1844, the day after Upshur's death aboard the *Princeton,* Henry A. Wise approached South Carolina Senator George McDuffie and wondered aloud whether the Senator's friend, John C. Calhoun, could be persuaded to fill Upshur's place as Secretary of State. If so, his name would "in all probability be sent to the Senate at once." Because of Wise's intimacy and almost daily contact with Tyler, McDuffie assumed that the suggestion was nothing less than an informal sounding from the President himself. Consequently, he immediately sat down and wrote Calhoun of Tyler's Cabinet offer. The fact is that the Wise action was in no manner authorized by Tyler, and Wise later confessed that he was "guilty of assuming an authority and taking a liberty with the President which few men would have excused and few would have taken." Yet he was convinced that the Texas question must be placed in "safe Southern hands." Nor was there any question where his selected instrument, John C. Calhoun, stood on the issue. Secretary of the Navy Thomas W. Gilmer had written Calhoun the preceding December. In that communication Calhoun was brought up to date on the secret negotiations then in progress with Texas, and was asked his confidential view of the matter. Calhoun replied on December 25 that annexation "in a political point of view ... could not more than compensate for the vast extension opened to the non-slaveholding States to the Pacific on the line of the Oregon ... it would extend our domestic institutions of the South...." [11]

Immediately after leaving McDuffie's parlor, Wise went to the White House for breakfast. There he met the President's brothers-in-law, Judge John B. Christian and Dr. N. M. Miller, the Second Assistant Postmaster General. Tyler was in a terrible emotional state that morning, breaking frequently into tears as he recounted to Christian and Miller the horrors he had witnessed on the *Princeton* the afternoon before. It was while the President was in this extremely distraught frame of mind that Wise calmly announced his presumptive offer of the Department of State to John C. Calhoun. Tyler fairly detonated at the news. "You are the most extraordinary man I ever saw!" he shouted at his old friend, "the most willful and wayward, the most incorrigible!" While Tyler fumed, Wise replied that if the two men were to remain friends Tyler must "sanction" his "unauthorized act." [12]

The last person Tyler wanted in his Cabinet was John C. Calhoun. On two earlier instances he had blocked movements seeking to elevate Calhoun to the Cabinet. Not only could Calhoun bring no political strength to the administration, but his aggressive pro-slavery views would only compromise and complicate the entire annexation question. On the other hand, the situation into which Wise had put him was frightfully embarrassing. To repudiate the conspiratorial arrangements the Virginian had made would simply antagonize Calhoun's friends in the Senate when he most needed their votes for Texas. Weighing all the factors involved, the emotionally upset President made a decision which marked the real beginning of his Texas troubles. "Take the office and tender it to Mr. Calhoun," he instructed Wise. "You may write to him yourself at once." [13]

By April 1, twelve days before the treaty was formally concluded by Calhoun, Tyler knew that his great design was in deep trouble. Two weeks earlier rumors of the secret Texas negotiations had leaked onto the front page of the Whig *National Intelligencer*. As slavocrat and abolitionist extremists began pounding their respective drums for and against the measure, many of the forty-two senators who had pledged Upshur their support of the treaty in December began melting discreetly into the shadows. Tyler had hoped that the very secrecy of the negotiations would permit him to present the Senate with a *fait accompli*, and that the completed treaty might slip quickly through the upper chamber without getting involved politically in the coming Presidential canvass.

This dream now blasted, there was no choice for Tyler save to push as rapidly ahead as possible with his third-party movement in the hope that its presence and function as a lever might force the Democracy to announce quickly for Texas annexation. For this reason, on April 1, 1844, he encouraged a group of his partisans, mainly postmasters and mail contractors, to meet at the Globe Hotel in Washington. There resolutions were adopted which praised his Bank vetoes, condemned Van Buren (who had a majority of Democratic delegates already pledged to his nomination) as a certain loser against Clay, called for the "reannexation" of Texas to the United States and the "re-election" of John Tyler to the Presidency. The Oregon question was carefully muted. Tylerite friendship feelers were extended to Andrew Jackson who had that week strongly come out for annexation.[14]

The treaty was signed on April 12 and Tyler hesitantly submitted it to the Senate ten days later. He had little hope now that it would pass. On April 27 Henry Clay's so-called Raleigh Letter of April 17 was published in the Washington papers. This communication placed him solidly in opposition to Texas annexation as "involving us certainly in war with Mexico and probably with other foreign powers, dangerous to the integrity of the Union, inexpedient in the present financial condition of the country, and not called for by any general expression of public opinion." This statement was followed a few days later by Clay's unanimous nomination at the Whig Baltimore convention on a platform which made no mention at all of Texas. More important politically, from Tyler's standpoint, was the fact that on the same day that Clay's Raleigh Letter saw print in the capital, Van Buren published a rambling statement on annexation that took essentially the same position. By April 27, then, both leading candidates for the White House in 1844 had announced against Tyler's Texas project.[15]

During the next week both Clay and Van Buren began to crack the whip to bring their supporters in the Senate to an anti-treaty position. Thus it became increasingly clear to Tyler, as the month of May wore on, that the treaty was doomed. In a final effort to force the treaty through, Tyler reluctantly reached for a political blackjack. It was the only weapon he had handy. He instructed his friends to organize a nominating convention which would meet in Baltimore on May 27, the same day the Democratic convention was scheduled to convene there. He had already decided that under no conditions would he permit his own name to be placed in nomination at the Democratic convention, for if Van Buren was chosen "then I became bound to sustain the nominee," and that "could not be." Instead, his Democratic-Republican third party would now be formally launched. "Go to Baltimore and make your nomination," he told his supporters, "and then go home and leave the thing to work its own results." His sole aim in all this was to create and "preserve such organization until the proper time should arrive for striking a decisive blow." Had the treaty been approved by the Senate in April, or had Van Buren embraced it prior to the Democratic convention on May 27, there would have been no Tyler candidacy in 1844 at all. As it was, he had prepared a political lever for just such a contingency and he would employ it now with all the vigor at his command.[16]

Tyler's third-party idea had had a long and uneven period of gestation. As early as December 1841 the renegade President and his new Cabinet had discussed the possibilities of forming a new party that might attract to Tyler's small political entourage moderates from both major parties. The new third party, as Tyler first conceived it, would eschew all sectionalism and factionalism and would work only for broad national goals. This course of action was strongly urged by Virginia Clique men like Upshur and Gilmer, who argued that Texas annexation would be a worthy aim around which to construct a new political grouping. But Tyler did not want Texas annexation as an issue on which to build a third party. Quite the reverse, he wanted Texas annexation for personal psychological reasons, for the "lustre" it would bring his battered administration historically. He also wanted it, as has been suggested, for the commercial advantages it would bestow upon the whole nation. The new party, if it had to be formed at all, would be subordinate to its goals. It would not feed on them. Since there seemed scant hope for annexation during the winter of 1841–1842, exploratory Cabinet conversations along these lines were abandoned.[17]

Instead, Tyler launched his ill-starred move toward an accommodation with the Conservative Democrats and the moderate Whigs. In April 1842 he specifically turned down an offer from Alexander Hamilton, Jr., to build a separate Tyler organization in New York City. Tyler's attempt to rally a center group, an effort revealed in his Exchequer Plan and in his acceptance of the 1842 Tariff Act, earned him little but the distrust and calumny of the extremists in both major parties. Clay and Botts talked impeachment, and the old nullifiers and extreme states' rights men looked with undisguised horror on the new tariff legislation. Upshur, meanwhile, patiently sought to outline to less ultra citizens the political policies of the administration. "We have *all* agreed," he explained, "without a single exception, that our only course was to administer the government for the best interests of the country and to trust the moderates of all parties to sustain us.... We came in *against all parties* ... without any support except what our measures would win for us.... Perhaps we have erred; the difficulties of our position rendered it difficult to avoid error." Errors notwithstanding, John Tyler honestly tried to organize the moderate center in 1842 and bring it to his support. As a gesture of conciliation toward Old Hickory and his followers, men who applauded his Bank vetoes and favored Texas annexation, the President saw that Amos Kendall got a government printing contract. For similar reasons Captain John C. Frémont, Benton's son-in-law, was appointed head of the Army Topographical Corps' projected expedition to Oregon.[18]

But by October 1842 Tyler felt that, save for the success of the Webster-Ashburton Treaty, his expiable tactics had accomplished little. Understandably, his new mood was one of despair. Thus he confided to his friend, Littleton W. Tazewell, that

So far the Administration has been conducted amid earthquake and tornado.... The *ultras* of both the prevailing factions will not consent to ground their arms.... Is there any other course for me to pursue than *to look to the public good irrespective of either faction?* ... My strong determination sometimes is to hold, as I have heretofore done, the politicians of both parties and of all parties at defiance.... But the difficulty in the way of administering the government without a party is undoubtedly great. From portions of the Democratic party I have received an apparently warm support; but while the *ultras* control in the name of *party*, I fear that no good would arise from either an amalgamation with them, or a too ready assent to their demands of office.[19]

If in October 1842 Tyler was beginning to think again in terms of a third party, the results of the November gubernatorial election in New York made the idea seem practical. As part of his campaign of rapprochement with the Conservative Democracy of the Empire State he instructed one of his partisans in New York City, Mordecai M. Noah, editor of the Tylerite New York *Union,* to support the candidacy of William C. Bouck, the Democratic nominee. This gesture of conciliation had little actual influence on Bouck's subsequent victory. Nevertheless, it was interpreted by the Van Buren machine in Albany as a crude attempt by Tyler to infiltrate and capture control of the badly divided Democracy in New York. The Van Buren organ in Washington, the *Globe,* made it perfectly clear to the President that if he was trying to return to the Democratic Party he would have to crawl back on his knees, his head covered with sackcloth. As editor Francis P. Blair sarcastically put it:

Mr. Tyler ... at the moment the fortunes of the Democracy were struggling with an accumulation of difficulties, separated himself from that party, and became, to a certain extent, the instrument of its overthrow. But he has now quarrelled with his new friends, and wishes to come back to his old.... If Mr. Tyler wishes to *return* ... *let* him return. But ... he must demonstrate the sincerity of his repentance in a more satisfactory manner than he has hitherto adopted. The treaty, the tariff, the bankrupt law, the exchequer ... the distribution bill, the repeal of the Independent Treasury and the composition of his cabinet are not sufficient pledges of his conversion.

This was not much of an invitation, especially since Tyler believed that his support of the Bouck candidacy in New York had proved the decisive factor in that race. So his friends in New York City informed him.[20]

As he carefully analyzed the sweeping Democratic victories in the midterm election of 1842, Tyler came to the conclusion that there did exist an anti-Van Buren Conservative Democratic bloc in the North, particularly in New York and Pennsylvania, to which he might appeal in a third-party movement. His plan was to ally this group with such states' rights Whigs and Democrats as he could muster in the South. At this moment the Texans were again pressing the annexation issue. As Tyler pondered the whole political situation in December 1842, he finally concluded that—to gain Texas or anything else that would redound to the lasting reputation of his administration—he would have to create his own political base of operation. His idea was not to form a third party on a truly national scale. He knew there was no chance for anything as ambitious as this. Instead, he would construct hardcore Tylerite factions in several crucial states, cadres large enough and well enough entrenched in federal patronage to tip the Presidential vote in these key states in any direction Tyler desired.

In New York City the foundations for such a cadre already existed although the Tylerites there were badly organized and politically ineffectual. Their leader was Paul R. George, a small-bore politician originally from New Hampshire, who was a close friend of Edward Curtis, Collector of the Port. Through Curtis, George had a direct connection with Daniel Webster, whose political protégé the shady Collector was. Webster's decision to remain in the Tyler Cabinet in September 1841 brought George and a small band of similar opportunists to the nominal support of the President, a relationship that remained cemented mainly in patronage favors. Chief among these Tylerites-by-proxy were John Lorimer Graham, Postmaster of the City of New York; Ogden Hoffman, District Attorney for New York; Silas M. Stilwell, Marshal of New York City; Collector Edward Curtis (chief patronage dispenser of the gang); Mordecai M. Noah; and such lesser lights as Louis F. Tasistro, Redwood Fisher, John O. Fowler, Robert C. Wetmore, William Taggart, and J. Paxton Hallet, all of whom held patronage jobs of some sort. As Alexander Gardiner correctly characterized them to Julia, they were people with whom one could take "no great pride" in being connected.[21]

The first major venture of this group was the launching of a pro-administration newspaper. An attempt by Robert Tyler to buy into the

New York *Herald* had failed in June 1841, and a subsequent working arrangement with John I. Mumford's New York *Standard,* effected by placing Post Office and Customs House announcements exclusively in the *Standard,* proved unsatisfactory. Mumford was for Lewis Cass. So it was that Paul R. George brought into being during the summer of 1842 the New York *Union* under the editorship of former Tammany brave Mordecai Noah. Noah was also appointed chairman of the Tyler General Committee. George ran the paper from behind the scenes, and it was largely financed by contributions from the faithful and by capital levies on civil servants owing their places to Tyler, Webster, and Curtis.[22]

Noah proved an unhappy choice. His Tylerite orthodoxy was suspect, and the fact that he was Jewish was thought to render him politically unsuitable for his responsibilities. In the fall of 1842 a factional struggle developed within the Tylerite clique to oust him. This pitted an anti-Noah splinter headed by Graham and Stilwell against a pro-Noah group headed by Paul R. George. In a series of letters and conversations with the President and with Robert Tyler, Graham argued that Noah's religious background was damaging the President's cause in New York and that unless he were ousted from his editorship the Empire State could not be captured. In direct conversations with Noah, Graham suggested that, were he gracefully to resign the editorship of the *Union,* he might expect to receive either the Surveyorship of the Port of New York or the Consul Generalship in Constantinople. In January 1843 Noah finally resigned under the mounting pressure, but no compensatory political plum was forthcoming. In his own words, he had been "most disgracefully and villainously cheated, swindled, bamboozled." In anger Noah dissolved the vest-pocket Tyler General Committee in March 1843 and returned to Tammany.[23]

With Noah's resignation and subsequent walkout, the New York *Union* was quietly merged into the New York *Aurora,* first brought out under Tylerite auspices in February 1843. The *Aurora* was an undistinguished sheet. Its main claim to fame had been a fleeting notoriety in charging Daniel Webster with the attempted rape of a lady visitor to the State Department. Webster was undoubtedly perturbed to learn that the irresponsible *Aurora* had become the Tyler outlet in New York; this knowledge may have hastened his exit from the Cabinet in May 1843. In any event, Robert Tyler and his friend Dr. Joel B. Sutherland, Collector of Customs and chief Tyler patronage dispenser in Philadelphia, persuaded Thomas Dunn English of Philadelphia to remove to New York and edit the paper. Under English the *Aurora* was well-conducted and respectable. It was dull and it always lost money, but it was skillfully pro-Tyler and there were no more rape stories. On two occasions, however, English and Graham were forced to carry out capital levies on Tyler officeholders to sustain the marginal sheet.[24]

One newspaper does not make a political faction, and Tyler still had no more than a small claque in New York. What was frequently headlined as a MONSTER TYLER RALLY or a GREAT TYLER MEETING in the *Aurora* (faithfully reprinted as such in the Washington *Madisonian*) was often no more than Graham, Hoffman, George, and a few of their cronies from the Customs House having a hot whiskey punch together in a private room at Delmonico's. In early January 1843, for instance, a GREAT TYLER MEETING IN CANAL STREET was attended by six of Graham and Curtis' hacks and four small boys who stopped by to heckle. A stirring speech was made, officers of the rally were elected, and resolutions were duly passed while the "surging crowd" lounged around on a few barrels, the adults smoking cigars.

Even when a legitimate throng could be gathered together the results could be disastrous. In February 1843, for example, Tyler's New York friends worked diligently to fill the Broadway Tabernacle for a major rally at which Corporal's Guardsmen Cushing and Wise were scheduled to speak. Chaired by Mordecai Noah, the widely advertised rally attracted hundreds of the Tyler faithful and near-faithful. The auditorium was packed. Delegations from the various wards marched noisily in, carrying Tyler portraits captioned "Old Veto." The crowd was disorderly and out of control from the very beginning. Drinking, laughing, whistling, stamping, and singing proceeded as Noah tried vainly to establish some measure of decorum. When Cushing finally rose to speak, the crowd began to clap and cheer for Henry Clay and show the proper Cushing "some evidences of disrespect." Cushing quickly quit the rostrum, the meeting, and the building in disgust, whereupon resolutions were passed which condemned a national bank, praised "Old Veto" for his vetoes, and called for the immediate annexation of Texas. The chaotic rally concluded with nine cheers for Henry Clay, nine cheers for Martin Van Buren, and three hurrahs for "a celebrated lady who conducted a harem in one of the streets which radiate from Broadway." The *Aurora* next day called this a GREAT ENTHUSIASTIC TYLER MEETING; its scrubbed account of the affair was duly reprinted in the *Madisonian*.[25]

Supported though he was by such motley legions, the President decided to plunge ahead with plans to organize Tyler factions in New York City and elsewhere. He cared not whether his supporters were Tidewater gentlemen or patrons of the "celebrated lady" off Broadway, only whether they could deliver a pro-Tyler vote when called upon. At a crucial White House strategy meeting with Noah early in January 1843, the President stated the opinion that his friends in New York City were numerous enough and dedicated enough to give him the balance of power in the Empire State. He pointed particularly to the work being carried on in his behalf there by loyal men like George, Graham, Fisher, Tasistro, and Fowler. At this enumeration of small-time political hacks, patronage bums, and Tammany opportunists, Noah was "struck dumb with amazement." But Tyler went on to argue, in a statistical analysis lasting several hours, that in addition to New York he had significant blocs of followers in Ohio, New Hampshire, Virginia, and Pennsylvania—enough in total to produce a third party large enough to exercise a controlling influence on the Democratic platform and on the ultimate success or failure of the Democratic nominee in 1844. Tyler made it plain to Noah during this lengthy interview that he "entertained no hopes of an election himself," only the aspiration that his party would be large enough to influence the behavior of the Democracy. A Tammany-trained professional and former editor of the New York *Courier and Enquirer,* Mordecai Noah knew his New York politics inside out. He agreed, he told the President, that

... the only hope you can have must rest on the chance of erecting a party of your own. This you cannot do. You possess patronage, to be sure; and you can use it, without violating any principle; but if it were ten times as extensive as it is it would not enable you to create a party of sufficient consequence to justify you in accepting a nomination even if you could obtain one. The whole Executive Patronage is but a drop in the ocean.[26]

It depended on the size of the drop and the extent of the ocean, and Tyler was satisfied that "the whole Executive Patronage" was a very large drop indeed. He was now sure he could construct a sizable political lever—one he would employ for the "sole purpose of controlling events by throwing the weight of that organization for the *public good.*" And by "the public good" John Tyler meant nothing less than the annexation of Texas. His decision made, his optimism keenly alive, it was not surprising that the confident President chased and kissed and flirted with young Julia Gardiner a few nights later at the White House. He was in a frisky mood. If he was a President without a party, he was still the nation's leading patronage dispenser. With the patronage, he believed, would come the party, and with the party would come the vehicle for annexing Texas and salvaging the historical reputation of his administration. As Corporal's Guardsman George H. Proffit of Indiana explained it to the House on January 10, the Tyler administration was "desirous and anxious to go out of power with a good name." No more, no less.[27]

Late in the spring of 1843 the President launched a vigorous purge of federal officeholders hostile to his administration and to his Texas ambitions. It was a long-overdue housecleaning. On May 12, from Charles City County, Tyler instructed Secretary of the Treasury John C. Spencer to grease the guillotine:

We have numberless enemies in office and they should forthwith be made to quit.... The movements ought to be numerous and decided. Let a number be made and announced on the morning of the same day and this will best be done by consulting with Mr. Wickliffe [Postmaster General] and sending on your commissions and his by the same mail.... In short the changes ought to be rapid and extensive and numerous—but we should have some assurances of support by the appointees. Glance occasionally at the Marshals and D[istrict] Attorneys and let me hear from you.... In short my D[ea]r Sir, action is what we want, prompt and decisive action, but what I say is that we ought to know whom we appoint.... One word more—Poor O'Bryan for a clerkship; the man is actually starving.

As a modest starter Tyler personally marked a dozen men for instant proscription, suggesting their replacements. Among the latter, for example, was his friend and neighbor Collier H. Minge, from whom he had purchased the Sherwood Forest property. Minge, he felt, should go to Mobile as Postmaster, while John Finley of Baltimore should be axed. Both men were related to Old Tippecanoe, but "Minge is Genl. Harrison's nephew, as true as steel," Tyler explained, "while Finley is [only] a 10th cousin." [28]

As the heads rolled regularly into the administration's spattered baskets, John Jones of the *Madisonian* sat by the blade demanding more victims. "Look at the collectors, naval officers, surveyors, appraisers ... marshals, dictrict attorneys, registers of the land office," he shouted, "the twelve or fifteen thousand postmasters ... the whole diplomatic corps abroad ... by whom are they filled? By the friends of the President or by his adversaries? Nineteen-twentieths of them are opposed to him, and a large proportion of that number are known to be the avowed advocates of his bitter revilers." [29]

So the bloodletting went forward, Tyler frequently and personally concerning himself with new personnel for the most obscure offices. Scarcely a sparrow fell from the federal firmament without the President's knowledge and encouragement. Whigs, Locofocos, Websterites, Van Burenites, and Clay men fell by the wayside in hundreds. Not surprisingly, the casualties roared and bellowed in pain like a herd of gored bulls. Even Webster, who knew the patronage game better than most politicians, wrote Tyler angrily from Boston in August 1843, charging that it would be "an unhappy thing if your Administration should be known and distinguished hereafter as one in which patronage of office was relied on for political and personal support ... your substantial and permanent fame as President of the United States is in no small peril...." [30]

The fact of the matter was that Tyler was actually engaged in salvaging the "substantial and permanent fame" of his administration after two years of ineffectual parleying with various political factions more powerful than himself. And if he had once said, "Patronage is the sword and cannon by which war is made on the liberty of the human race ... if the offices of the government shall be considered but as 'spoils' to be distributed among a victorious party ... all stability in government is at an end," he might now be forgiven youthful hyperbole. That unfortunate statement had been made a decade earlier, when Jackson was in power, and every politician had borrowed a little something from Old Hickory in the intervening years. Indeed, as John Minge of Petersburg reminded a now more politically realistic Tyler in 1844, the only road to political power and influence, as Jackson had proved, was through patronage. Why then, asked Minge, do you keep the important offices "too much out of the line of your personal friends?" [31]

Tyler needed no such *aide memoire* from his friend. Nor, actually, did he withhold office from his personal friends. On the contrary, he appointed many of them, including nine members of his family, to various posts. The heroic if ineffectual Corporal's Guard, all of whom had earned political isolation and exile for their support of the President, were also rewarded with federal appointments before Tyler left office. So too were the stalwarts of the Virginia Clique. Tyler did not, however, follow in Jackson's footsteps by stuffing friendly newspaper editors into office. This he had always considered a danger to the freedom and integrity of the press. In only two known instances did he appoint editors to government posts. More typically, he denied federal office to Mordecai Noah because Noah was an editor.[32]

In all his patronage appointments and proscriptions in 1843–1844 Tyler learned that for every new friend an enemy was made. A. G. Abell was rewarded with a consulship to Hawaii for a very favorable and still useful campaign biography, *Life of John Tyler* (1844). Hiram Cumming, on the other hand, failed to obtain a diplomatic appointment to St. Petersburg and slashed back in rage with his scurrilous *Secret History of the Tyler Dynasty* (1845). It was in this pamphlet that Cumming, onetime patronage hatchet-man for the Tylerites, conjured up the fable that the lustful old President had deceived the innocent young Julia, winning her fair hand by promising her he would enter and remain in the 1844 Presidential campaign. Coupled with this were other tales of gross political corruption, his "blasphemy and revelry" in the White House and his "bacchanalian" debauches with his sons. "It is a tissue of anathemas and so gross as to kill itself," snapped Julia when she read it. "He *wants* to be sued for libel and slander I have no doubt in order to bring himself into notoriety and further the sale of his book." Politics could be a dirty business.[33]

It was also a business in which not all the President's friends could hope to attain managerial positions. By September 1843 Tyler noted with dismay that the Tyler Club in New Orleans numbered four hundred supporters, all clamoring for public office. It was time to call a halt to the purge. Therefore on September 2 he instructed Secretary Spencer that "we have done enough and should pause. This I am pretty much resolved upon." He was convinced that he now had "a firm grasp on the reins." The purge, he felt, had nicely cleared the decks.[34]

The abrupt end of what Whigs called the "Reign of Terror" did not please John Jones. The *Madisonian* editor argued that too many of the President's new nominees had not or could not expect to receive Senate approval, and that much of the purgation had been wasted effort. Jones was right. An angry alliance of Clay Whigs and Van Buren Democrats in the Senate blocked more than a hundred of Tyler's appointments. Three of these were nominations to Cabinet posts. When a final count was made in 1845, it revealed that the Senate had rejected more of the appointees of John Tyler to federal office than those of any other President in American history. The record endures. "These men were rejected," wrote Tyler ruefully, only "because they supported my Administration." Jones also felt that the extent of the Tyler housecleaning had fallen far short of the need. "The enemies of the President are [still] at the head of almost every bureau in Washington ... out of six hundred clerks in the departments, scarcely fifty real Tyler men are to be found ... almost every important office in the great State of New York is in the hands of these anti-Texas gentlemen," he complained.[35]

Tyler was determined to do something about New York and the "anti-Texas gentlemen" there. His patronage manipulations meant little unless his friends could exercise a decisive role in the pivotal Empire State. His popular reception in New York City in June 1843, en route with Priscilla and Robert to Boston to attend Webster's speech at the dedication of the Bunker Hill monument, convinced him that the city was the key to his entire political strategy. Priscilla wildly exaggerated the size of his reception, but it was impressive:

When we arrived in New York [she wrote], there were four hundred thousand people assembled to greet us. You see, I won't allow it was only for the President. The bay was crowded with boats of every description. Seventy-four men-of-war down to thousands of club boats. The yards of the ships were all manned and cannons going off in every direction ... bands of music were playing and ten thousand troops [were] stationed round the Battery. I never saw so magnificent a spectacle in my life. ... The President had really showers of bouquets and wreaths thrown upon him everywhere. Windows of the houses ... [were] filled with the most beautiful women waving their handkerchiefs and casting flowers in his path. These latter demonstrations Mr. Tyler takes as intended solely for himself.[36]

In essence, Tyler's New York strategy was to effect an alliance with Tammany Hall, to infiltrate the Wigwam and bring Tammany to a pro-Texas annexation stand. He did not think this would prove difficult. Tammany and Van Buren's Albany Regency were at odds on many patronage fronts and, as everyone knew, the Tammany leadership was corruptible, usually for sale to the highest bidder. Tyler had much to bid with. In the Post Office, Customs House, and Brooklyn Navy Yard were hundreds of patronage jobs which the Chief Executive controlled. The President was in no hurry to capture Tammany in mid-1843, however. He would wait to see what happened to his Texas treaty in the Senate and what the nominating conventions the following spring would bring. He was perfectly willing to wait, to let other Democratic factions in New York weaken themselves in internecine combat before he stepped in. "Prudence, my D[ea]r Sir, prudence is the word," he instructed Jones in September 1843. "Let your fire be directed at Clay.... Use my name as little as possible in your paper." [37]

Tyler's decision in May 1844 to hold his own Democratic-Republican convention in Baltimore at the same time the Democrats held theirs there was no more subtle than open blackmail. The President wanted to force the Democracy, its nominee, and its platform to endorse his Texas project. So it was that one thousand of his friends, most of them officeholders in his administration, gathered at Calvert Hall in Baltimore on May 27, 1844. There were no grave problems, issues, or divisions. The stage was decorated with banners reading TYLER AND TEXAS and RE-ANNEXATION OF TEXAS—REJECTION IS POSTPONEMENT. The atmosphere was carnival. From every state in the Union they came to whoop it up for "Tyler and Texas!" and have a good time. "Large supplies of brandy and water, whisky and gin" were passed around to stimulate the enthusiasm. When it was suggested that the nomination be delayed until the Democrats had acted, delegate Delazon Smith of Ohio objected with the declaration, "Did you not come here to nominate John Tyler? Why then wait for the action of any other body? We will not wait; we will not allow any other body of men to steal our thunder, nor permit any other man to use our pick-axe. They shall not take our vetoes, neither shall they appropriate Texas to their own party uses." Tyler was nominated in less than an hour, the annexation of Texas was demanded in ringing tones, and many of the buoyant delegates drifted over to the Odd Fellows Hall on North Gay Street to see how the Democrats were doing. Tyler was the first into the field with a solid pro-Texas platform. Even the crusty old Adams admitted that Tyler had played his political hand "with equal intrepidity and address." [38]

The Tylerites discovered that the Democrats on North Gay were doing badly. While Van Buren had a clear majority of the delegates, he did not have the necessary two-thirds. By the seventh ballot Lewis Cass of Michigan had squeezed past him. There the voting and the convention deadlocked and a halt was called for the evening, the delegates adjourning into dozens of smoke-filled rooms in search of a compromise candidate. There over their shot glasses, surrounded by cigar haze, the Democracy discovered James Knox Polk of Tennessee—slaveowner, confidant of Old Hickory, former Speaker of the House, friendly with

Tyler, eager for Texas, and enough of a Locofoco on domestic policy to suit Van Buren. He was relatively obscure but he was a near-perfect candidate. On May 28, on the ninth ballot, he became the first dark-horse winner in convention history. The platform declared for "the re-occupation of Oregon and the re-annexation of Texas at the earliest practicable period." The Tyler strategy had worked.[39]

The President evaluated the Democratic candidate and surveyed the Democracy's Texas stand in a twinkling, as rapidly as Samuel Morse's new contraption had communicated the stunning news to the capital. On May 30 Tyler issued an acceptance-of-nomination statement to his own supporters that was a political masterpiece. In one breath it blasted both Clay and Van Buren, called for passage of the pending Texas treaty, and suggested to Polk that Tyler's withdrawal from the race was negotiable:

My name has become inseparably connected with the great question of the annexation of Texas to the Union. In originating and concluding that negotiation I had anticipated the cordial cooperation of two gentlemen, both of whom were most prominent in the public mind as candidates for the presidency. That cooperation would have been attended with the immediate withdrawal of my name from the question of succession. In the consummation of that measure, the aspirations of my ambition would have been complete. I should have felt that, as an instrument of Providence, I would have been able in accomplishing for my country the greatest possible good. . . . If annexation is to be accomplished, it must, I am convinced, be done immediately. Texas is in no condition to delay . . . . If the present treaty should be ratified . . . at the present session of Congress, you will leave me at liberty, gentlemen, to pursue the course in regard to the nomination . . . that my sense of what is due myself and the country may seem to require. . . . The question with me is between Texas and the presidency. The latter, even if within my grasp, would not for a moment be permitted to stand in the way of the first.[40]

There the matter stood until June 8. On that day the languishing Texas treaty was finally and decisively beaten in the Senate 35 to 16, two-thirds against rather than the two-thirds in favor Upshur had counted back in December; a crushing twenty-eight votes short. Many explanations were offered by Senators who switched their stands. Some complained that Tyler's secret diplomacy was un-American; others said the people should decide the question in November; still others responded to party discipline exercised by Clay and Van Buren. But over it all hung the slavery question. And while the various excuses and explanations were being made on Capitol Hill Santa Anna commenced what appeared to be serious war preparations. Calhoun was so discouraged over the vote he advised Tyler to give up the Texas project entirely. The nervous Texans, now on a very extended limb, asked that the military assurances guaranteed by the treaty be put into effect at once.[41]

His Texas treaty beaten, Tyler now entered into the campaign with zest. His plan was to convince Polk that he had enough power in a few key states to compel Young Hickory to purchase Tyler's withdrawal and endorsement with the coin of two basic guarantees: that the Democratic platform really meant what it said on Texas and that Tyler's friends would not be purged from office in the event of a Tyler-Polk amalgamation and a resulting Polk victory. Convinced that Polk had no choice but to come to Canossa, Tyler waited confidently for Young Hickory to make the first gesture toward an alliance. He did not have to wait long. On June 2 he received tentative feelers from the Democracy on a possible Polk-Tyler Union ticket. This pleased the President and convinced him he could play a cool and deliberate hand. "The Democrats ... are now looking to me for help," he told his daughter Mary. "I can either continue the contest or abandon it with honor." With his marriage to Julia but three weeks away, he was in fine fettle.[42]

Robert Tyler had joined his father's campaign with enthusiasm, giving up his two-month-old law practice in Philadelphia to manage Tyler's political affairs. This new political involvement by Robert suited Priscilla not at all. She wrote her husband from Philadelphia on June 4 that

> Of course the Polkites want a Union ticket.... They cannot succeed without Father's assistance. With that, I have no doubt the Democratic party will be successful, as they have stolen the Texas question, besides using the veto issue and all of Father's ammunition. I should consent to the Union ticket if I were in Father's place, but I should bargain for the protection of my friends if I did. But the next best thing is to withdraw and be disinterested and help the Democracie [sic] and get you a good foreign mission.... The first wish of my heart, my dearest husband, is that you may return [home] and decisively go into the practice of the law, giving up everything else.... My dear husband, you must return to Philadelphia, give up the life of political care and excitement in which you live [and] find your dearest happiness in your wife and children....

"The advice you give Robert is excellent," wrote Tyler in the margin.[43]

But the President needed his politically knowledgeable son awhile longer. Working with Dr. Joel B. Sutherland and all the patronage power at the command of the Philadelphia Customs House, Robert began building a Tyler organization in that city. On July 4, at a series of Tyler rallies in Philadelphia, the decision was made to run a separate Tyler slate for every office in Pennsylvania and thus split the Democratic vote in the Commonwealth. Similar divisive plans were already afoot in New Jersey and New York. When news of these developments reached Senator Robert J. Walker, the worried Mississippian reported to Polk that "Our friends in Philadelphia and also in New Jersey and New York have written to me in great alarm ... the greatest distraction and distrust in our ranks would be produced by running Tyler tickets in Pennsylvania."

As consternation spread throughout the Democracy, the President remained calm and confident. From his honeymoon retreat at Sherwood Forest he instructed Robert: "Our course is now a plain one. Make these men feel the great necessity of my co-operation." [44]

On July 9 Senator Walker appeared suddenly at Sherwood Forest. The time to open negotiations with Tyler had come, and Walker was the logical intermediary. While he was acting on his own initiative in this instance, his interest in Texas annexation on his Southern political conservatism in the Senate had made him *persona grata* to Tyler. At the same time, he stood high in the campaign councils of James K. Polk. Nevertheless, he came to Sherwood Forest as a suppliant, and his three-hour conversation with the President was a "disagreeable duty." Tyler, on his part, was relaxed and expansive. He spoke of Andrew Jackson "in terms of deep affection," expressed his "great anxiety that Polk and Dallas should be elected," and hoped that he might withdraw from the campaign and soon retire from the White House. Casually, in an almost offhand manner, he estimated his national strength at "about 150,000 ... chiefly Republicans who voted for the Whigs in '40," and he suggested that this considerable group could be added to the Polk total were he but to give the word. Walker did not dispute the estimate. Nor, given the stakes, did Tyler's terms for alliance with Polk seem outrageous or unreasonable. The President asked only that his political friends "be assured on reliable authority that they would be received with pleasure by you [Polk] and your friends into the ranks of the Democratic party, and treated as brethren and equals." That assurance given, Tyler pledged that he would "at once withdraw," throw his full support to Polk, and render his victory "certain." [45]

Walker assured the President that a bargain could be struck. He left Sherwood Forest that same day and returned to Washington. Immediately he wrote Polk that "the importance of this union and co-operation *cannot be over-rated*. In my judgment it would be *decisive* in your favor." Walker appreciated the fact that the face-saving element in any arrangement with Tyler was an important one. Therefore, he suggested that Polk write a private letter to a friend which might be shown confidentially to Tyler, a letter inviting the President and his supporters back into the Democracy "as brethren and equals." He thought Jackson might write a similar letter, one which could be published, attesting that on Tyler's withdrawal his followers would be joyfully received back in the Democratic bosom "on the same platform of equal rights and consideration" with all other Democrats.[46]

After consultations with Jackson, Polk chose the indirect approach. Were Polk to communicate in any way with Tyler his act, Jackson warned, would be interpreted "just as the Adams and Clay bargain" of 1828. It would be wiser if Jackson himself wrote the missive to be shown Tyler. Privately, Jackson rated Tyler's strength a "mere drop in the bucket," but he hastened to execute the Walker recommendation. Within a few weeks Tyler was shown a personal letter from Old Hickory to Major William B. Lewis which urged Tyler's withdrawal "as the certain means of electing Mr. Polk, and ensuring a consummation of all the leading measures" of the Tyler administration. In this circuitous manner Jackson assured the President of his "strong conviction" that the Tylerites "would be regarded as true friends of the country" by Polk and would be "as favorably looked upon as any other portion of the Democracy." Indeed, they would be "received as brethren...all former differences forgotten." And so in late July the bargain was well on the way to consummation.[47]

While these face-saving arrangements were being worked out in the Polk-Jackson camp, Tyler moved ahead with the organization of his friends in crucial New York City. If and when he did decide to withdraw, he wanted to be able to demonstrate in November that his self-sacrifice was the primary factor in Polk's election. He also reasoned that the no-purge promise would more likely be honored if the Tylerites could show that they had delivered the Empire State into the hands of Polk. The President turned the infiltration and seduction of Tammany Hall over to Alexander Gardiner and Robert Tyler.

On April 27, 1844, five days after the President's letter seeking Julia's hand had been received at Lafayette Place, Alexander had leaped eagerly to Tyler's political assistance. Within a month, under a variety of pseudonyms, he was bombarding New York editors with stinging criticisms of Van Buren's "craven" renunciation of Texas, predicting that the Democracy would meet defeat on the annexation issue. In these letters he noticed the "strong tide running in favor of reannexation," condemned Mexican dictator Santa Anna, called attention to British intrigue in Texas, and wondered where in all the history of mankind *"the people* anywhere [are] found adverse to any extension of territory." Over and over he called stridently for the "reannexation" of Texas and the election of John Tyler. He demanded "reannexation" on the grounds that Texas was American territory under the Louisiana Purchase. Tyler's election was urged with the argument that since annexation had been the President's special project from the start, he should be returned to power to carry it through.[48]

To assist Alexander in his labors for the Tyler cause in the Empire State, in mid-July the President made a basic change in the dispensation of patronage in New York City. On the urgent recommendation of Robert Tyler, Joel B. Sutherland, and Postmaster John Lorimer Graham, he purged Edward Curtis as Collector of the Port of New York, replacing him (on an interim appointment) with Judge Cornelius P. Van Ness, former governor of Vermont. Curtis had originally been a Harrison-Webster appointee and through the years had loaded the Customs House, the Post Office, and the Brooklyn Navy Yard with Websterites,

Clay men, and other Whigs of dubious loyalty to "Tyler and Texas."

Tyler first asked Curtis to resign his post on May 9. When the Collector bluntly refused, the President could do nothing but bide his time until the Senate adjourned in July. He knew that the Whig Senate was not likely to approve the dismissal of Curtis and the appointment of Cornelius Van Ness barely four months before the election. It was no secret in the capital that Judge Van Ness was a solid Tyler man. Onetime Minister to Spain and Collector of the Port of Burlington, Vermont, the Conservative Democrat was also the brother of the General John P. Van Ness so admired by the Gardiner family during their 1842–1843 Washington visit.

After the Senate adjourned and Curtis was summarily deposed, Collector Van Ness launched a ruthless "Reign of Terror" in New York City. On July 15 he began cutting away the Clay and Webster vines that clung to the walls of the federal agencies. Among the worthies marked for instant proscription was Paul R. George, whose connection with Curtis was his death warrant. In the first batch to go from the Customs House alone there were sixty men. These vacancies, together with the temporary three-dollar-per-day jobs created by Van Ness for the duration of the campaign, brought forth applicants "so numerous that they actually blocked up the streets leading to the Custom House... the out-pouring and out-scourings, of all the political parties that ever existed in this country." [49]

Most of the appointments to these minor sinecures were made from among various Roman Catholic immigrant groups—Irish, Polish, and German. Tammany was particularly powerful among these new Americans, and the Tyler leadership in New York wanted a foothold in their multilingual ranks for bargaining purposes in the Wigwam. More importantly, it was certain that the new Native American party, a passing phenomenon born in hatred, exclusionism, and anti-Catholicism, would combine with the Whigs in November in a joint effort to crush Tammany in the city. This opportunistic alliance represented a major threat to the Hall and the Tylerite strategists appreciated the problem. To attract the Irish vote to the projected Tyler-Tammany coalition, the President in March 1844 expressed the "liveliest interest" in the Irish struggle for freedom against England. Robert Tyler had also seen the political advantages of an identification with Roman Catholic immigrant groups. In the same month he became president of the Irish Repeal Association in Philadelphia on the eve of the bitter anti-Catholic riots that swept that city.[50]

Patronage distribution in New York devolved on Van Ness, Postmaster Graham, and Alexander Gardiner. A quick survey of the local political situation convinced Gardiner that he could be very useful to his new brother-in-law. He instructed Julia to advise the President "that no changes be made in the public offices here before I can ascertain that all is safe and to be trusted." It was indeed fortunate, he said, that a member of the immediate family was on the scene. "I think that I can make myself more useful in these matters than any other person in this city," he explained to Julia, "having most at stake ... in our family in the present and future honor and fame of the administration...."[51]

Alexander's newfound friends in the patronage-distribution business—men like John Lorimer Graham—were not the kind of New Yorkers with whom the Gardiners were in the habit of associating. When Julia complained that they were a seedy group, Alexander agreed that

> Although they are not persons of the best judgment, nor of very good reputation in pecuniary affairs, nor of any weight of character in the community, they are yet open and avowed friends of the President, and doubtless capable of making themselves useful in a public sphere. I hope therefore you have not given the President any particular concern about them.

Alexander was rapidly becoming a practical politician. As he sized up the Gotham political arena it was the end result that counted, not the means that had to be employed to attain it. For this reason he lent money to his lowbrow associates—generally small sums of fifty dollars or less—and he extricated them from various scrapes. He also saw to it that they were included in the wedding reception aboard the ferryboat *Essex* after Tyler's marriage to Julia on June 26.[52]

Alexander Gardiner had no illusions about the success of the Tyler faction in the November elections. He knew that the Tyler movement was a holding operation—nationally and in New York—created only to strike the best possible terms with the Democracy on Texas and patronage and then leave the field. Therefore, at a private meeting of Tyler leaders in Manhattan during the week of July 15 the decision was made to place a Tyler slate in the field for every elective office in New York state and to hold a public Tyler rally on July 23 at which the President's nomination by his Baltimore convention would be ostentatiously ratified.

This bold ploy galvanized the Tammany-dominated Democratic General Committee of New York City into immediate action. On July 20, a Tammany Hall delegation approached Alexander Gardiner, Collector Van Ness, and Postmaster Graham and suggested a Polk-Tyler alliance as the only hope of defeating Clay in New York. Specifically, they requested the establishment of a joint conference committee for the purpose of "arranging difficulties" between partisans of the two candidates. Alexander informed Tyler that an exploratory conference had been agreed upon, but that "no definitive action will be taken without approval at headquarters." Headquarters at that moment was the honeymoon cottage at Old Point Comfort.[53]

A few days later, on July 23, the Tyler ratification meeting was held, William Shaler presiding. It was a large, noisy, disorderly affair.

Strong-arm Tammany forces under colorful Mike Walsh arrived in numbers and attempted to disrupt proceedings. This tactic was defeated only when Delazon Smith of Ohio managed to seize the speaker's stand and hold it against all interruptions for two hours in an extemporaneous eulogy to Tyler. When the Walsh crowd finally gave up (*rigor mortis* must have set in), Thomas Dunn English and Judge Chesselden Ellis spoke briefly, and the rally then duly endorsed the Baltimore convention's nomination of Tyler. As Alexander explained the evening's excitement and its political significance to Julia, "My only hope now is, that the firm stand taken, may bring the friends of Polk to favorable terms; for I cannot believe that we have either the men or the means to make any general and effectual separate organization.... I rejoice that the nomination of the President has been ratified ... so that he may receive proposals on equal terms." [54]

Word came back to Alexander from honeymoon headquarters within the week. Tyler informed his brother-in-law that he was ready to withdraw, given a satisfactory patronage arrangement with the Polkites in New York. On the strength of this notification, Alexander circulated a confidential memorandum through the Democratic leadership in the city on July 29 calling for a Tammany alliance with the Tylerites. Speaking as a Tammany Democrat himself (he had been one for two years), he bluntly reminded the party professionals that Tyler's friends in New York were

...working politicians and hold offices of profit, and hence are able to give us at once valuable personal and pecuniary aid. How is it, now? They are kept in abeyance, and we holding no public patronage are now driven upon our private means for support. How inadequate a reliance! If the friends of Tyler are not embraced madness rides the land: we can lose nothing by it, but we may gain much.... Whigs in office would be immediately supplanted by Democrats ... the union acceded to *I have it on the best authority that the President will retire from the contest and throw his whole weight in favor of Polk*.... All that Mr. Tyler wants is justice and conciliation.... Let us act quickly: we should this day have the aid of the public patronage and be in the field with all our forces united! [55]

Tammany and the Polkites had little choice. It was win with Tyler's aid or lose without it. On the evening of August 2 the bargain was struck. Polk's spokesmen promised nothing less than equality of patronage opportunity and open patronage covenants openly arrived at. For these concessions they looked forward to the withdrawal of John Tyler from the field "with credit, honor, and upon terms of much prospective importance." With this agreement in hand, little more could be accomplished by the Tylerites in New York. "I speak with great diffidence," Alexander told the President, "[but] I cannot at present perceive that anything particularly desirable could be achieved by a continuance in the field, this point having been reached." Gardiner was right. Nothing more could be achieved, and a few days later at the Carleton House the eight members of the joint Polk-Tyler conference committee drew up resolutions praising the Tyler administration and pledging their common support of Young Hickory since "the Democratic friends of President Tyler are committed to the same general principles as the supporters of Mr. Polk." A Tammany delegation departed shortly afterward for Washington to urge Tyler's speedy withdrawal. Meanwhile, Joel B. Sutherland and Robert Tyler arrived at the White House from Philadelphia to press the same course. Letters from Democrats all over the country flooded into Washington pleading with the President to withdraw and join with Polk in the certain humiliation of Henry Clay. On August 20, 1844, John Tyler finally issued his withdrawal statement, but not before he got off a private letter to Andrew Jackson announcing that a statement was forthcoming and that he counted "40,000 friends in Ohio and a controlling power in Pennsylvania, Virginia and New Jersey, which if it can be brought to co-operate will decide the contest." [56]

Tyler's formal withdrawal statement, struck off hastily (in less than three hours), was an extensive defense of his administration in general, his vetoes in particular, his motives in the Texas matter, and his right as an American citizen "to think for myself on all subjects and to act in pursuance of my own convictions." He again denied the charge that his Texas treaty had any sectional bias. It was entirely a national measure, designed only to insure "the annual expansion of our coastwise and foreign trade, and the increased prosperity of our agriculture and manufactures." He admitted, however, that he felt personally "ambitious to add another bright star to the American constellation," and that the completion of annexation would furnish him "an unfailing source of gratification to the end of my life." The ratification of the Texas treaty, he confessed, was "the sole honor which I coveted, and that I now desire." For his personal role in advancing the issue toward some solution he could only "appeal from the vituperation of the present day to the pen of imperial history." [57]

Hailed by his followers as "decidedly one of the ablest productions from the Pen of our friend," the withdrawal statement was generally ridiculed in the Whig press, applauded by the Democratic press, and smiled at indulgently in some sectors of both. The cautious New York *Journal of Commerce* came closest to the contemporary significance of the decision when it noted on August 22 that

> Some have said the Tyler party is a *minus* quantity; and that its co-operation would be worse than its opposition. This will do for a joke, but in point of fact, the Polkites will rejoice, and the Whigs regret, to see this new accession, small though it be, to the ranks of the democratic nominee. In some of the Southern States where the votes of Whigs and Democrats are nearly balanced, a deduction of a comparatively small number from the latter, might entirely change the result.[58]

This too was the judgment of the Polk leadership. Andrew Jackson was satisfied that Tyler's withdrawal had strengthened Young Hickory significantly in Ohio, Connecticut, New York, Pennsylvania, and Michigan. *"All's well* in N. York and Pennsylvania . . . ," said the old General happily. Sutherland predicted a Polk majority in Virginia and a Polk sweep in the Keystone State. Indeed, when news of Tyler's withdrawal reached Philadelphia six thousand of his friends were crowded into the Chinese Museum and voted to go over to Polk and Dallas in a body.[59]

So smoothly and quickly did the alliance fuse that by mid-September Tyler was persuaded that a Polk administration would really be but "a continuation of my own, since he will be found the advocate of most of my measures." He was positive that his friends would be treated with "regard and attention," and he was pleased that they "rallied *en masse*" to Polk in Pennsylvania, New York, New Jersey, and New England. This unanimous rally, he predicted, would surely "secure the election" for Polk. In sum, John Tyler was satisfied with the bargain. Rumors that the arrangement involved his appointment to the Court of St. James's, or that Tyler had insisted that Franklin P. Blair's Washington *Globe* be cut off from any official connection with a Polk administration, were entirely without foundation. In fact, Tyler and Polk had no direct contact at any time during the campaign. All understandings were effected through intermediaries.[60]

In New York City the Tyler faction began vigorous efforts on behalf of the Polk ticket in early September. They, at least, would carry out their end of the transaction with Young Hickory. Julia received Alexander's instruction to send from Washington "a good bundle of the *Madisonian* pamphlet that I might distribute them here." This she quickly did, happy to contribute to the Polk campaign in any way she could. As the summer drew to a close Alexander dispensed increasing quantities of federal patronage in the city. Working through Van Ness and Graham, he placed deserving Democrats of all factions—Tyler's, Polk's, Tammany's, and even Van Buren's—into various jobs in the Customs House, Post Office, and Navy Yard. He took special care of the Long Island friends of his Uncle Samuel Gardiner. Gradually he came to control patronage distribution for the administration in all of Suffolk County. He also took a special interest in the seamen's vote on the docks in Manhattan and Brooklyn. Just before the polls opened on November 5 he circularized all Democratic ward leaders to the effect that if they knew of any "worthy Democrat" who needed employment, he could provide a full winter's work on the dry dock then building at the Brooklyn Navy Yard. The response to the dry dock work offer was, to say the least, heartening. Men came in droves, bringing their friends and relatives. All were votes for Polk. Alexander was busy with the Polk campaign from morning until night. "Alex has no peace with the constant demand upon his time and *purse,*" Margaret complained. "The door bell is nearly worn out with ringing." [61]

By the beginning of October Alexander Gardiner had become so enamored of the local political process that on Robert Tyler's suggestion he decided to run for the New York State Assembly. Robert pulled the strings within Tammany that assured Alexander a nomination on the Democratic ticket. To provide himself additional prestige and a closer personal connection with Tyler for campaign purposes, Alexander sought an appointment as the President's honorary aide-de-camp. When Tyler refused his request for a colonelcy the young lawyer complained to Julia that the President was slow to "give his relations situations." But in spite of Julia's pressure in her brother's behalf, the President stood firm. Enough of his relatives were already in office. Disappointed but unbowed, Alexander plunged into the campaign anyway. He came out strongly for Polk, Texas, and the "reoccupation" of Oregon. He was against the use of convict labor in competition with the HONEST MECHANICS OF THIS STATE.

This orthodoxy did not sway all the members of the nominations committee of the Democratic county convention. Young Gardiner had been a Democrat for only two years and his services to Tammany had not been noteworthy. As bread-and-butter professionals, some of Tammany's sidewalk sachems were not overly impressed with Alexander's argument that he had, after all, "supported the various measures of the party through the columns of the *Globe, Evening Post* and other papers." A strong effort was therefore made to block his nomination. Thanks to the labors of David H. Broderick, however, opposition to the Gardiner endorsement was beaten down in the nominations committee and upstart Alexander's name was sent along with the rest of the approved list to the county convention for ratification. Broderick was later rewarded by Tyler with a patronage job for his loyal efforts. The nominations-committee incident of October 11 convinced Alexander that "there is a great absence of friends in the Democratic Party." [62]

Alexander entered the Assembly race with scant hope of victory. He felt that the Whig-Native American alliance would likely defeat all Democratic candidates running, as he was, on a citywide ticket. Calculating his chances as "more possible than probable," he was half-angered, half-amused when a plot was sprung in the county convention in late October to deny him the nomination. He was not without warning that something of the sort was afoot. The New York *Herald* for October 13, commenting on his contested selection by the nominations committee, remarked that

The greatest possible commotion and excitement prevailed on Friday evening [October 11] in and around Tammany Hall, in consequence of the nomination of a highly respectable and wealthy young gentleman named Gardiner, as one of the thirteen members of the Assembly. It seems that Mr. Gardiner is wholly unknown in the Democratic party, and received his nomination mainly because he happens to be the brother-in-law of President Tyler, or as some of the nasty politicians will have it, the brother-in-law of the Custom House. Everybody seemed to be loud in the expression of disapprobation, and there will probably be difficulty at the County meeting on account of his nomination, and another made at the same time.

The maneuver to head Alexander was a crude one—typically Tammany. An anti-Tyler clique in the Wigwam, headed by Levi D. Slamm, hired a dim-witted gentleman named Joseph T. Sweet, a member of the nominations committee, to testify publicly that Alexander and Robert Tyler had used various improper methods—threats, bribery, and profanity—to suborn his vote. According to Sweet's charges, these Gardiner-Tyler importunities were aimed at denying Thomas N. Carr, a notorious anti-Tylerite, nomination to the State Assembly in Alexander's stead. Sweet, of course, was a liar, and he later signed a statement cheerfully admitting this fact (Carr, it turned out, was behind the plot), but his charges livened up the New York County Democratic convention meeting at Tammany Hall on the evening of October 28, reducing it to the usual state of chaos. In spite of Sweet's allegation, Alexander's nomination was upheld in a chorus of shouts, boos, cheers, and hisses. Nevertheless, his success did not lessen the outrage Juliana felt when Sweet's irresponsible allegations were hurled at her son. She was sure, for example, that her Alexander had "never made use of a profane word in his life." [63]

Following Alexander's baptism in mud, the family watched with interest as the Polk-Clay campaign entered its final phases. At best, it became a name-calling exercise punctuated by political hokum of the worst sort. Polk called for the "reannexation" of a Texas that had never been annexed and the "reoccupation" of an Oregon earlier inhabited by bears, beavers and other furry patriots. Clay, on the other hand, straddled the Texas question and struggled to avoid the very Bank issue with which he had joyfully smashed the Tyler administration three years earlier.

The main problem that confronted Tyler and his friends and family was how to interpret Polk's razor-thin victory when it ultimately materialized in November. Polk eased by Clay 1,337,000 to 1,229,000 in popular votes and 170 to 105 in the Electoral College. From the President's standpoint it was imperative to demonstrate that his August withdrawal had thrown the close election to Polk. In the first flush of family enthusiasm over the Democratic victory, Alexander argued that Young Hickory's slim margin of 5000 in New York state, nearly half of it from the city, could not have been possible had the President not purged Edward Curtis from the Customs House and applied the balm of Tylerite patronage to the Polk cause. At first Tyler adopted this satisfying interpretation without dispute. "That decisive act on my part secured the State for Polk," he declared confidently. Alexander further persuaded Tyler that the President's timely withdrawal had also tipped Pennsylvania and Virginia into the Polk column. "Mr. Polk is beyond question indebted to the President for his election," said Alexander with finality. True, had either New York or Pennsylvania gone for Clay, James K. Polk would have lost; and in Pennsylvania, thanks to Robert Tyler and Joel B. Sutherland, Tyler had a substantial bloc of supporters who had indeed gone over to Polk.[64]

The initial Gardiner-Tyler interpretation of Polk's victory in New York did not, however, take into account the fact that James G. Birney's strongly abolitionist and anti-Texas Liberty Party had polled 15,812 of its 62,300 national votes in the Empire State. Had Birney and his splinter group not been in the field, or had Clay campaigned strongly against Texas annexation, the Kentuckian might well have commanded enough of the Birney vote to have carried New York. Nor did the Gardiner-Tyler explanation account for the fact that the strongly antiannexationist Silas Wright led the winning Democratic ticket by 5000 votes in New York in his successful gubernatorial bid. Having earlier declined a Vice-Presidential nomination on the Polk ticket because he was anti-Texas, Wright had consented to run for governor only on the urging of Martin Van Buren, whose friend and ally he was. Since he ran so far ahead of the Democratic ticket, some observers argued that he actually dragged Polk in with him in New York. If this was a correct view of the matter, then Wright (and Van Buren) had delivered the Empire State to Polk. They therefore had a greater claim on his subsequent patronage favors than did Tyler. Daniel B. Tallmadge, a Tylerite leader in the city, admitted the logic of this interpretation in a confidential letter to the President. He carefully analyzed the returns in every ward and district in New York and concluded that many antiannexationist Democrats had split their tickets, voting for Wright for governor and Clay for President, cutting Polk. "It would in my judgment serve no good purpose to have this matter made the subject of newspaper discussion," he suggested to Tyler. "I deemed it proper however to bring it to the notice of yourself, because you have been so identified with the question of annexation and Polk's success." Polk's Texas annexationism probably hurt him in New York as much as it helped him. He very likely lost as many or more votes on the issue there than he gained from the alliance with Tyler.[65]

As these considerations became apparent to the President, he gradually abandoned the view that his withdrawal had swung New York to Polk. Instead, he pointed to those of his friends in Philadelphia (6000 by his count) who had gone over to Polk, and he maintained that their adherence to Young Hickory had swung Pennsylvania to the Democracy. "I say nothing of the elections elsewhere, nor is it necessary," he told Alexander. "The loss of Pennsylvania would have lost him the election." This comfortable thesis also contained loopholes. It did not take into account the possibility that the appearance of native son George M. Dallas on the Polk ticket as the Vice-Presidential candidate did more to tip Pennsylvania to the Democrats than had Tylerite support. In addition, the Pennsylvania Democracy took a decisive 23,000-to-19,000 licking in Tyler's Philadelphia stronghold from a Whig-Native American coalition ("Oh! the defeat in Philadelphia!" Margaret moaned). It could be argued, however, that Tyler's strength in the city, particularly among Roman Catholic immigrant groups, had reduced expected Democratic losses there enough to allow Polk to slide through by 6000 votes in the state as a whole. This, at least, became the Tyler-Gardiner view of the matter and it remains a reasonable though speculative opinion.

In other states where Tyler had predicted his withdrawal would exercise a decisive influence for Polk—Virginia, Ohio, and New Jersey—Polk carried only Virginia. Had Virginia's seventeen electoral votes gone to Clay, the outcome of the election would not have changed one bit. In the final analysis, then, Tyler's much-negotiated withdrawal from the canvass probably influenced the result in Virginia (and possibly that in Pennsylvania), and the decision in the Old Dominion was not crucial one way or the other. But dreams are not built on such pragmatic conclusions. In history, what actually happened is sometimes less important than what is *believed* to have happened, and John Tyler believed until the end of his days that his withdrawal from the 1844 campaign was the decisive factor in the unexpected victory of James K. Polk over Henry Clay. Whatever the truth of this belief, Polk undoubtedly owed Tyler something other than the ruthless and cynical proscription he carried out against Tylerite officeholders soon after he assumed power.[66]

Alexander Gardiner's try for elective office was not successful. All thirteen Democratic nominees for the Assembly in New York City went down to defeat. Alexander was beaten 27,487 to 26,183 by Harvey Hunt, the Whig-Nativist candidate. His altercation with the Slamm-Carr-Sweet clique in Tammany had certainly not helped his cause. Friends of the three conspirators had retaliated at the polls. In fact, Alexander ran well behind the Democratic ticket all the way. But the mild disappointment he experienced was buried in the general elation the Tylers and Gardiners felt over the election of James K. Polk. Like the President himself, they all remained convinced that Young Hickory owed his success entirely to John Tyler.[67]

From the President's point of view, Henry Clay had deliberately wrecked the Tyler administration to advance his own selfish political fortunes. The Bank issue with which he had accomplished the demolition was a manufactured one. The Whigs of 1844 had not even mentioned the fighting word *Bank* in their fuzzy platform. It was, therefore, with great satisfaction that Tyler saw Clay beaten by a political dark horse. In a larger sense, he viewed Polk's victory as a complete vindication of his own administration, and he would have been a very unusual human being had he not convinced himself that he had played the major role in Clay's humiliation. Both he and Julia joined enthusiastically in the victory celebrations in Washington at which "John Tyler was cheered with burst upon burst." They were delighted to hear that a Democratic victory rally in Charleston had hailed "Old Veto" with a "Well done! thou good and faithful servant." And when the Reverend Gregory Thurston Bedell told his predominately Whig congregation at the Episcopal Church of the Ascension on November 17 that the Whigs had tried to buy the election in New York but that Jesus Christ had tipped the scales for Polk, Juliana was convinced that she was in the presence of a truly great mind. Bedell, she decided, "deserves to be admired" because he always "aimed at truth.... It is a great privilege to hear him preach." Nor could young Julia contain herself. "Hurrah for Polk!" she exclaimed. "What *will* become of Henry Clay.... We shall have a very pleasant winter here I can now promise." [68]

A very pleasant winter was indeed being planned. As the Washington correspondent of the New York *Herald* informed his readers on November 21:

Had Mr. Clay been chosen by the people, gloom would have pervaded the social metropolis. Now, preparations are in progress to make this the most brilliant season Washington has ever beheld. A round of magnificent entertainments, commencing with the opening of Congress, will follow one another in rapid succession ... the Executive Mansion will be thrown open under the auspices of the President's bride, the most splendid and accomplished lady of the age. Possessed of the highest order of beauty and intellect, and of the most elegant and popular manners, she will draw about her a court circle rivaling in charms of mind and person, that of Charles II or Louis le Grand.

For all her enthusiasm, energy, and social poise, the twenty-four-year-old Julia was still a relatively young and inexperienced girl, and her mother was sure she would make mistakes playing her queenly role in the White House. "You must not mind any objections made of you in the newspapers," she warned her daughter. "You will not escape censure. Do your best. I should not be surprised at any ill nature." [69]

With a splendid social season to look forward to at the side of a beautiful young bride, Tyler could not remain angry at anyone very long, even the despicable Henry Clay. "Leave off abusing Mr. Clay altogether," he ordered the *Madisonian*. "He is dead and let him rest." As far as he was concerned, his long battle with Prince Harry was over.[70]

10

JULIA REGINA:
COURT LIFE IN WASHINGTON

> *I determined upon, and I think I have been successful, in making my Court interesting in youth and beauty. Wherever I go they form my train....*
> —JULIA GARDINER TYLER, 1845

F. W. Thomas, sometime Washington correspondent of the New York *Herald,* predicted in November 1844 that the coming social season would be the "most brilliant Washington has ever beheld"—for the penny press an understatement. Nevertheless, all the psychological and social conditions were favorable for an unusual display at the White House. Tyler's withdrawal from the campaign and Polk's victory over Clay had left the President "happy as a clam at high water." At his side was his vivacious bride, bubbling and bursting with all the energy and imagination that would make the Tyler administration long remembered for its social sophistication if not for its political accomplishments. "This winter," Julia breathlessly informed her mother, "I intend to do something in the way of entertaining that shall be the admiration and talk of the Washington world." Not only would there be the weekly White House levees and the usual formal receptions, but also several special grand functions that would be the marvel of all Washington. Julia planned to reign in truly regal style.[1]

The White House remained an unlikely castle. It was still a frightful mess. The chairs had been covered only once since the first Monroe administration and they were all in a state of "perfect explosion at every prominent point that presents contact with the outer garments of the visitors." An 1844 bill to provide a sorely needed $20,000 for refurbishing the moth-eaten furniture had predictably been defeated in Congress.

And since Tyler's private funds were now severely limited by the demands of the Sherwood Forest remodeling, it was up to the Gardiners to provide the cash for much of the planned brilliance. Julia was perfectly willing to bear any necessary expense. As her socially conscious mother advised her, there had to be a "change in the domestic economy of the establishment," an end to the marginal and near-threadbare standard of living in the President's Mansion. Needless to say, there was an instant change, one accomplished with Gardiner dollars. No sooner had Julia returned from her honeymoon in Virginia than she got her White House coachmen and footmen into expensive new livery—"a suit of black with black velvet bands and buckles on their hats." She was determined to "roll about very comfortably for a little while." [2]

As the opening of the new season approached with the return of Congress in early December, the First Lady busied herself with last-minute preparations for her "auspicious reign." She persuaded the President to obtain for her an Italian greyhound, a fashionable breed she believed would add Continental sophistication to the decor of her Court. Tyler dutifully placed an order for the animal through the American consul in Naples. Meanwhile, Margaret was instructed to procure a "Heron's plume" in New York. "For one kind of headdress this winter," Julia explained, "I intend to have a sort of velvet cap with a Heron's plume in front pinned on with my large diamond pin." She also thought Margaret had better send her diamond star feronia and her two strings of pearls to Washington. A rush order for a loose felt hat was quickly canceled, however, when the *au courant* Margaret reported that they were definitely out of style, "found nowhere but in the Bowery" and were now called "monkey caps." [3]

Definitely in style in New York was the new dance called the polka. Juliana reported it all the rage among the fashionable young set in Gotham, and Julia swiftly imported it to the White House in spite of David Lyon's comment that it was "half an Indian dance and half waltz." Aboriginal or not, both the polka and the suggestively daring waltz soon became *de rigueur* at all White House balls although Tyler, only a few years earlier, had found the waltz immoral and sternly forbidden his daughters to dance it or to associate with boys who did. John Tyler, it would seem, was mellowing. Also ordered for the White House at Julia's insistence was a quantity of good French wine and a number of pieces of expensive French furniture. Tyler hoped that these might arrive in time to be enjoyed at the President's Mansion before being sent on to Sherwood Forest in March 1845. But the winter passed without their appearance, and the President became increasingly anxious about his purchases. "With two such cargoes upon the water," wrote Margaret, "he compares himself to Antonio." [4]

As befitted a reigning queen, Julia set Saturday as her reception day. The first one she held, a *"recherche assemblage"* on November 23, attracted the French Minister and Madame Pageot, General John P. Van Ness, and many others "who all came in grand toilette." At the same time, the First Lady decided to have her portrait painted. This charge was executed by E. G. Thompson of New York at a cost of $250. But the finished product, thought Julia, was much too conservative. It showed too little of her neck and throat. She therefore commissioned an engraver, B. O. Tyler of New York, to execute a more décolleté version of the portrait. Fearing that the engraver might attempt to capitalize on his name and on his commission, she warned her family that "The President hopes you will not think B. O. Tyler is any *400th* cousin of his."[5]

With less monarchical detachment she wisely decided that her reign must have a good press, especially in socially decisive New York City. To effect this pioneer effort by a First Lady in White House public relations, she and the ladies of her Court were uncommonly agreeable to the *Herald*'s part-time correspondent, F. W. Thomas. Privately, they all found him a frightful bore and they were soon "quite sick of him." Thomas was a minor novelist and politician with no lasting claim to fame save through his friendship with Edgar Allan Poe. Indeed, Thomas had endangered his welcome at the White House in March 1843 when he brought Poe there in the hope of helping the rootless poet find a place in the Philadelphia Customs House. Poe had become dead drunk in the Presidential presence, an unseemly display that had ended his patronage prospects and embarrassed his patron. Thomas, however, had held on grimly to the outer fringes of the Tyler administration, and in late 1844 Julia moved him into the White House inner circle as her press agent. His job, as Margaret explained it, was to "sound Julia's praises far and near in Washington." This did not mean he was a political intimate of the President. On the contrary, Tyler would tell him nothing of his political plans. Thomas was made privy only to the social plans of the White House. This being the arrangement, Julia expected nothing less than rave notices from his pen, and when these fell below her considerable expectations she became quite upset. She did not appreciate, for example, Thomas' coy remark that "Her Excellency and Mistress President" looked as "rosy and as fat as ever, and, if my eyes did not deceive me, a little 'fatter.'" Nothing would have complicated her reign quite so much as a pregnancy, actual or rumored.[6]

Fortunately, Julia had several opportunities to practice being a queen before the new Congress convened on December 3. In late October she attended the launching of the new sloop-of-war *St. Mary* at the Washington Navy Yard. A large throng of people, "from prince to peasant," had gathered for the colorful event. When the First Lady finally arrived, a fashionable hour and a half late, she made a grand and impressive entry. Trailed by dozens of Cabinet officers, ambassadors, ministers, generals, commodores, and their ladies, she was, in her manner, like Elizabeth I bidding her fleet Godspeed against the Armada. By the time the little *St. Mary* had at last reached the water, Secretary of the Navy John Y. Mason and Secretary of War William Wilkins were bitterly arguing the relative military merits of ships versus militia, a debate spurred on by a laughing First Lady and the giggling ladies of her entourage. A century later the Pentagon would be built to provide decent housing for this venerable American forensic activity.[7]

A series of small dinner parties in honor of her recent marriage provided Julia additional opportunities to gain experience in her new role before the social season was fully under way. At Secretary of the Navy Mason's on November 26 (Tyler was not present) she found herself seated between Secretary of State Calhoun and Attorney General John Nelson. They were both "so exceedingly agreeable I cannot tell which was most so, but I like Mr. Calhoun the best," she happily reported to her mother. "He actually *repeated verses to me*. We had together a pleasant flirtation." The thought of the courtly John C. Calhoun whispering poetry of "infinite sweetness and taste" into Julia's ear was too much for the amused President. "Well, upon my word," he exclaimed to his bride when she recounted the incident, "I must look out for a new Secretary of State if Calhoun is to stop writing dispatches and go to repeating verses." Five months of marriage had not dulled Julia's sure feeling for provocative flirtation. Nor did she intend to discontinue her practice of the art form she knew so well. And yet it was true, as young Alice Tyler reported, that the President and Julia lived together on "dreams and kisses." They were indeed exceptionally happy. When, for example, they sat for a daguerreotype at the hands of Mr. Phimb of Washington, they were seated so "lovingly together" that Margaret was inclined to regard their cozy pose as a joke.[8]

By the time Tyler presented his fourth and final Annual Message to Congress on December 3 Julia felt herself ready for anything from dinner-table flirtation to Texas annexation. In his last Message, one of the great imperialist state papers of the nineteenth century, Tyler renewed his political offensive for the annexation of Texas, once again pointing out the benefits of the project to the entire nation. He demanded that the Congress, lame duck though it was, act swiftly and decisively on the matter:

> The great popular election which has just terminated afforded the best opportunity of ascertaining the will of the States and the people upon it.... The decision of the people and the States on this great and interesting subject has been decisively manifested. The question of annexation has been presented nakedly to their consideration.... A controlling majority of the people and a large majority of the States have declared in favor of immediate annexation.... It is the will of both the people and the States that Texas shall be annexed to the Union promptly and immediately. It may be hoped that ...all collateral issues may be avoided. Future legislatures can best decide as

to the number of states which should be formed out of the territory when the time has arrived for deciding that question. So with all others.... The two Governments having already agreed through their respective organs on the terms of annexation, I would recommend their adoption by Congress in the form of a joint resolution or act to be perfected and made binding on the two countries when adopted in like manner by the Government of Texas.[9]

Tyler's suggestion that the annexation of Texas could be effected by joint resolution, a device that neatly circumvented the specific demand of the Constitution that treaties be adopted by the advice and consent of two-thirds of the Senate, represented the Virginian's second major departure from the principle of strict construction. In April 1841 he had interpreted the imprecise language of the Constitution to read that he was really the President of the United States, not the "Acting President." Now he was willing to go a step further, saying that a treaty might become law by simple majority vote of both houses. John Tyler, like most states' rights devotees of strict construction, had again come upon a situation in which what he wanted as a person, as an American, and as a President could not be squared with the fundamentalist written word of the Constitution. When this happened, Tyler, like Jefferson before him on the Louisiana Purchase question, did not hesitate. He took the elastic road home; and in so doing he benefited the nation while compromising further the document to which the states' righters looked for salvation from the multiple evils of Federalist-Whig nationalism.

Whatever the constitutional questions involved—and they were numerous and complex—the joint-resolution tactic was a brilliant one. Ultimately it got Texas into the Union, although latter-day wags may argue that this was itself a national disaster. In any event, copies of the President's forthright Texas message were distributed throughout the Gardiner and Tyler families. Frank comments were invited. Julia remarked that it had created a "prodigious sensation" in Washington. "Oh! if it will only have the effect of admitting Texas!" she exclaimed. Alexander analytically surveyed the Northern press and informed the President that the newspapers there had "generally ... spoken very highly of the Message." Meanwhile, congratulatory letters reached the President from his friends in places as far removed from contemporary civilization as Birch Pond, Tennessee, assuring him that a majority of the American people stood solidly behind his annexation scheme. The public reaction to and the continuing family enthusiasm for the project were gratifying to the President. As he explained his deepest psychological motives in the Texas matter to Alexander, "if the annexation of Texas shall crown off my public life, I shall neither retire ignominiously nor be soon forgotten." [10]

Alexander, in support of his brother-in-law's dream, once again sharpened his facile quill and began composing pro-annexation pieces for the seaboard newspapers. "This piece of Alex's is glorious," said Tyler of one of the young lawyer's better efforts. "I had not perceived ... he was so strong a writer—why his *style is of the highest and richest kind!* ... [He] is destined to be a very distinguished man!" In his enthusiasm, the President even suggested that Alexander run for Congress. Julia demurred. "For my own part," she explained to her brother, "I prefer [for you] a foreign mission of some conspicuous sort, and everyday it occupies my mind and is often discussed by the President and myself." In the renewed excitement for the Texas project John Tyler, Jr., also contributed a few anonymous newspaper columns to the family effort for annexation.[11]

While her brother and her stepson thus urged Texas annexation with pen and ink, Julia fought for it with coquetry and persuasion. At a White House dinner party early in the season the conversation, as it inevitably did in those days, turned to Texas. When someone asked the views of Judge John McLean on the matter, Julia interrupted to say that she would "make it a matter of honor" with him that he support annexation.

"There is no honor in politics," said Calhoun, laughing.

"We will see," Julia replied.

Taking a small slip of paper she wrote "Texas and John Tyler" on it and passed it down the table to McLean with the request that he offer the slogan as a toast. The recently wed Justice, still not immune to Julia's charms, rose, bowed gallantly to her, raised his glass and said, "For your sake." The toast was accordingly rendered. Remarking later on the incident, Tyler was inclined to agree with Calhoun's cynicism. "His sentiment may not have appeared a very poetic one," the President told his wife, "but experience has taught me that politics is not the best school for the propagation of the purest code of morals!"[12]

Julia's personal identification with her husband's Texas ambition was complete. She was thrilled to be part of such a grand project without being overshadowed by it. One ditty which made the rounds in Washington in 1844–1845 gave her particular pleasure:

> Texas was the Captain's bride,
> Till a lovelier one he took;
> With Miss Gardiner by his side,
> He, with scorn, on kings may look.[13]

Julia worked diligently to create the social atmosphere she felt the administration must effect if it hoped to achieve Texas or anything else. She was a born ballroom lobbyist. No legislator was too obscure a target for her persuasive charm. Buckskin familiarity was not, however, her *modus operandi* any more than it was the President's. "Last evening I had a most brilliant reception," she informed her mother on one occasion. "At least fifty members of Congress paid their respects to me, and all at one time. I did not enter the room *until* they had assembled. It really presented an array, and it was imposing to see them all brought forward, and introduced one by one." It was a question of keeping everyone in his proper relationship to the "crown." She was determined to win friends and influence people for the greater glory of the Tyler administration, and she hoped to accomplish this by radiating a combination of regality and charm. Votes might be influenced by awe alone. In the spirit of Henry IV, Texas was worth a flirtation—or a reception.[14]

As First Lady, Julia was naturally the recipient of numerous gifts, prerogatives, and appeals which increased her sense of importance and heightened her feeling of usefulness to her husband. The President's franking privilege was used by all the Gardiners while Julia was in the White House. She received a fine Arabian steed from Commodore Jesse D. Elliot, USN, in appreciation of Tyler's personal intercession when the officer was under suspension from his command for having illegally transported horses on an American naval vessel. Hundreds of appeals reached her from citizens all over the country, begging clemency for their condemned sons, military transfers and emergency leaves for their husbands, patronage jobs for their luckless relatives. "One word from your good mouth would make us happy and comfortable, and would forever be remembered," wrote one East Hamptonian in search of a Customs House job. Condemned criminals also asked her to influence the President on their behalf. Julia carefully screened all these requests, passing what appeared to be the most deserving and legitimate to her husband or to the proper Cabinet officer.

Juliana was much disturbed to learn that her daughter would actually "receive letters and *read* them from condemned criminals. You must not read them," she ordered. "It is a most fearful responsibility, one that you should not have anything *whatever* to do with. The idea to my mind is really appalling." To Julia's mind it was rather appealing. She was never bored with pleas for her intercession or requests for her autograph. And when "The Julia Waltzes" appeared in New York she would not rest until she had procured copies of the sheet music.[15]

Julia was not entirely comfortable in her new station. She was still unsure of herself and unwilling to launch her social ship of state until she was surrounded by the young ladies of her family. These friendly faces would comprise her "Court." Their presence would give her confidence and their assigned functions would be roughly those of ladies-in-waiting to a queen. She began assembling the group as soon as Congress convened. Chief among them, of course, was her sister Margaret. The other ladies of the royal household were Julia's young first cousins, Mary and Phoebe Gardiner of Shelter Island, New York, daughters of her Uncle Samuel; and Alice Tyler, at eighteen the youngest of the President's daughters by Letitia. Julia and Margaret were both very fond of Mary and Phoebe and the four women remained lifelong friends.

Julia's relations with Alice were still tenuous but were improving. By late December 1844 Julia had gathered her coterie of Court ladies around her in Washington and felt much better prepared to commence the season.[16]

David Lyon arrived in the capital a few days before Christmas, in time to enjoy the holiday feast Julia placed upon the White House table. The food was "a la Virginia [with] immense hams, rounds of beef, veal, etc." Margaret had decorated the room and the table with wreaths of evergreen. A portrait of George Washington, clad in holiday greenery, gazed down on the festive scene. "We commenced the day with Egg Nog and concluded with apple Toddy," she reported. David Lyon was quite overwhelmed by the White House. "For the first week," Margaret informed Alexander, "he seemed to feel like the *last man,* wandering about the mansion first to study out his room and then the way out of doors. I am sure you would have been amused." Gradually, however, he became acclimated, and by New Year's Day he was "beginning to enjoy himself." His official White House function was that of general escort to the young ladies of Julia's Court. He learned his duties quickly, and performed them well. To provide him a suitable title for the occasion, Tyler appointed him aide-de-camp to the Commander-in-Chief. From that day forward David Lyon Gardiner proudly called himself "Colonel" Gardiner, a simulated rank he carried to his grave.[17]

Juliana appeared on the scene soon after New Year's to chaperon the First Lady's little retinue. Alexander remained in New York, happily involved in the politics of Texas annexation and the patronage problems of the Tyler faction there. The reign, it became clear, was almost exclusively a Gardiner show. Julia certainly did not want her husband's married daughters underfoot during her finest hour. Their initial reactions to her marriage had been so coldly formal Julia had actually been hurt, and she was not yet ready to forgive them or forget their hostility. "The President's daughters are all dying to come here this winter," Margaret reported, "but Julia says they *shan't come.*" Indeed, when William Waller arrived in Washington in mid-January, he stayed at Coleman's Hotel. There was no invitation to the President's Mansion, and it was the opinion within the Court that Lizzie Tyler Waller had dispatched her husband to the capital "purposely to report proceedings at the White House." Thus the Gardiners walked where Tylers feared to tread.[18]

If there was a single spot on earth less promising romantically for a young woman than East Hampton, Long Island, it was nearby Shelter Island. Remote, isolated, cold, it was hardly the place for an exciting winter—or for any excitement whatever. "We do nothing but read in winter here," Mary Gardiner had complained to Julia in 1840. "Do write [us] ... the news of the fashionable world.... The cold weather has *congealed* all my ideas...." Not surprisingly Mary and Phoebe

Gardiner leaped at the unexpected invitation to join their prominent cousin in Washington. Both girls had been polished and finished at the Albany Female Academy. If their minds had passed through this experience unmarred by serious thought, their manners had been highly refined. Like Julia before them, they too were ready for the final buffing a season in Washington could provide.[19]

Twenty-year-old Mary was the quieter and more reserved of the Shelter Island sisters. She was in love with and had half-promised herself to the man she would marry in 1847—Eben N. Horsford, from 1847 to 1863 Rumford Professor of the Application of Science to the Useful Arts at Harvard College. Awaiting his return from a trip to Germany, where he had gone to study chemistry, the patient Mary did not leap aboard the Washington marriage-go-round with the same abandon as her eighteen-year-old sister Phoebe. Mary was no wallflower. She was attractive, and she was open to a flirtatious exchange, but by and large she took Washington's fashionable young eligibles in stride while she pined for Horsford.[20]

Not so Phoebe. Phoebe liked boys—old boys, young boys, and boys in between, so long as they were taller than she and were competent dancers. She thought her sister a perfect dunce to sit around mooning and swooning for an absent man with whom she had no formal "understanding." A year earlier she had had a modest fling at young Horsford herself and the resulting "scandal" had rocked Shelter Island. News of it had spread into New York City, causing her alarmed father to assure the East Hampton branch of the family that "the report that Phoebe is engaged to Horsford or has countenanced his advances is without the least foundation." Shelter Island, it would appear, was not hard to rock.[21]

Phoebe was a delightful and engaging young lady, in temperament much like her cousin Julia. Robert Tyler called her "Phoebe the Coquette." She was vivacious, flirtatious, and bright. She danced beautifully, and she was always ready with a quick and clever retort. Privately, she liked to refer to herself as "The Poetess." This was a self-awarded title which grew out of the fact that in 1842 she had somehow won the annual poetry prize awarded by the Alumnae Association of the Albany Female Academy. Her effort was a 116-line nightmare titled "The Dream," which began:

> I looked into the miser's lonely lair,
> The yellow heaps were still secreted there;
> His icy hand, shriveled, and thin and old,
> Still clasped unconsciously the shining gold. . . .

What skill she lacked in writing verse was compensated for by her faculty for romance. Indeed, Phoebe Gardiner flirted so openly, captured beaux so easily, yet boasted of her emotional noninvolvement with men so convincingly, that Robert Tyler pictured her future as that of a shriveled old maid, despoiled of her charms by the passing years, while

> Silently she sips her tea
> Still boasting of her liberty.

Robert's prediction was almost correct. Phoebe did not marry until 1860, when she was thirty-four; then it was to her sister's widower, the same Professor Eben N. Horsford with whom she had flirted back in 1843.[22]

Phoebe had been a member of Julia's Court exactly one week when she received a proposal of marriage, a near-record for the Washington course. The eager suitor was Fayette McMullin of the Virginia state senate, a thirty-nine-year-old gentleman, later a United States representative from Marion, Virginia, and after that governor of the Washington Territory. McMullin was "desperately smitten" with Phoebe's "most interesting eyes." After a bare half-hour's conversation with her he *"offered himself in toto."* He apologized for such unseemly haste, but he explained to her that true Virginians always acted on heroic and hot-blooded impulse. Since he was leaving that very day for home, he begged Phoebe's permission to write her. Phoebe found him "very ordinary in his appearance" and gave him no encouragement. Tyler found the whole thing "exceedingly amusing," laughed heartily, and guessed it was just about "the speediest courtship on record." [23]

With the McMullin conquest safely behind her and with the collective romantic reputation of Julia's Court enhanced by its blinding speed and seriousness, "Phoebe the Coquette" turned her attention to a thirty-one-year-old congressman from Illinois—Judge Stephen A. Douglas. More accurately, Douglas turned his attention to Phoebe. He pursued her at various balls, receptions, and levees with such singleness of purpose that his campaign was remarked upon behind many a fluttering fan. Phoebe liked Douglas. She found him a fine and intelligent man, but she was convinced that he was much too short for her. He was just over five feet tall. Margaret assured her that it would "never do to be too fastidious for times 'isn't as they used to was'!" Margaret's analysis of the affair was that Douglas appeared "desperately smitten." She urged her flighty cousin to follow through toward something serious. But Phoebe considered "The Little Giant" too diminutive, and in spite of Margaret's continual goading that she could not expect "everything and ... might go a great deal farther and fare worse," she dropped Douglas and turned her charms on the President-elect's brother, Major William H. Polk of Tennessee. Douglas paired off with Miss Mary Corse of New York, and the Court soon learned that the New York belle, an old acquaintance of the Gardiners, was boasting of her "conquest, delighted beyond measure at having cut Phoebe out." [24]

The Polk interlude did not last long for Phoebe. The Major was in the capital only for a short visit while making arrangements for his brother's triumphal entry in late February. He too became interested in Mary Corse, the lady he subsequently married. When he left Washington in mid-January Margaret reported the entire Court dejected. "We are all in a terrible frustration here," she wrote Alexander. "Mary and I haint got no beaux at all. Mr. Polk has run off and left Phoebe brokenhearted and Mr. Cushing hasn't been heard of in two days. David hasn't found a mate—and something or another is the matter with John [Jr.] for he hasn't been seen for three days except at breakfast yesterday morning looking like a rowdy with Papa's wedding coat on." [25]

John Tyler, Jr., was involved at the time in the celebrated duel between Representatives William L. Yancy of Alabama and Thomas J. Clingman of North Carolina which briefly occupied the attention of official Washington and provided the ladies of the Court food for gossip. John's role was limited to carrying messages back and forth between the seconds, but in doing this he enjoyed acting in the most conspiratorial fashion. The duel was fortunately a bloodless fiasco, as inept in execution as it was foolish in origin. The principals spent most of their time eluding local police in their search for a peaceful spot in which to kill each other. The affair finally came off near Beltsville, Maryland. Each legislator fired one wild shot, no one was hit, and the seconds quickly stepped in and reconciled the dispute (which turned on an impugnation of personal honor). Both parties appeared satisfied with the result. John, Jr., thrived on excitement of this sort.[26]

Such excitement was denied well-bred ladies. For them it was beaux or nothing, and Margaret Gardiner lacked beaux. Charles Wilkins, son of the Secretary of War, flirted briefly with her but soon turned his attentions to Alice Tyler. Caleb Cushing was attentive, but he was "as awkward as ever" socially and in Margaret's view possessed "limited powers of gallantry." A Mr. Allen of Providence, Rhode Island, appeared briefly in her life. He was well-traveled and "positively worth over a hundred thousand dollars," but he and his checkbook soon departed the capital. For a short time a Mr. Piliot was "dead in love" with Margaret; this too came to nothing. "Never say die," Margaret sighed wearily. When Tyler impishly insisted that the ladies-in-waiting "must all be married this winter," Margaret laughingly retorted that she had settled upon the British Minister, the improbable Richard Pakenham, for her husband. "If you have fixed upon Pakenham," Alexander teased her, "don't fail to make sure of him!" [27]

Margaret would always have a problem with men. Her attitude toward them made it difficult for her to attract or hold them. She had a very quick sense of humor. More than that, she possessed a broad sense of the ridiculous which many potential suitors could not abide. She was too bright, too teasingly sarcastic, for most men. She enjoyed talking only with those "that have some sense," and this bias sharply reduced her choices. "I shall be very sure of what I am going to get before any engagement," she told Alexander, "and should advise you to do the same." Her standards in suitors were impossibly high. As she confided to Julia on one occasion, "After talking over the *supposition* of ... getting married I always conclude by saying nothing will satisfy [me] after having known the President!"[28]

Juliana's marital ambitions for her children were loftier than their own. Having married one daughter to the President of the United States, she became convinced that most of Margaret's beaux and all the young ladies in whom David Lyon and Alexander became interested were far beneath the new Gardiner norm. So insistently did she enforce her matrimonial views on her offspring that Alexander never married; Margaret finally married John H. Beeckman in 1848 over her mother's opposition (Juliana had talked her out of two better prospects); and David Lyon waited until 1860, when he was forty-three, to marry his distant cousin Sarah Gardiner Thompson, a New York lady of solid wealth and respectable blood line. Had Juliana had her way, David Lyon would not have married at all. Indeed, her possessiveness toward her children, her strong desire to keep them at her side and under perpetual maternal discipline, bordered on the compulsive.

Julia agreed with her mother's hymeneal standards. "I should like to see David married to a *rich*, pretty, fashionable girl," she remarked in December 1844. "But I don't know where except in the land of the Imagination he will win them all combined. The first essential would do better without the two last than the two last without the first— don't you think so for David?" David Lyon never discovered the elusive "land of Imagination." When he finally picked his wife he settled for wealth, "the first essential." Similarly, when Alexander evidenced a passing urge to wed in 1844–1845, Margaret joined with Julia and Juliana to ridicule his taste in women and suggest that he speedily get over such an absurd notion as matrimony. He got over it.[29]

Understandably, then, David Lyon's flirtations in Washington during his sister's reign were foredoomed to failure. A passing interest in the wealthy Miss Becky Delancy of nearby Alexandria ended quickly when Margaret pronounced her "short and not pretty" and criticized her tardiness in presenting herself "at Court." Alexander felt, however, that "if David does not better himself among the ladies now that he has every opportunity and ... leave no stone unturned to secure Miss Delancy I shall give him up. The golden moment is passing...." David Lyon admitted that young Becky was "not at all handsome," but he thought her reputed wealth of five millon dollars "very magnificent." He told Alexander that he had "promised Julia $100,000" if he were successful in his suit. Julia never collected. Becky had but one of the three essentials the First Lady and her watchdog mother deemed necessary in a wife, and that was that.[30]

Nannie Wickliffe, daughter of the Postmaster General, "made quite an impression" on David. She was pretty, fashionable enough, and she had been a maid of honor at Julia's wedding. Unfortunately she was penniless. Thus when David "began very seriously to comment upon her numerous attractions," his mother cut him off with one curt observation:

"She has no money."

"Pooh! I've got enough," replied the Colonel, with an unconvincing show of independence. But Mother had spoken and that was the end of the impoverished Nannie.[31]

David Lyon's interest in Mary Corse was also of brief duration, although he rushed her with considerable intensity during the season. Julia admitted that Miss Corse had a "passion for David" and that there was a certain "respectability in her Quakership." She certainly had numerous beaux and "numberless conquests." Even Uncle Samuel pronounced her "very rich," and he was something of an expert on such matters. She attracted the romantic attentions of both Stephen A. Douglas and Major William H. Polk ("on account of her money," said Margaret cattily). It was too bad that she had one of those faces for which the hands of time stand still. "Miss Corse will *never never* do," Margaret informed Alexander. "She is without exception the ugliest person I almost ever saw—a hundred thousand [dollars] could not cure it." Juliana thought her appearance quite "ordinary," and David himself admitted that his lady love was indeed *"very* plain looking." Exit Mary Corse.[32]

Miss Lucy Henderson, Miss Mary Wright, and Miss Caroline Bayard (daughter of the Senator from Delaware) all walked into and out of David Lyon's life that season in Washington. Invariably, something was found to be wrong with each of them, and David always deferred to the superior judgment of his mother and his sisters in matters concerning his romantic life. Juliana frequently reminded him that the basis for a suitable marriage, like Rome, was "not built in a day." She thought it wise that he remain a "general beau" for the duration of the White House reign. As she explained her reasoning to Alexander, "The more I see of Washington the more convinced I am that it is not all gold that glitters." Juliana was fearful that fashionable Washington was cluttered with chunks of iron pyrite, and she wanted no Gardiner stuck with inferior ore. "David has not found a mate yet," Margaret reported regularly. The whole family could laugh, however, over the rumor circulating in the capital in January 1845 that David Lyon and Alice Tyler were to be married within three weeks. That combination was simply ludicrous.[33]

Measured by sheer numbers of beaux and marriage proposals, Alice Tyler was the undisputed romantic champion of Julia's Court. At one levee she managed to collect six attentive escorts, and when the season was over she received three solid marriage offers, all of which she turned down. As Phoebe later remarked, with some show of jealousy, "After all we said of her unpleasing appearance she seems to have had more hearts than any of us at her control." Alice was not pretty, it is true. David Lyon found her "tall and fat." But her height permitted her to wear her clothes well, and both Julia and Margaret thought she generally made a fine appearance. Juliana counted her "exceedingly handsome." That her popularity was enhanced in some measure by her father's political position might be assumed.[34]

Alice posed a distinct personal problem for Julia. The First Lady was only six years older than her stepdaughter, and at first Julia did not know quite what their relationship should be. Her first instinct was to pack Alice off to school in Williamsburg and postpone the question until the few months of her reign had run out. Accordingly, Alice left for Virginia in early November. But her letters to her stepmother were so flattering to Julia, her desire to be friendly so apparent, that the First Lady relented and permitted Alice to return to the capital for the season. Juliana pointed out to her daughter that Alice had had "much reason to feel neglected" since the wedding. While she could see that Alice's presence in the White House "may be trying," she urged Julia to regard the President's daughter as a "companion" and be as "amiable" to her as possible. It was good advice. Not only did stepmother and stepdaughter begin to get along better together, but Alice contributed much to the gaiety of the Court.[35]

Alice Tyler spent most of her waking hours during Julia's reign trying to capture the affections of Charles Wilkins, son of the Secretary of War—and escape the attentions of the forty-four-year-old Caleb Cushing. Cushing, a widower since 1832, was very much in the marriage market after his return from China in December 1844. A distinguished linguist, legislator, diplomat and lawyer, member of Tyler's ill-fated Corporal's Guard, he was a suitable enough escort when one of the ladies-in-waiting needed a beau on short notice, but he was generally considered by all of them awkward, tongue-tied, and a bore. Alice had a difficult task avoiding him as she maneuvered for Wilkins. She had suitors other than Wilkins, to be sure, but she always came back to her "Charlie." Margaret allowed that Alice was "desperately in love" with young Wilkins, and had eyes for no one else "while Charlie is near her." The romance even continued for a time after Alice returned to Sherwood Forest. It finally sputtered out in late 1845 under the dual impact of the nearby William and Mary boys and the truism of "out of sight, out of mind." [36]

There were too many young girls in the White House and too much frivolity and noise there to suit Juliana. From the moment she arrived in Washington in early January she began anticipating her return to her quiet home on Lafayette Place. The recurrent migraine headaches bothered her terribly throughout her stay; she became cranky and short-tempered. Unimpressed by Washington society, she mixed in it as little as was politely possible. She was determined to remain above it. She was convinced, as she told Alexander, that Washington was "vastly inferior to New York in point of wealth. All agree that very little wealth exists here." The capital, she felt, was just not worth conquering. So Juliana McLachlan Gardiner kept to a large chair by the fire in her room all day while the din of the young people crashed around her throbbing temples. Although she was only forty-five, in many ways she was already becoming an old woman. She was certainly able to exercise no control over the high-spirited girls who raced through the rooms of the White House with such a fearful clatter. They enjoyed playing a noisy tag game which involved chasing "each other all day with red hot pokers, and as if that were not enough [then] throw the poker stands." In the middle of all the confusion would be Margaret, egging the others on, shouting such atrocious puns as "Phoebe has had the grandest *Polk* of all—Alice rejects the *pokes* and reclines on *Cushings!*" On more than one occasion the First Lady was forced to break off her letter-writing because "my room is quite too noisy with the many sallies of my little court to admit of my continuing further." [37]

Juliana simply could not tolerate the confusion, turmoil, giggling, and nonsense generated by four energetic young women, and she withdrew from it all. When she was not secluded in her chamber reading her Bible (she was convinced such devotion gave one "a very great advantage in society"), she was nagging Alexander by mail about losing his purse or hanging up his clothes properly. "You see I think you require a few cautions," she told him. To her, he was still a little boy. She did enjoy the occasional White House visits of a mesmerizer who was invited in to amuse and hypnotize the girls. This, at least, was a quiet activity. Juliana had a genuine interest in spiritualism, which she equated with dreams, hypnosis, unexplained noises, and other peculiarities on the fringe of the occult. Still, there was too much noise and excitement in the White House for her, and her forehead pounded in protest.[38]

On New Year's Day, her Court assembled, the duties and stations of each member assigned, Julia gave her first large public reception at the White House. The rooms were packed that afternoon. "It was indeed a glorious assemblage," exulted Margaret, "and all acknowledged with *tongues* and *eyes* that such a court and such a crowd was never before seen within the walls of the White House.... After the shaking of hands was over, the President and Julia made two circuits around the East Room followed by her maids of honor, the crowd gaping and pushing to see the show.... Mama did not go down but gazed at the multitude with wonder from the upper rooms." Julia was indeed at her regal best; so much so that "Judge McLean looked all sorts of ways at Julia ... and made the P[resident] as jealous as you please." As for Justice McLean, Mary Gardiner thought him "the handsomest man she ever laid eyes upon." Mary and Phoebe were understandably ecstatic over the opulence of Julia's display. It was, after all, a bit more stimulating than family teas on Shelter Island.[39]

The New York *Herald* correspondent naturally pronounced it a glorious success. "Well," wrote F. W. Thomas, "President Tyler will go out of the White House with drums beating and colors flying." He described Julia's Court as "very comely to look upon, indeed; an irresistible bodyguard of modesty and beauty." But for Julia herself Thomas pulled out all stops. She appeared

beautiful, winning, as rosy as a summer's morning on the mountains of Mexico, as admirable as Victoria, but far more beautiful, and younger, and more intelligent, and more Republican, and quite as popular with the people ... does John Tyler possess that ancient relic of fairyland, the lamp of Aladdin ... that such a spirit of youth, and poetry, and love, and tenderness, and riches, and celebrity, and modesty, and everything that is charming, should come forth as at his wish and stand at his side, the guardian angel of the evening of his days? ... John Tyler is no fool, and his selection of a bride clenches our assertions.[40]

The reception lasted from noon until midafternoon. If there was an element of failure in Julia's first major effort, it was because the Whig community in the capital studiously elected not to be present, repairing instead to a competing reception at the home of John Quincy Adams. It was probably just as well. There were more than two thousand people present without them. The Mansion became so crowded that the *Herald* commented in brisk doggerel:

> I beg your pardon, General G.,
> For trampling on your toes;
> And, Lady T., I did not see,
> My hat against your nose;
> And Holy Jesus! how they squeeze us,
> To that small room, where he,
> Old John, attends to greet his friends,
> This New Year's Day levee....
>
> And round and round,
> We wound and wound,
> Among the radiant belles,
> And high and low subordinates,
> And plain and fancy swells.
> And every soul did seem perplexed,
> And vexed as much as we,
> That the music of the red-coat band,
> And a single grip of Tyler's hand
> And a squeeze in the crowd,

And a place to stand,
For the best grin that you could command,
For the ladies' smiles so warm and bland,
And a stare at the would-be great and grand,
And a sigh and a look-out for the land,
Made up old John's levee....

Well done, Old Veto, after all,
And to his winsome wife;
But few responsibilities,
And a long and loving life.
God bless our land—land of the brave,
The beautiful and free;
But if next New Year, Uncle Sam
Don't treat his friends to something jam,
A bit to eat, and a genteel dram,
We would not give a Cape Cod clam,
Or a single continental damn
For the President's levee.[41]

It was an impressive beginning for the First Lady. Perhaps too impressive, for a week later at a private White House ball she smugly limited the guest list so severely that all present complained that the function was "unnecessarily select." (Her mother disagreed. She thought it "unusually pleasant" because it was so quiet and "select.") Nor did Julia's stunning appearance that evening entirely rescue the affair. She was dressed in black embroidered lace over white satin, set off with black and silver trim, and "a whole set of diamonds." A backwoods congressman from Ohio was literally transfixed at the sight of her. He stood, stared dumbly at her for several minutes, and finally exclaimed, "Well, now I'll go home and tell all about her." To be sure, there was nothing like Julia in Columbus.[42]

Whether it was unnecessarily select or not, the ball produced some useful gossip and information. The First Lady was relieved to learn from Mrs. Calhoun that widower Francis Pickens was being married in Charleston that very evening to Marion Antoinette Dearing, a lady who possessed "every advantage of beauty, fortune, family and piety, besides resembling very much his first wife." Tyler still showed evidences of jealousy over his wife's former suitors, and from Julia's standpoint the sooner they were all safely married off, the better. For the First Lady the evening was a success in one respect: McLean did not flirt with her, Pickens was being married, "Old Davis" was not present, Waldron was at sea, and John Tyler was happy.[43]

Like every aspiring and hardworking hostess, Julia had her failures. A White House dinner on January 10 was certainly in this category. The affair was designed to honor the justices of the Supreme Court and their ladies. An orchestra was engaged and invitations already extended when Julia learned to her chagrin that the Attorney General had scheduled a dinner for the same evening and had earlier invited more than half the First Lady's proposed guest list. Julia promptly extended her rival an invitation, "a hint... [that] he ought to yield to higher authority." Unhappily, the Nelsons did not take the hint. They returned their regrets ("either from ignorance or obstinacy," said Margaret), and their own dinner went off as planned. Tyler thought the Attorney General and Mrs. Nelson "extremely unmannerly." Julia was forced "to fill up the vacant seats with Senators and *visiting strangers*." It was a flop.[44]

Saturday, of course, was her regular reception day, and Julia could be much more certain of her arrangements on these occasions. The First Lady, or "Lady Presidentress" as Thomas of the *Herald* sometimes called her, was generally attended at these functions by six to twelve maids of honor all dressed alike in white. These vestal virgins included the members of her Court and other young ladies of good family drafted for the weekly spectacle. Julia stationed them beside and slightly behind her in matching banks. Then the Queen seated herself in front center on the raised platform. Wearing a headdress "formed of bugles and resembling a crown," she received such guests, friends, and tourists who chose to appear, file by, and pay their respects. Tuileries on the Potomac.[45]

By mid-January 1845, after various experiments, Julia had at last trained, composed, and deployed her Court as she thought eminently proper. She was now ready to exhibit the finished product at every opportunity. "I determined upon, and I think I have succeeded," she proudly told Mary Hedges, an old East Hampton friend, "in making my Court interesting in youth and beauty.... Wherever I go they form my train and their interest in the society which surrounds gives it an additional charm for me." At the public levee on January 21 she "upset all the forms" followed by previous First Ladies by ranging her entourage in a line along the Blue Room wall opposite the fireplace. This removed Tyler from the exposed center of the room and placed him at the head of a formal receiving line. "As each were [*sic*] introduced," Margaret explained, "they fell back facing us until we could see a crowd of admiring faces." It worked quite well.[46]

The President was in an exceptionally good mood on the evening of January 21. The Texas Resolution was moving along well in the House, and its prospects in the Senate gave him hope that annexation might be consummated before the session terminated. In addition, the "fine appearance of his family put him in excellent spirits." Many of the guests commented on his youthful appearance and relaxed mien. Margaret thought he looked "uncommonly handsome... better than I ever saw him." John Tyler was undoubtedly feeling mellow and self-satisfied as he contemplated his escape from the burdens of his office and his retirement to Sherwood Forest with his beautiful bride. And Julia, as usual, looked superb. She was wearing a new white satin dress overlaid with white lace, a white satin headdress with three white ostrich feathers, and her set of diamonds. "She did not look as if she belonged to this Earth," said Margaret breathlessly. All eyes were fixed on her. She was "perfectly splendid," and Tyler was so proud of her he nearly burst with delight.

The President was in ecstasies and in the fullness of his heart exclaimed to David, "How glad I am Judge McLean is not here tonight!" You can't imagine half how jealous he is of him—and actually made her stay home from Church Sunday afternoon because the Judge looked at her in the morning.

All the young ladies of the Court had admiring beaux, and all "received compliments flattering enough to make *ordinary* people vain." The red-coated Marine Band played polkas and waltzes. It was a gala evening. Julia immodestly pronounced it "dazzling," and called attention to "the lights, the beautiful faces, the court dresses of the foreign Ministers and the showy uniforms of the army and navy officers . . . delight seemed to pervade the rooms." [47]

Nor did the First Lady abandon her regal attitude when she left the White House to attend the parties around the capital that her opulent example at the White House had stimulated in conspicuous profusion. "Washington was never before so gay," said an exhausted Margaret; "two or three parties every night." If Julia arrived too late at these affairs to open the dancing, she declined to dance at all because "the ball had already been *opened*." The Continental forms were to be observed at all times. To these affairs away from the White House the First Lady transported her entire Court, and she bade them stay grouped about her during the evening. Her dress invariably occasioned much favorable comment.[48]

Following her triumphal levee of January 21, a success repeated with equal brilliance and éclat on February 4 and again on February 11, Julia began to consider and plan her final party—an affair so large and splendid it would leave Washington limp. She was determined to give "one grand affair"—one last magnificent fling before retiring to the bucolic pleasures of Sherwood Forest. In mid-January the preliminary planning for her swan song was well under way. It was important to her that her entire family be present. Alexander was encouraged to abandon his Customs House and Tammany intrigues for a few days and come to Washington for the event.[49]

Julia was thus pondering the timing and arrangements of her final levee when the President received the exciting news from New York that Robert and Alexander had forced strong pro-Texas annexation resolutions through Tammany Hall, an act which enhanced the political prospects of Tyler's great scheme. To Alexander Gardiner there were many things more important to do in January 1845 than dress up in white satin, diamonds, and ostrich feathers and dance the polka:

> For the last four or five nights I have had little rest [he wrote Tyler at midnight on January 24]: tonight I want not. We have had as glorious a triumph as was ever witnessed within the walls of Old Tammany. We put down triumphantly all luke warm resolutions, and all resolutions extraneous to the immediate subject and carried unanimously two in substitution which I enclose. Robert acquitted himself nobly well.... Van Buren's name was received with hisses and groans, in the very Hall of the Regency.... My part was probably prominent enough to lead to some public comment.... I enclose all our resolutions.... They were printed and distributed among our friends some hours before the meeting.[50]

Buoyed by Alexander's encouraging report from New York, reasonably sure now that Texas annexation would likely crown the political achievements of her husband's administration, Julia doubled her efforts on the social front. She selected Wednesday, February 18, as the date for her final ball. She was resolved that social Washington would never forget her or the Tyler tenure in the White House. For weeks the detailed planning proceeded apace, every member of the Court eagerly participating in the arrangements. Margaret was put to work compiling a guest list which came to number over two thousand. Hundreds of letters were dispatched to prominent Virginia and New York families requesting their presence. Close friends were asked to suggest the names of people in or near the capital who might reasonably be invited. In her laborious clerical task Margaret was assisted by F. W. Thomas. Margaret, in effect, became the First Lady's social secretary, carefully hand-copying each of the numerous invitations that went out. This employment of Margaret's chirographic skills was a tactical insight of the highest order, since Julia's own handwriting was so poor it was often illegible. (In fear that his wife would never learn to write properly, Tyler procured O. B. Goldsmith's text *Gems of Penmanship* for her, but Julia still failed the course.) Margaret's hand was clear and strong, and the invitations from her quill were duly delivered.[51]

Julia was disappointed that Alexander saw fit to remain in New York on the night of the ball. He was too busy with Texas and Tylerite politics, he said, to waste several days in the capital just then. He would arrive later, when the Texas Resolution was approaching its moment of truth in the Senate. But Samuel Gardiner arrived from distant Shelter Island to witness daughters Mary and Phoebe in their final White House action. And Juliana, who sorely wished to return to Lafayette Place, was persuaded to stay over until after the ball. She was not in the mood for much more frivolity and she had already made up her mind that she would not have a good time at her daughter's gala function. Not surprisingly, she had a wretched time. "I must confess it did not dazzle me," she later told Julia. Last-minute orders for lace and jewelry were sped northward to Alexander as the Court prepared for the coming jubilation. "Your ball to be is all the talk," Thomas informed Julia, "and ... many beautiful things said of the Lady Presidentress." [52]

The ball was a great success, although the irascible Juliana thought the assemblage "very republican." The fact that it was packed with officers, foreign diplomats, high government officials, and representatives of the fashionable set from Boston to Charleston did not impress her. She allowed only that it was "no doubt as select as so great a concourse would admit." Personally, she preferred "a few choice congenial spirits" to the mob that descended on the White House on February 18. With this judgment Margaret demurred. "Those 'congenial spirits,' where are they to be found?" she wondered. "No! no! I quite agree with you," she assured Julia, "the *grand* or nothing." [53]

Grand it was. Two thousand were invited; three thousand came. "We were," said Margaret, "as thick as sheep in a pen." A hundred additional lights were hung in the East Room, bringing to over six hundred the flickering candles which expensively illuminated the four rooms used for dancing and promenading. "The President reckons the cost at 350 dollars which ... is no trifling sum," Margaret confessed. A Marine band in scarlet uniforms supplied the music for waltzes, polkas, and cotillions. Margaret herself arranged the buffet supper and immodestly admitted that it was "superb ... wine and champagne flowed like water—eight dozen bottles of champagne were drunk with wine by the *barrels*."

Julia "opened" the ball with Secretary of War William Wilkins, then danced with the Postmaster General and Calderón de la Barca, the Spanish ambassador. Later in the evening the First Lady and the beautiful Madame Bodisco attracted great attention when they joined in a cotillion with the ambassadors from Austria, Prussia, France, and Russia. They were, said Thomas of the *Herald,* "two of the most beautiful women of that vast assemblage." As usual, Julia was magnificently clad in a "white satin underdress embroidered with silver with bodice en sailé and over that a white [cape] looped up all around with white roses and buds—white satin headdress hat embroidered with silver with three ostrich feathers and full set of diamonds."

The President, Julia, and the Court received their guests in the Blue Room. They were "arranged as usual along the side of the circular room and everyone was struck with the beautiful appearance of the Court." At 10 P.M. supper was announced, and "such a rush, crush and smash to obtain entrance was never seen before at a Presidential entertainment." But in all the confusion near the tables "only *two* glasses were broken," said Margaret, priding herself on her scientific deployment of the food and wine. Observed immersed in the human tide moving inexorably toward the meat and drink, trying to preserve some semblance of military dignity in the process, were General Winfield Scott, Commodore Charles Stewart, General Mirabeau B. Lamar, lately President of the Texas Republic, and Commodore Edwin Ward Moore, Chief of the Texas Navy. It was a rough voyage to the wine barrels. The tables were emptied and refilled many times, but "by due diligence and perseverance all were provided with the luxuries that flowed in abundance." Congratulated on the success of the affair, the President merely laughed and replied, "Yes, they cannot say now that I am *a President without a party!*"

The President-elect and Sarah Polk had been invited cordially but made no appearance. This was both a "surprise" and a disappointment to Tyler and his family. Mrs. Polk's announced "indisposition," Margaret felt, was little more than an attack of virulent Van Burenism brought on by pressure from Francis P. Blair and the Washington *Globe* clique. Vice-President-elect George M. Dallas was on hand, however. Not so the capital's prominent Whigs. With the exception of Maryland Senator William D. Merrick, whose son William Matthew had recently married Mary Wickliffe, few Whig politicians chose to attend. "They won't make up with Captain Tyler no how at all," explained Thomas. Their absence did not ruin the evening for Julia and her Court. The young ladies had beaux enough to staff a dozen balls, and a few hundred more guests would have collapsed the walls of the White House. "All acknowledge," concluded Margaret without exaggeration, "that nothing half so grand had been seen at the White House during any Administration, and fear nothing so tasteful would be again." It marked, agreed the *Herald,* "an era in Washington society." [54]

Thomas gave Julia a good press on her final social effort, but his kind treatment paled in comparison with the piece Alexander penned for the New York *Plebeian*. Working from notes supplied him by his sisters, he wrote a long "eyewitness" account (anonymously, of course) titled "Mrs. Tyler's Farewell Ball, or *Sic Transit Gloria Mundi*":

Whatever may be said of him, John Tyler always discharged the duties of such occasions with high bred propriety, and never was the dignity and urbanity of his manners more conspicuous. As to his beautiful bride, whom I a stranger saw from time to time in foreign parts, I can scarcely trust my pen to write of her. Burke apostropitized [*sic*] the Queen of France, whom he saw "just above the horizon"; but I have seen this lady above many horizons.... Tonight she looked like Juno and with her sister, cousins and Miss Alice Tyler constituted a galaxy of beauty, and I am told equal talent, which no Court of Europe could equal.... More diamonds sparkled than I have ever seen on any occasion in this country....[55]

Thanks to the cooperation of the *Herald,* the *Madisonian,* and the *Plebeian,* Julia's farewell ball attracted national interest and attention. Perhaps too much. Ten months later Tyler was still answering the criticisms of various prohibitionist Protestant churchmen who complained about the flow of spirits at Julia's farewell salute, the evil dancing that had taken place there, and the fact that the First Lady had sponsored such a conspicuous fling less than a year after her father's death. In a polite way, John Tyler properly told them all to go to the devil. Julia went out in a blaze of glory, in "a flood of light" shed by "a thousand candles from the immense chandeliers" of the East Room, and that was what counted even though the additional illumination had cost $350. To John Tyler, the success of his wife's last entertainment was almost as important as the achievement of his Texas dream two weeks later.[56]

~ 11 ~

ALEXANDER GARDINER:
SAG HARBOR TO THE RIO GRANDE

I am ready for any or all enterprises in love, politics, or business!
—ALEXANDER GARDINER, SEPTEMBER 1844

Julia flourished in a world of social display, glamorous gowns, personal flattery, and studied deference to rank. Her brother Alexander thrived in an environment of seedy politicians selling and reselling their political virtue. He understood that a few well-placed postmasters could be more valuable to a President than a dozen white-clad vestal virgins perched on a dais at a White House reception; he considered patronage more important than the polka. And if Julia labored to give "the President without a party" the kind of party her February 18 display had been, Alexander worked to give him a real political organization. Together, brother and sister, each in his own way, battled to give John Tyler the annexation of Texas—Julia from her ballroom and dinner table station on the Potomac firing line; Alexander from his Tammany foxhole in New York. None of the Gardiners wanted Tyler to "retire ignominiously nor be soon forgotten." His fame was their fame.

Alexander began combat anew in November 1844, convinced that John Tyler's role in the 1844 campaign had been the decisive one; that Polk owed Tyler his victory; and that a future Tyler-Polk alignment in New York might be used to contain the political aggression of the Albany Regency. The Van Buren Regency's antagonism to Texas annexation on antislavery grounds was opposition to a project Alexander considered vital to the nation's growth and welfare, important to the historical prestige of the outgoing administration, and material to the psychological well-being of his brother-in-law. He was certain, therefore, that if Tammany Hall could be induced to support Texas annexation the resulting political backlash would weaken the Van Buren-Silas Wright faction in New York and go far toward insuring the passage of the joint resolution in Congress. This analysis was correct. The way to seduce Tammany, of course, was through patronage favors; the old streetwalker was always willing. It was imperative also that Texas annexation be consummated before Tyler left the White House.

Alexander believed further that a separate Tyler political faction should be continued in existence in New York City. To be sure, the Tylerites had thrown their strength and their dry-dock jobs into the Polk candidacy after the President's withdrawal from the race in August. But one never knew to what extent a Polk administration would be impressed by these sacrificial oblations a year hence. Alexander was not certain that the recent Tyler-Polk alliance, insofar as patronage distribution was involved, could withstand the multiple pressures that would surely be brought to bear on Polk once he took office in March. To retain a Tyler faction within a larger Tyler-Polk anti-Regency alliance in New York seemed both prudent and foresighted. Such a faction might later be used as an anti-proscription lever in the Empire State. More important, a Tyler group could serve as a political enclave in New York if Tyler decided to make a try for the Presidency in his own right in 1848. As Alexander Gardiner thus evaluated the situation, it was obvious that men who were strongly pro-Tyler yet acceptable to Polk, men who favored Texas annexation and distrusted the Albany Regency, should be stuffed into as many key public offices in New York City as possible before March 4, 1845. Among these right-thinking citizens he naturally numbered himself, since only from such a vantage point could he maintain liaison with the Tyler faction in the city and help manipulate the terms of its continuing alliance there with the Polkites.

That this political analysis by young Gardiner seems hopelessly unrealistic in retrospect is not the point. In spite of the essential weakness of the Tylerites in New York vis-à-vis both the Polk and Van Buren factions, both Robert Tyler and Alexander Gardiner thought the scheme worth a try. Tyler himself went along with his son and his brother-in-law in the matter, although without anything approaching their excited optimism. Ultimately, the whole family joined in the design to maintain a Tyler faction in New York and use it to keep Polk honest on his pre-election patronage promises to Tyler. It was vital too to hold Polk to the Texas-annexation plank of the Democratic platform. Julia, Margaret, David Lyon, and Juliana all actively involved themselves in the patronage questions that arose. They also served as a post-election family lobby for "Tyler and Texas."

Within the family circle, Alexander was the ringmaster and disciplinarian. In his capacity as family politician extraordinary he objected to the levity of Julia's reign. He was dismayed by the numerous petty demands for dresses, laces, hats, yard goods, medicines, and garters that came from Washington in his sisters' letters. He complained that his communications to the White House concerning New York political affairs received inadequate attention, although he knew them to be "of more consequence than the purchase of hats and dresses." At times he thought Julia's regal approach to her duties "a little too dignified" and aloof. He urged her to mix more with the bread-and-butter politicians. At the same time, however, he sacrificed his private life to the Tyler cause so completely that Margaret chided him for being coldly "businesslike" in his relations with the ladies. "We live on hope [of love] and die fasting," she teased him, "and you live on Politics." Julia also thought him much too "full of business and politics." It distressed her that during his "flying visits" to Washington in mid-November 1844 and again for the White House levee of February 4, 1845, he spent all his time talking patronage. His refusal to attend Julia's February 18 farewell ball was bad enough. But his imperious demands for inside political information became tiresome to the White House ladies. "My goodness," exclaimed Juliana in reply to one of Alexander's impatient, fact-finding letters from New York, "we wish so much to tell you some news of importance, but we ladies know nothing politically unless canvassed before us." Actually, the ladies knew a great deal.[1]

Alexander's political activity and his narrow dedication to Tyler's career turned principally on his belief that the President should burn no political bridges behind him in his retirement from Washington to Sherwood Forest. On the contrary, he felt that Tyler should remain available and open to the possibility of the Democratic nomination in 1848. The convention might deadlock and lead to Tyler's nomination as a compromise candidate. There was always the possibility that middle-of-the-roadism would again be popular in the Democracy. And with the sensational Texas achievement behind the outgoing administration, lightning might well strike in Tyler's direction once more.

In spite of the President's desire to retire to the peace and quiet of Sherwood Forest with his young bride, there are several indications that he accepted Alexander's advice on remaining "available" for 1848. Having been constantly in public service since 1811, it was difficult for him to imagine life without public office. The call to political battle never left him unmoved. As late as 1860 he was actively pursuing the Democratic nomination. Indeed, when summoned again in April 1861, Tyler, at seventy-one, emerged from retirement and was elected to the Confederate Congress. He was a professional politician and remained one all his life. Thus his remark to Nathaniel P. Tallmadge in November 1844 that he had been "so rudely buffeted by the waves of Party politics for nearly four years past that I sigh for the quiet of my country residence" was a passing attitude built on temporary fatigue, not on an irrevocable decision to resign forever from the political process. More revealing was his statement to Margaret in July 1844, on the eve of his withdrawal from the Presidential canvass, about his "cherished hope of returning to the White House in '48." After the election he told Alexander confidently that the Polk and Van Buren factions of the Democracy would surely kill one another off in patronage struggles and that sooner or later "the country will look to a third person for peace" and he was quite willing to feed this factional fire to advance his own future political fortunes. By December 1844 Margaret was again alerting the family to Tyler's "political hopes for the future." And within a few months after his retirement to Sherwood Forest he was secretly at work trying to reorganize the old Tyler group in New Jersey. Thus when the New York *Herald* charged in March 1845 that "bargaining, and jobbing and corruption of the most flagrant character" had attended the filling of offices in New York City in the last months of the Tyler administration, and that this was designed "to make political capital for 1848," it came closer to the truth than it realized.[2]

With one eye on Tammany and the fate of the Texas Resolutions pending in Congress and the other on Tyler's political prospects in 1848, Alexander Gardiner returned to the odious New York City patronage business with undisguised enthusiasm. Soon after the election returns were in and it was certain that Polk had carried New York City and the Empire State, however small the margin, Alexander hastened to Washington for political consultations with Tyler. Returning to New York on November 20, he sent the President a summary of their conversations and a detailed patronage analysis of the local situation. "It is absolutely necessary," he concluded, "if we should retain our strength here in opposition to the Van Buren faction that the most important places should be filled by persons of sufficient insight to hold them hereafter." He suggested that District Attorney Hoffman, Surveyor of the Port Fowler, and U.S. Marshal Stilwell, among others, all be replaced with solid Tyler men acceptable to Polk. While these men had all supported Tyler in 1844, Alexander considered them too opportunistic and self-serving for the severe and perhaps discouraging trials that lay ahead. Further, they had all initially been appointees of the old Curtis regime in the Customs House. Gardiner urged the White House that the new appointments "be made immediately," and that there be no bargaining in New York with any faction but Polk's. It was also his view that "the prominent Judges of this state are very generally friendly ... one or more of them should be drawn out from the Bench into the field of active politics." Specifically, he seconded Robert Tyler's suggestion that Tyler kick Cornelius P. Van Ness upstairs to the United

States Supreme Court and make ex-Governor William C. Bouck Collector of the Port in his stead. The Conservative Democrat Bouck, he thought, was "doubtless a friend and it is desirable to keep him in position." Another possibility was to elevate New York Supreme Court Justice Samuel Nelson to the national Supreme Court, a promotion which would produce "much local satisfaction" in the city. Alexander also suggested that Tyler appoint Ely Moore to office. Moore, a former leader in the old Workingmen's Party in the 1830s, had anti-abolitionist and other Conservative Democratic views acceptable to the Tylerites. That he was a friend of Polk was an additional factor in his favor. By and large, Tyler agreed with his brother-in-law's wide-ranging analysis. He too saw the possibility and advantages of building a bloc of Tylerite Conservative Democrats in New York. He differed with Alexander only on specific names for specific jobs.[3]

Working with Robert Tyler and Collector Van Ness, Alexander made ready in late November to fill all available New York City offices with "persons of sufficient insight." As he evaluated the strength of the "various cliques" in Tammany and considered how each might react to given appointments, he began to suspect that Van Ness was not handling the purge and patronage front in the city with sufficient dash and decisiveness. He felt that the Collector was unduly nervous about Senate confirmation of his own interim appointment and that his anxiety in the matter had "somewhat deranged him." Alexander confided to the President his concern that the frightened Van Ness had "made but one appointment at my instigation." He could only hope that when the Collector's appointment was approved by the Senate "something better" would turn up. The longer he evaluated the New York scene the more convinced he became that the Tylerites there were "strongly established among the people and want only men of weight of character as leaders." It was vital, therefore, to get such men into office as quickly as possible.[4]

Throughout Alexander's correspondence and conversations with the President on patronage matters, Julia acted as intermediary. She relayed names, jobs, and patronage decisions back and forth between New York and the White House. Often she made clear her personal preferences. In this activity she was assisted by Margaret and by her mother, although Juliana's suggestions for specific appointments were usually worthless, too frequently guided by emotion. She realized, of course, that the President could not find appointments for "all his or your [Julia's] good friends," even though they were *"good democrats."* Yet she hoped a Supreme Court post could be found for her friend Judge Ogden Edwards because he was "very poor and I am sorry for it. I wish he might be relieved in some way. Oh! this poverty and pride is a trying thing indeed." Such economic considerations did not trouble Alexander. His viewpoint was much more businesslike and realistic than his mother's. Rich or poor, the prospective appointee had to be able to help Tyler and to have some reasonable chance of Senate approval. For this latter reason Alexander instructed Julia "to make as many friends as possible among the Senators" and gave her detailed advice on what politicians in Washington were worth cultivating socially and which ones were not.[5]

Julia's own analysis of the patronage process was not particularly complicated. Shortly after she returned from her honeymoon in Virginia she had been admonished by Margaret with the observation that the family had "not heard of any gifts of offices from you and I fear the time will slip by unheeded ... [and] you will not be able to look back with the satisfaction of having made a single person happy or grateful. You do not seem anxious to exhibit your power...." To make people happy and grateful, and to demonstrate that she did have power over her husband, the decisive influence that stems from the boudoir, Julia waded briskly into the patronage pool. She was not always sure of the more subtle political implications of her various recommendations, but what she lacked in cloak-and-dagger sophistication she made up for in enthusiasm. "I will make as many friends *as I can* among the Senators," she assured her brother.[6]

Armed with Tyler's support and Julia's assistance, Alexander began the task of creating a permanent Tyler faction in New York City. The Brooklyn postmastership, he told the President, should go to his Uncle Nathaniel Gardiner. "For political reasons, it is essential that we should have a Post officer beyond peradventure in this vicinity for the next four years...." Nathaniel Gardiner was certainly "beyond peradventure," as were several other men Alexander suggested for the job. But Tyler felt that Polk should have a free hand on the Brooklyn appointment, if for no other reason than to induce a fight there between the Van Buren and Polk factions.[7]

By December 1844 Alexander was managing all patronage appointments, removals, and forced resignations for the Tyler administration in Suffolk County. In addition, his iron hand, ill camouflaged by velvet glove, was involved in so much patronage dispensation in Brooklyn and New York that the Whig *Courier and Enquirer* bitterly compared him with Robert Tyler, long accused by the Whigs of exercising the real power behind his father's tottering throne:

Mr. Tyler's brother-in-law ... seems desirous to become a second Robert: he is endeavoring to distinguish himself in the manner the latter young gentleman was wont, before he went to Philadelphia to distinguish himself at the Bar. Vain and impotent will be the undertaking! For how can he hope, briskly as he may move in Robert's path, to rival the fame of that young Astyanax! that hope of modern Troy! Still, the ambition is a laudable one, and not to be resisted. We, therefore, must not be surprised to learn that the young gentleman ... is assuming the management of the Custom

House ... and requires the dismission of one inspector and the appointment of another, on no other ground but his individual pleasure. One would suppose he was part Tyler in blood, so naturally he falls into their agreeable habits! [8]

Whatever the patronage habits of the Tylers, father and son, Alexander freely admitted to Julia that "some of the applications made for these places, and they are numberless, exhibit strange hallucinations on the part of the applicants." He assured the White House, however, that he would recommend for appointments only those persons "most worthy of consideration." Still, in moving dozens of people into and out of office Alexander made errors in judgment, and for these he was sharply criticized by his closest friends. "The original friends of Mr. Tyler ought not to be sacrificed to make room for those who became good *'Tyler men' when no other party would have them*," protested Alexander L. Botts. "When needed most they fought against him, and not receiving the pay from the opposite party they shouted (all too late) lustily for Tyler." Alexander Gardiner's mistake (in this instance the accidental removal of a loyal Customs House supernumerary) was repaired and suitable apologies were speedily issued. More easily rectified was Alexander's appointment of a distant cousin, Egbert Dayton of East Hampton, to the United States Military Academy. In a sardonic note from Daniel Dayton, the boy's father, Alexander learned to his chagrin that Egbert was thirteen years old and scarcely ready to travel "the road to military fame." [9]

More embarrassing to the family, and certainly more public, was the patronage mess Julia and Alexander managed to create at Sag Harbor, Long Island, in their eagerness to get a few "safe" Gardiner and Dayton cousins into minor sinecures before the Tyler administration went out of power. In this instance, the in-fighting pitted Gardiners against Gardiners and Gardiners against Daytons. Before the nasty fight was over, Alexander and Julia were wondering whether they were really cut out for ward-level political manipulation at all.

The Sag Harbor confusion began in June 1844 when John D. Gardiner of that town, a cousin of Julia's, requested that Tyler appoint his son, Samuel L. Gardiner, to the Collectorship of the Port of Sag Harbor, replacing Henry T. Dering. At the time of the request young Samuel L. Gardiner was serving as Solicitor in Chancery for Suffolk County, a modest and unremunerative post. The Collectorship of the Port was neither. The solicitation of the office was channeled through Secretary of State John C. Calhoun, who had been at Yale with John D. Gardiner back in 1804 (Julia's father had been in the same class). Happy to accommodate another wearer of the Blue, Calhoun, with the President's approval, promised young Samuel the lucrative post. Julia seconded the arrangement enthusiastically. She had no love for Henry T. Dering. The man had no poetic soul. "I *really* think ... [Gardiner] deserves the Collectorship quite as much as Dering," she wrote her mother from the honeymoon cottage at Old Point Comfort. Dering, after all, "has never immortalized me in Rhyme," and he was also "a *thorough Whig.*" Alexander was soon informed of the family decision in the matter, and as Chief of the Tyler Patronage Distribution Bureau, Suffolk County Division, he heartily endorsed the appointment as a "very good one." Samuel L. Gardiner would be the next Collector of Customs of the Port of Sag Harbor.[10]

Sag Harbor was not an obscure port in 1844, nor was the collectorship there a mean post; sixty to seventy whaling ships operated annually from the town. As the New York *Herald* correspondent at Sag Harbor put it, "We are growing rich and oily," and "in a short time we shall outstrip New Bedford and Nantucket, as we have done all other whaling ports." It was even boldly predicted in the town that "in a short time we shall turn our attention to the arts, sciences and literature." While not yet a cultural center, Sag Harbor was the political and economic key to Suffolk County and the collector there controlled the turning of the key with his power of patronage. The projected appointment of Tylerite Conservative Samuel L. Gardiner to the office therefore threatened the position of the Van Buren Democrats in the county, a group headed by Dr. John N. Dayton (also a Gardiner cousin), Dr. F. W. Lord, and Peletiah ("The Duke") Fordham, Postmaster of Sag Harbor. News of Samuel's imminent elevation to the collectorship propelled this clique into a frenzy of activity.[11]

This exertion took in form nothing less than a bargain, a conspiracy, and a lie. In effect, the good doctors Dayton and Lord promised Fordham, in July 1844, that if he somehow managed to persuade Alexander Gardiner to substitute Dayton's name for Samuel L. Gardiner's in the nomination to the collectorship, the local Van Burenites would see to it that "The Duke" was not purged from his postmastership. As a "renegade Whig" and Webster appointee, Postmaster Fordham was in a precarious position. With Van Ness, Graham, and Alexander casually lopping off the heads of Van Burenites, Websterites, and Clay men to further the Tyler candidacy in New York and force the Polkites into an understanding with the President, Fordham had naturally begun to experience a feeling of insecurity. Consequently, when Alexander visited in East Hampton briefly in early August, two weeks before Tyler's formal withdrawal from the Presidential canvass, Peletiah Fordham hurriedly repaired there to speak with him. In the ensuing interview, Fordham represented Samuel L. Gardiner as being violently anti-Tyler and anti-Texas, unqualified for the office, unpopular in Sag Harbor, and ardently for the Van Buren Regency. On the other hand, he portrayed Dr. J. N. Dayton as vigorously pro-Tyler in action and deed, sound on every political issue of the day. He therefore urged Dayton's appointment as collector if the Tylerites had any interest in swinging Suffolk

273

County to Polk in the approaching elections. Meanwhile, the Dayton-Lord clique had circulated petitions in Sag Harbor demanding the nomination of Dayton.[12]

Alexander was bamboozled. Only in the most cursory fashion did he bother to check Fordham's characterizations of Samuel L. Gardiner. David Lyon stopped briefly in Sag Harbor in early September (after Tyler's withdrawal), spoke privately with the Dayton-Lord forces (now proclaiming themselves staunch Tylerites-for-Polk), and reported to Julia that Samuel L. Gardiner "has no influence whatever, nor have any of his relatives; no confidence can be placed in any of them." He informed his sister that he and Alexander would shortly "recommend someone who has *influence and character*." [13]

Not surprisingly, Dr. J. N. Dayton was soon recommended by Alexander for the Sag Harbor collectorship. As a distant cousin of the Gardiners he was eminently worthy. Nevertheless, Alexander's switch decision in the matter placed Tyler in a "quandary" because Secretary Calhoun had "gone so far" to secure Samuel L. Gardiner's appointment in the first place. Alexander admitted that his own handling of the problem had been equivocal, but he assured Julia that his actions had been prompted solely by his concern for the President's "advantage in Suffolk County." This concern took Alexander one step further. In October he was instrumental in obtaining Dayton's nomination to the New York State Assembly on the Suffolk County Democratic ticket. By election or appointment, Alexander was determined that Dr. Dayton would have a political position. Dayton was elected to the assembly in November.[14]

The President accepted his brother-in-law's spot judgment in the Sag Harbor affair. On December 1 Assemblyman-elect John N. Dayton was appointed Collector of the Port. In the meantime, the decision to substitute Dayton for Gardiner had been carefully concealed from the latter, young Samuel L. Gardiner assuming until the very last moment that the Presidential cornucopia would bathe him in the oil of office. At this point, seeking to minimize the explosion that was sure to come, Alexander made a crucial mistake. To propitiate Calhoun and the entire Sag Harbor Gardiner clan, Alexander recommended to Tyler that he appoint Ezra L'Hommedieu Gardiner Postmaster of Sag Harbor, replacing Peletiah Fordham. This arrangement, reasoned Alexander, would prevent "all difficulty and bad feeling" among the local Gardiners and would satisfy all parties.[15]

Ezra was John D. Gardiner's second son. His appointment to the postmastership was entirely an accident, a case of mistaken identity. In recommending another of John D.'s sons for the post, Alexander intended the appointment of John D. Gardiner, Jr., but he confused the numerous Sag Harbor Gardiner brothers and ended up submitting Ezra's name by mistake. He considered John D., Jr., "altogether the best of the family," but he informed Tyler in mid-December that "if however his brother Ezra has been already appointed the matter is not worth a second thought." A Gardiner is a Gardiner is a Gardiner.[16]

When it became apparent to Samuel in early December that he had been passed over for the Sag Harbor collectorship in favor of Dr. Dayton, that he had been stabbed in the back by the Dayton-Lord-Fordham clique, and that one of his brothers had been given the postmastership, he immediately set off loud salvos of outrage and anguish. A hurried trip to Washington and an interview with Tyler confirmed his worst suspicion—that Alexander had indeed abandoned him on the basis of Fordham's prevarications at East Hampton in August. No sooner had he returned home to Sag Harbor than he persuaded his mother, Mary Gardiner, to write to Julia and expose the whole plot. Within a few days a heart-rending letter was received at the White House demanding justice. The First Lady's intervention with her husband was urged in the most emotional terms. Mary Gardiner reminded Julia of the Calhoun-Tyler pledge of the office back in June; she assured Julia that her son had long been an enthusiastic supporter of Tyler; and she recalled that her husband "was a friend of your dear departed father, a fellow Townsman and a fellow Classmate, through their whole academic and collegiate course." [17]

All of this was very embarrassing to Julia, who had endorsed Samuel L. in the first place. No matter who got the appointment, one Gardiner cousin would remain terribly unhappy. In quiet desperation she contacted her brother to find out what had gone wrong at Sag Harbor. Alexander, in turn, confronted Peletiah Fordham with the charge that he had lied about Gardiner and Dayton during their August interview at East Hampton, Since he had lost his postmastership to Ezra L'H. Gardiner anyway, Fordham was quite willing to admit his fraud and deception. He claimed that he had been most cruelly used by Dayton and Lord. They were indeed Van Burenites, he confessed. Having used him, they had done nothing to save his postmastership. He admitted, further, that Samuel L. Gardiner was, as he had represented himself, a true friend of the President and his policies. Fordham's confession upset Tyler, who was distressed to learn that he had been a party to what he correctly labeled a "real piece of intrigue." Julia too was outraged. So was Juliana, who advised Alexander that "such people are dangerous to speak with—the very *least* you have to do with them the better. They are shocking." [18]

Alexander agreed with his mother's viewpoint, but it was decided within the family circle that John N. Dayton should not be openly antagonized—at least not for a while. As a newly elected New York assemblyman he could still help the cause of the Conservative Democracy in Albany. Tyler had earlier appointed his New York friend and ally, Senator Nathaniel P. Tallmadge, to the governorship of the Wisconsin Territory. In January 1845 the state legislature at Albany would select a new United States senator to fill Tallmadge's unexpired term. The legislature was also scheduled to fill the seat of Senator Silas Wright, elected governor of New York in November. It was this consideration of two vacant Senate seats that caused Alexander to importune Dayton not to resign as assemblyman to take his post as collector until he had first struck a blow for Tylerism in New York. Dayton agreed. On January 19, 1845, he reported to Alexander from Albany that "the long agony is over and our friend Mr. [Daniel S.] Dickinson elected to fill the unexpired term of Mr. Tallmadge." The selection of Conservative Democrat Dickinson was good news to Alexander, much better than the accompanying information that Van Buren Democrat John A. Dix had been chosen to fill the Senate seat of Silas Wright.[19]

Whatever Dayton's Van Burenite proclivities actually were, he had done for the Tylerites at Albany all Alexander had asked of him. He had voted consistently for Dickinson and against Dix. Still, his shady role in the Fordham misrepresentation marked him for proscription. When his nomination to the collectorship came before the Senate for consideration in early February, Tyler and Alexander quietly knifed him. By this time the President had decided to liquidate the Sag Harbor mess once and for all by restoring the nonpoetic Henry T. Dering to the post of collector. The whole family in the meantime had grown heartily sick of the Sag Harbor confusion. "I shall do nothing further respecting the vacant Collectorship at Sag Harbor," Alexander informed Margaret in disgust. For Juliana it provided an opportunity to make the larger point that "If the Sag Harbor business is a specimen of politics I should think you would be sick of the business. Don't pray place much confidence in anyone. I do not—no not one. All the best are selfish and politicians are intriguing. True honor is rarely to be found. *Poor politicians* have no idea of it." [20]

It did not take John Dayton long to realize that Peletiah Fordham's mid-January confession of chicanery had been supplied to the Senate by Tyler, or someone close to the White House, and that the administration's sudden loss of enthusiasm for his candidacy had caused his rejection by the upper chamber on February 10. Understanding the military dictum that a setback often provides the best opportunity for a renewed attack, he boldly suggested that the President send his name up to the Senate again, or at least the name of his compatriot in the deception, Dr. F. W. Lord. He blandly denied all complicity in the collectorship machination, charging instead that he was the innocent victim of a Fordham-Samuel L. Gardiner plot to discredit true Tylerism in Suffolk County. This was a bit farfetched. Whatever his degree of involvement with Fordham, his protestations of innocence were not rendered more creditable when F. W. Lord cheerfully confessed the whole conspiracy against Samuel L. Gardiner and again implicated Dayton as a charter member. Lord defended his own dishonest role in the matter on the grounds that in politics, as in war, the ends justified the means. The earlier Fordham confession he verified in all particulars. Since Samuel L. Gardiner already held the office of Solicitor in Chancery, it seemed fair, thought Lord, to ruin his chances for the collectorship, even if it meant telling a lie or two. While all this was relatively small-scale chicanery, it was still gutter politics. Juliana was humiliated that "Alexander's name should have been mixed up with all those people at Sag Harbor. You do not wonder," she told Julia, "your father avoided contact of any kind with them. I think they are shocking—so small." [21]

Well above the Sag Harbor political level in the projected postelection arrangement with Polk was the President's kindness to the President-elect and his wife. This went well beyond the usual social amenities, and it had a distinct bearing on Tyler's political look ahead to 1848. Not only did the President invite Polk to stay at the White House when he arrived in the capital, but Julia exchanged several friendly visits with Sarah Childress Polk after the Tennesseans reached Washington.[22]

It was through Tennessee State Senator Major William H. Polk, Young Hickory's brother, that Tyler attempted most assiduously to cement a permanent political and personal relationship with the new President. Major Polk arrived in Washington on December 20, 1844, to survey the political situation before the arrival of the President-elect. Margaret found him "very plain in his appearance and manners," but her mother was much impressed by the "tall respectable country men" who comprised the Polk entourage. As noted in another connection, Phoebe hurled herself romantically at the Major and for a brief time captured his romantic and terpsichorean attentions. David Lyon met him and thought him "a very clever man." He urged Alexander to call on Major Polk when he later reached New York—this on the chance that he "may be of some service to you hereafter." He also informed Alexander that the Major had been "introduced to the girls, danced with them at the Assembly, and has dined here and called upon the family several times. The President thinks of giving him a foreign mission, maybe to the south of Europe; you must not, however, mention it to anyone." Alexander took his brother's advice. He made himself known to the Major when he visited New York and took him to the opera. The two men got on excellently together. William H. Polk thus received the full Tyler-Gardiner treatment—from an armful of waltzing Phoebe to a box seat at the opera and an offer of a diplomatic appointment.[23]

Tyler first gave serious consideration to the appointment of Polk's brother as *chargé* to Naples as early as January 1, a few days after the Major's arrival in Washington. The initial idea was not Tyler's. The request for a diplomatic post for William H. Polk came from the President-elect himself in late December. Tyler, of course, was happy to comply. He wanted the President-elect indebted to him. Further, he was genuinely fond of the Major, who had skillfully served his brother during the early stages of the 1844 campaign as a liaison man with the Tylerites. Indeed, it was William H. Polk who had first suggested in June 1844 that Tyler's withdrawal from the race would be rewarded with a guarantee that no proscription of Tyler's friends would occur if Polk won the election in November. To remind Polk and his brother of this pledge; to accommodate and befriend the President-elect; and to provide additional protection for Tylerites remaining in federal office after March 4 (in this way salvaging a hard core of the Tyler faithful for future political battles) the President gladly nominated the Major to be American *chargé* in Naples.[24]

The nomination immediately revived baseless speculation that Tyler in turn would be appointed Minister to the Court of St. James's "where his young and blooming bride can receive the compliments of lorded nobility." Unfortunately, the Senate failed to act on Major Polk's appointment before March 4, and this forced the new President into the embarrassment of having to renominate his brother to the Italian post. Still, Tyler did the best he could for the President-elect. On the nepotistic surface of things a renomination looked a little better than a nomination.[25]

While the President and Julia were striving to accommodate the Polk family, Alexander was working diligently to purge Van Burenites from various federal offices in New York and replace them with pro-Polk Tylerites. Senate confirmation of Cornelius P. Van Ness as Collector of the Port of New York in early January quieted the jumpy nerves of the patronage dispenser in the Customs House and converted him into a more confident wielder of the pruning shears. Heads rolled and bodies twitched as he and Alexander lopped off the lower branches of the Albany Regency. By early February, however Alexander was calling on Tyler for more removals and new appointments than the President could possibly make and see through the Senate in the short time remaining to him. Even as the administration approached the last two weeks of its fading grip on power, the eager Alexander was bombarding the White House with demands and suggestions for dozens of "midnight" appointments. Only a few of these actually reached the stage of a formal Presidential nomination and fewer still ever came to a vote on the Senate floor. Alexander knew that only a handful of these last-minute nominations could possibly slip through. But his was the buckshot-against-the-barn-door theory: throw in enough names and a few might slide by in the rush of business at the end of a session. And if none did, the very fact of the nomination inflated the ego of the nominee and was often as valuable politically as a nomination that held real possibility of confirmation.[26]

As the Tyler administration approached the end of its allotted span, the inner circle in New York also debated the fate of its feeble printed voice. What to do with the *Aurora?* The newspaper had long gobbled up money faster than the Tylerites could raise it. On December 25, 1844, Postmaster John Lorimer Graham told Alexander that the journal had finally "come to a crisis," and that a heavy dose of new capital would be needed to keep the sheet afloat for as little as six more months. On January 9, 1845, Dr. N. T. Eldridge, one of the *Aurora*'s tiny band of angels, reported that the printer had not been paid for two weeks. He recommended "a collection from friends as early as possible" to meet the bill. Various contributions from Alexander Gardiner and editor Dunn English, a $2000 personal loan from Collector of the Port C. P. Van Ness, and a "forced loan" of $2000 from various loyal Tylerite officeholders in New York had already disappeared into the belly of the hungry *Aurora* with scarcely a trace. Debts mounted alarmingly. As much as the Tylerites desired and needed a newspaper outlet in New York City, there seemed no way to sustain the foundering journal. Thus when he was asked in early January whether he wanted to keep the paper going at any cost, Tyler responded bluntly that he did not "care a God damn about it." He had his own problems, and he had little time or disposition to worry about the *Aurora*'s. The decision was therefore made to merge the *Aurora* into Levi D. Slamm's New York *Plebeian*. There was apparently no other solution. At least the *Plebeian* was anti-Van Buren, although its pro-Tylerism was temporary, opportunistic, and quite rightly suspect. Nevertheless, in return for a guarantee of printing commissions from the Customs House and the Brooklyn Navy Yard, the *Plebeian* absorbed the *Aurora* and its numerous liabilities.[27]

At that moment, in mid-January, the loss of the *Aurora* seemed to the Tylerites more than compensated for by the progress of the Texas Resolution through Congress. Into this final fight for Texas the Tylers and Gardiners flung themselves with unity and vigor. For a brief period in January and February of 1845 the alliance of the two families functioned primarily as a lobby for Texas annexation. In Washington, the Gardiner and Tyler ladies cajoled, wheedled, flirted, danced, entertained, and otherwise stalked and buttonholed every walking vote that came within polka distance. In New York, Alexander and Robert Tyler labored to organize the Conservative Democracy for Texas annexation with patronage, persuasion, and pressure. In this effort the two young politicians had no difficulty distinguishing their friends from their enemies. As Alexander informed the White House, "The only division of the Democracy in this state, sensible and founded on principle, is with those who are favorably disposed to the Treaty of Annexation and those who are not. There is none which so clearly designates those who are with and those who are against us." [28]

Chief among those in New York City who were "favorably disposed" toward Texas was the colorful Captain Isaiah Rynders, leader of the Tammany Hall-connected Democratic Empire Club. It was through Rynders and his political roughnecks that Alexander and Robert worked most effectively to bring the whole of the Wigwam to a pro-annexationist point of view.

Isaiah Rynders was a thirty-eight-year-old, dark-complexioned, over-middle-height man who was built like a bull. Born in Waterford, New York, he grew up to the life of a deck hand on Hudson River sloops and steamers. Duelist, gambler, traveler, patriot, Democrat, expansionist, and soldier of fortune in the Texas Revolution, he eventually came to own two small river vessels on the Hudson. From this accomplishment he derived the title "Captain." In the words of the New York *Herald,* "women and wine, fighting, sporting, dancing, and free living, all receive his due attention." In July 1844 Rynders organized the Democratic Empire Club to protest a municipal ordinance prohibiting the use of fireworks and firewater in celebrations of the Glorious Fourth. The club quickly became a tough, patronage-hungry outfit comprised largely of free-swinging, hard-drinking Irish-American dock and river workers. During the 1844 Presidential campaign Rynders affiliated the club with Tammany Hall—for a modest ($3000) consideration. He served gallantly in the Polk cause, specializing in breaking up Henry Clay rallies with his roving squadrons of Empire Club street fighters. For somewhat more formal and official ceremonies he dressed his goons in snappy red jackets which attracted considerable attention. Mustering well over two hundred head-banging and often unemployed patriots (Rynders called them "The Boys"), the Empire Club was strongly anti-Van Buren and anti-abolitionist; it was pro-Polk, pro-Tyler, and pro-Texas. When Rynders went to Washington in late December to talk patronage, politics, and Texas annexation with Major William H. Polk, his presence in town stirred the *Herald* to remark that "important functionary as President Tyler is in Washington, we assure you that Mr. W. H. Polk is now the *lion* with Captain Rynders and the Empire Club —the lion of placemen and men for place." When patronage was involved, the dashing Captain was equally at home in either the Tyler or Polk camp.[29]

Alexander favored the Empire Club with as much patronage as he was capable of showering. The club, in turn, through member David H. Broderick, helped secure Alexander's nomination for the assembly in October 1844. More helpfully, Tammany Hall was packed with Rynder's strategically deployed "Red Jackets" on the crucial evening of January 24, 1845, when the New York City Democracy debated the Texas question in open convention. Robert Tyler treated the crowd to an emotionally charged speech on the subject. Alexander, however, had arranged the show. He drew up resolutions demanding the "immediate reannexation" of Texas and an end to "fruitless procrastination." These resolutions designated Polk's election victory a popular mandate for immediate annexation, and called for American intervention in the Mexican-Texan dispute under the provisions of the Monroe Doctrine. As Alexander phrased the Monroe Doctrine rationalization, the United States was "the parental source of the independence of every sovereignty in this hemisphere, [and] has a right to regard herself as the natural protector of their peace and welfare." These and similar propositions were offered the Tammany Hall gathering of January 24 by Alexander, and by Rynders and Broderick at Alexander's "instigation." The Gardiner resolutions were quietly circulated among the Tylerites, Polkites, and Red Jackets "some hours before the meeting," and when the time came to debate them they were cheered, shouted, and stamped through in a scene of pandemonium that concluded with "eight hearty cheers for Honest John Tyler." It was a beautifully organized *coup* for Alexander, and he was convinced that Tammany's action on Texas "had a material effect upon the action of Congress." Undoubtedly it did have some effect, although exactly how much cannot be determined. In any event, the next day, January 25, the Texas Resolution passed the House of Representatives with a twenty-two-vote majority, 120 to 98. "Rejoice with me," exulted Tyler on the fact and size of the House vote. "I entertain strong hopes that it will pass the Senate. A greater triumph was never achieved than that already accomplished." [30]

On January 26, Robert and Alexander hosted a lavish victory dinner at Howard's Hotel for Rynders and other leaders of the Empire Club and for various Tylerite functionaries from the New York Customs House and Post Office. The House had passed the Texas Resolution the preceding day and spirits around the banquet table were high. It was a happy occasion "marked by most delicious cookery—excellent wines—and the utmost brilliancy in the sentiments, toasts, speeches [and] songs." The political tone of the evening was set by Robert's opening toast to his father: "To John Tyler, President of the United States—an honest man is the noblest work of God." Other toasts and the speeches all cheered Texas annexation and hopefully linked the future political destiny of Tyler with that of Polk. The Van Buren-Silas Wright faction of the Democracy was roundly damned, hissed, and booed. The whole affair, remarked the *Herald*, "will have a most important and interesting bearing on the distribution of office under the new administration." [31]

Alexander did not relax his pursuit of Texas annexation after the House vote of January 25. On the contrary, he delivered speeches for annexation, manipulated patronage for annexation, prepared pro-annexation briefs for the use of Tylerite speakers (briefs which carefully avoided the slavery question), and urged Tylerite officeholders all over the country to bend their energies and their voices to promoting the great cause.[32]

In Washington the family fretted and worried as the joint resolution made its way through Congress. Julia and Margaret followed the course of the legislation with great care, reporting details of its daily progress to Alexander in New York. David Lyon frequently escorted the ladies of the Court to Capitol Hill to hear the Texas debate, most of which he evaluated as "very indifferent." Yet he was certain that any "Democrat who takes a stand in direct opposition to the wishes of the great mass of the Democratic party will have [not] much to hope for hereafter at their hands." Juliana, on the other hand, was fearful that the Van Buren element in Congress was too strong, and that the Senate would probably table the whole question as the session ended. The skillful floor fight for the measure conducted by Senator Robert J. Walker, the Fabian tactics of "Old Bullion" Benton in opposition to the resolution, the various amendments, counter-amendments, arguments, pleas, and subtle political exchanges on the issue were much too complex for the mother and her daughters to follow: "Politically all seems confusion," Juliana wrote Alexander. She was amazed at "how it seems to fluctuate—one day no doubt of annexation; the next, all doubt." [33]

After several weeks of alternate optimism and pessimism, Julia began to feel, by February 23, that the prospects for annexation now looked "very encouraging." She was ecstatic in anticipation of a triumphant outcome. "It is confidently expected to be passed this week," she told Alexander excitedly. "The prospect is quite bewildering; for it is the President's last remaining desire." Alexander immediately came to Washington to be on hand for the final push in the Senate. Happily for John Tyler and his battered ego, his "last remaining desire" became a reality on February 27 when the Senate approved the Texas Resolution by the tiny margin of 27 to 25. The shift of a single vote would have killed it. For this outcome Senator Walker was largely responsible. He saved the day for the President with a bit of very fancy parliamentary footwork. Specifically, he amended the House legislation to permit the Chief Executive the option either of dealing with Texas under the joint resolution or by negotiating an entirely new treaty of annexation. In so doing, he strongly intimated that the second course would be followed. Since Tyler's remaining time in office would obviously not permit him the luxury of the new treaty approach, Walker's shrewd amendment appealed alike to those anti-annexationists and anti-Tylerites who wanted to defeat the whole scheme by delay, and to those Polkites who would have been pleased to see Young Hickory receive the historical credit for the act however it was consummated. Walker's tactic influenced a few key votes. Thanks also to his compelling advocacy of his Texas "safety valve" slavery thesis, together with firm behind-the-scenes political pressure from President-elect Polk, enough Southern Whigs and Northern Democrats reversed the positions they had taken in July 1844 to assure the success of the measure. The House approved the Senate version as amended by Walker by a vote of 132 to 76.

It was a wonderful day for John Tyler. "All is glorification," Alexander reported from Washington. When Alexander's glad tidings reached New York (the Gardiner ladies had returned to Lafayette Place shortly after Julia's final ball on February 18), the reaction was explosive. "The girls [Mary and Phoebe] were here when news of the annexation of Texas arrived," Margaret wrote Julia. "We all cheered so vociferously in the dining room that Mama hastened downstairs with the sure conviction that we had quite run mad, and such an advent seemed the more natural to her from our continued merriment over the frothy events of our winter." [34]

Tyler signed the annexation measure into law on March 1, three days before he surrendered his office. It was, Julia recalled years later, "the great object of his ambition" and there was no hesitation on his part in rejecting the second of the Walker amendment options and completing annexation himself. His Cabinet approved his egocentric decision in this regard and Polk acquiesced in it. Tyler gave his wife the historic pen with which he signed the legislation and Julia wore the "immortal golden pen" around her neck like the Distinguished Service Medal it was. Meanwhile, the President's nephew, Floyd Waggaman, was dispatched to Texas with the documents necessary to consummate the final details of the annexation.

On the evening of March 2 a brilliant Cabinet dinner was held at the White House to celebrate the Texas victory. The Polks were present, Sarah Polk wearing "black velvet and a headdress with plumes." Julia was magnificently clad in "black blonde over white satin." The conversation, of course, was all Texas, as the outgoing and incoming Presidents congratulated and toasted each other on the success of annexation. Wine and champagne flowed. "Julia looked remarkably well," Alexander reported, "and carried off the whole affair with much effect, quite captivating Polk and Dallas." So it was that John Tyler left office in an atmosphere of euphoric triumph, Julia as usual "captivating" the right people right to the end.

No one in the family circle paid the slightest attention to the fact that on March 3, 1845, the Congress of the United States finally beat "Old Veto" at his specialty. For the first time in American history the Congress passed a bill into law over a Presidential veto. Even on this issue, a minor one concerning two revenue cutters, Tyler's position was sound. Still, who could get excited about revenue cutters when the Republic of Texas had just become part of the American Union? Not Tyler, certainly. To him, his administration was now a success. His enemies could have the revenue cutters; he would take Texas.[35]

To Alexander Gardiner the Tyler administration was a triumph in more ways than Texas. Indeed, as the annexation legislation wound its involuted way into law, Alexander secured from the President the patronage appointment in New York that would provide him a safe redoubt from which he could direct Tylerite political matters in the city after the Chief Executive left office. There were also financial considerations involved in Alexander's hunger for office. He and David Lyon were not successful lawyers in a financial sense. Their father, it will be recalled, had subsidized their struggling practice with regular cash infusions until shortly before his death in February 1844. After the Senator died, his sons were forced to draw on the principal as well as the income of the family estate to maintain a proper standard of living. In early 1844 David Lyon stopped practicing law altogether and left his brother to run the office alone. By January 1845 Alexander was complaining bitterly to Julia that his law business was very slack. He had received no legal commissions from the United States Circuit Court since the April 1844 term. What he was owed by the Circuit Court for work done prior to that term had not yet been paid. He was, of course, too involved in local politics to do full justice to what practice he had, and his mother frequently scolded him on this score. Thus, he wanted and needed a steady income for day-to-day expenses. He did not want to dip into Gardiner capital investments at a time when the 1837–1844 depression was lifting and stock and real estate values in New York were beginning to show hopeful signs of appreciation. For this reason, Juliana encouraged his quest for office, urging him not to become "discouraged about some appointment." [36]

Alexander first asked Tyler for a patronage post in May 1844, a month before the President's marriage to Julia. Tyler was willing to oblige the young lawyer, but he had nothing at that moment to confer, not even an assignment as a special diplomatic courier ("The rapid and facile intercourse by Steam Ships has almost entirely dispensed with the necessity of special dispatch agents," he explained), or a lowly secretaryship in an overseas consulate. "How would a trip to South America meet your views—the trip to last for some six months?" Tyler asked him. "I anticipate an occurrence which may shortly render an agent necessary." Unfortunately for Alexander, the "anticipated occurrence" did not transpire.[37]

Nevertheless, the idea of a romantic foreign mission fascinated him. In September 1844 he asked Julia about the vacant consulship at Marseilles:

What is the consulship at Marseilles *worth,* and what do you consider the dignity of the place? So far as health is concerned there could be no better location for me; and I have long had a desire to visit "foreign parts."... I presume that Marseilles is no *marrying* place, but I do not perceive that any immediate expectations in that way open upon me even here; unless, indeed, you may find me a southern lady, *rich and pretty.* I must have them both. High ho! Julia, what do you think of it?... I am ready for any or all enterprises in love, politics or business!

Julia encouraged his interest in a foreign mission "of some conspicuous sort," but she crushed the Marseilles idea with the information that the post paid no salary and *"to make it truly profitable [you] must be connected in commercial business.* It would *then* be very lucrative." Another drawback of the Marseilles appointment was that "Alex must run the chance of rejection by the Senate." [38]

Senate approval was a major consideration. So many of Tyler's end-of-administration appointees were being rejected by the Senate that Robert warned Alexander to seek only a position that did not require Senate consent. The scent of nepotism was already in the air, an odor Robert himself had raised in his unremitting efforts to get Priscilla's father suitably placed in office before the Tyler administration expired. Indeed, the Senate's stubborn refusal to confirm the old actor's nomination as Surveyor of the Port of Philadelphia could be traced to the fact that Robert had lobbied so crudely and openly on Cooper's behalf. Scalded on the Cooper appointment, Robert cautioned Alexander that "it would be bad to risk your name before the Senate." With this advice the President agreed, noting further that "if you [are] rejected it would be a death blow to your future prospects." Specifically, Robert suggested to Alexander that he take the post of Disbursing Agent of the dry dock at the Brooklyn Navy Yard, but the job did not appeal to Alexander. Nor was it on the patronage shopping list he had submitted to the White House on January 8. It had only the advantage of not being subject to Senate scrutiny:

As to office [he instructed Julia], the Liverpool Consulship would be highly agreeable if I could get it consistent with the President's interests; the Marshalship [of New York] I would not undertake; the Navy Agency I *would* take though it is scarcely of a *caste* to which I should aspire. The Navy Agency is worth in itself $2000 a year and is an easy, at least not a difficult office. If I am to remain in New York, it would be probably as good as any here excepting the clerkship of the U.S. Circuit Court.[39]

The Liverpool consulate was vacant, and at various times in January and February Julia and David Lyon suggested that Alexander take the post. He refused it, convinced now that Tyler's future political interests would better be served were he to remain in New York. The Navy Agency position was also a possibility. It would keep him in the city, but unfortunately it required Senate confirmation. Nonetheless, David Lyon thought Alexander might have a try at it if Tyler's initial nominee, James H. ("Cheap Jimmy") Suydam, was turned down by the Senate (he was). After a careful evaluation of the job, Alexander decided that the Navy Agency did not pay enough. With this belated discovery he announced flatly that he was not interested in it. Nor was he interested when William Gibbs McNeill, Chief Engineer of the Brooklyn dry dock and a Tyler leader in New York, suggested that he might become a

"Special Agent" for the dry dock; or, that not appealing, an Inspector of Live Oak for the Navy Department. McNeill informed Alexander, when offering him a sinecure in the dry dock, that Congress would have to come up with "a liberal appropriation and soon—for from the want of it I am already constrained to limit my operations." For this reason he urged Gardiner to "stir yourself among some of the Members on this point" when he next visited the capital. For a few weeks the dry dock appeared Alexander's best prospect, although his enthusiasm for the post remained low. When he finally learned from the White House in mid-February that neither a special agent nor a disbursing agent could be added to the already overloaded table of organization in the patronage preserve of the Brooklyn Navy Yard, he began to get panicky. Tyler had three weeks in office remaining and nothing had been decided. All the possible patronage doors seemed to be closing, and Alexander expressed his alarm to Julia. "I do not forget you," Julia calmed him, "and we shall see how things result." [40]

Things resulted quite neatly. Since early December Alexander had eyed the clerkship in the United States Circuit Court for the District of Southern New York, a "very good and lucrative office" held by Tylerite functionary J. Paxton Hallet. It required no Senate confirmation. When Hallet expressed interest in the vacant Liverpool consulship in December, Alexander hastily wrote Tyler suggesting Hallet's appointment—an appointment that would conveniently vacate the clerkship. In November, however, the President had nominated Judge Edward Douglass White for the Liverpool post in part payment for White's loyalty to him as chairman of the Tyler convention in Baltimore in May 1844. He did this in full knowledge that White's confirmation by the Senate was a dim prospect. White was indeed rejected by that body on February 8. By that date Alexander's anxiety for office had grown appreciably, and he was quick to urge Hallet for the Liverpool job once again.[41]

The clerkship was a plum. It paid a comfortable $2600 per annum. With various attached commissions, emoluments, perquisites, and opportunities for private practice outside business hours, it could be made to yield upwards of $10,000 a year. That, at least, was the value Margaret placed on it after careful research into the matter. Thus while Senate approval of Judge White's nomination was still pending, Julia urged her brother to "keep in view the Clerkship of the Court." She thought Robert might help Alexander make preliminary arrangements for the appointment at the New York end, and she wrote her brother that if he secured the lucrative post "I shall expect a handsome present." [42]

The day after White's rejection for the Liverpool consulate (February 9), Juliana assured Alexander that he was "likely to get the Clerkship" and she advised him that she thought "a very quiet course of politics will be the best policy for you at present." It was high time, she argued, that her son break off his "contact with the doubtful characters" who surrounded the Customs House and Post Office in New York. Alexander would not accept his mother's advice. Instead, he undertook to persuade Hallet, a very "doubtful character," to resign his clerkship and accept a nomination to Liverpool. This was no mean feat, since it was likely that even were Hallet to win Senate approval (as he did), he might swiftly be purged from his new post by Polk (as he was). Just how Alexander and the President accomplished this persuasive *coup* with Hallet is not known—probably by flattery, appeals to party loyalty, references to the great dignity of the Liverpool office, and perhaps even a small financial settlement. Hallet was a poor man, and he was uncommonly vain. In any event, at Alexander's urging, and with Hallet's consent, Tyler nominated him for the Liverpool consulate on February 18. Then with the help of Attorney General John Nelson and the intervention of New York Chief Justice Samuel Nelson, whose own nomination to the United States Supreme Court by Tyler had first been suggested by Alexander, the clerkship matter was arranged. Alexander took Hallet's place as Clerk of the United States Circuit Court for Southern New York on April 10, 1845.[43]

When he first occupied the clerkship Alexander found himself in an embarrassing financial condition. His law practice had lain neglected for over a year. He had poured money into the *Aurora* and into his own unsuccessful race for the New York Assembly. Contributions to the Tyler party and personal loans to various of its hacks had further reduced his reserves. Just how much covert financial grease he provided from his own pocket to lubricate the rusty axles of ward-level Tyler politics in New York cannot be determined. He was, however, frequently approached for party contributions, and his pursuit of the clerkship very likely required a dab or two of solvent. To ease his cash situation in 1845 he borrowed money from Julia (the exact amount is not known), promising her 25 per cent of the annual salary of his clerkship, or about $650 per year until the loan was repaid. These moneys belonging to his sister he carefully put aside, investing and managing them for her over the years. By the summer of 1850 he told her that if he could hold on to the clerkship for a while longer she would "soon be able to buy a fine estate on James River or any other residence I [Julia] pleased." When Alexander died suddenly in January 1851 without a will, leaving Julia only his Kentucky coal lands in a verbal deathbed distribution of his assets, she naturally protested Juliana's inheritance of that part of his estate (representing 25 per cent of his clerkship salary for five years) properly due herself.[44]

With the loan from Julia arranged, and his prospects for a comfortable future income from his clerkship assured, Alexander settled into the routine of his new office, keeping a critical eye on the New York political scene as Polk took charge of the nation. He beat off an intrigue by ex-consul Hallet to recover his clerkship, and he withstood several politically motivated attempts to slice into the economic fringe benefits of his office. Margaret hoped that "now that he has something else to occupy him ... he will abjure Politics which has only provided a *bill of expense* and from which no advantage has accrued *to him*." With this her mother agreed, returning to her old theme that the Gardiners had never before associated with the kind of people Alexander played politics with. "There is not one ... you are brought into contact with that I would be willing to endorse," she lectured him. To be sure, most of Alexander's political cronies would have cut less than acceptable figures at Newport, Saratoga, or White Sulphur Springs. But Alexander Gardiner could no more "abjure Politics" than his sister Julia could abjure a new dress, a glittering ball, or an innocently capricious flirtation.[45]

12

RETIREMENT TO SHERWOOD FOREST

The ball and the dance are all over. Goodnight to them, lady! Goodnight! Now you will have hours to indulge in that wonderful fancy of yours for the beauties of nature.
—MARGARET GARDINER, MARCH 1845

The brilliance of Julia's final ball and the triumph of Tyler's Texas treaty provided a magnificent valedictory to the administration of the tenth President. So successful were their last remaining weeks in the White House that it was difficult for Tyler and his bride to move so suddenly from the limelight of Washington to the relative political and social obscurity of rural Virginia. There is nothing quite so peripheral in American political life as a brand-new ex-President, a fact Tyler readily appreciated. After much discussion within the family circle, Julia's desire to remain in the capital for the Polk inaugural ball was vetoed. Instead, Tyler decided that they would depart immediately for Sherwood early on the morning of Inauguration Day, March 4. "The President," Margaret explained, "does not like the idea of our going from here [the White House] to a hotel." [1]

From the standpoint of the ladies of the Court, the few concluding days of the social season could only be anticlimactic after Julia's farewell ball had passed into history. It was determined, therefore, to dissolve the Court. Within a week after the levee of February 18, Juliana, David Lyon, and Margaret had returned to New York, and Mary and Phoebe were sadly en route home to the barren fastness of Shelter Island. To fill the void created by their departures Alexander appeared at the White House on February 24 in time to cheer Texas annexation through the Senate and help his sister pack and otherwise prepare herself physically and psychologically for the retreat to Sherwood Forest.

It had been a grand season, a wonderful social experience for the young ladies of Julia's entourage. "Together we have had a fund of merriment," concluded Margaret in retrospect. Phoebe agreed. "I cannot tell you how often I think of the joyous hours spent with you," she thanked Julia. "Scenes of such excitement and gaiety were something so new to me, and I mingled in them so constantly, that I now look back upon them as a dream, long and bright, from which I have been suddenly awakened. I cannot realize that they were over." Juliana feared that Julia, like Phoebe, would also have some difficulty awaking from the White House dream, of adjusting herself to the sudden shift from Washington to Sherwood Forest. She warned her daughter to accept the situation with grace and dignity. "I trust all things will go well with you, tho' it will probably take time to reconcile you to a life so new; perhaps you may find it pleasant."[2]

The departure was a sad one. A shipload of packing boxes, furniture, and personal effects was sent off to Sherwood Forest on March 1. Two of Tyler's slaves, Burwell and John, were sent ahead with the horses and carriage on the same day. Two days later, at 5 P.M. on March 3, the President and the First Lady officially said good-by to their many friends. Robert, Priscilla, and Alexander were on hand for this gloomy event, as were the Cabinet officers and their wives. Some three to four hundred people came to the Blue Room to bid the President and his lady farewell. Tears flowed freely. Even so hard-boiled a politician as John Lorimer Graham was seen dabbing his eyes with a large white handkerchief. Present also were a squad of Rynder's Red Jackets and a uniformed detachment from the Tammany Hall White Eagle Club. Both groups had come to Washington to cheer Tyler out and welcome Polk in. Julia was dressed in a "neat and beautiful suit of black with light black bonnet and veil." To Thomas of the *Herald* she was "charmingly beautiful.... I never saw any woman look more cheerful and happy." She seemed "as though she had been imprisoned within the walls of the White House, and was now about to escape to the beautiful country fields of her native Long Island." Julia played her parting role well.[3]

As the moment for the President's departure from the White House for Fuller's Hotel approached, General John P. Van Ness stepped forward and delivered a brief eulogy of the Tyler administration. He praised the President for his foreign-policy achievements and thanked him and the First Lady for their social hospitality during the recent months. He assured the visibly moved Chief Executive that the pen of history would surely justify his administration. To these remarks Tyler responded with a soft-spoken, extemporaneous speech:

In 1840 I was called from my farm to undertake the administration of public affairs, and I foresaw that I was called to a bed of thorns. I now leave that bed which has afforded me little rest, and eagerly seek repose in the quiet enjoyments of rural life.... I rely on future history, and on the candid and impartial judgment of my fellow citizens, to award me the meed due to honest and conscientious purposes to serve my country. I came to the Administration standing almost alone, between the two great parties which divide the country. A few noble-hearted and talented men rallied to my support, denominated a "corporal's guard," one of whom [Cushing] has just returned having concluded an important treaty with a vast empire, and thrown open the trade of more than one hundred millions of people to American commerce. Another [Wise] is at this time performing the most important services in Brazil for the prevention and extermination of the American slave-trade. The day has come when a man can feel proud of being an American citizen. He can stand on the Northeastern boundary, or on the shores of the Rio Grande del Norte and contemplate the extent of our vast and growing Republic, the boundaries of which have been settled and extended by peaceful negotiations. I am happy in leaving the government to know it has come into the hands of a successor who has been elevated by correct principles to take my place.... The acquisition of Texas is a measure of the greatest importance. Our children's children's children will live to realize the vast benefits conferred on our country by the union of Texas with this Republic....

There was, said Alexander, who witnessed the scene, "scarcely an eye which was not suffused—tears dropping upon the cheeks of men ... little given to the melting mood." It was an impressive moment.[4]

After shaking hands all around, especially with the ladies, many of whom were "bathed in tears," the President and Julia rode to Fuller's Hotel. There they were to spend the evening prior to departing for Richmond the next morning on the nine o'clock mail boat. At Fuller's the President was met and cheered by a large throng of well-wishers, among them members of the Empire Club and the White Eagle Club. Their rooms were filled all evening as their closest friends came to bid more lengthy and personal farewells. The early morning hours of Inauguration Day were disturbed by renewed cheers for John Tyler from a crowd gathered outside the hotel. A cannon salute from the playful White Eagle artillery unit broke several of Fuller's windows. Shortly after 9 A.M. the President and Julia, John, Jr., and Alice reached the dock, only to find that the mail boat had already departed downriver.

It was embarrassing to have to return again to Fuller's and wait for the night boat, but there was no alternative. Unfortunately for Julia, Letitia Tyler Semple and her husband James had arrived in town two days earlier to accompany Robert and Priscilla to Philadelphia. While Alexander found Letitia Semple a "fine looking and accomplished woman," her appearance in the capital severely discomfited Julia. The two ladies were scarcely on speaking terms, and the tense confrontation was awkward for both of them. The evening boat seemed a long way off. Conveniently, the President's rooms rapidly filled again with noisy well-wishers and the touchy situation was mercifully submerged. Professors and students of Georgetown College arrived in a body to thank Tyler for "having extended to the institution and the cause of learning in the District more attention than any of his predecessors." Other callers came and went. So the family remained occupied throughout the day. Only Alexander attended Polk's inauguration ceremony at noon. Young Hickory's cautious speech was delivered over the top of a sea of umbrellas, and Alexander remarked that he "would not go a half mile to see the ceremony repeated." Nor had any of the family attended the inaugural ball the previous evening, "the President deeming it more dignified and proper that himself and Julia should remain at home." [5]

At nine on the evening of March 4 the President and his family finally left the jam-packed capital and boarded the 3 A.M. boat for Richmond. No one accompanied their carriage as they rode to the pier, "not even the tenderhearted Postmaster of the city and county of New York was along," sneered Thomas of the *Herald*. The scene had quickly shifted to Polk, and the Tylers rode out alone. Julia's reign was over. "The ball and the dance are all over. Goodnight to them, lady! Goodnight!" Margaret wrote her sister. "Now you will have hours to indulge in that wonderful fancy of yours for the beauties of nature.... And when there's little to tempt you abroad, dance with the President to Alice's music." Still, Julia went out in a blaze. As she departed the town a huge fire which leveled the National Theater and a dozen surrounding buildings was at its height. Her last view of Washington was that of Captain Isaiah Rynders and his Empire Club Red Jackets, scarlet coats off, energetically fighting the blaze. It was a fitting symbol.[6]

Alexander remained in the capital for a few days to strengthen his personal ties with the new President and to complete a eulogistic account of Tyler's departure for publication in the *Madisonian* on March 6. He called twice at the White House to chat with Polk and found him "quite agreeable." He conferred also with those of "our political friends [who] are endeavouring to form a Central Executive Committee to give Mr. Polk a strong support" against the radical Van Buren wing of the Democracy. But he confessed to Julia that he was "heartily tired of Washington, which has lost almost every attraction since your departure. I hear the same remark made by many others." On March 8 he returned to New York. Margaret, meanwhile, demanded details of the family's "evacuation day" from the capital. "Tell Alice I am expecting a letter from her daily," she reminded Alexander on March 3. "She must not wait until she arrives at home and then discuss the pigs and chickens." [7]

The President and Julia reached Richmond at 2 P.M. on March 5 and went straight to the Powhatan House. Their presence there caused a delighted commotion among the guests. Following their return from a brief courtesy call at the Governor's Mansion ("where the President you know used to reside," Julia told her mother), they returned to the hotel to greet numerous friends and acquaintances who filled their parlor. Among these callers were editor Thomas Ritchie, his wife, and his daughters Ann Eliza and Margaret. Julia's campaign to charm the influential Tom Ritchie in the interest of Tyler's future political ambitions began at that moment.

Early the next morning the Tylers embarked in the small river steamer *Curtis Peck* for the short run down the James to Sherwood Forest. At noon they reached a landing opposite their destination, and the "agreeable company" on the boat gave them three loud cheers of farewell when their dinghy touched shore on the Sherwood Forest side. "How fortunate for us that Texas has passed and Clay is *not* President," remarked Julia of that scene. The annexation of Texas had salvaged the reputation of John Tyler along the James River. Or so it momentarily seemed. Actually, as he later told Edmund Ruffin, Tyler was "received coldly, or worse, by nearly all his former friends and neighbors, all such being his political opposers." Charles City was still strongly anti-Jackson Whig territory. Tyler's break with the Whigs and his subsequent endorsement of Young Hickory did not sit well with many of his aristocratic friends in the Tidewater. As a first order of business Julia was determined to break down this petty neighborhood irritation with her husband's politics. This she eventually did, employing in her effort weapons which had never failed her before—good food, good wine, and gracious entertainment.[8]

In the interim, however, Tyler spent many anxious moments worrying about his bride's adjustment to her new situation at Sherwood Forest. He need not have been concerned. Julia was an extremely resilient young woman and her initial reaction to her new life was one of delight and adventure. Two days after her arrival, as the packing boxes were being emptied and the draperies hung, she wrote her mother of her happiness, and of Tyler's concern for her comfort:

The house ... is neat and beautiful and in all the arrangements I am very much gratified. The house when we arrived was vacated and opened to us by the servants. Some bedrooms were in order, but I went immediately into the preparation of my own particular one commencing at two o'clock and before night the carpet was nailed down, the bedstead up and all the rest of the furniture in position.... I defy you to find so sweet a bedroom or chamber in every respect as *mine!* ... I assure you Mama my house outside and in is very elegant and quite becoming "a President's Lady." You will think it a sweet and lovely spot, and I am quite anxious to have you see it with your critical eyes.... It is clean and sweet, cheerful and lovely here, and you don't know how grateful the repose is to me. Perhaps it is the exciting and sometimes wearisome routine of gaiety I have experienced that throws such a charm around everything about me. The President is puzzling his wits constantly to prevent my feeling lonely, and if a long breath happens to escape me he springs up and says "What will you have," and "What shall I do" for "I am afraid you are going to feel lonely!" My little bird hangs in one of the piazzas and sings from morning until night....

Julia was as happy and content as "Johnny Ty," the little canary who sang from morning till dusk. She experienced moments of homesickness and she hungered for the political news and social gossip of Washington and New York, but by and large she found herself extremely pleased with Sherwood Forest.[9]

There was still much to be done in the house, and Julia attacked the problem of getting settled and arranging her belongings with characteristic energy. "I hope you will not go on too fast in Virginia nor undertake too much at once," her mother warned her, "as you will have nothing to do in time to come." There was little danger of that, and Julia hurried to make Sherwood Forest the showplace of all the estates on the James. "I wish I had a magic wand," she confided to Margaret. "I would make this place the most beautiful you ever saw by performing without delay what will now have to be gradually arranged." Since there was still much carpentry going on in and around the house, Julia daily supervised the workers, urging them forward with all possible speed. From Alexander she requested Andrew J. Downing's book on landscape architecture, and she began planning the grounds, gardens, fences, and gates of the estate. Two female statues were ordered from New York to "preside over the garden," and two large reclining cast-iron dogs were obtained for the north piazza. So many demands for rugs, curtains, furniture, yard goods, clothes, medicines, books, magazines—and even guitar music—went to the family in New York that she finally confessed to Alexander that "I suspect you think by this I will never cease to *want*." She never did cease to want. Over the next fifteen years much of her shopping for herself, her children, and her home was done by mail through members of her family in the city. "You will think my commissions neverending," she apologized to Margaret, "but I cannot help it." [10]

Among her New York purchases in 1845 was an expensive new carriage. To do it justice she put her Negro coachmen and footmen into resplendent new livery, "handsome light grey dress coats (livery cut) with black covered buttons (made in uniform style) white pantaloons and black hats." They cut dashing figures, almost as dashing as the hearty sailors of Julia's Navy, the four Negro oarsmen who manned her "Royal Barge."

This small boat was a farewell gift to Tyler from the family of Commodore Beverly Kennon. It arrived at Sherwood Forest already christened *Pocahontas*. Julia decided to rename the boat *Robin Hood*—"the Robin Hood of Sherwood Forest," but she gave up the idea when reminded that boats were "always of the feminine gender." Margaret wanted her to go one step further in nomenclature reform and drop the word *Forest* from the name of the plantation. (" 'Forest' seems associated with everything that is wild and unacclimated and remote," she argued.) After consultations with Tyler on the problem, Julia decided that "Forest" would stay and "Robin Hood" would go. Thus *Pocahontas* invaded "Sherwood Forest." Julia had the little craft painted a bright blue and she lined its seats and thwarts with damask satin cushions richly trimmed in matching blue. She had long had a weakness for colorful uniforms, one dating back to her prom week end at West Point in 1839. Her imagination was therefore at its creative height when she designed the garb of her oarsmen:

Bright blue and white check calico shirts—white linen pants—black patent leather belts—straw hats painted blue with Pocahontas upon them in white—and in one corner of the shirt collar (which is turned down) is worked with braid a bow and arrow (to signify the Forest) and in the other corner the President's and my initials combined.[11]

Julia was certain that the *Pocahontas* could "carry you across the ocean—she is so buoyant and light." On one of her first voyages, however, she barely made it across the James. Fitted with an American flag that rippled proudly from her prow, and a canopy that warded off the sun, *"a l'Italian"* [*sic*], the craft was made ready for Julia and the President to pay a mid-June call upon Mrs. George Harrison at Lower Brandon. Halfway across the river the trusty *Pocahontas* began leaking so badly that Julia found herself perched on top of her seat to keep dry. But her skilled oarsmen (*"sailors* and no mistake") brought the crippled vessel safely to shore. Subsequent caulking and painting properly tightened her seams, and on later social visits up and down the river to Brandon, Weyanoke, Lower Brandon, Shirley, and the other nearby plantations Julia, like Cleopatra, could in all security "stretch myself out on the cushions of a much sweeter boat than our Gondola in Venice." The *Pocahontas* survived all further challenges until 1864, when she disappeared during the fighting around Charles City, "liberated" no doubt by Union soldiers.[12]

Julia enjoyed visiting her new neighbors along the river. Whether she traveled to their homes in her new carriage or in her bright blue barge, she invariably arrived in style. She was soon integrated into the plantation society of the lower James. She was a new face in the neighborhood; pretty, young, vivacious, poised, she was the object of much local attention. Everyone—Carters, Harrisons, Douthats, Seldens —wanted to see the rich Yankee wife "Old Veto" had brought home with him. Tyler, of course, was pleased to show off his attractive bride. As Julia immodestly expressed his inordinate pride in her, "When he returns from visiting anywhere he is more and more enraptured with me and says I am 'different from everybody else in the world,' and formed to be the admiration of everyone who has taste and wit, and the wonder of all others—ahem! ... only a little bit of flattery!" Julia *was* different, and Tyler indulged her every wish and fancy. Her tastes, however, were expensive.[13]

By October 1845 the high cost of her numerous household purchases, combined with the expense of vacation trips to Old Point Comfort, White Sulphur Springs, and New York, had brought the former President into financial difficulty. These expenditures and the continuing outlays for the remodeling of Sherwood Forest finally forced a hard-pressed Tyler to negotiate a $2000 loan from Corcoran and Riggs, the Washington bankers. As security for the loan he put up one quarter of his interest in his coal and timber lands near Caseyville, Kentucky, which he had purchased as a speculation in 1837. At the same time he commenced preliminary negotiation for the sale of the property on the banks of the Ohio. His financial situation was not helped when a wandering note on which he had given surety for a friend came home to roost in July. This act of kindness and accommodation ultimately cost him $1400 he could ill afford. The friend had died and his creditors successfully sued co-signer Tyler for the full amount of the note. "Pray never go security for anyone," Julia warned Alexander. "The President has got to pony up pretty handsomely for that sort of generosity." In desperation for ready cash, Tyler began dunning his own debtors for sums as small as $3.56 still owed him for legal work performed years earlier. "These are small matters," he admitted to his nephew, "but the world is made up of atoms; and for myself I have incurred pretty heavy expenses in fixing up this place, and dollars whether few or many are important to me." In spite of his shaky fiscal situation, Tyler stinted on none of the expenses connected with Julia's desire to entertain her new friends and neighbors in the grand manner.[14]

In early May Julia gave a large dinner party, her first at Sherwood Forest. She was ostensibly pleased with the results. " 'The full extent or nothing' is almost my motto now," she told her mother in triumph. Only when the crusty Juliana expressed surprise that her daughter had really enjoyed the affair "as well as your grand ball at the White House," did Julia confess that the gaiety of social life along the river was a decided cut below that of Washington. "I ... have been almost spoiled by excitement and livelier scenes.... What dinner parties of the usual kind in country or city would not appear dull to me after all those brilliant ones we gave at the White House!" she admitted.[15]

More serious for Julia than this passing social disappointment was the badly infected throat (Tyler called it a "cold in the face") that sent her to bed for two weeks in mid-May 1845. Painful as this was to her, it gave her solicitous mother a splendid opportunity to indulge in her favorite hobby—medical diagnosis by mail. In fact,

Juliana spent most of her adult life practicing medicine without a license. No malady, large or small, escaped the attention of the family outpatient clinic she ran with the aid of the Post Office. In this typical instance, quantities of patent medicines were rushed southward to Sherwood Forest. She had discussed the symptoms of Julia's condition with Dr. Quin, the Gardiner family physician in New York, and she had decided upon the treatment to be employed. Having no confidence in any but New York doctors (who were medically as ignorant as she), Juliana confidently told her daughter exactly how throat infections should be treated. Alexander thought that Dr. Quin and his whole profession were engaged in "humbug," and Juliana agreed that "their knowledge is not perfect." But she was certain that a diet omitting wine and coffee would cure all infections if these dangerous liquids were replaced by tea and muffins and supplemented by massive doses of calomel. Eventually, Tyler's brother-in-law Dr. Henry Curtis, "an eminent physician," was called in from Richmond for consultation, and while he consulted and tinkered and speculated, Julia got well. She attributed her recovery to black tea. "I find that black tea is better for me than *coffee* which I thought I never could live without," she informed her mother. "I have acquired a fondness for black tea and scarcely regret the coffee." [16]

As Julia's health returned, her emotional attachment to Sherwood Forest and to Virginia deepened and matured. Soon after her arrival in Charles City she had complained about the *"peculiarity* of Virginia manners." The soft deference that characterized personal relations within the planter aristocracy seemed strange to her at first. She agreed with her mother's view that New York was still "the first city in our Country ... a bright and smiling city," even though she appreciated the fact that its elite social circles could not easily be breached unless one "grew up with it from earliest childhood." But after a few months at Sherwood Forest Julia came to love the studied chivalry of Old Dominion society. For the edification of her family she began to draw comparisons between Virginia and New York which became progressively more critical of the latter:

Yesterday I had a call from Mr. and Mrs. William Harrison of Lower Brandon across the river. They are of the first aristocracy of Virginia and amply did they meet my views of it. Her manner is very cultivated—great repose and finish. Her effect is that of one born a lady.... I was pleased with our interview and her soft manners.... I do not know any in New York society that would appear so elegant. I know she would feel herself far before the fashionable society there. I think there is every prospect of my being surrounded by an agreeable society and carry out your idea of exclusiveness in every particular ... but I think from what you write the first society in the State of New York is sadly declining.... I meet with more accomplishment among the ladies of Virginia than is usually met with in those of New York State. They have generally more talent and finer manners, more self-possession, which is owing I think to their priding themselves so much on their native state, "The Old Dominion"—the home or birthplace of so many Presidents.... I should think, Margaret, you were really tired of meeting *face to face* that same old set, *those same old coons*....[17]

In contrast with New York City, life at Sherwood Forest was pleasant, easy, and gracious. Tyler spent three or four hours a day on horseback among the slaves in the wheatfields "encouraging them by his presence." To protect himself from the sun while he was in the hot fields he purchased a huge Panama hat, which, in Julia's words, had a "brim so broad that his face was quite lost. I thought I should have killed myself with laughing. Since which he has been turning it up in every direction to lessen the size and made me also admire it." In the late afternoon Julia would join her husband, he on horseback, she on her pony, and they would ride across the flat acres. And in the early evening hours they would sit together on the piazza and "listen to the *corn song* of the work people as they come winding home from the distant fields." [18]

Tyler had managed to get "a few hundred acres" of wheat planted in the fall of 1844. From this modest effort he harvested two thousand bushels in June 1845. With wheat at one dollar a bushel that year, and only a fraction of the available land at Sherwood Forest yet under cultivation, the plantation gave great economic promise. Fifty acres of his best bottom land were capable of yielding from twenty-five to thirty bushels per acre. The remainder would produce considerably less, averaging little more than eight bushels to the acre. While this scarcely compared with the forty bushels an acre Nathaniel Gardiner harvested on Long Island, it would produce enough, Julia calculated, to "sustain all upon the estate in an abundance." Dollar wheat, she explained to Margaret, was "cash in hand" on a Virginia wheat plantation. She was quite certain, as was her husband, that "these James River lands are very highly esteemed and are susceptible of anything almost by improvement." In this she was correct. Under Tyler's expert management the productivity of the plantation rose steadily through the years.

John Tyler was a cautious farmer, devoted to careful and patient scientific experimentation. In August 1845 he ordered a copy of Liebig's *Chemistry in Its Application to Agriculture and Physiology* through Alexander in New York. Published first in 1841, this pioneer study in soil chemistry was the best in its field. He also read Edmund Ruffin's seminal *Essay on Calcareous Manures* (1831), and he followed Ruffin's later articles on the subject in the *Farmer's Reporter*. Tyler's study of Liebig and Ruffin convinced him that he must use marl (clay mixed with calcium carbonate) to correct the lime deficiency in his soil. He also experimented with South African wheat seed in 1847 and in 1850 with wheat seed from California in an attempt to develop a rust-resistant strain that would also better withstand frost. The seed experiments failed, but the marl applications worked so well in increasing his wheat and corn yields that he was slow to shift to the use of the much-superior guano as fertilizer. "The President's crop of wheat is the talk of Virginia," Julia boasted in June 1849:

> A notice of it even appeared in a Richmond paper as the most flourishing crop on James River. Some of his friends ... say "Ah ha! he's only been on his farm five years and is before his neighbors already." We cannot form the slightest idea how much he will make, but it is before by a great ways any of his former crops. The P—— rides down everyday to look at and admire it.

Following the failure of his 1850 crop, Tyler reluctantly abandoned marl for the more expensive guano. He selected thirty of his least promising acres for the experiment in 1851 and was astonished to see the wheat yield soar from three bushels to fifteen on this substandard land. From that point on he used guano almost exclusively. Until the drought of 1858–1860 struck all the James River plantations, Tyler generally had excellent crops. Nevertheless, he could never estimate the price his grains would bring in the Richmond and Baltimore markets. Wheat ranged from $1 to $2.50 a bushel during the decade 1845 to 1855. Corn fell as low as 50 cents and went as high as $1.50. Like all farmers of the period, Tyler produced blindly into an unstable market, one over which he had no control. The Mexican War of 1846–1848 shot prices upward for a time, and the Crimean War pushed wheat to a fantastic $2.50 a bushel in 1855. In 1850, however, corn stood at a mere 50 cents and Tyler was caught with 2500 bushels at a price "so low as scarcely to remunerate." Farming was like roulette. Still, guano fertilizer made an immense difference. As Juliana wrote from Sherwood during her annual visit there in September 1855:

> You see very few careworn faces here and I begin to think these planters lead comfortable, independent lives with less to annoy them than our city business men. Guano is making them rich quite rapidly. In driving around I am made sensible of this from the sight of their crops—wheat and splendid fields of corn.

Converted to the employment of guano in the early 1850s, Tyler was not eager to endanger his rising profit ratios with a heavy investment in farm machinery. Thus when he was invited to the Douthat plantation, Weyanoke, in June 1852 to witness the operation of "two soil machines, McCormick's and Hussey's," he was unmoved by the demonstration. While the mechanical reapers invented by Cyrus H. McCormick and Obed Hussey were destined to revolutionize American agriculture, the newfangled equipment caused little excitement and less interest when it was first exhibited on the James River wheat and corn plantations. Instead, Tyler and his neighbors piled on the guano and left the harvest to the labor of the Negro slaves in whom they already had such large financial investments.[19]

To harvest his first crop in 1845, however, the ex-President found it necessary to lease slave labor for the season. At the same time, he began adding to the permanent slave population of Sherwood Forest by outright purchase, financing these new acquisitions with long-term notes at Richmond banks. Since the Negroes, hired or purchased, usually came to the estate accompanied by their women and children, there was a built-in bonus for the owner. "The children and their work afford the interest upon the slaves," Julia explained to Margaret. "A pretty handsome interest is yielded for the amount invested." [20]

At Sherwood Forest plantation Julia found the good life. As she described it to her city-bound sister in June 1845 it seemed almost idyllic:

The President [is] in a large armchair near me on the piazza with feet raised upon the railing.... The reapers have come to their labors in the field about five hundred yards from us and their loud, merry songs almost drown the President's voice as he talks with me. Once in a while a scream from all hands, dogs and servants, causes us to raise our eyes to see a full chase after a poor little hare. This moment we have looked upon one, and I see they have caught it—there is a regular scuffle between dogs and men. With these hares and squirrels our place abounds. We are removed about a mile, in a direct line, from the river, that is to say the mansion—the estate runs down to it—and the trees on the bank that intercept the view have already been nearly cut away. Since I have been seated here I have noticed some five or six vessels pass up and down. Louisa and Fanny Johnston [house slaves] are sewing the carpet in the dining room—and now if you have any fancy you can picture us all.[21]

Nothing in the slave system disturbed Julia or shocked her sensibilities. As conducted by Tyler at Sherwood Forest it functioned easily and humanely. No whips or lashes, no brutal overseers were found on the President's property. The seventy-odd "servants" (as they were always politely called) were adequately clothed and housed, and if there was discontent among them it was not manifested by runaways or by recorded instances of "sassiness." Instead, slavery at Sherwood Forest was an example of Southern white paternalism at its best. No slave was ever "sold South," and Tyler saw to it that none of his slave "families" was broken and scattered. On the surface of things, the "servants" had a strong attachment and loyalty to the Tylers. In turn, the family saw to it that the slaves were instructed in the basic tenets of Christianity. And while neither Tyler nor his wife ever defended slavery as a positive moral good, Julia spent too many evenings sitting up with sick slaves (she treated their chills and fevers with strong doses of quinine laced with a jigger of whiskey), worried too many hours over their physical and material well-being, and witnessed too many evidences of her husband's kindness to them to be convinced that the institution was totally evil. Just how the slaves felt about it is not known. No one asked them. It is a fact, however, that from 1845 until the arrival of the Army of the Potomac at Sherwood in 1862 only one Negro deserted the property. He was drunk at the time, and he fled, of all places, to nearby Richmond, a city with no high reputation as an express stop on the Underground Railroad. He was scarcely a runaway in the *Uncle Tom's Cabin* sense.

Still, it is doubtful that the Tylers encouraged monogamy among their slaves. Negro children were shifted casually from one hut to another. Thus after Alexander visited the model plantation in November 1845 and complained that he had seen a Negro child there improperly clothed against the cold, Julia assured him that the boy had since been made comfortable. "Now he is like all the rest entirely fitted out in new warm clothes—coat, pantaloons, and shirt." She explained, "The truth of the matter is he was left to the care of one of the women who had other children—and she of course soon stripped him for them— but now he is transferred to a childless woman and finds himself very kindly treated." Nor is there any satisfactory evidence that the slaves were taught to read or write. And if they sang in the fields and played their banjos and bones in their quarters at night, the fact also remains that they speedily abandoned the plantation in 1862–1864 when opportunities to leave were presented them. Only four of the male Negroes remained on the estate after their liberation by the Union Army in May 1864—and these few joined in sacking the house and stealing the furniture.[22]

In spite of Julia's constant assurances that the slaves at Sherwood were content and happy, Juliana was concerned that her daughter was surrounded by so many Negroes. "Do inform me if you have any white people about you, or are all your servants colored?" she asked nervously. She pleaded with her daughter to employ a "respectable efficient white woman" as a housekeeper, someone Julia could turn to for sympathy and assistance in case of illness. To find such a person for Sherwood Forest Juliana undertook a thorough search in New York City. She soon located Catherine Wing. In November 1845 Catherine arrived by boat at Sherwood Forest to fill the station. She, like all the Gardiner servants in New York, was an Irish immigrant, and she accepted the situation in Julia's household for her room, board, and five dollars per month. "You must insist upon neatness and care and good order," Juliana lectured her daughter on the eve of Catherine's arrival. "You must learn to put your own things in order or I fear you will find no one to do it for you. I never did, that's a fact." Julia was pleased with the efficient Irish girl, whose many duties came to include general supervision of the house slaves.[23]

In February 1847 another white woman, twenty-five-year-old Harriet Nelson of Norfolk, joined the household staff as seamstress and nurse for Julia's baby. Harriet was of "good family with relations well to do," and she was "much brighter in mind than my Catherine and an experienced nurse" as well. "And what do you think her wages are?" Julia asked. "*$3 per month!* Did you ever hear anything so absurd—but that is all she has been in the habit of receiving. The reason that white labor is so low is this: Slaves are so general that a white person will only be hired as a favor almost—and a Virginia girl never thinks of leaving her state." Without quite sensing it, Julia had put her finger on one reason why so many urban workingmen in the North feared the economic implications of abolition.[24]

As Tyler's farming operations became increasingly extensive and his harvests larger, he continued the practice of leasing Negro labor from the slave brokers in Richmond for seasonal stints. He also hired free Negroes for field work at regular daily wages. A small settlement of freedmen at nearby Ruthville provided this particular labor source. Thus in the wheat- and cornfields of the plantation, resident slaves and leased slaves worked side by side with the Ruthville freedmen. In the main house slave women like Louisa and Fanny and Sarry worked alongside Catherine Wing and Harriet Nelson. This unusual mixture of race and status, indoors and out, was accomplished without incident.[25]

Contented slaves notwithstanding, not all was sweetness and light at Sherwood Forest during Julia's first year as mistress there. There were sharp tensions within the family circle that required patient handling. Neither Elizabeth Tyler Waller nor Letitia Tyler Semple was yet willing to accept Julia as a stepmother. And Julia became sick and tired of their studied insults and backbiting. As the collective blood pressure of the ladies mounted, an embarrassed Tyler worked diligently to soothe and placate all parties. He also had to deal firmly with eighteen-year-old Alice Tyler. The problem with Alice centered on the respect and deference she owed Julia. She was a headstrong and romantic girl who fell in and out of love so often and so completely that Julia questioned her indiscriminating romantic judgments. The bucolic life at Sherwood Forest bored young Alice, much as East Hampton had bored her stepmother at the same age. Her own success in Washington as a member of Julia's Court had given her a lively sense of independence and she did not accept Julia's effort to discipline her with good grace. "She is the most 'spoilt child' that ever existed," Julia concluded. Fortunately, Alice spent much of her time in Williamsburg visiting in the Waller home, a vantage point from which she could observe and be observed by the William and Mary collegians. This arrangement minimized her friction with Julia. But when their clashes did occur, Tyler strongly and plainly supported his young wife. He made it crystal-clear to Alice that she was to be guided entirely by Julia's "advice and opinions." The ideal solution to the problem, thought Julia, was to get Alice married off as quickly and as advantageously as possible. "I hope she will catch a beau who will love her dearly." But the contrary Alice refused to be rushed into matrimony. "You always tell me I'll marry a 'Mr. Nobody' (to use your expression) because I am so easy to please," she countered her stepmother. "But I have found out that I am not so easy to please as I thought myself. [I] have almost come to the conclusion it would be better to marry 'Nobody,' so you'll have to be contented with me as long as you live." From Julia's standpoint that was a grim prospect.[26]

With John Tyler, Jr., the family problem was quite different and much more serious. After his father left the White House he had nothing to occupy his time or his interest. His marriage was on-again, off-again—mostly off. For a time in 1844 he considered running for the Virginia House of Delegates from the Charles City district. This came to nothing. Then he came down with a severe case of mumps. Following this, he loafed around Washington looking vainly for a patronage job from the Polk administration. In late April 1845 he and his friend Louis F. Tasistro "got rather extensively corned" and were involved in a Washington street brawl in which they badly beat up a passing citizen. Much to the mortification of Tylers and Gardiners alike, the New York *Herald* ran an account of the disgraceful incident. Ordered to Sherwood Forest in May to explain his conduct, he was evasive and without contrition. Tyler finally decided that his foot-loose son was drinking too much, and he demanded that John adopt more temperate habits. The upshot of the President's stern counsel was John's decision to return to his wife and two children in Jerusalem, Virginia, stop drinking, and resume his study of law. By July 1845, Julia could report that he was temporarily sober and was determined to "keep out of debt if he has to dress in Virginia cloth and eat nothing else than cornbread." This reform was short-lived, one of many that marked a bacchanalian existence. No year passed that John, Jr., did not manage in some way to embarrass his long-suffering father. Julia finally gave up on him entirely. Not until the middle 1850s did he at last settle down in Philadelphia to practice law with Robert. By that date he had wasted nearly fifteen years of his life.[27]

Julia liked young John. She thought him good-natured and personable. When he visited at Sherwood Forest he always kept the table well supplied with fresh game and cheerful chatter. In her presence he was always a gentleman. Juliana's suspicious view that he was destined for perdition and that his affection for his stepmother improperly transcended the platonic and dutiful was unfair to John, as Julia frequently pointed out to her mother. Yet Juliana so strongly and narrowly detested the use of spirits in any form that she could not be objective about anyone who indulged a taste for liquor. Just how this God-fearing daughter of a wealthy brewer derived her prohibitionism from her Episcopalianism remains a theological mystery. Nevertheless she did, and it was for this reason that Juliana always disliked the irresponsible John. She was ever prepared to see or expect the worst in all his acts. He, in turn, thought her a cross between a prude and a battle-axe, and on one occasion he noted caustically that he had never "seen a Gardiner yet who could take a jest." By way of contrast, Tyler's approach to his son's use of liquor was more temperate. As Julia explained it to her mother: "The President has adopted a proper plan. To all those whom he thinks *care* for wine or for any sort of liquor he does not offer it." Thus when John, Jr., visited the estate after 1845 he found the sideboard and wine closet securely locked. When other visitors came the mellow liquids flowed.[28]

Visitors came often to Sherwood Forest. The most prominent in 1845 was the distinguished Caleb Cushing, who visited the James River country in May and June. Julia was certain that Cushing's motives in making the leisurely trip through Virginia were no more complex than the desire to find a wealthy wife from a politically prominent family. "I suppose if he married one of the Miss Ritchies he would be sent Minister to England right off," she observed. "He is getting to be notorious as a fortune hunter." Indeed, Cushing's effort to charm Ann Eliza Ritchie (who was visiting at Brandon) was less than subtle, as were similar romantic crusades designed to overpower suitable young ladies in Baltimore and Richmond. "He does not get disheartened by a few disappointments," said Julia. Yet when Cushing arrived at Sherwood Forest, Julia's graciousness could not have been faulted. She had eighteen to dinner to entertain and honor him, and he in turn toasted Tyler and his administration as the most "important and eventful administration... since the days of Washington." Julia thought it a "bold speech in these days" and "liked him for it more than I ever have done. Ann Eliza Ritchie will write it to her father I've no doubt." Julia's broad reminder that Cushing had promised to bring her a fan from China resulted a few months later in a far more impressive gift—two large blue-and-white Chinese vases. Cushing was not, said Julia, "particular to any *one* of the young ladies" while visiting at Sherwood Forest, although "he was frequently exposed and joked about the *fair ones* that report and newspaper paragraphs have attached him to which often made him quite nervous—much to my amusement."[29]

When Julia was not entertaining at home she found diversion in trips to various Virginia vacation spots. In late June 1845 she and the President visited Old Point Comfort to celebrate their first anniversary.

Julia hoped that her family had not forgotten the date—June 26—and that they had all toasted the absent couple with a bumper of ale. *"We did not forget it you may imagine,"* she wrote her mother. Army officers and prominent Virginians were present in quantity at the spa, among them the Ritchies, and Julia had an opportunity to catch up on the gossip of Richmond and Washington. She found Old Point Comfort particularly "agreeable for married ladies because the married society is of the best selection so far as it goes." But she informed Margaret that unmarried women would find it dull "excepting those that are content to become Officers' wives—which in my view is the last thing to be desired." In her contacts with editor Tom Ritchie she quickly discovered that "the sunset avenue" to his heart was "through kindness to his family." In traveling that avenue no possible kindness escaped her commission even though she discovered that Ritchie was a man of "very moderate circumstances." From the Washington gossip mill she was titillated to learn that George Bancroft, Polk's dignified new Secretary of the Navy, had been badly routed in a broadside gunnery exchange with Mrs. J. D. Stevenson of New York. According to the story that made the rounds at Old Point Comfort, the extroverted lady had playfully decided to observe his reactions were she to "jump up and kiss him." Dared to do so by her friends, she sprang toward Bancroft in her parlor one day and "sure enough *kissed him*." Bancroft immediately struck his colors, running "behind the door in fright and confusion and she cried out if he did not come out she would kiss him again!"[30]

Bancroft abandoned ship easily. Julia did not. It took a great deal more than an impetuous kiss to frighten her. When in late June Old Point Comfort was struck by a hurricane that ripped the roof and shingles off the hotel where Julia and the President were staying, the mistress of Sherwood Forest maintained her composure. While other ladies were fainting about her in droves, Julia calmly saw to the rescue of "Johnny Ty," the female canary she had brought back with her from Europe in 1841. "The first thing I did as I ran from the room was to seize the cage and place it in the hands of Sarry with the strict injunction she must save the bird's life with hers if possible." As the whole building trembled and shook, Julia and her body servant carried "Johnny Ty" to safety.[31]

The act was characteristic. Julia and John Tyler both loved animals. Throughout their married life they were surrounded by various horses, dogs, and birds, to all of which they became very attached. When one of Tyler's pet mockingbirds was mangled by a nondescript barn cat in June 1845 Julia was outraged. "The vile cat!" she exclaimed, as she undertook to nurse the unlucky bird through a broken leg, a torn breast, and a heavily depleted tail-feather collection. Julia was a better veterinarian than matchmaker. When, for example, Tyler purchased a mate for "Johnny Ty" in Norfolk, Julia was disturbed to observe that the male "treats her with the utmost contempt and ... does not deign to sit upon the same perch with her.... I fear it is not one of the marriages made in Heaven." The sudden death of the sexless "Johnny Ty" in November 1845 left Julia disconsolate for days. Dr. Wat Henry Tyler attributed the canary's death to a heart attack, but his knowledge did not erase the grief Julia sustained. "Such a delicate hold they have on life," she mourned. Similarly, the death of one of the President's favorite horses moved Tyler to erect over its grave in the grove of Sherwood Forest a wooden slab on which was inscribed the epitaph:

> Here lie the bones of my old horse, "General,"
> Who served his master faithfully for twenty-one years,
> And never made a blunder.
> Would that his master could say the same! [32]

Her intense love of animals caused Julia to look forward in great anticipation to the arrival of the Italian greyhound Tyler had ordered from Naples for her the preceding winter. The dog finally appeared at Sherwood Forest in November 1845 after spending several weeks with Juliana in New York. Julia was warned by her mother that "Le Beau," as he was called, was very rough on furniture and rugs and that he required constant attention and discipline. "I think a great deal of him, but I would not take such a pet for a gift," she decided. Le Beau arrived in Virginia accompanied by instructions from Lafayette Place that would do credit to a modern veterinarian. In fact, Juliana enjoyed practicing veterinary medicine when all the humans of her immediate acquaintance fell suddenly well. In the feeding and care of the handsome animal she left nothing to her daughter's imagination, and Julia responded by assuring her that "Little Le Beau is perfectly well and hearty and has the most unfailing attention. In the loss of my bird I have had a warning to keep my eye constantly on him." [33]

Compassion for animals at Sherwood Forest extended on one occasion to a hapless field mouse who fell accidentally into the foot tub in Julia's bedroom. She was awakened in the night by the creature's wild thrashing in the water, and she promptly woke the President and instructed him to investigate the strange noise. Candle in hand, he finally discovered the cause of the commotion and decided to let the little mouse drown. At breakfast the following morning the President was penitent. "I wonder," he said sadly, "if I had taken that mouse and put it in the woods whether it would have come back to the house again." Julia belatedly realized the enormity of the crime. "I felt like reproaching myself after that for the fate of Lady Mouse," she confessed to her mother.[34]

Following a suitable period of mourning for Lady Mouse, Julia prepared to assault White Sulphur Springs, the summertime citadel of fashionable Virginia society. Fashion alone did not dictate her decision to travel into the mountains. July and August was the malaria season along the James, and Julia was strongly encouraged by her family to depart for the Springs as soon as possible. There was also a political consideration. In choosing between the Virginia Springs and Newport for a vacation, Tyler felt he could "reap more political good" at White Sulphur than in Rhode Island. Preparations for what Julia called her "campaign in the Springs" required several strenuous shopping days in Richmond during which she "contrived to spend ... nearly two hundred dollars and yet got nothing very unusual or more than seemed absolutely necessary for a proper appearance for Alice and myself at the Springs." Actually, she was not too interested in making the long trip west to White Sulphur. To her the easy quiet of Sherwood Forest would be much more pleasant even though it was hot, humid, and fever-ridden. But she agreed that it was "improper and [a] *neglect of a duty* owed to society for anyone at *my* time of life to live in constant retirement." [35]

White Sulphur in 1845 was dull. A thoroughly bored Julia attended only one dance while she was there. "I went ... dressed in black," she wrote, "and have not attended again as I do not think the reasons that compelled me to enter in such scenes last winter exist now." During her stay she felt she had to "be dignified as an Ex-Queen, and sit with the Old Ladies, when I was dying to join in the mirth of the younger ones." Alice flirted with the skimpy manpower supply without success, and Tyler's planned political exposure was badly overshadowed by the unexpected arrival of Henry Clay. With Calhoun at nearby Sweet Springs, Tyler was sure that the two politicians were in the same area at the same time for only one reason—to strike an alliance that would put Clay in the White House in 1848. Yet, as Alice reported, Clay's arrival at White Sulphur had generated little political excitement among the guests. "He was not received as enthusiastically as one would have thought, and I fear greatly that he will never be President—So git-long, Clay." The continuing decline of Clay was the only hopeful note that the White Sulphur interlude produced. While Julia was "very flatteringly mentioned" in the "Letters from Sulphur Springs" column which appeared in newspapers all over the state, the reports "made me somewhat older than I *really* am, which was horrible to be sure." Thus after two disappointing weeks of inactivity the Tylers moved on to Sweet Springs for a week. From there they traveled northward to visit the Gardiners in New York.[36]

Meanwhile, Margaret and her mother had found Saratoga and Newport much gayer and more beaux-populated than the Virginia spas, in spite of Julia's pessimistic warning that there was "a painful scarcity of good beaux to be found anywhere." Those in Washington, she concluded, were a "contemptible, mean set." In New York, "few seek to marry at all." Margaret would have no luck at Newport or Saratoga either, Julia gloomily assured her. Nevertheless, Margaret had a wonderful time at Newport that summer, especially at the annual fancy-dress ball. At this function she was a sensation. She wore an elaborate white-and-silver dress topped by a "little opera hat with beautiful long drooping feather—the hat with silver gimp band and otherwise ornamented with silver—diamond on the forehead with pearls wound in the back of her head." Her costume was, said Juliana pridefully, "remarkably chaste and elegant":

...satin shirt trimmed with two rows of silver gimp, short tarletan dress trimmed with scalloped edging of silver, the silver flowers put on in chaplets in front of her dress, the silver Japonica on her bosom, all the silver bracelets on her arms, silver fringe upon her gloves and boots, a small train to her dress, pearl earrings, three balls and tassels of silver on her sleeves, [while] the butterflies confined her dress behind. The waist of her dress ornamented with silver gimp....

With Julia married and out of the husband market, Margaret was finally beginning to come into her own, although in this particular dress the wonder was that the weight of the silver ornamentation did not immobilize her. But the other young ladies were dressed in equally constraining costumes, so the beaux race was an even one (New York Senator Daniel S. Dickinson appeared at the ball in a sailor suit and "acted his part to perfection"). Margaret was quite a hit, and she had no dearth of admirers at Newport.[37]

Moving on to Saratoga, she was delighted to become the object of a ludicrous romantic struggle between a Mr. Gay of New York and a Mr. Watson of Baltimore. Gay, said Margaret, was "the oddest character you ever saw," a hopeless "piece of awkwardness." Nevertheless, he was "worth at least 150,000 dollars and was the most desperately in love man in the world." Watson was less wealthy and more awkward than his New York rival—and more captivated by the attractive Margaret. "How completely convulsed you would have been," she wrote Julia, "to have seen them as I did, at the Ball, one on each side of the same column casting despairing looks at me—both completely innocent of what the other was about." While Margaret sorely wanted a husband, she was not yet reduced to utter desperation. She gave neither of these wistful-eyed suitors any encouragement. "Yes, Julia, I killed two unhappy mortals—if not outright they are dead now to a certainty," she chortled. There were better beaux than these at Saratoga, and Margaret casually flirted with them. She did not hurl herself at the summertime Romeos. As Juliana explained it, "We are quiet people and stand a little upon dignity... [and] did not become so generally known to the multitude." Still, the United States Hotel at Saratoga was a matchmaker's paradise. "There never was such a scampering after young ladies that were thought rich," noted Margaret. "It was truly amusing to all lookers on."[38]

Her sense of feminine irresistibility restored by her modest success at Newport and Saratoga, Margaret was in excellent spirits when Julia, the President, and Alice arrived in New York from Sweet Springs in September. It marked the first reunion of the family since the evacuation from Washington. Julia had planned her homecoming with great care; she had looked forward to it eagerly for several months. It would give her an opportunity to purchase "the wardrobe I want *from* head downwards," as well as dozens of household articles for Sherwood Forest. The President, Julia informed her mother, would have to return to Sherwood Forest by October 1 to superintend the fall planting ("He is too good a planter to rely entirely on the judgment of an overseer"); but she hoped she might be able to stay on to shop and visit for a while longer, "though it would never do to breathe to him that I have any rebellious intentions." Her main concern on arrival in New York was that her mother secure a proper carriage for them while she and her husband were in town. "I don't like the idea of the President's riding in a hack on his first visit to Mama," she worried. Appearances should be maintained at all times, and to assure this Juliana was instructed to engage "a neat coachman with a velvet band round his hat."

Tyler, on the other hand, looked forward to the trip to the North as an opportunity to meet again with his political followers in Philadelphia and New York. Alexander and Robert arranged a series of conferences to this end. While Julia ran riot in the stores, Tyler quietly talked politics with his friends. A brief visit to East Hampton (Tyler's first appearance there) properly impressed the townspeople. Old friendships were renewed and gossip was exchanged by the ladies. Julia discovered, however, that an ex-First Lady did not attract anywhere near the attention and deference a reigning First Lady had. Her homecoming did not make nearly the social splash of her September 1844 visit.[39]

Julia returned to Sherwood Forest in mid-October. She found the plantation cool and healthy. The fever season had passed. The New York and East Hampton visits had given her a fresh opportunity to compare her former life as the "Rose of Long Island" and "Mrs. President Tyler" with her new role as mistress of Sherwood Forest. The longer she pondered the comparison, the more convinced she became that her former New York and Washington friends could not "affect our social position in any way although we may advance theirs." She was tired of their "obsequiousness" in her husband's presence, and she decided that in the future she would "play the Queen of the White

House among them." Seeing New York again had made Julia even more of a Virginian. Her contempt for New York society was sharply increased:

> Do you know I have a sort of disgust for New York [she confided to Margaret]. I do believe it is a place unequaled in selfishness.... I do not like nowadays to be anywhere where I am no mover or to have people move without me—*nous verrons*.... Half of N.Y. cares for the other half only so far as it is likely to advance their own interests... and those who can serve one another in life are those only who seem to be "Society," of which I think one must *be* or be unpleasantly situated in a City notwithstanding all the talk about philosophy and independence. A place ought to be shunned by one who finds his presence a matter of no moment and yet who has a right to influence somewhere... don't you say amen to all this?

Julia's judgment was as harsh as her question was rhetorical, and her emotional expatriation from New York was actually to be of short duration. She would visit often and pleasantly with her family in New York and East Hampton in the years ahead, usually in the early fall, and no winter passed at Sherwood Forest without protracted visits by her mother, sister, or one of her brothers. Indeed, when the Civil War enveloped the defenseless plantation she fled home with her children to Juliana.[40]

Her complaint to Margaret about New York society in late October 1845 was the offhand remark of a troubled woman. Julia had come to a feeling of remorse in having added heavily to her husband's financial burdens. She and Tyler had spent so much money since their departure from the White House on clothes, on travel, and on furnishing the plantation that for the first time in her life she was forced to undertake a minor economy program. As a start Alexander was instructed to cancel some of the more expensive New York purchases. She toyed with the idea of effecting a $250 economy by buying a "State Coach" carriage rather than the more costly "Modern Barouche." Only after an uneven match with her fiscal conscience did she decide that the barouche was really one of life's necessities, and she asked Alexander to lend the President the $250 difference in the price. "Do you venture his credit?" she asked him. "I think you had better, and I will *stand security* for him... you will be repaid and soon." At the same time, she told Alexander that insofar as income from the Gardiner estate was concerned, it was his duty to see that their mother was made entirely comfortable before any receipts were distributed among the children. She wanted no funds from her New York property until that condition had been met, although she did warn Alexander that she might "want possibly now and then a little *pin* money."[41]

Julia's petulant attitude toward Gotham society was also partly the product of her first pregnancy. By the end of October she knew that she had become pregnant on the New York trip. She was nauseated and irritable much of the time in November, and by year's end she was complaining to her mother that a new silk dress she had bought in New York was "the *most beastly fitting* thing you ever saw ... too large by a great deal about the bust and too small by a great deal about the waist and somewhat too short. ... I am really discouraged as to what shall be done with it." [42]

There was little Julia could do about her new silk dress. Until David Gardiner Tyler was born in July 1846 her fitting problem would grow progressively more hopeless. Her general mood, however, improved rapidly as her nausea decreased. By the time Margaret and Alexander visited Sherwood Forest in late November she was beginning to snap out of her depression. Save for the tragedy of her increasingly obsolete wardrobe, by Christmas she was more concerned with the health and welfare of her pets than she was with her own condition. Compared with Tyler's growing political disappointments, Margaret's inability to catch a husband, and the poverty and sickness which stalked the Robert Tyler home in Philadelphia, Julia had no serious problems. The death of "Johnny Ty" was her saddest personal experience in 1845. The difficult transition from the White House to life at Sherwood Forest had been effected with considerable ease if not with the strictest economy.

13

TYLER AND POLK:
A QUESTION OF REPUTATION

> *I know that after the struggles of the present day shall have passed away and those who have taken part in them shall have sunk into their graves, the greater part not even to be remembered, impartial history will not fail to write a faithful account of all my actions.... The impartial future will see the motive in the act; and the just historian will look to the good and evil only which will have been developed, and find in the one or the other cause of censure or of praise. To this ordeal I submit myself without fear.*
>
> —JOHN TYLER, JUNE 1847

Politics is an unsure business, but of one bit of political business John Tyler was sure. He was certain he had reached a firm understanding with James K. Polk on patronage. His friends would not be purged from their public offices. His withdrawal from the 1844 canvass following his conversation with Robert J. Walker, and his receipt of definite assurances on the patronage matter from Major William H. Polk and Andrew Jackson could sustain in his mind no other interpretation. His subsequent dispensation of patronage to strengthen the Conservative or "Hunker" Democracy in New York at the expense of the liberal Van Buren "Barnburner" Democrats there had been, as he viewed it, the maintenance of his part of a bargain with Polk. His willingness to appoint William H. Polk to a consular post, at Young Hickory's request, was further evidence to Tyler of a "gentlemen's agreement" with the new President on the whole patronage question.

And if Tyler had used his power of appointment from November 1844 to March 1845 to keep alive a Tylerite cadre within the Conservative Democracy in New York, that action was not aimed at the Polkites. On the contrary, it sought to strengthen the Polk faction vis-à-vis Van Buren; it was designed to advance the great issue on which both Tyler and Polk had staked a large measure of their political reputation—the annexation of Texas. True, Tyler's withdrawal from the 1844 canvass may not have proved a statistically decisive factor in Polk's victory, and for this reason Young Hickory may not have felt any special obligation to reward the Tylerites with additional offices. But he had no cause to purge those of Tyler's faction who already held sinecures.

The drift of Tyler's relations with Polk in 1845–1846 was not unrelated to Tyler's continuing political ambitions for 1848. He had decided to maintain his political contacts should talk of a Democratic nomination develop. It was therefore vital that his friends retain their offices in New York and elsewhere in the interests of his availability. Shortly after his return to Sherwood Forest he began corresponding with John R. Thompson of Princeton in an effort to strengthen the Tylerite faction in New Jersey. When this contact became known he was soon in receipt of "letters from several political friends about the country suggesting the propriety and advantage of taking a tour of the principal States . . . to extend his political and social acquaintance and acquaint himself with localities, etc. in a private manner." Meanwhile, Tyler's brother-in-law, Dr. N. M. Miller, and his old friend, Judge Edward Douglass White, busied themselves in a covert attempt to raise the $6000 necessary to buy up the influential Washington *Madisonian* as a permanent Tyler organ. From Philadelphia Robert reported that the President's friends in Pennsylvania had quietly gained control of the *Spirit of the Times*. Tyler very much wanted "a press in Richmond" through which his political views might be broadcast in Virginia, and it was largely in this desire that he sought a rapprochement with editor Thomas Ritchie in the summer and fall of 1845.[1]

John Tyler was certainly not willing to campaign openly in 1845–1846, but he did make an effort to remain in the political spotlight by keeping his name and his views of current affairs before the public. Robert and Alexander organized this effort and assisted him with it. Their function was to make certain that the ex-President's opinions and observations, and those of other commentators who were pro-Tyler, appeared in such influential papers as the New York *Journal of Commerce* and the *Wall Street Reporter*. Reprints of these articles were then distributed to key Tyler allies all over the nation as a sort of political newsletter from Sherwood Forest. At the same time, attempts were made to sustain and encourage those few newspapers which lauded Tyler's administration and fairly presented his views.[2]

In May 1845, shortly after he left the White House, it was decided within the family circle that the former President's most effective tactic would be to remain quietly available. He should maintain his New York City political position through Alexander and John Lorimer Graham, and he should effect a political and personal reconciliation with the powerful Thomas Ritchie, former editor of the Richmond *Enquirer*. Ritchie was now editor of the official Polk organ, the Washington *Union*. Suggestions from Virginia friends that Tyler run again for the United States Senate to secure a public platform from which to address the nation were never seriously considered at Sherwood Forest. Instead, it was felt that this object could be accomplished more conservatively and with more dignity through the columns of friendly newspapers.

All things considered, Tyler was hopeful, in Julia's words, that his friends might "unite to give him [an] abundance of support and increase thereby his influence." Many of them did. By September 1846 Robert Tyler could assure his father there was a Tylerite group in Philadelphia upwards of three thousand in size awaiting their marching orders from Sherwood Forest. Of course, they did not march, nor were they ever called to march again under the old banner of "Tyler and Texas!" When Tyler finally made the announcement in June 1848 that he had "no expectation of again entering public life," it was based on his firm conviction at that time that there was no moderate and conservative middle within the Democracy to which he might appeal. On the contrary, the Mexican War and the Wilmot Proviso had triggered the beginning of the sectional polarization of the Democratic Party that would lead in 1860 to its final disruption, the election of Lincoln, and the Civil War. By 1848, then, Tyler's aspirations were dormant. The Virginia Democrats, he complained, "have acted a more condemnable part towards me than any others, as I am to the manner born ... [but] I learn that they at last *talk* of a move in the way of invitation to dinner." A dinner invitation was a far cry from a Presidential nomination by the Old Dominion Democracy.[3]

In spite of his lingering political ambitions, it was not Tyler's intention in 1845-1846 to make war upon the Polkites in the Democratic Party. While he wanted to keep a Tylerite faction in existence for personal reasons, his larger desire was to employ it to sustain the new President and hold the party together at the national level. He wanted neither the Locofoco nor the nullifier extremists in any positions of power in the party. He hoped instead that a working alliance between Hunker Democrats and states' rights Democrats and Whigs might be forged under the spreading ideological tent that was the Democracy. This trans-sectional grouping of moderates, as Tyler visualized it, would center its program upon continental imperialism properly viewed as a national desideratum. It would, of course, be anti-abolitionist. That the leadership of the Van Buren Democracy and the Northern Whigs opposed territorial expansion on abolitionist grounds struck Tyler as a perverse sectionalization of the foreign-policy question. Slavery and expansion, he naïvely maintained, were issues which men of good will could keep separate and distinct. Linking them for political advantage he considered despicable.

Convinced, therefore, in 1845 that a bridge from the Tylerites to the new administration had been firmly anchored on the twin pillars of a patronage understanding and a joint commitment to Manifest Destiny, the tenth President was shocked to observe Polk's ruthless purge of Tylerite officeholders during the spring and summer of 1845. That the Van Burenites and Calhounites in the Democracy appeared initially to fare no better at Polk's patronage trough than the Tylerites was not the point. The point was that Polk used his power of appointment to surround himself with territorial expansionists who were not Tylerite expansionists. He favored many New York Conservative Democrats with appointments without recognizing the Tylerites among them. Of Tyler's Cabinet and top officialdom only John Y. Mason of Virginia and Charles A. Wickliffe of Kentucky were retained by Polk. Mason became Young Hickory's Attorney General and Wickliffe was sent as a special agent to Texas to counteract lingering Anglo-French antiannexationist influence there. Thus, while the new administration took on the character of a Dixie-Hunker Democratic operation, the Tylerites were scrupulously excluded from its patronage benefits. More disturbingly, they were actively removed to make way for Polkites who were no more anti-Barnburner or pro-annexationist than the Tyler partisans they replaced.

Tyler's disillusionment with Polk grew as reports of the first removals reached Sherwood Forest. As early as March 27, 1845, Julia's dressmaker in Washington inaccurately informed her that Army officers who had been close to the social life of the White House during Julia's reign were being transferred to remote stations. Four days later N. M. Miller told Alexander Gardiner that Polk's "work of decapitation" was under way in the capital. This action he attributed to the influence of the Democracy's Locofoco clique at the White House, particularly Francis P. Blair and the Washington *Globe*, who were "rabid and clamorous for the removal of every Tyler man." He felt that Tyler "would do well to profit by the moral of the fable of little Red Riding Hood and the wolf." The fact that Polk withdrew Tom Cooper's nomination for Surveyor of the Port of Philadelphia from the Senate produced great alarm within the family. "I am utterly at a loss to account for this," said Alexander, "for there was certainly a right to expect a very different course of action." [4]

Indeed there was. So upset was Alexander over these shocking developments that he composed a stiff letter to Polk recalling Tyler's aid in the 1844 campaign and arguing the right of *every* Democrat to be "retained in office until the expiration of his term." The Tylerites were Polk's friends, Alexander reminded the new President. "Turn them out they become *your enemies*. Do those by whom you supplant them *become your friends?* No. They are the friends of the partisans through whose influence they have become appointed—of Mr. Dallas, of Mr. Buchanan, of Mr. Walker, of Mr. Benton, of Mr. Wright, prominent gentlemen around the throne and candidates for the successor." [5]

Polk needed no gratuitous lecture on the patronage realities of factional politics. He had been in the business a long time. And nothing from Alexander Gardiner's pen could stay his decision to place into office and retain in office men loyal only to himself—not to John Tyler or anyone else. He did, however, relent in the case of Tom Cooper and appoint the sixty-nine-year-old actor to an inspectorship in the New York Customs House. But by April the other Tylerites in Gotham were reported by Alexander "resting quietly" and insecurely amid growing rumors of planned proscriptions. Only the *Plebeian* among the New York papers gave them "even a negative support." This dangerous situation led Alexander to the rueful conclusion that the support of the press was of more political consequence in the long run "than the most extensive patronage without it ... its value cannot be magnified." With the *Aurora* defunct and no Tylerite newspaper outlet in the city, the future for the ex-President's friends there looked grim. Not quite as grim as in Philadelphia, where the coming of May found all the Tylerites "decapitated," but black enough. The Philadelphia story, thought Margaret, was clear evidence of the "coldest ingratitude that one could be capable of." [6]

By May 1845 the New York City purge was also on in earnest and a worried Juliana informed Sherwood Forest that "the Tyler men meet but little quarter under the present administration." Among the first to go was William Gibbs McNeill. Pressure was also building up on Polk for the removal of John Lorimer Graham and Cornelius P. Van Ness. "The Van Buren and Anti-Texas men seem to be strong at headquarters," Alexander noted sadly. Whatever its ideological cutting edge, the anti-Tylerite axe struck Postmaster Graham on May 6 and he left the lush office amid a clamor of charges that his conduct of the New York City Post Office had not been without personal gain. The family was certain that his removal—and that of McNeill—demonstrated the Van Burenist leanings of Polk. Actually, Polk had no such clear-cut orientation; he was no Locofoco, but his abrupt removal of Collector Van Ness in June did nothing to disabuse the Gardiners and Tylers of that notion. "The conduct of Mr. Polk," opined Alexander, "appears to me to have been cold and ungrateful in the extreme and may lead to the defeat of the Democratic party in '48." [7]

A feeling of betrayal by Polk stalked the family circle as Nathaniel

P. Tallmadge fell in Wisconsin and Silas Reed in Missouri. Close personal and political associates of Tyler were also purged in Ohio and in Illinois. Tyler accurately termed it "an unrelenting war against the few sincere friends I left in office," noting to Alexander that "the blood of the martyr is said to be the seed of the church—*nous verrons*—I watch in silence the course of events."[8]

The longer Tyler watched, the more angry he became. Particularly humiliating to him was the way Polk toyed with his brother-in-law, N. M. Miller, first demoting him from Second Assistant Postmaster General to Third Assistant, then purging him altogether. At the same time, attempts by William Tyler, the ex-President's brother, and Robert Tyler to secure modest patronage positions from Polk met with cool indifference in the White House. Tyler had accommodated Polk's brother, it was recalled in the family, but the return favor seemed beyond Young Hickory's sense of moral obligation.[9]

Tyler's frustration increased daily. A rumor that Secretary Bancroft had unceremoniously removed the former President's portrait from a wall in the Navy Department disturbed the Sherwood Foresters a great deal, as did their growing realization that Polk was neither a man of his word nor a sagacious politician. Only Polk's Mexican policy reconciled Tyler at all to the new regime:

> I left some two hundred personal friends in office [Tyler noted in September] who were also the warm, active and determined friends of Mr. Polk in the late contest—a small number in comparison to the 40,000 officeholders. They have been for the most part removed or superseded. Some half dozen remain.... I cannot but sympathize with them—but I go no further. I shall neither seek to augment their discomfort or desire to encourage it—but I cannot but express the belief that Mr. Polk wars upon himself in permitting war on them. They were his true friends—men who would have battled for him at every step of his administration... they may still do so, and my hope is that they will.... I consider him entitled to the support of the whole country for his course on the Texas question as far as developments have gone....

The whole administration, General John P. Van Ness agreed, was politically "very contemptible."[10]

Not surprisingly, the prestige of the Polk administration sank rapidly and steadily within the Tyler-Gardiner family as Young Hickory snuffed out the precarious life of the Tyler faction. Tyler himself became persuaded that Polk's proscription of the Tylerites could only result in a Whig victory in 1848. "If Polk had played his game wisely," he confided to Robert in the summer of 1848, "he would have reconsolidated the old Republican party.... Such was my policy; but he destroyed, I fear, all that I built up, by the proscriptions of my friends." In this analysis Alexander concurred.[11]

As the sands of the arena soaked up the blood of Tylerite martyrs, Juliana and Margaret urged Alexander to disengage himself entirely from the sordid world of politics. He was simply wasting his time and his money because Polk was in "no way friendly to the Tyler party." "Oh! these politics," lamented Juliana, "I pity anyone who depends upon popular favor for preferment or happiness...it is indeed a broken reed." Alexander would not accept their well-meaning advice. He enjoyed politics whatever the cost, and he continued playing the game within Tammany Hall well into 1846. Letters from his busy quill praising the Tyler administration's patriotic sagacity in the annexation of Texas continued to appear in New York newspapers. Against increasing odds he struggled to maintain a hard core Tylerite cadre within Tammany Hall in the vain hope that the political roulette wheel would again come up with John Tyler in 1848. For this reason he held onto his Circuit Court clerkship with the tenacity of a boa constrictor.[12]

At least Alexander had a clerkship. Robert Tyler could point to no such lasting benefit from his own involvement with his father's political fortunes. He had given up his post in the Land Office in 1844 and had sought and secured no other office prior to Tyler's departure from the White House in 1845. He now had no prospect that Polk would bestow one upon him. In subordinating his Philadelphia law practice to Tylerite politics, he had reaped financial hardship and a distraught wife. Overwhelmed by poverty, family illnesses, and the tragic deaths of her babies (Mary Fairlee in 1845 and John in 1846), Priscilla, like Margaret and Juliana, viewed the alleged advantages of political life with reservation. In fact, the distressed woman suffered a complete nervous breakdown in 1846 under the impact of economic privation and personal sorrow. She was just beginning to recover her health and cheerfulness when her father died in April 1849. This blow was followed three months later by the death of her infant son, Thomas Cooper Tyler, at age one year. Again she was cast into gloom. Throughout these desperate years she pleaded with her husband to abandon politics and concentrate on his lagging law practice.

But Robert Tyler, like Alexander Gardiner, could not and would not disengage from the political process. Whatever its sacrifices, and for his family they were considerable, he gambled with politics until he died. And he died poor. In 1847 James Buchanan was instrumental in securing for him an appointment as Solicitor in the Philadelphia Sheriff's Office, a minor post which assured him a small annual income. After a discouraging start, his law practice gradually grew, although it never really prospered. In 1850 he was appointed Prothonotary of the Supreme Court of Pennsylvania, an office he held until the outbreak of the Civil War when he fled to Virginia to cast his lot with the Confederacy. This post finally brought Robert a modest measure of financial security and enabled him to move his family from the tiny cottage in Bristol into a new home on Rowlandson's Row in Philadelphia. By 1852 he was largely out of debt and Priscilla was occasionally able to entertain "the best people" in town. The Robert Tylers were never really well off, but during the 1850s they were comfortable and they managed to stay a short hop ahead of their creditors. Priscilla had three more children during the decade, all of whom lived.

Robert, of course, continued playing the political game. From 1848 until 1860 he was one of Buchanan's trusted political lieutenants in Philadelphia, specializing in mustering the Irish-American vote there for the greater glory of "Old Buck" and his Pennsylvania machine. Indeed, he played a major role in Buchanan's nomination in Cincinnati in 1856, and two years later he was named Chairman of the Democratic Executive Committee of Pennsylvania, a post which paid in the coin of prestige only. His political career, however, was solidly Buchanan-based after 1848. Polk did nothing for him and Robert returned the favor.[13]

Julia's attitude toward the Polk administration was no more enthusiastic than that of the other members of the family. It gave her a wry pleasure, of course, to learn that Sarah Polk's White House reign was considered in Washington social circles to be downright dull. It was, Alexander assured her, viewed with "general indifference." Sarah's narrow Methodism would not permit any drinking, card playing, or dancing in the White House. For this reason her four-year tenure in the President's Mansion was generally dubbed a social failure from beginning to end, though it was cheered by the prohibitionists and certain lunatic-fringe ecclesiastical groups as a great triumph of Christian virtue. When Alexander went to the capital in February 1846 to head off a Tammany raid on his clerkship, he found the President "excessively plain and equally devoid of manner and tact in conversation." From a strictly social standpoint, he told Julia, Washington was "not by any means what it was last winter." The only party he enjoyed was a jam-packed affair at the home of the John Y. Masons, where "the floor drank as much champagne as the guests, and it was an even chance whether the viands once lifted would reach the mouth or take some other direction." Nor was Julia convinced that the new President, whatever his shortcomings as a host, was a man of sound judgment. When she learned, for example, that Polk had offered the London mission to her old flame, Francis W. Pickens, she wondered at the common sense of Young Hickory. "What an incompetent Minister he would make at this crisis," she exclaimed. "His talents are quite too superficial for an emergency." She was relieved to hear a few days later that Pickens had turned down the post on Calhoun's urging, the South Carolinian wanting no such close connection with the new administration.[14]

Julia's disenchantment with Polk stemmed from her unquestioning acceptance of the family thesis that the new President was a Jacksonian mouthpiece, a Locofoco radical, who was purging the Tylerites because of their sane and patriotic political conservatism. Jackson had never been a favorite in the Gardiner family, and from Julia's standpoint Young Hickory was no improvement over Old Hickory. Both were dangerous levelers. Thus when the Old Warrior of the Hermitage finally died in June 1845 no tears were shed at Sherwood Forest or at 43 Lafayette Place. Indeed, when citizens in Norfolk and Portsmouth invited Tyler to deliver a eulogy to Jackson, Julia reported her husband "in a *complete dilemma* for he does not see how he can decline it without giving offense." Tyler, of course, did not decline. He was too much of a gentleman. He went through with it. Alexander also managed a gracious gesture to Jackson's memory at the Shelter Island Fourth of July celebration. Nevertheless, the family was not overcome by sorrow when Andrew Jackson was gathered unto his fathers. They had a strong suspicion, not unfounded, that the Polk purge of the Tylerites had been encouraged by the palsied hand of the aged General. Jackson had, in fact, written Polk soon after the 1844 election that "the offices are filling up by Tyler, so that all his partisans must remain in office or you be compelled to remove them ... give yourself elbow room whenever it becomes necessary." That Tyler had appointed Jackson's nephew, Andrew J. Donelson, United States *chargé* in Mexico in September 1844 did not temper the vindictiveness of the Hero of New Orleans. To the victors belonged the spoils.[15]

Nothing disturbed Julia quite so much as partisan attacks (she considered them Polk-inspired) on her husband's reputation, on his personal integrity, and on his political beliefs. His enemies were her enemies; and his struggle for Clio's accolade became her struggle. It was a time-consuming occupation during her first years at Sherwood Forest. Indeed, the entire family devoted considerable time and effort to the project of monitoring newspapers for references to the Tyler administration and its works. Pro-Tyler notices were happily circulated throughout the family circle and attempts were made to have them reprinted in other journals. Criticisms of the ex-President were vigorously contested in letters by Robert, Alexander and John Tyler himself to the editors involved. Hiram Cumming's exposé *The Secret History of the Tyler Dynasty* was branded the tissue of lies it was, and exception was taken to various statements and judgments in the generally accurate Mordecai Noah series on the Tyler administration which appeared in the New York *Sunday Dispatch* in early 1846. "He represents as facts things and affairs very new to the President," said Julia in some bewilderment. Many of the personal attacks on himself Tyler felt were "too gross to regard, still there are so many who are kept ignorant of facts it is hard to resist opening their eyes." Defenses of Tyler's administration penned by Robert and Alexander were sent first to Sherwood Forest, where they were edited and amended by Tyler before reaching print. Conversely, Tyler's own remarks in defense of his policies were placed in New York newspapers whenever possible by

Alexander. Reprints were obtained and then distributed to former Tylerite chieftains throughout the nation.[16]

The ex-President was particularly sensitive to the charge that his advocacy of Texas annexation had been a manifestation of slavocracy rampant. He was also easily upset by the slur that he had been a "President by accident." When, for example, Lord Brougham used the obnoxious phrase ("The miserable slang of Clay and his satellites," Tyler called it) in an 1845 House of Lords speech attacking Tyler on the Texas issue, the remark was challenged by the Philadelphia *Ledger* with the observation that Victoria herself was "Queen by accident." Tyler was delighted with the *Ledger*'s comment and sought to have it reprinted in other papers. After all, said the former President, Victoria had come to "the crown by the death of her predecessors as I to the Presidency by the death of the President."

Alexander was instructed to compose defenses of Tyler's Texas policy, emphasizing the point that Tyler had no interest in the slavery-expansion feature of annexation. These appeared, sometimes anonymously, under such titles as "The Voice of the Impartial as to the Administration of John Tyler." Julia made it clear to her brother precisely what Tyler wanted from him in these matters relating to his historical reputation:

I will tell you also what the President *I know* privately wishes; that you would not overlook the misrepresentations, when they appear in the papers, of him, to pass unnoticed. It cannot be best for no one to come forward in New York to notice them and let untruths as regards the acts, etc. of the President's administration be disseminated far and wide. When they appear in Philadelphia papers Robert T., I perceive, invariably corrects them over his signature, and why should not you do the same.... Whenever such misrepresentations as the one I enclose appear and another which the President himself noticed to you a few mails since, it is proper they should meet your attention ... with your own full signature at the bottom.[17]

Julia had no intention of being remembered as the First Lady of an administration history would count a failure. She was therefore unremitting in her efforts to set Clio straight before the histories were written. While the Tyler administration had not been as pure morally as driven snow, it had been uncommonly free of the petty corruption that had characterized previous administrations. Its foreign policy had been a series of dramatic successes and the failures of its domestic policies, however evaluated by future historians, had at least been founded on an honest effort to find areas of accommodation among moderate Whigs and Democrats. Its patronage record had been neither more nor less venal than those of the Jackson and Van Buren administrations. Compared with Polk's patronage ethics, Tyler's seemed almost pristine. Tyler's word was his bond in such matters. There was also the larger question of the constitutional status of the Vice-Presidency, the resolution of which could be counted a solid plus for Tyler. "If the tide of defamation and abuse shall turn," he told Robert in 1848, "and my administration come to be praised, future Vice Presidents who may succeed to the Presidency may feel some slight encouragement to pursue an independent course." The alternative to this would be Vice-Presidents so frightened by their accession to the Presidency that "the executive power will be completely in abeyance and Congress will unite the legislative and executive functions." [18]

Julia thought the nation should understand and appreciate these things, and she urged the active cooperation of the entire family in untangling the record before it was twisted further. She was not as concerned as were Robert and Alexander that her husband stay available for the 1848 Democratic nomination. She demanded only that he receive historical justice for what he had accomplished in the White House. Even her family complained sometimes that she was "too sensitive" to criticisms of the ex-President. She was pleased to note, therefore, that several newspapers long hostile to Tyler began in April 1846 to treat her husband more gently. "After exhausting their abuse, they have come to see that John Tyler's administration left the country in the most prosperous and happy condition... this is the language of the U.S. *Gazette* and other Whig papers of Philadelphia. Pray keep us *au fait* of any change of opinion in N.Y.," she instructed Alexander.[19]

The family was particularly pleased—grateful for small favors—when the good ladies of Brazoria County, Texas, saw fit to present Tyler a lovely silver pitcher in gratitude for his leading role in the annexation of the Lone Star Republic. The unexpected gift arrived at Sherwood Forest on New Year's Day 1846, and Tyler, deeply touched by the gesture, responded with a gracious letter of thanks which received as much national publicity as had the fact of the gift itself. Margaret impishly suggested that "a grant of a thousand or two acres of the best Texas land" would have made a somewhat more impressive gift, but the family was really much affected by the present.[20]

The Brazoria pitcher symbolized the fact that some of the old anti-Tyler passions were slowly dying out. Tyler did much to bank the partisan fires himself. In May 1846 he went to Washington (his first return visit there since March 1845) to appear as a witness before the House Foreign Affairs Committee. A month earlier, Democratic Representative Charles J. Ingersoll of Pennsylvania had charged Daniel Webster with a misuse of money from the Secret Service Fund in 1842. Secretary of State Webster, it was alleged, had employed the money to bribe newspaper editors and the Boundary Commissioners of Maine and Massachusetts. This, said Ingersoll, had been done to insure public acceptance of the Maine Boundary Treaty which Webster and Tyler had negotiated with Lord Ashburton in the full knowledge that American claims to the disputed territory were better cartographically and stronger legally than the final territorial settlement had reflected. In sum, the smell of treason permeated the Ingersoll charge, to say nothing of the Pennsylvanian's further imputation that Webster had also dipped money out of the Fund for his personal use.

As keeper of the Secret Service Fund in 1842 Tyler was by direct implication a party to the Ingersoll attack on Webster, and he hastened to the capital to support his former Secretary. Representative Thomas H. Bayley of Virginia, representing the Charles City district in Washington, defended Tyler on the floor of the House against any suggestion of wrongdoing, although his defense was not as vigorous as Alexander thought the situation demanded. Similarly, an attack on Tyler's honesty and integrity in the Fund matter by the alcoholic and unstable Virginia Representative George C. Dromgoole rankled the family circle a great deal. Webster in his own defense stated publicly that throughout the Maine Boundary negotiations he had acted under the constant counsel and direction of Tyler. Nonetheless, he said he was quite prepared to answer Ingersoll's charges without reference to that fact. He did, however, solicit Tyler's testimony on the question. The whole thing, said Julia, was merely additional evidence of calculated "injustice to John Tyler." She dismissed Dromgoole as an embittered antiannexationist and Van Burenite. "You may depend upon it the President will stand by Daniel Webster," Julia assured Margaret. "He alone directed [the treaty] and he alone deserves any credit or abuse attached to it." [21]

Tyler's heralded appearance before the Ingersoll committee was anticlimactic. With a sure grasp of the facts and figures of the Secret Service Fund, he demonstrated the mathematical impossibility of Ingersoll's charges. There just was not enough money in the Fund to finance all the alleged sins. It was an impressive, convincing, and dignified exposition, and the committee's deference to him increased proportionally as the charges against Webster slowly collapsed. Still, the partisan maneuverings of the politicians on the Fund issue disgusted him. "I turn my back upon the miserable set ... with indescribable pleasure," he told Robert as he prepared to return home to Sherwood Forest. With philosophic resignation he concluded that he would probably have to expect continued indirect attacks of the Ingersoll-Dromgoole sort until the campaign of 1848 when "the courtship for my friends will begin." [22]

The May 1846 trip to Washington did afford Tyler an opportunity to visit his friends in the capital. Dinner with Polk at the White House was uneventful. The table conversation centered on the Mexican War (which had begun two weeks earlier) rather than on domestic political developments. The purge of the Tylerites was not broached by the former President. Following this standoff with Young Hickory, the John Y. Masons, Daniel Websters, and Robert J. Walkers came forward to entertain him. The former President was wined and dined and called upon until he was fatigued. "One unbroken stream has flowed in upon me during the whole time that I have been here," he wrote Robert. "This has been gratifying... [but] my harvest is about beginning, and home is my place." So popular had John Tyler apparently become in Washington that N. M. Miller was moved to remark that "a stranger would have inferred that he was still the dispenser of patronage." Indeed, concluded John Lorimer Graham, "there is [now] a disposition to render unto Caesar the things that are Caesar's. A comparison is now drawn between the past and present administration of public affairs in almost every circle, greatly to the advantage of the former. We have always said that History would do justice to our friend...."[23]

If Clio had manufactured for Tyler the beginning of a Mona Lisa smile, the glad tidings were not conveyed to John C. Calhoun. The iron-jawed and iron-willed Carolinian, whose ego was exceeded only by his intellectual arrogance, decided in February 1847 that he and he alone had unilaterally annexed the Republic of Texas to the United States. "I may now rightfully and indisputably claim," said Calhoun without noticeable modesty, "to be the author of that great measure—a measure which has so much extended the domains of the Union; which added so largely to its productive powers; which promises so greatly to extend its commerce; which has stimulated its industry, and given security to our much exposed frontier." More alarming to Tyler, Calhoun's claim minimized the national economic advantages of annexation and identified the action with the South's interest in slavery expansion.[24]

Senator Calhoun's wild grab for the historical accolade of Texas annexation, an accolade properly Tyler's and one on which Honest John had painstakingly constructed his personal appeal to history, produced nothing less than outrage in the Tyler-Gardiner family. Alexander found very little "South Carolina chivalry" in Calhoun's speech, and he advised the former President to prepare a memoir of his administration which would put the Texas matter in its proper light. For a few weeks Tyler seriously considered his brother-in-law's suggestion. Even if an autobiographical exposition of his foreign policy would be "of no value to the great crowd," it might, he thought, be "acceptable to those who may come after me." He was extremely upset by Calhoun's impertinence. "Was there ever anything to surpass in selfishness the assumption of Mr. Calhoun?" he asked heatedly. "He assumes everything to himself, overlooks his associates in the Cabinet, and takes the reins of the government into his own hands.... He is the great 'I am,' and myself and Cabinet have no voice in the matter." Instead of an extensive personal memoir (the "building up and reclaiming an estate which had been permitted well nigh to run to waste" left him with no time to write an autobiography), Tyler dispatched two dignified letters to the Richmond *Enquirer* patiently explaining again the national character of annexation and the commercial and economic motives that had influenced his actions and thinking in the matter. At the same time, he assured Alexander that Calhoun's narrowing of the Texas question "to the comparatively contemptible ground of Southern and local interest" had distressed him more than the South Carolinian's arrogant claim of sole authorship, "for it substantially converted the executive into a mere Southern agency in place of being what it truly was—the representative of American interests... and if ever there was an American question, then Texas was that very question." Alexander and Robert were both urged to see to it that the Richmond *Enquirer* letters were reprinted in Northern papers, and that Tyler's interpretation of the national character of Texas annexation be brought once more to the attention of the Northern public.[25]

Julia thought Calhoun's February 24 Texas speech "the height of *impudence.*" She too was distressed that the South Carolinian had unnecessarily stirred up the slavery issue, and she advised Alexander that her husband could not let that phase of the matter pass unnoticed. Robert Tyler immediately challenged Calhoun's statement in a series of private letters to the senator. These produced no answers and no satisfaction. Juliana again threw up her hands in despair over the morality of politics and politicians. "It is rather late in the day for Mr. C. to be claiming the honor of it," she snorted. Where was Calhoun hiding in January 1844, she wondered, when the Texas measure was still unsettled and when "such heavy denunciations were pronounced against John Tyler for daring to effect it?" Calhoun had remained silent then. "As for President Tyler," she told Julia in disgust, "his laurels are destined I fear to be few if left to be awarded by his Cabinet. Webster in relation to the Ashburton treaty was much more courteous in admitting he acted under the instructions of the President. Indeed after this from Mr. Calhoun I think Mr. W[ebster] acted a much higher part." Toward Calhoun personally, the family decided finally to observe a "marked silence." There was little else they could do.[26]

The attempt to strip Tyler of his Texas laurels gathered momentum in 1847. Sam Houston began claiming that it was Andrew Jackson who had really engineered annexation. Tyler, in turn, attacked Houston for having slowed up the annexation process by his pro-British flirtations in 1844–1845. Meanwhile, Tyler was skewered by the Whig *National Intelligencer* for having been influenced in his Texas policy by "the speculators in Texas stocks and lands by whom he was surrounded, counseled and impelled to that unwise measure." Categorically denying the latter charge and the accompanying innuendo that he had personally profited by the annexation, Tyler insisted again that he "saw nothing but the country and the whole country, not this or that section, this or that local interest, but the WHOLE... the glory of the whole country in the measure."[27]

These were the opening salvos in a war for reputation that would rage for years as Tylers and Gardiners fought to assure John Tyler full historical credit for the one great accomplishment of his public life. In 1848 a nervous Tyler finally circularized the former members of his Cabinet, soliciting from them their recollections on the annexation question as these might pertain to the claims of Calhoun and Houston and to the charges leveled against him by the *National Intelligencer*. As he received their various written testimonials he was satisfied that his own mind had not played tricks on him, and that his point of view would be fully sustained in the eyes and judgment of history. Nevertheless, as late as 1856–1858 Tyler was still parrying threats to deprive him of the historical glory of his Texas accomplishment. Again he argued that Calhoun had played no important role in annexation ("Mr. Calhoun had no more to do with it than a man in Nova Zembla"). Upshur's role, under the President's daily direction, had been the vital one in preparing the treaty, Tyler maintained. Further, Texas annexation, by gravitational pull, had also brought California into the Union. The inclusion of California went well beyond what Tyler could reasonably claim for his Texas Annexation Treaty, even though he supported the Mexican War which Polk brought on to insure the additional acquisition of California. But there can be no doubt that Tyler's role in Texas annexation was the decisive one. And in boldly seeing it through he earned his place in American history, shaky as that niche seemed in the 1850s.[28]

Although at times Tyler felt he might truly detach himself from the sting of adverse public opinion, the fact was that every slight, every misrepresentation of his motives, cut his psyche deeply. Nor did it help much to tell himself that the opinions of the masses were worthless. "By far the greater part of them do not think at all," he argued. "The majority of those who do assert the reasoning facility conceal their opinion even from themselves from fear of inflicting self-injury." Even when he was criticized in what Alexander assured him were the "trash weeklies," newspapers with absolutely no circulation "among respectable classes," Tyler was upset. When Tyler was hurt, Julia was hurt. She therefore urged Robert and her brothers to continue their strict monitoring of the press and to report all evidences of anti-Tylerism to Sherwood Forest. Pro-Tyler references, of course, were still to be reprinted and circulated as widely as possible. So insistent and thin-skinned was Julia in this regard that her mother finally admonished her:

You must not think us so indifferent to the publications respecting the P. We were very sensitive at first and felt all the slanders cast upon him, but now we have become wiser and let all pass as something not worth regarding. When a good thing is said Alex and D[avid] are the first to see it, and speak of it at home and turn a deaf ear and blind eye to all that is bad. I should think by this time you had arrived at the same philosophical state.

Neither Julia nor her husband was ever able to reach that "philosophical state."²⁹

Tyler's position on the Mexican War produced new criticisms to which the family could close neither its ears nor eyes. The war split the opinion of the nation and brought James K. Polk under heavy attack from abolitionist Northern Whigs and Democrats who maintained that the President's war of conquest in the Southwest was designed for no purpose other than to conquer more land for slavery expansion—to secure bigger pens to put more slaves in. Ironically, Tyler suddenly found himself publicly defending an administration he personally disliked and a military venture in Mexico about which he had deep-seated reservations. In addition, this defense of Polk brought him under a brisk fire which once again linked him with the aggressive Southern slavocracy and with Texas land and stock speculations. It was a cruel dilemma. Tyler tried to solve it intellectually by refusing to admit the obvious fact that there was a causal connection between Texas annexation and the war itself. This too was Alexander's position, and about the best that can be said for it is that it had the advantage of separating the two men from the most blatant of the warmongers. "What does it matter whether it was caused by the annexation of Texas, or the marching of the American troops into the territory between the Nueces and the Rio Grande?" Gardiner asked in a speech written for a war rally in Tammany Hall. "The Historical or Antiquarian Society can settle this point on some long winter evening." Actually, it mattered a great deal. The Mexican government had long argued that the annexation of its province of Texas would be an overt act of war. True, no serious warlike preparations were launched in Mexico City after the annexation was formally completed by an exchange of treaty ratifications in July 1845. Nor were there any Mexican military preparations of significance until Polk provoked them early in 1846 in his eagerness for a war that would dismember the remnants of the Mexican Empire and secure California, New Mexico, and Arizona to the United States.

In this aggressive activity John Tyler played no part. He felt privately, however, that Polk's policy on the Rio Grande was unnecessarily provocative; and he insisted publicly that had the Senate passed his annexation treaty when he first submitted it to them in April 1844 there would have been no war at all. At that crucial moment in 1844, he explained, Anglo-American relations had been excellent, thanks in large measure to the 1842 Webster-Ashburton Treaty settlement of outstanding frictions between the two nations. A subsequent deterioration in these relations had occurred in late 1845, principally on the Oregon question. This decline Tyler traced to irresponsible Democratic demands for "Fifty-four Forty or Fight!" and to Polk's Annual Message of December 1845 which implied that the frosty latitude was the only settlement line in Oregon to which the United States could agree. This rising tension in Anglo-American affairs, Tyler further explained, had emboldened the Mexicans to cross the Rio Grande at Matamoros on April 24, 1846, and contest General Zachary Taylor's right to be encamped in the disputed territory between the Rio Grande and Nueces. The Mexicans, Tyler's analysis continued, had earlier had no "hope of succor, or aid from any quarter." In April 1846, however, they could look to London with some hope that British assistance would be forthcoming in their war with the Americans. More importantly, thought the former President, the war could only stimulate the rapid revival of the domestic slavery controversy and all the political and sectional dangers inherent in that smoldering subject. It was also clear to Tyler that in the contest between David and Goliath the American giant would annex vast reaches of new territory and the question of whether those areas would be organized slave or free could not long be avoided. He was therefore completely sincere when he said, on the eve of the conflict, "I should deprecate a war as next to the greatest of evils." [30]

Once Polk's crusade into Mexico and California had been set in motion in April 1846 Tyler joined Alexander in publicly proclaiming it the most "just war" ever fought by the American people. This was for the patriotic record. Privately, Tyler confessed to Alexander his concern over the morality of the unequal struggle. But he felt he could do nothing about it. Thus he noted with resignation that "even if the war be improper in its inception, there is no other mode by which we can get out of it with honor.... I go for whipping Mexico until she cries enough." Tyler, it will be recalled, had been perfectly willing to dismember the Mexican Empire in 1842, but he had hoped to accomplish his aim without bloodshed. There was too much blood and thunder in Polk's approach to suit him.[31]

As Floyd Waggaman, James A. Semple, and other Tyler-Gardiner kin marched off to fight the Mexicans, war fever swept through the entire family. John, Jr., willingly gave up his languishing law studies in a burst of patriotic fervor. Girding himself for combat, he implored his father to help him get a commission in the Army. Tyler agreed to try, but only on the condition that his son promise to forswear the use of liquor forever. John, Jr., accepted this condition, and Tyler reluctantly asked Polk for the favor. The President gladly obliged his predecessor and John, Jr., was soon Captain Tyler. He saw no action and quickly forgot his pledge, but he enjoyed army life immensely. "Excitement of some sort he must have," sighed Julia.

Not to be outdone by his younger brother, Robert Tyler raised a company of Philadelphia volunteers, mostly Irish-Americans, and pleaded with Pennsylvania authorities for an opportunity to march his unit off to kill Mexicans. The fact that there was a new baby in his household and that Priscilla strenuously opposed the idea did nothing to dull his ardor for service on the Rio Grande. When the honor of fighting was denied him by the governor, Robert was disconsolate. Tyler comforted him with the thought that the Rio Grande region was an unhealthy place and that "few laurels" could be won in such a war anyway. He was better off tending his struggling law business and advancing his political fortunes at home.

Julia, meanwhile, followed the war news avidly. She cheered each predictable victory and wrung her hands over the fate of the Mexican noncombatants. "What thrilling accounts every mail brings us from the seat of war," she wrote to Margaret. "The taking of Vera Cruz though glorious for our arms was ... terrible for the poor women and children." At the same time she devoutly hoped that neither of her brothers would "ever feel any martial fire glow in [their] veins," and that neither would join the glorious crusade to Mexico City. Neither did. Colonel David Lyon had no desire to leave the comforts of Lafayette Place, and Alexander felt he could do more for the war effort on the home front. Julia felt, however, that her brothers might at least show some patriotic enthusiasm for the unequal slaughter:

Are you not interested in, and do you never think of the war? It is full of thrilling interest in my opinion, but you do not seem even to think of it. What a glorious country is America! Who can recount such deeds of courage and valor as our countrymen? My opinion of them has never been half justice. I think that almost all are manly spirits. All nearly are capable of being heroes, and a coward constitutes the exception.[32]

Alexander actually thought a great deal about the war. In addition to delivering stirring pro-war orations inside and outside of Tammany Hall, he realistically evaluated some of the political and economic consequences of the conflict. He was hopeful that the "immense military patronage" the President held would ultimately be employed to break the backs of all the antiwar Whigs and Democrats. He saw also that the war-stimulated rise in wheat and corn prices was benefiting his kin at Sherwood Forest. When the conflict was over, he stood with his new brother-in-law, John H. Beeckman (Margaret's husband), and lustily cheered the returning New York Volunteers, "yielding to the enthusiasm of the moment somewhat to the damage of my hat." Within the family then, only Juliana could see no sense, profit, or glory in the war; nor could she generate any excitement for it. To her the whole thing "appeared quite improbable to my mind from the beginning." [33]

Alexander was much more critical of Polk's cautious diplomacy with Britain on the eve of the Mexican War than was John Tyler. Gardiner was particularly distressed to learn that the President was willing to settle the Oregon boundary dispute with England at the forty-ninth parallel. By February 1846 he had become fearful lest Polk's effort to compromise the boundary on that reasonable basis (thus wisely avoiding complications with Britain while he was preparing to despoil Mexico) "lose us a considerable portion of the territory—that portion of it north of forty-nine degrees." Alexander Gardiner was a thoroughgoing fire-eater. Unlike Tyler and Polk, he was quite willing to see the United States fight Mexico and Britain simultaneously. He seems to have believed the jingoistic nonsense about 54°40′ even though the American claim to territory north of the forty-ninth parallel was so dim legally as to be virtually nonexistent. His sister Margaret agreed with him, however, and promised him she would boycott all things English. "Until England accedes to '54°-40′,' " she told Julia, "I must eschew everything English." Robert Tyler likewise surrendered to Anglophobia in a violent form during the renewal of the Oregon controversy in 1846, although as head of Philadelphia's Irish Repeal Association and an active functionary in Irish-American politics there, his capitulation was perhaps predictable. In any event, he was a frequent and dedicated twister of the Lion's Tail on the Oregon boundary question, and he was all for raising a brigade to help drive the Redcoats from the Northwest.[34]

Tyler considered the views of his son and his brother-in-law on the Oregon problem shortsighted and dangerous. In a series of letters to Robert he explained his fear of an Anglo-American war over Oregon and the disadvantages of such a conflict for the United States:

I fear a war for the *whole* [of Oregon] will lose us the *whole*.... I go for peace if it can be preserved on fair terms. The United States require still a peace of twenty years, and then they hold in their hands the destiny of the human race. But if war does come, we shall fight on the side of right. Our claim to Oregon to the forty-ninth is clear; what lies beyond is attended with colorable title.... [But] should we be found at war, then every man should do his duty, and God forbid that a son of mine should be recusant. The brigade by all means! It gives you position and control. My thoughts, however, I must confess, are turned to peace.... For myself, I would much prefer success where you are.... Make but one speech in court equal to those you made at the [Irish Repeal Association] meetings, and all will be well.... Your Oregon meeting was certainly immense.... The resolutions which were adopted are sufficiently *ultra*.... But war! war! is the cry in which Democrats, Whigs, Abolitionists unite. Strange union, indeed. The objects of the last are easily understood. They seek not Oregon, but the Canadas, as means of overbalancing Texas. War, I also say, before one jot or tittle of the public honor be surrendered; but that is the very point to be decided.[35]

Happily for Anglo-American relations, a timely Cabinet crisis in London brought the muzzling of the imperialist Lord Palmerston by the peace-oriented Peel ministry. In addition, the successful repeal of the controversial Corn Laws in England, coupled with Polk's unwillingness to fight a war for 54°40′ while he was engaged on the Rio Grande, ultimately brought hotheads on both sides of the Atlantic under control. The responsible leaders of neither nation really wanted a war on the Oregon issue and the crisis passed safely into history. In June 1846 a treaty was concluded which divided the territory along the forty-ninth parallel.

For this Tyler was thankful. Peace was more sensible and much more profitable than war and he knew that the American claim for territory north of the compromise demarcation was "attended with colorable title." The repeal of the English Corn Laws, which abolished import duties on foreign grains, was "a measure of the greatest moment" for all American grain exporters, Tyler noted. With the assurance of peace, "The tide of prosperity will flow in upon us; the value of everything will be increased." Even war hawk Alexander had sober second thoughts about the Oregon matter toward the end of March 1846. "I have no doubt," he informed Sherwood Forest, that "the conclusion of a war [with Britain] would find the Whigs in power. I wonder whether England would not forego all her claims upon Oregon, in consideration of an amount equal to that which Polk calls for, for the increase of the Navy—Fifty millions! Whew!" The political and economic cost of an Anglo-American war was, he began to feel, too large a price to pay for martial glory in the frozen Northwest. A sharp drop in stock prices on the New York exchange contributed further to his loss of belligerency as it became increasingly apparent that his own market speculations were suffering as a direct result of the Anglo-American war scare. Julia had no direct economic motive in her desire for peace with England. She simply thanked God once again that the amorous Francis Pickens had not been sent to London as the American minister in the midst of such a complex and emotion-filled crisis.[36]

In the final analysis, the war with Mexico and the agitation for the whole of Oregon did produce, as Tyler feared it would, the revival of the slavery question. To see the abolitionists embracing 54°40′ "as a means of overbalancing Texas" disturbed Tyler as much as had Calhoun's narrowing of Texas annexation "to the comparatively contemptible ground of Southern and local interest." Tyler did not want to see the sectional issue drawn into either problem for political purposes. Yet when Congressman David Wilmot of Pennsylvania, a free-soil Democrat, introduced in the House in August 1846 his famous amendment to an emergency war appropriation bill, the sectional lines were firmly drawn. Tyler was forced to take a stand on a question he would have much preferred to see remain dormant. The so-called Wilmot Proviso asked for nothing more subtle than the exclusion of human slavery from any of the territories conquered from Mexico during the war. Administration forces sought to soften the Proviso by restricting its application to any territory acquired north of 36°30′. In brief, they would extend the old Missouri Compromise line to the Pacific. This maneuver was blocked, however, and the Wilmot Proviso was adopted by the House on August 8, 1846. Defeated in the Senate, the controversial Proviso never found its way into the law of the land. But its very existence as an idea tore the nation apart.

Once the issue was broached, Tyler swung to the Southern viewpoint on it. He was convinced, as he always had been, that the impact of climate would ultimately solve the question of slavery extension, and that the institution was destined to disappear in Delaware, Maryland, and Virginia as it already had in the North. Thus the former President's main criticism of the Wilmot Proviso was that it raised "a contest between the sections for the balance of power [that] is to render us in a foreign war the weakest nation of the world." Further, it seemed to say to the South, and to American soldiers from the South fighting in Mexico, that "You may toil and bleed and pay, and yet your toil and blood and money shall only be expended to increase our [the North's] power; you and your property being forever excluded from the enjoyment of the territory you may conquer." The Proviso was, as he put it in an anonymous letter to the Portsmouth (Va.) *Pilot,* "nothing less than a gratuitous insult on the slave-States." It would soon bring about the political subordination of the slave states to the free states within the Union. It would, in fine, raise new problems in America more dangerous than the one it sought to remedy. In these views both Alexander and Robert concurred, Alexander going one step further in his interpretation of the Proviso as part of a British abolitionist plot unfolding in the United States.[37]

As the sectional crisis deepened, the developing tension fortified the Tyler-Gardiner family in their opinion that the Polk administration was an unmitigated disaster in all its works. The fact that Polk had accommodated John, Jr., with a captaincy and Tom Cooper with an inspectorship of customs did little to soften this view. They disliked Polk's policies, foreign and domestic. Nothing he sought to do really suited them. His administration was, they unanimously agreed, undistinguished in every way. His financial policies disrupted the money market ("Money now commands two per cent a month in Wall Street, a rate of interest ruinous to regular business," Alexander complained). His foreign policies agitated the slavery question. That some of the old and true friends of the Tyler administration, notably former New York Congressman Roosevelt, had made their political peace with the Polk crowd seemed to the family evidence of the basest hypocrisy.[38]

Julia and Margaret could find but one redeeming feature in the whole Polk administration. Sarah Polk had at least shown the good sense not to disturb Julia's arrangement of the furniture in the White House bedrooms. But even in the peripheral area of home economics, the Polks, man and wife, did not measure up. When the *United States Journal* reported that in the interests of the *"strictest* economy" the new President and First Lady would spend only half of the 1845 appropriation designed for White House renovation and entertaining, Margaret was beside herself. "What monstrously small people they must be!" she exclaimed. She knew how desperately the President's Mansion needed a face-lifting and how expensive White House social functions, properly done, could be. The Gardiners had certainly paid for enough of them to know.[39]

From Julia's standpoint, Sahara Sarah was more than monstrously small. She was dull and uninteresting as a First Lady. Her nonalcoholic White House functions did save the taxpayers a few dollars, and the floors of the President's Mansion were undoubtedly protected from the wear and tear of waltzing feet. But her parties remained impossibly dreary. "I don't see or hear that Mrs. Polk is making any sensation in Washington," Julia remarked with ill-concealed cattiness in February 1846. Sarah Childress Polk was never a social sensation, and Tyler rarely missed an opportunity to encourage Julia's self-satisfied comparisons of the glories of her reign with the manifest failures of Sarah's. "The idea of her being able to follow after you," he assured her, was an impossible one. He was right. Whatever "impartial history" would say of John Tyler as President of the United States, it could only say of Julia that as First Lady she would have no real rival for one hundred and sixteen years.[40]

14

SHERWOOD FOREST: THE GOOD YEARS

> *We are raising up quite a large family, 3 boys and one girl and all fine children in intellect and mechanism.... Thus it is that my old age is enlivened by the scenes of my youth—and these precious buds and blossoms almost persuade me that the springtime of life is still surrounding me.*
>
> —JOHN TYLER, 1851

Within a year of her arrival at Sherwood Forest Julia began longing again for the bustle and activity of Washington. Especially during the winter months of 1846, when snow covered the plantation and confined the population indoors, she visualized a return to the scene of her triumph. Often she would while away an evening before the fire planning a reconquest of the capital that Sarah Polk had surrendered without firing a social shot. This was a harmless diversion Tyler encouraged. "I shall expect to meet with a good deal of attention and have no doubt every distinction which my *'position before the country'* has a right to command will be accorded me and therefore all of us," Julia said of one planned but never-realized return visit to Washington. As she well knew, however, these dreams would be many a year materializing. First she would have her seven babies. Indeed, she would not return to the capital until January 1861, when John Tyler emerged from retirement to serve as president of the Peace Convention called in a final abortive effort to save the nation from the stupidity of civil war.[1]

In the winter of 1846 Julia was anticipating the arrival of her first child—and her mother was bombarding her with obstetrical advice from New York. "Keep your mind in as easy and agreeable a state as possible and avoid all unpleasant sights," she counseled. Gentle exercise and clothes "comfortably loose" were also recommended. It had been willed for several months that Julia's first baby would simply have to be a boy and that his name would be "David Gardiner Tyler." Thus as she and John Tyler awaited the arrival of the son and heir, thoughts of social Washington and its superficial frivolity melted away. When her time of confinement finally approached in July, Tyler took her north to the fever-free climate of East Hampton where her mother and Margaret could be with her.[2]

Before the baby was born Julia encountered news from New York that made it difficult for her to preserve that "easy and agreeable" mental state recommended by her solicitous mother. On February 21, 1846, the New York *Morning News* carried an item to the effect that "A rumor is in circulation that Ex-President Tyler's wife has separated from him and returned to her home on Long Island, N.Y." Other papers, notably the New York *Ledger,* picked up the report, adding to it the innuendo that the May-and-December marriage had been a rocky one from the start. Alexander first heard the gossip in Washington in January, but he had not reported it to Sherwood Forest for fear of upsetting his sister. Actually, as former Attorney General John Nelson and Secretary of the Navy Mason had explained to Alexander, the rumor stemmed from the much-whispered-about marital difficulties of John Tyler, Jr., and his estranged wife Mattie. In its confused transmission from barber shop to Capitol Hill the rumor had settled somehow on the innocent shoulders of the ex-President and Julia. Since the family had no desire to see John, Jr.'s hymeneal problems further paraded through the newspapers, they could not publicly explain the origin of the story or the mistaken identities involved.

David Lyon experienced "great wrath" when he first saw the item in print; he was all set to "go direct to the office to give the man a regular blowing up for printing such a scandal." But a family conference decided on a more politic approach. Under the strategy adopted, David Lyon was assigned the delicate task of calling quietly on various editors to request that they run dignified retractions. Several papers did. Still, retractions are seldom so interesting or well remembered as the slanders they attempt to correct, and the subject remained common gossip in New York and Washington for several months. The incident did not, as David Lyon hoped it might, afford Tyler and Julia a "hearty laugh." On the contrary, as Juliana clearly understood, "such reports [are] very disagreeable because people are apt to think there must be some foundation for them." Julia agreed with her mother. She thought the entire thing

...more provoking than anything in the world and I should think you would have felt exactly like choking the perpetrator of the scandal. The way you managed its contradiction, however, was most proper, only the President thinks ... [that] the Editor in his contradiction should have been made to add also ... that no union could be more harmonious and happy for he is afraid that the world will think there must have appeared some foundation for the tale. Pray be on the alert for everything improper that may appear and let it not be unnoticed.

She was still upset about the divorce rumor when her baby was born.[3]

David Gardiner Tyler was born in East Hampton on July 12, 1846. At eighteen he would fight under Lee in the Army of Northern Virginia. During Reconstruction he would become a key figure in Charles City's successful struggle against the baneful influence of Carpetbagger government in Virginia. A fine lawyer and judge, he would also serve with distinction in the Congress of the United States in the 1890s. More important to Tyler and Julia than contemplation of his future was the fact that "Gardie" was from the beginning of his active life a healthy, happy baby. East Hampton friends crowded in to congratulate the parents on the birth of the "Little President" ("the only cognomen he is known by," explained Margaret), and Tyler was filled with pride and happiness. Barely a week after Gardie's arrival Tyler was forced to return to Virginia, having heard "unfavorable accounts of his harvest" at Sherwood Forest. But he soon hastened back to East Hampton to be with his family.[4]

With the aid of a nurse, a housekeeper, and at various times her sister, mother, brothers, and husband, Julia steadily regained her strength and health. By mid-August she was recovered enough to wish she could join Margaret in Newport "to see the maneuvers of the cliques." With Julia, this desire was as much a sign of her complete recovery as was her mournful discovery that she could no longer struggle into her old corsets. And while her postobstetrical ailments remained minor, they provided Juliana a fresh opportunity to practice medicine by mail. "You ought not to eat *hot* bread," she counseled on one occasion when Julia complained vaguely of a weak stomach. When her daughter experienced backaches (from carrying her new baby about so much), Juliana sent her a plaster to apply. This torturous device "occasioned such an intolerable itching, *irritation* it would be more elegant to say," that Julia could not bear it. As usual, much of Juliana's medical advice centered upon strictures against alcohol in any form. She rarely missed an opportunity to tell her daughter that wine was a debauching beverage—bad for her complexion, her back, her stomach, and all other parts of her anatomy. Julia did not discourage this well-intentioned medical intervention. She was so distressed by the amount of weight she retained after Gardie's birth she was ready "to try any diet or any prescription."[5]

Julia had her first baby with minimum difficulty and complication and with maximum assistance and advice from the family. When she and Tyler returned to Sherwood Forest in September, after the fever season on the James had passed, she discovered in her husband an excellent nurse and baby-sitter. The fact that Gardie was the first of a new set of children for the former President in no way dulled his enthusiasm for babies. "You would be amused to see what an excellent nurse the President has become," Julia told her mother.

> I devolve the whole charge in the morning upon him. The babe wakes at early dawn and he rises and sits with it before the fire until the horn arouses the plantation and its own proper nurse enters to relieve him. All this time I very calmly and *cruelly* go to sleep. This is really very right . . . to be broken of sleep *agrees* better with the President than with me. . . .

Tyler only lost sleep. For Alexander Gardiner the arrival of Gardie meant a new assignment to the servitude of baby shopping for Julia in New York, keeping her complex accounts straight, and generally providing her with the numerous things infants and young children constantly need. In the course of his life Alexander Gardiner probably did more shopping than any other man in the state of New York.[6]

Julia was wonderfully happy as a young mother. Indeed, little Gardie could emit no sound, cut no tooth, toddle no step, and take no bite that was not reported by Julia to Lafayette Place in the greatest and most breathless detail. Her baby was the most intelligent, precocious, and beautiful in the whole world. In appearance he was more Gardiner than Tyler, she thought, but in firmness of character and independence of spirit he was all Tyler. From the time he learned to walk and talk he had a mind and will of his own. "Wherever I go he puts all other children who are much older completely in the shade," Julia boasted. She loved bouncing him on her lap and playing with him on the bed. For hours on end she would sing him Mother Goose and other nonsense rhymes to the accompaniment of her guitar and his mellifluous gurgles:

> Rock-a-by baby, your cradle is green;
> Father's a nobleman, Mother's a queen.
> Betty's a lady and wears a gold ring,
> And Gardiner's a drummer and drums for the king.
>
> Ride away, ride away, Gardy shall ride;
> And he shall have pussy cat tied to his side.
> And he shall have pussy cat tied to the other;
> And Gardy shall ride and see his Grandmother.

To John Tyler, his new son was no less than "the noblest fellow in creation." Neither the war in Mexico nor the purges of the Tylerites in New York were as important to him as the baby. The former President delighted in predicting a "high destiny" for his son. Thus when whooping cough struck the plantation in November 1847, Gardie contracting it along with the other children, black and white, the entire family was alarmed.[7]

Whenever she was in doubt on some point relating to the care and feeding of infants Julia wrote to her mother, receiving back reams of detailed advice fresh from the New York pediatric front. "You must not allow the nurse to put anything she may be eating in his mouth," cautioned Juliana. "It is an old-fashioned practice entirely exploded. ... What food he takes let it be pure and properly prepared for the baby." Her mother also advised her to breast feed Gardie as long as she could. This, she assured Julia, would prevent her conceiving another child right away, a myth that was widespread in those days. In fact, Juliana thought one child quite enough for her daughter, and at one point she considered giving Tyler "the most severe lecture telling him he had children enough." [8]

This advice attracted absolutely no support at Sherwood Forest. On the contrary, Julia wanted another child as soon as possible. She was ecstatically happy in her new role as a mother, and she looked forward to having a large and handsome family. The only consideration that gave her any pause at all was the effect of childbearing on her petite figure. "It is the remark of everyone how *fat* I have become," she lamented a year after Gardie's birth. "I shall be a *fat old lady* I suppose. I cannot push my arm through any sleeve I used to wear." Like many attractive women who gaze self-consciously into their mirrors before breakfast each morning half expecting to see the final fall of Rome revealed, Julia's concern for her figure was more imagined than real. Juliana thought it mainly a question of posture and urged her daughter not to "allow your increase in size to make you *look* lazy— keep your figure erect, shoulders braced back." Actually, Julia remained a beautiful woman, a fact remarked upon by all her contemporaries. But when friends assured her that "they never saw me looking so well," Julia was not convinced. "I guess they have forgotten," she sighed wistfully.[9]

The birth of her second son, John Alexander Tyler, on April 7, 1848, at Sherwood Forest, brought Julia new joy and delight. "Alex" was destined to an unhappy life. On his seventeenth birthday he would find himself in the rain at Appomattox, cold, wet, and hungry, ankle-deep in red Virginia mud beside the gun he serviced. Two days later General Lee surrendered the remnants of his gallant and ragged army, Alex Tyler included, to the United States. It was a bitter moment for the boy. Trained as he later was in German universities Alex would become an engineer of considerable competence, but his entire life was scarred by the tragic events of April 9, 1865. His happiest days were those of his boyhood at Sherwood Forest—days of fishing in the James, hunting in the nearby woods, and playing with his older brother and with the Negro children of the plantation.

Again Julia had no difficulty in childbirth, although Alex weighed in at twelve pounds. Before his arrival, however, she heard that no less a personage than Queen Victoria was contemplating the use of chloroform when her sixth baby (Princess Louise) was delivered in March 1848. Thus she asked Margaret to find out in New York if the gas could "be safely used in confinements," pointing out that Norfolk doctors were already employing it in surgery with great success. Whatever her research into the value of chloroform revealed, there is no evidence that Julia ever used it herself in childbirth.[10]

As Alex grew straight and strong and devilish, Julia found him "the loveliest child that ever was seen." When he was a year old she decided that "Gardie has the *thinking* head and Alexander the *imaginative* one." Given this discovery, she could only pray that Alex's "imagination will be governed by discretion." Tyler was less worried about Alex's future discretion than he was pleased that his newest son had been born "a Virginian." In his satisfaction with this geographic circumstance he hastened to provide the nurse and the additional household help that would make Julia's recovery safe and rapid. Happily, her recovery was both, marked only by headaches and chills which were treated by "burning up my temples with hartshorn and deluging my head with bay water." Soon she was up and about again, busily dispatching eulogistic accounts of her two boys to Lafayette Place. In this motherly activity she was undeterred and unintimidated by Alexander's chiding that her children were, after all, like most other children. They were definitely *not* like other children, Julia stoutly insisted, reminding Alexander that she had magnanimously chosen his name for little Alex. Teasing aside, both of her brothers were terribly pleased that Julia had selected their names for her sons. "I think both babies of mine have been rightly named," she decided. Gardie, she felt, was very much like his Uncle David Lyon in temperament, while little Alex was more like his Uncle Alexander.[11]

Blessed as she was by two "goodly babies" and an exceptionally happy marriage, Julia was easily persuaded that Margaret, her brothers, and Alice Tyler should all experience the joys of the marital institution without further delay. To this end she appointed herself the family's official matchmaker and marriage-prospects consultant. Forming a loose partnership with her mother to deal with the problem systematically, she launched a campaign to marry David Lyon, Margaret, Alexander, and Alice to "suitable" mates at once. The mother-and-daughter marriage-brokerage firm did business entirely by mail, main office in Lafayette Square, branch office at Sherwood Forest. Tyler watched the firm's devious machinations with great amusement.

It was soon apparent to Julia that David Lyon would not be rushed to the altar. In fact, Alexander had long since given up on his bashful brother, his own efforts in matchmaking having produced no results. Juliana's most recent attempts had likewise been in vain. During Julia's reign the family had discouraged all of his flirtations with such caustic finality that he now approached women with a caution bordering on timidity. Nevertheless, every report from New York that mentioned his dancing with or even conversing with a young lady was hopefully construed by Julia as the beginning of a serious romance. She utilized his visits to Sherwood Forest to introduce him to various local belles, and she flattered his masculine ego by invariably interpreting these casual meetings as "really brilliant conquests" for him.

In the interests of his romantic aspirations she suggested that he become adept at the polka and understand clearly that "almost everything in the Polka depends upon the *fascinating expression* of countenance." It had to be danced, said Julia, "with a most bewitching smile and grace." She did not think David had nearly enough *savoir faire*, and she was sure that a firm mastery of the waltz and the polka would increase his opportunities. Her advice on dancing was sound, and David Lyon heeded it. He took dancing lessons at Madame Ferraso's studio in New York and gradually he acquired a ballroom conversational polish that brought him into an easier and more natural contact with a larger number of eligible women. At the same time, however, Julia worried lest David lose sight of the eternal verities of marriage as he spun around the dance floor. On one occasion she urged him to marry one homely young lady on no more than the practical grounds that it was his golden "chance for $100,000 planked down." Indeed, some of the names she came up with as possible mates for her oldest brother seemed so outlandish to Margaret that she finally scolded Julia with the observation that "You are continually insulting D. with your matchmaking and a few more such like proposals as the last will completely change his nose, with turning up." Julia was neither intimidated nor silenced by Margaret's criticism. Nonetheless, by 1851 she had become much discouraged. David's dancing lessons had accomplished little save teaching him to dance. By 1855 Juliana also began to fear that unless David soon married the Gardiner line was threatened with extinction. "I do not like the idea of the family name in our line becoming extinct either," Julia agreed. "If David remains a bachelor too long he will become an *inveterate* one." Discouraging as it seemed, she could still hope that someday her brother would "seem a blessing to the fashionable and rich young ladies when they become more aware of his steady and well regulated habits." That day would not arrive until 1860.[12]

Alexander had few of his brother's steady habits and none of his social shyness or humorless stolidity. Getting him safely into holy wedlock appeared to Julia an easy task. But in spite of his sister's elaborate plans for his happiness, Alexander had no interest in marriage. He was fascinated by the ladies and missed few opportunities to avail himself of their charms. Yet he never confused his desire for distaff companionship with the notion that he should marry. Instead, Alexander toyed with women as he played the stock market, acquiring and disencumbering himself of them as the situation demanded. He was an active young man about town with no desire to settle down. His legal duties, political interests, and business affairs were combined with the management of his mother's properties and, after 1845, with the direction of John Tyler's financial affairs. He was very busy. He enjoyed his cigars, his liquor, and his books, and he tolerated with good humor Julia's insistence that he make a *"rich* love match," settle down, and become a solid citizen. Attractive to women, his occasional "indiscreet and imprudent" involvements with them were handled with a skill and urbanity that avoided exposing the family to scandal. He had a fierce loyalty to his sisters and his mother, but his sense of family unity did not include their right to mess and muddle in his private affairs. Julia soon gave up on him. It was one of her few total defeats.[13]

All around Julia wedding bells were ringing for her friends and classmates, but they tolled not for David Lyon, Alexander, Margaret or Alice. In August 1847, however, a good omen appeared in the marriage of Mary Gardiner to Eben N. Horsford. Mary had waited three years for him, and her patience seemed to demonstrate that Gardiners were not by some strange hex inherently unmarriageable. The Horsford-Gardiner union was a love match, although Professor Horsford's friendly connection with industrialist-philanthropist Abbott Lawrence was not overlooked by the Gardiner family. Lawrence, indeed, was instrumental in obtaining for Horsford his post at Harvard College in 1847. For the vivacious but still untutored Phoebe her sister Mary's courtship was a revelation of another sort. "This love-making is so new to me," she wrote Julia a few days before the wedding. "I have been vastly amused, never having seen lovers together before... there is something going on for me to wonder at all the time!" Some excitement at last had come to remote Shelter Island.[14]

Mary Gardiner's good fortune caused Julia and her mother to worry more and more about Margaret's marital prospects, and they redoubled their efforts to provide her with a suitable husband. As early as November 1845 Juliana complained that it was foolish for Margaret to "waste her time" visiting Julia at Sherwood Forest when potential husbands were calling at 43 Lafayette Place every day inquiring after her. "She should keep her position here and not abandon her post," said Juliana. "Indeed I have been very careful not to mention her absence except for a very short time for fear it will go forth that she has gone South for the winter... there is nothing like being at one's post. The city is busy and gay in appearance this fall, a great deal of calling and walking is done." Margaret got the message. With Julia's urging she hastened home from a brief visit on the James to man her pillbox on the Lafayette Place social firing line.[15]

Margaret was an attractive girl, physically and financially. Her main drawback remained her intelligence and her absolute candor with men; and she had the additional bad habit of seeing the complex mating process of the 1840s as the superficial comedy of manners it was. She especially objected to having a wealthy husband captured, tied, branded, and delivered to her by her family like a side of Grade-A beef. Finding just any "suitable" husband for Margaret would have been no difficult task. She was a good catch. But she would not cooperate. She would not play the game as the rules of polite society demanded. She wanted a love match, not a corporate merger.

This made her an especially difficult problem for her mother and sister, who found "decent beaux" to be "lamentably scarce" in New York City anyway. There was, for example, Thompson S. Brown of New York, who would have been an adequate husband for Margaret. He clearly qualified as a "decent beau" by Gardiner standards. He was comfortably fixed and of good family. He called at 43 Lafayette Place often during 1845–1847, and he rushed Margaret at Newport and Saratoga during her summer visits there. But Margaret did not love him. She considered him physically unattractive and socially awkward in spite of her mother's exasperated view that he was "very genteel in his manners" and quite a good prospect.[16]

Margaret would probably have married George Samson in mid-1845 had family support for the match been unanimous. Although he was a widower with a small daughter, he owned some modest properties in the city and he was devoted to Margaret; she in time returned his affectionate interest. Julia thought him a good prospect and saw no reason why her sister should not marry him. "Were I Margaret," she explained to her mother, "and no chance of being Mrs. President Tyler (ahem!) I would most certainly devote my attention to Mr. Samson [whose] ... kind heart and good character and house in Broadway and Bond are not to be trifled with according to my thoughts." This, unfortunately, was not the majority view. Vetoes came from all sides. David Lyon's blunt "Not for the world!" and Juliana's conviction that Samson was not sufficiently possessed of the world's goods to make Margaret truly happy combined to defeat the project. Rumors within the family that a wedding was pending were quashed, and Margaret hid her evident disappointment in a frenzied round of Sunday School and Bible Association activities.[17]

When James Bruen walked suddenly into Margaret's life in December 1845 there was a new rustle of excitement within the family. "Is he rich?" Julia asked her sister. It was Alexander's job to discover the answer to this inevitable family question. A casual but pointed conversation with Bruen produced the information that he had "about $100,000 of his own and very much more in prospective." Another discreet investigation of the Bruen family by Judge Ogden Edwards corroborated Alexander's findings. Though Bruen had passed his Dun &

Bradstreet with flying colors the fact remained that Margaret was not in love with him. Only his considerable wealth tempted her at all. "I am rather *flurried*," she confessed to Julia, "and I don't know what to do. I shall have to come to a decision one way or the other—that's sure—and I would not for the world have an [engagement] take place that was to end in nothing.... To be or not to be, that is the question! Pray decide...." Not surprisingly, Julia had already decided. She wrote Margaret, strongly urging the match. And Alice Tyler humorously suggested that if Margaret did not want the wealthy Bruen she might at least have the good sportsmanship to pass him along to her. When Bruen actually proposed marriage in March 1846 Margaret put him off. She still could not make up her mind. As Juliana reported the breathless indecision of the Gardiner household to Sherwood Forest:

> We are in a peck of trouble, etc. about Mr. B[ruen] and M[argaret]. I dare not encourage or discourage—it is so serious. When we conclude upon what to do we shall write. Until then keep a closed mouth and talk about it to no one. Your letter almost decided M. it was so much in favor of it. She has begun to relapse a little now however and thinks it will not be agreeable to make a change just now. She wishes a little more time for reflection.[18]

Margaret's cautious reflectiveness on the Bruen proposal was typical of her basic honesty. She simply could not marry a man she did not love even if he did have "$100,000 of his own." At the same time it was becoming increasingly apparent to her that she was falling in love with the handsome though impecunious John H. Beeckman. She had known Beeckman for several years. She had first met him at East Hampton in 1842. She saw more of him during her romances with Samson and Bruen. By January 1846 he had become a regular caller at 43 Lafayette Place and Margaret's frequent escort to divine services at the Church of the Ascension and St. Thomas' Episcopal Church.

John Beeckman was an unusually tall and handsome young man of good family. His "glossy luxuriant" dark hair, sharply wrought features, and "genteel figure" commanded instant attention. Even the critical Juliana at first thought him an "excellent beau" for Margaret because he was "refined and gentlemanly in deportment...of good family, intelligent, well educated and well read." His mother had been Catherine Livingston, and that prominent New York name and connection placed the Beeckmans within the Gardiner social circle. The Beeckmans lacked none of life's necessities and few of its luxuries. The summer season usually found them at East Hampton, Saratoga, or Newport. But these displays did not conceal the fact that the Beeckmans were not truly wealthy. They all had to work for a living. At the time of John Beeckman's courtship with Margaret, his younger brother was clerking at Graham and Varnum's store (the Beeckmans and the Varnums were related by marriage), while John and his older brother Gilbert labored in a downtown mercantile house in which business was often so slow that one or the other would be laid off for several weeks at a time.

These economic realities were partly atoned for by the fact that Catherine Livingston Beeckman maintained a gracious home filled with mementos and curios attesting her ancestry and good breeding. She was extremely proud of her Revolutionary War heritage and delighted in displaying the war relics given her husband years earlier by Governor George Clinton. If the Gardiners were less than fascinated by Catherine Beeckman's tiresome excursions into her "Spirit of '76" genealogy (she only did it, said Margaret, to impress the Gardiners "with an idea of her importance"), their reaction could be traced to the fact that the Gardiners of the 1770s had not displayed an overpowering dedication to the great struggle for life, liberty and the pursuit of happiness. (They had been neutralists, selling their goods and services to both sides.) Future family genealogists, notably Curtiss C. Gardiner in his *Lion Gardiner and His Descendants,* would be hard pressed to find more than one or two members of the clan whose patriotic contributions during the Revolution far transcended profitable collaboration with the British occupation forces on Long Island. Catherine Beeckman, on the other hand, was an early prototype of a Daughter of the American Revolution, and her constant harping on the glorious events of 1776 did little more than confirm in the Gardiners a suspicion that the Beeckmans were stronger in blood line than in credit line. Margaret was threatening to accept half a loaf or no loaf at all in a marriage contract.[19]

Only when it was clear, by March 1847, that Margaret was genuinely in love with John Beeckman was Alexander detailed to discover how much of a loaf was actually there. A probing conversation with young Beeckman enabled him to report Beeckman's personal view that no man should marry unless he could support his wife "in the same style she has been accustomed to live" and the corollary observation that no lady should accept marriage "unless she was certain her position and enjoyments would be the same." On the basis of this meager information Margaret assured Julia that "the exposition of affairs was very satisfactory." Just how satisfactory, in cold round numbers, Alexander would not reveal. He favored the match and did not want to see Margaret denied the man she loved because of the money question. Nor did Beeckman himself offer any financial specifics. "If he had an income of some five or six thousand," Juliana complained to Sherwood Forest in March 1847, "we should know at once. That's the point of difficulty. Now what think you? Is it time to think of something and somebody else or keep the *status quo?*" [20]

Julia pondered the question and decided Margaret should marry Beeckman whether there was great wealth in the bargain or not. Both she and John Tyler had met the Beeckman family at East Hampton in 1845, and the ex-President had been particularly impressed with the young man. Still, she agreed with her mother that the economic element could not be entirely overlooked. "If I could only be sure of his independence I should not have any fears were the match concluded on," she said. "Margaret should refer him to you and then it would be his business to give sufficient assurance that he was able properly to support her." [21]

The sufficient assurance was never forthcoming and Margaret never insisted upon it. She was in love, not in high finance. When a panicky Juliana threatened to quash the whole thing in August 1847, Alexander finally stepped in and told her firmly that the marriage would take place. His sister's happiness must not be sacrificed to a misplaced decimal point. "I suppose it is perfectly understood that nothing [further] is to be said about it," he told his mother sharply. "You are yet to be satisfied as to manner, mode and extent, and that definitely. What one person may esteem abundant, another may not." It was the only time in her life that the strong-willed Juliana was thwarted by one of her children. Julia accepted her sister's judgment in the matter with better grace, noting only that Margaret would find Beeckman's *"manner* of wooing" more desirable were he wealthier and able to spend more money on her.[22]

The courtship was decidedly an economical one. It involved for Beeckman nothing more expensive or ostentatious than escorting Margaret to church and Sunday School and calling upon her in her heavily chaperoned parlor. An occasional stroll on Broadway completed the pattern. An engagement was agreed upon in August 1847 and the wedding planned for January 1848 in the Church of the Ascension. Not until the engagement was announced, daguerreotypes exchanged, and all the arrangements made, did Margaret inform her friends and her Shelter Island cousins of her plans. Nor did the usually talkative Julia let the secret out during her New York visit in September. To Phoebe Gardiner's chagrin, she was one of the last in the family to learn of her cousin's intentions. When she finally heard the news she eagerly demanded the *"whole* history" of the romance and asked Margaret especially to "devote a separate sheet to the confidential." Margaret's courtship had been a quiet one, devoid of all gossip and speculation, and she wanted to keep it that way. She did not oblige Phoebe with any of the details, confidential or other.[23]

That John Beeckman had no money ceased being a major conversation piece in the Gardiner family as Margaret began busily to make her wedding plans. While the financial suitability of the match was no longer talked about openly, it remained a concern in the minds of both Beeckman and his fiancée. Indeed, it was his fear of his inability to support Margaret in the manner to which she was accustomed as a Gardiner that drove John Beeckman to the California gold fields in April 1849—and to his death a year later near Sacramento. And it was apprehensiveness on Margaret's part that her husband would never feel comfortable in the Gardiner presence until he had made himself independently wealthy that persuaded her to acquiesce in his get-rich-quick scheme in the new El Dorado. The latent tragedy in the whole affair could not, of course, be appreciated as Margaret's wedding day approached.

It was Juliana's intention to give the twenty-five-year-old Margaret as nice a wedding and as expensive a trousseau as her sister Julia had had three and a half years earlier. She was determined also that the ceremony would be an exclusive affair involving the immediate families only. None of Alexander's seedy Tammany friends would be invited to *this* wedding. Julia endorsed her mother's decisions in these matters. "You need not regulate [Margaret's] wardrobe by mine," she volunteered. "*I hope it will be very nice*—but then I also hope there will be enough left to buy me a gold watch and Gardie a silver cup." A trip to New York in midwinter always posed grave transportation problems for Tidewater Virginians. Nonetheless, Julia assured her family that she and the President would "make the grand effort" even though Julia was six months pregnant with Alex at the time. Nothing, she vowed, could keep her from *"The Ceremony."* And while the President had just returned to Sherwood Forest in December from a fatiguing six-week trip with Alexander to view his coal and timber lands near Caseyville, Kentucky, he too was eager for the New York jaunt. "He is so happy *in being with me again* that he has rallied immediately and all the fatigued look ... has vanished," Julia explained.[24]

Margaret married John H. Beeckman at the Church of the Ascension on January 8, 1848. The Reverend Gregory T. Bedell performed the ceremony, as he had earlier for Julia and the former President. John Tyler gave the bride away. The service and reception went smoothly and with dignity, although Tyler was piqued that "there was no more particular mention made in the papers of [the] wedding." He expected, said Margaret, that "his giving me away would be *particularly announced.*" Priscilla wrote to congratulate Margaret on the event, observing that "if your husband is only one half as good as mine ... you cannot help being happy." With his usual organizational efficiency Alexander took upon himself the task of distributing the wedding cake to friends of the Tylers and Gardiners. With each piece of cake went the observation that Tyler could secure the Democratic nomination in 1848 if his many friends were properly rallied.[25]

Margaret and her husband returned to Sherwood Forest with the President and Julia for a month-long honeymoon visit. They were accompanied by Gilbert Beeckman, the bridegroom's brother. Alice Tyler immediately began a "desperate flirtation" with Gilbert. Julia arranged "two *blow outs*" to honor the newlyweds. For a few weeks Sherwood

Forest reeled under the impact of visiting, dancing, and merrymaking as friends and neighbors of the Tylers trooped in to pay their respects to the Beeckmans. During the clear crisp days of January 1848 Margaret rode horseback over the plantation while her city-bred husband tramped the woods and fields in a crash program to make himself into an outdoorsman and hunter. To educate and instruct him in the fine Virginia art of shooting and riding to hounds, Tyler organized several large fox hunts which filled the woods and meadows of the plantation with the sounds of horns and dogs. Beeckman tried, but he failed the test. His absolute inability to hit anything with a rifle was soon a broad family joke.[26]

It was a happy month for Margaret, and it was with real reluctance that she and John left Sherwood Forest on February 5 for Washington, the next stop on their honeymoon itinerary. Armed with letters of introduction from Tyler to various senators and Cabinet officers, the young couple looked forward to a pleasant visit in the capital. Julia envied her sister's return there. Much to Alice's dismay, Gilbert Beeckman preceded the honeymooners to Washington to make arrangements for their stay. Alice had "seriously encouraged" his attentions and his departure drove her to her room for a day of tears and fasting. "No girl ever courted so hard in this world.... I really think she was smitten," said Margaret. Also supplied with letters of introduction from the former President to prominent political figures in Washington, Gilbert hastened ahead to the capital to investigate the possibilities of a patronage appointment as well as to engage rooms for the oncoming travelers. The best he could manage for John and Margaret was cramped quarters in the Willard Hotel attic. This was better than he managed for himself. His Tyler connection was too tenuous to command patronage attention from the Polk administration, and by the time the newlyweds arrived on February 7 to claim their attic room, a crestfallen Gilbert had already departed for New York. Margaret reached town badly shaken with seasickness by a rough voyage up Chesapeake Bay and the Potomac. Nevertheless, she lost no time distributing her cards at the Polks', Calhouns', Walkers', Masons', Buchanans', John A. Dixes', and at Dolley Madison's. Her upset stomach was settled by drinking what she vaguely described to her teetotaling mother as "a wine of some description" Tyler had recommended that she take in such circumstances. Her health restored, she spent a few days pleasantly visiting, dining, and gossiping with old friends. She attended the third Assembly ball of the season. Her arrival at the ball, she reported,

... caused a general commotion among the dancers. Such a distingué couple couldn't be beat there, that's a fact. Nobody thought of dancing—but everybody was ogling and running after the bride. "There she is!" was echoed everywhere in my ears.... I wore my veil and therefore would not dance except with Robert Tyler who has been here since yesterday and is staying at this house... this morning I find myself not the least the worse for my frolic.[27]

No sooner had Margaret returned to New York in mid-February than she knew she was pregnant. Within a few weeks she was so uncomfortably ill she was forced to bed. By May 1848 she could no longer tolerate the noise and closeness of the city, and with her mother she moved out to East Hampton for the fresh sea air. While Julia experienced nothing more serious than "a sleepless humour" when Alex was on the way, Margaret's venture into motherhood was difficult throughout. At one point no fewer than three doctors were in attendance. During these troublesome months Beeckman remained at his office in New York and took his meals and lodging at a boardinghouse. He visited Margaret in East Hampton on week ends. His letters to her between these visits were filled with a passion and compassion that helped pull her through a critical period. His gift of a mockingbird also raised her spirits considerably. Still, she remained generally depressed and out of sorts until the birth of Henry Gardiner Beeckman on October 20, 1848. This glad release ended Margaret's travail for only a short time. The baby was weak and sickly and required constant attention during his first year. By the time "Harry" had fully caught hold of life, Margaret worrying and working herself half-sick over him all the while, John Beeckman had accidentally shot himself to death in California. Within two years, then, Margaret Gardiner was bride, mother, and widow. But at least her marriage, brief and tragic though it was, had been something more than a stock merger.[28]

Margaret's marriage encouraged Julia to hope that Alice Tyler's day of joy was also imminent. For a moment in February 1848 it appeared that Gilbert Beeckman would make Julia's fond wish ("I wish she was married to *somebody*") come true. It was high time, she thought, for Alice "to go seriously in search of a husband." Tyler agreed with his impatient wife. It was embarrassing, he felt, to have Alice running back and forth to Williamsburg and Richmond pursuing harmless flirtations when she should be thinking of settling down—especially when a perfectly good prospect appeared on the scene in 1848 in the person of Edward O'Hara of Williamsburg. He was twenty-six and eager to marry Alice. Juliana met him during her 1848 visit to Sherwood and found him "intelligent, well-educated, and pious. In all respects a most worthy and unexceptional character with an income between ten and twenty thousand a year and *no mistake*... thoroughly conversant with the Bible." O'Hara even appeared at Sherwood Forest on one occasion armed with a diamond ring and a firm proposal of marriage. Tyler discovered that the young man was "confounded shrewd" in business affairs and, supported by Julia, urged Alice to marry him. But Alice would have none of Mr. O'Hara. Her independent attitude left Julia frustrated. "He is... entirely too good for Alice," she finally snorted. "Any light laughing fellow suits her, but I perceive Mr. O'H. is altogether too serious and rational for one of her taste.... I fear it will be all to no purpose." [29]

The O'Hara interlude, as Julia feared, came to nought. Alice was only twenty-one and felt she had "not been a young lady long enough yet." She certainly did not want to be forced into marriage for the sake of marriage. She had overcome the adolescent awkwardness of her White House days, lost weight, and become a tall and attractive young woman. Rather than follow her father and Julia's advice in such matters as the O'Hara affair, she preferred to carry on the hopeless and unrequited flirtation with Gilbert Beeckman. She was still maneuvering for Beeckman's attention in 1849 when she met Henry Mandeville Denison.[30]

Denison was a tall, rugged, "very masculine looking" man of twenty-eight. A native of Wyoming, Pennsylvania, he was in 1849 the popular new Episcopal rector at Bruton Parish in Williamsburg. All the impressionable young ladies of the parish were soon hopelessly in love with him and Alice Tyler was no exception. As Julia quickly sized up the handsome clergyman, Denison was "very social in company and is ready to enter into the frolics of the wildest... of the girls—for he is altogether a ladies' man." Alice, of course, was wholly "captivated" by him. Soon he was a regular visitor at Sherwood Forest and Alice flirted with him "pretty freely." Julia thought her chances of landing Denison fairly slim, but Alice decided she wanted him and with the usual Tyler fortitude and singleness of purpose she set out to get him. The wedding took place at Sherwood Forest on July 11, 1850.[31]

Alice's married life, like Margaret's, was to be a series of tragedies. The wedding itself took place in an atmosphere of gloom. Scheduled for June 1850, it had been postponed a month when Tyler's second daughter, Elizabeth Tyler Waller, died suddenly of the after-effects of childbirth. Not yet twenty-seven, she left four young children behind her. When Alice's wedding party finally gathered at Sherwood Forest in July it comprised but a handful of the immediate family and the ceremony failed to dissipate the funereal depression that prevailed. Julia was not at all sure in her own mind that Alice was in love with Denison. With less than $6000 in savings and a new charge as Assistant Rector of Christ Church, Brooklyn, at $2000 a year, Denison was scarcely weighed down with material goods. Julia thought that a "wealthier match" with Gilbert Beeckman would have been of more advantage to the bride. Still, she was glad Alice had finally found a husband and would be leaving Sherwood, for "in whatever humor Alice was she did not possess real amiability." [32]

Whether she was really amiable or not, Alice's departure from home saddened John Tyler. A deeper shadow fell over Sherwood Forest when it was learned in April 1851 that Alice's first baby, born prematurely in Philadelphia while the Denisons were visiting Robert and Priscilla, had died after one fitful week of life. Her second baby, Elizabeth Russel Denison—"Bessy"—born in Louisville in March 1852, was more fortunate, although Julia thought the child "without any beauty, looking entirely unlike Alice." But long before little Bessy was able to do anything about her appearance, Alice herself died in June 1854 from the effects of "bilious colic." Her sudden passing nearly prostrated Tyler. Indeed, the sudden and unexpected deaths of three of his grown daughters within seven years (Mary in 1847, Elizabeth in 1850, and Alice in 1854) produced a fatalistic observation: "The ills of life are numerous enough without our dwelling on them too much. What best becomes us is to rest in the conviction that 'whatever is is right.' Altho my loss of three dear children has fallen in each instance heavily upon me, yet I am thankful to an over-ruling Providence for leaving me a larger share than falls to the general lot." [33]

Death came so quickly and with such frequency in the 1840s and 1850s that Americans of all classes had no choice but to learn to live with it philosophically. Yet with all the sorrow he bore, John Tyler's share of happiness was indeed much larger than that of the general lot of mankind. Although three of his daughters had died by 1854, a happy and healthy new family was growing around him. Sherwood Forest was a carefree, prosperous plantation. The house rang with the laughter of children and the sound of music, dancing, and entertaining. Interesting visitors and old friends stopped by whenever they were in Charles City, and these callers provided Julia numerous excuses for entertaining her neighbors with the elaborate balls and dinner parties for which she gained such well-deserved local fame.[34]

These, then, were good years for John Tyler. He was happy and his wife was happy. After she had borne him six of their seven children, he still referred to Julia as his "bride," and on one public occasion in 1858 he asked his embarrassed and delighted spouse "to bear testimony that the honeymoon has *not* passed with us." During his leisure moments nothing pleased Tyler more than to be asked to play his violin for his guests, for the dances of the young people, and for the children of the plantation. He was particularly proficient in playing "Washington's March," "Believe Me, If All Those Endearing Young Charms," and "Home Sweet Home." In 1848 Alexander presented him a new violin and he practiced regularly upon it, "night after night." His repertoire grew steadily. Often Julia sang to his accompaniment or joined him with her guitar in a string duet. The violin was a boyhood interest Tyler took up again with enthusiasm during his years at Sherwood Forest. "He plays with the same taste that he does everything else," said Julia. "It is better than his dancing of the Polka." Occasionally a family orchestra (Julia called it an "Ethiopian band") was formed to provide music for the dances at Sherwood Forest—Tyler on violin, son-in-law William Waller on banjo, Julia on guitar, and young Tazewell Tyler on bones. Alice, Belle Waller (William Waller's sister), Julia, and Margaret (if she happened to be visiting) often constituted themselves an all-girl choir and entertained their guests and themselves with Negro melodies, the Ethiopian band plunking happily away behind them. "The President is in good health, and cheerful, which is essential to good health," Juliana wrote of him in 1855. "He fiddles away every evening for the little children black and white to dance on the Piazza and seems to enjoy it as much as the children. I never saw a happier temperament than he possesses." [35]

The nearby woods were thick with deer, and Tyler shot venison for the table all winter. Ducks from the river added variety to the family diet and gave the former President countless opportunities to demonstrate himself an excellent marksman. Fox-hunting also provided good sport for the planters in the neighborhood and produced an occasional fur for Julia. Tyler enjoyed the chase immensely, and when any of the Gardiners, Tylers, or Beeckmans were visiting he arranged a hunt. The fox-hunting business, however, could be as gastronomic as it was athletic. As Julia explained its larger implications in 1846:

Yesterday the President joined the huntsmen around us in their sports and then made the party and their *hounds* come home and dine them for the which we were previously prepared and Catherine [Wing] dished us an elegant dinner I am sure of Maccaroni [sic] soup, Roast Turkey, Stew Venison, bacon and cold roast beef, celery, parsnips, Sweet and Irish potatoes—for dessert Transparent pudding, mince pie, apple tart, Damson tart, soft custard and preserves. Some of the company I presume never saw so fine a looking table in their lives before and it will be in consequence quite an era in their lives. A Fox was the result of their hunt.[36]

Julia always set a fine table. One never knew who would be dropping in for lunch or dinner. Tyler's birthday on March 29 called for something special, and Julia usually humored his sweet tooth with his favorite dessert—"pancakes, sweetmeats and ice cream." Good French wines also graced the table at Sherwood Forest. Of course, Julia had her disappointments—a December 1847 dinner party was in this category:

My own dinner was a failure in consequence of a pouring rain all day. My plum pound cake with its bunch of white roses and evergreens went for naught. Catherine sat up all night preparing the lemon puddings and pastries and I tired myself to death over *pigs feet* jelly until I got it as clear as crystal. ... My intended guests did not give up the hope of its clearing away until the eleventh hour when I received apologies. I however carried off the dinner and Mr. Jones, Mr. Tyler, Alice and myself sat down with formality and in costume while the lamp was lit in the drawing rooms and coffee handed around when we retired.[37]

Except on special occasions, life at Sherwood Forest was not particularly formal. Tyler insisted, however, that his wife be *"always* dressed proper for company." In April 1851, for example, Julia learned that the distinguished British diplomat Sir Henry Lytton Bulwer and Lady Bulwer were traveling through the county en route from Washington to Charleston. The Mistress of Sherwood immediately *"dressed for company* and [put] the rooms in order with a large bouquet of splendid tulips setting off the parlor. I presume they will not make their appearance but it is more agreeable not to be taken by surprise." Julia needed little urging about her dress. It was her intention "to keep nicely, *very* nicely dressed all the while," and she missed few opportunities to journey to Richmond to add to her considerable wardrobe. Like most women, Julia loved clothes, the more expensive the better.

But whether an occasion was formal or informal, she insisted on good manners in her home at all times. She became extremely annoyed when the basic civilities were not observed. Letitia Tyler Semple delighted in needling Julia in this respect. Returning from church one Sunday morning, Julia found Semple and his wife awaiting her in the parlor. "She was seated at one extremity of the room as we entered and did not rise to meet me, or rather us, until I walked quite up to her chair!" Julia expostulated. "Her ways until she went away this morning were what you would determine hateful [although] to her father she she was exceedingly coaxing." [38]

These moods passed quickly. There was so much genuine happiness and mutual respect within the family that the continuing Julia-Letitia feud never dominated the situation. And if there was tension with Letitia and with Alice (before her marriage to Denison), there was never any between Julia and young Tazewell. On the contrary, Julia loved Taz as though he were her own child. As he grew into young manhood (he was twenty in 1850), Julia delighted in teasing him about his various young lady friends, particularly the "pretty girl with a snug fortune of thirty thousand" who lived over near Williamsburg. The frequent balls at Sherwood Forest and at the other plantations along the river enabled Taz to pursue his interest in girls with considerable ease, and Julia followed the ups and downs of his romantic career with much encouragement and good advice.

When the snow lay deep upon the ground, clogging the dirt roads to Williamsburg and Richmond, the Sherwood Foresters were confined to more localized social activities. Nearby families joined the Tylers for winter sports, the neighbors visiting back and forth in their canoe sleighs:

Who should drive up in a canoe sure enough but the Douthats and Seldens [Julia wrote Margaret].... It was quite too funny for description. They were drawn by their carriage horses and they sat upon a thick carpet in Indian file in a long narrow canoe presenting as comfortable as curious an effect. It was a merry visit and they described to us the variety of their journey which consisted in floating in the most charming manner through all the runs that came by necessity in their way.... They took cake and wine and left full of spirits.[39]

Julia lacked nothing. The natural isolation of the plantation was easily overcome. The family experienced no difficulty entertaining themselves when special events were not scheduled. Thus a winter's evening like that of February 11, 1853, found Margaret visiting the plantation and the family engaged in experiments in levitation, magnetic power, and the conjuring up of spirits from the great beyond. On this particular instance, as Margaret reported the phenomenon to her spiritualist-inclined mother, Julia

assembled some four of the negroes and seated them around a table in the sitting room. They sat for an hour without effect and finally a sewing woman [Mrs. Adams] of Julia's placed her hand also upon it. In about ten minutes the table began to move—and [then] made the circumference of the room—with the combined influence of them all. What was singular, it would not move for [Mrs. Adams] alone nor for all the rest without her. Instead of being terrified, I was very glad I witnessed what is without doubt the magnetic influence of the body—and not supernatural agency.... As for the spirits having anything to do with the matter, we called upon them in vain. The more we called the more they would not come.[40]

It was much easier to raise a band of serenaders and revelers at Sherwood than the spirits of the departed. When Governor John B. Floyd and his wife visited the plantation in May 1851 the household was awakened at 2 A.M. by a wagonload of amateur musicians who came to serenade the governor and the Tylers. Musical instruments of all sorts blasted away with "Hail Columbia" and "Love Not." Tyler got up, called for light, and invited the noisy group indoors. "You know public men like manifestations of every sort," Julia explained to her mother. "The serenade was chiefly for us, but we ascribed it to the Governor ... and he was greatly pleased.... There was a violin and a guitar in the party and they sang after they entered the dining room, and after they had rested a little and conversed with the President and taken a *good drink* all around, they departed sending up three loud huzzas accompanied by a bugle blast as they drove off." There were few dull moments at Sherwood Forest. In fact, so many visitors came that it was a rare and welcome occasion when the family actually had the house to themselves. "I am luxuriating in a state of repose," Julia confessed to her mother in May 1852. "No *visitor* is here and I am breathing freely." [41]

In addition, Margaret and her mother kept Julia well supplied with

New York gossip so detailed in nature that it was the next best thing to being in the city. Such juicy tidbits as the Van Ness scandal (it was widely rumored that the old General had secretly had a young wife); the latest gaucheries of the Astor clan; the romantic death of Robert Mott, who "committed suicide by choking himself with a rope on his wife's bier"; and the social machinations of their Lafayette Place neighbors ("We stand upon our dignity and think it bad policy to be intimate with anyone," said Margaret. "It is the only way for us!") kept Julia in touch with the fashionable world. Frequently, however, she demanded more details of the various sins of omission and commission of the elite set in the city, and Margaret on more than one occasion had to apologize that she could not make her letters more "entertaining" in this regard because she was forced to be so prudent. "I can never take a pen in hand that my ears are not assailed from every quarter with 'Take care, Margaret, what do you intend publishing now!'"[42]

Detailed descriptions of the cultural events New York provided were also dispatched to Sherwood Forest, supplementing for Julia the newspaper reports of these activities and alerting her to what might be worth seeing and hearing when the attraction finally reached Richmond. The Gardiners especially urged Julia and John Tyler to see Tom Thumb when he appeared in Richmond in 1847. "He is the greatest curiosity in the *world* and no mistake," Juliana wrote. There was even some talk within the family of buying Tom Thumb's coach as a souvenir, but Juliana thought that would be going too far. The coach was simply not fashionable enough. Opinion in these matters was not always unanimous. Phoebe, for instance, found Barnum's money-making freak a revolting little man, a disgust engendered when the arrogant midget attempted on one occasion to seize and kiss her. Weighing the reported merits and demerits of the Tom Thumb exhibit, Julia said flatly that she would not go to Richmond or anywhere else to see such a nauseating creature. When Tyler was in Richmond in April 1847 buying summer supplies and had an opportunity one evening to see Tom Thumb, he too passed it up. Both Tyler and Julia thought it much more a curiosity that Mrs. John Selden of Westover had just given birth to her seventeenth child and was "still a very handsome woman." It was certainly a feat none of P. T. Barnum's freaks could match.[43]

When Jenny Lind came to Richmond to sing in December 1850 Julia and the President joined their James River neighbors in a trip to town to hear the celebrated Swedish Nightingale perform. Half the fun of going to Richmond for such events was the delight in seeing friends and neighbors aboard the riverboat and exchanging with them the news and gossip of the day. It was an opportunity for the planter families along the James, the "upper ten" as Tyler called them (the Harrisons, Tylers, Carters, Seldens, Douthats, *et al.*), to mingle casually and informally. The Jenny Lind excursion and others like it filled an important social purpose. Julia was disappointed with the concert, although she agreed with Margaret that the "angelic" soprano was "an interesting looking creation" even though her singing was "not exactly so melodious as we would expect from an angel." [44]

More enjoyable for Julia and the President was a trip to Richmond in February 1850 with Margaret and Juliana (then visiting at Sherwood) to be present at the ceremonies attending the laying of the cornerstone of the Washington Memorial and the great ball given by Governor Floyd to honor visiting President Zachary Taylor. Julia was happy to note that she still attracted much attention in such distinguished political company, and that there was a "great deal more interest shown to see 'Mrs. Tyler' than Gen. Taylor" at the ball. Indeed, the Gardiners found Old Zach wholly unimpressive. He was, said Margaret, an

indifferent specimen of the Lord of Creation. He is a short, thick-set man looking neither like the President of a great nation nor a military hero tho' he bears both honors and the last not undeservedly. If he had rested at that climax, history would have accorded him an unmodified distinction. Now the man-past is forgotten in the man-present, and if the party which elected him confessed themselves mortified and disappointed at his want of political tact ... the opposite one will have little conscience I fear in yielding him to the sacrifice. He has not the happy faculty of extemporaneous speech making....

The Gardiners and Tylers would take increasing comfort in the years ahead in the knowledge that in comparison with the likes of Taylor, Fillmore, Pierce, and Buchanan, the accomplishments of President Tyler looked impressive indeed.[45]

Julia never felt plantation-bound. She frequently accompanied Tyler on his speaking engagements around Virginia and to Baltimore and Philadelphia. No summer passed that she and her husband did not visit New York, East Hampton, Pittsfield, Saratoga, Newport, or the Virginia springs for at least a month at a time. She enjoyed the continuing deference paid her during these frequent public exposures. Her impact at Saratoga in 1847 was fairly typical. As David Lyon reported it:

I do not believe there has been any party here this season so much noticed as ours. Julia *in particular* on whom all eyes are centered and expressions of admiration are heard from every quarter. Everyone on our trip wanted to see Mrs. Tyler—she appeared to elicit universal admiration—and respect—*Old John* they said they were not so anxious to see.

Similarly, at a Richmond dinner party in 1849 Julia was toasted as "The Wife of Ex-President Tyler: the handsomest woman in the world" ("Was that not a *stretcher?*" she laughed); and at Charlottesville in June 1850 she was pleased that she and the former President "were the lions and treated accordingly." Her appearance was certainly a great deal more noticed than his pedestrian speech to the combined literary societies of the University of Virginia.⁴⁶

Preparations for her summer jaunts always involved heavy outlays for the proper clothes in Richmond and New York. Not infrequently these expenditures would exceed $500. In order to pay her clothing bills, Tyler, invariably cash poor between crops, would have to borrow the money from Alexander, or ask Alexander to go security for him on a note at a New York bank. "We have been out *shopping*," he wrote Alexander in 1849 from Richmond in semi-despair, "and I need not add the results." Julia could spend one hundred acres of wheat on a single costume and never bat an eye. To hold the summer-vacation cost line to something halfway reasonable, Tyler insisted that they avoid the posh hotels at the various spas and take rooms at the less expensive private boardinghouses in the area. At Mrs. Sylvia S. Rogers' house in Saratoga, for instance, the rents were relatively modest—four dollars a week for each adult, two dollars for each child and body servant, and three dollars for the coachman. The Tylers and the Gardiners occupied such accommodations at Saratoga and Pittsfield in 1849–1851.⁴⁷

The only thing that could keep Julia at all confined to the plantation and temporarily out of the social swim was advanced pregnancy and childbearing, and even this transitory inconvenience had the advantage of bringing Juliana and Margaret to Sherwood Forest for long and pleasant visits. None of her seven accouchements was accomplished without the aid of her sister or her mother. These creative experiences rarely slowed her down for more than a few months at a time, however, or interrupted planned excursions to New York or various fashionable spas.

Gardie and Alex were only the beginning of a large family. They were healthy, normal boys who cut teeth painfully, had flu, measles, chickenpox, and whooping cough, fell out of trees, and fought over their toys. Of the two, Alex was the more aggressive in spite of the fact that he had been baptized in genuine River Jordan water supplied Tyler by Navy Lieutenant Dominick Lynch. "You never saw such *fights* as he has with Gardie who takes away all his playthings and won't permit him to have a single thing," said Julia. "He kicks and *squeals* while I make Gardie give him up one or two." By December 1850 she had decided to employ a young French maid to ride herd on them and introduce them to the civilizing tendencies of the French language.⁴⁸

Julia loved her rowdy little boys, but she desperately wanted a daughter. Thus, when Julia Gardiner Tyler (she was usually called "Julie") was born at Sherwood Forest on December 25, 1849, Julia was overjoyed at the gift from St. Nicholas. Margaret and Juliana were on hand as usual to help out. After some hesitation Margaret pronounced Julie a beautiful baby with the possible exception of her "decided *Tyler nose*. I hope that organ will rest a while in its maturity, for its prominence is quite amusing." Fortunately, nature arrested the growth of the offending proboscis, and within a few months Julia was predicting that her daughter would become "the greatest belle of her day.... I am making very great calculations upon her." The birth of Julie was somewhat more difficult for Julia than those of her sons, and it was more than six weeks before she was again up and around. In the meantime, Gardie and Alex adjusted quickly to their little sister's presence and, said Margaret, "having fallen from their high estate upon Mama's knee by the recent innovation are making all haste to manhood." [49]

By the time Lachlan Tyler was born on December 9, 1851, Julia was beginning to weary of her biennial contribution to America's population explosion. Lachlan (Julia omitted the "Mc") was her most difficult pregnancy. This fact did not, however, prevent a grueling shopping trip to Richmond in July 1851, from which "she returned perfectly *foundered* in all her limbs so that she has fairly taken to her bed," or a jaunt to Saratoga in August. But a planned visit to Niagara Falls with Tyler, Margaret, and David Lyon in September proved quite beyond her strength, and she remained in New York with her mother and her children. The annual Northern trip had the advantage of removing the children from the mosquito, flea, tick, and fever season on the James and for this reason it was invariably undertaken, whatever the inconvenience. "The fleas are troublesome to Julie and the ticks to Gardie who *will* wander everywhere his Father goes," Julia explained. "If one flea finds its way to Julie before you know it she is spotted in many places and suffering greatly." While the children returned to Sherwood Forest in 1851 unmarked by insects, Julia reached the plantation badly fatigued and unusually apprehensive about her coming ordeal. She briefly considered the use of drugs or whiskey to ease her through the experience. This idea was sharply overruled by her friends and relatives. The puerperal advice she received from Mary Conger on the point was typical:

I do really feel sorry for you for you seem to be so ill beforehand which is certainly ungrateful work, as it does no good to anybody. I fear you do not take exercise enough in your Southern mode of life. I advise you to resume your old horseback [riding] habits. You were so healthy as a girl that you ought to be able to have children with little or no suffering besides the actual labor which is not to be got rid of anyhow. I have little faith in clouding one's perceptions by the use of any drug ... for myself I should have strong objections to entering eternity drunk, and in the character of a coward fleeing from the battle he was appointed to fight. I would sooner try all lawful means of strengthening mind and body to endure and conquer.[50]

Julia endured and she conquered. Within a few days of Lachlan's appearance at a husky nine and a half pounds, the delighted father could assure Henry Curtis that Julia was out of danger. Although she was "fatigued and overdone by nursing our little boy," all was well with her. "You perceive," Tyler added,

> that we are raising up quite a large family, 3 boys and one girl and all fine children in intellect and mechanism. The girl ... is as bright as her mother and is already the idolized of the Household. The boys by a sort of instinct, look upon her as one claiming their especial regard and in their conduct towards her manifest the deepest affection. Thus it is that my old age is enlivened by the scenes of my youth—and these precious buds and blossoms almost persuade me that the springtime of life is still surrounding me.[51]

John Tyler was sixty-one when Lachlan was born—still in the "springtime of life." His love for Julia and for his new "buds and blossoms" grew and deepened through the years and kept him young in heart and spirit. Thus Edmund Ruffin, Virginia's "celebrated agriculturist," could say of Tyler's second family during his March 1854 visit to Sherwood that "as *a lot* they would bear off the premium of any agricultural show." To which a gentleman present added: "With their mother at their head there would be no question about it!" Julia and John Tyler, in spite of the great age difference between them, were a happy and devoted couple. Ruffin remarked on this shortly after leaving the plantation:

> The mother of five living children, she [Julia] still looks as blooming and fresh as a girl of 20, and indeed I should not have guessed her to be older, if meeting her without knowing who she was. There was nothing in their manner to each other to indicate the relation of husband and wife. A stranger might have as soon supposed them to be father and daughter. But without any of the usual feeling (whether of real or pretended love) in such cases of disproportionate age, she really seemed to be her husband's devoted *admirer*, and a contented and happy wife.[52]

Only a few outsiders saw the John Tyler who rode his plantation, played his fiddle, struggled with his bank balance, smoked his cigars, sipped his wines, bounced his babies, teased his wife, and treated the family to poetry of his own composition. Julia finally made him give up the smelly black cigars for a pipe, but she could not still his iambic pen. Phoebe often received his poetic outpourings to cheer her dreary existence on Shelter Island, and after the Gardiners moved from Lafayette Place to Staten Island in 1852 Margaret was the subject and recipient of a piece titled "Margaret of the Isle" which began:

> The springtime has its violets,
>   The summer has its rose;
> The autumn has its varied tints,
>   But winter has its snows—
> But springtime's violet, summer's rose
>   Are not so sweet to see,

> Or autumn's tints or winter's snows
> So bright—so pure is she;
> As Margaret of the lovely Isle
> That is girt in by the sea....[53]

Difficult as Lachlan's arrival had been, Julia was content to bear Tyler's children. He derived so much pleasure from them and when he was happy she was too. Yet by the time her fifth child, Lyon Gardiner Tyler, was born on August 24, 1853, Juliana Gardiner was beginning to belabor her daughter with the notion that there was something rather indecent about families so large. She, of course, had had four children of her own in a space of six years. So Julia's five in nine years was scarcely a family frequency record. Still, when Julia informed Margaret in May 1853 of her new "predicament," she did so with the suggestion that Margaret break the glad tidings to her mother gently. "Her nerves might be too much shaken if taken by surprise," said Julia. Lyon Gardiner Tyler was destined to become the family biographer, a productive historian, and the distinguished president for many years of William and Mary College. But his arrival on the scene in August 1853 was for Julia an inconvenience. Mainly, it deprived her of her usual and much anticipated summer escape to Saratoga and East Hampton. For a moment she indulged in the luxury of feeling sorry for herself, something she rarely did. "I have it all to bear," she announced stoically, "[but] you may depend upon it I shall encourage no other state of mind than cheerfulness." She would, she said, "make the best of it." The arrival of another baby did have one peripheral advantage: it permitted Julia to break the routine of home and child management and take to her bed and rest. "I don't expect to get any rest or repose myself in mind or body until I am flat on my back," she had told her mother a month before "Lonie's" birth. Happily, she came through the ordeal well. "She has been a patient sufferer," Juliana reported. With five children now at Sherwood Forest, Tyler could proudly boast that he was "not likely to let the [family] name become extinct." [54]

Nevertheless, a family of five small children (later seven) made the annual pilgrimage to the North increasingly difficult for John Tyler and Julia to arrange. The sheer logistics of transporting so large a brood to East Hampton, Saratoga, or even to White Sulphur Springs was too much of a task despite the aid of several nurses and body servants. It was clear by 1853 that other summer plans would have to be made if the insect-and-fever season at Sherwood Forest was to be escaped.

So it was that Tyler began negotiating for the rental of a summer place at Old Point Comfort, Virginia. In October 1853 the arrangements were well advanced. Several years later, in 1858, Julia used $10,000 of her own money to buy a property at Hampton, Virginia, near Old Point Comfort, known in the family as "Villa Margaret." Here the family summered during the last years before the Civil War. The children loved the spot; its long wide beaches and ocean breezes were ideal. Julia and the President enjoyed the full social life that centered on nearby Fortress Monroe. Old Point Comfort thus became the delightful answer to the summer-vacation problem. It was near enough Sherwood Forest to permit Tyler to keep an eye on his fields, and close enough to the officers stationed at the Fortress to permit Julia to dance, flirt, and gossip. Juliana and Margaret approved the new summer-vacation arrangement wholeheartedly although they were not quite so impressed with the gallant West Pointers at the Fortress as was Julia. "Poor matches but the most *fascinating* of men," said Juliana of them. Nevertheless, she and Margaret visited the Tylers at Old Point Comfort during the summers of 1853-1856. As Juliana described the gala society there in July 1855:

There was no dearth of gentlemen at Old Point but I don't know who they all were.... I had not the means of ascertaining anything about their social position except those belonging to this state.... The ladies however found plenty to dance with which is more than they could do last season at Saratoga. I think for social enjoyment Old Point for the best, but for display Saratoga, as there is less dress. J[ulia] received with the P[resident] every attention at Old Point. A salute was fired and all the officers called together to pay their respects and were in turn presented to Julia. She was a decided belle ... and all pronounced her unchanged in appearance.

For Julia it was almost the recapture of her honeymoon.[55]

15

AND THE PURSUIT OF PROPERTY

> *Maybe our Argonauts, returned laden with the golden fleece, will be disposed to invest some of their riches on the banks of the Ohio. At any rate the land must become more valuable if gold becomes more abundant.*
> —ALEXANDER GARDINER, JUNE 1849

Sherwood Forest was an expensive plantation to maintain and scarcely a harvest season passed that John Tyler did not wish that he were a wealthy man. He wanted his young wife and growing family to have every luxury money could buy. For James River wheat planters, ready cash was always a scarce commodity, and Tyler spent most of his retirement years borrowing from one bank to pay notes due at another. He never missed a payment due, nor was he ever denied a loan. Nevertheless, he had many close calls. Had it not been for the Gardiners, particularly Alexander, financial embarrassment might well have overtaken him on several occasions. As he explained his predicament to Alexander on one occasion in 1849, "In a community so small as this, where every man's business is known to every other, I do not like it to appear that I substitute one note for another." This was, however, the way he was forced to operate, and although the Gardiners' role in his fiscal affairs was usually discreet to the point of secrecy, their function was the vital one. They served as co-signers and guarantors of his numerous notes and as his outright creditors. John Tyler, in sum, lived in a swirling sea of notes paid, notes negotiated, and notes due, and it was always a struggle for him to keep his chin above water. It was this unhappy way of fiscal life that caused him to get involved in a coal-and-timber speculation with Alexander Gardiner in Union County, Kentucky, a scheme which on the surface and at the outset had all the earmarks of get-rich-quick.[1]

Tyler had purchased the Kentucky land in the late 1830s. It amounted to three patents of 400 to 450 acres each, first issued to Lieutenant Colonel Holt Richardson of Virginia for his Revolutionary War services. From Richardson it had passed first into the hands of Patrick Hendren, and then from Hendren to the trustees of his estate, who offered it for sale to meet Hendren's debts. For a depression-level price he never disclosed, Tyler bought the property as a speculation, fought off several suits by disappointed Hendren creditors to attach the land, and subsequently rented it to two local farmers for a nominal annual fee of $100 pending a decision on what to do with it. Located about three miles due west of the small settlement of Caseyville, the plot fronted a mile and a quarter on the Ohio River. In July 1839 Tyler went to Caseyville to view his purchase and found it remote, heavily timbered, unsurveyed and unfenced. Save for two rude dwellings which stood in a small clearing and some fifty acres his tenants had cleared for farming, the property was an isolated jungle. Disappointed with the rugged appearance of the land, he put it up for sale at three dollars an acre and appointed Samuel Casey, a local realtor and jack-of-all-trades, his agent in the matter. There were no takers at this or any price. The panic and depression of 1837 had dried up all venture capital.[2]

Faced with a great need for cash during the months immediately following his departure from the White House, Tyler renewed his efforts to sell the Caseyville land. To effect this he appointed Captain John W. Russell his new agent. Russell was a well-known Ohio River snagboat operator and had served as the President's Superintendent of River Improvements in the West. His appointment as Tyler's realtor followed hard on the heels of his report to Sherwood Forest in June 1845 that coal of high quality had been discovered near the Tyler property line and was being mined commercially in the area. Ordered by Tyler to investigate this promising development further, Russell soon reported the likelihood of coal on the former President's land as well. Thus encouraged, Tyler promptly raised his asking price from three to five dollars an acre and urged Russell to find a buyer. At about the same time, in October 1845, in desperate need of cash he borrowed $2000 from Corcoran and Riggs, the Washington bankers. He secured this loan with a contract that gave the bank the option of calling the note when due or taking instead a deed to a quarter-interest in the coal lands. Meanwhile, he instructed his old friend John Lorimer Graham to look into the possibility of surveying the land and forming a joint stock company to exploit it. When Graham announced that the prospects at Caseyville would be well worth further analysis, Tyler decided to risk $200 in a detailed mineral survey. In this decision he was influenced by Alexander's optimistic prediction that "great profit" was to be made in the enterprise.[3]

While Tyler was making preliminary arrangements to have the real worth of the property assessed, Russell resigned as his agent to run for the Kentucky state senate. In so doing he turned Tyler's affairs over to two "young and poor, but strictly honest" Frankfort lawyers, Henry Tilford and R. G. Samuels. Tyler informed his new agents in April 1846 that while he still wanted to sell the land "at a fair price," he had "friends in New York" who would share in any reasonable plan to exploit the coal deposits. He made it clear to his new agents that it was their main responsibility to keep him "beyond the reach of fraudulent speculation." With this expression of the ex-President's intentions, Tilford and Samuels journeyed from Frankfort to Caseyville to look at the property. Their subsequent report pegged the value of the land at not more than five to eight dollars an acre and concluded that while there was indeed high-quality coal present, it was probably not in enough quantity to make mining it feasible. They did, however, recommend proceeding with a thorough exploration of the deposit on the off-chance that it might add "several thousand dollars" to the value of the land. This, of course, Tyler had already decided to do.[4]

The report of the coal survey undertaken by Thomas Wilson, a former English coalminer, led John Tyler to believe that his treasure ship had finally come in. Indeed, Corcoran and Riggs were so enthusiastic that they promptly exercised the option on their Tyler note and became one-quarter owners of the property. This optimism was occasioned by Wilson's survey analysis of October 1846 which announced the discovery of a three-foot seam of top-quality cannel coal, "all free from Sulpher [sic] ... superior to any coal we have in this part of the country ... superior to any coal for Grates I have ever seen tried." With these glad tidings, Tilford and Samuels informed Tyler they were unwilling to sell his land "even at $10 per acre." His coal deposit, they said, was "inexhaustible." They recommended an immediate investment of five or six thousand dollars to open a shaft and to build a spur railroad to the river which lay two miles distant. "Our idea would be to keep an extensive coal yard for Steamboats and woodyard also and let it be known as 'Capt. Russell's', then a Steamboat would scarcely ever pass, he being so very popular on the river...." Russell himself verified Wilson's encouraging report and guessed that Tyler's superior cannel coal would be worth eight to ten cents a bushel at the riverbank. He promised that he would use it himself and would also "persuade all of my acquaintances" on the river to buy exclusively at Tyler's coalyard. He noted further that Tilford and Samuels themselves had expressed an eagerness to work the mine on shares and he strongly urged such an arrangement.[5]

Confronted with the prospect of a great and lucrative coal operation that would solve his financial problems for life, Tyler sounded out Alexander in New York to ascertain his view of an initial six-thousand-dollar investment in opening a mine shaft. He also suggested a Tyler-Gardiner partnership to develop the coal land and urged Alexander to go to Union County and see for himself the great riches that awaited them both there. Although Julia assured her brother, the shrewdest businessman in the family, that "the President thinks this is a *fine chance for you*," Alexander backed politely away from the deal. He thought that if a substantial amount of stock in a development company could be sold to knowledgeable people on the scene, particularly optimistic souls like Russell, Samuels, and Tilford, it might be worth a gamble. Otherwise, he counseled extreme caution. The pressure of his clerkship and other affairs did not permit him, he said, an exploratory trip to Caseyville.

Instead, Tyler's brother-in-law, Dr. N. M. Miller of Columbus, Ohio, was asked to visit the property in December 1846 for a firsthand evaluation of its potential. Miller soon informed Sherwood Forest that a Memphis group headed by a Colonel David Morrison was interested in buying the land, although at a price well below the value Tilford, Samuels, and Russell had all placed upon it. This deflationary news aroused Tyler's suspicions, especially since Miller also noted in his letter that the new Farnum Iron Works had been established on the Cumberland River, and that "Caseyville is the best point to get their coal." The President's enthusiasm for the coal business dipped appreciably a few days later when Captain Russell turned down Tyler's offer of stock in a projected mining company on the grounds that he had just tied up all his available cash in a Frankfort tavern venture. Russell had belatedly discovered, he explained, that of Tyler's fourteen hundred acres, only fifty evidenced the presence of coal. When Alexander advised the sale of the land without deeper involvement and at the best price offered, Tyler accepted the suggestion without dissent. So discouraged had he suddenly become that he turned down a proposition offering him a seemingly low $2000 for every acre of coal dug on his land. This, as it turned out, he should have accepted.[6]

In February of 1847 Tilford and Samuels informed Tyler that they were, as instructed, drawing a contract to sell the land for $12,000. The potential buyer was reputed to be a company comprised of Messrs. Samuel Page, David Morrison, and Robert Winston. Tyler was delighted to have the matter so profitably disposed of, and he immediately agreed to the bargain. Actually, the contract, signed on August 16, 1847, showed Robert P. Winston, a Caseyville merchant, as sole purchaser. Before Tyler learned of this change, he was notified privately that the "company" to which he was selling his land did not in fact exist; that Winston alone was the buyer; and that Winston had never seen $12,000 in his life and never would. "Now my dear fellow I would advise this," wrote his friend Joseph L. Watkins from his Tylerite patronage job at the Memphis Navy Yard, "kick the bargain already made to hell, for I begin to suspect the buyers are men of straw.... I think there is now some disposition to swindle you." With justifiable alarm, Tyler confessed to Alexander: "I know the property to be valuable and I am almost persuaded that a fraudulent contract has been entered into to cheat me out of it."

Watkins' suspicions notwithstanding, the contract was not actually fraudulent. Robert Winston was simply financially incompetent to execute it. While discovering this sad fact for himself, Winston poured at least $3000 into a dauntless attempt to get a mine into operation. In this successful activity he discovered several new coal veins, which raised from fifty to three hundred the estimated coal acreage on the Tyler property. Meanwhile, he undertook to sell shares locally in his project in an attempt to meet the first of the three annual payments of $4000 due to Tyler on February 10, 1848. This little stockbroking effort failed completely. In September 1847 he therefore persuaded Samuel L. Casey to assume the burden of the Tyler contract. When, two months later, it became apparent that Casey could not make the first payment to Tyler either, Winston evidenced a willingness to cancel the contract altogether on repayment of the unwisely ventured $3000 capital investment he had put into the mine and property.[7]

Rather than begin tedious litigation at such distance, Tyler reluctantly decided to pay Robert Winston the $3000 morally due him, cancel the contract, and start over from the beginning. While he felt that he had been put upon by sharp Kentucky speculators, he became convinced once again that he could still make a fortune at Caseyville. Winston's discovery of additional veins brought a new flush of enthusiasm, a dream of great riches, which Tyler undertook to transmit to Alexander Gardiner. Privately, Alexander remained dubious about the entire speculation. But to accommodate his eager brother-in-law he became Tyler's active partner in the venture in November 1847. He purchased half interest in the President's share (Corcoran and Riggs still held their quarter) for $6000. He also agreed to put up half of the reimbursement to be paid Winston for his capital improvements. He did this, as Tyler described it, in the "belief that the property might be rendered available in some form at once and that at the earliest period the mines should be put into operation." With Alexander as his partner, Tyler explained to Corcoran and Riggs that the future would bring them all great profits. "So far as my own interests are involved ... you will see in all I have done security and not speculation." Alexander was never convinced. As he later confessed to Tyler, "My own chief inducement in becoming interested in the property was to preserve your interest from sacrifice." Nevertheless, he agreed to accompany Tyler to Caseyville in November 1847 to survey the situation at first hand and see what might be made of the operation.[8]

As a businessman Alexander Gardiner was no fool. He entered into the Caseyville speculation with his eyes open. He combined a flair for speculation with hard-headed business sense. In supervising the collection of Gardiner rentals in New York, for example, he allowed no feeling of sympathy to interfere with his duty. Judgments for back rent were quickly and regularly filed in the courts, and for the tenant it was either pay up in full and on time or get out on the street. Repairs and maintenance on the properties were held to a bare minimum, and then undertaken only under pressure from the Health Warden. Tenants were expected to effect their own repairs and improvements. That the downtown Gardiner properties were already well on their way toward slumhood was of no concern to him. If his mother complained that her "head requires everything of a business nature to be made plain," Alexander had no such problem. For him success in business boiled down to a simple philosophy—buy cheap and sell dear. And if he could bleed oratorically for the poor and the downtrodden of New York City at a Tammany rally, he never permitted that sentiment to interfere with his business acumen. By nature a plunger and speculator, he played the stock market with dash, investing thousands of dollars with cool, disdainful detachment. At various times he bought and sold stock of the United States Mining Company, the Hudson and Delaware Canal Company, the Long Island Railroad, and the British and Canadian Mining Company. He also gambled on New York City lots and on vacation properties in Newport. In all his financial speculations his methodology emphasized an icy calmness. "Do not be too anxious," he once counseled his brother. "Let results take care of themselves and if you lose make up your losses as well as you can without allowing yourself to be harassed. We have too much nervous susceptibility in our family... the weakness of a child in face of the smallest reverse." In spite of his coolness, Alexander never made very much money in the stock market. Nor did he lose money. When he died he was at about the break-even point. Certainly he never managed to elevate himself fully into New York's aristocracy of great wealth, the Astor-dominated clique he criticized but to which he subconsciously aspired:

The ball at the Astor's last week [he wrote in February 1843] was a very brilliant affair, more brilliant than any that has taken place this season. There was a great display of the precious metals. The Astors seem now at the head of fashionable society, and though they are laughed at privately, those that appear in such rich trappings must needs be treated with much deference. Money and impudence are the only essentials to such circles, but they are indispensable.... Of all aristocracies, that of wealth is the worst since it is the only kind that affords no incentive to virtue.[9]

How much incentive to virtue Alexander had as he set off for Caseyville with Tyler on November 15, 1847, is difficult to determine. Very likely he had motives no more complex than to convert their land into a profitable operation without delay. The trip itself was arduous and demanded a strong incentive of some sort. To reach Caseyville, Kentucky, one proceeded from Baltimore to Cumberland, Maryland, by rail, changing trains at Harpers Ferry, Virginia. There the President and Alexander met and chatted with Captain Robert Stockton, home from the war in California ("He looked like a Russian hussar hardened and bronzed by exposure—more military than naval"). Since Tyler was traveling "quite incognito ... not more than two or three persons recognized him" at Harpers Ferry. At Cumberland the travelers boarded a four-horse mail stage for Wheeling, Virginia, via the same National Road which Tyler, ironically, had fought against so vigorously as a young congressman. Forced to walk up each hill behind the stage, the two men were stunned by the magnificent views from the mountaintops. Or as Alexander reported it: "On the summit [Laurel Hill, Pa.] ... our eyes stretched far below and away over the Great West. It seemed as if a new world was bursting upon the vision." From Wheeling they proceeded down the Ohio by steamboat to Cincinnati. At the "Queen City of the West," they chanced upon and conversed with Mississippi Senators Henry S. Foote and Jefferson Davis, who were on their way to Washington. Davis was still on crutches, the result of his wounds at the Battle of Buena Vista. From Cincinnati a thirty-six-hour boat ride carried them down to Louisville, where Tyler was met and formally entertained by Governor Metcalf. Then came a punishing ten-hour carriage trip over to Frankfort to consult with Tilford and Samuels. Returning to Louisville, they boarded the boat for Caseyville where finally they "landed under the auspices of Hail Columbia, Yankee Doodle and the Star Spangled Banner. The passengers on board gathered at the side of the vessel, hats were raised by all, and the whole population of Caseyville was called out by the occasion." The trip took twelve days.[10]

Since Tyler's land was heavily timbered, Alexander saw at once that considerable money was to be made in the wood business. A week in Caseyville strengthened this view and convinced him that the coal deposits were also well worth exploiting. When he returned to New York in December he decided to form a joint stock company to capitalize and launch the coal venture. At the same time he began preliminary arrangements for the cutting of timber. With wood selling to steamboats on the river at $2 to $2.50 per cord, and with much of Tyler's property capable of yielding 150 cords an acre, he proposed to put six lumbermen to work cutting fuel. He was certain he could hire woodsmen for $75 to $100 per year and asked Samuel L. Casey to superintend the proposed lumbering operation for a 25 per cent commission. Casey, however, wisely refused the job, suggesting instead the employment of his deaf brother. Alexander admitted to Tyler that the handicapped sibling was "perhaps too deaf to be a safe conniver in mischief," but he decided to employ someone more experienced in business matters. Meanwhile, he assured Tyler that handsome profits would soon roll in from the forests. Under no conditions should the President divest himself of his interest in the enterprise. With upwards of $300,000 worth of timber on the property, Tyler agreed that the wood business might well be the answer to his financial problems.[11]

This point settled, Alexander pushed ahead with plans to form a joint stock company to mine the coal at Caseyville. Working with three retired veterans of the Tyler political wars—T. William Letson of Baltimore, General William G. McNeill of New York, and Major L. A. Sykes of New York—he undertook to sell 3000 shares at $20 each. Of the $60,000 thus raised, $45,000 would purchase the Tyler-Gardiner land. The remaining $15,000 would be used to build a spur line to the river, erect necessary utility buildings, purchase coal cars, mules, carts, river scows, and tools, and build a sawmill to process the timber. Employing somewhat optimistic arithmetic on production costs and probable sales, Alexander calculated a $27,000 net profit the first year, increasing to $45,000 the third. Letson estimated it even higher—$150,000 in the first three years, or $50 clear profit per share. By December 24, 1847, Alexander and Letson announced 2100 shares sold (to whom they did not reveal—probably to Tyler and themselves) and were urging McNeill and Sykes to pick up the remaining 900. McNeill assured Sykes that "this *is* a good thing," but Sykes did some rapid arithmetic of his own and concluded that "the reality does not exactly tally with the estimate." He figured that the known veins would yield 650,000 tons rather than Alexander's estimate of 30,000,000 tons. While he still thought the speculation a "good one," he decided he would have to "know more about it before engaging in it." The longer he looked at it the more harebrained it became, and he finally decided he would have no part of it. By mid-January 1848 the dubious project was virtually dead, Alexander explaining to Tyler that "the money market is so much oppressed that speculations find no favor."[12]

Whatever the reasons for the collapse of the joint stock venture, Corcoran and Riggs decided that they had had enough of speculative dreams along the beautiful Ohio. In March 1848 they offered to sell to either Tyler or Gardiner their one-quarter interest at Caseyville for $2100, or roughly what they had invested in the project. At first, Alexander was willing to buy the bankers' holding, but Tyler decided to retain it himself. A few months later, however, hard-pressed for cash as usual and determined to liquidate his Kentucky holdings entirely, he offered the Corcoran and Riggs share to Alexander. "My day for speculation and adventure is over; yours has just come," he told his brother-in-law. But at that moment Alexander was overextended in the stock market and in no position to purchase the additional interest. After much polite backing and filling, which occupied over a year, he finally informed Tyler bluntly in June 1849 that "matters are changed, expectations of the immediate return from the property have been scattered to the winds, all my cash means have been invested in other adventures, and the past has admonished me of the wisdom of having a little money on hand, keeping out of debt, and not expecting to make all the bargains in this world." Although he refused the proffered Corcoran and Riggs share, Alexander loyally retained his three-eighths interest in the uncertain venture.[13]

As his vision of a joint stock mining company gradually clouded, Alexander moved ahead with the lumber-cutting project. In May 1848 he signed a contract with Andrew J. Fenton of Gowanus wherein Fenton agreed to go to Caseyville for one year and supervise the cutting of timber. For this he would receive one-fourth of the net profits, the free use of such land as he and his wife might want to cultivate, and the use of either of the crude dwellings then standing on the property. To get matters off on a proper footing Alexander made a second trip to Caseyville in June 1848 to see that Fenton had arrived and to brief him on accepted business procedures. En route to Union County he stopped and visited pleasantly at Homewood, the estate of Tyler's former War Secretary William Wilkins, near Pittsburgh. When he finally reached Caseyville Fenton was still nowhere in evidence. It was symbolic of what the Gardiner-Fenton relationship would be during the next year. In a word, Andrew J. Fenton was one of history's tragic figures. Well-meaning and honest, he was also accident-prone, incompetent, and generally ill-starred. He could seemingly do nothing right, try as he might.[14]

When Fenton at last showed up, the two men surveyed the situation and discovered a tight local labor market. It was then decided that Fenton should return to Maryland and lease a dozen Negro slaves at $40 to $50 each per year, accompany them back to Caseyville, and set them briskly to chopping. With high hopes Fenton departed for the East. Within a few weeks he reported to Alexander that he had scoured eastern Maryland and the Eastern Shore without success. There were no slaves for hire at $50—or at any price. Alexander then ordered him back to Caseyville with instructions to hire whatever local white laborers were available and get started. "I know that you have too much courage and determination of purpose to be disheartened by trifles," he assured his manager.[15]

The "trifles" mounted alarmingly. Fenton's regularly submitted expense accounts soon demonstrated that more money was being poured into the forests than lumber was dribbling out. White labor was scarce, shiftless, and expensive, choppers demanding fifty cents per cord cut rather than the forty cents Alexander thought the work worth. Few of the men hired by Fenton stayed on the job for more than a few days. They would earn a few dollars, stock up on White Lightning, and disappear drunkenly and happily downriver. "If I could get all black men

I would prefer it," Fenton reported, "as the white men in this country are very lazy and have no desire to work. The man that I had last week cut 3½ cords and quit; he would not cut anymore for that price." While Fenton labored unsuccessfully to keep a token labor force in the woods, Alexander Gardiner's expenses mounted. The costs of building Fenton a habitable dwelling (the structures on the property were scarcely more than sheds), combined with the cost of tools, carts, and scows, were much higher than Alexander had anticipated or thought necessary. In addition, Fenton and his wife both fell ill with the malaria that raced through the community in August 1848. "All of our men are sick with fever and have been so this last ten days... everybody is sick, my wife included," he wrote. "I have had a bad beginning." Healthy labor, much less sober labor, became virtually impossible to procure. "If I can get Negroes by the month I shall get them," said Fenton, "for I can make them work, but the white men work one day and play the next and I think it will be more profitable to get Negroes." By September 1848 it was costing Alexander exactly $6.18 to get a cord of wood cut that sold from $1.75 to $2. This was not the royal road to the Seven Cities of Cibola that Alexander and John Tyler expected to travel.[16]

As Fenton fought his uneven battle against fever and trees on the banks of the distant Ohio, Alexander Gardiner lounged at Saratoga dancing, flirting, and boating with the ladies. Angered by what seemed to him sheer malingering on Fenton's part, he commenced sending off detailed instructions on just how a lumber business should be efficiently and profitably conducted. Alexander Gardiner had never chopped a stick of wood in his life, but he was certain that Fenton's force (such as it was) should be stockpiling 100 cords a week in preparation for winter demands from the steamboats. On the other hand, Fenton's patient explanations that he could obtain only a handful of choppers at any given time, Negro or white, and that fever felled them faster than they felled trees, elicited from Alexander little more than a demand for "proper perseverance"—and an unsolicited cure for malaria:

> The disease is now very easily managed in Virginia by active treatment [he told Fenton]. When first seized with it you should have taken ten grains of Calomel on going to bed at night, and a strong dose of castor oil upon getting up in the morning. As soon as this medium has operated, three doses of quinine of five grains each should be taken at intervals of four or five hours... the use of quinine should be continued... the dose being gradually reduced.... They give quinine in small doses in Kentucky and it is not so effectual.

If this advice proved any consolation or provided any cure, Fenton gave no evidence of it. As soon as he was up and around again he pleaded with Alexander to "send me more money, as much as you can spare, for I want teams and carts and boats and ropes and feed."[17]

As Alexander's expenses increased steadily, his belief that the cost of producing the fuel might be brought below its potential sale price waned. While Gardiner was complaining to Tyler that "the slowness of the proceedings in Kentucky passes all understanding," Fenton was complaining to Gardiner that he could not hold labor, and that he could not manage "without Negroes as the white men are not worth shooting." Nor was Alexander's growing frustration diminished when he learned that Fenton had named a small peninsula on the property "Gardiner's Point." This shrewd appeal to the Gardiner ego did not dull the darkening economic facts of the whole operation. Indeed, Alexander's desire to reduce operating expenses at Caseyville reached the ultimate extreme of instructing Fenton that "when your letters are heavy direct them (as it will save postage) to Ex-President Tyler, care of Alexander Gardiner, Esq., New York City." To this suggestion Fenton responded only with a plea for $500 to purchase additional equipment and as a personal advance on commissions to enable him to buy needed household provisions and pay his doctor's bills. "This is the last money that I shall want of you," he assured his employer. And for a week or so it was the last money he requested. Alexander, in turn, fired back a high-level lecture in Classical Economics, urging Fenton "cut on, and keep cutting constantly, and without flagging. There is no other way in which money can be made either to myself or to you." As Fenton cut on, Gardiner and Tyler continued throwing money into the deep woods. By mid-December 1848 the operation at last began to show dim signs of reaching the break-even point. At that hopeful juncture, however, came the rain, the flood, and the mud that bogged down Fenton's wagons, drove his meager and erratic labor supply to shelter, and swept away some 100 of the 600 cords of wood he had stacked on and near the riverbank.[18]

Tyler watched the trials and tribulations of poor Andrew J. Fenton with mounting dismay. With wood at $1.75 a cord, the venture had shown no profit whatsoever in its first six months. Indeed, Fenton had sold little of what he had cut, and over $1000 had already been invested in the project. Increasingly, Tyler began to think of the place as a future plantation site rather than a business location. Fenton was therefore instructed not to cut the pecan and other "highly ornamental" broad nut trees standing on the property. By February 1849 the President too had finally lost patience with Fenton. Flood and mud, cholera and malaria were bad enough, but when steamboats passed Gardiner's Point without stopping, Tyler was prepared to concede that the game was up. Not Alexander—at least not yet. "Keep the axe going," he ordered Fenton in late February, "the boats will all be in motion soon and you will have a brisk demand for wood." Nevertheless, he agreed with Tyler that Fenton's pessimistic reports were "discouraging, and to me... as unsatisfactory as they are indefinite." [19]

The April floods on the Ohio drowned forever the Gardiner-Tyler dream of a lumber empire. Inundating several hundred acres of the property, sweeping away much of the unsold stockpile of wood, the annual spring disaster convinced Tyler that Fenton should be fired for general inefficiency. He simply had not taken "those wise precautions which the knowledge of the constant liability to overflow... would properly have dictated." The only way the operation could be continued profitably, Tyler argued, was with a vigorous new overseer at the head of no less than four Negro slave workers. While the slaves would cost up to $2250 each, they would "do more and be less expensive than the casual white labour to be picked up by accident." This, of course, would mean pouring a great deal more capital into an already flooded rathole, and Tyler frankly preferred to fire Fenton, sell the jinxed property, and be done with it. With this evaluation Alexander reluctantly agreed. Fenton must go. But whatever modest satisfaction Tyler and Gardiner might have derived from discharging their hapless manager was denied them. In April 1849 Fenton and his wife simply pulled up stakes and disappeared from Caseyville, leaving their furniture behind them.

Following their hasty departure the ex-President and his partner decided to offer the land for sale again. This time they placed a price tag of $20,000 on the property. "I no more doubt the ultimate great value of the property than I do my own existence," Alexander assured Sherwood Forest. "The establishment of the Navy Yard at New Orleans dispels all doubt." As for the dream of great wealth which both partners had momentarily shared, Tyler philosophically told his brother-in-law to "set it down as a thing of the past, and let it no longer disturb." There was actually little else Alexander could do. Fenton, he concluded, was not a bad sort. "He is very stupid, but really seems to be honest." This opinion was strengthened when Fenton wrote him in May enclosing a final accounting of the disposition of the equipment at Caseyville. From a financial standpoint the operation had been a disaster, and Alexander agreed with his brother-in-law that the venture should be terminated and the property sold.[20]

Selling it was not an easy matter. On the contrary, it was still unsold when Alexander died in January 1851 and left his share to Julia. And it was not until September 1853, after such friends and agents as George Waggaman, General William G. McNeill, and Duff Green had worked on the problem, that Tyler and Julia finally disposed of the land to a group of Norfolk speculators for $20,000, Julia using her share of the proceeds in 1858 to purchase Villa Margaret, the summer house at Hampton. It was probably just as well that the property was not sold in 1849. "There could not be a worse time to sell than the present," said Alexander, "when the whole West is depressed by the floods and the cholera." There was also the possibility that David Lyon Gardiner and Henry Beeckman would return from the

California gold fields so laden with wealth that they would rush to invest it at Caseyville. As Alexander explained this final hope to Tyler:

> Maybe our Argonauts, returned laden with the golden fleece, will be disposed to invest some portion of their riches on the banks of the Ohio; at any rate the land must become more valuable if gold becomes more abundant, and next year will be an important one in regard to the ultimate value of the land.

Alexander's reverie that his brother and his young brother-in-law would return from California weighted with gold was destined to be dashed, as were the bright initial prospects of his own financial speculations in the Bear Flag Republic. But he turned eagerly from the Kentucky coal fields to the California gold fields, confident that great riches lay somewhere near his outstretched fingers.[21]

The discovery of gold on the American River near Coloma, California, in January 1848 produced as great an upheaval in the Tyler-Gardiner clan as it did in any family in the United States. Confirmed as a fact by Polk in his Annual Message of December 1848, news of the great strike raced from New York to Sherwood Forest and back with all the speed of a juicy scandal. Within a few months John H. Beeckman, David Lyon Gardiner, and Beeckman's cousin Henry B. Livingston of New York, had all departed for the gold fields, among the first in that vast tidal wave of humanity that began the frenzied trek to wealth and adventure in early 1849.

John Tyler's initial reaction to Polk's electrifying announcement was not an excited one. He had no desire to go to California or to speculate there. Burned by the collapsing Caseyville operation, he was in no humor to pour additional capital into the mountain streams of El Dorado County. "The President," Julia wrote on December 15, 1848, "has not expressed himself much about this California fever, but he says if gold is so plentiful it will be valueless. He thinks a good farm on James River with plenty of slaves is gold mine enough."

This mood quickly changed. By February 1849 the former President, along with millions of other Americans, had a severe case of California fever. More and more he came to regard California as "the only country worth living in," and he was persuaded that both John Beeckman and David Lyon Gardiner would make vast fortunes there. He agreed, however, with Samuel Gardiner that "it will not be the diggers of gold who will make the fortunes but the merchants." And he pointed out, as any good planter might, that the real wealth of California lay in the rich soil of the Sacramento and San Joaquin Valleys. Nevertheless, he was sure that John and David Lyon would quickly "line their pockets with the yellow dust" even though they had no interest in agriculture. Since both men were "mature and knowledgeable" in business matters, Tyler was confident that they would "not be led away from the true road to fortune by any will-of-the-wisp." Instead, they would sensibly mine the miners. As merchants and real estate operators, and even as moneychangers ("I hope that David carried with him a plentiful supply of 5 and ten cent pieces—each will be worth a pinch of gold and the Colonel's fingers are not the smallest"), they would make their fortunes in the new empire on the Pacific. "Will you believe it," he confided to Alexander, "that I ofttimes wish myself located on some choice spot of land on the Sacramento—and that in my imaginings I have fancied that country an Eden.... There is nothing like the elbow room of a new country." [22]

Tyler's growing enthusiasm for the California country was a direct product of the gold fever infection that swept Tidewater Virginia in 1849. The highly contagious virus did not spare Sherwood Forest. Even little Gardie began clamoring for adult members of the family to go to "Gattyformy to dig gold to buy Gardie tandy." Julia was far less interested in gold and candy for Gardie than she was in the great profits she was sure were to be made in California real estate and merchandising. She was "all for paying a person's passage and dividing the profits." Indeed, as shiploads of adventurers left Richmond and Norfolk, Julia pondered Alexander's suggestion that young Tazewell Tyler, not yet eighteen years old, be allowed to join the local Jasons bound for the gold fields, there to get a lucrative start in life. Taz was certainly eager to go, but Tyler put an end to his agitation with the firm decision that he would be better employed commencing the study of medicine with his uncle, Dr. Henry Curtis, in Hanover County.

Equally eager for adventure in the West was the foot-loose John Tyler, Jr., who enlisted his father's aid in his desire to join the migration to California. Working through Daniel Webster, Tyler attempted to secure for his second son a San Francisco patronage appointment. It was better, he reasoned, to have John, Jr., living his gay life in distant California than in nearby Richmond and Norfolk. Unfortunately the new Taylor administration refused to cooperate in effecting John, Jr.'s polite banishment to the Golden Gate. Tyler therefore considered Alexander's offer to grubstake any member of the immediate family who wished to seek his fortune, metallic, mercantile, political, or otherwise, in the new territory. But a moment's reflection convinced the President that it was well past the time when John should be made to "paddle his own canoe," and he turned down his brother-in-law's overture. Julia considered his decision a mistake. John, Jr., she argued, was "such an unsettled visionary fellow that for my part I shall jump for joy when he is 17,000 miles away ... the P[resident] will feel equally relieved. From first to last he has given him no end of annoyance.... The P. says he really believes him part a mad man...." Madman or not, John Tyler, Jr., never got to California. But then neither did

Julia's perfectly sane, gold-seeking cousin, Egbert Dayton of East Hampton, who died en route to the mines a few days out of Panama and was buried in a lonely Acapulco grave.[23]

First of the family Argonauts to depart for California was the handsome John Beeckman. His financial position had never been strong, and his marriage to Margaret in January 1848 had not improved matters. By December 1848 he was in serious economic difficulty. With a wife and a new baby to support, he found himself suspended hopelessly between underemployment and unemployment. Forced to move his small family into his mother-in-law's house on Lafayette Place, the humiliated young man had no prospect of ever maintaining Margaret in the accepted Gardiner manner. To Beeckman, therefore, the trumpet call of the gold fields was a summons to financial independence. Julia approved his judgment on the grounds that he had "a wife and child to be thinking of which gave a stimulus to the adventure." Juliana agreed. She had never really approved of Beeckman's marriage to her daughter, but she was willing to give her son-in-law his chance to become rich. She consented to lend him $2500 at 7 per cent that he might buy a stock of general merchandise for sale to miners in the Sacramento area. She made it clear to him, however, that the cost of supporting Margaret and the baby during his absence would obligate him to her for an additional $500 to $1000 annually. She would have her pound of flesh. With this unpleasant detail arranged, Margaret "screwed her courage to the breaking point" and finally assented to her husband's departure. In her reluctant decision she was assured by her sister that Beeckman would make a fortune, and that she would soon be "drawing on the 'Bank of California' for a few thousands." When this optimism was also echoed by John Tyler, Margaret's opposition collapsed. Beeckman shipped a cargo of merchandise ahead of him, worth perhaps $5000 retail in the mining camps, and left New York in early January 1849 for the arduous seven-month trip to San Francisco around the Horn.[24]

As a lonely and heartsick Margaret fought an unending battle with infant Harry's swollen gums, colic, and skin rash, reporting these hearthside difficulties in detailed and lengthy letters to her husband, Beeckman made his way slowly to California via Rio, Valparaiso, and Callao. Sporadic reports of his boredom at sea, his near-shipwreck off Cape Horn, and his hopes for the future in California drifted back to Sherwood Forest and Lafayette Place. In August 1849 he finally reached Sacramento. There he met David Lyon Gardiner, who had left New York several weeks behind him but had chosen the quicker trans-Panama route. There too was his cousin, Henry B. Livingston, who had reached El Dorado in early June. [25]

Beeckman's first report to Margaret from Sacramento in September 1849 described a lusty society dominated by diggers, some of whom had already "succeeded beyond all calculations" while others were nearly starving to death. "It all depends upon whether you are fortunate or not in the selection of your spot. One person may dig with all the assiduity in the world and find little or nothing for his pains; another, not three feet off may by a lucky stroke of his pick or turn of his shovel expose to view three or four hundred dollars' worth of the precious metal." This backbreaking pick-axe roulette was not for Beeckman. Instead, he sat

> in front of a small India rubber tent, my portfolio on my knee in the shade of a large oak surrounded by goods of every variety, looking keenly at every teamster as he passes on his way to the mines and anxiously inquiring his wants and scanning my ability to supply him on moment seen if a pair of shoes or boots will fit a very dirty pair of feet, the next instant called off to sell ½ barrel of pork or case of brandy and anon engaged in the more delicate and agreeable business of weighing a few dollars of gold dust received in payment in a small and nicely adjusted pair of scales.

He assured his worried wife that while Sacramento was little more than "a city principally of tents springing up in the wilderness amid the shade of large and spreading trees," bathed alternately in dust and mud, jammed full of Americans, Chinese, Europeans, Africans, and Polynesians ("every language is spoken that tongue can utter"), it was nonetheless an orderly community:

> No attention is paid to appearance... this is a community of men—no ladies —and very few women. Still everything is conducted in the most gentlemanly manner. No quarreling. Nor have I seen half a dozen drunken men since I have been in California. Indeed I am very much surprised at the extreme order which everywhere prevails. Goods left exposed in the streets are as safe as beneath your roof—this may perhaps be owing to Judge Lynch who deals out justice with most remarkable alacrity in this part of the world and the would be guilty stand greatly in fear of his summary mode of proceeding.... By the time I shall write you again... I hope to be able to send you some of the California dust as a token that I have not been idle or unemployed.[26]

So far as can be determined, Beeckman shipped none of the "California dust" to his waiting wife. Once his initial stock of merchandise was exhausted, he discovered that shipping schedules on the Coast were so unpredictable that regular replenishment of stock from New York was virtually impossible. In November 1849 he gave up retail merchandising and invested much of his capital, some $4000, in a real estate speculation in Sacramento in partnership with one Major Benjamin W. Bean. The Major (who supplied two thirds of the capital) and Beeckman bought a lot on J Street and spent $12,000 building a combination wooden frame store and residence on the property. They immediately rented the structure to two New York merchants for $2500 per month, a sum not considered excessive in the wild inflation of Sacramento in 1849. For a brief time it appeared that John Beeckman had struck it rich, that he would soon recoup his investment and enough in addition to repay Juliana and begin banking a sizable monthly income.

At this hopeful juncture in his affairs, floods swept down the Sacramento River in January 1850. Much of the tent city was inundated and the Bean-Beeckman property was damaged to the tune of $5000. By the time necessary repairs had been made and the tenants restored, a business slump struck the area, driving the rent down to $800 per month. As Beeckman explained the discouraging situation in February 1850, "most of those who have been engaged altogether in mercantile pursuits have failed or lost all they made last summer and fall. The high rates paid for store rents—most of them $1000 a month—and clerk hire make way with profits to a large amount so that at the end of the year one is little better off than at the commencement." In addition to this, a rowdy element was beginning to drift into the gold towns. "Numbers indeed of the most abandoned character have settled at San Francisco and Sacramento City and lead a life of the most shameful profanity." [27]

To escape the noxious immoral influences of Sacramento, and to exploit the now-obvious desirability of high ground along the river, Beeckman turned to land speculation at Butteville. In partnership with four other men, among them Benjamin Bean, the group hired a whaleboat and systematically explored a 600-mile stretch of the Sacramento River in search of high ground. They found what they were looking for and in March 1850 they purchased from Johann Augustus Sutter, for $3600, two square miles of high land on the Sacramento River about 175 miles above Sacramento City, near what is now called Butte City. Beeckman himself made the preliminary arrangements with the famous Sutter. Under the contract that was drawn Sutter retained half of the planned town site for his own use. He agreed, however, to bear half the cost of surveying the whole parcel. The idea was to divide the remaining square mile into 100 blocks of 36 lots each, six lots per partner, each block to be sold for $1000. Actually very little investment capital was involved. Sutter consented to take his $3600 from the initial sale of lots. The main cost would be that of a survey and the expense of a road linking Butteville with the immigrant wagon trail that passed nearby. The speculators were thus gambling on their belief that the town they would create at Butteville would become the supply and distribution point for diggers heading upriver into the Trinity Mine country north of Redding. As it turned out, the miners generally went up the west side of the river to Redding. This perverse habit caused them to bypass Butteville and property there was shortly reduced to virtual worthlessness.[28]

But Beeckman could not know this when he journeyed up the Sacramento in early April 1850 to examine the town site and arrange for a survey. On the contrary, he told Margaret that it would surely "prove a good operation and put money in our pockets." With the covered wagons of the overland immigrants beginning to reach California in great numbers, and with flood-prone Sacramento "once this winter all under water and ... momentarily in expectation of a similar catastrophe," Butteville could only prove a "profitable speculation." All the venture required was hard work. "Enterprise and *activity* alone are the watchwords to success in this stirring country ... and if industry and success are synonymous I shall have my reward."[29]

John H. Beeckman had his reward less than three weeks later. Following a ten-day evaluation of the Butteville site, John was returning downriver to Sacramento in a whaleboat when the accident occurred. At 7:30 A.M. on April 26, 1850, while passing Knights Landing ten miles above Verona, John attempted to shift his position in the boat. Somehow he joggled his loaded shotgun which was "resting [on the thwart] with the barrels turned towards his chest." One barrel discharged, the iron balls striking him solidly in the right lung. "My God I am shot!" he cried as he fell into the arms of one of the boatmen. He continued breathing for nearly half an hour; but he was dead, suffocated in his own blood, when the boat reached Verona. There the mayor of the settlement, a Doctor Weeks who had formerly practiced in New York City, took charge of the lifeless body and prepared it for burial. An item on the tragedy appeared in a Sacramento paper the next morning. Within an hour Henry B. Livingston was en route upriver to Verona. He arrived there that same afternoon.

Livingston arranged the final details, procuring a rude coffin, a Presbyterian clergyman, and a quiet lot in a cemetery a half-mile back from the unpredictable river. On Sunday morning, April 28, in a "beautifully retired grove," Margaret's unlucky young husband was buried. Hymns were sung by a small group of rough-looking men, an Indian, and a few women of the village. "On closing the lid of the coffin," Livingston reported, "John's countenance had not altered in the least and all remarked how placid and unchanged!" It was a "singularly solemn situation" for Livingston, who suddenly found himself "in a strange land 6000 miles from home performing the last rites of respect to the only relative in whose veins flowed my own blood, and I the solitary mourner." The lone Indian standing passively at the grave side caught something of Livingston's sorrow. As John's coffin was lowered into the ground, the Indian's eyes followed it slowly downward. "*Adiós, hombre,*" he said softly, "*adiós.*"

John Beeckman's dream of wealth, his ambition to achieve economic equality with the Gardiners, ended in a lonely grave on the Sacramento River. His estate, such as it was, added up to a $4000 interest in the J Street store, an option to purchase a one-twelfth interest in a large lot on J Street (value uncertain), a sixth interest in some undeveloped near-wilderness at Butteville (worth nothing), and a few personal effects. These included "his pocket book with 2 letters from Mr. Tyler, $25 or 30, his large ring with Margaret's initials and his own, his hunting watch, gun, pencil and a beautiful old silver cup which the men in the boat said he seemed to *prize* very much." His personal effects were worth, by Livingston's calculation, no more than $275. To be sure, the Bean-Beeckman store had a tenant for eight more months at a rent of $800, but aside from this immediate prospect of income the estate of John H. Beeckman was modest indeed. After ordering a headstone for the grave and sending a snip of his deceased cousin's hair to Margaret, Livingston undertook the thankless task of settling Beeckman's worldly affairs.[30]

News of her husband's death reached Margaret on June 8. Her reaction was very little less than traumatic. "Nothing could have been more distressing," Alexander noted. "The lamentations of Margaret were but overcome at last by exhaustion." To Alexander the tragedy was an object lesson in the careless use of firearms. But this irrelevant observation brought as little comfort to the widow as Julia's view that since Beeckman had died with little suffering Margaret would soon see the tragedy "in the right light" and "cease to mourn for *herself*." Juliana's initial reaction had the usual Gardiner decimal point in it. Revealing little of the "severe shock" that rocked Sherwood Forest, she immediately instructed Alexander to inform Henry Livingston in Sacramento that she had a solid $3000 claim on Beeckman's estate and that she wanted the matter settled without delay. With that practical demand made clear, she took her grief-stricken daughter to Saratoga for a month so that she might speedily regain her "cheerfulness." Margaret's cheerfulness was very slow to return. Years later she was still writing mournful lines that ran

> Would I were with him! To embrace
> The loved one lost long years before,
> What joy to gaze upon the face
> That never shall be absent more!
> There friends unite, who parted here
> At Death's cold river, oh! How sadly
> Forgotten are the sigh and tear
> Their hearts are leaping, oh! How gladly.

The disadvantages of marrying for love had at last become painfully apparent to Margaret Gardiner.[31]

Pain of another sort struck Lafayette Place when it became evident that Beeckman's estate was not destined to manufacture great riches. Increasing taxes, property assessments, repair and maintenance costs, combined with steadily decreasing rental income, effectively dissipated the Gardiners' optimistic expectation that the one-third interest in the jerry-built wooden store on J Street would prove a gold mine for Beeckman's distraught widow. By 1852 Sacramento was being transformed from a city of wood and canvas to one of brick and stone, and the less than desirable Beeckman-Bean property, when it had a tenant at all, brought Margaret only $100 a month. In 1853 the net rental income from the store amounted to only $538.19. Juliana's legal claim against the estate for $3000 was never upheld, filed as it was too late to meet the requirements of California law. There was not much to claim anyway. The Butteville land soon disappeared down the back-tax rathole, and the undeveloped lot on J Street, the purchase option which Margaret exercised in January 1853 for $2200, found no buyer. In spite of heroic legal efforts by John Tyler, acting as Margaret's agent and lawyer, John Beeckman's estate yielded precious little.

Indeed, family frustration in the matter produced caustic intimations and suspicions, wholly groundless, that Henry B. Livingston, Benjamin W. Bean, and other Gardiner agents on the scene were milking the estate. "He has either the hide of a Rhinoceros or a pocket with a very large hole in it," said Tyler ungenerously of Livingston. Insinuations of this sort, to say nothing of a threatened Gardiner lawsuit, finally persuaded a disgusted Henry Livingston to wash his hands of the whole mess and withdraw from further dealings with Lafayette Place. "For myself I have received nothing but the commissions allowed by law," he wrote them angrily, "charging nothing for my traveling expenses, etc., as I have wished to close up all transactions connected with my painful office as economically as possible." Actually, he had become involved in April 1851 in a creek-bed gold speculation at Oregon Bar which involved diverting the waters of the North Fork of the American River, and he was too busy with that extensive project to be troubled with insistent and ill-humored demands from New York and Sherwood Forest that he render instant and accurate accountings of every penny paid into and out of the John Beeckman estate.

The Gardiners also alienated Major Bean by bringing suit against him, forcing him to sell the J Street store and distribute the proceeds. This successful litigation eventually brought $2000 into the Beeckman estate, or roughly half of what John had put into the venture in the first place. Not surprisingly these short-tempered verbal and legal harassments from New York and Virginia ultimately caused the management of the Beeckman interests in Sacramento to be abandoned by acquaintances and kin of the deceased resident there. Instead, these matters fell into the hands of various local lawyers and rent collectors, strangers whose high charges and commissions further depleted Margaret's dwindling income from California.[32]

David Lyon Gardiner fared somewhat better in California than his brother-in-law. At least he got out alive, although his financial success was not nearly what his family had optimistically predicted for him. Unlike Beeckman, however, David Lyon did not have to go west for economic reasons. He went for adventure and out of a curiosity to see the new country. Practicing law bored him, and collecting Gardiner rents he found a demeaning and distasteful occupation. When it was agreed that Alexander would hire a law clerk to assist him with his clerkship and his growing private practice and also help manage the Gardiner rental properties (Richard E. Stilwell was engaged in April 1849), David Lyon felt free to leave New York. In February 1849 he shook off his usual lethargy long enough to board the *Eugenia*, bound for San Francisco via Veracruz and the Panama route. It would be, Tyler predicted, "an agreeable adventure" which would "improve him in every respect besides making him his fortune." He was supplied with letters of introduction to American military government officials in California by Tyler and Senator Robert J. Walker. Provided also with a $3000 stake by his mother and brother, David departed New York over Julia's objection and warning that he would find California rough and lonely. His absence, she warned him, would seriously distress their mother "however pleasured she might be to see you master of a large fortune." [33]

As in Beeckman's case, the "large fortune" was elusive. Arriving in San Francisco in April 1849, David went directly into merchandising. He quickly discovered that store rents were high and that dry goods shipped in from Australia, Canada, Hawaii, and South America were already glutting a very uncertain and unpredictable market, one which responded sharply upward and downward to the delay or arrival of a single shipload of a given commodity. When his profits failed to climb above a bare 10 per cent, Colonel David concluded that the Golden Fleece lay not in retailing. In August 1849 he headed into the gold fields near Sacramento to try his luck with pick and shovel. This unaccustomed labor blistered his hands and feet and hurt his back. So great was his pain that Julia wondered solicitously whether it would not be a good idea to send him a brace of "whalebones for him to wear around the hips and small of his back...when working in the mines." Although she hoped that her brother would "not give over his gold seeking for slight causes," David soon decided that he was no miner. Brushes with timber wolves frightened him. Sleeping in cramped cabins or in the open air with rough, dirty, and uncultured men degraded him. The loneliness and the monotony of heavy physical labor in the mining camps soon conspired to drive him swiftly back to San Francisco in September "to recruit his health," which, as Beeckman reported it, "had been severely tasked...at the mines."

As news of his various trials and tribulations filtered back to

Lafayette Place and Sherwood Forest, the ladies of the family decided that California was much too barbarous and sinful a place for "poor David." He should come home immediately. "Sleeping in a ravine produced his sickness no doubt," said his mother, "and being like the rest of us of a bilious constitution he will find it difficult to get rid of." With prostitutes, murderers, and thieves outnumbering the resident ladies, clergymen, and doctors, California was obviously no place for a well-bred and bilious young gentleman. Her thirty-three-year-old son, Juliana thought, was simply not suited for combat with such a hostile environment. "His exposure to wolves and fevers and bad climate is really quite too much to dwell upon," she concluded. "It is a fact men do not know how to take proper care of themselves. They require the attention of a mother all the days of their lives." To provide her little Argonaut with a touch of home she sent him preserves and jams and constant reminders that "there are many ways of making money here where you can be surrounded by family and friends and the comforts of civilization." [34]

In spite of these maternal urgings David Lyon decided to stick it out for a while longer in California, a decision Tyler approved and recommended because "no doubt a short period will make him rich if he will make up his mind to continue." Convinced that real estate speculation held the key to his counting room, David joined in partnership with the ineludible Major Bean and bought several pieces of Sacramento property in August 1849. A year later he sold the parcels at a $3000 profit. Having launched these Sacramento speculations, he returned to San Francisco in time to witness the first of the seven major fires that ravaged the city between December 1849 and June 1851. While his mother was hopeful that this disaster "would advance for the present the value of money very much," and suggested that Gardiner capital be rushed to the stricken community for near-usurious reconstruction loans, David felt that San Francisco would never transcend its incendiary nature. In February 1850, therefore, he decided to migrate to the nonflammable and more salubrious climate of San Diego, there to engage in merchandising, real estate speculation, and the warehousing and forwarding business.[35]

Tyler encouraged this shift, and David himself was confident that San Diego, riding the crest of a modest boom in 1850, would prove a more comfortable and profitable place to reside. Whoever bought San Diego real estate, thought Tyler, "will leave the estate of a millionaire." Alexander, on the other hand, considered the move foolish. Not only was San Diego (with its 650 inhabitants) a mere village compared to San Francisco, but it lay near no known gold fields and its population potential was, at best, dubious. "I take it that you left San Francisco just as the business season had commenced and that you arrived in San Diego just as the business season terminated," Alexander scolded him. Similarly, Juliana had no great confidence in the real estate future of San Diego, and in spite of encouragement from David Lyon she refused to put any of her own money into such an uncertain venture. "It would be absurd," she said flatly. "It is not safe on account of uncertain titles. A bird in hand is worth two in the bush and there is no mistake about property in and about New York." [36]

Alexander had more than a casual interest in his brother's new arrangement in San Diego. To be precise, he eventually had a $5000 stake in what David did in California, and the longer he watched his brother in action as a businessman and land speculator the more pessimistic he became that either of them would ever make a dollar. David Lyon Gardiner, in truth, was no businessman. He panicked easily, and he had little real feeling for business opportunities. He could not distinguish between a crazy speculation and a reasonable one. Nevertheless, his arrangement with Alexander made him his brother's partner and agent. Their agreement was that he would retail the general cargoes sent out from New York in both Alexander's name and in his own. The profits from this traffic would then be invested in California real estate and mining opportunities. From time to time Alexander shipped cured meats, blankets, kitchen utensils, wagons, hardware, wheelbarrows, furniture, doors, and even disassembled houses to California. "The freight of the house cost me as much as the house itself," he complained on one occasion. Plagued by bills of lading which often failed to reach their consignee, a thoroughly unpredictable consumer market, and the difficulty of doing business by mail at a distance of 6000 miles, Alexander concluded by January 1851 that merchandising in distant California was as speculative and profitless an operation as coal mining and lumbering had proved in Kentucky. David's removal to isolated San Diego and his general business inefficiency, together with Beeckman's tragic death at Sacramento, strengthened this conviction. And while he eventually recovered some of his investment in the form of gold dust (worth $17.50 per ounce in New York) and interest-bearing promissory notes remitted by David, Alexander Gardiner went to his grave in January 1851 knowing that his California operations had failed.[37]

It took David Lyon somewhat longer to realize his own inadequacies in the complex mercantile and real estate world of California. While San Diego in 1850 gave some signs of potential growth and prosperity, it soon began the rapid decline that resulted in the loss of its city charter in 1852 and left it with a population of scarcely a dozen souls in 1867. Ships did not often stop in a harbor that lacked a customs house. Mail and merchandise consigned to San Diego usually had to be transshipped by sloops back down the coast from San Francisco. For this reason, David spent much time and energy agitating for the establishment of a local customs house. Meanwhile he traveled up and down the coast between San Francisco and San Diego arranging for the purchase and shipment of dry goods to his store.

In this peripatetic enterprise he was assisted by his partner, John R. Bleeker, a transplanted New Yorker who was postmaster of San Diego. The firm of Gardiner and Bleeker, dedicated principally to the sale, storage, and forwarding of merchandise, also dabbled in San Diego real estate. Operating from a small combination store and warehouse located on the shore of San Diego Bay, the partners conducted what was at best a marginal enterprise. Later generations of San Diego Jaycees might acclaim them pioneer city fathers, but the 1850 truth of the matter was that Gardiner and Bleeker were situated in a town that had no economic *raison d'être*. By mid-1851 it was already moving back toward the sleepy settlement it had been under the Spanish and Mexican flags. The Cupeños Indian uprising in November 1851 (known locally as the Garra Rebellion, after Antonio Garra, chief of the Cupeños) created a confusion that was neither conducive to business enterprise nor productive of great confidence in the future stability and safety of the village. Only the vain hope that a major gold strike might be made in the nearby Laguna Mountains kept San Diego alive at all in 1851–1852. By 1853 some residents of the dying hamlet were so bored and foot-loose that they joined the first of William Walker's abortive filibustering expeditions into Mexico.

Others, like Bleeker himself, prayed "that the Rail Road route must come Southward and if so the Port on the Pacific must be San Diego." Indeed, the prospect that the projected transcontinental railroad would terminate at San Diego persuaded Gardiner and Bleeker in June 1850 to purchase a lot on San Diego Bay (at the foot of Spring Avenue, now Broadway) in the hope that they would achieve a great financial *coup* if and when the railroad bought it up as a right of way or elected to build a terminal on it. Their purchase was thus based on the gamble that the transcontinental railroad, when it was authorized by Congress, would follow a southern route. The question of routing became one of the great sectional political issues of the mid-1850s and enlisted on the Southern side of the argument such outstanding spokesmen as Robert Tyler. The onset of the Civil War suspended this rancorous debate. Not until 1869 was the transcontinental railroad completed—along the central route.

Gardiner and Bleeker did eventually make a killing on their Spring Street lot. They sold it in 1887 for $35,000, after the Sante Fé Railroad system reached San Diego and the town began its renaissance. But by this late date the aging David Lyon Gardiner had long since lost all interest in the speculations of his youth, and was devoting his time to an enjoyment of his own and his wife's money while he dabbled in family genealogy.[38]

Unfortunately, no railroad was to rescue San Diego in the early

1850s. Gardiner and Bleeker collapsed with the town while David pleaded fruitlessly with Alexander and his mother to send more family capital from New York for his real estate operations. Tyler consistently encouraged all of David's projects in California (including a wild scheme to build and operate a flour mill in San Diego), but Julia did not. She feared that her brother was going "native" in California, and she urged him to stop throwing good money after bad in San Diego and come home to a civilized way of life. "So you have taken to *cooking* for yourself!" she exclaimed. "Well, many *stranger* things have occurred, but I should like to know who washes the *china?* ... I hope you keep up your civilized habits, shave and dress in neat apparel every day." [39]

Faced with the gradual realization that the Midas touch was not to be learned in a warehouse-store on San Diego Bay or by buying up local property sinking rapidly in value, David Lyon did what came naturally to the Gardiners after their Tyler connection had been made fast. He wrote to John Tyler in October 1850 and asked the former President to use his influence in Washington to secure him the collectorship of customs in San Diego when the new Fillmore administration got around to establishing a customs house in the town. He had voted for Taylor and Fillmore in the 1848 campaign (the only member of the family who had voted Whig), and to his way of thinking this demonstrated dedication enough to Old Zach to secure the post. Tyler immediately wrote to William McKendree Gwin, California's first senator. He identified "Colonel Gardiner" as his wife's brother, a man of "high honor and business talents," whose appointment to the San Diego post would be considered by Tyler a "personal favor." Alexander, meanwhile, contacted James Brooks, owner of the New York *Express,* and Senator Daniel S. Dickinson of New York and interested them in his brother's newfound political aspirations. Unfortunately for David, Gwin reported that Fillmore and Congress had simultaneously established and filled the $3000 post. This sad news was communicated to David by Julia. "I cannot tell you by words how great was our regret the Collectorship of San Diego had not earlier been thought of," she apologized. Alexander, political realist that he was, thought it "exceedingly doubtful" that David Lyon could expect any appointment from the Fillmore administration "sufficiently valuable to be worthy of your acceptance." He was right. Nothing "sufficiently valuable" was forthcoming, and when David was offered the unpaid post of mayor of San Diego in November 1850 by the local citizenry he declined it.[40]

Disappointed in politics and business, David Lyon Gardiner was contemplating his next predictably unsuccessful move when news reached him in San Diego on March 4, 1851, that his brother Alexander had died suddenly in New York in late January. The sad tidings stunned him, as it had the rest of the family. Although he briefly considered remaining in San Diego for a few more months on the strength of rumored gold strikes in the Sierra Madre, anguished pleas from home and from Sherwood Forest that he return to New York immediately became so insistent and were couched in such piteous terms that he could not resist them. Turning his business affairs over to John Bleeker, he departed San Diego on April 4 and arrived back in New York on June 7. Again he used the shorter trans-Panama route. When he reached New York he was so sun-tanned, ragged, and bearded that Juliana and Margaret scarcely recognized him. It was clear to them that his personal habits had indeed deteriorated. But they welcomed him with enthusiasm, happy that he had returned at last from the degrading influences of distant California.[41]

It was probably well that he left California when he did. Within a few months he was receiving from Bleeker news of San Diego's demise. "Sales are remarkably dull and money exceedingly scarce, and our Indian excitement has not bettered matters.... Our New Town lots will probably not sell for their cost," his partner reported. By March 1852 Bleeker had nearly given up all hope that San Diego would ever amount to anything. Employing his vague connection with John Tyler, he attempted to secure the vacant collectorship of customs in San Diego. The emoluments of the sinecure would enable him, he argued, to remain on the scene until the transcontinental-railroad-route question was settled one way or the other. "Good bye to the prospects of old San Diego until it is made the terminus of the Rail R.," he told David Lyon flatly in June 1852. The population of the town, he reported, had decreased 50 per cent in the past year, and local real estate values had plunged to near-worthlessness. Tyler did all he could for Bleeker's pursuit of office, writing Senator Gwin in his behalf, but nothing came of the collectorship idea. Nor did a modest coal discovery on the shores of San Diego Bay in 1856 arrest the decline of the town. Water filled the shaft at 100 feet and the Mormons involved in the venture gave it up. In 1857 the discouraged Bleeker sold the store and the remaining merchandise for a pittance and returned to New York. Without a railroad, San Diego had become a ghost town. With neither coal nor gold to sustain it, it could not continue.

So ended the Gardiner quest for wealth in California. While the liquidation of the Gardiner-Bleeker enterprise eventually brought David Lyon a $5000 rebate on his San Diego investments, the short-term economics of the family speculation in El Dorado added up to little more than death, frustration, and litigation. One grave on the banks of the Sacramento and some worthless lots in Butteville, San Francisco, and San Diego were about all the family could show in 1854 for a cash investment of nearly $12,000. It was a gloomy chapter in the history of the Gardiner-Tyler connection.[42]

16

BLACK MEN AND BLACK REPUBLICANS

It is quite sensibly felt by all that the success of the Black Republicans would be the knell of the Union.
—JOHN TYLER, JULY 1856

The unexpected death of Alexander Gardiner momentarily unhinged the entire Gardiner-Tyler family alliance. Serving as its lawyer, broker, banker, rent collector, speculator, and political analyst, and as Tyler's appointed biographer, his sudden departure from the scene produced lamentations, confusion, and, finally, the necessity of reorganizing the administration of all family affairs. John Tyler was particularly upset by his young brother-in-law's passing. "The President feels as if he had lost his chief prop," Julia wrote of the shock experienced at Sherwood Forest. "Alexander and he alone understood his thoughts and feelings entirely. Upon him he depended for his posthumous fame. He was literally the chosen friend of his bosom, and he felt for him a deeper affection than he had ever felt for an own brother." [1]

Alexander fell ill on Friday, January 17, 1851, following a strenuous round of midwinter social activities which had kept him out late and brought him home inebriated for three successive evenings. He complained initially of sharp abdominal pains, later diagnosed as "severe bilious colic which terminated in inflammation of the bowels." He had had several such attacks before, the most recent during his second trip to Caseyville in June 1848. Three prominent doctors were called into the boardinghouse room at Houston and Crosby streets in which he was living at the time. With David Lyon and John Beeckman absent in California, Juliana and Margaret had given up the Lafayette Place house in April 1850, auctioned some of the furniture, and moved back to East Hampton. At the time of Alexander's final illness, however, the ladies were at Sherwood Forest for their annual midwinter visit. News of his serious condition was telegraphed to Charles City on January 21. Thoroughly alarmed by this report, Juliana and Margaret departed Sherwood Forest the same afternoon to hurry to Alexander's bedside. They had barely reached Baltimore the following day when they read a newspaper account that their son and brother had died on the evening of January 21.

During his last hours Alexander was quiet and rational, although he suffered severe pain. He seemed to know that he was dying and he spoke calmly of his imminent fate to his uncle Nathaniel Gardiner, his cousin Dr. William Henry Gardiner of Brooklyn, the Reverend Henry M. Denison, Richard M. Stilwell, his law clerk, and others who visited his sickbed near the end. Having no disposition to draw up a formal will, he told Stilwell exactly how he wanted his estate distributed. Julia was to receive his three-eighths interest in the Caseyville lands "on account of her associations and position in society she will naturally be more expensive in her mode of living." David Lyon was released from all financial obligations to him from their joint California speculations. His mother was to receive everything else, his share of his father's estate, and some $15,000 worth of stocks, bonds, and real estate parcels in New York City. Margaret, he told Stilwell, would be looked out for by her mother. With these details attended to, he assured his anxious friends that he was not afraid to die. Indeed, his last words were: "I don't know if I care whether I live or die. I am not particularly fond of the world. I believe in the Christian religion. I would not take one word from it." At 7 P.M. on Tuesday, January 21, 1851, Alexander Gardiner, aged thirty-two, died of a ruptured appendix as three of New York's "most skillful physicians" stood helplessly by his bedside. "He died as peacefully as an infant would lie down to sleep," said Margaret.

The funeral was held in the Church of the Ascension by the Reverend Gregory Thurston Bedell on January 28 with members of the United States Circuit Court, the New York bar, and the old Tyler party in New York City present in numbers. On the following day Alexander was buried at East Hampton. Obituaries were carried in important newspapers from New York to Richmond. Since one of his last official acts as a Clerk of the Circuit Court had been the handling of the controversial James Hamlet fugitive slave case in such a way as to "create a feeling of great respect for him at the South," his passing was noted with more than casual interest in that section.[2]

Alexander's sudden departure emotionally overwhelmed the women of the family. Juliana felt that had she been with him at the end her longstanding knowledge of his physical condition might have helped him. While Margaret and Julia assured her that this was an unreasonable and masochistic attitude, that nothing known to medical science could have saved Alexander, they did agree with her that David Lyon should be urged to return speedily from California to take charge of family affairs. Awaiting his return, Juliana and Margaret rented rooms in a private home on Clinton Avenue in the Bedford section of Brooklyn. "It looks like a delightful country village," said Juliana; "I like it much better than living in the City." They also procured a French nurse, "who cannot speak a word of English," to help with little Harry, turned over the complete management of the Gardiner properties in New York to Richard Stilwell, and fired the first salvos in the long battle to settle John H. Beeckman's estate in California as quickly and profitably as possible.

At the same time, Sherwood Forest was assured that the President's various personal notes would be underwritten and secured as they had been in the past when Alexander handled Tyler's financial affairs in New York. Indeed, Tyler discovered within a month of Alexander's death that his seasonal cash shortage and the necessity of juggling his notes and bills of credit from one New York bank to another would become insoluble problems without continuing Gardiner aid. For this reason he spent some anxious moments until Juliana's assurances on the subject reached him. Julia diplomatically arranged this touchy situation with her mother, explaining that

The President will require someone to take Alexander's place in giving him the free use of their name for his accommodation in his worldly matters ... I hope therefore you will at once offer your name to him to continue matters as they stood between him and A. *Your name* only is required and he meets everything else ... when I hear from you I shall tell the President that I had written you to propose you should take Alexander's place in assisting him in his affairs and you unhesitatingly consented. I shall look for your reply to ease the perplexity the President I see is feeling—and, of course, myself also.

Less diplomatically, Julia made clear to her mother her doubts that Alexander meant to exclude her from that part of his estate above and beyond the Caseyville property. She was certain he had not regarded the Kentucky bequest a full settlement of the 25 per cent portion of the income of his clerkship due her under their 1845 agreement. "I know that no one in the family as yet requires so much as myself, with my three children," she reminded Juliana. "It seems to me that if anything remains after the payments of debts and bequests it should be divided between yourself, D., M., and myself and ... if you would throw in your part for our benefit it would add much to our comfort while it would be of small value to you. As far as I am concerned, it would leave a smaller amount of the President's notes to be paid." [3]

While these fiscal matters were being settled to Julia's satisfaction, though not without strained feelings all around, David Lyon returned to New York from San Diego. He took charge of meeting the small claims against his brother's estate, and he confirmed the arrangement under which Stilwell would manage the family rental properties in town. Meanwhile, Juliana, Margaret, and Harry left Brooklyn and returned to East Hampton to live. They soon decided, however, that the place was far too lonely and isolated. Since Juliana was determined to take a more active personal interest in the administration of her New York properties, she decided to move closer to the city.

In 1852 the house and several lots in East Hampton were sold, some of the furniture there was disposed of at auction, and the bulk of the funds realized was invested in a large house and eleven-acre property on Staten Island (what is now West New Brighton) known as Castleton Hill. Juliana, Margaret, and her three-year-old son moved there in May 1852. When David Lyon had recovered several thousand dollars of his California investment from Bleeker's liquidation of their San Diego partnership, he too located on Staten Island, purchasing a seventy-three-acre farm at Northfield, about two and a half miles from his mother's property. He made this decision only after John Tyler and Julia, working through State Supreme Court Judge James I. Roosevelt, had failed in their attempt to procure for him the patronage job of Marshal of the Circuit Court of the Eastern District of New York.

Beginning in March 1853 David Lyon Gardiner reluctantly became a gentleman farmer on Staten Island, a casual pursuit varied by occasional attention to the legal problems of the Gardiner properties in the city. The actual labor on his farm was done by a series of tenants. None of these hired hands suited David any more than a steady stream of various Irish domestics suited his meticulous mother. Consequently, throughout the remainder of the decade Gardiner servants and tenants on Staten Island came and went by the platoon. In the city, Stilwell undertook the day-to-day work that the family's real estate holdings required. The livability of the Gardiner houses in New York gradually deteriorated, but their value mounted steadily as the city grew and prospered. The Gardiner philosophy of landlordism had long been that the tenant was always wrong, and Juliana did nothing to disturb this hoary tradition. "All embellishments must be at the cost of the tenant," she decreed. And at no time did she consider young Stilwell quite firm enough in dealing with the destructive, complaining malingerers who invariably inhabited her premises.[4]

During none of these trials, disappointments, and crises in the family circle did John Tyler or his in-laws lose interest in or surrender an active connection with American politics. Tyler was not convinced that his own political career was over. He even derived some wry satisfaction when the Charles City Whigs selected him overseer of roads for the county in 1847. Designed to humiliate him, his election was considered a great joke by the local Whigs. But so hard and long did Tyler keep the slaves requisitioned for this work at road duty (this at the height of the harvest season) that the jokesters were soon pleading for his resignation and an end to road-building. "Offices are hard to obtain in these times," he teased them in reply, "and having no assurance that I will ever get another, I could not think under the circumstances of resigning." Work on the roads continued. Less humorous to Tyler was the realization that his political influence in Washington had waned so much by 1848 that he could do nothing effective to help Robert Tyler's vain quest for appointment to a proposed diplomatic mission to Rome. Similarly, a trip to New York in December 1847 conclusively demonstrated to him that there was no remaining interest in that quarter for another Tyler attempt at Presidential politics. Instead of rallying the old Tylerite hosts in Gotham, his visit did little more than stimulate newspaper speculation that Tyler had come to the city to marshal his friends behind the Whig candidacy of General Zachary Taylor—a charge Tyler hotly denied. "I am wholly unconnected with the political intrigues of the day and cloak myself under no secret movements whatever," he wrote the editor of the New York *Journal of Commerce*. His statement was accurate, although the former President might have wished it otherwise. Tyler *was* detached from the national political scene. The time had come, said the New York *Herald* patronizingly, to forget about John Tyler as a force in American politics, "for that once distinguished man, whom the steamboat left on the wharf—lady, trunk, and all—has long since ceased to possess any influence for either good or evil." [5]

The time would again come when Tyler would have influence, but in early 1848 his political role was reduced to remaining "entirely passive until election day." He watched the Presidential boom for the Virginia-born, slaveowning Zachary Taylor with neutrality and disinterest. In March 1848 he learned from Juliana and Margaret that Clay demonstrations in New York and Philadelphia had fizzled as the Kentuckian's last bid for the White House ran head-on into the hard fact that most Whigs preferred an inept old general who could win an election to a brilliant and controversial two-time loser who could only lose again. This news of Clay's embarrassment pleased Tyler, as did a report from Alexander in February 1848 that all the old Tylerites in New York were for Lewis Cass of Michigan because of his sturdy opposition to the Wilmot Proviso. The pro-Proviso Van Buren Democrats, opposed as they were to the further extension of slavery in the territories, continued to command as little support at Lafayette Place and Sherwood Forest as did Clay and the Whigs.

From the standpoint of the Tyler-Gardiner family, the nomination of Taylor and Cass to head the two tickets was perhaps the best the country could hope for, since both men were basically "safe" on the slavery issue. Robert Tyler embraced Cass reluctantly—only when it became apparent that his friend and mentor James Buchanan was beaten for the nomination in the Baltimore convention in May 1848; then he endorsed Lewis Cass. "If Genl. Cass be *defeated,* as *entre nous* he will certainly be," Robert wrote Buchanan pessimistically in July, "the very foundations of the party will be swept up as with a deluge." When the Whigs in June passed over the controversial Clay and nominated Zach Taylor and Millard Fillmore to oppose Cass and General William O. Butler of Kentucky, the entire family (except David Lyon) unenthusiastically supported the Democratic nominee while freely predicting the inevitability of Old Zach's election. These predictions involved no psychic insights. The Democracy was badly split on the Wilmot Proviso, and a divided Democracy could not win. With Van Buren running on a third-party Free Soil ticket in the North, it was certain that the Cass vote there would be badly fractured, as indeed it was.

On the whole, the 1848 campaign was an exercise in political tiptoeing. Both major party candidates submerged the slavery question as best they could and both took moderate positions on all other issues that threatened further to divide their respective followers into the internal sectional contradictions inherent in each group. The result was never in doubt. Cass could not win, and Taylor had only to remain studiously vague on all issues to keep from losing. This he managed to do without trying. Tyler voted quietly for the lackluster Cass, and privately blamed the Democracy's expected defeat on Polk. Young Hickory, said Tyler, had commenced his

> administration by a war on all my friends. I have sustained them as well as I was able in a quiet way, and I have voted for Cass, but Mr. Polk inflicted the *immedicable vulnus* on the Democratic party in the onset, by rejecting the aid which had brought him to power. Van Buren and the men of no principle were courted and the true men thrown off.... Now all things have to become new. The end we shall probably live long enough to see.

If the election statistics failed to support the Tyler analysis that Polk was the evil genius of the piece (the Van Buren candidacy, not Polk's treatment of the Tylerites, had cost Cass New York state and the 36 electoral votes there that would have spelled a Democratic victory), the ex-President could take comfort in the fact that the Democratic press began treating him more gently after the Cass debacle. While this new orientation in no way helped him secure midnight patronage positions from the outgoing Polk for son Robert or for nephew M. B. Seawell, it did encourage him to believe that he was no longer living entirely outside the Democratic pale. Nor did Taylor's success at the polls really disturb him. "I shall not shed many tears at the result," Tyler concluded. "Poor Van! He is literally a used-up man; and Clay, let him shed tears over the fact that anybody can be elected but himself." [6]

The Taylor administration was not a brilliant one. The old General had never voted prior to 1848, his personal political views ranged from the confused to the obscure, and the Whig Party had again, as in 1840, carefully refrained from adopting or running on a platform. The new President had no program. When in his Inaugural Address the fuzzy-minded hero seriously suggested that California was too distant to become a state and might well become an independent nation instead, some Americans wondered about his sanity. Jarred from this quaint view by William H. Seward and other antislavery Northern Whigs and Democrats who wanted California in the Union as a free state, Taylor quickly reversed himself and announced that he would welcome California into the Union, with the slavery question there to be decided on the basis of "squatter sovereignty." This controversial idea, advanced by Lewis Cass in the 1848 campaign, sought to remove the question of slavery extension into new territories from congressional control and politics. Instead, the inhabitants of a territory would decide the slavery question for themselves locally and democratically, and then apply for admission to the Union either as a free state or a slave state. Under this concept California applied for entrance as a free state in March 1850, and in so doing threatened to upset the numerical balance of free and slave states. But well before this crisis over the future status of slavery in the vast territories wrested from Mexico split the nation and threatened civil war, the Tyler-Gardiner family had passed harsh judgment on the fumbling Taylor administration.

Indeed, Tyler took one look at the Cabinet Taylor assembled around him after the election and told Alexander that he was "ready to admit the complete ascendancy of old-fashioned Federalism in the U.S." Taylor's appointment of "that scoundrel Ewing" to the new Department of the Interior particularly upset him. He interpreted it as nothing less than a Clay maneuver to "reward" Thomas Ewing "for his perfidies to me." This was a thin-skinned and inaccurate view of the appointment of Tyler's former Secretary of the Treasury to Taylor's Cabinet. Nevertheless, Tyler was never able to forgive or forget those men who had participated in the Cabinet resignation "plot" of September 1841, and on this point his conspiracy theory of history never changed. "I rejoice most heartily now in my vote for Cass," he finally decided.

In spite of his hostility to Taylor, Tyler was not averse to supporting the patronage importunities of his friends and relatives. In fact, both the ex-President and Alexander Gardiner thought their chances of getting something from Taylor "somewhat more promising" than from Polk. Thus John Tyler, Jr., John Lorimer Graham, David Lyon Gardiner, William Bray Gardiner (Julia's first cousin), and other Tylerites were strongly recommended to the new administration for patronage jobs. Needless to say, none of these stalwarts received appointments.[7]

Patronage matters faded quickly into the background for John Tyler when California's application for admission into the Union as a free state triggered sharp sectional animosities and led to the introduction of Henry Clay's third and last great compromise measure. Amid much talk of secession and civil war during the spring and summer of 1850, Congress hammered Clay's resolutions into a series of legislative acts collectively known as the Compromise of 1850. Under these, California was to be admitted as a free state; the New Mexico and Utah territories were to be organized on the basis of "squatter sovereignty" ("popular sovereignty," as Stephen A. Douglas more elegantly dubbed it) with the understanding that all questions regarding slavery in these territories would be reviewed by the Supreme Court; a new Fugitive Slave Act placed the pursuit and recovery of runaway slaves under federal legal jurisdiction; and the slave trade in the District of Columbia was to be abolished.

As these controversial suggestions emerged from committee and into law, Tyler concluded that the main hope for avoiding civil war lay in the ability of the Democratic Party to maintain its unity across sectional lines and avoid support of any and all extreme solutions to the nation's problems. He was no more impressed, therefore, with William H. Seward's denunciation of the Compromise as "radically wrong and essentially vicious" than he was with Jefferson Davis' demand that Congress not interfere with slavery anywhere or under any conditions. He objected to Ohio Senator Salmon P. Chase's view that it was the moral duty of Congress to prohibit slavery in the territories, and he regarded as dangerous extremism the dying Calhoun's demand on March 4 that the South be given virtually an autonomous status within the Union. Instead, he warmly supported Cass, Douglas, and Mississippi Senator Henry S. Foote in their endorsement of the Clay compromise proposals. These moderate Democrats Tyler saw as the true saviors of the party and of the nation, a vision which caused him to argue that the expulsion of lunatic-fringe free-soil and abolitionist elements from the Democracy would have to be accomplished if the party was to endure:

The Democratic party [he wrote Robert] can only hope for success by discarding from among them the Free-Soilers, Abolitionists, and all such cattle. Let the Whigs, if they please, court them, and take them to their embraces; but let the true lovers of the Union repudiate them as unworthy of their association. They do, indeed, deserve the deepest curses of the patriot for having put in jeopardy the noblest and fairest fabric of government the world ever saw. When I think of it, all the milk of my nature is turned to gall.... Calhoun's speech does him no credit. It is too ultra, and his ultimata impracticable.... I regard his speech as calculated to do injury to the Southern cause....[8]

Given these attitudes, it is not difficult to understand why Tyler welcomed Daniel Webster's famous Seventh of March speech, which fervently appealed for the preservation of the Union and a spirit of compromise. Denounced by Northern fire-eaters as a "traitor" to his section for criticizing the excesses of the abolitionist societies, Webster argued persuasively in his great address that there was really no need for congressional action on slavery in the New Mexico and Utah territories. The twin impact of hostile soil and climate made the institution wholly impracticable there, he pointed out. These views squared with those Tyler had long held, and Webster was soon in receipt of a letter from Sherwood Forest praising his patriotism and sagacity and thanking him for his exposure of the "machinations" of the organized abolitionists. At the same time, however, Tyler felt it necessary to counter Webster's Seventh of March suggestion that the Texas annexation movement of 1843–1845 might indeed have been launched by Southerners interested only in slavery expansion. Tyler hastened to assure his former Secretary of State that this charge was partly in error. Whatever the motives of Upshur, Calhoun, and other Southern fire-eaters had been in supporting annexation, Tyler's own decisive role in the matter had turned entirely upon an honest desire to achieve a cotton monopoly for the whole United States.[9]

By late May 1850 Tyler was prepared to accept the Compromise of 1850 as the only reasonable alternative to splitting the Democratic Party and risking a civil war. In endorsing the compromise he knew full well that slavery could never successfully be carried into the arid wastelands of New Mexico and Utah. He also appreciated the fact that the admission of California as a free state, together with the whole principle of "popular sovereignty," would soon doom the South to an inevitable and lasting inferiority in its political-power balance with the North. Clearly, popular sovereignty would result in more free states being carved from the remaining territories than slave states. Yet he was prepared to accept the containment of slavery and the political inferiority of the South as preferable to civil war. These views he freely incorporated into a letter solicited from him by Senator Henry S. Foote of Mississippi. The letter was widely circulated by Foote on Capitol Hill in his successful effort to bring moderate Southern elements to the support of Clay's compromise proposals. Later it was published. As Tyler told Alexander Gardiner on May 21, "I go for the compromise."[10]

The unexpected death of General Taylor in July 1850 and the elevation of Vice-President Millard Fillmore to the White House momentarily threatened the progress of the compromise bills through the Congress. Suspicions swept moderate circles, North and South, that Fillmore's long antislavery background in New York might upset the delicate arrangements being made. Happily, the new President announced his willingness to support the legislation and preserve the Union, and in September the compromise package became law over his signature. In both sections moderate Union parties, and Union committees within the Democracy, sprang into existence dedicated to the preservation of the Compromise of 1850 as the "final solution" to the trying sectional-slavery issue. In New York City both Alexander Gardiner and John

Lorimer Graham took active roles in the Union Committee there, and the group enlisted in its ranks many of the old Conservative Democrats and Tylerites of 1843–1845.

In spite of his patriotic stand on the compromise, Millard Fillmore did not command the support of the Tyler-Gardiner family. To begin with, the failure of David Lyon's patronage safari into the San Diego Customs House was not accepted by the clan with exceptionally good grace. Not only did Tyler have no patronage influence with the new administration ("of the administration I can ask nothing," he lamented), but he also became increasingly worried lest Fillmore not throw the full power and prestige of the federal government behind the Fugitive Slave Act. This particular portion of the 1850 legislation had done much to marshal Southern support behind the compromise package. At the same time, it was this very section of the compromise that most infuriated the Northern abolitionists. They regarded it as bestial and inhumane and in violation of a higher moral law that completely transcended the Constitution. While Tyler himself had no problem with runaway Negroes at Sherwood Forest, he had assumed, in publicly supporting the compromise, that the Act would be administered with "impartial justice" and that the recovery of Southern slave property from the North would be accomplished with speed and decision by federal authorities. As he phrased his view of this point in his letter to Senator Foote, "what I should chiefly desire to see would be the ... effectual delivery of the fugitive by some means to prevent recapture. There is so solemn an obligation resting on the government to carry faithfully into execution the provision of the Constitution on this point, that I cannot believe that an objection will be made to the most stringent provision." [11]

By December 1850 there was so much agitation by abolitionist extremists for the overthrow of the Fugitive Slave Act, much of it from the pen of George Thompson, the celebrated British abolitionist, that Tyler was prepared to blame the entire anti-Fugitive Slave movement on self-serving English interference in American internal affairs. He even toyed momentarily with the irresponsible idea that provoking a war with Britain on the Thompson intervention issue might serve to heal the sectional split in an excited burst of American patriotism. As seen through Tyler's Anglophobic window on the world, the rascally Redcoats had fastened slavery on America in the first place. Now they might perform a really useful service to the United States by obliging the nation with a therapeutic war. "An earthquake of some sort would seem to be necessary," he told Alexander, "[for] unless a new direction is given to the public mind, I cannot augur results." The censure of Senator Foote by the Mississippi legislature for his moderate stance on the Compromise of 1850 strengthened Tyler's belief that the very fabric of the compromise was being torn to shreds by extremists on both sides. Only in the flames of a foreign war "might the disturbers of our harmony be consumed." At no time did he agree with John Tyler, Jr.'s view that instant Southern secession was the answer to the problem. Tyler did not want a civil war. An Anglo-American war would do. This bellicose mood eventually passed, however, and the former President vented his ire instead in an anonymous letter to John S. Cunningham, editor of the Portsmouth *Pilot*. It was an indignant and ill-considered communication dashed off in less than an hour on December 10, 1850. In it he demanded that Fillmore support the Fugitive Slave Act firmly and vigorously:

It is the law of the land.... Let him discharge it faithfully, boldly and unflinchingly. No half-willing marshalls, no doubting commissioners..... No prying about for a subterfuge under which to escape, no honeyed words.... Let the President ... pledge the army and navy to sustain them if needs be. The time for fair words, easily spoken, has passed. The time for decision and action is at hand. Let him begin the work of seriousness with "the Hon." George Thompson, member of Parliament ... by remonstrance to the British govt ... and then he is ready for the Garrisons and their allies.[12]

For an old enemy of the 1833 Force Bill these were ironical words. But Tyler felt that the Fugitive Slave Act alone had reconciled Southern moderates and unionists to the total compromise deal. Destroy the effectiveness of that mollifying sweetener, he argued, and the secessionist extremists in Dixie would ultimately force the slavery question to civil war. Tyler fully appreciated the difficulties a Vice-President had in coming suddenly to power, but he feared that the Buffalo politician would prove too weak to parry abolitionist pressure to repeal the legislation. "There are but few men in the world who have the moral boldness to face all odds and encounter all hazards in the honest discharge of duty, and we must express the fear that Millard Fillmore is not one of them," he told the readers of the *Pilot*.[13]

The slavery controversy was brought home even more forcefully and personally to the Gardiner-Tyler family when Alexander, in the last months before his death, found himself in the heated middle of the controversial James Hamlet case. Serving as a federal commissioner in New York under the Fugitive Slave Act, Alexander was involved in a much-criticized action which saw James Hamlet, a porter in the store of Tilton and Maloney on Water Street, and allegedly a runaway slave from Baltimore, arrested and given over to Mary Brown of Baltimore, his master. Unfortunately for Alexander, the case was not so clear-cut as it might have been, nor were the legal procedures he employed beyond criticism.

In the first place, instead of taking the depositions himself, Alexander permitted his deputy, Charles M. Hall, to collect the initial data on Hamlet's legal status. Hall was a competent young upstate lawyer, but not a qualified commissioner under the meaning and wording of the Fugitive Slave Act and thus not empowered to take depositions. In the formal hearings over which Alexander did preside personally, in September 1850, there was also much to fault. As the American and Foreign Anti-Slavery Society charged in its subsequent pamphlet on the matter, Hamlet "was taken into a retired room in the second storey of the old City Hall, and the Commissioner, without any notice to any acquaintance of the prisoner, without assigning him any counsel, or giving him a moment's opportunity to send for assistance, proceeded with hot haste, *ex-parte,* to take the testimony of [Thomas J.] Clare, the son-in-law of the alleged claimant, and young Gustavus Brown, her son, in proof that the prisoner was her slave." A bystander happened to overhear what was going on and sent immediately for a lawyer to appear for Hamlet. The lawyer arrived in time to elicit by cross-examination the fact that Mary Brown was not Hamlet's owner of record as defined by the Fugitive Slave Act. She had leased Hamlet to the Baltimore Shot Company, which Clare served as clerk, prior to the Negro's "escape" from Maryland in 1848. Hamlet insisted during the hearing he was a free man and that his mother was a free woman. "But the law prohibited his testimony from being taken, and Commissioner Gardiner, upon the testimony of two family witnesses ... decided that the prisoner was a slave of the claimant, and doomed him to perpetual bondage ... not by verdict of a jury but by the fiat of a mere clerk whom the law has constituted slave-catcher for Southern masters."

Within a few days Commissioner Gardiner's office became the swirling storm center of a concerted abolitionist effort to hamstring the operation of the hated Fugitive Slave law. "The affair," said Alexander, "kept my office in confusion more than a week and gave me more trouble than any one nigger was worth." The fact that the law permitted no Negro who claimed to be a freedman (as Hamlet vigorously did) the right to a trial by jury, or even the right to give testimony in his own behalf, outraged the abolitionists. So too did the fact that a simple affidavit by a claimant was regarded as sufficient proof of his ownership of an alleged fugitive. The Fugitive Slave Act, whatever its purely political merits as part of the Compromise of 1850, flew foolishly in the face of everything the American judicial system represented in the area of responsible trial procedures. Common fairness was found nowhere in it. Instead, it established star-chamber techniques which mocked, on racial grounds alone, the basic rights of the individual under traditional Anglo-Saxon law.

The abolitionists were handed a strong moral argument, and they lost no time making the most of it. The crusade for James Hamlet was led by William Jay, son of the former Supreme Court Chief Justice and one of New York City's most active and dedicated abolitionists. Jay centered his criticism of Alexander's handling of the Hamlet case on the technical question of Charles M. Hall's competence in taking the depositions. He argued that Alexander's deputy was not a bona fide commissioner under the law and had no business being involved in the case at all. The whole procedure before Gardiner's bench had therefore been an improper one from start to finish. Alexander's surrender of Hamlet to his alleged owner, concluded Jay, was both immoral and illegal.[14]

Alexander Gardiner was strongly antiabolitionist and had been so since his undergraduate days at Princeton. To him, a slave was private property, and a master had as much right to recover a fugitive as he did a strayed horse. Not surprisingly, he considered Jay's arguments irrelevant and he went through with the Hamlet transfer to Baltimore. He was stung, however, by abolitionist letters vehemently condemning his role in the case, some of them addressed to him from as far away as Rockton, Illinois. Under the impact of these attacks his patience gave way, and he struck back at the intervention of the New York abolitionists in the Hamlet case. In an unsigned New York *Herald* article titled "The Question of the Day," he pointed out that the letter of the law had been faithfully complied with and that the whole issue had been artificially manufactured and blown up by William Jay, "pretty well known in this community for some years past in connection with the negro race. He is an abolitionist of the darkest shade, and one of the most fanatical and persevering agitators." Defending every provision of what he preferred calling the "Fugitive From Service Act," Alexander concluded with the biting observation that

> We do not entertain the idle expectation that truth or reason can make any impression on the commingled freesoil, abolition, Fourierite, infidel and woman's rights party. From Martin Van Buren and William H. Seward, the arch demagogues, who are looking to a Northern Presidency, to Frederick Douglass and Samuel Ward (black men) ... through the host of such inferior lights as Abby Kelley, Horace Greeley, Sojourner Truth, Ward Beecher, Rosa Lee, William Jay, Lucretia Mott ... and others ... these people and their followers constitute a formidable party, espousing one side of the only substantial question now dividing the country. These are the abolition party, engaged in an effort to abolish—first the union of these States, and then the distinctions of color, and those social institutions which are a result of the wisdom of the ages. Against them is arrayed a party most properly designated as republican, composed of men of established moral views, who keep in sight the imperfections of our nature, and whose habits of thought and action are founded on the old continental school. The sooner the empty party distinctions of Whig and Democrat are abandoned ... the sooner we will have a clear field and a fair fight on the only substantial topic of the day— the better for ourselves, even though it be too late to save the Union.[15]

Alexander Gardiner did not live to discover how the slavery question was finally resolved. Hamlet himself achieved his freedom when a public subscription was collected in New York to buy him out of slavery. But the emotionalism engendered by the explosive Hamlet affair was still reverberating throughout the nation when Alexander died. As mentioned earlier, his sudden passing was prominently noted in Southern newspapers, and his obituaries in the South were tributes to his patriotic steadfastness in the face of the abolitionist provocations of the American and Foreign Anti-Slavery Society. There was even talk for a time that the Union Committee of New York would erect a monument over his grave in East Hampton. "The South," said Julia, "would be more convinced by that act than by anything they could do to show their patriotism and real desire to see the laws of their country upheld—and it would create here one universal sentiment of approval and satisfaction." No Union Committee monument ever materialized, but Sherwood Forest was later pleased to learn that Governor John B. Floyd of Virginia had been in private correspondence with Alexander during the Hamlet case. Floyd regarded the young New York lawyer's passing a great loss to the South. "His conduct as United States Commissioner," agreed Cunningham of the Portsmouth *Pilot*, "showed him to be a very proper man." [16]

The Fugitive Slave question would continue to trouble the political waters of the nation until the onset of the Civil War. Tyler's stand on so incendiary an issue (as expressed in his public letter to Senator Foote) brought him again into the national political limelight. En route to join Julia at Saratoga in September 1850, he was hissed at an address he gave a group of law students in New York City, an incident gleefully reported in the local abolitionist and free-soil press. On the other hand, his Fugitive Slave attitudes earned him a favorable hearing among those elephant-memoried Virginia Democrats who had roundly condemned him when he identified himself with the Whigs in 1836-1840.

Indeed, Tyler felt that the sectional crisis of 1850 had actually benefited and "purified" the Democratic Party by shaking out both the Northern abolitionists and Southern secessionists in a single snap. For this reason Tyler gave ear to Robert's suggestion that he support James Buchanan's renewed quest for the Democracy's nomination in 1852. Actually, the master of Sherwood had little love for Buchanan ("he had none for me in my severe trials"), but he sensibly realized that as long as Virginia and Pennsylvania moderates remained united on their Presidential candidates, the Democratic Party as a whole could probably be held together.[17]

A severe case of flu which developed into pneumonia prevented Tyler from participating in the usual preconvention maneuverings that occupied the politicians during the early months of 1852. During this illness Julia spent many nights "holding his head and giving him warm drinks," while her mother argued for massive doses of "German pills" and "alum water." By April the former President was recovered enough to take an active interest in politics again, and he was much restored and buoyed when the Virginia State Democratic Convention retroactively endorsed the acts of his administration and welcomed him once again into full political brotherhood. There was even some talk in Richmond, Julia reported, that his "friends stand ready to throw in his name" as a compromise candidate if the coming Democratic convention should fail to reach a decision among its half-dozen hopefuls.

This endorsement of his administration by the Virginia Democracy ended at last John Tyler's long battle for the recovery of his political reputation. "I began to fear," he confessed to Henry A. Wise, "that I was to descend to my grave without any shadow of justice being done to me in public places." The rest of the family was equally cheered by this happy turn in Tyler's psychological fortunes. "The endorsement of Father and his Administration," said John, Jr., "is certainly gratifying. The time is surely rapidly coming when the whole country will acknowledge his just and meritorious claims upon its opinions. I think he will live long enough to die happy in the consciousness of the fact realized...." [18]

At the Democracy's Baltimore convention in June 1852 delegate Robert Tyler labored diligently (down to "the *very last* ballot") for the nomination of James Buchanan. Tyler encouraged his son's activity, and he was willing to accept Old Buck as the party standard-bearer himself. He was not unhappy, however, when dark horse Franklin Pierce of New Hampshire was nominated on the forty-ninth ballot. In fact, several days before Pierce's selection Tyler informally polled his "own family circle" and announced that Pierce was the solid family choice. He was certain that Pierce, a Northern man with Southern principles, would defeat General Winfield Scott, latest and last of the Whig soldier-hero candidates. And he was encouraged by the prospect that Pierce would attempt to knit the Democratic Party firmly together across sectional lines and preserve the Union. Robert, of course, was disappointed that Buchanan had not received the prize at Baltimore, but once the convention's decision was made he gave himself wholly over to the Pierce campaign. As in the past, he concentrated on his political specialty, mustering the Roman Catholic vote for the Democracy in Philadelphia.[19]

The campaign of 1852, a dull and listless affair, was highlighted by the embarrassing pomposity of hero Scott and the gutter tactics of both Whigs and Democrats. Both party platforms stood solidly for the Compromise of 1850, but to many voters in the South Pierce seemed "safer" on slavery and on the Fugitive Slave Act than did Scott. Southern Whigs by the thousands thus renounced their own candidate, streamed into the Democracy, or went fishing on election day. The result, as Tyler predicted, was never in doubt. Supported by a unified if not honeymooning Democratic Party, Pierce won in a landslide. Scott carried only four states, the disaster marking the end of the Whig Party as a major force in American politics. The Whigs, it would seem, had finally run out of available generals. With their Northern wing split on the Compromise of 1850 and their Southern wing defecting into the Southern Democracy, no single personality, certainly not the egocentric Scott, could hold the eclectic Whig coalition together any longer. The timely death of the Whig Party produced no tears at Sherwood Forest.[20]

As the Pierce administration took office in March 1853 John Tyler was confident that all was right in the world again. Pierce's appointment of former Corporal's Guardsman Caleb Cushing as Attorney General gave the ex-President a personal pipeline to the new administration which he immediately filled with patronage suggestions. "The ultras of the Democratic party are already restless," he warned Cushing soon after the election. The Attorney General should therefore work to "conciliate as large a body of true friends as you can ... the person, whoever he may be, who hands you a letter from me is *your true friend*, and no mistake." Tyler promised Cushing he would recommend for federal office men who were "old tried friends who have stood by us in past times and have never wavered since." Among these old, tried friends was his nephew, William Waggaman, whom Tyler hoped Pierce would "provide for comfortably." When Pierce offered Henry A. Wise any Cabinet job the Virginian wanted, Tyler was further persuaded that the new President was indeed a discriminating judge of political talent. This view was strengthened in May 1853 when Robert Tyler was signally honored by Pierce with a White House dinner invitation followed by an ostentatious two-hour "arm-in-arm" stroll down Pennsylvania Avenue. And when John Tyler met the President at White Sulphur Springs in August of that year the mutual exchanges of greeting and respect could not have been more cordial. Buchanan's appointment to the Court of St. James's, Jefferson Davis' selection as Secretary of War, and rumors that Robert Tyler would sooner or later secure the London consulate all contributed to Tyler's belief that Franklin Pierce would bring new strength and unity to the Democratic Party. With Pierce in the White House and the Compromise of 1850 on the books, the whole question of slavery in the territories, thought Tyler, had become an academic abstraction. "I do not see to what Free-soilism can [now] attach itself, or upon what food it can longer live. It is at this moment but a mere abstraction." [21]

In the midst of this emerging euphoria over the Pierce administration the slavery controversy struck Sherwood Forest with full force. As might have been expected, the storm center of the excitement was Julia. In the February 1853 issue of the *Southern Literary Messenger*, a Richmond monthly of broad circulation, appeared Julia's letter defending slavery. First printed in the New York *Herald* and the Richmond *En-*

quirer in January, the article was a spirited rebuttal to an open letter from the Duchess of Sutherland, the Countess of Derby, the Vicountess Palmerston, the Countess of Carlisle, and Lady John Russell urging Southern ladies of quality and moral sensitivity to take the lead in demanding an end to the immoral slave institution. Although Tyler's thoughts on the subject ran prominently through the piece, Julia actually wrote it. Indeed, she labored over it for a full week until she was exhausted by the close concentration and attention it demanded. "Authorship does not agree with her," Margaret reported, "and what with intense thinking and excitement on the subject it has quite upset her usual current of health. She has been obliged to take some *blue pills in consequence*." [22]

The slave system Julia knew intimately at Sherwood Forest and saw functioning among the James River wheat plantations bore little resemblance to the view of slavery the English ladies had evidently derived from reading Harriet Beecher Stowe's *Uncle Tom's Cabin* when it first appeared in March 1852. Julia's response to the Duchess was thus an attack on the Stowe image of the Southern plantation slave as well as a restatement of the positive paternalistic features of the system. She knew perfectly well that the Sherwood Forest slaves were well treated and that they had a deep emotional attachment to their master. She had witnessed too many evidences of this to permit the Sutherland charges to go unanswered.[23]

As recently as June 1852, for example, she had seen Henry, a body slave who had "run away" from Sherwood Forest in 1844, return voluntarily to the plantation to explain to Tyler that he had not really been a runaway. Henry's story was that his desertion had been no more than an attempt to rejoin Tyler at the White House after being left behind at Sherwood Forest when the President and Julia had returned to Washington from their honeymoon. Whatever the truth of his account, Henry had been arrested, classified as a runaway, and had been sold by Tyler to a new master in Georgia. There in the intervening years he had learned the barber's trade, saved his money, and in 1852 he had purchased his freedom and journeyed to Washington to secure manumission papers which were legally unobtainable in Georgia. On his way back to Georgia, papers in hand, he stopped at Sherwood to see his old master. On greeting Tyler again, reported Julia, "he could not restrain his tears—and said . . . he never could be a contented man or die happy unless the time should come when he might see and talk with his master once again." After cutting Gardie and Tazewell's hair, he left for Georgia. This was not the stuff of *Uncle Tom's Cabin*.[24]

The only other runaway incident recorded at Sherwood Forest (it could scarcely be classed as a serious attempt at escape) occurred in December 1855 when the slave Roscusis got drunk, became impertinent with John Tyler, Jr., and was knocked to the ground for his attitude.

In fear and panic the bewildered Negro picked himself up and "ran out of the front gate" and away—to nearby Richmond. Immediately apprehended, roughed up, and slapped in a Richmond jail, he would, said Julia, "have had punishment enough before he sees home again to disgust him with *traveling*." [25]

In her lecture to "The Duchess of Sutherland and the Ladies of England" Julia did not attempt to defend slavery as a positive moral good. She admitted too that it had grave political disadvantages and was the "one subject on which there is a possibility of wrecking the bark of this Union." But she denied that the slave system was by definition a form of bestiality run amuck and she questioned the right of British critics, male or female, to intervene in what was essentially an American domestic problem. Warming to her task, Julia pointed out that—compared to the depressed white laborers of London—the Southern Negro "lives sumptuously," enjoying warm clothing, plenty of bread, and meat twice daily. The separation of slave families was "of rare occurrence and then attended by peculiar circumstances." In addition, she praised the work in Liberia of the American Colonization Society, called attention to the steady statistical increase in the numbers of free Negroes in Virginia, and noted that in helping Negro freedmen return to Africa "we seek to retribute the wrongs done by England to Africa, by returning civilization for barbarism, Christianity for idolatry." Negro slaves attended church in great numbers, Julia maintained. They had their own pastors, and they were encouraged to undertake religious instruction. To charge that their masters cruelly denied them this spiritual boon (as the Duchess of Sutherland had) was to parrot "some dealer in, and retailer of, fiction." [26]

By 1853 these arguments were standard, mechanical defenses of the slave institution. The main force of Julia's article rested in her well-mounted attack on British abolitionist interference in American internal affairs. Charging that the Duchess and her co-signers were merely mouthing the abolitionist opinions of their powerful husbands, Julia reminded the English ladies that slavery was first fastened on America by British colonial administrators. It came with singular bad grace for the English now to shed great "crocodile" tears for the poor slaves. If the ladies of England demanded an object for their tears, their mercy, and their frustrated sense of humanitarianism, Julia suggested that they concentrate on the destitute and impoverished people of their own country, particularly on the miserable conditions of their merchant and naval seamen and the plight of their starving Irish:

Spare from the well-fed negroes of these States one drop of your superabounding sympathy to pour into that bitter cup [Ireland] which is overrunning with sorrow and with tears.... Go, my good Duchess of Sutherland, on an embassy of mercy to the poor, the stricken, the hungry and the naked of your own land—cast in their laps the superflux of your enormous wealth; a single jewel from your hair, a single gem from your dress would relieve many a poor female of England, who is now cold, and shivering and destitute. ... Go, and arrest the proceedings of your admiralty! Throw your charities between poor Jack and the press gang!... I reason not with you on the subject of our domestic institutions. Such as they are, they are ours.... We prefer to work out our own destiny.... The African, under [English] policy and by her laws, became property. That property has descended from father to son, and constitutes a large part of Southern wealth.... We meddle not with your laws of primogeniture and entail although they are obnoxious to all our notions of justice, and are in violation of the laws of nature.... We preach no crusades against aristocratic establishments.... We are content to leave England in the enjoyment of her peculiar institutions; and we must insist upon the right to regulate ours without her aid. I pray you to bear in mind that the golden rule of life is for each to attend to his own business, and let his neighbor's alone! [27]

Within a fortnight of Julia's appearance in print Sherwood Forest was showered with congratulations and letters of support from all over the country. For a brief moment Julia Gardiner Tyler became a national figure and a Southern heroine. Sarah Polk sent congratulations. Resolutions of thanks were received from various women's organizations all over the South. More than fifty newspapers, North and South, were received at Sherwood Forest containing favorable notice of the article. The Boston *Times* pronounced it "powerful," as did the New York *Journal of Commerce*. The Philadelphia *Pennsylvanian* praised it, and such Whig papers as the Petersburg (Va.) *Gazette* crowed that Julia's effort had "knocked the Duchess's document into the middle of next week." Robert Tyler and John Tyler, Jr., wrote that it had "created an immense sensation in Philadelphia circles and added greatly to her fame." Washington was "loud in commendation," reported Colonel John S. Cunningham from the capital. Some argued that Julia had squashed Harriet Beecher Stowe in one blow, but Margaret demanded better and more tangible evidence for this broad claim. "I think the good people of our Union had better unite in subscribing a sum at least equal to the amount of Mrs. Stowe's publication. This would be a substantial evidence of the favor with which it has been received." Still, Tyler opined that "there was never a public document in the annals of our history which has received such universal approval and admiration." As Julia happily dispatched reprints of her effort to old Washington friends and acquaintances—Mesdames Polk, Webster, Calhoun, Wickliffe, and Wilkins—the music halls in Richmond began enjoying the fun and excitement. When Tyler took Gardie to town in September to hear the Kimble Band he learned that the organization was preparing a new song titled "The Duchess," the refrain for each verse ending with the sassy lines:

> Oh, Lady Sutherland,
> To comfort you I'll try.
> Mrs. Tyler gave you what was right,
> But Duchess don't you cry.[28]

Tyler's Anglophobic appetite was not entirely sated by Julia's rebuke to the good Duchess and her circle. The onset of the Crimean War in 1854 raised briefly the hope at Sherwood Forest that Britain would be crushed by Tsarist Russia in the contest and that such a defeat would obviate for many years any English plans for a military intervention in America's domestic slavery problem. "The allied armies find they have caught a Tartar," Julia exulted. Tyler had no love for Tsarist Russia. He recognized it for the senseless despotism it was. Indeed, when Tsar Nicholas intervened in the Hungarian Revolution in June 1849 Tyler had been loud in his praise of the courage and democratic idealism of Louis Kossuth and his heroic Hungarian patriots. But the advantage of the Crimean War to Americans, as he saw it, lay in the possibility of the mutual military exhaustion both of the autocratic Tsar and the meddlesome John Bull.

As the ill-managed slaughter progressed, however, Tyler expressed his willingness as a humanitarian (and as a politician not averse to a comeback attempt) to head an American peace mission to negotiate an end to the conflict. "These views are for your own eye," he informed Robert in January 1855 after his son sounded him out on the idea with a view to reporting Tyler's reaction to Ambassador Buchanan in London. "If such a thing as a tender of such mission should be made me, accompanied with such outfit as the occasion would demand, I might take its acceptance under serious advisement." Tyler was not summoned from his bucolic retirement to head a peace mission. Instead, he remained on his farm and enjoyed the rise in grain prices occasioned by the Crimean War. With wheat up to $2.50 per bushel and applications of guano steadily increasing the yield of his corn- and wheatfields, Tyler could regard the continuing combat with a certain equanimity.[29]

He could not regard the sharp renewal of the slavery controversy in the same detached manner. On the contrary, the introduction of the Kansas-Nebraska Bill in January 1854 threatened again to break asunder the Democratic Party and lead the nation down the shortening road to war. Proposed by Senator Stephen A. Douglas of Illinois, the controversial bill provided for the organization of territorial governments for Kansas and Nebraska, both of which lay north of the 36°30' line set by Congress in the Missouri Compromise of 1820 as the dividing line between slave and free territory. Whatever Douglas' personal motives in submitting the legislation (they included his interest in a central route for the projected transcontinental railroad, his private ambition for the White House, and his attempt to remove the slavery controversy football once and for all from the fumbling hands of Congress), the feature of the proposal that produced the greatest national turmoil was the provision that the slavery question in each territory was to be solved democratically by popular sovereignty. In sum, the Missouri Compromise would be repealed and slavery in the territories, now no longer contained by congressional fiat, could legally expand north of the old 36°30′ boundary. Southern supporters of the legislation, denying that these proposals necessarily meant "squatter sovereignty," pointed defensively to the provision in the legislation that permitted all legal disputes over slavery in the two territories to be carried to the Supreme Court. This, however, did not still the uproar. Although it was not likely that more slaveowners than free-soil advocates could be moved into Kansas in time to win the territory for slavery, the fact that the institution might now legally metastasize brought fierce attacks in Northern free-soil and abolitionist circles on the "aggressive slavocracy" of the South and the Pierce administration. Aggressive or not, the fact was, of course, that the slavery forces could not long compete in Kansas with the antislavery advocates who ultimately rushed into the territory in far greater numbers. In Nebraska the slavocracy had no chance at all. When this became apparent, the initially agreeable doctrine of popular sovereignty soured suddenly in the South and the suspicion grew that the wily Douglas had advocated the principle in the full knowledge that slavery, unable to compete in any of the still unorganized territories, would be confined forever within its 1854 boundaries.

Tyler had opposed the Missouri Compromise limitation on slavery. As a young congressman he had argued in 1820 that Congress had no constitutional prerogative to interfere with slavery in the territories one way or another. While he had never been particularly interested in slavery expansion as such (indeed, he had regarded this as the least relevant argument for Texas annexation in 1844–1845), he still believed slavery should be legally *permitted* to expand into regions where the climate and soil conditions were particularly favorable to the institution. He had never been militant on the subject; he had accepted the hydrological limitations on expansion implicit in the Compromise of 1850. He knew that the slave institution could not flourish in arid New Mexico or Utah. He correctly saw that the alleged victory for the South in those desert sections was far outweighed by the political advantages the North achieved through the admission of California as a free state. Nor did he think that more than a few Missouri planters would want to carry their "domestics" into neighboring Kansas. Nevertheless, he thought they should have the *right* to do so until such time as the settlers of Kansas Territory declared against the institution in a democratic and orderly manner. He therefore publicly favored the passage of the Kansas-Nebraska Bill as recognition of the legal "equality" of Southern and Northern institutions in the unorganized territories. It would mark an end to three and a half decades of "busy intermeddling of Congress" in the slavery question in those areas. Popular sovereignty, as conceived by Douglas, publicly received his support in 1854 as a reasonable solution to the question of slavery expansion in the territories. Nevertheless, he remained fearful in his own mind that the revival of the whole issue would lead only to the ultimate "despoilment of the South." He was certain that "these agitations cannot end in good." For these reasons he devoutly wished that the whole question had never come up. Privately, he defended the judgment of his own congressman, John Singleton Millson, in voting against the measure.[30]

With confusion enough abroad in the land, it particularly galled Tyler to observe that some segments of the Northern clergy were willing to interject theological and ecclesiastical considerations into the Kansas-Nebraska debate. As he wrote Margaret:

I am especially vexed with the Northern Clergy who have left their appropriate sphere of peace on Earth and good will to men to enter upon the battlefield of politics—an arena from which they cannot depart without bearing all the marks of a wretched and unhallowed conflict about them. Mr. Bedell even is of the number. Alas, alas! I thought him so absorbed in the saving of souls, as to have no time to devote to us *poor devils of the South* as their learned and very pious men of the pulpit would have us. Don't ask me to accompany you to any church in which any one of these busybodies may have to preach. I should have to deny your request altho' to do so would give me pain.[31]

The Kansas-Nebraska Bill passed Congress in May 1854 and was duly signed by South-leaning Pierce. Hailed initially in the South as a triumph for the future health and welfare of Southern institutions, the measure immediately set into motion a series of dangerous reactions, which, as Tyler had feared, brought civil war a step closer. Within two years a coalition of Northern Whigs, abolitionists, Free Soilers, and antislavery Democrats had organized the new radical Republican Party; Kansas had become a bloody battleground fought over by pro-slavery and abolitionist guerrilla forces; the Democratic Party began disintegrating in a great centripetal motion; and in the midst of the growing social and political disorder the short-lived Know-Nothing Party made its wild bid for government by hate.

John Tyler watched these tragic developments with consternation. It distressed him to see the Roman Catholic issue hurled into the political arena. He had condemned the intolerant Nativist movement in the 1840s, and with equal vigor and consistency he attacked its anti-Catholic and anti-immigrant Know-Nothing offspring in 1854. To Tyler, the Roman Catholic Church, above all others, was to be commended for its noninvolvement in the slavery controversy. Catholicism, said Tyler in July 1854, "seems to me to have been particularly faithful to the Constitution of the country, while their priests have set an example of non-interference in politics which furnishes an example most worthy of imitation on the part of the clergy of the other sects at the North, who have not hesitated to rush into the arena and soil their garments with the dust of bitter strife." In defending the Roman Church against

Know-Nothing charges of treason, un-Americanism, and worse, Tyler saw that the hate crusade fed principally on the broader sectional confusion engendered by the Kansas-Nebraska controversy and the threatening breakup of the two party structure. Thus he felt that the new party's real danger turned on its bid to "unite the malcontents of all parties" and compromise the prospects of a victory for moderate Democrats in 1856. For these views he was heavily indebted to Robert Tyler whose war against the Know-Nothings in Philadelphia on behalf of James Buchanan's continuing candidacy for the Democratic nomination was reported to Sherwood Forest in great detail. As for the future of the Know-Nothing movement, Tyler could only hope that

The intolerant spirit manifested against the Catholics, as exhibited in the burning of their churches, etc., will, so soon as the thing becomes fairly considered, arouse a strong feeling of dissatisfaction on the part of a large majority of the American people; for if there is one principle of higher import with them than any other, it is the principle of religious freedom.

Tyler predicted that the madness would eventually run its course. The Know-Nothings would soon split helplessly into their own pro- and antislavery sectional components and with that division the church-burners and immigrant-beaters would play but a small role in the 1856 canvass.[32]

In the meantime, Tyler supported the gubernatorial aspirations in Virginia of his old friend Henry A. Wise. Not only did former Guardsman Wise "denounce and satirize by turn the Know Nothings" in the Old Dominion, but his campaign included as well a vigorous *ex post facto* defense of the accomplishments of the Tyler administration. "The Democratic press, in order to sustain him," observed Tyler, "has to eulogize me; and thus Mr. Wise's nomination has been better for me than any other incident which has occurred." Wise's impressive victory in May 1855 over an ideologically rudderless Whig–Know-Nothing coalition smashed the anti-Catholic movement in Virginia and elated the Sherwood Foresters. "The opponents to that miserable know-nothingism are *so* anxious to bring in Wise," Julia wrote on the eve of the election. Even little Alex, barely seven, was reported to have declared he did "not wish to live a day longer in the world if Henry A. Wise is defeated." Not only was Wise victorious; the size of his sweep was enough to bring his name prominently before the South as a possible candidate for the Democratic nomination in 1856. John Tyler, his personal struggle for reputation over, hastened into Governor Wise's corner. With Republican, Democratic, Whig, and Know-Nothing parties now in the national political picture, all save the Republicans badly divided on the slavery issue, the election of 1856 loomed as one of the most unpredictable in American political history. Nor would the task facing the victorious candidate, Wise or otherwise, be enviable. As Tyler saw the immediate political future in November 1855:

Rely upon it, that the next four years will prove to be the turning point of our destiny, and that it requires no ordinary man at the head of affairs to weather the storm. I even doubt whether the presidency would be desirable. He would be but a wreck in history, whose administration should witness a destruction of the government. But I must here end my gloomy reflections....[33]

Never had the former President been so clairvoyant. President James Buchanan turned out to be a very "ordinary man," and his administration, a "wreck in history," did little more than preside paralytically over the steady erosion of the Union. Tyler, of course, was not an enthusiastic partisan of Buchanan in 1856, even though his son Robert continued to labor loyally in the Buchaneer cause. Tyler favored the Democracy's nomination of Wise, Pierce, and then Buchanan—in that order. When it was apparent that Governor Wise could hope to command little or no Northern support, Tyler "inclined strongly" toward Franklin Pierce, who had "on the absorbing question of the times been true as steel." This attitude toward Pierce, whose administration had proved something less than a glorious success, was in part determined by Tyler's unwillingness to trust Buchanan fully. As the Democratic convention in Cincinnati in June 1856 came to its end, he worried that Old Buck was still "wedded to the men who most figured as partisans during General Jackson's administration." About the only thing that reconciled him to Buchanan at all was the thought that a Pennsylvania-Virginia alliance within the Democracy might serve to preserve the transsectional integrity of the party and with it "the integrity of the Union and the Constitution." [34]

The various nominations, counternominations, walkouts, endorsements, divisions, and deals of the politicians turned the preconvention and convention activities of the several parties into near-chaos. The Know-Nothings, meeting in Philadelphia in February 1856, had no difficulty condemning immigrants and Catholics to hell, but they promptly split on the slavery issue. In the confusion the Northern antislavery delegates walked out, leaving the remainder to nominate Millard Fillmore and launch the so-called American Party. The ex-President was available. Since Fillmore's moderate role in the Compromise of 1850 assured him some following among Southern Whigs, the fanatics who ran the Know-Nothing rump decided that he was the man of the hour. His only other support came from a scattering of conservative Whigs in upstate New York who were not militant on the slavery question. This attempt by the Know-Nothings to attach Southern and New York Whigs to the hard core of anti-Catholic and anti-immigrant lunatics who dominated the Americans stimulated talk in Virginia that the Democracy might well bring Tyler forward again to lure the Southern Whigs away from the Fillmore standard. But Tyler scotched this talk with the statement in mid-May 1856 that he had "neither longings or ardent desires" for the White House. At this point he was still for Pierce and he was now sure the Know-Nothings would disintegrate in the sectional heat of the campaign.[35]

The antislavery Know-Nothing secession group nominated Speaker of the House N. P. Banks with the understanding that he would withdraw in favor of John C. Frémont if the new Republican Party nominated the Pathfinder. Since Frémont's nomination on a strong antislavery platform was a possibility if not a probability, the threat of that prospect hung over the Democratic convention in Cincinnati. By the time the Democracy's delegates reached the Queen City on June 1, the influential Virginia delegation was strongly—though not unanimously—for Buchanan. Thanks in part to tireless liaison work of Robert Tyler between the Virginia and Pennsylvania delegations, Wise's own ambitions for the nomination had been blunted and his sensibilities in the matter salved. Indeed, both Wise and John Tyler had swung over to a reluctant acceptance of Old Buck. Tyler's shift was dictated largely by the realization that much of Pierce's support within the Northern Democracy had seeped away to Stephen A. Douglas during the months before the convention, a point employed by Robert with telling effect at Sherwood Forest in his successful effort to bring his father around to Buchanan. Old Buck, absent in London for two years, had the additional advantage of not having taken a public stand on the popular-sovereignty feature of the Kansas-Nebraska question. Thus when the convention met in Cincinnati, Buchanan, Pierce, and Douglas (in that order) were the front runners.[36]

As one of Buchanan's floor managers at Smith and Nixon's Hall in Cincinnati, Robert Tyler was in the thick of Old Buck's fight for the nomination. Speaking, cajoling, banqueting, and buttonholing, the Tyler touch was so prominent among the delegates that there were rumors of Robert's nomination for the Vice-Presidency should Buchanan fail to receive the top spot. "Think of that," he informed his father. "But I laughed it off, when mentioned to me, as a good joke. If I were a rich man, and the Union does not 'slide,' I might be something yet. But as it is I float helplessly in the waves of doubt and debt." As it turned out, the efforts of Wise and Robert Tyler were decisive for Buchanan. Leading all the way, he was nominated on the seventeenth ballot after Pierce had withdrawn and thrown his support to Douglas. Virginia held firm for Buchanan during this maneuver. As a result, the Pierce vote (largely Southern) that went over to Douglas at the crucial juncture did not trigger a general stampede to the Little Giant. When the expected rush failed to materialize, Douglas also withdrew rather than see the convention hopelessly deadlocked.

The platform on which Buchanan and Vice-Presidential nominee John C. Breckinridge of Kentucky were pledged to stand upheld the Compromise of 1850, the Kansas-Nebraska Act, the concept of popular sovereignty, the Fugitive Slave Act, and states' rights generally. For Virginia's constancy in his cause Buchanan was extremely grateful. As he had said to Robert a week before the convention, "Should the Old Dominion stand firm, it is my opinion that my friends will succeed at Cincinnati." Succeed they had, and Robert was soon in receipt of the "warmest sort of letter" of thanks from Buchanan who had assured him earlier that his many services to the Buchanan candidacy over the years were eternally "recorded in my heart." Elated by the vital role he had played in the Buchanan nomination, Robert was momentarily overwhelmed by the patronage implications of the nominee's debt to him. "After all, I do not know what he can do for me," he remarked in some bewilderment. Margaret experienced no such hesitation. She knew exactly what Buchanan could do for Robert. He could bestow the "good fat office" which Robert had obviously earned and "ought to have." [37]

When Tyler received the news of Buchanan's nomination he pronounced the selection "fortunate," although the feeling still nagged him that if "anyone ever deserved a renomination it was General Pierce, especially at the hands of the South." Nonetheless, he realized correctly that "the great game is the *Union*, and with Pennsylvania sound the Union is safe." He was hopeful that Buchanan would win in November, and that the Know-Nothings would "entirely melt away" during the campaign. That latter prospect being likely, the "Black Republicans," he said, "will either have to rush into the embraces of the Abolitionists, and recognize the lead of Garrison and Phillips, or go into so violent and rabid a course as to abandon and disgust all reflecting men." [38]

When on June 17 the "Black Republicans" predictably nominated John C. Frémont at Philadelphia on a frankly sectional platform that opposed the extension of slavery in the territories and called boldly for the admission of Kansas as a free state, the distress felt throughout the Tyler-Gardiner family was profound. Similarly, when what remained of the broken Whig Party endorsed the Know-Nothing nomination of Fillmore at Baltimore in September, on a platform appealing vaguely for national unity, the concern at Sherwood Forest increased to ill-disguised alarm. With three major candidates now in the field, the anti-Republican vote could conceivably split so badly between Buchanan and Fillmore that Frémont might slip into the White House by the side door. That result, thought the Tylers, would lead straight to the disruption of the Union. As Tyler pointed out to David Lyon, "it is quite sensibly felt by all that the success of the Black Republicans would be the knell of the Union." [39]

As a momentary panic developed within the family, Robert Tyler argued that in the event of a Republican victory the South should immediately secede lest the "infidels, atheists and rascals" who ran the Frémont crusade undertake to reduce the section to a "tributary people." His father's views were more moderate, but Tyler's sense of imminent doom reached a new peak of intensity. Sanguine that Buchanan would somehow squeeze through to victory, Tyler was still forced to admit that some Southern Whigs, among them many Virginians, were so hostile to the Democracy that they were willing to take "Frémont or the Devil in preference to Buchanan." The Know-Nothings, he predicted, unimportant in themselves, would bend every effort to "divide and distract us here at the South." Their unholy alliance with the Whigs behind Millard Fillmore and his American Party might well cast the election into the House of Representatives.

Were this to occur, reasoned the former President, the South could be certain "of the union of the malcontents upon Frémont over Buchanan." If Frémont were elevated to the White House in this manner, the South would find itself in serious trouble. Tyler rejected Robert's radical concept of immediate secession, just as he turned his back on similar recommendations from Henry A. Wise and other Southern fire-eaters. But he admitted to his eldest son that Frémont's election would force the South into some sort of collective regional action. The alternative was to stand by helplessly and watch the Republican abolitionists legislate the South's slave property out of existence:

> I know not what to say about the course... Virginia will pursue in the event of Frémont's election [he wrote in September 1856]. The Democracy looks the danger in the face, and is prepared to meet it; and there is a large minority who are entirely indisposed to any action. They wish to see the inaugural, and to await some hostile movement. For myself, I scarcely know what to counsel. To await the inauguration is to find ourselves under the guns of every fortification and our trade at the mercy of our enemies. It is, therefore, the dictate of prudence that the Southern States should understand each other at once. A concentrated movement would control the fate of the country and preserve the Constitution. I believe that such measures are looked to by those in high places in the South. A call of all of the legislatures of this section to make a distinct avowal of their sentiments and to place their States in a condition to maintain their resolves would not fail to roll back the tide—or at least to restrain all arbitrary legislation.[40]

This, in broad outline, would be Tyler's reaction to Lincoln's election four years later. In 1856, however, he need not have been so nervous or concerned. Buchanan ran well throughout the campaign, and he looked the probable winner when the first returns began coming in in late October. This happy outcome was in no small measure a result of the labors of Robert Tyler who became the work horse of the Pennsylvania-Virginia alliance within the Democracy and served as a roving ambassador of good will between Buchanan and the Wise faction during the campaign. Patiently he undertook to explain the politics of each man to the other. He calmed the mercurial Wise's suspicions that Old Buck was not sound on the popular-sovereignty concept the Southern extremists now so clearly feared. In addition, Robert stumped Philadelphia and mustered the Irish-American vote there for Buchanan. In fact, Robert was on the verge of a nervous breakdown, so complete was his physical exhaustion as the campaign drew to a close. But his effort was rewarded when the first returns reached Sherwood Forest. Buchanan outpolled the combined Frémont and Fillmore vote in both Pennsylvania and Indiana. To an elated John Tyler this news from the North and West filled the "Democratic people with unspeakable joy." To his daughter, Letitia Tyler Semple, then touring in Europe, he expressed the belief that Buchanan's now-certain election would "forever strangle the monster which has threatened to devour the Confederacy." Returning again to a long-standing and deep-seated Anglophobia, Tyler informed Letitia that

I can enjoy the confusion and mortification of our foreign enemies if the B. ticket shall prevail by a large majority. The *Westminster Review* had chuckled in anticipation of Frémont's election, and had pronounced it the knell of the Union. Old Mother Britain may yet put on sackcloth and ashes before the epitaph of this Republic is written.[41]

Whether Buchanan's narrow election in 1856 preserved the Union or merely postponed its dissolution and whether the subsequent paralysis of the Buchanan administration actually contributed to the catastrophe of 1861 remain moot points. Certainly Tyler's view of the Republican Party as a "treasonable sectional movement" contributed more heat than light to a political situation already burdened with excessive emotion. Tyler did not ponder the fact that Buchanan's success was by plurality rather than majority vote. The combined Frémont-Fillmore vote exceeded Old Buck's by some 400,000. Nor did the former President seem to appreciate the fact that the Democracy, now moving toward the status of a minority party, had been forced, like the Whigs before them, to purchase sectional unity at the price of nominating a faceless man who posed as all things to all Democrats.

These fundamental problems apparently disturbed Sherwood Forest not at all. In the general elation over Buchanan's victory the Tyler-Gardiner family speculated mainly on the bread-and-butter issue of just what "good fat office" the struggling Robert had earned with his heroic effort for Old Buck. Much to their evident and bitter dismay they quickly discovered that Buchanan would set no speed records in rewarding Robert with a patronage appointment commensurate with the value of his years of labor for the President-elect. Although Buchanan told him he could have "anything he wanted," the specific tender of the ministry to Switzerland in November 1856 had to be rejected. Desirable as this post was from a prestige standpoint, it paid little and Robert therefore had no choice but to turn it down. This decision was a "dreadful blow" to Priscilla, who considered it a "very nice, quiet and dignified" job that would "take Mr. Tyler away from all the din and fury of party politics, from personal hostilities, and from this vulgar, hurried turmoil of city life." She agreed, however, that her husband's economic situation would not permit him the luxury of the Swiss post. As Robert explained his postelection financial status to Wise, "I have never yet for fifteen years known one day free from pecuniary embarrassments and the most painful." And, although he thought he saw a "dawning political future" ahead of him, this dawn could scarcely be pursued in the mountains of distant Switzerland. Just what Robert had in mind for himself, just how glorious a political sunrise he anticipated, cannot be determined. When, for example, his brother John undertook after the election to enlist Henry Wise's influence with Buchanan to secure Robert a Cabinet post, Robert dismissed the attempt with the observation that "I would not think of accepting a place in Mr. Buchanan's Cabinet. I am wanting in the specific information and talents for the only two Cabinet positions of any value, and I regard the others as mere clerkships."

There is no evidence, of course, that Buchanan considered offering Robert a Cabinet appointment. Nevertheless, a full year and a half passed before he again offered Robert anything, and when the offer finally came it evidenced a rather pronounced deflation in the Chief Executive's estimation of his obligation to the Philadelphia lawyer. Thus in May 1858 Robert disdainfully declined a clerkship in the United States Circuit Court for Eastern Pennsylvania, informing Buchanan testily that he was "distinctly my own master and no office seeker." He was still burdened with "debt and poverty," but he let the President know that he expected political favors from no man, at least not at the clerkship level. "While I am by no means insensible to political honors and advancement, I do not want them unless they come to me unsolicited and unquestioned," he told Buchanan. Nor during these lean months of waiting could his father aid him financially. "I am as hard put up, to use a vulgar phrase, as any one," Tyler confessed in 1859. In November of that year Robert turned down the offer of a paymastership in the Navy Department on the advice of Sherwood Forest. The job itself, like the Circuit Court clerkship, was almost an insult. "Give up politics," Tyler finally urged him, "by which no man profits other than a knave; retrench, as far as retrenchment be practicable, and wait for political preferment to reach you at its own gait." Tyler firmly believed that Robert's long devotion to the President's career should be handsomely rewarded, but he certainly wanted no Tyler to have to beg a minor sinecure from the likes of James Buchanan. The independent and haughty attitude of the Tylers, father and son, ended the patronage matter and Robert had to be content with the chairmanship of the Democratic Executive Committee in Pennsylvania, to which Buchanan appointed him in 1858. While this post had considerable prestige it had no salary, and Robert's modest income continued to be derived from his job as Prothonotary of the Pennsylvania Supreme Court and from his marginal law practice in Philadelphia.

Similarly, John, Jr.'s attempt to land a patronage job from Buchanan came to grief. With little else to occupy his time, John, Jr., had worked as hard for Buchanan's election as Robert had. He vigorously supported the administration after it took office, frequently placing articles in Virginia newspapers designed to explain and rationalize the decisions and policies of the President. Yet by June 1858 Tyler saw there would be no reward for his second son either. "The people in Washington seem to be resolved to give him nothing," the former President complained. "That a man of his fine talents and accomplishments should not be able to earn his daily bread, or should fail to set about the task of doing so, is to me incomprehensible. I had rather see him following the plough than doing nothing."

By July 1860 John Tyler was quite upset by the treatment his sons had received at Buchanan's hands. As he told Robert:

He has been uniformly polite to you... but he is altogether *your debtor.* No one has been so true to him or rendered him greater service... but now his political days are numbered, and his sand nearly run. He might now reciprocate by rendering you service. Will he volunteer to do it, or, having squeezed the orange, will he throw the rind away? I may do him injustice in regarding him as a mere politician without heart. I hope I am mistaken.

Tyler was not mistaken. Robert was squeezed dry and cast aside. The Confederate States of America would do much better by him politically than had the United States under James Buchanan.[42]

17

RUMORS OF WAR:
AN END TO NORMALCY, 1855-1860

> *We have fallen on evil times. The day of doom for the great model Republic is at hand. Madness rules the hour.... I sigh over the degeneracy of the times.*
> —JOHN TYLER, NOVEMBER 1860

On the surface of things life at Sherwood Forest reflected little of the confusion and turmoil that gripped the nation during the last years before the Civil War. As the country proceeded steadily down the road to sectional conflict, the Tylers and Gardiners continued their normal habits. They enjoyed their extensive social life at various fashionable spas during the summers and they advised one another on the complex problems of health and longevity throughout the winters. Julia continued having babies, and John Tyler continued to tend his wheat- and cornfields, confident that whatever the nation's agony on the slavery question it would surely be solved short of the idiocy of civil strife. Visits back and forth between New York and Charles City also marked these final innocent years in the history of the family. Julia still thrilled to hear that her reign as First Lady had not been forgotten. She applauded the sagacity of the Ohio riverboat captain who, with more persistence than imagination, named all of his boats *The Gentle Julia*. Indeed, when Henry M. Denison reported seeing *The Gentle Julia No. 17* near Louisville, the mistress of Sherwood Forest was confident that an immortality of sorts was hers. Only under the impact of the John Brown raid at Harpers Ferry in October 1859 did normalcy flee Sherwood Forest.[1]

Until then, Julia and her husband enjoyed the pleasant existence afforded by the plantation and their frequent exposures at Saratoga,

Old Point Comfort, or the Virginia springs. "It is but reasonable," Tyler held, "that Julia should like to look out on the great world once a year." Whether they journeyed to the Virginia mountains (Tyler's preference) or to the North (which his wife preferred), Julia was invariably "all agog to go." True, Tyler's increasingly precarious health in the late 1850s limited the duration of these excursions, on occasion threatening to cancel them entirely, but he was generally able to summon the necessary strength and energy for Julia's forays into the outside world.[2]

Visits with Robert and Priscilla in Philadelphia and with Juliana, Margaret, and David Lyon on Staten Island and at the New England watering holes were combined with joint family gatherings at Old Point and the Virginia springs. Margaret and her mother enjoyed these escapes to Virginia's beaches and mountains from the heat of New York. For Tyler, the occasional journey to New York or New England had the additional advantage of allowing him to test the political opinions of the area, to say nothing of the medicinal advantages he thought he derived from "taking the waters" at Saratoga or Sharon Springs. Still, the "numerous retinue of servants and children" involved in such northerly operations increasingly dictated the logic of vacationing in Virginia. In 1855 and 1856, for example, the summer vacation was confined to a month at Old Point Comfort and a month touring White Sulphur Springs, Rockbridge Alum Springs, and Warm Springs. Margaret, Harry Beeckman, and Juliana came down to Sherwood Forest in June and the ladies then took turns tending the children while the adults proceeded to Old Point Comfort or to the Virginia springs. On one occasion, in August 1855, Julia sent Gardie, Alex, and Julie to Staten Island to visit their grandmother while she, Tyler, and Margaret casually toured the Virginia spas. This arrangement was a failure. Julia spent much of her vacation time nervously bombarding her harassed mother with detailed instructions on child care.[3]

Whether they had any therapeutic value or not, the Virginia mineral springs were the nerve center of the Old Dominion's ante-bellum society. Like the Tylers and the Gardiners, those wealthy and socially prominent Americans who could afford the luxury of taking the waters believed that their health was improved by the experience. "The company is now so good and the waters agree so well with me I have very little disposition to move," Margaret wrote from Alum Springs in August 1856. Indeed, Margaret reported the Rockbridge County resort so crowded that summer that guests of the hotel were packed five to a room and were reduced to sleeping on mattresses in the drawing and reception rooms. But the salutary effect of drinking and bathing in the waters was thought to be well worth the inconvenience. "I am now fairly under the influence of the waters," Margaret informed her city-bound brother. "They have taken hold of me pretty severely." Tyler also felt rejuvenated by the sulphuric ingestions.

In addition, the family found the company good and the social activities pleasant at the western Virginia spas they frequented. Old friends were invariably present, and old recollections and new gossip could be exchanged. When, for example, the families of Commodore Beverly Kennon and Thomas W. Gilmer arrived at Rockbridge Alum Springs in August 1856, Margaret thought it singular that three of the five prominent families connected with the *Princeton* disaster should again have been brought accidentally together. The somber remembrance and recounting of that tragedy did not dull the merrymaking of the survivors. On the contrary, dances and picnics were the order of the day. The appearance of Governor Wise added the inevitable political touch. Tyler, however, preferred not to mix his politics with his sulphur, and all efforts to persuade him to speak to the guests on the issues of the day proved unavailing.[4]

In her frequent travels to Virginia, winter and summer, Margaret was searching for health and recreation, not for another husband. She had developed a nagging cough in 1854, and she was more interested in treating that condition than she was in finding a new father for young Harry. Julia could only dimly perceive this fact. With all the matchmaking power and instinct at her command she persistently endeavored to involve Margaret in a serious romance. Thus when the young widow visited Sherwood Forest during the winters of 1854–1856, Julia and her neighbors sponsored numerous dances and dinner parties for her entertainment. These gave Julia an opportunity to nudge a bewildering array of unattached Tidewater men toward the comely Margaret in her campaign to find the husband she was sure her sister sorely needed. Not surprisingly, Margaret responded no more positively to Julia's new effort than she had to her sister's matchmaking in 1845–1847. She did, of course, enjoy the attentions of the men and the excitement of the various neighborhood "blowouts" immensely. "The F.F.V.s of Charles City are not so bad," she had confided to her mother in 1854. "You must try to appreciate them better. They improve upon acquaintance ... but I find many of them have as *extensive* ideas as their lands are.... Here's this young Wilcox, heir apparent to his uncle's estate and half heir to his father's. Both are rich ... [and] his father who is a widower took quite a fancy in this direction and wishes very much to pay a visit. Don't laugh!"[5]

Margaret had "no little fun" at Sherwood Forest among her "many admirers." She danced, teased, and flirted with all of them although most of the eligible men were quite a bit older than she. Her most loyal suitor, Dr. Henry Wilcox, was "upwards of sixty" by Julia's frank reckoning. Margaret also made it clear that a classic May-and-December match, however well it had worked for Tyler and her sister, was not her idea of torrid romance. Julia was quick to admit that many of the aging land-rich local beaux left much to be desired as "eligible matches for fashionable ladies unless the lady can produce a good part of the cash." But she was certain that this condition was not a Charles City phenomenon. In her opinion it was a universal malady. Margaret was foolish, therefore, not to grab whatever she could get—rich, poor, old, or young. After all, Julia reasoned, Margaret was fortunate to be able to meet a variety of "Colonels, Doctors, Lawyers, planters, Honorables and ex-Presidents" in Virginia. "Won't that do? To dress up for? ...if one is going to be always looking for a suitable offer and *nothing but that* they will waste a good deal of time." Nevertheless, during the winter of 1855–1856 Margaret managed to work her merry way through "no less than eight balls, eleven dinner parties, a countless number of tea drinkings," and a flock of fox hunts without rewarding Julia's romantic interests in her behalf. Tyler better understood Margaret's feelings in the matter, and he flatly informed one of her suitors that "the lady in question is not to be won even by a Prince Alton or a Duke of Brunswick." [6]

Margaret never did remarry. She still mourned for John Beeckman. It is not certain, however, that she would have remained content with widowhood for the rest of her life. She died before the question could be tested, before Beeckman's memory had dimmed. On June 1, 1857, while visiting at Sherwood Forest preparatory to a visit to the Virginia springs with Julia and the ex-President, the thirty-five-year-old widow suddenly passed away. Death came as quickly to her as it had to Alexander in 1851, and as it had to her young Shelter Island cousin Mary Gardiner Horsford in November 1855. It would come with equal celerity to Henry Mandeville Denison, Alice Tyler's widower, in October 1858. But to the lovely Margaret it came inexplicably. Mary died at the age of thirty-one, "without a struggle or a groan," in the grim gamble that was childbirth in 1855. That was normal. The thirty-six-year-old Denison was predictably, almost suicidally, carried away by yellow fever in Charleston after he refused to leave his stricken parishioners at the height of an epidemic there. Margaret, on the other hand, was alive and healthy one day and dead within the week. Her last letter, dated May 28, 1857, indicated the mystery of her ailment as well as the unwitting contribution of the medical profession to her sudden demise:

Dr. Giddeon Christian... appeared to understand my ailing better than anyone I have seen yet. Said at once I had sneaking chills with torpor of liver and deranged digestion—all of which I believe to be true. He gave me right off a dose I shan't soon forget. It made me *so sick*. I think it must have been antimony mingled with a good quantity of quinine and a nervine. However I believe it was a good dosing. He does not go for small doses of quinine. It must be taken until the *ears ring*, and to this end I have taken some thirty grains since yesterday—and with fine effect.

The initial "fine effect" was compromised by continued ear-ringing quantities of dangerous drugs, and a few days later the gay Margaret was gone, probably from a heavy overdose of morphine. The funeral was held at Sherwood Forest on June 3. Harry Beeckman and Juliana came down to Virginia for the melancholy amenities. When these were completed Tyler and Julia returned with them to New York that they might all attend graveside ceremonies for Margaret at East Hampton. It was "our most sad and bitter mission," said Julia. It was decided during this crisis that Margaret's orphaned nine-year-old son would be reared by his grandmother in her Staten Island home.[7]

The death of her beloved sister removed from the earth Julia's closest and dearest confidante. "We were always in such close communion. She was included in all my arrangements past, present and future." Julia went into deep mourning for a year. She tormented herself with the thought that perhaps "the skill of Margaret's physician was at fault." She derived only a bit of consolation from the fact that her sister had passed away "under the influence of a dose of morphine." At least "Death stole upon her without producing a dread or a pang." In mid-July the sorrowing Tylers and their children went to Staten Island to be with Juliana for the remainder of that desolate summer.[8]

For Julia it marked the end of an era. After 1857 she did not visit the Virginia springs or travel north for casual vacations on Staten Island and at the New England watering places. For the mourning Julia these once-happy excursions were meaningless without Margaret's cheerful presence. Not until November 1862 did she appear again at Castleton Hill—this time to deposit four of her children in the safety of her mother's home for the duration of the Civil War. Until the outbreak of that conflict the reunions of the family brought Juliana and Harry to Sherwood Forest or to Old Point Comfort. A summer place at Hampton was purchased in 1858, and named Villa Margaret in Margaret's memory. It provided a stationary vacation spot for the clan. Here Harry could swim and fish and play with his first cousins while Julia visited with her mother.

David Lyon did not visit in Virginia during the last five years before the war. Julia had always felt less close to him than she had to either Margaret or Alexander, and the tragic upheaval that would mark their relations during the Civil War had seeds that germinated in their long separation on the eve of the conflict. Settled, self-satisfied, and lazy, the Colonel had all he could do to muster the strength to override his mother's opposition and get married in 1860. Traveling to Virginia was apparently well beyond his energy, and Julia was too busy with too many children and an aging husband to dash off to New York. And so brother and sister drifted gradually apart. They seldom corresponded. Only a new baby at Sherwood Forest seemed important enough to produce an exchange of letters.

The birth of Robert Fitzwalter Tyler, Julia's sixth child and fifth son, on March 12, 1856, was accomplished without incident save that the sturdy expectant mother had, in her husband's words, "a violent pneumonia" accompanied by a cough "so severe and violent and of such long continuance as much to have enfeebled her, a circumstance particularly unfortunate at this time as the period is near at hand for her regular confinement." (Tyler reconsidered the sentence for a moment and then primly struck through the word *regular*.) But Julia coughed her way through the ordeal and was soon out of danger. Juliana was on hand for the blessed event, as usual, and nothing connected with the arrival of little Fitz was allowed to disturb the normal flow of visitors and dinner parties at Sherwood Forest. Childbirth had indeed become a regular thing for Julia.[9]

Fortunately, her children were as healthy as she. They passed through their various adolescent diseases without serious difficulty. The most severe of their illnesses was Gardie's "bilious attack" in October 1856. Julia was on Staten Island at the time. For a time Tyler feared he would lose the boy, but the ten-year-old responded to opiates and extensive cupping and somehow pulled through. He was pronounced out of danger the same day Tyler learned that Buchanan had carried Indiana and Pennsylvania. The former President was thus "in the happiest condition to enjoy the good political news." By the time a panicky Julia had rushed home to Virginia, Gardie had entirely recovered. Nevertheless, she was so frightened by the incident that she determined never again to leave her children. To be sure, they continued to have their bouts with boils, mumps, measles, and chicken pox, but they survived these childhood shocks just as they managed to survive the beginnings of their formal educations. Chicken pox was no worse than arithmetic and composition, and it was over and done with a lot faster. The Tyler children were not bad scholars. Like most children, however, they were less than entranced by the beauties of irregular French verbs and Latin conjugations—especially when the fish were biting and the rabbits were jumping.[10]

They were happy, active children who lacked nothing. Christmas at Sherwood Forest was their day, and Tyler had all he could do to prevent them from finding the presents and opening them before the appointed hour. As he described the scene on December 25, 1855:

The children last night hurried to bed at an early hour in order to sleep away the tedious hours which were to elapse before the dawning of day, but I went to Gardie and Alex's room at near eleven o'clock, and sleep had not visited their eyes. They were watching for Santa Claus, and complained of his tardiness. Being told that Santa Claus objected to being seen, and did not like boys to watch for him, they finally went to sleep; but the day had not fairly dawned when their exclamations filled the whole house. Having dispatched the sweet things, they then opened their toy boxes: Gardiner is still (eleven o'clock) carrying on the siege of Sebastopol; Alex is busily engaged with "Whittington and his Cat"; Julia arranges her furniture; Lachlan spurs his hobby horse; and Lionel ... calls for his drummer. A happier concern you rarely ever saw.

Nor was the Christmas season at the plantation entirely a children's festival. It was an opportunity for Julia to entertain her neighbors and their holiday houseguests. "Before midnight," said Tyler of one of these gatherings, "the fun grew fast and furious." [11]

As the years sped by Tyler had more and more difficulty keeping up with his spirited children and with the "fast and furious" parties sponsored by his socially zealous wife. Unlike the other members of his hearty family, the aging Tyler complained increasingly of his health after 1854. His late sixties found him with numerous aches and pains located in a variety of inaccessible organs. His medical problem centered chiefly in his digestive tract, as it had since his early thirties. After his sixty-fifth birthday he was also prone to heavy colds and influenza, arthritic attacks, and kidney disturbances. When in 1854 he threatened to try homeopathy for his "dyspepsia" (as all gastric problems were then termed), Julia urged him to go instead to Baltimore and place himself under the care of competent physicians there. Tyler rejected this advice, preferring to rely on local medical talent. He also rejected his wife's various home medical remedies (for example, her standard cure for flu—small doses of morphine combined with the copious drinking of "chicken water"). He always objected to extensive and experimental self-medication, and he spent much of his life with Julia cautioning her against the persistent tinkering with her body she (and her mother) so thoroughly enjoyed. While he was not slow to summon a doctor, he had little confidence in the medical profession. He was, however, no faith healer. On the contrary, he spent some $700 a year for four long years procuring his talented son Tazewell an expensive medical education at the Philadelphia Medical College. It was just that the diagnoses and nostrums of the medical fraternity seemed to vary so widely on the same set of symptoms. "I wish that I could entirely cure myself," he wrote in February 1856, "for I am never perfectly clear of pain. There is a great difference between 32 and 65—especially in cold weather.... What a delight it would have been to have fled [to Florida] from this oversevere winter." He was sure his illnesses were God's will. "I am the oldest and most infirm and cannot move about much," he complained in 1856. "I have many aches and pains. They will attend upon a sexagenarian, however, and so be it, for I am convinced that all is wisely ordered by Providence." Taking the waters at the Virginia springs seemed to ease these multiple aches and pains for a time, and, as has been noted, Tyler became a devotee of sulphuric hydrotherapy. Frequent and massive doses of calomel also became standard with him. Nevertheless, he was often rendered "quite feeble" by digestive upheavals, and his continuing war against this "old enemy" was one of attrition. In November-December 1856 he became so ill he "despaired at times of recovery."[12]

During this two-month crisis in late 1856 he began planning for a "fair history" of his administration. Too ill and weak to complete a biographical account of his public service he had commenced in the late 1840s, he ordered his public and private papers turned over to his old friend Caleb Cushing. He had heard that the distinguished lawyer was contemplating a scholarly reminiscence of the Tyler administration after his stint as Pierce's Attorney General had ended. Alexander Gardiner had originally been selected for this task, but his death in 1851 had caused the project to be abandoned. Now Tyler was anxious to see the book launched before death overtook him. "That a fair history of my administration should be written by a competent person is a matter very near to my heart," he told John, Jr., in January 1857. "Whatever time might be assigned for the publication of such a work, whether during my life or after my death, I feel it to be important that it should be written while I live. My own explanations might be wanting to render the narrative clear and perfect." Unfortunately, Cushing turned to other pursuits in 1857, and Tyler's unfinished manuscript, with most of his private papers, was burned in 1865 when the retiring Confederate defenders set fire to Richmond. Nor was the former President's health ever again robust enough prior to his death in 1862 to permit him to finish the work himself.[13]

By 1858 Tyler was loath to leave Sherwood Forest for very long for fear he would take ill and die in strange surroundings. In January-February of that year he again very nearly joined his fathers. Weakened by severe gastric upset and crippled by arthritis, he was confined to bed for two months. But on March 29, 1858, his sixty-eighth birthday, he was able to report to David Lyon that

> I now walk about the house and take my seat at the table with the rest of the family, but I cannot adventure out of doors except in a closed carriage—then I ride over the estate and see how matters are going on. I have had a terrible winter, and when I look back upon it I am at a loss to know how I have survived. Nothing but the kind providence of our heavenly Father could have saved me. For an entire month I remained suspended between life and death without perceptible change. I am at this time laboring under one of my old attacks which has I hope nearly run its course. Today I am better. It is my birthday and I now number 68 years—my three score and ten nearly attained and I can well appreciate what the Psalmist says of living to three score and ten—aches and pains, etc. etc. But I do not mean to sermonize.

Shaken by his close brushes with death in 1856 and again in 1858, Tyler drew up his will in 1859, leaving everything he owned to Julia and her children. His private papers were left to his sons Robert, John, Tazewell, and Gardie, and to his sons-in-law James A. Semple and William N. Waller, all of whom were to serve as his literary executors.[14]

As he contemplated the provisions of his will and the approaching end of his allotted days, Tyler became more attached to the scenes of his youth. William and Mary College received a good deal of his time and interest in the late 1850s. As Rector of its Board of Visitors and Governors he concerned himself with the details of faculty appointments, the renovation of the physical plant, and institutional finances. Awarded an LL.D. by the college in 1854, he was named its Chancellor in 1860, a post held before only by George Washington. Both of these honors pleased him immensely, and he frankly confessed his "egotism" in being so conspicuously signalized. William and Mary, with its solid academic emphasis on the Greco-Roman classics and states' rights, was, he felt, the "nursery of the great principles" which had contributed to the "glorious" elevation of his lifelong friend, Henry A. Wise, to the Governor's Mansion in Richmond in January 1856. The William and Mary LL.D. he therefore considered a real "feather in his cap." The chancellorship was an honor of which he was "quite as proud as any other ever conferred upon me by my fellow men." As often as his health permitted and his presence on campus was needed, he journeyed to Williamsburg to attend to his official duties or to address commencement exercises and other college gatherings. At these he was always enthusiastically received. "The cheering was immense," he wrote of one of his better performances in October 1859. "I never spoke better. Every sentence was followed by loud applause. I was twice after toasted with rapturous applause." [15]

His few public speeches during these years of increasing infirmity also demonstrated a growing tolerance of conflicting political and sectional viewpoints. Gone was the sharp and sarcastic invective of his great free-trade orations in the Senate. Gone was the absolute certainty of his ringing Presidential messages on states' rights, the Bank of the United States, and Manifest Destiny. Departed too was the self-conscious sense of moral righteousness that had often characterized his political outlook and tiresomely manifested itself in his public pronouncements. Instead, John Tyler, his own political wars apparently concluded, sought to pour soothing oil on the troubled waters of the Buchanan administration. To him states' rights as a concept seemed not nearly so important now as the reality of continued national unity. His almost-compulsive need to defend the total record of his administration before the altar of Clio and in the memories of his fellow men also became less evident. While he still felt obliged to counter and correct the more obvious distortions of his Presidential motives and acts, particularly those casting shadow on his personal honesty in office and on his motives in the Texas matter, he no longer lashed out at his tormentors with the wounded pride and savagery of 1845–1852. "I am almost indifferent to what others think," he told Robert in 1859.[16]

His speech at the Maryland Mechanics Institute in Baltimore

on March 20, 1855, to an overflow audience of five thousand, reflected something of his newfound political peace of mind and his interest in pacifying sectional passions. Titled "The Prominent Characters and Incidents of Our History from 1812 to 1836," the address sought to bury the factional and sectional rancors of the immediate past in an appeal to the glories of the Union. It was, said Margaret, who heard it, "considered magnanimous in its bearing towards those who had not spared the P—— politically." A gratuitous tribute to the departed Henry Clay particularly impressed Henry M. Denison as the beginning of a whole new orientation in Tyler's political life—one in which "you have attained the cool eventide of life where the meridian heats of party spirit and indiscriminating passions have passed away." To Tyler's delight, the Maryland Institute address was well received by all who heard it, and the Baltimore trip was marred only by the circulation of a story that the former President had suddenly died in Barnum's Hotel the following night. Some eight hundred persons called at the hostelry during the evening hours to make "anxious inquiries" about the report which, Julia hastily assured her mother, "had not the slightest foundation ... he is remarkably well at present." Nevertheless, the rumor blighted an otherwise gay round of shopping, parties, and receptions that the journey to Baltimore had provided Julia.[17]

Similarly, Tyler's "The Dead of the Cabinet" speech delivered in Petersburg on April 24, 1856, was designed to calm troubled sectional waters roiled by the bitterness of the 1856 Presidential campaign. On the advice of Thomas Ritchie, and by his own inclination, he scrupulously avoided any mention of the growing menace of "Black Republicanism." Instead, he was resolved to maintain a "dignified silence and graceful non-interference in the political questions of the day." Widely published in newspapers North and South, the Petersburg address was the plea of an elder statesman to the nation to bury the animosities of the past. Eulogizing the deeds, patriotism, and memory of men as different in their attitudes and politics as Hugh Swinton Legaré, Abel P. Upshur (who "failed not to see in virtual monopoly of the cotton plant what the annexation of Texas would accomplish"), Daniel Webster, John C. Calhoun, John C. Spencer, and Henry Clay, Tyler asked his audience to view these dead patriots as he did—as Americans

undisturbed by the ravings of faction or the roar of the political tempest, intent only on the public good, and earnest to record their names on the pages of history as public benefactors.... We were comrades—sat at the same table —brake bread and ate salt together, bared our bosoms to the same storms, and when the angry clouds so far parted as to admit a ray of sunshine, we basked in it together.... Let no man fear that I shall ... introduce into my address anything that can excite party feeling. I shall do no such injustice to the memory of those of whom I design to speak....[18]

Having made his peace with the American political spectrum from Webster to Calhoun, Tyler lovingly tackled the history of his native state in a major speech in Jamestown on May 14, 1857. Eight thousand Virginians were present to celebrate two and a half centuries of the white man's presence in the Old Dominion. Tyler was the featured orator. Of the hundreds of speaking invitations he received annually, the Jamestown address was one of the very few he felt obliged to accept. The remainder were declined, usually because his health was "too precarious." To the Jamestown speech he devoted weeks of preparation, attempting to cram a two-hundred-fifty-year survey of Virginia history into a two-and-a-half-hour eulogy to the glories of the Old Dominion. "They have not given me time enough," he complained. In spite of the careful preparation, the final result was not satisfactory. It was a tedious, rambling, superficial effort which taxed his health and the attention span of his audience with equal severity. Nevertheless, the ancestor worship in it strongly appealed to those Virginia Shintoists near enough the platform to hear it over the din of crying babies, lost children, and mint-julep merrymaking that characterized the carnival atmosphere of the celebration.[19]

In spite of his various physical infirmities, John Tyler had much to live for as the 1850s came to a close. His growing children brought him great joy, and he enthusiastically continued bringing more of them into the world. His marriage to Julia remained the honeymoon it had been since 1844. On his sixty-fifth birthday his doting wife could lovingly tell him:

> I would that I could add, love,
>   To wreaths that deck thy brow
> A leaf of brighter hue, love
>   Than shines among them now.
>
> But if my *fondness* serves, love,
>   To *gild* those wreaths of thine,
> Then will thy path be marked, love,
>   By radiance divine!
>
> On this thy natal day, love,
>   I will renew the vow
> Always to keep undimmed, love,
>   The lustre on thy brow! [20]

Luster John Tyler had achieved. His sincere efforts to stay the sectional whirlwind seemed to him neither a mean nor a hopeless task, and as he approached his seventieth birthday he could take pride in the fact that his had been a firm voice for moderation on the slavery question for a solid decade, a "wreath" not to be scorned. If his autobiography remained unwritten, if his speeches lacked the intellectual power and incisiveness of bygone days, if the patronage-stingy Buchanan commanded little of his respect, Tyler's psyche had healed from the rude buffeting of 1841–1845. He was content.

Little did he suspect in 1859 that the final storm was about to break in all its fury. The summer of 1859 was a relaxed and happy one. The family spent three wonderful months at Villa Margaret. Juliana and Harry visited there in August and found the six-acre retreat a "gem of a place," its peach trees "filled with peaches not yet ripe but large and fine looking." The children rode their ponies, swam, and fished, Tyler accompanying them on their excursions and fish fries. For the adults there were dances and masquerade balls at the Fortress. Tyler commuted back and forth between Hampton and Sherwood Forest, keeping one eye on his sickly wheat and the other on his vacationing family. When the trek back to Sherwood Forest commenced in early October Julia was happy, relaxed—and pregnant again. She saw Julie race eagerly off to her first day of school "as blithe as a bird," and she busied herself with supervising the setting out of new shrubs, evergreens, and fruit trees purchased from a nursery at Staunton. Although Tyler's wheat crop had been a disappointing one for the second successive year, the plantation had never been more beautiful in its colorful fall clothing.[21]

Then it happened. The three days that shook the South. On October 16, 1859, John Brown and his desperate little band struck at Harpers Ferry, Virginia, briefly seized the federal arsenal, and called for an armed insurrection of all Virginia slaves. Faced with this challenge to domestic peace, order, and safety, to say nothing of the seizure of government property, Buchanan had no alternative under the Constitution but to send a company of United States Marines and two artillery units into Harpers Ferry. Taken prisoner by federal troops on October 18, Brown was turned over to the hastily mobilized Virginia militia and brought to trial in Charles Town on October 25 for treason against the Commonwealth of Virginia. Speedily convicted on this charge and for criminal conspiracy to incite a slave uprising, the psychopathic murderer of Pottawatomie fame was hanged on December 2. Northern abolitionists and "Black Republicans" who had financed and encouraged the confused liberator's ill-starred venture now eulogized their unstable pawn as a hero, martyr, and latter-day Christ. They wept and screamed and gnashed their teeth in frustrated anguish. They demanded an early end to the infamous slavery institution in the most incendiary terms, disunion and civil war foremost among them. "I feel," said Tyler in shocked response to the abolitionist outcry,

great concern about the present condition of things in the Country. Matters have arrived at such a pass disunion must soon come. A few years ago a man to have dared to utter such treasonable discourses as proceed from so many lips at the North now would have been at once mobbed, stoned, and put down instead of listened to—and they would have been pointed at as objects of disgust—but how is it now? They are *lions,* and soon they will have followers enough to overthrow the government or create more terrible mischief.[22]

The audacity of the Brown raid, the mental picture it generated of hundreds of thousands of slaves rising in armed revolt against the handful of white masters who owned them, sent waves of panic through the Southern aristocracy. Visions of widespread Nat Turner rebellions, organized, coordinated, and directed from the North, even caused moderates among Southern plantation owners, Tyler among them, to begin stockpiling arms and preparing local defenses against an expected black revolution. Whatever sophisticated historians of another century would say "caused" the Civil War, the primary issue at Sherwood Forest during the final months before the deluge turned on Negro slavery—not on states' rights, Southern nationalism, Free-Soilism, the semantics of the Constitution, or on any of the other reasons separately and in combination since adduced to explain the origin of the 1861 catastrophe. To John Tyler, who labored as diligently and selflessly as any man to prevent civil war, the fundamental question was nothing more complex than the status of the Negro slave and the grim prospect that the abolitionism sponsored by Northern Republicans would eventually produce in Tidewater Virginia, and throughout the South, tiny islands of privileged whites isolated in angry seas of shiftless, liberated blacks. All other issues were subordinate to this, all other arguments became mere rationalizations and extensions of this primary fear of ultimate racial inundation. Especially was this true at Sherwood Forest after the John Brown raid on Harpers Ferry.

In Charles City County, where Negroes outnumbered whites more than two to one, the alarmed citizenry quickly began organizing an armed mounted patrol for "general security." As Julia explained its function to her mother in mid-November, "if it does no other good it will prevent stealing and keep the black people where they ought to be at night." By December 1, as the date for John Brown's execution neared, Tyler's friend and neighbor Robert Douthat of Weyanoke plantation had completed the mustering of the volunteer "Charles City Cavalry" which he captained. At the same time, the "Silver Greys," a mounted unit of older men "who cannot leave home to do active service," was raised. Tyler was offered the captaincy of this second-line security force. It was an honor he promptly accepted. Meanwhile, his son Dr. Tazewell Tyler joined the New Kent County militia as its surgeon and marched with the outfit to Richmond to tender his services to Governor Wise in the emergency. The Governor's energetic mobilization of the Virginia militia, and his deployment of several of its units to Charles Town during the trial and execution of Brown, was vigorously supported by the former President and his neighbors. "Wise's energy," Tyler reported to Robert in Philadelphia, "receives unqualified approval." [23]

On other aspects of the crisis, however, the Tylers differed. John, Jr., wrote Wise two letters urging him to spare Brown's life on the ground of political expediency. Robert, on the other hand, wanted Brown and his little army of "thugs," murderers, and horse thieves hung promptly and without a backward glance. "Why they should incite the least sympathy is very surprising to all Virginians and I may say to most conservative men," he fumed. Unless abolitionism were speedily crushed root and branch, Robert predicted the South would be forced to "establish a separate Confederacy in less than two years." John Tyler was less pessimistic than his eldest son, although for a moment in late December 1859 he gave ear to Ohio congressman C. L. Vallandigham's proposal for three separate confederacies in the event of dissolution. "If broken up, the fragments would collect around three centers, the North, the West, and the South," Tyler explained. "You may rely upon it that Virginia will prepare for *the worst*." [24]

Tyler expected local slave uprisings would follow the hanging of Brown. Fortunately, all remained quiet along the lower James. The Sherwood Forest Negroes remained docile throughout the crisis. They went about their usual routines without incident. They gave no evidence that they understood what the furor at Charles Town was all about. Very likely they had been carefully shielded from all information about the events in Harpers Ferry. "They are a strange set, are they not?" Julia asked her mother. "Generally kind and happy and don't want to have anything to do with *poor white people*." Nevertheless, local and state security measures were pushed energetically forward. "Virginia is arming to the teeth," Tyler pointed out, "more than fifty thousand stand of arms already distributed, and the demand for more daily increasing. Party is silent, and has no voice. But one sentiment pervades the country: security in the *Union*, or separation.... I hope there is conservatism enough in the country to speak peace, and that, after all, good may come out of evil." [25]

Enough conservatism was mustered to prolong peace, although little lasting good came out of the Harpers Ferry evil. At the outset of the Brown crisis Julia was positive that disunion was near at hand unless there was an immediate and "important demonstration of good feeling on the part of the North toward the South." Southerners, she warned, "are now completely wrought up and will not be tampered with any longer." Only when she learned that Americans as prominent as Edward Everett and Caleb Cushing had spoken out at Boston's Faneuil Hall for peace and conciliation did she decide that the Union could probably be saved. "The best minds are really with the South," she said of the Faneuil Hall rally. Still, she supported a movement originating in Richmond to boycott the use of Northern textiles in the hope that such pressure on the Yankee pocketbook would awaken businessmen in that section to the economic implications of "forcing" the South out of the Union on the Negro question. The "Wear-Virginia-Cloth" campaign, and the fashionable "Calico Balls" in Richmond that launched it, would, Julia calculated, compel New York City to "follow the example of Boston and Philadelphia in making such demonstrations as will soothe the wounded South." [26]

In spite of young Gardie's prediction that "the times are very threatening and I do not think there is much hope of a reconciliation between the North and the South," the "wounded South" was gradually soothed. "Old Brown" went to his doom, reaping, said the angry Julia, "the miserable consequence of his shameful outrage." Conservative Democratic newspapers in the North, like the pro-Southern New York *Express*, mounted shrill attacks on Brown and the abolitionists. The *Express*, said Tyler, "is really battling the cause for the South bravely." Julia was pleased to learn that unionist meetings and rallies in New York City and on Staten Island had received the full support of her mother. The Shelter Island branch of the family also followed the Southern line during the Harpers Ferry crisis, urging sectional conciliation and an end to abolitionist provocations. On the other hand, Julia was disturbed to hear from her mother that David Lyon had refused to sign the call for a union meeting held on Staten Island in mid-December. Inexplicably, he had also refused to endorse a formal denunciation of abolitionist excesses emerging from the rally. This meeting, sponsored by Virginia expatriate W. Farley Grey and an organization called "Friends of the Union and Constitution," convinced Sherwood Forest, nevertheless, in Grey's words, that "the feeling here in New York is all we could wish. An army of fifty thousand, I am persuaded, could be raised here at the tap of a drum to march to your aid if necessary. Many are as violent as any Southern man could be." Whatever David Lyon's refusal to sustain incipient Copperheadism on Staten Island boded for the future harmony of the family, Julia and Tyler were confident by February 1860 that the threat of actual secession had passed.[27]

Neither Tidewater Virginia nor Sherwood Forest was ever again quite the same after the Harpers Ferry upheaval. The relative merits of union and secession were debated with such emotional fury throughout Charles City and in nearby Richmond that few social functions could be held without the sectional crisis injecting itself into the gaiety. Everywhere nervous Virginians looked they saw abolitionist plots unfolding. A Richmond reception held in February 1860 at the Exchange Hotel in honor of Commissioner Christopher G. Memminger of South Carolina (dispatched to Virginia to address the state legislature on joint Southern defense plans against future Brown raids) was ruined when one of the guests, a spurious Roman Catholic "priest" from Massachusetts, was detected circulating among the Negro waiters, encouraging them to enter the ballroom and dance with the ladies present. This, he whispered to them, was their "right." The sham ecclesiastic was challenged and severely beaten by outraged gentlemen at the reception. He barely managed to flee the building before the police arrived, and he was run out of town the next day. As Julia evaluated the incident, it conclusively proved that "Northern intermeddlers have not ceased their mischief." [28]

Even polite parlor conversation could produce explosions. In March 1860, for example, the drawing room at Sherwood Forest very nearly became the scene of a fist fight when two of Tyler's neighbors, the Reverend Dr. Wade, the local Episcopal clergyman, and planter John Clopton angrily exchanged words on Governor Wise's handling of the Brown affair. Wade, an outspoken Whig and unionist, argued that Wise had over-reacted to the Harpers Ferry incident, needlessly contributing to the tension by placing Virginia on a virtual war footing. The governor had, Wade charged, misrepresented the relative calm prevailing at Harpers Ferry after Brown's capture in order to whip up support throughout the state for a militant policy of anti-abolitionism. At this point Clopton sprang from his chair, fists clenched, shouting: "I have no opinion of clergymen coming from the pulpit to make themselves Sunday evening politicians and slander and accuse of perjury such a man as Governor Wise whose honor and word I have never heard doubted by his bitterest political opponents." Fortunately, no blows were struck. Tyler and his wife clearly sided with Clopton, however. Julia thought he had acted with "a spirit and independence truly becoming," while Tyler dismissed the thrust of Wade's arguments with the observation that the clergyman was a fuzzy-minded Federalist who had "married for his second wife one of the granddaughters of Chief Justice Marshall." Obviously a bad sort.[29]

Parlor heroics of the Wade-Clopton type pointed up the fact that Virginians were badly divided on the political issues of the hour after the John Brown affair. The most dangerous legacy of the Brown incident was its tendency in Virginia, and throughout the South, to polarize and then freeze opinions; to reduce complex sectional questions to the deceptive either-or simplicity of union or secession, abolitionism or civil war. These post-Harpers Ferry pressures drove many Southern moderates, caught in a no man's land of verbal cannonading between sectional extremists, into frightened silence or pell-mell into the South's extremist camp.

Other moderates, like Tyler, were fearful that if the Republicans managed to win the election of 1860 that event alone would trigger a civil war by converting thousands of Southern moderates into secessionists overnight, particularly if the new party nominated and elected abolitionist William H. Seward as President. Seward's October 1859 statement that the sectional controversy was an "irrepressible conflict" which could only lead to a United States "either entirely a slaveholding nation or entirely a free-labor nation" provided Dixie moderates few straws to grasp in their desire for a long-range sectional accommodation.

To John Tyler the main question in 1859–1860 was no longer whether slavery could or could not expand legally into the territories. Although the Dred Scott decision of March 1857 declared that the institution could expand, the controversial Supreme Court ruling had elated Tyler not at all. Southern extremists, of course, cheered it as a great victory. The whole argument over the legal status of slavery in the territories remained to Tyler a "mere abstraction" since from a practical standpoint the further expansion of slavery was topographically, climatically, and politically impossible. He had not been outraged by the popular-sovereignty concept espoused as an article of political faith by Douglas and the Northern Democracy at the time of the Kansas-Nebraska controversy. Nor in 1858 did he share the South's horror when Stephen A. Douglas, in his famous debate with Lincoln, announced his so-called Freeport Doctrine, that politically motivated clarification of popular sovereignty which argued that the people of a territory could, in spite of the Dred Scott decision, lawfully exclude slavery from their midst *prior* to drawing up a state constitution and applying for admission to the Union. That Douglas was prepared to subordinate legalistic abstractions to practical realities ("Slavery cannot exist a day or an hour anywhere unless it is supported by local police regulations," he maintained) infuriated Southern extremists and undoubtedly cost the Little Giant the nomination of a united Democracy in 1860.

Tyler did not support Douglas' final bid for the White House. But neither was he infected by the divisive anti-Douglas hydrophobia that broke out south of the Potomac as the Presidential campaign got under way. On the contrary, his political behavior immediately before the crucial election of 1860 was conditioned almost entirely by his belief that abolitionist radicals would eventually seize control of the overtly sectional and rapidly growing Republican Party. By exercising a tyranny of the majority in Congress, and ultimately in the Supreme Court, they would soon be in a position to legislate and adjudicate slavery out of existence in Southern states, where it had long been an economically viable and constitutional institution.

Tyler was willing to go far toward adjusting the slavery controversy peacefully. He was willing to surrender a great deal to prevent a civil war. He had accepted the ominous upset of the Free State-Slave State political balance of power inherent in the Compromise of 1850 and in the popular-sovereignty basis of the Kansas-Nebraska Act of 1854. He strenuously opposed Southern demands in the late 1850s that the infamous African slave trade be revived and legalized. In this unpopular stand (among the extremists at least) he defended the rightness and morality of the antislave trade article of his Webster-Ashburton Treaty when it came under severe attack by Southern fire-eaters in 1857–1858. But Tyler could not accept the prospect of a Charles City County dominated by emancipated Negroes, with or without financial compensation to their owners. Nor could he accept the risk of a "Black Republican" Congress or an abolitionist-oriented Supreme Court depriving him at some future date of his private property while it subjugated the owners to the owned. He did not want secession or civil war, but at the same time he could not abide the social and economic dislocations implicit in abolition.

As viewed from the quiet of the Sherwood Forest piazza, the only sure bulwark between these multiple dangers and the maintenance of the *status quo* along the lower James was the continued unification of the Democratic Party under the permissive leadership of its pro-slavery Pierces and Buchanans, however innocuous and inefficient these men might prove to be as Presidents. The long-range solution, as Tyler saw it, was essentially political. The Republicans must not win the Presidency in 1860—or for that matter, ever. At the same time, he was realistic in believing that no Southern Democrat could ever again hope to gain the White House. "I am the last of the Virginia Presidents," he lamented in July 1858. "The times indicate that the South has but little out of the line of commerce to give the North but the patronage of government to ensure the support of the latter." Instead, the South would have to pin its future hopes on Northern or border-state Democrats who leaned safely southward. This was the best the beleaguered section could expect.[30]

In spite of these realistic views and his accurate impression that Virginia's Governor Henry Wise was far too ultra on the slavery issue to capture the White House, Tyler privately supported Wise for the Democratic Presidential nomination during the spring of 1859. More than anything else this gesture was an act of personal loyalty. He still felt a substantial personal debt to Wise for his enlistment in the Corporal's Guard of 1841–1842. And in the Wise-Letcher gubernatorial campaign of 1859 the governor, as he had in 1856, took special pains to praise Tyler for Texas annexation and his bank vetoes. "My acts while in the White House and my course of conduct in office has been extensively canvassed ... my name has become more familiar to the lips of the many than since I left Washington," he told Robert proudly. Convinced that Buchanan himself had no chance of renomination (Bloody Kansas and Dred Scott had settled that), Tyler in May 1859 began urging a Henry Wise-Robert Tyler ticket. Indeed, the former President argued that his eldest son should take advantage of his longstanding connection with the politically doomed Buchanan and, utilizing his chairmanship of the Pennsylvania Democratic State Central Committee, commence a serious campaign for the Vice-Presidential nomination. Were this drive successful (and Tyler dispatched much unsolicited political advice to Philadelphia to insure its success), Robert would anchor to northward a sectionally balanced ticket. This would re-create the Virginia-Pennsylvania coalition that had held the disintegrating Democracy together in 1856. "The only possible objection to the union of *your* two names at Charleston is in the fact of the birthplace of both being Virginia—but that objection is easily met." Just how, Tyler did not say.[31]

Wise's ultraism on the slavery question was, however, approaching outright secessionism. This and his increasingly angry attacks on the wishy-washiness of the Buchanan administration caused dismay at Sherwood Forest. Wise was talking himself out of any possible consideration for the Democratic nomination. Thus when Robert told his father that a Wise-Tyler ticket was "totally out of the question" because there were "forty men the Democratic Party would sooner take," Tyler quietly abandoned the extremist governor and gave ear to the faint rumblings of a tiny boomlet for the squire of Sherwood Forest himself.

In response to Robert's conviction that "Virginia can make *you* the President if she will," Tyler admitted in July 1859 that he was receiving "daily assurances from plain men of an anxious desire on their part to restore me to the presidency." At first he paid little attention to these unorganized importunities. "I could not improve upon my past career," he declared flatly. But by October 1859 his popularity in Virginia seemed so solid and enthusiasm for his moderate approach to the slavery issue seemed so broadly based that he began seriously to weigh his prospects as a compromise nominee should the Charleston convention, scheduled for April 1860, reach a deadlock. "I verily believe," he said somewhat immodestly, "that I should at this day meet with more enthusiasm from the rank and file than has occurred since Jackson's time." Fearful that a divided convention might well prove "the grave of the Democratic party," he therefore encouraged the formation of a small committee to direct the Tyler movement. And in the classic manner of all American politicians seeking to project a disinterested availability, he began cautiously to tell those of his friends who asked him whether he would accept the nomination that "it will be time enough to respond when it takes place." To a certain extent he coveted a nomination for the contribution it would make to his historical reputation. It would be valuable to Clio's recollection of John Tyler whether he won the White House or not. "The historic page is the most that I look to," he told Robert on October 6, "and that would be embellished by the thing and would impart to it value." The thought of actually sitting in the Presidential chair once again gave him pause. "Things are, too, terribly out of sorts, and he who undertakes to put them right would assume or have thrown upon him a fearful responsibility." Nevertheless, he pushed forward with what he called his "movement." There was the barest possibility that the Virginia delegation to Charleston, unable to unite on either Wise or Senator R. M. T. Hunter as the Old Dominion's favorite-son candidate, might toss his name into the ring as Virginia's compromise favorite-son nominee for a compromise Democratic nomination.[32]

The Tyler movement of 1859 was headed by A. Dudley Mann of Washington, editor James D. B. De Bow of the influential *De Bow's Review*, and the Reverend Father James Ryder, S.J., former president of Georgetown College in the District of Columbia. De Bow opened the columns of his magazine to John Tyler, Jr., and John, under the pseudonyms *Python* and *Tau*, supplied articles which praised his father's administration while suggesting that only John Tyler was experienced enough and moderate enough to cope with the gathering storm. Father Ryder served the minuscule Tyler crusade as liaison with the Northern Roman Catholic community long assiduously wooed by Robert Tyler in his capacity as president of the Irish Repeal Association in Philadelphia. This, then, was the politically obscure triad which planned to make "Honest John" Tyler "available" for the Democratic nomination should a fortuitous combination of factors and flukes at Charleston produce another lucky turn of the wheel for "His Accidency." These men, said Tyler, should plan to be on hand at Charleston when the convention met. When the iron of deadlock was hot they could strike.

Tyler meanwhile did all the things a dark-horse candidate was expected to do. He let it be known that he would certainly support Buchanan if the President was renominated by the party; he reminded the friends of Henry Wise that his longstanding political obligation to the governor had not weakened; he remained scrupulously quiet in public on the controversial issues of the moment; and he predicted that a Democratic split in 1860 would surely bring the hated and feared "Black Republicans" to power. Under no conditions, thought Tyler, should the Democracy therefore risk adopting a platform at its forthcoming Charleston convention. Not only was a platform "at most a useless thing," but it would surely atomize the party. "We had in 1839–'40 far greater dissensions at Harrisburg, and a platform would have scattered us to the winds," he recalled.[33]

The Harpers Ferry crisis in Virginia did nothing to harm the Tyler movement. It did however severely damage extremist Wise's favorite-son prospects for the nomination while strengthening those of Senator Hunter and Tyler. More significantly, the resulting talk of secession in the South stimulated speculation in New York City, within Tammany and among various old-line Conservative Democrats in Gotham, that the Democracy could bring forward no stronger compromise candidate in 1860 than experienced John Tyler. With visions of a Virginia-New York political alliance that might sustain Democratic conservative principles and prevent a party split, Robert Tyler, Prosper M. Wetmore, and other former Tyler leaders in New York began working to transform this casual talk into something politically solid. For a brief and exciting moment the ambitious Julia was encouraged to believe that her husband's public career was about to bloom again. The serious illness of Stephen Douglas' wife in November 1859 would, she felt, "check Douglas' wish for the Presidency" and open the field to a Southern candidate. The distaff optimism at Sherwood Forest was further encouraged when editor John S. Cunningham of Portsmouth came to the support of the Tyler cause in Virginia. While Julia did not go to the extreme of planning the details of another White House reign, she did inform her mother, in March 1860, that her husband was being talked of "very freely as being the second choice of at least three candidates. Wise, Hunter and Douglas, *they say*, will all turn to him if they each find there is no chance for themselves, and all these you know, are bitterly opposed to one another.... The President seems to have outlived the abuse of his enemies, and is every day more and more properly appreciated by all parties." [34]

Unfortunately for Julia's renewed dream of the Presidential Mansion, the Tyler "boom" collapsed as quickly and quietly as it had been launched. Wise's loss of the governorship to the moderate if not outright unionist John Letcher in the fall of 1859 brought R. M. T. Hunter gradually to the fore as Virginia's most likely favorite-son candidate at the Charleston convention. His skillful direction of the compromise 1857 tariff bill through the Senate had won Hunter many friends and supporters in the North, and his relative temperateness on the sectional controversy commended him to many Virginia Democrats who, like Governor-elect Letcher, saw no future in political extremism. With the decline of the fire-eating Henry A. Wise and the emergence of the obviously more available Hunter, nothing more was heard of the possible candidacy of John Tyler. At a banquet in Richmond on April 12, 1860, honoring the memory of Henry Clay, Tyler removed himself from any further consideration as Virginia's candidate for the Democratic nomination, citing (and slightly doctoring to fit the situation) those lines from Poe's "To One in Paradise" which ran:

> Alas! alas! for me!
> Ambition all is o'er;
> No more—no more—no more—
> (Such language holds the solemn sea
> To the sands upon the shore)
> Shall bloom the thunder-blasted tree;
> Or stricken eagle soar.[35]

On April 23, the day the Democracy convened at Charleston for the purpose of committing political suicide, the Stricken Eagle left his

437

Sherwood Forest aerie for what would be his last trip to the North. The occasion was the belated marriage of David Lyon Gardiner to Sarah Griswold Thompson, a respectable New York lady whose humorlessness was exceeded only by her considerable wealth. Julia, seven months pregnant, was not well enough to make the trip. Nor was her enthusiasm for the match high. She therefore confined her modest contribution to suggesting what prominent Virginians David Lyon might invite to the ceremony. The marriage was also opposed by the matriarchal Juliana, who consented to it only when her forty-three-year-old son promised to move with his bride into the Gardiner home at Castleton Hill. Two earlier engagements had been broken off by David Lyon when the ladies in question had categorically refused to accept such an arrangement. The thirty-year-old Sarah Thompson consented to the cloying conditions involved. She knew nothing whatever about housekeeping or cooking. She had never even dressed herself for a formal occasion without the aid of a servant. She was quite willing, therefore, to have her mother-in-law usurp her function as housewife. She and David Lyon also consented to having Juliana bear the entire cost of maintaining them at Castleton Hill. Needless to say, this capitulation to rampant momism gave the lonely Juliana an opportunity to manage the private lives of the couple literally down to and including detailed instructions on how best to put the cat out for the night. To make matters even more difficult, the sixty-one-year-old Juliana had, by 1860, come under the influence of spiritualism and was beginning to "talk" regularly with her departed husband and with Alexander and Margaret. Her migraine headaches also became worse and more frequent with her advancing years. Were this not enough, additional tensions were introduced into the West New Brighton household when it became evident that David Lyon and Sarah were as pro-Northern as Juliana and the Tylers were pro-Southern.[36]

By the time John Tyler returned to Sherwood Forest from the wedding in early May the political situation had taken an ominous turn. Unable to agree on either platform or candidate, the Democratic convention in Charleston had broken up in chaos and confusion. Northern Democrats would not accept a platform plank declaring it the *duty* of the federal government to protect slavery in the territories, and Southern Democrats would accept nothing less. Enough delegates from the Deep South finally walked out to make it mathematically impossible for Stephen A. Douglas, the leading candidate for the nomination, to amass the necessary two-thirds majority for selection. Fifty-eight ballots availed the Little Giant nothing. Before adjourning, the delegates voted to convene again in Baltimore on June 18 and have another try at nominating a candidate acceptable to all factions. Meanwhile, the seceders from the shattered convention moved to another hall in Charleston, chose Delaware Senator James A. Bayard their chairman, and adopted a platform that was uncompromisingly pro-slavery. They decided, however, to withhold a Presidential nomination until the reconvened Democratic convention had acted in Baltimore in June. To insure the choice of a man acceptable to the extremist South they voted to hold their own watchdog convention in Richmond on June 11.

The centrifugal developments in Charleston struck Tyler as extremely dangerous and unwise. The Democracy's bitter split filled him with "apprehension and regret," and he could only hope that the Baltimore convention would somehow magically produce a reunified party able to salvage American conservatism and prevent the election of a radical Republican. The strategy of the Southern delegates at Charleston he considered stupid and self-defeating. Either they should have *all* remained in the convention hall and pressed for the nomination of "someone whose name would have constituted a platform in itself," or they should have *all* walked out together and instantly nominated a South-leaning Northerner like Joseph Lane of Oregon or James Bayard of Delaware. They had done neither. Instead, they had "played the game badly by throwing away their trump card," their unity of action as a solid sectional bloc.[37]

That unity of action would be needed to prevent the triumph of "Black Republicanism" became more apparent on May 9 when a polyglot group of moderate Northern and Southern Whigs combined with a body of Union Democrats and the remnants of the shattered Know-Nothing sect in the South to launch the Constitutional Union Party. The new group nominated John Bell of Tennessee and Edward Everett of Massachusetts on a purposely vague platform calling for the Union, the Constitution and the enforcement of the laws. Designed as it was to rally moderates on both sides of the Mason-Dixon line with a call for peace and patriotism, particularly moderates in the border states, the Constitutional Union Party, whatever its ideological fuzziness, was definitely more acceptable to Tyler than was the Republican Party which met in Chicago on May 16 and nominated Abraham Lincoln.

The Republican platform, demanding as it did an end to slavery expansion in the territories, the admission of Kansas as a free state, and the revocation of the Dred Scott decision, struck Southern extremists as little less than a call to arms. Tyler's reaction was much calmer and more reasonable than this. After all, the Republican platform also called for the preservation of the Union, disavowed abolitionism, and condemned armed attacks on the South in the John Brown manner. Too, the Republicans had passed over the (by Southern lights) wild-eyed abolitionist William H. Seward, and had nominated instead the moderate and relatively unknown Abraham Lincoln. No missionary for the radical notion of racial equality, Lincoln was mainly opposed to the further extension of Negro slavery into the territories. In spite of his rather inflammatory "House Divided" speech of June 1858 he was willing to accept the institution where it legally and traditionally existed. In this sense, he was certainly no recruit to the abolitionist stand on the Negro question.

For these reasons Tyler did not panic when news of the Republican platform and Lincoln's nomination reached Sherwood Forest. He was not happy about it, but he did not fly off in all directions as did so many Southern slaveowners. Instead, he worried principally about the reaction of the lunatic fringe in the Deep South should Honest Abe be elected. "The consequences of Lincoln's election I cannot foretell," he wrote Robert in July. "Neither Virginia, nor North Carolina, nor Maryland (to which you may add Kentucky, Tennessee and Missouri) will secede for that. My apprehension, however, is that South Carolina and others of the cotton States will do so, and any attempt to coerce such seceding States will most probably be resisted by all the South." [38]

The probability of Lincoln's election loomed large when the Democracy failed to heal its wounds at the reconvened Baltimore convention in June. Once again the Southerners present walked out in anger, leaving the Northern Democracy to nominate Stephen A. Douglas on a platform which reaffirmed the 1856 Cincinnati platform and assigned the specific problems of slavery and slaves in the territories to Supreme Court adjudication. This was neither a radical nor an anti-Southern program. But because it failed to demand that the federal government actively protect slavery in the territories, the Southern extremists bolted the convention and the party. The dissidents promptly convened nearby and, with Caleb Cushing in the chair, nominated the conciliatory John C. Breckinridge of Kentucky for President and the pro-Southern Joseph Lane of Oregon for Vice-President. Vigorous federal protection of slavery in the slave states and in the territories was demanded by the splinter party in its platform. The Breckinridge-Lane ticket, more moderate in personnel than in the platform it was forced to transport as baggage, was promptly endorsed by the rump Democratic convention meeting simultaneously in Richmond. With this action the Democracy was hopelessly and irretrievably split.

Tyler surveyed the shambles of the Democratic Party first with alarm, then with stoic resignation. "I fear that the great Republic has seen its last days," he worried in August. Nevertheless, throughout the summer of 1860 he supported attempts in Virginia to create a Breckinridge-Douglas fusion ticket and similar efforts in New York to fashion a Bell-Douglas alliance. He deplored the sniping back and forth between Northern and Southern Democrats during the campaign, and between Douglas and Breckinridge he found "nothing to approve on either side." The defeat of Lincoln was "the great matter at issue," and he saw no hope for this "unless some one of the so-called free States is snatched from him." New York, he felt, was the great hope. As he explained the situation to David Lyon in October,

There is a deeper gloom resting on the country than I ever expected to see. Should New York rise up in her might, and declare against Lincoln, all will unite in ascribing to her great glory. She will, in truth, be hailed as the great conservative State. She will have rebuked the disorganizers, and imparted new vitality to our institutions. Should, however, the picture be reversed, and her great popular voice unite to swell the notes of triumph for the sectional hosts, then indeed will a dark and heavy cloud rest upon the face of the country.... Property has already fallen in value amongst us, and there is an obvious uneasiness in the minds of all men. I will not permit myself to abandon the hope that the cloud which hovers over us will be dispersed through the action of your large and powerful State. I am busily engaged in seeding a large crop of wheat. Shall I be permitted to reap it at its maturity in peace? Time will decide! [39]

Tyler reluctantly supported the Breckinridge candidacy, embarrassed in so doing to find himself making common cause with some of the worst fist-shakers in Dixie. While the logic of his convictions dictated his support of Bell and the Constitutional Unionists, he endorsed Breckinridge on the practical and arithmetical grounds that a vote in Virginia for John Bell was a wasted and divisive vote. If the Southern and border states could all be swung to Breckinridge, he reasoned, and if Lincoln should lose either New York or Pennsylvania to Douglas, the election would then be thrown into Congress, where practical politicians might successfully negotiate a peaceful solution. It was Tyler's fervent hope that neither Lincoln, Douglas, nor Breckinridge would secure the 152 electoral votes constituting a majority, and that Joseph Lane would somehow emerge from the trial in Congress as the compromise President of the United States. By this analysis, any electoral votes that Bell received would weaken both Douglas and Breckinridge, strengthen Lincoln, and frustrate Tyler's prayer that the November balloting would result in a neat standoff.[40]

In July and August 1860 this thinking was not unreasonable. Bell narrowly carried Virginia, Tennessee, and Kentucky, although in all three of these border states the combined Douglas-Breckinridge Democratic vote well exceeded the Constitutional Unionists' tally. Had Bell's 39 electoral votes been added to Breckinridge's 72, the Southern Democracy would have secured 111. And had the Douglas-Bell fusion ticket won in New York (it lost by 50,000 popular votes of the 775,000 cast), Lincoln's electoral count would have been reduced to 145, seven shy of a majority. It was the logic of this Electoral College numbers game that caused Tyler to deplore Southern attacks on Douglas ("You are too bitter on Douglas," he scolded Robert) and promote Douglas-Breckinridge fusions that would frustrate the divisive Bell movement. At the same time, he refrained from any attack on Lincoln. Instead, he concentrated his fire on Seward ("a more arch and wily conspirator does not live") and the Northern abolitionist extremists around Lincoln in the hope "that a defeat of the negro-men now will dissolve their party." He also attempted to link Seward to alleged British machinations to "foment sectional divisions among us" by sending over abolitionist agents and provocateurs. This, of course, was sheer campaign nonsense.[41]

The confused political situation cast a distinct pall of anxiety over the last summer vacation the family enjoyed together in peace at Villa Margaret. In the epicurean spirit of Phoebe Gardiner Horsford, who advised Julia that "we may as well have *good times* as long as we can," a determined effort was made to function normally and happily in the midst of loud predictions of secession and civil war should Lincoln be elected. Julia had made careful plans for the summer season and for her seventh accouchement that would open it. A change in personnel at Fortress Monroe assured a ready supply of new officers, "all equally agreeable and accomplished." Juliana and Harry Beeckman, now an active eleven-year-old, were expected to visit the Villa, Harry to join the play of Julia's own brood of six (she called them "my troop"), whom she pronounced "pictures of health and happiness ... all fat and rosy, gay as larks ... progressing and improving in all respects." In the meantime, Tyler's niece Patty, who had lived for several years at Sherwood Forest as Julia's companion, would be married in May 1860 and her place in the family circle would be taken by her sister Maria Tyler. This assured Julia a "useful intimate" as the time for her confinement approached in early June. She was determined to hold off the event until all had been made ready for her comfort at the Villa. "You may depend upon it I shall try to reach the seaside before the event transpires with me," she informed her mother. In mid-May Tyler was dispatched to Hampton with furniture and household goods and a knocked-down frame house that he erected on the property for the use of the body servants and house slaves making the trip.[42]

All was in readiness for Julia at Villa Margaret when she arrived there on May 25. Juliana reached Hampton on June 12; her presence was a signal that labor could officially begin. Julia therefore promptly delivered herself of a nine-and-a-half-pound baby girl at 9 A.M. on June 13. Save for a "nervous blind sick headache" the birth was accomplished without incident. At first it was decided to name the infant "Margaret Gardiner Tyler," but this nostalgic idea was dropped and the child was christened Pearl. Within a few days the hardy mother was up and around, the older children were happily shouting, playing, fishing, and crabbing again, and Tyler was commuting up to Sherwood Forest to supervise his wheat harvest.

Gardie and Alex, now fourteen and twelve respectively, accompanied their father to the harvest and while at Sherwood Forest took several hours' instruction each day at Mr. Ferguson's school in Charles City where they were in regular attendance during the winter months. Harry Beeckman and the school-age younger Tyler children attended as part-time students a small private school in Hampton during the summer months. It was conducted by a "well educated lady" from Baltimore, for young ladies seeking to become well educated. Harry strenuously objected to being sent to a "girls' school." He would have much preferred attending the highly regarded Hampton Academy nearby. Tyler was an honorary "Old Boy" of the institution, and in 1858 Julia had considered wintering at Hampton so that Gardie and Alex might attend the Academy as day pupils. Tyler did not "fancy staying at Sherwood alone," and he vetoed the idea with the clinching argument that the "air would be too severe for his health—the plantation being inland is milder." The Academy was military in its discipline, and from the porch at Villa Margaret the hundred-odd cadets, clad in gray uniforms, could be seen drilling and exercising. Occasionally Gardie and Alex would stroll over to watch the cadets perform, but neither of them gave any evidence at this time of a yearning for the military life.[43]

While the children combined vacations with educations, harvesting with French verbs, the adults picnicked, danced, and visited at the Fortress. Colonel Justin Dimick, USA, later brigadier general in command at Fort Warren Prison in Boston, was senior officer present that summer, and he did everything in his power to see that the former Commander-in-Chief, his wife, and his mother-in-law were entertained royally. In mid-August the British liner *Great Eastern,* largest iron ship ever built, visited Hampton Roads and provided the family a "merry and exciting" day of shipboard tourism. Julia, only eight weeks from childbed, clambered up and down the steep ladders with cautious indecision. But she managed it.[44]

By the time the family returned to Sherwood Forest in early October it appeared to Tyler that Lincoln would very likely win the election. The former President did not feel, however, that such an outcome would necessarily mean disunion. Indeed, on November 5 he advised his grandson, Cadet William G. Waller, not to resign from the plebe class at West Point "until Virginia had distinctly and plainly marked out her course after the election." Disunion was not inevitable, he instructed Waller, and there was also a practical military consideration involved in remaining at West Point: "May it not prove very injurious to the interests of the South for all the Southern young men to leave, thus giving exclusive command of the army, at least to the extent of the present classes, to the North? My advice is to stay where you are until events have fully developed themselves."[45]

Five days later, however, John Tyler was cast into gloom. "So all is over, and Lincoln elected. South Carolina will secede.... Virginia will abide developments.... For myself, I rest in quiet, and shall do so unless I see that my poor opinions have due weight." He was right. Lincoln was elected, receiving 180 electoral votes on 39.8 per cent of the popular vote. The South Carolina legislature immediately called for a state convention which, several weeks later, on December 20, passed an ordinance of secession without a dissenting vote. In a "Declaration of Immediate Causes" issued on December 24 the aroused Carolinians called attention to Lincoln's 1858 "House Divided" speech as damning evidence of the President-elect's intractability on the slavery question. "A house divided against itself cannot stand," Lincoln had remarked. "I believe this government cannot endure permanently half slave and half free. I do not expect the Union to be dissolved; I do not expect the house to fall; but I do expect it will cease to be divided. It will become all one thing, or all the other." This enigmatic utterance which carefully avoided any specifics on the how or the when, was (and has since been) interpreted in a variety of ways. Suffice it to say here that the South Carolina radicals in December 1860 preferred to view it as a virtual declaration of sectional war. Their action in Charleston was also justified with the further argument that the North had long attacked the slavery institution and that a crudely sectional party had finally seized power under the leadership of a President-elect "whose opinions and purposes are hostile to slavery." That Lincoln's opinions were not hostile to slavery as such, that his purposes with regard to it were far from formed, was not the point. The lunatic fringe in South Carolina took the bit in its teeth and ran crazily away. From Northern abolitionists came shrill demands for instant and bloody retaliation against the South Carolina secessionists.

In the midst of the immediate postelection confusion, Tyler attempted to maintain some degree of emotional and intellectual equilibrium. He found this increasingly difficult to do as extremist bleatings in one section triggered extremist counterblasts in the other. Writing to his old friend Dr. Silas Reed on November 16, he lamented that

We have fallen on evil times ... the day of doom for the great model Republic is at hand. Madness rules the hour, and statesmanship ... gives place to a miserable demagogism which leads to inevitable destruction.... The fate of the Union trembles in the balance. Ever since a senator, regardless of his oath to sustain the Constitution, set up a law for each man above the Constitution, I foresaw that the game of demagogism and treason was fairly started, and that unless arrested it would end in ruin.... In the midst of all this I remain quiescent. No longer an actor on the stage of public affairs, I leave to others younger than myself the settlement of existing disputes... sometimes I think it would be better for all peaceably to separate.... I sigh over the degeneracy of the times....

As the sigh escaped his lips Tyler did not lose sight of what the sectional controversy was at bottom all about. To be sure, states' rights was part of the problem, but only because it was related to the more deeply rooted slavery question. Concluding his letter to Reed was a paragraph, omitted from the 1885 version printed by his biographer, Lyon G. Tyler, which indicated Tyler's primary concern with the Negro problem in Charles City County and throughout Virginia:

Nor can I say what course Virginia will adopt.... On one thing I think you may rely, that she will never consent to have her blacks cribbed and confined within proscribed and specified limits—and thus be involved in all the consequences of a war of the races in some 20 or 30 years. She must have expansion, and if she cannot obtain for herself and sisters that expansion in the Union, she may sooner or later look to Mexico, the West India Islands and Central America as the ultimate reservations of the African race. But now everything is reversed, and no more Slave States has apparently become the shibboleth of Northern political faith.[46]

Earlier, of course, Tyler had been quite willing to accept the prospect of "no more Slave States." His position on the Compromise of 1850 and on the Kansas-Nebraska Act demonstrated that beyond question. That he was now, for the first time, seriously proposing slavery expansion as a fundamental condition for the preservation of the Union provides an accurate barometric measure of the panic that swept Charles City County in the first weeks following Lincoln's election. Relatively speaking, Tyler remained less agitated than some of his neighbors, but he too began evidencing signs of the political hypertension that seized Tidewater Virginia as South Carolina prepared to secede. Within four months Tyler himself would become a leader in Virginia's secession movement. His conversion to this position was dictated by military rather than political considerations. Nevertheless, the metamorphosis in his thinking began shortly after South Carolina departed the Union on December 20.

Virginia, to be sure, was predominantly unionist in sentiment during these trying months. The state had gone for Bell over Breckinridge by 74,681 to 74,323 in November. Douglas had polled 16,290, mainly in the western counties, and even Lincoln had commanded 1929 votes. The election of 1860 in the Old Dominion was no mandate for secession, no call for radical experimentation with the organic structure of the federal government. In the Tidewater counties, however, particularly in Charles City where the Negroes so decisively outnumbered the whites, there was alarm. Renewed visions of John Browns descending upon Virginia produced nightmares along the lower James. To these fears Tyler was not immune. Indeed, he frankly advised his neighbors to prepare for the worst. They should sell their slaves outright or move with them into the Deep South, where the germs of Northern abolitionism would be less likely to infect the master-slave relationship. This was advice for others, advice he would not follow himself. He considered his obligation to his own slaves based on something more elevated than a mere property relationship. For this reason he felt a strong and continuing moral obligation to stand by and protect their physical and material welfare, come what may. He was determined, therefore, neither to sell his servants south nor abandon his plantation, although given the severe drought and bad harvests of 1858–1860 it would have been to his financial advantage to have liquidated his slave property at the high prices then prevailing in the lower South. Instead, John Tyler stood firm, hoping that some compromise political solution to the sectional controversy would appear, one that would guarantee the private property of the plantation aristocracy from abolitionist expropriation and in so doing preserve the social and racial *status quo* of the Charles City neighborhood.[47]

Firsthand reports reaching Sherwood Forest from the Deep South permitted little optimism that such a compromise would be allowed to emerge. In mid-December 1860 Tyler's neighbor and physician, Dr. James Selden, returned to Charles City from a survey trip through Alabama, Georgia and South Carolina. He had gone there, on Tyler's advice, to study prospects for moving his plantation and his slaves to the cotton belt. He brought back to Sherwood Forest the disturbing news, as Julia relayed it, that "the South is perfectly ripe for secession. ... The South Carolina ladies say they would rather be widows of secessionists than wives of submissionists! and that they will never again attend a ball in the *United States*. Blue cockades are as thick as *hops*...." Still, the mistress of Sherwood hoped that "the Union on a right and just basis will be preserved," and Tyler took pen in hand to plead anew for sectional harmony. "It is the duty of every citizen," he wrote, "however profound his retirement from public affairs, and whatever may have been his position in relation to them and the country in other days, to contribute his best efforts to restore harmony when discord prevails, and aid in rescuing the country from danger." By December 14, less than a week before South Carolina finally seceded, Tyler had matured a tentative plan for sectional unity, although by this date he was beginning to blame the deepening crisis more on the Northern extremists than on the Charleston hotheads. As he explained the tragic situation to Caleb Cushing,

I confess that I am lost in perfect amazement at the lunacy which seems to have seized the North. What imaginable good is to come to them by compelling the Southern States into secession? I see great benefits to foreign governments, but nothing but prostration and woe to New England. Virginia looks on for the present with her arms folded, but she only bides her time. Despondency will be succeeded by action. My own mind is greatly disturbed. I look around in every direction for a conservative principle, but I have so far looked in vain. I have thought that a consultation between the Border States, free and slaveholding, might lead to adjustment. It would embrace six on each side. They are most interested in keeping the peace, and if they cannot come to an understanding, then the political union is gone.... When all things else have failed, this might be tried. It would be a *dernier ressort*.[48]

It was.

18

FROM PEACE TO PARADISE
1861–1862

These are dark times, dearest, and I think only of you and our little ones.... I shall vote secession.
—JOHN TYLER, APRIL 16, 1861

John Tyler was not the only American casting about for a *dernier ressort* to stave off civil war. In his last Annual Message to Congress on December 3, 1860, Buchanan blamed the crisis on the "long-continued and intemperate interference of the Northern people with the question of slavery in the Southern States" and offered a three-point pacification proposal to this end in the form of an amendment to the Constitution which would recognize slavery as a property right where it already existed, provide federal protection of slavery in the territories until such time as a given territory elected to enter the Union as a free state, and uphold the right of a master to have his runaway slave promptly returned to him through the police action of the federal government. In the same breath, the nervous Buchanan (desiring little more than to get safely out of office before the dam broke) confessed his belief that the "Executive has no authority to decide what shall be the relations between the Federal Government and South Carolina.... He possesses no power to change the relations heretofore existing between them." Not surprisingly, these tired proposals from a supine administration caused little stir among the political literati of the North. Still, they struck Tyler as reasonable. Encouraged by Buchanan's modest example, he offered on December 14 his own proposal for a peace convention of the twelve border states, six slave and six free.[1]

As the former President matured his plan and began soliciting support for it in Richmond political circles, Senator John J. Crittenden of Kentucky offered a peace resolution in the Senate on December 18, two days before South Carolina formally seceded. The resolution contained as its central feature the legalization and recognition of slavery in all territories south of 36°30′. Under the proposed Crittenden amendment to the Constitution, states formed from territories below 36°30′ could enter the Union slave or free as their inhabitants decreed, but until such decision was rendered by the territorials themselves, slavery was legal in and could extend into areas south of 36°30′. This projected revitalization of the Missouri Compromise which had been repealed by the Kansas-Nebraska Act and declared unconstitutional in the Dred Scott decision, Lincoln could not accept. He was unalterably opposed to any further extension of slavery even if extension was accomplished by democratic means. The Republican platform had been clear on this point, and Lincoln had campaigned on the platform. Consequently, the joint Senate committee appointed to consider the Crittenden proposal was hopelessly deadlocked by December 31. "No ray of light yet appears to dispel the gloom which has settled upon the country," Tyler wrote David Lyon on New Year's Day. "A blow struck would be the signal for united action with all the slave States, whereas the grain States of the border are sincerely desirous of reconciling matters and thereby preserving the Union. . . . They are so deeply interested in preserving friendly relations. . . ."[2]

Events moved swiftly as the new year opened. Between January 9 and January 19 Mississippi, Alabama, Georgia, and Florida all seceded and, following South Carolina's example, seized federal forts and arsenals as they departed the Union. On January 5 Buchanan dispatched the unarmed *Star of the West* to Charleston harbor to reinforce and provision the small garrison at Fort Sumter, still in federal hands. The ship was fired upon and turned back on January 9, and a confused Buchanan resumed playing the role of an undulating cobra transfixed by secessionist flutes. This nonprovocative White House policy, virtually paralytic in its effect, Tyler considered a "wise and statesmanlike course." He was willing to appease the South Carolina radicals without shame if such a policy would buy cooling-off time, however little. On January 15 his advocacy of appeasement seemed justified when the Virginia General Assembly proposed that a peace convention of all the states convene in Washington on February 4. Although this mitigatory gesture was largely the legislative work of Governor John Letcher and William C. Rives, Tyler's behind-the-scenes work in the Virginia peace movement was so prominent that in a very real sense he was the father of the peace convention.[3]

Paternity has its problems as well as its joys. The specific proposal passed by the General Assembly seemed to Tyler a horribly misshapen child. Unfortunately, Virginia had called for a convention of *all* the states. Tyler, conversely, favored a convention of commissioners from twelve "border" states— New Jersey, Pennsylvania, Ohio, Indiana, Illinois, and Michigan from among the free states; Delaware, Maryland, Virginia, Kentucky, Tennessee, and Missouri to represent the slave states. Correctly seeing that a convention of all the states would merely add to the number of extremists present from both sections and would produce an administratively unmanageable bedlam, the former President marched into the columns of the Richmond *Enquirer* for January 17 to call loudly for the smaller, more efficient convention. If the twelve border states could agree, Tyler argued, "I think their recommendation will be followed by the other States and incorporated into the Constitution.... If they cannot agree, then it may safely be concluded that the restoration of peace and concord has become impossible." The bloody alternative to speedy accommodation Tyler also outlined to his fellow Virginians:

If the Free and Slave States cannot live in harmony together... does not the dictate of common sense admonish to a separation in peace? Better so than a perpetual itch of irritation and ill feeling. Far better than an unnatural war between the sections.... Grant that one section shall conquer the other, what reward will be reaped by the victor? The conqueror will walk at every step over smoldering ashes and beneath crumbling columns.... Ruin and desolation will everywhere prevail, and the victor's brow, instead of a wreath of glorious evergreen... will be encircled with withered and faded leaves bedewed with the blood of the child and its mother and the father and the son. The picture is too horrible and revolting to be dwelt upon.[4]

The picture was horrible and revolting. For this reason Tyler suggested that should a convention fail, the secessionist states should be permitted their exit from the Union in peace. These departed states, he felt, might then convene, adopt the United States Constitution as their own constitution, amend it with "guarantees going not one iota beyond what strict justice and the security of the South require," and then invite the other states "to enter our Union with the old flag flying over one and all." This interesting if wholly impractical idea had the advantage of confusing the question of just who would be seceding from whom, and Tyler apparently offered it to delay and complicate the formulation of a legal basis for federal military coercion should the sectional crisis come to that. In mid-January 1861 he was still willing to buy peace at nearly any price and he was anxious to frustrate any prospect of armed intervention.[5]

On the very day Tyler's appeal for a twelve-state peace convention saw print in Richmond, the legislatures of Pennsylvania and Ohio, two of Tyler's "border" states, were reported in Virginia papers as having offered troops and funds to the federal government to subjugate the seceded states. At the same time, the General Assembly in Richmond rejected Tyler's convention concept and voted for a conference of all the states. "The course of the Pennsylvania and Ohio Legislatures...

leaves but little hope of any adjustment," he wrote Robert in dismay. "The Legislature of Virginia have so trammelled their [peace] convention bill that I fear that we shall have a doubtful result." Since none of the five already seceded states would be likely to send delegates to such a conference (they did not), the rump conclave could scarcely be expected to restore the Union. Further, the free states would have such a pronounced majority in the convention that no truly meaningful dialogue could be expected to take place.[6]

Gloomy as the future seemed, Tyler reluctantly accepted appointment as one of Virginia's five commissioners to the peace convention. His colleagues were James A. Seddon, William C. Rives, John W. Brockenbrough, and George W. Summers. Summers and Rives were moderate Constitutional Unionists; Seddon was a fire-eating Virginia secessionist; Brockenbrough was more moderate than Seddon but tended to lean toward the secessionist point of view. Tyler, of course, was still a moderate, albeit a frightened one, in search of some panacea that would prevent federal military coercion of the seceded states. If that happened, he reasoned, Virginia's secession was inevitable and with it a civil war. He wanted to preserve the Union and keep Virginia in it, but not at the price of having his slave property liberated around his ears, or at the cost of having to watch federal troops march through Virginia en route to slaughter South Carolinians and Georgians. His, it will be remembered, was the only vote against Jackson's Force Bill in 1833.

Given the temper and confusion of the times, Virginia's delegation to the peace convention was remarkably well-balanced in attitude. It fairly represented a state in which sectional opinions ranged from predominantly secessionist in the eastern Tidewater to predominantly unionist on the Ohio River. All shades and intensities of viewpoint were to be found between these terminal points and even at both ends of the geographic scale. Nor did the General Assembly's instructions to the Virginia delegates manifest overt extremism. They were directed to work for peace along the general lines of the Crittenden compromise resolutions, the principles of which Tyler had already endorsed.[7]

On the day Tyler was named a peace commissioner, January 19, he was also appointed Virginia's special commissioner to President Buchanan. Similarly, Judge John Robertson was dispatched to Charleston as special commissioner to the seceded states. Both men were instructed to persuade their respective charges to "agree to abstain... from any and all acts calculated to produce a collision between the States and the government of the United States," pending the convening of the Peace Conference on February 4, the day Alabama had chosen for the seceded states to meet in Montgomery to establish the Confederate States of America. News of his two appointments and the details of his instructions reached Tyler at Sherwood Forest on January 20. He was feeling quite unwell at the time, but Julia gave him heavy doses of *hydrargyrum cum creta* (mercury with chalk), and by the morning of the twenty-second he was feeling shaky but strong enough to depart for Richmond for a conference with Governor Letcher prior to taking the train to Washington that afternoon. "The P—— started off very unwell," Julia informed Staten Island, "but he felt that *go he must*, and I hope as the excitement of convention always agrees with him he will improve and not grow worse." On the eve of his departure a family conference had determined that Gardie would accompany his father to Washington as a bearer of dispatches between Brown's Hotel (where Tyler would stay) and the White House; it was also decided that Tyler would return briefly to Sherwood Forest before the peace convention officially opened. Julia would then accompany him back to Washington.[8]

Julia was elated at the prospect of a return to the capital. When she learned, on January 22, that her husband had also been elected by Charles City, James City, and New Kent counties to serve as their representative in the emergency Virginia State Convention called for February 13 in Richmond, she knew that her return to Washington would be as the wife of a very important man indeed. She immediately instructed her mother to send her Margaret's silk evening dresses, and she promised her family that with her husband serving as special Virginia commissioner to Buchanan, Virginia commissioner to the Peace Conference, and Charles City delegate to the state convention, all would be well: "The seceding States on hearing that he is conferring with Mr. Buchanan will stay, I am sure, their proceedings out of respect to him. If the Northern States will only follow up this measure in a conceding Union, peace will be insured. The South asks no other than *just* treatment, and this she must have to be induced to remain in the Union." Juliana needed no such propaganda from Sherwood Forest. She was already a convert to the Southern line. The problem was with David Lyon and Sarah.[9]

While Tyler had received, in Julia's words, "honor enough to gratify the most ambitious," his mere presence in the capital did not cause the rumbling glacier of secessionism suddenly to stand still, respect or no respect for the tenth President. Within ten days of his arrival Louisiana and Texas seceded, and Virginia, Arkansas, Tennessee, and North Carolina had all warned Buchanan they would oppose any federal attempt to coerce a seceded state militarily. But Buchanan, as Tyler quickly discovered during an interview on January 24, was in no condition, psychologically or emotionally, to coerce anybody. The man was in a daze, and he whined to the former President that "the South had not treated him properly; that they had made unnecessary demonstrations by seizing unprotected arsenals and forts . . . acts of useless bravado which had quite as well been let alone." Tyler could see that his job in Washington was going to be quite a bit easier than Judge Robertson's in Charleston. He assured Buchanan that these Southern actions were minor things, calculated only "to fret and irritate the Northern mind ... the necessary results of popular excitement which, after all, worked no mischief in the end if harmony between the States was once more restored." Grasping at any straw floating past, Buchanan accepted this strained interpretation without comment.[10]

A few days later the Virginia commissioner scored another success in the reduction of tensions when Buchanan cooperatively helped him quash two groundless rumors which had inflamed many Virginians. Had either been true, the whole purpose of Tyler's mission to Washington as a special commissioner would have collapsed instantly. The rumor mill had it, first, that the USS *Brooklyn* had been sent to Charleston with a load of federal troops; and, secondly, that the guns of Fortress Monroe had been trained menacingly inland upon the Virginia countryside. Buchanan, pressed by a nervous Tyler, assured the commissioner that the *Brooklyn* had sailed for Pensacola on an errand of mercy and relief, and that the guns of Fortress Monroe still pointed peacefully seaward. Tyler's relief at these assurances turned to positive gratification on January 28. On that date the President, at the Virginia commissioner's request, sent a special message to Capitol Hill communicating to Congress the resolutions of the Virginia General Assembly calling for peace and compromise. To these resolutions Buchanan added the personal plea that Congress refrain from any hostile act against the South. "What he recommends Congress to do he will do himself," Tyler reported with satisfaction. "His policy obviously is to throw all responsibility off of his shoulders." Given the appeasing paralysis of the Buchanan administration, Tyler felt free to return to Sherwood Forest on January 29. There would be no federal military coercion of the South so long as nervous Old Buck was still in the White House.[11]

The question now, however, was whether South Carolina would militarily coerce the United States. On January 31 the Charleston government dispatched Colonel I. W. Hayne to Washington to demand formally of Buchanan the surrender of Fort Sumter. Hayne's request took the form of a "highly improper letter" which Buchanan refused to receive. The President stalled and fretted for a few days, but finally on the advice of Secretary of War Joseph Holt he rejected the Gamecock ultimatum with the argument that since the fort was federal property he had no power to sell it or otherwise divest the federal government of its possession without authorization from Congress. Because the fort was still legally a federal military installation he maintained the right, as Commander-in-Chief, to reinforce its garrison if the situation called for such a step. He did not, however, contemplate this necessity. Delivered to Colonel Hayne on February 6, two days after the Peace Conference convened, the Holt-Buchanan rejection of the South Carolina demand (which the agitated Hayne termed "highly insulting" to him personally) brought the nation to the brink of war.

This was the immediate crisis Tyler would face shortly after he returned to the capital for the peace convention. He arrived on February 3, accompanied by Julia, Alex, baby Pearl, and the body servant Fanny.

No sooner had the Tylers settled into their suite at Brown's Hotel than their rooms were filled with a throng of milling, frightened people all looking to John Tyler, the probable president of the Peace Conference, to work some quick miracle to save the Union. Letters and telegrams poured in pleading for peace, many offering plans and formulae to accomplish this end. Julia described the chaotic scene, heavy as it was with portents of disaster. "Perhaps I am here during the last days of the Republic," she told her mother on February 3.

> The President has been surrounded with visitors from the moment he could appear to them.... It would interest you to see how deferentially they gather around him. They will make him President of the Convention, I presume, from what I hear.... All of the South or border States will enter upon the deliberations with very little expectation of saving the Union, I think. There seems such a fixed determination to do mischief on the part of the Black Republicans. General Scott's absurd and high-handed course here in Washington is very much condemned. The rumor today is afloat that he is collecting here troops to overawe Virginia and Maryland. If the President concludes so, upon observation, I think he will recommend the Governor of Virginia to send five thousand troops at once to Alexandria to stand on the defensive side and overawe General Scott's menacing attitude; but this is *entre nous* and a "State secret."... There seems to be a general looking to him by those anxious to save the Union. I wish it might be possible for him to succeed in overcoming all obstacles. They all say if through him it cannot be accomplished, it could not be through any one else.[12]

Julia did not accompany her husband to Washington solely to satisfy her "most intense interest" in all things political. Instead, she planned the trip as a social reconquest of the capital she had left to the dry mercies of Sarah Polk sixteen years earlier. Nor was she disappointed in her ambition. With her husband "the great center of attraction" as the nation's political Moses, Julia tripped happily through the social bulrushes to the point of physical exhaustion. Parties, receptions, dinners, and balls broke out like measles as proper Washingtonians made one last effort to drown the throb of martial drums in a sea of alcohol and in the lulling swish-swish of dancing slippers. This suited Julia. "You ought to hear the compliments that are *heaped* upon me.... I haven't changed a *bit* except to improve, etc., etc.," she boasted to her mother. At forty Julia had energy to burn; at nearly seventy-one Tyler had difficulty keeping up with her, although Julia assured her mother that her aging husband was "quite bright, bearing up wonderfully and *looking* remarkably well." His ego sustained by the thought that he was "looked to to save the Union," his stomach disorder made endurable by massive doses of *hydrargyrum cum creta*,

John Tyler rode boldly forth to grapple with all dragons, sectional and social, while Julia danced on. "I have not been allowed a moment's leisure," she wrote her mother on February 13:

> Within the hotel it has been an incessant stream of company, and then I have had visits to return, the Capitol to visit, etc., etc. Last night I attended, with the President, the party of Senator Douglas.... I paraded the rooms with the handsomest man here, Governor Morehead of Kentucky—one of the best likenesses to Papa you ever saw in appearance, voice, laugh and manner. I suppose I may conclude that I looked quite well. No attempts at entertainment have succeeded before, I was told, this winter, and to the hopes that are placed upon the efforts of this Peace Convention is to be attributed the success of this. People are catching at straws as a relief to their pressing anxieties, and look to the Peace Commissioners as if they possessed some divine power to restore order and harmony.[13]

John Tyler had no divine power. Instead, he had a bad stomach and a socially ambitious wife; the combination rendered his role at the Peace Conference a difficult one. Convening in Willard's Hall on February 4, the convention adjourned to the following day to permit more delegates time to arrive. On the fifth, as expected, Tyler was unanimously elected president of the gathering. As he mounted the rostrum to deliver his welcoming address he could see the faces of several old political friends—Robert F. Stockton of New Jersey, Charles S. Morehead and Charles A. Wickliffe of Kentucky. There were also ancient enemies in the hall—Francis Granger of New York, David Wilmot of Pennsylvania, and Thomas Ewing of Ohio. He could also see that the free states outnumbered the slave states fourteen to seven. Of the 132 delegates assembled most of them were as old, tired, and sick as himself. John C. Wright of Ohio was blind and feeble and would die within the week; Charles A. Wickliffe was lame; the lungs of Missouri's Alexander W. Doniphan were "so much inflamed that I deem it unsafe to go out in the damp atmosphere." To some, Tyler himself appeared a "tottering ashen ruin." But there was much political skill and experience present. The group numbered six former Cabinet officers, nineteen former governors, fourteen ex-United States senators, fifty former congressmen, and a scattering of former ambassadors, ministers, state supreme court justices, and circuit court judges.[14]

Tyler's speech to this distinguished if spent assemblage was not one of his better forensic efforts. Calling attention to his own "variable and fickle" health and to his personal ambition to be numbered among those history would remember as saviors of the Union, Tyler devoted the major part of a cliché-ridden address to pleading in general terms for peace, compromise, reconciliation, and adjustment. In eulogistic detail he recalled the past historical glories of each state with a delegation present. For the first time in his life, however, he admitted that the Founding Fathers had "probably committed a blunder" in not rendering the Constitution more easily amendable. He began dimly to see that the document was a living, growing thing, not the dead fossil strict constructionists had for years insisted it remain. Unfortunately, said Tyler, the Fathers "have made the difficulties next to insurmountable to accomplish amendments to an instrument which was perfect for five millions of people, but not wholly so as to thirty millions." This defect he thought the assembled delegates might remedy by their patriotism and by their willingness to "accomplish but one triumph in advance . . . a triumph over party." The convention applauded enthusiastically.[15]

February 6, 1861, was an eventful day. As the twenty-one-member resolutions committee under the direction of Kentucky's James Guthrie settled down to the task of hammering out a proposed constitutional amendment that would stave off civil war, Tyler, encouraged by the almost-universal acclaim his speech the preceding day had generated, hurried with Julia to the White House to snuff out the sputtering Fort Sumter fuse. He pleaded with Buchanan to accept the South Carolina ultimatum of January 31 and abandon Sumter. The government, after all, had already given up other forts and arsenals in the seceded states. Furthermore, the fort could not possibly be defended by "that noble boy," Major Robert Anderson, and his tiny garrison of eighty-odd men. Indeed, the very presence of Anderson in the fort, Tyler insisted, was a provocation that imperiled the prospects of the peace convention. In daily threatening an overt collision at Charleston it risked precipitating the nervous border states headlong into secession. Why not, Tyler suggested, reduce the garrison to a token guard of six men and thereby appease the South Carolinians who "in spite of the Northern bluster that denounces them as rebels in arms thirsting for blood are bent on peace." Buchanan would not agree to a reduction in force. There was really no force to speak of in Sumter. But he did authorize Tyler to enter into direct communication with South Carolina Governor Francis W. Pickens, Julia's old admirer, to assure the governor that the administration was interested only in peace. His refusal of South Carolina's ultimatum was in no manner intended, in tone or wording, to "insult" Colonel Hayne or anyone else, Buchanan averred. This important task Tyler immediately undertook. Within a few days he and Judge Robertson had calmed Pickens and Hayne and had snipped the fuse of the crisis in Charleston Harbor. For this service Buchanan was extremely grateful. On the evening of February 11 he showed his appreciation by paying Tyler the singular compliment of calling at his parlor to thank him personally. "I suppose it is the first visit he has paid since being the nation's chief," Julia exclaimed, thrilled at the social *coup*.[16]

Scarcely had this small blow for peace and sanity been struck when Tyler began to realize that the deliberations of the Peace Conference were destined to end in abject failure. Not only was debate on the floor often a raucous and disorderly affair (Tyler occasionally lost control of the proceedings entirely), but the dissension within Guthrie's resolutions committee became so severe Tyler despaired that any proposal would emerge from it at all. Northern extremists in the committee and on the floor of the convention argued that any concession to the South's position on slavery extension in the territories would be a rank betrayal of the Republican platform of 1860 and would stand no real chance of ratification before Republican-dominated state legislatures in the North. Southern spokesmen argued that unless the North at least accepted the possibility of slavery extension along the democratic, popular-sovereignty lines of the Crittenden proposal, the seven seceded states could not possibly be enticed peacefully back into the Union. From February 6 to February 15 the matter stood thus deadlocked in the resolutions committee while the convention as a whole marked time. There were sincere men of good will on both sides, men dedicated to genuine compromise, but Tyler soon saw, as he had earlier feared, that the convention had attracted too many delegates and too many extremists to function either harmoniously or efficiently.[17]

By February 13, two days before the resolutions committee finally reported, Tyler's thinking had undergone a significant change. Despairing that there could be any workable or acceptable compromise, he began to consider the sectional problem in military terms. Specifically, he began to worry about Virginia's military security should the convention fail and war result. Tyler came to the convention in search of peace through *political* compromise; he left it wedded to a plan for peace through a *military* balance of power. This fundamental change in his thinking had taken place by the end of the ninth stormy day of the Conference. Publicly, he still urged the Virginia State Convention, which convened in Richmond on the thirteenth, to adjourn its deliberations from day to day until the Peace Conference in Washington had acted one way or another. Privately, he began toying with the idea of secession. Julia, who invariably reflected her husband's thinking in her own, told Staten Island on the afternoon of February 13 that

All is suspense, from the President down. The New York and Massachusetts delegation will no doubt perform all the mischief they can; and it may be, will defeat this patriotic effort at pacification. But whether it succeeds or not, Virginia will have sustained her reputation, and in the latter event will retire with dignity from the field to join without loss of time her more Southern sisters; the rest of the slave Border States will follow her lead, and very likely she will be able to draw off, which would be glorious, a couple of Northern States. It is to be hoped that this state of suspense, which is bringing disaster to trade everywhere, will soon be removed in one way or another.

If this result could be counted upon to follow on the heels of Virginia's secession, if "a couple of Northern states" could indeed be drawn out of the Union by the Old Dominion, the weakened North would likely not feel itself strong enough militarily to crush so powerful a confederacy. There would therefore be no war. Or so Tyler reasoned. Instead, a peaceful balance of power would be created—two scorpions in a bottle—and Virginia would be spared invasion and bloodshed. This calculation was, of course, a wild gamble. It was based on a dangerous overestimation of Virginia's prestige and pulling power, a disastrous underestimation of South Carolina's urge to lunacy when the Fort Sumter crisis was resumed in April 1861, and a tragic misevaluation of the temper of Abraham Lincoln. Nevertheless, Tyler embraced it as preferable to either civil war or a supine acceptance of the occupation of Virginia by the armed forces of an abolitionist regime.[18]

The proposed constitutional amendment brought in by the Guthrie committee on February 15 was an eight-section proposal which closely followed the Crittenden plan. Section 1, the key clause, permitted slavery south of 36°30′, prohibited it north of that line, and allowed slaveowners to carry their property into a territory anywhere south of the designated boundary until such time as the inhabitants of the territory drew up a state constitution specifically prohibiting involuntary servitude. However unacceptable this slavery-expansion program was to President-elect Lincoln and to the Republican Party in general, it was not from the Southern standpoint a radical proposal. For this reason Tyler might well have supported it. That he did not was in sharp contradiction to what he had been advocating, publicly and privately, for nearly a year. Instead, Tyler supported James A. Seddon's disruptive minority report. This would have amended the Constitution to permit the South a virtual veto on Executive appointments south of 36°30′. Not only did the Seddon amendment visualize the South as a state within a state, it also maintained the constitutional *right* of any state to secede from the Union whenever it wished.

There is some evidence that Tyler had a Machiavellian hand in forging the extremist Seddon amendment, acceptable only to the most rabid secessionists. Whether he did or not, it is clear that Virginia's subsequent vote against the resolutions committee's majority report was largely Tyler's doing. He joined with Seddon and Brockenbrough to outvote Rives and Summers on each test within the Old Dominion's delegation. In the end, Virginia's unit vote was not found on the side of conciliation and adjustment. Tyler's motives in his apostasy were dual. He had arrived at his hopeful peace-through-secession-and-balance-of-power idea; in this plan he had growing confidence; and he could see immediately that the resolutions committee's proposed constitutional amendment, however conciliatory, had no mathematical chance whatever of adoption. With seven states already out of the Union, every one of those still remaining in would have to approve it to command the necessary three-fourths majority required under the Constitution. Realistically, this could not be expected to happen.[19]

The final vote on the Guthrie committee's majority resolution and

Seddon's minority report did not take place until February 26. In the interim, a period characterized by parliamentary chaos and a floor debate that often threatened to degenerate into blows, Tyler maintained public silence on the issues. On the eighteenth the Confederate States of America was proclaimed in Montgomery and Jefferson Davis inaugurated President. This, however, brought no new sectional incidents and Tyler continued as before his close liaison with Buchanan in their joint efforts to maintain peace until the convention had officially spoken. Although he was seen increasingly in the company of secessionist delegates, he did not step down from the neutrality of the chair and openly support the radical Seddon proposal on the floor of the convention until February 25, two days *after* his interview with Lincoln. Following that revealing experience Tyler's muted secessionism came loudly, positively, and publicly to the fore.[20]

The confrontation with Lincoln took place at 9 P.M. on February 23, fifteen hours after the President-elect had arrived secretly in the capital. Tyler and other delegates to the Conference waited upon Lincoln in his Willard Hotel suite. It was a tense moment which Lincoln sought to relieve with a show of sincere good will, even jocularity. Then the fire-eating James A. Seddon began to bait him, accusing him of supporting in the past the most extreme abolitionist excesses—from the John Brown raid to the distribution throughout the South of William Lloyd Garrison's incendiary pamphlets. Lincoln's mood suddenly hardened.

"I beg your pardon, Mr. Seddon," he said. "I intend no offense, but I will not suffer such a statement to pass unchallenged, because it is not true. A gentleman of your intelligence should not make such assertions."

As the political temperature in the room cooled, delegate William E. Dodge, New York merchant-capitalist, said, "It is for you, sir, to say whether the whole nation shall be plunged into bankruptcy, whether the grass shall grow in the streets of our commercial cities."

"Then I say it shall not," replied Lincoln. "If it depends upon me, the grass shall not grow anywhere except in the fields and meadows."

"Then you will yield to the just demands of the South. You will not go to war on account of slavery!" Dodge pressed him.

"I do not know that I understand your meaning, Mr. Dodge," Lincoln answered stiffly. "If I shall ever come to the great office of President of the United States, I shall take an oath . . . that I will, to the best of my ability, preserve, protect, and defend the Constitution of the United States . . . not the Constitution as I would like to have it, but as it *is*. . . . The Constitution will not be preserved and defended until it is enforced and obeyed in every part of every one of the United States. It must be so respected, obeyed, enforced and defended, let the grass grow where it may."

With that declaration some of the Southern delegates stalked out of the room in anger. But Tyler stayed to hear Lincoln say further, in answer to a question whether territories democratically choosing and legalizing slavery could ever again hope to enter the Union as slave states, "It will be time to consider that question when it arises.... In a choice of evils, war may not always be the worst." [21]

Tyler had heard enough. This ugly, rawboned man was no Buchanan. Rumors reaching him next day that Lincoln might be persuaded to withdraw federal troops from Fort Sumter if Virginia would promise to stay in the Union failed to stay Tyler's decision on secession. Assurances from Secretary of State-designate Seward that there would be no coercion, that Sumter would very likely be abandoned, likewise had no effect on his now single-track thinking. He was completely convinced that Virginia must secede quickly, pulling the border states "and perhaps New Jersey" with her into the Southern Confederacy. Only this could insure a lasting peace. Only this could produce the military balance of power that would give Lincoln pause in his coercive instincts and intents.

For Tyler, then, the last three days of the Peace Conference were entirely anticlimactic. From the enforced detachment of the chair he descended onto the floor to support the disruptive Seddon amendment. When it was overwhelmingly disapproved by 16 to 4, Virginia then voted against Section 1 of the resolutions committee's majority report. The crucial section similarly went down to an 11-to-8 defeat. A period of panicky logrolling followed. Demands for another vote were voiced. Fear and confusion stalked the convention, on the verge now of accomplishing absolutely nothing. Thanks in part to New York's angry abstention from the second vote, Section 1 was finally approved by a narrow 9-to-8 count, with Virginia still in stubborn opposition. With that shaky decision made, the remaining sections of the proposed constitutional amendment slipped through with small majorities.

In his farewell address to the delegates Tyler promised he would submit the Conference's decisions to Congress with a "recommendation" for their adoption. He had no heart for this task, however. In his eagerness to return to Richmond and enter into the secession debates of the state convention, he merely forwarded the suggested constitutional amendment to Congress with the laconic comment that he had been instructed to do so. There, as Tyler expected, it reposed without action. Ridiculed and unsung, it was a blank cartridge fired by a spiked gun into an angry mob. Several Northern state legislatures immediately denounced it, as did both of Virginia's senators. Within a few weeks it was dead and buried as a live option, hastened to its grave by Northern extremists, Southern fire-eaters—and by John Tyler himself. As he would say nine months later of the failure of the Peace Conference, "No man could have been more earnest to avert the sad conditions of things which now involve us in the terrible realities of war than myself, but at the Peace Conference I had to address 'stocks and stones' who had neither ears to hear or hearts to understand. Blinded by lust of power, they have heedlessly driven the ship of state upon rocks and into whirlpools which have dashed it to pieces." [22]

Memories are short. On the foundered ship of state John Tyler was one of the chief pilots. Arriving back in Richmond on February 28, he delivered an incendiary speech from the steps of the Exchange Hotel—denouncing the Peace Conference and all its works and calling for Virginia's immediate secession as the only means of preserving the general peace and the safety of the Old Dominion. The following day he took his seat in the Virginia State Convention meeting in the hall of the Mechanics' Institute. There he began working actively with extremists Henry A. Wise and Lewis E. Harvie for secession. He had been elected to the state convention on January 22 as a moderate who would make "every effort in his power to effect a reconciliation." He had returned from the peace convention breathing fire and brimstone. For a few days he worried that he had betrayed his constituents. "Have you any information of what is the sentiment of Charles City?" he asked Julia nervously. Whatever her answer, Tyler learned a few days later that Robert and Priscilla's eldest daughter, nineteen-year-old Letitia Tyler, had hoisted the new Confederate flag to the top of the Capitol at Montgomery in ceremonies on March 5. The Tylers were seceding with commendable dash.

Not until March 13 did Tyler gain the floor of the state convention to deliver his slashing speech for secession. Lincoln's Inaugural Address of March 4 had breathed a mixed spirit of menace and adjustment, and Tyler was fearful that the latter element in it might seduce the Old Dominion into a policy of continued inaction. True, Lincoln had announced his intention to enforce the Constitution. He had defined secession as unconstitutional. But he had also rejected a violent solution to the nation's sickness "unless it be forced upon the national authority," and he declared he had no "purpose directly or indirectly to interfere with the institution of slavery in the States where it exists." While Tyler complained that the speech had certain grammatical deficiencies, he could not deny its impact in Virginia, where unionist sentiment was still running strong. A large bloc of delegates in the state convention, well over half, was willing to endorse either the Peace Conference compromise or the Crittenden compromise. Anything but secession and war.[23]

The Tyler who rose to his feet on March 13 to begin a speech that lasted well into the next day was the oratorical Tyler of old. Although the pain in his abdomen was intense, it did not still a voice filled with equal measures of indignation, pathos, morality, derision, and bitter sarcasm. The address had everything: an arithmetical analysis which demonstrated the impossibility of the adoption of the Peace Conference's proposed constitutional amendment; a point-by-point semantic and legal demolition of the amendment itself; a healthy twist of the British Lion's tail; a eulogy of Henry Clay; a gratuitous defense of the Tyler administration; the coronation of King Cotton; a review of the glories of Colonial Virginia; a defense of the Seddon amendment; the economic need for slavery expansion; the Heaven-ordained racial suitability of the African Negro for work in hot fields; an attack on the abolitionists, their murderous plans, and their underground railroad; and an assault on Abraham Lincoln for ordering home the Pacific and Mediterranean squadrons for the sole hostile purpose of "intimidating" the South. Let Lincoln abandon Fort Sumter and Fort Pickens in Pensacola, suggested Tyler. Let him recognize the Confederate States and begin to negotiate commercial and defensive alliances with the Montgomery government and all would be well. But this the stubborn Lincoln would probably not do. Virginia, Tyler concluded, must therefore secede. Her long frontier, stretching from Norfolk on the Atlantic to Wheeling on the Ohio, was indefensible. Only by seceding and drawing the border states, New Jersey, Pennsylvania, and New York City ("the South is her natural ally, and she must come with us") out of the Union with her could Virginia hope to preserve peace and avoid invasion and subjugation:

Brennus may not be yet in the Capitol, but he will soon be there, and the sword will be thrown into the scale to weigh against our liberties, and there will be no Camillus to expel him.... I look with fear and trembling to some extent, at the condition of my country. But I do want to see Virginia united. ...I have entire confidence that her proud crest will yet be seen waving in that great procession of States that will go up to the temple to make their vows to maintain their liberties, "peacefully if they can, forcibly if they must." Sir, I am done.[24]

Powerful as it was, Tyler's speech triggered no stampede toward secession. Instead, the former President was forced to sit and listen, hour after hour, day after day, to speeches variously advocating union, secession, or continued inaction. It was clear that there was yet no majority for secession in Virginia. On week ends Tyler left his room at the Ballard House and visited with Julia and the children at Sherwood Forest. Gardie stayed with him for a few days at the Ballard, and while he was in town father and son visited Julie, boarding at Miss Pegram's school. If secession were not large enough a problem for Tyler to handle, Julie got measles, gave them to Gardie, and he democratically spread them to all his brothers and sisters at Sherwood. And to make quite sure Tyler had enough to keep him busy between convention sessions and the innumerable dinners to which the delegates

461

were invited ("Dinner party succeeds dinner party," he complained), Julia loaded him down with shopping commissions.

Meanwhile, Tyler fretted that the Richmond *Enquirer* was slow in printing his secession speech, which, he told Julia, had been called the "great speech of the session." When it finally saw print on March 30 he immediately sent a copy to David Lyon in Staten Island. Copies were also distributed throughout his Charles City-New Kent-James City district in an effort to bring his constituents to the level of his own fever-pitch secessionism. Through Julia he kept David Lyon and Juliana informed on the course of the debates at the Mechanics' Institute. For example, he characterized Professor James P. Holcombe's speech for secession a "magnificent effort. His invective against Seward was one of the most terrible invectives I ever heard. The Convention and galleries were greatly moved." On the other hand, when a group of Richmond "Union Ladies" came into the chamber to present Staunton delegate John B. Baldwin a floral tribute for his powerful three-day antisecessionist speech, Tyler was so "disgusted with the proceeding I left the room as did many others." Similarly, the debate on and the demise of the Peace Conference's proposal, the vain attempts of the state convention to create an alternative based upon it, and the progress of Tyler's own fly-by-night plan to create a separate Union comprised of seceded states and border states were reported to Castleton Hill. "A number of the Northern States will come into the plan which he proposes," Julia assured her mother. Not mentioned in these reports to Staten Island was the fact that on April 3 the state convention firmly voted down a secession resolution 90 to 45. On the eve of Lincoln's call for 75,000 volunteers on the fifteenth, the convention, in a secret vote, again divided 60 to 53 against secession. Although Tyler spoke of "great changes" in the public mind and predicted that Virginia would "adopt an ultimatum.... The people of the State are becoming very restless," there was no majority for secession in Richmond until after Lincoln's call for troops.[25]

Lincoln's April 6 decision to provision the helpless little garrison at Fort Sumter triggered the great carnage of 1861–1865. The guns of General P. G. T. Beauregard's Confederate artillery, in noisy rejoinder to the President on April 13, blew Virginia out of the Union just as decisively as they reduced the Fort to untenable rubble. Whether Lincoln provoked South Carolina's angry response, or whether he was merely responding to the four-month-old provocation inherent in South Carolina's unconstitutional act of secession, cannot be decided here. A century later it remains an open question in historical interpretation. Tyler, however, solved it neatly and quickly to his own satisfaction with the observation that "Mr. Lincoln, having weighed in the scales the value of a mere local Fort against the value of the Union itself resolved to send ships of war and armed men to bring on that very collision which he well knew would arise." Tyler admitted that Lincoln's strategy at Charleston had been brilliant. The whole purpose of the provocative Sumter provisioning had been "to rally the masses of the North around his own person and to prevent the faction which had brought him to power from falling asunder. In this he has succeeded. The upheaving of the people of the North fully attests to this." Whatever the truth concerning Lincoln's motives, it is certain that his decision to punish the Confederacy for the Fort Sumter outrage by calling 75,000 volunteers to the colors on April 15 gave Virginia little choice but to defend her soil. Quickly meeting in secret session on April 16, the state convention debated a new ordinance of secession. That evening Tyler wrote Julia that

> The prospects now are that we shall have a war, and a trying one. The battle at Charleston has aroused the whole North. I fear that division no longer exists in their ranks, and that they will break upon the South with an immense force.... Submission or resistance is only left us. My hope is that the Border States will follow speedily our lead. If so, all will be safe... do not understand me as saying an ordinance will be passed. On the contrary, it will be in doubt until the vote.... These are dark times, dearest, and I think only of you and our little ones.... I shall vote secession.[26]

Tyler's theory that peace could be preserved through a balance of power had collapsed overnight, although he still hung grimly to a shadow of it. By being maneuvered into firing the first shot, the Charleston hotheads had effectively unified the North, leaving Tyler only the faint hope that the immediate secession of Virginia and all the border states might still provide safety for the Old Dominion by creating a balance of power which would preserve peace or, at worst, an initial military stalemate from which a negotiated peace might emerge. But he was realistic enough to see now that the coming war would likely be more *blitzkrieg* than *sitzkrieg* and he warned Julia accordingly.

Julia regarded it at the outset as a medieval tournament fought by Southern White Knights against Northern Black Knaves. The Charles City Cavalry, under Captain Robert Douthat, comprising "eighty well-horsed, well-armed, and well-drilled and brave, true, high-toned gentlemen, who love the right and scorn the wrong," could only be victorious in any engagement it fought. She heard heavy cannonading all day on the seventeenth from the direction of Richmond and assumed, correctly, that the vote in the state convention there had been for secession. She immediately wrote her mother the glad tidings, thanking her for her past pro-Southern views and expressing the hope that like-minded New Yorkers would "now make a demonstration and form a party against coercion." Juliana needed no urging. From the moment the war began she was a full-fledged, charter-member Copperhead.[27]

Julia soon learned from her husband in Richmond that secession from "the Northern hive of abolitionists" had indeed been voted by a margin of 88 to 55 (adjusted to 103 to 46 when some members later changed their vote for the record) on the afternoon of the seventeenth. Virginia troops, she was informed, were already marching to seize the arsenal at Harpers Ferry and the Navy Yard at Norfolk. More importantly, she heard from her husband that Robert Tyler had been threatened with "mob violence" in Philadelphia. "Do, dearest," Tyler pleaded with her, "live as frugally as possible in the household—trying times are before us." This, of course, was like asking a hurricane to stop hurrying.[28]

The excitement of the final secession vote and the unrestrained celebrations in Richmond which followed it were too much for John Tyler's ailing stomach. He accepted membership on a state commission to negotiate a union with the Confederate States government and he personally drafted the agreement placing Virginia's armed forces under the direction of Jefferson Davis. Nevertheless, he turned down an appointment to the Provisional Confederate Congress at Montgomery. He was simply too "debilitated from a protracted participation in the exciting scenes of the convention" to make the long journey to Alabama. He thus missed an opportunity to see John, Jr., who, commissioned major in the Confederate Army, was attached to the War Department at Montgomery. Fortunately, the mountain was brought to Mohammed. When the seat of the Rebel government was moved from Montgomery to Richmond in May, John Tyler was unanimously elected by the Virginia State Convention to serve in the Provisional Congress of the Confederate States of America.[29]

During the first few weeks of confusion following Virginia's secession one of the family's main concerns was the safety of Robert Tyler. Robert's outspoken defense of the Southern position in the early months of 1861 had made him less than popular in Philadelphia. He had publicly criticized the Peace Conference as a plot to "demoralize the people of the Southern section." The Crittenden proposals were designed, he charged, "to prepare the South ... for final submission to Squatterism or Abolitionism, or both." On several occasions he had loudly predicted that Pennsylvania "will assuredly wish to secede from the Northern Confederacy..." in the event of civil war. Not surprisingly, a speaker at a mass patriotic meeting in Independence Square on April 17 condemned him as a traitor, and cries of "He ought to be lynched!" sent one of his friends hurrying to Robert's office to warn him that a Vigilance Committee mob was stirring. Quickly hiring a hack, Robert escaped to Frankford. There he caught a train to Bristol, where he hid for a day in the attic of a friend's house while a mob of his neighbors burned him in effigy in his own front yard. On April 19 he managed to slip aboard a steamer for New York, where he was taken in by Priscilla's sister, Julia Cooper Campbell. A few days later Priscilla joined him in New York to plan their next move. It was decided that Robert should proceed alone to Richmond. He arrived there on May 8, thankful that he had left "no *creditors* among the savages" back in Pennsylvania. "Poor Bob Tyler!" lamented Buchanan when he learned of Robert's flight to Richmond and his subsequent employment by the Confederate government. "He was a warm hearted and eloquent man, and a true and faithful friend. I am truly sorry he went so far astray from his line of duty. I knew he was as poor as a church mouse...."

Priscilla returned to Bristol with her sisters Julia and Louisa. The ladies closed up the old Cooper homestead while Priscilla procured a pass through the lines from General Robert Patterson. Gathering up her children and a few personal items, she proceeded to Richmond via Washington. Departing Bristol was a wrenching experience. "The grief of my children is more than I can stand," she wrote her sister Mary Grace. "I can't tell you how many people accompanied us to the landing.... Poor Major [the family dog] ran along with the children, evidently knowing something to be wrong. And the last thing I saw while the boat steamed away was Major held by two or three boys, and the last thing to be heard was the crying of the children on the shore and mine in the boat responding." By May 28, after a brief stopover at the Exchange Hotel in Richmond, Priscilla and her children were safe at Sherwood Forest. "How terrible the times are," she lamented. "Richmond and Washington both bristling with bayonets. I saw a S.C. Regiment pass the hotel while I was there. Such a splendid looking set of men! With a bouquet, thrown by the ladies, upon every bayonet. Every man you see is in uniform. Even Father [John Tyler] talks of fighting.... I very much fear that Mr. [Robert] Tyler will go into the army. He is exceedingly anxious to do so himself, and Father also wants it. The thought of it gives me the greatest agony." [30]

At seventy-one John Tyler could only talk of fighting. Even the forty-four-year-old Robert was considered a little advanced in age for combat duty. Therefore he accepted from President Davis an appointment as Register of the Treasury of the Confederacy at $3000 per annum, and he satisfied his martial spirit by enlisting as a private in the "Treasury Regiment." Composed of civil servants, it was a second-line unit organized especially for the defense of Richmond. In this he saw action on several occasions during the war. The rest of the family also speedily mobilized when the trumpets sounded in Richmond. Major John Tyler, Jr., served as an assistant to the Secretary of War. Tazewell Tyler became a surgeon in the Confederate Army. James A. Semple resigned his purser's commission in the United States Navy, moved from Brooklyn to Richmond with his wife Letitia, and took a post in the Confederate States Navy Department. Henry and Robert

Jones, sons of Henry L. Jones and the deceased Mary Tyler Jones, entered the Army of Northern Virginia. Both were mentioned in orders for gallantry, and young Robert was awarded a field commission for bravery at Gettysburg, where he received three wounds. William Griffin Waller, son of William and Elizabeth Tyler Waller, resigned from West Point when Virginia seceded and joined the Confederate Ordnance Department. His younger brother, John Tyler Waller, "a gallant but rash young officer," fell in combat during the conflict. The Long Island Gardiners, on the other hand, did not rush forward to save the Union with quite so much enthusiasm as the Tylers came forward to destroy it, although John Lyon Gardiner, later the eleventh proprietor of Gardiners Island, did serve as a colonel in the New York Sixth Brigade, National Guard. No one in the family on either side of the fight surpassed Julia in her eagerness for the war. She joined various local ladies' volunteer groups to help the war effort, and she encouraged Gardie and Alex to enlist in the Charles City Junior Guard, in which the thirteen-year-old Alex served as second lieutenant. The boys, in turn, solemnly warned their cousin Harry Beeckman in Staten Island that they would have nothing further to do with him "if he countenances the invasion of Southern homes." [31]

David Lyon Gardiner did countenance the "invasion." When Julia learned from her mother on May 6 that her own brother supported the North, she was beside herself with rage:

I think D. has been bitten by the rabid tone of those around him and the press. It seems he belongs to a different school of politics from his experienced friend, the President, and is ready to deny State-sovereignty. Therefore he opposes the movement of the South to save itself from destruction through an abolition attack, and sympathizes with the dominant power of the North. I was so unprepared for his views that I read his letter aloud to the President without first perusing it, which, if I had done, I should not have committed so decided [a] mistake. He says the government at Washington will not invade, but will only reclaim its *property,* and take by force the forts now in possession of Southern States. What is that but invasion, I should like to know? The government at Washington has no business with the forts that were built for the protection of the States that have seceded.... For my part, I am utterly ashamed of the State in which I was born, and its people. All soul and magnanimity have departed from them—"patriotism" indeed! A community sold to the vilest politicians. The President tells me ... to ask D. if he does not recognize the existing blockade a *positive war* upon the South. Even our river boat would be fired at and taken, if that impudent war steamer, lying off Newport News could get the chance.[32]

Juliana was entirely sympathetic with her daughter's Southern nationalism. The other New York Gardiners, however, remained loyal to the Union and this fact produced complications. A chill wind soon blew into Juliana's relations with her eldest son and his wife, and the home at Castleton Hill, like so many others in America, became a house divided. Her first worried reaction to the commencement of hostilities was to suggest to Sherwood Forest that Julia bring her children to the safety of Staten Island. Tyler vetoed this idea. Virginia, he told her confidently, was "clad in steel" and had more troops in the field "panting for conflict" than could readily be armed and trained. Given the recent secession of Tennessee and North Carolina, and a Southern population "filled with enthusiasm" for war, he was certain his children were in no danger. "In a week from this time," he told his mother-in-law on May 2, "James River will bristle with fortifications, and Charles City will be far safer than Staten Island." [33]

Convinced this was true, Julia called loudly for the blood of the Yankee aggressor. She reported as great Confederate victories battles that never took place and she repeated as gospel truths war rumors that bordered on the fantastic. A group in Massachusetts was said to have offered $20,000 for the severed head of Henry A. Wise, for example. Tyler demanded in the Confederate Congress that a strong cavalry force be immediately sent to seize Washington. Considering the chaos in the capital at that moment, this was not a bad idea. But the suggestion was voted down on grounds that the state should take no offensive military action until the ordinance of secession had been ratified by the voters. By a 96,750-to-32,134 count this formality was finally accomplished on May 23.

Julia was slow to realize that war was not a delightful game played by "high-toned gentlemen." She seemed to feel that it should take place in a large field, distant from Camelot, where it might be observed and enjoyed as an exciting spectacle without its interfering in the normal routine of the castle. She was disturbed, therefore, to discover that it unsettled her regular correspondence with her mother and otherwise upset her accustomed pattern of life. Moreover, it was no respecter of private property. This insight she began to grasp in late April when a Massachusetts outfit ("these scum of the earth," Julia called them) landed at Old Point Comfort to reinforce Fortress Monroe and promptly seized Villa Margaret for use as a barracks. The loss of the Villa earned for the Tylers the dubious distinction of being among the first Southerners to lose their property by act of war.

As the Union garrison at Fortress Monroe was gradually increased, fear momentarily swept Sherwood Forest that a Yankee foray into Charles City County might be attempted. Sherwood Forest itself might even fall to the "fiendish" invaders. By early May there was nervous talk at the plantation of an evacuation "into the mountains." While flight did not become necessary, thanks to the rapid fortification of the river below Richmond, the loss of Villa Margaret to the Yankees infuriated Julia. "Was there ever such a savage wicked war?" she fumed. To make the Villa Margaret matter more disturbing, Julia learned in June that Quartermaster T. Bailey Myers of New York had proudly exhibited before the City's Union Defense Committee a Confederate flag which he claimed he had "captured from Villa Margaret." The New York *Commercial Advertiser* described the alleged trophy as "a dirty looking affair of red, white and blue flannel with eight stars ... roughly made, the sewing having been done by half-taught fingers." That Quartermaster Myers was a tradesman with whom Juliana had done business in peacetime suggested that war was also no respecter of socially prominent persons.[34]

Unlike her mother, who felt that the North could not lose the war ("My fears are they will overpower the South with numbers and their Blockade"), Julia never for a moment doubted Southern victory. She had absolute faith that the invaded South was "favored of Heaven." She had complete confidence in President Davis and General Lee. They were both "splendid" men of proper social background, a judgment strengthened after she had met and mingled with them socially in Richmond in 1862. So desperately did she want to believe in military myths that she had no difficulty converting the little skirmish at Big Bethel in York County on June 10 into a major Confederate victory. When the myth momentarily took on the flesh of reality at Manassas on July 21 she was nearly overcome with glee. "What a brilliant victory for the South has been the battle at Manassas!" she exulted. "[We] may talk *now* of the revival of feudal times, for never in the days of chivalry were there such knights as this infamous Northern war has made of every Southern man." Tyler, sick abed at the time, was equally elated. When he heard the news of Manassas, he raised himself up in bed, "called for champagne, and made his family and friends drink the health of our generals." Big Bethel and Manassas convinced Julia that the South was unconquerable. Excitement over the victories ran so high in Richmond that Gardie and Alex ("all fired up with enthusiasm for ... such a sacred cause as the defense of their soil from the wicked and cruel invader") wanted to join the army at once. "It makes the heart beat and the eyes fill to witness such noble resolution on the part of all," Julia told her mother. "In particular on the part of those who, bred in ease and luxury, still cheerfully accept every and any hardship that comes with a soldier's life. ... The men have become heroes. ... An unlawful war has been waged against them, and if the possession of every warrior trait will enable them to 'conquer a peace,' there will soon be one for us." [35]

Sustaining Julia's confidence in Southern victory at the outset of the conflict were frequent reports from her mother that England might enter the war on the Confederate side. "England will and must have Southern cotton and war with her is threatened by the Government if she tries to enter the [blockaded] ports," read one hopeful pronouncement from Staten Island. Similarly, Juliana assured the Tylers that there was much Southern sentiment in New York City, and this news cheered Sherwood Forest considerably.

This horrible war keeps me excited and harassed all the time [she said]....
I can give slight attention to anything else. I do not pretend to visit friends
or neighbors. I have such a *dread* of opposition. I understand, however, there
are a great many Southern sympathizers on this [Staten] Island who are
entirely opposed to this war. I have no doubt there will be a great reaction in
public sentiment, but I fear nothing will be effected before another dreadful
battle will be fought. How much I wish such a dire calamity could be prevented.

The calamity could not be averted and the "dreadful battle" was the first fight at Bull Run.[36]

Three and a half months later Tyler swept the field of the Virginia Third Congressional District with equal élan. Running in November 1861 for a seat in the Confederate House of Representatives on a platform of patriotism and more patriotism until the enemy was crushed, the old politician signally defeated two of his devoted personal friends, William H. Macfarland and Richmond attorney James Lyons, brother-in-law of Henry A. Wise. In his last race for public office, Tyler flanked both his opponents and amassed twice their combined vote. His record of never having been defeated in a public election remained intact.

His success at the polls and the joy it occasioned within his family and among his neighbors could not conceal the fact that after six months of war and blockade a pinch was already beginning to be felt at Sherwood Forest and throughout Charles City. Julia began to "miss a few luxuries." But she bore up bravely and carried on at home as if all were normal. Gardie, Alex, Lachlan, and Lonie (Julia sometimes called him Lionel at this age) were in school as usual in Charles City. Julie was withdrawn from Miss Pegram's in Richmond "until better times," and was being tutored at home. Fitz was still underfoot, too young to go to school but not too young to begin his instruction in French conversation. Pearlie was still in arms. Discouraged by the three-year drought which had cut severely into his corn and wheat yields, Tyler shifted some of his acreage to potatoes in an effort to help feed the Southern armies. The 1861 potato crop was "truly astonishing." This, Julia admitted, was "fortunate under the circumstances." The two older boys, meanwhile, made their contribution to the South's wartime economy by trapping the rabbits of the plantation ("Their skins are in great demand," Julia noted) and selling the pelts in the Richmond market. In spite of shortages of luxury items, optimism prevailed at Sherwood Forest as the first winter of the war began.[37]

During the week of January 5, 1862, Tyler left Sherwood Forest and went up to Richmond to take his seat in the Confederate House of Representatives. Julia planned to join him in town the following week, pausing first for brief New Year's visits at Brandon and Shirley. On the night of January 9, however, she had a singular dream which caused her to abandon her plans to visit the Harrisons and the Carters and to proceed straight to Richmond. She dreamed that her husband had fallen dangerously ill and had taken to his bed at the Exchange Hotel. Unlike her mother, who took séances, levitation, and other manifestations of the occult seriously, Julia thought spiritualism ridiculous, the celebrated Fox sisters fraudulent, and levitation no more than a parlor game. Nonetheless, she had long put great store in dreams. So had Margaret. Julia believed, in a vague way, in what a later generation would call extrasensory perception. While she made no fetish of these alleged psychic phenomena, she felt that dreams served as vehicles for thought-transference. For this reason and in this belief, she gathered up Pearl and hastened to Richmond to tend her "fallen" spouse. She arrived at the Exchange Hotel on Friday evening, January 10—and found Tyler entirely well.

On Sunday morning, January 12, Tyler arose early. He felt nauseated and dizzy and he soon began vomiting. Julia was half awakened by the sound of his retching and he told her to go back to sleep. He had only a slight "chill," he said, and he would go down to the hotel dining room for a cup of hot tea. The tea seemed to restore him. Rising to leave the table, he suddenly staggered and fell unconscious. He was carried to a sofa in the parlor and regained consciousness in a few minutes. Assuring the early diners who had gathered around him that he was quite all right, he somehow managed to stumble back upstairs to his room. Julia, still abed, saw him totter into their chamber, his collar open, cravat in hand. "I would not have had it happen for a good deal," he exclaimed, still badly shaken by the experience. "It will be all around the town." True to his foreboding, friends were soon streaming into the parlor to help. Before Julia could get out of bed and get dressed, he had been persuaded to lie down again on the sofa. Dr. William Peachy arrived and pronounced his condition "a bilious attack, united with bronchitis." This did not come very close to the cerebral vascular accident he had had, but at least he was seen by a doctor.

Save for frequent and severe headaches and a persistent cough, Tyler seemed well enough for the next few days. He sat in his parlor and received his political friends, lucidly discussing with them the affairs of the new nation. Peachy treated his cough with morphine, and the former President slept well. Robert Tyler moved onto the sofa in the parlor to be near his father at night, and his brother Dr. Tazewell Tyler, stationed in Richmond, looked in on the patient from time to time. When neither the headaches nor the cough responded to treatment, however, Peachy ordered the congressman to return to Sherwood Forest for a complete rest. It worried Tyler that he was missing the opening sessions of the Confederate Congress, but he finally decided he would go home on Saturday, the eighteenth.

During the night of January 17–18, Julia suddenly awoke to the sound of her husband's gasping for air. The vascular thrombosis had spread, paralyzing the respiratory center. Robert was awakened and immediately ran to summon a Dr. Brown who had a room on the same floor of the hotel. Pearl, who occupied a cot on Julia's side of the bed, awoke and began crying. "Poor little thing, how I disturb her," Tyler apologized. While the nurse was comforting the baby, Julia rubbed her husband's head and chest with alcohol. Brown arrived and prescribed brandy and mustard plasters. "Doctor, I think you are mistaken," said Tyler, refusing the plasters. But he took a sip of brandy. At that moment Dr. Peachy also appeared.

"Doctor, I am going," Tyler sighed when he saw Peachy at his bedside.

"I hope not, Sir," replied the physician.

"Perhaps it is best," said the former President.

Julia moved to put the brandy glass again to his lips. His teeth chattered on the rim. Then he looked at her and smiled, and, "as if falling asleep," he died. It was 12:15 A.M., January 18, 1862. The bed in which he died, Julia recalled, "was exactly like the one I saw him upon in my dream, and unlike any of our own." [38]

It was Tyler's last wish that Julia continue to make Sherwood Forest her home. This at least was Julia's recollection of his final request after the Civil War, when she was fighting so desperately to hold onto the plantation. But in May 1865 when she was being criticized by Tazewell for having abandoned the estate to flee to the safety of Staten Island with her children, she challenged her stepson's version of his father's last entreaty. "Julia, let no consideration induce you to go North," Tazewell remembered Tyler's having said. This, Julia retorted, was a faulty recollection. What her husband had actually said, "only a few hours before my trembling fingers closed the lids of his departing sight," was "Ah, dearest, you will go North—[but] don't bring up the children there. I prohibit it." And she had answered him, "Dearest, I will never do anything that you do not approve." Then the President had smiled and said quietly to her, "Love piled on love will not convey an idea of my affection for you. It is idolatrous." [39]

Whatever his final wishes about Sherwood Forest, John Tyler's death left his forty-one-year-old widow frightened and unsettled. With seven children to rear, one still in arms, a plantation of sixteen hundred acres and seventy slaves to manage, Tyler's debts to face, and a savage war still to be reckoned with, Julia was understandably shaken. Her religious ideas had never transcended the moralistic, anthropomorphic Protestant Christianity of the mid-nineteenth century, nor had she ever penetrated theologically beneath the beautiful rote of the Book of Common Prayer. She did not, therefore, turn to her Anglican God in lamentations. She turned instead to her mother in New York, and to

Robert and Priscilla in Richmond. But most characteristically, she dried her eyes, put on mourning clothes, and fell back upon her own considerable inner strength.

On January 20 Tyler's body lay in state in the black-draped hall of the Confederate Congress. The Stars and Bars covered him, and on his chest rested a wreath of evergreens and white roses. Several thousand citizens filed mournfully by his open casket to "take a last look at his well-known features." The business of Congress that day was devoted entirely to eulogies to the former President of the United States. Funeral services were held the following day in St. Paul's Episcopal Church, the Reverend Dr. Charles Minnigerode and the Right Reverend John Johns, Bishop of Virginia, officiating. The church was jammed with Confederate dignitaries headed by President Jefferson Davis. After the ceremony a solemn train of 150 carriages, stretching a quarter of a mile, followed the hearse through the drizzling rain to Hollywood Cemetery. There on a knoll overlooking the James River he loved so much, John Tyler was buried beside the tomb of James Monroe.[40]

Although his will specified his wish to be buried simply and unostentatiously in the grove at Sherwood Forest, his funeral had been conducted with great pomp and circumstance in Richmond. No official notice was taken of his passing in Washington by the nation he had served for half a century. John Tyler had died a rebel and a "traitor." Julia must have winced at the high-flown obituaries, the political eulogies, and the propaganda-laden tributes that drummed her departed husband into his grave. None caught the spirit of the man. None captured his wry humor, his selfless devotion to his wife and children, his stubborn loyalty to his friends. None saw the soft, human side of his personality—the John Tyler struggling to meet a payment due, or riding through his fields in his floppy straw hat; or the Tyler who laughed and danced and bounced his babies and fiddled on his piazza for the children of the plantation. None saw John Tyler the man, the husband, the father, the poet, or the planter. Virginia unfurled her battle flags, sounded her bugles, shook a mailed fist at the Yankees—and buried a Confederate caricature of the real man. He was, said Henry A. Wise, "an honest, affectionate, benevolent, loving man, who had fought the battles of his life bravely and truly, doing his whole great duty without fear, though not without much unjust reproach." The flag-draped patriotic ceremony that was his funeral caught little of this.[41]

19

MRS. EX-PRESIDENT TYLER
AND THE WAR, 1862-1865

> *Will President Lincoln have the kindness to inform Mrs. Ex-President Tyler whether her home on the James River can be withdrawn from the hands of the negroes who were placed in possession of it by Gen. Wild and restored to the charge of her manager... even though her estate has been subjected to wreck and devastation within doors and without?*
> —JULIA GARDINER TYLER, AUGUST 1864

Juliana Gardiner made every effort to procure a pass through the lines to reach her daughter's side during the melancholy weeks following John Tyler's death. She even bearded old General Winfield Scott in the lobby of the Brevoort Hotel and demanded that he help her reach the South. But her request was denied in Washington "for military reasons," and Julia discouraged further efforts in this direction for fear her mother's health was not up to the rigors of a wartime journey to Sherwood Forest. Nevertheless, Juliana kept trying to obtain a pass to the South. To accomplish this she worked through an old New York friend, Louise Ludlow, wife of Major William H. Ludlow, who was then in charge of prisoner exchange at Fortress Monroe. Unfortunately, she had no success. The preliminary movement of Union soldiers assigned to McClellan's Peninsula campaign had begun and civilian travel into and out of Virginia was sharply restricted.[1]

That a great battle was developing below Richmond, near Sherwood Forest, worried Juliana considerably. Great concern for Julia's welfare and safety, and that of her children, ran strongly through the Gardiner family as McClellan made ready to end the war in one crushing blow against the Confederate capital in the spring of 1862. Although Phoebe and Eben Horsford were "strong Union people" (Horsford resigned his Harvard science professorship in 1863 to manage the explosives division of the Rumford Chemical Works near Providence), they were not insensitive to Julia's plight. Being for the Union "does not make us love our friends the less," Phoebe said. This too was the feeling of Mrs. James I. Roosevelt and other of Julia's prewar friends in New York. They did everything in their power to help her.[2]

Julia was frightened as McClellan's advance up the Peninsula in April threatened to engulf the plantation. To make matters more difficult, she and all her children fell seriously ill with influenza that month. Fitzwalter's life "hung by a thread for days," and Pearl experienced "two shocking convulsions." Priscilla rushed down to the plantation from Richmond to help the stricken household, and Doctors John Selden and James B. McCaw interrupted busy practices in town to journey to Sherwood Forest and treat the immobilized family. The Reverend Dr. Wade also stayed with Julia and her children at the plantation at night, as did various of the neighbors. By the end of April the disease had run its course and the family was functioning again.

Fortunately, Julia was able to communicate with her worried mother during this crisis. She worked out a system of sending letters by private hand to occupied Leesburg in Loudoun County. From Leesburg they were transmitted regularly to Baltimore and on to the North by United States postal authorities. In this manner she kept her mother informed of her situation at Sherwood Forest and her determination to stay at the plantation, come what may. Thus on April 28, two months after Tyler's funeral, she told Juliana:

Though we shall be within hearing of the roaring battle when it takes place on the Peninsula at Yorktown I do not intend to desert my home whichever army carries the day. If I am molested by brutal men it will be more than I expect in this civilized age though it would seem as if we had collapsed into barbarism from the quantity of kindred blood that has already flowed upon the battlefield. I cannot flee and leave all my servants who would consider it a cruel act to desert them. If I leave they wish me to take them along, but how would it be possible to remove so many women and children? No, I have concluded to remain where I am and have the worst, and as you know my timidity you can judge I do not anticipate much inconvenience ... would that the better class at the north would have the sense and feeling to put a stop to this war. I know I am dreadfully tired of it.[3]

Not only was Julia finding the war an increasing inconvenience and bore, she became aware of the fact that people were killed in combat. When the Reverend Peyton Harrison, a kinsman of the Harrisons at Brandon, lost one son at Manassas and another at Fort Donelson, Julia soberly concluded that knighthood was no longer in flower. War, she finally decided, was "sad, sad, cruel and melancholy." More and more she gave heed to her mother's pleas to bring her children to the safety of Staten Island. At one point she even began considering a European trip "for the sake of educating the children."

Juliana, meanwhile, continued her efforts to secure a pass into Virginia, and she praised her daughter's spunk in staying with the plantation during the Peninsula fighting. "Under the circumstances," she told Priscilla's sister, "I think it would be cruel to run away and I am glad she is determined to remain. I shall make all haste to join her, but I must get well first to prepare, and we are now in the midst of house cleaning which renders everything confused here." First things first.[4]

While Juliana finished her spring cleaning, the war swirled around Sherwood Forest. Moving steadily up the Peninsula toward Richmond, McClellan's patrols reached the plantation shortly after the Union occupation of Yorktown and Williamsburg on May 5–6, 1862. By May 14 Sherwood Forest lay well behind Union lines as McClellan established his headquarters at White House on the Pamunkey River twenty miles from the Confederate capital. No harm befell Julia or the estate during these troop movements. Thanks to the direct intercession of Mrs. James I. Roosevelt through her friend General John E. Wool of Newburgh, New York, McClellan placed a protective guard at Sherwood Forest. There was no looting, raping, or burning of buildings. Save for the disappearance of the plantation's fencing into a hundred soldiers' campfires, nothing of substance was destroyed. Julia was quite safe during the great battle for Richmond, although she was cut off from her kin and friends in the city and was entirely dependent on the protection of the invader. To keep the plantation going during these trying months the inexperienced Gardie was given the task of overseeing the harvest and the planting. Although he worked hard at his new responsibility, he managed to get in but a "meager crop of wheat" that summer. Crop or no crop, Julia and her brood were secure.

They were also thoroughly isolated. Julia did not learn until later that Robert had taken up a rifle in the defense of the capital. Nor could she assist the gallant Richmond ladies who furiously made sandbags for the breastworks. She was not present to cheer the Confederate soldiers from the Shenandoah Valley as they were deployed through the city to do battle with the Yankees on the Peninsula. She could not comfort the nervous Priscilla. Nor was she on hand to witness the patriotic self-assurance of sixteen-year-old Grace Tyler, Priscilla's daughter:

When I think of the rivers of blood that must flow in a few days from now [Priscilla wrote], my heart sinks and faints within me. Our soldiers, our noble soldiers, travel-worn and weary, have been arriving here from Manassas and going down to Yorktown for the last two weeks. Thousands and tens of thousands of them have passed within a few yards of our door. Every encouragement that waving handkerchiefs, smiles, tears and prayers could give them... bunches of flowers, and kisses blown from fair fingers, they have received. And sometimes warmer words and wishes than are usual upon a first acquaintance. Imagine Grace, for instance, with all her reserve, beckoning a young lieutenant from the ranks of the gallant Georgia 7th, leaning over a bank, handing him a bunch of flowers and saying with the tears flowing over her cheeks, "God bless you. I shall pray for you every night." He with an earnest look of gratitude, "While you ladies do the praying, be sure we shall do the fighting." Then joining his ranks and looking back at Grace till his column passed out of sight.[5]

Julia was wholly cut off from her family until Lee's counterattacks in the Seven Days' battles of late June drove the invaders back down the Peninsula toward Hampton. Her main problem during these uncertain days of bloodshed was the unheard-of behavior of two of the Negro women of the plantation, one a "free negress whom charity alone, from pity for her friendless condition, had induced me to give a home," the other a slave, "my supposed faithful maid and seamstress." On the evening of May 24 the two women gathered up as many of Julia's and the children's clothes as they could carry and made off in the night. Julia was outraged to lose several of her best dinner gowns, and she immediately dispatched a strong letter to the commanding officer at Williamsburg demanding that federal authorities arrest and punish the thieves, then return them to Sherwood Forest lest "the success of the expedition be apt to produce a restless feeling among the rest of my hitherto happy family of Negroes who are in fact blessed in being situated above every want with a very moderate effort on their own part." The women were not apprehended.[6]

The incident did produce a "restless feeling" among the slaves. The Negroes on the plantation remained relatively quiet and in place during McClellan's campaign. But when it was over the young male slaves began to drift away one by one, making their way to Hampton and the protection of the Union forces at Fortress Monroe. Julia could do nothing about this leakage. She fell quite ill again in July, this time with malaria, and her mother could "almost wish her negroes would decamp as she would then feel more at liberty to join me. If the war continues I suppose her plantation would not avail her much for a house, and she will be obliged to come to me for safety.... I shall use every effort to join Julia.... I go to try to save the life of Julia if possible. I shall endeavor to bring her North. The climate during the summer is all but *death* to her." Try as she might, and in spite of the helpful efforts of Major Ludlow at Fortress Monroe and General Egbert L. Viele, Military Governor of Norfolk, Juliana could still procure no pass into Virginia. She did manage to work out a way of getting an occasional letter to her daughter through a commercial forwarding service in Franklin, Kentucky. Aside from that, she could only wait and worry and console herself with the observation that "the *fashion* of Washington are secessionists—this must be uncomfortable to the occupants of the White House." Weeks became months at Castleton Hill without word of Julia and her children. Rumors reaching her that Villa Margaret had been burned, that the Sherwood slaves had decamped en masse, and that eastern Virginia lay desolated turned her in a desperate search for assistance to her old New York friend from Tyler administration days and before, General John A. Dix, Chief of the Seventh Army Corps of the Department of Virginia. Dix promised her a pass to Virginia just as soon as the military situation permitted. Thus she stewed and fretted and waited for news of the second great battle pending at Bull Run, which, she hoped, would clear Virginia of Yankees and permit her to reach Sherwood Forest.[7]

Julia survived the fever as well as the departure of the first of her field hands. By October 1862 she decided that Charles City County was destined to become a great battlefield in all future campaigns around Richmond. It would therefore be wise to begin removing her children to the safety of Staten Island. In November 1862, through the cooperation of General Dix and various officers of his staff, principally Captain Wilson Barstow, whose wife was one of Juliana's friends, Julia procured a federal pass which permitted her to board the weekly flag-of-truce boat on the James River and proceed with her children to Hampton. There she was authorized to board a bay steamer to Baltimore. Leaving Sherwood Forest to the management of sixteen-year-old Gardie and his cousin Maria Tyler, Julia's personal companion, she took Alex, Julie, Lachlan, Lyon, Fitzwalter, and Pearl to Staten Island.

The homecoming was not particularly pleasant although Juliana was overjoyed to see her daughter at long last. The house was crowded with adults and noisy children. It was so crowded, Julia told David Lyon, that he and his family would certainly have to seek other quarters before she returned in the near future for the duration of the war. To this declaration her brother replied testily that he would leave his mother's house only when she ordered him out. Brother and sister also argued bitterly about politics and the war. Fortunately, her tense visit was a short one. Before leaving for Virginia, however, Julia transferred the ownership of Villa Margaret to her mother, who in turn instituted correspondence designed to secure indemnification and compensation from federal authorities for the occupation and use of the property by Union soldiers.[8]

Soon after New Year's Day Julia, Fitz, and Pearlie returned to Virginia, arriving at Hampton by bay steamer from Washington on January 8, 1863. Again General Dix and Captain Barstow saw to it that the former First Lady received every consideration. Barstow even managed to get Julia and her two small children off the packed little steamer and into a room at Willard's Hotel in Old Point Comfort. The remainder of the passengers were confined to the boat for the night, "huddled together like so many animals." After a comfortable night ashore, Julia was put aboard the flag-of-truce boat on the morning of January 9 and deposited safe and sound at her own landing that afternoon. Happily, she found everything in order at the plantation and in the county:

> Everything in the Southern Confederacy is most auspicious [she wrote Juliana]—a more hopeful, determined community cannot be imagined. Separation is the one thing believed in and all their deprivations are borne without a murmur so far as they themselves are concerned, but oh! how the wickedness of the North is stamped upon their very souls! It is a perfect *surprise* to them when I assure them there is some good feeling there. They are hardly prepared to believe in the exceptions.... It is well I am back. Many persons were beginning to murmur at my wishing to be North.... Property is selling very high.... You may depend upon it I shall not hold back Sherwood if I consider it best not to do so.... I passed without search—thanks to Capt. Barstow, Capt. [John E.] Mulford, and last but not least Gen. Dix. Do not take the charge of the children entirely upon yourself. It worries me very much to think how much care I left upon your hands—but how could I have helped it!!... The negroes are well disposed and in order. There are [Confederate] soldiers dispersed all over the County so that we were never more safe....[9]

Julia's return home signaled a round of visits and modest celebrations. The war in the Virginia theater was going well for the South. Patriotism ran high and the Charles City neighborhood ignored the presence of the Union garrison at Fortress Monroe and the federal gunboats on the river. The flag-of-truce boats plied regularly up and down the river, bringing in the mail and news of the outside world. On the lower James, at least, the war was temporarily stalemated. The Yankees controlled most of the river and the Confederates controlled most of the hinterland, and both sides had learned for the time to live with the other's tactical situation.

With four of her children safe in New York, Julia began to plan for the immediate future. It was her determination, regardless of those who might "murmur at my wishing to be North," to place Gardie in school in Virginia, sell Sherwood Forest if possible, and go with her two youngest children to Staten Island for the duration. Julia was thoroughly fed up with the conflict and the thought of another fever-ridden summer at Sherwood Forest was too much to contemplate. Berkeley plantation had recently sold for $50,000 although it was "in its present horrible state," and Julia was confident that Sherwood could be also disposed of without sacrifice—indeed, at a considerable profit.

With these thoughts in mind, Julia entered her husband's will in probate at the Charles City courthouse on January 15 and let it be known that the plantation was for sale. The following month she took Gardie to Lexington and enrolled him in Washington College (now

Washington and Lee University). She was distressed at having to leave him by himself "away off there among entire strangers," but he adapted well to the new situation, socially and academically. Within two months he was elected to membership in the school's select Washington Literary Society, and by October 1863 he decided he really "preferred College to Farming." [10]

Attempts to find a buyer for Sherwood Forest were not successful, although Julia did manage to sell the plantation's well-stocked wine cellar for an inflationary $4000 and dispose of two fine riding horses for $800. But both transactions were made for rapidly depreciating Confederate dollars. No buyer for the estate itself came forward. Even had there been one, the plantation was so encumbered by various claims, large and small, against John Tyler's estate that it would have been difficult to have effected transfer of a clear title in 1863. To pay these claims, totaling at least $2000 in sound pre-Civil War United States currency, and the principal and interest on several notes Tyler had left unpaid behind him, Julia deposited $5000 in Confederate money (the proceeds from the wine and horse sale, no doubt) in the Farmer's Bank of Virginia in March 1863.

Unable to sell the plantation, she reluctantly decided to continue operating it during her projected absence in the North. To this purpose she hired John C. Tyler, her deceased husband's nephew, son of Dr. Wat Henry Tyler, as her plantation manager; she also engaged two white men ("the only two white men about here") as farm laborers. She decided to hold on to the remaining slave population, especially the younger Negroes. But she left instructions that they should be sold south immediately or hired out to the Confederate government for service in labor battalions should the reappearance of the Union Army in the neighborhood give them notions of freedom and flight. "I should not keep them even now," she explained to her mother in April, "but release myself of all anxiety concerning them . . . but it is impossible to hire free labor. There are no working free people around, either black or white, and at Richmond the wages of the common whites are so high they would not come into the country for any consideration a farmer would be willing to pay." [11]

By mid-May Julia could report that she was ready to leave again for Staten Island. Inflation had by this juncture become a major problem in Virginia. With calico and cotton goods at $2.50 to $3 per yard, "homespun will soon be entirely worn by at least the country people. I am spinning altogether for the servants," she confessed. Still, inflation had its advantages and the "immense prices we get for everything," even the "meager" 1862 wheat crop, encouraged Julia to believe that she might pay off all the claims against the Tyler estate in cheap Confederate dollars. "What a fortunate thing I came home when I did," she boasted to her mother, "for no one could have managed as I have done."

Much to her dismay she discovered that Tyler's creditors were in no hurry to press their claims against the estate. Better to wait and collect in sound dollars, they reasoned.

Working with "the small force we have left," John C. Tyler began seeding oats and planting corn at Sherwood Forest as Julia departed the plantation on May 15 for Richmond. She had decided to stay in the Confederate capital until the necessary arrangements could be made with Union authorities for another pass to the North. On the eve of her removal to the city she informed her mother that inflation, however inconvenient for the poorer classes, had not disturbed the Virginia aristocracy or the Southern war effort. Even the death of Stonewall Jackson at Chancellorsville was not regarded an insurmountable disaster among Richmond fashionables:

Ladies and gentlemen dress as well and tastefully as ever and calico is rarely purchased. It is not considered worth wasting money upon ... rich things direct from Paris are worn as much as ever in dress at prices of course enormously high. A wedding took place in Petersburg the other day at an expense of ten thousand dollars ($10,000) for the wedding supper and other hospitalities—everything imported from France, the rarest confectionery, etc. ... The South has lost a beloved General, but no difficulty is found in supplying his place as heroism and skill is the rule, not the exception.[12]

Julia's return to Staten Island could not come too soon to suit Juliana. Five children (including Harry Beeckman) were more than she could handle. And with David Lyon and Sarah's two infants also in the house, the din and confusion were considerable. Grandmother Catherine Beeckman died in May 1863 and with her passing the entire responsibility for Harry devolved upon Juliana, who found to her consternation that the mere "keeping of these five children in a *comfortable wardrobe* has reduced me to the dimensions of a skeleton." Clothing bills, dental bills, and tuition bills (the children attended Mr. Major's private school near Castleton Hill) steadily mounted. In August 1863, at a great expense of money and energy, she transported the entire "little troop" to the Catskills for a vacation. At other times she consoled Alex and Harry when they were intimidated by neighborhood children ("rowdy ... untrusted Irish children," Juliana called them) for articulating their pronounced Southern views. Indeed, she had all she could do to keep the two little Rebels from running away from home to join the Confederate Army. "Alex appears to be resolved upon a desperate determination to return South and Harry equally earnest to prepare for a *gunning excursion*," Juliana exhaustedly reported in April 1863.[13]

In addition to her energy-draining obligations to Julia's children, Juliana's spirits were steadily beaten down by the unfavorable war news from the South. The Union victories at Gettysburg and Vicksburg in July 1863 she correctly interpreted as the disasters they were for the

Confederacy. "The cause of the Confederacy looks gloomy," she confessed to Julia in August. "When will this awful war end? It is horrible. The next thing, they will have Gardie in the Army unless you can all come North. Do try to send him to Europe." The crushing of the draft riots in New York City also distressed her, since for a short time during the summer of 1863 they gave much aid and comfort to the South and encouraged some of New York's more optimistic Copperheads to hope that the city might be wrenched out of the Union. "Many think this is the commencement of civil war at the North," Juliana remarked hopefully in July. "I hear from all quarters that the Irish in particular are opposed to the introduction here of Negro labor and are resolved to do no more fighting as they are dissatisfied with the objects of the war." The death of the brilliant Stonewall Jackson further saddened her and her Copperhead friends, as did their realization that the federal blockade, for all the times it was successfully run, was slowly crushing the South to death. Only the hope of Anglo-French intervention on the Confederate side gave Juliana any comfort at all. And this too had faded for her as a real prospect in mid-1863. But the situation that gave her the greatest concern in 1863 was Julia's tardiness in coming North. "I sometimes think it is destined that we shall never meet again," she worried.[14]

Julia stopped at the Ballard House in Richmond while she worked on the increasingly difficult problem of obtaining a federal pass to New York. She had no trouble securing permission from the Confederate government to leave Virginia. She had easy access to both President and Mrs. Davis. She knew them socially and she visited them frequently. Indeed, William G. Waller, Tyler's grandson, was engaged to Mrs. Davis' youngest sister, Jenny Howell (they were married in the Confederate White House in November 1863), and the South's First Lady already delighted in calling Julia "my beautiful step mother," even though Julia's actual connection with the Davis family would be that of step-grandmother-in-law to the First Lady's sister. However remote the relationship, Varina Howell Davis thought Julia "positively did not look one day over twenty" and always appeared "so fresh, agreeable, graceful and exquisitely dressed."

The problem with the pass stemmed therefore not from high Richmond officials but from Union authorities, who insisted that all Virginia applicants for passes take an Oath of Allegiance to the United States at Fortress Monroe before receiving clearance north. This oath Julia would not and, in all honesty, could not take. Letters from Juliana in Staten Island to President Lincoln requesting that the degrading requirement be waived for "Mrs. Ex-President Tyler" were unavailing. Julia told General Dix that "while I would be ready to give my *parole d'honneur* to be inoffensive in all respects to the U.S. Govt. I wish to be spared the presentation of any other oath—which I could not take." Since she was a female noncombatant and only wanted to "see the faces of my darling mother and my little children who are with her," she was certain an old Washington friend like former New York Senator Dix would not insist on "forms and ceremonies which I learn are imposed on others." Old friend or no, Dix could do nothing for Julia (save graciously forward her mail to New York) without the oath.[15]

All hope of leaving Virginia legally dashed, Julia began making arrangements to depart illegally—from Wilmington, North Carolina, by blockade runner. From his post in the Confederate Navy Department James A. Semple was instrumental in helping Julia make the necessary plans. Actually, his task was not a difficult one. It was complicated, however, by Julia's desire to take a few bales of cotton out of the country with her for speculative purposes and to travel with the shipment to Bermuda, where she could personally dispose of it. Working through William G. Waller, who was attached to the Confederate Ordnance Department's arsenal at Augusta, Georgia, and through Colonel Josiah Gorgas, Chief of Confederate Ordnance, Julia finally secured an Ordnance Department authorization, dated August 10, 1863, directing "J. M. Seixas, Esq., Special Agent of the War Department, at Wilmington, N.C., to furnish free passage to yourself, two young children and one servant on the Govmt. *R. E. Lee,* as requested, with permission to take out also on same Str. Five bales of Cotton." Since the *R. E. Lee,* Captain John Wilkinson, had just sailed, Julia was told she would have to wait for her next voyage "probably early in September." Unfortunately, when the *R. E. Lee* was ready to depart Wilmington again in late September, Julia had not yet completed arrangements for the cotton she wanted to take with her. Her tardiness in leaving the South was due entirely to her inability to get herself and her cotton allotment together on the same ship. While trying to solve this logistic problem she was constrained to turn down passage for herself, her children, and her Negro servant Celia Johnson on vessels leaving port in early and middle October. While the delay afforded her an opportunity to press a niggling claim against the Confederate War Department for a horse and some oats commandeered from Sherwood Forest by a cavalry foraging party, Semple urged her to leave as quickly as possible for Bermuda, permit him to handle the claim, and let Seixas consign the cotton to Nassau. To this importunity Julia finally agreed. She sailed, therefore, from Wilmington on October 28 aboard the CSS *Cornubia,* Captain R. H. Gayle, and arrived in Bermuda on November 2. The five bales of cotton were shipped to Nassau in December aboard the steamer *Eugenie.* There an agent sold them for Julia to a Spanish buyer for the handsome sum of £225.11.6d. So handsome was the sum, in fact, that Julia would attempt, unsuccessfully, in May 1864 to get another profitable cotton lot through the ever-tightening blockade.[16]

Scarcely had Julia settled down to enjoy briefly the pleasant society that peacetime Bermuda afforded, while waiting for passage to New York, than she learned of the capture of the gallant Captain Gayle and the *Cornubia* on the vessel's return trip to Wilmington. Gayle, who was in his early thirties, had treated his distinguished passenger with great kindness on the outward voyage to Bermuda, and it may be assumed that the eligible and still attractive widow did not discourage his flattering attentions. In any event, his capture distressed her terribly. Not until January 1864, after she had safely reached Staten Island, did she learn that he had heroically stayed with his ship, attempting to burn the vessel, while his panicky crew fled to the boats in a vain attempt to escape. He was the only man remaining on deck when the Union boarding party came over the side. "If Capt. Gayle's commands had been obeyed," Jefferson Davis was reported to have said, "the ship could have escaped." Whatever the truth of the loss of the *Cornubia* and the responsibility for it, the dashing Gayle, member of a distinguished Richmond family, was sent to Fort Warren Prison in Boston.[17]

Equally disturbing to Julia was news from Gardie in Lexington that the Washington College students had marched off to war, or at least in eager search of war. Under the emergency-manpower provisions of a proclamation by Governor Letcher, the college had formed a reserve infantry company which was attached to the Rockbridge Regiment of the Virginia Home Guard, Colonel Thomas Massey commanding. Actually trained for less than two weeks, the Washington College boys, together with the more experienced Virginia Military Institute Cadets, were ordered to Alleghany County in late October 1863 to help repel a federal cavalry raid in the area. Under the command of Professors Alexander Nelson and John L. Campbell, the civilian undergraduates hiked the forty-five miles into the mountains " 'spiling' for a fight." It was a lark. Passing through the Rockbridge Alum Springs, Gardie and his mates "found the place entirely deserted and *drank alum water to our heart's content free of cost!*" Marching on, the column learned that the enemy was at Covington. "We immediately began to advance against them," wrote Gardie. "Everybody expected a fight and while on our way an old woman came out of her house and commenced cheering us on saying that the Yanks were only two miles ahead. This greatly excited us and we marched ahead with loud cheers." The information from the small Rebel cheering section proved wrong. Only when they reached the vicinity of Clifton Forge did they learn that General J. D. Imboden's Cavalry Brigade had already driven the Federals out of Covington and back toward the West Virginia line. There would be no fight. So the boys and their professors turned around and marched back to Lexington, arriving there "pretty well worn out." To seventeen-year-old Gardie the whole experience was wonderful. "I liked camp life amazing," he told his mother. "I try to study as much as possible but I find it quite hard to do so as everything is so full of war fever." [18]

With all her worries about Captain Gayle and her eldest son, Julia nonetheless found a pleasant life awaiting her among congenial friends in peaceful, booming Bermuda. She immediately attached herself to the gay community of Confederates who for various reasons—business, pleasure, escape, adventure—had established themselves in St. George. Confederate officers and civil servants, Confederate purchasing agents and ship's captains, Confederate speculators, transients, and tourists were present in number in Bermuda, many in the company of their ladies —or someone else's lady. Along with the British officers and officials stationed on the island, they peopled the numerous dances and dinner parties, the opulence of which made wartime Richmond with its growing shortages and inflation seem another world. The British 39th Regimental band generally played for these gala affairs and there were always plenty of "Red coats to liven the scene." Mrs. Norman J. Walker, wife of a Confederate Army purchasing agent, became Julia's principal friend during her two-week stay in St. George prior to her voyage to New York on the British ship *Harvest Queen* in mid-November. The Walkers' Christmas party was a typical Southern function of the time and place. It was dedicated more to the birth of the Confederacy than to the birth of Christ:

We are becoming quite gay in our little Island home [Mrs. Walker wrote Julia in January 1864]; that is the civilians and military are.... The Confederate Flag gaily decorated my little cottage [on Christmas Day], and at supper, I myself, proposed the health of "Our President" which was drunk with a hearty good will; and then went up one cheer after another, which resounded to every corner of the house. We were body, and heart, and soul *Confederates;* and I laughingly remarked to the [British] Colonel at my side, "*Now* we may cheer our own Flag and abuse, if we choose, all the rest of the governments of the earth." ... I had made them forget the war, and that was certainly *next* to spending their Xmas night in Dixie! Of course, we had our own national drink, "egg-nog," made in the old Virginia style.[19]

Fortunately, Julia, Fitz, and Pearlie were quite safe at Castleton Hill on Christmas Day, 1863. And if their arrival there on November 24 brought the resident population of the Gardiner homestead to four adults, nine children, Juliana's nurse, and Julia's maid (four other servants lived out), there was, at first, general satisfaction that the family was united again. Juliana, old and sick, more often confined to her room than not, was relieved to have her daughter with her again. But the premises were terribly crowded. In December Mr. Ralph Dayton of New York was introduced into the already bursting household as private tutor to the children.

By Christmas Day, while Southern patriots celebrated in Bermuda, there was little peace on earth at Castleton Hill. Tension between Julia and her brood of Rebels and David Lyon and his Union family increased during the holiday season and became almost unbearable during

January 1864. Political arguments raged incessantly. With so many children underfoot there was also constant confusion. Alex and Harry enjoyed playing harmless pranks on their Yankee uncle and, predictably, the humorless David Lyon, "very much tried by the children," retaliated. On at least three occasions he cuffed Alex and Julie around severely, actions which produced screams of bloody murder from the children and angry exchanges between Julia and her brother. During one of these scenes with David, Julia was struck and knocked to the floor. Sarah Thompson Gardiner was caught in the middle of this acrimony. "My position is a most unpleasant one," she told Juliana. "I cannot take sides against my husband or his Mother.... It makes me sick to think of what has taken place." Juliana experienced no mixed loyalties. She sided completely with Julia and she protected Julia's children from David Lyon's abuse. On one occasion she told her nurse that she "didn't feel safe in the house when Mr. Gardiner was with the children." Indeed, so angry did she become with her son that on February 10, 1864, with Julia's urging, she removed all her business affairs from his hands and summarily ordered him and his family from her house. He returned to his own farm at nearby Northfield and never saw his mother alive again. He made no effort to.[20]

There is little doubt that underlying this tragic family split was the sectional emotion engendered by the Civil War. No sooner had Julia arrived in Staten Island and treated herself to a series of shopping sprees in the well-stocked New York City stores, notably Lord & Taylor, than she began involving herself in local Copperhead activities. These were subversive enterprises to which the patriotic David Lyon strenuously objected.

Julia's first and most extensive, certainly her most trying and dedicated, project was to secure the exchange and release of Captain R. H. Gayle from Fort Warren Prison. At this task she worked throughout 1864 and into 1865. Gayle was no ordinary war prisoner. His sister was Mrs. Josiah Gorgas, wife of the capable Chief of the Confederate Ordnance Department. Another of his brothers-in-law was Brigadier General H. K. Aiken of the Sixth South Carolina Cavalry. Nor was Gayle, as he himself disdainfully put it to the military commission examining his exchange status in April 1864, a mere "blockade runner." He was, he told the commission proudly, "an officer in the Navy of the Confederate States, and am consequently a 'prisoner of war.'" The fact that the *Cornubia* had been operated by the Confederate government, Gayle being paid according to his naval rank, elevated the Captain above the status of the free-enterprising Rhett Butlers of the South and legally placed him in a prisoner-exchange category. Julia thus had great hopes that she might hasten his passage to freedom through the red-tape blockade.

Meanwhile he was allowed to receive a single-page letter a week from each of his correspondents on the outside, and no week passed that Julia did not send him a cheering missive. She also made arrangements regularly to send him books, cigars, food, wine, and small sums of money. Fort Warren was no Andersonville. But mainly she worked directly through and on General John A. Dix, now stationed in New York, to effect Gayle's exchange. She also listened patiently and understandingly to the complaints and frustrations of an active man, cooped up in prison, dreaming of freedom and a return to the wars. "When I read in the papers of all the bustle and busy life that is sweeping over the land," he wrote his benefactress in March 1864, "I almost am tempted to attempt the leap of Fort Warren's high walls." Julia, of course, was permitted to write him no politically oriented letters—these were subject to confiscation. But Gayle and his fellow prisoners kept abreast of the war through the Boston newspapers and he interpreted for Julia the military implications of passing events. "We can tell what Grant will do, and know what Lee ought to do," he laughed. "To hear us talk, one would think the combined military talent of the country was wasting itself within these walls."

By May 1864 the bored and lonely prisoner's letters to Julia were becoming increasingly personal. He asked her for her picture, received it, and sent one of himself in return. "Photographs seldom do justice to their subject," he told her, "but he must indeed be a poor artist, who in your case, could make a failure with such a model." Her picture helped him pass the lengthening months of his captivity. "I feel no longer alone," he thanked her. His boredom became unbearable when exchange negotiations were suspended during Grant's 1864 summer campaign around Richmond. Gayle began to wonder whether he would ever leave Fort Warren: "I shall consider the loss of my liberty for a whole year as equal to the loss of a leg," he complained to Julia. "I might have been a Commodore by this time." The weeks and months dragged on.

On August 28, 1864, the claustrophobic Gayle finally learned from Colonel Robert Ould, Confederate agent for prisoner exchange in Richmond, that he would soon be exchanged for Lieutenant Commander Edward P. Williams, USN. Julia shared his joy and excitement. At the beginning of October the necessary papers had been arranged, and Gayle, in company with other Confederate naval officers from the *Tennessee, Selma, Atlanta,* and *Tacony,* left Fort Warren for City Point, below Richmond. There on October 20 he was duly exchanged. "For my part," he wrote Julia before leaving Boston, "I should look back upon the last ten months as a hideous nightmare, to be remembered only with a shudder, were it not for the bright beams which you, my dear Madam, have occasionally darted within these frowning walls." [21]

Within a few weeks Gayle had another ship, the steamer *Stag*, and was "employed again" on the Wilmington-Bermuda run. "I ran her out of Wilmington while the fleet was thundering at Fort Fisher," he happily wrote his "ministering angel" from Bermuda on New Year's Day. Leaving Bermuda for Wilmington on January 14, 1865, the *Stag* reached the Cape Fear River around midnight on the nineteenth. There she was captured, the last Confederate ship attempting to run the Union blockade to be taken in the war. Her captain could not appreciate the historical uniqueness of the event. "Imagine, my dear Madam," Gayle fumed from Fort Warren in February,

how astonished I was when, fancying myself safely at home, I found myself a prisoner. No intimation of the fall of Fort Fisher had ever reached me, and without a suspicion of anything being wrong I confidently ran my ship up to the usual anchorage. At the entrance to the harbor there was no suspicious appearance—the usual lights were properly set, and I unsuspectingly ran into the trap so cleverly laid ... and here I am once more, as quietly settled down in my old quarters as if I had never left them.... I find it somewhat difficult to realize that I have had a holiday. I was exchanged on the 20th of Oct. and captured again on the 20th of Jan.—only three months. Had my ship been shot to pieces, or fairly run down at sea, I would not mind it so much; but to have deliberately walked into a trap purposely prepared for me makes me feel so foolish that I can hardly look anyone in the face. Most of the prisoners whom I left behind me are still here, and you can imagine what a commotion there was when I made my appearance within the sally-port. Upon my word, Mrs. Tyler, I felt as if I had been caught in a theft.... Tell Pearly that I appreciate her sympathy....

And so Julia again took up her Fort Warren-Gayle project.[22]

Other war ventures had meanwhile been pressed with vigor. With her inflated Confederate money Julia loyally purchased sinking Confederate war bonds. She sent money and clothes to needy friends in the South and to Confederate soldiers of her acquaintance who were languishing in Union prison camps. She became a working member of a small cell of Staten Island Copperheads, a group of women who distributed peace pamphlets, conducted relief activities in Southern cities occupied by the Union Army, cheered Confederate victories and plugged for General George B. McClellan's election to the Presidency in 1864. In these activities she was assisted by her mother and by Louisa Cooper (Priscilla's sister) who lived in the city.[23]

Throughout 1864 Julia held as an unimpeachable article of faith the belief that the Confederacy would eventually win the war even though all the private information she could gather from her Southern friends and correspondents told her otherwise. She knew that inflation was completely out of hand in Virginia; she realized that the blockade was squeezing the Confederacy to death; she knew also that the struggling nation was split militarily in twain, and that Union armies and cavalry units were plunging deeper into the vitals of the South with less and less opposition. Yet she preferred to believe that somehow all would turn out well. She believed in slogans, not facts; and this at a time when the history of Charles City County alone told her all was lost, that the Old South was dying. "The news from home certainly gives us no occasion for rejoicing," Mrs. Walker wrote her from Bermuda in February 1864. Julia simply would not believe it.²⁴

The last full year of the war opened quietly in Charles City. Maria Tyler reported everything at Sherwood Forest in excellent condition as of January 1864, "all the servants are well and their clothing attended to." Only a single Union cavalry raid, which destroyed the county courthouse in November, had disturbed an otherwise peaceful winter in the neighborhood. The Confederate Congress had passed a new draft act extending the military age from eighteen to fifty-five and this promised, in Maria's words, to "swell our army it is thought to two hundred thousand." Except for complaints about the soaring inflation from the poverty-ridden Richmond masses, confidence in the future was generally high in the Tidewater. "Things look brighter for our cause," Maria told Julia. "Our soldiers here are perfectly confident of success and Gen. Lee is the same good Christian and great General." The local Charles City Cavalry was disbanded and its personnel, in search of rest and relaxation, whiled away the time jousting for the hands of fair maidens at mock medieval tournaments. "Charles City has been unusually gay this winter, party after party, dinners and even Tournaments," John C. Tyler wrote Julia. He had great hope that a normal crop would be planted and harvested at Sherwood Forest. At the end of March 1864, then, the only winter casualty sustained by the plantation was one raided smokehouse and the theft of the meat therein.²⁵

At Lexington Gardie remained impatiently in college, struggling unequally with Tacitus and Xenophon. "The truth is my mind is so full of war and rumors of war that I cannot study with any sort of plan." The march to Covington had whetted his martial appetite and filled him with the most intense patriotism. He spent most of the winter of 1863–1864 trying to decide which branch of the Confederate service to join when he became eighteen in July. The thought of slaughtering Yankees filled him with delight. "Come one, come all," he crowed to Alex, "we are ready for them.... Our army was never in such a fine condition as it is now. With the exception of a few delicacies we live as well as we ever did. Never believe a word about our starvation, etc." ²⁶

Heralded in early April 1864 by Union cavalry raids through the county and gunboat reconnaissance along the river, the opening of Grant's spring campaign in May struck Charles City and Sherwood Forest like a thunderclap. Striking south from Culpeper through the Wilderness, Grant's 100,000-man Army of the Potomac coordinated a massive attack on Richmond with General Benjamin Butler's 36,000-man Army of the James, which moved up the south side of the river from Norfolk to hit the Confederate capital from the east and south. In the Shenandoah Valley Franz Sigel's force of 20,000 began to advance southward toward Staunton and Lynchburg in a twin effort to pin Jubal A. Early in the Valley and strip Virginia's granary of food and supplies that might otherwise reach Lee at Richmond. In the west Sherman departed Chattanooga on his celebrated march to the sea. The Confederacy was coming apart at the seams. Or so it seemed.

Once again Sherwood Forest was in the midst of a Peninsula campaign as Butler drove toward Richmond along the south bank of the James. This time, however, the plantation was not spared. On May 7, 1864, the 1st Brigade, Hink's Division, XVIII Corps, Negro troops commanded by Brigadier General Edward A. Wild, crossed the river at Kennon's Landing and occupied Sherwood Forest and the surrounding countryside. Save for a sharp scrap at Wilson's Landing with roving units of Fitzhugh Lee's cavalry, the Negro troops easily took possession of Charles City County. It was during this fighting, however, that some of the outbuildings were burned at Sherwood Forest, probably by retreating Confederate cavalrymen. A reign of terror was soon unleashed against the defenseless county by the conquerors. Mr. Lamb Wilcox was shot dead in his yard by Negro soldiers for refusing to salute them. George Walker was shot down by colored soldiers for resisting their plunder, although he was more fortunate than Wilcox and lived to go to prison. Throughout the county plantations were plundered, homes sacked, livestock driven off, and outbuildings burned. Slaves were "liberated" and carried away by their dusky emancipators. William H. Clopton, reported by "some of my negro women" for being a "most cruel master," was seized by Wild's troopers, stripped naked, and lashed while his slaves stood by and cheered. John C. Tyler was arrested. He, Clopton, G. B. Major, A. H. Ferguson, R. J. Vaiden, J. C. Wilson, Thomas Douthat, and other civilian planters and professional men of the neighborhood were hauled down to Fortress Monroe where they were imprisoned. "My wife and family are at Weyanoke," said Douthat sadly, "everything lost on the farm and themselves surrounded by U.S. Colored troops. God will protect them I feel assured, and in his hands I leave them." As at Weyanoke, the Sherwood Forest farm buildings were raided, meat seized and livestock expropriated. Fortunately, James A. Semple and John C. Tyler had managed to get most of the deceased President's papers and all of the family silverware and portraits to a warehouse and bank vault in Richmond during the cavalry raids in April. On the farm, however, "they have not left five dollars worth," John C. informed Julia on May 20. So brutal was the Yankee visitation in Charles City that even the infamous General Butler was shocked. General Wild was reprimanded and his rampaging troops finally brought under control. The detained planters were treated with "marked respect" at Fortress Monroe by Butler and formal charges against the most vicious of the looters, plunderers, and lashers were entertained by Butler's Provost Marshal. Clopton promptly preferred charges against General Edward A. Wild. Needless to say, nothing came of them.[27]

When Julia learned of the Yankee deluge in Charles City she immediately wrote letters to General Butler and to President Lincoln, signed "Mrs. Ex-President Tyler," asking that her friend, William Clopton, and her plantation manager, John C. Tyler, be released from prison and returned to their farms. They were needed at home to protect what property remained. The presence of John C. Tyler was especially required at Sherwood Forest to give comfort, succor and protection to Miss Maria Tyler, "the delicate orphan girl ... exposed to a fate I dread even to think of." Julia pleaded with Lincoln: "By the memory of my Husband, and what you must be assured would have been his course in your place, had your Wife appealed to him, remove from me these causes for anxious suspense." Benjamin Butler may have been the "Beast" of New Orleans, but he promptly responded to Julia's entreaty and saw to it that Maria Tyler was made safe. "For your prompt action in this respect I owe you many thanks," Julia admitted.[28]

Her plea to the President was less expeditiously processed. Lincoln referred Julia's letter to General Butler and he in turn forwarded it back to Colonel Joseph Holt, Judge Advocate General, in Washington with a request for instructions. Holt, meantime, had received a direct tongue-lashing from Julia protesting the whipping of Clopton and the "complete dismantlement of Sherwood Forest." She demanded, as the widow of a former President of the United States, immediate restoration of "the resources of which I have been suddenly and violently deprived." Thanks in part to the former First Lady's paper barrage, John C. Tyler and Clopton were finally released, Clopton in late June, Tyler in mid-July.

But while this round-robin correspondence was in progress, Sherwood Forest was turned over to local Negroes and they sacked its interior. Early in June General Wild placed the plantation house in the possession of two of the Tyler slaves, Randolph and Burwell. Within a few days the house furnishings had disappeared. Beds were carted off, marble table tops were smashed, and furniture was removed to the open-air Negro camp Wild had established near his command post at Kennon's Landing. Sofas were stripped of their velvet and "mirrors crushed all to atoms." Busts and windows were broken. "Old Fanny was the leader in tearing down the curtains and gathering things up generally," Clopton reported. Randolph, Burwell, and some half-dozen other Negroes from surrounding plantations (the remaining Tyler slaves had run aimlessly off) temporarily moved their women and children into the debris. Under Wild's orders the Sherwood Forest barns and smokehouses still standing were opened to the drifting neighborhood Negroes and the last of the livestock was seized and distributed among them. "They kill a hog nearly every day. The negroes have eaten all the sheep that were left and the hogs and are now going on upon the neighbor's stock." Structurally, the main house was not harmed beyond a few smashed windows and a split door or two, but the plantation itself was rendered a wasteland. The white laborer, Oakley, was "no better than the negroes," and he joyously joined in the plunder. When John C. returned to Sherwood in mid-July the Negro occupants sassily refused to vacate the main house. "Give up nothing to anyone," Wild had instructed them.[29]

When she received the news of General Wild's arrogance Julia wrote the White House: "Will President Lincoln have the kindness to inform Mrs. (Ex-President) Tyler whether her home on the James River can be withdrawn from the hands of the negroes, who were placed in possession of it by Gen. Wild, and restored to the charges of her manager, Mr. J. C. Tyler ... [even] though her estate has been subjected to wreck and devastation within doors and without...." While she was in the letter-writing mood she also demanded of Lincoln that the government either vacate Villa Margaret or begin paying rent for using it. These requests were also referred by the President to General Butler, who had already received similar missives directly from Julia. Under this bombardment of pen and ink from Staten Island and Washington, Butler undertook an investigation into Julia's complaints. General Wild assured his commanding officer that he had placed no impediment in the way of John C. Tyler's recovery of the estate. As for the Negroes living there, they were, said Wild, merely "three colored men (two old and one middle-aged) with their families, said to be claimed by Mrs. Tyler as her servants, who now live as they have done for many years upon the estate of the late Mr. Tyler.... They have cultivated some portion of the estate and I suppose desire to reap where they have sown." This view, endorsed by Butler, became the official one and was made known to Julia in September.[30]

The federal authorities at Fortress Monroe did not see fit to inform Julia that the downstairs rooms of Sherwood Forest had been converted into a temporary schoolhouse for "negroes and whites" in June. This distressing information came from William H. Clopton, whose release from the Fortress Julia had been instrumental in securing and whose wife, Lu Clopton, had given Maria Tyler refuge in her home during the upheaval in Charles City in May. "It is occupied yet as a School house," William wrote Julia on July 1. "The trees are nearly all destroyed and a good many houses erected around the lot. The land is all ploughed up and cultivated pretty close to the Dwelling. The house looked to be in very good repair outside as far as I could see from the road." [31]

Sherwood Forest was not unique under the new order of things in Charles City County. An entire social system had disappeared overnight. The two-to-one Negro majority in name had become a two-to-one

491

majority in fact. King Numbers was enthroned. The whites were stunned and bewildered by the swiftness of the revolution. When planter Clopton's slaves denounced him and had him thrashed by Negro soldiers, his reaction was outrage. But when his servants fled his property, his feeling was indifferent. "The loss of my negroes gives me no concern.... My feelings have been so changed in regard to them that I don't feel that I ever care to see another." Julia felt much the same way. When Celia Johnson, her Negro maid on Staten Island, asked to be sent home to Charles City, Julia did nothing to dissuade her. She arranged the necessary pass with Butler's headquarters. She too had had enough of Negroes. The benevolent paternalism of the plantation system was dead, casually abandoned by the very people it had sought to civilize. Julia felt that, having bitten the hand that fed them, the ungrateful Negroes could begin looking after themselves on a free-enterprise basis. She was through with them.[32]

Among the numerous tidings of disaster that wended north to Julia from Charles City during the summer of 1864, none distressed her so much as the sudden marriage of Maria Tyler to a Yankee soldier. Soon after the Union Army overran Charles City and turned Sherwood Forest over to the local Negroes, Julia received a pitiful letter from the frightened woman asking to be allowed to come to Staten Island. She was sick and she was panicky, and with Clopton and John C. Tyler both incarcerated in Fortress Monroe she was also helpless. "I do not know what is to become of *me*," she moaned to Julia. "My health is feeble, very [and] ... I am surprised that you do not seem yet to understand the complete wreck at Sherwood.... Wish I could have an interview if only of one hour's duration with you, *dearest of all friends*—perhaps you could then form a more correct idea of my desolate condition ... provisions are scarce I assure you—almost to starvation. The prospect is gloomy in the extreme." Julia had a lively imagination when it came to THE FATE WORSE THAN DEATH. In a letter to the New York *Evening Post* on June 26 she pictured the twenty-seven-year-old Maria as "a delicate orphan girl ... deprived of her protector and exposed to the terrible vicinity of an unscrupulous colored soldiery." She was naturally much relieved when Mrs. Clopton took Maria in at Selwood, more relieved when she later learned that Generals Butler and Wild had consented to Maria's departure for the North whenever she wished to go. Further, the Union officers assured Julia the girl would be shielded from THE FATE; she could also receive any clothes or money Julia wished to send to her through Federal lines. Thus when General Wild informed Staten Island in mid-June that Maria had suddenly decided not to leave Charles City, Julia was puzzled. But she accepted Wild's explanation that Maria was "liable to haemorrage [*sic*] and troubled with rheumatism."[33]

The real reason for Maria's hesitancy soon became apparent.

"Maria is married to a little Dutchman," Clopton informed Castleton Hill in shock on August 2,

who will be twenty one in August from Buffalo, N.Y., entirely without any of the civilities of life about him. He sits in the parlor or dining room and spits on the floor as though he was outdoors. When I got home [to Selwood] she had made it all up to suit herself. He was left at Mr. Major's in hire for a guard.... Lu thinks it awful she did not consult anyone about it, John [C. Tyler] nor me.... She passed herself off for 23.... Mr. James Christian came and married them.... He spits on the floor and piles fish bones on the table around his plate—but enough! I feel that I am lowered in the world by being compelled to admit such a thing to take place in my house. But the force of circumstances could not be overcome.

"Beast" Butler filled in the harrowing details for Julia a few days later. The happy groom who spat on the floor was Private John Kick of Company F, 2nd Regiment, New York Mounted Rifles. If Julia was to see no humor in the marriage, Butler did. He had been extremely polite to Julia and to all her kin in Charles City. Every possible consideration had been extended them by his headquarters, even while he was brilliantly botching up Grant's campaign before Richmond. Benjamin F. Butler was one of the most incompetent general officers ever to wear a United States Army uniform. But he knew something of the intense Gardiner-Tyler concern with proper marriage alliances, and he could not resist the comment that Julia need no longer worry about Maria's virtue. In Private John Kick, Maria Tyler had at last found "a natural protector."

I have just taken measures to give the bridegroom a furlough to spend the honeymoon in. This step of Miss Tyler's may tend to relieve your mind of any anxiety as to her health which you have suffered for some time past. Allow me my dear Madam to congratulate you upon so loyal an alliance of your relative and so happy a recovery of her health.

Julia was no amateur in the barbed-words game. Declining Butler's offer of a pass to come to Charles City to visit the newlyweds, she testily informed him that poor Maria had for some weeks been

bordering on insanity. The terrible scenes she depicted [in her last letter] have evidently banished reason from its throne. Otherwise I think she would have braved the starvation which by her account stared her in the face, or met death in any form rather than have taken the step of which you inform me. It is to be hoped, however, that the loyalty of her husband to which you particularly allude will soon promote him to high military rank....[34]

The Cloptons would not let Maria bring her Yankee husband to live with them at Selwood, and they ordered her from their home. Mrs. Henry Holt of Charles City at last took the girl in, but she would not accept Maria's bridegroom in her house either. It did not matter in the long run. Private Kick was shortly arrested by Union military police and sent out of the area when it was discovered he already had a wife in New York state. The "marriage" therefore was bigamous and illegal from the beginning.

While the marital exploitation of the hapless Maria was under way, Julia in New York and Major John Tyler, Jr., in Richmond wrote various newspapers in the North and South announcing to one and all that Maria Tyler was neither the daughter nor the "adopted daughter" (as the New York *Herald* had identified her) of the tenth President. James A. Semple advanced the theory that Maria had married the Yankee soldier as part of a plot to seize Sherwood Forest: "Maria's plan was to marry and then quietly settle at Sherwood as owner of it and if the war lasted long enough possession would have given her the right.... She is a bigger goose than I gave her credit for." This thesis, wrongheaded as it was, was generally accepted within the embarrassed family. That Maria was a frightened, insecure, half-sick, hungry, confused, unmarried twenty-seven seems not to have occurred to anyone as a possible explanation of her strange behavior. But the initial shock of the thing was a little too much to absorb. Virginia ladies normally did not marry common Yankee soldiers in the middle of the Civil War.[35]

The opening of Grant's spring campaign of 1864 in Virginia put an end to Gardie's helpless struggle with Tacitus and Xenophon at Washington College. Franz Sigel's drive up the Shenandoah in May produced a manpower crisis in western Virginia of serious proportions. To help stem the Union tide in the Valley the young Cadets of the Virginia Military Institute, boys fifteen to seventeen, were hastily marched north to New Market and attached to General John C. Breckinridge's command. At the Battle of New Market on May 15 they "behaved splendidly, driving the enemy off the field and capturing 6 pieces of artillery." Gardie watched them form up and march out of their barracks the night they left Lexington for New Market, hopes high, drums throbbing. So many of his friends were among them. "I would have liked so much to have been with them," he lamented to his mother. "None of the Cadets were killed that I was acquainted with. Only five were killed and forty wounded."[36]

The defeat of the hapless Sigel at New Market and his retreat north to Cedar Creek seemed for a moment to write *finis* to the Valley campaign of 1864. A large segment of General Breckinridge's force in western Virginia was confidently deployed to the Richmond area to reinforce the beleaguered Lee. Brigadier General William E. Jones was left in the Valley, headquarters in Lynchburg, with little more than a scratch army to keep an eye on the battered enemy. The replacement of Sigel by Union General David Hunter caused no particular alarm in Jones' undermanned camp. Hunter was known to be no Bonaparte even though he could muster, all told, some 18,000 men to oppose the 6000 Rebels left in the Shenandoah. It was therefore a matter of some surprise to Confederate commanders in the Valley to learn in late May that the unskilled Hunter actually harbored notions of offensive warfare and was preparing an advance south from Woodstock into the Staunton-Harrisonburg area.

On May 26 the Rockbridge reserves, old men and young boys, including among the boys Gardie Tyler and a number of other Washington College students, were called to the colors and marched north to Staunton on what was identified at the outset as a routine "training operation" in the field. They reached Staunton on May 29, the same day Hunter's army of 8500 departed Woodstock for Harrisonburg. This ominous movement of the Yankees put an end to all prospects of a training exercise. Instead, General Jones ordered the attachment of the untried Rockbridge troops to his force as combat reinforcements while he hastily moved his meagerly supplemented little army northward from Lynchburg to stem the Yankee plunge up the Valley. For nearly a week, from May 29 to June 4, the Rockbridge soldiers marched, countermarched and prepared fortifications near Mount Crawford, Virginia, under Jones' command, as the Confederate general maneuvered to stay between Hunter and Staunton. Into this exciting real-war situation Gardie joined enthusiastically. He had learned of the sacking of Sherwood Forest before leaving Lexington, and he burned with vengeance as he waited impatiently to come to grips with Hunter's despicable Yankees.

Unhappily for young Tyler, he reported sick with "ague and fever" on June 2 and was ordered by the surgeon to a military hospital in Staunton. He therefore luckily missed the disastrous Battle of Piedmont (variously called Mount Meridian and New Hope) eleven miles northeast of Staunton on Sunday, June 5. Here a superior Union force of 8500 flanked the Confederate right, crushed it, rolled it up, and drove the stunned Confederates streaming from the field in disarray. It was Hunter's finest hour. General Jones himself died in the fight. In addition to 460 Confederates killed and some 1450 wounded, more than 1000 Rebels were taken prisoner. Jones' mixed army of 5600 regulars and reserves practically disintegrated under the shock of the Union attack. "Gen. Wm. E. Jones was in command on our side," Gardie dejectedly wrote his mother, "and altho' he was a brave man and a fine cavalry officer yet he showed himself to be no infantry leader. He was killed in the battle while gallantly striving to rally his men. The reserves fought with the steadiness of regular troops and were the last to give way. They suffered severely. We lost 1 killed, 3 wounded and two captured out of our company."

The decisive defeat at Piedmont opened Staunton to the enemy.

At eleven o'clock on the night of June 5 Gardie hastily fled the hospital there and made his way by carriage to nearby Waynesboro, where he managed to rejoin his retreating comrades. He narrowly missed being captured by Hunter's victorious army when it entered Staunton at 2 A.M. on the sixth and took prisoner 400 sick and wounded Confederate soldiers caught in the town. Dispirited and dejected, and somewhat disabused of the widespread Southern myth that one Rebel soldier in the field was somehow worth ten Yankees, Gardie straggled southward through Rockfish Gap toward Lynchburg with his unit, now temporarily under the command of Brigadier General John C. Vaughn. Meanwhile, Lee detached General Breckinridge and his division from the Army of Northern Virginia and rushed them by forced marches to the defense of crucial Lynchburg, the southern anchor of the entire Valley defense system.

Fortunately for the Confederate cause in the Shenandoah, the conquering Hunter suddenly developed a severe case of hesitancy, the peculiar tactical malady that so frequently debilitated Union generalship throughout the Civil War. Instead of vigorously pursuing the beaten and retreating Confederates directly south through Rockfish Gap toward Lynchburg, Hunter rested a day in Staunton and then marched obliquely southwestward to Lexington. There he casually frittered away another two days accomplishing little but the vindictive burning of V.M.I. and the home of Governor John Letcher on June 12–13. Washington College was also sacked by Hunter's soldiers. Its science equipment was destroyed, its library scattered, doors and windows were broken, geological and fossil specimens were thrown around the campus like rocks, and army horses were stabled in the college dormitory. By the time the dilatory general finally appeared before Lynchburg on June 17, Breckinridge had reached the town. Jubal A. Early and his Second Corps, also detached by Lee from the Richmond theater and rushed to Lynchburg, were arriving in the area, elaborate trenches and fortifications had been dug, and Confederate forces in the Valley had been thoroughly reorganized. A frontal assault by Hunter on the Lynchburg trenches on June 18 produced no more than a small-scale Union blood bath and an opportunity for young Gardie Tyler to shoot at the hated Yankees at last—and from the relative safety of a shoulder-deep rifle pit at that. Following his predictable repulse at Lynchburg, the confused Hunter withdrew westward through Salem and into West Virginia, hotly pursued by Early. This foolish tactic abandoned the entire Shenandoah Valley to the Confederates and virtually ended the summer campaign in the region. What had opened brilliantly for the Union commander at Piedmont ended in a gloom rivaling that which gripped the Yankee army following Sigel's disaster at New Market.

By the time Gardie's unit returned again to Lexington to be demobilized in late June the inadequate Hunter was wandering aimlessly and ineffectually through the West Virginia mountains. He had, however, left his mark on Lexington. Gardie found the proud V.M.I. reduced to "a mass of ruins." The Yankee visit to the little town had also terminated the semester at Washington College. The institution was in no fit condition to function, although some students stayed on to complete the disrupted term. The desolation of the rifled campus and the excitement of the jaunt to Staunton and Lynchburg and back combined to convince Gardie that he could not return to the stricken college in the fall. "I am going to join the Drewry's Bluff battery," he told his mother firmly. "You must get over the notion that I am only a child for indeed I feel fully able to take care of myself." David Gardiner Tyler had become a soldier and a man simultaneously. On July 12, 1864, he turned eighteen.[37]

Gardie arrived in Richmond from Lexington on July 23 and moved into a flat occupied by James A. Semple. The capital was quiet and confident still, and young Tyler expressed to Harry Beeckman something of its defiant mood:

From present appearances one would infer that the war is fast drawing to an end, but appearances are deceitful sometimes; God grant it may be so this time. Still, if our enemies are determined on war we are better prepared than ever before to meet the shock. Our cry will be, and is: "Come one, Come all!" This is not the language of a few enthusiasts only but of the whole nation.... The Northern people are at last coming to their senses and begin to see the war in its true light. They have only two alternatives upon which to decide and those are: peace or subjugation of, not the South, but of the North itself, for they are fast losing every vestige of their former boasted freedom and are lapsing into a despotism worse than that of Russia.[38]

There were, more persuasively, solid military reasons for the optimism felt in Richmond that the war might yet be brought to an end by a negotiated peace recognizing Confederate independence. By September 1864 Grant's casualties in the Wilderness, at Spotsylvania, and at Cold Harbor had added up to a total so staggering that the bloody record had been introduced into the 1864 Presidential campaign as an anti-Lincoln issue. Unable to take Richmond by frontal assault, Grant had slipped around the city to the east and south in June and laid siege to Petersburg in an attempt to enter Richmond by the back door. By the end of July this maneuver had bogged down in the trenches before Petersburg. Butler's Peninsula campaign had also come to grief. Badly mauled by an inferior force under General Beauregard in June, the incompetent Butler had managed to get himself locked up in the Bermuda Hundred Peninsula on the James River some thirty miles below Richmond where, in the words of one historian, his army was "actually as much out of the war as if they had been transported bodily to South America." In the Shenandoah Valley Sigel's defeat at New Market in May, followed by the containment of Hunter before Lynchburg in June, might not have been such a Union disaster had not Hunter stupidly withdrawn from Lynchburg to the west. This uncovered the Valley and permitted Jubal Early's daring and psychologically satisfying raid to within five miles of Washington on July 11. Only Sherman in Georgia had met with success in the 1864 summer campaigns. But if Atlanta was under his guns on September 1, Richmond, for the moment at least, was safe. Ringed by powerful entrenchments and batteries, the Confederate capital appeared inviolable.[39]

After discussing the matter thoroughly with Semple, Gardie decided to join one of the artillery units protecting Richmond. As a soldier in the Virginia Home Guard, he had been assigned duty guarding prisoners at the Libby Prison shortly after his arrival in town in late July. This he found to be uninteresting and unheroic work. Therefore on September 1 he volunteered for service in the Rockbridge Battery, a distinguished artillery unit which had earned much glory earlier in the war when attached to the famous Stonewall Brigade under Jackson. At one time it had been commanded by Lee's son, G. W. C. Lee. It was now under the direction of Captain Edward Graham. Former Maryland Senator William D. Merrick's son and other young men of quality served in its enlisted ranks. When Gardie joined it the outfit was attached to A. P. Hill's command and was stationed fourteen miles below Richmond at Deep Bottom. The unit, as Gardie assessed its multiple advantages, was "so convenient to Richmond" and was "composed of gentlemen of the best standing belonging to the F.F.V.'s." Several of Gardie's classmates had also joined the Rockbridge Battery, so there was something of the atmosphere of a Washington College alumni reunion about the whole enlistment venture.

For the next few months David Gardiner Tyler served with the Battery in various defensive positions around Richmond. During these months he quieted Julia's fears with constant assurances that he was in no danger whatever. Save for shelling an occasional Federal gunboat on the river, the Battery had little to do. The food served the gunners was good. There was ample coffee and sugar in the battery mess. Guard duty was light and leaves into town were frequent. "My dear mother do not be anxious about me," he wrote her, "for you know that I am just as safe where I am as I would be were I at a peaceful home.... The artillery is by far the easiest service.... I would have been ashamed to show my face if, after we had gained our independence, it should be said that I did not assist to establish it.... Furthermore I like soldiering first rate."[40]

His brother Alex thought he would like soldiering first-rate, too. As early as April 1864 he began nagging Julia to be permitted to go south and join his brother so that he too might "take my stand in Dixie's land, to live, fight and die in Dixie's land." Translating Sallust bored him. It was no decent occupation for a red-blooded, 110-per-cent

Confederate patriot all of sixteen years old. He wanted to massacre Yankees. Julia pleaded with her son not to go. But he insisted, and she finally gave way—after Alex had run away from home in mid-April and gone to Baltimore, determined to leave for Virginia whether his mother approved or not. Brought back to Staten Island, he was punished for disobedience. This formality attended to, Julia then reluctantly helped him make plans to leave for the South. She made him promise her, however, that he would join the Confederate Navy rather than the high-casualty-rate infantry. For a moment in July 1864 she considered going south with him. She was at this juncture very much worried about Maria Tyler (whose "marriage" to Private Kick had not yet taken place), and she thought she might be able to salvage something from the reported chaos at Sherwood Forest. But Semple strongly advised her against the trip. "I do not want you to run the risk even of being maltreated by the Feds, much less by the abominable *Yankee darkies* who would be all around you," he warned. So Alex departed New York for Halifax alone in July, determined to join the Confederate Navy when he reached Richmond. Arriving in Bermuda from Halifax on July 31, he contacted Major Norman Walker, who saw that he got aboard the speedy CSS *Mary Celestia*, Lieutenant Arthur Sinclair, CSN, sailing for Wilmington on August 3. As he observed Confederate naval officers strolling in the streets of St. George, Alex decided the makeshift naval uniform Julia had fitted him out with in New York "will *not do at all.*" He told his mother to send him gold lace, gray cloth, a Bowditch Navigation text, and, most important, a dress sword. And to do it promptly.[41]

By his own account, Alex had a perfectly "bully time coming through the blockade, and boy the old Yanks were as thick as bees round a man's head when he goes to get the honey; but they didn't happen to see us ere they were all after the privateer *Tallahassee* who was agoing out when we was acoming in." For sixteen days, however, the grammatically retrograde patriot was quarantined aboard the *Mary Celestia* "because we had the yaller fever on board." Not until August 26 did Alex walk casually into his brother's tent at Camp Lee where Gardie was living while he was attached to the Libby Prison guard detail.

It was a happy reunion, and it called for a family conference. Semple made it clear to Alex, and later in a letter to Julia, that the boy would have great difficulty securing a midshipman's warrant. Few midshipman appointments were being made in September 1864 as the Confederate Navy fast disappeared from the seas. Nevertheless, Semple arranged personal interviews for Alex with President and Mrs. Davis and with the Confederate Secretaries of the Navy and the Treasury. "Strong influences" were thus brought to bear in behalf of Alex's naval ambitions, but to no avail. He was, Semple argued, "entirely too young to enter the Army and it is not desirable that he should do so." And since he could not get into the Navy, Semple recommended to Julia that the youngster be sent to Washington College for the fall semester. In October 1864 the embryonic Confederate admiral found himself right back at his Latin translations. He was one of the tiny band of twenty-two students the battered institution enrolled that term. He remained in Lexington until December, when the threatened closing of the college for lack of students brought him back again to Richmond to resume his vain quest for a midshipman's commission.[42]

The appearance in Richmond of Gardie in July and of Alex in August 1864 swelled to nine the number of adult Tylers in the city who had taken their stands "in Dixie's land." Present in the beleaguered Confederate capital for the last Christmas of the war were Robert and Priscilla, John, Jr., Dr. Tazewell Tyler and his wife, Nannie Bridges Tyler, and James A. Semple and his spouse, Letitia Tyler Semple. If they disagreed on other questions, they were all vigorous Rebels. They kept the remainder of their relatives and in-laws informed of their activities and the progress of the war. The shared hardships of life in a city virtually cut off from what was left of the Confederacy gave them a strong degree of adhesion. From Gardie and Alex's standpoint, Semple was the linchpin in the group. He gave the boys their room and board when they reached Richmond, arranged their financial affairs, and helped them with their military ambitions. "The kindness of Brother James," Alex told his mother, "we will *never* be able to repay. He is the best man that *ever lived* without *any* exception. I love him next to yourself and the children." Semple did all he could for the Tyler boys, and through him Julia maintained close contact with her sons and stepsons. It was a liaison she desperately needed after Juliana died in October 1864 and as Julia's relations with her brother came to a point of showdown in December 1864. "I am so sorry to hear that you are likely to be troubled by that man, Mr. G.," Gardie sympathized with her. "I have heard of his cowardly course towards you. But perhaps one of these days he will have occasion to repent it." [43]

David Lyon's course toward Julia involved his decision to contest the deathbed will Juliana left when she expired on October 4, 1864. It was, indeed, a controversial will which raised the legal question of whether Julia exerted "undue influence" on her rapidly failing mother when Juliana formally executed the document a bare four hours before her passing. The case was a long and stormy one. Following hearings before the Surrogate Court of Richmond County, New York, hearings demanded by David Lyon, the will was denied admission to probate on August 29, 1865, on the ground that undue influence had been exercised by the chief beneficiary, Julia, on the testatrix. Julia promptly carried this ruling to the New York Supreme Court. There, on May 18, 1866, by a vote of 4 to 0, the Surrogate's decision was reversed and the will ordered admitted to probate. David Lyon, in turn, appealed the Supreme Court decision to the New York Court of Appeals, the Empire State's highest tribunal. On January 2, 1867, the Court of Appeals ruled, in a controversial 5-to-3 decision, that the will was void because of undue influence. Lacking a valid will, both parties then went back into the Supreme Court to fight over the actual division of the estate. A compromise was eventually hammered out on October 3, 1868. This gave Julia the Castleton Hill house and three eighths of the Gardiner real estate in downtown New York; David Lyon got three eighths of the city property; and Harry Beeckman received one quarter. The financial burdens of the various assessments, taxes, and mortgage payments on and against the estate were fairly distributed along these fractional lines, as was the income from the inheritance. Personal and household items of sentimental value were also divided equally. To help heal the family breach opened by three years of bitter litigation, the 1868 compromise agreement, on its face, accepted the principle that "the last will and testament of Juliana Gardiner shall be deemed and adjudged a valid instrument." In broad outline, this was true. The fractional grants were similar, but the severe restrictions on David Lyon's enjoyment of his three-eighths share, written into his mother's 1864 will, were properly abolished.

Actually, the final compromise in 1868 hewed closer in spirit to an earlier will Juliana had drawn in 1858, after Margaret's death, than it did to her deathbed testament six years later. Under the prewar 1858 will, David Lyon, Julia, and Harry were each to have received one third of the Gardiner properties in New York City. David Lyon, however, was given the Castleton Hill property, then valued at $20,000, in special consideration for having managed his mother's legal and financial affairs in the city after his return from San Diego in 1851. But since he was also saddled with carrying the $5000 mortgage on the Staten Island house, this extra boon under the original will was not unreasonable—even though he had been a poor manager of his mother's interests. Julia, after all, would eventually inherit Sherwood Forest and have it for her own home as long as she lived.

The deathbed will of 1864, however, was quite different in orientation from the equitable 1858 document. Under its provisions Julia received Castleton Hill, now valued at $27,000, while David Lyon was charged with carrying the mortgage payments on the property. Harry Beeckman received one quarter instead of one third of the residue of the estate. The remaining three quarters were divided equally between Julia and David Lyon, three eighths each, but with the proviso that all of the rental income and interest from David Lyon's portion was to go to Julia "until her losses in the rebel States should be made up to her" by the federal government or until such time as she died. Nevertheless, David Lyon was expected to shoulder three eighths of the taxes, maintenance, and mortgage payments on the downtown Gardiner rental properties. These discriminatory provisions disappeared in the final compromise of 1868—as indeed they should have. In addition, under the 1864 will Julia was named Harry's trustee with the power to control the income from his one-quarter inheritance until he attained his majority in 1869. The estate, including Castleton Hill, was valued at roughly $180,000 in 1864. Outstanding mortgages on the rental parcels amounted to about $35,000. Steadily increasing in market value under the impact of Civil War prosperity, it was an estate worth fighting over.

The tragedy of the contested 1864 will was that it was unfair; so unfair that it raised the suspicion (however untrue) of a dark conspiracy, mired in greed, carried out by a Copperhead subversive against a dutiful and patriotic son over the expiring body of a foolish old woman as she attempted to make psychic contact wth relatives beyond the grave toward which she herself was hastening. The will might have been challenged on the moral ground of rank inequity rather than on the tricky undue-influence proposition. This latter emphasis admitted into consideration, implicitly and explicitly, numerous political, psychic, and economic irrelevancies. Juliana fully appreciated the fact that the 1864 arrangement was inequitable. In the language of the will she pointed to Julia's army of dependent children and noted that her daughter, whom she admitted she was consciously favoring, had been "subjected to much injury and loss during the existing war." Sherwood Forest, she announced, was "in ruins" and "could afford her no income—none whatsoever."

Actually, Sherwood Forest's physical wounds were more superficial than real, a fact better appreciated in 1866 than in 1864. The main house remained intact. Only the fences and outbuildings had been destroyed. The furniture, livestock, and farm implements, to be sure, had been carried off. It was true, therefore, that the plantation might no longer be expected to produce a livable income for a family the size of Julia's. Still, the garbled and excited reports on the condition of the plantation which Julia received from Charles City in the late spring and early summer of 1864 were grim enough to convey the impression of near-total destruction that found its way into the will. As Juliana told Louisa Cooper three months before she died: "Julia is poor, has a large family and is unprotected. She cannot afford to be poor. She must have enough. David is a man and he has one of the handsomest farms on the island. His wife's father is rich. Don't think that I don't care for David, but I must take care of Julia."

That David Lyon had married well and was capable of sustaining himself with Thompson money was but one of the irrelevancies dragged into the case. Julia's lawyers, among them the brilliant William M. Evarts, later Secretary of State in the Hayes administration, made much of the point that David Lyon had managed his mother's business and legal affairs in the city from 1851 until his expulsion from her household in February 1864 with an indifference and inefficiency bordering on the chaotic, and that he really deserved no more than the will allowed him. This charge was true. David Lyon never was much of a businessman or a lawyer. But the argument was scarcely germane to the undue-influence charge. Similarly irrelevant was the fact that during a family quarrel in January 1864 Gardiner had struck his sister and knocked her senseless to the floor.

The entire case was also conditioned, if not actually influenced, by Julia's arrant Copperheadism and by the converse fact that David Lyon and Sarah were loyal Unionists as well as old-line citizens of wealth and social standing in New York City. Newspaper accounts of the litigation, as it made its weary and bitter three-year journey through the courts, invariably emphasized Julia's connection with the deceased President and identified him as one of Virginia's leading slavers and secessionists. On the other hand, David Lyon was pictured as a staunch American patriot. Indeed, in December 1864 he threatened to have the rest of the members of the Staten Island Board of Supervisors, on which body he served, shipped to Fort Lafayette for Copperhead disloyalty. He was a patriot's patriot.

Finally, the whole question of undue influence was not nearly so clear in the law of 1865–1867 as it would be a century later. Not that it is an open-and-shut proposition today. The conflicting legal precedents offered by opposing counsel in their attempts to define the term were inconclusive to the point of mutual cancellation. The plaintiff's case thus turned essentially on specific evidences of Julia's actual physical interference in the drawing and signing of the will, with a view toward demonstrating that the degree of this influence constituted circumstantial evidence of a premeditated conspiracy. The main contentions of the plaintiff did not center on the emotional and psychological *intent* of the parties to the alleged conspiracy.

At the risk of pronouncing a gratuitous *obiter dictum* on the case a full century after it was argued, it must be pointed out that there was on Julia's part no conscious intent to conspire. While her actions did, in fact, manifest some evidence of "influence" over her dying mother, Juliana clearly wanted her 1864 will to read exactly as it did. The deep personal relations between mother and daughter, the intimate tone of their private correspondence during the Civil War, their long concern for each other's health and welfare, the identity and similarity of their political views, their mutual concern for the financial fate of Julia's young children after Tyler's death and after Sherwood Forest was plundered and its labor force militarily manumitted all support the contention that the provisions of the overturned will were exactly what the dying Juliana wished them to be. The fact that she was desperately ill (organically, not mentally) when she authorized Julia to have the document drawn did not necessarily uphold David Lyon's argument that she was incapable of straight thinking because disease had reduced her will power to jelly. On the contrary, Juliana McLachlan Gardiner died at the age of sixty-five with her considerable will power still intact. And while she imagined herself in communication with her husband and her departed children, that quaint notion did not establish her as mentally incompetent in a legal sense. Much, however, was made of her psychic peculiarity by David Lyon's counsel and this irrelevancy found its way into the majority opinion of the Court of Appeals.

It was the specific manner in which the will was executed that brought ultimately the undue-influence decision that negated it. On the surface it looked bad. For several months prior to the drawing of the will Julia had been writing all her mother's letters for her. She also spent a great deal of time closeted with her mother in Juliana's sickroom. Indeed, Juliana spoke to no one else. She relied exclusively on her daughter for her every need and want. She appeared to be, as the plaintiff later argued, under Julia's "influence" during her last months on earth.

On Saturday, October 1, when it appeared Juliana had taken a bad turn, Julia wrote out certain provisions her mother wished incorporated in a new will. On Monday morning, October 3, tutor Ralph Dayton carried these suggestions to Mr. Clark, Juliana's lawyer. Clark called at Castleton Hill early that evening and said he could not prepare a new will without personal instructions from the devisor. Julia told him to return the following morning for an interview with her mother. Accordingly, at 9:30 A.M. on Tuesday, October 4, Clark reached the house and spoke with Juliana. He found her at this time cogent, but "exhausted, vomiting, weak, signifying her wishes and assent sometimes by words and sometimes by nods." Nevertheless, a rational conversation ensued during which the lawyer suggested some minor changes from Julia's written list of provisions. He promised to return that afternoon at five o'clock with the finished document.

At noon, however, Clark was instructed by a messenger from Julia to complete the work at once and come quickly to the house, as Juliana was dying. The lawyer arrived at 2 P.M. and found Juliana attended by Dr. Rice, an Islip, Long Island, physician who had treated her the preceding summer. Julia had called Rice into the case on Monday, October 3. That evening she had been informed by the doctor that in his opinion her mother's illness was terminal. When Clark reached the bedside Juliana was indeed so far gone that Julia had to hold her head for her while she coughed and vomited. She could not speak. Clark read the finished will to her after asking Dr. Rice whether in his judgment his patient still possessed the ability and capacity to make a will. The physician said he thought so. As Clark read, Juliana nodded her head in assent to the provisions. Julia then raised her mother up and held her steady while Juliana affixed her signature. Rice and Dayton then signed as witnesses. Juliana slumped back in the bed. Four hours later, at 6 P.M. on October 4, 1864, the powerful matriarch of the Gardiner family passed silently away. "I am so happy to see with what Christian fortitude you stand the blow," Gardie sympathized from Richmond. "Oh! how I wish that I could have seen her before her death." David Lyon probably wished the same thing.

At no time during these final crucial days and hours was David Lyon told that his mother was dying, or summoned to her house, or informed that she had executed a new will. It seems clear, as David Lyon argued and as the Court of Appeals later held, that Julia had persuaded, or influenced, her mother to order her eldest son and his family away from Castleton Hill in February 1864. It may also be true (the evidence is not quite so conclusive) that Julia somehow induced, or influenced, her mother to believe that David Lyon had purchased his Northfield farm in 1853 with her money. If so, this false accusation on the part of the daughter, whatever its morality, merely compounded a split between mother and son produced earlier by political differences and the tension of too many people of unlike mind and habit living together under the same roof. In any event, the precise relevance of these two evidences of Julia's "influence" over her mother remains obscure in a case turning on the physical execution of a will several months later. To argue, as the majority opinion of the New York Court of Appeals subsequently did, that this puissant matron was "infirm of purpose, sick and old ... imbued with false impressions, and brought to a condition of nervous and causeless suspicion and alarm" by a Machiavellian daughter under whose nefarious influence she supinely ordered and executed her will, is, in retrospect, difficult to accept. More reasonable is Justice Peckham's minority opinion that

undue influence within the meaning of the law ... must be an influence exercised by coercion or by fraud to set aside the will of a person of sound mind. ... This undue influence cannot be presumed, but must be proved to have been exercised, and exercised in relation to the will itself and not merely to other transactions. ... This will was executed according to law when the mind of the testatrix was sound and clear. It was carefully read over to, and fully understood by, her. She expressed her gratification that it was made. It was also prepared by her own personal directions and instructions. It was in substance in accordance with her wishes expressed in New York, when her daughter was not present, several months prior to its execution. There is nothing rising to the dignity of evidence, to show any undue influence over the testatrix.[44]

Be that as it may, Julia ultimately lost her battle. The will was formally overturned in January 1867. And for a period of nearly three years after the Civil War, while Tyler *vs.* Gardiner was being fought, the income from the estate was held in escrow and dribbled out by a court-appointed referee pending the final decision. During these grim Reconstruction years Julia was, by Gardiner standards at least, poor. She borrowed to the hilt to make ends meet in the style to which she had been long accustomed. Sherwood Forest was almost lost for back taxes. The education of her children at home and abroad was deficit-financed. Old mortgages were extended and second mortgages were negotiated to cover these expenses. And the bitterness she developed for her brother was absorbed in all its intensity by her progeny. It split the Gardiner-Tyler family alliance to the bone, creating a gaping wound that could not be bandaged with a compromise settlement, however fair, four years after the event. In the final analysis Tyler *vs.* Gardiner was a small-scale Civil War.

Julia began her long legal battle in October 1864 by warning her brother that a will contest could only expose Gardiner dirty linen to a sensation-hungry public and bring discredit upon the whole family. She pleaded with him not to undertake a suit. His response to her plea was to force his way into Castleton Hill, armed with a search warrant and in company with a policeman "bearing a club," to gather evidence to sustain his side of the contest. Julia's 1864 winter campaign thus opened rather inauspiciously.

One thing was clear to her, however. She would have to hold on to Castleton Hill in the legal trials that lay ahead. Continuing reports from Charles City gave her little confidence that Sherwood Forest would ever again suffice the needs of her family. To be sure, a few of the former Tyler slaves—Bennett, Burwell, Randolph, Randall, and their women—had drifted back and settled down on the place. "In connection with some free negroes" they had even harvested a "tolerable crop of corn" in the fall of 1864. Having always lived at Sherwood Forest they had no other home. Emancipation as an idea came through to them only dimly. And without tools or money they could not begin repairs on the demolished farm buildings or on the house they had foolishly helped sack. So they squatted on the land and waited, and pleaded for their old mistress to return and help them. Her former servant, Celia Johnson, reported to Julia in November 1864, however, that the house was completely uninhabitable. Only two carpets had been salvaged. "One or two tables I think are whole but they are the ends of dining tables." In the early winter Julia again sought a Union Army pass to return to the plantation, if only "for a day," to evaluate for herself its livability and bring away whatever was left worth saving. Again she was dissuaded. "Don't you let mother *think* of *coming south*," Alex told his sister Julie. "If she goes anywhere let it be England or the Continent." News that "Confed scouts" had burned some of the outbuildings during the confusion in May and June made the estate no more livable than if the hated Union Army had set the fires. And as Julia and everybody else with clear vision could see, the sands of the Confederacy were running out. She decided therefore to heed her son's objections and not return to the plantation.[45]

Increasing inflation, shortages of raw materials, and widespread desertions from the Confederate Army badly compromised the South's ability to carry on the unequal struggle. President Davis' desperation proposal in November 1864 to arm the Negro slaves was an oblique announcement of the gathering disaster staring the Confederacy full in the face. The fall of Fort Fisher in January 1865 (which landed the unlucky Captain Gayle back at Fort Warren for his sophomore year and closed Wilmington, the South's last open port) raised the curtain on the final act of the bloody drama. As Sherman slashed boldly up through the Carolinas in February and March, Lee and his Army of Northern Virginia, outnumbered 115,000 to 54,000, made their last heroic attempts to break through Grant's lines and lift the siege of Petersburg and Richmond. These efforts failing, Lee had no choice but to abandon Petersburg and Richmond on April 2, 1865, and begin his last march westward toward Lynchburg away from the jaws of the closing Yankee trap. The Confederate government fled to Danville, where, it was hoped, the Army would eventually catch up with the politicians and then, somehow, all would join General Joseph E. Johnson's battered forces in North Carolina and carry on the fight in the mountains. It was, of course, a hopeless prospect.

But the Tylers caught in Richmond at the end refused to abandon hope. Convinced that the collapsing government still had prospects, Major John Tyler, Jr., announced himself a candidate for the Confederate Congress in February and commenced a brisk campaign. Until late March, Alex Tyler kept working for a midshipman's commission in the Navy even though there were no Confederate ports left from which to sail. In early April, when Lee's evacuation of the capital began, Alex joined the Virginia First Artillery Battalion and together with his older brother began the last, sad march to Appomattox, "tugging and pulling at the cannon" all the way. As the lower city rose in the flames set by the retreating army, neither he nor Gardie could know that the Moncure and Dunlap building where John Tyler's papers and the family portraits were stored would go up in the holocaust. The bank where the family silver was vaulted also caught fire and burned, badly scarring the metal. Before leaving Richmond, Gardie, Alex, Semple, and Robert all forwarded their trunks to Danville, determined to fight on for the Confederacy as long as any semblance of a government or an army remained.[46]

The end came with merciful suddenness. Surrounded at Appomattox Court House on April 7, Alex's seventeenth birthday, Lee had no choice but to surrender his starving, wet, and bedraggled army of 30,000 thoroughly beaten men and boys—among the latter the dispirited Tyler brothers. On April 9, 1865, it was over. Grant paroled Lee's veterans to their homes, and the once-mighty Army of Northern Virginia disappeared into song and legend down a hundred country roads. For Alex it had been a very short war. As he described his two-week experience to Ralph Dayton, his old Staten Island tutor, from occupied Richmond on April 19,

> I arrived on "Parole" three days ago after a weary march of 14 days—sometimes up in mud to my knees, tugging and pulling at the cannon and fighting nearly every day and rations of two ears of corn a day with no where to parch and burn it. It is true we had two days "rest," but then it was no rest for both days it was raining "pitchforks" and we had nothing to cover with but our blankets which were soon wet through which you can readily perceive was far from making us more comfortable—but pish! I am telling only what will worry you so I'll stop. I was sorry to hear of the death of Mr. Lincoln for I expect it will be very hard for us "Rebels." ...

A conference between the paroled brothers was held at Appomattox immediately after the surrender. It was decided that Gardie should proceed to Lexington and re-enter Washington College; Alex would go to Sherwood Forest and "try to fix things up there." And so the boys separated, Alex reaching Richmond again on April 16 "completely in rags." Brigadier General John E. Mulford, USA, the polite New Yorker who had done Julia several favors during the war in his capacity as a prisoners-exchange officer at Fortress Monroe, befriended the lad, helping him cash a check on his mother's account in the Manhattan Bank and providing him with a pass to New York City. But Alex was determined to return to Sherwood Forest. This he did, reaching the plantation on May 1. Meanwhile, Robert Tyler had returned to Richmond via Danville from Charlotte, North Carolina, where he and Semple had gone with Jefferson Davis in the last-ditch stand of the Confederate government.[47]

As the Confederacy breathed its last, Julia experienced her own Appomattox, a degrading and humiliating defeat that clouded her expectations of receiving judicial impartiality in the "Yankee Courts" on the status of her mother's will. At ten o'clock on the rainy Saturday evening of April 15, fifteen hours after Abraham Lincoln's tragic death in Washington, three inflamed and vengeful local toughs, armed with "swords and clubs" and led by one Bertram Delafield of Staten Island, burst suddenly into the parlor at Castleton Hill and demanded that Julia give up the "Rebel flag" she was "known" to be displaying somewhere in the house. Spying a flag of sorts hanging over a picture in the parlor, the muddy-booted invaders climbed up on chairs, ripped it down, knocked over some furniture, and made off into the night with their trophy. "Secessionism, open or secret, will not be tolerated here," boasted one of the patriotic trespassers in an anonymous letter to the New York *Herald* two days later. "You are aware that we are blest with having as a resident among us, Mrs. Tyler, widow of the deceased rebel ex-President John Tyler. She seems to be successful in passing the lines of our army, and of returning at her pleasure, and with her two eldest sons in the rebel army would seem to be a privileged person." Other city newspapers picked up the story, playing it as a timely blow against latent Copperheadism as the martyred Lincoln went to his Rebel-dug grave. None of the published accounts pointed out that Julia's "Rebel flag" was actually a small piece of nondescript, tricolored bunting sewn by Margaret ten years earlier as a handkerchief for Harry and sentimentally retained in the family as a souvenir of Margaret's handicraft. Julia was an out-and-out secessionist and Copperhead, but she was not so foolish in her sentiment as to have risked displaying an actual Confederate flag in her parlor.

She strongly suspected that David Lyon was behind the violation of her home. Delafield later implied this much, confessing that a "near relative" of Julia's had told him of a Confederate flag hanging in the subversive den that was Castleton Hill. She muted these suspicions of her brother, and in her angry protests to the newspapers and to Union Army authorities in New York she emphasized only the cowardly audacity of the Delafield gang in its raid on a parlor inhabited by helpless women and children. She demanded the return of the souvenir, and she pointed out that the only flag at Castleton Hill was an American flag. But what the newspapers referred to casually as a "spirited little affair" that had rid Staten Island of a "secesh banner" Julia saw as a preview of dark things to come for Confederate sympathizers caught in the North during the emotional period following Lincoln's assassination. Anonymous threats to burn down her house were received. So frightened did she become that she moved her family into a New York hotel for a few days for safety. Simultaneously, she pressed charges against Delafield for trespass through General Dix's headquarters, asking also that the general protect her from future mob violence. Dix investigated her complaint and admitted that Julia had indeed been "subjected to insult and calumny without in the slightest degree deserving it." Little more came of it than that. Margaret's handkerchief was not recovered and Delafield was not punished.[48]

From Fort Warren prison Captain Gayle wrote Julia a gentle note expressing sympathy for her in her harrowing experience with the superpatriot fringe. From Lexington came an outraged expression of Gardie's frustrated desire to have been present in the parlor to thrash the rascals when they pushed their way in. To Alex the Delafield incident argued for but one decision: "Now my dear mother," he advised her as he was leaving Richmond for Sherwood Forest,

> I cannot see for my life how you can live North where you endure such insults. It is the wish, and I pray of you, for both Gardie and myself to sell out directly all your property and go to Europe—anywhere so that you leave and take the children from the U. States. I would even sell Sherwood, for if the South is conquered, which with the help of God it never will be, neither G—— or A—— will ever live here under Northern rule. My mother, grant our prayer.[49]

As Julia considered Alex's suggestion she wondered what there was left of the old way of life worth struggling to preserve. The prospect of Europe was appealing. The Old South was dead. Her husband, her father, and her mother were all dead. Alexander and Margaret were gone. Her plantation was destroyed and its labor force forever scattered. Her two oldest sons, bitter and disillusioned in defeat, advised her flight. Her surviving brother had broken with her entirely and ahead lay a rigorous and expensive legal battle with him. Her Copperhead sympathies actually endangered her younger children and threatened to bring down on their heads the fiery destruction of her Castleton Hill refuge. From Gardie in particular, and from her friends in the conquered South generally, came a picture of despair and hopelessness. "Here I am," Gardie wrote from Washington College in June,

> without home, without means and, I may almost say, without hope. Sometimes I begin to think that I will have to hire myself out as a day-laborer. My clothes are entirely played out and I have had them patched. So you see I am a perfect "rag, tag and bobtail." How much happier I was in the army than I am now. I would rather have remained in it twenty years than be in the situation that we are now in. No country, no home, no freedom. What a deplorable case we present. I will not be able to come to you as I (even if I could get the necessary funds) have only my uniform which I am not permitted to wear.[50]

Julia pondered, then she decided. She would stay in the United States and fight—for the Gardiner estate, for Sherwood Forest, for her children's educations, for the standard of living to which the Gardiners were accustomed, for the social and political principles her husband had embraced, and for the sheer cussedness of it. This was what John Tyler would have wanted her to do.

20

RECONSTRUCTION AND EPILOGUE
1865–1890

> *Desolation has set its seal upon all around us, and the gloom like the veil of the grave has settled upon the land.... It can never again be as it was.*
> —DAVID GARDINER TYLER, JUNE 1868

The first bleak months following Lee's surrender found Julia hard at work trying to help old friends in the conquered South who had lost everything in the "late political contest." Pleas for clothes, money and food could not go unanswered. The situation of Varina Davis was particularly piteous. The former First Lady of the Confederacy was destitute. Her husband had been arrested as a traitor and was imprisoned in Fortress Monroe. While his fate was still uncertain, there was much wild talk in the North of a firing squad. His wife was desperate. Because of her relationship to Julia through Jenny Howell Waller she felt no embarrassment asking her "beautiful step mother" for help. "We are very poor," she wrote Julia in July from Savannah. "In what a maze of horrors we have been groping for these two months. ... I sometimes wonder if God does not mean to wake me from a terrific dream of desolation and penury...." To Mrs. Davis' plea Julia promptly responded with gifts of shoes and clothing for her and for those of her children who were bound to school in Canada away from "Yankee influences." Julia had been thinking along the same educational lines herself. All over the South schools and colleges were closed. She knew her children would not accept education under Yankee auspices. Therefore, like Varina Davis, she started investigating Canadian and German institutions.[1]

Simultaneously, she undertook to ease Captain Gayle's last boring months in Fort Warren Prison with packages of food and tobacco. "We have become assured that under no circumstances will a man of us be liberated without taking the amnesty oath," Gayle sadly informed her. "As the Confederacy has ceased to exist, I do not see what else remains for us to do . . . but to accept with as good a grace as possible the existing condition of affairs and subscribe to the 'oath.' " Julia agreed there was no other choice.

Gayle's realism was not as widespread among some defeated Confederates as it might have been under the blunt new circumstances of the post-Appomattox world. Thousands, like Gardie and Alex Tyler, could not absorb the idea that the war was really over and that the gallant South had been beaten. It was as though personal bravery, suffering, dedication, and devotion had counted for nothing—that God had somehow made a frightful mistake in permitting the Yankees to win. "Sometimes I think," said Gardie, "that the heroes who fell during the war are ten thousand times better off than the survivors. All the future is dark and cheerless before us, our sorrows can only end in the grave." At first, the confused and dejected nineteen-year-old thought he might join the stream of high-ranking Confederate officers and officials who were fleeing the South for lives of exile in Brazil and Mexico. Certainly he could not accept the prospect of living under the flag of the invader; nor could he abide the humiliation of having to take the "damnasty oath" and come crawling back "like a whipped cur" into the United States. For a brief time in August 1865 he prayed to God that the diplomatic crisis over the Emperor Maximilian's continued presence in Mexico would lead to a rousing war between the United States and Napoleon III's government. "You would know *very well* which side I'd be apt to join in such an event," he told his cousin Harry.[2]

When a war with France failed to materialize, Gardie reluctantly decided that his mother's idea of sending him, Alex, and Harry Beeckman to college in Germany was a good one. After all, the season for "slaughtering larger game such as Yankees" was over, and he did not think he could accustom himself to watching the former Sherwood Forest slaves riding around Charles City in their own buggies free and sassy as you please. Alex, meanwhile, had had no luck getting the plundered plantation functioning again during the late spring and early summer of 1865. The job was much too big for him and Julia had matured other plans for farming the estate anyway. Discouraged and beaten, he too was ready for a change of occupation and scenery.

So it was that in September 1865 the two Tyler boys and their cousin Harry were aboard the SS *Hansa* bound for Europe and for college in Karlsruhe, Germany. They sailed in the company of the Reverend John Fulton and his wife, old Copperhead associates of Julia's from Staten Island. It was Fulton's plan to open a boardinghouse in Karlsruhe and take in British and American students there for a livelihood. "Our crowd is a jolly one," Gardie wrote his mother from shipboard, "all except five being southerners. We talk 'Secesh' as much as we please and sing Southern songs on deck every evening." Behind him Gardie Tyler left an iambic record of his attitude toward the Yankees and all their works, a parting salvo into the Union positions as the youthful artilleryman retreated into distant Baden. It was schoolboyish verse, but it made crystal-clear the fact that David Gardiner Tyler, former Confederate gunner, future Virginia farmer, lawyer, state senator, Circuit Court judge, and United States congressman, would live and die proudly "unreconstructed."

> Yes, we'll fight them again,
> Tho' vanquished as before;
> We'll break the tyrant's chain,
> Or die 'mid cannon's roar.
> Better die as they have done,
> Than live as we do now;
> With no rights beneath the sun,
> And shame upon our brow....
> We fought for four long years,
> For liberty and fame;
> Our flag went down 'mid tears,
> Shed for our country's shame.
> But we'll up at them once more,
> With Jehovah for our shield;
> This time we'll whip the foe,
> Or be left upon the field.[3]

It was one thing to anathematize the hated Yankees in verse. It was quite another to learn to function normally again under their heavy-handed occupation of the South, to try to reclaim something of the ante-bellum way of life from the junkpile of defeat and subjugation. To this difficult if not impossible task Julia turned during the summer of 1865 in an effort to get Sherwood Forest once again into production.

Shortly after Appomattox she hired Sievert von Oertzen as her farm manager and dispatched the immigrant Swede, cousin of a Staten Island acquaintance, to Sherwood Forest to begin the restoration of the plantation. Julia had read many novels of castle and manor life in the Middle Ages, Walter Scott's *Ivanhoe* and kindred works, and it was her plan to reproduce something resembling the medieval manorial system in Charles City. But instead of employing freed Negroes as her peasant labor force she contemplated the hiring of Swedish immigrant farmers and their families on an informal contract basis. Under her verbal agreement with Oertzen and the four Swedish farmers and their families who were subsequently recruited in New York in June and sent down to Sherwood, each immigrant was given a "few acres" of ground for his personal use. In return, the farmers agreed to work four days each week on Sherwood land and two days on their own. Julia, in turn, paid the transportation costs for each family from New York to Virginia, and she agreed to supply her Nordic laborers with food and clothing, seed and tools, until the first crop was harvested. After this they were to be on their own until the three-year agreement had expired. John C. Tyler thought this an excellent arrangement, "the best scheme I have had presented to my mind; for as to the negroes, they, so far, are perfectly worthless." Similarly, other Charles City plantation owners, faced with the same labor problem as Sherwood Forest, watched the Swedish experiment with considerable interest. "Everyone who has heard of it thinks it excellent," Alex wrote his mother in July.[4]

The Swedish interlude began on July 3, 1865, when the first of the immigrant families arrived at Sherwood. Oertzen had purchased two "condemned" U.S. Army horses at Fortress Monroe and his small labor force immediately began plowing the caked and long-neglected earth in an attempt to get turnips, beans, and potatoes into the ground before undertaking the major job of planting a wheat crop. In addition to the funds sent to Oertzen for the horses, Julia dispatched the first of several shipments of beef, flour, sugar, salt, nails, and tools from New York to the plantation to feed and provision her Swedes.

What began in optimism ended in gloom. By the beginning of September Oertzen was demanding more and more cash for groceries, horses, harnesses, seed wheat, and farm equipment. "We are doing nothing," he confessed. "It is so very dry here that everything is dying away. The ground so hard that not two horses are able to get a plough through the ground, and so we are waiting for rain or money or both. . . . We are living already on milk and peaches and peaches and milk mornings, noons and nights. The meat is nearly all gone . . . we do not know how sugar looks." Julia did not respond very sympathetically to this urgent appeal for "a few hundred dollar now," coming as it did within a week of the Surrogate Court's ruling that her mother's will was inadmissible to probate. Still, she sent $400 to John C. Tyler with instructions to purchase mules, plows, fencing, and other farm gear for Sherwood. In the same mail, however, she summarily discharged Oertzen and ordered him from her property. She was fortified in this precipitate action by John C. Tyler's opinion that the Swede "is of no earthly account. None of the persons you sent here have earned their salt since they have been here . . . it would be to your interest to get rid of all of them." Julia agreed, and the Swedish experiment ended a few months after its inception.

To fill the labor void and keep something growing on the old plantation, the mistress of Sherwood Forest accepted the pattern into which most of the postwar agricultural South was gradually drifting. She followed John C. and Gardie's advice to let out various parcels of Sherwood land to the "damned niggers" on a straight sharecrop basis. "I have applications from several persons to work portions of it on shares," her former manager informed her in late September 1865, "and have no doubt but the whole or nearly all the plantation could be worked that way. I let out a part of [your] land this year to two persons to cultivate in corn. They will make about eighty barrels and they are to pay one half of what they make."[5]

Von Oertzen did not accept his summary discharge in good spirit. On the contrary, he calculated the value of the work he had already done at Sherwood Forest at $20 per month and suggested that Julia pay him $100 or "what you think proper." Julia did not think more than half that amount "proper," and her decision in the matter prompted the Swede to sue her for $100 in March 1866. The suit was eventually thrown out of court, but not before Julia had spent nearly the amount of Oertzen's claim in legal fees.[6]

Thanks to David Lyon Gardiner and Sievert von Oertzen among others, Julia was rapidly becoming one of the most sued women in America. From 1865 until 1874 she was almost constantly before the courts in one capacity or another and for one reason or another. There was the long struggle over Juliana's will, the numerous claims against her husband's estate, various suits involving tax liens and real estate transfers, the attempt to regain control of Villa Margaret, and a desperate struggle to hold onto Sherwood Forest in 1870–1874.[7]

The fight to regain possession of Villa Margaret, if not typical of Julia's multiple legal tribulations, revealed something of the difficulties encountered by a "Rebel lady" in securing satisfaction from the federal government during the Reconstruction years, and the massive amounts of sheer patience the process demanded. Actually, Julia anticipated no conscious obstructionism from the Johnson administration in the Villa Margaret matter. Shortly after hostilities ended and Andrew Johnson of Tennessee had taken office, she dispatched a strong letter to the new President lecturing him on how he should run the distracted country. Only a policy of kindness and conciliation toward the conquered South, she assured him, would earn him the everlasting plaudits of Southerners like himself:

Now, President Johnson, you can redeem yourself in the hearts of your real fellow countrymen, your brave and noble fellow citizens of the South, whose blood runs in *your* veins, for whom you *must* have a mellow feeling, a *natural* sympathy.... You have only to move in the *right way*—the way of righteousness, peace and mercy—with a memory of the terrible trials and sufferings that have rent the hearts and souls of your own people in flesh and blood to be blessed thrice by them.... May your heart be the abode of gentle mercy, so that when your last hour shall come you can hope to be forgiven, even as you forgave.[8]

Since one of the "terrible trials and sufferings" Julia herself had sustained during the war was the loss of Villa Margaret, she began a heavy pen-and-ink bombardment of the White House and Washington officialdom demanding the return of her Hampton property. Unfortunately, the problem was complicated by the fact that the Tyler house was occupied in early 1866 by white schoolteachers from the North sent down to Virginia by the Freedmen's Bureau to instruct the emancipated Negroes in the Hampton area. The Bureau, however, did not directly control or administer the property, so Julia's protesting letters to General O. O. Howard, Bureau chief in Washington, fell on fallow ground. Instead, the Villa was managed by the American Missionary Society in New York under an authority secured directly from the Secretary of War. The Missionary Society provided room and board at the Villa for the "school marms" and other Freedmen's Bureau officials in the area. Julia therefore began a correspondence with the Reverend George Whipple, Secretary of the American Missionary Society, asking that he clear the Negro squatters and their ugly little shacks from the six acres surrounding the main house. She suggested also that the Society either begin paying a fair rent for the continued use of the property ($250 per year was mentioned) or commence evacuating it altogether. Whipple referred her demands to the Freedmen's Bureau and to the War Department. They in turn passed Julia's complaints around Washington and then threw them back into Whipple's lap. As the bureaucratic buck-passing became an exact science, Julia and her lawyers tried to ascertain whom to sue, in what court, and on what charge. For three frustrating years this merry-go-round spun around while the property deteriorated alarmingly in appearance and value. "They have never yet surrendered willingly one foot of property real or personal that they could possibly make use of," lawyer Charles B. Mallory had accurately warned her in August 1866.

In October 1868 the War Department did authorize the not overly generous payment of four dollars rent per month for the property, but when Julia at last obtained control of the once-beautiful Villa in 1869 it was in dreadful condition. It was, she protested angrily to President Ulysses S. Grant, "shorn of its beauty—the furniture gone, the outbuildings destroyed and the grounds covered with negro huts." Since she had no available funds with which to restore it herself, she suggested to Grant that the government buy it. "The house which is of the Italia gothic style can be restored without much cost to good condition," she informed him. "It seems to me a desirable piece of property for the government to possess being near the Artillery School which you have instituted." The government was not interested. Julia was therefore forced to sell the unsightly Villa Margaret privately in September of the depression year 1874 for a mere $3500, less than a third of its 1860 value. She was lucky to get that for it.[9]

As the former First Lady became suffocatingly immersed in the complex world of wills, suits, depositions, tax claims, and real estate transfers, she did not lose sight of or sympathy for the difficult adjustments, emotional and economic, faced by all the Confederate Tylers during Radical Reconstruction. Sending her oldest sons and Harry Beeckman off to college in Germany and putting her plantation into marginal operation were but the first evidences of her determination to do all she could to help the Tyler family regain its ante-bellum status and dignity. To be sure, some members of the proud family responded better to the challenge of the new order than others and needed her assistance not at all. Some were nearly helpless and clung to her bounty and psychological support tenaciously.

Robert Tyler, for example, adjusted quickly. He moved with Priscilla to Montgomery, Alabama, after the conflict. There he did what had long come naturally to Tyler men. In November 1866 he became a candidate before the state legislature for the office of Adjutant General and Inspector General of Alabama. "To live at all is a great struggle to us," he told his stepmother in October 1866. "This country is almost unredeemable. The negroes are violent politicians and I look forward with dread to the election next month, not that I would mind much the *dying*, but I hate the idea of being murdered." Robert neither won the election nor was he murdered. Too proud to accept financial assistance graciously offered him by James Buchanan and some of his old prewar Pennsylvania political friends (he returned a check for $1000 to Buchanan), he accepted instead a loan of $1000 from Priscilla's brother-in-law, Allan Campbell, to sustain his family until he secured the editorship of the Montgomery *Advertiser* in 1867. As editor of the influential newspaper and as chairman of the State Democratic Executive Committee and a leader in the racist White Man's Party, Robert spent the last years of an active life successfully fighting the Radical Republican-Negro domination of Alabama. He died of a stroke on December 3, 1877, but not before he had seen the Carpetbagger power broken in 1874 and suffering Alabama freed of corrupt and venal Radical rule. Montgomery, Priscilla wrote in 1866 when she and her husband first arrived there, was a town where

> Negro women sit along the sidewalks with their baskets of provisions while the men fill the street. They never move an inch to let a lady pass and actually at times I walk into the streets to get around them. They are dirty and ragged, looking unhappy, restless and hungry.... The Negro is the inhabitant of the town, the arbiter of its destinies, while over all floats in every direction the Stars and Stripes, a hollow mockery! God only knows where it will all end.

Thanks in part to editor Robert Tyler, it all ended in White Supremacy, a racial despotism as morally corrosive as the one it replaced.[10]

If Robert Tyler found the key to his personal reconstruction in a crusade against Negro rule in Alabama, King Numbers in Black, James A. Semple found his in mental fantasy and political make-believe. He was incapable of absorbing psychologically the reality of the South's defeat. For the first year and a half after Appomattox he spent most of his time attempting to organize Confederate underground cells in Canada. Dedicated to the dubious proposition that the South would somehow rise again militarily, these little expatriate groups, as short-lived as they were ineffectual, maintained contact with Confederate officials who had fled the country, opposed the Union military occupation of the South, fought Radical Republican political policy, attempted to get unreconstructed Confederates into public office (Semple worked hard, for example, to secure Robert Tyler's election in Alabama in 1866), sought the release of Jefferson Davis from Fortress Monroe, and generally labored to maintain focal points of Southern resistance pending the arrival again of *Der Tag*. In this pathetic comic-opera cause Semple functioned as liaison man, courier and propagandist, and as a working scribe in an unofficial Confederate Committee of Correspondence patterned after the Colonial models of 1772–1773. Throughout this period he teetered dangerously on the brink of a complete psychological crack-up, occasionally drifting across the thin dividing line into moments of irrationality.

Refusing to take the amnesty oath in 1865, Semple went underground. He changed his name, first to John Doe and then, with a shade more imagination, to Allan S. James, took a disguise, and became a cloak-and-dagger fugitive from the Union occupation. "So far I am free and have no fears," the forty-four-year-old conspirator informed Julia in November 1865, "as I am pretty well by this time acquainted with my own powers of adroitness, courage, etc., and can provide pretty well for emergencies." He helped Julia maintain contact with Varina Davis, and Julia in turn gave him shelter when he passed through New York en route to and from Canada.

Semple soon discovered with considerable disgust that the Confederate sympathizers in Montreal were mutually suspicious of one another and hopelessly split in doctrine and policy. "There is the devil to pay among the 'tribe' here," he informed Julia from Canada in August 1866. "No one speaks to the other and I have heard the most astounding reports and been questioned by a member of the 'tribe' and had no hesitation in at once answering all questions in writing, and I tell you now that by my own volition I will never pass another word with one of the members here.... I shall write to Mrs. Davis and inform old Jeff of the circumstances... at the same time, I am ready to engage in any matter which will further the interests of the South." But after eighteen months' work he was ready to quit the whole futile business. Old friends wrote him that his work for the defunct Confederacy was really hopeless. The South, said one, "should yield at once to inevitable fate and accept the Constitutional Amendment [Fourteenth] which it is shown that nothing can defeat. It seems to me all idle to prolong the struggle, especially after the sword has proved so worse than useless.... Would that all had your wise and manly views!" Semple finally agreed that the lost cause was beyond resurrection. "I am tired of being hunted down," he confessed to Julia in November 1866. Thus when Jefferson Davis, Semple's "Fortress Monroe correspondent," asked him to visit Mississippi on a "confidential matter," Semple declined the commission. With that decision, James A. Semple, alias John Doe, alias Allan S. James, acknowledged at last the Civil War victory of the United States of America.[11]

It was a decision dictated by a near-total nervous breakdown in October-November 1866 and by the final rupture at that time of his never very satisfactory marriage to Letitia Tyler Semple. Indeed, while Semple was playing cat and mouse with the Yankees in 1865–1866, Letitia left him, moved to Baltimore, and opened a private school there called the Eclectic Institute. During his mental illness in late 1866 Julia nursed him, worried about him, and gave him shelter at Castleton Hill. She paid for his room and board in a New York hotel while he was convalescing in 1867. She also urged the purser to abandon the sea of alcohol on which the South's defeat, the failure of the Confederate underground, and his own despair had launched him. He did not heed her advice. Wine, women, and cards temporarily became his life's work. And he worked hard. Tazewell Tyler saw him in New York in October 1866 "constantly around the Theaters, traveling about the country with actresses, gallivanting them to Central Park." January 1867 found him in New Orleans, drinking and gambling heavily, threatening suicide. For a time the confused Semple even imagined himself in love with Julia. "You are good, *I know,* and beautiful to my eyes, *but you are not mine!!* My love you know you have taken, one day share my lot . . . my Sister darling," he wrote her in March 1866. Julia was mildly flattered by all this, but she quickly put Semple straight on her feeling for him. "Shall I admit," she asked,

that it gave me pleasure to read your professions of ardent affection? Perhaps it should have been otherwise, and I shall rather chide you for avowals that do not entirely agree with the abiding *friendship* I wish should grow up between us—but it is so sweet to be caressed when the heart finds little difficulty in responding that I will forgive you the mere expressions of a letter and reproach only myself for suffering their influence to be so agreeable and soothing. But why should I not regard you most tenderly? To that question there are many answers in my heart, each one so satisfactory that I shall not under any circumstances strive to weaken the tie which I trust with time will rather grow firmer between us. . . . [But] if necessary Cestorus himself must be invoked to stand guard between us. I will become your mentor to guide you into the right path whenever there is danger of your needing [guidance]. Thus I am sure our *friendship* will be unmistakable. . . .

Nevertheless, reports of Semple's debauchment in New York and New Orleans and Julia's patient attempts to snap him out of his moral and mental decline reached Letitia in Baltimore and convinced her that her errant husband and her still-attractive stepmother were up to no good. She had never liked Julia anyway. To be sure, Julia owed Semple a great debt of gratitude. He had done much for Gardie and Alex in Richmond during the war, and for Julie after the war. Julia fully repaid this debt to him, but not in the fashion the suspicious Letitia imagined. And while Semple had indeed "led a wild, roving and checkered life," Julia had not figured in that side of it. She was never the "other woman" in any triangle, and she strenuously objected to Letitia's insinuations that she was. Semple also challenged those insinuations after he emerged from his illness and intemperance in July 1867 and was able to see clearly and sensibly the sad drift of affairs.

Your remarks relative to Mrs. T. are not worthy of a daughter of John Tyler [he told his estranged wife]. No matter what I may think of a lady, I rather think I would keep it to myself. I was suffering and Mrs. T. offered me a home (I have never had one before) and I accepted it and passed many pleasant hours there. As to your terms relative to her I throw them back with the scorn which they deserve, a lady she is and always will be. As to "carrying my name" to save it from disgrace, it is incredulous. I am the custodian of my own honor.... You are yet on the sunny side of maidenhood. Take your own steps and resume your own name.

There was no formal divorce. Semple never lived with his wife again, however. The acrimonious Letitia sought to punish Julia for her innocent role in Semple's erratic postwar behavior by instituting a petty legal fight with her stepmother over possession of some family portraits Semple had salvaged from Sherwood Forest during the war.[12]

If the various emotional problems of Semple and Letitia distressed Julia, the outward adjustment of John Tyler, Jr., to the new order of things in the South gave her cause for great happiness. Psychologically the least stable of the deceased President's children by his first wife, John's maturation was hastened and fixed by the trauma of the conflict. Forty-six years old when the organized bleeding stopped, he left Richmond and his post in the collapsed Confederate War Department for Baltimore. For a short time he lived with his sister Letitia on Mount Vernon Place while he began building a law practice. He brought his drinking habits under control. He did not, however, resume his marriage with Martha Rochelle Tyler, who died January 11, 1867, at the age of forty-six. In 1869 he was appointed to a position in the Internal Revenue Office in Washington. By 1872 he was in Tallahassee, Florida, at work in the Assessor's Office of the Internal Revenue Bureau there, a patronage post that required him to announce publicly for Grant in the 1872 campaign. Julia defended his shocking defection from Rebel orthodoxy with the argument that "the political parties are so mixed that one should not be judged harshly for any course he chooses or sees fit to take." She thought Republican Grant terrible, but not much worse than former abolitionist editor Horace Greeley, nominee of both the Democratic and Liberal Republican parties. Privately, of course, John Tyler, Jr., remained politically unreconstructed until his death in 1896. He was always a Rebel patriot and eager secessionist ready to join in a new civil war. In the late 1880s he was known as "General" John Tyler, his military rank having increased more rapidly as a Confederate veteran than it had while he was on active duty in the Confederate Army. His only reconstruction was in the spiritual realm. Finding the Episcopal Church in Tallahassee weighed down with dogmatism and ritualism, he converted to Methodism in 1873. For a time he even considered entering the Methodist ministry in order better "to hammer the wicked and denounce sin." This urge fortunately passed. General John was simply not the ecclesiastical type.

Still, John adjusted better to the postwar world in the South than his younger brother, Dr. Tazewell Tyler. Taz broke angrily with Julia after the conflict, accusing her of cowardly running away from Sherwood Forest to the comforts of Staten Island during the war. Embittered by the collapse of the Confederacy, refusing to live under the Yankee occupation of Virginia, he drifted to California in 1867. There he attempted to mix the practice of medicine with the "wine cup." The compound was not stable. Divorced in 1873 for his "dissipation" by Nannie, his wife of sixteen years, the broken Taz found surcease at last in an early grave. He died in California on January 8, 1874, at the age of forty-three. In a real sense he was as much a casualty of the Civil War as if he had fallen in combat in the Wilderness.[13]

While Julia sympathized with the postwar problems of her stepchildren and their families, she was naturally more concerned with the fate of her own children. After sending Gardie and Alex off to Germany in September 1865 she realized that something would also have to be done with her sixteen-year-old daughter Julie, who was already very much a woman and "as wild as the waves that dash upon the shore." Actually, Julie was not that wild. She was just boy-crazy, and, as she put it herself, "only a little *gay*." West Point Cadets and young Army officers particularly captivated her. Flirtation came naturally to her. Julia decided the time had come to curb her romantic activities with at least one semester in a boarding school. She had long considered Roman Catholic schools "generally very thorough—much better than any other." Thus when she learned something about the Convent of the Sacred Heart in Halifax, Nova Scotia, she decided to enroll Julie there for a few months. It was inexpensive, cultured (classes were conducted in French), and located in Canada, well removed from Yankee educational influences.[14]

On March 31, 1866, young Julia Gardiner Tyler left New York for Halifax in the care of James A. Semple, who was bound in that direction on one of his clandestine voyages for the Confederate underground. Just as Juliana Gardiner had once lectured her daughter when

Julia had departed East Hampton for the Chagaray Institute in New York City, so now, thirty years later, Julia introduced Julie to the ways of the world and to the expected deportment of young ladies therein:

Do cultivate your voice to the best of your ability and do not waste your time as you have done. People do blame *me* so much for letting you flirt around among the beaux and neglect all your studies. I am particularly sorry you ever wrote to any of them. Miss Julia Tyler is expected to hold herself in *reserve*.... I wish you could see the carriage bill from Quarantine of your various drives from there and back! It mounts up nicely. You must buy nothing in Halifax that is not absolutely necessary for your school.... You must write every week to me, telling me everything, and write to very few others—and to *no gentlemen*. I shall be very much offended if you disobey me. I wish you to attend particularly to your spelling and arithmetic in your English studies. You must learn to be a good accountant.

Julia had great ambitions for her daughter in society and was certain Julie would be "a great belle one of these days judging from her commencement." Like her mother at the same age, Julie was an incorrigible flirt. Indeed, on the ship to Halifax she took a young West Pointer "in tow" and soon had his photograph on her dresser. "She certainly has 'Army' on the brain," Semple reported to Julia in amazement. Amazed for quite different reasons was Gardie, who thought it positively seditious that his sister could become interested in West Pointers. "They may be *very brave boys,* as you say," he snorted, "but it would be a source of much unhappiness to me to see a sister of mine hanging on the arm of one of those *mighty heroes* who are being bred up now for the express purpose of tyrannizing over the South.... I hope never to see an infernal Yankee in the house. They have ruined our country and we are, morally speaking, bound to hate every one of 'em without exception, which I *do* with an intensity you can't understand." [15]

That heated statement from Karlsruhe ended Julie's West Point phase and she began concentrating on the civilian youth of Halifax. At the same time she settled down to the challenge of being a Protestant student in a Roman Catholic school. She liked the Roman Church immediately. "Don't be *astonished* if in the course of three or four months you hear of my becoming a *nun,*" she warned her mother. "I don't know what may happen, I like everything in the convent so much." Even Semple, who believed in very little beyond the divinity of Jefferson Davis, was impressed with what he saw of the school. "Say what you will," he told Julia, "these Romish Bishops are the best educated and smartest men you can find anywhere almost, and on all subjects are agreeable and entertaining." All in all, the brief experience at Sacred Heart was a good one for the young Tyler lady. She became no nun, of course. She studied diligently and responded constructively to the mild discipline of the convent. And when she returned to New York in July

1866, leaving behind her a small blizzard of unpaid bills in various Halifax stores, she also left at least one broken-hearted male admirer in Nova Scotia. It was not all prayer and no play at the *Sacre Coeur,* and she experienced no difficulty resuming her flirtatious ways in New York.[16]

For the Tyler boys in Germany, formal education was a more difficult matter. Arriving in Karlsruhe in late September 1865 after a brief sightseeing trip through northwestern Germany, the Confederate innocents abroad took counsel with John Fulton, their guide and mentor, and made their educational plans. At first they did little except study German intensively with private tutors. Within a few months, however, they were all taking formal courses—Gardie in the sixth class of the local Lyceum, Harry and Alex in the fourth and sixth classes respectively at the Karlsruhe Burger Schule. Gardie quickly abandoned his interest in engineering and settled down instead to a not overly successful study of modern languages and classics with a view toward entering law. The German language came very slowly to him and he often felt he was wasting his time and his mother's money sitting in classes in which he barely understood what was going on. By October 1866 he was discouraged enough with his lack of linguistic progress to think seriously of returning home. "I have never believed that I could do as well here as in an American College," he confessed to Julia.[17]

Alex, on the other hand, did extremely well at the Burger Schule. He leaped the language barrier easily and decisively. When, therefore, in the spring of 1866 it threatened to come down to the simple financial question on Staten Island of which son Julia could afford to maintain in Germany, both boys agreed it should be Alex. He had a flair for math and science, and his desire to become a mining engineer was no passing fancy. "I am told that I have first rate talents for Mathematics," he boasted to his mother in September 1866. "Well, if I haven't, I haven't talents for anything." Fortunately, he did have scientific talents, and his academic ambitions carried him far beyond wanting to become an "educated country gentleman" in Virginia. The Burger Schule would ready him for the mathematics curriculum at the Karlsruhe Polytechnic, and this in turn would prepare him for the engineering course at Freiburg. And a Freiburg education in mining engineering would, he reasoned, be worth "an income of from five to six thousand yearly in gold." [18]

Harry Beeckman did not belong in Germany at all. Deprived of a father in infancy and a mother at the age of nine, raised first by a crotchety grandmother and now by his Aunt Julia, the seventeen-year-old boy possessed neither emotional stability nor professional goals. He was a good enough student, but he much preferred the beer halls and the friendly *fräulein* of Karlsruhe to the disciplined quiet of the study and the library. He gave up engineering before he really tried it. Instead, he began to study for a business career with the vague idea of someday entering his Uncle Gilbert Beeckman's retail dry goods store in New York City. Gardie did not think the Beeckman store "at all fit for a young man to commence his career in" and he soon came to feel that Harry was by and large wasting his time in Karlsruhe. Had Margaret lived it might have been different. As it was, Harry's decline began before his rise was completed.

It was a decline to which Julia unwittingly contributed when she empowered Fulton to dole out very little spending money to her sons and nephew. Possessing little conception of currency-exchange ratios, Julia put the boys on an allowance which came to about twenty cents a week in German money. This scarcely covered the cigars, beer, late suppers, and other pleasures to which the student community of Karlsruhe was addicted. Even haircuts were well beyond the economic competence of the Tylers. The bare trickle of allowance money through Fulton's spigot produced much tension between the clergyman and his charges, and it eventually led to a flurry of bitter protests to Julia demanding more money and the discharge of the penurious Fulton. Fulton, of course, was not to blame. He merely carried out his instructions from Staten Island. Julia knew this and she supported him. "His sympathies with the South cover a multitude of faults," she told her sons. Nevertheless, she did finally promise more realistic currency dispensations, although several thin months passed before the new allowance schedule went into effect.

Julia had grave money problems herself during her long will fight with David Lyon. But severe as these were, she managed in May and June 1866 to find $768.15 for the purchase of four dresses and one $40 black silk petticoat at Mme. Gigon-Russell's exclusive New York shop preparatory to vacationing in Newport. "You must spend as little as you can," she pleaded with her sons and nephew, "for you must remember your expenses are enormous, or at least will seem so to me until my affairs are fully settled." Her entreaties did not influence young Beeckman. So desperate did Harry become for funds that he sold his gold watchchain in February 1866. Punished by Fulton for the deed by having his meager allotment suspended altogether, he enlisted Gardie's aid with Julia. "Money makes the mare go here as well as elsewhere," Gardie told his mother patiently. "It is all very well for you to tell us we make ourselves unnecessarily uneasy but a fellow is very apt to incline that way when he puts his hand in his pocket and finds no comfort thar!" [19]

Before Julia eased the boys' financial agony Harry foolishly took money matters into his own hands. Unable to buy cigars or borrow them from Gardie ("How can I supply the whole school with cigars on twenty cents a week?" his cousin snapped), he approached a breaking point. This craving and Julia's refusal to let him purchase a guitar and take instruction on it at forty cents a lesson finally conspired to force his hand into Fulton's locked desk and remove forty florins (about $15) from it. For a few days he was the big-spending sport of the school, treating the other boys to billiards, beer, and cigars. Promptly found out, he contritely returned most of the money to Fulton. Still, Harry's unthinking act was reported to Julia and she immediately removed him from the school. With Fulton escorting him as far as Bremen, Harry was returned to New York in August 1866. Gardie and Alex were much embarrassed by their cousin's indiscretion. They were gratified to learn, however, that their mother had decided to send the wayward lad to Washington College in Lexington. "It is much better than a Yankee college and he will be less liable to be led astray," said Gardie.[20]

Harry's disgrace notwithstanding, the Tyler boys found Germany an interesting experience. If their studies were difficult, if pangs of homesickness occasionally seized them, there were the compensating educational and social advantages of Karlsruhe's extensive cultural life. The city of some 30,000 population was a delightful one, strewn with beautiful walks and parks. Its band was "superior to any I ever heard in the United States," admitted Gardie. The palace of the Grand Duke of Baden was the local architectural and political attraction. Old wine cellars vied with older churches for the boys' attention. Schiller's *Joan of Arc* was only one of the first-rate plays the Karlsruhe theater ran during their stay in Baden (its main impact on Gardie was to make him "feel like eating something after coming out").[21]

The Germans even thoughtfully provided a war against the Austrians in June 1866 to amuse the militant young Confederates during their residence in Karlsruhe. This brief and decisive conflict disturbed the flow of funds from Staten Island, put an end to plans for a summer-vacation tour of Central Europe, and threatened for a time to force them to seek refuge in Switzerland. Nevertheless, it provided the Tylers with a look into the Prussian character and an opportunity to play amateur war correspondent. They were impressed with what they saw and heard of the war, and they reported its course with mounting excitement to Staten Island. Prussian efficiency and military precision truly amazed the young veterans of Appomattox. They had brought with them to Karlsruhe the curious notion that all German soldiers were like those ill-trained Cincinnati and New York immigrant troops under Franz Sigel who had been routed at New Market by Breckinridge. "Great people for talking and not much for acting, except in the running away style," Gardie had sized up German soldiery in April 1866. The smashing Prussian victory over Austria changed his opinion radically. The Seven Weeks' War was over almost before it fairly commenced, so brilliantly did the well-honed Prussian army sweep each field of combat against the hopelessly outclassed Austrians and their German Catholic allies (Baden among them) in the doomed Germanic Confederation. The boys could not, however, understand the stolid manner in which the Germans seemed to make war and alliances with one another.

These folks over here [Gardie reported in July] don't act in regard to military matters like we do in America, that is, pitch in with immense enthusiasm, fight six or seven battles in so many days, then gradually cool down 'til we fight on a certain line all the summer, more with spade than musket.... Instead ... these Germans go at it with a great deal of circumspection and deliberation, whetting their swords with as much care as a butcher does his knife, listening now to what this nation [and that] has to say in regard to their little family quarrel, not being the least offended at an outsider's meddling in family matters ... and on the whole acting with astonishing coolness and not at all disturbed by patriotic appeals ... but looking on with a calm and composed air deliberating whether it would be more for their interest to go with sister Austria or cousin Prussia. As a general thing most of them have determined to take sides with their nearest relation "not because they hated Prussia more but because they loved themselves the best."

The young Confederates could only conclude, therefore, that the Germans were an impassive, mechanical people devoid of all emotion, all values save that of calculating self-interest. "Confound the Germans," Harry cursed them, "they are in fact good for nothing but to work out mathematical problems and that they are really good at." Or as Gardie put it: "Just suppose these thick-skulled Germans could hear a regular Confederate yell; wouldn't that make them open their eyes in wonder!" [22]

The German girls certainly elicited no Rebel yells from the Confederate expatriates in Baden. "The ladies are passing up and down our street this morning in great numbers," Gardie told his sister with mock salaciousness, *"but the wind isn't blowing strong enough,* so it isn't worth the trouble to look out the window." Sex, when it reared its ugly head at all in 1866, reared it no higher than a well-turned ankle—at least not for the Tyler boys. By their critical standards there wasn't much to look at anyway. "I haven't seen a pretty girl since I have been in Germany," said Gardie disgustedly to his mother. "They are without exception the ugliest set of *beer-barrels* you ever heard or read of. I am nearly dying to see a pretty face again. If I conclude to settle down here I will have to import my wife ... I will let you know when I want her ... so you can send her on, 'right side up with care.'" Harry, less difficult to please, or less bashful in such matters, found a "great many pretty girls" in Karlsruhe, "and between the girls and the Lager Beer we are *half tipsy all the time.*" This was an exaggeration, obviously, since Julia had exacted strict prohibition pledges from her sons and nephew prior to their departure for Europe. She had, however, excluded beer and egg-nog from the promises so that Karlsruhe was not entirely transported to the Gobi Desert for the thirsty young men. Still, Gardie considered the maternal prohibition on wine and hard liquor an unrealistic one and he begged to be released from it, "For you will know that I am cut off from all social enjoyment.... The Germans consider it really a breach of etiquette not to partake of the jovial bowl.... It is the last temperance pledge you will ever get from me." Julia was unmoved by his arguments.

Even without wine and liquor the social enjoyments in Karlsruhe were considerable. American Consul George F. Kettell of Massachusetts and his young wife ("She is quite pretty, but, ye heavenly powers, what a foot and ankle!") often entertained the American students resident in town. Frau Steinbach, Gardie and Alex's landlady after Harry's departure in August 1866, saw to it that they met young German girls of good bourgeois background. It was a pleasant enough life. "The theaters and music of Karlsruhe are splendid," Gardie admitted, "and with ten thousand a year how a fellow could live. Life in Germany is certainly very pleasant if one has the where-with-all to enjoy it." [23]

Other leisure hours were filled with sports. With the dozen or so other American students in Karlsruhe, most of them Confederate expatriates like the Tylers, the boys formed an American baseball club in February 1866, the first of its kind, surely, in Germany. Together with some English students they also helped organize a local cricket club. In addition, Gardie absorbed the German passion for gymnastics and urged his mother to put up parallel bars for his younger brothers at home to exercise on. He also joined a student shooting fraternity. He and Alex both took up boxing so that "during leisure moments we may scientifically bung up each other's peepers. It is a pleasant and healthy amusement and saves the expense of calling in a doctor for bleeding purposes." Julia put her foot down when it came to fencing, fearful that it would lead her combat-happy sons straight into the dangerous student dueling clubs. But Gardie assured her that he would eschew fencing and dueling completely. "When I fight it will be with 'pistol and coffee for two,' or perhaps with the 'Arkansas Toothpick' [bayonet]. I ain't perticklar, anything from a cannon to a pen knife!" Alex complained that both his athletic and social life was being compromised by the lingering "camp itch" he had picked up during his brief tour with the Army of Northern Virginia. "I don't like to go to a Doctor here," he told his mother, "for it is considered dreadful, so please send me by first opportunity a good remedy." [24]

With all the academic, social, cultural, and athletic advantages Karlsruhe afforded, Gardie still wanted to come home. "Notwithstanding all these attractions I would rather be in 'Old Virginia,' " he told his mother. He was disturbed with the way the fight against David Lyon was going in the courts, and he found it frustrating to be able to contribute nothing more to the family effort than harmless anathemas hurled at his uncle from a distance of four thousand miles. He followed the will suit closely and was alternately elated and depressed as the direction of his mother's cause was first up and then down. As he expressed his deep concern to Julia in April 1867:

> He [David Lyon] seems to be lost to all feeling of gentleness and moderation and deserves to be branded as a public coward and woman-insulter.... Never mind, we'll have a settlement with the gent one of these days or I'm a Dutchman. I am sorry that I am not with you. I don't relish this idea of your being eternally troubled by a pack of villains and we over here at our ease. I'd feel much more satisfied if I could share your troubles or do something to mitigate them.... I feel savage about the way those dogs have treated you.... I know we have never heard half of what you have suffered since that confounded lawsuit commenced. However, the calm follows the storm and we'll have a good time together yet.... The whole concern has been bribed and you are among the meanest people in the world—and no good will ever come out of Nazareth.[25]

Similarly, Gardie was distressed at reports of what was happening in the South under the Reconstruction program of the Radical Republicans. So angry did he become over his mother's treatment in the "bribed" Yankee courts, and over the South's treatment by the Yankee occupation, he could hardly study or think about anything save returning home to take a stand against such slings and arrows of outrageous fortune. He hoped that President Johnson and the Radicals would come to such an impasse that civil war would again break out. "It would be my duty to be with Gen. Lee (God bless him) again. How I would like to meet my old comrades once more under the 'Bonnie Blue Flag,'" he sighed. News of the Reconstruction Act of March 1867, which divided the South into five military districts, and the subsequent stationing of federal troops (including Negro militia) throughout the section to supervise the registering and voting of Negroes, filled the Tyler boys with sadness. "Our poor South," Gardie mourned. " 'Tis too dreadful to contemplate.... It absolutely makes one sick. Farewell to States' rights and liberty! Triumph, Puritans and negro-worshippers! But remember, *we bide our time.*" Threats of the Radicals to impeach Johnson struck them as insane. They cheered the President's courage in vetoing Radical Republican legislative excesses, just as they hailed the good news of Jeff Davis' parole from Fortress Monroe. "We yelled with joy," Gardie reported. "That Andy Johnson is *something.*" There was actually very little to yell about. The passage of the Thirteenth and Fourteenth amendments cast the boys into despair. The Report of the Joint Committee of 15 in June 1866, recommending that the former Confederate states be denied representation in Congress, impressed them as the beginning of a "yoke of servitude, for in reality we are nothing else but *slaves,* however we may hate to say the degrading word." The only encouraging news reaching them from the South was a much exaggerated report from Lexington of riots there in March 1867. White boys had smashed and looted a Negro school, and the V.M.I. cadets had teamed up with Washington College students to "turn the Yankee Garrison out of the town." Or so it was said. "By Jove!" exulted Gardie, "there's life in the old Land yet!" [26]

David Gardiner Tyler could not sit safely on the sidelines in faraway Karlsruhe forever. His agitations to return home, begun as early as February 1866, increased in tempo and intensity. He procured catalogues from the University of Virginia and from Washington College. He carefully compared the schools and decided he would re-enter the Lexington institution, now under the direction of Robert E. Lee. "To be under Gen. Lee is . . . one of the greatest honors, whether in war or peace," he told Julia in October 1866. Also, the professors there were "among the most enlightened men of the South." Julia finally consented, and on September 24, 1867, just two years from the time he had arrived in Karlsruhe, he left for home. Five hundred students were expected at Washington College for the 1867–1868 session and Gardie was sure that "with so many young Southerners together 'twill be the freest place in America. The Yanks won't dare to try their negro equality politics there!" [27]

Alex remained behind in Germany by choice. He was subsequently graduated from both Karlsruhe and Freiburg as a mining engineer, and not until March 1873 did he return to the United States. He arrived home speaking fluent German and French and displaying a "magnificent physical development and . . . all the polish and address of a foreigner." In the intervening years he had run up a series of monumental debts. On one occasion his creditors saw him into a Baden "dungeon keep" where he spent several defiant weeks. Julia painfully paid off enough of these longstanding obligations for Alex to escape Germany for home.

She was not at all happy about his free-spending ways in college. But she thought he had completely lost his mind when he volunteered to fight for the Germans in the Franco-Prussian War. Failing in an attempt to join the Baden Army in October 1870 because he was too well known in Karlsruhe as an American citizen, he dropped out of school for a semester, took an assumed name, and finally, in December 1870, managed to enlist in the 1st Company, 15th Regiment of the Saxon Army. Two weeks under Lee had not been enough war to suit him. While he missed the heavy fighting at Mars-la-Tour, Gravelotte, and Sedan in August and September 1870, he did serve as a Uhlan trooper in the occupation of France for several months early in 1871. For this modest military contribution he was awarded a ribbon by the Kaiser for "faithful service" in the German Army. He admitted his enlistment had a "romantical" cast about it, but he enjoyed himself thoroughly. It was quite an adventure and he managed to amass some wonderful new debts in occupied France. "You know how excitable I am," he told his mother, "and then I think Germany perfectly right." [28]

The war Gardie saw after his return to Staten Island was of a quite different sort. Andrew Johnson was locked in mortal struggle with the Radical Republican Congress over the Tenure of Office Act and the related question of Edwin M. Stanton's status in Johnson's Cabinet. As Gardie observed the political situation from Castleton Hill in January 1868, "a very serious collision between the President and Congress is anticipated ... the Dogs of War are very like being loosed again, and this time we can look on and rub our hands with great satisfaction." While this bitter contest between the President and the Congress was approaching the showdown of the unsuccessful Radical attempt in February to impeach the Chief Executive, Gardie left Staten Island for Lexington to enroll in Washington College for the spring semester.[29]

There he found a distinguished student body of unreconstructed young Rebels like himself. Among them were Henry Clay's grandson, a cousin of John C. Calhoun, two nephews of General Lee, General John C. Breckinridge's son, and many others "from the best families" of the South. Harry Beeckman was there too. "Look out, ye Yanks," Gardie shouted in glee, "we are a-coming." Mainly he was impressed with Robert E. Lee, the revered president of the college who had already become a folk hero in the South. His matriculation interview with the general left Gardie misty-eyed:

I found the Old Hero as erect and noble looking as ever [he told Julia], and affable and kind and—but it is no use to attempt to describe him; all the adjectives in the English language could not begin to do him justice. He is universally beloved and revered by all the students, and his word is law with them. His influence and energy alone have made what was formerly a simple Academy one of the finest colleges in America; aye, I believe in the world.... The European plan has been adopted, and everything is carried on with the most perfect order. "Old Marse Bob" is *good* at everything he turns his hand to.

Under the stimulus of Lee's kindness and encouragement ("I never meet the General but that he asks after you," Gardie wrote his mother) young Tyler became a hard-working student of the law, classics, and modern languages. He saw his beloved general frequently on campus, and Mrs. Lee, who had known Julia in Richmond in 1862–1863, occasionally invited Gardie and other students into her home for tea. While Gardie was constantly forced to dun his mother for money to meet the most obvious college expenses—tuition, board, clothes, books—he remained in good spirits until his graduation in 1869 very near the top of his class. White rule had by that time been firmly re-established in Lexington. "No news except the knocking down of an African by a Student last week, which is no unusual occurrence," he informed Julia in June 1868.[30]

Even before he was graduated Gardie was fighting against any form of political accommodation with the carpetbagging Radical Republicans and their scalawag allies who ran the Old Dominion with the aid of Negro votes. Instead, he preached resistance and nothing but resistance to the Yankee occupation. "If we remain quiet," he exploded to Julia on the eve of the 1868 election, "and submit to... Radical enormities, allow ourselves to be insulted, knocked down, and spit upon without resistance," the South would never escape its bondage. Similarly, the Radicals' proposed new state constitution, the so-called Underwood Constitution, which enfranchised the Negro and permitted him to hold public office, was to young Tyler nothing more than a "political monster, born of Radical malignity and scalawag negrophilism." The idea of the Negro's voting in Virginia or receiving any of the normal rights of citizenship there was a notion Gardie (in common with most other white Southerners) could not readily absorb. "No true Virginian is going to give an assenting vote to his own degradation. I for one will *never* by my vote allow the Negro to exercise such a right." In spite of Gardie's opposition the Underwood Constitution was overwhelmingly ratified in June 1869.[31]

These views, as politically unrealistic as they were emotionally sincere, were partly conditioned by Gardie's visit to Sherwood Forest during his vacation from college in the summer of 1868. There he looked out over weed-choked fields and saw that

Desolation has set its seal upon all around us, and the gloom like the veil of the grave has settled upon the land. Sherwood looks as forlorn as ever, everything is going to yet greater ruin. With the exception of some one hundred acres which are being cultivated by negroes on shares, all the plantation is fast growing up in scrub pine, sassafras, and red oak bushes. The house... is gradually rotting, and in a few years longer it will be beyond the possibility of repair. Deserted, tenantless, forsaken, the once beautiful home of our then happy family! Can I ever forgive or forget the fiendish wretches who have wrought this work of desolation? If I should ever affiliate or stand on a friendly footing with a single one of this foul brood, may the direst vengeance of the Omnipotent fall upon me and mine.... It can never again be as it was ... when the negroes work merely on shares they are so indolent that they often entirely neglect what little they have under cultivation, and the whites have now no authority over them unless they are hired monthly as in the North....[32]

Julia twice visited the decaying plantation in 1866–1867, but she had virtually given up on the place after the failure of her Swedish experiment in 1865. In 1866 she again made up her mind to sell the property. Only the pained protests of Gardie and Alex from Karlsruhe and the knowledge that depressed farm land on the peninsula was selling for $40 to $50 per acre caused her to procrastinate. "I really think that the loss of our working population has decreased the real value of the land at least one fourth to one third," Semple correctly informed her at the time. The boys, of course, had strong sentimental attachments to the scene of their childhood. Gardie was determined to restore the estate and live on it.

After reading law in the Richmond offices of family friend James Lyons in 1869–1870 and gaining admission to the Virginia bar in June 1870, Gardie moved back to Sherwood Forest to do what his father and grandfather before him had done (and what his son is now doing)—combine the practice of law in Charles City with farming and local politics. He turned down an appointive county judgeship on the sensible ground that he first needed actual experience in the law. He was, after all, only twenty-four years old in 1870 and he had never practiced law a day. Not that the stipend for the post would not have been welcome. Ready cash was so tight in the Tyler family in 1870 that to satisfy a tax lien of $58.09 on the plantation the Sherwood cattle (three cows) were ordered put up to public auction by the local sheriff. Fortunately Julia, who hastened to Charles City to attend to this crisis, managed to buy the cows herself, and she picked up three heifers in addition, all for $79.00. "If I had not been present I do not suppose anyone could have made so good a bargain for me," she boasted happily.[33]

Her good luck in this single instance did not conceal the fact that Sherwood Forest, like almost all the other Tidewater plantations, remained in serious financial trouble throughout the entire Reconstruction period. The price of guano, seed wheat, and hired labor was so high in 1870—and the potential market for wheat so uncertain—Gardie decided it would not pay to put in a wheat crop at all. Brother Lonie was scheduled to enter the University of Virginia that year, and to Gardie it did not seem a good gamble to have his mother "strain and scuffle" to raise two or three hundred dollars to invest in a wheat crop that would probably bring in no more than three or four hundred. Better to invest the money in college tuition in the fall and plant oats in the spring, a crop for which guano was not required. A wheat crop would simply tie up too much capital. "The negroes will not work unless they are paid punctually every Saturday night, dependent as they are on the proceeds of their daily labor for sustenance," he explained to his mother in September 1870. "You already find it very difficult to throw up temporary dams to keep back the tide of debt... [and] as matters now are, a bird in the hand, let him be ever so poor a one, is certainly worth two in the bush."[34]

Julia agreed. Cash was extremely scarce. Overwhelmed with lawyers' fees, tuition payments, taxes, the everyday expenses of her smaller children, the maintenance of Castleton Hill, and claims against the Tyler estate, she was in no mood to gamble two hundred dollars in the unpromising Sherwood fields to win, at best, three hundred and fifty in return. Nor did her financial situation improve. In 1871 the little herd of livestock almost went on the sheriff's block again to satisfy a $85 tax bill. Judgments totaling $2000 against the plantation kept Gardie frequently in court after 1870 and nearly resulted in the forced sale of the estate in 1872 to satisfy the creditors. In that desperate year of 1872 Gardie had but one lone worker on the place, David Brown. "He has a mule, and supplies the labor and I have the land and my mule on terms of ½ the product. This is the best I can do, and has the merit of avoiding the outlay of money." As he looked out upon the snowy Christmas season of 1872 it pained him to see his "poor cattle standing shivering on the dreary hillside, and no feed to warm the poor beasts in the barn. I hope this will be the last winter our herd will be forced to endure, unsheltered and uncared for, the piercing blasts of winter. Christmas greetings...."[35]

Gardie's political career in Charles City County began almost as inauspiciously as did his attempt to re-enter the ranks of the landed gentry astride a long-neglected farm. The Old Dominion political arena contained more lions than Christians. The Republican governor of Virginia in 1870 was Gilbert C. Walker of Norfolk. He had been elected to the office in 1869 by an informal coalition of relatively moderate white Radical Republicans and old-line white Virginia Democrats. The latter group had opportunistically supported him because he was a lesser evil than Radical Republican New Yorker Henry H. Wells, the demagogic candidate of the militant Negro bloc. General Wells had served as Virginia's governor from 1867 to 1869 under a federal military appointment. While Walker was a great improvement over the rabble-rousing Wells (the Norfolk *Journal* crowed that Virginia had been "redeemed, regenerated and disenthralled" by Walker's victory), to Gardie Tyler he was no more than a "superb apollo and guttermanly carpetbagger." This harsh view was conditioned by the fact that twenty-seven Negroes had also been elected to the General Assembly in the June 1869 state canvass that swept the new governor in and approved the Underwood Constitution. In October, soon after the Walker regime took power in Richmond, the Republican-dominated General Assembly, to Gardie's disgust, formally ratified the Fourteenth and Fifteenth amendments. Only by this action could Virginia comply legally with federal requirements leading to the restoration of her statehood. There was, therefore, no practical or sensible (or moral) alternative to this belated decision in Richmond. Gardie nonetheless viewed Governor Walker as a carrier of bubonic plague because he was committed to a policy of sectional reconciliation.

His reluctant decision to run for Commonwealth's Attorney of Charles City County in the November 1870 elections seemed the only way he could contribute in some small manner to the downfall of the governor and his scalawag and carpetbagger friends. He believed that if he ran as an independent on a platform of "political neutrality and residence in the County," he might draw enough local Negro votes to slip into office. He certainly could not run as a white-supremacy candidate in a heavily Negro county, and he knew he could not win at all unless the Charles City whites united solidly behind his candidacy. "Unless an out-and-out Radical is run by the Negroes my chances for election are good," he decided. Unfortunately for Gardie's ambition and for the logic of his nonracist tactics, the Republicans ran in John Talley an extremist Radical. Nor did the whites fall in solidly behind young Tyler. They were unimpressed with his moderate position on race relations and Radical Reconstruction, and they failed to see that it was mainly a campaign stance designed to "split the Black vote." They stayed home from the polls in droves. Only a third of the eligible whites bothered to vote at all, and Gardie attracted but forty scattered Negro ballots. Talley pulled the Negro bloc and beat Tyler by an "overwhelming" majority. "This is the last time that I shall run as an Independent," Gardie told Julia in disgust, "with one foot on shore and one at sea. I was opposed to it all along and yielded at the expense of my feelings and better judgment to the advice of *soi-disant* friends. From this day forth I am a Rebel, Democrat, or whatever you choose to call it here, but never more a Trimmer." [36]

The national political scene of the early 1870s cast a light no more bright by Tyler standards than Radical rule in Charles City. Julia railed bitterly against military Reconstruction in the South, condemned the venal and corrupt Grant administration, and did what she could in the way of letters of recommendation to help her politically correct friends obtain patronage appointments. The Democratic Party, however, seemed to offer the distracted nation little more than did the corrupt Republican regime of the bewildered Grant. The plunders of Boss William M. Tweed's infamous Ring in New York City, and Tweed's cynical use of Tammany Hall as a vehicle for municipal piracy on a classic scale, struck Julia and Gardie as the end of the Democracy John Tyler had loved. "It is rotten to the core," Julia proclaimed in full exasperation. "Let the cry be reform anywhere.... New York seems like a paralyzed city—so dull is business." [37]

A breath of political fresh air in Virginia, the first since Appomattox, seemed to stir in the "refreshing victory" the white Conservative Democracy achieved in the state elections of November 1871. Thanks to "a complete fusion of old-line-Whigs and dyed-in-the-wool Democrats," the white-supremacy party captured Richmond. Though the Radicals continued their local domination of Charles City, Gardie was now hopeful that an anti-Grant, anti-Radical Reconstruction, anti-Tweed coalition reform movement on the national level, crossing party lines North and South, might save "what little there remains of constitutional liberty by a defeat in '72 of the stupid dog that kennels in the White House." The stunning defeat of the Democracy in the Empire State in November 1871, a setback occasioned by the unsavory Tweed exposés in New York City, dashed this momentary optimism at Sherwood Forest. It was, Gardie argued, "the severest blow that has befallen the South since the downfall of the Confederacy, because it insures us four years more (perhaps a perpetuation) of carpet-baggers, ku klux legislation and military tyranny.... Grant's hands are strengthened and the bulwark of *our* safety overthrown."

Nor did the emergence of the Liberal Republican movement in 1872 impress Gardie. Although it was dedicated to reform, the interment of the "bloody shirt," and an end to the military occupation of the South, its nomination of former abolitionist Horace Greeley seemed "a nasty dose to take even to get rid of Butcher Grant." The Tylers thus strenuously opposed Democratic Party endorsement of the Liberal Republican ticket of Greeley and B. G. Brown. Indeed, Gardie was instrumental in seeing that Charles City delegates to the Virginia Conservative [Democratic] Convention on June 27, 1872, went to Richmond committed to no endorsement of "such a vile concoction as Greeley." When, however, the national Democratic convention, meeting in Baltimore on July 9, did accept and endorse the Greeley-Brown ticket, Gardie reluctantly came out for old Horace with the rationalization that *anybody* would be an improvement over Grant. Greeley had, after all, helped bring about Jefferson Davis' release from prison, and his election would encourage some hope of an end to carpetbag rule in the South. The Democratic-Liberal Republican coalition ticket was a "nauseous emetic," but Gardie held his nose and swallowed it. He was not surprised, however, when Grant, "bloody shirt" flying in the political breeze, overwhelmed "Horace of the White Hat" with a popular majority of 763,000 and an electoral vote margin of 286 to 66. "In our County," Gardie reported to his mother, "the negroes thronged ... to the polls, voting nearly as a unit for Grant; the white vote was small, many refusing to take Greeley, casting their ballots only for County officers and Congressional candidates.... Many of the lower classes of whites voted for Grant." The Democratic Party, concluded Julia after the election, "is at present defunct and I pity all wedded to it." [38]

The institutional problems of the Democratic Party in the early 1870s were no more complicated than the personal problems of Julia Gardiner Tyler. Nor were they any more susceptible to ready solution. On the surface of things, however, Julia seemed to have more effective stabilization machinery in her hull than did the floundering Democracy. In her early fifties, she was still a very attractive woman. She had started getting plump, but she remained quite pretty and she enjoyed excellent health throughout the decade. To James Lyons she was "the best as well as the loveliest of women." She could still race in and out of Richmond stores with a speed and a determination that left her sturdy children trailing far behind. "A few more days of shopping," Gardie complained to her in 1870, "would, I have no doubt, have made me a fit inmate of the Lunatic Asylum at Staunton." Her flying visits to

Washington were invariably noted in the papers of the capital. In March 1872, with considerable newspaper fanfare and much to Gardie's dismay, she visited Julia Dent Grant in the White House. Her correspondence with Laura Holloway promised her a secure historical niche in that author's forthcoming *Ladies of the White House*. Her portrait had been hung in the President's Mansion with appropriate ceremony. She was not obscure. News that Henry A. Wise was writing a eulogistic memoir of her husband (published in 1871 as *Seven Decades of the Union*) pleased her a great deal even though the crusty Wise had "once told the President that he did very wrong to marry me!" Wise laughed at her sally and promptly assured her that she had "certainly proved exceptional in making the President the most discreet and winning of wives on whom he doted to the last." [39]

But with all of these safety nets separating her from sickness and obscurity, Julia was by 1872 a very distraught woman. Entirely aside from her multitudinous legal and financial worries, she was unhappy and rootless. She was pained to learn in 1870, for example, that she was still considered "a bitter enemy of the Government" in Internal Revenue circles. More importantly, she watched the continuing decline of Harry Beeckman with sadness. She had always felt a special responsibility for Margaret's child. After he reached his twenty-first birthday in 1869 he withdrew from Washington College, moved to Sherwood Forest, and began a life of aimless dissipation. Julia lost all control over him. He was a pleasant, generous young man. On several occasions he loaned his Aunt Julia money, income from his quarter of the Gardiner estate, that she might remain a tiny step ahead of her creditors. But all attempts by Julia and Gardie to persuade him to buy land in Charles City and settle down to the stable life of the planter failed. "He is *irreclaimable* and neither affection nor duty demands that you should trouble yourself about him more than you have already done," Gardie told Julia. "Let him run his course . . . between us, I am tired of him as a dweller under the same roof." [40]

Of all Julia's postwar experiences nothing elated her quite so much as the marriage of the nineteen-year-old Julie to William H. Spencer in 1869; and nothing broke her so decisively as the young bride's death in childbirth at the age of twenty-one on May 8, 1871. Little is known of Will Spencer's background or of his courtship with Julie save that he was an impecunious, debt-ridden young man who wrote insipid love letters to his intended. But Julie loved him and that was what mattered. They were married in the Church of the Ascension in New York City on June 26, 1869, exactly twenty-five years to the day after Julia's wedding there to John Tyler. Following their marriage, they moved to Tuscarora, New York, where Spencer had a mortgaged farm. Not surprisingly, Julia packed her newlywed daughter off to her new home with the reminder that she must "do your duty in society. . . . You should not hold back when an occasion presents itself *worth* your exertions." To encourage this exertion and to instruct Julie further in the nuances and ramifications of her social duties, Julia visited the young couple at Tuscarora in 1869. The three of them also vacationed together at Saratoga Springs in the summer of 1870. Then, without warning, Julie died in May 1871 following the birth of a daughter, Julia Tyler Spencer, nicknamed "Baby." No death in the family struck Julia so powerfully—not even Margaret's or John Tyler's. She was absolutely crushed. She spent the rest of her life mourning Julie while she provided a home for and raised Baby Spencer as her own child. For several years she loaned Will Spencer money, made good his bad debts, and settled his overdue notes (one of them for $2650). Will, in turn, wandered aimlessly to the silver mines of Colorado and the citrus groves of California, and back again, in search of fame and fortune. He found neither, and Julia was that much the poorer. In the mid-1880s he disappeared from the family's sight forever.[41]

The death of young Julie brought Julia back to Washington. In 1871 she decided to quit Staten Island, sell Castleton Hill, the upkeep and taxes on which were becoming oppressive, and move to Georgetown in the District of Columbia. There she could be near the scene of her great triumph of 1844–1845 and closer to Sherwood Forest. Equally important in her decision was the prospect of placing fifteen-year-old Fitz and eleven-year-old Pearlie in the excellent Roman Catholic schools the District afforded. She had been very well impressed with Julie's earlier experience at the Sacred Heart in Halifax, and she was persuaded that the Roman Church ran better and less expensive schools than were generally to be found under other auspices. Accordingly, she moved into a flat on Fayette Street in Georgetown in January 1872. Pearlie was immediately enrolled in the nearby Georgetown Academy of the Visitation, and Fitz entered Georgetown College the following fall. Julia was delighted with both institutions and with the friendliness and kindness of the priests and nuns with whom she soon came in contact.[42]

Her return to Washington permitted Julia to involve herself once more in the social swirl of the capital. The newspapers again became "frequent in their allusions to me" as she happily made the social rounds. A friendly reception by Grant at the White House caused James Lyons to remark that "your witchery—your beauty ... have enlightened the President and softened him to the South." Julia, of course, had nothing but contempt for the Grant administration and it is doubtful that anybody could have enlightened the dull-witted Chief Executive. But the more she was entertained in Republican homes in Washington, some of them the homes of Radical Republicans, the more developed became her Paris-is-worth-a-Mass social philosophy. In January 1873 she described one of these Radical Republican affairs and her reaction to it to her son Lyon, who was then at the University of Virginia:

I went, and the consequence was the handsomest attentions ... as the ladies crowded in at the reception and were introduced to me as "Mrs. Ex-President Tyler." I was enthusiastically received by those who had formerly met me.... I was taken by surprise ... at the warmth of my old acquaintances—with the gulf of so many years between. The fact is, dear Lonny, the only way now to get along is to take the world as you find it and to make the best of it. It will be the means of satisfying your feelings much better than by *showing* them your dislike or opposition. That is the way to *triumph* and to make your enemies even speak well of you. People can hold to all their opinions without pressing them forward on unnecessary occasions.... And so I was glad I went, though it was as much as I could do to have the spirit to dress myself for it beforehand.

When Gardie heard that his mother was consorting with the Republicans he gave her a proper tongue-lashing:

Were I in your place, and remembering circumstances *past* and *present*, I should have nothing to do with the present Administration or any of its satellites. Our family have suffered so much from the acts of those people as any in the North or South, and *nationally* and *privately* we would have too much to forgive and forget to ... benefit from association with them.... Before the public *you* occupy a position similar to that of Mrs. Gen'l Lee, the widow of one of the leading men in a dead cause, and that position must be *exclusive*. ... Think of the widow of Marco Bazzan's entertaining a Turkish governor of Athens.

After that explosion from Sherwood Forest, Julia began choosing her Washington friends with more care.[43]

Her recaptured social life did not put to flight her basic loneliness or bring young Julie back from the grave. The social adulation her personality had long fed upon for its psychological nourishment no longer sufficed to make her happy or contented. Julia needed something else to sustain her in her middle years, something more substantial than party dresses, pretty compliments, crowded ballrooms, dependent babies, and loving relatives. During this period of financial crisis and mourning for Julie she began reading deeply in the history and theology of the Roman Catholic Church. She also began a serious investigation of spiritualism in the hope that it might give her an answer to the meaning of human existence and permit her to "talk" with the departed Julie. For the first time in her life she searched frantically for God and for some means of approaching the Godhead. She desperately needed spiritual comfort. As her search progressed she quickly and sensibly rejected the spiritualists and their spurious séances and table tremblings. Instead, she gravitated more and more toward the rigid ideology and discipline of the Roman Church in the belief that Rome's ancient dogmas and mystical ceremonies might provide an anchor to a life that had become increasingly storm-tossed since John Tyler's death in 1862.

Much to the surprise of her children and some of her oldest and dearest friends, she finally made up her mind to convert to Roman Catholicism in March 1872. The following month she formally embraced the Roman Church and took Pearlie into the new faith with her. Bishop, later Cardinal, James Gibbons performed the appropriate rituals in Washington. Guiding her study and instruction as she prepared for this important transition was the Reverend Father Patrick F. Healy, S.J., Professor of Philosophy and Vice-President (later President) of Georgetown College. Sister Loretto of the Convent of the Visitation and Father Daubresse of Georgetown also helped Julia with her search, advising her and answering her theological questions. During this preliminary period of instruction and preparation for conversion no pressure of any kind was exerted on the former First Lady. No emotional appeals to her despair for the dead Julie were made or suggested. On the contrary, Julia came willingly and eagerly into the Roman communion. The Church neither pursued her, manipulated her, nor promised her pie in the sky. She was treated honestly, fairly, and intelligently throughout the catechistical process. Indeed, Sister Loretto tried to talk Julia out of the idea of rebaptism that possessed her. "The fact of another baptism will avail nothing—it will be but an empty ceremony," said the Sister. Nevertheless, Julia firmly insisted on a second baptism and it was granted her in May 1872. In August Pearlie Tyler was also rebaptized. Julia demanded this when her twelve-year-old daughter fell ill that month, and she stuck to the demand even though Father Healy saw no reason why the "empty ceremony" should be visited upon the child.

Julia's conversion was a spiritual *coup* for the Roman Catholic Church. Much favorable newspaper publicity was derived by the often-persecuted Church in America and Julia began receiving letters from other troubled women all over the United States asking her to help them find their way into the Roman communion. Even Father Healy, who became Julia's "godfather," was not unmindful of the pleasant realization that his convert and new godchild was none other than "Mrs. Tyler, widow of the late John Tyler, President of the United States." It was about as close as the Roman Church would come to the White House until Alfred E. Smith threatened its Protestant doors in 1928 and John F. Kennedy finally battered them down in 1960. When newspapers in New York and Richmond carried accounts of her conversion and rebaptism, Julia assured her politely skeptical family and friends that it was all her own idea. As she explained to Lonie in May:

I suppose you see by all the papers that I have turned Roman Catholic. I have indeed, and much to my satisfaction. No Priest or nun had anything to do with it. It was simply from my conviction of its being the best and truest religion as well as the oldest. There is unity and system in it, as well as beauty and real Christianity. The other sects I came to see were like ships at sea without anchor or rudder, though until one comes to understand this one is not to blame for continuing with them.[44]

Julia seldom did things halfway. Once converted to the "unity and system" she so desperately craved, she began heavy mailings of Roman Catholic literature to her friends and kinsmen. This pamphlet and letter-writing crusade was blessed by Father Healy. "To disarm people of prejudice is the first step toward inculcating sound principles," he told her. "May our good God bless your efforts with success." To Phoebe Gardiner Horsford "it seemed very natural ... [that] left alone as you have been you should seek shelter in the protecting arms of the Church"; and Julia's friend Belle Chalmers of Nyack, New York, agreed she "did perfectly right to become a living member of the church that roused you from a life of coldness." But almost all Julia's heretical Protestant intimates soon wearied of the stream of Roman Catholic propaganda from her escritoire. Gardie put the matter to her most forcefully in May 1872:

Of course, such an addition to their Church Catholics will not fail to express their jubilant satisfaction over, and the knowledge thereof will soon be diffused over the Continent. Well, *ma chère*, if you feel all right about it I shall not deprecate the step. It doesn't clash with any sectarian feelings of my own.... Don't fear an argument from me.... I wouldn't take any great satisfaction in roasting a fellow-mortal because he happened to differ with me as to what kind of fish swallowed the unquenchable Jonah, nor would I care to be grid-ironed myself.... I have learned too well ... how unavailing and futile it is to talk logic with you Catholics.... What are you going to do about your embryo Spiritualism? ... In fact, my dear mother ... I have some curiosity to see what sort of a Catholic you will make. All those I have yet seen are so supremely complacent about their dogmas that I could find no other name for their state of mind but bigotry.... You threaten to convince me. That is an utter impossibility. If I am ever to be a Christian the Church of my Fathers will fully satisfy [me].... I place no sort of value upon forms ... and if a man is conscientious and obeys moral law, the Church is simply a house for the soul to worship in, and whether its style of architecture is that of the cathedral or of a chapel is not of the slightest importance....

Gardie's curiosity was soon satisfied. Julia turned out to be an excellent Roman Catholic, although she finally did give up trying to proselytize the rest of her family. Only Pearlie among the Tylers embraced Roman Catholicism and she did not bring up her own children in the Church. She remained a "very mild" Catholic all her life.[45]

Julia's newfound faith in the Church carried her safely through the serious economic crisis that confronted her when the great Panic of 1873 and the long, deep depression that followed it struck the nation. Income from her rental properties in Manhattan quickly dropped from a monthly average of $750 to less than half that amount. By 1878 there was scarcely any income from this source at all. Mortgage payments, taxes, and assessments on the properties remained the same. The Tyler tenants either ducked out without paying or asked for extensions and moratoriums on their rent. New York City itself ground to an economic standstill. "You cannot by any means calculate safely that the tenants of any property in New York are to pay their rent when it becomes due under present circumstances," Julia's New York agent informed her. "We would be glad to get $2000 per annum for property formerly bringing $4000. There is scarcely a full building in the neighborhood [Chatham St.]. Landlords are ready to take anything they can get in preference to having empty places." Julia decided she too had better take what she could get. Lachlan, now studying medicine at the New York College of Physicians and Surgeons on Fourth Avenue, reinforced this decision with his report of "terrible times in Wall Street." He told his mother she had no idea "how hard up everybody here is.... I can't imagine where the mischief so much [of our] money goes to! Every little five cents seems to amount up to so many dollars, though at the time it seems to be almost nothing!"

Indeed, cash dried up so rapidly in the Tyler family after the onset of the Panic of 1873 that the purchase of the simplest necessities of life often had to be postponed. At Sherwood Forest the financial situation became critical. In July 1873 the Bank of Virginia finally entered suit against the estate for payment of the longstanding Tyler note due it. On top of this new threat to the plantation, disease decimated the small herd of cows in September. "The spirits of deceased cattle are ascending in battalions towards the bovine Heaven all over this section," Gardie sadly informed his mother.[46]

On the eve of these financial difficulties Alex returned from Germany in March 1873, penniless but happy. Thanks to Julia's efforts and to those of William M. Evarts and Priscilla's brother-in-law, railroad executive Allan Campbell, Alex immediately found work in the Floyd Aspinvale mines near Salt Lake City. But within a few months he too joined the growing army of American unemployed made jobless by the Panic and depression. For nearly a year he could find nothing suitable to do in spite of Julia's intercession with various Washington politicians to secure a government job for him. In October 1874 Allan Campbell finally found him a modest position with the Southside Railroad Company at $800 per annum. Between these jobs the impoverished Alex lived at the still-unsold Castleton Hill. Physically he was a handsome man, cultured and well educated, and he soon became quite a social lion on Staten Island. Known as "Captain" Tyler, "much to the gratification of his vanity," said Lachlan, Alex attended all the right balls and receptions. He found Staten Island a miserable place to live yet he agreed it was a good place to hide from his German creditors while searching for employment. "What a treadmill they make of me. I would think the dogs would weary." His sense of humor never deserted him during these jobless months. "I am penniless," he told Julia, "but I suppose golden days will yet come. Lachlan says I laugh too much; I'm always laughing." [47]

Julia was not laughing. So dangerous had her economic situation become in late 1873 she was fearful the hard-pressed Lachlan might have to drop out of medical school. The simple fact of the matter was that Julia was badly overextended financially. With Lachlan at Physicians and Surgeons, Lyon at the University of Virginia, Fitz at Georgetown College, and Pearlie in boarding school, she had an immense room, board, tuition, books, and clothing load to carry. There was also Baby Spencer to support. In addition, she was trying to maintain Castleton Hill, Sherwood Forest, Villa Margaret, an apartment in Georgetown, and all her rental properties in New York. Her hotel bills, as she flitted back and forth between New York, Washington, and Richmond, were enormous. She could not and would not economize on her own clothes. Her personal appearance had to be maintained at all costs and for Julia the costs were invariably high, even by modern standards. Sherwood Forest had long since become economically marginal. The Castleton Hill house leaked badly and extensive repairs were needed. Villa Margaret was in appalling condition. Alex was unemployed, his German creditors pressing him vigorously. Faced with this situation, Julia had no choice but to accept the advice of her sons, her New York agent, A. J. Mathewson, and her lawyers and effect a radical consolidation of her entire financial position.[48]

Castleton Hill, Villa Margaret, and the Tyler property on Greenwich Street in New York City were all advertised for sale in 1873–1874. Castleton Hill, offered privately to the Roman Catholic Church for $20,000, attracted no buyers, secular or ecclesiastical. The Greenwich Street property, placed on the market at $60,000, found no takers at that depressed price. Villa Margaret produced no stampede of eager realtors. For a period in the spring of 1874 Sherwood Forest was therefore in grave danger. The Charles City sheriff again stalked the insecure (and presumably not contented) Sherwood milch cows for a $60 overdue tax bill. Even the animal kingdom conspired to bring the plantation to ruin. The "enormous expenditures of this family have been still more increased by the recent addition of three blind kittens," Gardie wrote in dismay. Finally, a Richmond court ordered the plantation sold in May 1874 to satisfy the Bank of Virginia's $1300 judgment against the Tyler estate. Although Harry Beeckman helped out with a small loan, the proud plantation was actually advertised for public sale. Indeed, Julia had already received a letter from Father Healy expressing Jesuit interest in buying the historic property when, *Deo gratias,* salvation came. Villa Margaret suddenly and unexpectedly found a buyer, and the $3500 realized in the sacrifice transaction lowered the Damoclean sword hanging over Sherwood Forest. "I am so glad you have dear old Sherwood secure," wrote Alex with joy from Staten Island. "At all events we have a place to 'retire' to!"[49]

As part of Julia's economy-and-retrenchment program, she gave up her Georgetown apartment in the spring of 1874 and moved with Baby Spencer to Sherwood Forest. She refused, however, to withdraw Pearlie from the Academy of the Visitation and place her in the less costly and not so fashionable St. Joseph's Academy in Richmond. Still, the responsible Gardie could now watch his mother's personal accounts more closely. Seldom did she venture forth to visit Pearlie in Georgetown without his warning ringing in her ears: "And, Madam, be careful about your own expenses while in Georgetown and beyond my restraining control.... Economy must be the watchword for, as I regard it, this is our last chance for recuperation."

Gradually the family financial situation improved. Lachlan began the practice of medicine in Jersey City in 1876 and became more or less self-sufficient. He also married Georgia Powell of Richmond that year. Lyon finished college at Charlottesville in 1874, took a master's degree there in 1875, and, after a brief stint on the William and Mary faculty, moved to Memphis to continue his teaching career. In November 1878 he married Annie Baker Tucker, daughter of the gallant Colonel St. George Tucker of the Confederate cavalry, and began raising his own family. "I do not know how we could teach nine long months if we were not cheered by the prospect of our summer visit to Sherwood," Annie wrote from distant Memphis in 1881. Still, a job was a job in these depression years. While there was no money to waste in the Tyler family, Gardie complained in April 1878 that his farm "hands are clamorous for their wages." At least he had "hands"—plural. And while "every dollar" remained to him "as precious in my sight as the ruby drops that visit my sad heart," he had sufficient credit in 1878 to secure a Riggs Bank loan of $5000 and he was creditor for $2000 to a neighbor. Also by 1878 Julia was able to employ a governess at Sherwood for seven-year-old Baby Spencer. By the end of the decade the Tylers had gradually struggled back from the twin blows of Reconstruction and the Panic of 1873, and from the depths of the financial crisis of May–June 1874 when, for a time, everything had seemed lost. All Julia's children had, in the meantime, been educated. Tuition had proved, after all, a better investment than seed wheat and guano. Nor in 1880 was David Gardiner Tyler any longer poor. Like his father before him, the master of Sherwood Forest had recaptured the status of being seasonally cash poor in the manner of all American farmers in the 1870s and 1880s. In terms of respect and self-respect it was a vastly different kind of poverty.[50]

Julia's return to Sherwood Forest in 1874 allowed her without gratification to witness the final chapter of Harry Beeckman's ill-starred life. Disappointed in love, the income from his inheritance reduced to near zero by the Panic of 1873, Harry took the liquid way out. By April 1874 the twenty-six-year-old playboy was on "a continuous debauch for an indefinite period." He had, said the disgusted Gardie, "squandered enough to have insured the happiness of a prudent man." Early in August 1875 the rootless Harry was killed one night while riding back to Sherwood Forest. The party he had attended had lasted late into the evening and Harry was in no condition to ride a horse. Galloping along homeward at high speed, he struck his head accidentally on a low-hanging branch. The impact broke his neck instantly and pitched him to the ground dead. Julia was heartsick. She blamed herself for Harry's death. His will left her his quarter share of the Gardiner estate in Manhattan, but that economic balm did little to salve her deep sense of guilt at his death.[51]

Happily, the unexpected blow was softened somewhat by the joy she experienced when her son Alex married his third cousin, Sarah Griswold Gardiner. The ceremony was performed by the Reverend Mr. Charles Gardiner in the Presbyterian Church in East Hampton on August 5, 1875. It was a good match for Alex. Sarah—or Sally, as she was called—was the daughter of the prominent Samuel Buell Gardiner, tenth proprietor of Gardiners Island and a New York State Assemblyman. Alex had met her on Staten Island before leaving Castleton Hill for Richmond in 1864 to fight the Yankees. He had kept in touch with her during his eight years in Germany and upon his return in 1873 a serious romance flowered. Sally was not a beautiful woman, nor was she extroverted like so many of the Gardiners, but she did have (as Phoebe Horsford described her) a great deal of style. "I think her appearance, especially in some of her elegant dresses, is exceedingly aristocratic." Alex was very much in love with her. Following a wedding and reception for five hundred people, he brought her to Sherwood Forest for part of the honeymoon.[52]

Sally Tyler was not to have a very happy life. She lost her first baby at birth in June 1876. Within a year of her marriage her husband was again unemployed, and for two years he remained jobless. The first of her children to survive infancy, Gardiner Tyler, born in January 1878, died in March 1892 at the age of fourteen. Her second child, Lillian Horsford Tyler, called Daisy, contracted an unfortunate marriage in August 1910 with Alben N. Margraf, a German naval officer, and divorced him before the birth of their daughter in March 1912. She died in May 1918 at the age of thirty-nine. Most tragically, Sally lost her husband on September 1, 1883.[53]

Julia moved heaven and earth in Washington in 1877–1879 to get the idle Alex a job with the Department of the Interior as an engineer or surveyor. Working through her old friend and lawyer, William M. Evarts, President Hayes' Secretary of State, Julia made several trips to the capital seeking her son's appointment to a government post. She also buttonholed various legislators in a campaign for larger Interior Department appropriations in the hope that Alex might secure employment of some kind in an expanding department. During this dogged quest she was several times entertained in the White House by Lucy Webb Hayes. "That's right," Alex cheered when he learned of his mother's social contact with the First Family, "go it while you can!" Fortunately, she and Evarts were successful in securing from Congress a $20,000 appropriation for one Daniel G. Major to survey Indian lands in the Dakota Territory. Major was an experienced surveyor; he had executed similar contracts for the Department of the Interior for many years. The private understanding behind this particular appropriation was that Major and Alex would form a partnership to execute the contract. Crews would have to be hired and supplies for months in the wilderness would have to be purchased. This took capital, and Alex agreed to supply $4000 to cover the initial operating costs of the partnership. "Hurrah for Mr. Evarts!" Alex shouted when Major's contract finally came through in November 1878; "God knows I have struggled to get employment in every way I could.... What a wonderful friend in need he has been!" Julia, of course, supplied the money for Alex to buy into the deal with Major. "I only want four thousand dollars ($4000)—three thousand ($3000) cash and one thousand ($1000) to hold in reserve...," Alex told her blandly. Without his investment the agreement with Daniel Major was void. Alex was certain he would make a $5000 profit on the Dakota venture. Thanks to his energetic mother's influence and money, and the intercession of Secretary of State Evarts ("God bless him!"), J. Alexander Tyler was launched into the Indian lands surveying business in the summer of 1879. Sally saw him infrequently after that.[54]

After he had gained experience in the desolate Indian country, Alex was appointed United States Surveyor in the Department of the Interior. On September 1, 1883, while serving as Government Inspector of Surveys in New Mexico, the thirty-five-year-old Alex Tyler, graduate of Karlsruhe and Freiburg, Uhlan for the Kaiser, artillerist for Robert E. Lee, died suddenly at the Governor's Palace in Santa Fé. He apparently ran out of fresh water on a surveying expedition in the nearby desert, drank alkaline water in desperation, and contracted the dysentery that killed him. But Julia learned in Richmond in April 1884 from a Virginia engineer and surveyor named Coleman, "lately arrived from Santa Fé," that "Alex was murdered." This is a much more poetic version of his demise than the alkaline-water story, but it is untrue. The sorrowing Sally was left with two small children, both of whom she outlived, and the prospect of a lengthy widowhood. When she died in East Hampton on September 25, 1927, at seventy-nine, she had been a widow for forty-four years.[55]

Julia had as much success getting Lachlan on the public payroll as she did finding Alex a position in the federal government. After practicing medicine for a year in Jersey City, Lachlan discovered he had few patients, fewer dollars, and a bride to support. In June 1877 he sought his mother's aid in an application for the job of Police Surgeon of the town. Julia had no influence in Journal Square and that hope died aborning. Disgusted with Jersey City, Lachlan moved to Washington to seek federal employment. So pinched for funds did he become by early 1878 that he was forced to consider the then-radical idea of permitting his wife, Georgia Powell Tyler, to seek work in the Department of Agriculture. Indeed, several Virginia congressmen were sounded out on this and they agreed to help Georgia find employment. Meanwhile, Lachlan began working for a surgeoncy in the Navy Department. He knew his medical knowledge was adequate for the post, but he feared that his grasp of grammar, orthography, geography, history, and modern languages was insufficient to win the stiff comprehensive competitive examination for one of the Navy's "soft berths." He could only hope that "perhaps they *modified* things to those applicants who came forward highly recommended, or were undoubtedly *gentlemen*." Under no circumstances did he want to risk the "discomfiture and degradation of a failure." He therefore asked Julia to find out if "my name and the 'Peace Policy' of the [Hayes] Government towards the South will go a sufficient way in the examination to almost certainly insure my success." Urged to enlist the aid of the ever-helpful Evarts ("Ask Mr. Evarts point blank if influence amounts to anything in the matter"), Julia again approached the Secretary of State on behalf of one of her children. He was helpful and sympathetic. Unfortunately, Lachlan failed the Navy's preliminary physical examination in October 1878 for reasons of "general debility" which, he explained to Julia, "means in the medical vocabulary everything and nothing." Dr. Tyler also ruefully discovered that on the Board of Medical Examiners he had "no friends or influence as you [Julia] supposed I would have, and I had to tell the Board who I was and everything." It was a shock.

Nevertheless, Lachlan and his mother persisted. Julia went to work on Evarts and Evarts spoke with Secretary of the Navy R. W. Thompson. Both Cabinet officers led Lachlan to understand confidentially, through Father Patrick F. Healy, that if he could pass the Navy physical the remainder of the examination would "present no difficulty." Lachlan promptly began a body-building regimen and in July 1879 he passed both the physical and the academic examinations and was certified for appointment as a surgeon in the United States Navy. Combined with an outside private practice the post afforded Lachlan a secure future. Straightway he called on Evarts to thank him for his help and encouragement. He found the Secretary to be "the same grand gentleman, ever attentive and kindly disposed to me." Evarts suggested that if Lachlan preferred not to take the Navy post, he might be interested instead in a position in the Pension Office or on the District of Columbia Board of Health. But the struggling young physician demurred. The Board of Health post paid very little, and "a certainty, however small, is more than an uncertainty, and I have a certainty of some kind here [with the Navy]." Julia had again prevailed in Washington. You are, Lachlan confessed to his patronage-wise mother, "a remarkable woman in all respects." [56]

Julia's own campaign for a federal pension as a President's widow also ended in success. The precedent for such a pension was established in July 1870 when Congress passed legislation giving Mary Todd Lincoln an annual stipend of $3000. Needless to say, Julia saw no reason, particularly after her friend Evarts became Secretary of State, why she, Sarah Childress Polk, and Caroline Fillmore should not receive the same consideration from the Congress. The Hayes administration was embarked on a policy of burying the "bloody shirt" of the Civil War which Grant and the Radicals had waved so frantically from the White House staff for eight corruption-sodden years. Consequently, former Rebels were in somewhat better repute in the capital. By Julia's reckoning, 1879 seemed a propitious year for the launching of her pension campaign.

Enlisting the assistance of Secretary Evarts and former Colonel Robert E. Withers, CSA, now Senator from Virginia and Chairman of the Senate Committee on Pensions, and the aid of various Old Dominion congressmen, principally Representative John Goode of Norfolk, Julia manned her trusty desk and began firing letters at Capitol Hill designed to enlist legislative support for the pension proposition. These she combined with occasional trips to the capital to beard the lawmakers in their dens. It was a maximum effort in every respect.

First, however, she claimed the $8 per month allowed the widows of all veterans of the War of 1812 who had served actively for over fourteen days. This she received without contest. Her claim that the payments should be made retroactive to January 1862, when the legislation was passed, was denied. Nonetheless, her argument that she was entitled to the retroactive pay because "Captain" Tyler had died before the legislation came into law and had never been placed on the disallowed list as a "traitor" had a certain ingenuity. The War of 1812 pension payments to Julia commenced in March 1879 and included five months' accumulated benefits in the first payment. It was a modest triumph, but one "gratefully received."

"Do you not think now would be a favorable time to suggest that the only two other Presidents' widows now living shall be generously allowed the same pension that Mrs. Lincoln receives?" she inquired of Evarts. This rhetorical interrogatory was followed by letters to Representative Goode in January 1880 asking him to prepare, introduce, and manage the necessary legislation on the floor of the House when it convened again in March. In her instructions to Goode she asked only for the same $3000 treatment Mary Lincoln had received. Letters to Representative James B. Garfield of Ohio and other legislators stressed her "impatience to be heard" and produced still another version of John Tyler's deathbed wish: "With my pension of three thousand dollars my days will be made comfortable.... I now remember the exclamation of my Husband when he was so suddenly taken with his last illness to the group around him and when he thought he was passing away immediately: 'I leave my wife and young children to God and my country.' Well, the time has come when the necessity arises for me to turn to the country he spent his life in serving for relief...."[57]

Gardie was very much opposed to his mother's quest for a federal pension. It was, he thought, degrading to have to appeal to former Union Army officers like Generals Rutherford B. Hayes and James A. Garfield for charity. Evarts and Senator Withers also advised her against pushing the pension campaign in 1880. They feared that to agitate the question in a Presidential election year would hand the Radical Republicans in Congress another "bloody shirt" political issue with which to flail the Democracy. Rebel John Tyler had been the only American President who seceded with his state from the very Union he had governed. "The stalwarts of the Republican party are ready to catch at anything out of which political capital can be made," Withers informed Sherwood Forest. So the matter was temporarily dropped, even though Julia was assured by her Washington friends that she had strong support on Capitol Hill for the pension concept.[58]

In 1881 she was resolutely back in action. She had carefully drawn up a petition in 1879 detailing her financial needs and pointing out the extent of her property losses during the Civil War at Sherwood Forest and Villa Margaret. This petition was now formally submitted to the Congress. In it she outlined the heavy costs of four years of litigation in the will fight with her brother, and argued that she simply could not live on the income "from the remnant of my mother's estate," in spite of the fact that "my distinguished counsel Hon. Wm. M. Evarts (present Secretary of State), Judge Edwards Pierrepont (now Minister to England) and Hon. James Lyons of Richmond, Va., proposed to forego their claims for arduous and indefatigable services rendered me." She concluded her plea with the heartrending observation that

By great effort and economy I have continued to struggle up to this period—have educated my children as far as it was possible, and paid many debts for which I was not originally accountable. But now, so depressed have my fortunes become, I am forced, though reluctantly, to appear before you to seek that aid that was not denied Mrs. Lincoln.... The continued financial depression permeating the remotest corners of the country has deprived me for two years of the rents I depended upon, foreclosures of mortgages are threatening, and executions on judgments will leave me without means to satisfy the most necessary expenditures. Against this torment of misfortune I can no longer contend without assistance.... Surely the Widow of a President who served his country so arduously and successfully during fifty years, and held every position in its councils, deserves your consideration.[59]

The appeal was successful. In 1881 Julia was awarded by Congress an annual pension of $1200, less than half that being paid Mary Todd Lincoln. Before she had time to protest this inequity, the death by assassination of President Garfield on September 19, 1881, added a fourth "Mrs. Ex-President" to the group of widowed former First Ladies—Julia Gardiner Tyler, Sarah Childress Polk, Mary Todd Lincoln; and now Lucretia Rudolph Garfield. Caroline Fillmore had died on August 11, 1881. The tragic addition of Mrs. Garfield to the trio solved Julia's pension problem quickly.

On March 31, 1882, Congress awarded all four annual pensions of $5000 each and ordered payments made retroactive to September 19, 1881, the date of Garfield's death. The Pension Act canceled Mary Lincoln's earlier award of $3000 and Julia's lesser stipend of $1200. Julia's small War of 1812 pension was not affected. Although she had covertly written the Washington *Post* in October 1881 (signing herself "A Lady Subscriber") suggesting a $10,000 annual payment to the widowed First Ladies, "that they may be placed above want and enabled in some measure to meet the requirements their actual position in the society of the country imposes upon them—and let there be no invidious distinctions," she was delighted with the 1882 legislation as it stood. She immediately thanked Evarts for his influence on the passage of the bill. But he informed her, through Lachlan, that "its success was so certain that any movement of [mine] would have been unnecessary." He playfully warned his former client, however, that she should "not indulge in any extravagance" with her windfall. The advice came too late. The sixty-two-year-old Julia had already overcelebrated her good fortune. At Shirley and Westover dinner parties she had "crammed" herself with "good and rich things" and suffered a bad attack of indigestion. This indisposition passed swiftly and June 1882 found her healthy and happy once again in Newport, as in days of yore, enjoying the summer season there in grand style. More importantly, the pension permitted her to lease a town house in the Church Hill section of Richmond. Later she moved into a house on the corner of Grace and Eighth, opposite St. Peter's Roman Catholic Cathedral. There she lived peacefully and comfortably the last few years of her life. At the same time, the nation gradually emerged from the great depression and the New York real estate and rental situations steadily improved. Not all her income in the 1880s was received from Congress.[60]

Paradoxically, the Hayes administration, which through William

M. Evarts had done so much for Alex, Lachlan, and Julia, commanded none of Gardie's respect. He remained as unreconstructed as ever. True to his resolve in 1870, he had held himself aloof from all elective office. In 1873 he turned down a chance to run for the state senate. With a predictable Radical majority of nearly 5000 against any white Conservative Democratic candidate who might be put up for the state senate the prospect of election seemed hopeless anyway. So Gardie politely passed up the "glorious but extremely profitless honor of leading a forlorn hope" in Charles City. Importunities from Julia and from Samuel Buell Gardiner in 1875 to change his mind and run for public office failed. Instead, he campaigned occasionally for Conservative Democrats who were leading less hopeless crusades against Radical domination elsewhere in the Old Dominion. While affecting this politically detached stance he watched in disgust as the Republicans made off with the Presidential election of 1876.[61]

When the votes were counted in November, Samuel J. Tilden of New York, the Democratic nominee, emerged with a 250,000 popular margin over Rutherford B. Hayes of Ohio. He also had 184 electoral votes, one short of the necessary majority. Hayes had 165 undisputed electoral votes. Twenty electoral votes, centering in South Carolina, Florida, and Louisiana, were vigorously contested. Hayes needed all twenty of these disputed votes to win the election. A Republican-dominated fifteen-man Electoral Commission was finally appointed in January to investigate and certify the confused electoral returns in the contested states, and by February 1877 the Commission, along straight 8-to-7 party lines, had awarded every one of the controversial votes to Hayes. Hayes therefore "won" the canvass of 1876 by an Electoral College count of 185 to 184 and was duly declared elected March 2. Behind the scenes during this critical period stalked chicanery, corruption, and multiple other pressures.

The main thing that reconciled the Democrats to being "counted out" of the White House was a series of Republican promises to remove the last of the federal troops from the South, appoint a Southerner to the Cabinet, and appropriate substantial sums for Southern internal improvements. Also promised by the Republicans was the construction of the Texas and Pacific Railroad from East Texas to San Diego. This would provide the transcontinental rail route for which Dixie legislators had been agitating since the 1850s. These guarantees seemed to many Democrats substantial—as good as anything they might secure for themselves were they actually in the White House. And so the bargain was struck. The Democracy accepted the Republican arithmetic, and Hayes in turn delivered on most of the Republican commitments.[62]

Gardie considered this deal a supine surrender to the Yankees in every respect, even though a Hayes administration gave every prospect of following pro-Southern policies. He urged his mother, en route to

Georgetown in February 1877 to visit Pearlie, to "use your influence with the Southern Congressmen and get them to prevent Hayes' inauguration by every possible means." He was certain that "the people would consider any evil preferable to the success of fraud and the Radical Party. But I have long since despaired of seeing anything like backbone among the Dems, Dem 'em!" Julia did not agree with her angry son. When she learned that her friend Evarts would be named Secretary of State in the Hayes Cabinet, her personal reconciliation to the fraud developed speedily and realistically. She could not therefore accept Gardie's extremism when he declared in March 1877 that

My hatred, prejudice or whatever you may choose to call it, against Yankees of whatever sort, Democrat or Radical ... grows greater every day.... My greatest wish is that I may live to strike another blow for Southern Independence, with "Old Bob" God bless him, in the lead. If I did not live in hopes of this, I'd be desperate. The idea of being forever under Yankee thralldom ... ! The bare thought is enough to set me crazy! Excuse this effusion, but if I didn't put my thoughts on this subject on paper sometimes I verily believe I would burst with concentrated emotion. 'Tis such a luxury to curse one's enemies! [63]

It was a luxury Julia no longer indulged after her federal pension was voted and she moved to Richmond in 1882. Her last days there were spent pleasantly although she was in failing health. In 1883 she fractured an arm and the recurrent pain of it was with her until her death. In 1885, and again in 1887, she had what was diagnosed as a serious "congestive chill" that forced her to bed for several weeks. The 1885 attack rendered her unconscious for five days and nearly ended her life then and there. But she struggled back. During these twilight years Julia visited frequently with her friends in town and in Charles City. Until Lachlan moved his medical practice from Washington to Elkhorn, West Virginia, in 1887, she visited him regularly in the city she loved so much. She was still "the subject of great attention from the society people" when she returned to Washington. In spite of her enthusiastic traveling about she invariably clothed herself in deep mourning. She had so many dead to lament. The lines in her face deepened, her hair grayed, and she put on a great deal of weight. In the house on Grace Street the aging First Lady raised Baby Spencer to young womanhood. She pursued her Roman Catholicism without ostentation at St. Peter's. No longer did she feel it her bounden duty to convert anyone else to her faith, however.

During these final years she kept in close touch with her children. She saw Fitz begin the difficult life of a Virginia farmer on leased land near Ashland in Hanover County. She urged Gardie toward marriage so that Sherwood Forest might have a new mistress, and she became impatient with his lack of enterprise in the matter. "I still sport in unfettered freedom amid my unhooked brothers of the deep although there never swam a fish who made lustier efforts to get hooked," he teased her. Not until June 6, 1894, did he "hook" the attractive Mary Morris Jones. More rewardingly, Julia saw her beloved Pearlie married in St. Peter's Cathedral to Major William Mumford Ellis of Shawsville, Virginia. He had formerly served as a Montgomery County representative to the Virginia House of Delegates. The family that eventually numbered eight Ellis children commenced its expansion almost immediately. Julia and Baby Spencer often visited Pearlie and the Major at Madison, their home near Roanoke, in the years that followed.

Julia was particularly proud when her scholarly son, Lonie, brought out in 1885 his massive two-volume *The Letters and Times of the Tylers*, and she was glad to have the author and his family in her home while the extensive work was in preparation. Not surprisingly, Lyon Gardiner Tyler's book was a detailed defense and justification of his father's political career in every regard. For this reason it did much to quiet the anger of Julia's other children when they happened on memoirs that threatened to demote their revered father in the eyes of Clio. "Poor old fools," Lachlan fretted when he read a less than eulogistic article about John Tyler in the January 1880 *Southern Farmer and Planter* by former Governor William Smith.

They thought that father was courting their wisdom whereas he was just using them as old brooms to sweep [forward] his own and original ideas.... What would have become of Wise, Smith, *et al.* if they hadn't in some way or another been in association with John Tyler? It is the light from his name that casts a glow upon theirs in the ... remote corners of History.

Julia did not enlist again in the family crusade for her husband's reputation. She had already served her tour of duty in that enterprise. She now had sturdy sons to carry the banner for her. Indeed, Lonie spent the remainder of his days, until his death in 1935, fighting and refighting his deceased father's battles. In dozens of books and articles the distinguished president of William and Mary College maintained the political, moral, and intellectual superiority of President John Tyler over every one of his contemporaries—Abraham Lincoln prominently and specifically included.[64]

Julia also watched Sherwood Forest gradually returned to its antebellum beauty under Gardie's sure touch. And though she frequently visited the plantation in the 1880s, she tried to avoid the place in the summer months. "How I do wish Sherwood agreed with me," she sighed in July 1886, in one of the last of her letters that has survived. "I think I would never care to leave it for I do love farm life. But there is death in the ague and fever for me and for Baby Spencer too. Gardie is young enough now to rise from such attacks, but they will injure him yet.... The great remedy [for malaria] there no doubt is calomel and quinine." [65]

During these last years in Richmond Julia had no contact with brother David Lyon or his wife Sarah. Their estrangement was complete. The marriage of Alex Tyler to Sally Griswold Gardiner in 1875 had done nothing to heal the Tyler-Gardiner breach. Indeed, if the pro-Confederate inscription on Alex Tyler's monument in the East Hampton cemetery is any indication, Sally had accepted her husband's sectional politics when she accepted his wedding ring. Lyon had some correspondence with his Uncle David in 1882–1883 relative to collecting family-held materials for inclusion in his biography of John Tyler. In this effort David Lyon cooperated. "The letters arrived in the nick of time," Lonie thanked him, "and I find them of immense importance in supplying missing links and suggesting new ideas." This was the only contact between the Long Island Gardiners and the Virginia Tylers in the 1880s.[66]

While the Tylers suffered severely (though never in silence) under the dual blow of Black Reconstruction and the Panic of 1873, David Lyon Gardiner remained comfortable. Armed with his own inheritance and Sarah's, he experienced no difficulties. In 1878 he took his family to Europe for a casual tour of the Continent. Through his New York agent, William Cruikshank, he managed his New York City properties with casual competence. He also sold his long-valueless San Diego lots to excellent advantage when the Texas and Pacific finally pushed its tracks into the reviving town. By 1885 he owned a large yacht and employed a crew to sail her. His politics were, and remained until his death on May 9, 1892, conservative and "bloody shirt" Republican.[67]

The older David Lyon grew, the more concerned he became with defending the purity of the Gardiner name. His interest in family history and genealogy became a passion, and he devoted his leisure time (which was all the time) to its study. He soon became the family expert on all Gardiner matters. In 1871 he saw his father's unfinished *Chronicle of the Town of East Hampton* posthumously into print. Thus when Curtiss C. Gardiner of St. Louis published in the Brooklyn *Eagle* and other Long Island papers in 1885 excerpts from his planned *Lion Gardiner and His Descendants,* David Lyon, defender of the faith, erupted in anger. Curtiss Gardiner had the temerity to suggest that not *all* the descendants of Lion Gardiner were equal combinations of Cincinnatus, Sir Galahad, George Washington, and thrifty Ben Franklin. Perhaps eleven generations of Gardiners in America had produced fewer failures, wastrels, alcoholics, and wartime pacifists than other prominent families over a comparable period of two and a half centuries. But they had produced some. No family has been wholly perfect. In a sharp letter to Curtiss Gardiner, David Lyon informed the wayward genealogist that his vicious work was a failure. "You have shown yourself to be entirely unfitted for literary work...your object is notoriety." Curtiss Gardiner was not intimidated by this blast. "I have received your letter...and placed it in our file for reference," he replied wearily.

This did not suit David Lyon. To stem the poison flowing from distant St. Louis he encouraged the circulation of pro-Gardiner articles and book reviews prepared by Martha J. Lamb, editor of the *Magazine of American History* in New York City. "Concerning the St. Louis *assaulter*...your letter to him was excellent and I thank you warmly," said the more malleable Martha. Her always-charitable accounts of the Gardiner clan swiftly earned her the imprimatur of David Lyon. There was never any suggestion in any of her work that "Gardiners Island was never a manor, nor its early proprietors *Lords*." In fact, she believed this nonsense implicitly. David Lyon believed it too, and in 1888 he was a leading force within the family to provide an elaborate tomb in the East Hampton cemetery for the remains of the magnificent Lion, builder of towns, victor over the Pequots, founder of the family in America. A reclining marble statue of the seventeenth-century fortifications engineer portrayed him impressively decked out in fourteenth-century armor. Sergeant Lion Gardiner became a medieval knight at last.[68]

The *ex post facto* knighting of Sir Lion in East Hampton, Long Island, produced no flourish of trumpets on Grace Street in Richmond. In many ways Julia was no longer a Gardiner. When she seceded from the Union she seceded from the family. Juliana's death and the court battles with David Lyon had virtually ended her connection with the other descendants of the immortal Lion. Julia was thus more interested in the election of son Lyon to the presidency of William and Mary College in 1888 than she was with the elevation of forebear Lion to some mythical Round Table. It was with great pride in Lonie's accomplishment that she attended the first commencement exercise over which he presided in Williamsburg, in June 1889. She attended the ball that preceded it, and seemed in good health and excellent spirits. She visited in Lonie's home in Williamsburg for a few days after the graduation, and on Sunday, July 7, she returned to Richmond. Since her own house had been closed up during the hot days of her absence, she and eighteen-year-old Baby Spencer took a room in the Exchange Hotel. It was her intention to consult with Dr. Hunter McGuire on Monday morning about the pain her previously fractured arm was giving her and then take the river boat down to Sherwood Forest that afternoon for a visit with Gardie.

But on Monday morning, July 8, she felt so ill and her arm hurt so much she summoned McGuire to her room. She complained of chills, fever, and biliousness and the physician treated her accordingly. To this therapy she did not respond. On Wednesday morning, the tenth, she asked Baby to go for Dr. McGuire at his office. The young girl left her grandmother with a chambermaid and set out on the errand. During her brief absence, at about 11 A.M., Julia suffered a stroke. When Baby returned she found Room 27 crowded with hotel employees. Julia was nearly unconscious. A porter who lifted her from her chair into bed said, "I believe she is dying." Baby immediately had telephone messages sent to several physicians; Dr. Edward McGuire responded first. He diagnosed Julia's ailment as "congestive chill" and summoned his uncle, Dr. Hunter McGuire. Dr. J. B. McCaw, Julia's regular family physician, was also called in. When someone at Julia's bedside suggested that she be given a sip of liquor, she shook her head slightly and whispered, "Tea." It was her last word. A moment later she lapsed into unconsciousness. In midafternoon Father Dinneen was called from St. Peter's to administer extreme unction. At 5:15 P.M., on July 10, 1889, Julia Gardiner Tyler died without regaining consciousness. Three doctors worked over her until the end. At her bedside were Baby Spencer and three Richmond ladies who were old friends of the former First Lady. Room 27, the scene of her death, was only a few doors down the hall from where John Tyler had died in 1862.

At noon on July 10 all of Julia's five living children were notified of her illness by telegraph. Lonie was the first to reach the Exchange Hotel. He left Virginia Beach where he was participating in an educational convention and reached Richmond at 11 P.M., too late, of course, to see his mother alive. On July 11 Pearlie arrived from Shawsville in Montgomery County, Fitz came on from Ashland, and Gardie arrived from Sherwood Forest. The funeral was held in St. Peter's Cathedral at 11 A.M. on Friday, July 12, Bishop-elect A. Van de Vyver officiating. Julia's body, "with thoroughly natural features, was in a neat casket covered with black." Reverend Father Charles E. Donahoe of Fredericksburg celebrated the Requiem Mass for the dead. In the middle of the service, Lachlan and his wife arrived at the church from Elkhorn, West Virginia. The Cathedral was packed with Richmond notables and fashionables, mostly Protestants. Indeed, Father Van de Vyver could not resist the golden opportunity to instruct the captive Protestants, several clergymen among them, in the meaning and symbolism of the Roman Catholic service for the dead, and it was to this educational subject that the Bishop-elect devoted much of his eulogy to Julia. Neither David Lyon nor any of the New York Gardiners attended Julia's funeral. When it was all over, "Mrs. Ex-President Tyler," Confederate patriot, the "Rose of Long Island," was taken to Hollywood Cemetery and buried beside her distinguished husband and her beloved Julie. Father Donahoe conducted the graveside prayers. At the age of sixty-nine the former First Lady's energetic "reign" was over.

There in Hollywood Cemetery she lies today, beside John Tyler, under the tall marble shaft belatedly erected by Congress in 1915 to the memory of the tenth President of the United States. Within a few feet of her grave rest such prominent Virginians and Americans as President James Monroe and Matthew Fontaine Maury, "Pathfinder of the Seas." It is a fashionable and accomplished group—"altogether select" —just as Julia would have wanted it to be.[69]

NOTES

Key to frequently cited footnote abbreviations:

GPY: *Gardiner Family Papers*, Yale University Library
LTT: *Letters and Times of the Tylers*, by Lyon G. Tyler
TFP: *Tyler Family Papers*
TPLC: *Tyler Papers*, Library of Congress

Footnote citations have generally been placed at the end of paragraphs in the text (sometimes at the end of two or three paragraphs in sequence) with a view toward grouping the relevant citations to a particular point, argument or series of interrelated facts in one place. References within each footnote have been arranged in series corresponding to the order of the data each supports in the text above. For this reason the pagination in a given citation may appear numerically out of sequence.

CHAPTER I

¹ [Benjamin T.] Onderdonk to [Alexander] Gardiner, Memorandum of Appointment, n.d. [June 20, 1844], *Gardiner Papers,* Manuscript Division, Yale University Library. Hereafter cited as GPY (*Gardiner Papers, Yale*).

² John Tyler to Juliana Gardiner, Washington, April 20, 1844, GPY. An offset print of this letter has been published in the Yale University Library *Gazette*. It is accompanied by an excellent article analyzing the historiographical importance of the Gardiner Papers at Yale by Howard Gotlieb and Gail Grimes. See their "President Tyler and the Gardiners: A New Portrait," Yale University Library *Gazette*, XXXIV (July 1959), 2–12.

³ Juliana Gardiner to John Tyler, New York, April 22, 1844, *Tyler Family Papers*. Hereafter cited as TFP (*Tyler Family Papers*).

⁴ The account of the wedding is taken from the New York *Herald*, June 27, 1844. Two accounts of the ceremony appeared in that issue, the principal and most detailed version being based on facts supplied by someone quite close to the family, probably Alexander Gardiner. See also "Interview with Julia Gardiner Tyler," Washington, Winter, 1888–1889, in Philadelphia *Press*, July 11, 1889; reprinted in Richmond *Dispatch*, July 12, 1889.

⁵ New York *Herald*, Nov. 17, 1844.

⁶ Alexander Gardiner to Margaret Gardiner, New York, June 28, 1844; also David L. Gardiner to Julia Gardiner Tyler, New York, June 30, 1844, TFP.

⁷ New York *Herald*, June 27, 1844.

⁸ *Ibid.*

⁹ Alexander Gardiner to Julia Gardiner Tyler, New York, June 28, 1844. Juliana Gardiner confessed that "we have had something to laugh at you may suppose although the effect upon the public never occurred to us in making our arrangements." Juliana Gardiner to Julia Gardiner Tyler, New York, June 28, 1844; Margaret Gardiner to Julia Gardiner Tyler, New York, July 11, 1844, TFP.

¹⁰ Juliana Gardiner to Julia Gardiner Tyler, New York, July 10, 1844. Margaret reported "a general stir among the congregation" when the usual Episcopal prayer was read in church on Sunday, Aug. 11, 1844, blessing the President of the United States. "They gave a sly glance at me to see the effect." Margaret Gardiner

to Julia Gardiner Tyler, East Hampton, N.Y., Aug. 11, 1844, *TFP;* see also David L. Gardiner to Juliana Gardiner, East Hampton, N.Y., July 7, 1844, *GPY;* and Alexander Gardiner to Juliana Gardiner, New York, July 14, 1844, *Tyler Papers,* Manuscript Division, Library of Congress, Washington, D.C. Hereafter cited as *TPLC (Tyler Papers, Library of Congress).*

[11] John Tyler to Mary Tyler Jones, Washington, June 4; 28, 1844, *TPLC.*

[12] Elizabeth Tyler Waller to Julia Gardiner Tyler, Lynchburg, Va., Sept. 11, 1844, *TFP.*

[13] Julia Gardiner Tyler to Juliana Gardiner, Washington, June 30, 1844, *TFP.*

[14] *Ibid.* So great were the demands for souvenir bits of the wedding cake that Julia had a replica baked in New York for distribution to her friends and relatives there. On the insistence of Priscilla Cooper Tyler, the President instructed Wilkins, the White House cook, to prepare still a third replica for distribution in the Philadelphia area. Elizabeth Tyler Coleman, *Priscilla Cooper Tyler and the American Scene, 1816–1889* (University, Ala., 1955), 112.

[15] Juliana Gardiner to Julia Gardiner Tyler, [New York], July 4, 1844, *TFP.*

[16] Margaret Gardiner to Juliana Gardiner, Washington, July 3, 1844, *TFP.*

[17] Juliana Gardiner to Julia Gardiner Tyler, New York, [July 6], 1844, *TFP.*

[18] Margaret Gardiner to Julia Gardiner Tyler, New York, July 8, 1844; *see also* Juliana Gardiner to Julia Gardiner Tyler [New York], July 10 [1844]; Julia Gardiner Tyler to Juliana Gardiner, Old Point Comfort, Va., July [3], 1844, *TFP.*

[19] New York *Herald,* Nov. 12, 1844; Julia Gardiner Tyler to Juliana Gardiner, Old Point Comfort, July 1844, *TFP.*

[20] *Ibid.,* July 13, 1844; Sherwood Forest, July 14, 1844, *TFP.* The honeymoon cottage was a one-story affair consisting of a living room, dining room, bedroom, and pantry-kitchen. Colonel De Russy later served as brigadier general in the Union Army during the Civil War and was cited for gallantry in action.

[21] *Ibid.; see also* Juliana Gardiner to Julia Gardiner Tyler, New York, July [8], 1844, *TFP.* William Compton Bolton began life as William Bolton Finch, changing his name in 1831.

[22] Julia Gardiner Tyler to Juliana Gardiner, Old Point Comfort, July [5], 1844; Juliana Gardiner to Julia Gardiner Tyler, New York, July [8], 1844, *TFP.*

[23] Julia Gardiner Tyler to Juliana Gardiner, Old Point Comfort, July [5], 1844; Juliana Gardiner to Julia Gardiner Tyler [New York], July 10 [1844], *TFP.*

[24] Julia Gardiner Tyler to Juliana Gardiner, Sherwood Forest, July 14, 1844, *TFP.*

[25] *Ibid.,* Old Point Comfort, July 13, 1844; Sherwood Forest, July 14, 1844, *TFP.* Today Sherwood Forest is a Registered National Historic Landmark, so designated by the United States Department of the Interior. It is located on Virginia Route 5 midway between Williamsburg and Richmond. Open to the public, it is a unique house in that it is not a formal monument to a bygone era. It is the home of Mr. J. Alfred Tyler and his family. Mr. Tyler is the grandson of John and Julia Gardiner Tyler, the son of David Gardiner Tyler.

[26] Julia Gardiner Tyler to Margaret Gardiner, Washington, Oct. 14, 1844. Julia sent the ballad to Alexander in New York urging him to see that it was published. Apparently it never was. Julia Gardiner Tyler to Juliana Gardiner, Sherwood Forest, July 14, 1844, *TFP.* A copy of the verse in Tyler's handwriting is found in *TPLC.* The music has not survived. The verse was written for Julia shortly after her father was killed on board the U.S.S. *Princeton* in Feb. 1844.

[27] Juliana Gardiner to Julia Gardiner Tyler, New York, July [8], 1844, *TFP;* Juliana Gardiner to Alexander Gardiner, East Hampton, June 6, 1843; Margaret Gardiner to David L. Gardiner, Washington, Dec. 25, 1842, *GPY;* Margaret Gardiner to Julia Gardiner Tyler, New York, Nov. 17, 1845; *see also ibid.,* Oct. 12, 1845, in which Margaret says, "I believe I have a greater penchant for old people than young. What does this augur? That I shall follow in the footsteps of my

illustrious predecessor? Heigh ho! it will never do to print this"; and also *ibid.*, n.d. [1844], *TFP,* in which she remarked that a daguerreotype of Tyler made him "look as if he had put his *veto* upon everything but *age."*

[28] Henry A. Wise, *Seven Decades of the Union* (Philadelphia, 1881), 233.
[29] Julia Gardiner Tyler, "A Birthday Song," March 1852, *TFP.*
[30] Wise, *Seven Decades of the Union,* 235.
[31] Julia Gardiner Tyler to Juliana Gardiner, Washington, Sept. 8, 1844, *TFP.*

CHAPTER 2

[1] Allan Nevins and Milton H. Thomas (eds.), *The Diary of George Templeton Strong,* 3 vols. (New York, 1952), I, 238.
[2] Pierre S. R. Payne, *The Island* (New York, 1958), 17; W. F. Williams to David Gardiner, Norwich, Conn., Feb. 13, 1839, *GPY.*
[3] Payne, *The Island,* 22-23; Curtiss C. Gardiner, *Lion Gardiner and His Descendants* (St. Louis, Mo., 1890), 3, 48-49; Lion Gardiner, *Relation of the Pequot Wars* (East Hampton, 1660), reprinted in C. C. Gardiner, *op. cit.,* 9-13, 55, 24, 17, 65, 21, 19.
[4] *Ibid.,* 57-58; Payne, *The Island,* 77-82.
[5] Lion Gardiner to John Winthrop, Isle of Wight (Gardiners Island), Apr. 27, 1650, in C. C. Gardiner, *Lion Gardiner and His Descendants,* 34; *ibid.,* 3. Lion Gardiner's East Hampton period, 1653-1663, is fully treated in David Gardiner, *Chronicle of the Town of East Hampton, County of Suffolk, N.Y.* (New York, 1871); William S. Pelletreau, *History of East Hampton Town* (New York, 1882); and Benjamin Thompson, *History of Long Island,* 2 vols. (New York, 1843), Vol. I.
[6] Will of David Gardiner (1691-1751), fourth proprietor, May 16, 1751, in C. C. Gardiner, *Lion Gardiner and His Descendants,* 108.
[7] *Ibid.* The herds on the island at this time numbered 200 cows, 40 horses and 3000 sheep. Sarah Diodati Gardiner, *Early Memories of Gardiners Island* (East Hampton, 1947), 73, 79-80.
[8] New York *Herald,* Nov. 17, 1844. On the slavery issue in New York at this time, 1810-1820, see Dixon Ryan Fox, *The Decline of the Aristocracy in the Politics of New York* (New York, 1919), 269-70. For Alexander Gardiner's pro-slavery views see his "An Oration Delivered At Princeton College, July 4, 1838," *GPY.* See also Sarah D. Gardiner, *Early Memories of Gardiners Island,* 73-74.
[9] No two versions of John Gardiner and the Captain Kidd treasure agree in details or in the degree of John's complicity, if any, in hiding the treasure on the island. Compare Payne, *The Island,* 111-49; Sarah D. Gardiner, *Early Memories of Gardiners Island,* 63-64, 17-18; C. C. Gardiner, *Lion Gardiner and His Descendants,* 98-101. The Payne account is the most detailed and best researched. See also W. F. Williams to David Gardiner, Lebanon, Conn., Mar. 18, 1839, *GPY;* Sarah D. Gardiner, *Early Memories of Gardiners Island,* 64-67; 75-87; C. C. Gardiner, *Lion Gardiner and His Descendants,* 101; Thomas Hardy to John Lyon Gardiner, HMS *Ramillies,* off Gardiners Island, July 31, 1813; Charles Paget to John Lyon Gardiner, British Squadron off New London, n.d., *GPY.*
[10] C. C. Gardiner, *Lion Gardiner and His Descendants,* 108-26. Abraham Gardiner married Phoebe Dayton in 1781. Their five children were Abraham (1782-1827), Julia's father David (1784-1844), Mary (1786-1858), Samuel (1789-1859), and Nathaniel (1792-1856). Julia's aunt and her three uncles all married and had large families. Julia thus had twenty-two first cousins who survived infancy. She was on intimate terms with only three of them, however: Mary, Phoebe, and Frances (Fanny), daughters of her Uncle Samuel, who lived on Shelter Island, L.I., N.Y. Captain Abraham Gardiner (1763-1796) and his father, Colonel Abraham

Gardiner (1722–1782), were both residents of East Hampton. Gardiner family genealogies list the marriage of David Gardiner to Juliana McLachlan as 1816. Their first son, however, was born on May 23, 1816. Hence the wedding year was very likely 1815.

[11] David Gardiner to Mary Smith Gardiner, New York, May 27, 1805; July 31, 1809; and David Gardiner to Mary Smith Gardiner Van Wyck, Croton, N.Y., Aug. 25, 1814, *GPY*.

[12] David Gardiner to Mary Smith Gardiner, New York, July 31, 1809; *see also* David Gardiner to Phoebe Dayton Gardiner, New York, Dec. 18, 1809, *GPY*.

[13] C. C. Gardiner, *Lion Gardiner and His Descendants*, 149; Franklin B. Dexter, *Biographical Sketches of the Graduates of Yale College* (New York, 1911), V, 659–60; *David Gardiner Account Book*, 1841–1844. These properties were located at numbers 181, 183, 185, 187 Chatham St.; 1, 3, 5, 7, 9 Oliver St.; 349, 351, 353 Greenwich St.; and 22 Harrison St. Juliana Gardiner to David L. Gardiner, New York, Dec. 9, 1850, *GPY*.

[14] Julia Gardiner Tyler, "Reminiscences of Mrs. Julia G. Tyler," Cincinnati *Graphic News,* June 25, 1887. Reprinted in Lyon G. Tyler, *Letters and Times of the Tylers*, 3 vols. (Richmond, Va., 1884; 1894), III, 194–201. Hereafter cited as *LTT* (*Letters and Times of the Tylers*). Alexander Gardiner to Samuel Gardiner, New York, Feb. 19, 1849, *GPY*. The Gardiner home in East Hampton was purchased in 1822 from a Mr. Jones who had bought it in 1819 from Abraham Smith.

[15] Sarah D. Gardiner, *Early Memories of Gardiners Island*, 91; "The Guardians of David J. Gardiner in Account with David Gardiner, 1818–1822," *GPY; Assets and Liabilities of David Gardiner* (March 1844), *TFP;* D. S. Gardiner to David Gardiner, Gardiners Island, Mar. 22, 1828; David Gardiner to D. S. Gardiner, New York, Apr. 19, 1828, *GPY; East Hampton Cemetery Records,* East Hampton Free Library. Julia apparently did not know exactly when she was born. John Tyler's son and biographer, Lyon G. Tyler, listed her birthday as May 4, 1820. Julia's tombstone in Hollywood Cemetery, Richmond, uses the July 23, 1820 date. Julia often mentioned, however, as did newspaper accounts of her wedding at the time, that she was twenty-four when she married John Tyler on June 26, 1844. She never mentioned her birthdate in any of her many letters.

[16] *Journal of the Senate of the State of New York,* Forty-Seventh Session (Albany, 1824) 28–29, 121, 129, 354–55, 364; *ibid.,* Forty-Eighth Session (1825), 118, 205, 338, 554–56; *ibid.,* Forty-Ninth Session (1826), 212, 245, 546; 482–83; *ibid.,* Fiftieth Session (1827), 29, 51–52, 92–93, 315–16, 354–55, 544–45, 576–77; Jabez D. Hammand, *Life and Times of Silas Wright* (Syracuse, N.Y., 1848), 56–59; De Alva S. Alexander, *A Political History of the State of New York*, 3 vols. (New York, 1906), I, 334–56.

[17] John Donley to David Gardiner [New York], Apr. 30 [1834]; J. R. Hobbie to David Gardiner, Washington, Oct. 26, 1832; George B. Hanley to David Gardiner, New Haven, Conn., Jan. 11, 1834, *TFP;* Margaret Gardiner to Alexander Gardiner, East Hampton, June 8, 1840, *GPY*. His work on East Hampton was first published in article form in the Sag Harbor (N.Y.) *Corrector* and posthumously in book form as the *Chronicle of the Town of East Hampton* in 1871. See Benjamin F. Thompson to David Gardiner, Hempstead, N.Y., Dec. 1, 1838; W. F. Williams to David Gardiner, Norwich, Conn., Feb. 13, 1839; Lebanon, Conn., Mar. 18, 1839; Juliana Gardiner to Alexander Gardiner, East Hampton, May 17, 1840; Alexander Gardiner to David Gardiner, New York, June 3, 1840. David Gardiner's interest in Clinton Academy, particularly in the hiring of teaching personnel, is seen also in David Gardiner to David L. Gardiner, East Hampton, Sept. 6, 1835; N. D. Chagaray to Julia Gardiner [New York], Dec. 8, 1838, *GPY*.

[18] Jonathan Thompson to David Gardiner, New York, Sept. 14; Oct. 2; 27, 1832; E. Hand to David Gardiner, New York, Nov. 4, 1832; John A. King to David

Gardiner, Jamaica, N.Y., Nov. 9, 1832, *GPY*. Jonathan Thompson, former Collector of the Port of New York during the John Quincy Adams administration, was a cousin of David Gardiner. He provided the $200 which Gardiner disbursed. Sarah Frances Dering to Eliza Gardiner Brumley, Sag Harbor, Nov. 7, 1832, *Gardiner Papers*, Long Island Collection, East Hampton Free Library.

[19] J. G. Dychman to David Gardiner, New York, Jan. 2, 1834, *TFP;* H. Ketchum to David Gardiner, New York, July 30, 1834, in [Lyon G. Tyler (ed.)], "Letters From Tyler Trunks, Sherwood Forest, Virginia. Political Letters—1832-1834," *Tyler's Quarterly Historical and Genealogical Magazine*, XVII (January 1936), 156. (Hereafter cited as *Tyler's Quarterly*). Ketchum was Clerk, Whig General Committee of New York City. Thurlow Weed to David Gardiner, New York, Dec. 14, 1837; L. Bassedill to David Gardiner, Albany, N.Y., Feb. 21, 1838; David Gardiner to [N. N. Hunt], n.p., n.d. [East Hampton, Dec. 1838]; N. N. Hunt to David Gardiner, Sag Harbor, Dec. 25, 1838; Jan. 12, 1839; Margaret Gardiner to David L. Gardiner, East Hampton, July 16, 1840, *GPY*.

[20] Joseph G. Albertson to David L. Gardiner, New Haven, Conn., Jan. 8, 1834; David L. Gardiner to Juliana Gardiner, Princeton, N.J., n.d. [1834]; Samuel B. Gardiner to David L. Gardiner, East Hampton, Dec. 1, 1833; David Gardiner to James Carnahan, East Hampton, May 24, 1834; David Gardiner to David L. Gardiner, New York, Mar. 25 [1835], *GPY;* David L. Gardiner to Juliana Gardiner, Princeton, N.J., Aug. 7, 1834, *TFP;* David Gardiner to David L. and Alexander Gardiner [East Hampton], May 31, 1835; David Gardiner to David L. Gardiner, East Hampton, Aug. 3, 1835; Alexander Gardiner to Margaret Gardiner [Princeton], July 15, 1837, *GPY*. David Gardiner built a new home in East Hampton in 1835-1836 which placed a temporary strain on the family resources.

[21] Juliana Gardiner to Julia and Margaret Gardiner, Princeton, Mar. 1836, *GPY;* David L. Gardiner to David Gardiner, Princeton, Dec. 13, 1833; Nov. 16, 1834; Alexander Gardiner to David Gardiner, Princeton, Nov.; Dec. 18, 1834, in Lyon G. Tyler, "Letters From Tyler Trunks," *loc. cit.*, 157-58, 161-62; Alexander Gardiner to Juliana Gardiner, Princeton, Nov. 22, 1835, *TFP;* David L. Gardiner to Alexander Gardiner, Princeton, Aug. 24, 1834, in Lyon G. Tyler, "Letters From Tyler Trunks," *loc. cit.*, 160-61; Alexander Gardiner to Juliana Gardiner, Princeton, Jan. 1, 1835, *GPY;* David L. Gardiner to David Gardiner, Princeton, Dec. 13, 1833, in Lyon G. Tyler, "Letters From Tyler Trunks," *loc. cit.*, 158; Alexander Gardiner to Professor Alexander, East Hampton, Feb. 28, 1837, *GPY*. See also Alexander Gardiner, *Princeton Diary*, 1834-1838, *passim, GPY*. Alexander Gardiner to Julia Gardiner, Princeton, Dec. 28, 1836; Alexander Gardiner to David and Juliana Gardiner, Princeton, July 12, 1837, *GPY;* Alexander Gardiner to Juliana Gardiner, Princeton, Nov. 22, 1835, *TFP;* Alexander Gardiner to David Gardiner, Princeton, Dec. 18, 1834; David L. Gardiner to David Gardiner, Princeton, Jan. 5, 1834, in Lyon G. Tyler, "Letters From Tyler Trunks," *loc. cit.*, 163, 158; Alexander Gardiner to Margaret Gardiner [Princeton], July 15, 1837, *GYP*.

[22] David L. Gardiner to David Gardiner, Princeton, Jan. 5; Mar. 2; Mar. 1834, in Lyon G. Tyler, "Letters From Tyler Trunks," *loc. cit.*, 158-59, 161.

[23] Alexander Gardiner, "Notes For an Essay in Classical History," Princeton College, May 16, 1837; Alexander Gardiner, "An Oration Delivered at Princeton College, July 4, 1838," *GPY*. A marginal note on this manuscript states that portions of the speech "were suggested by Father." See also Alexander Gardiner, *Princeton Diary*, 1834-1838, *GPY, passim*.

[24] Juliana Gardiner to Julia Gardiner, East Hampton, Feb. 12, 1837, *TFP;* David L. Gardiner to David Gardiner, New York, May 23, [1835], in Lyon G. Tyler, "Letters From Tyler Trunks," *loc. cit.*, 160; Julia Gardiner to Juliana Gardiner, New York, May 22, 1835; Alexander Gardiner to Juliana Gardiner, Princeton, Nov. 22, 1835, *TFP*. Eliza Packer Gardiner Brumley (1788-1863) was the wife

of Reuben Brumley (1799–1860). They had no children. *East Hampton Cemetery Records,* East Hampton Free Library.

[25] Juliana Gardiner to Julia Gardiner, East Hampton, Apr. 1; 5, 1835; May 1, 1837, *TFP.*

[26] Julia Gardiner to Juliana Gardiner, New York, Apr. 23; May 22, 1835, *TFP. Minunet* was Julia's phonetic spelling of the flower mignonette. This horticultural information made available to the author by Helen Hales Seager, Granville Garden Club, Granville, Ohio.

[27] Juliana Gardiner to Julia Gardiner, East Hampton, May 7, 1835; Feb. 12, 1837, *TFP.* Just where Margaret attended school is not known.

[28] David L. Gardiner to C. F. Jones [Princeton], June 1836. David Lyon read law and clerked in the offices of Richard and Emerson, 70 Wall St. Alexander studied in the Anthon firm. Alexander Gardiner Notebooks—1839; Julia Gardiner to David L. Gardiner, East Hampton, May 19, 1842; Julia Gardiner to Alexander Gardiner, East Hampton, May 30, 1842, *GPY.*

[29] Alexander Gardiner to David Gardiner, New York, June 15, 1839; Margaret Gardiner to Alexander Gardiner, East Hampton, May 20; June 19, 1840; David Gardiner to Alexander Gardiner [East Hampton], July 16, 1840; Alexander Gardiner to David L. Gardiner, East Hampton, June 28, 1842; David L. Gardiner to Alexander Gardiner, East Hampton, Jan. 2, 1843; David L. Gardiner to David Gardiner, New York, Jan. 24, 1843; David L. Gardiner to Alexander Gardiner, New York, Mar. 7, 1843; East Hampton, May 4, 1843; Margaret Gardiner to Alexander Gardiner, East Hampton, May 11, 1843, *GPY.* The Gardiner law office at 14 Wall St. rented for $70 per month. When the rent was raised to $90 per month they moved to 49 Williams St.

[30] Juliana Gardiner to Alexander Gardiner, East Hampton, Oct. 31 [1842]; Alexander Gardiner to David Gardiner, New York [Oct. 1842]. A large room with small attached bedroom on the second floor, adequate for two, could be had for $13 per week at Madame Garcia's. Board was included. Juliana Gardiner to Alexander Gardiner, East Hampton, May 4 [1840], *GPY.* This warning was delivered on the occasion of the move of her sons to Mrs. Boyd's house at 422 Houston St., a few doors from Madame Chagaray's Institute.

[31] Alexander Gardiner to [Julia Gardiner], [New York], June [1839] (draft copy of a letter); Julia Gardiner to Alexander Gardiner, East Hampton, June 14, 1839; Alexander Gardiner to Julia Gardiner, New York, June 2; May 24, 1839; Alexander Gardiner to [David L. Gardiner] [New York], June 9, 1841 (fragment of draft copy of a letter). In 1843 the connection with the Livingston family was broken when Julia informed Alexander: "Ma says she would prefer you not to visit the Livingstons again this summer—No reason only no *object.*" Julia Gardiner to Alexander Gardiner, June 4, 1843; Julia Gardiner to David L. Gardiner, East Hampton, May 31, 1840; Alexander Gardiner to J—— L—— [Julia Lane] [New York], June 14, 1841, *GPY.*

[32] David L. Gardiner to Margaret Gardiner [New York], May 1840; Alexander Gardiner to Julia Gardiner, New York, May 24; June 2; 15, 1839; Alexander Gardiner to Margaret Gardiner, New York, June 2, 1840, *GPY; see also* Caroline Clarkson to Julia Gardiner, New York, June 2, 1840, *TFP.*

[33] Alexander Gardiner to Margaret Gardiner, New York, June 2, 1840; Margaret Gardiner to Alexander Gardiner, East Hampton, June 8, 1840, *GPY.*

[34] Julia Gardiner to David L. Gardiner [East Hampton], April 5, 1840; *see also* Margaret Gardiner to Alexander Gardiner, East Hampton, May 10, 1840; Julia Gardiner to Alexander Gardiner, East Hampton, May 12, 1840; David L. Gardiner to [Margaret Gardiner] [New York], May 1840, *GPY.*

[35] Margaret Gardiner to Alexander Gardiner, East Hampton, May 10, 1840; Julia Gardiner to David L. Gardiner, East Hampton, May 31, 1840; *see also* Margaret Gardiner to Alexander Gardiner, East Hampton, June 8, 1840; Margaret Gar-

diner to David L. Gardiner, East Hampton, June 29, 1840. Juliana did not dispute this characterization, but she softened it considerably in her view that "he is not very great as a preacher." Quoted in *ibid.* He was to become a good, loyal, and dear friend of the Gardiners. Julia Gardiner to Alexander Gardiner, East Hampton, June 14, 1840, *GPY.*

[36] Margaret Gardiner to David L. Gardiner, East Hampton, June 29, 1840, *GPY;* printed invitation from Corps of Cadets, United States Military Academy, to Ball given August 28, 1839, with notation: "Will Miss Gardiner be so good to fill up the enclosed invitations at her pleasure and much oblige Cadet Rogers." That Julia corresponded with beaux in New York and that on occasion she would receive poetry from them is indicated in Alexander Gardiner to Margaret Gardiner, New York [May], 1840, *GPY.*

[37] Alexander Gardiner to Julia Gardiner, New York, May 24, 1839; Julia Gardiner to David L. Gardiner, East Hampton, May 31, 1840; Julia Gardiner to Alexander Gardiner, East Hampton, July 27; Aug. 1; 2, 1842; [Summer] 1843, *GPY.*

[38] *Ibid.,* June 14; May 4; 10; 12; June 29, 1840; May 30; July 27, 1842, *GPY.*

[39] P. S. R. Payne recounts this incident interestingly in *The Island,* 202–3, but adds some colorful speculation not warranted by the facts. He guesses, for instance, that the strange man present "looks suspiciously like" David Gardiner "disguised with mustache and chin whiskers." That Julia posed voluntarily would seem indicated by David Gardiner's failure to press a lawsuit against Bogert and Mecamly.

[40] Julia Gardiner to Alexander Gardiner, East Hampton, May 17, 1840, *GPY.* Julia guessed that the author of the poem was a "Mr. G.," otherwise unidentified.

[41] Nathaniel Gardiner to David Gardiner, New Haven, July 8, 1840; Benjamin F. Butler to Lewis Cass, New York, Sept. 22, 1840; Charles King to Georges W. Lafayette, New York, Oct. 1, 1840, *GPY.* Charles King was the son of Rufus King of New York, Federalist Vice-Presidential nominee in 1808; Georges Washington Lafayette was the son of the celebrated marquis.

[42] Juliana Gardiner to Alexander Gardiner [New Haven], Aug. 3, 1840; Juliana Gardiner to David L. Gardiner, New York, Washington, Aug. 9 [1840]; Philadelphia, Aug. 27, 1840, *GPY.*

[43] Margaret Gardiner, *Leaves From a Young Girl's Diary, 1840–1841,* Sarah D. Gardiner (ed.), (privately published, 1926), Sept. 28; Nov. 3, 1840, 8, 24–25. Hereafter cited as Margaret Gardiner, *Diary.*

[44] David Gardiner to Samuel Gardiner, London, Nov. 2, 1840, *GPY.*

[45] Margaret Gardiner, *Diary,* Nov. 10, 1840, 29–30.

[46] *Ibid.,* Nov. 28; Dec. 2, 1840; Jan. 6, 1841, 38–40, 49–50.

[47] David Gardiner to Editor, New York *American,* Paris, Jan. 14, 1841; Alexander Gardiner to Samuel Gardiner, [New York], Mar. 28, 1841, *GPY;* New York *American,* Mar. 25, 1841. The piece in the *American* was captioned "Presentation at Court."

[48] Juliana Gardiner to David L. and Alexander Gardiner, Rome, Feb. 21, 1841; David Gardiner to Nathaniel Gardiner, Florence, Apr. 20, 1841, *GPY;* Margaret Gardiner, *Diary,* Apr. 13; July 4, 1841, 97–98, 135; Margaret Gardiner to [David L. and Alexander Gardiner], Rome, Feb. 23, 1841, *GPY;* Margaret Gardiner, *Diary,* Feb. 21, 1841, 70; Leonard Wood to Julia Gardiner Tyler, Brunswick, N.S., Dec. 2, 1872; J. Alexander Tyler to Julia Gardiner Tyler, Karlsruhe, Baden, Jan. 10, 1867; David Gardiner Tyler to Julia Gardiner Tyler, Karlsruhe, Oct. 19, 1866, *TFP.* Wood, who had served as an intermediary in the romance, recalled it as "that conquest of yours of which I became a witness." David Gardiner Tyler feared that if he and his brother Alex did find the baron he might become "so far wrought up as to 'kiss us for our mother.'"

[49] Margaret Gardiner, *Diary,* Mar. 12, 1841, 84–85; David Gardiner to Nathaniel Gardiner, Florence, Apr. 20, 1841; John J. Bailey to Andrew Stevenson, Genoa, Apr. 15, 1841, *GPY;* Margaret Gardiner, *Diary,* Apr. 15–July 3, 1841, 100–35; Julia

Gardiner Tyler, "Reminiscences," in *LTT*, III, 194; Margaret Gardiner Beeckman to Julia Gardiner Tyler, [New York], Aug. 2 [1849], *TFP*. A brief romantic fling with a Belgian count was so successful for Julia that according to Margaret the gentleman was on the verge of leaving Brussels for America to ask for her hand when he learned of her marriage to Tyler.

[50] Juliana Gardiner to David L. and Alexander Gardiner, Leamington, Aug. 27, 1841, *GPY*.

[51] Julia Gardiner Tyler, "Reminiscences," in *LTT*, III, 194.

[52] Alexander Gardiner to David Gardiner, New York, Apr. [9], 1841, *GPY*.

[53] [Alexander Gardiner] to the Editor of the New York *Courier and Enquirer*, Oct. 11, 1841 (Private), *GPY*.

[54] Julia Gardiner Tyler, "Reminiscences," in *LTT*, III, 195.

[55] *Ibid.*, 194-95.

[56] Coleman, *Priscilla Cooper Tyler*, 93; Margaret Gardiner to Alexander Gardiner, Washington, Jan. 21, 1842, *GPY*.

[57] *Ibid.*; Julia Gardiner Tyler, "Reminiscences," in *LTT*, III, 196-97.

[58] Julia Gardiner to Alexander Gardiner, East Hampton, Mar. 6, 1842; Margaret Gardiner to Alexander Gardiner, East Hampton, Nov. 9; 13, 1842, *GPY*. John Griswold Gardiner (1812-1861), ninth proprietor of Gardiners Island, died unmarried.

[59] Juliana Gardiner to David L. Gardiner, East Hampton, June 26, 1842; Margaret Gardiner to Alexander Gardiner, East Hampton, Nov. 13, 1842; Julia Gardiner to Alexander Gardiner, East Hampton, July 27, 1842; Julia Gardiner to David L. Gardiner, East Hampton, May 19, 1842; Julia Gardiner to Alexander Gardiner, East Hampton, July 27, 1842; Margaret Gardiner to Alexander Gardiner, East Hampton, Nov. 13, 1842; Julia Gardiner to Alexander Gardiner, East Hampton, July 27; May 30, 1842, *GPY*.

[60] *Ibid.*, Aug. 1, 1842; J. J. Bailey to David Gardiner, New York, Sept. 12, 1842; David Gardiner to Alexander Gardiner, East Hampton, Mar. 6; Nov. 13, 1842; Alexander Gardiner to David Gardiner, n.p., n.d. [New York, Nov.-Dec. 1842], *GPY*.

[61] Moses Yale Beach, *Wealth and Pedigree of the Wealthy Citizens of New York City. Comprising... Persons Estimated to be Worth $100,000 and Upwards*, Third Edition (New York, 1842), 2. Beach was the editor of the New York *Sun*.

[62] *Ibid.*, 8. Following his death in 1844, David Gardiner was listed in the 1846 edition as "Estate of $200,000." The figure was a bit high. Gardiner's brother Nathaniel of Sag Harbor (Julia's Uncle Nathaniel), did not make the 1842 edition of Beach, but he was included in the 1846 version at a comfortable $100,000. Julia Gardiner to Alexander Gardiner, East Hampton, June 21, 1842, *GPY*. The surprised lady whose parlor was violated was Sarah Griswold Gardiner (1781-1863), wife and widow of John Lyon Gardiner (1770-1816), seventh proprietor of Gardiners Island, and mother of John Griswold Gardiner.

[63] *Ibid.*; David Gardiner to David L. Gardiner, East Hampton, June 21, 1842; Juliana Gardiner to David L. Gardiner, East Hampton, June 19, 1842, *GPY*; Beach, *Wealth*, 6, 9, 19.

[64] Alexander Gardiner to David L. Gardiner, Norwich, Conn., June 27, 1842; Margaret Gardiner to Alexander Gardiner, East Hampton, Nov. 13, 1842; Alexander Gardiner to David Gardiner, n.p., n.d. [New York, Nov.-Dec. 1842], *GPY*.

CHAPTER 3

[1] Oliver P. Chitwood, *John Tyler: Champion of the Old South* (New York, 1939), 10, 202-3; *LTT*, I, 198-200; John S. Wise, *Recollections of Thirteen Presidents* (New York, 1906), 13-16; Julia Gardiner Tyler to David Gardiner Tyler, Staten Island, N.Y., Oct. 30, 1869, *TFP*; A. G. Abell, *Life of John Tyler* (New York,

1844), 1–10; Rudolph Marx, *The Health of the Presidents* (New York, 1960), 134; Katherine Tyler Ellett, *Young John Tyler: A True Story for Boys and Girls* (Richmond, Va., 1957), 10–12, 29–33. In the Ellett book for children (ages 8–10) the story is told that Tyler had memorized large passages of Patrick Henry's "If this be treason" speech at the age of eight. *See also* W. Burlie Brown, *The People's Choice: The Presidential Image in the Campaign Biography* (Baton Rouge, La., 1960), *passim,* for a delightful discussion of the hokum surrounding the youthful years of American Presidents. For some inexplicable reason the marbles-at-dawn story found its way into the otherwise excellent Hugh Russell Fraser, *Democracy in the Making: The Jackson-Tyler Era* (Indianapolis, 1938), 152.

[2] John Tyler to William Tyler, Sherwood Forest, Oct. 29, 1854, *TPLC;* *LTT,* I, 200; Chitwood, *Tyler,* 17–18; Wise, *Seven Decades of the Union,* 32–33.

[3] Over the years Tyler served as William and Mary's benefactor, legal adviser, Rector of its Board of Visitors, and Chancellor. He spoke frequently on the campus and in 1825 he blocked an ill-considered scheme to move the college to Richmond. See *LTT,* I, 344; Henry A. Wise to John Tyler, Onancock, Va., Aug. 7, 1855; John Tyler to ———, Sherwood Forest, Oct. 22, 1860; John Tyler to Robert Tyler, Sherwood Forest, Feb. 1, 1851; Prof. W. E. Hopkins to John Tyler, Williamsburg, Aug. 21, 1850; John Tyler to Prof. George F. Holmes, Sherwood Forest, Jan. 31, 1848; Williamsburg, Feb. 22, 1847; John Tyler to Prof. Ewell, Sherwood Forest, Feb. 11, 1859, *TPLC.* For Tyler's legal training see Abell, *Tyler,* 136; Chitwood, *Tyler,* 20–21; *LTT,* I, 280–81, 204, 272; John Tyler to Henry Curtis, Washington, Dec. 8, 1820, in *ibid.,* 336.

[4] *Ibid.,* 55–56, 70; John Tyler to William Tyler, Sherwood Forest, Jan. 12, 1852; Dec. 23, 1859. For additional evidence of Tyler's genealogical interests see *ibid.,* Feb. 15, 1848; Nov. 12, 1850, *TPLC;* Julia Gardiner Tyler to Juliana Gardiner, Sherwood Forest, Dec. 14, 1859, *TFP.*

[5] *LTT,* I, 41–42; Chitwood, *Tyler,* 10, 64–65, 122; John Tyler to John C. Hamilton, Sherwood Forest, July 14, 1855, *TPLC.*

[6] *LTT,* I, 142–143, 149–50; John Tyler, Sr., to George Tucker, Greenway, July 10, 1795, *TPLC;* John Tyler to William Tyler, Sherwood Forest, Jan. 12, 1852; May 22, 1854, in *LTT,* II, 496, 510; John Tyler to Robert Y. Hayne, Gloucester, Va., June 20, 1831, *TPLC.*

[7] *LTT,* I, 154, 567–70; John Tyler to Henry S. Foote, Sherwood Forest, May 21, 1850, in *ibid.,* II, 489; *see also* John Tyler's speech at Jamestown on May 13, 1857, in which the point is made concerning slavery in British colonial policy, *ibid.,* I, 10–11; Chitwood, *Tyler,* 154; *LTT,* I, 266–67; Margaret Gardiner Beeckman to Juliana Gardiner, Niagara Falls, Sept. 21, 1851, *TFP.*

[8] John Tyler to Henry Curtis, Woodburn, Sept. 30, 1821, *TPLC;* John Tyler to Mary Tyler Jones, Washington, Jan. 20, 1836, in *LTT,* I, 531; *ibid.,* 280–81; III, 183; Anon., *John Tyler: His History, Character and Position* (Pamphlet; New York, 1843), 11; Chitwood, *Tyler,* 20–21.

[9] Richard B. Morris (ed.), *Alexander Hamilton and the Founding of the Nation* (New York, 1957), 266; for a brief history of the first Bank of the United States see Davis R. Dewey, *Financial History of the United States* (New York, 1903), 98–101.

[10] John Tyler to Hugh Blair Grigsby, Sherwood Forest, Jan. 16, 1855, *TPLC;* Chitwood, *Tyler,* 27–28; *LTT,* I, 274. The Tyler resolution was introduced on Jan. 14, 1812.

[11] [Lyon G. Tyler (ed.)], "Will and Inventory of Hon. John Tyler," *William and Mary College Quarterly Historical Magazine,* XVII (April 1909), 231–35. The estate of John Tyler, Sr., also included 40 slaves. John Tyler to Letitia Christian, Richmond, Dec. 5, 1812, in Laura C. Holloway Langford, *The Ladies of the White House; Or, In the Home of the Presidents* (Philadelphia, 1881), 309–10.

[12] John Tyler to Henry Curtis, Greenway, Mar. 23, 1813; Richmond, May 18, 1813, in *LTT,* I, 276, 277; Chitwood, *Tyler,* 22–23.

[13] Letitia Tyler to Letitia Christian Tyler, Parsonage, Jan. 7, 1837, *TFP;* John Tyler to Mary Tyler, Washington, Dec. 26, 1827; Feb. 24; Apr. 30, 1828; Mar. 4; Apr. 28; Dec. 24, 1830, in *LTT,* I, 389–92, 546, 549, 551–52; Armistead C. Gordon, *John Tyler: Tenth President of the United States. An Address at the Dedication of the Monument Erected by Congress in Hollywood Cemetery, Richmond, Va., in Memory of President Tyler, Oct. 12, 1915* (Pamphlet; [Richmond], 1915), 19; Anne Royall, *Letters From Alabama* (Washington, 1830), 189; *LTT,* I, 550; Margaret Gardiner to David L. and Alexander Gardiner, Washington, Mar. 9, 1843, *GPY;* Langford, *Ladies of the White House,* 312–17.

[14] Priscilla Cooper Tyler to Mary Grace Cooper Raoul, Williamsburg, Oct. 1839, in Coleman, *Priscilla Cooper Tyler,* 73–75; Langford, *Ladies of the White House,* 325–26.

[15] Abell, *Tyler,* 59; *LTT,* I, 266–67, 280–81.

[16] *Ibid.,* 278–79; Chitwood, *Tyler,* 29–30; Abell, *Tyler,* 13.

[17] John Tyler to Margaret Gardiner Beeckman, Sherwood Forest, June 14, 1855, *TPLC;* Rufus Stone to Julia Gardiner Tyler, Sioux City, Iowa, June 8, 1869, *TFP.*

[18] John Tyler to Henry Curtis, Washington, Apr. 13, 1832, in *LTT,* I, 439.

[19] Abell, *Tyler,* 13–14; Chitwood, *Tyler,* 34; *LTT,* I, 296–97; John Tyler to Letitia Christian Tyler, Washington, Feb. 1, 1817, in *ibid.,* 288.

[20] Chitwood, *Tyler,* 41–44; *LTT,* I, 316–17, 334.

[21] Abell, *Tyler,* 18–19.

[22] John Tyler to Henry Curtis, Washington, Feb. 22, 1830, in *LTT,* I, 408; Chitwood, *Tyler,* 318.

[23] John Tyler to Robert McCandlish, Sherwood Forest, Feb. 22, 1851, in *LTT,* I, 402–3; John Tyler to Littleton W. Tazewell, Washington, June 23, 1834, in *ibid.,* 499; Chitwood, *Tyler,* 254.

[24] John Tyler to Henry Curtis, Philadelphia, Dec. 18, 1818; Washington, Jan. 19, 1819, in *LTT,* I, 303, 305.

[25] Abell, *Tyler,* 34–52.

[26] Carl Brent Swisher, *American Constitutional Development* (New York, 1943), 175–76; John Tyler to Littleton W. Tazewell, Washington, June 23, 1834, in *LTT,* I, 499.

[27] Abell, *Tyler,* 65–74.

[28] *Ibid.*

[29] *Ibid.,* 55–62; John Tyler to Henry Curtis, Washington, Jan. 19, 1818, in *LTT,* I, 305.

[30] *Niles' Weekly Register* (Aug. 8, 1818), XIV, 399.

[31] Claude C. Bowers, *John Tyler: An Address at the Unveiling of the Bust of President Tyler in the State Capitol, Richmond, Va., June 16, 1931* (Pamphlet; Richmond, 1932), 8–9; Chitwood, *Tyler,* 53; *LTT,* III, 26–27; I, 319–20.

[32] John Tyler to Henry Curtis, Washington, Feb. 5, 1820, *TPLC; LTT,* I, 319–20.

[33] Abell, *Tyler,* 64; *LTT,* II, 540.

[34] *Ibid.,* I, 318–19; Chitwood, *Tyler,* 49–50; Gordon, *John Tyler: Tenth President,* 20.

[35] *LTT,* I, 329.

[36] *Ibid.,* 335–36; Marx, *Health of the Presidents,* 133–34.

[37] John Tyler to Henry Curtis, Charles City, July 20, 1821, *TPLC.*

CHAPTER 4

[1] John Tyler to Henry Curtis, Charles City, June 21, 1822, *TPLC.*

[2] *Journal of the Virginia House of Delegates, 1823–1824 Session* (Richmond, 1824), 55, 74–76, 95; Chitwood, *Tyler,* 60–61; *LTT,* I, 341–42.

³ Eugene Roseboom, *A History of Presidential Elections* (New York, 1959), 82; *LTT,* III, 28–29.
⁴ Roseboom, *A History of Presidential Elections,* 84; Samuel Flagg Bemis, *John Quincy Adams and the Union* (New York, 1956), 11–57; Charles M. Wiltse, *John C. Calhoun: Nationalist, 1782–1828* (Indianapolis, 1944), 304–6; Glyndon G. Van Deusen, *The Life of Henry Clay* (Boston, 1937), 219–22.
⁵ John Tyler to Henry Clay, Charles City, Mar. 27, 1825, in Calvin Colton (ed.), *The Private Correspondence of Henry Clay* (Cincinnati, 1856), 119–20.
⁶ Chitwood, *Tyler,* 64; Abell, *Tyler,* 78–84; Chitwood, *Tyler,* 67–69; Abell, *Tyler,* 85–86; Chitwood, *Tyler,* 60, 70; *LTT,* I, 345; Bowers, *Tyler,* 9.
⁷ H. S. Foote, *A Casket of Reminiscences* (Washington, 1874), 58; *LTT,* I, 356.
⁸ *Ibid.,* 69.
⁹ The cautiously worded letters between Tyler and the committee of anti-Randolph legislators urging the Tyler candidacy are reproduced in Abell, *Tyler,* 87–89; *see also* Wise, *Seven Decades of the Union,* 86–87; John Tyler to Henry Curtis, Greenway, Sept. 4, 1827, *TPLC;* Chitwood, *Tyler,* 76; W. C. Bruce, *John Randolph of Roanoke,* 2 vols. (New York, 1922), I, 513, 543; Chitwood, *Tyler,* 74–75, 78–79; *LTT,* I, 357–62; Chitwood, *Tyler,* 82.
¹⁰ Bemis, *John Quincy Adams and the Union;* 69; Abell, *Tyler,* 92; Wise, *Seven Decades of the Union,* 88–89.
¹¹ The tariff policies of the 1820s and the Jacksonian tariff plot of 1828 are treated in many standard sources, principally F. W. Taussig, *The Tariff History of the United States* (New York, 1909), 70–102; George Dangerfield, *The Era of Good Feelings* (New York, 1952), 396–409; and Bemis, *John Quincy Adams and the Union,* 87–91.
¹² John Tyler to John Rutherfoord, Washington, Dec. 8, 1827, *John Rutherfoord Papers,* Duke University Library; John Tyler to Henry Curtis, Washington, Mar. 18; May 1, 1828, in *LTT,* I, 384–85, 387; Apr. 23, 1828, *TPLC.*
¹³ John Tyler to Henry Curtis, Washington, Dec. 16, 1827; Mar. 18, 1828; Greenway, Sept. 4, 1827, in *LTT,* I, 379, 386, 375; *ibid.,* 365.
¹⁴ John Tyler to John Rutherfoord, Washington, Dec. 8, 1827, *John Rutherfoord Papers,* Duke University Library; John Tyler to Henry Curtis, Washington, Dec. 16, 1827, in *LTT,* I, 379.
¹⁵ Roseboom, *A History of Presidential Elections,* 90–91.
¹⁶ John Tyler to John B. Clopton, Washington, Dec. 14, 1828, *Tyler Papers,* Duke University Library.
¹⁷ Claude C. Bowers, *The Party Battles of the Jackson Period* (Boston, 1928), 37.
¹⁸ *Ibid.,* 48.
¹⁹ Arthur M. Schlesinger, Jr., *The Age of Jackson* (Boston, 1946), 67–73, 104.
²⁰ James D. Richardson (comp.), *A Compilation of the Messages and Papers of the Presidents* (Washington, 1902), II, 448–49; Schlesinger, *The Age of Jackson,* 46–47.
²¹ *LTT,* I, 408–9; John Tyler to John B. Seawell, Washington, Jan. 25, 1832, *TPLC;* John Tyler to Robert Tyler, Washington, Feb. 2, 1832, in *LTT,* I, 426–27.
²² Abell, *Tyler,* 102, 105–7; *LTT,* I, 421.
²³ John Tyler to John Rutherfoord, Washington, Mar. 14, 1830, *John Rutherfoord Papers,* Duke University Library.
²⁴ *LTT,* I, 412; Abell, *Tyler,* 97–99.
²⁵ Wiltse, *John C. Calhoun: Nationalist,* 390–98; Richard M. Hofstadter, "John C. Calhoun: The Marx of the Master Class," in *The American Political Tradition and the Men Who Made It* (New York, 1949), 67–91; Margaret Bayard Smith, *The First Forty Years of Washington Society.* Gaillard Hunt, (ed.) (New York, 1906), 252–53; Charles M. Wiltse, *John C. Calhoun: Nullifier, 1829–1839* (Indianapolis, 1949), 26–38.
²⁶ John Tyler to Littleton W. Tazewell, Gloucester, May 8, 1831, in *LTT,* I,

422–23; Thomas Hart Benton, *Thirty Years' View*, 2 vols. (New York, 1889), I, 219, 215; for Tyler's continued distrust of Van Buren *see* John Tyler to James Iredell, Jr., Washington, Jan. 10, 1835, *James Iredell, Jr., Papers*, Duke University Library. In this letter Tyler characterizes Van Buren as Jackson's "sweetest little fellow," the "Sejanus of the mighty Tiberius."

[27] John Tyler to Mary Tyler, Washington, Apr. 20, 1832, in *LTT*, I, 429–30.

[28] J. S. Bassett, *Life of Andrew Jackson* (New York, 1928), 599; Schlesinger, *The Age of Jackson*, 87.

[29] J. C. Fitzpatrick (ed.), *Martin Van Buren, Autobiography* (*American Historical Association Annual Report for the Year 1918*), II, 625.

[30] Abell, *Tyler*, 132; *LTT*, I, 474–75.

[31] Nicholas Biddle to Henry Clay, Philadelphia, Aug. 1, 1832, in Colton, *The Private Correspondence of Henry Clay*, 341; Richardson, *Messages and Papers of the Presidents*, II, 590; Schlesinger, *The Age of Jackson*, 91.

[32] John Tyler to Henry Curtis, Washington, Apr. 13, 1832, in *LTT*, I, 439.

[33] Roseboom, *A History of Presidential Elections*, 104–5.

[34] Wiltse, *John C. Calhoun: Nullifier*, 171–72, 173.

[35] Wise, *Seven Decades of the Union*, 122–23; Henry T. Shanks, *The Secession Movement in Virginia, 1847–1861* (Richmond, 1934), 21.

[36] John Tyler to Mary Tyler, Washington, Apr. 26, 1832; John Tyler to John B. Seawell, Washington, June 15, 1832; John Tyler to Henry Curtis, Washington, Apr. 13, 1832, in *LTT*, I, 559, 437, 439; Abell, *Tyler*, 113, 121–23; *Congressional Debates*, 1831–1832, VIII (Washington, 1832), 355–67; *LTT*, III, 69.

[37] Henry St. George Tucker to Nathaniel B. Tucker, Richmond, Jan. 24, 1833, in *William and Mary College Quarterly Historical Magazine*, XII (October 1903), 91–92; Shanks, *The Secession Movement in Virginia*, 21; Arthur C. Cole, *The Whig Party in the South* (Washington, 1913), 20–21. The quotation is Duff Green's in a letter to Richard K. Crallé, dated Dec. 15, 1832.

[38] John Tyler to John Floyd, Washington, Jan. 16, 1833; John Tyler to Littleton W. Tazewell, Washington, Feb. 2, 1833, *TPLC*.

[39] John Tyler to John B. Seawell, Washington, Jan. 25, 1832, *TPLC*; John H. Pleasants to John Tyler, Richmond, Jan. 1, 1833, in *LTT*, I, 452; John Tyler to Littleton W. Tazewell, Washington, Feb. 2, 1833; John Tyler to John Floyd, Washington, Jan. 16, 1833; John Tyler to William F. Pendleton, Washington, Jan. 19, 1833, *TPLC*; *LTT*, I, 454; Abell, *Tyler*, 135–46.

[40] *LTT*, I, 444, 447, 461; II, 143.

[41] Chitwood, *Tyler*, 119; *LTT*, I, 467; John Tyler to John Floyd, Washington, Jan. 16, 1833, *TPLC*.

[42] John Tyler to Littleton W. Tazewell, Washington, Feb. 2, 1833, *TPLC*; Abell, *Tyler*, 145; John Tyler, Speech at a Banquet Honoring Henry Clay, Richmond, Virginia, April 12, 1860, in *LTT*, I, 467.

[43] *Ibid.*, 462; John Tyler to John Floyd, Gloucester, Nov. 21, 1833, *TPLC*.

[44] Schlesinger, *The Age of Jackson*, 97–105; Benton, *Thirty Years' View*, I, 374.

[45] John Tyler to Littleton W. Tazewell, Washington, Dec. 3; 25, 1833; John Tyler to Thomas W. Gilmer, Washington, Jan. 7, 1834; John Tyler to Littleton W. Tazewell, Washington, Dec. 25, 1833, *TPLC*; Schlesinger, *The Age of Jackson*, 106–7, 109; Van Deusen, *The Life of Henry Clay*, 279–81.

[46] John Tyler to Littleton W. Tazewell, Washington, Jan. 9, 1834, *TPLC*; *LTT*, I, 484; John Tyler to Letitia Christian Tyler, Washington, Feb. 17, 1834, in *ibid.*, 485; Abell, *Tyler*, 149–56. Abell produced the entire Tyler speech on the deposits question as he did most of Tyler's important addresses in Congress and out. Apparently he had access to the original manuscript copies of Tyler's pre-1842 utterances. These documents, it may be assumed, were among those burned in Richmond in April 1865.

[47] *Ibid.*

⁴⁸ *Ibid.; LTT,* I, 489, 597; Abell, *Tyler,* 158.
⁴⁹ John Tyler to Thomas W. Gilmer, Washington, Jan. 7, 1834; John Tyler to Littleton W. Tazewell, Senate Chamber, Washington, May 9, 1834, *TPLC; LTT,* I, 484-85.
⁵⁰ John Tyler to William Patterson Smith, Washington, Mar. 31, 1834, *William Patterson Smith Papers,* Duke University Library; John Tyler to Henry Curtis, Washington, Mar. 28, 1854; John Tyler to Littleton W. Tazewell, Washington, June 23, 1834, *TPLC.*

CHAPTER 5

¹ John Tyler, "Oh Child of My Love," *TPLC.*
² John Tyler to Henry Curtis, Charles City, July 20, 1821; Oct. 9, 1820, *TPLC.*
³ *Ibid.,* Washington, May 1; 16, 1828, *TPLC.*
⁴ *Ibid.,* Greenway, Sept. 4; Oct. 26; Nov. 16, 1827, *TPLC.*
⁵ John Tyler to John B. Seawell, Washington, Jan. 25, 1832; John Tyler to Elizabeth Tyler Waller, Washington, Jan. 16, 1843, *TPLC;* John Tyler to John B. Seawell, Washington, June 15, 1832; John Tyler to Littleton W. Tazewell, Richmond, May 2, 1826, in *LTT,* I, 437, 331.
⁶ *Ibid.,* 575-77.
⁷ John Tyler to Letitia Christian Tyler, Washington, Feb. 1, 1835; John Tyler to John Tyler, Jr., Washington, Feb. 19, 1834; John Tyler to Mary Tyler, Washington, June 15, 1832; Dec. 26, 1827; Feb. 8, 1831; Dec. 24, 1830; Jan. 20, 1832; John Tyler to Robert Tyler, Washington, Feb. 6, 1834; John Tyler to Letitia Christian Tyler, Washington, Feb. 1, 1835, in *ibid.,* 510, 563, 562, 390, 552, 551, 554, 562-63, 510.
⁸ John Tyler to Henry Curtis, Greenway, Nov. 23, 1827, *TPLC;* John Tyler to Mary Tyler, Washington, Apr. 30, 1828; Dec. 24, 1830; Mar. 11, 1832, in *LTT,* I, 392, 552, 555; Chitwood, *Tyler,* 18; John Tyler to Mary Tyler, Washington, Mar. 4; 18; Apr. 28, 1830, in *LTT,* I, 546, 547, 549; Letitia Tyler to John Tyler, [Williamsburg], Jan. 21, 1837, *TFP.*
⁹ John Tyler to Mary Tyler Jones, Washington, Jan. 20, 1836; John Tyler to Robert Tyler, Gloucester, Nov. 28, 1836; Dec. 11, 1834. John Tyler, Jr., received similar academic pep talks from his father in Washington. See John Tyler to John Tyler, Jr., Washington, Feb. 19, 1834; John Tyler to Henry Curtis, Washington, Mar. 28, 1834; John Tyler to Robert Tyler, Washington, Dec. 11, 1834; Jan. 24, 1835, in *LTT,* I, 531, 564, 514, 563, 491, 514, 564.
¹⁰ *Ibid.,* Gloucester, Nov. 28, 1836, in *ibid.,* 564-65.
¹¹ John Tyler to Mary Tyler, Washington, Dec. 28, 1831; Jan. 20; June 15, 1832; John Tyler to Mary Tyler Jones, Washington, Jan. 20, 1836, in *ibid.,* 428-29, 554, 562, 531.
¹² John Tyler to Mary Tyler, Washington, Dec. 26, 1827; Feb. 16, 1831; Mar. 11, 1832; Mar. 4; May 13, 1830; Feb. 8, 1831. The Jeffersonian anger adage was also urged upon Robert. See John Tyler to Robert Tyler, Washington, Jan. 16, 1836, in *ibid.,* 390, 553, 555, 547, 550, 553, 530; John Tyler to James Iredell, Jr., Gloucester, Nov. 16, 1836, *James Iredell, Jr., Papers,* Duke University Library; John Tyler to Mary Tyler Jones, Mar. 25, 1836, *TPLC;* John Tyler to Robert Tyler, Washington, Feb. 15, 1836, in *LTT,* I, 535; Royall, *Letters From Alabama,* 178.
¹³ John Tyler to Mary Tyler, Washington, Apr. 30, 1828; John Tyler to Robert Tyler, Washington, Feb. 2, 1832; Jan. 16; Feb. 15, 1836; John Tyler to Mary Tyler Jones, Washington, Feb. 18, 1836; John Tyler to Letitia Christian Tyler,

Washington, Feb. 1, 1835; John Tyler to Robert Tyler, Washington, Feb. 23, 1835; Dec. 11, 1834, in *LTT*, I, 392, 427, 530, 535, 535, 510, 511, 514; John Tyler to John B. Seawell, Washington, June 13, 1832, *TPLC;* John Tyler to Henry Curtis, Washington, May 1, 1828; John Tyler to Mary Tyler, Washington, Feb. 16, 1831, in *LTT*, I, 387, 553; *ibid.*, II, 22; John Tyler to George G. Waggaman, Williamsburg, Feb. 15, 1838; John Tyler to John H. Waggaman, Williamsburg, Aug. 30, 1839, *TPLC*.

[14] John Tyler, Speech at the Memorial Service for Thomas Jefferson, Richmond, July 11, 1826, in Chitwood, *Tyler*, 66; John Tyler to Mary Tyler, Washington, Dec. 26, 1827; Feb. 24, 1828, in *LTT* I, 390, 390–91; John Tyler, Speech to the Virginia Colonization Society, Richmond, Jan. 10, 1838, in *ibid.*, 567–69.

[15] John Tyler to Mary Tyler, Washington, Jan. 20, 1832, in *ibid.*, 554–55; John Tyler to Henry Curtis, Washington, Jan. 25, 1844, *TPLC;* John Tyler to Mary Tyler, Washington, Dec. 28, 1831; June 15, 1832; Mar. 4, 1830, in *LTT*, I, 429, 561–62, 547.

[16] John Tyler to Robert Tyler, Washington, Jan. 16, 1836, in *ibid.*, 530.

[17] Benton, *Thirty Years' View*, I, 471; *LTT*, I, 503–5; Chitwood, *Tyler*, 129–32; Benton, *Thirty Years' View*, I, 481–87. Besides Tyler, the antiadministration members of the committee were Senators Daniel Webster, Thomas Ewing of Ohio, and Willie P. Mangum of North Carolina. The lone pro-Jacksonian was Senator William Wilkins of Pennsylvania, later Tyler's Secretary of War. He boycotted the committee and would have nothing to do with its work or its subsequent December 1834 report.

[18] *Ibid.*, 483, 487.

[19] John Tyler to Col. Thomas Smith, Washington, Dec. 16, 1835, in *LTT*, I, 525. The offer was made to Tyler by the Reverend William S. Morgan, member of Congress from Virginia. Col. Thomas Smith was Gloucester delegate in the Virginia House of Delegates.

[20] Benjamin W. Leigh to John Tyler, Richmond, July 5, 1835, in *ibid.*, 523.

[21] John Tyler to Robert Tyler, Washington, Jan. 16, 1836, in *ibid.*, 529–30. Tyler had sounded out his friend William F. Gordon on the idea of appealing to the people in order to "put our adversaries on the defensive." John Tyler to William F. Gordon, Washington, Jan. 8, 1836, *James Rochelle Papers*, Duke University Library.

[22] William F. Gordon to John Tyler, Albemarle, Jan. 15, 1836, *TPLC;* John H. Pleasants to John Tyler, Richmond, Jan. 13, 1836; James Barbour to John Tyler, Richmond, Jan. 14, 1836; in *LTT*, I, 526, 527; *see also* Robert Allen to John Tyler, Mt. Jackson, Va., Dec. 22, 1835, *TPLC*.

[23] John Tyler to Mary Tyler Jones, Washington, Jan. 20, 1836, in *LTT*, I, 531.

[24] Col. Thomas Smith to John Tyler, Richmond, Feb. 11, 1836; William Crump to John Tyler, Powhatan County, Va., Feb. 14, 1836; D. F. Slaughter to John Tyler, Richmond, Feb. 28, 1836, in *ibid.*, 532, 533–34, 536–37. The key test vote in the House of Delegates to instruct Tyler and Leigh to vote for the Benton expunging resolution showed a Jacksonian-Democratic majority of only 14. On the more general proposition of the right of the legislature to instruct and the duty of the representative to obey, or resign, the affirmative margin was an overwhelming 114 to 14. In the Virginia senate the Jacksonian-Democratic working majority was only 6, yet the right of instruction proposition, which carried 114 to 14 in the House of Delegates, was carried 25 to 5 in the senate. The instructions issue transcended faction.

[25] John Tyler to Robert Tyler, Washington, Feb. 15, 1836, *TPLC;* John Tyler to Mary Tyler Jones, Washington, Feb. 18, 1836, in *LTT*, I, 535. Tyler told Robert that his decision to resign "seems to be the wish of my friends in Richmond," a rather strange misreading of the bulk of the advice he seems to have received. John Tyler to William F. Gordon, Washington, Jan. 8, 1836, *James Rochelle Papers*,

Duke University Library. He was also worried that the Jacksonians would carry his own Gloucester County in the state elections in April. "It is necessary that you should put everything in motion at once for the election in April," he wrote William Patterson Smith at Gloucester Courthouse. "Success always, as you know, depends on diligence and industry. The Expungers would rather carry Gloucester than any other County." John Tyler to William Patterson Smith, Washington, Mar. 7, 1836, *William Patterson Smith Papers,* Duke University Library.

[26] John Tyler to Hugh Blair Grigsby, Sherwood Forest, Jan. 16, 1855, *TPLC.*

[27] John Tyler to the General Assembly of Virginia, Washington, Feb. 29, 1836, in Abell, *Tyler,* 166-71.

[28] John Tyler to William F. Pendleton, Gloucester, Oct. 27, 1836, *TPLC.*

[29] *LTT,* I, 541-42.

[30] The standard work on the emergence of the Whig Party is E. Malcolm Carroll, *Origins of the Whig Party* (Durham, N.C., 1925), *passim.* See also Cole, *The Whig Party in the South,* 20, 69; Barton H. Wise, *The Life of Henry A. Wise of Virginia, 1806-1876* (New York, 1899), 178. An excellent account of the origin of the Whig Party in Virginia is found in Henry H. Simms, *The Rise of the Whigs in Virginia, 1824-1840* (Richmond, 1929), *passim.*

[31] Schlesinger, *The Age of Jackson,* 284. For a detailed history of Anti-Masonry see Charles McCarthy, *The Antimasonic Party, 1827-1840* (Washington, 1903), *passim;* see also the chapter on Anti-Masonry in William B. Hesseltone, *The Rise and Fall of Third Parties, From Anti-Masonry to Wallace* (Washington, 1948).

[32] John Tyler to William F. Gordon, Gloucester, Nov. 9, 1834, *James Rochelle Papers,* Duke University Library; John Tyler to James Iredell, Jr., Washington, Jan. 10, 1835, *James Iredell, Jr., Papers,* Duke University Library.

[33] Freeman Cleaves, *Old Tippecanoe: William Henry Harrison and His Times* (New York, 1939), 202-4, 294.

[34] John Tyler to Col. Thomas Smith, Gloucester Place, May 8, 1835, in *LTT,* I, 516-17. Throughout 1835 such papers as the Richmond *Virginia Free Press,* the Washington *Sun,* and the Richmond *Whig* boomed Tyler's Vice-Presidential nomination. See *LTT,* II, 517-18.

[35] Cleaves, *Old Tippecanoe,* 45-49, 351, 240-41, 247-48, 252, 254-55, 263, 266-67, 269, 274-75, 282, 284, 291; Henry Clay to John Bailhache, Ashland, Sept. 13, 1835, in Colton, *The Private Correspondence of Henry Clay,* 400; Nicholas Biddle to Herman Cope, Philadelphia, Aug. 11, 1835, in R. C. McGrane (ed.), *Correspondence of Nicholas Biddle Dealing with National Affairs* (Boston, 1919), 255; Cleaves, *Old Tippecanoe,* 305-8.

[36] Robert Allen to John Tyler, Mt. Jackson, Va., Dec. 22, 1835, *TPLC;* John Tyler to Mary Tyler Jones, Washington, Jan. 20, 1836, in *LTT,* I, 531; Chitwood, *Tyler,* 149-50; John G. Miller to John Tyler, Columbus, O., Feb. 23, 1836; *see also* Robert Ware to John Tyler, Columbus, Feb. 24, 1836, in *LTT,* I, 520-22.

[37] Chitwood, *Tyler,* 149-50.

[38] John Tyler to William F. Pendleton, Gloucester, Oct. 27, 1836, *TPLC;* John Tyler to James Iredell, Jr., Gloucester, Nov. 16, 1836, *James Iredell, Jr., Papers,* Duke University Library.

[39] John Tyler to William F. Pendleton, Gloucester, Oct. 27, 1836, *TPLC;* Chitwood, *Tyler,* 155-56; John Tyler to Henry A. Wise, Gloucester, Jan. 23, 1837, in *LTT,* III, 70-71.

[40] John Tyler to Thomas Ritchie, Williamsburg, Mar. 21, 1840, *TPLC;* John Tyler to Henry A. Wise, Gloucester, Jan. 23, 1837, in *LTT,* III, 70-71.

[41] Robert Tyler, *Poems* (Richmond, 1839), *passim;* Robert Tyler, *Ahasuerus. A Poem* (Richmond, 1842), *passim;* and Robert Tyler, *Death; Or, Medorus' Dream* (Richmond, 1843), *passim;* Priscilla Cooper Tyler to Mary Grace Cooper, Williamsburg, Oct. 1839, in Coleman, *Priscilla Cooper Tyler,* 75; John Tyler to Mrs. Martha Rochelle, Williamsburg, Oct. 20, 1838; John Tyler to John Tyler, Jr., Williamsburg,

Nov. 4, 1838; John Tyler to Mrs. Martha Rochelle, Washington, Sept. 4, 1841; Oct. 22, 1843, *James Rochelle Papers,* Duke University Library. See also Priscilla Cooper Tyler to Mary Grace Cooper, Williamsburg, Oct. 1839, in Coleman, *Priscilla Cooper Tyler,* 75. John, Jr., returned to Jerusalem in early May 1844 to see the new baby daughter Mattie had given birth to. A son, James Rochelle Tyler, had been born in 1841. Tyler's letters to Mattie in May 1844 sent "Many kisses to the little stranger" and apologized for his son's tardy departure from Washington. John Tyler to Mrs. Mattie Rochelle Tyler, Washington, May 1, 1844, *TPLC* (photostat). Midshipman James H. Rochelle became Passed Midshipman on Aug. 10, 1847; Master on Sept. 14, 1855; Lieutenant on Sept. 15, 1855. When the Civil War came he went with the Confederacy and Navy records list him as "dismissed, 17 April, 1861."

[42] Coleman, *Priscilla Cooper Tyler,* 1-6, 8-10, 26-27, 31-37, 38-58. The only good house they had on the 1837-1838 tour was in Charleston on Dec. 19, 1837. They played *Much Ado About Nothing.* Happily, the great Florida Indian Chief Osceola was in the audience and a curious crowd paid in $1200 to see him react to the Coopers' presentation of Shakespeare. *Ibid.,* 60.

[43] *Ibid.,* 65-66.

[44] *Ibid.,* 69-73. Mrs. Coleman in her excellent study of Priscilla Cooper Tyler cites passages from ten of Robert's love letters to Priscilla written during the spring and summer of 1839. Details of the romance during 1837 and 1838, and the letters of that period, have apparently not survived.

[45] *Ibid.,* 78-79, 81-82.

[46] *Ibid.,* 79-80, 81, 84-85.

CHAPTER 6

[1] John Tyler to Nathaniel B. Tucker, Williamsburg, Sept. 26, 1837; John Tyler to James Lyons, Williamsburg, Dec. 29, 1838; John Tyler to George G. Waggaman, Williamsburg, Feb. 15, 1838, *TPLC;* William C. Preston to John Tyler, Washington, Dec. 20, 1837, in *LTT,* I, 587; Cole, *The Whig Party in the South,* 56; Carter Beverley to John Tyler, Westmoreland County, Jan. 28, 1839, *TPLC;* John Tyler to Henry A. Wise, Williamsburg, Dec. 26, 1838, in *LTT,* III, 74.

[2] Schlesinger, *The Age of Jackson,* 217-26; Robert Gray Gunderson, *The Log Cabin Campaign* (Lexington, Kentucky, 1957), 13-19; Van Deusen, *The Life of Henry Clay,* 301-4; William C. Preston to John Tyler, Washington, Dec. 30, 1837, in *LTT,* I, 586.

[3] *LTT,* I, 596; Wise, *Seven Decades of the Union,* 162-63, 167-69. Wise dates these important interviews and commitments only as occurring "one evening in the session of 1838-1839." Internal evidence, however, would indicate that the Clay-White exchanges took place in late January or early February 1839. For further evidence of Clay's accommodation with the states' rights viewpoint *see* Henry Clay to Nathaniel B. Tucker, Ashland, Oct. 10, 1839; William C. Preston to John Tyler, Washington, Dec. 20, 1837; John Tyler to Henry A. Wise, Williamsburg, Dec. 26, 1838, in *LTT,* I, 601-2, 587; III, 73-74.

[4] Henry Clay to Francis Brooke, Washington, Dec. 26; 20, 1838, in Colton, *The Private Correspondence of Henry Clay,* 435, 432; John Tyler to Henry A. Wise, Williamsburg, Dec. 26, 1838, in *LTT,* III, 73; John Tyler to James Lyons, Williamsburg, Dec. 29, 1838, *TPLC.*

[5] Chitwood, *Tyler,* 157-58; *LTT,* I, 591-93; Wise, *Seven Decades of the Union,* 158-60.

[6] Chitwood, *Tyler,* 160, 162-63, 170-71; *LTT,* I, 587-93; Cole, *The Whig Party in the South,* 56; Simms, *The Rise of the Whigs in Virginia,* 141.

[7] John Tyler to Henry Clay, Williamsburg, Sept. 18, 1839, in *LTT*, III, 75-77; John Tyler to John H. Waggaman, Williamsburg, Aug. 30, 1839, *TPLC*.
[8] John Tyler, Speech in the Virginia House of Delegates, Feb. 14, 1839, in *LTT*, II, 140-48; *ibid.*, I, 608; John Tyler to the Whigs of Louisville, Ky. [Williamsburg], July 19, 1839, in *ibid.*, 618.
[9] [Lyon G. Tyler], "John Tyler and the Vice Presidency," *Tyler's Quarterly*, IX (October 1927), 89-95.
[10] Gunderson, *Log Cabin Campaign*, 45-47, 52; T. W. Barnes, *Memoirs of Thurlow Weed*, 2 vols. (Boston and New York, 1884), I, 480-82; II, 75-77; Wise, *Seven Decades of the Union*, 165-66.
[11] Gunderson, *Log Cabin Campaign*, 57-62; Harriet A. Weed (ed.), *Autobiography of Thurlow Weed* (New York, 1883), 481; *LTT*, I, 593-94.
[12] Horace Greeley, *Recollections of a Busy Life* (New York, 1868), 131; Chitwood, *Tyler*, 166-67; *LTT*, I, 595. Greeley suggested that the tear-shedding story actually brought Tyler the Vice-Presidential nomination. Tyler later told Julia Gardiner Tyler, however, that the story was "the greatest of the falsehoods propagated" against him.
[13] Wise, *Seven Decades of the Union*, 170-72; *LTT*, I, 595.
[14] Gunderson, *Log Cabin Campaign*, 62-64; [Lyon G. Tyler], "John Tyler and the Vice Presidency," *loc. cit.*, 89-95; Chitwood, *Tyler*, 169-71; *LTT*, III, 36; Barnes, *Memoirs of Thurlow Weed*, II, 76-77; Cleaves, *Old Tippecanoe*, 318.
[15] *LTT*, I, 596, 618; Chitwood, *Tyler*, 172-73; Appendix B, 472-73. Professor Chitwood carefully analyzes the charge that Tyler quietly made pro-Bank noises at Harrisburg to improve the chances of his nomination. He demonstrates that the evidence for the charge ranges from the weak to the imaginary. Gunderson, *Log Cabin Campaign*, 65-66; Allan Nevins (ed.), *The Diary of Philip Hone*, 2 vols. (New York, 1927), II, 553; Abraham Lincoln to John T. Stuart, Jan. 20, 1840, in John G. Nicolay and John Hay, *The Complete Works of Abraham Lincoln*. 12 vols. (New York, 1905) I, 39-40.
[16] *LTT*, II, 1-2; Gunderson, *Log Cabin Campaign*, 176-77, 239-40; Nathan Sargent, *Public Men and Events*. 2 vols. (Philadelphia, 1875), II, 115-16; Gunderson, *Log Cabin Campaign*, 25, 114-15, 101-7, 154-55, 133-34, 141, 128.
[17] Cleaves, *Old Tippecanoe*, 303, 312-13, 316, 319; Gunderson, *Log Cabin Campaign*, 51, 73-75, 170-71, 225; *LTT*, I, 620; Abell, *Tyler*, 181.
[18] John Tyler to James Iredell, Jr., Williamsburg, June 5, 1840, *James Iredell, Jr., Papers*, Duke University Library; *see also* John Tyler to Henry A. Wise, Williamsburg, Apr. 28, 1840, *TPLC*.
[19] Abell, *Tyler*, 181; Wise, *Seven Decades of the Union*, 177-78; *LTT*, I, 619-20.
[20] Chitwood, *Tyler*, 184-88, 195; Gunderson, *Log Cabin Campaign*, 195-97; *LTT*, I, 620, 621-22; Abell, *Tyler*, 181; Chitwood, *Tyler*, 191-92; Appendix C, 475-77. In a speech in the House on Sept. 10, 1841, Rep. John Minor Botts of Virginia, a bitter enemy of the Tyler administration, quoted an excerpt from the Wheeling *Gazette* of August 21, 1840, which declared that Tyler had advocated a national bank in a Wheeling address. According to the extract Botts cited, Tyler "pulled from his pocket an empty purse, and, shaking it at the multitude, ridiculed the idea of a metallic currency, abused the Sub-treasury [i.e., Independent Treasury], and avowed a preference for 'good United States bank notes.'" An attempt by Professor Chitwood in the 1930s to locate a copy of the Wheeling *Gazette* for Aug. 21, 1840, failed, as did an effort by this writer in 1959. The Botts charge is thus impossible to check one way or the other. It might be pointed out, however, that the Botts speech of Sept. 10, 1841, was otherwise filled with factual inaccuracies.
[21] The letter of the Henrico, Virginia, Democrats to Tyler is dated Henrico, Oct. 3, 1840; Tyler's answer is dated Williamsburg, Oct. 16, 1840. Both letters are published in Abell, *Tyler*, 176-80.
[22] Gunderson, *Log Cabin Campaign*, 187-91, 198-200; *LTT*, I, 597-98, 609, 612, 615-16; II, 60.

[23] Gunderson, *Log Cabin Campaign*, 5, 78–83.
[24] *Ibid.*, 3–4, 6, 219–21, 242–46, 249–51; Roseboom, *A History of Presidential Elections*, 122.
[25] Gunderson, *Log Cabin Campaign*, 254–58; Roseboom, *A History of Presidential Elections*, 122–23; *LTT*, I, 629–32.
[26] Alexander Gardiner to ——, New York, Sept. 26, 1840; Alexander Gardiner to David Gardiner, New York, Jan. 1841, *GPY*.
[27] *LTT*, I, 600; John Tyler to Henry A. Wise, Williamsburg, Nov. 25; Dec. 20, 1840, in *ibid.*, III, 84–88. For a similar view see Virginia Governor Thomas W. Gilmer's open letter to Louisa County, Va., Whigs, in *ibid.*, I, 609–10.
[28] Cleaves, *Old Tippecanoe*, 333.
[29] Charles F. Adams (ed.), *Memoirs of John Quincy Adams.* 12 vols. (Philadelphia, 1874–1877), X, 372; *LTT*, II, 9, 95, 127; III, 52–53; Alexander Gardiner to David Gardiner, New York, Apr. [9], 1841, *GPY;* Cleaves, *Old Tippecanoe*, 331.
[30] *Ibid.*, 333; *LTT*, II, 10–11; Benjamin Perley Poore, *Reminiscences*, 2 vols. (New York, 1886), I, 245–46; Wise, *Seven Decades of the Union*, 179–80; E. F. Ellet, *Court Circles of the Republic* (Hartford, 1869), 284; John Tyler to Mr. Higgins, Sherwood Forest, Feb. 26, 1853, in *LTT*, II, 163.
[31] George R. Poage, *Henry Clay and the Whig Party* (Chapel Hill, 1936), 18–20; *LTT*, II, Appendix E, 704; III, 89–91; Gunderson, *Log Cabin Campaign*, 265; Cleaves, *Old Tippecanoe*, 330–31.
[32] John Tyler to Thomas W. Gilmer, Williamsburg, Jan. 7, 1841, in *LTT*, II, 14; *ibid.*, III, 86–87; Cleaves, *Old Tippecanoe*, 335.
[33] Ellet, *Court Circles of the Republic,* 286; Gunderson, *Log Cabin Campaign*, 266; Cleaves, *Old Tippecanoe*, 336. For text of Tyler's speech see Washington *Madisonian,* Mar. 6, 1841; also Chitwood, *Tyler*, 200–1.
[34] Cleaves, *Old Tippecanoe*, 229, 336–37; Peter Harvey, *Reminiscences and Anecdotes of Daniel Webster* (Boston, 1890), 160–63; Poore, *Reminiscences*, I, 250; Richardson, *Messages and Papers of the Presidents*, IV, 5–21.
[35] Cleaves, *Old Tippecanoe*, 339; *LTT*, II, 11; Gunderson, *Log Cabin Campaign*, 269.
[36] Poage, *Henry Clay and the Whig Party*, 30–31.
[37] *Ibid.*, 31; Sargent, *Public Men and Events*, II, 115–16; Henry Clay to William Henry Harrison, Washington, Mar. 15, 1841, in Colton, *Private Correspondence of Henry Clay*, 432; Ellet, *Court Circles of the Republic*, 287.
[38] Cleaves, *Old Tippecanoe*, 342–43; Gunderson, *Log Cabin Campaign*, 273; *LTT*, II, 11; Marx, *Health of the Presidents*, 130–131; Wise, *Seven Decades of the Union*, 180.

CHAPTER 7

[1] *LTT*, II, 11–12; Chitwood, *Tyler*, 202. The myths relating to Tyler's tears and to his attempt to borrow money from lawyer William S. Peachy are found in Fraser, *Democracy in the Making: The Jackson-Tyler Era*, 152–57. Where they originated is anyone's guess.
[2] Chitwood, *Tyler*, 203; John Tyler to James Buchanan, Sherwood Forest, Oct. 16, 1848, in *LTT*, II, 13.
[3] Robert J. Morgan, *A Whig Embattled: The Presidency under John Tyler* (Lincoln, Neb., 1954), 59–60; Chitwood, *Tyler*, 270; Abel P. Upshur to Nathaniel B. Tucker, July 28, 1841, in *LTT*, II, 115.
[4] John Tyler to Nathaniel B. Tucker, Washington, July 28, 1841; John Tyler to William C. Rives, Washington, Apr. 9, 1841, in *ibid.*, 53, 20.
[5] Duff Green to Abel P. Upshur, Washington, Dec. 29, 1842, in *ibid.*, 25–26;

John Tyler to [?] Lord, Pittsfield, Mass., Sept. 7, 1849, in *Tyler's Quarterly,* VIII (January 1927), 181.

⁶ Chitwood, *Tyler,* 204–5; John Tyler to Nathaniel B. Tucker, Washington, Apr. 25, 1841; John Tyler to Henry Clay, Washington, Apr. 30, 1841, in *LTT,* II, 32; III, 93–94.

⁷ Henry Clay to Nathaniel B. Tucker, Ashland, Apr. 15, 1841, in *ibid.,* II, 30; Mordecai N. Noah [pseud. "Horace Walpole"], "Reminiscences and Random Recollections of the Tyler Administration," New York *Sunday Dispatch,* May 10, 1846. Hereafter cited as Noah, "Reminiscences." Chitwood, *Tyler,* 212; John Tyler to William C. Rives, Washington, May 8, 1841, in *Tyler's Quarterly,* XII (October 1930), 85–86.

⁸ Daniel Webster, *The Writings and Speeches of Daniel Webster* (Nat. Ed.), 18 vols. (Boston, 1905), XV, 187.

⁹ Chitwood, *Tyler,* 210; Thomas W. Gilmer to George Stillman, Richmond, Apr. 13, 1841, in *Tyler's Quarterly,* VII (October 1925), 106; Henry A. Wise to Nathaniel B. Tucker, Washington, May 29, 1841; Abel P. Upshur to Nathaniel B. Tucker, Washington, Aug. 11, 1842, in *LTT,* II, 34, 178–79.

¹⁰ Poage, *Henry Clay and the Whig Party,* 43; James H. Hopkins, *Political Parties in the United States* (New York, 1900), 66; Chitwood, *Tyler,* 217; R. P. Letcher to J. J. Crittenden, Frankfort, June 21, 1842, in *LTT,* II, 5; Morgan, *A Whig Embattled,* 39–40.

¹¹ Waddy Thompson to John Tyler, Mexico City, Jan. 30, 1843; Henry A. Wise to Leslie Coombs, Washington, Dec. 29, 1842, in *LTT,* II, 15–17; III, 106.

¹² John Tyler to Nathaniel B. Tucker, Washington, July 28, 1841, in *ibid.,* II, 54; John Tyler to William C. Rives, Washington, May 8, 1841, in *Tyler's Quarterly,* XII (October 1930), 85; John Tyler, *Statement Published in the Washington Madisonian,* Apr. 23; 26, 1845, in *LTT,* II, 68–69, 33–34.

¹³ Chitwood, *Tyler,* 221; *LTT,* II, 33–34; Alexander Gardiner to [David Gardiner], [New York], June 9, 1841, *GPY* (fragment of draft letter).

¹⁴ John Rutherfoord to John Tyler, Richmond, June 21, 1841, *John Rutherfoord Papers,* Duke University Library; John Tyler to John Rutherfoord (Confidential), Washington, June 23, 1841, *Tyler Papers,* Duke University Library.

¹⁵ Chitwood, *Tyler,* 223–24; *LTT,* III, 39.

¹⁶ John Tyler to Nathaniel B. Tucker, Washington, July 23, 1841, in *ibid.,* II, 54; George Poindexter to John Tyler, New York, July 16, 1841, *TPLC.*

¹⁷ Chitwood, *Tyler,* 225–26; New York *Herald,* Aug. 5, 1841; Thomas W. Gilmer to Franklin Minor, Washington, Aug. 7, 1841, in *LTT,* II, Appendix E, 706–9; Poage, *Henry Clay and the Whig Party,* 70–72; John B. Christian to Nathaniel B. Tucker, Washington, Aug. 10, 1841, in [Lyon G. Tyler (ed.)], "Correspondence of Judge N. B. Tucker," *William and Mary College Quarterly Historical Magazine,* XII (January 1904), 143–44; A. H. H. Stuart Statement, in *LTT,* II, 78; John M. Botts to John Tyler, Washington, Aug. 10, 1841, in anon., *A Defense of the President Against the Attacks of Mr. Botts and the Clay Party* (Pamphlet); n.p., n.d. [1842]), 5–6.

¹⁸ *LTT,* II, 71–72, 101; Carl Schurz, *Life of Henry Clay,* 2 vols. (Boston, 1887), II, 207; Benton, *Thirty Years' View,* II, 328–30; Chitwood, *Tyler,* 228–29; New York *Herald,* Nov. 22, 1841; Amos Kendall to John Tyler [Washington], Aug. 21, 1841; J. Johnson to John Tyler, Philadelphia, Aug. 23, 1841, *TPLC.* Jackson's initial opinion of Tyler as President was low—"an imbecile in the Executive Chair," he designated Tyler. But after the first Bank veto one of Jackson's friends wrote him that "it will do Old Hickory's heart good when he hears of the veto. It is said that Tyler got hold of one of Jackson's pens and it wouldn't write any other way but plain and straightforward." Oscar D. Lambert, *Presidential Politics in the United States, 1841–1844* (Durham, N.C., 1936), 37.

¹⁹ *LTT,* II, 92, 166; *Congressional Globe,* 27 Cong., 1 Sess., 368–69; Poage, *Henry Clay and the Whig Party,* 75–78.

[20] The Coffee House Letter is printed in *LTT*, II, 112.

[21] Professor Chitwood had carefully examined these charges in great detail and categorically rejected them. See Chitwood, *Tyler*, 218, 237, 172-73, 191-92; Appendix B, 472-73; Appendix C, 475-77. Similarly, this writer has found no evidence of even a circumstantial sort that would lend credence to the Botts allegations. See also *LTT*, II, 105-6; and *A Defense of the President Against the Attacks of Mr. Botts and the Clay Party*, passim.

[22] *LTT*, III, 39-40, 53; II, 86-87; Chitwood, *Tyler*, 241-42, 258-59; Poage, *Henry Clay and the Whig Party*, 83-84.

[23] Henry A. Wise to Nathaniel B. Tucker, Washington, Aug. 29, 1841, in *LTT*, II, 91; Lyons is quoted in *ibid.*, 41.

[24] Adams, *Memoirs*, X, 544-45; Poage, *Henry Clay and the Whig Party*, 88-89; Chitwood, *Tyler*, 244.

[25] *LTT*, II, 102, 111; Duff Green to Abel P. Upshur, Washington, Dec. 29, 1842, in *ibid.*, 25; John J. Crittenden to [John Tyler], *Draft Book of Notes, Speeches and Letters*, n.d., *John J. Crittenden Papers*, Duke University Library.

[26] Richardson, *Messages and Papers of the Presidents*, IV, 68-72; Chitwood, *Tyler*, 244-46; Wise, *Seven Decades of the Union*, 190; Abell, *Tyler*, 202; John Tyler to Daniel Webster, Washington, Oct. 11, 1841, in *LTT*, II, 126.

[27] See editorial comments collected in *TPLC*, Book V, Items 95, 101, 152.

[28] Chitwood, *Tyler*, 277; *LTT*, II, 81, 115-16; III, 41; John Tyler, Jr., to Lyon G. Tyler, Washington, Jan. 29, 1883, in *ibid.*, 122; Chitwood, *Tyler*, 274; *LTT*, II, 94-95; 110-11; John J. Crittenden, *Draft Book of Notes, Speeches and Letters, John J. Crittenden Papers*, Duke University Library; John J. Crittenden to John Tyler, Washington, Sept. 11, 1841; and John J. Crittenden to Chapman Coleman, Washington, Sept. 10, 1841, *John J. Crittenden Papers*, Duke University Library; John Tyler to J. S. Cunningham, Sherwood Forest, Oct. 26, 1851, *TPLC*; John Tyler, Letter to Norfolk [Va.] Democratic Association [Washington], Dec. 2, 1844, in *LTT*, II, 96; John Tyler to Alexander Gardiner, Sherwood Forest, May 6, 1845, *TPLC*; John Tyler, *Statement in Answer to the Report of the House Committee, in August, 1842*, in *LTT*, II, 100.

[29] *Diary of Philip R. Fendall*, Sept. 23, 1841, *Philip Richard Fendall Papers*, Duke University Library; Nevins, *Diary of Philip Hone*, Sept. 11, 1841, II, 560.

[30] *The Andover Husking: A Political Tale, Suited to the Circumstances of the Present Time, and Dedicated to the Whigs of Mass.* (Pamphlet; Boston, 1842), 14-15; Henry A. Wise to Nathaniel B. Tucker, Washington, Aug. 29; Sept. 5, 1841, in *LTT*, II, 90, 120; John B. Christian to Nathaniel B. Tucker, Washington, Aug. 10, 1841, in [Lyon G. Tyler]. "Correspondence of Judge N. B. Tucker," *loc. cit.*, 143; Chitwood, *Tyler*, 279-80; Daniel Webster to Nicholas Biddle, Washington, Mar. 2, 1843, in McGrane, *The Correspondence of Nicholas Biddle*, 345-46.

[31] John Tyler to Thomas A. Cooper, Washington, Oct. 8, 1841; John Tyler to Daniel Webster, Washington, Oct. 1, 1841; John Tyler to Littleton W. Tazewell, Washington, Oct. 11, 1841, in *LTT*, II, 125, 123, 128; John Tyler to Daniel Webster, Washington, Oct. 11, 1841, in *Tyler's Quarterly*, VIII (July 1926), 18; John Tyler to John C. Spencer, Washington, Mar. 13, 1843, *TPLC*; John Tyler to Littleton W. Tazewell, Washington, Aug. 26, 1842, in *LTT*, II, 184.

[32] George T. Curtis, *Life of Daniel Webster*, 2 vols. (New York, 1870), II, 207-9; [J. P. Kennedy], *Defense of the Whigs* (New York, 1844), 122-24; *LTT*, II, 102-3; *New York Herald*, Apr. 9, 1842.

[33] For a sampling of these pamphlets see *John, the Traitor; or, the Force of Accident. A Plain Story by One Who Has Whistled at the Plough* (New York, 1843), 1-43; Anti-Janius, *Who and What is John Tyler* (New York, 1843), 1-16; see also Anon., *John Tyler: His History, Character, and Position* (New York, 1843), 1-40; John L. Dorsey, *Observations on the Political Character and Services of President Tyler and His Cabinet*. By a native of Maryland (Washington, 1841), 1-131; *The Andover Husking*, 1-27.

[34] John B. Christian to Nathaniel B. Tucker, Washington, Aug. 10, 1841, in [Lyon G. Tyler], "Correspondence of Judge N. B. Tucker," *loc. cit.*, 143-44; Washington Seawell to Maria Tyler Seawell, Fort Micanopy, Fla., Sept. 18, 1841, in *Tyler's Quarterly,* II (October 1920), 111. Major Seawell (1802-1888) was the brother of John Boswell Seawell, a prominent attorney of Gloucester, Va., who had married Maria Henry Tyler, the President's sister. *LTT,* II, 98-102; Alexander Gardiner to Julia Gardiner Tyler, New York, Dec. 15, 1844; Margaret Gardiner to Julia Gardiner Tyler, New York, July 11, 1844, *TFP;* Alexander Gardiner to Julia Gardiner Tyler, New York, July 14, 1844, *TPLC;* New York *Herald,* May 5, 1843; Oct. 23, 1844; Margaret Gardiner to Robert Tyler, East Hampton, May [7], 1843, *TFP;* Noah, "Reminiscences," New York *Sunday Dispatch,* Mar. 29, 1846.

[35] E. Littell to Daniel Webster, Philadelphia, Sept. 14, 1841; John Tyler to Daniel Webster, Washington, Oct. 11, 1841; John Tyler to Littleton W. Tazewell, Washington, Oct. 11, 1841; Williamsburg, Nov. 2, 1841, in *LTT,* III, 97; II, 126, 127, 129-31.

[36] Richardson, *Messages and Papers of the Presidents,* IV, 84-87; Abell, *Tyler,* 213-15; *LTT,* II, 131-34; Abel P. Upshur to Nathaniel B. Tucker, Washington, Dec. 23, 1841, in *ibid.,* 155.

[37] John Tyler, Letter to the Philadelphia Fourth of July Committee, Washington, July 2, 1842, in *ibid.,* 171; *see also* Dorsey, *Observations on the Political Character and Services of President Tyler,* 128-29; John Tyler to Nathaniel B. Tucker, Washington, June 16, 1842, in *LTT,* II, 168.

[38] John Tyler, Letter to the Philadelphia Fourth of July Committee, Washington, July 2, 1842; John Tyler to Robert McCandlish, Washington, July 10, 1842; Abel P. Upshur to Nathaniel B. Tucker, Washington, Mar. 6; 13; 28, 1842 in *ibid.,* 171, 173, 156-58, 165.

[39] David Gardiner to Alexander Gardiner, Washington, Jan. 11; 20; Feb. 6, 1843; David Gardiner to David L. Gardiner, Washington [Feb. 13, 1843]. Gardiner's political friends in New York had decidedly less sympathetic views of Tyler. See J. J. Bailey to David Gardiner, New York, Sept. 12, 1842, *GPY.*

[40] *LTT,* II, 150-51.

[41] J. J. Crittenden to Henry Clay, Washington, July 1842, in Anna M. B. Coleman (ed.), *The Life of John J. Crittenden,* 2 vols. (Philadelphia, 1871), I, 199; John Tyler to Littleton W. Tazewell, Washington, Aug. 26, 1842, in *LTT,* II, 184; Daniel Webster to John Tyler, Washington, Aug. 8, 1842, in *Tyler's Quarterly,* VIII (July 1926), 21; *LTT,* II, 174-75; Abel P. Upshur to Nathaniel B. Tucker, Washington, Aug. 11, 1842, in *ibid.,* 179; Chitwood, *Tyler,* 298-301.

[42] *Ibid.,* 301-2.

[43] The bill passed the House 105 to 102 and the Senate 24 to 23. *LTT,* II, 182; see also *The Andover Husking,* 18-21. There is some speculation that Tyler felt honor-bound to sign the controversial "Black Tariff" because he had based his earlier veto of the 1842 tariff measure on the fact that it contained a distribution clause. The bill he signed at least contained no distribution proviso. There is no specific evidence for this interpretation of Tyler's motives, although it is not an improbable one. In any event, the President's acceptance of the high tariff measure (it went far beyond the revenue needs of the moment) was later a major impediment to his return to the Democratic party.

[44] Chitwood, *Tyler,* 303; Henry Clay to J. J. Crittenden, Ashland, July 16, 1842, in Coleman, *Crittenden,* I, 199. It was Upshur's opinion that the "Clay-men are *afraid* to impeach the President. I daresay that Botts will attempt it, but even his own party will not sustain him." Abel P. Upshur to Nathaniel B. Tucker, Washington [July] 1842; John Tyler to Robert McCandlish, Washington, July 10, 1842, in *LTT,* II, 174, 173.

[45] *Ibid.,* 189; Chitwood, *Tyler,* 303; Abell, *Tyler,* 242; David Gardiner to Alexander Gardiner, Washington, Jan. 11, 1843, *GPY.*

[46] Abel P. Upshur to Nathaniel B. Tucker, Washington, Mar. 28, 1842, in *LTT,*

II, 165; Poore, *Reminiscences,* I, 271-72; [Alexander Gardiner] to Editor of the Washington *Globe* [New York], Nov. 15, 1842; *LTT,* II, 150-51; Abell, *Tyler,* 204.

[47] John Tyler to Alexander Gardiner, East Hampton, July 11, 1846, in *LTT,* II, 341; *ibid.,* 188; Abel P. Upshur to Nathaniel B. Tucker, Washington [July] 1842; John Tyler to Mr. Higgins, Sherwood Forest, Feb. 26, 1853, in *ibid.,* 174, 163-64.

[48] John Tyler to Alexander Gardiner, East Hampton, July 11, 1846; John Tyler to Daniel Webster, Williamsburg, Oct. 11, 1841, in *ibid.,* 341, 254.

[49] *Ibid.,* 374-79, 383.

CHAPTER 8

[1] Langford, *The Ladies of the White House,* 330-31; Coleman, *Priscilla Cooper Tyler,* 86-88. In the Langford book the details of life in the White House during Priscilla's tenure as hostess and much of the surviving information on Letitia Christian Tyler's illness there are taken from two letters made available to Mrs. Langford years later by John Tyler, Jr. They are: Letitia Tyler Semple to John Tyler, Jr., Baltimore, Mar. 27, 1869; and John Tyler, Jr., to Laura Holloway Langford, n.p., n.d. (late 1870s). Both letters, particularly the latter, contain factual inaccuracies, mistaken recollections, and confused chronology and must be treated with extreme care.

[2] *Ibid.,* 89.

[3] Langford, *The Ladies of the White House,* 331-32; Coleman, *Priscilla Cooper Tyler,* 87, 99; John Tyler to Robert Tyler, Sherwood Forest, Nov. 1, 1850, *TPLC.*

[4] Coleman, *Priscilla Cooper Tyler,* 88-89.

[5] *Ibid.,* 89-91; Chevalier de Bacourt, *Souvenirs of a Diplomat* (New York, 1885), 191, 209, 214; Adams, *Memoirs,* XI, 174; *LTT,* II, 177.

[6] Coleman, *Priscilla Cooper Tyler,* 101.

[7] *Ibid.,* 101-2.

[8] *Ibid.,* 92.

[9] *Ibid.,* 93.

[10] *Ibid.,* 93-94, 90-91.

[11] *LTT,* II, 311-12; New York *Herald,* Nov. 12, 1844.

[12] *Ibid.,* Nov. 27, 1844; John Tyler to Mr. Benson, Washington, Nov. 5, 1842; John Tyler to Mary Tyler Jones, Washington, Dec. 20, 1843, *TPLC.*

[13] Coleman, *Priscilla Cooper Tyler,* 84-85, 98.

[14] John Tyler to Mary Tyler Jones, Washington, July 6, 1842, in *LTT,* II, 172; John Tyler to Elizabeth Tyler Waller, Washington, Jan. 16, 1843, *Tyler Papers,* Duke University Library.

[15] Coleman, *Priscilla Cooper Tyler,* 99; Langford, *The Ladies of the White House,* 329; H. March to John Tyler, Trades, [Va.], Dec. 25, 1841, *Tyler Papers,* Duke University Library.

[16] Coleman, *Priscilla Cooper Tyler,* 99; *LTT,* II, 189; Letitia Tyler Semple to Norma Doswell, Washington, Mar. 29, 1897, *TFP.* Letitia Christian Tyler was buried at Cedar Grove in New Kent County, Va.

[17] Priscilla Cooper Tyler to Juliana Gardiner, Washington, n.d. [Dec. 1842-Jan. 1843], *GPY.*

[18] Emmie F. Farrar, *Old Virginia Houses Along the James* (New York, 1957), 123-25; John Tyler to Mary Tyler Jones, Washington, July 6, 1842, in *LTT,* II, 172; *ibid.,* Dec. 20, 1843; June 4, 1844, *TPLC;* Mary Tyler Jones to John Tyler, Sherwood Forest, n.d. [early 1843], *TFP;* Julia Gardiner to Alexander Gardiner, East Hampton, June 4, 1843, *GPY.*

[19] *Ibid.*, Washington, Dec. 13, 1842, *GPY*.
[20] *Ibid.;* Juliana Gardiner to David L. Gardiner, Washington, Dec. 19-23, 1842, *GPY*.
[21] *Ibid.*, Juliana Gardiner to [Alexander Gardiner], Washington, Feb. 12, 1843, *GPY*.
[22] Margaret Gardiner to Alexander and David L. Gardiner, Washington, Dec. 26, 1842; Jan. 7, 1843; Julia Gardiner to Alexander Gardiner, Washington, Dec. 27; 29, 1842; David Gardiner to David L. Gardiner, Washington, Dec. 25 [1842], *GPY*.
[23] Margaret Gardiner to David L. Gardiner, Washington, Jan. 29, 1843; Juliana Gardiner to [Alexander Gardiner], Washington, Feb. 12. 1843, *GPY*.
[24] Julia Gardiner to Alexander Gardiner, Washington, Dec. 13, 1842; Margaret Gardiner to Alexander and David L. Gardiner, Washington, Dec. 26, 1842; Juliana Gardiner to David L. Gardiner, Washington, Dec. 19-23, 1842, *GPY*.
[25] Margaret Gardiner to David L. Gardiner, Washington, Jan. 29, 1843; Juliana Gardiner to Alexander and David L. Gardiner, Washington, Feb. 17, 1843, *GPY*.
[26] *Ibid.*, Feb. 12; 15; 17, 1843; Margaret Gardiner to Alexander Gardiner, East Hampton, Apr. 7, 1843; Juliana Gardiner to Julia and Margaret Gardiner, New York, May 28, 1843, *GPY*.
[27] Julia Gardiner to Alexander Gardiner, Washington, Dec. 13, 1842, *GPY*.
[28] Margaret Gardiner for his David L. Gardiner, Washington, Dec. 18, 1842; Jan. 1; 7; Feb. 5; 14, 1843; Julia Gardiner to David L. Gardiner, Washington, Dec. 29, 1842, *GPY*.
[29] Julia Gardiner to Alexander Gardiner, Washington, Jan. 6, 1843; Margaret Gardiner to David L. Gardiner, Washington, Jan. 29, 1843, *GPY*. Margaret had excellent recollective powers. In this letter she quoted with surprising accuracy a humorous section of McDuffie's speech given four days earlier.
[30] Julia Gardiner to Alexander Gardiner, Washington, Dec. 27; 29, 1842; Margaret Gardiner to David L. Gardiner and Alexander Gardiner, Washington, Jan. 14, 1843; Margaret Gardiner to David L. Gardiner, Washington, Jan. 29, 1843; Margaret Gardiner to Alexander Gardiner, Washington, Mar. 7, 1843, *GPY*.
[31] New York *Herald*, Dec. 18, 1842. Congressmen and senators who regularly called on the Gardiners at Peyton's included Senators Richard H. Bayard (Del.) and Nathaniel P. Tallmadge (N.Y.); Representatives Caleb Cushing (Mass.), Edmund W. Hubard (Va.), Ira A. Eastman (N.H.), Francis Marion Ward (N.Y.), Richard D. Davis (N.Y.), Henry Van Rensselaer (N.Y.), Daniel D. Barnard (N.Y.), John B. Thompson (Ky.), Augustus O. Sollers (Md.) Francis W. Pickens (S.C.), and John Thompson Mason (Md.). Julia and Margaret attended the debates in the House or Senate on Dec. 12, 16, 21, 29, 1842; Jan. 1, 3, 6, 11, 25; Feb. 7, 15; and on Mar. 3, 1843. See *Gardiner Papers,* Dec. 13, 1842 to Mar. 7, 1843, Yale University Library, *passim*. One congressional caller, John T. Mason of Md., had roomed with David L. Gardiner at Princeton. This gave him an entree some of the others did not have. But Margaret thought Mason "a common looking man, and, as you say, not clean." Nor was Julia particularly overwhelmed when Mason rushed her at dances and sent her valentines. Margaret Gardiner to David L. and Alexander Gardiner, Washington, Jan. 7; 14; Feb. 15, 1843, *GPY*.
[32] *Ibid.*, Dec. 26, 1842; Jan. 1, 1843. David Gardiner chatted with Calhoun from time to time in December and January 1842-1843, and received from him the distinct impression that he planned to run in 1844. He hoped to establish a Northern anchor for his aspirations in New York state, counting on a break there between Van Buren's Albany Regency machine and that of Tammany Hall in New York City as an entree for his ambitions. See David Gardiner to David L. Gardiner, Washington, Dec. 25 [1842], *GPY*.
[33] Julia Gardiner to Alexander Gardiner, Washington, Dec. 13, 1842, *GPY*.
[34] *Ibid.;* Margaret Gardiner to David L. Gardiner, Washington, Dec. 18, 1842; Julia Gardiner to Alexander Gardiner, Washington, Dec. 27, 1842; Jan. 6, 1843;

Margaret Gardiner to Alexander Gardiner, Washington, Jan. 1; Feb. 5; 8, 1843; Julia Gardiner to Alexander Gardiner, East Hampton, Apr. 23, 1843; Juliana Gardiner to David L. Gardiner, Washington, Dec. 19–23, 1842, *GPY*. For the few sparse facts on the career of Richard R. Waldron see Daniel C. Haskell, *The United States Exploring Expedition, 1838–1842, and Its Publications, 1844–1874* (New York, 1942), 139; R. R. Waldron to Charles Wilkes, USS *Vincennes*, at Sea, Jan. 31, 1840, in Charles Wilkes, *Narrative of the United States Exploring Expedition*, 5 vols. (Philadelphia, 1844), II, 490. Waldron's Island is found on a chart in Charles Wilkes, *United States Exploring Expedition*, Vol. XXIII. Hydrography (Philadelphia, 1861), opp. p. 7. Waldron died Oct. 20, 1846, causes unknown, at the age of twenty-seven.

[35] Julia Gardiner to Alexander Gardiner, Washington, Dec. 29, 1842; Jan. 6, 1843; Margaret Gardiner to David L. and Alexander Gardiner, Washington, Jan. 7, 1843; Margaret Gardiner to Alexander Gardiner, Washington, Jan. 10, 1843, *GPY*.

[36] Julia Gardiner to Alexander Gardiner, Washington, Jan. 6, 1843, *GPY*.

[37] Juliana Gardiner to [Alexander Gardiner], Washington, Feb. 12, 1843; Margaret Gardiner to David L. and Alexander Gardiner, Washington, Feb. 15; 16, 1843; Juliana Gardiner to David L. Gardiner, Washington, Dec. 19–23, 1842; Margaret Gardiner to Alexander Gardiner, Washington, Mar. 7, 1843, *GPY*.

[38] *Ibid*.

[39] Pickens' letter of proposal dated Edgewood, May 8, 1843, has not survived. The section quoted is taken from Julia Gardiner to Alexander Gardiner, East Hampton, May 21, 1843, *GPY*. For her reply see Julia Gardiner to Francis W. Pickens, East Hampton, May 25, 1843. Margaret's view of the matter is found in Margaret Gardiner to Robert Tyler, East Hampton, Apr. 6, [1843], *TFP*.

[40] Margaret Gardiner to Alexander Gardiner, East Hampton, Apr. 3; June 12, 1843, *GPY;* Alexander Gardiner to Juliana Gardiner, New York, Aug. 6, 1843; Woodhouse Stevens to Julia Gardiner, Devonshire, England, July 16, 1843, *TFP;* Francis W. Pickens to David Gardiner, Edgewood, S.C., near Edgefield, Nov. 20, 1843; Feb. 11, 1844, *GPY*.

[41] Margaret Gardiner to Alexander Gardiner, Washington, Feb. 5; Mar. 7, 1843; Margaret Gardiner to David L. Gardiner, Washington, Mar. 14, 1843, *GPY*.

[42] McLean's first letter to Julia was posted in Cincinnati around Mar. 30, 1843. It was enclosed in a cover letter addressed to Alexander Gardiner at 14 Wall St. with instructions to forward it to Julia in East Hampton. In this way McLean hoped to keep the correspondence confidential from the gossipy post-office officials in East Hampton. For the same reason Julia sent her letters to Tyler, Pickens, and McLean through Alexander in New York and received their replies to her in like manner. She invariably insisted that Alexander pay the postage on all her letters to her beaux. As the intermediary in all this, Alexander financed a rather expensive correspondence—there was a twenty-five-cent charge on a letter from New York to Cincinnati, for example. Until this arrangement was worked out, however, there could be no certainty of privacy. Julia Gardiner to Alexander Gardiner, East Hampton, Apr. 3 [1843]; Alexander Gardiner to Julia Gardiner, New York [Apr. 1843]; Margaret Gardiner to Alexander Gardiner, East Hampton, Apr. 7, 1843; Julia Gardiner to Alexander Gardiner, East Hampton, Apr. 30, 1843, *GPY;* John McLean to Julia Gardiner, Cincinnati, Apr. 19, 1843, *TFP*.

[43] Julia Gardiner to Alexander Gardiner, East Hampton, May 21, 1843, *GPY*.

[44] Margaret Gardiner to David L. Gardiner, Washington, Jan. 14, 1843; Juliana Gardiner to David L. and Alexander Gardiner, Washington, Feb. 17, 1843, *GPY*.

[45] Margaret Gardiner to Alexander Gardiner, Washington, Feb. 8, 1843; Margaret Gardiner to David L. Gardiner, Washington, Feb. 11; 14; 28, 1843; Margaret Gardiner to David L. and Alexander Gardiner, Washington, Feb. 15, 1843, *GPY*.

At the Webster ball on Feb. 13 Julia was squired by Francis P. Granger, Harrison's Postmaster General, while Margaret was escorted by Arkansas Senator Ambrose H. Sevier until rescued by Robert Tyler. It was at this function that Henry A. Wise flirted so openly with Margaret. At General Easton's on Feb. 14 the girls were waltzed and otherwise rushed by Representative Edward D. White of Louisiana, Senator John Sargeant of Pennsylvania (Henry A. Wise's brother-in-law), Senator James Buchanan of Pennsylvania, and Representative Henry Van Rensselaer of New York. At the Wickliffe party of Feb. 28, Julia was handed in by John Tyler, Jr., and Margaret by Robert Tyler. "You have no idea how much attention this attracted," wrote Margaret. At most of the private functions the President's sons were particularly attentive to the Gardiner ladies.

[46] Juliana Gardiner to Alexander Gardiner, Washington, Jan. 27, 1843; Margaret Gardiner to David L. and Alexander Gardiner, Washington, Dec. 26, 1842; Jan. 7; 14; Mar. 11, 1843, *GPY*.

[47] Margaret Gardiner to David L. Gardiner, Washington, Dec. 18, 1842; Julia Gardiner to Alexander Gardiner, Washington, Dec. 27; 29, 1842, *GPY*.

[48] *Ibid.*, Dec. 27, 1842; Margaret Gardiner to Alexander Gardiner, Washington, Jan. 1, 1843, *GPY*.

[49] Julia Gardiner to Alexander Gardiner, Washington, Jan. 6, 1843. Juliana's Jan. 31 opinion of the celebrated Madame Bodisco was a minority one: "...a healthy fair looking woman well featured and good teeth, but not an interesting expression. Her manners are plain without any marked elegance or refinement. She is comely but destitute of the spirit and ate plateful upon plateful until your father thought Mr. [James I.] Roosevelt must be tired of serving her at supper." Juliana Gardiner to David L. Gardiner, Washington, Feb. 1, 1843, *GPY*.

[50] David Gardiner to Alexander Gardiner, Washington, Jan. 20, 1843; Juliana Gardiner to Alexander Gardiner, Washington, Jan. 27, 1843; Margaret Gardiner to Alexander Gardiner, Washington, Feb. 5, 1843; Juliana Gardiner to David L. Gardiner, Washington, Feb. 1, 1843, *GPY*.

[51] Robert Tyler, *Death; or, Medorus' Dream;* see also Robert Tyler, *Ahasuerus. A Poem,* and Robert Tyler, *Poems;* Margaret Gardiner to Alexander Gardiner, Washington, Feb. 5; 8, 1843, *GPY*.

[52] *Ibid.*, Feb. 8, 1843, *GPY*.

[53] *Ibid.*

[54] Margaret Gardiner to David L. and Alexander Gardiner, Washington, Feb. 15, 1843; David Gardiner to Alexander Gardiner, Washington, Feb. 6, 1843; Margaret Gardiner to Alexander Gardiner, Washington, Feb. 10, 1843, *GPY*.

[55] Juliana Gardiner to [Alexander Gardiner], Washington, Feb. 12, 1843, *GPY*.

[56] Margaret Gardiner to David L. Gardiner, Washington, Feb. 14, 1843, *GPY*.

[57] "Interview with Julia Gardiner Tyler," Washington, Winter, 1888–1889, *loc. cit.*

[58] Margaret Gardiner to David L. Gardiner, Washington, Feb. 15, 1843; Margaret Gardiner to Alexander Gardiner, Washington, Mar. 7, 1843, *GPY;* J. J. Bailey to Julia Gardiner [New York], May 12, 1843, *TFP;* Margaret Gardiner to David L. Gardiner, Washington, Feb. 14, 1843; Alexander Gardiner to [Margaret Gardiner], New York, Feb. 16, 1843; Margaret Gardiner to Alexander Gardiner, East Hampton, Mar. 30, 1843, *GPY*.

[59] Constance M. Green, *Washington: Village and Capital, 1880–1878* (Princeton, N.J., 1962), 153; Alexander Gardiner to [Margaret Gardiner], New York, Feb. 16, 1843; Juliana Gardiner to David L. Gardiner, Washington, Feb. 17, 1843; Margaret Gardiner to David L. Gardiner, Washington, Feb. 26; 28, 1843, *GPY*.

[60] *Ibid.*, Feb. 26, 1843, *GPY*.

[61] Margaret Gardiner to David L. and Alexander Gardiner, Washington, Mar. 9, 1843; Margaret Gardiner to Alexander Gardiner, East Hampton, June 12, 1843; copy of poem in Margaret Gardiner to Alexander Gardiner, Washington, Mar. 11,

1843; Margaret Gardiner to David L. and Alexander Gardiner, Washington, Mar. 9; 14, 1843; Margaret Gardiner to Alexander Gardiner, East Hampton, Apr. 7, 1843. The poem concludes:

>It speaks in praise of holy shrine;
>Of eyes upturned to Him divine,
>By whom are sins forgiven.
>
>II
>
>It tells the rose, which blooms so gay
>And courts the Zyphers kiss today,
>As if t'would never die;
>Its leaves, which perfume all around,
>Strew'd on the earth shall soon be found;
>Unnoticed, there to die.
>Unwelcome truth it tells to thee,
>Lovely in Beauty's majesty,
>The roses fate—is thine:
>Unlike in this—thy soul, so pure,
>Through endless ages shall endure.
>Kneel thou at Holy Shrines!

Margaret, her poetic ear trained by the serious efforts of Robert Tyler, did not think much of this as poetry. In relaying it to her brothers she made them "promise you won't laugh." Margaret Gardiner to David L. and Alexander Gardiner, Washington, Mar. 9, 1843, *GPY*.

[62] Margaret Gardiner to Alexander Gardiner, Washington, Mar. 7, 1843; Margaret Gardiner to David L. Gardiner, Washington, Mar. 14, 1843, *GPY*.

[63] Margaret Gardiner to Alexander Gardiner, Washington, Mar. 15, 1843, *GPY*. (Emphasis added.)

[64] Julia Gardiner Tyler to Juliana Gardiner, Old Point Comfort [July 1844], *TFP;* Margaret Gardiner to David L. Gardiner, Washington, Mar. 14, 1843, *GPY*.

[65] *Ibid.,* Feb. 14, 1843, *GPY;* Margaret Gardiner to Robert Tyler, East Hampton, May [6–8], 1843, *TFP;* Margaret Gardiner to Alexander Gardiner, Washington, Jan. 1; Mar. 7, 1843; Margaret Gardiner to David L. and Alexander Gardiner, Washington, Dec. 26, 1842, *GPY*.

[66] Julia Gardiner to Alexander Gardiner, East Hampton, Apr. 30, 1844; Margaret Gardiner to Alexander Gardiner, East Hampton, May 3, 1843; Juliana Gardiner to Julia and Margaret Gardiner, New York, May 28, 1843, *GPY*.

[67] Margaret Gardiner to David L. and Alexander Gardiner, Washington, Mar. 9; 14, 1843; Julia Gardiner to John Tyler [East Hampton, May 1843], quoted in Julia Gardiner to Alexander Gardiner, East Hampton, May 21, 1843; Julia Gardiner to Alexander Gardiner, East Hampton, May 21, 1843, *GPY*.

[68] Margaret Gardiner to Alexander Gardiner, East Hampton, May 3, 1843; John Tyler to Julia Gardiner, Sherwood Forest, May 28, 1843; Washington, Apr. [14], 1843, quoted in Julia Gardiner to Alexander Gardiner, East Hampton, June 4, 1843; Apr. 17, 1843; Julia Gardiner to Alexander Gardiner, East Hampton, June 4, 1843; John Tyler to Julia Gardiner, Washington, *GPY*.

[69] *Ibid.,* Apr. 3, 1843; J. J. Bailey to Julia Gardiner [New York, Apr. 1843], quoted in Julia Gardiner to Alexander Gardiner, East Hampton, May 21, 1843, *GPY*.

[70] *Ibid.,* Apr. 30; 23, 1843; Juliana Gardiner to Alexander Gardiner, East Hampton, June 6, 1843; Alexander Gardiner, Draft Tyler Article, Apr. 1843, *GPY*.

[71] David L. Gardiner to Alexander Gardiner, East Hampton, May 4, 1843; David Gardiner to Alexander Gardiner, East Hampton, May 11, 1843; Margaret

Gardiner to Alexander Gardiner, East Hampton, June 14, 1843; Julia Gardiner to Alexander Gardiner, East Hampton, May 21, 1843; David L. Gardiner to Alexander Gardiner, East Hampton, May 4; 11, 1843; Juliana Gardiner to Julia and Margaret Gardiner, New York, May 28, 1843, *GPY*.

[72] Juliana Gardiner to Alexander Gardiner, Troy, N.Y., Aug. 3, 1843; Julia Gardiner to Alexander Gardiner, East Hampton, June 4, 1843. At this time Julia wore her dresses 43½ inches in the front and 47 inches in the back; her height therefore was around 5'3". Her riding hat was 20¾ inches around the forehead with a 6-inch crown and a 3-inch brim. Alexander understandably had trouble keeping all these data straight. *Ibid.;* Margaret Gardiner to Alexander Gardiner, East Hampton, Nov. 2; 4, 1843; Julia Gardiner to Alexander Gardiner, East Hampton, Nov. 21, 1843, *GPY*. The house on Lafayette Place still stands. It is the current site of a restaurant and seems well beyond the possibility of restoration.

[73] *Ibid.*, June 4, 1843, *GPY*.

[74] Margaret Gardiner to Alexander Gardiner, Saratoga [Aug. 1843]; East Hampton, June 12; Oct. 31, 1843; David L. Gardiner to Alexander Gardiner, East Hampton, Aug. 6, 1843; Alexander Gardiner to Juliana Gardiner, New York, Aug. 3, 1843; Juliana Gardiner to Alexander Gardiner, Troy, N.Y., Aug. 3, 1843, *GPY*.

[75] John Tyler to Julia Gardiner, Washington, Oct. 25, 1843, quoted in Margaret Gardiner to Alexander Gardiner, East Hampton, Oct. 31, 1843; Julia Gardiner to Alexander Gardiner, East Hampton, Nov. 21, 1843; Leonard Wood, Jr., to David Gardiner, Steamship *Columbia,* approaching Halifax, Aug. 17, 1844, *GPY*. The mortgages, held by James Van Antwerpt, were for $2500, dated Dec. 27, 1843, and for $4342, dated Jan. 3, 1844. Both were at 6 per cent, to be paid off in full, principal and interest, by Jan. 3, 1849. See *Assets and Liabilities of David Gardiner* (March 1844), *TFP*.

[76] New York *Herald*, Oct. 27, 1845.

[77] See Alfred H. Miles, "The 'Princeton' Explosion," United States Naval Institute *Proceedings*, LII (November 1926), for an excellent study of the *Princeton* affair; also an attractively illustrated condensation of Miles in the Lynchburg (Va.) Foundry Company, *The Iron Worker*, XXI (Spring 1957), 1–11. The account herein of the *Princeton* explosion is based primarily upon an extensive recounting of it set down within a week of the disaster by Alexander Gardiner in a letter to the Reverend S. R. Ely of East Hampton, dated New York, Mar. 7, 1844, *GPY*. While in general it is similar in broad outline to previously reported accounts of the tragedy, it differs in the important details of the exact time of the explosion and in the movements and the sequence of movements of the principals on board the *Princeton* at that moment. With Alexander's version have been correlated various eyewitness and other accounts taken from Miles, "The 'Princeton' Explosion." Tyler's own recollection of the *Princeton* disaster did not appear until his "The Dead of the Cabinet" speech delivered at Petersburg, Va., Apr. 24, 1856, printed in *LTT*, II, 390–91. This too has been utilized. *See also* John Tyler to Mary Tyler Jones, Washington, Mar. 4, 1844, in *ibid.,* 289.

[78] Alexander Gardiner to S. R. Ely, New York, Mar. 7, 1844; Alexander Gardiner to Juliana Gardiner, Philadelphia, Feb. 29, 1844, *GPY*.

[79] Alexander Gardiner to S. R. Ely, New York, Mar. 7, 1844, *GPY;* John Tyler, "The Dead of the Cabinet," speech in Petersburg, Va., Apr. 24, 1856, in *LTT*, II, 390–91. The expenses of the public funeral were paid for by the United States. See Thomas Hart Benton, *Abridgment of the Debates of Congress from 1789 to 1856,* 16 vols. (New York, 1857–1861), XV (June 12, 1844), 151.

[80] S. R. Ely to Juliana Gardiner, East Hampton, Mar. 5, 1844, *GPY;* "Stranger Friend" to Gardiner Family, Mountains of Virginia, Mar. 3, 1844, *TFP;* John Tyler to Mrs. Thomas W. Gilmer, Washington, Mar. 4, 1844, *TPLC;* John Tyler to Alexander Gardiner, Washington, Mar. 15, 1844; Alexander Gardiner to John Tyler, New York, Mar. 30, 1844, *GPY*.

[81] David Gardiner was buried in East Hampton during the week of March 25, 1844, probably on Tuesday, March 26. Pallbearers at the funeral were former New York Governor Silas B. Wright, Charles H. Canott, Silas B. Strong, and Richard D. Davis—the same "Old Davis" who so recently had pursued Julia. In July 1846 an obelisk monument of polished granite was erected over the grave at a total cost of $700 for cutting, polishing, hauling, and setting. The lengthy inscription was worked out by Alexander. The family had some difficulty raising the cash to pay for it, so tied up in real estate was the Gardiner money. Julia said, however, she would not "consent to have one of less value erected." At the time of his death, David Gardiner held title deeds on Juliana's property—Lots 181, 183, 185, 187 on Chatham St., and Lots 1, 3, 5, 7 and 9 on Oliver St., New York City. These formed a solid block of property, since the Chatham St. lots backed onto those on Oliver St. The assessed value for these properties and for the house and lot in East Hampton for tax purposes was $30,500. They were worth, of course, much more (over $100,000), and they began rapidly appreciating again as the 1837–1843 depression wore off. The Gardiner furniture and personal belongings added an additional $5000 to the estate. Juliana still held in her own name three lots on Greenwich St. and one on Harrison St. Gardiner's children inherited the East Hampton and Greenwich and Oliver Sts. property in equal shares under his will. They deeded their shares to Juliana on April 18, 1844, for a consideration of $1 until her death. However, they apparently got some income from their portions. Gardiner's liabilities in the form of mortgages (most of the obligations had already been paid off) on his various properties came to $21,842. Of this $8000 had been borrowed in 1826 at 6 per cent and would be fully retired Jan. 3, 1849; $2500 had been borrowed in Dec. 1843 and $4342 in Jan. 1844 at 6 per cent and would be fully retired Jan. 3, 1849. For the remaining $7000 at 7 per cent there are no details. In sum, it was often difficult for the Gardiners to procure hard cash quickly. On these and related points, see Alexander Gardiner to John Tyler, New York, Mar. 30, 1844; Alexander Gardiner to Hon. Silas Wright, Hon. Charles H. Canott, Hon. Silas B. Strong, Hon. Richard D. Davis [New York, Mar.–Apr. 1844]; David L. Gardiner to Alexander Gardiner, East Hampton, Apr. 2, 1846; Lenny Gibson to David L. Gardiner, New York, June 22, 1846; Alexander Gardiner to Benjamin F. Thompson, New York, July 11, 1846, *GPY;* Juliana Gardiner to Julia Gardiner Tyler, New York [Feb. 1846]; Julia Gardiner Tyler to Juliana Gardiner, Norfolk [Sept.–Oct. 1845]; Gardiner Property Deed, Apr. 18, 1844; *Assets and Liabilities of David Gardiner* (March 1844), *TFP.*

[82] Juliana Gardiner to Julia Gardiner Tyler, East Hampton [Summer 1844]; Julia Gardiner to [David L. Gardiner, New York], Mar. 27, 1844, *TFP;* Coleman, *Priscilla Cooper Tyler,* 109; John Tyler to Juliana Gardiner, Washington, Apr. 20, 1844, *GPY;* "Interview with Julia Gardiner Tyler," Washington, Winter, 1888–1889, *loc. cit.*

[83] John Tyler to Mary Tyler [Jones], Washington, Mar. 24, 1844, *Pequot Collection,* Yale University Library.

[84] Juliana Gardiner to Julia Gardiner Tyler, New York [Nov. 1844]; Julia Gardiner Tyler to Juliana Gardiner, Sherwood Forest, Mar. 9; June 12, 1845, *TFP;* "Interview with Julia Gardiner Tyler," Washington, Winter, 1888–1889, *loc. cit.*

[85] Alexander Gardiner to [Editor ?], New York, Apr. 27, 1844, *GPY;* John Tyler to Mary Tyler Jones, Washington, Mar. 4, 1844, in *LTT,* II, 289.

CHAPTER 9

[1] *LTT,* II, 310; Isaac Van Zandt to Anson Jones, Washington, Mar. 15, 1843, in *ibid.,* III, 129. This conversation took place around March 10. It may be doubted

the language Van Zandt put in Tyler's mouth was exact. Tyler would never have split the infinitive. Van Zandt reported to his government in the same letter that "the President, though much abused, is gaining ground; the Democrats and moderate Whigs are falling into his ranks and coming to his support. Our principal strength in this country is with the Democrats."

² *Ibid.*, II, 273-80; III, 116-22; Chitwood, *Tyler,* 344-45; John Tyler to Editor, Richmond *Enquirer,* New York, Sept. 1, 1847; John Tyler to Alexander Gardiner, Sherwood Forest, Dec. 25, 1848, in *LTT,* II, 428-31, 433.

³ Abell, *Tyler,* 129; *LTT,* I, 436. Speech against the Tariff Bill of 1832, Feb. 12, 1832; John Tyler, Draft of Speech to Virginia Convention, Sherwood Forest [March 1861], *TPLC;* John Tyler to John Rutherfoord, Washington, Feb. 4, 1831, *John Rutherfoord Papers,* Duke University Library. In his letter to Rutherfoord he cheered the Polish uprising against Czarist Russia. Abell, *Tyler,* 127; John Tyler, "Letter of Withdrawal From the Campaign of 1844," Washington, Aug. 20, 1844; on the Zollverein Treaty see Henry Wheaton to John Tyler, Berlin, Mar. 27, 1844; Andrew Jackson to James K. Polk, Hermitage, Sept. 2, 1844, in *LTT,* II, 347, 326-27; III, 148-49; Minister von Geralt to John Tyler, Washington, Mar. 19, 1845. For Tyler's thoughts on and hopes for a free-trade arrangement with the Kingdom of the Two Sicilies, see William Boulware to John Tyler, Naples, Oct. 30, 1844, *TFP.* John Tyler to John S. Cunningham, Sherwood Forest, Nov. 4, 1855, in *LTT,* II, 200-1; Julia Gardiner to Alexander Gardiner, Washington, Dec. 13, 1842, *GPY;* John Tyler to Hugh S. Legaré, Charles City County, May 16, 1843, in *LTT,* III, 111; John Tyler, Special Message to Congress on Hawaii, Dec. 30, 1842, in Richardson, *Messages and Papers of the Presidents,* IV, 212; Julia Gardiner Tyler to Margaret Gardiner, Washington, Dec. 5, 1844, in *LTT,* II, 358; Caleb Cushing to John Tyler, Macao, July 18, 1844; Alexander Gardiner to Julia Gardiner Tyler, New York, Dec. 8, 1844, *TPLC.* Cushing's gift to the Tylers on his return from China, two lovely blue Chinese vases, are still to be seen at Sherwood Forest. John Tyler to Caleb Cushing, Charles City, Oct. 14, 1845, in *LTT,* II, 445.

⁴ John Tyler to Robert McCandlish, Washington, July 10, 1842; John Tyler to Daniel Webster, Washington, July 10, 1842, in *ibid.,* 173, 257; Daniel Webster to Waddy Thompson, Washington, June 27, 1842, in C. H. Van Tyne (ed.), *Letters of Daniel Webster* (New York, 1902), 269-70; John Tyler to Robert Tyler, Sherwood Forest, Dec. 11, 1845; John Tyler to Daniel Webster (two letters), Washington [Jan. 1843]; Silas Reed to Lyon G. Tyler, Boston, Apr. 8, 1885, in *LTT,* II, 448, 261; Appendix D, 696; Chitwood, *Tyler,* 336-37.

⁵ John Tyler to Littleton W. Tazewell, Washington, Oct. 24, 1842, in *LTT,* II, 248; *ibid.,* 225-26; Abel P. Upshur to Nathaniel B. Tucker, Washington, Mar. 6; Aug. 11, 1842, in *ibid.,* 157, 179. Tyler and Webster worked as a well-coordinated team on this treaty. Webster undertook the daily negotiations under Tyler's immediate and detailed supervision. The drafts of all Webster's correspondence with Ashburton were brought to Tyler for revisions, corrections, and suggestions. According to Julia, these were "always adopted by Mr. Webster word for word." The President was also responsible for some definite improvements in the finished document, and the tact and charm with which he handled Ashburton were remarked upon by many observers. Tyler was a smooth diplomat. Julia claimed in 1846 that he was "the direct and Webster only the *passive* agent in every act and every line of correspondence" relating to the treaty, a view embraced by Robert Tyler—who was at his father's side during the negotiations. Julia Gardiner Tyler to Margaret Gardiner, Sherwood Forest, Apr. 16, 1846; Robert Tyler to Julia Gardiner Tyler, Montgomery, Ala., Mar. 22 [1866]; Julia Gardiner Tyler to [Eben N.] Horsford, Sherwood Forest, n.d. [but probably 1868], *TFP.* Most of Tyler's correspondence with Webster on the treaty was consumed in the 1865 Richmond fire. This loss, said Robert, was "a great national calamity." *See also* Chitwood, *Tyler,* 314-15.

⁶ Isaac Van Zandt to Anson Jones, Washington, Mar. 15, 1843, in *LTT,* III,

129; *ibid.*, 152–53; II, 441; John Tyler to Robert Tyler, Sherwood Forest, Dec. 11, 1845, in *ibid.*, 447.

[7] Richardson, *Messages and Papers of the Presidents,* IV, 258, 261–62.

[8] The American-Texan diplomatic correspondence of January–February 1844 on the deployment of 500 American dragoons, 1000 infantry, and an undetermined force of naval vessels is reproduced in *LTT,* II, 282–90; as is the correspondence relating to Texan demands for operational control over these forces and Tyler's rejection of the request on constitutional grounds.

[9] As early as Mar. 7, 1820, Ritchie's Richmond *Enquirer* had denounced the Missouri Compromise and instructed the South to keep its eyes "firmly fixed on Texas. If we are cooped up on the north, we must have elbow room to the west." Quoted in *LTT,* I, 325–26; see also Abel P. Upshur to [Nathaniel B. Tucker], Washington, Nov. 5, 1842; Abel P. Upshur to W. S. Murphy, Washington, Jan. 16, 1844; John C. Calhoun to Thomas W. Gilmer, Fort Hill, Dec. 25, 1843; Thomas W. Gilmer to John C. Calhoun, Washington, Dec. 13, 1843, in *ibid.*, II, 268, 284, 296; III, 131; Wise, *Seven Decades of the Union,* 221–22; *LTT,* III, 116–17; John Tyler to Robert Tyler, Sherwood Forest, Apr. 17, 1850, in *ibid.*, II, 483; John Tyler, Message to the Senate of the United States, Washington, Apr. 22, 1844, in Richardson, *Messages and Papers of the Presidents,* IV, 308–9; John Tyler to "Mr. Editor" [Sherwood Forest, Mar. 1847], *TPLC;* John Tyler to Hamilton Smith, Sherwood Forest, Feb. 5, 1849, printed in Richmond *Enquirer,* Mar. 23, 1849; John Tyler to Daniel Webster, Sherwood Forest, Apr. 17, 1850; John Tyler, Draft Speech to Virginia Convention [Sherwood Forest, March 1861], *TPLC.* To Robert Tyler he wrote in 1850: "The monopoly of the cotton plant ... now secured, places all other nations at our feet. An embargo of a single year would produce in Europe a greater amount of suffering than a fifty years' war. I doubt whether Great Britain could avoid convulsions." John Tyler to Robert Tyler, Sherwood Foest, Apr. 17, 1850, in *LTT,* II, 483.

[10] John Tyler, Message to the Senate, Washington, Apr. 22, 1844, in Richardson, *Messages and Papers of the Presidents,* IV, 310, 312.

[11] Wise, *Seven Decades of the Union,* 221–22; Thomas W. Gilmer to John C. Calhoun, Washington, Dec. 13, 1843; John C. Calhoun to Thomas W. Gilmer, Fort Hill, Dec. 25, 1843, in *LTT,* III, 131; II, 296.

[12] Wise, *Seven Decades of the Union,* 223–24.

[13] *Ibid.*, 224–25; *LTT,* II, 293–95.

[14] *Democratic Tyler Meeting at Washington* (Pamphlet; n.p., n.d. [April 1844]), 1–24; *LTT,* II, 285–86, 305–6. Tyler had offered Jackson protégé James K. Polk the Cabinet post of Secretary of the Navy after Gilmer was killed on the *Princeton.* Polk refused it, he being an announced Vice-Presidential hopeful at the time, but the gesture was not wasted on Old Hickory. James K. Polk to Theophilus Fisk, Columbia, Tenn., Mar. 20, 1844, in *ibid.*, III, 133–34. Polk, a confirmed expansionist, endorsed Calhoun's appointment to the Cabinet, "especially in reference to the Texas and Oregon questions."

[15] John Tyler, Message to the Senate, Washington, Apr. 22, 1844, in Richardson, *Messages and Papers of the Presidents,* IV, 311; *LTT,* II, 298; Roseboom, *A History of Presidential Elections,* 128, 127; Glyndon G. Van Deusen, *The Jacksonian Era* (New York, 1959), 182–83.

[16] *LTT,* II, 324–25, 331; III, 122–23; John Tyler to Henry A. Wise, Sherwood Forest, Apr. 20, 1852, in *ibid.*, II, 317. This letter was published again in Vol. III a few years later; in this version Lyon G. Tyler rendered the word *scheme* to read *theme.* John Tyler to Henry A. Wise, Sherwood Forest, Apr. 20, 1852, in *ibid.*, III, 170–71; John Tyler to Alexander Gardiner, East Hampton, July 11, 1846, in *ibid.*, II, 341.

[17] Abel P. Upshur to Nathaniel B. Tucker, Washington, Oct. 30; Dec. 23, 1841;

Mar. 6, 1842, in *ibid.,* 308, 153–54, 156–58; *ibid.,* 256; III, 116–22; Chitwood, *Tyler,* 344.

[18] Abel P. Upshur to Nathaniel B. Tucker, Washington, Dec. 23, 1841, in *LTT,* II, 153–54; Alexander Hamilton to John Tyler, New York, Apr. 23, 1842, *TPLC; LTT,* II, 291–92; Andrew Jackson to John Tyler, Hermitage, Sept. 9, 1842; Amos Kendall to [John Tyler], Washington, Oct. 20, 1843, *TPLC;* John Tyler to Andrew Jackson, Rip Raps, Va., Sept. 20, 1842, in Lyon G. Tyler, "Some Letters of Tyler, Calhoun, Polk, Murphy, Houston and Donelson," *Tyler's Quarterly,* VI (April 1925), 225. Tyler's decision to appoint Frémont came in March 1842 on the urging of Silas Reed. "You have it in your power to touch his [Benton's] heart through his domestic affections," suggested the then Surveyor-General for Illinois and Missouri. Silas Reed to Lyon G. Tyler, Boston, Apr. 8, 1885, in *LTT,* II, Appendix D, 697. Tyler's later decision to promote Frémont for his exploits in the West was less politically motivated. *See* William Wilkins to John Tyler, War Dept., Washington, Jan. 16, 1844, *TPLC.* Kendall needed his printing commission badly. "The emoluments of this station," he thanked Tyler, "would be an inexpressible relief to me under existing circumstances."

[19] John Tyler to Littleton W. Tazewell, Oct. 24, 1842, in *LTT,* II, 248–49.

[20] Washington *Globe,* Nov. 29, 1842, quoted in *LTT,* II, 303–4; *ibid.,* 249–50; Noah, "Reminiscences," New York *Sunday Dispatch,* Dec. 21, 1845; *LTT,* II, 188, 250; John Tyler to Alexander Gardiner, East Hampton, July 11, 1846, in *ibid.,* 341.

[21] William Taggart was Surveyor of the Port of New York; George himself served variously as Naval Storekeeper at the Brooklyn Navy Yard, Military Storekeeper on Governors Island, and Secret Inspector in the N.Y. Customs House. Hallet was a clerk of the U.S. Circuit Court for the District of Southern New York; Fowler was a small shop tailor in the Bowery who was vice-president of an organization called the Tyler State Convention. He aspired to employment in the Customs House but obtained instead the Surveyorship of the Port. Robert C. Wetmore served as Navy Agent in Brooklyn until removed by Tyler for corruption. A former Whig, he had been prominently involved in a vote-fraud case in New York in 1838. Gunderson, *Log Cabin Campaign,* 249–51; New York *Herald,* Feb. 9, 1845. This account of the Tyler party in New York City in 1843–1844 is based largely on Noah, "Reminiscences," New York *Sunday Dispatch,* Dec. 21; 28, 1845; Jan. 11; 18; 25; Feb. 1; 8; 22; Mar. 15; 22; 29; Apr. 5; 12; 26; May 10, 1846. While Noah's account is biased and must be regarded with care, its main outline may be substantiated by reference to the New York *Herald* and the Washington *Madisonian* for the 1842–1844 period and to the *Gardiner Papers,* 1842–1844, Yale University Library, *passim.*

[22] Noah, "Reminiscences," New York *Sunday Dispatch,* Mar. 29; Jan. 25, 1846. Robert Tyler worked through the Washington correspondent of the *Herald,* N. T. Parnelle, in his attempt to bring the paper solidly over to Tyler. James Gordon Bennett, editor of the *Herald,* would have none of this, although his paper was, and remained, reasonably friendly to the administration. John I. Mumford later (Jan. 1845) sought from Tyler an appointment as Surveyor of the Port of New York. Needless to say, he got nothing. New York *Herald,* Jan. 25, 1845; Noah, "Reminiscences," New York *Sunday Dispatch,* Jan. 25; Mar. 15, 1846. Curtis put up $500, Graham $200, Taggart $200. Other contributors were Wetmore, Hoffman, Stilwell, Fisher, Fowler, and some dozen others who held offices in New York City salaried in the $1500-to-$2500 bracket.

[23] *Ibid.,* Jan. 25, 1846. Noah never blamed Tyler for his disappointment. He blamed John Lorimer Graham and Robert Tyler.

[24] *Ibid.,* Mar. 15, 1846. Noah's suggestion that Webster actually left the Cabinet because of the Tylerite absorption of the *Aurora* is not substantiated by any other evidence.

²⁵ New York *Sunday Dispatch*, Dec. 28, 1845; Jan. 11; Mar. 22, 1846.
²⁶ *LTT*, II, 250; Lyon G. Tyler, *Parties and Patronage in the United States* (New York, 1891), 82.
²⁷ *LTT*, II, 250; John Tyler to Alexander Gardiner, East Hampton, July 11, 1846, in *ibid.*, 341; Rep. George H. Proffit quoted in *ibid.*, 225.
²⁸ John Tyler to John C. Spencer, Charles City County, May 12, 1843, *TPLC*.
²⁹ Washington *Madisonian*, July 21, 1843.
³⁰ Daniel Webster to John Tyler, Boston, Aug. 29, 1843, in *Tyler's Quarterly*, VIII (July 1926), 25–26. For a standard Whig scream of anguish over the Tyler proscription, see the pamphlet *John, the Traitor; or, the Force of Accident. A Plain Story*, 30, 36–37, 42.
³¹ Abell, *Tyler*, 154–55; 107; *see also* John Tyler to Robert Tyler, Washington, Feb. 2, 1832, in *LTT*, I, 427. This delicate feeling about the unrestrained use of the appointing power persisted in Tyler until June 1841. See *ibid.*, II, 310–11. By October 1842, however, the President was hard at work building a Tyler group in Missouri by patronage appointments. Silas Reed to John Tyler, St. Louis, Oct. 1, 1842, *TPLC*; John Minge to John Tyler, Petersburg, Mar. 18, 1844, in *LTT*, II, 404.
³² Tyler kin appointed to various posts: *Thomas A. Cooper* was appointed Military Storekeeper at the Frankford, Pa., Arsenal in 1841. When Congress abolished that job in 1843 (to strike at the President), Tyler nominated him as Surveyor of the Port of Philadelphia (1844). Failing Senate confirmation for that post in 1845, the President and son Robert got the old actor placed finally by Polk in the New York Customs House, where he remained until senility overtook him in 1846 and he retired. Coleman, *Priscilla Cooper Tyler*, 84–85, 111–12, 120–21; Noah, "Reminiscences," New York *Sunday Dispatch*, Feb. 1, 1846; New York *Herald*, Feb. 9, 1845; Margaret Gardiner to Alexander Gardiner, Washington, Feb. 8, 1845, *GPY; ibid.*, Feb. 14, 1845; Margaret Gardiner to Julia Gardiner Tyler, New York, May 16, 1845, *TFP;* Alexander Gardiner to N. M. Miller, Washington, Mar. 13, 1845, *GPY*.

Robert Tyler was appointed to a clerkship in the Land Office in 1841. He remained in that job until March 1844, resigning to begin a law practice in Philadelphia. In May 1844 he abandoned his practice to manage his father's campaign. From May 1844 to April 1845 Tyler virtually supported Robert and his family. Robert later unsuccessfully sought office from the Polk, Pierce and Buchanan administrations. Coleman, *Priscilla Cooper Tyler*, 84–85; John Tyler to Robert Tyler, New York, Dec. 30, 1847, *TPLC*.

John Tyler, Jr., served as his father's private secretary until 1844 when he was discharged for inefficiency. His salary was apparently paid from the President's own pocket, however. Langford, *The Ladies of the White House*, 330–31; John Tyler to Martha Rochelle, Washington, Oct. 22, 1843, *James Rochelle Papers*, Duke University Library.

James Rochelle, John Tyler, Jr.'s young brother-in-law, received a midshipman's appointment in the Navy; *James A. Semple*, the President's son-in-law, received a purser's berth in the same service. John Tyler to Martha Rochelle, Washington, Sept. 4, 1841, *James Rochelle Papers*, Duke University Library; Langford, *The Ladies of the White House*, 331; Julia Gardiner Tyler to Margaret Gardiner, Washington, Oct. 14, 1844, *TFP*.

John H. Waggaman and his brother *Floyd Waggaman*, Tyler's nephews, both received minor appointments—John in the Treasury Department, and Floyd as a diplomatic courier. John Tyler to Thomas Ewing, Washington, Mar. 5, 1841, *TPLC;* Margaret Gardiner to Julia Gardiner Tyler, New York, Mar. 7, 1845, *TFP*.

Dr. N. M. Miller of Ohio, the President's brother-in-law, was first appointed a clerk in the Appointment Office and then Second Assistant Postmaster General. Polk demoted him to Third Assistant and finally purged him altogether. New York Herald, Nov. 21, 1844; Mar. 30, 1845.

Alexander Gardiner's appointment to a clerkship in the U.S. Circuit Court for the Southern District of New York was an appointment the President arranged through Attorney General John Nelson of Maryland and Chief Justice Samuel Nelson of the New York Supreme Court. Tyler elevated Samuel Nelson to the United States Supreme Court just before he left office.

Most of the Corporal's Guardsmen were also appointed to the diplomatic service or to the Cabinet: Proffit and Wise to Brazil, Cushing to China; Virginia Cliqueman Gilmer and Upshur of course were brought into the Cabinet. *LTT*, II, 162–64; New York *Herald*, Feb. 19; Mar. 5, 1845; John Tyler to [Henry A. Wise], Clarke County, Va., Sept. 13, 1843, *TPLC*. Charles Cody of the Palmyra (Mo.) *Courier*, on the strong recommendation of Silas Reed, Tylerite patronage chief in St. Louis, was given a post in St. Louis. This act, said Reed, would "add strength to our Cause in Missouri.... It would aid us much in presenting a bold and strong front to our V[an] B[uren] rivals here, to have the *Courier* at Palmyra warmly on our side." George Roberts, editor of the Boston *Times*, was appointed Naval Officer of the Port of Boston. "He is a well known friend of President Tyler," said the New York *Herald*. Silas Reed to John Tyler, St. Louis, Oct. 1, 1842, *TPLC;* New York *Herald*, June 27, 1844; Noah, "Reminiscences," New York *Sunday Dispatch*, Mar. 29, 1846; *LTT*, III, 49. In 1832 Tyler had voted against an attempt by Jackson to appoint Noah to office because Noah was then editor of the New York *Courier and Enquirer.*

[33] Abell was first nominated for consul to Marseilles in December 1844. Rejected by the Senate, he was stubbornly nominated again by Tyler—to the Sandwich Island post. For this spot he gained Senate approval. New York *Herald*, Dec. 13, 1844; Jan. 18, 1845.

Hiram Cumming, a Vermont teacher and lawyer, sometime friend of Robert Tyler and frequent visitor at the White House in 1842–1843, was a high-pressure (and corrupt) founder of fly-by-night pro-Tyler newspapers in various New England villages. These were financed by capital levies on Tylerite officeholders in these backwater locales. Cumming was, said Noah (praising Tyler for never having "knowingly appointed a disreputable man to office"), one of the "bunch of charlatans, vagabonds, leeches, vampires and scoundrels" who attached themselves to the skirts of the Tyler movement. Noah, "Reminiscences," New York *Sunday Dispatch*, Jan. 11, 1846; Hiram Cumming, *Secret History of the Perfidies, Intrigues, and Corruptions of the Tyler Dynasty* (New York, 1845), *passim;* Julia Gardiner Tyler to Alexander Gardiner, Sherwood Forest, Oct. 23, 1845, *TFP.*

[34] John Tyler to [Henry A. Wise], Clarke County, Va., Sept. 13, 1843; Bodie Peyton to John Tyler, New Orleans, Dec. 17, 1843; John Tyler to John C. Spencer, Jordans Springs, Va., Sept. 2, 1843, *TPLC.*

[35] *LTT*, II, 313–14. The Washington correspondent of the New York *Herald*, a journalist generally friendly to the Tyler administration, kept a tally of the Senate rejections of Tyler appointees. The number he reported was 102. New York *Herald*, Feb. 19; Mar. 8, 1845. Those rejected for Cabinet posts were Caleb Cushing as Secretary of the Treasury (three times!), David Henshaw of Massachusetts as Secretary of the Navy, and James M. Porter of Pennsylvania as Secretary of War. Henshaw and Porter were Conservative Democrats. Wise, *Seven Decades of the Union*, 213–14.

[36] Priscilla Cooper Tyler to Frederick Raoul, Boston [June 1843] in Coleman,

Priscilla Cooper Tyler, 103–4; Juliana Gardiner to Julia Gardiner, New York, May 28, 1843, *GPY.* Tyler was also flatteringly received in Princeton, N.J., where he was the houseguest of Captain Robert P. Stockton, USN. The Grand Marshal of the New York reception for Tyler was Prosper M. Wetmore whose brother, Robert C. Wetmore, was a leading figure in the Tyler group in New York City.

[37] John Tyler to John B. Jones [Clarke County, Va.], Sept. 13, 1843, in *LTT,* III, 113–14.

[38] Noah, "Reminiscences," New York *Sunday Dispatch,* Apr. 12, 1846; *LTT,* II, 314–16; Washington *Madisonian,* June 1, 1844; Lambert, *Presidential Politics in the United States,* 159–60. Delegations were present from 18 of the 26 states. Individuals were present from all the states.

[39] Roseboom, *A History of Presidential Elections,* 128–29.

[40] John Tyler, Letter of Acceptance, Washington, May 30, 1844, in *LTT,* II, 319–21.

[41] Van Deusen, *The Jacksonian Era,* 186; *LTT,* II, 324–25, 331, 334–37; III, 47, 121–22. There were 28 Whigs in the Senate; 27 voted against the treaty, as did 7 agrarian Democrats, Benton among them, against the expressed wishes of Jackson.

[42] John Tyler to Mary Tyler Jones, Washington, June 4, 1844, *TPLC.*

[43] Priscilla Cooper Tyler to Robert Tyler, Philadelphia, June 4, 1844, in Coleman, *Priscilla Cooper Tyler,* 110–11.

[44] Robert J. Walker to James K. Polk, Washington, July 10, 1844; John Tyler to Robert Tyler [Sherwood Forest], July 6, 1844, in *LTT,* III, 139, 141; II, Appendix G, 710; Jay A. Micheals to John Tyler, New York, Nov. 7, 1844, *GPY.*

[45] Robert J. Walker to James K. Polk, Washington, July 10, 1844, in *LTT,* III, 139–41.

[46] *Ibid.*

[47] John Tyler to Alexander Gardiner, East Hampton, July 11, 1846, in *ibid.,* II, 342; see also *ibid.,* 337–38; III, 49, 56, 124–25. Jackson's letter was published in *Niles' Register,* LXVI, 416. See also New York *Herald,* Jan. 7, 1845, for influence of the Jackson-Lewis letter on Tyler's decision to withdraw; also Lambert, *Presidential Politics in the United States,* 204.

[48] Alexander Gardiner to [Editor ?], New York, Apr. 27, 1844; Alexander Gardiner [pseud. "Cyrus Smith"], to [Editor ?], New York, May 19, 1844; John Lorimer Graham to Alexander Gardiner, New York, Aug. 20, 1844; Alexander Gardiner, Draft Manuscript Speech on Texas Annexation, [July 1844], *GPY.* Most of Alexander's Texas propaganda appeared in the Washington *Madisonian,* the New York *Herald,* and the New York *Aurora.*

[49] Noah, "Reminiscences," New York *Sunday Dispatch,* Feb. 1; 8; 22, 1846. At this time George was a Secret Inspector in the Customs House, a do-nothing job paying $3 per day.

[50] John Tyler to the St. Patrick's Anniversary Celebration Committee, Washington, Mar. 15, 1844, *TPLC; LTT,* II, 645.

[51] Alexander Gardiner to Julia Gardiner Tyler, New York [Late June–early July 1844]; David L. Gardiner to Julia Gardiner Tyler, New York, July 29, 1844, *TFP.*

[52] Alexander Gardiner to Julia Gardiner Tyler, New York, July 14, 1844, *TPLC;* Margaret Gardiner to Julia Gardiner Tyler, New York, Apr. 14; June 5; Dec. 10, 1845; Juliana Gardiner to Julia Gardiner Tyler, New York, n.d. [1845], *TFP.* In these letters his mother and sister complained regularly of Alexander's advancement of money "for political purposes." When Alexander lent *Aurora* editor Thomas Dunn English the sum of $50 in June 1845, Margaret was certain that this was but a "small portion of the [political] demands upon his funds.... Duce take the Politics," she snapped angrily.

[53] Alexander Gardiner to [John Tyler], New York, July 21, 1844, in *LTT,* II, 338.

[54] Alexander Gardiner to Julia Gardiner Tyler, New York, July 23, 1844, *TPLC*. Delazon Smith (1816–1860) was virtually unique in the Tyler party. He was the editor of a small Ohio newspaper, the Dayton *Western Empire*, who had attended the Baltimore convention in May as a Tyler delegate from Ohio. He believed that Tyler could actually be re-elected and became an enthusiastic Tyler supporter. In June he had, at his own expense, toured Maryland and Virginia holding Tyler rallies and drumming up Tyler sentiment. In July he arrived in New York City, where he launched a series of indifferently attended sidewalk Tyler meetings. His utterings saw print in both the *Aurora* and the *Madisonian*. He asked nothing of Tyler. Tyler, however, appointed him Commissioner to Ecuador (1842–1845). His later career carried him to Oregon. From Feb. 14, 1859, to Mar. 3, 1859, he served as a U.S. senator from Oregon (Democrat), a very short term indeed. See Noah, "Reminiscences," New York *Sunday Dispatch*, Apr. 5; 12, 1846. William Shaler was a more typical Tylerite. His modest contribution to the Tyler cause led to his nomination as consul to Hong Kong in January 1845. The appointment still pending before the Senate when Tyler left office, Shaler was renominated by Polk (one of the few Tylerites so honored), but was finally rejected by the Senate. See New York *Herald*, Jan. 18; Mar. 12; 21, 1845. Mike Walsh had the gall to solicit an office from Tyler in Dec. 1844. Understandably, Tyler refused. See Margaret Gardiner to Alexander Gardiner, Washington, Dec. 30, 1844, *GPY*.

[55] Alexander Gardiner, Draft of Memorandum [New York, July 29, 1844], *GPY*. The Tyler letter to Alexander from Old Point Comfort has not been found. Its existence and content can be inferred, however, from the chronology of the situation, Tyler's known political concerns that week at Old Point Comfort, and internal evidence in Alexander Gardiner's memorandum. It was probably written July 26, 1844.

[56] Alexander Gardiner to [John Tyler], New York, Aug. 2, 1844; Abraham Hatfield, Cornelius P. Van Ness, *et al.* to John Tyler, New York, Aug. 6, 1844; John Tyler to Alexander Gardiner, East Hampton, July 11, 1846; Joel B. Sutherland to Andrew Jackson, Philadelphia, Aug. 20, 1844; John Tyler to Messrs. Hatfield, Van Ness, *et al.*, Washington, Aug. 22, 1844, in *LTT*, II, 338, 339, 342; III, 147; II, 339–40; John Tyler to Andrew Jackson, Washington, Aug. 18, 1844, in Lyon G. Tyler (ed.), "Some Letters of Tyler...," *loc. cit.*, 232. The Tylerites who signed the Carleton House treaty of Aug. 2 were Van Ness, J. Paxton Hallet, George D. Strong, and John O. Fowler.

[57] John Tyler to "Friends Throughout the Union," Washington, Aug. 20, 1844, in *LTT*, II, 342–49. "I never saw a person who could write more rapidly," exclaimed Julia in amazement at the speed with which Tyler produced his withdrawal statement. Julia Gardiner Tyler to [Juliana Gardiner] [Washington], Aug. 22, 1844, in *ibid.*, 342, fn.

[58] John Lorimer Graham to Alexander Gardiner, New York, Apr. 20; 24, 1844; *GPY;* New York *Journal of Commerce*, Aug. 22, 1844; *see also* New York *Herald*, Aug. 22, 1844; New York *Evening Express*, Aug. 22, 1844; New York *Democrat*, Aug. 22, 1844; New York *Daily Plebeian*, Aug. 22, 1844. Tyler himself thought the statement quite bold. "You know," he told a friend, "that I can neither talk nor write upon any subject without doing so frankly and somewhat boldly." John Tyler to M. S. Sprigg, Washington, Aug. 20, 1844, *TPLC*.

[59] Andrew Jackson to Joel B. Sutherland, Hermitage, Sept. 2, 1844; Andrew Jackson to James K. Polk, Hermitage, Sept. 2, 1844; Joel B. Sutherland to Andrew Jackson, Philadelphia, Aug. 20, 1844; John Tyler to Alexander Gardiner, East Hampton, July 11, 1844, in *LTT*, II, 341, 342; III, 147–48, 150–51. Tyler further cemented his relations with Jackson in early September, appointing Major A. J. Donelson, Old Hickory's nephew, U.S. Minister to Texas. At the same time he warned Santa Anna that any invasion of Texas would mean war with the United States. "This is the true, energetic course," Jackson told Polk.

[60] John Tyler to Elizabeth Tyler Waller [Washington], Sept. 13, 1844, in *ibid.*,

155; *ibid.*, Sept. 4, 1844, *TPLC; see also* New York *Herald,* June 27, 1844; Alexander Gardiner to John Tyler [New York], Dec. 9, 1844, *TPLC;* John Tyler to Thomas Ritchie, Sherwood Forest, Jan. 9, 1851, in Richmond *Enquirer,* Jan. 17, 1851. Tyler was stunned to learn, however, that William Waller, his son-in-law, was leaning toward Clay. "I am still abused as the violent wretch by all the newspapers in his advocacy.... I hope Mr. Waller will seriously ponder this before he commits himself for Clay." John Tyler to Elizabeth Tyler Waller, Washington, Sept. 5, 1844, *TPLC.*

[61] Alexander Gardiner to Julia Gardiner Tyler, New York, Sept. 3, 1844; R. M. Price to Alexander Gardiner [New York], Sept. 16, 1844; Samuel Gardiner to Alexander Gardiner, Shelter Island, N.Y., Aug. 16; Sept. 17, 1844; Vanbrugh Livingston to Alexander Gardiner, New York, Oct. 3, 1844; John Lorimer Graham to Alexander Gardiner, New York, Oct. 13, 1844; John Pierce to Nathaniel Gardiner (forwarded to Alexander Gardiner), Brooklyn, Oct. 28, 1844; T. W. Letson to Alexander Gardiner, Dry Dock Office, Brooklyn, Oct. 29; 30, 1844; Garrit H. Stukes, Jr., to Alexander Gardiner, New York, Oct. 30, 1844; John E. Ross to Alexander Gardiner, New York, Nov. 18, 1844, *GPY;* Margaret Gardiner to Julia Gardiner Tyler, New York, Oct. 18, 1844, *TFP.*

[62] Garrit H. Stukes, Jr., to Alexander Gardiner, New York, Oct. 30, 1844, *GPY;* Margaret Gardiner to Julia Gardiner Tyler [New York], July 22, 1844; Alexander Gardiner to Julia Gardiner Tyler, New York, Oct. 15; 16, 1844, *TPLC;* Margaret Gardiner to Julia Gardiner Tyler, New York, Oct. 18, 1844. On this trip to New York Robert and Priscilla Tyler were the houseguests of Surveyor Henry C. Atwood. Priscilla had given birth to her third child, a son, in July. See *ibid.,* July 10; Aug. 5, 1844, *TFP;* Samuel Osgood to Alexander Gardiner, Tammany Hall, Oct. 5, 1844; Alexander Gardiner to [Samuel Osgood] [New York, Oct. 6, 1844]; [Alexander Gardiner], Statement of Qualifications [New York, Oct. 1844]; Committee of Stone Cutters to Alexander Gardiner, New York [Oct. 1844]; Alexander Gardiner to Committee of Stone Cutters, New York, Oct. 28, 1844, *GPY;* Alexander Gardiner to Julia Gardiner Tyler, New York, Oct. 15, 1844. For his labors on Alexander's behalf, Broderick ("an invaluable friend") was later (December) rewarded by Tyler with an appointment as Secret Inspector in the Customs House, replacing Paul R. George. *See* Alexander Gardiner to Julia Gardiner Tyler, Oct. 11, 1844, *TFP;* Alexander Gardiner to John Tyler, New York, Nov. 23, 1844, *TPLC;* David H. Broderick to Alexander Gardiner, New York, Nov. 12, 1844, *GPY;* Alexander Gardiner to John Tyler, New York, Dec. 6, 1844, *TFP.*

[63] Fox, *The Decline of the Aristocracy in the Politics of New York,* 431–35; Alexander Gardiner to Julia Gardiner Tyler, New York, Oct. 11; 16; 14, 1844, *TFP;* Alexander Gardiner, Memorandum of a Conversation with Joseph T. Sweet, New York, Oct. 31, 1844, *GPY;* Alexander Gardiner to Julia Gardiner Tyler, New York, Oct. 31, 1844, *TPLC;* Juliana Gardiner to Julia Gardiner Tyler, New York, Oct. 29, 1844, *TFP;* New York *Herald,* Oct. 29, 1844; Alexander Gardiner, Notice, New York *Evening Post,* New York, Oct. 30, 1844.

[64] Roseboom, *A History of Presidential Elections,* 131–35. Polk: 1,337,243; Clay: 1,229,062; Birney: 62,300. Electoral votes: Polk, 170; Clay, 105. Clay carried Ohio, N.C., Tenn. (by 113 votes), Ky., Md., Del., Mass., R.I., Conn., Vt., and N.J. Polk carried Virginia, the entire Deep South, the West save Ohio, and, most significantly, N.Y. and Penna. John Lorimer Graham to Alexander Gardiner, New York, Dec. 6, 1844, *GPY;* Unsigned Letter to Editor [James Watson Webb] of New York *Courier and Enquirer,* Washington, Dec. 4, 1844; Alexander Gardiner to Julia Gardiner Tyler, New York, Nov. [9], 1844, *TFP.* This too was the view of former New York Senator Nathaniel P. Tallmadge, Tyler's appointee as governor of the Wisconsin Territory. N. P. Tallmadge to Robert J. Walker, Faycheedah, Wis., Dec. 9, 1844, in *LTT,* III, 153–54. *See also* Jay A. Micheals to John Tyler, New York, Nov. 7, 1844, *GPY.*

[65] Andrew Jackson to James K. Polk, Hermitage, Sept. 2, 1844, in *LTT*, III, 150; D. B. Tallmadge to John Tyler, New York, Nov. 14, 1844. This was also the reasoned view of George F. Thompson. George F. Thompson to Robert Tyler, New York, Nov. 11, 1844, *GPY*. That many Van Burenites had cut Polk was agreed to by Alexander Gardiner but he did not carry the implications of this to Tallmadge's conclusion. Alexander Gardiner to Julia Gardiner Tyler, New York, Nov. [9], 1844, *TFP*.

[66] John Tyler to Alexander Gardiner, East Hampton, July 11, 1846, in *LTT*, II, 342; Margaret Gardiner to Julia Gardiner Tyler, New York [Nov. 1844], *TFP*; John Tyler to Andrew Jackson, Washington, Aug. 18, 1844, in Lyon G. Tyler (ed.), "Some Letters of Tyler...," *loc. cit.*, 222, 232; Edward Stanwood, *A History of Presidential Elections* (New York, 1892), 158; W. Dean Burnham, *Presidential Ballots, 1836-1892* (Baltimore, 1955), 704, 716, 820.

[67] *See* election returns in New York *Herald*, Nov. 12, 1844. Clarkson Crolius, running as a straight Whig for the Assembly, polled 947 votes. Compare Alexander Gardiner's 26,183 votes to Polk's 28,402, Wright's 29,220 and Lt. Gov. Addison Gardiner's 29,117. Alexander even ran behind Henry Clay, who polled 26,518 in New York City. Alexander Gardiner to Julia Gardiner Tyler, Nov. 7; [9], 1844, *TFP*.

[68] New York *Herald*, Nov. 11; 21, 1844; Julia Gardiner Tyler to [Juliana Gardiner], Washington, Nov. 27; 29, 1844, in *LTT*, II, 356; Mary Gardiner to Margaret Gardiner, Shelter Island, Dec. 5, 1844; Julia Gardiner Tyler to Margaret Gardiner, President's Mansion [Washington], Nov. 13, 1844; Juliana Gardiner to Julia Gardiner Tyler, New York, Nov. 17; 19, 1844. *TFP*.

[69] New York *Herald*, Nov. 21, 1844; Juliana Gardiner to Julia Gardiner Tyler, New York, Nov. 19, 1844, *TFP*.

[70] John Tyler to John Jones, Washington [Nov. 1844], *TPLC*.

CHAPTER 10

[1] New York *Herald*, Nov. 21; Oct. 23, 1844; Julia Gardiner Tyler to Juliana Gardiner, Washington, Nov. 17, 1844, *TFP*.

[2] New York *Herald*, Nov. 27, 1844; Feb. 20, 1845; Juliana Gardiner to Julia Gardiner Tyler, New York [Nov. 1844]; Julia Gardiner Tyler to Juliana Gardiner, Washington, Sept. 9, 1844, *TFP*.

[3] William Boulware to John Tyler, Naples, Oct. 30, 1844, *TFP;* Julia Gardiner Tyler to Juliana Gardiner, Washington, Nov. 25, 1844, *GPY;* Margaret Gardiner to Julia Gardiner Tyler, New York, July 13, 1844, *TFP*. The consul insisted that such a dog was "exceedingly delicate and particularly sensitive to cold" and suggested that shipment be delayed until March 1845. Tyler agreed.

[4] Juliana Gardiner to Julia Gardiner Tyler, New York, Nov. 21, 1844, *TFP;* Margaret Gardiner to Alexander Gardiner, Washington, Dec. 28, 1844, *GPY; LTT*, I, 390. The wines were shipped from France on the *Marietta Burr* on December 5. Tyler feared that the vessel had gone down in one of the heavy gales reported in the Atlantic that winter. The *Marietta Burr* happily came through, although far behind schedule. *See* David L. Gardiner to Juliana Gardiner, Washington, Dec. 21, 1844, *GPY*. The furniture included French mirrors, rugs, chandeliers, wallpapers, occasional tables, etc. They were later transshipped from New York to Sherwood Forest. Somewhat over $1000 worth of dry goods and furniture was ordered from New York to be shipped directly to Kennon's Landing, James River, near Sherwood Forest. *See* John Tyler to Alexander Gardiner, Washington, Dec. 8, 1844, in *LTT*, II, 358-59; Farrar, *Old Virginia Houses Along the James*, 124.

[5] Julia Gardiner Tyler to Juliana Gardiner, Washington, Nov. 25, 1844. Neither

the Thompson painting nor the Tyler engraving based on it has survived. Thompson also executed a portrait of Senator David Gardiner, dunning Alexander for payment with the artist's age-old observation, "O! This painting business is *bad!*" E. G. Thompson to Alexander Gardiner [New York], n.d., *GPY*.

[6] Margaret Gardiner to Alexander Gardiner, Washington, Jan. 11, 1845, *GPY;* New York *Herald,* Oct. 31, 1844; Hervey Allen, "Special Biographical Introduction," in *The Works of Edgar Allan Poe* (New York, 1927), xvii; Margaret Gardiner to Juliana Gardiner, Washington, Dec. 23, 1844, *TFP.*

[7] New York *Herald,* Oct. 27, 1844.

[8] Julia Gardiner Tyler to Juliana Gardiner, Washington, Nov. 25, 1844, *GPY; ibid.,* Nov. 27, 1844, in *LTT,* II, 356; Margaret Gardiner to Alexander Gardiner, Washington [Jan. 1845], *GPY;* Julia Gardiner Tyler, "Reminiscences," in *LTT,* III, 199; Margaret Gardiner to Alexander Gardiner, Washington, Feb. 12, 1845, *GPY*. The Phimb daguerreotype unfortunately has not survived.

[9] Richardson, *Messages and Papers of the Presidents,* IV, 341-45.

[10] Julia Gardiner Tyler to Margaret Gardiner, Washington, Dec. 5, 1844, in *LTT,* II, 358; Alexander Gardiner to Julia Gardiner Tyler, New York, Dec. 8, 1844; Joseph S. Watkins to John Tyler, Birch Pond, Tenn., Dec. 21, 1844, *TPLC;* John Tyler to Alexander Gardiner, Washington, Dec. 8, 1844, in *LTT,* II, 359.

[11] Julia Gardiner Tyler to Alexander Gardiner, Washington, Dec. 8, 1844; Alexander Gardiner to Julia Gardiner Tyler, New York, Dec. 7; 15, 1844, *TFP*. By this time the behavior of John Tyler, Jr., had become so erratic and his personal habits so unpredictable that the President replaced him in September 1844 as his private secretary and gave the duties to a Mr. C. B. Moss. Said the New York *Herald* of Moss: "This gentleman...is decidedly a very civil and worthy young man—always at his post during office hours, ready and willing to attend to all business matters coming within the range and scope of his official duty." New York *Herald,* Oct. 23, 1844.

[12] Julia Gardiner Tyler, "Reminiscences," in *LTT,* III, 198.

[13] *Ibid.,* 197.

[14] Julia Gardiner Tyler to Juliana Gardiner, Washington, Dec. 6, 1844, in *ibid.,* II, 358.

[15] The *Gardiner Papers,* Yale University Library, show much evidence for this statement on the franking privilege, particularly during the period August 1844 to March 1845. Margaret Gardiner to Alexander Gardiner, Washington, Jan. 2, 1845; Juliana Gardiner to Julia Gardiner Tyler [New York, 1844]. For typical clemency, etc., requests see Cornelius Dreslane to Julia Gardiner Tyler, New York, Jan. 10, 1845; Mary de John to Mrs. President Tyler [Washington], Jan. 31, 1845; Lucy Marie Murphy to Julia Gardiner Tyler, Chillicothe [Ohio], Feb. 14, 1845; Calvin Durphree to John Tyler, East Walpole, Mass., Jan. 13, 1845; L. D. Dewey to Julia Gardiner Tyler, New York, Sept. 16, 1844; Mary Smith to Julia Gardiner Tyler, Fort Monroe, Va., July 21, 1844; Esther M. Gibbons to Julia Gardiner Tyler, Albany, N.Y., July 13, 1844; Tris P. Coffin to Julia Gardiner Tyler, Granville [Ohio], Jan. 15, 1845, *TFP;* Mrs. William Lynde to Mrs. John Tyler, New York, Dec. 11, 1844, *GPY*. For Julia's role in Tyler's pardoning of one "Babe," a New York seaman under sentence of death for alleged piracy, see N.Y. *Herald,* Jan. 31, 1845. For "The Julia Waltzes" see Margaret Gardiner to Julia Gardiner Tyler, New York, Oct. 31, 1844; Feb. 27, 1845; and Julia Gardiner Tyler to Juliana Gardiner, Washington [Dec. 1844]. "The Julia Waltzes were composed by Lovel Purdy... dedicated to Mrs. Tyler," and published by Firth and Hall at No. 1 Franklin Square and 239 Broadway, New York City. Julia heard that they were "so popular" that the first edition of 1400 copies had been sold out quickly. "I understand they are very pretty," she told her mother. She instructed Margaret to promote knowledge of the music among friends of the Gardiners in New York. "She must...say to her friends, 'Have you seen the Julia Waltzes which are just out? dedicated to

Mrs. Tyler. They are quite beautiful.'" *See also* Margaret Gardiner to Julia Gardiner Tyler, New York, May 16, 1845, *TFP*, wherein Margaret dubs Lovel Purdy "the last of Pea-Time" and notes his interest in procuring a consulship. Margaret did not think the "Julia Waltzes" very pretty, nor Purdy much of a human being.

[16] Phoebe Gardiner to Julia Gardiner Tyler, Shelter Island, Dec. 3, 1844, *TFP*. Julia was very close to her Uncles Samuel and Nathaniel, her father's younger brothers. Samuel, a lawyer by profession, lived most of his life on Shelter Island, L.I., and was prominent in N.Y. state politics, having served at various times as Secretary of the N.Y. State Constitutional Convention (1821), Member of the N.Y. State Assembly from N.Y.C. (1823–1824), and Deputy Collector of the Port of New York (1825–1828). Julia was particularly close to his daughters, Mary (1824–1855), Phoebe (1826–?), and Francis Eliza (1832–?). Julia's Uncle Nathaniel married Elizabeth Stensin (1793–1842), and by her he had six children. The eldest, John Bray Gardiner (1821–1881) was Yale 1840 and became a lawyer in N.Y.C. The next eldest was William Henry Gardiner (1822–1879), NYU 1844, who became a physician in Brooklyn. Julia liked neither of these cousins and indeed had little to do with any of Nathaniel's children. The Nathaniel Gardiners lived in Sag Harbor, L.I., during Julia's childhood. Soon after Julia's Aunt Elizabeth died in June 1842 her Uncle Nathaniel married a young Miss Howell, a match which generally horrified the family. Nothing is known of Miss Howell save the family opinion that she was a fortune-hunter. For these and other genealogical facts about the extensive Gardiner family *see* C. C. Gardiner, *Lion Gardiner and His Descendants, passim.*

[17] Margaret Gardiner to Alexander Gardiner, Washington, Dec. 27, 1844, *GPY;* *ibid.,* Jan. 2, 1845, *TFP.*

[18] *Ibid.,* Dec. 30, 1844; Jan. 11, 1845, *GPY*. Dr. Wat Tyler, the President's brother, was, on the other hand, quite welcome at the White House and he was graciously entertained there in January 1845. *See ibid.,* Jan. 25, 1845, *GPY.*

[19] Mary Gardiner to Julia Gardiner, Shelter Island, Feb. 6, 1840; Nov. 27, 1839; Margaret Gardiner to Julia Gardiner Tyler, New York [Nov. 1844], *TFP*. Alexander Gardiner, a stern judge of women, said of Mary and Phoebe when they were sixteen and fourteen respectively: "They altogether lack matter of conversation and hide their talents under a bushel [but] they are somehow interesting." Alexander Gardiner to Juliana Gardiner [New York, Summer 1840], *GPY.*

[20] Margaret Gardiner to Alexander Gardiner, Washington, Jan. 1; 8; 22, 1845, *GPY*. Horsford was A.M., Union College, 1843; A.M. (Hon.) Harvard College, 1847; and M.D., Castleton Medical College (Vt.), 1847. In 1861–1862 he served as Dean, Lawrence Science School, Harvard University.

[21] Samuel Gardiner to Alexander Gardiner, Shelter Island, June 2, 1843; Alexander Gardiner to Samuel Gardiner, New York, June 5, 1843, *GPY.*

[22] Unidentified newspaper clipping; Margaret Gardiner to Alexander Gardiner, Washington, Jan. 8, 1845, *GPY;* Robert Tyler, "Phoebe the Coquette," poem quoted in Margaret Gardiner to Julia Gardiner Tyler, New York, Feb. 27, 1845, *TFP.*

[23] Margaret Gardiner to Alexander Gardiner, Washington, Jan. 5; 10, 1845, *GPY.*

[24] *Ibid.,* Jan. 22; Feb. 12; 20, 1845, *GPY*. In 1847 Douglas married Martha Martin, daughter of Col. Robert Martin of North Carolina. Her death in 1853 very nearly broke him psychologically. In 1856 he married Adele Curtis, a Maryland belle and grandniece of Dolley Madison. Adele Curtis Douglas later became the undisputed leader of Washington society, especially during the winter of 1857–1858, when bachelor President James Buchanan was in the White House.

[25] Margaret Gardiner to Alexander Gardiner, Washington, [Mid-Jan. 1845], *GPY.*

[26] *Ibid.*, Jan. 10, 1845, *GPY;* New York *Herald,* Jan. 15, 1845.

[27] Margaret Gardiner to Alexander Gardiner, Washington, Dec. 29, 1844; Jan. 5; 11; 22; Feb. 8; Jan. 10; 1, 1845, *GPY;* Alexander Gardiner to Julia Gardiner Tyler and Margaret Gardiner, New York, Jan. 8, 1845, *TFP.*

[28] Margaret Gardiner to Alexander Gardiner, Washington, Jan. 22; 23, 1845; Margaret Gardiner to Julia Gardiner Tyler, New York, Feb. 28, 1845, *GPY.*

[29] Julia Gardiner Tyler to Juliana Gardiner, Washington [Dec. 1844], *TFP;* Margaret Gardiner to Alexander Gardiner, Washington, Dec. 29, 1844; Jan. 23, 1845; Juliana Gardiner to Alexander Gardiner, Washington, Feb. 11, 1845, *GPY.*

[30] Margaret Gardiner to Alexander Gardiner, Washington, Dec. 27, 1844; Jan. 1, 1845, *GPY;* Alexander Gardiner to Julia Gardiner Tyler, New York, Jan. 8, 1845, *TFP;* David L. Gardiner to Alexander Gardiner, Washington, Jan. 9, 1845, *GPY.*

[31] Margaret Gardiner to Alexander Gardiner, Washington, Jan. 5, 1845, *GPY.*

[32] Julia Gardiner Tyler to Juliana Gardiner, Washington [Dec. 1844]; Juliana Gardiner to Alexander Gardiner, Washington, Feb. 11, 1845, *TFP;* Margaret Gardiner to Alexander Gardiner, Washington, Feb. 12; 20, 1845; Margaret Gardiner and Juliana Gardiner to Alexander Gardiner, Washington [Feb. 12, 1845]; David L. Gardiner to Alexander Gardiner, Washington, Feb. 14, 1845, *GPY.*

[33] Juliana Gardiner to Alexander Gardiner (two letters), Washington, Feb. 11, 1845, *GPY;* and *ibid., TFP;* Margaret Gardiner to Alexander Gardiner, Washington, Jan. 11, 1845; *see also ibid.,* Jan. 10; Feb. 12; 20, 1845, for further data on David Lyon's relations with the Misses Henderson, Wright, and Bayard. For the Alice Tyler-David L. Gardiner rumor, *see ibid.,* Jan. 22, 1845, *GPY.*

[34] *Ibid.,* Jan. 23, 1845; Phoebe Gardiner to Julia Gardiner Tyler, Shelter Island, Mar. 28, 1845, *TFP.* (Alice Tyler's proposals came from a Mr. Lawrence of New York, a Dr. Esselman of Tennessee, and a Judge Irvin of Virginia.) David L. Gardiner to Juliana Gardiner, Washington, Dec. 21, 1844, *GPY;* Julia Gardiner Tyler to Mary Hedges, Washington [Jan. 22, 1845], *TFP.*

[35] Alice Tyler to Julia Gardiner Tyler [Williamsburg], Nov. 6, 1844; Juliana Gardiner to Julia Gardiner Tyler [New York], n.d. [probably mid-Nov. 1844], *TFP.*

[36] Margaret Gardiner to Alexander Gardiner, Washington, Jan. 22, 1845; Dec. 29, 1844; Feb. 12, 1845, *GPY;* Margaret Gardiner to Phoebe Gardiner, New York, Mar. 27, 1845; Phoebe Gardiner to Julia Gardiner Tyler, Shelter Island, Mar. 28, 1845, *TFP.* Cushing had married Caroline Elizabeth Wilde in Newburyport, Mass., in November 1824. She was frail, her health was poor, and she was often confined indoors until her death in August 1832. Her passing left Cushing truly griefstricken. Claude M. Fuess, *The Life of Caleb Cushing,* 2 vols. (New York, 1923), I, 58–59, 129–30. His interest in Alice Tyler seems to have been the first in any other woman since the death of his wife.

[37] Juliana Gardiner to Alexander Gardiner, Washington, Feb. 12, 1845; Margaret Gardiner to Alexander Gardiner, Washington [mid-Jan. 1845], *GPY;* Juliana Gardiner to Alexander Gardiner, Washington, n.d. [*circa* Jan. 25, 1845]; Julia Gardiner Tyler to Mary Hedges, Washington [Jan. 22, 1845], *TFP.*

[38] Juliana Gardiner to Julia Gardiner Tyler, New York, Dec. 1 [1844]; Juliana Gardiner to Alexander Gardiner, New York, Feb. 25; 28, 1845, *TFP;* Margaret Gardiner to Alexander Gardiner, Washington, Feb. 8, 1845, *GPY.*

[39] *Ibid.,* Jan. 1, 1845, *GPY; ibid.,* Jan. 2, 1845, *TFP.*

[40] New York *Herald,* Jan. 3, 1845.

[41] *Ibid.,* Jan. 12, 1845.

[42] Margaret Gardiner to Alexander Gardiner, Washington, Jan. 8, 1845, *GPY.*

[43] Juliana Gardiner to Alexander Gardiner, Washington, Jan. 8, 1845, *GPY.*

[44] Margaret Gardiner to Alexander Gardiner, Washington, Jan. 10; 11, 1845, *GPY.*

[45] Bess Furman, *White House Profile* (Indianapolis, 1951), 129.

⁴⁶ Julia Gardiner Tyler to Mary Hedges, Washington [Jan. 22, 1845], *TFP;* Margaret Gardiner to Alexander Gardiner, Washington, Jan. 22, 1845, *GPY.*
⁴⁷ *Ibid., GPY.*
⁴⁸ *Ibid.,* Jan. 11; 24, 1845, *GPY.*
⁴⁹ Juliana Gardiner to Alexander Gardiner, Washington, Jan. 8, 1845, *GPY.*
⁵⁰ Alexander Gardiner to John Tyler, Post Office, New York, midnight, Jan. 24, 1845, *GPY.*
⁵¹ Margaret Gardiner to Alexander Gardiner, Washington, Jan. 22; 25; Feb. 7, 1845, *GPY;* F. W. Thomas to Julia Gardiner Tyler (two letters), Washington, n.d. [*circa* Feb. 10-12, 1845]; O. B. Goldsmith to John Tyler, New York, Jan. 15, 1845, *TFP.*
⁵² David L. Gardiner to Alexander Gardiner, Washington, Feb. 14, 1845; Margaret Gardiner to Alexander Gardiner, Washington, Feb. 12, 1845, *GPY;* Juliana Gardiner to Alexander Gardiner, Washington [Feb. 9, 1845]; Juliana Gardiner to Julia Gardiner Tyler, New York, May 19, 1845; F. W. Thomas to Julia Gardiner Tyler, Washington, n.d. [Feb. 10-12, 1845], *TFP.*
⁵³ Juliana Gardiner and Margaret Gardiner to Julia Gardiner Tyler, New York, May 19, 1845, *TFP.*
⁵⁴ This account of the Feb. 18 ball is based primarily upon Margaret Gardiner to Alexander Gardiner, Washington, Feb. 20, 1845, *GPY;* and upon Thomas' account in the New York *Herald,* Feb. 22, 1845; *see also LTT,* II, 361.
⁵⁵ Alexander Gardiner, "Mrs. Tyler's Farewell Ball," Washington, Feb. 20, 1845, *TFP;* David L. Gardiner to Alexander Gardiner, New York, Feb. 26, 1845, *GPY.*
⁵⁶ John Tyler to Editors of the *U.S. Journal,* James City, Va., Dec. 27, 1845, in Noah, "Reminiscences," New York *Sunday Dispatch,* Jan. 11, 1846.

CHAPTER II

¹ Margaret Gardiner to Alexander Gardiner, Washington, Jan. 5; 8; 10; Feb. 11; 12, 1845, *GPY;* Juliana Gardiner to Julia Gardiner Tyler, New York [Nov. 1844]; Dec. 1, 1844, *TFP;* Margaret Gardiner to Alexander Gardiner, Washington [Jan. 1845], *GPY;* Julia Gardiner Tyler to Mary Hedges, Washington [Jan. 22, 1845], *TFP;* Juliana Gardiner to Alexander Gardiner, Washington, Feb. 12, 1845, *GPY.*
² John Tyler to N. P. Tallmadge, Washington, Nov. 7, 1844, in Lyon G. Tyler (ed.), "Some Letters of Tyler ...," *loc. cit.,* 9; Margaret Gardiner to Juliana Gardiner, Washington, Dec. 23, 1844, *TFP;* New York *Herald,* Mar. 8, 1845.
³ He suggested that the District Attorney, Ogden Hoffman ("The fact is he is a Webster man") be replaced by R. H. Morris; that Surveyor Jonathan O. Fowler give way to Charles G. Ferris, a protégé of Robert Tyler and onetime Tyler nominee for the collectorship but rejected by the Senate; and that U.S. Marshal Stilwell be replaced by William Shaler. He was not convinced, however, that Shaler would gain Senate approval, and suggested for him the alternate job of consul at Havana, a post once held by Shaler's father under Jackson. Alexander Gardiner to John Tyler, New York, Nov. 27, 1844, *TFP; ibid.,* Nov. 23, 1844, *TPLC.* Tyler had no use for Hoffman or Stilwell and was quite ready to purge them. But largely on the advice of Gen. William Gibbs McNeill, a frequent White House visitor during these months and according to Margaret "not at all afraid to speak *his thoughts,*" Tyler nominated Henry C. Atwood as Surveyor and James H. Suydam as Navy Agent. When Suydam was rejected by the Senate, thanks in large measure to the hostile intervention of James Watson Webb, editor of the New York *Courier and Enquirer,* Tyler nominated Prosper M. Wetmore as

597

Navy Agent. Wetmore's brother, Robert C., had earlier been removed from the same job by Tyler for corruption. He had, however, the strong support of the New York mercantile community. Margaret Gardiner to Alexander Gardiner, Washington, Jan. 10; Feb. 12, 1845; Cornelius P. Van Ness to John Tyler, New York, Jan. 4, 1845, *GPY;* John Tyler to Alexander Gardiner, Washington, Dec. 1, 1844, in *LTT,* II, 357. See also New York *Herald,* Dec. 13, 1844; Jan. 14; 15; 18; Feb. 9, 1845; New York *Courier and Enquirer,* Dec. 4, 1844. On the Ely Moore appointment, *see* Alexander Gardiner to Julia Gardiner Tyler, New York, Jan. 8, 1845, *TFP.*

[4] David H. Broderick to Alexander Gardiner, New York, Nov. 12, 1844; Thomas Dunn English to Alexander Gardiner, New York, Nov. 20, 1844; William Shannon to Alexander Gardiner, New York, Nov. 20, 1844, *GPY;* Alexander Gardiner to John Tyler, New York, Dec. 6; Nov. 28, 1844, *TFP; ibid.,* Nov. 23, 1844, *TPLC;* David Palmer to Alexander Gardiner, Brooklyn, Nov. 24; Dec. 5, 1844; David Palmer to John Tyler, Brooklyn, n.d.; Alexander Gardiner to David Palmer [New York, Nov. 26, 1844]; William Gibbs McNeill to Alexander Gardiner, Brooklyn, Dec. 13, 1844, *GPY.*

[5] Alexander Gardiner to Julia Gardiner Tyler, New York, Dec. 8, 1844, *TPLC;* Juliana Gardiner to Julia Gardiner Tyler, New York [Nov. 27, 1844]; Margaret Gardiner to Julia Gardiner Tyler, New York, Nov. 27, 1844, *TFP;* Judge Ogden Edwards to David L. Gardiner, New York [Nov. 1844], *GPY.*

[6] Margaret Gardiner to Julia Gardiner Tyler, East Hampton, Aug. 18, 1844; Julia Gardiner Tyler to Alexander Gardiner, Washington, Nov. 25, 1844; Mrs. William Lynde [*née* M. P. Stimson] to Julia Gardiner Tyler, New York, Dec. 11, 1844, *GPY.*

[7] Alexander Gardiner to John Tyler, New York, Nov. 30, 1844; Alexander Gardiner to Julia Gardiner Tyler, New York, Jan. 8, 1845; Julia Gardiner Tyler to Alexander Gardiner, Washington, Dec. 10, 1844, *TFP;* John Tyler to Alexander Gardiner, Washington, Dec. 8, 1844, in *LTT,* II, 359.

[8] Southampton Citizens Petition to Charles A. Wickliffe, Forwarded to Alexander Gardiner, Southampton, N.Y., Dec. 11, 1844, *GPY;* John Tyler to Alexander Gardiner, Washington, Dec. 1, 1844, in *LTT,* II, 357; Judge R. J. Church to Alexander Gardiner, Brooklyn, Dec. 4, 1844; Amos Palmer to the Appriser's [*sic*] Office, Forwarded to Alexander Gardiner, New York, Dec. 30, 1844; John Lorimer Graham to Alexander Gardiner, New York, Dec. 6, 1844, *GPY;* Alexander Gardiner to Julia Gardiner Tyler, New York, Dec. 15, 1844, *TFP;* New York *Courier and Enquirer,* Dec. 4, 1844. The criticism from the *Courier and Enquirer,* sent to Alexander by John Lorimer Graham, was found carefully preserved among his papers a century and a quarter later. He apparently got a wry pleasure from it. Better notoriety than anonymity.

[9] Alexander Gardiner to Julia Gardiner Tyler, New York, Dec. 15, 1844, *TFP;* Alexander L. Botts to Alexander Gardiner, New York, Dec. 2, 1844; Daniel Dayton to Alexander Gardiner, East Hampton, Feb. 15, 1845. The appointment of distant cousin Charles Gardiner of Brooklyn to a clerkship in the Brooklyn Navy Yard was somewhat more smoothly handled. David L. Gardiner to Alexander Gardiner, Brooklyn, June 11, 1844, *GPY.*

[10] John D. Gardiner to John Tyler, Sag Harbor, Dec. 6, 1844, *TFP;* Mary L'Hommedieu Gardiner [Mrs. John D. Gardiner], to Julia Gardiner Tyler, Sag Harbor, Dec. 18, 1844, *GPY;* Julia Gardiner Tyler to Juliana Gardiner [Old Point Comfort], July [5], 1844; Margaret Gardiner to Julia Gardiner Tyler, East Hampton, Aug. 8, 1844, *TFP.*

[11] New York *Herald,* Apr. 27, 1845; [David L. Gardiner?] to James Gordon Bennett, Apr. 7, 1845, (draft fragment of a letter), *GPY.*

[12] Samuel L. Gardiner to David L. Gardiner, Sag Harbor, Jan. 19, 1845, *GPY.*

[13] David L. Gardiner to Julia Gardiner Tyler, East Hampton, Sept. 3, 1844, *TFP*.
[14] Julia Gardiner Tyler to Juliana Gardiner, Washington, Sept. 8, 1844; Alexander Gardiner to Julia Gardiner Tyler, East Hampton, Sept. 3, 1844; New York, Oct. 14, 1844, *TFP*.
[15] *Ibid.*, Dec. 7, 1844; Jan 8, 1845, *TFP;* Ezra L'H. Gardiner to Alexander Gardiner, Sag Harbor, Jan. 2, 1845, *GPY;* New York *Herald,* Feb. 11, 1845; Alexander Gardiner to John Tyler, New York, Nov. 23, 1844, *TPLC.*
[16] *Ibid.,* Nov. 28; Dec. 15, 1844, *TFP; ibid.,* Nov. 23, 1844, *TPLC.*
[17] *Ibid.,* Dec. 15, 1844, *TFP;* Mary L'H. Gardiner to Julia Gardiner Tyler, Sag Harbor, Dec. 18, 1844, *GPY.*
[18] Samuel L. Gardiner to David L. Gardiner, Sag Harbor, Jan. 19, 1845; Alexander Gardiner, Memorandum, n.p., n.d. [New York, *circa* mid-Jan. 1845], *GPY;* Juliana Gardiner to Alexander Gardiner, Washington, Feb. 9, 1845; David L. Gardiner to Alexander Gardiner, Washington, Jan. 19, 1845, *TFP.*
[19] George D. Strong to Alexander Gardiner, Washington, Jan. 4, 1845, *GPY;* Alexander Gardiner to Julia Gardiner Tyler, New York, Oct. 14, 1844, *TFP;* New York *Herald,* Feb. 11, 1845; John N. Dayton to Alexander Gardiner, Albany, Jan. 19, 1845, *GPY.*
[20] Juliana Gardiner to Alexander Gardiner, Washington, Feb. 9, 1845, *TFP;* Alexander Gardiner to Margaret Gardiner [Washington, Feb. 27, 1845], *GPY;* Juliana Gardiner to Alexander Gardiner [Washington, *circa* Jan. 25, 1845], *TFP.*
[21] John N. Dayton to Alexander Gardiner, Albany, Feb. 12; 15, 1845, *GPY;* New York *Herald,* Apr. 27, 1845; Juliana Gardiner to Julia Gardiner Tyler, New York, Apr. 10, 1845, *TFP.*
[22] Margaret Gardiner to Alexander Gardiner, Washington, Dec. 29, 1844, *GPY;* Juliana Gardiner to Alexander Gardiner, Washington, Feb. 11, 1845, *TFP.* Juliana thought Sarah Polk "looked very well and acted her part well."
[23] Margaret Gardiner to Alexander Gardiner, Washington, Dec. 29, 1844, *GPY;* Juliana Gardiner to Alexander Gardiner [Washington, Feb. 9, 1845; mid-Jan. 1845], *TFP;* David L. Gardiner to Alexander Gardiner, Washington, Jan. 9, 1845, *GPY;* New York *Herald,* Dec. 30, 1844.
[24] Margaret Gardiner to Alexander Gardiner, Washington, Jan. 1, 1845, *GPY;* J. George Harris to George Bancroft, Nashville, Sept. 13, 1887, in Lyon G. Tyler, "Some Letters of Tyler...," *loc. cit.,* 14–15; Silas Reed to Lyon G. Tyler, Boston, Apr. 8, 1885; A. V. Brown to James K. Polk, Washington, Jan. 24, 1845, in *LTT,* II, Appendix D, 698; III, 157–58; New York *Herald,* Jan. 15; 16, 1845.
[25] *Ibid.,* Jan. 18; Mar. 12, 1845.
[26] *Ibid.,* Jan. 14, 1845; David L. Gardiner to Alexander Gardiner, Washington, Feb. 8; 26, 1845; Juliana Gardiner to Alexander Gardiner, Washington, Feb. 11, 1845, *GPY;* New York *Herald,* Mar. 6, 1845; Alexander Gardiner to Julia Gardiner Tyler, New York, Jan. 2, 1845, *TPLC.*
[27] John Lorimer Graham to Alexander Gardiner, New York, Dec. 19; 22; 25, 1844; Jan. 4, 1845; N. T. Eldridge to Alexander Gardiner, New York, Jan. 9, 1845, *GPY;* New York *Herald,* Jan. 14, 1845. Tyler's use of profanity was often commented upon. "The People here make a great fuss about the President's *swearing,*" Margaret wrote Julia soon after the Old Point Comfort honeymoon. "If so, you must bid him read *St. Matthew....*" Margaret Gardiner to Julia Gardiner Tyler, New York, n.d. [*circa* Nov. 1844], *TFP.*
[28] Alexander Gardiner to Julia Gardiner Tyler, New York, Dec. 8, 1844, *TPLC.*
[29] New York *Herald,* Jan. 31; Feb. 2; 6; Jan. 29; Mar. 6; Jan. 2, 1845.
[30] Alexander Gardiner, Texas Resolutions and Memorandum, n.p., n.d. [New York, Jan. 24, 1845]; Alexander Gardiner to John Tyler, New York, midnight, Jan. 24, 1845, *GPY; LTT,* II, 360. An account of Tammany's "Great Texas Meet-

ing" and Robert Tyler's speech there is found in the New York *Herald,* Jan. 25, 1845. Also addressing the rally were Cornelius P. Van Ness, John I. Mumford, and David H. Broderick.

[31] *Ibid.,* Jan. 27; 29, 1845; New York *Express,* Jan. 28, 1845.

[32] Alexander Gardiner, Draft Memorandum on Texas Annexation, n.p., n.d. [New York, Nov. 1844–Feb. 1845], *GPY;* Margaret Gardiner to Julia Gardiner Tyler, New York, Dec. 16, 1845, *TFP;* Interview with Judge J. Randall Creel and his wife, Alexandra Gardiner Creel, Oyster Bay, Long Island, N.Y., Aug. 28, 1959. Judge Creel summarized for the author the contents of some dozen Alexander Gardiner and Julia Gardiner Tyler letters bearing on the Texas annexation question. These letters, held apart from those deposited by Mrs. Creel in the Manuscript Collection of Yale University Library, support the statement on Alexander Gardiner's considerable propaganda and pressure activities on behalf of Texas annexation during the period November 1844 to February 1845. They also point up Julia's flirtations and social machinations for annexation at various White House functions in greater detail than do those letters in the *Gardiner Papers* at Yale. Unfortunately, these crucial letters became lost, were misplaced in moving, or were accidentally burned during the winter of 1958–1959.

[33] Margaret Gardiner to Alexander Gardiner, Washington, Dec. 28; Jan. 10; 25, 1845; David L. Gardiner to Alexander Gardiner, Washington, Jan. 9, 1845, *GPY;* Juliana Gardiner to Alexander Gardiner, Washington, Feb. 11; 28, 1845, *TFP.*

[34] Julia Gardiner Tyler to [Alexander Gardiner] [Washington], Feb. 23, 1845. in *LTT,* II, 361; Alexander Gardiner to Margaret Gardiner [Washington, Feb. 27, 1845], *GPY;* Margaret Gardiner to Julia Gardiner Tyler, New York, Mar. 7, 1845, *TFP; LTT,* II, 362–65.

[35] Julia Gardiner Tyler, "Reminiscences," in *ibid.,* III, 200; Julia Gardiner Tyler to Juliana Gardiner, Richmond, Mar. 6, 1845, in *ibid.,* II, 369; Margaret Gardiner to Julia Gardiner Tyler, New York, Mar. 7, 1845, *TFP;* New York *Herald,* Mar. 4, 1845; Alexander Gardiner to Margaret Gardiner, Washington, Mar. 4, 1845, *TPLC; LTT,* II, 365–66.

[36] Alexander Gardiner to Julia Gardiner Tyler, New York, Jan. 2, 1845, *TPLC;* Juliana Gardiner to Alexander Gardiner, Washington, n.d. [mid-Jan. 1845], *TFP.*

[37] John Tyler to Alexander Gardiner, Washington, May 11, 1844, *GPY.*

[38] Alexander Gardiner to Julia Gardiner Tyler, East Hampton, Sept. 3, 1844; Julia Gardiner Tyler to Juliana Gardiner, Washington, Sept. 8, 1844; Julia Gardiner Tyler to Alexander Gardiner, Washington, Dec. 8, 1844, *TFP.*

[39] Robert Tyler and John Tyler, quoted in Margaret Gardiner to Alexander Gardiner, Washington, Jan. 23, 1845, *GPY;* Alexander Gardiner to Julia Gardiner Tyler, New York, Dec. 9, 1844, *TPLC; ibid.,* Jan. 8, 1845, *TFP.*

[40] David L. Gardiner to Alexander Gardiner, Washington, Jan. 9; Feb. 9, 1845; Margaret Gardiner to Alexander Gardiner, Washington, Feb. 12, 1845; Juliana Gardiner to Alexander Gardiner, Washington, Feb. 11, 1845; William Gibbs McNeill to Alexander Gardiner, New York, Feb. 4; 6, 1845; Julia Gardiner Tyler to Alexander Gardiner, Washington, n.d. [*circa* Feb. 10–13, 1845], *GPY.*

[41] Alexander Gardiner to Julia Gardiner Tyler, New York, Dec. 8, 1844, *TPLC;* Joel B. Sutherland to Andrew Jackson, Philadelphia, Aug. 20, 1844, in *LTT,* III, 147; Alexander Gardiner to John Tyler, New York, Nov. 27, 1844, *TFP;* David L. Gardiner to Alexander Gardiner, Washington, Feb. 8, 1845, *GPY.*

[42] Alexander Gardiner to Julia Gardiner Tyler, New York, Apr. 11, 1845, *TFP;* Margaret Gardiner to Alexander Gardiner, Washington, Jan. 23, 1845, *GPY.*

[43] Juliana Gardiner to Alexander Gardiner, Washington, Feb. 9, 1845, *TFP;* New York *Herald,* Feb. 20, 1845; Margaret and Juliana Gardiner to Alexander

Gardiner, Washington [Feb. 12, 1845]; John Tyler to Alexander Gardiner, Sherwood Forest, July 13, 1847, *GPY;* Alexander Gardiner to Julia Gardiner Tyler, New York, Apr. 1; 15, 1845, *TPLC.* Judge Samuel Nelson's appointment to the Supreme Court was strongly urged by author James Fenimore Cooper. Tyler later (1847) said that Cooper's endorsement of Nelson most influenced his nomination of Nelson to the Court. Margaret thought Justice Nelson "not very remarkable in any way—about equal to what one might expect [from] such a village as Cooperstown." He was, she told Julia, "quite a handsome man but not particularly neat in his dress." *See* on Nelson, John Tyler to Alexander Gardiner, Sherwood Forest, July 13, 1847, *GPY;* Margaret Gardiner to Julia Gardiner Tyler, New York, May 16; June 13, 1845, *TFP.*

[44] The financial history of the Gardiner-Tyler family alliance is discussed and documented further in various following chapters. For details of the Alexander-Julia loan of April 1845 *see* Julia Gardiner Tyler to Juliana Gardiner, Sherwood Forest, Feb. 14; 28, 1851, *TFP.*

[45] Alexander Gardiner to Julia Gardiner Tyler, Washington, Feb. 13, 1846, in *LTT,* II, 451; Alexander Gardiner to David L. Gardiner, New York, July 2, 1847; Robert Tyler to Alexander Gardiner, Philadelphia, July 18, 1847; John Tyler to Alexander Gardiner, Sherwood Forest, July 13, 1847, *GPY;* Julia Gardiner Tyler to Juliana Gardiner, Sherwood Forest, July 13, 1847; Margaret Gardiner to Julia Gardiner Tyler, New York, Apr. 14, 1845; Juliana Gardiner to Alexander Gardiner, Washington [Feb. 9, 1845], *TFP.*

CHAPTER 12

[1] Margaret Gardiner to Alexander Gardiner, Washington, Feb. 20, 1845, *GPY.*

[2] Margaret Gardiner to Julia Gardiner Tyler, New York, Feb. 28, 1845, *GPY; ibid.,* Feb. 27, 1845; Juliana Gardiner to Alexander Gardiner, New York, Feb. 25, 1845 (Juliana left Washington in such haste that she did not return some dozen calls she owed. She instructed Alexander to present her apologies to those she had neglected); Phoebe Gardiner to Julia Gardiner Tyler, Shelter Island, Mar. 28, 1845; Juliana Gardiner to Julia Gardiner Tyler, New York, Feb. 28, 1845, *TFP.*

[3] John Tyler to Elizabeth Tyler Waller, Washington, Mar. 1, 1845, *TPLC;* Julia Gardiner Tyler to Mary Gardiner, Washington, n.d. [Mar. 1845]; Julia Gardiner Tyler to Juliana Gardiner, Richmond, Mar. 6, 1845; Alexander Gardiner to Margaret Gardiner, Washington, Mar. 4, 1845, in *LTT,* II, 365–66, 368–69, 368; New York *Herald,* Mar. 4; 5, 1845.

[4] Tyler's farewell speech in the Blue Room as recorded here is based on a composite of several published and unpublished eyewitness accounts, principally those found in Alexander Gardiner, Memorandum, Washington, n.d. [Mar. 5, 1845], *GPY;* New York *Journal of Commerce,* Washington, Mar. 3, 1845, reprinted in *LTT,* II, 366–67; New York *Herald,* Mar. 5, 1845; and on evidence found in Julia Gardiner Tyler, "Reminiscences," in *LTT,* III, 200. The author has changed verb tenses and the person of pronouns to cast it in the present tense.

[5] Alexander Gardiner, Memorandum, Washington, n.d. [Mar. 5, 1845], *GPY; ibid.,* Mar. 4, 1845; Julia Gardiner Tyler to Juliana Gardiner, Richmond, Mar. 6, 1845, in *LTT,* II, 367–68, 368–70.

[6] Margaret Gardiner to Julia Gardiner Tyler, New York, Mar. 9, 1845, *TFP;* New York *Herald,* Mar. 6, 1845.

[7] Alexander Gardiner to Julia Gardiner Tyler, Washington, Mar. 7, 1845,

TPLC; Margaret Gardiner to Alexander Gardiner, New York [Mar. 3, 1845], *TFP.* "Alas!" mourned Margaret, "I can direct no more [letters] under cover to the President of the United States."

[8] Julia Gardiner Tyler to Juliana Gardiner, Richmond, Mar. 6, 1845, in *LTT*, II, 368–70; Julia Gardiner Tyler, "Reminiscences," in *ibid.,* III, 201; Julia Gardiner Tyler to Alexander Gardiner, Richmond, Mar. 6, 1845; Julia Gardiner Tyler to Juliana Gardiner, Sherwood Forest, Mar. 9, 1845; Edmund Ruffin to Jane M. Ruffin, Marlbourne, Mar. 21, 1854 (copy), *TFP.*

[9] Julia Gardiner Tyler to Juliana Gardiner, Sherwood Forest, Mar. 9, 1845; Julia Gardiner Tyler to Alexander Gardiner, Sherwood Forest, Apr. 1, 1845; Margaret Gardiner to Phoebe Gardiner, New York, Mar. 27, 1845; Julia Gardiner Tyler to Margaret Gardiner, Sherwood Forest, Mar. 18, 1845; Julia Gardiner Tyler to Juliana Gardiner, Sherwood Forest, Apr. 3, 1845, *TFP.* "Your descriptions of Broadway and its promenades made me feel indeed like *two years ago,*" she confessed to her mother. "How I should like to have been with you in your walk just for the sake of Auld Lang Syne."

[10] Juliana Gardiner to Julia Gardiner Tyler, New York, Apr. 30, 1845; Julia Gardiner Tyler to Margaret Gardiner, Sherwood Forest, Apr. 10, 1845; Alexander Gardiner to Julia Gardiner Tyler, New York, Mar. 27, 1845; Julia Gardiner Tyler to Alexander Gardiner, Sherwood Forest, Apr. [16], 1845, *TFP;* Julia Gardiner Tyler to Margaret Gardiner, Sherwood Forest, Apr. 25, 1845, *GPY.* The reclining iron dogs may still be seen at Sherwood Forest, guarding the main entrance. Family tradition has it that they were procured from the Manor House on Gardiners Island. Julia's guitar music has not survived. "Collect *all* my guitar music that is left at home," Julia instructed Margaret on April 25, "and get me besides—'Come Sing That Simple Air Again' and 'The Origin of the Harp' if it is set easy to the guitar."

[11] Julia Gardiner Tyler to Alexander Gardiner, Sherwood Forest, Apr. [16], 1845; Margaret Gardiner to Julia Gardiner Tyler, New York, n.d. [*circa* Apr.–May 1845]; Julia Gardiner Tyler to David L. Gardiner, Sherwood Forest, Apr. 16, 1845. Juliana thought that "liveries in our country are bad taste. I have always thought so." Her daughter, obviously, did not agree. Juliana Gardiner to Julia Gardiner Tyler, New York, Nov. 18, 1845, *TFP.*

[12] Julia Gardiner Tyler to Margaret Gardiner, Sherwood Forest, n.d. [June 1845]; June 10, 1845; Julia Gardiner Tyler to Gen. Benjamin Butler, Staten Island, N.Y., Nov. 7, 1864, *TFP.*

[13] Julia Gardiner Tyler to Margaret Gardiner, Sherwood Forest, June 10, 1845, *TFP.*

[14] John Tyler to Messrs. Corcoran and Riggs, Sherwood Forest, Oct. 6, 1845, *TPLC;* Julia Gardiner Tyler to Alexander Gardiner, Sherwood Forest, July 22, 1845, *TFP;* John Tyler to Machen Boswell Seawell, Sherwood Forest, Nov. 11, 1845, in *Tyler's Quarterly,* XIII (October 1931), 76–77.

[15] Julia Gardiner Tyler to Margaret Gardiner, Sherwood Forest, Mar. 18, 1845; Julia Gardiner Tyler to Juliana Gardiner, Sherwood Forest, n.d. [*circa* May 15, 1845]; Juliana Gardiner to Julia Gardiner Tyler, New York, May 19, [1845]; Alexander Gardiner to Julia Gardiner Tyler, East Hampton, June 5, 1845, *TFP.*

[16] Julia Gardiner Tyler to Juliana Gardiner, Sherwood Forest, n.d. [mid–May 1845]; Juliana Gardiner to Julia Gardiner Tyler, New York, May 19; 22, 1845, *TFP;* John Tyler to Alexander Gardiner, Sherwood Forest, May 21, 1845, *TPLC;* Julia Gardiner Tyler to Juliana Gardiner, Sherwood Forest, June 17, 1845, *TFP.*

[17] *Ibid.,* Mar. 26, 1845; Juliana Gardiner to Julia Gardiner Tyler, New York, n.d. [May 1845]; Julia Gardiner Tyler to Margaret Gardiner, Sherwood Forest, Apr. 10; 16, 1845; Julia Gardiner Tyler to Alexander Gardiner, Sherwood Forest, June 17, 1845. Margaret had written her sister the latest New York scandal—a messy adultery case involving members of the prominent Dow and Van

Rensselaer families. This probably produced Julia's sharp view of the decline and fall of New York society. Margaret Gardiner to Julia Gardiner Tyler, New York, Mar. 22, 1845, *TFP*.

[18] Julia Gardiner Tyler to Margaret Gardiner, Sherwood Forest, June 19, 1845; Julia Gardiner Tyler to Alexander Gardiner, Sherwood Forest, June 17, 1845, *TFP*.

[19] For Tyler's farming operations at Sherwood Forest, 1845–1855, see Julia Gardiner Tyler to Margaret Gardiner, Sherwood Forest, June 19, 1845, *TFP;* Julia Gardiner Tyler to Margaret Gardiner Beeckman, Sherwood Forest, June 25, 1852, *TPLC;* Julia Gardiner Tyler to Juliana Gardiner, Sherwood Forest, June 6, 1849; Mar. 24; Apr. 9; June 19, 1851; Julia Gardiner Tyler to Alexander Gardiner, Sherwood Forest, June 17, 1845, *TFP;* Julia Gardiner Tyler to David L. Gardiner, Sherwood Forest, Jan. 14; Mar. 19, 1851, *GPY;* Alexander Gardiner to Julia Gardiner Tyler, New York, Aug. 6, 1845, *TPLC;* Juliana Gardiner to David L. Gardiner, Sherwood Forest, Mar. 10; 17, 1850; Sept. 27, 1855, *GPY; ibid.*, Aug. 25, 1853, *TFP;* David L. Gardiner to Julia Gardiner Tyler, East Hampton, Apr. 20, 1847, *GPY;* John Tyler to Philip R. Fendall, Sherwood Forest, Apr. 19, 1845, *Philip R. Fendall Papers,* Duke University Library; John Tyler to Alexander Gardiner, Sherwood Forest, Nov. 10, 1846, *TPLC; ibid.,* Feb. 21; Apr. 9, 1849, *GPY;* John Tyler to H. A. Cocke, Sherwood Forest, June 21, 1848, *Tyler Papers,* Duke University Library; John Tyler to Robert Tyler, Sherwood Forest, Apr. 17, 1850, in *LTT,* II, 482.

[20] Julia Gardiner Tyler to Margaret Gardiner, Sherwood Forest, June 19, 1845, *TFP*. For further details of Sherwood Forest agriculture prior to 1845, see John Tyler to Mary Tyler Jones, Washington, Dec. 20, 1843; June 4, 1844, *TPLC*.

[21] Julia Gardiner Tyler to Margaret Gardiner, Sherwood Forest, June 19, 1845, *TFP*.

[22] Julia Gardiner Tyler to Juliana Gardiner, Sherwood Forest, Dec. 16, 1845, *TFP*. See Chapter 19.

[23] Juliana Gardiner to Julia Gardiner Tyler, New York, Apr. 10; May 27; Oct. 29; Nov. 2; 18, 1845; David L. Gardiner to Julia Gardiner Tyler, New York, Nov. 10, 1845, *TFP*. Catherine left Sherwood Forest in the summer of 1847 to be married. Alexander was sure her husband would "scatter her earnings in a very brief period," and that she would be back again. But she never returned. Alexander Gardiner to Julia Gardiner Tyler, New York, June 1, 1847, *TPLC*.

[24] Julia Gardiner Tyler to Juliana Gardiner, Sherwood Forest, Feb. 17, 1847, *TFP*.

[25] *Tyler Family Papers*, 1845–1860, *passim*.

[26] Julia Gardiner Tyler to Juliana Gardiner, Sherwood Forest, Apr. 3, 1845; Elizabeth Tyler Waller to John Tyler, Williamsburg, May 19, 1845; Julia Gardiner Tyler to Margaret Gardiner, Sherwood Forest, Dec. 25; [Dec.] 1845, *TFP;* John Tyler to Elizabeth Tyler Waller, Sherwood Forest, Oct. 18, 1845, *TPLC*. For data on Julia's relations with Alice Tyler, see Julia Gardiner Tyler to Juliana Gardiner, Sherwood Forest, n.d. [July]; July 8, 1845; Julia Gardiner Tyler to Margaret Gardiner, Sherwood Forest, Mar. 18; Apr. 15; [Summer] 1845; Phoebe Gardiner to Margaret Gardiner, Shelter Island, June 26–28, 1845; Alice Tyler to Julia Gardiner Tyler, Williamsburg, May 29, 1845, *TFP*.

[27] David L. Gardiner to Alexander Gardiner, Washington, Jan. 9, 1845, *GPY;* New York *Herald,* Apr. 7; 30, 1845; Margaret Gardiner to Julia Gardiner Tyler, New York, Apr. 4; May 2, 1845; Julia Gardiner Tyler to Juliana Gardiner, Sherwood Forest, May 8; July 22, 1845, *TFP*. For the sad career of John Tyler, Jr., 1845–1855, see *Gardiner Papers,* 1845–1855, Yale University Library, *passim;* and *Tyler Family Papers,* 1845–1855, *passim*.

[28] Juliana Gardiner to Julia Gardiner Tyler, New York, May 19 [1845]; Julia Gardiner Tyler to Juliana Gardiner, Sherwood Forest, May 8, 1845, *TFP*.

²⁹ *Ibid.,* June 2, 1845; Julia Gardiner Tyler to Margaret Gardiner, Sherwood Forest, May 29; June 5; Oct. 9, 1845; Margaret F. Ritchie to Julia Gardiner Tyler, Brandon, n.d. [June 3, 1845]; Alexander Gardiner to Julia Gardiner Tyler, East Hampton, June 5, 1845; Julia Gardiner Tyler to Alexander Gardiner, Sherwood Forest, Dec. 9, 1845, *TFP; ibid.,* Richmond, Aug. 3, 1845, *GPY.* Cushing at various times on this trip south pursued Miss Ritchie, Miss Harper of Baltimore, Miss Bromlee of Richmond, and Miss Bruce of Richmond. "Miss Bruce has rejected, so they say, the Minister of China," Julia reported. "All his laurels were not quite enough for her or Miss Harper it seems. Perhaps he will distinguish himself another time and then try somewhere else again." Julia thought the Chinese vases were "magnifico... [though] what they are intended for I do not know except to look at, and so I have placed them before each mirror."

³⁰ Julia Gardiner Tyler to Juliana Gardiner, Old Point Comfort, June 27, 1845; Julia Gardiner Tyler to Margaret Gardiner, Old Point Comfort, June 29, 1845; Julia Gardiner Tyler to Alexander Gardiner, Sherwood Forest, Dec. 9, 1845, *TFP.* The campaign to propitiate the Ritchies paid handsome dividends. By February 1846 the Richmond *Enquirer,* now edited by Ritchie's son Robert, was carrying "flattering notices" of Tyler. Julia Gardiner Tyler to Margaret Gardiner, Sherwood Forest, Feb. 5, 1846, *TFP.*

³¹ *Ibid.,* Old Point Comfort, June 29, 1845, *TFP.*

³² Julia Gardiner Tyler to Juliana Gardiner, Sherwood Forest, June 12; 23; Nov. 20, 1845; *ibid.,* Norfolk, n.d. [Fall 1845], *TFP; LTT,* II, 466. There are several versions of the "General" epitaph. *See also* Joseph N. Kane, *Facts about the Presidents* (New York, 1959), 125.

³³ Juliana Gardiner to Margaret Gardiner, New York, Nov. 2, 1845; Juliana Gardiner to Julia Gardiner Tyler, New York, Oct. 29; [Nov. 1], 1845; Julia Gardiner Tyler to Juliana Gardiner, Sherwood Forest, Nov. 20; Dec. 5, 1845, *TFP.*

³⁴ *Ibid.,* June 23, 1845. For Julia's constant struggle against ticks, fleas, mosquitoes, and other insects at Sherwood Forest, *see ibid.* Needless to say, her compassion for God's creatures did not extend to these miserable pests. The insect problem was a continuing one for families along the James. Constant war raged between the human and insect kingdoms with honors about even. *See also* Juliana Gardiner to Julia Gardiner Tyler, New York, n.d. [1846], *TFP.*

³⁵ Alexander Gardiner to Julia Gardiner Tyler, New York, July 14, 1845; Julia Gardiner Tyler to Margaret Gardiner, Sherwood Forest, May 29, 1845, *TFP;* Julia Gardiner Tyler to Alexander Gardiner, Richmond, Aug. 3, 1845, *GPY.*

³⁶ Alice Tyler and Julia Gardiner Tyler to Margaret Gardiner, White Sulphur Springs, Va., Aug. 23, 1845, *TFP.*

³⁷ Julia Gardiner Tyler to Margaret Gardiner, Sherwood Forest, Apr. 16, 1845; Juliana Gardiner to Julia Gardiner Tyler, Newport, R.I., Aug. 20, 1845; Margaret Gardiner to [Alice Tyler], New York, Aug. 28, 1845, *TFP.*

³⁸ Margaret Gardiner and Juliana Gardiner to Julia Gardiner Tyler, New York, Aug. 19, 1845, *TFP.*

³⁹ Julia Gardiner Tyler to Juliana Gardiner, Sherwood Forest, June 17, 1845; Julia Gardiner Tyler to Alexander Gardiner, Sherwood Forest, June 17, 1845, *TFP; ibid.,* Richmond, Aug. 3; Sherwood Forest, Oct. 16, 1845; John Tyler to Alexander Gardiner, Philadelphia, Sept. 15, 1845; Robert Tyler to Alexander Gardiner, Philadelphia, Sept. 22, 1845, *GPY.*

⁴⁰ Julia Gardiner Tyler to Juliana Gardiner, Sherwood Forest, June 2, 1845; Julia Gardiner Tyler to Margaret Gardiner, Sherwood Forest, Oct. 23, 1845, *TFP.*

⁴¹ Julia Gardiner Tyler to Alexander Gardiner, Sherwood Forest, Oct. 16, 1845, *GPY.*

⁴² Julia Gardiner Tyler to Juliana Gardiner, Sherwood Forest, Dec. 4, 1845, *TFP.*

CHAPTER 13

[1] Julia Gardiner Tyler to [Margaret Gardiner], Sherwood Forest, n.d. [1846]; Margaret Gardiner to Juliana Gardiner, Washington, July 3, 1844, *TFP;* John Tyler to Alexander Gardiner, Washington, Dec. 8, 1844, in *LTT,* II, 359; Margaret Gardiner to Julia Gardiner Tyler, New York, May 1845; Julia Gardiner Tyler to Juliana Gardiner, Sherwood Forest, June 2, 1845; Julia Gardiner Tyler to Margaret Gardiner, Sherwood Forest, June 5, 1845; Julia Gardiner Tyler to Alexander Gardiner, Sherwood Forest, July 24, 1845, *TFP.*

[2] Robert Tyler to Alexander Gardiner, Philadelphia, July 25, [1846], *GPY;* Alexander Gardiner to Julia Gardiner Tyler, Rockaway, L.I., N.Y., Aug. 6, 1845, *TPLC.* Among papers which were generally pro-Tyler and were financially aided and otherwise sustained by Tyler, Robert, and Alexander were Dunn English's *Aristidean* in New York, Col. John S. Cunningham's Portsmouth (Va.) *New Era,* the Philadelphia *Truth-Teller,* and the Richmond (Va.) *Old Dominion.* The Norfolk (Va.) *Pilot* was also in this category. On this point *see* Julia Gardiner Tyler to Margaret Gardiner, Sherwood Forest, May 29, 1845, *TFP;* Julia Gardiner Tyler to Alexander Gardiner, Sherwood Forest, Mar. 17; Apr. 23, 1846; Robert Tyler to Alexander Gardiner, Philadelphia, Mar. 30, 1846, *GPY;* Alexander Gardiner to Julia Gardiner Tyler, New York, Apr. 17, 1846, *TPLC; LTT,* II, 411-12.

[3] Margaret Gardiner to Julia Gardiner Tyler, New York, May 4, 1845; Juliana Gardiner to Julia Gardiner Tyler [New York], Mar. 22 [1846]; Julia Gardiner Tyler to Margaret Gardiner, June 29, 1845; J. Holbrook to John Tyler, Boston, Nov. 9, 1844, *TFP;* New York *Herald,* Jan. 7, 1845; Robert Tyler to John Tyler, Philadelphia, Sept. 22 [1846], *TFP;* Julia Gardiner Tyler to Alexander Gardiner, Sherwood Forest, Apr. 23, 1845, *GPY;* John Tyler to Robert Tyler, Sherwood Forest, June 14, 1848, in *LTT,* II, 460; John Tyler to John Tyler, Jr., Sherwood Forest, Jan. 23, 1848, *Tyler Papers,* Duke University Library.

[4] Susan [?] to Julia Gardiner Tyler, Washington, Mar. 27, 1845, *TFP;* N. M. Miller to Alexander Gardiner, Washington, Mar. 31; 20, 1845; Alexander Gardiner to N. M. Miller, New York, Mar. 13, 1845, *GPY;* Margaret Gardiner to Julia Gardiner Tyler, New York, May 15, 1845, *TFP.*

[5] Alexander Gardiner to [James K. Polk], New York, n.d. [*circa* Mar.-May 1845] (two draft letters), *GPY.*

[6] Margaret Gardiner to Julia Gardiner Tyler, New York, May 9, 1845; Alexander Gardiner to Julia Gardiner Tyler, New York, Apr. 11, 1845, *TFP; ibid.,* Apr. 15, 1845, *TPLC;* Coleman, *Priscilla Cooper Tyler,* 111-12; 120-21. Tom Cooper retired from his inspectorship in the summer of 1846. He was then 71 and had become quite senile.

[7] Juliana Gardiner to Julia Gardiner Tyler, New York, May 9, 1845; Julia Gardiner Tyler to Juliana Gardiner [Sherwood Forest], n.d. [*circa* May 1845], *TFP;* Alexander Gardiner to Julia Gardiner Tyler [New York, Apr. 1, 1845], *TPLC;* Margaret Gardiner to Julia Gardiner Tyler, New York, May 6, 1845, *TFP;* George D. Strong to Alexander Gardiner, New York, Mar. 13, 1845, *GPY;* Alexander Gardiner to Julia Gardiner Tyler, East Hampton, June 5, 1845; Margaret Gardiner to Julia Gardiner Tyler, New York, June 23, 1845, *TFP.* On the question of Graham's honesty in office see the printed brochure of his December 1848 correspondence with Matthew St. Clair Clarke, former Auditor of the Post Office Department in *GPY.* The evidence is inconclusive.

[8] John Tyler to Alexander Gardiner, Sherwood Forest, May 21, 1845; N. P. Tallmadge to Robert J. Walker, Faycheedah, Wisconsin Territory, Apr. 15, 1845, in *LTT,* II, 445; III, 159; New York *Herald,* Apr. 14, 1845; Lyon G. Tyler, "The Annexation of Texas," *Tyler's Quarterly,* VI (October 1924), 88, 92-93.

[9] N. M. Miller to Alexander Gardiner, Washington, Mar. 20, 1845, *GPY;* Margaret Gardiner to Julia Gardiner Tyler, New York, Mar. 27, 1845; Alexander Gardiner to Julia Gardiner Tyler, New York, Mar. 27, 1845; Julia Gardiner Tyler to Juliana Gardiner, Sherwood Forest, Apr. 10, 1845, *TFP;* New York *Herald,* Mar. 22; 30, 1845; William Tyler to John Tyler, Washington, June 2, 1845; Robert Tyler to [Robert J.] Walker, Philadelphia, Oct. 17 [1845], *TPLC.*

[10] William Tyler to John Tyler, Washington, June 2, 1845, *TPLC;* John Tyler to William Collins, New York, Sept. 17, 1845, in Lyon G. Tyler, "Some Letters of Tyler...," *loc. cit.,* 10–11.

[11] John Tyler to Robert Tyler, n.p., n.d. [Sherwood Forest, Summer 1848], in *LTT,* II, 461–62; Alexander Gardiner to Julia Gardiner Tyler, East Hampton, June 5, 1845, *TFP;* Lyon G. Tyler, "The Annexation of Texas," *loc. cit.,* 92–93.

[12] Margaret Gardiner to Julia Gardiner Tyler, New York, June 5; 12; Dec. 16, 1845; Juliana Gardiner to Julia Gardiner Tyler, New York, n.d. [May 1845; 1846], *TFP;* John Lorimer Graham to Alexander Gardiner, New York, July 14, 1845; June 30, 1846; A. B. Conger to Alexander Gardiner, Sept. 20, 1846; N. M. Miller to Alexander Gardiner, Washington, June 5, 1846, *GPY.*

[13] Coleman, *Priscilla Cooper Tyler,* 113, 116–17, 122–23; James Buchanan to Robert Tyler, Washington, Dec. 13, 1847, *TPLC.* In May 1846 Priscilla's daughter Grace was born. When he began his Philadelphia law practice in 1845 Robert lived in Bristol, Pa., and commuted by train to his office every morning at six o'clock. His commuter's fare was $10 per year. He rented a small house in Bristol for $60 per year. With some justification for the view, Julia thought that he tended to live beyond his means. See Julia Gardiner Tyler to Alexander Gardiner, Sherwood Forest, July 22, 1845; Julia Gardiner Tyler to Juliana Gardiner, Sherwood Forest, n.d. [May 1845], *TFP.* Robert made extra money lecturing on such topics as "The Conflict Between Monarchial and Republican Principles" and "The Oregon Dispute." Alexander helped him engage halls for this activity in New York. *See* Alexander Gardiner to Julia Gardiner Tyler, New York, Feb. 22, 1846, *TPLC;* Alexander Gardiner to Robert Tyler, New York, Feb. 27, 1846, *GPY.* For concern for the plight of Robert and Priscilla felt within the family as a whole, *see* Julia Gardiner Tyler to Margaret Gardiner, Washington, Dec. 9, 1844; Juliana Gardiner to Julia Gardiner Tyler, New York, Apr. 30, 1845; Priscilla Cooper Tyler to Margaret Gardiner, Fire Island, N.Y., Aug. 29, [1845]; Juliana Gardiner to Julia Gardiner Tyler, New York, July 10, 1844; Margaret Gardiner to Julia Gardiner Tyler, New York, May 6, 1845; Mar. 26, 1846; Priscilla Cooper Tyler to Julia Gardiner Tyler, Philadelphia, Dec. 7 [1849]. Shortly after the death of Mary Fairlee in 1845, Priscilla's sense of sorrow and her feeling of economic privation caused her to explode in a jealous rage one day while visiting at 43 Lafayette Place. This unfortunate but human outburst against the Gardiners introduced some tension in her later relations with Julia and Margaret. Julia accused the distraught Priscilla of having an unrealistic amount of pride. *See* Julia Gardiner Tyler to Juliana Gardiner, Sherwood Forest, n.d. [*circa* June–July 1845], *TFP;* Coleman, *Priscilla Cooper Tyler,* 114, 122–23. For a brief biography of Robert Tyler, *see LTT,* II, 645–46, 684–87. Priscilla's children and their birthdates were: Mary Fairlee (Dec. 1840–June 1845); Letitia Christian (Spring, 1842); John IV (July 1844–July 1846); Grace (May 1846); Thomas Cooper (Summer 1848–July 1849); Priscilla Cooper (Oct. 1849); Elizabeth (Jan. 1852); Julia Campbell (Dec. 1854); Robert, Jr. (Dec. 1857).

[14] Alexander Gardiner to Julia Gardiner Tyler, Washington, Feb. 13, 1846, in *ibid.,* 451–53; Furman, *White House Profile,* 136; New York *Herald,* Mar. 16, 1845; Juliana Gardiner to Julia Gardiner Tyler, New York, Jan. 25, 1846; Julia Gardiner Tyler to Juliana Gardiner, Sherwood Forest, May 8, 1845, *TFP;* Alexander Gardiner to Julia Gardiner Tyler, Washington, May 7, 1845, *TPLC;* Julia Gardiner Tyler to Juliana Gardiner, Sherwood Forest, May 8, 1845; Juliana

Gardiner to Julia Gardiner Tyler, New York, n.d. [May 1845]; Margaret Gardiner to Julia Gardiner Tyler, New York, May 2; 9, 1845, *TFP.*

[15] Julia Gardiner Tyler to Juliana Gardiner, Sherwood Forest, n.d. [June 1845]; Julia Gardiner Tyler to Margaret Gardiner, Sherwood Forest, June 19, 1845; Juliana Gardiner to Margaret Gardiner, New York, July 7, 1845; Julia Gardiner Tyler to Alexander Gardiner, Sherwood Forest, Oct. 17, 1845; Alexander Gardiner to Julia Gardiner Tyler, New York, July 9, 1845, *TFP;* Andrew Jackson to James K. Polk, Hermitage, Dec. 13, 1844, in *LTT,* III, 155; Julia Gardiner Tyler to Juliana Gardiner, Sherwood Forest, June 23, 1845, *TFP.*

[16] Margaret Gardiner to Julia Gardiner Tyler [New York], July 18, 1845; Julia Gardiner Tyler to Alexander Gardiner, Sherwood Forest, July 22, 1845, *TFP; ibid.,* Richmond, Aug. 3, 1845, *GPY; ibid.,* Sherwood Forest, Oct. 23, 1845; Julia Gardiner Tyler to Juliana Gardiner, Sherwood Forest, Apr. 14, 1846; Margaret Gardiner to Julia Gardiner Tyler, New York, May 4, 1845; Julia Gardiner Tyler to Juliana Gardiner, Sherwood Forest, n.d. [May 1845], *TFP;* Alexander Gardiner to Julia Gardiner Tyler, Rockaway, L.I., N.Y. Aug. 6, 1845, *TPLC;* Julia Gardiner Tyler to Juliana Gardiner, Sherwood Forest, July 8, 1845, *TFP.*

[17] John Tyler to John Jones, Charles City, Sept. 11, 1845, *TPLC;* Julia Gardiner Tyler to Margaret Gardiner, Sherwood Forest, Apr. 16, 1846, *TFP;* Julia Gardiner Tyler to Alexander Gardiner, Sherwood Forest, Apr. 4; Jan. 27, 1846, *GPY.*

[18] John Tyler to Robert Tyler, Sherwood Forest, Mar. 12, 1848, in *LTT,* II, 107.

[19] Julia Gardiner Tyler to Alexander Gardiner, Sherwood Forest, Mar. 17; Apr. 23, 1846; Robert Tyler to Alexander Gardiner, Philadelphia, Mar. 30, 1846, *GPY;* Margaret Gardiner to Julia Gardiner Tyler, New York, Mar. 25, 1846, *TFP;* Julia Gardiner Tyler to Alexander Gardiner, Sherwood Forest, Apr. 7, 1846, *GPY.*

[20] Sarah A. Wharton to John Tyler, Brazoria County, Texas, July 22, 1845; John Tyler to Sarah A. Wharton, Sherwood Forest, Jan. 1, 1846, in Richmond *Enquirer,* Jan. 29, 1846. The pitcher, manufactured by Ball, Tompkins and Black of New York (formerly Marquand and Co.), was badly burned and blackened in the Richmond fire of April 1865. The inscription today can barely be read: "Presented by the Ladies of Brazoria County, Texas, to Ex-President Tyler as a small token of their gratitude for the benefits conferred upon their Country by procuring its Annexation to the U. States." Margaret Gardiner to Julia Gardiner Tyler, New York, Jan. 6; 9, 1846, *TFP.*

[21] Julia Gardiner Tyler to Juliana Gardiner, Sherwood Forest, Apr. 22, 1846, *TFP;* Alexander Gardiner to Julia Gardiner Tyler, New York, Apr. 17, 1846; May 4, 1847, *TPLC;* Juliana Gardiner to Julia Gardiner Tyler, New York, Apr. 12, 1846; Julia Gardiner Tyler to Margaret Gardiner, Sherwood Forest, Apr. 16, 1846, *TFP.*

[22] John Tyler to Robert Tyler, Washington, June 1, 1846; Sherwood Forest, Apr. 21, 1846. For additional details on the Ingersoll hearings and Tyler's role, *see* John Tyler to Daniel Webster, Sherwood Forest, Mar. 12; Apr. 21, 1846; John Tyler to Robert Tyler, Washington, May 30, 1846. When the Maine Boundary bribery charges were aired again in 1857 Tyler was forced to repeat his denials. *Ibid.,* Sherwood Forest, Sept. 17, 1857, in *LTT,* II, 457; 455; 228-29; 456; III, 172-73.

[23] John Tyler to Robert Tyler, Washington, May 30, 1846, in *ibid.,* II, 456; N. M. Miller to Alexander Gardiner, Washington, June 5, 1846; John L. Graham to Alexander Gardiner, Washington, June 30, 1846, *GPY.*

[24] Calhoun's speech of Feb. 24, 1847, quoted in *LTT,* II, 417.

[25] Alexander Gardiner to John Tyler, New York, Mar. 4, 1847, *GPY;* Alexander Gardiner to Julia Gardiner Tyler, New York, Mar. 11, 1847, *TPLC;* John Tyler to

Alexander Gardiner, Sherwood Forest, Mar. 11; June 17, 1847; John Tyler to Robert Tyler, Sherwood Forest, Mar. 11, 1847, in *LTT*, II, 420–22. The *Enquirer* letter of June 5, 1847, was reprinted in the New York *Herald*, June 7, 1847.

[26] Julia Gardiner Tyler to Alexander Gardiner, Sherwood Forest, Mar. 4, 1847, *GPY;* Juliana Gardiner to Julia Gardiner Tyler, New York, Feb. 27, 1847; n.d. [*circa* Mar. 6, 1847]; Alexander Gardiner to Julia Gardiner Tyler, New York, n.d. [*circa* June 1847], *TFP*.

[27] *LTT*, II, 427; John Tyler, Letter to the Editor of the Richmond *Enquirer*, Sherwood Forest, June 5, 1847; New York, Sept. 1, 1847; John Tyler to Alexander Gardiner, Sherwood Forest, Dec. 25, 1848, in *LTT*, II, 424–31, 433; New York *Herald*, June 7, 1847.

[28] Alexander Gardiner to John Tyler, New York, Nov. 6, 1848, *GPY;* John Tyler to Alexander Gardiner, Sherwood Forest, Dec. 25, 1848, *TPLC;* Julia Gardiner Tyler to Juliana Gardiner, Sherwood Forest, Nov. 1848; Julia Gardiner Tyler to Alexander Gardiner, Sherwood Forest, Jan. 2, 1849, *TFP;* John Tyler to Robert Tyler, n.p., n.d. [Sherwood Forest, 1856]; May 9, 1856; John Tyler to John S. Cunningham, Sherwood Forest, May 8, 1856; John Tyler to Thomas J. Green, Sherwood Forest, Feb. 28, 1856; Robert Tyler to John Tyler, Philadelphia, Aug. 27, 1858, in *LTT*, II, 297, 413–15; III, 171–72; II, 239–40.

[29] John Tyler to Robert Tyler, New York, Dec. 30, 1847; Alexander Gardiner to Julia Gardiner Tyler, New York, May 4; June 1, 1847, *TPLC;* John Tyler to Alexander Gardiner, Philadelphia, June 23, 1847, *GPY;* Juliana Gardiner to Julia Gardiner Tyler, New York, Apr. 27 [1847], *TFP*.

[30] John Tyler, Letter to Editor of Richmond *Enquirer*, Sherwood Forest, June 5, 1847, in *LTT*, II, 424; Margaret Gardiner to Julia Gardiner Tyler, New York, Mar. 25, 1846, *TFP;* Alexander Gardiner, Speech to Tammany Hall Meeting in Support of the War, Mar. 1, 1847, *GPY*. (Illness prevented Alexander from delivering this, a rabble-rousing address.) The same position on the origin of the Mexican War has been taken by the family biographer, Lyon G. Tyler. See *LTT*, II, 416–17; *see also* John Tyler to Caleb Cushing, Sherwood Forest, Oct. 14, 1845, in *ibid.*, 446.

[31] John Tyler to Editor of [Richmond *Enquirer*], n.p., n.d. [Sherwood Forest, Mar. 1847]; Alexander Gardiner to John Tyler, New York, Mar. 12, 1847, *TPLC;* John Tyler to Robert Tyler, Sherwood Forest, Apr. 14, 1846, in *LTT*, II, 455.

[32] Julia Gardiner Tyler to Juliana Gardiner, Sherwood Forest, Mar. 11, 1847, *GPY;* Juliana Gardiner to Julia Gardiner Tyler, New York, Mar. 23, 1847, *TFP;* John Tyler to Robert Tyler, Washington, May 30; June 1, 1846, in *LTT*, II, 456–57; Julia Gardiner Tyler to Margaret Gardiner, Sherwood Forest, May 6, 1847, *TFP;* Julia Gardiner Tyler to Alexander Gardiner, Sherwood Forest, n.d. [May 1847], in *LTT*, II, 433. When Purser Semple called at Sherwood Forest after the war, appearing "quite a Mexican with mustache and large beard," and bearing war-trophy gifts for Tyler, principally a suit of armor, Julia gave him a friendly reception. She had little regard or respect for him normally because she could not tolerate his wife, Letitia Tyler Semple. But in this instance the returning hero "behaved so well and complimented me so highly ... that I was not sorry I consented to see him." Julia Gardiner Tyler to Juliana Gardiner, Sherwood Forest, May 2, 1848, *TFP*.

[33] Alexander Gardiner, Speech to Tammany Hall Meeting in Support of the War, Mar. 1, 1847, *GPY;* Alexander Gardiner to Julia Gardiner Tyler, New York, Feb. 19, 1847, in *LTT*, II, 457–58; *ibid.*, Jan. 27, 1847, *TPLC;* John H. Beeckman to Margaret Gardiner Beeckman, New York, July 28, 1848, *TFP;* Alexander Gardiner to David L. Gardiner, New York, July 27, 1848, *GPY;* Juliana Gardiner to Julia Gardiner Tyler, New York, Mar. 1 [1847], *TFP*.

[34] Alexander Gardiner to Julia Gardiner Tyler, New York, Feb. 22; Apr. 6, 1846, in *LTT*, II, 453, 454; Margaret Gardiner to Julia Gardiner Tyler, New York, Jan. 21; Mar. 26, 1846, *TFP*. Robert lectured on the Oregon question before

Roman Catholic Irish groups in New York. Alexander and David Lyon often shared the platform with him. On one of these occasions, in March 1846, Juliana and Margaret "had a merry laugh" over David Lyon's account of his entrance into one of the Irish filled lecture halls "arm in arm with a *catholic Priest!*... D[avid] looked most sober."

[35] Quotation is a composite of John Tyler to Robert Tyler, Sherwood Forest, Dec. 23, 1845; Jan. 1; 26, 1846, in *LTT*, II, 449–50.

[36] *Ibid.*; Julia Gardiner Tyler to Margaret Gardiner, Sherwood Forest, Feb. 26, 1846; Alexander Gardiner to Julia Gardiner Tyler, New York, Mar. 29, 1846; Julia Gardiner Tyler to Juliana Gardiner, Sherwood Forest, May 8, 1845, *TFP;* Julia Gardiner Tyler to Alexander Gardiner, Sherwood Forest, Jan. 27, 1846, *GPY*.

[37] John Tyler to Alexander Gardiner, Sherwood Forest, Mar. 2, 1847; [John Tyler] to Editor of Portsmouth [Va.] *Pilot*, Sherwood Forest, n.d. [Feb. 1847], in *LTT*, II, 479, 478; Alexander Gardiner to Julia Gardiner Tyler, New York, Mar. 11, 1847, *TPLC;* Alexander Gardiner, Draft Ms. on Political Questions, n.d. [1847]; Alexander Gardiner, Speech to Tammany Hall Meeting in Support of the War, Mar. 1, 1847, *GPY*. The Proviso, in stirring up criticism of pro-Wilmot Van Burenism from the Conservative Democracy in New York, did have the effect of widening further the gap in that intraparty struggle in the Empire State. This Tyler regarded as a political benefit. John Tyler to Alexander Gardiner, Sherwood Forest, Nov. 1, 1847, *TPLC*.

[38] Robert Tyler to John C. Calhoun, Philadelphia, Apr. 19, 1845; Alexander Gardiner to Julia Gardiner Tyler, New York, Feb. 22, 1846, in *LTT*, III, 160–61; II, 453–54; *ibid.*, New York, Apr. 17, 1846, *TPLC;* Margaret Gardiner to Julia Gardiner Tyler, New York, Apr. 26, 1845, *TFP*.

[39] *Ibid.*, Mar. 31; May 26, 1845, *TFP*.

[40] Julia Gardiner Tyler to Margaret Gardiner, Sherwood Forest, Feb. 5, 1846, *TFP*.

CHAPTER 14

[1] Julia Gardiner Tyler to Margaret Gardiner, Sherwood Forest, Feb. 5, 1846, *TFP*.

[2] Juliana Gardiner to Julia Gardiner Tyler, New York, n.d. [February 1846]; Margaret Gardiner to Julia Gardiner Tyler, New York, Jan. 21, 1846, *TFP*.

[3] David L. Gardiner to Julia Gardiner Tyler, New York, Feb. 22, 1846, *TFP;* New York *Morning News*, Feb. 21; 22, 1846; Juliana Gardiner to Julia Gardiner Tyler, New York, n.d. [Mar.]; Mar. 1; Feb. 21, 1846; Margaret Gardiner to Julia Gardiner Tyler, New York, Feb. 20; 27; Mar. 6; Apr. 17, 1846; Julia Gardiner Tyler to Alexander Gardiner, Sherwood Forest, Mar. 3, 1846, *TFP*.

[4] Margaret Gardiner to Alexander Gardiner, East Hampton, July 17, 1846, *GPY;* Julia Gardiner Tyler to Juliana Gardiner, East Hampton, Aug. 17, 1846; Phoebe Gardiner to Margaret Gardiner, Shelter Island, July 1846; David L. Gardiner to Alexander Gardiner, New York, Aug. 7, 1846; Alexander Gardiner to Juliana Gardiner, New York, Sept. 20, 1846, *TFP*. Phoebe called the baby "His Little Excellency." Everyone else in the family at first called him "The Little President."

[5] Julia Gardiner Tyler to Juliana Gardiner, East Hampton, Aug. 17, 1846; Sherwood Forest, Dec. 28, 1846, *TFP; ibid.*, Mar. 11, 1847, *GPY;* Juliana Gardiner to Julia Gardiner Tyler, New York, Dec. 18, 1846; Mar. 23, 1847, n.p., n.d. [New York, Mar. 1847]; Julia Gardiner Tyler to Juliana Gardiner, East Hampton, Aug. 21, 1846, *TFP*.

[6] *Ibid.*, Sherwood Forest, Dec. 10, 1846; Alexander Gardiner to Julia Gardiner Tyler, Nov. 28, 1846, *TFP*.

[7] Julia Gardiner Tyler to Juliana Gardiner, Sherwood Forest, Mar. 11, 1847, *GPY;* John Tyler to Alexander Gardiner, Sherwood Forest, Mar. 11, 1847, in *LTT*, II, 420. For proud references to the excellence of her offspring, *see* Julia Gardiner Tyler to Alexander Gardiner, Sherwood Forest, Mar. 4, 1846; July 13, 1847, *GPY;* Julia Gardiner Tyler to Juliana Gardiner, Sherwood Forest, June 20, 1848; Julia Gardiner Tyler to Margaret Gardiner, Sherwood Forest, Feb. 2, 1847; Alexander Gardiner to Juliana Gardiner, Baltimore, Nov. 14, 1847, *TFP.*

[8] Juliana Gardiner to Julia Gardiner Tyler, n.p., n.d. [New York, 1847]; May 25, 1847, *TFP.*

[9] Julia Gardiner Tyler to Margaret Gardiner, Sherwood Forest, June 3, 1847; Juliana Gardiner to Julia Gardiner Tyler, New York, June 8, 1847, *TFP;* Julia Gardiner Tyler to Alexander Gardiner, Sherwood Forest, Mar. 4, 1847, *GPY.*

[10] Julia Gardiner Tyler to Margaret Gardiner Beeckman, Sherwood Forest, Feb. 27, 1848, *TFP.*

[11] Julia Gardiner Tyler to Alexander Gardiner, Sherwood Forest, Dec. 15, 1848, *GPY;* Alexander Gardiner to Julia Gardiner Tyler, New York, May 4, 1847; John Tyler to Dr. W. A. Patterson, Sherwood Forest, Apr. 9, 1848, *TPLC;* Julia Gardiner Tyler to Alexander Gardiner, Sherwood Forest, Nov. 24, 1848; Julia Gardiner Tyler to Juliana Gardiner, Sherwood Forest, May 1, 1848, *TFP.*

[12] Alexander Gardiner to Julia Gardiner Tyler, New York, July 9, 1845; Juliana Gardiner to David L. Gardiner, Newport, Aug. 28, 1845, *TFP;* Julia Gardiner Tyler to David L. Gardiner, Sherwood Forest, Jan. 14, 1851; Jan. 29, 1846, *GPY;* Julia Gardiner Tyler to Margaret Gardiner, Sherwood Forest, Jan. 15; Apr. 16, 1846; Margaret Gardiner to Julia Gardiner Tyler, New York, Jan. 1846; Julia Gardiner Tyler to Juliana Gardiner, Sherwood Forest, Feb. 26, 1851; Feb. 8, 1855; Juliana Gardiner to Julia Gardiner Tyler, New York, Jan. 18, 1846, *TFP;* Robert Tyler to Alexander Gardiner, Philadelphia, July 18, 1847; Julia Gardiner Tyler to David L. Gardiner, Sherwood Forest, June 9, 1858, *GPY.*

[13] Julia Gardiner Tyler to Alexander Gardiner, Sherwood Forest, Dec. 13, 1850, *TFP;* Alexander Gardiner to [John Tyler], New York, Sept. 28, 1849, *GPY;* Alexander Gardiner to Margaret Gardiner, New York, July 12, 1847, *TFP;* Margaret Gardiner to Alexander Gardiner, Washington, Jan. 1, 1843; Alexander Gardiner to Samuel Gardiner, New York, Feb. 19, 1849; Alexander Gardiner to David L. Gardiner [New York], Jan. 11, 1851, *GPY.*

[14] Margaret Gardiner Beeckman to Julia Gardiner Tyler, New York, Apr. 10, 1848; Phoebe Gardiner to Julia Gardiner Tyler, n.p., n.d. [Shelter Island, Summer 1847]; Phoebe Gardiner to Margaret Gardiner, Shelter Island, July 14; 28; Oct. 13, 1847, *TFP.*

[15] Juliana Gardiner to Julia Gardiner Tyler, New York, Nov. 11, 1845, *TFP.*

[16] Margaret Gardiner to Julia Gardiner Tyler, New York, Apr. 22, 1845; May [1846]; Julia Gardiner Tyler to Margaret Gardiner, Sherwood Forest, Apr. 10, 1845; Juliana Gardiner to Julia Gardiner Tyler, Newport, Aug. 20, 1845; New York [March]; Apr. 27, 1847, *TFP.*

[17] Margaret Gardiner to Julia Gardiner Tyler, New York, June 3, 1845; Feb. 24, 1846; May 4, 1845; Feb. 27, 1847; Julia Gardiner Tyler to Juliana Gardiner, Sherwood Forest, June 12; July 8, 1845; Priscilla Cooper Tyler to Margaret Gardiner, Fire Island, N.Y., Aug. 29, 1845; Phoebe Gardiner to Margaret Gardiner, Shelter Island, June 26; 28, 1845; Juliana Gardiner to Julia Gardiner Tyler, New York, Jan. 18, 1846, *TFP.*

[18] Julia Gardiner Tyler to Margaret Gardiner, Sherwood Forest, Dec. 25, 1845; Feb. 26, 1846; Margaret Gardiner to Julia Gardiner Tyler, New York, Feb. 27; Mar. 6, 1846; Juliana Gardiner to Julia Gardiner Tyler, New York, Mar. 1; 26, 1846, *TFP.*

[19] *Ibid.*, Feb. 27, 1847, *TFP;* Margaret Gardiner to David L. Gardiner, East Hampton, June 21, 1842; Margaret Gardiner to Alexander Gardiner, East Hampton, June 14, 1843, *GPY;* Margaret Gardiner to Julia Gardiner Tyler, New York, n.d.

[May 1845]; John H. Beeckman to Margaret Gardiner Beeckman, New York, June 23, 1848; Catherine L. Beeckman to Margaret Gardiner Beeckman, New York, n.d. [1848]; David L. Gardiner to Juliana Gardiner, New York, Aug. 17, 1847; Alexander Gardiner to Margaret Gardiner, New York, Sept. 27, 1847; Margaret Gardiner to Julia Gardiner Tyler, New York, n.d. [1845-1846], *TFP.*

[20] *Ibid.*, Mar. 6, 1847; Juliana Gardiner to Julia Gardiner Tyler, New York, Mar. 23, 1847, *TFP.*

[21] Julia Gardiner Tyler to Juliana Gardiner, Philadelphia, Oct. 12, 1845; Sherwood Forest, Mar. 24, 1846, *TFP.*

[22] Alexander Gardiner to Juliana Gardiner, New York, Aug. 30, 1847; Julia Gardiner Tyler to Margaret Gardiner, Sherwood Forest, May 6, 1847, *TFP.*

[23] Margaret Gardiner to Julia Gardiner Tyler, New York, Jan. 9, 1847; Julia Gardiner Tyler to Juliana Gardiner, Sherwood Forest [Feb. 9, 1847]; Juliana Gardiner to Julia Gardiner Tyler, New York, May 15; 18; June 8, 1847; David L. Gardiner to Juliana Gardiner, New York, Aug. 29, 1847; Phoebe Gardiner to Margaret Gardiner, Shelter Island, Aug. 27; Oct. 13, 1847, *TFP.*

[24] Julia Gardiner Tyler to Juliana Gardiner, Sherwood Forest, Dec. 1847, *TFP.*

[25] Margaret Gardiner Beeckman to Juliana Gardiner, Sherwood Forest, Jan. 26, 1848; Priscilla Cooper Tyler to Margaret Gardiner Beeckman, Bristol, Pa., Jan. 8, 1848; Clarissa Dayton to Juliana Gardiner, East Hampton, Jan. 25, 1848; George L. Huntington to Alexander Gardiner, East Hampton, Jan. 25, 1848, *TFP.*

[26] Julia Gardiner Tyler to Juliana Gardiner, Sherwood Forest, Jan. 27, 1848, *TFP;* John Tyler to Alexander Gardiner, Sherwood Forest, Jan. 27, 1848, *TPLC.*

[27] Julia Gardiner Tyler to Juliana Gardiner, Sherwood Forest, Feb. 8; 17, 1848; Gilbert Beeckman to John H. Beeckman, Washington, Jan. 22, 1848; Margaret Gardiner Beeckman to Juliana Gardiner, Sherwood Forest, Jan. 20, 1848; Richmond, Feb. 5; Washington, Feb. 8; 11, 1848, *TFP.*

[28] Julia Gardiner Tyler to Juliana Gardiner, Sherwood Forest, June 20; May 1, 1848; John H. Beeckman to Margaret Gardiner Beeckman, New York, May 31; June 5; 19; July 28; [July]; Aug. 31; [Sept.–Oct.] 1848, *TFP;* Alexander Gardiner to John Tyler, New York, Oct. 21, 1848, *GPY.*

[29] Julia Gardiner Tyler to Juliana Gardiner, Sherwood Forest, May 8, 1848; Julia Gardiner Tyler to Alexander Gardiner, Sherwood Forest, Nov. 12, 1846, *TFP;* John Tyler to Elizabeth Tyler Waller, Sherwood Forest, Apr. 21, 1846, *Tyler Papers,* Duke University Library; Juliana Gardiner to Margaret Gardiner Beeckman, Sherwood Forest, n.d. [Apr. 1848]; Julia Gardiner Tyler to Juliana Gardiner, Sherwood Forest, Nov.; Feb. 10; 18, 1848, *TFP.*

[30] *Ibid.*, Feb. 17, 1848, *TFP;* Julia Gardiner Tyler to David L. Gardiner, Sherwood Forest, July 24, 1850, *GPY;* Margaret Gardiner Beeckman to John H. Beeckman, Sherwood Forest, Dec. 7, 1849, *TFP.* Gilbert Beeckman became a smallstore owner in New York City in 1850, investing a small inheritance from his father, Henry Beeckman, who died in June 1850, in the enterprise. In 1851 his business was adequate enough to permit his engagement and marriage to Miss Margaret Foster, a nineteen-year-old whose father was an auctioneer in Fourteenth St. "We do not believe she will prove an heiress," said Juliana quite correctly. The wedding was celebrated on June 4, 1851. Margaret Foster Beeckman soon died, however, just why and when is not known. In 1857 Gilbert married again. The name of his second wife and details of his life after 1857 are also not known, save that he continued in the dry goods business in New York during and after the Civil War. He died in August 1875. *See* Julia Gardiner Tyler to David L. Gardiner, Sherwood Forest, July 24, 1850; Juliana Gardiner to David L. Gardiner, New York, Mar. 10, 1851, *GPY;* Julia Gardiner Tyler to Juliana Gardiner, Sherwood Forest, Mar. 24, 1851; May 7, 1857; Julia Gardiner Tyler to Margaret Gardiner Beeckman, Sherwood Forest, June 4; 22, 1851; David Gardiner Tyler to Julia Gardiner Tyler, Karlsruhe, June 7, 1866, *TFP.*

[31] Julia Gardiner Tyler to Juliana Gardiner, Sherwood Forest, Dec. 1848, *TFP.*

[32] *Ibid.*, Feb. 18, 1851, *TFP;* Juliana Gardiner to David L. Gardiner, New York, Mar. 1851; Julia Gardiner Tyler to David L. Gardiner, Sherwood Forest, July 24, 1850, *GPY*.

[33] Julia Gardiner Tyler to Juliana Gardiner, Sherwood Forest, Apr. 2; 11; 23; 1851; May 7, 1852, *TFP;* Juliana Gardiner to David L. Gardiner, Brooklyn, Apr. 26, 1851, *GPY;* Julia Gardiner Tyler to Margaret Gardiner Beeckman, Sherwood Forest, June 15, 1854; Margaret Gardiner Beeckman to Juliana Gardiner, Sherwood Forest, Feb. 1, 1855, *TFP;* John Tyler to James A. Semple, Sherwood Forest, Dec. 29, 1854, *TPLC; see also Tyler's Quarterly*, XII (January 1931), 194–95, for additional genealogical material on Tyler's children and in-laws. William M. Denison was serving as assistant to the Bishop of Kentucky in Louisville when Bessy was born and Alice died. A row with the vestry of Christ Church, Brooklyn, had caused him to resign that post a year after he began in it. Following Alice's death in 1854 he took a parish in Charleston, S.C., where he remained until his own death in 1858.

[34] Juliana Gardiner to David L. Gardiner, Sherwood Forest, July 27, 1855, *GPY*.

[35] Julia Gardiner Tyler to David L. Gardiner, Sherwood Forest, June 9, 1858, *GPY;* Julia Gardiner Tyler to Alexander Gardiner, Sherwood Forest, Dec. 2, 1846; Julia Gardiner Tyler to Juliana Gardiner, Sherwood Forest, Dec. 1, 1848; Julia Gardiner Tyler to Margaret Gardiner Beeckman, Sherwood Forest, Jan. 24, 1849; Margaret Gardiner Beeckman to Juliana Gardiner, Sherwood Forest, Feb. 23, 1853, *TFP;* Juliana Gardiner to David L. Gardiner, Sherwood Forest, July 27, 1855, *GPY*.

[36] Julia Gardiner Tyler to Alexander Gardiner, Sherwood Forest, Dec. 2, 1846; Julia Gardiner Tyler to Juliana Gardiner, Sherwood Forest, Feb. 17, 1848; Dec. 11, 1854; Dec. 28, 1846, *TFP;* John Tyler to Alexander Gardiner, Sherwood Forest, Dec. 20, 1850, *TPLC*.

[37] Julia Gardiner Tyler to Juliana Gardiner, Sherwood Forest, Mar. 29, 1849; Juliana Gardiner to Julia Gardiner Tyler, New York, Mar. 23, 1847; Julia Gardiner Tyler to Margaret Gardiner, Sherwood Forest, Apr. 2, 1846; Dec. 8, 1847, *TFP*.

[38] Julia Gardiner Tyler to Margaret Gardiner Beeckman, Sherwood Forest, n.d.; Julia Gardiner Tyler to Juliana Gardiner, Sherwood Forest, Dec. 11, 1845; Apr. 19, 1851, *TFP*.

[39] Juliana Gardiner to Margaret Gardiner Beeckman, Sherwood Forest, June 11, 1853; Julia Gardiner Tyler to Margaret Gardiner, Sherwood Forest, Mar. 5, 1846, *TFP*.

[40] Margaret Gardiner Beeckman to Juliana Gardiner, Sherwood Forest, Feb. 12, 1853, *TFP*.

[41] Julia Gardiner Tyler to Juliana Gardiner, Sherwood Forest, May 28, 1851; May 24, 1852, *TFP*.

[42] Margaret Gardiner to Julia Gardiner Tyler, New York, Oct. 12, 1845; Mar. 6; Nov. 21; 27; Apr. 17, 1846; Alexander Gardiner to David L. Gardiner, New York, Sept. 15, 1846; Juliana Gardiner to Julia Gardiner Tyler, New York, Dec. 18, 1846; Jan.; May 18, 1847; Julia Gardiner Tyler to Margaret Gardiner, Sherwood Forest, Jan. 7; Dec. 8, 1847, *TFP*.

[43] Margaret Gardiner to Julia Gardiner Tyler, New York, Dec. 10, 1845; Juliana Gardiner to Julia Gardiner Tyler, New York, Nov. 11, 1845; Mar. 23; June 8, 1847; Phoebe Gardiner to Margaret Gardiner, Shelter Island, Apr. 16, 1847; Julia Gardiner Tyler to Juliana Gardiner, Sherwood Forest, Apr. 20, 1847, *TFP*.

[44] John Tyler to Alexander Gardiner, Sherwood Forest, Dec. 20, 1850, *TPLC;* Julia Gardiner Tyler to Juliana Gardiner, Sherwood Forest, May 16, 1851, *TFP*.

[45] Julia Gardiner Tyler to Alexander Gardiner, Sherwood Forest, Feb. 27, 1850; Margaret Gardiner Beeckman to John H. Beeckman, Sherwood Forest, Mar.; Mar. 8, 1850, *TFP*.

[46] David L. Gardiner to Juliana Gardiner, Saratoga, Sept. 12, 1847; Julia Gardiner Tyler to Juliana Gardiner, Richmond, Mar. 20, 1849; Julia Gardiner Tyler to David L. Gardiner, Sherwood Forest, July 24, 1850, *TFP;* John Tyler, *An Address*

Delivered Before the Literary Societies of the University of Virginia on the Anniversary of the Declaration of Independence By the State of Virginia, June 29, 1850 (Pamphlet; Charlottesville, 1850), *passim*.

⁴⁷ John Tyler to Alexander Gardiner, Richmond, Mar. 22, 1849; Alexander Gardiner to John Tyler, New York, Nov. 9, 1849, *GPY;* Sylvia S. Rogers to Juliana Gardiner, Saratoga Springs, May 11 [1850], *TFP*.

⁴⁸ Julia Gardiner Tyler to Juliana Gardiner, Sherwood Forest, Mar. 29, 1849; Alexander Gardiner to Juliana Gardiner, New York, Apr. 18, 1849, *TFP;* John Tyler to Alexander Gardiner, Sherwood Forest, Apr. 9, 1849; May 21, 1850; Pittsfield, Mass., Sept. 18, 1849; Julia Gardiner Tyler to David L. Gardiner, Sherwood Forest, Jan. 10, 1849, *GPY;* Julia Gardiner Tyler to Alexander Gardiner, Sherwood Forest, Dec. 13, 1850, *TFP*.

⁴⁹ Margaret Gardiner Beeckman to [Alexander Gardiner], n.p., n.d. [Sherwood Forest, Dec. 1849]; Margaret Gardiner Beeckman to Clarissa [Dayton], n.p., n.d. [Sherwood Forest, Dec. 1849]; Julia Gardiner Tyler to Alexander Gardiner, Sherwood Forest, Feb. 27, 1850, *TFP;* Julia Gardiner Tyler to David L. Gardiner, Sherwood Forest, July 24, 1850, *GPY;* Margaret Gardiner Beeckman to Josephine [Metcalfe], Sherwood Forest, n.d. [Jan. 1850], *TFP*.

⁵⁰ John Tyler to Margaret Gardiner Beeckman, Sherwood Forest, July 17, 1851, *TPLC;* Julia Gardiner Tyler to Juliana Gardiner, Sherwood Forest, Apr. 2; June 26; Aug. 5, 1851; Margaret Gardiner Beeckman to Juliana Gardiner, Niagara Falls, Sept. 21, 1851; Juliana Gardiner to Margaret Gardiner Beeckman, Sherwood Forest, Dec. 10, 1851; Mary [Conger] to Julia Gardiner Tyler, Grassy Point, N.Y., Jan. 15, 1852, *TFP*. The date of Lachlan's birth is given as December 2, 1851, on his tombstone in Hollywood Cemetery, Richmond, Va. But Juliana's letter to Margaret, clearly dated Sherwood Forest, December 10, notes that "last night at half-past eleven" Julia give birth to Lachlan.

⁵¹ John Tyler to Henry Curtis, Sherwood Forest, Dec. 17, 1851; John Tyler to Margaret Gardiner Beeckman, Sherwood Forest, June 25, 1852, *TPLC*.

⁵² *Ibid.*, Mar. 18, 1854, *TPLC;* Edmund Ruffin to Jane M. Ruffin, Marlbourne, Mar. 21, 1854, *TFP*.

⁵³ Phoebe Gardiner to Margaret Gardiner, Shelter Island, May 19, 1847, *TFP;* John Tyler to Margaret Gardiner Beeckman, Sherwood Forest, Oct. 23, 1856, *GPY;* Margaret Gardiner Beeckman to Mrs. [?] Harris, n.p., n.d. [Sherwood Forest, Dec. 1856], *TFP*. For Tyler's smoking habits *see* Julia Gardiner Tyler to Alexander Gardiner in John Tyler to Alexander Gardiner, Sherwood Forest, Dec. 20, 1850, *TPLC*.

⁵⁴ Julia Gardiner Tyler to Margaret Gardiner Beeckman, Sherwood Forest, May 24, 1853; Julia Gardiner Tyler to Juliana Gardiner, Sherwood Forest, July 1, 1853, *TFP;* Juliana Gardiner to David L. Gardiner, Sherwood Forest, Aug. 25, 1853, *GPY;* John Tyler to Mrs. Henry Waggaman, Sherwood Forest, June 8, 1853, *TPLC*.

⁵⁵ Julia Gardiner Tyler *vs.* The Bank of Virginia, Legal Deposition, Aug. 3, 1868, *TFP;* Juliana Gardiner to David L. Gardiner, Sherwood Forest, July 9; 25, 1855, *GPY*.

CHAPTER 15

¹ John Tyler to Alexander Gardiner, Richmond, Mar. 22, 1849; Richard E. Stilwell to Alexander Gardiner, New York, July 26, 1849, *GPY*.

² John Tyler to Alexander Gardiner, Richmond, Mar. 22, 1849; John Tyler to Tilford and Samuels, Lawyers, of Frankfort, Ky., Sherwood Forest, Apr. 14, 1846; George Stealy, Memorandum on Size and Value of Tyler Land in Union County,

Ky., Frankfort, Ky., Aug. 16, 1847; R. G. Samuels to John Tyler, Frankfort, Ky., Dec. 24, 1847, *GPY;* John Tyler to John H. Waggaman, Williamsburg, Aug. 30, 1839, *TPLC.*

[3] John W. Russell to John Tyler, Frankfort, Ky., Sept. 12, 1845, *GPY;* John Tyler to Messrs. Corcoran and Riggs, Sherwood Forest, Oct. 6, 1845, *TPLC;* Alexander Gardiner to Julia Gardiner Tyler, New York, Nov. 29, 1845, *TFP.*

[4] John W. Russell to John Tyler, Frankfort, Ky., Mar. 23; Apr. 27, 1846; John Tyler to Tilford and Samuels, Sherwood Forest, Apr. 14, 1846; Tilford and Samuels to John Tyler, Frankfort, Ky., Aug. 6, 1846, *GPY.*

[5] Thomas Wilson, Nicholas Casey, Sanford Conelly, Coal Survey Report to Tilford and Samuels, Caseyville, Ky., Oct. 9; 14, 1846; Tilford and Samuels to John Tyler, Frankfort, Ky., Oct. 9, 1846; John W. Russell to John Tyler, Frankfort, Ky., Oct. 15, 1846, *GPY.*

[6] Julia Gardiner Tyler to Alexander Gardiner, Sherwood Forest, Nov. 26, 1846; Alexander Gardiner to Julia Gardiner Tyler, New York, Nov. 28, 1846, *TFP;* N. M. Miller to John Tyler, Louisville, Dec. 1, 1846; John W. Russell to John Tyler, Frankfort, Ky., Dec. 16, 1846, *GPY;* Alexander Gardiner to Julia Gardiner Tyler, New York, Dec. 5, 1846, *TFP;* John Tyler, Memorandum of G. H. Peck Letter, dated Caseyville, Ky., Jan. 18, 1847. It was estimated at Caseyville in August 1847 that a 5' vein of coal yielded about 42 bu. a foot, or about 200,000 bu. per acre. Delivered to the river bank from Tyler's mine two miles away at 4¢ cost per bu., the profit in one vein per acre was estimated at $8000, assuming 8¢ per bu. sale price to passing steamboats. For this reason the G. H. Peck offer seemed much too low to Tyler and his agents advised him to reject it. *See* George Stealy Memorandum, Aug. 16, 1847, *GPY.*

[7] John Tyler to John W. Russell, Sherwood Forest, Oct. 25, 1847; John Tyler to Tilford, New York, Oct. 4, 1847; Joseph L. Watkins to John Tyler, Memphis, Oct. 10, 1847, *GPY;* John Tyler to Alexander Gardiner, Sherwood Forest, Nov. 1, 1847, *TPLC;* Articles of Sale of Tyler Land in Union County, Ky., Between Robert P. Winston and Samuel L. Casey, Dated Sept. 9, 1847, *GPY.*

[8] John Tyler to Messrs. Corcoran and Riggs, Sherwood Forest, Feb. 23, 1848; Alexander Gardiner to John Tyler, New York, Mar. 7, 1848, *GPY.*

[9] Alexander Gardiner to David L. Gardiner, East Hampton, Aug. 6, 1848; Richard E. Stilwell to Alexander Gardiner, New York, May 29; June 8; Aug. 25, 1849; Apr. 20; Aug. 9; Aug. 12; Sept. 4, 1850; Juliana Gardiner to David L. Gardiner, East Hampton, July 6, 1848, *GPY;* Andrew Harris to Alexander Gardiner, Detroit, Apr. 1, 1846; Juliana Gardiner to Alexander Gardiner, Sherwood Forest, Jan. 14, 1846, *TFP;* Alexander Gardiner to David L. Gardiner, Washington, Feb. 7, 1846; Juliana Gardiner to David L. Gardiner, Mar. 10, 1851; Alexander Gardiner to John Tyler, New York, Mar. 4, 1847; Alexander Gardiner to David L. Gardiner, Newport, Aug. 21, 1847, *GPY; ibid.,* New York, June 1850, *TFP;* Alexander Gardiner to Juliana Gardiner, New York, Jan. 30, 1843, *GPY.*

[10] Alexander Gardiner to Juliana Gardiner, Steamboat *Hibernia,* No. 2, On the Ohio, Nov. 17, 1847; Louisville, Nov. 21, 1847; Caseyville, Nov. 23, 1847, *GPY.*

[11] George Stealy, Memorandum, Frankfort, Ky., Aug. 16, 1847; Alexander Gardiner to Samuel L. Casey, Baltimore, Dec. 7, 1847; Alexander Gardiner to John Tyler, New York, Feb. 19, 1848; Baltimore, Dec. 8, 1847; New York, Feb. 11, 1848, *GPY;* John Tyler to Alexander Gardiner, Sherwood Forest, Jan. 27, 1848, *TPLC.*

[12] Alexander Gardiner, Proposition to Form a Company to Purchase Lands of Coal Mines and Work the Same Near Caseyville, Union County, Kentucky, n.d.; T. William Letson to Maj. L. A. Sykes, Baltimore, Dec. 20, 1847; T. William Letson to Alexander Gardiner, Baltimore, Dec. 12, 1847; Jan. 22, 1848; Maj. L. A. Sykes to Gen. William G. McNeill, New York, Dec. 27, 1847; Alexander Gardiner to John Tyler, New York, Jan. 15, 1848, *GPY.*

[13] John Tyler to Corcoran and Riggs, Sherwood Forest, Feb. 23, 1848; Corcoran and Riggs to John Tyler, Washington, Mar. 10, 1848; Alexander Gardiner to John Tyler, New York, May 30, 1848; John Tyler to Alexander Gardiner [Sherwood Forest], Nov. 14, 1848, quoted in Alexander Gardiner to John Tyler, New York, June 2, 1849 (draft letter heavily struck over); Alexander Gardiner to John Tyler, New York, June 2, 1849, *GPY*.

[14] Agreement Between Alexander Gardiner and Andrew J. Fenton, May 22, 1848; Alexander Gardiner to John Tyler, New York, May 20, 1848; Alexander Gardiner to David L. Gardiner, Caseyville, June 10, 1848, *GPY*; Alexander Gardiner to David L. Gardiner, Pittsburgh, June 1, 1848, *TFP*.

[15] *Ibid.*, Caseyville, June 21, 1848; Andrew J. Fenton to Alexander Gardiner, Baltimore, July 8, 1848; Alexander Gardiner to Andrew J. Fenton, Telegram, New York, July 10, 1848; Alexander Gardiner to John Tyler, New York, July 11, 1848; Alexander Gardiner to Andrew J. Fenton, New York, July 12, 1848, *GPY*.

[16] Andrew J. Fenton to Alexander Gardiner, Caseyville, July 18; 28, 1848; Alexander Gardiner to Andrew J. Fenton, New York, Aug. 2, 1848; Andrew J. Fenton to Alexander Gardiner, Caseyville, Aug. 10; 24; Sept. 2, 1848, *GPY*.

[17] Alexander Gardiner to David L. Gardiner, New York, Sept. 1, 1848; Alexander Gardiner to Andrew J. Fenton, New York, Sept. 4; 11; 18; Oct. 4, 1848; Andrew J. Fenton to Alexander Gardiner, Caseyville, Sept. 12; Oct. 21, 1848; Alexander Gardiner to John Tyler, New York, Oct. 21, 1848, *GPY*.

[18] *Ibid.*, New York, Nov. 6, 1848; Andrew J. Fenton to Alexander Gardiner, Gardiner's Point, Ky., Nov. 10; 22; 25; Dec. 15, 1848; Louisville, Dec. 22, 1848; Alexander Gardiner to Andrew J. Fenton, New York, Nov. 20; 28; Dec. 2; 5; 28, 1848; Alexander Gardiner to Samuel L. Casey, New York, Nov. 30, 1848, *GPY*.

[19] John Tyler to Alexander Gardiner, Sherwood Forest, Feb. 2; 21, 1849; Alexander Gardiner to Andrew J. Fenton, New York, Feb. 23, 1849; Alexander Gardiner to John Tyler, New York, Feb. 26, 1849, *GPY*.

[20] John Tyler to Alexander Gardiner, Sherwood Forest, Apr. 9; May 10, 1849; Alexander Gardiner to John Tyler, New York, June 2, 1849, *GPY*; *ibid.*, Sherwood Forest, Dec. 25, 1848, *TPLC*.

[21] Alexander Gardiner to John Tyler, New York, June 2, 1849, *GPY*. For the subsequent history of the Caseyville property, including the crude attempt by land speculators in the Kentucky legislature in 1850 to seize the property under eminent-domain legislation, the legal problems involved in Alexander's deathbed assignment of his share to Julia, the various offers, near-sales, and boundary survey suits and difficulties, and the growing family concern to secure good title to Julia's share and to be rid of the Kentucky holdings, etc., see John Tyler to Alexander Gardiner, Sherwood Forest, May 29, 1850, *TPLC*; *ibid.*, Saratoga, Sept. 18, 1850; Juliana Gardiner to David L. Gardiner, New York, Jan. 30, 1851, *GPY*; John Tyler to Juliana Gardiner, Sherwood Forest, Feb. 13, 1851, *TPLC*; Julia Gardiner Tyler to Juliana Gardiner, Sherwood Forest, Feb. 1, 1851, *TFP*; Julia Gardiner Tyler to David. L. Gardiner, New York, Mar. 10, 1851, *GPY*; Julia Gardiner Tyler to Juliana Gardiner, Sherwood Forest, Mar. 7, 1851, *TFP*; John Tyler to Margaret Gardiner Beeckman, Sherwood Forest, June 5, 1851; John Tyler to Samuel Page, Sherwood Forest, June 6, 1851, *TPLC*; Julia Gardiner Tyler to Margaret Gardiner Beeckman, Sherwood Forest, July 9, 1851; Julia Gardiner Tyler to Juliana Gardiner, Sherwood Forest, Mar. 30, 1852, *TFP*; *ibid.*, Sherwood Forest, Jan. 14, 1853, *GPY*; Margaret Gardiner Beeckman, to Juliana Gardiner, Sherwood Forest, Jan. 31, 1853; Deed of Sale and Trust Between John Tyler, David L. Gardiner, Julia Gardiner Tyler and C. H. Mathias, N. J. M. Smith, Wilson Carpenter, For Tyler Property in Union County, Ky., Dated Oct. 4, 1853; Julia Gardiner Tyler to Juliana Gardiner, Sherwood Forest, Dec. 16, 1855, *TFP*.

[22] *Ibid.*, Sherwood Forest, Dec. 15, 1848; Margaret Gardiner Beeckman to John H. Beeckman, Sherwood Forest, n.d. [Jan.-Feb. 1849]; Julia Gardiner Tyler to

Margaret Gardiner Beeckman, Sherwood Forest, Jan. 24, 1849, *TFP;* Samuel Gardiner to Alexander Gardiner, Shelter Island, Jan. 31, 1849; John Tyler to Alexander Gardiner, Sherwood Forest, Feb. 21; Mar. 9, 1849, *GPY.*

[23] Julia Gardiner Tyler to David L. Gardiner, Sherwood Forest, Jan 10, 1849; July 24, 1850, *GPY;* Julia Gardiner Tyler to Margaret Gardiner Beeckman, Sherwood Forest, Jan. 24; May 25, 1849, *TFP;* John Tyler to Alexander Gardiner, Sherwood Forest, Feb. 2; 21, 1849; Alexander Gardiner to David L. Gardiner, New York, Aug. 15, 1849; Juliana Gardiner to David L. Gardiner, East Hampton, Dec. 9, 1850; Julia Gardiner Tyler to David L. Gardiner, Sherwood Forest, Jan. 14, 1851; Jan. 10, 1849, *GPY.* For details of Egbert Dayton's voyage and death see Juliana Gardiner to Alexander Gardiner, New York, Oct. 21, 1849, *GPY;* Margaret Gardiner Beeckman to Clarissa Dayton, n.p., n.d. [Sherwood Forest, Dec. 1849], *TFP;* Alexander Gardiner to Dayton Family, New York, Jan. 17, 1850, *GPY;* Clarissa Dayton to Margaret Gardiner Beeckman, East Hampton, Feb. 13, 1850, *TFP.* John Tyler, Jr., actually joined a Richmond company scheduled to depart for California in February 1849 but when he failed to secure a patronage job in California he withdrew from the enterprise. For John Jr's. frequent comings and goings into and out of the Temperance Society see Julia Gardiner Tyler to Juliana Gardiner, Sherwood Forest, Oct. 18, 1847, *TFP;* and *Tyler Family Papers,* 1845–1860, *passim.*

[24] Julia Gardiner Tyler to Alexander Gardiner, Sherwood Forest, Dec. 15, 1848, *GPY;* Alexander Gardiner to David L. Gardiner, New York, June; June 28, 1850, *TFP;* Julia Gardiner Tyler to David L. Gardiner, Sherwood Forest, Jan. 10, 1849; John Tyler to Alexander Gardiner, Sherwood Forest, Feb. 2, 1849, *GPY;* John Tyler to Margaret Gardiner Beeckman, Sherwood Forest, May 16, 1851, *TPLC.* Tyler later estimated Beeckman's cargo at worth $10,000, but Beeckman's subsequent financial history in California would suggest its value at nearer half that.

[25] Margaret Gardiner Beeckman to John H. Beeckman, Sherwood Forest, n.d. [early 1849]; Margaret Gardiner Beeckman to Catherine Beeckman, East Hampton, May 6, 1849, *TFP;* Alexander Gardiner to David L. Gardiner, New York, Aug. 15, 1849; Julia Gardiner Tyler to Alexander Gardiner, Sherwood Forest, Feb. 21, 1849, *GPY;* Gilbert Beeckman to Margaret Gardiner Beeckman, New York, May 3, 1849; Margaret Gardiner Beeckman to John H. Beeckman, n.p., n.d. [New York, Mar.–Apr. 1849]; Henry B. Livingston to John Tyler, Sacramento, Apr. 12, 1851, *TFP.*

[26] John H. Beeckman to Margaret Gardiner Beeckman, Sacramento, Sept. 23, 1849, *GPY.*

[27] Margaret Gardiner Beeckman to Juliana Gardiner, n.p., n.d. [Sherwood Forest, Jan.–Feb. 1850]; Alexander Gardiner to David L. Gardiner, New York, June 1850; Alexander Gardiner to Henry B. Livingston, New York, June 13, 1850, *TFP;* Margaret Gardiner Beeckman to Alexander Gardiner, Saratoga Springs, Sept. 1, 1850, *GPY;* Margaret Gardiner Beeckman to John H. Beeckman, Sherwood Forest, March 1850; John H. Beeckman to Margaret Gardiner Beeckman, Sacramento City, n.d. [Feb. 1850]. On Beeckman's disillusion with high water and the future of merchandising in Sacramento see John H. Beeckman to Catherine Beeckman, quoted in Catherine Beeckman to Margaret Gardiner Beeckman, New York, May 13, 1850, *TFP.*

[28] Beeckman's partners in the venture were, in addition to Sutter, Samuel Moss, Edwin Herrick, Benjamin W. Bean, and Anson V. H. LeRoy. For the details of the deal see Contract Between John A. Sutter and Samuel Moss, Jr., *etal.,* Sacramento, Mar. 6, 1850; Edwin Herrick and Samuel Moss to B. W. Bean, San Francisco, Apr. 18, 1850 (copy); John H. Beeckman to Margaret Gardiner Beeckman, Sacramento, n.d. [Apr. 10, 1850]; Catherine Beeckman to Margaret Gardiner Beeckman, New York, May 13, 1850; Henry B. Livingston to John Tyler, Sacramento City, Apr. 12, 1851, *TFP.*

[29] John H. Beeckman to Margaret Gardiner Beeckman, Sacramento City, n.d. [Apr. 10, 1850], *TFP*.

[30] Henry B. Livingston to Gilbert Beeckman, Fremont, 30 Miles Above Sacramento City, Saturday and Sunday, Apr. 27–28, 1850; Henry B. Livingston to Gilbert Beeckman, quoted in Gilbert Beeckman to Alexander Gardiner, New York, July 12, 1850; Edwin Herrick to David L. Gardiner, San Francisco, Apr. 30, 1850, *TFP*. A version of Beeckman's death by Anson LeRoy, somewhat scrambled in transmission, had the shotgun discharge as Beeckman tossed it into the boat preparatory to shoving the craft into the stream on the morning of Apr. 26. This version emphasized the point that the gun was loaded because Beeckman thought he "might shoot some ducks possibly" that morning on the river.

[31] Alexander Gardiner to David L. Gardiner, New York, June 1850; Julia Gardiner Tyler to Juliana Gardiner, Sherwood Forest, June 15, 1850; Alexander Gardiner to Henry B. Livingston, New York, June 13; July 27, 1850, *TFP*; Julia Gardiner Tyler to David L. Gardiner, Sherwood Forest, July 24, 1850, *GPY*; Margaret Gardiner, Poem on the Death of John H. Beeckman, n.p., n.d. [circa 1855–1856], *TFP*. See also sympathy letters to Margaret, *viz.*: Catherine Beeckman to Margaret Gardiner Beeckman, Sharon (Conn.), Aug. 29, 1850; Newport, R.I., July 8, 1851; Robert Tyler to Alexander Gardiner, Philadelphia, June 9, 1850; Clarissa Dayton to Margaret Gardiner Beeckman, June 9, 1850, *TFP*; Samuel L. Gardiner to Alexander Gardiner, June 17, 1850, *GPY*.

[32] On the Beeckman estate issue *see* particularly John Morgan to David L. Gardiner, Sacramento, Aug. 13, 1850; Alexander Gardiner to Margaret Gardiner Beeckman, New York, Nov. 22, 1850; Josiah H. Drummond to David L. Gardiner, Sacramento, Jan. 28, 1851, *GPY*; David L. Gardiner to Henry B. Livingston, New York, July 10, 1851; Margaret Gardiner Beeckman to Henry B. Livingston, New York, May 26, 1851; Alexander Gardiner to Henry B. Livingston, New York, July 27, 1850, *TFP*; Margaret Gardiner Beeckman to Alexander Gardiner, Saratoga Springs, Sept. 1, 1850; Alexander Gardiner to David L. Gardiner, New York, Nov. 11, 1850; Juliana Gardiner to David L. Gardiner, East Hampton, Dec. 9, 1850; New York, Jan. 11; 30, 1851, *GPY*; Henry B. Livingston to Margaret Gardiner Beeckman, Accounting of Beeckman Estate, May 1850 to Sept. 1851 [Sacramento, Sept. 1851]; Julia Gardiner Tyler to Juliana Gardiner, Sherwood Forest, Feb. 8, 1851, *TFP*; John Tyler to Margaret Gardiner Beeckman, Sherwood Forest, May 16, 1851, *TPLC*; Henry B. Livingston to John Tyler, Sacramento, Apr. 12, 1851; Charles Smith to Margaret Gardiner Beeckman, Sacramento, July 13; Aug. 29, 1852; Mar. 12, 1854; Charles Smith to Juliana Gardiner, Sacramento, July 11, 1852; Juliana Gardiner to Charles Smith, New York, Apr. 15, 1852; Benjamin W. Bean to Margaret Gardiner Beeckman, Sacramento, Jan. 31; Oct. 30, 1853; *ibid.*, Accounting of Beeckman Estate, 1853, Sacramento, n.d. [Jan. 1854]; Margaret Gardiner Beeckman to Benjamin W. Bean, Staten Island, Nov. 3, 1853, *TFP*; John Tyler to Margaret Gardiner Beeckman, Sherwood Forest, June 5, 1851, *TPLC*; Henry B. Livingston to David L. Gardiner, Oregon Bar, North Fork, American River, Oct. 20, 1852; Deed of Sale of John H. Beeckman Property, Lot. No. 3, J. Street, Sacramento, Jan. 6, 1853, *TFP*.

[33] John Tyler to Alexander Gardiner, Sherwood Forest, Feb. 21; Mar. 9, 1849, *GPY*; Julia Gardiner Tyler to Alexander Gardiner, Sherwood Forest, Jan. 26, 1849, *TFP*; John Tyler to General Persifer F. Smith, Sherwood Forest, Mar. 5, 1849; Robert J. Walker to General Persifer F. Smith, Washington, Jan. 15, 1849, enclosed in Robert J. Walker to Alexander Gardiner, Washington, Jan. 15, 1849, *GPY*; Alexander Gardiner to David L. Gardiner, New York, June 28, 1850, *TFP*; Julia Gardiner Tyler to David L. Gardiner, Sherwood Forest, Jan. 10, 1849. For details of Richard E. Stilwell's engagement and duties *see* Richard E. Stilwell to Alexander Gardiner, New York, May 25; 26; 29; 31, 1849, *GPY*.

[34] [David L. Gardiner], "Extract of a Letter Dated San Francisco, June 15,

1849," New York *Journal of Commerce,* Aug. 14, 1849; John Tyler to Alexander Gardiner, Pittsfield, Mass., Sept. 18, 1849; Alexander Gardiner to David L. Gardiner, New York, Aug. 15, 1849, *GPY;* Julia Gardiner Tyler to Juliana Gardiner, Sherwood Forest, Mar. 29; Apr. 3, 1849; Julia Gardiner Tyler to Alexander Gardiner, Sherwood Forest, Nov. 10, 1849; John H. Beeckman to Margaret Gardiner Beeckman, Sept. 23, 1849, *TFP;* Juliana Gardiner to Alexander Gardiner, Sherwood Forest, Feb. 15, 1850; New York, Jan. 11, 1851; East Hampton, Oct. 22; Nov. 12, 1849; Dec. 9, 1850; Juliana Gardiner to Alexander Gardiner, Pittsfield, Mass., Sept. 15; 27, 1849, *GPY;* Margaret Gardiner Beeckman to Alexander Gardiner, Sherwood Forest, n.d. [Jan. 1850], *TFP.*

[35] John Tyler, quoted in Juliana Gardiner to Alexander Gardiner, Pittsfield, Mass., Sept. 15, 1849; John Morgan to David L. Gardiner, Sacramento, Aug. 13, 1850; Benjamin W. Bean to David L. Gardiner, New York, Nov. 11, 1850; Juliana Gardiner to Alexander Gardiner, Sherwood Forest, Feb. 15, 1850; Margaret Beeckman to Alexander Gardiner, Sherwood Forest, Feb. 13, 1850, *GPY.*

[36] Julia Gardiner Tyler to Juliana Gardiner, Sherwood Forest, Feb. 8; 21, 1851; John Tyler to John H. Beeckman, Sherwood Forest, n.d. [*circa* Feb. 1850], *TFP;* Alexander Gardiner to David L. Gardiner, Sherwood Forest, Apr. 21, 1850; Juliana Gardiner to Alexander Gardiner, Sherwood Forest, Mar. 20, 1850; Juliana Gardiner to David L. Gardiner, New York, Mar. 10, 1851, *GPY;* Julia Gardiner Tyler to Margaret Gardiner Beeckman, Sherwood Forest, n.d. [*circa* mid-1851], *TFP.*

[37] Julia Gardiner Tyler to Margaret Gardiner Beeckman, Sherwood Forest, Jan. 24, 1849, *TFP;* Alexander Gardiner to John Tyler, New York, Feb. 26, 1849; Alexander Gardiner to David L. Gardiner, New York, Mar. 13; Aug. 15, 1849 (2 letters); Sept. 26, 1850, *GPY; ibid.,* June 28, 1850; Alexander Gardiner to Edwin Herrick, New York, June 13, 1850; Michael Mullone to Juliana Gardiner, Jersey City, N.J., May 7, 1851, *TFP;* John R. Bleeker to Alexander Gardiner, San Diego, Jan. 2, 1851; Alexander Gardiner to David L. Gardiner, New York, Jan. 11, 1851, *GPY.*

[38] John R. Bleeker to David L. Gardiner, San Diego, Feb. 25; Mar. 2; 14; 20, 1851. For the subsequent history of the Spring Street lot and the Gardiner-Bleeker reaction to the growth of modern San Diego occasioned by the coming of the railroad, *see* John R. Bleeker to David L. Gardiner, New York, Apr. 19; May 26; June 18, 1873; Dec. 4, 1878; Apr. 11; May 2, 1883; Jan. 2; Apr. 29; May 5; 15; Oct. 6; Nov. 18; Dec. 24, 1886; Jan. 8; Apr. 15, 1887; E. W. Morse to John R. Bleeker, San Diego, Dec. 17, 1885; Apr. 19, 1886, *GPY. See also* David L. Gardiner and John R. Bleeker to Charles A. Wetmore, Deed of Sale [Photostat], New York, Dec. 21, 1887. Wetmore, in turn, deeded a right of way to the California Central Railway Company on Sept. 27, 1888. Lewis B. Lesley, "A Southern Transcontinental Railroad Into California: Texas and Pacific versus Southern Pacific, 1865-1885," *Pacific Historical Review* (March 1936), 52-60. The Santa Fé Railroad Station now stands on the Gardiner-Bleeker property. Details of the Garra Rebellion and its impact on San Diego may be found in Joseph J. Hill, *The History of Warner's Ranch and Its Environs* (Los Angeles, 1927), 135-42; James Mills, "San Diego— Where California Began," *San Diego Historical Society Quarterly,* VI (January 1960), Special Edition, 1-34.

[39] Alexander Gardiner to David L. Gardiner, New York, June 28, 1850, *TFP;* Julia Gardiner Tyler to David L. Gardiner, Sherwood Forest, July 24, 1850; Jan. 14, 1851, *GPY.*

[40] John Tyler to Alexander Gardiner, Sherwood Forest, Dec. 20, 1850, *TPLC;* Julia Gardiner Tyler to Alexander Gardiner, Sherwood Forest, Dec. 13, 1850, *TFP;* William McK. Gwin to John Tyler, Washington, Dec. 13, 1850; Juliana Gardiner to David L. Gardiner, East Hampton, Dec. 9, 1850; New York, Mar. 26, 1851; Alexander Gardiner to David L. Gardiner, New York, Dec. 28, 1850; Jan. 11, 1851; John R. Bleeker to David L. Gardiner, San Diego, Feb. 25, 1851, *GPY.*

[41] David L. Gardiner to Margaret Gardiner Beeckman, San Francisco, Mar. 15, 1851; Julia Gardiner Tyler to Juliana Gardiner, Sherwood Forest, June 7, 1851, *TFP;* John Tyler to Margaret Gardiner Beeckman, Sherwood Forest, June 5, 1851, *TPLC;* Julia Gardiner Tyler to Margaret Gardiner Beeckman, Sherwood Forest, Apr. 24; May 15; June 22, 1851, *TFP;* Juliana Gardiner to David L. Gardiner, Brooklyn, Mar. 10; 12, 1851; Julia Gardiner Tyler to David L. Gardiner, Sherwood Forest, Mar. 19, 1851, *GPY.*

[42] John R. Bleeker to David L. Gardiner, San Diego, Sept. 3; Oct. 3; 17; Nov. 30; Dec. 15, 1851; Feb. 1; 15; Mar. 17; Apr. 17; May 15; 17; 28; June 3; July 16; Aug. 16; Oct. 18, 1852; May 28, 1854, *GPY;* John Tyler to David L. Gardiner, Sherwood Forest, Feb. 26, 1852, *TPLC.* With the $3000 realized from his Sacramento lot speculation David L. Gardiner bought a property on 14th Street in New York City. *See* Office of Receiver of Taxes, New York City Hall, Tax Bill, Nov. 1858; and Julia Gardiner Tyler, Deposition in Gardner *vs.* Tyler, n.p. (Staten Island, N.Y.), n.d. [1866], *TFP;* John R. Bleeker to David L. Gardiner, San Diego, July 20, 1856, *GPY.*

CHAPTER 16

[1] Julia Gardiner Tyler to Juliana Gardiner, Sherwood Forest, Jan. 26, 1851, *TFP.*

[2] Juliana Gardiner to David L. Gardiner, New York, Jan. 30; Mar. 10, 1851; Margaret Gardiner Beeckman to David L. Gardiner, New York, Jan. 26, 1851, *GPY;* Richard Stilwell to John Tyler, quoted in Julia Gardiner Tyler to Juliana Gardiner, Sherwood Forest, Feb. 14; 21, 1851; Julia Gardiner Tyler to Margaret Gardiner Beeckman, Sherwood Forest, Apr. 4, 1849, *TFP.* Typical of the New York obituaries was that run in the *Journal of Commerce,* Jan. 23, 1851. John Tyler himself wrote the obituary that appeared in the Richmond *Enquirer.* The New York doctors who attended Alexander were Clark, Bulkly, and Joseph Smith, "all standing at the head of the profession." A graveside service was held in East Hampton, the Rev. Mr. Winans reading the appropriate passages from the Book of Common Prayer. Margaret and her Uncles Nathaniel and Samuel accompanied Alexander's body to East Hampton for burial.

[3] Juliana Gardiner to David L. Gardiner, New York, Jan. 30; Mar.; Mar. 26, 1851; Julia Gardiner Tyler to David L. Gardiner, Sherwood Forest, Mar. 19, 1851, *GPY;* Julia Gardiner Tyler to Juliana Gardiner, Sherwood Forest, Jan. 24; 26; Feb. 1; 8, 1851; Feb. 14; 28; Mar. 7; 28; July 4, 1851, *TFP.*

[4] David L. Gardiner to Juliana Gardiner, New York, July 13, 1851, *TFP.* The East Hampton house and its thirteen acres sold for $5000. After passing through the hands of several "strangers" (as Julia called them) the East Hampton property was purchased by Mrs. Samuel L. Gardiner in 1864. Castleton Hill cost $9500, $4500 of which was put down in cash, the remaining $5000 being in the form of a mortgage held by Judge James I. Roosevelt. David paid $13,250 for his farm, $5000 in cash and $8250 in the form of a mortgage held by Patrick Houston. The Castleton Hill property rapidly increased in value and in 1864 Juliana turned down an offer of $20,000 for it. For the details of these financial and real estate arrangements *see* Gardiner *vs.* Tyler in John Tiffany, Comp., *Reports of Cases Argued and Determined in the Court of Appeals of the State of New York.* (Albany, 1867), VIII, "Gardiner *vs.* Tyler." Cited as Gardiner *vs.* Tyler, *35 New York Reports,* 563–65; Julia Gardiner Tyler, Deposition in Gardner *vs.* Tyler, n.p., n.d. [New York, 1866], *TFP;* David L. Gardiner—Patrick Houston Mortgage Agreement, Mar. 25, 1853; Tax Assessment, School District No. 2, West New Brighton, Staten Island, N.Y., July 23, 1875, *TFP;* B. Piesrigg to David L. Gardiner, New York,

Nov. 18, 1858; Juliana Gardiner to David L. Gardiner, New York, Mar. 12, 1851; Old Point Comfort, Va., July 25, 1855; David L. Gardiner to Juliana Gardiner, East Hampton, May 5, 1852, GPY; John Tyler to Margaret Gardiner Beeckman, Sherwood Forest, June 25, 1852, TPLC; Julia Gardiner Tyler to Juliana Gardiner, Sherwood Forest, Mar. 20, 1852, TFP; S. R. Ely to David L. Gardiner, Roslyn, L.I., N.Y., Mar. 25, 1864, GPY; Richard E. Stilwell to Juliana Gardiner, New York, July 31, 1850; Juliana Gardiner to Margaret Gardiner Beeckman, Sherwood Forest, Dec. 31, 1851; Jan. 29, 1852, TFP.

[5] David L. Gardiner to Alexander Gardiner, New York, Aug. 9, 1847, TFP; LTT, II, 465; John Tyler to Robert Tyler, New York, Dec. 30, 1847, TPLC; Alexander Gardiner to David L. Gardiner, East Hampton, Aug. 6, 1848, GPY; John Tyler to the Editor, New York Journal of Commerce, New York, Jan. 8, 1848, reprinted in New York Herald, Jan. 12, 1848; John Tyler to Alexander Gardiner, Sherwood Forest, Jan. 27, 1848, TPLC.

[6] John Tyler to John Tyler, Jr., Sherwood Forest, Jan. 23, 1848, Tyler Papers, Duke University Library; Juliana Gardiner to Margaret Gardiner Beeckman, Philadelphia, Mar. 1848; Margaret Gardiner Beeckman to Juliana Gardiner, New York, Mar. 10, 1848, TFP; Alexander Gardiner to John Tyler, New York, Feb. 19; Nov. 6, 1848; Alexander Gardiner to David L. Gardiner, New York, Sept. 10, 1848, GPY; John Tyler to M. Boswell Seawell, Sherwood Forest, Nov. 13, 1848, in Tyler's Quarterly, XIII (October 1931), 78; Juliana Gardiner to Margaret Gardiner Beeckman, Sherwood Forest, Jan. 14, 1849, TFP; John Tyler to Alexander Gardiner, Sherwood Forest, Nov. 14, 1848, LTT, II, 462. For Robert Tyler's relationship to the Buchanan candidacy see Philip G. Auchampaugh, Robert Tyler: Southern Rights Champion, 1847–1866 (Duluth, Minn., 1934), 13–16; Stanwood, A History of Presidential Elections, 161–76; Roseboom, A History of Presidential Elections, 137–42.

[7] John Tyler to Alexander Gardiner, Sherwood Forest, Mar. 21; 9, 1849; Alexander Gardiner to John Tyler, New York, Feb. 26, 1849; John Lorimer Graham to Alexander Gardiner, New York, May 25, 1849; Alexander Gardiner to Jacob Collamer, New York, Mar. 14, 1849, GPY; Julia Gardiner Tyler to Juliana Gardiner, Sherwood Forest, Mar. 20, 1849; George L. Huntington to John Tyler, East Hampton, Mar. 1, 1849, TFP; Alexander Gardiner to ———, Pittsfield, Mass., June 25, 1849, GPY.

[8] John Tyler to Robert Tyler, Sherwood Forest, Mar. 12, 1850, in LTT, II, 481.

[9] John Tyler to Daniel Webster, Sherwood Forest, Apr. 17, 1850, TPLC; John Tyler to Robert Tyler, Sherwood Forest, Apr. 17, 1850, in LTT, II, 483.

[10] John Tyler to Henry S. Foote, Sherwood Forest, May 21, 1850; John Tyler to Alexander Gardiner, Sherwood Forest, May 29, 1850, in LTT, II, 485–89, 484; John Tyler to Alexander Gardiner, Sherwood Forest, May 21, 1850, GPY. See also Margaret Gardiner Beeckman to Josephine Metcalfe, Sherwood Forest, n.d. [circa May 1850], TFP.

[11] John Tyler to John S. Cunningham, Sherwood Forest, Feb. 5, 1851; John Tyler to Henry S. Foote, Sherwood Forest, May 21, 1850, in LTT, II, 412, 489.

[12] John Tyler to Alexander Gardiner, Sherwood Forest, Dec. 5, 1850, in LTT, II, 490; John Tyler, Jr., to Henry A. Wise, Philadelphia, Nov. 18, 1850, in Auchampaugh, Robert Tyler, 20–21; Julia Gardiner Tyler to Alexander Gardiner, Sherwood Forest, Dec. 13, 1850; Samuel Gardiner to John Tyler, Shelter Island, Jan. 1, 1851, TFP; John Tyler, Letter to the Editor of the Portsmouth Pilot, Sherwood Forest, n.d. [Dec. 10, 1850], TPLC.

[13] Ibid.

[14] Alexander had engaged Hall as his deputy in November 1850 largely on the strength of a strong recommendation from Samuel J. Tilden. See Charles M. Hall to "Evidence," New York Herald Office, New York, Oct. 23, 1850; Alexander

Gardiner to Margaret Gardiner Beeckman, New York, Nov. 22, 1850, *GPY*. Hall was 29 years old and came from Chatham, Columbia County, N.Y. Alexander Gardiner to David L. Gardiner, New York, Dec. 28, 1850; Jan. 11, 1851, *GPY*. Details and testimony in the Hamlet case may be found in the pamphlet, *The Fugitive Slave Bill: Its History and Unconstitutionality: With an Account of the Seizure and Enslavement of James Hamlet and His Subsequent Restoration to Liberty* (New York, American and Foreign Anti-Slavery Society, 1850), 1–5, and *passim*. See also the New York *Journal of Commerce*, Dec. 30, 1850; and Jan. 7, 1851; and Louis Filler, *The Crusade Against Slavery, 1830–1860* (New York, 1960), 202.

[15] "Justice" to Alexander Gardiner, Rockton, Ill., Oct. 21, 1850, *GPY*; [Alexander Gardiner], "The Question of the Day," New York *Herald*, Nov. 10, 1850. See also Judge Samuel E. Johnson to Alexander Gardiner, Brooklyn, Oct. 26, 1850, *TFP*.

[16] John Lorimer Graham to John Tyler, New York, Feb. 14, 1851; Julia Gardiner Tyler to Juliana Gardiner, Sherwood Forest, Feb. 1; 21, 1851, *TFP*; John S. Cunningham to John Tyler, Portsmouth, Jan. 27, 1851, in *LTT*, II, 412; John Tyler to John S. Cunningham, Sherwood Forest, Feb. 5, 1851, in *ibid.*, 413.

[17] John Tyler to Robert Tyler, Saratoga, Sept. 11, 1850, *TPLC*; Alexander Gardiner to J. W. Footh, New York, Sept. 12, 1850, *GPY*; John Tyler to Robert Tyler, Sherwood Forest, Mar. 17, 1851, in *LTT*, II, 494; John Tyler, Jr., to Henry A. Wise, Philadelphia, Apr. 16, 1852, in Auchampaugh, *Robert Tyler*, 38–39.

[18] Julia Gardiner Tyler to Juliana Gardiner, Sherwood Forest, Mar. 17; Apr. 3; May 24, 1852, *TFP*; John Tyler to M. B. Seawell, Sherwood Forest, Mar. 29, 1852, in *Tyler's Quarterly*, XIII (October 1931), 79; Julia Gardiner Tyler to Juliana Gardiner, Sherwood Forest, Apr. 17, 1852, *TFP*; John Tyler, Jr., to Conway Whittle, Philadelphia, Apr. 8, 1852; John Tyler to Henry A. Wise, Sherwood Forest, Apr. 20, 1852; John Tyler to John S. Cunningham, Sherwood Forest, Apr. 20, 1852, *TPLC*. Attacks on the Tyler administration from outside Virginia were still carefully monitored and challenged by Robert Tyler. See Robert Tyler to John W. Forney, Philadelphia, July 20, 1852, in Auchampaugh, *Robert Tyler*, 45–47.

[19] Philip G. Auchampaugh, "John W. Forney, Robert Tyler and James Buchanan," *Tyler's Quarterly*, XV (October 1933), 76; John Tyler to John S. Cunningham, Sherwood Forest, June 10, 1852, in *LTT*, II, 497–98; *ibid.*, Apr. 20, 1852, *TPLC*; James Buchanan to Robert Tyler, Wheatland, Penna., June 8, 1852, in *LTT*, II, 498; Auchampaugh, *Robert Tyler*, 43–45; Coleman, *Priscilla Cooper Tyler*, 129.

[20] Roseboom, *A History of Presidential Elections*, 144–48; Stanwood, *A History of Presidential Elections*, 178–91.

[21] John Tyler to Caleb Cushing, Sherwood Forest, Mar. 17, 1853, in *LTT*, II, 505–6; John Tyler to Mrs. John Waggaman, Sherwood Forest, June 8, 1853, *TPLC*; Henry Wise to John Tyler, Onancock, Va., Apr. 5, 1853, in *LTT*, II, 505; Robert Tyler to Julia Gardiner Tyler, Washington, May 18, 1853, in *ibid.*, 505 Coleman, *Priscilla Cooper Tyler* 129; Julia Gardiner Tyler to [Juliana Gardiner], White Sulphur Springs [Aug. 1853], in *LTT*, II, 505; Roy Franklin Nichols, *Franklin Pierce* (Philadelphia, 1958), 421; John Tyler to William Tyler, Sherwood Forest, May 22, 1854, in *LTT*, II, 509–10; *ibid.*, 506.

[22] Margaret Gardiner Beeckman to Juliana Gardiner, Sherwood Forest, Jan. 25, 1853, *TFP*.

[23] Julia Gardiner Tyler to Juliana Gardiner, Sherwood Forest, Dec. 16, 1845, *TFP*; Juliana Gardiner to Alexander Gardiner, Sherwood Forest, Mar. 6, 1850; Margaret Gardiner Beeckman to Alexander Gardiner, Pittsfield, Mass., July 7, 1849, *GPY*; Julia Gardiner Tyler to Juliana Gardiner, Sherwood Forest, July 2, 1851, *TFP*; John Tyler to John S. Cunningham, Sherwood Forest, Dec. 15, 1852;

Robert Tyler to John Tyler, Philadelphia, June 13, 1856, in *LTT*, II, 500, 527; Margaret Gardiner Beeckman to Juliana Gardiner, Sherwood Forest, Feb. 15, 1855, *TPLC*.

[24] Julia Gardiner Tyler to Juliana Gardiner, Sherwood Forest, June 18, 1852, *TFP*.

[25] *Ibid.*, Jan. 23, 1856, *TFP*.

[26] Julia Gardiner Tyler, "To the Duchess of Sutherland and the Ladies of England," *Southern Literary Messenger*, XIX (Richmond, Feb. 1853), 120-26. Article originally written at Sherwood Forest, Jan. 24, 1853, and published in the Richmond *Enquirer*, Jan. 28, 1853.

[27] *Ibid.*

[28] Margaret Gardiner Beeckman to Juliana Gardiner, Sherwood Forest, Feb. 5; 12; 19; 23, 1853; Josephine Metcalfe to Margaret Gardiner Beeckman, Chicago, Aug. 12, 1853, *TFP;* John Tyler to William Tyler, Sherwood Forest, Mar. 29, 1853, in *LTT*, II, 507; John Tyler to Juliana Gardiner, Sherwood Forest, Sept. 19, 1853, *TPLC*.

[29] Julia Gardiner Tyler to Juliana Gardiner, Sherwood Forest, Jan. 17, 1855, *TFP;* John Tyler to William Tyler, Sherwood Forest, Oct. 29, 1854, *TPLC; ibid.*, Sherwood Forest, May 22, 1854; John Tyler to Robert Tyler, Sherwood Forest, Jan. 20; Nov. 19, 1855; John Tyler to Robert Tyler, Sherwood Forest, Jan. 8, 1855, in *LTT*, II, 510, 522, 517, 515. For Tyler's view of the Hungarian Revolution *see* John Tyler to Robert Tyler, Sherwood Forest, July 16, 1849, in *ibid.*, 491; Sanka Knox, "A Tyler Letter," New York *Times*, Dec. 7, 1958.

[30] John Tyler to David L. Gardiner, Sherwood Forest, Feb. 2, 1854; John Tyler to William Tyler, Sherwood Forest, May 22, 1854, in *LTT*, II, 509, 510; Margaret Gardiner Beeckman to Juliana Gardiner, Sherwood Forest, Nov. 13, 1854; Julia Gardiner Tyler to Margaret Gardiner Beeckman, Sherwood Forest, June 5, 1854, *TFP*.

[31] John Tyler to Margaret Gardiner Beeckman, Sherwood Forest, Mar. 23, 1854, *TPLC*.

[32] John Tyler to Robert Tyler, New York, Dec. 30, 1847; Saratoga, Aug. 11, 1854; Gov. William Bigler to Robert Tyler, Harrisburg, July 6, 1854, *TPLC;* John Tyler to Robert Tyler, Sherwood Forest, July 17, 1854; James Buchanan to Robert Tyler, London, Jan. 18, 1855; John Tyler to Robert Tyler, Sherwood Forest, May 19; June 10, 1856; Robert Tyler to John Tyler, Philadelphia, Dec. 23, 1855, in *LTT*, II, 513, 516-17, 416, 527, 523.

[33] John Tyler to Robert Tyler, Sherwood Forest, Jan. 20, 1855, in *ibid.*, 517-18; Wise, *Seven Decades of the Union*, 244-45; Julia Gardiner Tyler to Margaret Gardiner Beeckman, Sherwood Forest, May 12, 1855, *TFP;* John Tyler to Robert Tyler, Sherwood Forest, Nov. 19, 1855, in *LTT*, II, 522.

[34] John Tyler to Robert Tyler, Sherwood Forest, May 19; June 10, 1856, in *ibid.*, 416, 527.

[35] John Tyler to Robert Tyler, Sherwood Forest, May 19, 1856, in *ibid.*, 416.

[36] For Robert Tyler's crucial liaison role in the political relations between Buchanan, Wise, and John Tyler *see* the Wise-Buchanan, Buchanan-Robert Tyler, and Wise-Robert Tyler correspondence in *LTT*, II, 518-26; and in Auchampaugh, *Robert Tyler*, 74-75, 77, 80-82, 86-88, 109, 113, 115, 117, 119. See also John Tyler to John S. Cunningham, Sherwood Forest, Apr. 28, 1856, *TPLC;* Robert Tyler to Henry A. Wise, Philadelphia, Mar. 17, 1856, *TFP*.

[37] Robert Tyler to John Tyler, Philadelphia, June 13, 1856, in *LTT*, II, 527; Robert Tyler to Henry A. Wise, Philadelphia, June 9, 1856, in Auchampaugh, *Robert Tyler*, 103; Robert Tyler to John Tyler, Philadelphia, June 13, 1856, *TPLC;* James Buchanan to Robert Tyler, Wheatland, May 23, 1856, in *LTT*, II, 526; Margaret Gardiner Beeckman to Juliana Gardiner, Sherwood Forest, May 12, 1856, *TFP*.

[38] John Tyler to Robert Tyler, Sherwood Forest, June 10, 1856; John Tyler to John S. Cunningham, Sherwood Forest, July 14, 1856, in *LTT,* II, 527, 530.
[39] The details of the conventions and nominations are drawn from Roseboom, *A History of Presidential Elections,* 157–64; and Stanwood, *A History of Presidential Elections,* 192–213. John Tyler to David L. Gardiner, Sherwood Forest, July 21, 1856, in *LTT,* II, 532.
[40] John Tyler to Robert Tyler, Sherwood Forest, July 25, 1856, *ibid.*, 531; Auchampaugh, *Robert Tyler,* 127–29; Henry A. Wise to Robert Tyler, Richmond, Aug. 15, 1856; John Tyler to Robert Tyler, Sherwood Forest, Sept. 27, 1856, in *LTT,* II, 531–32.
[41] Henry A. Wise to Robert Tyler, Richmond, July 6, 1856; John Tyler to Robert Tyler, Sherwood Forest, Oct. 22, 1856, in *ibid.*, 530, 534; Auchampaugh, *Robert Tyler,* 130; John Tyler to Letitia Tyler Semple, Sherwood Forest, Oct. 29, 1856, *TPLC.*
[42] Coleman, *Priscilla Cooper Tyler,* 131–32; Auchampaugh, *Robert Tyler,* 143–44, 165–66, 237; John Tyler, Jr., to Henry A. Wise [Philadelphia, Nov. 1856], in Auchampaugh, "John W. Forney, Robert Tyler and James Buchanan," *loc. cit.*, 76; *LTT,* II, 645–46; John Tyler to Robert Tyler, Sherwood Forest, June 3, 1858, *TPLC; ibid.,* Nov. 23; Dec. 6, 1859; July 22, 1860, in *LTT,* II, 554–55, 559–60.

CHAPTER 17

[1] Julia Gardiner Tyler to Juliana Gardiner, Sherwood Forest, May 21; Dec. 16, 1855, *TFP.*
[2] John Tyler to Robert Tyler, Sherwood Forest, July 17, 1854; John Tyler to ———, Sherwood Forest, Apr. 21, 1857, in *LTT,* II, 513, 537.
[3] Julia Gardiner Tyler to Margaret Gardiner Beeckman, Sherwood Forest, May 1854; Margaret Gardiner Beeckman to Juliana Gardiner, Saratoga, Aug. 1854, *TFP;* John Tyler to Robert Tyler, Saratoga, Aug. 11, 1854; John Tyler to Julia Gardiner Tyler, Saratoga, Aug. 15, 1854, *TPLC;* Julia Gardiner Tyler to Juliana Gardiner, Sherwood Forest, Oct. 1854, *TFP;* Margaret Gardiner Beeckman to David L. Gardiner, Sherwood Forest, July 17, 1855; Juliana Gardiner to David L. Gardiner, Sherwood Forest, July 27, 1855, *GPY;* Julia Gardiner Tyler to Juliana Gardiner, Sherwood Forest, Aug. 5, 1855, *TFP.*
[4] Margaret Gardiner Beeckman to David L. Gardiner, Alum Springs, Aug. 2; 12; 14; 25, 1856, *GPY.*
[5] Margaret Gardiner Beeckman to Juliana Gardiner, Sherwood Forest, Nov. 30, 1854, *TFP.*
[6] *Ibid.*, Jan. 5; Mar. 2, 1855; Julia Gardiner Tyler to Juliana Gardiner, Sherwood Forest, Feb. 8, 1855; Mar. 1, 1856, *TFP;* John Tyler to Margaret Gardiner Beeckman, Sherwood Forest, Apr. 27, 1855, *TPLC.*
[7] Daniel M. Lord to John Tyler, Shelter Island, Nov. 25, 1855, *TFP.* Mary L'Hommedieu Gardiner Horsford (1824–1855) gave birth to four daughters: Lillian (1848), Mary Catherine (1850), Gertrude (1852), and Mary Gardiner (1855). Her sister, Phoebe Gardiner, married her widower, Eben N. Horsford, in 1860 and had one child, Cornelia, by him in 1861. Denison's death left his daughter Bessie an orphan. She was brought up by her aunt, Letitia Tyler Semple. Denison left her an estate of $10,000, and some lots in Kansas City and Wilkes-Barre. A few slaves were also in the inheritance. Although an Episcopal clergyman and a Pennsylvanian by birth, Denison was a strong supporter of the slavery system. He wrote Tyler in September 1858 that he had just been aboard a slaver brought into Charleston harbor and "for the first time saw naked savages in their primitive condition. It was a sad spectacle. Slavery would elevate them many degrees."

W. M. Denison to John Tyler, Charleston, Sept. 1, 1858, *TPLC;* Juliana Gardiner to David L. Gardiner, Hampton, Va., Oct. 1858, *GPY;* James A. Semple to John Tyler, New York, Mar. 3, 1859; Feb. 28, 1860, *TFP*. For details of the death of Margaret Gardiner Beeckman (1822–1857) see Margaret Gardiner Beeckman to Juliana Gardiner, Sherwood Forest, May 28, 1857; Phoebe Gardiner to Juliana Gardiner, Cambridge, Mass., June 7, 1857; John A. Belvin (Funeral Director) to John Tyler, Richmond, Oct. 21, 1857, *TFP;* Julia Gardiner Tyler to Eliza Gardiner Brumley, Sherwood Forest, July 5, 1857, *Gardiner Papers, Long Island Collection,* East Hampton Free Library. The funeral bill of $174.25 had not been paid by October 21. A family tradition is that Margaret died of tuberculosis. She probably had the disease, but it is doubtful that it killed her in 1857. Interview with J. Alfred Tyler, Sherwood Forest, Jan. 27, 1960.

[8] Julia Gardiner Tyler to Eliza Gardiner Brumley, Sherwood Forest, July 5, 1857, *Gardiner Papers, Long Island Collection,* East Hampton Free Library.

[9] John Tyler to Henry A. Wise, Sherwood Forest, Mar. [8–10]; 17, 1856, *TPLC;* Juliana Gardiner to David L. Gardiner, Sherwood Forest, Mar. 27, 1856, *GPY*. Robert Fitzwalter Tyler spent his entire life farming in New Kent County. He married a Fannie Glinn and died in Richmond on Dec. 30, 1927.

[10] John Tyler to Robert Tyler, Sherwood Forest, Oct. 22, 1856, in *LTT,* II, 534; John Tyler to Margaret Gardiner Beeckman, Sherwood Forest, Oct. 21; 24, 1856, *TPLC*. For the health, growth, and education of the Tyler children, particularly Gardie and Alex, during this period, *see* John Tyler to Margaret Gardiner Beeckman, Sherwood Forest, July 3, 1856, in *LTT,* II, 529 ("I . . . reached home, finding Julia well and the children with the chicken-pox; and so ends my catechism"); David Gardiner Tyler to David L. Gardiner, Sherwood Forest, Apr. 15, 1857, *GPY* ("I go regularly to school studying Dictionary, Latin, Geography, English grammer [*sic*], and Arithmetic besides reading"); Julia Gardiner Tyler to Margaret Gardiner Beeckman, Sherwood Forest, May 12, 1855, *TFP;* John Tyler to Margaret Gardiner Beeckman, Sherwood Forest, June 14, 1855; *TPLC;* Julia Gardiner Tyler to David L. Gardiner, Sherwood Forest, June 9, 1858; Juliana Gardiner to David L. Gardiner, Hampton, Oct. 19; 26, 1858, *GPY*.

[11] John Tyler to Margaret Gardiner Beeckman, Sherwood Forest, Dec. 25, 1855; John Tyler to Robert Tyler, Sherwood Forest, Jan. 6, 1855, in *LTT,* II, 523–24; 514–15.

[12] Julia Gardiner Tyler to Juliana Gardiner, Sherwood Forest, Nov. 17, 1854; Margaret Gardiner Beeckman to Juliana Gardiner, Sherwood Forest, Nov. 22, 1854, *TFP;* John Tyler to Henry Curtis, Sherwood Forest, Feb. 14, 1855; John Tyler to Margaret Gardiner Beeckman, Sherwood Forest, June 23, 1855; Feb. 17; 20; 24, 1856, *TPLC;* John Tyler to John Tyler, Jr., Sherwood Forest, Jan. 5, 1857, in *LTT,* II, 109. For Tazewell Tyler's medical education and practice in Williamsburg and in New Kent County *see* John Tyler to Margaret Gardiner Beeckman, Sherwood Forest, Jan. 8, 1853; John Tyler to Robert Tyler, Sherwood Forest, Nov. 6, 1854; John Tyler to Letitia Tyler Semple, Sherwood Forest, Dec. 8, 1857, *TPLC;* Julia Gardiner Tyler to Juliana Gardiner, Sherwood Forest, July 1, 1853, *TFP*.

[13] John Tyler to John Tyler, Jr., Sherwood Forest, Jan. 5, 1857, in *LTT,* II, 109.

[14] Julia Gardiner Tyler to Margaret Gardiner Beeckman, Philadelphia, Oct. 18, 1856; Margaret Gardiner Beeckman to David L. Gardiner, Alum Springs, Aug. 2, 1856, *TFP;* Julia Gardiner Tyler to David L. Gardiner, Sherwood Forest, June 9, 1858; Hampton, Oct. 26, 1858, *GPY;* John Tyler to Silas Reed, Sherwood Forest, Apr. 7, 1858, in *LTT,* II, 541; John Tyler to David L. Gardiner, Sherwood Forest, Mar. 29, 1858, *TPLC;* Will of John Tyler, Sherwood Forest, Oct. 10, 1859 (photostat), entered for probate in Charles City County Court (by Julia) on Jan. 15, 1863, *TFP*.

[15] John Tyler to Margaret Gardiner Beeckman, Sherwood Forest, June 14, 1855; Henry A. Wise to John Tyler, Onancock, Va., Aug. 7, 1855; William Green to John Tyler, Culpepper, Va., Aug. 13, 1855, *TPLC;* Julia Gardiner Tyler to Juliana Gardiner, Sherwood Forest, July 6, 1854, *TFP;* Juliana Gardiner to David L. Gardiner, Hampton, July 12, 1860, *GPY;* John Tyler to Professor Ewell, Sherwood Forest, Feb. 11, 1859; John Tyler to ———, Sherwood Forest, Oct. 22, 1860, *TPLC;* John Tyler to Robert Tyler, Sherwood Forest, Oct. 19, 1859, in *LTT,* II, 547; John Tyler, "Early Times of Virginia—William and Mary College," *De Bow's Review,* XXVIII (August 1859), 136–49.

[16] John Tyler to Robert Tyler, Sherwood Forest, Oct. 6, 1859, in *LTT,* II, 553.

[17] Margaret Gardiner Beeckman to Juliana Gardiner, Sherwood Forest, Mar. 2, 1856; Mar. 26, 1855, *TFP;* Henry M. Denison to John Tyler, Louisville, July 2, 1855, *TPLC;* Julia Gardiner Tyler to Juliana Gardiner, Baltimore, Mar. 22, 1855; Sherwood Forest, Mar. 7, 1855, *TFP.*

[18] Thomas Ritchie to John Tyler, Richmond, Mar. 14, 1856; John Tyler to John S. Cunningham, Sherwood Forest, Apr. 28, 1856, *TPLC.* The speech is reprinted in *LTT,* II, 384–99, and in the *Southern Literary Messenger* for August, 1856.

[19] *LTT,* II, 537–38; John Tyler to David L. Gardiner, Sherwood Forest, Apr. 6, 1857, *TPLC;* David Gardiner Tyler to David L. Gardiner, Sherwood Forest, Apr. 15, 1857, *GPY;* Ralph H. Rives, "The Jamestown Celebration of 1857," *The Virginia Magazine of History and Biography,* LXVI (June 1958), 259–71.

[20] Julia Gardiner Tyler to Juliana Gardiner, Sherwood Forest, Mar. 31, 1855, *TFP.*

[21] Juliana Gardiner to Julia Gardiner Tyler, Hampton, Aug. 10; 24; Sept. 24, 1859, *GPY;* Julia Gardiner Tyler to Juliana Gardiner, Sherwood Forest, Nov. 14, 1859, *TFP;* John Tyler to Robert Tyler, Sherwood Forest, Nov. 23, 1859, in *LTT,* II, 554.

[22] Quotation reconstructed from a detailed paraphrase found in Julia Gardiner Tyler to Juliana Gardiner, Sherwood Forest, Nov. 10, 1859, *TFP.*

[23] *Ibid.,* Nov. 14; Dec. 1, 1859; J. Alexander Tyler to Harry Beeckman, Sherwood Forest, Dec. 1, 1859, *TFP;* John Tyler to Robert Tyler, Sherwood Forest, Dec. 6, 1859, in *LTT,* II, 555. The 1850 census showed Charles City County with 1664 whites, 772 Negro freedmen, and 2764 Negro slaves.

[24] Auchampaugh, *Robert Tyler,* 275–76, 363; John Tyler to Robert Tyler, Sherwood Forest, Dec. 23, 1859, *TPLC.*

[25] Julia Gardiner Tyler to Juliana Gardiner, Sherwood Forest, Dec. 1, 1859, *TFP;* John Tyler to Robert Tyler, Sherwood Forest, Dec. 6, 1859, in *LTT,* II, 555.

[26] Julia Gardiner Tyler to Juliana Gardiner, Sherwood Forest, Dec. 8; 14; 19; 1859, *TFP.*

[27] David Gardiner Tyler to Harry Beeckman, Sherwood Forest, Jan. 7, 1860; Julia Gardiner Tyler to Juliana Gardiner, Sherwood Forest, Nov. 28; Dec. 28, 1859; Samuel Gardiner to John Tyler, Shelter Island, Nov. 29, 1858, *TFP;* W. Farley Grey to John Tyler, New York, Dec. 22, 1859, in *LTT,* II, 556; Julia Gardiner Tyler to Juliana Gardiner, Sherwood Forest, Feb. 8, 1860; Nov. 10, 1859, *TFP;* John Tyler to Robert Tyler, Sherwood Forest, Oct. 19, 1859, in *LTT,* II, 547; Julia Gardiner Tyler to Juliana Gardiner, Sherwood Forest, Nov. 8, 1859, *TFP.*

[28] *Ibid.,* Feb. 14, 1860, *TFP.*

[29] *Ibid.,* Mar. 13, 1860. At the same time, the Tylers made a special effort to entertain Judge Richard Parker when he visited in the county in February 1860. See *ibid.,* Feb. 29, 1860, *TFP.*

[30] *LTT,* II, 549; 236–39; John Tyler to Robert Tyler, Sherwood Forest, Sept.

6, 1857, *TPLC; ibid.,* Villa Margaret, Aug. 28, 1858; John Tyler to John Tyler, Jr., Sherwood Forest, Sept. 7, 1858; John Tyler to Robert Tyler, Sherwood Forest, July 14, 1858, in *LTT,* II, 241–42, 242–43, 544.

³¹ *Ibid.,* May 26, 1859, *TPLC.*

³² Robert Tyler to John Tyler, Philadelphia, July 13, 1859, *TPLC;* John Tyler to Robert Tyler, Villa Margaret, July 16; Aug. 1, 1859; Sherwood Forest, Oct. 6; 19, 1859, in *LTT,* II, 551, 552, 547, 553.

³³ *Ibid.,* Oct. 6, 1859, in *ibid.,* 553; *ibid.,* Dec. 23, 1859, *TPLC; ibid.,* Jan. 19, 1860, in *LTT,* I, 596; II, 557; John Tyler, Jr. [pseud. "Python"], "The History of Party, and the Political Status of John Tyler," *De Bow's Review,* XXVI (March 1859), 300–9; John Tyler, Jr. [pseud. "Tau"], "The Relative Status of the North and the South," *De Bow's Review,* XXVII (July 1859), 1–29.

³⁴ Julia Gardiner Tyler to Juliana Gardiner, Sherwood Forest, Dec. 28; Nov. 8; 10, 1859; Feb. 8; Jan. 3, 1860, *TFP;* Mar. 20, 1860, in *LTT,* II, 546–47.

³⁵ *Ibid.,* I, 467; John Tyler to H. B. Grigsby, Sherwood Forest, Apr. 16, 1860, in *Tyler's Quarterly,* XI (April 1930), 236–37.

³⁶ *Ibid.;* Mary Conger to Julia Gardiner Tyler, Waldberg, July 24, 1869; Sarah Thompson Gardiner to Juliana Gardiner, Staten Island, June 1860, *TFP;* Tyler vs. Gardiner, *35 New York Reports,* VIII, 600–1; Receipts from Tiffany and Co. to David L. Gardiner, New York, Apr. 23; 25, 1860, *GPY;* Julia Gardiner Tyler to David L. Gardiner, Sherwood Forest, Apr. 12, 1860, *TFP;* Juliana Gardiner to David L. Gardiner, Hampton, June 13; 14; 16; 23; July 12; 26, 1860, *GPY;* David L. Gardiner to Juliana Gardiner, Staten Island, Aug. 6, 1860, *TFP;* Sarah Thompson Gardiner to David L. Gardiner, Pomfret, Conn., Aug. 25, 1886, *GPY.* Three children were born to David Lyon and Sarah Thompson Gardiner: David in April 1861, Sarah Diodati in July 1862, and Robert Alexander in 1864. Robert married Norah Loftus in 1908. Their children were Alexandra Diodati Gardiner (Mrs. J. R. Creel) (1910–   ); and Robert David Lion Gardiner (1911–   ). Sarah Diodati Gardiner died unmarried in 1953, as did David in 1927. Robert Alexander died in 1919. *See* John Tyler to Juliana Gardiner, Richmond, May 2, 1861, in *LTT,* II, 664; Juliana Gardiner to L. F. Cooper, New York, Aug. 2, 1862, *TFP;* Interview with Judge J. Randall Creel and Alexandra Gardiner Creel, Oyster Bay, L.I., N.Y. Aug. 28, 1959; *East Hampton Cemetery Records,* East Hampton Free Library.

³⁷ John Tyler to John S. Cunningham, Sherwood Forest, May 30, 1860; John Tyler to Robert Tyler, Villa Margaret, July 22, 1860, in *LTT,* II, 558, 559.

³⁸ *Ibid.;* Roseboom, *A History of Presidential Elections,* 173–80.

³⁹ John Tyler to Robert Tyler, Villa Margaret, Aug. 14, 1860; Sherwood Forest, Aug. 27, 1860; John Tyler to David L. Gardiner, Sherwood Forest, Oct. 27, 1860, in *LTT,* II, 559, 560, 561, 563.

⁴⁰ John Tyler to Robert Tyler, Villa Margaret, July 22; Aug. 14, 1860; Sherwood Forest, Aug. 27, 1860, in *ibid.,* 559, 560, 561–62.

⁴¹ John Tyler to Robert Tyler, Sherwood Forest, Aug. 27, 1860; Villa Margaret, Sept. 14, 1860; John Tyler to H. S. Foote, Sherwood Forest, Aug. 26, 1860, in *ibid.,* 562, 561.

⁴² Phoebe Gardiner Horsford to Julia Gardiner Tyler, Cambridge, Mass., n.d. [Sept.–Oct. 1860], *TFP:* Juliana Gardiner to David L. Gardiner, Villa Margaret, June 9, 1858; June 23, 1860, *GPY;* Julia Gardiner Tyler to Juliana Gardiner, Sherwood Forest, Jan.; Feb. 23; 29; May 15, 1860, *TFP.*

⁴³ Juliana Gardiner to David L. Gardiner, Hampton, June 13; 14; 23; July 12; 26, 1860, *GPY;* Fanny Gardiner to Juliana Gardiner, Staten Island, July 17, 1860, *TFP;* Juliana Gardiner to David L. Gardiner, Hampton, Oct. [20–26], 1858, *GPY;* Society of the "Old Boys" of Hampton Academy to John Tyler, Hampton, Jan. 3, 1860, *TPLC.*

⁴⁴ Juliana Gardiner to David L. Gardiner, Villa Margaret, Aug. 15, 1860; Sarah Thompson Gardiner to Juliana Gardiner, Staten Island, June 29, 1860, *TFP*.
⁴⁵ John Tyler to William G. Waller, Sherwood Forest, Nov. 5, 1860, *TPLC*.
⁴⁶ John Tyler to Robert Tyler, Sherwood Forest, Nov. 10, 1860, in *LTT*, II, 563; John Tyler to Silas Reed, Sherwood Forest, Nov. 16, 1860, *TPLC*. Compare with the version printed in *LTT*, II, 574-75.
⁴⁷ J. Selden to Julia Gardiner Tyler, Baltimore, Dec. 26, 1874, *TFP*.
⁴⁸ Julia Gardiner Tyler to Juliana Gardiner, Sherwood Forest, Dec. 14, 1860, *TFP;* John Tyler to ———, Sherwood Forest, Dec. 3, 1860, *TPLC;* John Tyler to Caleb Cushing, Sherwood Forest, Dec. 14, 1860, in *LTT*, II, 577.

CHAPTER 18

¹ *LTT*, II, 576.
² John Tyler to David L. Gardiner, Sherwood Forest, Jan. 1, 1861, in *ibid.*, 578.
³ *Ibid.*, 580-81; Robert Gray Gunderson, *Old Gentlemen's Convention: The Washington Peace Conference of 1861* (Madison, Wis., 1961), 24-25.
⁴ Richmond *Enquirer,* Jan. 17, 1861; John Tyler to ———, n.p., n.d. [Sherwood Forest, Jan. 10-17, 1861], *TPLC*.
⁵ Richmond *Enquirer,* Jan. 17, 1861; *LTT*, II, 580, Philadelphia *Pennsylvanian,* Jan. 26, 1861, quoted in Auchampaugh, *Robert Tyler,* 320-21.
⁶ John Tyler to Robert Tyler, Sherwood Forest, Jan. 18, 1861, in *ibid.*, 578-79; *ibid.*, 581.
⁷ *Ibid.;* John Tyler to Robert Tyler, Sherwood Forest, Jan. 18, 1861, in *ibid.*, 579; Gunderson, *Old Gentlemen's Convention,* 25-26. Gunderson links Tyler to the extremist Seddon viewpoint at this time. While Tyler later did identify himself with Seddon at the Peace Conference, he was clearly no secessionist in mid-January 1861. Nevertheless, the Gunderson study is by far the best on this subject.
⁸ *LTT*, II, 581; Julia Gardiner Tyler to Juliana Gardiner, Sherwood Forest, Jan. 22, 1861, *TFP*.
⁹ *Ibid.; LTT*, II, 619-20.
¹⁰ *Ibid.*, 589-90.
¹¹ John Tyler to Wyndham Robertson, Washington, Jan. 26, 1861; John Tyler to James Buchanan, Washington, Jan. 28, 1861, in *ibid.*, 590-91, 592.
¹² *Ibid.*, 610; James D. Halyburton to John Tyler, Richmond, Jan. 25, 1861; Robert Winthrop to John Tyler, Boston, Feb. 12, 1861; Robert Dale Owen to John Tyler, Indianapolis, Feb. 14, 1861, *TPLC;* Julia Gardiner Tyler to Juliana Gardiner, Washington, Feb. 3, 1861, in *LTT*, II, 596-97.
¹³ Julia Gardiner Tyler to Juliana Gardiner, Washington, Feb. 4; 13, 1861, in *ibid.*, 597-98, 612-13; Gunderson, *Old Gentlemen's Convention,* 55, 58.
¹⁴ *Ibid.*, 10-11, 105-6; Alexander W. Doniphan to James Guthrie, Washington, Feb. 14, 1861, *Tyler Peace Collection,* Alderman Library, University of Virginia.
¹⁵ Unidentified Newspaper Clipping, Feb. 6, 1861, *Tyler Peace Collection,* Alderman Library, University of Virginia.
¹⁶ *LTT*, II, 610-12; Julia Gardiner Tyler to Juliana Gardiner, Washington, Feb. 13, 1861, in *ibid.*, 613.
¹⁷ Gunderson, *Old Gentlemen's Convention,* 49, 63-64, 70, 50-60, and *passim.*
¹⁸ Julia Gardiner Tyler to Juliana Gardiner, Washington, Feb. 13, 1861, in *LTT*, II, 613.
¹⁹ Gunderson, *Old Gentlemen's Convention,* 62-64, 107-9, 141; *Speech of John*

Tyler, Delivered March 13, 1861, in the Virginia State Convention (Pamphlet; Richmond, 1861). For the wording of the radical Seddon proposal *see LTT*, II, 606. The question and degree of Tyler's complicity in drafting the Seddon proposal rests on an interpretation of a semantically obscure, undated [February 1861], John Tyler to James A. Seddon note in the *Tyler Peace Collection*, Alderman Library, University of Virginia. It reads: "Here is my suggestion thrown into form. I cannot but regard it as important. It avoids propagandism and secures us in our territories. The distribution clause appropriately follows—so it seems to me. If you concur present it at the proper time. If you incline against it [this phrase struck through but legible] I cannot but consider it as well calculated to heal discontents both North and South." If indeed the wording of this informal note refers to the most extreme section of Seddon's proposal (most of it ran along Crittenden compromise lines), then a knowledge of its date would have great significance in detailing Tyler's shift to the radical secessionist position. Given Tyler's changing frame of mind on February 13–15, 1861, it is quite conceivable that he actually helped Seddon draw up the proposal in the hope that its very extremism would bring the convention to grief and a speedy adjournment. If so, one might hazard Feb. 14 as the date of the letter.

[20] James Buchanan to John Tyler, Washington, Feb. 21, 1861, *TPLC*; *LTT*, II, 613–14; Gunderson, *Old Gentlemen's Convention*, 68.

[21] Carl Sandburg, *Abraham Lincoln: The War Years*, 4 vols. (New York, 1939), I, 87–90.

[22] *LTT*, II, 615–16, 633; Gunderson, *Old Gentlemen's Convention*, 86–94, 107; John Tyler to Talbot Sweeney, Richmond, Nov. 30, 1861, *TPLC*.

[23] Gunderson, *Old Gentlemen's Convention*, 95–97; *LTT*, II, 616, 620, 622, 629; Coleman, *Priscilla Cooper Tyler*, 135–36; Sandburg, *Lincoln*, I, 125–37.

[24] *Speech of John Tyler, Delivered March 13, 1861, in the Virginia State Convention*, 1–32; *LTT*, II, 621–28; *Richmond Enquirer*, Mar. 30, 1861.

[25] John Tyler to Julia Gardiner Tyler, Richmond, Mar. 24, 1861, *TPLC*; *ibid.*; Julia Gardiner Tyler to Juliana Gardiner, Sherwood Forest, Mar. 19, 1861, in *LTT*, II, 629, 627; John Tyler to Julia Gardiner Tyler, Richmond, Mar. 19–20, 1861, *TPLC*; John Tyler to David L. Gardiner, Richmond, Apr. 5, 1861, in *LTT*, II, 630; John Tyler, "To the People of the Northern States," Richmond, n.d. [Mar. 13–25, 1861], *TPLC*; Sandburg, *Lincoln*, I, 222; *LTT*, II, 630.

[26] John Tyler to [Benjamin Patton], Sherwood Forest, May 7, 1861, *TPLC*; John Tyler to Julia Gardiner Tyler, Richmond, Apr. 16, 1861, in *LTT*, II, 640.

[27] Julia Gardiner Tyler to Juliana Gardiner, Sherwood Forest, Apr. 18, 1861, in *ibid.*, 646–47.

[28] John Tyler to Julia Gardiner Tyler, Richmond, Apr. 18, 1861, in *ibid.*, 641–42.

[29] *Ibid.*, 642–43, 647, 658–59.

[30] Coleman, *Priscilla Cooper Tyler*, 136–40; Deran Green, *Old Houses on Radcliff Street* (Bristol, Pa., 1938), 151; Auchampaugh, *Robert Tyler*, 342; 306–13; 336–39; Priscilla Cooper Tyler to Juliana Gardiner, New York, Apr. 27, 1861, *TFP*; Julia Gardiner Tyler to Juliana Gardiner, Sherwood Forest, Apr. 25; May 7; 11, 1861, in *LTT*, II, 648, 649, 650–51. For Robert Tyler's escape from Philadelphia and the subsequent confiscation of his Bristol, Pa., property in September 1861, *see* New York *Tribune*, Apr. 16, 1861, and Philadelphia *Inquirer*, Sept. 14, 1861, reprinted in Frank Moore (ed.), *The Rebellion Record. A Diary of American Events*, 3 vols. (New York, 1862), I, 26; III, 28. Priscilla's sister, Julia Cooper Campbell, was the wife of Allan Campbell, president of the New York and Harlem Railroad. They lived at 44 E. 39th St., in 1861. Still at home with Priscilla at the time of her flight were these of her children: Grace Raoul, 15; Priscilla, called "Tousie," 11; Elizabeth, 9; Julia Campbell, 5; and Robert, called "Robbie," 3. Daughter Letitia Christian, the Confederate flag-raiser, was then with her aunt,

Priscilla's sister, Mary Grace Cooper Raoul, in Montgomery. She was 19. Three other of Priscilla's children died young, *viz.:* Mary Fairlee (1840-1845); John IV (1842-1846); and Thomas Cooper (1848-1849). When she fled Philadelphia Priscilla left her daughter Elizabeth with her sister Julia Cooper Campbell.

[31] Coleman, *Priscilla Cooper Tyler,* 142-43; L. F. Campbell to Juliana Gardiner, Albany, N.Y., Sept. 9, 1863, *TFP; LTT,* II, 684-85; Langford, *Ladies of the White House,* 327-29; Sarah D. Gardiner, *Memories of Gardiners Island,* 97; Julia Gardiner Tyler to Juliana Gardiner, Sherwood Forest, May 11; 7, 1861, in *LTT,* II, 651, 650. William G. Waller survived the war and later served as assistant editor of the Savannah *News* and managing editor of the Richmond *Times.* His first wife was Jenny Howell, his second was Bessie Austin. See Richmond *Dispatch,* July 11, 1889.

[32] Julia Gardiner Tyler to Juliana Gardiner, Sherwood Forest, May 7, 1861, in *LTT,* II, 649-50.

[33] John Tyler to Juliana Gardiner, Richmond, May 2, 1861, in *ibid.,* 643.

[34] Julia Gardiner Tyler to John Tyler, Sherwood Forest, Apr. 27, 1861, *TPLC;* Julia Gardiner Tyler to Juliana Gardiner, Sherwood Forest, Apr. 25; May 2; 4; 7, 1861, in *LTT,* II, 644, 647-48, 649, 650; *ibid.,* 659; Juliana Gardiner to Julia Gardiner Tyler, Staten Island, June 10, 1861; Julia Gardiner Tyler to Juliana Gardiner, Sherwood Forest, Jan. 11, 1860, *TFP.* The Villa Margaret flag incident of June 3, 1861, is recounted in the New York *Commercial Advertiser,* June 4, 1861, reprinted in Moore, *Rebellion Record,* I, 91.

[35] Juliana Gardiner to Julia Gardiner Tyler, Staten Island, June 10, 1861, *TFP;* Julia Gardiner Tyler to Juliana Gardiner, Sherwood Forest, May 4; June 16; July 2, 1861, in *LTT,* II, 649, 653; 651-52. The champagne celebration of Manassas story is found in Moore, *Rebellion Record,* III, 11.

[36] Juliana Gardiner to Julia Gardiner Tyler, Staten Island, June 10, 1861; Juliana Gardiner to —— Cooper, Staten Island, Aug. 9, 1861, *TFP.*

[37] *LTT,* II, 658-65; Julia Gardiner Tyler to Juliana Gardiner, Sherwood Forest, Nov. 4, 1861, *TFP.*

[38] This account of John Tyler's death is Julia's. It is very likely a recollection from the distance of the late 1870s or early 1880s when her son, Lyon G. Tyler, was working on *The Letters and Times of the Tylers.* It is found in *LTT,* II, 670-72. Wise, *Seven Decades of the Union,* 283; *LTT,* II, 667. For a medical interpretation of the cause of his death see Marx, *Health of the Presidents,* 136-37.

[39] Julia Gardiner Tyler to Judge Fitzhugh, Sherwood Forest, n.d. [Summer 1865]; Julia Gardiner Tyler to Tazewell Tyler, Staten Island, n.d. [May 1865], *TFP.*

[40] *LTT,* II, 673-84; Will of John Tyler (photostat), Sherwood Forest, Oct. 10, 1859, *TFP;* Richmond *Whig,* Jan. 21; 22, 1862, cited in *LTT,* 674-76, 681-84.

[41] Wise, *Seven Decades of the Union,* 283.

CHAPTER 19

[1] Juliana Gardiner to L. F. Campbell, Staten Island, Jan. 31, 1862; Julia Gardiner Tyler to Juliana Gardiner, Sherwood Forest, Apr. 1, 1862; Louise Ludlow to Juliana Gardiner, Baltimore, Mar. 23; 28, 1862, *TFP.*

[2] Phoebe Gardiner Horsford to Juliana Gardiner, Shelter Island, Aug. 21, 1863; Cambridge, Mass., Jan. 27; Sept. 9, 1862; Juliana Gardiner to Julia Gardiner Tyler, Staten Island, May 18, 1862, *TFP.*

[3] Coleman, *Priscilla Cooper Tyler,* 143; Julia Gardiner Tyler to Juliana Gardiner, Sherwood Forest, Apr. 28, 1862; Juliana Gardiner to Julia Gardiner Tyler, Staten Island, May 18, 1862; Juliana Gardiner to L. F. Campbell, Staten Island, Apr. 21, 1862, *TFP.*

⁴ Julia Gardiner Tyler to Juliana Gardiner, Sherwood Forest, Apr. 1, 1862; Juliana Gardiner to L. F. Campbell, Staten Island, May 18, 1862, *TFP*.

⁵ Coleman, *Priscilla Cooper Tyler*, 143–45; Juliana Gardiner to Julia Gardiner Tyler, Staten Island, May 18, 1862, *TFP*.

⁶ Julia Gardiner Tyler to Commanding Officer, U.S. Forces at Jamestown and Williamsburg, Sherwood Forest, May 30, 1862, *GPY*.

⁷ Juliana Gardiner to L. F. Campbell, New York, Aug. 2; n.d. [Aug.]; July 13, 1862; L. F. Campbell to Juliana Gardiner, New Rochelle, N.Y., July 22; Aug. 20, 1862; Phoebe Gardiner Horsford to Juliana Gardiner, Cambridge, Sept. 9, 1862, *TFP*.

⁸ See n. 20, below, for references to the tensions emerging during this visit to Staten Island.

⁹ Julia Gardiner Tyler to ———, n.p., n.d. [Staten Island, early 1863]; Julia Gardiner Tyler to Juliana Gardiner, Old Point Comfort, Jan. 8, 1863; Sherwood Forest, Jan. 12, 1863, *TFP*.

¹⁰ Julia Gardiner Tyler to Juliana Gardiner, Richmond, Feb. 17, 1863; Juliana Gardiner to Louisa Cooper, Staten Island, Mar. 8, 1863; Julia Gardiner Tyler to Juliana Gardiner, Sherwood Forest, May 12, 1863; William H. Clopton to Julia Gardiner Tyler, Charles City, Oct. 18, 1863; David Gardiner Tyler to Julia Gardiner Tyler, Lexington, Oct. 2, 1863; Dec. 24, 1863, *TFP*.

¹¹ Chitwood, *Tyler*, 255–56; Julia Gardiner Tyler to Judge Fitzhugh, Sherwood Forest, n.d. [Oct. 1862]; Julia Gardiner Tyler to Tazewell Tayler, Sherwood Forest, Sept. 21, 1863; L. C. Crump to Julia Gardiner Tyler, Winslow, New Kent County, Va., Sept. 24, 1863; Julia Gardiner Tyler to L. C. Crump, Sherwood Forest, Sept. 4, 1863, *TFP*. The deposit slip for $5048.25 is dated Mar. 19, 1863, and is found in *TFP*. James A. Semple to Julia Gardiner Tyler, Drewry's Bluff, Va., Oct. 31, 1863; Julia Gardiner Tyler to Juliana Gardiner, Sherwood Forest, Apr. 8, 1863, *TFP*. The two white laborers Julia was "lucky" to hire were named Harod and Oakley. Harod, a mason by trade, was to run the plantation mill for which he was paid $150 annually plus board. He took the job in order to feed his family and hold it together. Oakley, an "old man," had been the last overseer at nearby Weyanoke plantation and wanted to remain in the area. His services were purchased for $144 and board annually. Both men lived in "tenements on the place," probably abandoned slave quarters.

¹² Julia Gardiner Tyler to Juliana Gardiner, Sherwood Forest, Apr. 8; May 12, 1863, *TFP*.

¹³ Gilbert Beeckman to Harry Beeckman, New York, May 20, 1863; May 23, 1863; Juliana Gardiner to Louisa Cooper, Staten Island, Aug. 13, 1863; Phoebe Gardiner Horsford to Juliana Gardiner, Cambridge, Mass., Dec. 26, 1863; John B. Gardiner to Juliana Gardiner, Brooklyn, Apr. 8, 1863; Juliana Gardiner to Julia Gardiner Tyler, Staten Island, July 19; Aug. 19, 1863; Harry G. Beeckman to Juliana Gardiner, Gardiners Island, Aug. 27, 1864; David Gardiner Tyler to Julia Gardiner Tyler, Richmond, Sept. 6, 1864; Julia Gardiner Tyler to Juliana Gardiner, Sherwood Forest, Apr. 8; May 12, 1863; Julia Gardiner Tyler, Deposition, in Gardiner *vs.* Tyler, n.p., n.d. [Staten Island, 1865]; Juliana Gardiner to Mrs. Crane, Staten Island, Apr. 14 [1863], *TFP*.

¹⁴ Juliana Gardiner to Julia Gardiner Tyler, New York, Aug. 19; July 19; 20, 1863; J. Meta L. to Juliana Gardiner, Staten Island, May 22; Sept. 9, 1863; Juliana Gardiner to Mrs. Crane, Staten Island, Apr. 14 [1863], *TFP*.

¹⁵ Louisa Cooper to Julia Gardiner Tyler, Montgomery, n.d. [May 13, 1863], quoted in Julia Gardiner Tyler to Juliana Gardiner, Sherwood Forest, May 12, 1863, *TFP*; Coleman, *Priscilla Cooper Tyler*, 147–48; Langford, *The Ladies of the White House*, 329; James A. Semple to Julia Gardiner Tyler, Drewry's Bluff, Nov. 9, 1863; Juliana Gardiner to Julia Gardiner Tyler, New York, July 20, 1863; Julia Gardiner Tyler to Gen. John A. Dix, Sherwood Forest, July 20, 1863, *TFP*.

¹⁶ Major Thomas L. Bayne to Julia Gardiner Tyler, Ordnance Bureau, Rich-

mond, Aug. 10, 1863; James A. Semple to Julia Gardiner Tyler, Drewry's Bluff, Sept. 23; Oct. 31, 1863; H. J. Miller to Julia Gardiner Tyler, Bank, Va., Oct. 8, 1863; David Gardiner Tyler to Julia Gardiner Tyler, Lexington, Nov. 14, 1863; L. Heyligery to Julia Gardiner Tyler, Nassau, Dec. 29, 1863; Jan. 16, 1864; Norman J. Walker to Julia Gardiner Tyler, St. George, Bermuda, Oct. 19, 1863; J. M. Seixas to Julia Gardiner Tyler, Wilmington, July 10, 1864. For Julia's claims against the War Department for the horse and oats, prosecuted in the main by Semple, see James A. Semple to Julia Gardiner Tyler, Drewry's Bluff, Nov. 9, 1863; Feb. 10; Apr. 3, 1864, *TFP*. Brig. Gen. A. R. Lawton, CSA, handled the claim for the government. There is no evidence that it was ever paid. The *R. E. Lee* was a long, narrow, fast, Clyde-built iron steamer operated by the Confederate Ordnance Department; Wilkinson, a former U.S. naval officer and native of Norfolk, was one of the Department's most skillful and successful skippers; he was paid as a naval officer in the grade of lieutenant. He was not, in this sense, a free-enterprising blockade runner, but an officer in the Confederate States Navy. This too was the status of Captain R. H. Gayle of the *Cornubia*.

[17] David Gardiner Tyler to Julia Gardiner Tyler, Lexington, Nov. 14, 1863; Mrs. Norman J. Walker to Julia Gardiner Tyler, St. George, Bermuda, n.d. [early January 1864]; Jan. 10, 1864, *TFP*. Gayle was taken on Nov. 7, 1863. See R. H. Gayle to Julia Gardiner Tyler, Fort Warren, Boston, Aug. 7, 1864, *TFP*. Gayle's exact age is not known. He was appointed midshipman in the U.S. Navy in 1848 (resigned in 1853), which would probably put his year of birth around 1830–1831.

[18] Professor Nelson served as Captain of the Washington College Company with Professor Campbell as First Lieutenant. The Washington College Company paused or bivouacked at Millerstown, Jordan's Furnace, Rockbridge Alum, California Furnace, and Shirkey's during the three-day march which took them to within eight miles of Covington. David Gardiner Tyler to Julia Gardiner Tyler, Lexington, Nov. 14, 1863. Several weeks later the Washington College Company marched off on another "Quixotic expedition ... but we did not succeed in coming to blows with the enemy. I had a good deal of fun in camp, as my company was a jolly one." David Gardiner Tyler to Harry Beeckman, Lexington, Feb. 4, 1864, *TFP*.

[19] Mrs. Norman J. Walker to Julia Gardiner Tyler, St. George, Bermuda, Feb. 18, 1864; n.d. [early Jan. 1864]. Major Norman J. Walker, CSA, was a purchasing agent for the Confederate government. He had helped Julia with her cotton transaction. Norman J. Walker to Julia Gardiner Tyler, St. George, Bermuda, Oct. 19, 1863, *TFP*.

[20] The residents of the Castleton Hill house, and their ages as of Christmas 1863 were: Juliana (64); Julia (43); Alex (15); Julie (14); Lachlan (12); Lyon G. (10); Robert Fitzwalter (7); Pearl (3); Harry Beeckman (15); David Lyon Gardiner (47); Sarah Thompson Gardiner (34); and their two children: David (2) and Sarah Diodati (1); (their third child, Robert Alexander, was not born until 1864). Julia's maid Celia, of course, was a freed Negro. Details of these difficult months, Dec. 1863 to Feb. 1864, in the Gardiner household and during Julia's earlier visit in Nov.–Dec. 1862 may be found in Gardiner *vs.* Tyler, *35 New York Reports*, VIII, 561–65; and *passim*, 559–616; and also in various draft depositions relating to this case, in the handwriting of Julia Gardiner Tyler, found in *TFP*. Sarah Thompson Gardiner to Juliana Gardiner, note, n.d. [Jan.–Feb. 1864]; Julia Tyler, Draft Deposition in Gardiner *vs.* Tyler, New York, Apr. 1867; Nurse [name unknown] to Julia Gardiner Tyler, Statement in a Deposition in Gardiner *vs.* Tyler, New York, n.d. [Spring 1867]; Julia Gardiner Tyler, Draft Depositions in Gardiner *vs.* Tyler, New York, n.d. [Spring 1867], *TFP*. Juliana Gardiner to David L. Gardiner, Staten Island, Feb. 10, 1864, in Gardiner *vs.* Tyler, *35 New York Reports*, 569.

[21] R. H. Gayle to Julia Gardiner Tyler, Fort Warren, Boston, Mar. 10; 26;

Apr. 12; May 3; 14; 19; June 4; 9; Aug. 7; 18; 22; 28; Sept. 30, 1864; City Point, Va., Oct. 18, 1864; Julia Gardiner Tyler to Gen. John A. Dix, Staten Island, Mar. 23, 1864; Dr. W. Tucker to Julia Gardiner Tyler, Brooklyn, Feb. 18, 1864; Mrs. Norman J. Walker to Julia Gardiner Tyler, St. George, Bermuda, Feb. 18; Apr. 17, 1864; Major Norman J. Walker to Julia Gardiner Tyler, Halifax, N.S., Aug. 15, 1864, *TFP*.

[22] James A. Semple to Julia Gardiner Tyler, Richmond, Dec. 18, 1864; R. H. Gayle to Julia Gardiner Tyler, St. George, Bermuda, Jan. 1, 1865; Mrs. Norman J. Walker to Julia Gardiner Tyler, Halifax, N.S., Jan. 11, 1865; R. H. Gayle to Julia Gardiner Tyler, Fort Warren, Boston, Feb. 10; 17; Mar. 24; Apr. 10, 1865, *TFP*.

[23] David Gardiner Tyler to Julia Gardiner Tyler, Lexington, Mar. 29, 1864; Julia Gardiner Tyler to Juliana Gardiner, Staten Island, Sept. 1, 1864; L. C. Clark to Julia Gardiner Tyler, New York, Dec. 21, 1864; Anna M. Atwood to Julia Gardiner Tyler, Pittsburgh, Feb. 21, 1865; Lucy Trowbridge to Harriet Francis, New York, Jan. 15, 1865; J. Meta L. to Juliana Gardiner, Staten Island, Sept. 9, 1863; M. F. Vaiden to Julia Gardiner Tyler, U.S. Prison, Point Lookout, Md., July 28, 1864; Thomas Douthat to Julia Gardiner Tyler, U.S. Prison, Point Lookout, Md., May 31, 1864; William H. Clopton to Julia Gardiner Tyler, Roseland, Va., June 20, 1864; Mrs. D. E. L. Carter to Capt. Blake, Philadelphia, July 21, 1864; Lt. T. J. King to Julia Gardiner Tyler, Military Prison, Fort Delaware, Del., Mar. 30, 1865; William P. Ballard to Julia Gardiner Tyler, Prisoners' Camp Hospital, Apr. 26, 1864, *TFP*. Coleman, *Priscilla Cooper Tyler*, 146.

[24] Mrs. Norman J. Walker to Julia Gardiner Tyler, St. George, Bermuda, Feb. 18; Jan. 10; Mar. 18; Apr. 17, 1864; C. A. L. to Julia Gardiner Tyler, n.p., n.d. [Spring 1864]; R. H. Gayle to Julia Gardiner Tyler, St. George, Bermuda, Jan. 1, 1865; Anna M. Atwood to Julia Gardiner Tyler, Haywind Springs, Pa., July 22, 1864; N. Ilewish to Julia Gardiner Tyler, Clarksville, Tenn., June 30, 1864; Jane Selden to Julia Gardiner Tyler, Reswick, Va., May 4, 1864; James A. Semple to Julia Gardiner Tyler, Richmond, Feb. 10, 1864, *TFP*.

[25] Maria Tyler to Julia Gardiner Tyler, Charles City, Jan. 2, 1864; John C. Tyler to Julia Gardiner Tyler, Sherwood Forest, Feb.; Feb. 27, 1864; David Gardiner Tyler to Julia Gardiner Tyler, Lexington, Mar. 29, 1864; Thomas Douthat to Julia Gardiner Tyler, Point Lookout, May 31, 1864, *TFP*.

[26] David Gardiner Tyler to J. Alexander Tyler, Lexington, Feb. 24, 1864; David Gardiner Tyler to Julia Gardiner Tyler, Lexington, Feb. 3; Mar. 29, 1864; David Gardiner Tyler to Harry Beeckman, Lexington, Feb. 4, 1864, *TFP*.

[27] Maria Tyler to Julia Gardiner Tyler, Sherwood Forest, Apr. 10, 1864; David Gardiner Tyler to Julia Gardiner Tyler, Lexington, May 22, 1864; William H. Clopton to Julia Gardiner Tyler, Bermuda Hundred, May 17; 24; 1864; Roseland, Charles City County, June 20, 1864 (Clopton reported in this letter that "Wild and his horde" had been removed from Kennon's Landing, but he was mistaken.); John C. Tyler to Julia Gardiner Tyler, Fort Hamilton near Fortress Monroe, May 20, 1864, *TFP*.

[28] Julia Gardiner Tyler to Gen. Benjamin F. Butler, Staten Island, May 21; June 2, 1864; Julia Gardiner Tyler to Abraham Lincoln, Staten Island, May 21, 1864, *TFP*.

[29] John G. Nicolay to Mrs. Ex-President Tyler, Washington, Aug. 19, 1864; Julia Gardiner Tyler to Col. Joseph Holt, Staten Island, June 8, 1864 (Holt was a close friend of the Charles A. Wickliffe family and Julia did not hesitate to mention their mutual connection in her demand for the "attention to which under any circumstance I should certainly conceive myself to be entitled"); David Gardiner Tyler to Julia Gardiner Tyler, Richmond, July 19, 1864; Capt. John Cornell, Office of the Provost Marshal, Fortress Monroe, Va., July 16; Aug. 2, 1864; James A. Semple to Julia Gardiner Tyler, Richmond, July 30, 1864; **William H. Clopton to**

Julia Gardiner Tyler, Selwood, Charles City County, Aug. 2, 1864; Roseland, June 30, 1864; Julia Gardiner Tyler to Gen. Benjamin F. Butler, Staten Island, Aug. 23, 1864, *TFP*.

[30] Julia Gardiner Tyler to Abraham Lincoln, Staten Island, Aug. 15, 1864; Julia Gardiner Tyler to Gen. Benjamin F. Butler, Staten Island, Aug. 23, 1864; John G. Nicolay to Mrs. Ex-President Tyler, Washington, Aug. 19, 1864; [Gen. Edward A. Wild] to Headquarters District, Army of the James, Wilson's Landing, Va., Sept. 11, 1864, *TFP*. Julia's Aug. 23 letter to Butler was referred to Wild on Sept. 8; returned by Wild with the quoted notation on it to HQ on Sept. 11, it was endorsed by Gilman Marston by order of Gen. Benjamin F. Butler on Sept. 21, 1864; and returned to Julia on Sept. 23.

[31] William H. Clopton to Julia Gardiner Tyler, Roseland, Charles City County, July 1, 1864, *TFP*.

[32] *Ibid.*, Office of the Provost Marshal, Fortress Monroe, Va., Nov. 12, 1864, *TFP*.

[33] Maria Tyler to Julia Gardiner Tyler, Selwood, June 20; July 9, 1864; Julia Gardiner Tyler to William H. Clopton, Staten Island, July 2, 1864; Julia Gardiner Tyler to William Cullen Bryant, Editor, New York *Evening Post*, Staten Island, June 27, 1864; Brig. Gen. Edward A. Wild, to Julia Gardiner Tyler, Wilson's Wharf, Va., June 16, 1864; Julia Gardiner Tyler to Brig. Gen. Edward A. Wild, Staten Island, n.d. [late June 1864], *TFP*.

[34] William H. Clopton to Julia Gardiner Tyler, Selwood, Charles City County, Aug. 2, 1864; Capt. Hale Clarke to Julia Gardiner Tyler, Headquarters, Dept. of Va. and N.C., In the Field, Aug. 3, 1864 (Pass to Wilson's Wharf but not valid "beyond the Federal pickets"); Gen. Benjamin F. Butler, Headquarters, Dept. of Va. and N.C., In the Field, Va., to Julia Gardiner Tyler, Aug. 6, 1864; Julia Gardiner Tyler to Gen. Benjamin F. Butler, Staten Island, n.d. [Aug. 1864], *TFP*.

[35] New York *Herald*, Aug. 12, 1864; Julia Gardiner Tyler to the Editor, New York *Herald*, Staten Island, Aug. 12, 1864; James A. Semple to Julia Gardiner Tyler, Richmond, Sept. 7; 10, 1864; David Gardiner Tyler to Julia Gardiner Tyler, Richmond, Sept. 6, 1864, *TFP*.

[36] *Ibid.*, Lexington, May 22, 1864, *TFP*.

[37] *Ibid.*, Lexington, May 22; June 29, 1864; Richmond, July 24, 1864, *TFP*. Accounts of the Valley Campaigns of Sigel and Hunter in May–June 1864, particularly the battles at New Market and Piedmont, may be found in Charles H. Porter, "The Operations of Generals Sigel and Hunter in the Shenandoah Valley, May and June, 1864," in *Papers of the Military Historical Society of Massachusetts. The Shenandoah Campaigns of 1862 and 1864; and the Appomattox Campaign of 1865* (Boston, 1907), 61–82; George E. Pond, *The Shenandoah Valley in 1864* (New York, 1883), 9–45. The destruction of Washington College is found in Walter Creigh Preston, *Lee: West Point and Lexington* (Yellow Springs, Ohio, 1934), 48–49.

[38] David Gardiner Tyler to Harry Beeckman, Richmond, Sept. 2, 1864, *TFP*.

[39] Bruce Catton, *This Hallowed Ground* (New York, 1956), 328–29.

[40] David Gardiner Tyler to Julia Gardiner Tyler, Richmond, July 24; Aug. 29; Sept. 2; 16; Oct. 24; Nov. 28, 1864; James A. Semple to Julia Gardiner Tyler, Richmond, Sept. 7, 1864, *TFP*.

[41] J. Alexander Tyler to David Gardiner Tyler, Staten Island, Apr. 10, 1864; J. Alexander Tyler to Harry Beeckman, Baltimore, Apr. 17, 1864; Andrew Reid to Julia Gardiner Tyler, Baltimore, May 5, 1864; Julia Gardiner Tyler to ———, n.p., n.d. [Staten Island, July 1864]; Julia Gardiner Tyler to [William H. Clopton], Staten Island, July 17, 1864; James A. Semple to Julia Gardiner Tyler, Richmond, Sept. 7, 1864; J. Alexander Tyler to Julia Gardiner Tyler, St. George, Bermuda, July 31, 1864; Major Norman J. Walker to Julia Gardiner Tyler, Halifax, N.S., Aug. 15, 1864, *TFP*.

[42] J. Alexander Tyler to ———, Richmond, Sept. 2, 1864; David Gardiner Tyler to Julia Gardiner Tyler, Richmond, Aug. 29; Oct. 24; Dec. 13, 1864; J. Alexander Tyler to Julia Gardiner Tyler, Richmond, Aug. 27; Dec. 14, 1864; James A. Semple to Julia Gardiner Tyler, Richmond, Sept. 7; 10; Dec. 18, 1864, *TFP*.

[43] James A. Semple to Julia Gardiner Tyler, Richmond, Apr. 3; May 27; July 5; 30; Dec. 18, 1864, *TFP;* J. B. Jones, *A Rebel War Clerk's Diary* (Philadelphia, 1866), 294, 229; David Gardiner Tyler to Julia Gardiner Tyler, Richmond, Oct. 24; Dec. 13, 1864; J. Alexander Tyler to Julia Gardiner Tyler, Richmond, Dec. 14, 1864, *TFP*. Tazewell Tyler married Nannie Bridges in 1857. A son was born to them in Richmond in December 1864. Priscilla and her children fled Richmond during Grant's approach to the capital in May–June 1864 and took refuge with Priscilla's sister Mary Grace Cooper Raoul at Longwood plantation at Mt. Meigs, Alabama. She returned for Christmas during this crisis. Robert again took up arms and marched out with the "Treasury Battalion" to defend the city. At no time did he surrender hope that the South would win the war and he spent considerable time and energy combating defeatism and defeatist criticisms of the Davis administration in Richmond. Coleman, *Priscilla Cooper Tyler*, 150–52.

[44] The record of the case, Tyler vs. Gardiner, is found in *35 New York Reports,* 559–616. William Watson represented David Lyon; William M. Evarts and James I. Roosevelt represented Julia. Voting to overturn the will were Court of Appeals Justices Porter, who wrote the majority opinion, Chief Justice Davies, and Justices Wright, Leonard, and Morgan. Voting to sustain the will were Justices Peckham, who wrote the minority opinion, and Justices Hunt and Smith. A reading of the precedent cases cited by both sides leads this writer, not a lawyer, to conclude that the definition of "undue influence" had historically been both vague and variable and that precedent alone served one side as well as the other. At the time of the court fight David Lyon was a member of the Board of Supervisors of Richmond County, N.Y., and a Trustee of the Staten Island Savings Bank. See S. Clift to David L. Gardiner, New York, Aug. 16, 1864, *GPY;* L. C. Clarke to Julia Gardiner Tyler, New York, Dec. 21, 1864. In April 1864 Juliana Gardiner had had herself appointed Harry's legal guardian. See H. B. Metcalfe, Surrogate, to Juliana Gardiner, Richmond, N.Y., April 8, 1864, *TFP*. For opinions, family reactions and legal details of the Surrogate phase of the case in mid-1865 see A. W. W. H. to Julia Gardiner Tyler, n.p., n.d.; James I. Roosevelt to Julia Gardiner Tyler, Bill for Professional Services Covering Period April 1864 to April 1865 (bill was for $245); James A. Semple to Julia Gardiner Tyler, Augusta, Ga., Nov. 14, 1865 (expressing Mrs. Jefferson Davis' support of Julia's legal fight); Edward B. Merville to Julia Gardiner Tyler, New York, July 19, 1865; L. C. Clarke to Julia Gardiner Tyler, New York, July 31, 1865. For similar data on the Supreme Court reversal of the Surrogate in May 1866 see James A. Semple to Julia Gardiner Tyler, n.p., May 27, 1866; Julia Gardiner Tyler to David G. and J. Alexander Tyler, New York, May 16; Apr. 6, 1866; Julia Gardiner Tyler to Julia Tyler, Staten Island, June 4, 1866 ("I have won my suit in one Court—but they are taking it to another Court I believe.... I am still busy with the law and oh! I shall so rejoice when it is all off my hands"); David Gardiner Tyler to Julia Gardiner Tyler, Karlsruhe, Germany, June 15, 1866; J. Alexander Tyler to Julia Gardiner Tyler, Karlsruhe, June 18, 1866; July 9, 1866; Charles B. Mallory to Julia Gardiner Tyler, Hampton, Va., July 24, 1866, *TFP*. The New York Supreme Court by a 4 to 0 decision ordered the will admitted to probate on May 18, 1866. Judges William W. Scrugham, Joseph F. Barnard, John A. Lott, and Jasper W. Gilbert all held that the Surrogate's decision was "erroneous, illegal and improper." Copy of order found in *TFP*. When the Court of Appeals reversed the Supreme Court in January 1867 Julia and her friends interpreted it as punishment for her Copperhead views during the Civil War. Armed with this decision, and as Court-appointed administrator of Juliana's personal belongings, David Lyon put up the Castleton Hill furniture at

public auction in February 1867, forcing his sister to buy back the items she needed. On these points *see* A. S. Johnston to William H. Evarts, Albany, Jan. 4, 1867; Tazewell Taylor to Julia Gardiner Tyler, Norfolk, May 6, 1867; Julia Gardiner Tyler to David G. and J. Alexander Tyler, New York, Mar. 29, 1867, *TFP*. Julia was forced out of Castleton Hill as a result of the Court of Appeals decision and took temporary residence at 170 Broadway. Throughout the fight and after, both sides worked to build suitable public-relations "images" for themselves. For this and for various newspaper references, including "inspired" letters to editors, *see* "A Subscriber" [Julia Gardiner Tyler] to Horace Greeley, Editor, New York *Tribune*, n.p., n.d. [New York, Apr. 2, 1868], *TFP;* New York *Tribune*, Apr. 4, 1868; John A. Taylor to David L. Gardiner, Brooklyn, June 19; Oct. 19, 1868; David L. Gardiner to John A. Taylor, New York, June, 1868, *GPY*. Taylor was a Wall Street lawyer who worked with David Lyon on a project designed to acquaint the newspaper-reading public with a proper view of the Tyler *vs.* Gardiner will case. "I am quite disposed to do what I may to keeping the channels of public opinion running in the right direction," Taylor told David Lyon. For the details of the compromise settlement of Oct. 3, 1868, *see* various documents and financial statements and personal letters relating to it, including copies of the settlement itself, in *GPY* and in *TFP*. Additional Tyler *vs.* Gardiner legal actions, dealing with court costs, etc., and the action leading to the compromise agreement may be found in "Gardiner *vs.* Tyler and Beeckman," in Benjamin V. Abbott and Austin Abbott, *(comps.)*, *Abbotts Practice Reports, New Series,* Vol. IV of *Reports of Practice Cases Determined in the Courts of the State of New York* (New York, 1869), 463–69; and "Gardiner *vs.* Tyler," New York Common Pleas, General Term, January, 1868, in *ibid.,* V, 33–39. When Harry Beeckman reached his majority in 1869 he drew up a will, dated Nov. 20, naming his Aunt Julia his sole beneficiary. *See* Will of Henry G. Beeckman (copy), Nov. 20, 1869, entered in Surrogate's Court, County of New York, *GPY*. For Gardie's lament over his grandmother's death, *see* David Gardiner Tyler to Julia Gardiner Tyler, In Camp Near Richmond, Nov. 28, 1864, *TFP*.

[45] Julia Gardiner Tyler to David L. Gardiner, n.p., n.d. [New York, Oct. 1864]; Julia Gardiner Tyler to Judge Michael Laughten, n.p., n.d. [New York, Nov. 1864]; Judge Michael Laughten to Julia Gardiner Tyler, n.p., n.d. [New York, Nov. 1864]; James A. Semple to Julia Gardiner Tyler, Richmond, Sept 10, 1864; David Gardiner Tyler to Julia Gardiner Tyler, Richmond, Sept. 6; Nov. 28, 1864; Celia Johnson to Julia Gardiner Tyler, Charles City, Nov. 16, 1864; Julia Gardiner Tyler to Gen. Benjamin F. Butler, Staten Island, Nov. 7, 1864; J. Alexander Tyler to Julia Gardiner Tyler, Richmond, Dec. 14, 1864; Col. John E. Mulford to Julia Gardiner Tyler, Lowell, Mass., Feb. 8, 1865; J. Alexander Tyler to Julia Tyler, Richmond, Feb. 24, 1865, *TFP*.

[46] James A. Semple to Julia Gardiner Tyler, Richmond, Feb. 24; Mar. 25, 1865; J. Alexander Tyler to Julia Gardiner Tyler, Richmond, Jan. 10, 1865; n.p., n.d. [Richmond, Apr. 1865]; William H. MacFarland to Julia Gardiner Tyler, Richmond, July 3, 1865, *TFP;* Coleman, *Priscilla Cooper Tyler,* 156.

[47] J. Alexander Tyler to Ralph Dayton, n.p., n.d. [Richmond, Apr. 19, 1865]; J. Alexander Tyler to Julia Gardiner Tyler, n.p., n.d. [Richmond, Apr. 1865]; Sherwood Forest, May 5, 1865, *TFP;* Coleman, *Priscilla Cooper Tyler,* 156.

[48] Staten Islander, "Incident on Staten Island," New York *Herald,* Apr. 17, 1865; New York *World,* Apr. 17, 1865; Julia Gardiner Tyler to Editor, New York *World,* Apr. 19, 1865; Henry A. Curtis to Editor, New York *Tribune,* June 2, 1865; Julia Gardiner Tyler to ———, Staten Island, n.d. [Apr. 16, 1865] (draft letter), Julia Gardiner Tyler to Major Wilson Barstow, Staten Island, n.d. [Apr. 1865]; Julia Gardiner Tyler to General John A. Dix, Staten Island, n.d. [Apr. 1865]; John Dean to Julia Gardiner Tyler, Staten Island, Apr. 16, 1865; Julia Gardiner Tyler to ———, Staten Island, n.d. [Apr. 1865] (draft letter), *TFP*.

⁴⁹ R. H. Gayle to Julia Gardiner Tyler, Fort Warren, Boston, Apr. 28; June 1, 1865; David Gardiner Tyler to Julia Gardiner Tyler, Lexington, June 26, 1865; J. Alexander Tyler to Julia Gardiner Tyler, Richmond, Apr. 29, 1865, *TFP*.

⁵⁰ David Gardiner Tyler to Julia Gardiner Tyler, Lexington, June 26, 1865, *TFP*.

CHAPTER 20

¹ E. G. Points to Julia Gardiner Tyler, Richmond, Oct. 19, 1865; Catherine P. Speed to Julia Gardiner Tyler, Lynchburg, July 21, 1865; G. Christian to Julia Gardiner Tyler, Charles City, June 20, 1865; Lt. T. J. King, 42nd Batt., Va. Cavalry, to Julia Gardiner Tyler, Ft. Delaware, Del., Mar. 30, 1865; S. F. Bunch, Company C, 1st S.C. Regiment, 15th Div. to Mrs. John Tyler, Fort Delaware, Del., May 12, 1865, *TFP;* Coleman, *Priscilla Cooper Tyler,* 147-48; Varina H. Davis to Julia Gardiner Tyler, Savannah, Ga., July 24, 1865, in *Tyler's Quarterly,* XVII (July 1935), 24; Julia Gardiner Tyler to Varina H. Davis, n.p., n.d. [Staten Island, August 1865], *TFP*.

² R. H. Gayle to Julia Gardiner Tyler, Fort Warren, Boston, May 12; June 1; Apr. 10, 1865; David Gardiner Tyler to Julia Gardiner Tyler, Lexington, June 5; July 12, 1865; David Gardiner Tyler to Harry Beeckman, Lexington, July 30, 1865; Staten Island, Aug. 22, 1865; David Gardiner Tyler to J. Alexander Tyler, Lexington, July 28, 1865, *TFP*.

³ David Gardiner Tyler to Harry Beeckman, Lexington, July 30, 1865; Staten Island, Aug. 22, 1865; Harry Beeckman to Julia Gardiner Tyler, East Hampton, Aug. 7, 1865; David Gardiner Tyler to Julia Gardiner Tyler, SS *Hansa,* At Sea, Sept. 17, 1865; J. Alexander Tyler to Julia Gardiner Tyler, Karlsruhe, Feb. 27, 1866 (Fulton had thirteen students living in his home in Feb. 1866); David Gardiner Tyler, "Yes, We'll Fight 'Em Again," n.p., n.d. [Lexington, July 1865], *TFP*.

⁴ Sievert von Oertzen to Julia Gardiner Tyler, Sherwood Forest, Sept. 23, 1865; John C. Tyler to Julia Gardiner Tyler, Sherwood Forest, July 10, 1865; J. Alexander Tyler to Julia Gardiner Tyler, Sherwood Forest, July 4, 1865, *TFP*.

⁵ *Ibid.;* John C. Tyler to Julia Gardiner Tyler, Sherwood Forest, July 10; Sept. 28, 1865; John H. Lewis, Ships Chandler, to Julia Gardiner Tyler, New York, June 26, 1865; A. E. Godeffroy to Julia Gardiner Tyler, New York, Nov. 28, 1865; Sievert von Oertzen to Julia Gardiner Tyler, Sherwood Forest, Sept. 3, 1865; David Gardiner Tyler to Julia Gardiner Tyler, Karlsruhe, Dec. 26, 1865, *TFP*.

⁶ Sievert von Oertzen to Julia Gardiner Tyler, Sherwood Forest, Sept. 23, 1865; Julia Gardiner Tyler to David Gardiner Tyler, Staten Island, Apr. 6, 1866; J. Buchanan Henry to Julia Gardiner Tyler, Receipt for Professional Services in von Oertzen *vs.* Tyler, n.p., n.d. [1866], *TFP*.

⁷ The Bank of Virginia *vs.* Julia Gardiner Tyler, 1868, turned on prewar Tyler notes amounting to $2155.07 held by the bank. Tazewell Taylor of Norfolk at first represented Julia in this action. But in the middle of the case he abandoned her cause and became counsel for the bank. Julia was indignant at Taylor's "treachery" and told him so in no uncertain language. James Lyons of Richmond, brother-in-law to Henry A. Wise, then became Julia's attorney in the case, which Julia eventually lost, the courts not substantiating her contention that the statute of limitations negated the notes. The bank attempted to attach Villa Margaret to satisfy the debt. Lyons' argument was that the property was Julia's, purchased with her own money, and could not be seized to satisfy a claim against Tyler's estate. So hard-pressed for cash did Julia become in 1866-1867 that she again investigated the possibility of selling Sherwood in April 1867. Under the second codicil of Tyler's will, dated Oct. 29, 1860, this could only be done with approval from Robert Tyler and David Lyon Gardiner. Robert opposed the idea. For these

and other problems relating to various suits and claims, large and small, against Tyler's estate, *see* Tazewell Taylor to Julia Gardiner Tyler, Baltimore, Oct. 25; Dec. 22, 1865; Norfolk, May 7, 1866; Mar. 8, 1867; Apr. 22, 1868; Dr. J. McCaw to Julia Gardiner Tyler, Richmond, Sept. 12, 1865; Julia Gardiner Tyler to Tazewell Taylor, n.p., n.d. [Staten Island, 1867]; James Lyons, Deposition in Bank of Virginia *vs.* Julia Gardiner Tyler, Richmond, Aug. 3, 1868; Julia Gardiner Tyler to William M. Evarts, n.p., n.d. [Staten Island, 1868]; Charles B. Mallory to Julia Gardiner Tyler, Hampton, July 24, 1866; John P. Pierce to Julia Gardiner Tyler, New Kent C.H., Va., Apr. 15, 1867; Richard M. Graves to Julia Gardiner Tyler, Charles City, Nov. 22, 1865; David Gardiner Tyler to Julia Gardiner Tyler, Staten Island, Sept. 2, 1869. Julia allowed 160 acres of land in Sioux County, Iowa, in what is now Sioux City (Section 36, Block 94, Range 48), to pass out of her hands for back taxes in 1869, although these taxes amounted to little more than $8 to $12 per year. Tyler had acquired the land granted him as a veteran of the War of 1812. *See* Thomas J. Stone to Julia Gardiner Tyler, Sioux City, Iowa, Jan. 25; Apr. 18, 1866; Apr. 5, 1869; Rufus Stone, Treasurer of Sioux County, Iowa, to Julia Gardiner Tyler, Sioux City, June 8, 1869; J. Alexander Tyler to Julia Gardiner Tyler, Karlsruhe, June 18, 1866, *TFP*. In 1866 she rejected advice to purchase real estate at rock-bottom prices in what is now downtown Galveston, Texas, Apr. 15, 1866, *TFP*.

[8] Julia Gardiner Tyler to Andrew Johnson, n.p., n.d. [Staten Island, Summer 1865], *TFP*.

[9] David Gardiner Tyler to Julia Gardiner Tyler, Karlsruhe, Apr. 30, 1866; Jan. 24, 1867; Richmond, June 6, 1872; Charles B. Mallory to Julia Gardiner Tyler, Hampton, Aug. 2, 1866; G. William Semple to Julia Gardiner Tyler, Richmond, Nov. 5, 1866; T. P. McElrath to Wilson Barstow, Office of the Post Quartermaster, Fortress Monroe, Feb. 18, 1867; Tazewell Taylor to Julia Gardiner Tyler, Norfolk, Apr. 17, 1867; May 7, 1866; May 22, 1867; G. M. Peek to Julia Gardiner Tyler, Hampton, July 12, 1869; Julia Gardiner Tyler to President U.S. Grant, n.p., n.d. [1874]; Thomas Tabb to Julia Gardiner Tyler, Hampton, Sept. 23, 1874, *TFP*.

[10] James A. Semple to Julia Gardiner Tyler, Albany, N.Y., Nov. 27, 1866; Robert Tyler to Julia Gardiner Tyler, Montgomery, Oct. 3, 1866, *TFP*; James Buchanan to Robert Tyler, Wheatland, Aug. 3, 1865, in *LTT*, II, 685; Robert Tyler to James Buchanan, Richmond, Aug. 14, 1865, in *ibid.*, 686; Coleman, *Priscilla Cooper Tyler*, 162–69. Robert served as editor of the *Advertiser* in 1867–1874 and editor of the Montgomery *News*, 1874–1877. He was Chairman of the State Democratic Executive Committee in 1872–1874, and worked for the White Man's Party in 1874. During these financially thin Reconstruction years in Alabama Robert's daughter Letitia taught school in Montgomery; daughter Priscilla ("Tousie") went to Baltimore in 1867 and taught in Letitia Tyler Semple's private school, The Eclectic Institute; daughter Julia Campbell was maintained by Allan and Julia Cooper Campbell in New York City. After Robert's death, Priscilla remained in Montgomery and was supported by the prosperous Campbells until her own death on Dec. 29, 1889, at the age of 73. Campbell employed her youngest child, Robbie, as his secretary. *See* Coleman, *Priscilla Cooper Tyler*, 171–75.

[11] James A. Semple to Julia Gardiner Tyler, Augusta, Ga., Nov. 14, 1865; Montreal, Canada, Jan. 3, 1866; Savannah, June 17, 1866; New York, Aug. 3, 1866; Montreal, Aug. 13, 1866; New York, Sept. 6, 1866; V. B. Rittenhouse to James A. Semple, Panama, Oct. 1, 1866; James A. Semple to Julia Gardiner Tyler, Albany, Nov. 27, 1866, *TFP*.

[12] James A. Semple to Julia Gardiner Tyler, New York, Mar. 28; Aug. 3; Sept. 6; Nov. 7; Oct. 19; Nov. 24; 27, 1866; Jan. 12, 1867; New Orleans, Feb. 5; 15; 25, 1867; New York, Aug. 1; 12, 1868; James A. Semple to Letitia Tyler Semple, New York, July 27, 1867; J. Alexander Tyler to Julia Gardiner Tyler,

Karlsruhe, Feb. 13, 1867; Lachlan Tyler to David Gardiner Tyler, New York, Feb. 22, 1867; Letitia Tyler Semple to Julia Gardiner Tyler, Baltimore, July 11, 1867; Julia Gardiner Tyler to Letitia Tyler Semple, Staten Island, July 18, 1867; Julia Gardiner Tyler to James A. Semple, n.p. [Sherwood Forest], July 1868; [Mar. 1866], *TFP*. In March 1866 Semple gave Julia control of his financial affairs, fearing that one of his attacks of "brain fever" (as it was called) would carry him suddenly to his grave. In December 1866 he made out a will leaving some acreage he owned in Texas to little Pearlie Tyler, whom he called "Birdie." James A. Semple, Last Will and Testament, New York, Dec. 20, 1866, *TFP*. The portraits at stake in 1867–1868 were those of John Tyler's mother and father and of Mary Tyler Jones and Alice Tyler Denison. Semple's career after his break with Letitia is obscure. In 1870 he was working for the York Railroad Company at Turnstalls Station in New Kent County, Va.—in what capacity is not known. In 1875 he was apparently engaged in farming in New Kent County. In April 1881 he visited Julia in Richmond and was reported "looking so well." The date of his death is not known. Letitia Tyler Semple died in Baltimore on Dec. 28, 1907, at 86. She had raised Elizabeth Russel Denison (1852–1928), orphan daughter of Alice Tyler and Henry M. Denison, to womanhood and had seen her married to William Gaston Allen (1849–1891) and then widowed. *See* James A. Semple to Julia Gardiner Tyler, New Kent Co., Va., Sept. 24, 1875; Julia Gardiner Tyler to Pearl Tyler, Sherwood Forest, Apr. 27, 1881, *TFP;* Richmond *Dispatch,* July 11, 1889.

[13] Langford, *The Ladies of the White House,* 323; John Tyler, Jr., to Rep. John Critchen of Va., Tallahassee, Fla., Nov. 28, 1872; John Tyler, Jr., to Sen John W. Johnston, Tallahassee, Nov. 28, 1872, *Tyler Papers,* Duke University Library; Julia Gardiner Tyler to Lyon G. Tyler, Georgetown, Jan. 18, 1873; James A. Semple to Julia Gardiner Tyler, Norfolk, Jan. 1; Nov. 30, 1873; John Tyler, Jr., to David Gardiner Tyler, Washington, Apr. 7, 1877; Julia Gardiner Tyler to Tazewell Tyler, n.p., n.d. [Staten Island, late 1865]; David Gardiner Tyler to Julia Gardiner Tyler, Sherwood Forest, Apr. 24, 1873, *TFP*.

[14] Julia Tyler to Etta ———, Staten Island, Sept. 26 [1865]; Marcia C. Roosevelt to Julia Tyler, n.p., n.d. [New York, Nov. 2, 1865]; Julia Gardiner Tyler to Juliana Gardiner, Sherwood Forest, Apr. 8, 1863, *TFP*. Julia's high opinion of Roman Catholic schools was in part derived from prewar conversations with artist G. P. A. Healy, official portraitist of so many nineteenth-century Presidents. A brochure of the Convent of the Sacred Heart at Halifax found in *TFP* listed tuition, room, and board at £30 quarterly (or $120 American in 1866). Private singing lessons were £10. Needlework, map drawing, and French lessons were free. Each girl brought her own bedclothes, veils, and tableware. A uniform was required only for Sunday wear. Regular clothes were worn at other times. The school had been founded by a Mother Barat who had died in 1865 at the age of 85.

[15] Julia Tyler to Julia Gardiner Tyler, Halifax, Apr. 5, 1866; Julia Gardiner Tyler to Julia Tyler, New York, Apr. 18, 1866; Julia Gardiner Tyler to David Gardiner Tyler, Staten Island, Apr. 6, 1866; James A. Semple to Julia Gardiner Tyler, Halifax, Apr. 6, 1866; David Gardiner Tyler to Julia Tyler, Karlsruhe, June 12, 1867, *TFP*.

[16] Julia Tyler to Julia Gardiner Tyler, Sacre Coeur, Halifax, Apr. 29, 1866; James A. Semple to Julia Gardiner Tyler, Halifax, May 2, 1866; Julia Gardiner Tyler to David G. and J. Alexander Tyler, New York, May 16, 1866; David Gardiner Tyler to Julia Gardiner Tyler, Karlsruhe, June 15, 1866; George L. Sinclair to Julia Tyler, Halifax, July 1866; Julia Gardiner Tyler to Julia Tyler, Newport, R.I., Aug. 10, 1866; Burton H. Harrison to Julia Gardiner Tyler, New York, Jan. 8, 1869; Sally Ruddel to Julia Gardiner Tyler, New York, Dec. 31, 1866, *TFP*.

[17] J. Alexander Tyler to Julia Gardiner Tyler, Karlsruhe, Sept. 27, 1865; John Fulton to Julia Gardiner Tyler, Karlsruhe, Oct. 9, 1865; J. Alexander Tyler to

Julia Tyler, Karlsruhe, Feb. 27, 1866; David Gardiner Tyler to Julia Gardiner Tyler, Karlsruhe, Apr. 5; Spring; June 6; Oct. 31, 1866, *TFP*.

[18] John Fulton to Julia Gardiner Tyler, Karlsruhe, Oct. 9, 1865; J. Alexander Tyler to Julia Gardiner Tyler, Karlsruhe, Sept. 27, 1865; May 24; Aug. 28; Sept. 6, 1866; J. Alexander Tyler to James A. Semple, Karlsruhe, June 1, 1866; David Gardiner Tyler to Julia Gardiner Tyler, Karlsruhe, June 7; Oct. 31, 1866, *TFP*. Alex calculated that he could stay on in Germany and complete his education for $450 to $600 per year gold, including the cost of German-language tutors. Gardie reckoned it at $600 if one wanted to "live like a gentleman"; $200 to $300 if one lived like an "Italian artist or German student dragging out a miserable existence."

[19] J. Alexander Tyler to Julia Tyler, Karlsruhe, Dec. 20, 1865; Feb. 27, 1866; David Gardiner Tyler to Julia Gardiner Tyler, Karlsruhe, Nov. 28; Dec. 14, 1865; June 6; Sept. 17; June 7, 1866; Harry Beeckman to Julia Gardiner Tyler, Karlsruhe, Oct. 2, 1865; Jan. 24; 28; Feb. 25, 1866; Julia Gardiner Tyler to David Gardiner and J. Alexander Tyler, New York, May 16, 1866; Julia Gardiner Tyler to David Gardiner Tyler, Staten Island, Apr. 6, 1866; Bill from Mme. Gigon-Russell to Julia Gardiner Tyler, New York, July 1866 (Julia customarily spent from $150 to $200 for a dress); Julia Gardiner Tyler to Julia Tyler, Willow Cottage, Newport, R.I., Aug. 10, 1866, *TFP*.

[20] David Gardiner Tyler to Julia Gardiner Tyler, Karlsruhe, Nov. 21, 1865 (Gardie estimated that their total expenses in Karlsruhe came to about $100 gold per month); June 25; Dec. 20, 1866; Harry Beeckman to Julia Tyler, Karlsruhe, Dec. 13, 1865; Harry Beeckman to Julia Gardiner Tyler, Karlsruhe, June 2; July 21, 1866; John Fulton to Julia Gardiner Tyler, Karlsruhe, June 18, 1866; J. Alexander Tyler to Julia Gardiner Tyler, Karlsruhe, Sept. 6, 1866. While Fulton was conducting Harry to Bremen, Gardie and Alex moved into the home of Frau Steinbach at No. 2 Stephanienstrasse, Karlsruhe. She charged them $300 gold each for a year's room and board. The board was more than ample: "What would you homefolks think of having two or three courses nearly every day at dinner," Gardie asked. "Roast-beef, fish, veal; then fruits of different varieties, and often pies, cakes and dough-nuts? I can just see the children's eyes open in mute wonderment, as you read this to them.... Just think and ponder on that, ye eaters of salt-codfish and cold potatoes!" J. Alexander Tyler to Julia Gardiner Tyler, Karlsruhe, Sept. 6, 1866; David Gardiner Tyler to Julia Gardiner Tyler, Karlsruhe, July 11, 1867, *TFP*.

[21] J. Alexander Tyler to Julia Gardiner Tyler, Karlsruhe, Sept. 27, 1865; David Gardiner Tyler to Julia Gardiner Tyler, Karlsruhe, Oct. 25, 1865; Oct. 31, 1866; David Gardiner Tyler to Julia Gardiner, Karlsruhe, Sept. 12, 1866, *TFP*.

[22] For really quite pertinent comments on the Austro-Prussian, or Seven Weeks' War of 1866, *see* David Gardiner Tyler to Julia Gardiner Tyler, Karlsruhe, Apr. 20; June 7; 15; 18; 25; July 14, 1866; J. Alexander Tyler to Julia Gardiner Tyler, Karlsruhe, June 13; July 9, 1866; Harry Beeckman to Julia Gardiner Tyler, Karlsruhe, July 21, 1866. "These Germans are a queer set," said Gardie in bewilderment. "Sunday is to them as any other day. They go to Church in the morning and to the Theater at night. That is a mixing of Godliness and worldliness which I have no great admiration for." David Gardiner Tyler to Julia Gardiner Tyler, Karlsruhe, n.d., *TFP*.

[23] David Gardiner Tyler to Julia Tyler, Karlsruhe, June 12, 1867; David Gardiner Tyler to Julia Gardiner Tyler, Karlsruhe, Oct. 7; 19; Dec. 20, 1866; Harry Beeckman to Julia Tyler, Karlsruhe, Oct. 19; Dec. 21, 1865; David Gardiner Tyler to Julia Tyler, Karlsruhe, Nov. 22, 1865; J. Alexander Tyler to Julia Gardiner Tyler, Karlsruhe, Sept. 6; Nov. 14, 1866, *TFP*.

[24] Harry Beeckman to Julia Gardiner Tyler, Karlsruhe, Feb. 25, 1866; David Gardiner Tyler to Julia Gardiner Tyler, Karlsruhe, Apr. 5; June 15; 18, 1866; J.

Alexander Tyler to Julia Gardiner Tyler, Karlsruhe, Nov. 14, 1866. Among the Confederate Americans in Karlsruhe in 1865–1866 were Bryan, Pickett, and MacCreary, all sons of former Confederate Army officers. See Henry Beeckman to Julia Gardiner Tyler, Karlsruhe, Dec. 6, 1865; David Gardiner Tyler to Julia Gardiner Tyler, Karlsruhe, Sept. 11, 1866, TFP.

[25] David Gardiner Tyler to Julia Gardiner Tyler, Karlsruhe, Oct. 25, 1865; Apr. 4, 1867. For similar remarks, and others happily cheering their mother's 4-to-0 victory in the New York Supreme Court, see David Gardiner Tyler to Julia Gardiner Tyler, Karlsruhe, Apr. 5, 1865; Jan. 10, 1866; Jan. 30; May 8, 1867; n.d. [1866]; J. Alexander Tyler to Julia Gardiner Tyler, Karlsruhe, Dec. 20, 1865; J. Alexander Tyler to James A. Semple, Karlsruhe, June 1, 1866; Harry Beeckman to Julia Gardiner Tyler, Karlsruhe, June 2, 1866, TFP.

[26] David Gardiner Tyler to Julia Gardiner Tyler, Karlsruhe, Dec. 26, 1865; Feb. 14; n.d. [Feb.]; Apr. 30; June 15; July 14; Dec. 17, 1866; Jan. 17; Apr. 4, 1867; J. Alexander Tyler to Julia Gardiner Tyler, Karlsruhe, Dec. 20, 1865; July 9, 1866, TFP. The Negro school was sacked on March 22, 1867. President Lee promptly expelled the student ringleader and placed his cohorts on disciplinary probation. The story of the Yankee garrison's being turned out of Lexington was false. See Preston, *Lee: West Point and Lexington*, 82–83.

[27] David Gardiner Tyler to Julia Tyler, Karlsruhe, Feb. 27; July 18, 1866; David Gardiner Tyler to Julia Gardiner Tyler, Karlsruhe, Oct. 31, 1866; May 8; July 11, 1867; J. Alexander Tyler to James A. Semple, Karlsruhe, June 1, 1866; J. Alexander Tyler to Julia Gardiner Tyler, Karlsruhe, Oct. 2, 1867, TFP.

[28] David Gardiner Tyler to Julia Gardiner Tyler, Sherwood Forest, Mar. 23, 1873; Julia Gardiner Tyler to ———, n.p., n.d. [Georgetown, D.C., Mar. 1873]; J. Alexander Tyler to Julia Gardiner Tyler, Karlsruhe, Feb. 24, 1869; Beauvais, France, Feb. 27, 1871; A. Baudman to Julia Gardiner Tyler, New York, Apr. 6, 1874; A. J. Mathewson to Julia Gardiner Tyler, New York, Feb. 8, 1874; David Gardiner Tyler to Julia Gardiner Tyler, Sherwood Forest, Apr. 9, 1874; Alfred Schmidt, Consul General of Baden in New York, to Gen. Wilcox Barshaw, New York, Nov. 17, 1868; David Gardiner Tyler to Julia Tyler, Lexington, Jan. 26, 1869; David Gardiner Tyler to Lachlan Tyler, Lexington, Feb. 5, 1869. While languishing in a Karlsruhe jail in November 1868 for his debts, Alex would not demean himself by begging a pardon from the Grand Duke of Baden. The Germans were naturally embarrassed to have an American citizen in their prison but Alex would not help them liquidate their problem. So he was released anyway. "I applaud his *obstinacy*," Gardie told Julie, "and admire his pluck.... He's a glorious fellow and worth a thousand of your milk-and-water men." For Alex's Franco-Prussian War experience see J. Alexander Tyler to Julia Gardiner Tyler, Freiburg, Saxony, Dec. 3, 1870; Beauvais, France, Feb. 27, 1871; Liancourt, France, Mar. 19, 1871; Lachlan Tyler to David Gardiner Tyler, Rochester, N.Y., Feb. 16, 1871; David Gardiner Tyler to Lyon G. Tyler, Sherwood Forest, Mar. 4, 1871; Julia Gardiner Tyler to Hon. William W. Belknap, n.p., n.d. [Georgetown, D.C., 1874]; Julia Gardiner Tyler to Hon. Hamilton Fish, n.p., n.d. [Georgetown, D.C., 1874]. In these 1874 draft letters to the Secretaries of War and State, in which Julia was trying to get Alex a government job, Alex's Franco-Prussian War decoration from the Kaiser was variously described as "a medal and ribbon for faithful service" (to Fish) and as "a ribbon—a medal for gallantry" (to Belknap). Since Alex apparently saw no combat, the "gallantry" award is highly unlikely. Julia was constantly dunned for his German debts. In May 1872, when she had little cash to spare, she learned that Alex had one debt for 346 florins, or about $142, two years old, most of it for cigars alone. "How many a dollar here ends in smoke," Gardie gasped in shock. See Veit and Nelson, Importers, to Julia Gardiner Tyler, New York, May 20, 1872, TFP.

[29] David Gardiner Tyler to J. Alexander Tyler, Staten Island, Jan. 15, 1868, *TFP*. During his brief visit with his mother, Gardie reported to Alex that "Lachlan has grown to be a big fellow, measuring five feet nine in his boots.... Pearlie is going to be the belle of the family from present appearances. Julie is as pretty as ever, and smashes the hearts of her admirers all to flinders." Actually Julie was far from pretty. She had protruding eyes, a somewhat concave or "dishpan" face, and large, protruding ears. Her hair, a reddish brown, was, however, quite beautiful.

[30] David Gardiner Tyler to Julia Gardiner Tyler, Lexington, Feb. 10, 1868. The college faculty of twenty included Colonel William Preston Johnson, professor of history and English literature, son of "that bravest of the brave," General Albert Sidney Johnson. *Ibid.*, Jan. 7, 1869; June 8; Oct. 1, 1868; May 30; Feb. 20, 1869; David Gardiner Tyler to Lyon G. Tyler, Lexington, Jan. 2, 1869; Washington College, Grade Report for David Gardiner Tyler, Lexington, May 30, 1868, *TFP*. Gardie estimated his college expenses at about $600 annually. Lee's tenure as President (1865-1870) and his status with the students is adequately discussed in Preston, *Lee: West Point and Lexington*, 50-93.

[31] David Gardiner Tyler to Julia Gardiner Tyler, Sherwood Forest, Sept. 1868; Lexington, Mar. 4, 1869, *TFP*.

[32] *Ibid.*, June 27, 1868, *TFP*.

[33] *Ibid.*, Karlsruhe, Apr. 30; June 18, 1866; J. Alexander Tyler to Julia Gardiner Tyler, Karlsruhe, May 24; June 18, 1866; James A. Semple to Julia Gardiner Tyler, Albany, N.Y., Nov. 27, 1866; David Gardiner Tyler to Julia Gardiner Tyler, Richmond, Oct. 1869; Sherwood Forest, Dec. 2, 1870; Julia Gardiner Tyler to Julia Tyler Spencer, Richmond, May 15, 1870; Harry Beeckman to Julia Gardiner Tyler, Sherwood Forest, Feb. 16, 1870; Julia Gardiner Tyler to David Gardiner Tyler, Sherwood Forest, Feb. 25, 1870, *TFP*.

[34] To put in 20 acres of wheat in 1870, Gardie calculated the costs as follows: 25 bu. of seed wheat @ $1.50 bu., or $37.50; Negro farm laborers, $35.00; 2 tons of guano, $148.00 cash. Total—$220.00. David Gardiner Tyler to Julia Gardiner Tyler, Sherwood Forest, Sept. 16; 19; n.d. [Sept.]; Dec. 19, 1870. A good mule sold for $175 in Charles City in 1870. In addition to these problems, one Sam Brown, a local Negro minister, demanded, and got, $50 for some seed wheat he had sold John C. Tyler in 1864 when John C. was managing the estate. Fearing another suit against the plantation, Gardie paid the debt promptly. Lyon entered the University in February 1870. "Study hard and be a great man like Papa was and you will astonish the world," Julia assured him. See Julia Gardiner Tyler to Lyon [Lionel] Tyler, Tuscarora, N.Y., Apr. 1, 1870, *TFP*.

[35] David Gardiner Tyler to Julia Gardiner Tyler, Sherwood Forest, Mar. 8, 1871; Mar. 22; Dec. 9; 28, 1872. For legal action relative to the threatened forced sale of Sherwood Forest in 1872 and the general financial plight of the family in 1870-1872, see Julia Gardiner Tyler to David Gardiner Tyler, Staten Island, Dec. 16, 1869; James A. Semple to Julia Gardiner Tyler, Tunstalls Station, New Kent Co., Va., June 19, 1870; David Gardiner Tyler to Julia Gardiner Tyler, Richmond, Nov. 3, 1870; Sherwood Forest, May 6, 1872; Richmond, June 6, 1872; George L. Christian, Clerk's Office, Supreme Court of Appeals, to David Gardiner Tyler, Richmond, Jan. 30, 1872, *TFP*.

[36] David Gardiner Tyler to Julia Gardiner Tyler, Richmond, June 22; 12, 1870; Sherwood Forest, Sept. 19, 1870; Richmond, Nov. 3, 1870; Sherwood Forest, Nov. 11; Dec. 19, 1870; James A. Semple to Julia Gardiner Tyler, New Kent Co., Va., Nov. 5, 1870, *TFP*. For the larger background of Reconstruction politics in Virginia, 1869-1870, see Hamilton J. Eckenrode, *The Political History of Virginia During the Reconstruction* (Baltimore, 1904), 116-28.

[37] Julia Gardiner Tyler to David Gardiner Tyler, Staten Island, Nov. 6, 1870;

New York, Nov. 15, 1871; Staten Island, Dec. 4, 1871; Rep. Henry A. Reeves to Julia Gardiner Tyler, Washington, Apr. 7; 10, 1869; David Gardiner Tyler to Julia Gardiner Tyler, Sherwood Forest, Nov. 17, 1871, *TFP*.

[38] *Ibid.*, Nov. 17; Sept. 5, 1871; May 6; June 23; Nov. 7; 17, 1872; Julia Gardiner Tyler to Lyon G. Tyler, Georgetown, Jan. 18, 1873, *TFP;* Roseboom, *A History of Presidential Elections,* 222–34.

[39] James Lyons to Julia Gardiner Tyler, Richmond, May 1, 1873; David Gardiner Tyler to Julia Gardiner Tyler, Richmond, June 8, 1870, *TFP; Frank Leslie's Magazine,* "Washington Items," Apr. 6, 1872; David Gardiner Tyler to Julia Gardiner Tyler, Sherwood Forest, Mar. 3, 1872; Laura C. Holloway to Julia Gardiner Tyler, Brooklyn, May 17, 1870; Julia Gardiner Tyler to Messrs. Samuel Walker and Co., n.p., n.d. [1870]. (When Laura C. Holloway Langford's book appeared in 1881 only two pages were devoted to Julia and these were studded with factual errors. Julia made Holloway privy to an extensive autobiographical account of her life, detailed and correct, but the author could scarcely have employed it in constructing her account of Julia.) Julia Gardiner Tyler to Gen. Michler, n.p., n.d. [Richmond, Aug. 1874]; James Dailey, Office of Public Buildings and Grounds, Washington, Aug. 29, 1874. On the Wise memoir of Tyler, to which Julia contributed her own recollections, *see* Julia Gardiner Tyler to David Gardiner Tyler, Staten Island, Oct. 30, 1869; Henry A. Wise to Julia Gardiner Tyler, Richmond, Mar. 6, 1872; David Gardiner Tyler to Julia Gardiner Tyler, Sherwood Forest, Mar. 22, 1872, *TFP*. "In some way or other," Gardie confided to his mother, "his book—*entre nous* strictly—*grated*. But on second thought I think we owe him thanks for his vindication of Father. If there is *brusqueness* and a vein of egotism running through it, we must remember that the style is but a true reflex of the writer—and the truth and strength of the book redeems its faults." The Tylers were particularly proud of Wise's unreconstructed postwar stand. He steadfastly refused to take the amnesty oath and in so doing he forfeited his political and civil rights. His third wife, Mary Elizabeth Lyons, was sister to Julia's good friend and legal counselor James Lyons. Wise died in Richmond in 1876, age 70, still unreconstructed; still cursing the "damn Yankees." "They [Congress] have never been able to bend or break his spirit," said Julia in admiration in October 1869. "He stands like a rock."

[40] William R. Cummings to Julia Gardiner Tyler, U.S. Internal Revenue, Long Island City, N.Y., Jan. 21, 1870; Julia Gardiner Tyler to David Gardiner Tyler, Staten Island, Dec. 11, 1869; Nov. 16, 1870; Geneseo, N.Y., Sept. 20, 1870; Julia Gardiner Tyler to Harry Beeckman, Staten Island, Nov. 28, 1871; *ibid.,* I.O.U. for $1000, Jan. 31, 1873; William Evarts to Julia Gardiner Tyler, New York, Mar. 17, 1871; David Gardiner Tyler to Julia Gardiner Tyler, Sherwood Forest, July 12; Nov. 17, 1871. In 1872 Harry had an unrequited courtship with the niece of Abel P. Upshur. *See* James A. Semple to David Gardiner Tyler, Waterloo [N.Y.], Aug. 13, 1872; Harry Beeckman to Julia Gardiner Tyler, Farmer's Rest [N.Y.], May 13; Sept. 19, 1873, *TFP*.

[41] David Gardiner Tyler to Julia Gardiner Tyler, Lexington, Mar. 4, 1869; William H. Spencer to Julia Tyler, n.p., n.d. [early June 1869]; Mrs. John Tyler, Wedding Invitation to Marriage of Julia Tyler to William H. Spencer, New York, June 26, 1869; Card: Mr. and Mrs. William H. Spencer, At Home, Tuscarora, [N.Y.], July 5, 1869; Julia Tyler Spencer to Julia Gardiner Tyler, Tuscarora, N.Y., Jan. 27, 1871; Phoebe Gardiner Horsford to Julia Gardiner Tyler, Cambridge, Mass., May 10, 1871; Belle B. Chalmers to Julia Gardiner Tyler, New York, n.d. [May 1871]. *See* Lachlan Tyler to Julia Gardiner Tyler, New York, Mar. 15; Apr. 3, 1872; Feb. 8; 10, 1875; Julia Gardiner Tyler to Lyon G. Tyler, Staten Island, May 13, 1872. For the subsequent unprofitable (for Julia) financial relations between Julia and the wandering Will Spencer, *see* Fimmer and Weill, Pawnbrokers, to Julia Gardiner Tyler, New York, Feb. 14, 1873 (Spencer had pawned Julie's

jewelry to these people); William Evarts to Julia Gardiner Tyler, New York, Jan. 24, 1874; S. M. Barton and Co. to Julia Gardiner Tyler, San Francisco, July 19, 1875 (Spencer had used Julia's name as surety on personal notes for $200 without her authorization); William H. Spencer to Julia Gardiner Tyler, Lone Pine Ranch, Colorado, Feb. 12, 1875; Fort Collins, Colo., Aug. 11, 1875, *TFP;* John A. Taylor, Lawyer, to David L. Gardiner, New York, Jan. 28, 1870, *GPY.* Julia Tyler Spencer later married George Fleurot.

⁴² James I. Roosevelt to Julia Gardiner Tyler, New York, Mar. 16, 1872; Lachlan Tyler to Julia Gardiner Tyler, Staten Island, Apr. 3, 1872; West New Brighton, L.I., N.Y. School District No. 2 to Julia Gardiner Tyler, Tax Bill for 1871; Georgetown College to Julia Gardiner Tyler, Washington, Nov. 25, 1872; Georgetown Academy of the Visitation to Julia Gardiner Tyler, Bill for First Semester, 1872–1873; Julia Gardiner Tyler to Louise ———, Georgetown, D.C., Feb. 16, 1872, *TFP.* Pearlie's room, board, tuition, and books cost but $116 per semester; Fitz's charges amounted to but $170 per semester.

⁴³ James Lyons to Julia Gardiner Tyler, Richmond, May 1, 1873; Julia Gardiner Tyler to Lyon G. Tyler, Georgetown, Jan. 18, 1873; David Gardiner Tyler to Julia Gardiner Tyler, Sherwood Forest, Jan. 19, 1873, *TFP.*

⁴⁴ J. Selden to Julia Gardiner Tyler, Baltimore, Mar. 21, 1872; Lachlan Tyler to Julia Gardiner Tyler, Georgetown, Mar. 30, 1872; David Gardiner Tyler to Julia Gardiner Tyler, Sherwood Forest, May 12, 1872; Pearl Tyler to Julia Gardiner Tyler, Georgetown, Mar. 14; Nov. 7, 1875; D. Anna Cook to Julia Gardiner Tyler, Baltimore, Apr. 8; Nov. 27, 1872; Belle B. Chalmers to Julia Gardiner Tyler, n.p., n.d. [Nyack, N.Y., Apr. 1872]; May 10, 1872; Sister Loretto to Julia Gardiner Tyler, Georgetown, Aug. 9, 1872; P. F. Healy to Julia Gardiner Tyler, Boston, July 24; Aug. 8, 1872; John P. ——— to Julia Gardiner Tyler, New York, June 19, 1872; P. F. Healy to the Rev. Father Daubresse, Georgetown, May 20, 1872; Mother Superior of the Convent of the Visitation to Julia Gardiner Tyler, Georgetown, July 4, 1872; Betty B. Walthall to Julia Gardiner Tyler, Tarboro, N.C., Jan. 15, 1874; Julia Gardiner Tyler to Lyon G. Tyler, Staten Island, May 13, 1872, *TFP.*

⁴⁵ P. F. Healy to Julia Gardiner Tyler, Boston, Aug. 8, 1872; Phoebe Gardiner Horsford to Julia Gardiner Tyler, Cambridge, Mass., Sept. 1, 1872; Belle C. Chalmers to Julia Gardiner Tyler, Nyack, N.Y., May 10; Nov. 12; Dec. 15, 1872; David Gardiner Tyler to Julia Gardiner Tyler, Sherwood Forest, Dec. 9; May 12, 1872. For something of Julia's flirtation with spiritualism in 1871–1872, *see* Belle B. Chalmers to Julia Gardiner Tyler, n.p., n.d. [Nyack, N.Y., 1871 or 1872]. A clipping of William J. Venable's spiritualist poem, "Spirit Visitants," is found carefully preserved in Julia's papers in *TFP.* Pearl Tyler Ellis (1860–1947) was a "very mild" Roman Catholic. Julia Tyler Wilson to Robert Seager, Charlottesville, Va., Aug. 1, 1962.

⁴⁶ A. J. Mathewson and Son to Julia Gardiner Tyler, New York, Apr. 3, 1872; Dec. 19; July 19; Sept. 16, 1873; Mar. 24, 1877; Lachlan Tyler to Julia Gardiner Tyler, New York, Sept. 24; Nov. 3; Dec. 10, 1873; David Gardiner Tyler to Julia Gardiner Tyler, Sherwood Forest, June 13; Sept. 20; 21; Oct. 9, 1873; Thomas J. Evans, Lawyer, to Julia Gardiner Tyler, July 15, 1873. A groceries and sundries bill for $82.97 from W. D. Blair and Co., Richmond, could not be met at Sherwood Forest in October 1873; similarly, a coal bill for $65.12 from C. W. Hunt and Co., Staten Island, could not be met at Castleton Hill in October 1873. These and additional evidences of financial difficulty in 1873–1875 may be found in *TFP,* 1873–1880, *passim.*

⁴⁷ Julia Gardiner Tyler to the Hon. William W. Belknap, n.p., n.d. [Georgetown, 1874]; Julia Gardiner Tyler to Hamilton Fish, n.p., n.d. [Georgetown, 1874]; Julia Gardiner Tyler to ———, n.p., n.d. [Georgetown, Mar.–Apr. 1873]; William M. Evarts to Julia Gardiner Tyler, New York, Apr. 5, 1873; Lachlan Tyler to Julia Gardiner Tyler, New York, Dec. 10, 1873; Staten Island, May 4;

Oct. 6, 1874; J. Alexander Tyler to Julia Gardiner Tyler, Staten Island, June 10; Aug. 17, 1874, *TFP*.

⁴⁸ Lachlan Tyler to Julia Gardiner Tyler, New York, Sept. 29; 30; Oct. 1; 6, 1874, *TFP*.

⁴⁹ William M. Evarts to Julia Gardiner Tyler, New York, Apr. 5; June 21; Dec. 26, 1873; Lachlan Tyler to Julia Gardiner Tyler, New York, Oct. 8; Nov. 3, 1873; Staten Island, May 4, 1874; Julia Gardiner Tyler to Hon. Peter Cooper, n.p., n.d. [1873]; Leonard Caryl to Julia Gardiner Tyler, New York, July 31, 1874; Julia Gardiner Tyler to Leonard Caryl, Sherwood Forest, Aug. 10, 1874; David Gardiner Tyler to Julia Gardiner Tyler, Sherwood Forest, Mar. 20; Apr. 14; 17; May 7; Oct. 9, 1874; Abbott and Sill to Mortimer Seaver, Geneseo, N.Y., Apr. 18, 1874; Harry Beeckman to Julia Gardiner Tyler, Farmer's Rest, N.Y., May 8, 1874; P. F. Healy to Julia Gardiner Tyler, Boston, May 1, 1874; J. Alexander Tyler to Julia Gardiner Tyler, Staten Island, June 10, 1874, *TFP*.

⁵⁰ David Gardiner Tyler to Julia Gardiner Tyler, Sherwood Forest, Sept. 21, 1873; Apr. 6, 1876; Feb. 27, 1877; Mar. 21; Apr. 8, 1878; Lachlan Tyler to Julia Gardiner Tyler, Jersey City, N.J., Jan. 6, [1877]; Annie Baker Tyler to Julia Gardiner Tyler, Memphis, Mar. 13, 1881; Julia Gardiner Tyler to Virginia Parker, Sherwood Forest, Aug. 28, 1878, *TFP*. "I wish to give my little girl who is only seven years suitable companionship and propose to take four or five other little scholars into my family between the ages of six and ten," Julia told Miss Parker, a friend of Priscilla in Bristol, Penna.

⁵¹ James A. Semple to David Gardiner Tyler, Waterloo, N.Y., Aug. 13, 1872; David Gardiner Tyler to Julia Gardiner Tyler, Sherwood Forest, June 13, 1873; Apr. 3; 29; Oct. 9, 1874; Lachlan Tyler to Julia Gardiner Tyler, New York, Sept. 30, 1874; Madeleine Beeckman to Julia Gardiner Tyler, Cornwall, [N.Y.], Aug. 11, 1875; Phoebe Gardiner Horsford to Julia Gardiner Tyler, Shelter Island, Sept. 5, 1875; William M. Evarts to Julia Gardiner Tyler, Windsor, Vt., Aug. 28, 1875; William Cruikshank to Julia Gardiner Tyler, New York, Oct. 6, 1875; M. D. Rockwell to Julia Gardiner Tyler, Elizabeth, N.J., Oct. 25, 1875, *TFP;* Interview with J. Alfred Tyler, Sherwood Forest, Jan. 27, 1960; Will of Henry Gardiner Beeckman, Nov. 20, 1869, *GPY*. Gilbert Beeckman's death also occurred in 1875.

⁵² Samuel Buell Gardiner (1815–1882) was the youngest of three sons (there were also two daughters) of John Lyon Gardiner (1770–1816), seventh proprietor. His oldest brother, David Johnson Gardiner (1804–1829) had served as eighth proprietor. David Johnson Gardiner's death in 1829 brought in the second brother, John Griswold Gardiner (1812–1861), the colorful and erratic ninth proprietor mentioned in these pages. John's death by dissipation in 1861 brought Samuel Buell Gardiner in as the tenth proprietor of Gardiners Island. He married (1837) Mary Gardiner Thompson, his brother-in-law's sister. Their children were five, Sarah Griswold Gardiner (1848–1927) being the youngest. Sarah's blood relationship to her husband, Alex Tyler, was actually that of third cousin, Senator David Gardiner, Julia's father, and Samuel Buell Gardiner having been first cousins. For the courtship and marriage of J. Alexander Tyler and Sarah Griswold Gardiner, *see* Invitation to the Wedding of Sarah Griswold Gardiner to J. Alexander Tyler, East Hampton, L.I., N.Y., August 5, 1875; David Gardiner Tyler to J. Alexander Tyler, Staten Island, Jan. 15, 1868; Phoebe Gardiner Horsford to Julia Gardiner Tyler, Cambridge, Mass., Jan. 31, 1875; Shelter Island, Sept. 5, 1875; J. Alexander Tyler to Julia Gardiner Tyler, New York, June 7; 8, 1875; Sarah Griswold Gardiner Tyler to Julia Gardiner Tyler, The Ebbitt, Washington, Aug. 13, 1875; Madeleine Beeckman to Julia Gardiner Tyler, Cornwall [N.Y.], Aug. 11, 1875; Pearl Tyler to Julia Gardiner Tyler, Georgetown, Nov. 7, 1875; Samuel Buell Gardiner to Sarah Griswold Gardiner Tyler, Albany, Feb. 13, 1876. Ironically, when Sally was born on May 24, 1848, Julia had written Juliana: "To think of Sam's wife having *another,* and a daughter. Suppose Sam should ever be a widower,

he would not be in *much demand,* would he?" Julia Gardiner Tyler to Juliana Gardiner, Sherwood Forest, June 11, 1848, *TFP.*

[53] Coralie Gardiner to Sarah Griswold Gardiner Tyler, East Hampton, June 23, 1876; E. G. Martston to Julia Gardiner Tyler, Providence, R.I., Feb. 23, 1879, *TFP; East Hampton Cemetery Records,* East Hampton Free Library; Julia Tyler Wilson to Robert Seager, Charlottesville, Va., Aug. 1, 1962.

[54] David Gardiner Tyler to Julia Gardiner Tyler, Sherwood Forest, Nov. 28, 1877; J. Alexander Tyler to Julia Gardiner Tyler, Sherwood Forest, Feb. 27, 1878; New York, Nov. 21, 1878; East Hampton, Jan. 20; Feb. 24, 1879; New York, May 5, 1879; Rosebud Agency, Dakota Territory, Oct. 23; Nov. 6, 1879; Daniel G. Major to J. Alexander Tyler, San Francisco, Mar. 22, 1878; Daniel G. Major to Julia Gardiner Tyler, Utica, N.Y., May 13, 1879; Julia Gardiner Tyler to Daniel G. Major, n.p., n.d. [Sherwood Forest, May 1879], *TFP.*

[55] J. Alexander Tyler to Julia Gardiner Tyler, Durango, Colo., Oct. 3, 1881; David Gardiner Tyler to Julia Gardiner Tyler, Sherwood Forest, Dec. 20, 1881; Julia Gardiner Tyler to David Gardiner Tyler, Richmond, Apr. 18 [1884], *TFP; East Hampton Cemetery Records,* East Hampton Free Library. *See also* dates and inscriptions on the gravestones of J. Alexander Tyler (1848–1883), Sarah Griswold Gardiner Tyler (1848–1927), Gardiner Tyler (1878–1892), and Lillian Gardiner Horsford Tyler [Margraf] (1879–1918). Details of J. Alexander Tyler's death and supporting documents are found in Margaret Gardiner Tyler Costello to Robert Seager, Sahuarita, Ariz., Oct. 9, 1962.

[56] Lachlan Tyler to Julia Gardiner Tyler, Jersey City, N.J., June 9, 1877; Sherwood Forest, Feb. 24; Mar. 1, 1878; Washington, Oct. 15; Aug. 5, 1879; Julia Gardiner Tyler to William M. Evarts, n.p., n.d. [Sherwood Forest, Feb.–Mar. 1878]; P. F. Healy to Julia Gardiner Tyler, Georgetown College, Washington, Oct. 27, 1878, *TFP.*

[57] James A. Semple to Julia Gardiner Tyler, York R.R., Feb. 15, 1879 ("I have seen Mrs. Lincoln's application for means to live as befitting the widow of a President; the woman is insane or a miser.... I have known her for years and always thought her very common and low in all her tastes and actions...."); Julia Gardiner Tyler to William M. Evarts, n.p., n.d. [Sherwood Forest, Feb.–Mar. 1879; Dec. 1879–Jan. 1880]; A. F. Posey to Julia Gardiner Tyler, Greenville, Ala., Apr. 13, 1878; Julia Gardiner Tyler to Rep. John Goode, n.p., n.d. [Sherwood Forest, Jan.; Apr. 7, 1880]; Julia Gardiner Tyler to A. H. Stevens, n.p., n.d. [Sherwood Forest, Jan.–Mar. 1880], *TFP.*

[58] Julia Gardiner Tyler to James Lyons, n.p., n.d. [Sherwood Forest, Apr. 1880]; Julia Gardiner Tyler to Sen. Robert E. Withers, Sherwood Forest, Jan. 31, 1880; Sen. Robert E. Withers to Julia Gardiner Tyler, Washington, Feb. 7, 1880 (copy in Julia's handwriting); Rep. John Goode to Julia Gardiner Tyler, Washington, Apr. 15 [1880], *TFP.*

[59] Julia Gardiner Tyler, A Petition to the Senate and House of Representatives, n.p., n.d. [Sherwood Forest, 1879], *TFP.*

[60] "A Lady Subscriber" [Julia Gardiner Tyler] to the Editor, Washington *Post,* n.p., n.d. [Sherwood Forest, Oct. 1881]; Lachlan Tyler to Julia Gardiner Tyler, Washington, Apr. 27; 29, 1882; M. D. R. to Julia Gardiner Tyler, % E. G. Hartshorn, Newport, R.I., n.p., June 5, 1882, *TFP;* Kane, *Facts About the Presidents,* 398–99; Julia Tyler Wilson to Robert Seager, Charlottesville, Aug. 1, 1962.

[61] David Gardiner Tyler to Julia Gardiner Tyler, Sherwood Forest, Oct. 2; 8, 1873; Oct. 3, 1875; Samuel Buell Gardiner to Julia Gardiner Tyler, East Hampton, Dec. 5, 1875, *TFP.*

[62] Roseboom, *A History of Presidential Elections,* 243–49.

[63] David Gardiner Tyler to Julia Gardiner Tyler, Sherwood Forest, Feb. 11; 22; 27; Mar. 7; 21, 1877, *TFP.*

[64] David Gardiner Tyler to Pearl Tyler, Sherwood Forest, May 15, 1880; David

Gardiner Tyler to Julia Gardiner Tyler, Sherwood Forest, July 28, 1881; Lachlan Tyler to Julia Gardiner Tyler, Washington, Mar. 7, 1880; Julia Gardiner Tyler to Annie Ellis, Shawsville, Montgomery Co., Va., July 27, 1886, *TFP*. Lonie returned to Virginia in 1881 from Memphis, determined to abandon teaching and study law. This he did in 1882–1883, combining it with work on the Tyler biography. He practiced law in Richmond for several years, but in 1886 he drifted back into teaching at William and Mary although his mother reported him at the time as having "an intense distaste for teaching in any form."

[65] *Ibid.*

[66] Lyon G. Tyler to David L. Gardiner, Sherwood Forest, July 25, 1882; Richmond, Jan. 16; Aug. 13, 1883, *TFP*. The papers David Lyon controlled in 1882 were given to Yale University Library by his grandniece, Alexandria Gardiner Creel, in 1959. Lyon G. Tyler saw only a handful of them when he was preparing his study.

[67] Sarah D. Thompson to Sarah Thompson Gardiner, New York, Mar. 9, 1877; William Cruikshank to David L. Gardiner, New York, July 30; Aug. 8, 1883; Feb. 9, 1881; May 29, 1882; Oct. 8; 22; Dec. 1, 1883; Jan. 31, 1884; Oct. 13, 1885; Nov. 9, 1886; Frederick Thompson to David L. Gardiner, New York, Mar. 15, 1884; Francis H. Lee to David L. Gardiner, Petersham, Mass., July 14, 1885; John R. Bleeker to David L. Gardiner, New York, Dec. 4, 1878; Dec. 2, 1884; Jan. 2; Oct. 6, Nov. 18; Dec. 24, 1886; Jan. 8, 1887; Jonathan T. Gardiner to David L. Gardiner, East Hampton, Oct. 4, 1888, *GPY*.

[68] David L. Gardiner to Curtiss C. Gardiner, New Haven, Conn., Jan. 16, 1885; Curtiss C. Gardiner to David L. Gardiner, St. Louis, Mo., Jan. 19, 1885; Martha J. Lamb to David Lyon Gardiner, New York, Jan. 3; Mar. 15, 1885, *GPY*. In his later years David Lyon changed the Lyon to "Lion," and this spelling appears on his ostentatious tomb at East Hampton with the inscription: *Beati mundo corde quoniam ipsi deum videbunt.*

[69] Julia Tyler Wilson to Robert Seager, Charlottesville, Va., Aug. 1, 1962. For details of Julia's death, funeral, and burial, *see* Richmond *Dispatch*, July 11; 12; 13, 1889; Richmond *State*, July 11; 12, 1889.

BIBLIOGRAPHY

A. *Manuscript Sources*
  Henry Clay Papers, Library of Congress, Washington, D.C.
  John Clopton Papers, Duke University Library, Durham, N.C.
  John J. Crittenden Papers, Duke University Library, Durham, N.C.
  East Hampton Cemetery Records, East Hampton Free Library, East Hampton, N.Y.
  Philip Richard Fendall Papers, Duke University Library, Durham, N.C.
  Gardiner Family Papers, Yale University Library, New Haven, Conn.
  Gardiner Papers, Long Island Collection, East Hampton Free Library, East Hampton, N.Y.
  James Iredell (Sr. and Jr.) Papers, Duke University Library, Durham, N.C.
  Pequot Collection, Yale University Library, New Haven, Conn.
  James Henry Rochelle Papers, Duke University Library, Durham, N.C.
  John Rutherfoord Papers, Duke University Library, Durham, N.C.
  William Patterson Smith Papers, Duke University Library, Durham, N.C.
  John Tyler Papers, Library of Congress, Washington, D.C.
  John Tyler Papers, Duke University Library, Durham, N.C.
  Tyler Collection, Alderman Library, University of Virginia, Charlottesville, Va.
  Tyler Collection, William and Mary College Library, Williamsburg, Va.
  Tyler Family Papers, scattered; copies in possession of Author.

B. *Tyler-Gardiner Primary Sources*
  1. BOOKS
     Abbott, Benjamin V. and Abbott, Austin (comps.), *Abbott's Practice Reports, New Series,* Vol. IV and Vol. V of *Reports of Practice Cases Determined in the state of New York.* Albany, N.Y., 1869. (Briefs and depositions in Tyler vs. Gardiner).
     Congressional Debates, Vol. VIII, 1831–1832. Washington, 1832.
     Gardiner, Alexander, *Princeton Diary, 1834–1838.* Gardiner Papers, Yale University.
     Gardiner, Curtiss C. (ed.), *The Papers and Biography of Lion Gardiner.* St. Louis, 1883.
     Gardiner, Sarah D. (ed.), *Margaret Gardiner, Leaves from a Young Girl's Diary, 1840–1841.* Privately published, 1926.
     Journal of the Senate of the State of New York, 1824–1827. Albany, N.Y., 1825–1828.
     Journal of the Virginia House of Delegates, 1823–1824. Richmond, Va., 1825.
     Richardson, James D. (comp.), *A Compilation of the Messages and Papers of the Presidents.* Vol. IV, 1841–1849. Washington, 1902.
     Tiffany, John (comp.), *Reports of Cases Argued and Determined in the Court of Appeals of the State of New York.* Vol. VIII. Albany, N.Y., 1867. (Briefs and depositions in Tyler vs. Gardiner).
     Tyler, Lyon Gardiner, *Letters and Times of the Tylers.* 3 vols. Richmond, Va., 1884; 1894.
     Tyler, Robert, *Poems.* Richmond, Va., 1839.
     ———, *Ahasuerus. A Poem.* Richmond, Va., 1842.
     ———, *Death; or Medorus' Dream.* Richmond, Va., 1843.

2. ARTICLES AND PAMPHLETS

Anon., "Interview with Julia Gardiner Tyler," Washington, n.d. [Winter 1888–1889], Philadelphia *Press,* July 11, 1889; reprinted in Richmond *Dispatch,* July 12, 1889.

Gardiner, David Lyon, "Extract of a Letter Dated San Francisco, June 15, 1849," New York *Journal of Commerce,* Aug. 14, 1849.

Gotlieb, Howard and Grimes, Gail, "President Tyler and the Gardiners: A New Portrait," Yale University Library *Gazette,* XXXIV (July 1959).

Knox, Sanka, "A Tyler Letter, New York *Times,* Dec. 7, 1958.

Noah, Mordecai M. [pseud. "Horace Walpole"], "Reminiscences and Random Recollections of the Tyler Administration," New York *Sunday Dispatch,* Dec. 1845 to May 1846.

Tyler, John, "Early Times of Virginia—William and Mary College," *De Bow's Review,* XXVIII (August 1859).

———, *An Address Delivered Before the Literary Societies of the University of Virginia on the Anniversary of the Declaration of Independence by the State of Virginia, June 29, 1850.* Charlottesville, Va., 1850.

———, *Lecture Delivered Before the Maryland Institute... Baltimore, Md., March 20, 1855.* Richmond, 1855.

———, Miscellaneous Tyler Letters. *Tyler's Quarterly Historical and Genealogical Magazine,* II (October 1920); VII (October 1925); VIII (July 1926); VIII (January 1927); XI (April 1930); XII (October 1930); XII (January 1931); XIII (October 1931); *William and Mary College Quarterly Historical Magazine,* XII (October 1903); XVII (July 1935).

———, *Speech Delivered March 13, 1861, in the Virginia State Convention.* Richmond, 1861.

Tyler, John, Jr. [pseud. "Python"], "The History of the Party, and the Political Status of John Tyler," *De Bow's Review,* XXVI (March 1859).

———, [pseud. "Tau"], "The Relative Status of the North and the South," *De Bow's Review,* XXVII (July 1859).

Tyler, Julia Gardiner, "To the Duchess of Sutherland and the Ladies of England," *Southern Literary Messenger,* XIX (February 1853).

———, "Reminiscences," Cincinnati *Graphic News,* June 25, 1887; reprinted in Richmond *Dispatch,* July 21, 1889.

Tyler, Lyon G. (ed.), "Correspondence of Judge N. B. Tucker," *William and Mary College Quarterly Historical Magazine,* XII (January 1904).

——— (ed.), "Will and Inventory of Hon. John Tyler," *William and Mary College Quarterly Historical Magazine,* XVII (April 1909).

——— (ed.), "Some Letters of Tyler, Calhoun, Polk, Murphy, Houston and Donelson," *Tyler's Quarterly Historical and Genealogical Magazine,* VI (April 1925); VII (July 1925).

———, *John Tyler and Abraham Lincoln.* Richmond, 1927.

———, "John Tyler and the Vice Presidency," *Tyler's Quarterly Historical and Genealogical Magazine,* IX (October 1927).

——— (ed.), "Letters from Tyler Trunks, Sherwood Forest, Virginia. Political Letters, 1832–1834," *Tyler's Quarterly Historical and Genealogical Magazine,* XVII (January 1936).

Tyler, Robert, *A Reply to the Democratic Review.* New York, April 1845.

C. *Newspapers*
New York *American*
New York *Aurora*
New York *Courier and Enquirer*

New York *Daily Plebeian*
New York *Democrat*
New York *Evening Express*
New York *Herald*
New York *Journal of Commerce*
New York *Morning News*
New York *Post*
New York *Sunday Dispatch*
New York *Tribune*
New York *World*
Niles' Weekly Register
Philadelphia *Pennsylvanian*
Philadelphia *Truth-Teller*
Richmond, Va. *Dispatch*
Richmond, Va. *Enquirer*
Richmond, Va. *Times*
Washington *Globe*
Washington *Madisonian*
Washington *Union*

D. *Tyler-Gardiner Secondary Sources*
   1. BOOKS
      Abell, A. G., *Life of John Tyler*. New York, 1844.
      Auchampaugh, Philip G., *Robert Tyler: Southern Rights Champion, 1847–1866*. Duluth, Minn., 1934.
      Chitwood, Oliver P., *John Tyler: Champion of the Old South*. New York, 1939.
      Coleman, Elizabeth Tyler, *Priscilla Cooper Tyler and the American Scene, 1816–1889*. University, Ala., 1955.
      Cronin, John W., *A Bibliography of...John Tyler*. New York, 1935.
      Cumming, Hiram, *The Secret History of the Perfidies, Intrigues, and Corruptions of the Tyler Dynasty*. New York, 1845.
      Ellett, Katherine Tyler, *Young John Tyler*. Richmond, 1957.
      Gardiner, Curtiss C., *Lion Gardiner and His Descendants*. St. Louis, 1890.
      Gardiner, David, *Chronicle of the Town of East Hampton, County of Suffolk, N.Y.* New York, 1871.
      Gardiner, John Lion, *The Gardiners of Gardiners Island*. East Hampton, N.Y., 1927.
      Gardiner, Lion, *Relation of the Pequot Wars*. East Hampton, N.Y., 1660.
      Gardiner, Sarah D., *Early Memories of Gardiners Island*. East Hampton, N.Y., 1947.
      Ireland, Joseph N., *A Memoir of the Professional Life of Thomas Abthorpe Cooper*. New York, 1888.
      Lambert, Oscar D., *Presidential Politics in the United States, 1841–1844*. Durham, N.C., 1936.
      Marx, Rudolph, *The Health of the Presidents*. New York, 1960.
      Morgan, Robert J., *A Whig Embattled: The Presidency under John Tyler*. Lincoln, Neb., 1954.
      Payne, Pierre S. R., *The Island*. New York, 1958.
      Perling, J. J., *The President Takes A Wife*. Middleburg, Va., 1959. (Fiction)
      Reeves, Jesse S., *American Diplomacy under Tyler and Polk*. Baltimore, 1907.
      Tyler, Lyon G., *Letters and Times of the Tylers*. 3 vols. Richmond, 1884; 1894.

———, *Parties and Patronage in the United States.* New York, 1891.
Wise, Henry A., *Seven Decades of the Union. Illustrated by a Memoir of John Tyler.* Philadelphia, 1881.

2. ARTICLES AND PAMPHLETS

Anon., *A Defense of the President Against the Attacks of Mr. Botts and the Clay Party.* N.p., n.d. [Washington, 1842].
———, *Brief Sketch of the Life of John Tyler.* N.p., n.d. [1842].
———, *Democratic Tyler Meeting at Washington.* Washington, 1844.
———, *John, the Traitor; or, the Force of Accident. A Plain Story by One Who Has Whistled at the Plough.* New York, 1843.
———, *John Tyler: His History, Character and Position.* New York, 1843.
———, *The Andover Husking: A Political Tale Suited to the Circumstances of the Present Time, and Dedicated to the Whigs of Massachusetts.* Boston, 1842.
Anti-Junius [pseud.], *Who and What Is John Tyler?* New York, 1843.
Auchampaugh, Philip G., "John W. Forney, Robert Tyler and James Buchanan," *Tyler's Quarterly Historical and Genealogical Magazine,* XV (October 1933).
Bowers, Claude C., *John Tyler: An Address at the Unveiling of the Bust of President Tyler in the State Capitol, Richmond, Va., June 16, 1931.* Richmond, 1932.
Bradshaw, Herbert C., "A President's Bride of 'Sherwood Forest,'" *Virginia Cavalcade,* VII (Spring, 1958).
Dorsey, John L., *Observations on the Political Character and Services of President Tyler and His Cabinet.* Washington, 1841.
Gardiner, Alexander, "Lion Gardiner," *Collections of the Massachusetts Historical Society,* Series 3, Vol. X. Boston, 1849.
Gardiner, Sarah D., *The Gardiner Manor.* Baltimore, 1916.
Gordon, Armistead C., *John Tyler: Tenth President of the United States. An Address at the Dedication of the Monument Erected by Congress in Hollywood Cemetery, Richmond, Va., in Memory of President Tyler, Oct. 12, 1915.* Richmond, 1915.
Kennedy, J. P., *Defense of the Whigs.* New York, 1844.
Leslie, Lewis B., "A Southern Transcontinental Railroad Into California: Texas and Pacific versus Southern Pacific, 1865-1885," *Pacific Historical Review* (March 1936).
Miles, Alfred H., "The Princeton Explosion," United States Naval Institute *Proceedings,* LII (November 1926).
———, "The Princeton Explosion," Lynchburg (Va.) Foundry *Iron Worker,* XXI (Spring 1957).
Mills, James, "San Diego—Where California Began," *San Diego Historical Society Quarterly,* VI (January 1960), Special Edition.
Peterson, Helen Stone, "First Lady At 22," *Virginia Cavalcade,* XI (Winter, 1961-62).
Rives, Ralph H., "The Jamestown Celebration of "1857," *The Virginia magazine of History and Biography,* LXVI (June 1958).
Tyler, Lyon G., "The Annexation of Texas," *Tyler's Quarterly Historical and Genealogical Magazine,* VI (October 1924).

E. *General Studies and Related Monographic Works*

Adams, Charles F. (ed.), *Memoirs of John Quincy Adams.* 12 vols. Philadelphia, 1874-1877.
Alexander, De Alva S., *A Political History of the State of New York.* 3 vols. New York, 1906.

Alexander, Holmes, *The American Talleyrand*. New York, 1935.
Allen, Hervey, "Special Biographical Introduction," in *The Works of Edgar Allan Poe*. New York, 1927.
Ambler, Charles H., *Thomas Ritchie: A Study in Virginia Politics*. Richmond, 1913.
American and Foreign Anti-Slave Society, *The Fugitive Slave Bill: Its History and Unconstitutionality: With an Account of the Seizure and Enslavement of James Hamlet and His Subsequent Restoration to Liberty*. New York, 1850.
Auchampaugh, Philip G., *James Buchanan and His Cabinet on the Eve of Secession*. Lancaster, Pa., 1926.
Bacourt, Chevalier de, *Souvenirs of a Diplomat*. New York, 1885.
Ballagh, James C., *A History of Slavery in Virginia*. Baltimore, 1902.
Barnes, Gilbert H., *The Antislavery Impulse, 1830–1844*. New York, 1933.
Barnes, T. W., *Memoirs of Thurlow Weed*. 2 vols. Boston, 1884.
Bassett, J. S., *Life of Andrew Jackson*. New York, 1928.
Beach, Moses Y., *Wealth and Pedigree of the Wealthy Citizens of New York City*. 3rd ed., New York, 1842.
Bemis, Samuel F., *John Quincy Adams and the Foundations of American Foreign Policy*. New York, 1949.
———, *John Quincy Adams and the Union*. New York, 1956.
Benton, Thomas Hart, *Abridgment of the Debates of Congress From 1789 to 1856*. 16 vols. New York, 1857–1861.
———, *Thirty Years View*. 2 vols. New York, 1889.
Billington, Ray, *The Protestant Crusade, 1800–1860*. New York, 1938.
Boucher, Chauncy S., *The Nullification Controversy in South Carolina*. Chicago, 1916.
Bowers, Claude C., *The Party Battles of the Jackson Period*. Boston, 1928.
Bradsher, Earl L., *Matthew Carey, Editor, Author, Publisher*. New York, 1912.
Brown, W. Burlie, *The People's Choice; The Presidential Image in the Campaign Biography*. Baton Rouge, La., 1960.
Bruce, W. C., *John Randolph of Roanoke*. 2 vols. New York, 1922.
Burnam, W. Dean, *Presidential Ballots, 1836–1892*. Baltimore, 1955.
Callahan, James A., *American Foreign Policy in Mexican Relations*. New York, 1932.
Capers, Gerald M., *Stephen A. Douglas*. Boston, 1959.
Carroll, E. Malcolm, *Origins of the Whig Party*. Durham, N.C., 1925.
Catterall, Ralph C. H., *The Second Bank of the United States*. Chicago, 1903.
Catton, Bruce, *This Hallowed Ground*. New York, 1956.
Chambers, William N., *Old Bullion Benton, Senator from the New West*. Boston, 1956.
Cleaves, Freeman, *Old Tippecanoe: William Henry Harrison and His Times*. New York, 1939.
Cole, Arthur C., *The Whig Party in the South*. Washington, 1913.
Coleman, Anna M. B. (ed.), *The Life of John J. Crittenden*. 2 vols. Philadelphia, 1871.
Colman, Edna M., *Seventy-five Years of White House Gossip*. New York, 1925.
Colton, Calvin (ed.), *The Private Correspondence of Henry Clay*. Cincinnati, 1856.
Craven, Avery, *The Civil War in the Making, 1815–1860*. Baton Rouge, 1959.
Crawford, Mary C., *Romantic Days in the Early Republic*. Boston, 1912.
Crenshaw, Ollinger, *The Slave States in the Presidential Election of 1860*. Baltimore, 1945.
Curtis, George T., *Life of Daniel Webster*. 2 vols. New York, 1870.

Dangerfield, George, *The Era of Good Feelings*. New York, 1952.
Davis, Varina, *Jefferson Davis, A Memoir*. New York, 1890.
Dewey, Davis R., *Financial History of the United States*. New York, 1903.
Dexter, Franklin B., *Biographical Sketches of the Graduates of Yale College*. New York, 1911.
Donovan, Herbert, *The Barnburners*. New York, 1925.
Dumond, Dwight, L., *Antislavery Origins of the Civil War in the United States*. Ann Arbor, 1939.
———, *The Secession Movement, 1860–1861*. New York, 1931.
Eckenrode, Hamilton J., *The Political History of Virginia During the Reconstruction*. Baltimore, 1904.
Ellet, E. F., *Court Circles of the Republic*. Hartford, 1869.
Elliott, Charles W., *Winfield Scott*. New York, 1937.
Farrar, Emmie F., *Old Virginia Houses Along the James*. New York, 1957.
Filler, Louis, *The Crusade Against Slavery, 1830–1860*. New York, 1960.
Fitzpatrick, J. C. (ed.), *Martin Van Buren, Autobiography*. Washington, 1920.
Fleming, Walter L., *Civil War and Reconstruction in Alabama*. Cleveland, 1911.
Foote, H. S., *A Casket of Reminiscences*. Washington, 1874.
Fox, Dixon R., *The Decline of the Aristocracy in the Politics of New York*. New York, 1919.
Fraser, Hugh R., *Democracy in the Making: The Jackson-Tyler Era*. Indianapolis, 1938.
Fuess, Claude M., *The Life of Caleb Cushing*. 2 vols. New York, 1923.
Furman, Bess, *White House Profile*. Indianapolis, 1951.
Garraty, John A., *Silas Wright*. New York, 1949.
Glover, Gilbert C., *Immediate Pre-Civil War Compromise Efforts*. Nashville, 1934.
Goebel, Dorothy B., *William Henry Harrison*. Indianapolis, 1926.
Going, David B., *David Wilmot, Free-Soiler*. New York, 1924.
Govan, Thomas P., *Nicholas Biddle*. Chicago, 1959.
Graebner, Norman A., *Empire on the Pacific*. New York, 1955.
Gray, Wood, *The Hidden Civil War: The Story of the Copperheads*. New York, 1942.
Greeley, Horace, *Recollections of a Busy Life*. New York, 1868.
Green, Constance M., *Washington: Village and Capital, 1800–1873*. Princeton, N.J., 1962.
Green, Deran, *Old Houses on Radcliff Street*. Bristol, Pa., 1938.
———, *A History of Bristol Borough*. Bristol, Pa., 1911.
Gunderson, Robert G., *Old Gentlemen's Convention: The Washington Peace Conference of 1861*. Madison, Wis., 1961.
———, *The Log Cabin Campaign*. Lexington, Ky., 1957.
Hamilton, Holman, *Zachary Taylor, Soldier in the White House*. Indianapolis, 1951.
Hammand, Jabez D., *Life and Times of Silas Wright*. Syracuse, N.Y., 1848.
Hammond, Bray, *Banks and Politics in America*. Princeton, N.J., 1957.
Harvey, Peter, *Reminiscences and Anecdotes of Daniel Webster*. Boston, 1890.
Haskell, Daniel C., *The United States Exploring Expedition, 1838–1842, and Its Publications, 1844–1874*. New York, 1942.
Hesseltine, William B., *The Rise and Fall of Third Parties*. Washington, 1948.
Hill, Joseph J., *The History of Warner's Ranch and Its Environs*. Los Angeles, 1927.
Hofstadter, Richard M., *The American Political Tradition and the Men Who Made It*. New York, 1949.
Hopkins, James H., *Political Parties in the United States*. New York, 1900.

Houston, David F., *A Critical Study of Nullification in South Carolina.* Cambridge, Mass., 1896.
James, Marquis, *Andrew Jackson, Portrait of a President.* Indianapolis, 1937.
Jones, John B., *A Rebel War Clerk's Diary.* Philadelphia, 1866.
Kane, Joseph N., *Facts about the Presidents.* New York, 1959.
Kennedy, John F., *Profiles in Courage.* New York, 1956.
Klein, Philip S., *President James Buchanan.* University Park, Pa., 1962.
Langford, Laura Holloway, *The Ladies of the White House.* Philadelphia, 1881.
Levin, Peter R., *Seven By Chance: The Accidental Presidents.* New York, 1948.
Lynch, Jeremiah, *Life of David C. Broderick.* New York, 1911.
McCarthy, Charles, *The Antimasonic Party, 1827-1840.* Washington, 1903.
McCormac, Eugene I., *James K. Polk.* Berkeley, 1922.
McGrane, R. C. (ed.), *Correspondence of Nicholas Biddle Dealing with National Affairs.* Boston, 1919.
Meyer, L. W., *Life and Times of Col. Richard M. Johnson.* New York, 1932.
Moore, Frank (ed.), *The Rebellion Record: A Diary of American Events.* 3 vols. New York, 1862.
Morris, Richard B. (ed.), *Alexander Hamilton and the Founding of the Nation.* New York, 1957.
Myers, Gustavus, *History of Tammany Hall.* New York, 1901.
Nevins, Allan, *Ordeal of the Union.* 2 vols. New York, 1947.
────── (ed.), *The Diary of Philip Hone.* 2 vols. New York, 1927.
────── and Thomas, Milton H. (eds.), *The Diary of George Templeton Strong.* 3 vols. New York, 1952.
Nichols, Alice, *Bleeding Kansas.* New York, 1954.
Nichols, Roy F., *Franklin Pierce.* Philadelphia, 1958.
──────, *The Disruption of American Democracy.* New York, 1948.
──────, *The Stakes of Power, 1845-1877.* New York, 1961.
Nicolay, John G. and Hay, John, (eds.), *The Complete Works of Abraham Lincoln.* 12 vols. New York, 1905.
Overdyke, W. D., *The Know-Nothing Party in the South.* Baton Rouge, La., 1950.
Paul, James C. N., *Rift in the Democracy.* Philadelphia, 1951.
Pelletreau, William S., *History of East Hampton Town.* New York, 1882.
Phillips, Mary E., *Edgar Allan Poe—the Man.* 2 vols. Philadelphia, 1926.
Poage, George R., *Henry Clay and the Whig Party.* Chapel Hill, N.C., 1936.
Pond, George E., *The Shenandoah Valley in 1864.* New York, 1883.
Poore, Benjamin Perley, *Reminiscences.* 2 vols. New York, 1886.
Porter, Charles H., "The Operations of Generals Sigel and Hunter in the Shenandoah Valley, May and June, 1864," *Papers of the Military Historical Society of Massachusetts. The Shenandoah Campaigns of 1862 and 1864; and the Appomattox Campaign of 1865.* Boston, 1907.
Potter, David, *Lincoln and His Party in the Secession Crisis.* New Haven, 1942.
Preston, Walter C., *Lee: West Point and Lexington.* Yellow Springs, Ohio, 1934.
Quaife, Milo M. (ed.), *The Diary of James K. Polk.* 4 vols. Chicago, 1910.
Rantoul, R. S., *Personal Recollections.* Cambridge, Mass., 1916.
Rayback, Robert J., *Millard Fillmore.* Buffalo, N.Y., 1959.
Remini, Robert V., *Martin Van Buren and the Making of the Democratic Party.* New York, 1959.
Rives, George L., *The United States and Mexico, 1821-1848.* 2 vols. New York, 1913.
Roseboom, Eugene, *A History of Presidential Elections.* New York, 1959.
Royall, Anne, *Letters From Alabama.* Washington, 1830.
Sandburg, Carl, *Abraham Lincoln: The War Years.* 4 vols. New York, 1939.
Sargent, Nathan, *Public Men and Events.* 2 vols. Philadelphia, 1875.

Schlesinger, Arthur M., Jr., *The Age of Jackson.* Boston, 1946.
Schurz, Carl, *Life of Henry Clay.* 2 vols. Boston, 1887.
Scisco, Louis D., *Political Nativism in New York State.* New York, 1901.
Scrugham, Mary, *The Peaceable Americans of 1860–1861.* New York, 1921.
Sellers, Charles G., *James K. Polk, Jacksonian, 1795–1843.* New York, 1957.
Seward, William H., *An Autobiography.* New York, 1891.
Shanks, Henry T., *The Secession Movement in Virginia, 1847–1861.* Richmond, 1934.
Shepard, Edward M., *Martin Van Buren.* Boston, 1889.
Simms, Henry H., *A Decade of Sectional Controversy, 1851–1861.* Durham, N.C., 1942.
———, *Emotion At High Tide: Abolition as a Controversial Factor, 1830–1845.* Richmond, 1960.
———, *Life of Robert M. T. Hunter.* Richmond, 1935.
———, *The Rise of the Whigs in Virginia, 1824–1840.* Richmond, 1929.
Singleton, Esther, *Story of the White House.* New York, 1907.
Smith, Arthur D. H., *Old Fuss and Feathers.* New York, 1937.
Smith, Justin H., *The Annexation of Texas.* New York, 1941.
———, *The War With Mexico.* 2 vols. New York, 1919.
Smith, Margaret Bayard, *The First Forty Years of Washington Society.* New York, 1906.
Smith, W. B., *Economic Aspects of the Second Bank of the United States.* Cambridge, Mass., 1953.
Stampp, Kenneth M., *The Causes of the Civil War.* New York, 1959.
Stanwood, Edward, *A History of Presidential Elections.* New York, 1892.
Stillwell, Lucille, *John Cabell Breckinridge.* Caldwell, Id., 1936.
Strode, Hudson, *Jefferson Davis.* 2 vols. New York, 1955, 1959.
Swisher, Carl B., *American Constitutional Development.* New York, 1943.
Taussig, F. W., *The Tariff History of the United States.* New York, 1909.
Thompson, Benjamin, *History of Long Island.* 2 vols. New York, 1843.
Van Deusen, Glyndon G., *The Jacksonian Era.* New York, 1959.
———, *The Life of Henry Clay.* Boston, 1937.
———, *Thurlow Weed: Wizard of the Lobby.* Boston, 1947.
Van Tyne, C. H. (ed.), *The Letters of Daniel Webster.* New York, 1902.
Webster, Daniel, *The Writings and Speeches of Daniel Webster.* 18 vols. (National Edition) Boston, 1905.
Webster, Fletcher, *The Private Correspondence of Daniel Webster.* Boston, 1857.
Weed, Harriet A. (ed), *Autobiography of Thurlow Weed.* New York, 1883.
Weinberg, Albert K., *Manifest Destiny: A Study of Nationalist Expansionism in American History.* Baltimore, 1935.
Wellington, Raynor G., *The Political and Sectional Influence of the Public Lands, 1828–1842.* Cambridge, Mass., 1914.
Whitton, Mary O., *First First Ladies, 1789–1865.* New York, 1948.
Wilkes, Charles, *Narrative of the United States Exploring Expedition.* 5 vols. Philadelphia, 1844.
———, *United States Exploring Expedition.* Vol. XXIII. Hydrography. Philadelphia, 1861.
Wiltse, Charles M., *John C. Calhoun.* 3 vols. Indianapolis, 1944–1951.
Wise, Barton H., *The Life of Henry A. Wise of Virginia, 1806–1876.* New York, 1899.
Wise, John S., *Recollections of Thirteen Presidents.* New York, 1906.
Woodburn, James A., *Political Parties and Party Problems in the United States.* New York, 1924.
Woodford, Frank B., *Lewis Cass, the Last Jeffersonian.* New Brunswick, N.J., 1950.

INDEX

Abell, A. G., 226; *Life of John Tyler*, 226; patronage appointment, 589
Abolitionists, 104–105, 302; in Democratic Party, 394; reaction to Fugitive Slave Act, 396; James Hamlet case and, 398–400; English, 404; John Brown's trial, 428–430; 1860 election, 439–441
Adams, John Quincy, 25, 74, 142, 167, 170; nationalism, 79; "Corrupt Bargain" charge, 82; renomination, 82
Adams-Onís Treaty with Spain, 214
African Colonization Society, 109
African slave trade, 433–434
Agrarianism vs. capitalism, 66
Aiken, Gen. H. K., 485
Alabama, 446, 448
Albany Regency, 227–228, 266, 278
Allen, William Gaston, 637–638n
Ambrister, Robert C., 67–68
American and Foreign Anti-Slavery Society, 398, 400
American Missionary Society, 516
American Party, 410, 413
American Colonization Society, 404
American System, 62–63, 110; national economic self-sufficiency and, 63; Tyler's opposition, 65–66, 71, 80, 85; Adams and, 74–75
Anderson, Major Robert, 455
Animals, Tyler's fondness for, 305–306, 357, 593n, 604n
Annapolis (Md.) Convention, 51
Anti-Masons, 109, 117
Appointment power of Presidents, 83–85
Appomattox (Va.) battle, 507–508
Arbuthnot, Alexander, 67
Arbuthnot, British Admiral Marriot, 22
Arkansas, 451
Articles of Confederation, 51
Ashburton, Lord, 175, 322–323
Assembly balls in Washington, 191–192
Astor family, 354, 366
Atwood, Henry C.; entertains Tyler, 592, 597–598

Bacourt, Chevalier de, 175
Badger, George E., 143
Bailey, J. J., 14, 197
Baldwin, Judge Henry, 189, 198
Baldwin, John B., 462
Baltimore, Md., Convention of 1835, 118; depression of 1837, 129; nominating conventions, 218–219; 1844 Democratic Convention, 228–229; Democratic Convention of 1848, 392; 1852 Democratic Convention, 401; Democratic Convention of 1860, 438
Bancroft, George, 305, 317
Bank crisis of 1841, 151–156
Bank of the United States, 425; first, 54–55; chartered by Congress, 55; second, 63–64, 65, 88; charter renewal in 1832, 88–89; investigations of, 88, 111; Jackson's veto message, 89; government deposits removed by Jackson, 97–101; Tyler disliked, 88, 97–98; campaign of 1840, 137–139
Bankruptcy Act of 1842, 169–170, 183
Banks, N. P., 411
Banks, Sir Thomas, 18
Banks and banking; Fiscal Corporation Bill, 157–159
(*See also* Bank of the United States; National Bank question)
Barnard, Daniel D., 579
Barnum, P. T., 354
Barston, Capt. Wilson, 477–478
Bayard, Caroline, 255
Bayard, James A., 438–439
Bayard, Richard H., 579
Bayley, Thomas H., 323
Beach, Moses Y., 45
Bean, Major Benjamin W., 376–377, 380, 382, 616n
Beauregard, General P. G. T., 462, 497
Bedell, Dr. Gregory Thurston, 1, 4, 242, 346, 388
Beeckman, Catherine Livingston, 343–344

655

Beeckman, Gilbert, 343–344, 346–347, 348–349, 524, 611; desire for patronage appointment, 347; letters about Sacramento, Calif., 375–376

Beeckman, Henry Gardiner ("Harry"), 348, 418, 421, 428, 442–443, 466, 480, 485, 497, 611n, 642n; inheritance from grandmother, 502; education in Germany, 512, 523–530; indiscretion in money matters, 524–525; decline and death of, 536, 543–544

Beeckman, John H., 254, 329, 343–348, 420; family background, 344–345; death, 346, 348, 378, 617n; financial position, 375, 379–380; California experiences, 376–380, 616n; estate of, 378–380, 389

Beeckman, Margaret Foster, 611n

Beeckman, Margaret Gardiner; on Tyler-Julia Gardiner age difference, 14, 558n; recollective powers, 183, 579n; low opinion of Tyler's poetry, 198, 581n; marriage, 346; birth of son, 348; return to Lafayette Place house, 375; death of husband, 379; death of Alexander, 388–389, 619n; on Julia's health, 403; on Buchanan, 412; vacations with the Tylers, 418–419; Julia's attempt at matchmaking, 419; death, 420–421, 623n; laments loss of franking privilege, 601–602n

(*See also* Gardiner, Margaret)

Bell, John, 143, 439, 441, 445

Benton, Thomas Hart, 101, 110–111, 156, 185, 205, 282

Bermuda during the Civil War, 482–484, 499

Bertrand, Henri, 175–176

Biddle, Nicholas, 88, 97–98, 111

Big Bethel (Va.), battle, 468

Bill of Rights, 52

Bills, passed over Presidential veto, 283

Biographies of Tyler, 226, 320, 536, 589n, 642n; *Secret History of the Tyler Dynasty* (Cumming), 226, 320, 589n; Tyler's plan for, 424

Birney, James G., 239–240

"Black Republicans," 412, 426, 428, 434, 436

(*See also* Republican Party)

Blair, Francis P., 83, 191, 220–221, 237, 264, 315

Bleeker, John, 384–386, 390; political aspirations, 386

Blockade during Civil War, 482–483, 487

Bodine, Polly, 5

Bodisco, Russian Ambassador, Count de, 193

Bodisco, Madame de, 42, 177, 263, 581n

Bogert and Mecamly, 35

Bolton, Commodore William C., 11, 558

Border states, 448–449

Boston, Massachusetts, depression of 1837, 129; Civil War causes and, 430–431

Boston (Mass.) *Times*, 405

Botts, Alexander L., 272

Botts, John Minor, 154–157, 169; attacks Tyler, 138, 573n

Botts Compromise, 154

Bouck, William C., 220–221, 270

Boycott of Northern textiles, 431

Brazoria (Tex.) pitcher given to Tyler, 322

Breckinridge, John C., 440–441, 445; Vice-Presidential nomination, 411–412; in command of Confederate troops, 494, 496, 525

Brent, Richard, 55–56

Brockenbrough, John W., 450, 457

Broderick, David H., 238, 280; patronage appointment, 592n, 599–600n

Brooklyn, New York, 271; patronage appointments at Navy Yard, 285–286; Christ Church, 349; Gardiner family resides in, 389

Brooklyn, USS, 452

Brooklyn (N.Y.) *Daily News*, 36

Brooklyn (N.Y.) *Eagle*, 553

Brooks, James, 385

Brougham, Lord, 321

Brown, B. G., 535

Brown, Gustavus, 398

Brown, John, 428–432; raid at Harpers Ferry, 417, 428–432

Brown, Mary, 398

Brown, Thompson S., 342

Bruen, James, 342–343

Brumley, Eliza Gardiner, 30, 561–562

Brumley, Reuben, 561–562

Buchan, Sir John, 38, 450

Buchanan, President James, 156, 180, 185, 318, 355, 452, 455, 458, 465, 580–581n; Baltimore Convention of 1848, 392; quest for Democracy's nomination in 1852, 400; Robert Tyler

656

worked for nomination of, 401; Ambassador to England, 402, 406; administration, 410, 414; nomination in 1856, 411-412; Tyler supported, 411; platform, 411-412; election of, 413-415; patronage appointments, 414-416; Cabinet, 415; sent troops to Harpers Ferry, 428; renomination possibility, 436; pacification proposals of 1860, 447; role in secession, 448; aid offered Robert Tyler, 517
Budget, national, 166
Bull Run (Va.) battles, 469, 477
Bulwer, Sir Henry Lytton and Lady, 352
Bunker Hill monument, 200, 227
Butler, Benjamin F., 37
Butler, Gen. Benjamin, 488-493, 497
Butler, William O., 392
Butteville (Calif.) land speculation, 377-378, 380

Cabinets, 1841, 164; Tyler's, 393; resignation of, 160-161, 393; Buchanan, 415
Calhoun, John C., 8, 22, 74, 94, 156, 272, 324, 426; Vice-Presidential candidate, 75, 82; States' rights advocate, 82, 87; break with Jackson, 87; resignation from Vice-Presidency, 90; on nullification and secession, 92-96; compromise tariff settlement, 95-96; "South Carolina Exposition and Protest," 96; member of Whig coalition, 117; political talks with Sen. David Gardiner, 184-185, 579n; slavery views, 215; appointed Secretary of State, 217-218; Texas treaty vote, 229; social affairs, 246; takes credit for Texas annexation, 324-325
Calhoun, Floride, 87
"Calico Balls," 431
California, 521; admittance to Union, 326, 393, 407; annexation plan, 210-212; gold mining, 381; merchandising 381, 383; slavery question, 393
California gold rush, 345-346, 373-386; announced by Polk, 373; gold fever, 373-374; John H. Beeckman, 373-380; David Lyon Gardiner, 381-386; real estate speculations, 382-386

Campaigns, Presidential, of 1840, 135-140; of 1844, 237-40, 266, 280, 312; of 1852, 401-402; of 1856, 426 (*See also* Elections)
Campbell, Allan, 517, 541, 606, 628-629, 637
Campbell, John L., 483
Campbell, Julia Cooper, 465, 606, 628-629, 637
Canada, Confederacy efforts conducted from, 518
Canott, Charles H., 584
Carlisle, Countess of, 403
Carpetbaggers, 530, 535
Carr, Thomas N., 239
Casey, Samuel, 362, 365, 367-368
Caseyville, Kentucky, coal and timber land, 296, 361-372; attempts to sell, 362-365, 372; mineral survey, 362-363; land purchased by Tyler, 362; Tyler-Gardiner partnership to develop, 363-364; Tilford and Samuels agent for, 363-364; land evaluated by N. M. Miller, 364; Alexander purchased half of Tyler's interest, 365, 368; trip of Tyler and Alexander to, 366-367; coal deposits, 367; timber-cutting operations, 367-368; joint stock company formed, 368; Alexander's second trip, 369; Fenton placed in charge, 369; lumber-cutting project, 369-372; damage done by floods, 371-372; operating expenses, 371; legal problems, 372-373, 615n; Alexander left interest to Julia, 388
Cass, Lewis, 37, 38, 117, 193, 222, 228, 391, 393; Presidential nomination, 391-392
Castleton Hill, Staten Island, 542, 619-620n, 637n; Tyler children evacuated to, 421, 471-472, 477, 484-485; Delafield incident over Confederate flag, 508-510; Semple cared for, 519
Caucus system of nominating Presidential candidates, 74
Chagaray Institute for young ladies, 29-30
Chalmers, Belle, 540
Chancellorsville (Va.) battle, 480
Charles City, Virginia, 336, 431, 445-446, 451, 460, 467, 488; Tyler studied law, 50; Tyler elected overseer of roads, 390-391; John Brown's trial,

657

428–432; Union destruction, 489–490
Charles City County (Va.) Cavalry, 429, 463
Charles City County, Virginia, 48, 293, 626n; panic following Lincoln's election, 445; John Brown's trial, 428–432
Charleston, South Carolina, 448, 452; 1860 Democratic Convention, 435–438; Fort Sumter, 462–463
Charlottesville, Virginia, 118
Chase, Salmon P., 394
China, trade treaty with, 211
Christian, Judge John B., 131, 155, 163
Christian, Letitia, 56–57
(See also Tyler, Letitia Christian)
Christian, Robert, 56
Christmas holidays at Sherwood Forest, 250, 422–423
Chronicle of the Town of East Hampton (Gardiner), 553
Cincinnati, Ohio, Democratic Convention of 1856, 410–412
Civil War, threat of, 94; Tyler's attempts to stave off, 394, 447–472; events leading to, 417–446; John Brown's raid, 427–432; causes, 452; Fort Sumter, 462–463; participation by Tyler-Gardiner families, 465–466; Peninsula campaigns, 475–485; federal blockade, 481; Anglo-French intervention, 481; campaigns of 1864, 488–500; amnesty oaths after, 512, 518
(See also Confederate States of America; Reconstruction)
Clare, Thomas J., 398
Clark, Matthew St. C., 605
Class privilege, 83, 122
Clay, Henry, 12, 62–63, 74, 78, 80, 86, 90, 94, 107, 116, 156, 307, 437; on the tariff of 1820, 66; appointed Secretary of State, 75–76; "corrupt bargain" charge, 75–76, 78; Tyler's letter of congratulation (1825), 76, 81; campaign for Bank charter renewal, 88–89; campaign for Presidency, 90, 129–134, 236; compromise tariff settlement, 95–96; Tyler's personal feelings for, 97, 152, 426; resolutions to censure Taney and Jackson, 98–101; Granger nominated by, 120; Great Compromiser, 130; supported Rives for Senate seat, 131; attempts to dominate Harrison, 142–146; struggle with Tyler for power, 150–171; Bank plan, 150–156; attempt to seize control of Whig leadership, 151–152; power position, 152–153; Tyler castigated by, 156–157; planned walkout of Tyler's Cabinet, 160–161; Congress dominated by, 165; Distribution Act of 1841, 166–167; nomination of, 218; "Raleigh letter," 218; defeat, 241–242; election of 1848, 391; Compromise of 1850, 394; tribute to, 426
Clayton, John M., 134, 143
Clingman, Thomas J., 253
Clinton, Governor DeWitt, 81
Clinton, Governor George, 344
Clinton Academy, East Hampton, N.Y., 22, 24, 26
Clopton, John, 432
Clopton, William H., 489–493
Coal and timber speculations, 361–372
Cody, Charles, 588–589
"Coffee House Letter" written by Botts, 156–157, 159
Commercial agreements signed by Tyler, 211
Compromise of 1850, 394–397, 410–411, 433, 445; extremists and, 396–397
Compromise Tariff Bill of 1833, 96, 116, 129, 132, 138, 166–167
Confederate "Committee of Correspondence," 518
Confederate Congress, 469, 488; election of Tyler to, 268
Confederate States of America, 450, 458, 461, 464; boycott of Northern textiles, 431; in 1863, 478–481; inflation, 487–488; defeat of, 489–510; hope for negotiated peace, 497; last days, 507–510; Julia accused of possessing flag, 508–510; attitudes after end of war, 511–512; adjustments during Reconstruction, 517
Confederacy (*see* Confederate States of America)
Conger, Mary, 46, 357
Congress, first Bank of the United States chartered by, 55; doctrine of "implied powers," 55, 65; regulation of slavery, 71; stalemate between

Tyler and (1842), 165–166; debates, 182–184; slavery controversy and, 407
(*See also* House of Representatives; and Senate)
Connecticut Company, 2, 18, 19
Conservative Democrats, 46, 219, 279 312–313, 396, 534, 550; Tyler's rapprochement with, 220; anti-Van Buren bloc, 221; New York, 270
(*See also* Democratic Party)
Constitution, Tyler's views on, 50, 51–52, 148, 247, 455; checks and balances, 52; ratification opposed by Judge Tyler, 52; Tyler's speech on, 61; *M'Culloch v. Maryland* decision, 65; Jackson's interpretation, 81; Tyler as strict constructionist, 148, 247, 455; Lincoln on, 458
Constitutional Amendments, Thirteenth, 528; Fourteenth, 518, 528, 533; Fifteenth, 533; on slavery expansion, 447–460
Constitutional history, Texas Resolution and, 247
Constitutional Union Party, 439, 441, 450
Conventions, 1835 in Baltimore, 118; Whig (1839), 132–135; 1844 Democratic in Baltimore, 228–229; 1848 Democratic, 392; 1852 Democratic, 401; Virginia State Democratic, 401; 1856 Democratic in Cincinnati, 410–412; 1860 Democratic in Charleston, 435; 1860 Democratic in Baltimore, 438; 1872 Democratic in Baltimore, 535
Cooper, James Fenimore, 600–601
Cooper, Louisa, 487, 502
Cooper, Priscilla, 123–126
(*See also* Tyler, Priscilla Cooper)
Cooper, Thomas A., 124–126, 162, 178, 194, 195; patronage appointment, 226, 315–316, 332, 588*n*; retirement, 316, 605*n*
Copperheads, 431, 463, 481, 487, 502–503, 509–510
Corcoran and Riggs, bankers, 362, 365; option on Caseyville land, 362–363; sold land back to Tyler, 368–369
Corn Laws in England, 330–331
Cornubia, CSS, 482–483, 485, 631*n*
"Corporal's Guard," 152, 159, 164, 170, 226, 256, 402, 434; patronage appointments, 588–589*n*
Corse, Mary, 46, 253, 255
Cotton-monopoly and Texas annexation, 215–216
"Court" ladies, 249–257, 289
Covington (Va.) episode, 483, 488
Crawford, William H., 74–75, 78
Creel, Alexandra Diodati Gardiner, 626*n*, 646*n*
Creel, Judge J. Randall, 626*n*
Crimean War, 299, 406
Crittenden, John J., 143, 158–159, 167, 447–448
Crittenden amendment, 448, 456–457, 464
Crolius, Clarkson, 593*n*
Cruikshank, William, 553
Cumming, Hiram, 226, 320, 589*n*; *Secret History of the Tyler Dynasty*, 226, 320, 589*n*
Cunningham, John S., 397, 400, 405, 437
Currency question, 164
Curtis, Christiana Tyler, 64
Curtis, Edward, 145, 201, 221, 232–233, 239
Curtis, Dr. Henry, 297, 358, 374; Tyler's letters to, 57, 64, 69, 71–72, 81, 103, 358
Cushing, Caleb, 41, 164, 170, 183–184, 200, 211, 253, 256, 430, 440, 579*n*; gift to Tyler, 211, 585*n*; marriage, 256, 596*n*; romantic endeavors, 304, 604*n*; visit to Sherwood Forest, 304–305; appointed Attorney General, 402; Tyler gives papers to, 424; letters to, 446; rejected for Cabinet post, 589*n*
Cushing, Caroline Wilde, 596*n*

Dallas, George M., 264
Dances, 244, 340; Assembly balls, Washington, 191–192
Daubresse, Rev. Father, 539
Davis, Henry, 44
Davis, Jefferson, 54, 367, 394, 402, 458, 464–465, 468, 472, 483, 499, 507–508; in prison, 511, 518, 535; parole, 528
Davis, Richard D., 41, 184, 186–187, 579*n*, 584*n*
Davis, Varina Howell, 481, 518, 578*n*, 634–635*n*; during Reconstruction, 511
Dayton, Daniel, 272

Dayton, Egbert, 272, 375, 616n
Dayton, Dr. John N., 273–277
Dayton, Ralph, 484, 504, 508
"Dead of the Cabinet, The," speech by Tyler, 426
Dearing, Marion Antoinette, 259
De Bow, James D. B., 436
Delafield, Bertram, 508–510
Delancy, Becky, 254
Democratic Empire Club, 280
Democratic Executive Committee, 415–416, 434
Democratic Party; Conservative Democrats, 46, 117, 129, 161, 163, 396; Jacksonian Democracy, 46, 53, 81, 100–101; Virginia, 81, 400–401; renounced by Tyler, 100; Jeffersonian Democracy, 116; Locofocoism, 117, 128–129, 136; nomination of Van Buren, 118; radical element, 129, 394; renomination of Van Buren, 138–139; Southern, 162–163; convention in Baltimore (1844), 228–229; sectionalism, 314–315, 400; Van Buren faction, 391; 1848 split, 392; must maintain unity, 394; Tyler urges expulsion of extreme elements, 394; Union committees, 395; campaign of 1852, 401–402; election of Pierce, 402; effect of Kansas-Nebraska Bill on, 406; disintegration of, 408, 414; divided on slavery issue, 409; 1856 Convention in Cincinnati, 410–412; Pennsylvania-Virginia alliance, 410–411, 435; need for unification in 1860, 434–446; 1860 Convention at Charleston, 435; 1860 split, 436–440; 1860 Baltimore Convention, 440; corruption in early 1870s, 534; defeat in 1871, 534–535; election of 1872, 535; election of 1876, 550 (*See also* Conservative Democrats)
Democratic Republican (Tyler) third party, 218–219; convention in Baltimore (1844), 228
Denison, Alice Tyler, 349–350, 610n, 637–638n; marriage, 349
Denison, Elizabeth ("Bessy"), 350, 610n, 623–624n, 637–638n
Denison, Rev. Henry M., 349–350, 388, 417, 420, 426
Denison, William M., 610, 623–624, 637–638
Depressions, 65, 127, 129–130

Derby, Countess of, 403
Dering, Henry T., 272–273
Dering, Sarah, 26
De Russy, Col. Gustavus A., 10, 558n
Dew, Thomas R., 106–107
Dickinson, Daniel S., 308, 385
Dimick, Justin, 443
Dinneen, Rev. Father, 555
Distribution Act of 1841, 166–167, 170
Divorce rumor, 335–336
Dix, Gen. John A., 477–478, 481–482, 486, 509
Doctrine of "implied powers," 55, 65
Doctrine of Instructions, 110–115, 570n
Dodge, William E., 458
Donahoe, Rev. Father Charles E., 555
Donelson, Andrew J., 83, 89, 320, 591n
Donelson, Emily, 107
Doniphan, Alexander W., 454
Douglas, Stephen A., 252, 255, 394, 433, 437; Kansas-Nebraska Bill, 406; popular sovereignty doctrine, 406–408; debate with Lincoln, 433; Freeport Doctrine, 433; nomination, 438, 440; marriages, 595n
Douthat, Robert, 429, 463, 489
Downing, Andrew J., 294
Dred Scott decision, 433, 439
Dromgoole, George C., 323
"Duchess, The," popular song, 405
Duels, 253
Dychman, Jacob G., 24

Early, Gen. Jubal A., 489, 496, 498
East Hampton, Long Island, New York, 348, 359, 544; residence of Gardiners, 2, 388; news of the wedding, 6; Gardiner family, 17–47; Clinton Academy, 22, 24, 26; reaction to Julia Gardiner's romance, 200–203; Tyler's visit to, 309, 335; cemetery, 400, 553–554
Eastman, Ira A., 184, 579n
Eaton, John H., 87
Eaton, Peggy O'Neale, 87
Edwards, Judge Ogden, 197, 270, 342
Eldridge, Dr. N. T., 279
Elections, of 1824, 75, 171; of 1828, 82; of 1832, 90; of 1836, 120–121; of 1840, 140; of 1842, 170, 220–221; of 1848, 391–392; of 1852, 401–402; of 1856, 410–416; of 1860, 432–433, 436, 438–441; of 1872, 535; of 1876, 550
Electoral College, 75, 441
Elliot, Commodore Jesse D., 249
Ellis, Judge Chesselden, 235

Ellis, Pearl Tyler (Pearlie), 552, 643n
Ellis, Maj. William Mumford, 552
Ely, Rev. Samuel R., 34, 220
Empire Club, 280–281, 291
English, Thomas Dunn, 222–223, 235, 279, 590n
English-American relations, 327–331, 468 (*See also* Great Britain)
Equal Rights Party, 128–129
Erie Canal, 81
Essex, ferryboat, 5
Evarts, William M., 503, 541, 544–551, 634–635n
Everett, Edward, 430, 439
Ewing, Thomas, 143, 152, 158, 393, 454
Executive role, 83, 144
Expunging Act, 132
Expunging resolution, 110–115, 570n

Fairlee, Major James, 124
Farmer's Reporter, 298
Farming operations, Sherwood Forest, 298–300
Farnum Iron Works, 364
Federalist principles, 50, 163, 393
Fenton, Andrew J., 369–372
Ferguson, A. H., 489
Ferris, Charles G., 597–598
Fillmore, Caroline, 547, 549
Fillmore, President Millard, 41–42, 116, 133, 355, 410, 413; administration, 385, 396; Vice-Presidential nomination, 392; accedes to the Presidency, 395; patronage appointments, 396; election of 1856, 412
Finley, John, 225
Fiscal Corporation Bill, 157–159; veto by Tyler, 159–160
Fisher, Redwood, 221, 224
Fitzwalter, Robert, 18
Fleurot, George, 642–643n
Florida, 448; invasion by Jackson, 67, 87
Floyd, Governor John, 92–94
Floyd, Governor John Buchanan, 353, 355, 400
Foote, Henry S., 367, 394–396, 400
Force Bill of 1833, 91–94, 132, 397, 450; Tyler's speech against, 93–94
Fordham, Peletiah ("The Duke"), 273–277
Forrest, Edmund, 124
Fort Fisher (N.C.), 487, 507
Fort Sumter (S.C.), 448, 462; South Carolina demands surrender, 452–453; surrender of, 455; crisis, 457
Fort Warren Prison, Boston, 483, 485–486
Fortress Monroe (Va.), 360, 442, 452, 467, 476, 481, 489, 491
Fowler, John O., 221, 224, 269, 587n, 591n, 597–598n
Fox hunting at Sherwood Forest, 347, 351
France, 50, 481; Louisiana territory acquired from, 69–70
Frankford, Pennsylvania, Arsenal, 178, 464
Frankfort, Kentucky, 367
Franking privilege, 249, 601–602n
Free Soil Party, 392, 394, 402
Free trade, 50, 65–66, 210–211
Freedmen's Bureau, 516
Freemasonry, 117
Freeport Doctrine, 433
Frémont, John C., 220, 411
"Friends of the Union and Constitution," 431
Fugitive Slave Act, 394, 396, 412; James Hamlet case, 397–400
Fuller's Hotel, Washington, 291
Fulton, Rev. John, 512–513, 523

Gage, General Thomas, 21
Gardiner, Col. Abraham (1722–1782), 559n
Gardiner, Capt. Abraham (1763–1796), 22, 559n
Gardiner, Abraham (1782–1827), 559n
Gardiner, Alexander, 4, 6, 25, 206–207, 266–288, 466; makes arrangements for sister's marriage, 1–2; temperament and character, 27–28; political interests, 27, 40, 197, 208, 266–288; education, 28–32; law training, 31–32, 202, 284, 287, 562n; joined Democratic Party, 46–47; social life in New York, 32–33; for Whigs in 1840, 140–141; on bank bills, 154; forwards Julia's love letters, 190, 580n; account of USS *Princeton* explosion, 204–205, 583n; patronage matters handled by, 226, 266, 269–272, 278, 283–288, 588–589n; New York City politics, 232–234, 250; Polk campaign, 237–238; try for elective office, 238–239, 241; pro-Texas annexation writings, 247–248, 281, 600n; relationship with mother, 254; pro-Tyler defenses in news-

papers, 264, 320–321; political analyses, 267; dedication to Tyler, 268–269, 341, 368, 387, 619n; saves hostile clipping, 271–272, 598n; financial condition, 284, 287; Circuit Court clerkship, 286, 318; loan from Julia, 287–288; visits to the White House, 289–290; contacts with Polk, 292; shopping commissions from Julia, 294, 337; Tammany Hall politics, 318; Mexican War, 328–330, 608n; hears false rumors of Tyler's marital difficulties, 335; romantic aspirations, 340–341; directed John Tyler's financial affairs, 341; coal and timber speculations, 361–372; business ability, 365–366; managed New York properties, 366; stock and real estate speculations, 366; social life, 370; death of, 372, 385–388, 400, 619n; interest in David Lyon's California business, 381, 383; Hamlet fugitive slave case, 388, 397–400; disposition of estate, 388; commissioner under Fugitive Slave Act, 397; views on slavery, 399; letters to the newspapers, 399; obituaries, 400; planned to do Tyler's biography, 424; financial relations with Thomas Dunn English, 590n

Gardiner, Charles, 598
Gardiner, Curtiss C., 344, 553–554
Gardiner, David (1691–1751), 20–21
Gardiner, Senator David (1784–1844), 22–47, 204, 559n; death of, 1–2, 205–208, 584n; marriage, 24; State Senator, 25–26; political ambitions, 25–27; wealth of, 45, 564n; on Congressional inactivity, 166; political talks with Calhoun, 184–185, 579n; estate, 207, 584n; *Chronicle of the Town of East Hampton*, 553
Gardiner, David (son of David Lyon Gardiner), 626n
Gardiner, David Johnson, 24, 644
Gardiner, David Lyon, 4, 25, 202, 206–207, 480; temperament and character, 27–28; education, 31–32, 562; political interests, 40, 385; visits to White House, 250; romantic interests, 254–255, 339–340; marriage, 254, 384, 421, 438, 502; financial condition, 284, 381; reaction to false rumors of Tyler's marital difficulties, 335; dancing lessons, 340; New York property managed by, 381; California adventures, 353, 381–390; real estate speculations, 382–386, 619–620n; agitated for customs house at San Diego, Calif., 383, 396; interest in family genealogy, 384, 553–554; death of Alexander, 385–386, 388; desired patronage appointment, 383, 385, 393, 396; home on Staten Island, 390, 505; supported Northern cause, 431, 451, 466; family quarrels, 477–478, 485, 553; litigation over Juliana's will, 500–507, 634–635n; Delafield affair, 509; during Reconstruction, 553; children, 626n
Gardiner, Elizabeth Stensin, 595n
Gardiner, John (1661–1738), 21, 559n
Gardiner, John Bray, 595n
Gardiner, John D., 272
Gardiner, John Griswold (1812–1861), 43–45, 564n, 644n
Gardiner, John Lyon (1770–1816), 21, 22, 466, 564n, 644n
Gardiner, Julia, marriage to President John Tyler, 1–16; reigning belle, 2; courtship of John Tyler and, 2, 192–208; education, 29–31; social debut, 30–31; poise and sophistication, 30–31; guitar playing, 34–35; European tour, 35–41; advertising lithograph of, 35–36; "Rose of Long Island" incident, 35–36; trip to Washington, 37, 41–43, 172–200; invitation to White House, 42–43, 192–200; first meeting with John Tyler, 43; social position, 45–46; birth, 72, 560; financial assistance, 103; romantic triumphs in Washington, 172–200; political views, 184–185; impression created by, 191; Tyler's proposals of marriage, 198–199; gifts and prerogatives, 249 (*See also* Tyler, Julia Gardiner)
Gardiner, Juliana McLachlan, 186, 242; gives permission for Julia's marriage, 2–3; letters to Julia, 9–11; temperament, 10, 24, 254; family background, 23–24; rental properties in New York City, 23, 287, 366, 381, 390, 540–541; contest over will, 23, 27, 485, 500–507; advice

to children, 9–11, 30; impressions of Washington society, 192–193, 581n; informed of husband's death, 206; visits to the White House, 250, 255–257; marital ambitions for children, 254–255, 339–340; possessiveness toward children, 254; desire to return to New York, 262–263; patronage suggestions, 270; inheritance, 287; on liveries, 295, 602n; medical diagnosis by mail, 296–297, 306, 336, 338; Margaret's marriage, 345; loaned Beeckman money for California trip, 375, 379–380; death of Alexander, 388; financial assistance to Tyler, 389; moves to Staten Island, 390; Tyler's visits to, 418; death of Margaret, 421; visits with the Tylers, 428, 442; opposition to David Lyon's marriage, 438; interest in spiritualism, 438; Southern sympathies, 451, 463, 466; during the Civil War, 473–475; care of Tyler children, 477, 480; family split, 485; death of, 500, 595n; relations with Julia, 503–504; on Sarah Polk, 599n
Gardiner, Lion (1599–1663), 2, 18, 51, 553–554
Gardiner, Margaret, 9–10, 25; bridesmaid, 4; accompanied newlyweds, 5; on Julia's marriage, 14; temperament, 27–28; European trip, 38–41; presentation at court of Louis Philippe, 38; marriage, 46, 254, 346; Washington season (1842–1843), 180–200; romantic attachments, 199–200, 253–254, 308–309, 341–348; life at the White House, 243–265, 289–292; political activity, 269–270; on Major W. H. Polk, 277; at Saratoga and Newport, 202–203, 307–309, 359, 418
(*See also* Beeckman, Margaret Gardiner)
Gardiner, Mary, 249–251, 420; marriage to Eben N. Horsford, 341
Gardiner, Mary Gardiner Thompson, 644n
Gardiner, Nathaniel, 36–37, 45, 388, 559n, 564n, 595n, 619n
Gardiner, Norah Loftus, 626
Gardiner, Phoebe, 249–252, 289–290, 341, 345
(*See also* Horsford, Phoebe Gardiner)
Gardiner, Phoebe Dayton, 559n
Gardiner, Robert Alexander, 626
Gardiner, Robert David Lion, 626
Gardiner, Samuel, 34, 45, 237, 249, 262, 272–277, 373, 559–560n, 595n, 619n
Gardiner, Samuel Burell, 544, 550, 644n
Gardiner, Sarah Diodati, 626n
Gardiner, Sarah Griswold, 24, 544, 553, 564n, 644n
Gardiner, Sarah Thompson, 626
Gardiner, William Bray, 393
Gardiner, Dr. William Henry, 388, 595n
Gardiner family, 17–47; wealth of, 17; genealogy of, 18, 26, 384, 553–554, 559n; New York City property, 23, 287, 366, 381, 390, 540–541; Washington season, 1842–1843, 180–200; calls at the White House, 192–200; in East Hampton (1843), 200–203; lobby for Tyler and Texas, 267–268; dissatisfaction with Polk administration, 312–318; background, 344; service during the Civil War, 466; books about, 553–554
Gardiners Island, 2, 17–18; history and folklore, 20–21; managed by Sen. David Gardiner, 24–25
Gardner, J. McLean, 203
Gardner, James B., 84
Garfield, James A., 548, 549
Garfield, James B., 548
Garfield, Lucretia Rudolph, 549
Garra Rebellion, 384
Garrison, William Lloyd, 458
Gayle, Capt. Robert H., 482, 484–487, 507, 509, 511–512, 631n
Gentle Julia, The (river boat), 417
George, Paul R., 221, 222, 224, 233, 587n, 590n, 592n
Georgetown College, 292, 436, 537
Georgetown home of Julia Tyler, 537, 543
Georgetown Visitation Academy, 537, 539
Georgia, 446, 448
German treaty, 211, 517
Germany, Tyler boys educated in, 512, 523–530; social life, 525–527; military successes, 525
Gettysburg (Pa.), 466, 480
Gibbon, James Cardinal, 539
Giles, William B., 55–56
Gilmer, Thomas W., 143, 152, 161, 205, 215, 217, 219, 417
Gloucester County (Va.) farm, 103
Godwin, William, 124
Goode, John, 547–548

Gordon, William F., 92, 570n
Gorgas, Col. and Mrs. Josiah, 482, 485
Graham, John Lorimer, 197, 221, 222, 224, 232–233, 237, 279, 290, 316, 324, 362, 598n, 605n; attends Tyler wedding, 3–4, 6; request for patronage, 393
Granger, Francis P., 117, 120, 121, 133, 143, 454, 580–581n
Grant, Julia Dent, 536
Grant, Ulysses S., 507; campaigns, 486, 488, 494–500; Julia Tyler's pleas to, 516; Julia's opinion of, 520–521; election of, 534–535; administration, 534–535, 537; "bloody shirt," 535
Great Britain, 468; Tyler's distrust of, 54, 67, 332, 396–397, 404–406; War of 1812, 58–59; diplomatic negotiations, 161; activities in Mexico, 210, 212; machinations in Texas, 216; Oregon question, 327–328; interference in U.S. domestic affairs, 396–397, 404–405; letter from English ladies on slavery, 402–406; Crimean War, 406; Webster-Ashburton Treaty (*See* Webster-Ashburton Treaty)
Great Eastern (British liner), 443
Greeley, Horace, 520, 535
Green, Duff, 82, 83, 150, 159, 181, 372
Greene, Gen. Moses, 59
Greenway (Tyler family estate), 48, 56, 58, 103
Grey, W. Farley, 431
Guthrie, James, 455–456
Gwin, William McKendree, 385–386

Haines, John, 181
Hall, Charles M., 397–399, 619–620n
Hallet, J. Paxton, 5–6, 221, 286–288, 587n, 591n
Hamilton, Alexander, 91; on national bank question, 55; doctrine of implied powers, 65
Hamilton, Alexander, Jr., 219
Hamiltonian Federalists, 82, 116
Hamlet, James (fugitive slave case), 388; hearing before Alexander Gardiner, 397–400
Hampton, Virginia, 421; Villa Margaret, 372
(*See also* Villa Margaret)
Hampton (Va.) Academy, 443
Haolilio, Prince Timoleo, 185, 211

Harpers Ferry, Virginia, 367, 428–432, 464
Harrisburg, Pennsylvania, Whig convention, 132–135
Harrison, Mrs. George, 295
Harrison, Peyton, 474
Harrison, Mr. and Mrs. William (Brandon, Va.), 297–298
Harrison, President William Henry, 40, 116, 118, 132; Presidential nomination, 114, 119–120, 132–134; legend of Old Tippecanoe, 119, 140; Tyler and the election of 1836, 120–122; campaign of 1840, 136–140; Clay's attempt to dominate, 142–146; patronage controversies, 142–144; Cabinet, 142–143; health, 142; inauguration, 144; opposes abuse of executive power, 144; death of, 146–148; funeral, 149–150
Harvard College, 251, 341
Harvie, Lewis E., 460
Hate groups, 109; Know-Nothing Party, 408–413
Hawaiian Islands, 185, 211, 226
Hayes, President Rutherford B., 546, 548; administration, 547–550; election of, 550
Hayes, Lucy Webb, 545
Hayne, Col. I. W., 452–453, 455
Hayne, Robert Y., 90, 117
Healy, G. P. A., 638n
Healy, Rev. Father Patrick F., S.J., 539–540, 546
Henderson, Lucy, 255
Hendren, Patrick, 362
Henry (Tyler slave), 403–404
Henshaw, David, rejected by Senate for Cabinet post, 589n
Herrick, Edwin, 616
Hill, Gen. A. P., 498
Hill, Isaac, 83, 84
Hoffman, Ogden, 221, 269, 597–598n
Holcombe James P. 462
Holloway, Laura, 536, 642n
Holt, Mrs. Henry, 493–494
Holt, Col. Joseph, 452, 490, 632–633n
Hone, Philip, 135
Horsford, Cornelia, 623–624
Horsford, Eben N., 251–252, 341, 474, 595n, 623–624n; attitude toward slavery, 623–624n
Horsford, Gertrude, 623–624n
Horsford, Lillian, 623–624n

Horsford, Mary Catherine, 623–624*n*
Horsford, Mary L'H. Gardiner (1824–1855), 249–251, 420, 559–560*n*, 595*n*, 623–624*n*
Horsford, Phoebe Gardiner, 442, 540, 544, 559–560*n*, 595*n*, 623–624*n*
House of Representatives, 413; hostility to Tyler, 10; Tyler's election (1816), 60–61; Texas Resolution passed by, 281
Houston, Sam, 210, 213–214, 325
Howard, D. D., 4
Howard, Gen. O. O. 516
Howell, Jenny, 481, 511, 629*n*
Hubard, Edmund W., 41, 184, 196–197, 579*n*
Hungarian Revolution, 406
"Hunker" Democracy, 312, 314
Hunt, Harvey, 241
Hunter, Gen. David, 494–496
Hunter, R. M. T., 436–437, 497–498

Impeachment talk, 167–169; Andrew Johnson, 528, 530
"Implied powers," doctrine of, 55, 65
Independent Treasury plan, 128–130, 132, 164; repeal of, 150–151, 156, 170
Indian land survey, 545
Indian wars, 18–19
Inflation, of 1835–1837, 128; during the Confederacy, 479–480, 487
Ingersoll, Charles J., 322
Instructions, doctrine of, 110–115, 570*n*; Tyler resigned Senate seat, 110–115
Internal-improvements program, 77; Adams administration, 79; veto of Maysville Road Bill, 85–86; government-financed, 86
Iredell, James, Jr., 118, 121, 137
Irish Repeal Association, 330, 436
Irish vote, 136, 233, 401, 436
Irving, Washington, 107, 171

Jackson, Andrew, 46, 60–62, 75, 575*n*; popular democracy of, 26, 74; removal of the Treasury deposits, 28–29, 97–101; on Constitution, 52; invasion of Spanish Florida, 67, 87; feared by Tyler, 67, 74; hero of New Orleans, 68; Tyler's motion to censure, 68; vote-catching image, 74; Tariff Bill of 1828, 79–80; Tyler's decision to support, 80–81; administration, 82–101; election of 1828, 82;
Calhoun nominated as Vice-President, 82; appointment policy, 83–84; Inaugural Address, 83; "Kitchen Cabinet," 83; social graces, 85; vetoed the Bank Bill in 1832, 87–89; break with Calhoun, 87; Proclamation to the People of So. Carolina, 90–91; election of 1832, 90; policy of armed coercion (Force Bill), 91–97; Tyler's indictment of, 98–100; Clay's resolution to censure, 98; political patronage, 99; political techniques, 100; Jeffersonian Democrats dislike of, 116; criticism of, 117; fiscal policies, 127–128; annexation of Texas, 218, 325; letter concerning Tyler and Polk, 232; Tyler's withdrawal, 236–237; assurance to Tyler on patronage, 312; death of, 320
Jackson, Rachel, 82
Jackson, Gen. Thomas J. (Stonewall), 480–481
Jacksonian Democracy, 46, 53; renounced by Tyler, 100–101; upheaval of 1828, 25–26
"James, Allan S." (pseud. of Semple James A.), 518–519
James City, Virginia, 451
James River, 293, 403
Jamestown (Va.) speech of Tyler's, 427
Japan, trade policy, 211
Jay, William, 398–399
Jefferson, Thomas, 51, 107; on national bank question, 55; political patronage, 83–84
Jeffersonian Democrats, 116
Jerusalem, Virginia, 303
Johnson, Gen. Albert S., 641
Johnson, President Andrew, 515; Julia Tyler writes to, 515; threat of impeachment, 528, 530; and Tenure of Office Act, 530
Johnson, Celia (Negro servant), 482, 492, 506
Johnson, Gen. Joseph E., 507
Johnson, Richard M., 60, 118, 121, 138, 139
Johnson, Col. William Preston, 641
Joinville, Prince de, 175
Jones, Henry Lightfoot, 12, 108, 465–466
Jones, John, 6, 227
Jones, Mary Morris, 552
Jones, Mary Tyler, 7–8, 12, 108, 125, 172, 466
Jones, Brig. Gen. William E., 494–495

"Julia—The Rose of Long Island" by "Romeo Ringdove," 36
"Julia Waltzes," 594n, 595n
Kansas-Nebraska controversy, 406–409, 433, 445
Karlsruhe, Germany, 522–527; social life, 526–527
Kean, Edmund, 124
Keating, James, 180
Kendall, Amos, 83, 84, 89, 220, 587n
Kennedy, President John F., 539
Kennon, Commodore Beverly, 205, 294, 419
Kentucky, coal and timber speculations, 361–362
Kettell, George F., 527
Kick, John, 493
Kidd, Capt. William, 21
King, Charles, 37, 563n
King, Thomas Butler, 41
"King Numbers" and "King One," Tyler's opinion on as political dangers, 62, 75, 82, 100, 122
"Kitchen Cabinet," 83, 89
Know-Nothing Party, 109, 408–413; 1856 Convention in Philadelphia, 410
Kossuth, Louis, 406
Kremer, George, 75–76
Kruder, Baron von, 39, 563n

Labor problems, lumber-cutting operation, in Caseyville, Ky., 369–372 (*See also* Slaves and slavery)
Ladies of the White House (Holloway), 536
Lafayette, Georges W., 563n
Lafayette Place (N.Y.C.) town house of Gardiners, 1–2, 5, 202–203, 342, 387, 583n; Margaret's return to, 375
Lamar, Mirabeau B., 264
Lamb, Martha J., 554
Lane, Frances ("Fanny") Gardiner, 559–560, 595
Lane, Joseph, 439–441
Langford, Laura C. Holloway, 536, 642n
Lawrence, Abbott, 145, 341
Lawton, Brig. Gen. A. R., 631
Lee, Henry, 84
Lee, General Robert E., 468, 476, 488, 494, 496, 507; president of Washington College, 529–530
Lee, Robert E., CSS, 482, 631n
Legaré, Caroline, 4
Legaré, Hugh Swinton, 4, 426

Leigh, Benjamin W., 101, 110–115, 132, 134–135
LeRoy, Anson V. H., 616–617n
Letcher, Gov. John, 437, 448, 451, 483, 496
Letcher, R. P., 153
Letson, T. William, 368
Letters and Times of the Tylers, The (Tyler), 552
Lewis, William B., 83
Lexington, Virginia, 478, 494, 496; riots, 528–529
Libby Prison, Richmond, 498–499
Liberia, 404
Life of John Tyler (Abell), 226
Lincoln, Abraham, 93, 135, 448; Tyler's reaction to election of, 413; debate with Douglas, 433; "House Divided" speech, 439–440, 444; nomination, 439; electoral count, 441; election of, 443–446; Tyler's views on, 457–458; Inaugural Address, 460–461; call for volunteers, 462; motives for Fort Sumter, 463; letters from Juliana Gardiner, 481; pleas from Julia Tyler, 490–491; assassination, 508–509
Lincoln, Mary Todd, pension received by, 547–549
Lind, Jenny, 354–355
Lion Gardiner and His Descendants (Gardiner), 344, 553
Livingston, Catherine, 343–344
Livingston, Henry B., 373, 375, 380; handled John H. Beeckman's estate, 378–379
Livingston, Mary, 32–33, 562
Locofocoism, 117, 128–129, 136
"Log Cabin and Hard Cider," slogan, 135
Lord, Dr. F. W., 273–277
Louis Philippe, 37; Gardiner presentation at court of, 38, 44
Louisiana, 451
Louisiana Purchase, 69–71, 214
Low, Sarah, 182
Ludlow, Louise, 473
Ludlow, Maj. William H., 473, 476
Lynch, Lt. Dominick, 356
Lynchburg, Virginia, 489, 496–497, 507
Lyons, James, 158, 469, 532, 535, 537, 636–637n

McCaw, Dr. J. B., 555
McClellan, Gen. George B., 473–476, 487; campaigns, 475–476

McClellan, Robert, 192
McCormick reapers, 299–300
M'Culloch v. Maryland, 65
McDowell, James, 93
McDuffie, George, 183, 216
Macfarland, William H., 469
McGuire, Dr. Edward, 555
McGuire, Dr. Hunter, 554–555
McKeon, John, 41, 180
McLachlan, Juliana, 23–24; marriage, 24
(*See also* Gardiner, Juliana McLachlan)
McLachlan, Michael, 23
McLean, Justice John, 117, 184, 188–191, 248, 257–258; romantic correspondence with Julia Gardiner, 190, 580n
McMullin, Fayette, 252
McMurdo, Mr., Scottish schoolmaster, 49
McNeill, William Gibbs, 285, 316, 368, 372, 507–508, 597–598n
Macon, Colonel John, 73
Madison, Dolley, 178, 204
Madison, President James, 60
Madisonian, The (Tyler newspaper in Washington), 6, 225, 227, 237, 242, 292, 313
Magazine of American History, 554
Maine, admission to the Union, 69; boundary question, 161, 212, 322–323
Major, Daniel G., 545
Majority principle in government, 61–62, 75, 82, 100–101, 122
Malaria, 370
Mallory, Charles B., 516
Mallory, Francis, 41, 170
Manassas, Virginia, 468
Manchonake (Gardiners) Island, 17, 19
Mangum, Willie P., 116, 135
Manhattan Bank in New York, 26
Manifest Destiny, 210, 214, 315, 425
Mann, A. Dudley, 436
Margraf, Alben N., 544
Marriage of President Tyler to Julia Gardiner, 1–16; secret arrangements, 1–2, 5–6; ceremony, 4–5; guests, 4, 6; effect of news of the wedding, 5–6; reaction of Tyler's family, 6–8; difference in ages, 14; gossip concerning, 14; honeymoon, 5–16; White House reception, 8–9
Marseilles, Alexander's interest in consulship at, 284–285

Marshall, Justice John, 52, 65, 91, 432
Marshall, Thomas F., 184
Mary Celestia, CSS, 499
Maryland Mechanics Institute, Baltimore, 425–426
Mason, John Thompson, 579n
Mason, John Y., 131, 246, 315, 319, 323
Mathewson, A. J., 542
Maury, Matthew Fontaine, 556
Maxcy, Virgil, 205
Maysville (Ky.) Turnpike Road Company, 85–86
Memminger, Christopher G., 431
Memphis (Tenn.) Navy Yard, 364
"Mere majority principle" in government, 62, 101
Merrick, William D., 264
Merrick, William Matthew, 264
Metcalf, Governor Robert, 367
Mexican War of 1846–1848, 299, 314, 323, 327–330; New York Volunteers, 329
Mexico, annexation of Texas and, 214–215; Emperor Maximilian, 512
Military career of John Tyler, 58–60
Miller, John G., 120
Miller, Dr. N. M., 313, 317, 324; patronage appointments, 226, 588–589n; Caseyville land evaluated by, 364
Miller, Sylvanus, 22
Millson, John Singleton, 408
Minge, Collier H., 225
Minge, John, 226
Mississippi, 448
Missouri, admission to the Union, 69
Missouri Compromise, 331, 406–407; debate, 69–71; Thomas Amendment, 70–71; Tyler opposed limitation on slavery, 407
Monroe, President James, 472, 556
Monroe Doctrine, 211, 281
Montgomery (Ala.) *Advertiser*, 517
Moore, Edwin Ward, 264
Moore, Ely, 270
Morehead, Gov. Charles S., 454
Morgan, William S., 570n
Morris, R. H., 597–598n
Morris, Richard, 78
Morrison, David, 364
Morse, Samuel F. B., 229
Moss, C. B., 594n
Moss, Samuel, 616n
Mott, Robert, 354
Mulford, Burnet, 25

667

Mulford, Brig. Gen. John E., 508
Munford, John I., 222, 587n, 599–600n
Myers, T. Bailey, 467

Napoleonic Wars, 66; American involvement, 63
Nat Turner slave revolt, 103, 429
National bank question, 54–55, 63; action of Giles and Brent, 55–56; depository for government funds, 55; opposition of Tyler, 63–65; Congressional investigation, 64–65; constitutional amendment proposed, 99; Jackson destroyed, 127–128; Tyler and, 147–171; White Plan for District Bank, 153–156; Botts compromise, 154–155; branching process, 154; Fiscal Corporation Bill, 157–159
National Intelligencer, 217, 325–326
National Republicans, 82, 86, 116, 119
Native American Party, 109, 233, 238, 241, 408
Nebraska, slavery controversy, 406–409 (*See also* Kansas-Nebraska controversy)
Negroes, Charles City, Va. plantations taken over by, 491–492; effect of Emancipation on, 506; during Reconstruction period, 532; elected to Virginia General Assembly, 533 (*See also* Slaves and slavery)
Nelson, Alexander, 384
Nelson, Harriet, 302
Nelson, Judge John, 259–260, 270, 287, 335, 588–589
Nelson, Samuel, 287, 588–589; appointment to Supreme Court, 287, 600–601n
New Jersey, Tyler faction, 269, 313
New Kent, Virginia, 451
New Market (Va.) battle, 494, 496, 525
New Mexico, Compromise of 1850, 394; slavery question, 395, 407
New Orleans, Tyler Club, 226–227
New York *American*, 38
New York *Aurora*, 222, 279, 316
New York City, social life, 3, 32–33, 45–46, 297–298, 309–310; machine politics 117; Locofocoism, 128; patronage appointments, 145, 233–235, 237, 266–288; Tyler organization, 219, 223–224, 232, 234, 237, 267, 271, 313, 391, 437; politics, 224; Tyler political strategy, 227–242; popularity of Tyler, 227; Irish vote, 233; pro-annexation resolutions, 261–262; visit of Tylers, 307–309; Conservative Democracy, 312–313; purge of the Tylerites, 315–316, 337; gossip, 354; cultural events, 354; Gardiner properties, 23, 287, 366, 381, 390, 540–541; Union Committee, 395–396, 400; sectional controversy, 431; Democratic Party in 1860, 436; 1860 election, 440–441; Southern sentiment, 468–469; draft riots, 481; Boss Tweed, 534; Panic of 1873, 541
New York College of Physicians and Surgeons, 541
New York *Courier and Enquirer*, 271
New York *Evening Post*, 492
New York *Express*, 431
New York *Herald*, 4, 5, 155, 160, 184, 203, 222, 238–239, 242, 243, 258, 280, 290, 385, 391, 399, 402, 494, 509
New York *Journal of Commerce*, 236, 313, 391, 405
New York *Ledger*, 335
New York *Morning News*, 335
New York *Plebeian*, 264, 279, 316
New York *Post*, 197
New York *Standard*, 222
New York State, Albany Regency, 227–228, 266, 278; Tyler-Polk alignment, 266–267; Van Buren-Silas Wright faction, 267; 1848 election, 392
New York *Union*, 220, 227
Newport, Rhode Island, 307–309, 549
Newspapers, pro-administration, 221–222, 313; appointing editors to federal jobs, 226; pro-Tyler communications, 320–321; treatment of Tyler after 1848, 392; reaction to Julia Tyler's defense of slavery, 405; on Tyler administration, 409; on sectionalism, 431; accounts of litigation over Juliana's will, 503
Niagara Falls, New York, 54
Noah, Mordecai M., 84, 201, 220–222, 226, 320, 587–588n; conversation with Tyler, 224
Nomination of Presidential candidates, 74–75, 100 (*See also* Conventions)
North, Fugitive Slave Act and, 396; participation of clergy in Kansas-Nebraska controversy, 408 (*See also* Civil War)
Northwest Ordinance, 69
Nullification doctrine, 87–96

Oertzen, Sievert von, 513–515

O'Hara, Edward, 348-349
Ohio River, 370-371
Old Point Comfort, Va., 10, 296, 304-305, 359-360, 372, 418, 421, 467; Tyler honeymoon cottage, 10-13 (*See also* Villa Margaret)
Onderdonk, Bishop Benjamin Treadwell, 1-2, 4
Oregon, boundary problem, 161, 183, 212-213, 327-331; expedition to, 220; slavery question and, 331
Ould, Col. Robert, 486

Page, Samuel, 364
Pageot, French Minister and Madame, 245
Pakenham, Richard, 253
Palmerston, Lord, 330
Palmerston, Viscountess, 403
Panic of 1873, 540-543
Papers, Tyler's public and private, 168, 425, 507; destroyed during Civil War, 168, 489; administrators, 424
Parker, Judge Richard, 625
Parker, Virginia, 644
Partisan attacks on Tyler, 320
Patronage, 83-84, 224-229; purge of federal officeholders, 224-225; dispensed by Jackson, 226; friends and relatives appointed, 226; "Reign of Terror," 227; Senate approval needed, 227, 271, 285, 287; New York City, 233-234, 266-288; Alexander Gardiner and, 226, 266, 269-272, 278, 283-288, 588-589*n;* Tyler's understanding with Polk, 312-313; Polk's purge of Tyler officeholders, 315
Parnelle, N. T., 587
Patterson, General Robert, 465
Payne, John Howard, 171
Peace Conference of 1861, 334, 447-460; Tyler's proposals for, 447; Tyler's speeches, 454-455, 459-460; Tyler's plan for twelve-state, 449-450; Tyler elected president, 453-454; membership, 454; Guthrie resolution, 457; denounced by Tyler, 460
"Peacemaker," firing of, 204-205
Peachy, Dr. William, 470-471
Peachy, William S., 574*n*
Peck, G. H., offers to lease Tyler coal lands, 614*n*
Peckman, Judge, 505
Pennsylvania, Tyler faction, 240; Robert Tyler's political activities, 313-314, 318, 328-330, 401, 410-411, 415-416, 434, 436; Democratic Executive Committee, 415-416, 434
Pennsylvania, USS, 11
Pennsylvania-Virginia political alliance, 410-411, 435
Pension Act of 1882, 549
Pensions, Julia Tyler's campaign for, 547-549
Pequot Indians, 18-19
Perry, Matthew C., 211
Petersburg, Virginia, 426, 497, 507
Petersburg (Va.) *Gazette*, 405
Peyster, Captain de, 37-38
Peyton's boardinghouse, Washington, D.C., 41-42, 179, 181-182
Philadelphia, 128; patronage, 222, Tyler organization, 230, 237; anti-Catholic riots, 233; Irish Repeal Association, 330, 436; Roman Catholic vote, 401; Robert Tyler's political activities, 313-314, 318, 328-330, 401, 410-411, 414, 436; Know-Nothings in, 409-410 (*See also* Pennsylvania)
Philadelphia Medical College, 423
Philadelphia *Pennsylvanian,* 405
Pickens, Francis W., 117, 184, 187-189, 259, 319, 331, 455, 579-580*n*
Piedmont (Va.) battle, 495-496
Pierce, Franklin, 355, 401-402, 410, 412; election of, 401-402; administration, 402; patronage, 402
Pirates visit Gardiners Island, 21-22
Pleasants, John H., 160
Pocahontas, small boat, 294-295
Poe, Edgar Allan, 245
Political organizations, 77, 82, 100, 117 (*See also* Tammany Hall)
Political parties, 82 (*See also* Democratic Party; Repubican Party; Third Tyler Party movement)
Polk, President James K., 4, 11, 116, 264; on Calhoun's appointment to Tyler Cabinet, 217-218, 586*n;* nomination for Presidency, 228-229; negotiations with Tyler, 230-232; New York City followers, 235-236; Tyler's withdrawal, 236; election of, 239-240; Tyler-Gardiner interpretation of victory, 239-242; Tyler's kindness to, 277; Texas victory dinner, 283; inauguration ceremony, 289, 292; administration, 312-333; Tyler's dissatisfac-

tion with, 312–318; patronage appointments, 312–317, 332, 392; purge of Tylerite officeholders, 315, 323; Mexican War, 327–330; Annual Message announcing California gold discovery, 373; blamed for Cass's defeat, 392
Polk, Sarah Childress, 277, 334, 405, 453, 547, 549; dull social functions, 319, 332–333
Polk, Maj. William H., 252–253, 255, 277–278, 280; assurances on patronage, 312
Pope Gregory XVI, 39
Popular sovereignty concept, 394, 406–407, 411, 413, 433
Porter, James M., Senate rejects for Cabinet post, 589n
Portsmouth (Va.) *Pilot*, 397, 400
Powell, Georgia, 543, 546
Power, Tyrone, 124
Powhatan House, Richmond, 292–293
Preston, William C., 117, 129, 135
Princeton, USS disaster, 1–2, 5, 204–206, 419
Princeton University, 26, 28–29
Proffit, George H., 158, 164, 170, 224
Protectionism, 66–67, 210–211
Public lands, 129; distribution scheme, 166–167
Purdy, Lovel, 594–595

Quin, Dr., 297

Radical Republicans, 517, 528; Southern resistance to, 530–531 (*See also* Republican Party)
Railroad, transcontinental, 384, 406, 550
Randolph, Edmund, 50
Randolph, John, 76, 78–79
Raoul, Mary Grace Cooper, 628–629n, 634n
Reconstruction Act of 1867, 528
Reconstruction period, 506, 511–556; difficult adjustments for Southerners, 517; amnesty oath, 512, 518; rule of Radical Republicans, 528
"Red Jackets" political group, 280, 290
Reed, Dr. Silas, 317, 444, 587n
Relation of the Pequot War (Gardiner), 19
Religious issues, 140; views of Tyler, 108–109
Republican Party, 409, 433; organization of, 408; 1856 Convention, 411; Frémont nominated in 1856, 412;

Tyler's views of, 414, 434–446; election of 1860, 432–433, 436, 438–439; platform, 448, 456; Radical Republicans, 517; Liberal movement, 535; election of 1876, 550
Revolutionary War, 22, 344
Richardson, Holt, 362
Richmond, Virginia, 291, 307, 354–355, 424, 451, 481, 507; War of 1812, 59; Washington Memorial, 355; boycott of Northern textiles, 431; sectional crisis, 431; political activities in 1860, 447, 460–462; Robert Tyler's flight to, 464–465; vote for secession in, 464; defense of, 465; Civil War period, 469–470; Peninsula campaigns, 475–485; attack on, 488–489; life during the war, 488; Tyler family during war, 500; evacuation of, 507; postwar politics, 534–535; town house leased by Julia Tyler, 549–550; Hollywood Cemetery, 555–556
Richmond (Va.) *Enquirer*, 91, 115, 139, 325, 403, 449, 462
Richmond (Va.) *Whig*, 160
"Ringdove, Romeo," 36
Ritchie, Ann Eliza, 304
Ritchie, Thomas, 91, 115, 139, 293, 305, 313–314, 426, 604n
Rives, William C., 94, 101, 115, 130–131, 141, 149–150, 448, 450
Robert E. Lee, CSS, 482, 631n
Roberts, Daniel G., 34
Roberts, George, 588–589n
Robertson, Judge John, 450–451, 455
Rochelle, James H., 571–572n, 588–589n
Rochelle, Mattie, 123, 192
Rockbridge (Va.) Alum Springs, 418–419, 483
Rockbrige County (Va.) reserves, 495–496, 498
Roman Catholic Church, Julia Tyler's conversion, 538–540
Roman Catholic vote, 136, 323, 401, 408, 436
Rome, Italy, 38–39
Roosevelt, James I., 170, 180, 194, 581, 619–620, 634–635
Roosevelt, Mrs. James I., 474–475
"Rose of Long Island" incident, 35–36
Royall, Anne, 108
Ruffin, Edmund, 62, 293, 298
Rumford (R.I.) Chemical Works, 474
Rush, Richard, 82

Russell, James M., 160
Russell, Capt. John W., 362–363
Russell, Lady John, 403
Russia, 406, 585n
Rutherfoord, John, 85, 154
Ruthville, Virginia, 302
Ryder, Rev. Father James, S.J., 436
Rynders, Capt. Isaiah, 279–280, 290

Sacramento City, Calif., 376–377, 380; social life, 375–376
Sacramento (Calif.) Valley, 373–374
Sacred Heart Convent, Halifax, N.S., 521–522, 537, 648n
Sag Harbor, Long Island, 26, 37, 44; patronage appointments, 272–277
St. Mary, launching of USS, 245–246
Samson, George, 342
Samuels, R. G., 363, 364
San Diego, Calif., 382–386; attempt to establish customs house, 383
San Francisco, Calif., 377, 381, 383–384
San Jacinto (Tex.) battle, 211
San Joaquin (Calif.) Valley, 373
Santa Anna, Gen. Antonio López de, 165, 211, 214, 229
Sante Fe Railroad system, 384
Saratoga, New York, 202–203, 307–309, 359, 418; vacation trips to, 355–356; Alexander's visits to, 370
Sargeant, John, 580–581n
Saybrook, Conn., 18, 19
Schools and colleges, 511–512; Germany, 512, 523–530
(*See also* William and Mary College)
Scott, Gen. Winfield, 116, 133, 209, 264, 401, 473
Seawell, John B., 87, 108, 577n
Seawell, M. B., 392
Seawell, Maria Henry Tyler, 577n
Seawell, Maj. Washington, 163, 577n
Secession, 445–472; threat by South Carolina, 90–96, 431; Compromise of 1850 and, 394, 397; Tyler's views, 412–413; threat of, 431; Tyler's decision on, 459–460; Tyler's speech for, 460–461
Secret History of the Tyler Dynasty (Cumming), 226, 320, 589n
Secret Service Fund, 322–323
Sectional-balance-of-power concept, 70
Sectional controversy, 331–332, 384, 417–446; Tyler's views, 80–81; Oregon question, 331; California's application for admission and, 393–394; Tyler's

efforts to solve, 427–428, 446; Southern line on, 430–431; Tidewater Virginia, 431–432; treatment in press, 431; moderates in 1860, 432–433; Tyler's views, 444–445; secession of South Carolina, 444
Seddon, James A., 450, 457–458
Seixas, J. M., 482
Selden, Cary, 107
Selden, Dr. James, 446
Semple, Judge James, 50
Semple, James A., 122, 328, 424, 465, 482, 489, 494, 497, 499–500; moral and mental decline, 518–520, 637–638n; work in underground Confederate cells in Canada, 518; returns from Mexican War, 608n
Semple, Letitia Tyler, 8, 172–173, 291–292, 352, 500, 519; relations with Julia Tyler, 302, 520n, 608n, 623–624n; Tyler's letters to, 414; later life and death, 500, 519, 637–638n
Senate, United States, Tyler's election to (1827), 78–79; "advice and consent," 84; Tyler resigned seat over instruction question, 110–115; on veto of District Bank Bill, 155–156; approval of Presidential appointments, 227; approval of patronage appointments, 271; approval of Texas Resolution, 282–84
Senate *Journal*, 101, 110; Expunging Resolution, 114–115
"Serenade Dedicated to Miss Julia Gardiner," 13–14
Seven Decades of the Union (Wise), 536, 642n
Sevier, Ambrose H., 580–581n
Seward, William H., 117, 132, 140, 234, 393–394, 432, 439, 441–442, 462
Shaler, William, patronage appointment, 591, 597–598n
Sharecroppers at Sherwood Forest, 514–515
Sharon Springs, Conn., 418
Shelter Island, New York, 34, 249–251, 258, 341
Shenandoah Valley (Va.) campaigns, 489–490, 495–496
Sheridan, packet ship, 37
Sherman, General William Tecumseh, 489, 498, 507
Sherwood Forest, Charles City County, Virginia, 5, 11–13, 179–180, 201, 558; slaves, 54, 103–104, 300–302, 403–406,

430; transition from White House to, 289–311; furnishings, 293–294, 593, 602, 604; boat and oarsmen, 294–295; social activities, 295–298, 304–305, 347, 350–353, 421–423; remodeling of, 296; Julia's emotional attachment to, 297; farming operations, 298–300, 302, 361, 641*n;* wheat crop, 298–300, 361, 406; white labor, 301–302, 631*n;* family circle, 302–304, 334–360; visits of Margaret and Juliana to, 388; during the Civil War, 465, 488; potato crop, 469; after death of Tyler, 471–472; Julia's desire to sell, 478–479; occupation and damage, 489–490, 495, 502; destruction wrought by Negroes, 502; Reconstruction years, 506; during Reconstruction period, 512, 531; Swedish immigrants hired for, 513–515; restoration of, 532–533, 552–553; Panic of 1873, 541–543; financial problems in 1874, 542–543; property losses, 548
Sierra Madre (Calif.) mountains, 386
Sigel, General Franz, 489, 494, 497, 525
Sioux City, Iowa land grant, 60, 636–637*n*
Sister Loretto, 539
Slamm, Levi D., 239, 279
Slaves and slavery, 12, 20–21; attitude of Gardiner family, 21; Tyler's treatment of, 53–54, 103–104, 300–302, 403–406, 423, 427–428, 430, 444–445, 476; Sherwood Forest, 54, 300–302, 403–406, 430, 506; opposition to continuation of African slave trade, 53; African colonization scheme, 53; Missouri Compromise debate, 69–71; Congressional regulation, 71; abolitionist propaganda, 104–105; leasing, 302; Wilmot Proviso, 331–332, 609*n;* at Caseyville, Ky., 372; 1848 campaign, 392; "Squatter sovereignty," 393; Compromise of 1850, 394; James Hamlet case, 397–400; Julia Tyler's letter defending slavery, 402–406; Kansas-Nebraska Bill, 406–409; Tyler's moderation on, 427–428; Tyler's views in 1860, 433, 444–445
Smith, Adam, 50, 67
Smith, Alfred E., 539
Smith, Delazon, 228, 235; relations with Tyler Party, 591*n*
Smith, Col. Thomas, 119, 570*n*
Smith, William, 121

Smith, Gov. William, 552
Social life of the Tylers, 417; in the White House, 172–208; Sherwood Forest, 295–298, 304–305, 347, 350–353, 421–423; Virginia mineral springs, 418–419; Villa Margaret, 442–443
Sollers, Augustus A., 579*n*
South, reaction to Fugitive Slave Act, 396; plans for secession, 412–413; reaction in the event Frémont elected, 413; Union occupation, 513
(*See also* Confederate States of America)
South Carolina, 446–447; nullification issue, 90–96; nullification and secession acts, 91–96; suspended Ordinance of Nullification, 95–96; threat of secession, 440, 443; secession of, 445, 448; ultimatum on Fort Sumter, 452–455, 457
Southard, Samuel L., 160
Southern Farmer and Planter, 552
Southern Literary Messenger, 402
Specie Circular, 128
Speeches of John Tyler, 54, 93–96, 138, 425–428, 460; on national bank question, 65; motion to censure Jackson, 68
Spencer, John C., 224–225, 426
Spencer, Julia Tyler ("Baby"), 537, 542–543, 550–555, 642–643*n*
Spencer, William H., 536, 642–643*n*
Spirit of the Times, 313
"Spoils" System, 83–84
"Squatter sovereignty," 393–394, 407
Stag, CSS, 486–487
Stage travels, 367
Star of the West, steamer, 448
Staten Island, New York, Gardiner homes on, 390, 471–472
(*See also* Castleton Hill)
States' rights, 50, 52, 60, 444; position on national bank question, 65; Tyler's views, 73–101, 136, 148, 425; Calhoun advocate of, 82, 86–87; Democrats, 314; 1856 election, 412
Staunton, Va., 489, 495–496
Steinbach, Frau, 527, 639*n*
Stevens, Thaddeus, 132–133
Stevenson, Andrew, 60, 72
Stevenson, Mrs. J. D., 305
Stewart, Charles, 264
Stilwell, Richard E., 381, 388–389, 597–598*n*
Stilwell, Silas M., 5, 192, 221–222, 269

672

Stock market, 331
Stockton, John Potter, 205
Stockton, Capt. Robert F., 204–205, 367, 454, 589–590n
Stowe, Harriet Beecher, 403, 405
Strong, George D., 5, 591n
Strong, George Templeton, 17
Strong, Silas B., 584n
Stuart, A. H. H., 155
Suffolk County, New York, 26; patronage appointments, 271–277
Summers, George W., 450
Sumter, Thomas Delage, 41–42, 182, 187, 192–193
Supreme Court, to settle territorial slavery disputes, 394, 407, 433; slavery questions, 433
Sutherland, Duchess, 403–404
Sutherland, Dr. Joel B., 222, 230, 232, 236–237
Sutter, Johann Augustus, 377, 616
Suydam, James H., 285, 597–598
Sweet, Joseph T., 239
Sweet Springs, Virginia, 307
Sykes, L. A., 368

Taggart, William, 221, 587
Taliaferro, John, 160
Talley, John, 534
Tallmadge, Daniel B., 240
Tallmadge, James, 70
Tallmadge, Nathaniel P., 117, 129, 131, 134, 135, 268, 317, 579n, 592n
Tammany Hall, 46–47, 129, 232, 436, 534; patronage arrangements, 235, 267; Tyler strategy and, 227–242; Alexander Gardiner and, 239, 318; Texas annexation resolutions, 261–262, 280–281; Democratic Empire Club, 280; White Eagle Club, 290
Taney, Robert B., 89, 97–98
Tariff Act of 1828, 79–80, 82, 86, 91
Tariff Act of 1832, 90–91
Tariff Act of 1842, 168–169
Tariff compromise movement, 94–96
"Tariff of Abominations" (1828), 80, 82, 86, 91
Tariffs, Tyler's views on, 50, 65–67, 210–211; free trade vs. protectionism, 66–67, 210–211; revenue-raising intent, 166–167
Tasistro, Louis F., 5, 6, 221, 224, 303
Taylor, John A., 634–635n
Taylor, President Zachary, 116, 328, 355; patronage appointments, 374, 393;
Presidential candidate, 391–392; election of 1848, 392; death of, 395
Tazewell, Littleton W., 93, 98, 100–101, 105, 122, 142, 163, 220; Presidential boom, 117–118
Tecumseh, Indian chief, 118
Telegraphy, 171
Tennessee Resolution, 74
Texas and Pacific Railroad, 550, 553
Texas annexation, 5–6, 16, 168, 171, 209–219; slavery issue and, 209, 215, 321, 395; secret negotiations, 213–214, 218; economic advantages, 215–216, 219, 324–325, 395, 425; British machinations, 216; Jackson in favor of, 218; Clay's opposition, 218; treaty signed, 218; treaty defeated in Senate, 229; Tyler's Annual Message (1844), 246–247; joint resolution instead of treaty, 247, 260–261, 269, 279–283; resolutions passed by Tammany Hall, 261–262; accomplished, 265; Alexander Gardiner's attitude toward, 266–267; signed by Tyler, 283; national character of, 324–325; Tyler's role, 324–326; Calhoun tries to take credit for, 324–325; Tyler's desire to achieve a cotton monopoly, 395; Tyler's motives, 395, 425
Texas Republic, recognition of, 214
Texas Resolution, 260–261, 269; passage through Congress, 279–283
Texas Revolution, 214
Thames (Ont.) battle, 118
Third (Tyler) Party movement (1843–1844), 170–171, 201, 209, 218; planned by Tyler, 161, 179; purpose, 210; Democratic Republicans, 218–219; platform, 218; following in New York City, 221–224; anti-Van Buren bloc, 221
Thomas, F. W., 243, 258, 262, 290; press agent for Julia Tyler, 245
Thomas, Jesse B., 70
Thomas Amendment, Missouri Compromise, 70
Thompson, E. G., 593–594n
Thompson, George, 396
Thompson, George F., 593n
Thompson, John B., 579n
Thompson, John R., 313
Thompson, Jonathan, 560–561n
Thompson, Sarah Gardiner, 254
Thompson, Sarah Griswold, 438
Thompson, Judge Smith, 189

673

Tidewater Virginia, sectional controversy, 431–432; after Harpers Ferry, 431; after Lincoln's election, 445; plantations plundered, 489–490 (*See also* Sherwood Forest)
Tilden, Samuel J., 550, 619–620
Tilford, Henry, 363–364
"Tippecanoe and Tyler Too," 40, 135
Tom Thumb exhibit, 354
Trade, Tyler's views on, 50, 65–66, 210–211
(*See also* Tariffs)
Travels and traveling, to Kentucky, 366–367; to California, 375, 386
Tucker, Annie Baker, 543
Tucker, Henry St. George, 92
Tucker, Nathaniel Beverley, 125, 150, 155, 161, 165
Tuscarora, New York, 536–537
Tweed, William M. ("Boss"), 534
"Two dollars a day and roast beef," 128–129, 136
Tyler, Alex (*see* Tyler, John Alexander)
Tyler, Alice, 172, 246, 249; romantic interests, 253, 255–256, 346–348; relations with Julia, 302–303; marriage to Henry M. Denison, 349
Tyler, B. O., 245, 593–594n
Tyler, Chancellor Samuel, 50
Tyler, Christiana, 64
Tyler, David Gardiner ("Gardie"), 311, 335–336, 422, 442–443, 451, 461, 466, 488; birth of, 311, 335; during Civil War, 475, 483, 496–499, 510; supervisor of Sherwood Forest, 477, 532; education, 478–479, 508, 529–530; military service, 483, 496–499, 510; at Washington College, 478, 483, 495–497, 500, 508, 529–530; dedication to the Confederacy, 512–513, 550–551; education in Germany, 512, 523–530, 639n; postwar problems, 521; interest in sports, 527; feelings about David Lyon Gardiner, 528; law practice, 532; political activity, 532–534, 550, Panic of 1873, 543; on Julia Tyler's pension request, 548; marriage, 551–552; on H. A. Wise memoir of Tyler, 636, 642n
Tyler, Elizabeth, 102, 172–173, 178–179, 606n, 628–629n
(*See also* Waller, Elizabeth Tyler)
Tyler, Fannie Glinn, 624n
Tyler, Fitz (*see* Tyler, Robert Fitzwalter)

Tyler, Gardie (*see* Tyler, David Gardiner)
Tyler, Gardiner (1878–1892), 544
Tyler, Georgia Powell, 543, 546
Tyler, Grace Raoul, 475–476, 606n, 628–629n
Tyler, Henry, 51
Tyler, James Rochelle, 571–572
Tyler, Judge John, 48–51; father of the President, 48–49; political and social views of, 50–51; elected Governor of Virginia, 50; Revolutionary career, 51
Tyler, President John, marriage to Julia Gardiner, 1–16, 57, 189–190, 337, 350, 358, 427, 580n; campaign for reelection, 5; children of first marriage, 6–7; poetic composition, 13–14, 102, 198, 358–359, 581n; "A Serenade Dedicated to Miss Julia Gardiner," 13–14; children, 16, 57, 71, 102, 105–107, 122–123, 178–179, 357–358, 427; temperament and character, 43, 62, 74, 147, 472, 599n; philosophy, 40–41, 50–54, 61, 88–89, 108–110, 148, 219–242; death of Harrison, 40, 49, 147–148; first meeting with Julia Gardiner, 43; childhood, 48–72; education, 48–50; birth, 48; myths concerning, 49, 148; William and Mary College, 49–50, 106–107, 425, 565n; love for music, 49, 350–351; law practice, 50, 54, 114, 122–123; Governor of Virginia (1825), 50, 57, 76–78; family background, 51; views on the extension of slavery, 53–54, 394–395, 427, 433; political career, 54–57, 102; hatred of Great Britain, 54, 332, 396, 406; oratorical ability, 54, 93–96, 138, 425–428, 460; marriage to Letitia Christian, 56–57; Congressional service, 57, 60–61, 65–66, 71–72, 78–79, 93, 110–115; delegate to House of Delegates, 57, 65–66, 71–72, 74, 127; military career, 59–60; War of 1812, 58–60; Sioux City, Iowa, land grant, 60, 636–637n; lacked the "common touch," 61–62; feared the power of the people, 61–62; efforts to preserve Constitution, 62–63, 71; re-elected to the House in 1819, 65–66; on tariff of 1820, 65–66; Jackson distrusted by, 67, 74–75, 108; resignation from House, 71–72; health, 72, 418, 423–424, 427, 450, 453–454; dilemmas, 73–101; states' rights views, 73–101, 136,

148, 425; re-elected to House of Delegates, 74; support of Adams-Calhoun administration, 74–76, 79; financial affairs, 77, 102–103, 112, 115, 177–178, 296, 310, 341, 356, 361; political organization, 77; public school bills, 77; canal- and road-building program, 77; election to the Senate (1827), 78–79; congratulatory letter sent Clay, 76, 81; decision to support Andrew Jackson, 80–81; appointment of Donelson, 83, 89, 320, 591*n*; attack on Jackson's appointment policy, 84–85; support of Jackson, 85–90; on Jackson's veto of Bank Bill in 1832, 87–88; grasp of banking economics, 88–89; So. Carolina's nullification bill, 91–96; speeches, 93–96, 138, 425–428, 460; against the Force Bill, 93–96; re-election to the Senate (1833), 93; break with Jackson, 97–100, 108; comes to support Clay, 97, 591–592*n*; Whig sympathies, 97, 122; renounces the Democratic Party, 97, 100; middle years, 102–126; political advancement, 102; slaves, 103–104, 300–302, 403–406, 430; lent money to friends and relatives, 103; education of children, 105–107, 442–443; member of Board of Visitors, William and Mary College, 106–107; social life in Washington, 107–108; use of franking privilege, 108; nickname of "Honest John," 108; religious toleration, 108–109; political honesty, 108; resigned Senate seat over the Instruction question, 110–115, 570–571*n*; nominated for Vice-Presidency by Whigs, 111–115; letter of resignation, 114–115, 570–571*n*; censure of Giles and Brent, 114; moved family to Williamsburg, 115; Presidential boom for Tazewell, 117–118; endorses nomination of White, 118–119; Vice-Presidential nomination, 120–121, 127–146, 571*n*; election of 1836, 120–121; multiple candidates of Whig Party, 120; vote polled by, 121–122; did not campaign personally, 121; class bias, 122; election of 1840, 122, 432–433; return to politics in 1838, 127–132; elected to Virginia House of Delegates (1838), 127; contest for Senate seat (1838), 130–132; supported Clay, 130–134; precampaign speeches, 132;

nomination for Vice-Presidency, 134–135; campaign of 1840, 135–139; tear-shedding story, 132, 573*n*; speech at Columbus, 138; on the Whig coalition, 141; sworn in as Vice-President, 144; notification of Harrison's death, 147–148; administration, 147–171, 331–332, 392–393, 401, 409; struggle with Clay and the Whigs, 147–171; training in government, 147; adherence to principles, 147; strict constructionist, 148; Cabinet, 149, 155, 160–162, 164; oath of office, 149; fiscal changes, 150–171; inaugural address, 150; expulsion from the Whig Party, 151, 162–163; resignation of Cabinet, 151, 160–161; personal feelings for Clay, 97, 152, 426; veto of District Bank Bill, 153–156; bank views, 153–154; signed bill repealing Van Buren's Independent Treasury, 156; burnt in effigy, 156; castigated by Clay, 156; Fiscal Corporation Bill vetoed by, 159–160; personal vilification, 160; foreign policies, 161; Third party movement, 161, 170–171, 218–242; Exchequer Plan, 163–165; veto of tariff-distribution bill, 166–167; impeachment talk about, 167–169; Whig attacks, 167–168; public and private papers, 168, 425, 489, 507; domestic program, 170; social life in the White House, 172–208; personal life, 172–180; nepotism, 178; love letters from Julia, 189–190, 580*n*; courtship, 192–208; dedication of Bunker Hill monument, 200, 227; patronage, 201, 218, 226–227, 385, 588*n*; use of appointing power, 201, 218, 226–227, 385, 588*n*; asks Juliana for Julia's hand, 207; Texas annexation, 209–219, 283, 324, 586*n*; role in Webster-Ashburton treaty negotiations, 212, 323, 585*n*, 607*n*; appointment of Frémont, 218, 586*n*; appointment of Kendall, 218, 586*n*; offers Polk Cabinet post, 218, 586*n*; conversation with Noah, 223–224; purge of federal officeholders, 224–225; attacks on, 226; opposes Noah appointment, 226, 588*n*; nomination in 1844, 228–229; withdrawal from 1844 campaign, 229–242, 312; withdrawal statement, 236–237; interpretation of Polk victory, 239–242; final Annual Message, 246–247; relationship with Alexander Gardiner, 268–269, 341, 368, 387, 619n; "availability" for 1848, 268–269; future political ambitions, 268–269, 293, 307, 313, 322; election to Confederate Congress (1861), 268; professional politician, 268; kindness to President-elect Polk, 277; annexation measure signed by, 283; on Samuel Nelson's appointment to Supreme Court, 287, 600–601n; departure from the White House, 289–292; foreign-policy achievements, 290; concern for Julia's comfort at Sherwood Forest, 293–294; proud of Julia, 295–296; farming operations, 298–300; treatment of slaves, 300–302, 403–406, 430, 445–446; fondness for animals, 305–306, 357, 593n, 604n; conferences in New York and Philadelphia, 309; disenchantment with Polk administration, 312–333; power of appointment, 313; political appointments, 320; partisan attacks on, 320; "President by accident," slur, 321; visit to Washington (1846), 322–324; appearance before Congress (1846), 322–323; receipt of Brazoria pitcher, 322, 607n; dinner with Polk (1846), 323; credit for Texas annexation challenged, 324–326; position on the Mexican War, 327–330; on impact of Wilmot Proviso, 332, 609n; president of the Peace Convention, 334; life at Sherwood Forest, 334–360; love for Julia, 337, 350, 358; Margaret's wedding, 346; fox hunting, 347, 351; happiness enjoyed by, 337, 350, 358; deaths of three daughters, 350; political reputation, 355, 401, 409, 425, 435, 552; Caseyville coal and timber speculation, 361–372; enthusiasm for California, 373–374; financial assistance from Gardiners, 389; elected overseer of roads, 390–391; connection with politics, 390–391; on Taylor's candidacy, 391–393; political influence in Washington, 391; 1848 political role, 391; blamed Polk for Cass's defeat, 392; patronage requests, 393; letter to Webster on slavery, 394–395; supported Compromise of 1850, 394–395, 407; views on Fillmore, 396; views on Fugitive Slave Act, 397, 400; views on Buchanan, 400–401, 411, 414, 416; attack of pneumonia, 400–401; on Pierce, 401–402, 410; administration endorsed by Virginia Democracy, 401; on Czarist Russia, 406, 585n; on Kansas-Nebraska Bill, 407–408; opposition to Missouri Compromise limitation on slavery, 407; defense of Roman Catholics, 408–409; political future in 1855, 409–410; support of Buchanan, 411, 414, 416; on secession, 412–413; reaction to election of Lincoln, 413; events leading to Civil War, 417–446; will, 424–425, 472, 478; plans for biography, 424; honorary degree, 425; Bank of the United States, 425; "The Dead of the Cabinet" speech, 426; Maryland Institute address, 426; moderation on slavery issue, 427, 440; Julia's poem on 65th birthday, 427; speech at Jamestown, 427; Virginia history love of, 427; Presidential "boom" in 1860, 435–437; on 1860 split of the Democratic Party, 439–441; on Lincoln's nomination, 440; views on election of 1860, 445–446; pleas for sectional harmony, 446; attempts to stave off the Civil War, 447–472; appointed to Peace Conference, 450, 453–454; complicity in Seddon amendment, 450, 457, 627–628n; elected to the Virginia State Convention, 451; elected president of Peace Conference, 453–454; urges Buchanan to surrender Fort Sumter, 455; sought peace through balance of power, 456–460, 463; change to prosecessionism, 456–460; interview with Lincoln, 458; forwarded suggested constitutional amendment to Congress, 459–460; Peace Conference denounced by, 460; speech for secession, 460; elected to Provisional Congress of the Confederate States, 464, 469; never defeated in a public election, 469; last illness and death, 470–472, 548; funeral, 472, 556; claims against estate of, 515, 532, 636–637n; warns Waller on Clay, 591–592n; warns Santa Anna, 591n; use of profanity, 599n

Tyler, John, Jr., 4, 8, 11, 71, 106, 123, 160, 163, 303–304, 401, 405, 424, 464, 500, 507; escorts Julia Gardiner, 191, 580–581n; discharged as Presidential secretary, 226, 588–589n, 594n; newspaper articles by, 248, 436, 494; and Yancy-Clingman duel law practice, 303; Mexican War, 328–329; desire to go to California, 374–375, 616n; personal habits, 374–375, 616n; patronage appointment, 393, 520–521; worked for Buchanan's election, 416; service during Civil War, 465; post-Civil War adjustment, 520

Tyler, John Alexander ("Alex"), 338–339, 442–443, 485, 509–510; birth of, 338–339; desire to join Confederate Navy, 498–500; military service, 508; during Reconstruction, 512; education in Germany, 512–530, 541–542; scientific ability, 523; fought in Franco-Prussian War, 529–530, 640n; patronage appointment, 544–545; marriage, 544, 553; death, 545

Tyler, John C., 479–480, 488–490

Tyler, John IV, 628–629n

Tyler, Julia Campbell, 606n, 628–629, 637n

Tyler, Julia Gardiner, marriage to John Tyler, 1–16, 246, 358; appearance, 4, 189, 352, 355–357, 542, 583n, 641n; reign as First Lady, 8–9, 38, 208, 243–265, 268, 302, 417; social and political ability, 12; on "Sweet Lady Awake," 13, 558n; poem written by, 15, 427; temperament and character, 20, 27, 246, 538; attitude toward slavery, 21; guitar playing, 34–35, 294, 351, 602n; Bogert and Mecamley advertisement, 35, 563n; romance with Belgian Count, 39, 563n; court life in Washington, 243–265, 302; clothes, 244, 263–264, 307–308, 352, 356, 542; portraits, 245, 536; Texas annexation promoted by, 247–248, 268, 281–283, 600n; mail received by, 249; receptions and levees, 257–265; farewell ball, 261–265; patronage matters and, 270–271; transition from White House to Sherwood Forest, 289–311; social hospitality, 290; strained relations with Tyler's daughters, 291–292, 302–304, 352, 606n; homesickness for New York City, 294, 602n; shopping commissions, 294, 337; life at Sherwood Forest, 297, 334–360; fondness for animals, 305–306, 357, 593n, 604n; economy program, 310; visit to New York, 308–309, 480; pregnancies, 311, 334–339, 356–359, 421–422, 428, 442; birth of David Gardiner Tyler, 311, 335; attitude toward Polk administration, 319–320; sensitive to criticism, 321–322; divorce rumors, 335–336; happiness with President, 337, 350, 358; children, 337–338, 350, 359, 422; birth of John Alexander Tyler, 338–339; matchmaking activities, 339–350, 419; Margaret's wedding in New York, 346; vacations, 353–356, 417–418, 421, 442–443; birth of daughter, 356–357; effect of Alexander's death on, 387; letter in defense of slavery, 402–406; attack on British interference in domestic affairs, 404–405; congratulatory letters received, 405; song "The Duchess," 405; children sent to New York during war, 421, 471–472, 477, 480; effect of Margaret's death on, 421; poem on Tyler's 65th birthday, 427; return to Washington, 451, 453, 455; social successes, 453–454; Civil War period, 463–469, 475–510; death of husband, 470–472; at Sherwood Forest after Tyler's death, 474; sickness of children, 474; return to Staten Island, 480; attempt to secure pass, 481; departs on blockade runner, 482; split with David Lyon Gardiner, 485, 500–507; attempts to secure release of Capt. Gayle, 485–487; pleas to Lincoln, 490–491; litigation over mother's will, 500–507, 524, 634–635n; relationship with mother, 503–504; attack by Delafield, 508–510; postwar decisions, 510; Reconstruction period, 511–517; friendship with Varina Davis, 511; Swedish immigrants hired by, 513–515; letter to Andrew Johnson, 515; Semple cared for by, 518–520; marriage and death of Julie, 536–537; visits to Washington, 536; social life in Washington, 537–538; conversion to Roman Catholicism, 538–540; during Panic of 1873, 540–543; financial problems, 540–543; attempts to get Alex a government appointment, 544–545; campaign for a federal pension, 547–549; last days in Richmond, 551–556; death and funeral, 554–555; exact date of birth uncertain, 560; "The Julia Waltzes," 594n, 595n

Tyler, Julia Gardiner ("Julie"), 356–

677

357, 461, 469; birth of, 356–357; education at Sacred Heart Convent, Halifax, 521, 522, 537, 648n; advice given by mother, 522; marriage and death, 536–537

Tyler, Lachlan, 357, 543, 551–552, 555, 613n; study of medicine, 541; seeks federal employment, 546–547

Tyler, Letitia, 71, 102, 106, 123, 460; (*See also* Semple, Letitia Tyler)

Tyler, Letitia Christian, 7, 43, 77; death of, 2, 168, 178–179, 578n; children, 7, 57, 102; temperament and character, 57–58; paralytic stroke, 58, 172–173

Tyler, Letitia Christian II, 606n, 628–629n, 637n

Tyler, Lillian Horsford, 544

Tyler, Lyon Gardiner ("Lonie"), 51, 168, 359, 444, 537–538, 542–543, 555; education, 537, 641n, 645–646n; *The Letters and Times of the Tylers*, 552; president of William and Mary College, 552, 554

Tyler, Maria, 442, 447, 488, 490, 492–494

Tyler, Martha Rochelle, 520, 571–572n

Tyler, Mary, 71, 87, 107–108, 350; marriage to Henry L. Jones, 107, 112

Tyler, Mary Armistead, 48

Tyler, Mary Fairlee, 628–629n

Tyler, Nannie Bridges, 500, 634n

Tyler, Patty, 442

Tyler, Pearl ("Pearlie"), 442, 537, 542; conversion to Catholicism, 539; married to Major Ellis, 552

Tyler, Priscilla Cooper, 43, 58, 148, 163, 192–193, 227, 414–415, 465, 500, 517; marriage, 123–126; White House hostess, 172–175; children, 318–319, 606n; Julia Gardiner Tyler's wedding cake, 558n; economic privations, 415, 606n; death, 637n

Tyler, Priscilla ("Tousie"), 606n, 628–629n, 637n

Tyler, Robert, 8, 42, 44, 58, 71, 106, 148, 163, 173, 175, 178, 194, 236, 251–252, 311; marriage to Priscilla Cooper, 123–126; New York politics, 221–222, 270; campaign of 1844, 230; efforts to promote Texas annexation, 279; departure from the White House, 290; political activities in Philadelphia, 313–314, 318, 328–330, 401, 410–411, 414, 436; patronage appointments and disappointments, 317, 391–392, 414–416, 588–589n; family, 318, 628–629n, 637n; law practice, 318, 416; monitoring of the press, 326–327; Mexican War, 328–329; on route of transcontinental railroad, 384; supported Cass, 391; worked for Buchanan's election, 401, 411–416; on Julia's letter in defense of slavery, 405; war against the Know-Nothings, 409; hope for patronage appointment from Buchanan, 414–416; on Democratic Executive Committee, 415–416; financial status, 415, 606n; visits by Tylers, 418; private papers of President left to, 424; Vice-Presidential possibility, 434–435; service to the Confederacy, 460, 464–465, 500, 508; Bristol, Pa., residence, 464–465, 606n, 628n; death of John Tyler, 470–471; during Reconstruction, 517, 637n; Buchanan's offer of aid, 517; editor of Montgomery *Advertiser*, 517; death, 517; escorts Margaret Gardiner, 580–581n; on Oregon question, 606n, 608–609n; serves in "Treasury Battalion," 634n

Tyler, Robert, Jr. ("Robbie"), 628–629n, 637n

Tyler, Robert Fitzwalter, 18, 421–422, 537, 542, 551, 555, 624n

Tyler, Sally Gardiner, 546–547

Tyler, Sarah Griswold Gardiner ("Sally"), 24, 544, 553, 564n, 644n

Tyler, Tazewell, 8, 49, 102, 105, 351–352, 423–424, 429, 470–471, 500, 519, 636–637n; education, 374, 624n; surgeon in the Confederate Army, 465; marriage, 500, 634n; postwar adjustments, 521

Tyler, Thomas Cooper, 628–629n

Tyler, Wat, English revolutionist, 51

Tyler, Dr. Wat Henry, 306, 595n

Tyler, William, 317

"Tyler and Texas," 208

Tyler Doctrine, 211

Tyler family, 51, 105–107; background, 17; anti-Tyler campaign and, 163; service to the Confederacy, 465–466; during Reconstruction period, 517

Tyler-Gardiner family alliance, effect of Alexander Gardiner's death on, 387; legal trouble over Juliana's estate, 500–507

Uncle Tom's Cabin (Stowe), 301, 403
Underground Railroad, 301
Underwood Constitution (Va.), 531, 533
Union, Tyler's speeches on, 425–426
Union County, Kentucky, 361–362, 364
Union political parties, 395
United States Circuit Court, 415; Alexander Gardiner appointed to clerkship, 286–288, 388
United States Telegraph, 118
Upshur, Abel P., 149, 152, 161, 164, 165, 170, 205, 212–213, 219, 326, 426, 577n; negotiations with Texas, 210; death, 216
Utah, Compromise of 1850, 394; slavery question, 395, 407

Vacations, Tyler and Gardiner family, 353–356, 417–418, 421, 442–443 (*See also* Villa Margaret)
Van Antwerpt, James, 583n
Van Buren, Martin, 25, 37, 40, 46, 86–87, 90, 113, 129, 132, 240; joins with Jackson, 87; leader of New York Democrats, 87; opposition to, 117; nomination of, 118; election to Presidency, 121; administration, 128–129; Independent Treasury plan, 128–129; defeat, 140–141; opposition to Texas annexation, 218; Albany Regency, 227–228, 266, 278; loss of renomination, 228; ran on Free Soil ticket, 392
Van Buren Democrats, 391
Van Buren-Silas Wright faction, 281
Van de Vyvew, Bishop-elect A., 555
Van Ness, Cornelius P., 232–233, 269–270, 278–279, 316, 591, 599–600
Van Ness, Gen. John P., 42, 180, 245, 290, 354
Van Rensselaer, Henry, 579–581n
Van Wyck, Mary Gardiner, 559–560n
Van Zandt, Isaac, 209, 584–585n
Vetoes, use of Presidential, 283
Vice-Presidency, 121; ascendancy to Presidency, 148–149; status, 322; Breckinridge, 411–412
Vicksburg (Miss.) battle, 480
Victoria, Queen, 339
Viele, Gen. Egbert L., 476
Villa Margaret, Hampton, Va., 372, 421, 428, 442, 467–468, 491, 515, 542; attempts to regain, 515–516; property losses, 548

Virginia, House of Delegates, 51, 54, 56, 58, 74, 110, 113–114, 552; Democrats, 81, 400; Jacksonians, 81; General Assembly, 100–101, 448, 452, 533; Convention of 1831–1832, 104; Jackson Democrats, 110–115; Whigs, 113; contest for Senate seat (1838), 130–132; vacation spots, 304–305; society, 309–310; anti-Catholic movement, 409; Pennsylvania-Virginia alliance, 410–411, 435; mineral springs, 418, 423; Tyler's speech on history of, 427; sectional crisis, 431–432; policy of antiabolitionism, 432; election of 1860, 445; secession controversy, 450; delegation to the Peace Convention, 450; secession of, 457, 464; State Convention, 451, 460; Home Guards, 498; Radical Republicanism in, 530–533, 550; Underwood Constitution, 531, 533; restoration of statehood, 533; Conservative Convention of 1872, 535
Virginia, Bank of, 636–637n
Virginia, University of, 356, 529
"Virginia Clique," 152, 159, 161, 219, 226; patronage appointments, 588–589n
Virginia Military Institute, 483, 494, 496

Wade, Reverend Dr., 432, 474
Waggaman, Floyd, 283, 328
Waggaman, George, 372
Waggaman, Henry, 103
Waggaman, John H., 108, 132; patronage appointment, 588–589n
Waggaman, William, 402
Waldron, Richard R., 42–43, 180, 184–186, 192–193, 196, 579–580n
Walker, Gov. Gilbert C., 533
Walker, Maj. and Mrs. Norman J., 484, 631n
Walker, Robert J., 215, 230–232, 282, 323, 381
Walker, William, 384
Wall Street lobby, 164
Wall Street Reporter, 313
Waller, Bessie Austin, 629n
Waller, Elizabeth Tyler, 7–8, 14, 250, 349–350, 466, 578n; strained relations with Julia, 302
Waller, Jenny Howell, 481, 511, 629n
Waller, John Tyler, 466
Waller, William Griffin, 443, 466, 481–482, 578, 629n

679

Waller, William N., 173, 178–179, 204, 250, 351, 424, 591–592n
Walsh, Mike, 235, 591n
War of 1812, 22, 25, 58–60; causes, 58–59; Tyler's participation, 58–60
Ward, Gen. Aaron, 42
Ward, Francis Marion, 184, 579n
Warm Springs, Virginia, 418
Washington, President George, 55, 425
Washington, D.C., living conditions, 57, 60–61; Mrs. Peyton's boardinghouse, 105, 179, 181–182; social and political life, 107–108, 172–208, 243–265; police force, 156; meeting of Tyler's followers, 218; burning of National Theater, 292; Julia Tyler visits to, 334, 536–537; Margaret Beeckman's honeymoon, 347–348; Confederate raids near, 498
Washington College, 478, 483, 495–497, 500, 508, 529–530; Reserve infantry unit, 483, 631n; Robert E. Lee president of, 529–530
Washington (D.C.) *Globe*, 220, 237, 315
Washington (D.C.) *Madisonian*, 6, 225, 227, 237, 242, 292, 313
Washington Memorial (Richmond, Va.), laying cornerstone of, 355
Washington (D.C.) *Union*, 314
Watkins, Joseph L., 364–365
Watkins, Col. Joseph S., 112
Watson, William, 634–635
Wealth and Pedigree of the Wealthy Citizens of New York City (Beach), 45
Wealth of Nations (Smith), 50
Webb, James Watson, 597–598
Webster, Daniel, 80, 83, 91, 116, 132, 134, 139, 143, 145, 158–159, 323, 374, 426; on nullification and secession, 92; Presidential nomination, 119; Bank crisis of 1841, 152; in Tyler's Cabinet, 160–162; social life, 174–175; protégés, 221; gossip concerning, 222; Ingersoll charges, 322–323; Seventh of March speech, 394–395
Webster, Mrs. Daniel, 180
Webster, Fletcher, 147–148
Webster-Ashburton Treaty, 161, 212, 220, 325, 327, 434; Tyler's role in negotiations, 212, 585n; bribery charges, 323, 607n
Weed, Thurlow, 41, 117, 132, 135
Wells, Henry H., 533
West Point, New York (U.S. Military Academy), 34, 295, 443

Wetmore, Prosper M., 437, 589–590, 597–598
Wetmore, Robert C., 221, 587n, 589–590n, 597–598n
Wheat, 298–300, 361, 406
Whig Party, 26, 40, 116; Tyler Vice-Presidential nominee, 111; coalition (1836), 115–122; Southern, 116, 129–130, 410, 413; Old Dominion, 118; campaign strategy, 119; multiple-candidate approach, 120; Congressional election, 1838, 129; convention at Harrisburg (1839), 132–135; campaign of 1840, 135–140, 393; National faction, 141; Northern wing, 141; Tyler expelled from, 151, 158, 162–163; 1842 elections, 170; alliance with Native American Party, 238, 241; attempts to humiliate Tyler, 390; elections of 1848, 391–392; antislavery Northern, 393; election of 1836, 400; 1852 elections, 401–402; end of, 402; slavery issue, 409; New York, 410; endorsed Fillmore in 1856, 412
Whipple, George, 516
White, Edward C., 580–581n
White, Edward Douglass, 286, 313
White, Hugh L., 113, 116, 118–119, 129; Tyler's support of, 122; District Bank plan, 153–156
White Eagle Club, 291
White House, Tyler's honeymoon at, 5–6; condition, 10, 177–178, 243–244; rebuilding of, 60; social life, 172–208, 243–265; receptions and levees, 173–177, 244–245, 257–265; furnishings, 177–178, 243–244; New Year's Day reception, 257–259; Tyler's farewell ball, 261–265; Texas victory dinner, 283; end of Tyler's administration, 289–292; Polk administration, 332–333; Julia Tyler's visits to, 536, 545
White Man's Party (Ala.), 517, 534
White Sulphur Springs, Virginia, 37, 296, 307, 359, 402, 418
Wickliffe, Charles A., 4, 42, 143, 203, 315, 454, 632–633
Wickliffe, Nannie, 4, 254–255
Wilcox, Dr. Henry, 419
Wilcox, Lamb, 489
Wild, Brig. Gen. Edward A., 489–490, 492–493, 632n
Wilderness (Va.) battle, 497
Wilemson, Mary, 18, 264
Wilkes Expedition, 180, 185

Wilkins, Charles, 253, 256
Wilkins, William, 246, 263, 369, 570*n*
Wilkinson, Capt. John, 482
Will of John Tyler, 424–425, 472, 478
Willard, Capt. Abijah, 21
William and Mary College, 59, 359;
   Tyler's academic career, 48–50;
   Tyler's service to, 106–107, 425, 565*n*;
   Robert and John, Jr., attended, 106–107; Lyon G. Tyler president of, 552, 554
Williams, Edward P., 486
Williams, Capt. Paul, 21
Williamsburg, Virginia, 425, 475, 554;
   Tyler educated in, 50; War of 1812, 59–60; Tyler's home, 115, 163
Wilmington-Bermuda blockade run, 486, 507
Wilmot, David, 331, 454
Wilmot Proviso, 314, 331–332, 391–392, 609*n*; Tyler on impact of, 332, 609*n*
Wilson, J. C., 489
Wilson, Thomas, 363
Wilson, Woodrow, 61
Wing, Catherine, 301–302, 351, 603*n*
Winston, Robert, 364–365
Wise, Henry A., 14–15, 91, 122, 130–131, 139, 146–147, 152, 158, 161, 164, 170, 183, 200, 215–217, 401–402, 410, 413, 460, 472; flirts with Margaret Gardiner, 183, 580–581*n*; letters to, 127, 141; Governor of Virginia, 409, 419, 425, 437; Presidential aspirations, 410–411, 434–436; mobilization of Virginia militia, 429–430; John Brown affair, 432; supported by Tyler, 434–435; biographer of Tyler, 536, 642*n*; *Seven Decades of the Union*, 536, 642*n*; postwar career, 642*n*
Witchcraft, 19
Withers, Col. Robert E., 547–548
Wood, Fernando, 42–43
Wood, Leonard, 563*n*
Woodbury, Levi P., 180, 182
Woodbury, Ruth, 182
Woodhill, Maxwell, 181
Wool, Gen. John E., 475
Workingmen's Party, 46, 128, 270
Wright, John C., 454
Wright, Mary, 255
Wright, Silas, 42, 129, 240, 281, 584*n*

Yale University, 22
Yancy, William L., 253
Yellow fever, 420
Yorktown, Virginia, 475

ABOUT THE AUTHOR

The son of an Episcopal missionary, Robert Seager II was born in Nanking, China, in 1924. He graduated from the United States Merchant Marine Academy in 1944, received his A.B. and M.A. degrees in American history from Rutgers and Columbia Universities and, in 1956, the Ph.D. in history from Ohio State University. After teaching for several years at Denison University in Ohio, he joined the civilian faculty of the United States Naval Academy in 1961, where he is presently an assistant professor of history. In addition to his teaching responsibilities, he has served as Consulting Historian to the Ohio Civil War Centennial Commission and as National Councillor of Phi Alpha Theta, the national honor society in history. His scholarly historical articles, which have appeared in the *Mississippi Valley Historical Review* and the *Pacific Historical Review*, won him early recognition, and in 1959 he was the recipient of the Louis Knott Koontz Prize for historiography, presented by the Pacific Coast Branch of the American Historical Association.

And Tyler Too is Dr. Seager's first book, and with its publication he proves himself to be a gifted young historian who has the exciting ability to make obscure characters and times leap vividly and amusingly to life.